THE OXFORD ENCYCLOPEDIA OF

BIBLICAL INTERPRETATION

THE OXFORD ENCYCLOPEDIA OF
BIBLICAL INTERPRETATION

Steven L. McKenzie
EDITOR IN CHIEF

VOLUME 1

African American Interpretation–Materialist Criticism

OXFORD
UNIVERSITY PRESS

OXFORD
UNIVERSITY PRESS

Oxford University Press is a department of the University of Oxford.
It furthers the University's objective of excellence in research,
scholarship, and education by publishing worldwide.

Oxford New York

Auckland Cape Town Dar es Salaam Hong Kong Karachi
Kuala Lumpur Madrid Melbourne Mexico City Nairobi
New Delhi Shanghai Taipei Toronto

With offices in

Argentina Austria Brazil Chile Czech Republic France Greece
Guatemala Hungary Italy Japan Poland Portugal Singapore
South Korea Switzerland Thailand Turkey Ukraine Vietnam

Oxford is a registered trademark of Oxford University Press
in the UK and certain other countries.
Published in the United States of America by

Oxford University Press
198 Madison Avenue, New York, NY 10016

Library of Congress Cataloging-in-Publication Data

The Oxford encyclopedia of biblical interpretation / Steven McKenzie, editor in chief.
pages cm
Includes index.

ISBN 978-0-19-983226-2 (set : alk. paper) — ISBN 978-0-19-999335-2 (v.1 : alk. paper) —
ISBN 978-0-19-999336-9 (v.2 : alk. paper)

1. Bible–Criticism, interpretation, etc.–Encyclopedias. 2. Bible–Hermeneutics–Encyclopedias.
I. McKenzie, Steven L., 1953–
BS511.3.O88 2013
220.603—dc23
2012041156

3 5 7 9 8 6 4 2

Printed in the United States of America on

Editorial and Production Staff

ACQUIRING EDITOR	Grace Labatt
DEVELOPMENT EDITORS	Mary Funchion Jennifer Carlson
EDITORIAL ASSISTANTS	Lauren Konopko Diana Fang
PRODUCTION EDITOR	Mark O'Malley
COPYEDITORS	Jan A. Maas Mary Sutherland
PROOFREADERS	Lynda Crawford Nancy Wolitzer
INDEXER	Katharyn Dunham
COMPOSITOR	SPi Global
MANUFACTURING CONTROLLER	Genieve Shaw
COVER DESIGN	Caroline McDonnell
PRODUCTION MANAGER	Mary Araneo
SENIOR EDITOR, DEVELOPMENT	Alixandra Gould
PUBLISHER	Damon Zucca

CONTENTS

THE OXFORD ENCYCLOPEDIA OF BIBLICAL INTERPRETATION

List of Articles

Series Introduction

The importance of the Bible cannot be overstated. For Jews and Christians, it is the supremely authoritative text, which has guided and inspired them for more than two thousand years. It has also profoundly affected Western culture, influencing not just religious belief and practice, but also the arts, literature, law, politics, and many other fields. In the twentieth century especially, it has also had an impact on cultures worldwide, and scholars, writers, and artists from those cultures have in turn influenced the interpretation of the Bible everywhere.

Several years ago, when editors at Oxford University Press and I discussed producing a new biblical encyclopedia, we first thought along traditional lines: a comprehensive, up-to-date multivolume reference work that would provide a wide audience with comprehensive information about everything in the Bible and about the Bible. We wanted to do this in part because our online reference tool, *Oxford Biblical Studies Online,* needed constant feeding, and in part because it had been almost 20 years since such a work had been produced. As we began to work on the early stages of the project, however, we began to think more creatively. This was prompted in part by the appearance of just such a comprehensive dictionary, and also by our experience in producing some entries for the website. We realized that the amount of effort necessary to duplicate what was already available, about, say, every minor Levite in the book of Chronicles, would not be proportionate to the result, and in many such cases there was little or nothing new to be said.

Biblical studies, however, is not static: new discoveries, new approaches, new insights make the discipline of biblical interpretation dynamic, and it is difficult to communicate these developments in the format of a comprehensive encyclopedia of the Bible. So, we changed the template: instead of a collection of relatively brief articles even on important topics, we decided to produce *The Oxford Encyclopedia of the Bible* in two-volume sets, each of which is devoted to a particular subject or approach. Within each set, entries several thousand words long explore specific topics in depth.

The cumulative result is a monumental reference work, consisting of more than a dozen volumes containing hundreds of comprehensive essays by scholars from many countries and with a wide variety of perspectives. The simultaneous publication of the articles in these sets in *Oxford Biblical Studies Online* enhances their use and reach. It makes them accessible to scholars and students in a wide variety of places, and it enables us to revise entries on a regular basis. As a whole then, the series is a worthy addition to the innumerable distinguished reference works produced by Oxford University Press, both as printed books and, more and more, in digital format.

Michael D. Coogan
General Editor

Preface

Critical Biblical Interpretation: An Overview This encyclopedia is a tribute to the vibrancy of the field of biblical studies and the creativity of its members. As a critical, academic enterprise, biblical studies is a relatively young discipline. A product of the Enlightenment in the eighteenth and early nineteenth centuries, it initially focused on questions of the Bible's historical veracity and the discernment of various sources and contributing writers behind its composition (source criticism). This focus continued well into the twentieth century, abetted by the developing field of archaeology (and later sociology and anthropology) and a growing collection of inscriptional materials from the ancient world. The advent of other methods—especially form criticism in the last quarter of the nineteenth century—changed this focus slightly, but form criticism was still very much in the historical-critical paradigm, as illustrated by how readily it lent itself to tradition-historical and redaction criticism, which were hybrids of "literary" (source) and form criticisms. These remained the primary methods employed by biblical scholars into the late 1960s and early 1970s.

During these decades, though, there arose a growing unease with the limitations of these methods and their tendency to concentrate on historical questions to the neglect of literary and aesthetic ones. James Muilenburg's 1968 Presidential Address to the Society of Biblical Literature sparked a methodological revolution in this respect as he launched a new approach—"rhetorical criticism"—that proposed exploring biblical literature *qua* literature. The address and the approach would have a far-reaching impact in liberating scholars to move beyond purely historical questions and to apply newer modes of literary analysis and criticism to the Bible. Shortly afterwards, canonical criticism, launched in different trajectories by James Sanders and Brevard Childs, created similar bridges between the historical and the literary paradigms.

Following upon the paths blazed by these pioneers, methods and approaches began to multiply in the later 1970s and throughout the 1980s. Driven largely by revolutions that had taken place in the fields of literary theory and philosophy, scholars started to apply a spate of experimental techniques to the Bible. These included structuralism, deconstruction, narrative criticism, reader-response theory, and poststructuralism, among others. Moreover, in what would become the most influential and most fertile new direction in biblical studies, explicitly ideological approaches began to surface in the form of feminist, socioeconomic, and ethnic (African American, Hispanic) criticisms that were often, though certainly not always, postcritical in nature. The result was tension throughout the 1980s and 1990s as older, more traditional historical-critical approaches and more recent approaches representing a paradigm shift vied for ascendancy in the field, eventually settling into a sometimes uneasy coexistence.

It would be naïve to claim that the rivalry between paradigms has dissipated across the dawn of the new millennium. Tensions certainly remain and occasionally flare. At the same time, a new spirit of mutual recognition and tentative cooperation has begun to surface, even if it has not displaced the rivalry. The new movement is coupled with and evident in a proliferation of critical approaches across the abutting paradigms and is fueled by at least three interrelated factors that all grow out of a growing appreciation of diversity. The first of these is acknowledgment of the advantages to be gained from interdisciplinary approaches and from the application to the Bible of insights gained in other fields of inquiry. Going back at least to Adolf Deissmann's errant attempt to distinguish epistles from letters (1895), there has been an awareness that the Bible did not appear in a vacuum and that insights from fields such as Greco-Roman studies were invaluable for biblical interpretation. But there has also been a trend toward isolationism in Biblical studies and one-sidedness about its dialogue partners. The paradigm shift brings with it an eagerness to converse with many other fields of study in the humanities (e.g., literary theory and philosophy, as noted) and social sciences (anthropology, cultural studies, linguistics, psychology, etc.) especially. In addition to providing new ways of examining the biblical text, other disciplines have led more traditional approaches to the Bible to become increasingly sophisticated, with results that are sometimes radically divergent from those of a few decades past. For instance, theories about the composition of the Pentateuch (source criticism) and the Gospels (redaction criticism) are being transformed by insights gained from orality and folklore studies and from improved understandings of literary and scribal practice in the ancient Near Eastern and Greco-Roman worlds. These insights are further enhanced and developed by recent approaches such as performance and mimetic criticisms. In some cases, this has shown itself in a return to older areas of interest but with a new orientation that recognizes the paradigm shift of the postmodern world. One might point to renewed interest in psychological criticism, the rise "new historicism," and the emergence of queer theory as examples. Biblical studies is coming of age and taking its place without embarrassment or isolation as an academic discipline that intersects with, benefits from, and contributes to its peers.

The second factor is globalization. There is much greater dialogue than ever before among biblical scholars from different parts of the world. This is largely the result of technology, which greatly facilitates communication around the globe and has brought with it greater and closer attention to the voices of people outside of Western Europe and North America, who have just as much of a stake and interest in biblical interpretation. Globalization has effected awareness of the gaps that exist between different continents and cultures when it comes to assumptions and approaches about the interpretation of biblical literature. It has also brought with it an interest in issues of global concern reflected in interpretations dealing with such topics as ecocriticism, postcolonialism, economics, and classism.

A third important factor fueling the proliferation of approaches to the Bible is the recognition of the significance of the reader's location in the process of interpretation. To put it another way, one's interpretation of the Bible is significantly influenced if not determined by one's social, ethnic, and national identity. Recent scholarship has cultivated not just an awareness of interpretive location but also a positive appraisal of it as an element to be embraced rather than embarrassingly shunned or denied. The result is an ever expanding list of interpretations exploring the particular vantage point of interpreters of various nationalities, ethnic origins, genders, sexual orientations, physical states, and combinations of these. In addition, interest in how the Bible has been and is received and interpreted has spawned specific interpretive approaches in their own right. A clear, if subtle, indication of this shift is the language about interpretive *approaches* rather than interpretive *methods*. The latter term implies regimentation and consistency across practitioners, who come to the text with a checklist of "measurements" to be taken of it. The term "approach," in contrast, acknowledges the "situatedness" of the reader and the role that context plays in the interpretive enterprise. It is more comfortable with the identity of biblical studies as a discipline in the Humanities rather than aspiring to the model of Natural-Scientific *Wissenschaft*. This move is not at all a diminishing of academic rigor in critical interpretation. Rather, it is another sign of biblical studies coming into its own in academe and becoming comfortable with itself—its strengths and its limitations.

The Need for an Encyclopedia of Biblical Interpretation Some readers of this work will remember when there were only two approaches to the critical study of the Bible: "lower" and "higher" criticism. The former was another name for textual criticism; the latter included "literary" (source), form, tradition-historical, and redaction criticisms. These were all treated as methods with step-by-step instructions for carrying them out, and up-and-coming scholars were trained to become practitioners of them all. As noted, this situation began to change gradually after 1968.

By 1993 the number of methods and approaches to the Bible had more than doubled. A guidebook to them was warranted, not just for students but also for professors struggling to maintain some kind of familiarity with their swiftly changing discipline. A colleague and I put together just such a guidebook in that year (Steven L. McKenzie and Stephen R. Haynes, *To Each Its Own Meaning: An Introduction to Biblical Criticisms and their Application* [Westminster/John Knox]). Aimed primarily at seminary and undergraduate students, it compiled a set of articles graciously contributed by leading exponents of the predominant approaches. Even so, the volume contained only thirteen essays. Six years later when a second edition with fourteen essays appeared, so did the two-volume, 1,328-page *Dictionary of Biblical Interpretation* (*DBI*) edited by John Hayes (Abingdon). While the *DBI* contained articles on interpretive approaches, they were not its sole focus; it ambitiously included treatments of biblical and noncanonical books, specific topics within the Bible (e.g., covenant), genres of biblical literature (genealogy, parable), and even biographies of leading scholars in the field.

In the more than a dozen years since the publication of the *DBI*, the number and variety of academic approaches to the Bible has proliferated exponentially, as described above. And the number is still growing. It is no longer possible for any one scholar to maintain expertise in every approach available. It is a struggle just to be aware of all the choices, must less to understand the sophistication and contribution that each of them brings to the discipline. Yet some familiarity with the techniques outside of one's specialization is crucial for dialogue and for retaining some sense of the direction of the field at large. The *Oxford Encyclopedia of Biblical Interpretation* (*OEBI*) is created to meet this need.

Resources for information about the contents of the Bible—the books and topics it contains—are readily available in the form of dictionaries (e.g., *Anchor Bible Dictionary, New Interpreter's Dictionary of the Bible*) and handbooks (e.g., the *Oxford Companion to the Bible*). But the only comparable, up-to-date resource for interpretation is W. Randolph Tate's *Interpreting the Bible: A Handbook of Terms and Methods* (Hendrickson 2006). This book is impressive for its breadth of coverage—all the more so, since it is the work of a single author—and is a highly useful resource for definitions of terms used in biblical interpretation. The *OEBI* seeks to build on Tate's work (and the *DBI* before it) by covering fewer topics in greater depth. The focus is not on broader terminology but more specifically on approaches and strategies for reading and interpreting the Bible, with entries authored by expert practitioners of those approaches. The purpose is to afford biblical scholars of all stripes a sympathetic and comprehensive presentation of available approaches that will foster appreciation across diverse perspectives and perhaps even dialogue and cooperation among them. The detail requested of the authors in explicating their approaches requires that the complete project constitute a multivolume encyclopedia—something of the length of the *DBI*—but again with a focus exclusively on interpretive approaches. The simultaneous publication of the *OEBI* in both hard copy and electronic form is a crucial part of the project as well, since this will allow for adjustment and augmentation as approaches continue to evolve and to multiply, thus making it possible for scholars to keep pace with the rapidly changing field of biblical scholarship. The electronic format will also facilitate access to the *OEBI* by scholars on a global scale, thereby further enhancing communication in the field without compromising diversity.

The Configuration of the *OEBI* The decision was made early on to exclude topics on biblical books, scholars' biographies, and the like and to focus on interpretive approaches. This decision was based partly, as just indicated, on the ready availability of other reference works focused on those topics. This is best illustrated by the *Oxford Encyclopedia of the Books of the Bible* (*OEBB*), which rendered explicit treatment of biblical books in the *OEBI* unnecessary. The *OEBB* is the first of a family of encyclopedias dealing with the Bible and Bible-related topics. Other family members in preparation will deal with the Bible and the arts, the Bible and archaeology, and the Bible and ethics, so that it was deemed unnecessary for the *OEBI* to include entries dealing with these topics as well. The decision not to include biographies of scholars was made on practical grounds. While a comprehensive, updated set of biographies is not available elsewhere and would enrich our field, such an effort lies beyond the real scope of the *OEBI*.

Once the general parameters of the *OEBI* were established, an initial set of topics was drafted. Paul Ricoeur's rubric of the worlds behind the text, of the text, and in front of the text was adopted as the categorical framework for the entries. These categories were also useful as one consideration among several for identifying potential board members. Beyond that, however, the categories were purely heuristic and served no function in organizing the entries in the *OEBI*, which, as an encyclopedia, follows alphabetical order. The initial set of topics was enlarged and refined by the developing board and consultants. The objective was to be as comprehensive and inclusive as possible in compiling topics. At the same time, there was a pragmatic side to this decision making. Certain approaches were not yet ready for inclusion because they were still in the process of being formulated or because they had yet to develop a community of practitioners strong enough to establish their viability in the discipline. More regretable, and admittedly reflective of the North American orientation of this encyclopedia, is the fact that in certain entries, most notably African Biblical Interpretations and Central/South American Interpretation, the work of entire continents was lumped together. We are grateful to the authors of these articles, Professors Musa Dube and Néstor Míguez, for describing the growing diversity of interpretation within these settings. One of the reasons for such large-scope entries was the logistical difficulty of finding contributors for each of the constituencies within Africa and Central and South America. This problem is illustrated even within the North American setting by the article on Cuban Interpretation. The search for someone to write an entry on biblical interpretation within the Cuban context in order to accompany and balance Francisco García-Treto's fine article on "Cuban Interpretation in the Cuban Diaspora" proved unsuccessful. We hope that the online publication and maintenance of the *OEBI* will produce more detailed coverage of these areas in the future than has been possible here.

A small number of other entries (e.g., Native American Interpretation) fell victim to unanticipated circumstances that prevented authors from completing their assignments when it was too late to replace them. Tragically, Ada María Isazi-Díaz, who was slated to write the entry on "Mujerista Interpretation," passed away during the preparation of this encyclopedia. The fact that we were unable to find an author to replace her testifies to her significance as the leading proponent of this approach. We are grateful to Professors García-Treto and Leticia Guardiola-Sáenz, author of the entry on "Latina/o Interpretation," for their help in trying to compensate for these losses. Again, it is our hope that future editions of the *OEBI* will be able to include these and other intended entries that were waylaid in process.

The People behind the *OEBI* Recognition is due first and foremost to the authors who contributed articles to the *OEBI*. An encyclopedia of this nature could not exist without the cooperation of scholars across the guild, their passion for the approaches they practice and promote, and their willingness to share their expertise and insights with their colleagues and with interested readers at large.

The astuteness of the directors and editors of Oxford University Press in recognizing the need for an encyclopedia on biblical interpretations is due in large measure to Michael Coogan, whose production of such works with OUP is prodigious. He is the umbrella editor of the family of encyclopedias relating to the Bible and biblical studies mentioned earlier that are recently minted or currently in production. I am grateful to him for his perception of the need for such a work as this and for his recommendation of me to be its editor in chief, but also for the freedom he has allowed me in executing its design—all of which increases a large debt already owed to a former teacher. He sometimes said, "The Bible is bigger than all of us," and I have carried that wise observation—well illustrated in the present encyclopedia—throughout my career.

The editorial board as ultimately constituted was made up of five scholars in addition to the editor in chief. These five are (in alphabetical order, of course):

Colleen Conway, Professor of New Testament, Seton Hall University, whose work has focused on the construction of gender in the New Testament and the Greco-Roman world with special attention to the Gospel of John.

David G. Garber Jr., Associate Professor of Old Testament and Hebrew, McAfee School of Theology, who has specialized in issues of trauma theory and social justice, particularly as they relate to the book of Ezekiel.

John Kaltner, Virginia Ballou McGehee Professor of Muslim-Christian Relations, Rhodes College, whose teaching, research interests, and publications encompass the Bible and the Qurʾan individually and as lenses for one another.

Elizabeth Struthers Malbon, Professor of New Testament, Virginia Tech, is best known for her narrative-critical studies of the Gospel of Mark, particularly in relation to narrative space and characterization in the Gospel at large.

W. Randolph Tate, Professor of Humanities, Evangel College, shares an interest in the Gospel of Mark and particularly in the literary-critical interpretation of it; he is best known as the author of *Interpreting the Bible: A Handbook of Terms and Methods* described above.

These brief sketches fall far short of the recognition due to each of these fine scholars and individuals. It has been a genuine honor and pleasure to work with them because of the traits of editorial proficiency (often for entries outside of their immediate expertise), patience, and affability that they have in common. Their persistent and tireless labors on behalf of this project have vastly improved the nature of the *OEBI* beyond its initial design.

The board (and the editor in chief particularly) was helped especially early on in the conception and design of the *OEBI* by Professors Amy-Jill Levine and Stephen Moore. Their names kept coming up as "must haves" for any project dealing with biblical interpretation. So it was with great relief that I greeted the news of their gracious acceptance to serve as consultants for the *OEBI*. Their advice along the way has been indispensable, especially when needs for replacement authors arose.

Finally, I wish to thank the two managing editors at Oxford University Press for their guidance. Mary Funchion got the project off to a good start; Jennifer Carlson energetically saw it through to completion.

Steven L. McKenzie
Professor of Hebrew Bible/Old Testament
Spence L. Wilson Senior Research Fellow
Rhodes College

Abbreviations Used in This Work

// or ||	parallel passages
§	Section
Acts	Acts of the Apostles
Add Dan	Additions to Daniel
Add Esth	Additions to Esther
Ag. Ap.	Josephus, *Against Apion*
Amos	Amos
Ant.	Josephus, *Jewish Antiquities*
B. Bat.	*Baba Batra*
Bar	Baruch
B.C.E.	Before the Common Era (= B.C.)
Bel	Bel and the Dragon
C.E.	Common Era (= A.D.)
cf.	*confer,* compare
ch./chs.	chapter/chapters
1–2 Chr	1–2 Chronicles
Col	Colossians
col./cols.	column/columns
1–2 Cor	1–2 Corinthians
d.	died
Dan	Daniel
Deut	Deuteronomy
DH	Deuteronomistic History
DSS	Dead Sea Scrolls
Dtr	Deuteronomist
E	Elohist source in the Pentateuch

Eccl	Ecclesiastes
ed.	editor (pl., eds.), edition
1 En.	*1 Enoch*
Eph	Ephesians
Ep Jer	Letter of Jeremiah
1–2 Esd	1–2 Esdras
Esth	Esther
Exod	Exodus
Ezek	Ezekiel
Ezra	Ezra
4 Ezra	*4 Ezra*
Gal	Galatians
Gen	Genesis
Gen. Rab.	*Genesis Rabbah*
Hab	Habakkuk
Hag	Haggai
HB	Hebrew Bible
Heb	Hebrews
Hos	Hosea
Isa	Isaiah
J	Yahwist source in the Pentateuch
Jas	James
Jdt	Judith
Jer	Jeremiah
Job	Job
Joel	Joel
John	John
Jonah	Jonah
Josh	Joshua
Jub.	*Jubilees*
Jude	Jude
1–2 Kgs	1–2 Kings
KJV	King James Version
Lam	Lamentations
Lev	Leviticus

Lev. Rab.	*Leviticus Rabbah*
lit.	literally
Luke	Luke
LXX	Septuagint
1–2 Macc	1–2 Maccabees
3–4 Macc	3–4 Maccabees
Mal	Malachi
Mark	Mark
Matt	Matthew
Mic	Micah
ms/mss	manuscript/manuscripts
MT	Masoretic Text
NAB	New American Bible
Nah	Nahum
n.d.	no date
NEB	New English Bible
Neh	Nehemiah
Nid.	*Niddah*
n.p.	no place
NRSV	New Revised Standard Version
NT	New Testament
Num	Numbers
Num. Rab.	*Numbers Rabbah*
Obad	Obadiah
OG	Old Greek
OL	Old Latin
OT	Old Testament
P	Priestly source in the Pentateuch
p.	page (pl., pp.)
1–2 Pet	1–2 Peter
Phil	Philippians
Phlm	Philemon
Pr Azar	Prayer of Azariah
Pr Man	Prayer of Manasseh
Prov	Proverbs

Ps(s)	Psalm(s)
Q	*Quelle*, a hypothetical source used by Matthew and Luke
Q	Qumran
Qoh	Qoheleth
r.	Reigned
Rab.	*Rabbah*
Rev	Revelation
rev.	Revised
Rom	Romans
RSV	Revised Standard Version
Ruth	Ruth
1–2 Sam	1–2 Samuel
Sanh.	*Sanhedrin*
Sir	Sirach
Song	Song of Solomon
SP	Samaritan Pentateuch
supp.	Supplement
Sus	Susanna
1–2 Thess	1–2 Thessalonians
1–2 Tim	1–2 Timothy
Titus	Titus
Tob	Tobit
v./vv.	verse/verses
vol.	volume (pl., vols.)
Vulg.	Vulgate
Zech	Zechariah
Zeph	Zephaniah

THE OXFORD ENCYCLOPEDIA OF
BIBLICAL INTERPRETATION

A

African American Interpretation

Historical criticism attempts to read texts in their original situations, informed by literary and cultural conventions reconstructed from comparable texts and artifacts. African American interpretation extends this approach to questions about race and social location for the ancient text, its reception history, and its modern readers. It arose as a corrective and alternative to white supremacist use of the Bible in moral and political arguments regarding race, civil rights, and social justice. Accordingly, African American interpretation has combined the insights of abolitionists and activists with academic tools to demonstrate how biblical interpretation can function as an instrument of oppression, obfuscation, or opportunity. Of course, most of these developments have occurred in the larger framework of American Christianity. Yet, its analyses reach beyond that specific setting, touching on the connections between the Bible and race in public discourse generally, whether in government, academia, or popular culture.

White Supremacy, Slavery, and the Bible. The importance of African American interpretation is evident when viewed in light of white supremacy's development in the United States. When propertied white men during the seventeenth and eighteenth centuries were deliberating about their freedoms, they were also creating rationales for not extending those liberties to others—poorer white men, white women, indigenous people, and enslaved blacks from Africa. There were some who saw the hypocrisy of such thinking; some even articulated aspirations for a better day, but such hopes for others were left to the invisible hand of Providence. Meanwhile, their own freedom required immediate protest, collective action, and even war (Fredrickson 2002, pp. 1–47).

Nevertheless, white supremacy did not reach its zenith in the United States until the period stretching from the middle of the nineteenth century to the first half of the twentieth century. This era included a series of episodes centered on the control of African Americans: (a) the debates about slavery before the Civil War, accompanied by a variety of violent incidents; (b) the unconscionable carnage of the Civil War; (c) a hopeful yet eventually ruined Reconstruction; and (d) a time of unchecked terrorist violence to enforce *de jure* and *de facto* segregation (Fredrickson 2002, pp. 49–138).

In each episode, the Bible's interpretation played a central role in arguments for and protests against white supremacy. In arguments over slavery, for instance, defenders and opponents alike confidently cited the Bible (Noll 2006, pp. 31–50). Slavery's supporters could easily point to multiple passages where slavery is regulated and slaves are commanded to submit to their masters (e.g., Exod 21:1–11; Deut 20:10–18; 1 Cor 7:21; Col 3:22; 4:1; 1 Tim 6:1–2; 1 Pet 2:18–25). Thus, for those who considered the Bible a divinely inspired rule book, slavery was obviously morally permissible and its opponents possessed by impiety. Moreover, the belief in black inferiority blinded many to the immorality of this race-based system, not to mention its innumerable abuses such as family breakup and rape.

Conversely, slavery's opponents contended that larger biblical principles should guide the reading of particular passages. These included creation in God's image (Gen 1:26), Jesus's admonitions on mutuality, love, and care for the vulnerable (Matt 7:12; 22:34–40; 25:31–46), human unity before God (Acts 17:26), and the absolution of social barriers for fellow believers in Christ (Gal 3:28). Because of the self-interests of some, the simple view of the Bible for many, and the white supremacy of most, these latter arguments proved unpersuasive. Instead, the resolution "was left to those consummate theologians, the Reverend Doctors Ulysses S. Grant and William Tecumseh Sherman, to decide what in fact the Bible actually means" (Noll 2006, p. 50).

Antebellum Ancestors. One development, however, would have lasting, constructive consequences: the emergence of African American interpretation of the Bible in disputes about their humanity and societal standing (Noll 2006, pp. 64–72). In 1810 Daniel Coker, a founding minister of the African Methodist Episcopal Church, published *A Dialogue between a Virginian and an African Minister*, where he set forth seven arguments from the Bible against slavery. In 1813 Lemuel Haynes, a Congregationalist minister in Vermont, pointed out the contradictions between the outrage over the forced service of American sailors in the War of 1812 and the quiet acceptance of slavery's injustices. David Walker published his famous *Appeal* in 1829, where he argued passionately against slavery on biblical, moral, and historical grounds. Preferring their exegetical arguments, Mark Noll, a historian and an evangelical, concludes that Coker and Haynes "demonstrated that African American biblical reasoning could match in theological acumen the most profound arguments that any white put forward in that period" (p. 73).

Frederick Douglass, marching to the beat of a different drum, mustered unequalled eloquence against biblical and theological defenses of slavery. Although he taught himself and others literacy with the Bible, Douglass understood that it was a treacherous tool of oppression in the hands of racist, pro-slavery whites. So much so that Douglass once publicly argued against raising money for smuggling Bibles to Southern slaves (Callahan 2006, pp. 21–26). "He knew that some people reading the Bible under the slave regime remained tone-deaf to its message of justice" (p. 24). Thus, he found pro-slavery use of the Bible simply loathsome. Indeed, he refused to "play the game" of so-called civil debate. Douglass concluded that the obvious duplicity of slavery's defenders must only be met with derision.

> It would be insulting to Common Sense, an outrage upon all right feeling, for us, who have worn the heavy chain and felt the biting lash to consent to argue with Ecclesiastical Sneaks who are thus prostituting their Religion and Bible to the base uses of popular and profitable iniquity. They don't need light, but the sting of honest rebuke. They are of their father the Devil, and his works they do, not because they are ignorant, but because they are base. (Noll 2006, p. 66)

Still, Douglass did not advocate slave revolt. Other African Americans, however, were unwilling to limit their protests to advocacy in activism, oratory, and print. In 1810, slave brothers in Virginia, Gabriel and Martin, orchestrated a revolt before it was discovered and stopped. Trial testimony indicates that the Bible was a fundamental inspiration for them. In the neighboring state of South Carolina, moved by Bible reading among black Methodists, Denmark Vesey planned a slave revolt on Bastille Day, 14 July 1822. His plot was foiled, and he and thirty-six others were executed. Nine years later in August 1831, back in Virginia, Nat Turner's revolt killed sixty whites, and nearly as many blacks were executed for that uprising. In the aftermath, several states passed laws not only prohibiting African American education but severely restricting unsupervised gatherings. Obviously, when these African Americans considered their circumstances, they did not perceive the Bible as pointing to their perpetual compliance. Instead, they saw themselves as similar to the Israelites in Egypt, awaiting emancipation, and like the Maccabees under Seleucid rule, they considered human agency a legitimate means of freedom (Callahan 2006, pp. 6–10).

Of course, these men were not alone in their protests and revolts against slavery. African American women also resisted the repeated denial of their humanity. Instead of viewing the Bible as a handbook for hierarchy, many of these women saw liberty in its pages. In the latter half of the eighteenth century, Phillis Wheatley, the first African American woman to publish a book of poetry, foresaw redemption in biblical references to salvation for Ethiopia (e.g., Ps 68:31; Callahan 2006, p. 141). Harriet Tubman, who escaped from slavery, was inspired by the account of Israel's exodus from Egypt and was called "Moses" for her work in the Underground Railroad (Callahan pp. 94, 121, 189). Sojourner Truth, a former slave and, later, an abolitionist and advocate for women's rights, contended for the simple truth that she, too, was a woman, worthy of the same recognition given to others. Thus, like Tubman, she anticipated God saving American slaves similar to the stories of deliverances in the Bible (p. 122).

These women and men saw through the prevalent self-serving use of the Bible by the privileged whites of their day. Life experience and keen observation apparently taught them the importance of social location for how one interpreted the Bible. They discerned the interpretive double standard: one approach applied to one set of human beings for the sake of "inalienable rights" and state sovereignty. Yet, a different approach applied to this other set, those deemed subhuman due to skin pigmentation, and whose labor had become essential for the others' economic gain.

Despite learned sophistry to the contrary, these antebellum African Americans knew they were deserving of the same respect as any other human being. For a minister like Coker, a doctorate was not required to understand that more learned theologians like Moses Stuart and James Henley Thornwell were obfuscating the clear meaning of Matt 7:12 in the King James Version: "Therefore all things whatsoever ye would that men should do to you, do ye even so to them: for this is the law and the prophets" (Noll 2006, pp. 56–64, 66). Indeed, three decades before the Civil War, David Walker asked a pointed rhetorical question: "Now, Americans! I ask you candidly, was your sufferings [*sic*] under Great Britain, one hundredth part as cruel and tyrannical as you have rendered ours under you?" (p. 68).

Yet, the resistance of these men and women is only part of the larger picture. The Bible was more than a site of contest in arguments about slavery. African Americans in this era also employed the Bible in creative ways for religious encouragement in song and sermon (Callahan 2006, pp. 10–20). Its language and symbolism were pervasive, providing the threads with which various tapestries were woven as expressions of weal and woe:

> African Americans found the Bible to be both healing balm and poison book. They could not lay claim to the balm without braving the poison. The same book was both medicine and malediction. To afford themselves its healing properties, African Americans resolved to treat scripture with scripture, much like a homeopathic remedy.... Their cure for the toxicity of pernicious scripture was more scripture. The antidote to hostile texts of the Bible was more Bible, homeopathically administered to counteract toxins of the text. (p. 40)

There were also African Americans in this period who did not subscribe to the sentiments of David Walker, Frederick Douglass, or Harriet Tubman. Some heard and understood the Bible in the terms provided by their masters. They were willing to consider that it was indeed their lot to be slaves in submission to a divinely sanctioned system. Perhaps some who took this position were simply looking out for their self-interests, knowing that rebellion was risky, preferring the known over the unknown. Still, whatever their motivations, whether sincere or cynical, some conducted themselves as if they did indeed believe that the Pauline commands of obedience applied directly to them.

In fact, some slaves were so committed to the status quo that they were informants on others plotting insurgence. In one infamous example, several slaves subverted the Stono Rebellion of South Carolina in 1739. One slave named July was so important in stopping that rebellion that he was commended by the state legislature and emancipated with clothes and shoes. Likewise, a house slave named Peter Prioleau helped squelch Denmark Vesey's revolt in 1822. Prioleau was emancipated on Christmas and given an annual pension, which he used for slave purchase (Kennedy 2008, pp. 32–37). These examples illustrate why someone like Douglass was unwilling to raise funds for contraband Bibles sent to Southern slaves. He lamented, "I have met many religious colored people, at the South, who are under the delusion that God requires them to submit to slavery and to wear chains with meekness and humility" (Callahan, p. 23).

The Bible's interpretation among African Americans before the Civil War demonstrates how thoroughly so many of them understood the importance of social location. Many of the best black thinkers in this period were creative and critical "masters of suspicion" in their scrutiny of the complex relationship between text, reader, and community. They modeled what would become the subject of academic debate decades later: the Bible (like any text) does not necessarily have a definitive, discernable meaning, which is universally accessible and applicable. Rather, its meaning is largely determined by a community of interpreters who are morally accountable for how they arrange and apply that interpretation. This is particularly the case with an anthology of discrete books like the Bible, whose texts do not literally speak without the agency of human interpreters. Thus, appeal to the text as an independent authority is simply a way of obscuring, intentionally or unintentionally, the decisive role of interpreters. Long before literary theorists like Stanley Fish were raising critical questions about the role of interpretive communities in determining textual meaning (Fish 1982), African Americans were asking, "Is there a text on this plantation?"

Social Location after Slavery. This stance of suspicion toward the predominate interpretation of the Bible continued as racism became worse and more violent in the first half of the twentieth century. After the Civil War, white terrorism included the lynching of more than 3,400 African Americans from 1882 to 1944 (Dray 2002). In addition, as Douglas Blackmon argued in his Pulitzer Prize–winning book *Slavery by Another Name* (2008), in many respects slavery did not cease with the war in 1865. Instead, a vast public/private system was orchestrated to virtually re-enslave a significant segment of African American men. Blackmon concludes that slavery was not effectively over until the 1940s.

In fact, after the celebrated struggles and successes of the civil rights movement, culminating with landmark legislation in 1964–1965, the power of racism over the lives of African Americans still did not come to an end. It did become more oblique, however. This shows up in paradoxical developments after that pivotal period. On the one hand, American society has made tremendous progress in reducing societal impediments based on race. The opportunities that became available for African Americans have been significant and should not be minimized. This progress recently reached a symbolic plateau unforeseen by many with the election in 2008 and re-election in 2012 of Barack Obama, the first African American president.

On the other hand, these strides were often marked by setbacks. The setbacks were, in fact, reactions to the progress. In response to employment gains for African Americans in government, educational, and privates sectors, for instance, there was a significant controversy around affirmative-action policies, a related rise in resentments by whites, and concomitant complaints by African Americans about subtle racial bias among professionals and police. These tensions set the stage for momentous turmoil in the 1990s, as seen in the riots that occurred in Los Angeles in 1992 after police were acquitted of criminal charges despite video recording of their beating of Rodney King. Likewise, substantial racial strife arose after O.J. Simpson was acquitted in 1995, also in Los Angeles. These racially tinged events in the American West some three decades after the civil rights movement led one white biblical scholar to write a brief critique of racism. In his judgment, "The O.J. trial . . . exploded the myth that racism in America is confined to the South. And the truth is that his trial is only the most public example of the racism and racial division that exist nationwide" (McKenzie 1997, p. vii).

The conflicting perceptions around the presidential election in 2008 also illustrate the dilemma of racial progress. Many political observers contend that reactions to that presidential campaign were clearly imbued with overt racism and indirect racial bias. Further, some argue that President Obama's racial identity has actually made it more difficult for him to address race-related issues. Thus, even an event of this magnitude becomes a two-edged sword, revealing stirring progress and persistent prejudice, simultaneously (Kennedy 2011).

This dynamic is not limited to political elections, either. In other areas, it is actually more troubling and consequential but admittedly more difficult to discern. For one willing to look closely, though, one can observe how social policies significantly affecting urban areas after the late 1960s were reactions to the gains of the civil rights movement. These urban centers, such as Detroit, Cleveland, and, again, parts of Los Angeles, have become more dilapidated and dysfunctional, with the influx of illegal drugs, a corresponding increase in prison sentencing for drug-related crimes, and an extensive exodus in jobs and taxes by middle-class whites and blacks.

These debilitating aspects have had a disproportionate impact on poorer African Americans who inhabit these spaces. Several social scientists, in fact, contend that these dysfunctional sites are the outgrowth of a segregationist past coupled with the evolution of a nuanced racial stigma, now augmented and diffused by socioeconomic class. Incomparable incarceration rates for African American men demonstrate the depth of these deleterious factors. The numbers have skyrocketed since the civil rights movement, the Black Power movement, and the race riots in the late 1960s. "The US prison population is larger than at any time in the history of the penitentiary anywhere in the world. Nearly half of the more than two million Americans behind bars are African Americans, and an unprecedented number of black men will likely go to prison during the course of their lives" (Muhammad 2010, p. 1).

Inheritance in the Academy. These larger sociohistorical developments provide the setting for academic interpretation of the Bible among African Americans. Yet, no African American held a doctorate in biblical studies before World War II. In 1945, though, Leon Edward Wright became the first African American to earn a PhD in New Testament from Harvard. He went on to serve as a professor for more than thirty years at Howard University in Washington, D.C. Two years later, Charles B. Copher earned a PhD in Hebrew Bible from Boston University. He joined the faculty at the Interdenominational Theological Center (ITC) in Atlanta, teaching there for more than five decades. In 1953 Joseph A. Johnson was the first African American student in the Vanderbilt Divinity School in Nashville and received his PhD in NT five years later, the third African American to earn a doctorate in biblical studies. Johnson also taught at ITC, later becoming president of its Christian Methodist institution, Phillips School of Theology (Wimbush 2010, p. 8, n. 4).

As these pioneers instructed seminarians at historically black institutions in the 1960s, they witnessed young African Americans moving away from the integrationist emphasis of the civil rights movement. Instead, there was a turn to Black Nationalism, which included a focus on the contributions of African Americans, an affirmation of physical blackness, and a celebration of origins in Africa. During this time, many African American Christians were criticized heavily by other African Americans and often told that their religion was "the white man's religion." This accusation came from Black Nationalists generally and from the Nation of Islam in particular, perhaps most powerfully expressed by Malcolm X before his split with Elijah Muhammad.

James Cone articulated a response with the publication of *Black Theology and Black Power* in 1969 and *A Black Theology of Liberation* in 1970. Cone created a theological approach that addressed African Americans and their societal concerns. He emphasized "black theology" as an affirmation of black suffering and in opposition to white oppression. This blackness was not just about skin color; it was about a condition in a society still characterized by white supremacy despite premature self-congratulations after the civil rights movement. This was a theology of "blackness" in terms of the downtrodden, those left to languish in cities wrecked by riots just a few years earlier. Accordingly, there would be no salvation for white American Christians until they rejected the privilege of whiteness and identified with blackness instead. For Cone, that is the meaning of the Christian cross at that particular moment in American history.

Black biblical scholars began to argue for a "black presence" in the Bible as a complement to and support for the aims of black theology. Moreover, in the larger setting of Black Nationalism, African Americans sought to identify black heroes as a source of pride as well as a counter to claims of inferiority. In this logic, if black people are equal, then history should be replete with examples of black greatness, examples that have been denied, suppressed, or stolen by a distorted history. Given the place of the Bible in American religion and culture, it became an important site of contest about race and misrepresentations. To a certain degree, this was entirely appropriate given the pervasiveness of white images in biblically focused movies, books, and art. Too often, Jesus looked like a man from Norway rather than from Nazareth (Blum and Harvey 2012).

Charles Copher can be identified as "the parent of modern day scholarly study of 'Blacks in the Bible'" (Bailey 2000, p. 697). Writing in the 1970s and under the influence of John Bright's historiography, Copher assumed a general reliability for the biblical accounts, beginning with the list of nations in Genesis 10. He endeavored to show that several of the places mentioned there and in the rest of the Bible could be identified as locations in Africa and thus the inhabitants should be considered black. In ironic contrast to the disparaging deployment of Ham by white supremacists, Copher identified Ham in Genesis 10:6–14 as a black African, and the sons of Ham delineated there—Egypt, Cush, Put, and Canaan—were also black. Thus, blacks were not cursed for slavery but were important, respected, and valued (Bailey 2000, pp. 697–698; Brown 2004, pp. 24–34).

Cain Hope Felder employed a similar approach in the 1980s and 1990s, noting that Southwest Asia and North Africa are generally populated by people of color, however dark or light in complexion. The people who lived in those areas were not white Europeans. Thus, the Egyptians with their great accomplishments should be understood as people of color (Felder 1989). Similarly, the Ethiopian queen and her official mentioned in Acts 8:26, for instance, were people of color. When Joseph, Mary, and Jesus had to flee for safety, they fled to Egypt in North Africa (pp. 12–14). Again and again, one can see the presence and importance of people of color in the Bible.

Felder's approach dovetailed nicely with an emphasis on multiculturalism in education during the 1990s. As he traveled and explained these issues, he often found receptive audiences; his success was complemented by editing an important collection of essays by African American scholars (Felder, 1991). In addition, Felder published *The Original African Heritage Study Bible* (KJV) in 1993, with annotations addressing the black presence in the Bible.

The impact of this study Bible was as much about psychological uplift as it was about scholarly specifics. To be sure, Felder could argue his point. Yet, in some respects, that was not the most important effect, at least not on a sociocultural level. African Americans had seen nothing but images of whites in biblical depictions for centuries. Now, finally, credentialed scholars were saying that such a picture was incomplete at best, and racist at worse. Felder's Afrocentric approach resonated and provided a helpful psychosocial defense against persistently negative images of African Americans. Understood in these terms, one can appreciate the efforts of Felder, and of Copher before him. In retrospect, one can also recognize legitimate criticisms and preferable alternatives (Bailey 2000, pp. 698; Brown 2004, pp. 35–53).

For African American scholars entering biblical studies in the 1990s and since, the conversation has changed significantly. For one, it was important to extend the conversation beyond a male-centered one on race and identity. A full picture of how the biblical text has been and can be employed must address gender as well as race and interrogate how gender and race may be intertwined or separated to different effects. This applies to the ancient biblical text as well as its interpretation by modern men and women. Attempting to take account of these complexities is one distinctive aspect of womanist interpretation compared to feminist criticism (Martin, 1991; Weems, 1991).

African American biblical scholars are also asking larger historical and cultural questions about the function of the Bible in diverse black communities, past and present. How has the Bible functioned? To what effect? To whose benefit? Moreover, does the Bible even deserve its sacred standing? Randall Bailey, Hugh Page, Brian Blount, and Vincent Wimbush have consistently pressed these and other questions. Besides their individual publications, each of these scholars has edited an impressive collection of essays on African American biblical interpretation. Each collection pushes past traditional conceptions of what constitutes biblical scholarship. In chapter after chapter in these edited volumes, biblical interpretation is engaged alongside literature, art, politics, music, and larger sociopolitical issues.

Brian Blount has also published several books on biblical interpretation and the African American church (1998; 2001; 2005). In addition, he is now the first African American president of Union Theological Seminary in Richmond, Virginia. In 2010 Vincent Wimbush became the first African American to serve as president of the Society of Biblical Literature. Characteristically, he pressed the guild "to start and to sustain 'talkin' 'bout somethin'" (2010, p. 9).

The Contribution of African American Interpretation. In sum, contemporary African American scholars of the Bible have adapted their antebellum inheritance in diverse ways, while remaining faithful to key aspects of it. They continue to employ biblical interpretation as a community-centered counter to various forms of bias and marginalization. Accordingly, they have resisted the strictures of so-called mainstream scholarship and its definition of what constitutes valuable contributions. They have repeatedly demonstrated an awareness of and some allegiance to the pressing needs and concerns of the African American communities that produced them. They have understood that calls from the guild to do "typical" scholarship certainly have their place, especially for professional advancement and security. Yet, such calls can also come from privilege and detachment, luxuries that many African American scholars feel they cannot afford.

[*See also* African Biblical Interpretation; Asian American Biblical Interpretation; Class Criticism; Cross-Cultural Exegesis; Cultural Studies; Race, Ethnicity, and Biblical Criticism; *and* Womanist Interpretation]

BIBLIOGRAPHY

Bailey, Randall C. "Academic Biblical Interpretation among African Americans in the United States." In *African Americans and the Bible: Sacred Texts and Social Textures,* edited by Vincent Wimbush, 696–711. New York: Continuum, 2000.

Bailey, Randall C. "Beyond Identification: The Use of Africans in Old Testament Poetry and Narratives." In *Stony the Road We Trod: African American Biblical Interpretation,* edited by Cain Hope Felder, 165–184. Minneapolis, D.C.: Fortress, 1991.

Bailey, Randall C., Tat-siong Benny Liew, and Fernando F. Segovia, eds. *They Were All Together in One Place? Toward Minority Biblical Criticism.* Atlanta: Society of Biblical Literature, 2009.

Blackmon, Douglas A. *Slavery by Another Name: The Re-Enslavement of Black America from the Civil War to World War II.* New York: Doubleday, 2008.

Blount, Brian K. *Can I Get a Witness?: Reading Revelation through African American Culture.* Louisville, KY.: Westminster/John Knox, 2005.

Blount, Brian K. *Cultural Interpretation: Reorienting New Testament Criticism.* Minneapolis: Fortress, 1995.

Blount, Brian K. *Go Preach!: Mark's Kingdom Message and the Black Church Today*. Maryknoll, N.Y.: Orbis, 1998.
Blount, Brian K. *Revelation: A Commentary*. The New Testament Library. Louisville, KY.: Westminster/John Knox, 2009.
Blount, Brian K. *Then the Whisper Put on Flesh: New Testament Ethics in an African American Context*. Nashville: Abingdon, 2001.
Blount, Brian K., ed. *True to Our Native Land: An African American New Testament Commentary*. Minneapolis: Fortress, 2007.
Blum, Edward J., and Paul Harvey. *The Color of Christ: The Son of God and the Saga of Race in America*. Chapel Hill: University of North Carolina Press, 2012.
Brown, Michael Joseph. *Blackening of the Bible: The Aims of African American Biblical Scholarship*. New York: Trinity Press International, 2004.
Callahan, Allen Dwight. *The Talking Book: African Americans and the Bible*. New Haven, Conn.: Yale University Press, 2006.
Dray, Philip. *At the Hands of Persons Unknown: The Lynching of Black America*. New York: Random House, 2002.
Felder, Cain Hope, ed. *Stony the Road We Trod: African American Biblical Interpretation*. Minneapolis: Fortress, 1991.
Felder, Cain Hope. *Troubling Biblical Waters: Race, Class, and Family*. Maryknoll N.Y.: Orbis, 1989.
Fish, Stanley. *Is There a Text in This Class? The Authority of Interpretive Communities*. Cambridge, Mass.: Harvard University Press, 1982.
Fredrickson, George M. *Racism: A Short History*. Princeton N.J.: Princeton University Press, 2002.
Kennedy, Randall. *The Persistence of the Color Line: Racial Politics and the Obama Presidency*. New York: Vintage, 2011.
Kennedy, Randall. *Sellout: The Politics of Racial Betrayal*. New York: Vintage, 2008.
Martin, Clarice. "The Haustafeln (Household Codes) in African American Biblical Interpretation: 'Free Slaves' and 'Subordinate Women.'" In *Stony the Road We Trod: African American Biblical Interpretation*, edited by Cain Hope Felder, 206–231. Minneapolis: Fortress, 1991.
McKenzie, Steven L. *All God's Children: A Biblical Critique of Racism*. Louisville, KY.: Westminster/John Knox, 1997.
Muhammad, Khalil Gibran. *The Condemnation of Blackness: Race, Crime, and the Making of Modern Urban America*. Cambridge, Mass.: Harvard University Press, 2010.
Noll, Mark A. *The Civil War as a Theological Crisis*. Chapel Hill: University of North Carolina Press, 2006.
Page, Hugh R., ed. *The Africana Bible: Reading Israel's Scriptures from Africa and the African Diaspora*. Minneapolis: Fortress, 2010.
Weems, Renita J. "Reading *Her* Way Through the Struggle: African American Women and the Bible." In *Stony the Road We Trod: African American Biblical Interpretation*, edited by Cain Hope Felder, 57–77. Minneapolis: Fortress, 1991.
Wimbush, Vincent, ed. *African Americans and the Bible: Sacred Texts and Social Textures*. New York: Continuum, 2000.
Wimbush, Vincent. "Interpreters—Enslaving/Enslaved/Runagate." *Journal of Biblical Literature* 130 (2010): 5–24.
Wimbush, Vincent. "We Will Make Our Own Future Text: An Alternate Orientation to Interpretation." In *True to Our Native Land: An African American New Testament Commentary*. edited by Brian Blount, 63–72. Minneapolis: Fortress, 2007.

Joseph Scrivner

African Biblical Interpretation

African biblical interpretation is a thriving enterprise in and out of the academy, from the ancient past to contemporary times and is best articulated in the volumes edited by West and Dube (2000), Dube (2001), and Dube, Mbuvi, and Mbuwayesango (2012) that largely inform all the sections of this article. From the earliest Bible translations, such as the Septuagint/LXX of Alexandria (ca. third century B.C.E.) and the Ethiopian Ge'ez Bible of the fourth century C.E., to multiple biblical translations of modern times attest that the Bible has been read and interpreted in the African continent in various frameworks as Christianity continues to grow. While we are yet to fully capture all the frameworks of African biblical interpretations, some of its characteristics include: (1) reading the Bible with and through African cultural perspectives; (2) reading the Bible for liberation; (3) reading the Bible within the African context and addressing the communal issues of well-being; (4) studying various Bible readers for possible frameworks of interpretation;

(5) addressing the link between the Bible and colonialism; (6) utilizing both African and Western ways of reading the Bible; and (7) collaborating with people of African descent in the Diaspora (Dube, Mbuvi, and Mbuwayesango 2012, pp. 63–84). Given the historical link of the Bible with colonialism in Sub-Saharan Africa and the continuing challenges confronting the continent, African biblical interpretation is at once a postcolonial practice and a quest for emancipation. Gosbert Byamungu thus underlines, "It is the task of the African scholar to engage the world in a hermeneutic of emancipation" (2006, p. 228). This article highlights some frameworks of interpreting the Bible in the African continent under the following subheadings:

1. The Saharan Bible,
2. The Inculturation Bible,
3. The Black Liberation Bible,
4. The Reconstruction Bible,
5. The Community Bible,
6. The HIV and AIDS Bible,
7. The Indigenous African Bible,
8. The Oral Bible,
9. The African Earth Bible,
10. The Gendered African Bible,
11. The Colonized Sub-Saharan Bibles, and
12. The Pentecostal Bible.

These subheadings, underline that both the method and context of study are not only used to illuminate the biblical texts but interactively illuminate each other. Further, these listed frameworks of interpretation are not exclusive as attested by the above listed cross-cutting common features and concerns.

The Saharan Bible. The Saharan Bible is a framework that consists of several reading practices. It may involve underlying African historical involvement with biblical history. Interpretation in the Sahara highlights African lands and characters in the Bible. These characters' depiction by Western scholars in translations, commentaries, maps, and scholarly books are studied to expose the racist and colonial ideologies that have informed their depiction, as well as to give new readings. Consequently, studies may explore such characters as Hagar, Ham, Moses, Queen of Sheba, the Ethiopian Eunuch, and such geographical locations as the Nile and the ideological construction of the Saharan Africa as separate from the rest of the continent. That the Matthean Jesus and his parents are presented as having sought refuge in Egypt until Jesus was fully grown, underlines the centrality of African lands and contribution to the biblical thought. This approach serves several ends. First, it counteracts the colonial and racist position of denying people of African descent any history. Second, it highlights how racist and colonial ideologies have permeated Bible translations by informed commentators among Western scholars of the Bible. Third, it contests the tendency for academic biblical studies to focus on Greco-Roman history and philosophy as the normative context for biblical interpretation as a Eurocentric approach, which is consistent with racist perspectives of erasing Africa and Africans in the Bible and history in general. Fourth, it seeks to give new translations, commentaries, and scholarly interpretations of the Bible that are not Eurocentric. This framework has been pioneered by African Americans, but African scholars in the continent have also warmed up to the approach as evidenced by Tuesday Adamo's work, among others (2001).

The Saharan Bible framework also highlights the contribution of African people to biblical interpretation by pointing out that some of the major church fathers were people of African descent. The Bible, Christianity, and biblical interpretation were not newly introduced to Africa in modern times as claimed by eighteenth- and nineteenth-century colonizers. Justin S. Ukpong holds that:

> Africa can rightly be referred to as the cradle of systematic biblical interpretation in Christianity. The earliest such attempt can be traced to the city of Alexandria and to such names as Clement of Alexandria, Origen, and others who lived and worked there. The foundations laid by this tradition, which were largely allegorical and uncritical in the modern sense, lasted in the Western Church until the onset of

> the Enlightenment. It was replaced by the historical critical method in the eighteenth century. (2000, p. 11)

Further, the Saharan Bible contributes to translation studies. It has become increasingly clear that translation is a form of interpretation, and any interpretation derives from a particular context, perspective, and agenda. These ancient Bible translations provide us with case studies for observing interpretation at work in translation as well as investigating the ideologies and power relations that informed the project. Given the proliferation of African Bible translations that occurred during the modern colonial period, this area is vital (see The Colonialized Sub-Saharan Bibles).

The Inculturation Bible. An inculturation framework locates the Bible within African cultures where it is read or heard. This approach was pioneered by the African Instituted Churches, which broke away from the colonially founded churches because of being denied leadership on the basis of their race and alienated from their African cultures. The colonial missionary gospel required converts to turn their backs on their cultures, for the latter were regarded as incompatible with biblical religion and Western civilization. African converts did not share the same view. Kimba Vita (1684–1706), a Congolese woman, is held to be the founder of African Instituted Churches. Not only did she revert to the oral canon by claiming to be possessed by the spirit of Saint Anthony, she also proclaimed that biblical characters, such Jesus and his disciples, were black, at the same time insisting that the white, blond images of biblical figures in her Roman Catholic Church should be dismounted because they were idolatry. Kimba Vita not only interpreted biblical characters as black—thus resisting the colonial ideology that associated whiteness with godliness while constructing blackness as its counterforce—she also contextualized biblical places by locating them within her own country. Kimba Vita also held that God will restore the subjugated kingdom of Congo, thereby taking an openly political stance. Her approach led her to crucifixion. Placing the inculturation framework of reading within this history is to acknowledge its oppositional and postcolonial foundation (Antonio 2006, p. 1). This historical practice of mixing African cultures with biblical scriptures highlights its hybridity.

African biblical scholars, who were and still work largely in a postcolonial context, began to tour the inculturation path of African Instituted Churches in a quest to be relevant to their contexts and communities of readers. According to Antonio (2006, pp. 28–56), the scholarly inculturation approach has taken various practices, ranging from conservative to reformative and even to radical ways of reading. The approach was sometimes comparative, highlighting continuities, discontinuities, and cross-fertilization between the two traditions. The conservative inculturist's approach sought to highlight African cultures as the preparatory stage for establishing the gospel. They approached the Bible and African cultures through the metaphor of clothing, holding that African cultures are needed for dressing up and presenting the Bible in an acceptable manner to African people. Sometimes the metaphor of marriage between the gospel and African cultures was used. Generally, African indigenous cultures were subjugated to biblical texts and served the purpose of advancing the latter. The inculturation framework for reformatives who seek to make some modest changes from within, was seen as an expression of the incarnation, for the Word did dwell among us, within our cultures. The radical inculturists insisted that African cultures and the Bible are treasures of the same weight. Canaan Banana, for example, called for the rewriting of the Bible to include other religious traditions, maintaining that God's revelation did not begin and end with the biblical traditions but was also experienced in various other traditions (Banana 1993). Seratwa Ntloedibe-Kuswani has also insisted on reading the figure of Christ and the African indigenous doctor as compatriots (Ntloedibe-Kuswani 2000, pp. 498–510). Yet more than just resistance, the inculturation framework signifies that the Bible in Africa exists and is read with the canon of African cultures—the Bible has not and will not displace African cultures, but it must coexist with them. The challenge confronting the inculturation approach is the need to transcend the sometimes dualistic and comparative approaches to capture the hybridity of the Bible in African cultures as championed by African Instituted Churches.

African women readers have made important contributions to the inculturation framework by introducing the category of gender. While African male scholars tended to construct inculturation readings that were patriarchal, African women insisted on a gender-sensitive practice. A good example was the reading of Jesus as an African male ancestor while most African cultures recognize a community of ancestors as intermediaries, which embrace both genders. Counteracting the patriarchy of African Christianities, women readings constructed gender-inclusive and communal Christologies. In 2002 Musimbi Kanyoro published a book on gender-sensitive inculturation, which she named as "feminist cultural hermeneutics." The work of Mercy A. Oduyoye (2004) in general represents one of the best articulations of inculturation interpretations.

The Black Liberation Bible. The black biblical framework of interpretation is associated with the South African history of the struggle for liberation from colonial and apartheid structures. Given their race-based economic oppression, this framework identified with the African American biblical readings expressed in black theology. Itumeleng Mosala (1989) best illustrates this reading. Given that apartheid was a racist ideology, which sought to justify the economic exploitation of black people by creating classes on the basis of color, black biblical interpretation drew from black consciousness to construct emancipatory reading and utilized Marxist theory to understand and highlight the relationship between various classes, thus empowering the oppressed to seek transformation. In his chapter "Ownership or Non-Ownership of Land" Mosala holds that:

> A Black Theological reading of the Bible is at the same time an ideological reading.... The real question is: in the interest of which social class, race, culture, and gender is the reading conducted?... Black Theology insists on a critical historical and biblical hermeneutics of liberation. No culture of the Bible is automatically liberating. No culture of black society is automatically liberation. The task of the biblical cultural worker involved in the struggle for freedom from poverty is to liberate the Bible so that the Bible can liberate us. (1997, pp. 62–63)

The Black Liberation Bible was not just an academic discourse but was drawn from the history and context of oppression experienced by the black majority on the basis of their color. It sought to usher concrete change into the lives of the oppressed and the history of South Africa as a whole. The champions of black biblical interpretation were, therefore, community leaders such as Allen Boesak and Desmond Tutu. The Bible's commitment to a justice-loving society and to reading in solidarity with the oppressed communities is best characterized by the Kairos Document (1985, pp. 61–81). In the post-apartheid context, black biblical interpretation must be sought among those who read the Bible from the perspective of truth and reconciliation, in the context of a rainbow nation, and with the attempt to learn from the inculturation biblical hermeneutics.

Given the gender-insensitive Marxist theory and the patriarchal Bible, black biblical interpretation discourse was class- and race- conscious but was not always committed to gender justice. South African women biblical scholars such as Madipoane Masenya, Sarojini Nadar, and Gloria Plaatjie (see Dube 2001, pp. 114–158; Dube, Mbuvi, and Mbuwayesango 2012, pp. 43–62, 283–298, 389–408) have made commendable efforts to articulate gender-inclusive black biblical interpretation through perspectives that restore experiences of South African women of color and their participation in the struggle for liberation. Pushing the button for a liberation-oriented reading, Gloria Plaatjie argues that the South African inclusive constitution should become a canon that should be read together with the Bible in order to educate and empower South African women to live out their hard-earned liberation from oppression (Dube 2001, pp. 134–140).

The Reconstruction Bible. Reconstruction biblical readings highlight a time of hope for the future in the African continent. The perspective arose at the end of apartheid and the emergence of globalization. The latter was seen, by some, as creating a level playing field. With all African countries liberated from their colonial rule, it was the end of colonialism and a time for reconstruction. The framework of liberation that drew from the Exodus story was no longer appropriate. Instead, a new scriptural framework, which represented the new context of rebuilding after long exploitation and sometimes destructive wars, was necessary. The books of Ezra–Nehemiah and their call for rebuilding the walls of Jerusalem were seen as more suitable, hence the reconstruction framework of interpretation. Some of the weaknesses, however, are in the foundation of this framework; for example, the assumption that the end of colonial rule meant freedom from former colonial domination; that globalization meant a level playing field for all parties; and its uncritical reading of Ezra–Nehemiah books (Dube, Mbuvi, and Mbuwayesango 2012, pp. 331–388).

The Community Bible. The African community Bible explores various strategies that underline the agency of African readers and highlights the frameworks of reading they provide or seek to read in solidarity with the disempowered communities (West and Dube 1996). It covers readers from the past centuries to the present and from outside the academic biblical guild, such as creative writers and artists. Works that explore readers from the past and the structures they provide include the analysis of Kimba Vita and women in African Instituted Churches for articulating a postcolonial feminist reading of Batswana kings' oppositional response to colonial missionary biblical interpretations, descriptions of Queen Mmahutu and Shembe, and the exploration of the first literate Basotho readers of colonial times, featured in West and Dube (2000, pp. 221–235) and Dube, Mbuvi, and Mbuwayesango (2012 pp. 1–28, 75–154). As more archival documents become available in various regions and countries, more work must be done to analyze the first African interpretations of the Bible. A significant area, perhaps best exemplified by the work of John and Jean Comaroff (1991; 1997), is the need to comprehend the modern colonial biblical interpretations. The Comaroff's work in historical anthropology (reading modern missionary documents of Southern Africa) highlights that biblical interpretation was a contested practice engineered through the school, the hospital, the plow, the well, architecture, and clothes; in effect, more like David Livingstone's promotion of the gospel of three Cs—Christianity, civilization, and commerce. Examples of explorations of biblical interpretations among creative writers and artists are featured in West and Dube (2000, pp. 163–183) and Dube, Mbuvi, and Mbuwayesango (2012, pp. 115–154, 389–440). This framework includes those contemporary readers in search of liberating strategies, those in solidarity with the disadvantaged, as well as addressing the power relations between the academic and nonacademic readers (West and Dube 1996).

The HIV and AIDS Bible. Reading the Bible within the HIV and AIDS context is reading for liberation and in solidarity with the oppressed members and communities, for it is an epidemic that largely attacks the poor and the socially discriminated members of our world. Worldwide documentations of HIV and AIDS indicate that it is an epidemic within other social epidemics. Thus statistics indicate that the most vulnerable members are women, black people, youth, third-world nations, populations in conflict zones, drug addicts, and gay men. Two-thirds of the millions infected and those who have died of HIV and AIDS are counted within the African continent. The rest of the uninfected African populations are affected by grief, loss, burdens of caregiving for sick or orphaned children, and the crisis of the meaning of life where the future can no longer be taken for granted.

Reading the Bible in the light of HIV and AIDS thus became imperative as affected and infected communities sought meaning and healing. The approach includes identifying how biblical texts, alone or in conjunction with other traditions, are part of the problem and making efforts to re-read for healing. Basic techniques such as reading the Bible for prevention, reducing HIV and AIDS stigma and discrimination, quality care, and access to treatment in solidarity with those infected and affected are applied. In particular, HIV and AIDS biblical interpretation underlines that exposure to injustice is also exposure to ill health. It demands creation of healing communities as creation of justice-oriented relationships. In addition, HIV and AIDS biblical interpretation calls for a socially engaged scholarship that seeks and dreams with the wider community for a healing and healed world. For an evaluative work, see the chapter "'*Go tla Siama. O tla Fola*': Doing Biblical Studies in an HIV and AIDS Context" in *Postcolonial Perspectives* (Dube, Mbuvi, and Mbuwayesango 2012, pp. 483–508).

The Indigenous African Bible. The indigenous Bible features vernacular frameworks of reading. It highlights some African philosophical frameworks of knowledge production and analysis of social relations, and how they have been and can be put to work in interpreting biblical texts. Some of the methods include storytelling, divination, proverbs, sayings, and songs. Storytelling has been a significant mode of communication in teaching, commenting, and analyzing social situations in African communities as attested by the role of folktale. The Bible has been received among African communities as another set of stories in addition to the prevailing canon of African indigenous stories. The African Instituted Churches also champion biblical interpretation through storytelling (Dube, 1996, 111–129), and African biblical scholars are in the process of theorizing storytelling and applying it as a mode of biblical interpretation. The edited volume *Other Ways of Reading: African Women and the Bible* set out to document and theorize indigenous ways of reading, featuring a number of examples. These include the interpretation of the story of Esther through and with Northern Sotho folktales and proverbs; the reading of Mark 5:21–43 through a Ndebele folktale, and African stories of living with colonialism and HIV and AIDS; an analysis of the assumptions and processes of divination in Southern African indigenous thinking and theorizing it as a framework of reading and an exploration of African proverbs, sayings, and concepts for reading the biblical texts (Dube 2001, pp. 27–52, 145–158, 179–178). Jeremy Punt (2004, pp. 83–101) explores the concept of *Ubuntu* (humanness as measured by the capacity to treat other people with respect and dignity) and its communal ethics as articulated in popular phrase, *uMuntu ngu muntu ga bantu* ("a person is only human with and through other people") and how its philosophy can inform biblical reading. The concept has also been explored for reading the Bible for building compassionate communities in the context of HIV and AIDS stigma.

The Oral Bible. African communities and cultures are largely oral. The Bible is thus read in, with, and through African oral cultures and their frameworks of knowledge production, storage, and analysis. How does the orality of African communities inform the interpretative practices? Field work among African Instituted Churches (Dube 1996, pp. 111–126) indicated that some church members read the text aloud to those who could not read but who indeed heard it. Those who hear the Bible demonstrate a high skill of memorizing biblical references and recounting the stories almost word for word. Recounting passages, repeating particular phrases for emphasis, interjecting thematically relevant songs, community participation, and performance are all integral techniques of interpretation.

The sub-Saharan oral Bible bursts the pages of the written Bible and often subverts the written texts. Examples include women leaders who say they are able to assume leadership, despite the patriarchal Bible because, when God speaks to them, God does not open the Bible! Thus, the women refer to dreams, visions, and hearing God speaking and authorizing them to undertake leadership (Dube, p. 194). Similarly, readers from the African Instituted Churches resorted to the oral culture to subvert the colonial translation that had equated ancestors with demons, by reinstating ancestors to their divine status through using the Bible for divination, and by continuing to maintain veneration of the ancestors in their healing practices (Dube 1999, pp. 55–56). African oral interpretation is also applied to analyze how the first biblical recipients may have heard and interpreted the text.

The African Earth Bible. Given that the sub-Saharan Bible is undeniably a postcolonial Bible, it is inseparably entwined with the land question. Pointing out that the Bible "was used to justify the conquest and dispossession of people of their land," Paul Germond asks, "How often has it been said in African history: 'when the missionaries came we had the land and they had the Bible. They taught us how to pray. When we opened our eyes they had our land and we were left holding their Bible?'" (Germond 1997, pp. 190). Takatso Mofokeng thus asks, "Can the Bible . . . that has been used to attack black lives and land also serve as trustworthy and credible source for the struggle to reverse that attack? If so, what kind of reading . . . will produce the needed weapons?" (Mofokeng 1997, p. 50). The postcolonial quest for return of land to the dispossessed is by no means anthropocentric activity, for with colonial dispossession and the creation of poverty among the colonized, the environment was subjugated to oppression, when indigenous people and their domestic animals were overcrowded in already infertile areas, leading to overgrazing, deforestation, soil erosion, and pollution. The colonized earth is thus exploited and oppressed.

Given that the colonial enterprise was to separate, alienate, and dispossess African people from their lands, an important part of reclaiming the land is to reunite with it. This is best captured by Thabo Mbeki's speech, associated with African Renaissance, which begins:

> I am an African! I owe my being to the hills and the valleys, the mountains and the glades, the rivers, the deserts, the trees, the flowers, the seas and the ever-changing seasons that define the face of our native land. My body has frozen in our frosts and in our latter day snows. It has thawed in the warmth of our sunshine and melted in the heat of the midday sun. The crack and the rumble of the summer thunders, lashed by startling lightening, have been a cause both of trembling and of hope. (2004, pp. 9–13)

The modern colonial discourse that constructed African people as meshed and inseparable from nature sought to justify dispossession. The construction, however, sought to present them as underdeveloped infants, stuck at the very beginning of time, hence in need of their colonizing parents to nurse them to maturity. Mbeki's construction, on the other hand, serves to reclaim what was stolen partly through the Bible. The Zimbabwean case of the past two decades shows that the question of land has not been solved for many African countries that have gained independence from the former colonizers. Several articles in *Postcolonial Perspectives in African Biblical Interpretations* focus on the land, highlighting that the African Earth Bible is read through the land and the land is read through the Bible (Dube, Mbuvi, and Mbuwayesango 2012, pp. 221–248). Yet the oppression of the earth is closely related to the oppression of women, who are closely related to the land. Consequently, Oduyoye is one of the best in centering the earth in her reading of the Bible and theological construction (Oduyoye 2004).

The Gendered African Bible. Factoring gender in African biblical interpretation has been championed by the founding of the Circle of Concerned African Women Theologians, launched in 1989 by Mercy A. Oduyoye. The academic association sought to create a space for African women studying any religious faith to research, write, and publish together from perspectives of liberation as well as to create a space for mentoring younger women interested in this scholarship. Not only have African women biblical scholars been pushing and crossing the boundaries of prevailing African frameworks of reading the text such as inculturation, black biblical interpretation, and Western feminism, they have also been in the forefront of articulating new ways of reading the Bible.

Postcolonial Perspectives in African Biblical Interpretations opens with the a section that highlights African women's contribution: Oduyoye and Kanyoro have developed a feminist inculturation perspective; Masenya has developed the *Bosadi* (womanhood) reading framework; Teresa Okure has constructed a theory of reading for and from a position that ethically supports life in its fullness; and Dube has constructed a postcolonial feminist way of reading the Bible for decolonization and liberating interdependence (Dube, Mbuvi, and Mbuwayesango 2012, pp. 1–74). Collectively, through the Circle agenda, African women have been at the forefront of constructing perspectives of reading the Bible through the HIV and AIDS story—since women are at the center of the storm of this epidemic (Dube and Kanyoro 2004). Given the proliferation of Pentecostal churches and their influence on women's lives, the construction of Pentecostal feminist ways of reading the Bible are being articulated (Nadar 2005).

One area that needs attention in the gendered African Bible is the articulation of Queer African biblical interpretations. Some work toward this end has already begun. Paul Germond explores the six problematic biblical texts (Gen. 19:1–29; Lev. 18:22, 20:13; Rom. 1:18–32; 1 Cor. 6:9 and 1 Tim. 1:8–11) concerning homosexuality, problematizes reading practices that assume normativity of heterosexuality, and suggests a liberating, inclusive framework of reading (1997, pp. 186–232); Jeremy Punt reads Romans 1:18–32, searching for interpretative options (2007, pp. 965–982) and explores theoretical convergences and divergences of postcolonial and queer theory (2007, pp. 965–982); HIV and AIDS have opened the space for discussing sexuality in sermons in the African continent (Dube, 2003, 202–206). The International Network of Religious Leaders Living with AIDS (INERELA+) was founded by Gideon Byamugisha, a Ugandan Anglican priest, to mobilize HIV+ priests to play an active role in destigmatizing the disease. INERELA+ is another space for producing queer-sensitive biblical readings (Chitando and Nikkles 2010). Similarly, African masculinities are beginning to be studied in relation to HIV and AIDS, religion, and the biblical text (Chitando and Chirongoma 2012).

The Colonized Sub-Saharan Bibles. While the Saharan Bible consists of ancient Bible translations, the sub-Saharan Bibles (save for the Ethiopian Ge'ez Bible) were translated, for the most part, during the modern colonial period by missionaries who regarded African cultures as deserving annihilation. On average these Bibles have been in, and read by, African communities for some two hundred years; although some new editions have been produced, colonial Bible translations are still read in most African communities. It has taken almost a century for sufficiently equipped mother-tongue biblical scholars to begin re-reading these Bibles, along with Greek and Hebrew Bibles, and through established translation theories. The assessment of these translations is best captured by Aloo Mojola, who states:

> Postcolonial translation theory disputes the proposition that translation has to do with the question of textual equivalence, or faithfulness or fidelity of target text to the original source: On the contrary, postcolonial approaches to translation take it as an axiom that translation has much more to do with macropolitics of empire and promotion of the interest and well-being of the empire. (Mojola 2004, p. 10)

In *Postcolonial Perspectives in African Biblical Interpretations,* the section on Bible translation in colonial contexts highlights that sub-Saharan Bible translations were packed with colonizing ideology as means of providing sacred textual evidence to indigenous readers that African cultures were evil and not worth retaining (2012, pp. 157–220). For example, the word for "ancestors" was translated as "demons" in the Setswana Bible; the reluctance to use indigenous East African divine concepts in the Swahili Bible and the tendency to draw such words from Arabic; listing key communal rituals among catalog of vices that are abhorent before God in the Shona Bible; and a general aversion to the use of indigenous names for God, characterized by creating new words and borrowing meaningless ones from foreign ethnic groups.

African women have pushed the boundaries even further in re-reading colonized Bibles, as attested by "Patriarchal and Colonizing Translations" in *Other Ways of Reading: African Women and the Bible* (Dube 2001, pp. 63–67). Dora Mbuwayesango's chapter on the Shona Colonial Bible in this volume has shown that colonial ideology is not only at work when the indigenous divine names are avoided; instead a much more alienating and colonizing impact happens when they are used. For Seratwa

Ntloedibe-Kuswani, the colonial ideology is not only apparent in the Bible translations but also in the long-standing and still widely used translations theories that suggest that the so-called target languages and cultures must be subjugated to the source text and its cultures. She advocates treating both cultures as equals (Dube, pp. 78–97). The articles have also highlighted that when the indigenous divine names of God were finally admitted in the colonial African Bibles, they were transformed from their gender-neutral identities to a male-gendered patriarchal identity.

Re-reading the colonized sub-Saharan African Bibles ushers translations studies into African biblical studies. The studies mentioned only scratch the surface of entire re-readings that must occur in scrutiny of colonial ideologies that shaped the translations and in order to articulate translations of liberating interdependence. This includes re-reading the revisions to study how indigenous translators are revising or maintaining the colonized Bible and patriachalized African God/s. Major studies are also needed to assess how the indigenous communities circumvented the colonial bombs planted in their cultures by reverting to the oral cultures and creating hybrid coexistence of biblical and indigenous cultures (Dube 1999, pp. 53–57). Long before African biblical scholars came onto the scene, the first educated African readers of the Bible had an articulated response to what they perceived as the distortion of their languages and cultures. An analysis of their response and strategies of resistance needs to be undertaken. Similarly, the long-term impact of these translations on African languages (for example the patriachalization of gender-neutral concepts of God) needs to be studied, and postcolonial and gender-sensitive theories must be articulated and put to use. Re-reading colonized sub-Saharan Bibles is an important upcoming area in African biblical interpretation.

The Pentecostal Bible. The Neo-Pentecostal movements in the African continent, as elsewhere, are new and thriving. They represent the face of the future worldwide church. What are the emerging frameworks of reading the Bible? Much has already been documented about their gospel of prosperity, deliverance, healing, and spirit. It is also clear that the Bibles, songs, and preaching that Pentecostals use are not in indigenous languages. The Holy Spirit, on the other hand, has taken a decidedly male gender in Pentecostal biblical reading. But how are such interpretations generated? And what kinds of interpretations are generated by reading the Bible through an overhead projector on the screen? Finally, how is the Pentecostal Bible related to the frameworks described earlier and how are they applied, if at all, to Pentecostal biblical interpretations? Some work toward this end has already begun (Nadar 2005, pp. 60–69; Togarasei 2011) but much more must be undertaken.

[*See also* African American Interpretation; Central and South American Interpretation; Cross-Cultural Exegesis; Cultural Studies; Feminist Biblical Interpretation; Liberation Hermeneutics; Pentecostal Interpretation; Postcolonial Biblical Interpretation; Race, Ethnicity, and Biblical Criticism; Theological Interpretation; *and* Womanist Interpretation.]

BIBLIOGRAPHY

Adamo, David T. *Africa and Africans in the Old Testament.* Eugene, Ore: Wipf and Stock, 2001.

Antonio, Edward P. *Inculturation and Postcolonial Discourse in African Theology.* New York: Peter Lang, 2006.

Banana, Canaan. "The Case for a New Bible." In *Re-Writing the Bible: The Real Issues,* edited by James L. Cox, Isabel Mukonyora, and F. J. Vestrelen, 17–32. Gweru, Zimbabwe: Mambo Books, 1993.

Byamungu, Gosbert. "Postcolonial Discourse and the Use of the Hebrew Bible in African Theology: The Case of Joshua 9." In *Inculturation and Postcolonial Discourse in African Theology,* 209–240. New York: Peter Lang, 2006.

Chitando, Ezra, and Chipo Chirongoma. *Redemptive Masculinities: Men, HIV, and Religion in Africa.* Geneva, Switzerland: World Council of Churches, 2012.

Chitando, Ezra, and P. Nikkles. *What's Faith Got to Do With It? A Global Multi-Faith Discussion on HIV Response.* Oslo, Norway: Nowegian Church AID, 2010.

Comaroff, John L., and Jean Comaroff. *Of Revelation and Revolution: Christianity, Colonialism and Consciousness in South Africa.* Vol. 1. Chicago: University of Chicago Press, 1991.

Comaroff, John L., and Jean Comaroff. *Of Revelation and Revolution: The Dialectics of Modernity on a South African Frontier.* Vol. 2. Chicago: University of Chicago Press, 1997.

Dube, Musa W., ed. *Africa Praying: A Handbook of HIV/AIDS Sensitive Sermon Guidelines and Liturgy.* Geneva, Switzerland: World Council of Churches, 2003.

Dube, Musa W., ed. "Consuming A Colonial Cultural Bomb: Translating *Badimo* into 'Demons' in the Setswana Bible." *Journal for the Study of the New Testament* 73 (1999): 33–59.

Dube, Musa W., ed. *Other Ways of Reading: African Women and the Bible.* Atlanta: Society of Biblical Literature, 2001.

Dube, Musa W., ed. "Readings of *Semoya*: Batswana Women's Interpretations of Matt. 15:21–28." *Semeia* 73 (1996): 111–113.

Dube, Musa, and Musimbi Kanyoro, eds. *Grant Me Justice! HIV/AIDS and Gender Readings of the Bible.* Maryknoll, N.Y.: Orbis, 2004.

Dube, Musa W., Andrew Mbuvi, and Dora Mbuwayesango, eds. *Postcolonial Perspectives in African Biblical Interpretations.* Atlanta: Society of Biblical Literature, 2012.

Germond, Paul, and Stephen De Gruchy. eds. *Aliens in the Household of God: Homosexuality and Christian Faith in South Africa.* Cape Town: David Phillip, 1997.

"Kairos Document." *Journal of Theology for Southern Africa* 53 (1985): 61–81.

Kanyoro, Musimbi. *Introducing Feminist Cultural Hermeneutics: An African Perceptive.* Sheffield: Sheffield Academic Press, 2002.

Mbeki, Thabo. "I Am an African." *African Renaissance* 1/2, September/October (2004): 9–13.

Mofokeng, Takatso. "Land is Our Mother: A Black Theology of Land." In *An African Challenge to the Church in the Twenty-first Century,* edited by M. Guma and L. Milton, 57–72. Cape Town, South Africa: Revelation Desk Top, 1997.

Mojola, Aloo, O. "Post-colonial Translation Theory and the Swahili Bible." In *Bible Translation and African Languages,* edited by Gosnell Yorke and Peter M. Renju, 77–104. Nairobi, Kenya: Acton, 2004.

Mosala, J. Itumeleng. *Biblical Hermeneutics and Black Theology in South Africa.* Grand Rapids: Eerdmans, 1989.

Mosala, J. Itumeleng. "Ownership or Non-Ownership of Land." In Guma and Milton, *An African Challenge,* 57–72. Cape Town, South Africa: Revelation Desk Top, 1997.

Nadar, S. "On Being the Pentecostal Church: Pentecostal Women's Voices and Visions." In *On Being Church: African Women's Voices and Visions,* edited by Isabel A. Phiri and Sarojini Nadar, 60–79. Geneva, Switzerland: World Council of Churches, 2005.

Ntloedibe-Kuswani, Seratwa. "The Case of Modimo in the Setswana Bible." In *Other Ways of Reading: African Women and the Bible,* edited by Musa W. Dube, 78–100. Atlanta: Society of Biblical Literature, 2001.

Ntloedibe-Kuswani, Seratwa. "Ngaka and Jesus as Liberators: A Comparative Reading." In *The Bible in Africa: Transactions, Trajectories and Trends,* edited by Gerald West and Musa W. Dube, 498–510. Leiden, The Netherlands: Brill, 2000.

Oduyoye, Mercy A. *Beads and Strands: Reflections of an African Woman on Christianity in Africa.* Maryknoll, N.Y.: Orbis, 2004.

Punt, Jeremy. "Value of Ubuntu for Reading the Bible in Africa." In *Text and Context in New Testament Hermeneutics,* edited by Jesse Mugambi and Jannie A. Smit, 83–101. Nairobi, Kenya: Acton, 2004.

Punt, Jeremy. "Romans 1:18–32 Amidst the Gay Debate: Interpretative Options." *Hervormde Theological Studies* 63/3 (2007): 965–982.

Togarasei, Lovemore. "The Use of the Bible in HIV and AIDS Contexts: Case Study of Some Botswana Pentecostal Churches." In *The Faith Sector and HIV/AIDS in Botswana, Responses and Challenges,* edited by Lovemore Togarasei; Sannah Mmolai, and Fidelis Nkomazana, 117–137. Cambridge, UK: Cambridge Scholars Publishing, 2011.

Upkong, Justin. "Developments in Biblical Interpretation in Africa: Historical and Hermeneutical Directions." In West and Dube, *Bible in Africa,* 11–29. Leiden, The Netherlands: Brill, 2000.

West, Gerald, O., and Musa W. Dube, eds. *The Bible in Africa: Transactions, Trajectories and Trends.* Leiden, The Netherlands: Brill, 2000.

West, Gerald, O., and Musa W. Dube, eds. "*Reading With: An Exploration of the Interface between Critical and Ordinary Readings of the Bible: African Overtures. Semeia* 73 (1996). This volume of *Semeia* includes an introduction, eleven essays, and four responses.

Musa W. Dube

Allegory and Allegorical Interpretation

"Allegory" means discourse that speaks of one thing by means of another. Among nonbiblical forerunners, this appears to have occurred for the first time when a certain number of passages in Homer's *Iliad* and *Odyssey* simply made no sense at the level of the words' obvious meanings, even after recourse to interpretation in the light of other passages in Homer (*Homeron ex Homerou saphênizein: to clarify Homer by Homer*). Instead, such passages came to be understood as communicating higher truths. The alternative view is that allegory began when interpreters moved to find sense for the text from *another*, even a "foreign" frame of reference, because the work *as a whole* was suggestive of being read that way, for *it was intended to mean something other than what it meant at face value.* These were two quite different reasons for going beyond the face value of texts in interpreting them. The Latin technical term for allegory as used by Isidore of Seville in the early seventh century was *alieniloquium*, which he illustrated from *Aeneid* 1.191.

In the centuries before the Christian era, Stoics such as Crates at Pergamum had been quick to turn to allegory. Hence the depiction of Hephaestus manufacturing Achilles's shield in the *Iliad* was understood as having to do with the ten circles of the heavens. The Alexandrians Aristarchus and Apollodorus as philologists resisted this and insisted that the Homeric stories are accounts of a real heroic age, to be read "straight." Apollodorus insisted that the gods do not "represent" material things, as the Stoics say. However, for many Stoics allegory meant that texts said something about nature, or heroes (Euhemerism), with some moral lessons for the reader to learn, whereas neoplatonists tended to see metaphysical rather than moral truths to be discerned behind stories.

In the Bible. As for the Bible itself—in a way reminiscent of Homeric epic—allegory does not seem to be its first intention. The Hebrew Bible, when it relates history, relates it in terms of at least verisimilitude, somewhere between historical fiction and reportage. Judges 9:8–15 contains a story told by Jotham, in which trees are in the business of anointing a king. As Isidore of Seville in his *gloss* observed, the varieties of trees represent different kinds of men, a fairly obvious interpretation. The story has no historical sense of its own, and so one is driven to find a "mystical" sense. Yet this is a small section in a text that is otherwise narrative of a genre akin to history writing.

Where the Hebrew Bible really turns to allegory is in Proverbs, where there is an extended metaphor of Lady Wisdom (Prov 1–8). Allegory may also be present to some degree in Job, and in the Song of Songs. (Indeed neither of these is a long, full-scale story.) Assuming that the Song contains some allegory—it often uses simile instead, where one is aware that the "ordinary world" of the protagonists has not been left behind—it is not so much interested in charting another world of spiritual realities, but in the possibilities of love in this one.

Regarding the New Testament, H.-J. Klauck (1978) argues that, in the handing down of Jesus's parables, some words gave hostage to fortune in that they were suggestive of, or open to, allegorical readings. Klauck traced a trajectory of allegorizing, which meant saying that "this" means "that," from the visions of Zechariah 1–6 and their explanation to those of Daniel, through to the approach of *The Manual of Discipline* (6, 3–10) of the Dead Sea Scrolls. For Klauck, the same method takes place in the Evangelists' accounts of Jesus's parables. There is a clear difference between the parables being examples of "allegory" and their offering opportunities to be read allegorically; failing to see this was Jülicher's problem in his famous rejection of traditional Christian parable interpretation. "*Allegorisierung*" means the constant interpreting of a text in the sense of its allegorical understanding. This is legitimate when the text already has metaphorical elements. The redactor hence solves the enigma set up in the tradition, and text-critical variants are a clue to further attempts at this. As Dan Via observed, Mark and Matthew regarded the parable of the Sower as an allegory that needed a key to be unlocked, like a *mashal* or riddle whose meaning is not obvious: it "needs to be translated into what it represents, in order to have some sense made of it" (Via 1967, p. 6). The Evangelists encouraged allegorical interpretation to make sense of unclear texts by giving a "key" to one (parable of the Sower).

More than one point was to be made in such stories. In fact, the evangelists may have both obscured and oversimplified the parables of Jesus, although if this procedure focuses on "one point" (e.g., God has rejected "Pharisaic" religion), then something of the point of allegory is lost, in that allegory does not serve to get across one truth but to map relationships of invisible *truths*. Via's point is that parables serve to reconfigure our view of reality, whereas allegories simply reaffirm a standard view. Nevertheless, no less a scholar than Jean Pépin can conclude that in the Synoptic Gospels one senses "l'expression allégorique" (Pépin 1976, p. 253). Like allegory, a parable is a story whose truth does not reveal itself at first telling. Its material is the stuff of everyday life rather than of heroic deeds. In addition, the idea of reward for merits, foreseen (but denied) in the parable of the Sower, gives the story its ironic form—and subverts rather than confirms expectations. Pépin concludes that, whoever composed them, the parables are cases of authentic allegories in the most classical sense of the term (Pépin, p. 256). They are allegories with a twist.

Some think that Paul in Galatians 4 gave encouragement to Christians to allegorize other parts of the Hebrew Bible. However, it is unlikely that he was giving his readers such a model to follow. Paul's usage is a rhetorical device, not a theological hermeneutic. It is a rhetorical symbol, to give picture-form to the theological principle. The Sarah-Hagar story of Genesis 16, which Paul alludes to, contributes little; even the keywords "free/slave" are imported from elsewhere. (Hagar is a maidservant-concubine rather than slave; Gen 16 is silent about Sarah's status.) The parallel exists between the two stories of election and non-election, of promise and non-promise. Sinai does not need Hagar. For Philo, who thought the stories were historical, Abraham signified the mind that will have Sarah/virtue for "wife," while Hagar denoted "the whole range of false pagan virtue" (*De Congressu* 23). "Paul's argument is based rather on a christologically informed authoritative *interpretation* of Scripture" (De Boer 2011, p. 287). "According to the flesh" in Galatians 4:23 allegorically means "circumcision," whereas the "free" begetting in the gospel that produces spiritual children is what was practiced by Paul the Apostle. "It remains unclear, however, whether Paul regards the Genesis story he is now interpreting as in fact an allegory (as a literal translation of v. 24a would suggest), whether he effectively makes the story into an allegory through the addition of new elements (as the characterization of Sarah as 'the free woman' in v. 23 might suggest), or whether he simply gives it an allegorical interpretation" (De Boer, p. 295). All of these are possible.

Early Christian Interpretation: Greek Speaking Irenaeus distrusted those who would try to see what scripture narrated as in any sense parabolic (*Against Heresies* II, 27), not least those who offered obscure interpretations of the parables, or who would build their doctrines of God upon anything other than texts that can be understood according to their "plain grammatical sense." Origen inherited both traditions, the Stoic and the Alexandrian, as well as Jewish methods, especially from his time at Caesarea. The literal sense of what the words mean at face value came first, but he was also clear that a transcendent reality is signified in a way that did not happen with Jewish midrash (Boyarin 2010, p. 52). One is able to know God by faith from bottom up (p. 50) since an "incarnational" principle works both ways (downwards and upwards), although to some extent this is also perhaps Origen's own Stoic influence at work, noticeable in his use of the term *to hegemonikon* (for Stoic philosophers, the seat to the soul with four powers: *phantasia*, reason, impulse, and assent) to identify the bride's true character in the Greek fragments of his Song of Songs commentary.

This process differs from Philo, for whom only God and the heavens are truly real. (Although spiritualizing interpretation may be seen in the Targums and midrashim, "allegory" did not develop as an interpretive category in Judaism.) Readers of David Dawson's work might add that Origen's process of allegorizing differs from Clement's as well. For Clement, "(A)llegorical interpretation is a necessary if not sufficient condition for a reading of scripture that revises rather than endorses the status quo.... Clement appealed to an ontological norm (*Logos*) that guided readers to form judgments concerning texts, pushing at the constraints of meaning" (Dawson 1992, pp. 237–240). For Origen allegorizing meant that readers needed to have the mind of Christ, or a "Luke 24" (Emmaus Road) experience of illumination. Texts become paschal as they are read "upwardly." Allegory then should not be seen as having been simply a "last resort" for puzzling texts—that is a misinterpretation of *De Principiis* IV, 2, 9, for which J. Pépin among others might be held accountable. For in that text Origen is talking simply about interruptions in the text of historical books, which indicates that these books as a whole are not to be seen primarily as recounting a story, but as getting in touch with "divine wisdom." Origen in *De Principiis* is giving a further justification for the belief that all scripture has a spiritual sense beyond what the words mean at face value. Paul served as an example to Origen in treating the law as "spiritual."

In the hands of Gregory of Nyssa, reading the Bible became about spiritual self-transformation (Heine, 1984). To any protest that one must not do away with the historical basis, Gregory's reply is something like: the problem is not with the events (whether they happened or not) but with the plain meaning of many of the words in scripture. For example, theological truth demands that Proverbs 8:22 ("The Lord created me at the beginning of his work, the first of his acts of long ago") simply cannot be taken literally. Gregory asserted that the spiritual sense within the text seemed to touch a spiritual sense in the reader.

The task of unmasking meaning can be seen on display in Maximus the Confessor who, with Gregory the Great, stands at the end of the patristic era. In his *Commentary on the Our Father*, 361–371 (translated by G. C. Berthold, in *Maximus Confessor: Selected Writings*, Classics of Western Spirituality, New York: Paulist Press, 1985, pp. 108–109), the mantle Elijah gave Elisha in 2 Kings 2:6–14 signifies "the mortification of the flesh in which the magnificence of the good moral order is firmly grounded" (Krueger 2010, p. 215). Thus the mantle, which signifies the mortification of the flesh, is interpreted as "an ally of the spirit in the struggle against any enemy force and as a blow against the unstable and flowing nature figured by the Jordan so that the disciple be not held back from crossing over to the Holy Land by being swamped in the mud and slipperiness of the craving for matter" (Krueger, p. 215). When one stops to consider, it is hard to think of any other way in which the mantle could be interpreted: it is the giving over of an office, of course, but more than that—of a power.

Early and High Medieval Western Biblical Interpretation. As well as a Greek way of reading, allegory became in later Latin-speaking circles a way of speaking, for pagans and Christians alike. Famously, Augustine tried to suggest that employing scripture in an imaginatively interpreted way was indeed a way of embellishing an argument. In *On Christian Teaching* II, 6, Augustine comments on Song of Songs 4:2:

> that there exist holy and perfect men by whose lives and conduct the church of Christ tears away those who come to it from their various superstitions, and somehow, by inspiring them to imitate their goodness, incorporates them into itself; and that there exist servants of the true God, good and faithful men who putting aside the burden of this life, have come to the holy font of baptism, arise from it born again with the Holy Spirit, and then produce the fruit of a double love. (*On Christian Teaching*, translated by R. P. H. Green, Oxford and New York: Oxford University Press, 1997, p. 33)

The point is that here he seems to be employing a verse from Song of Songs rhetorically rather than providing an exegesis of the passage: "Your teeth are like a flock of shorn ewes ascending from the pool, all of which give birth to twins, and there is not a sterile animal among them" (Song 4:2). This scriptural verse is a text that gives Augustine pleasure; it helps him to remember lessons: obscurity delights those whose faith is long in the tooth. It is an exercise in the imagination of a playful sort. It is not meant to be "commentary."

The Byzantium-educated Gregory the Great is perhaps the most significant figure to establish a

Greek reading in the West. He took Ezekiel's visions to mean that he saw Jesus on the throne, exalted above all others. For Gregory, however, the Gospel does not clarify everything: "See when we want to untie the meaning of Ezekiel, we re-tie the same question from the Gospel. We must ask in what way he also enters and enters through himself (as God and 'door' of John 10:1): it is for the Church as Christ's body to enter through the scriptures and faith" (Gregoire Le Grand, *Homélies sur Ézéchiel*, *Sources Chrétiennes* 360, Paris: Cerf, 1990, p. 126). The Gospel does not give us an answer but makes Ezekiel even more mysterious. In the same monastic tradition, Psalm 121 (LXX 120) encouraged the reader of "I lift my eyes to the hills" to contemplate angels or prophets and apostles, with Christ himself as Zion above all. The Songs of Ascents (Pss 120–134) lifted Bruno of Cologne upwards in contemplation (Pradié 2006, 77–97).

Allegory then meant seeing through the biblical text to the meaning beneath, not adding a layer of poetic embellishment. One can speak of a more general spiritualizing hermeneutic at work in the medieval Christian worldview: places of pilgrimage, the liturgy, sacred spaces all pointed to invisible realities "above." Allegorical interpretation came to occupy a position somewhere between what should be believed and what should be done. Ralph of Flaix's view of Leviticus was that the accounts of the ritual sacrifices in that book taught the monastic reader which dispositions to cultivate (Elliott 2011, p. 25). Origen had already suggested that in Ezekiel's vision, revealed to him in the midst of "Chaldea," which was the headquarters of the astrologers, three of the "faces" stood for the rational, the irascible, and the concupiscent parts of the soul, but the eagle's face signified "the soul's presiding spirit" (*Sources Chrétiennes* 352, 94). Ambrose glossed this faculty as discernment or the capacity for justice (Christman 2005, p. 112), and that is what matters for guiding the soul into flight. Contemplation is both cause and effect of this purification, as Gregory the Great would emphasize. The allegorical sense is really the contemplative one: it will deal, as Hugh says in *Didascalion* VI, iv, with the mystery of the Trinity, or the mystery of free will and the origin of sin. It rises up from the foundation of sound faith and must be consonant with it. As the reader contemplates, the imagination is filled and captivated.

"The exegetical method whereby the unity of the Bible was established was allegory. . . . As described in the *Glossa Ordinaria* and in other commentaries, the *materia* of the Psalter is not—as is usually the case with the *material* of a secular work—the subject-matter understood literally, but rather its central allegorical referent, the whole Christ" (Minnis and Scotta 1988 p. 46). Peter Lombard in his *Prologue* to the Psalter writes: "Note that the soliloquies (in the Psalms) deal with the whole Christ, that is, both the head and the body. So, the subject-matter (*material*) of this book is the whole Christ, that is, the betrothed and His spouse. Its intention (*intentio*) is to remake men" (Minnis and Scott, p. 110). So what one finds is allegory in the sense of christological fulfillment, followed by the fairly sobering "moral sense" and the even more sobering "anagogical sense" (as understood in terms of final judgment).

Allegory mattered also because it was the doorway to the other two spiritual senses of scripture—and because it allowed the text to be part of the living economy of God in his church. Bonaventura writes in the *Breviloquium* (Prologue):

> So the Scriptures, given by the Holy Spirit, take up the book of creation, and adapt it to the final end by a threefold method: by tropology, they teach us how to act as men; by allegory, show us what to believe with faith; by anagogy, reveal to us what to desire for our eternal delight. (*The Works of Bonaventure II: The Breviloquium*, translated by Dominic Monti. Patterson, N. J.: St. Anthony Guild Press, 1963, p. 5)

Although not every passage is to be allegorized, (just as pagan critics such as Donatus had said about the *Aeneid*), "[s]cripture, then, deals with the whole universe, the high and the low, the first and the last, and all things in between. It is, in a sense, an intelligible cross in which the whole organism of the universe is described and made to be seen in the light of the mind" (Bonaventura, *Breviloquium*, Prologue, 6). As De Lubac insisted, there could be no moral actualizing of a scriptural pattern without assimilating the fully Christian "allegorical" worldview first. In the maturing of this hermeneutic, allegory was *typological* allegory built on the foundation of establishing correspondences between testaments, and it in turn served to found the Christian moral life and the hope for the life to come.

Allegory became so strong from the Middle Ages onward that Christian writers, having seen Christ and the economy of salvation at every turn in the Old Testament (OT), subsequently moved on to allegorizing pagan classics, from the *Timaeus* to the *Aeneid*, in the direction of Christian truth, and eventually on to Dante's Christian *Commedia*, before creating new allegories such as Spenser's *Faerie Queene*. In part this trajectory illustrates the view that, if creation as God's second book could speak of him and his salvation in some mediated way, then Christian scholars were ready to show how.

"An approach to visionary texts like Ezekiel 1, Isaiah 6, or the Apocalypse that stipulates a later reader to 'see again' what the biblical prophet saw in his vision might in fact offer an understanding of the text that is more faithful to the text than the results of patient historical exposition" (Kovacs and Rowland 2004, p. 13). Where the meaning of the text is unclear, then it is open. Hence when Peter of John Olivi (ca. 1270) took "the beast rising from the sea" (Rev 13:1) to symbolize the bestial life of carnal Christians, any constructive moralizing that ensued was only made possible by the allegorical sense, which is the "universe lit up and made comprehensible by Christ and the Spirit" (Kovacs and Rowland, p. 151). Yet Joachim of Fiore (ca. 1183) wanted to see the spiritual meaning of texts like the Apocalypse as fulfilled in church history, or more accurately, New Testament history extended, which would last the same length of time as the OT history from Adam to Zerubabel had: "Allegoria is a similitude of a thing from small to large, such as a day to a year, or a person to an order or a city. It is a spiritual understanding (*spiritualis intellectus*)" (Daniel 1983, p. 65). It is the spiritual understanding that counts (2 Cor 3:6, "the letter which kills," was Joachim's favorite text), but life in the New Age meant that the church of monks would take over Christendom. This transformation meant a new law that went beyond the Gospel of Christ. De Lubac was only half right to comment: "the whole exegesis proceeds from an extreme literalism" (De Lubac 2009, p. 343), for Joachim did indeed allegorize, such as when he interpreted "Bathsheba" to be the Benedictine institution pleasing the papal Master (p. 356). Joachim looked for a "concord of the two testaments" that fused spiritual and earthly. Insight into the perfect law of heaven is what believers will gradually enter into on this renewed earth: that is the meaning of "eternal gospel" in Revelation 14:6 (Kovacs and Rowland, p. 151). Joachim saw the concord of the two taking place in the life of a spiritual movement that enveloped the world.

Medieval historicist literalism, or anti-allegorical approaches, can be seen as a conservative political reaction to Joachim's interpretation (Buc 1994, p. 392). Nicolas of Lyra (1270–1349) refused to allow 2 Samuel 24:1 to work as an encouragement for popular uprising against corrupt power, as Stephen Langton had done a century earlier, but took the story to intend the very opposite: the protection of the common good. Added to this growing resistance to "spiritualizing" was the awareness, sounded by Thomas Aquinas (1225–1274), that allegory "is not a semantic property of the *words* of scripture, but is the meaning of the actual *events*, more generally the *res*, that scripture literally narrates through those words whether poetically or prosaically" (Turner 2010, p. 80). This view of allegory meant that one could trace some arc of providence linking the Testaments. Allegorical interpretation, or theological allegory, shows the links between the events of the dispensations and communities of faith under the old covenant and those under the new covenant, as distinguished from literary allegory, the "allegory of the poets." "The allegorical sense is that whereby those things which are of the Old Law signify things of the New Law. The moral sense is that whereby those things which are done in the person of Christ or those things which prefigure Christ are guides to what we ought to be doing. But insofar as they signify what lies ahead in eternal glory, that is the anagogical sense" (Aquinas, *Summa Theologiae* Ia q.1, art 10, resp.). Thus allegorical interpretation is a Christian theological approach to the biblical tradition.

Allegorical Interpretation on the Wane. One can trace the decline of the "allegorical sense" in scriptural interpretation from the time of Thomas Aquinas onward, although in some monastic, contemplative settings it held on. "Augustine's exploitation of the riotous metaphoricity of the Song of Songs as allegory is no more sensitive of the text's own literary qualities than is the wooden and po-faced commentary of Denys the Carthusian" (Turner, p. 81). Turner points out that the "breasts" of the Song of Songs 1:2 are equated by Denys to "the secrets hidden in the heart or bowels of Christ, that is, they are the treasures of wisdom and knowledge, by which he nourishes the hearts of the faithful. But it is also possible to interpret as the two commandments of charity." Such interpretation happens where the world of things signified and that of things signifying have grown far apart. There is a cold metaphysics in Denys, against which the Romantic poets' preference for "symbolism" later protested.

According to Minnis (1984, p. 243), among the scholastics, Henry of Ghent (1217–1293) fought a rear-guard defense of allegory. "According to the *Glossa Ordinaria*, as Henry notes, David represents Christ whereas Uriah represents the devil . . . events or characters which, considered literally, are good can, considered allegorically, turn out to be bad" (Minnis and Scott, p. 207). This interpretation goes back at least as far as Honorius of Autun in his 1155 Psalms commentary. William of Auvergne was not so sure that one could permit this manner of interpretation without offending the literal sense of the story. Henry of Ghent had to concede that Uriah was not really "the devil," but David could still be "Christ," because the substance of taking a wife as king is good, even if his method was not. Henry believed such moves were crucial for preachers. Hence his Article 16 asserts:

> the allegorical exposition is that which among the essential elements of our belief teaches the hidden sacraments [mysteries] of primary truth, upon which, through faith, the Church of Christ is founded. Therefore the allegorical interpretation is centred on Christ and the church, because within the trinity of divine persons the knowledge of essential elements of belief is likened to the Son, because wisdom is assigned to him as His particular attribute. (Minnis and Scott, p. 259)

As the Renaissance matured, the literal sense became privileged, as Christopher Ocker (2002) shows in tracing a synthesis of the spiritual and the literal in the later Middle Ages. Alfonso Tostado de Madrigal (1410–1455) claimed that the literal sense was greatest because it was "immediate, determinate, verifiable, capable of being fulfilled, and it can furnish proof in argument." The moral sense also mattered, although Tostado did fulminate against any obscuring of the literal sense. Over time the "mode" of scriptural rhetoric, that is, how the text communicated, did seem to triumph over an interest in a plurality of what the text might mean. There was more concern with how scripture got its message across than how it is read according to the senses of the readers. For Giles of Rome, the "Song of Songs had a special mode: *affectivus, desiderativus et contemplativus* [pertaining to emotions, desire, and the mystical]." In other words, it concerned the heart, not the head. Thus biblical science is charged with molding the will (Minnis and Scott, p. 199).

Another problem for allegorical reading when it came to the Bible was a dawning awareness that the Bible was literature. The more one emphasized human cooperation in the production of these texts, the more it was tempting to see their producers as authors in their own right. "By the late Middle Ages, Christians increasingly sense that despite their invocation of the scriptural *historia*, their own multilevel method tends to break the biblical narrative into isolated passages of schematic analysis" (Whitman, 2003, p. 11). Against this, the masters of the School of St. Victor in twelfth-century Paris had always stressed continuity within the biblical narrative, and this "narrative" reading was rediscovered in the later Renaissance.

Episodic and esoteric-seeming books like the Apocalypse and the Song of Songs cannot be read easily from start to finish, and so allegorical interpretation of these continued long after the historical books became free from it. Indeed the attempt to see the Song of Songs as having a smooth diachronic plot, say as the Jewish Targum did, seemed artificial. In recent times Robert Jenson (2005, p. 6) is convinced that the Song invites a reading that relates the personae to the Lord and his people. It was "sexy poetry about the Lord" (p. 7), and that was what those who received it as scripture thought. Jenson adds: "an observable affinity with the literature of Wisdom, reflected in the Christian ordering of the Old Testament, generally inhibits finding narrative of actual sequences of saving history. Like Wisdom, the Song is about what is foundationally the case between God and his people" (p. 12). He seems to see grace not as a specific historical act of God, but rather as an atmosphere in which the personae move. Divine *eros* (God's desire for "us") is primary, and *agape* (God's acting on that love) is secondary. This Romantic reaction means that this kind of interpretation is more properly called "symbolic" than allegorical. The goal is less ascending to divine meaning, than going down into the depths of human meaning.

The reappearance of "typology," and the coining of that term in the modern era, is associated with J. C. K. von Hofmann (d. 1877) and L. Goppelt (d. 1973). Showing correspondences between types and their antitypes was a way of keeping the Christian Bible together as a unity at a time when the fulfillment of multiple prophecies connecting the two testaments seemed harder to defend. These correspondences were less between, for example, David as messiah in the OT and Christ in the NT, as between corresponding states of affairs for the respective "peoples of God" in each Testament. What drives this interpretation is not so much the realization of a surplus of divine meaning in each stage of revelation but a lack, in light of what is yet to come. The later would not be what it is without the earlier, which had shaped its possibilities, yet as "antitype" it will be something fuller than what has gone before. This "progressive" yet sober understanding was seen in L. Goppelt's work, *Typos*, for instance, in his discussion of the Gospel of John's use of Old Testament symbols. The OT was no collection of proof texts but was a "word that was living in their hearts and intended for their time" (Goppelt 1982, p. 198).

It was Goppelt's view that, for all there is mutuality of type and antitype, there can be no type without the antitype that heightens it. It is not just a question of seeing repetitions, as was R. Bultmann's criticism of it. The concern was not to see everything that Moses did as Christlike, but to notice that some of the situations Moses and Israel found themselves in were suggestive of Christ. This seems rather literary, until one remembers that the relationship exists in experienced events. "God dealt in a typical way (τύπικως) with Israel in the wilderness, in a manner that is a pattern for his dealing with the church in the last days" (Goppelt, p. 4).

Allegory and Theological Interpretation Today. It is not for the commentator or the theologian to make statements that make the revealed text *more* obscure, nor should they try to empty this obscurity, as if they could. But they should honor the mystery that is that of the text's meaning. Yet, it has seemed right, from at least Jerome onward, only to admit this once the task of textual, linguistic, and historical work has been attempted. Johann Gerhard (d. 1637) in *Commonplaces* I, 69 was keen to say that allegory helped to draw out doctrine from exegesis.

Allegory recognizes that there is more to the meaning of a narrated text than its historical truth content. In Christian allegorical interpretation, the theology is just as important. It reminds one not to read the Bible as any other book, but to follow the text in its function as witness to God's action (Watson 1998, p. 308). In the movement that is often referred to as "theological interpretation," typology is often preferred to allegory as a way of reading scripture because it contains the idea of moral example as a way of encouraging action that mirrors God's saving action. The "force" of the type hence carries on into the life of the church today. This was a concern already in Goppelt's work (p. 90). One also finds this concern in the typological interpretation of Hans Frei. More recently, Daniel Treier reminds us that biblical typology is not just prophetic but is also imperative (Treier 2005, p. 826), or prophetic in a fuller sense of that term, given that the prophets were arguably messengers of a covenantal morality before anything else. The point of 1 Corinthians 10 is that Christ was present long ago in the desert; thus Thiselton (2000) thinks that "formative model" is the best way to translate *typos* in 10:6, and he agrees with R. Hays that the note of ethical responsibility is clearly sounded in this interpretation. However, the idea of divine wisdom as protector across the Testaments is also important.

From a Roman Catholic perspective, Christoph Jacob (1992) rhetorically asks: who complains when a theatre play is performed differently from its author's intention? Just as the saints' lives drew on biblical tropes and expressions, so too, more generally, salvation, as it works itself out in the church up until today, provides the norm for the interpretation of the OT and NT. There was for Ambrose (d. 397) a sense of the ongoing fulfillment of types in the church. Allegory allows that fulfillment to happen; it stretches beyond "biblical theology" and its descriptions of past beliefs. So allegory is fuller, not lesser than typology. Allegorical interpretation is unashamedly "presentist" and ecclesially focused. It insists that a theological aesthetic needs forming, in engagement with contemporary culture. It is countercultural in an era of "deconstruction" and suspicion of any metaphysics of presence. Ambrose, writing on Cain and Abel, deconstructed the Heracles myth and replaced it with the peaceable one of a banquet and the delicious "bread with honey" from Song of Songs 5:1. Proverbs 9:5 invites all to Wisdom's banquet, through Christian initiation, into the very real life of the church.

Jacob argues that the fathers did not have a concept of a text's "real" meaning, to which an allegorical sense must then be added. And yet, as we have seen throughout the medieval maturity of the method, allegorical interpretation is best when the literal sense is the base or foundational sense. (This stage was reached with Aquinas rather than with Hugh of St. Victor a century earlier, for whom the controlling foundations were those of doctrine, not the plain sense of the text as such.) In what way is allegory of any use for Bible reading today? Is it the sort of thing Hans Frei accused Ricoeur of, trying to escape into a world of one's own imagination, even while claiming to honor the text and its symbols? Anne-Marie Pelletier places the emphasis on meaning for our everyday world, since the older scriptures (OT) are fulfilled not by the new scriptures (NT) but in the moral activity of Jesus Christ (Pelletier 2004, p. 97). Yet allegory has the advantage of pointing upwards toward God in Christ, and not only to Christ as guide to virtue and ethical living or Christ as sharer of religious experience. It reminds the church of the liturgical Christ, transcendent in his presence. A better way of putting it might be to say that the OT is echoed in the NT, and what resounds is a witness to the reality of Jesus Christ today.

It is not straining at authorial intentions to think that Job could be read and probably should be read as an (ultimately comic) story of "humanity": not for nothing is he "pre-patriarchal," almost prehistoric and hence "universally human." The Song of Songs can be read as about divinely led covenantal love leading us somehow to consider God's descending and ascending love. The Apocalypse can be read as contemplation of the state of affairs "now" and "to come," after Christ's victory over everything. If allegory gives meaning "beyond" the NT, then it is that which points to the Lord exalted above creation, caring for it, being ready to return for it, proleptically present in church and sacrament. It might suggest a Christian philosophical way of seeing things, an imaginative framework, as required when approaching the Bible, in order to read it with the grain.

[*See also* Authority of the Bible; Dispensationalist Interpretation; Inner-biblical Interpretation; Intertextuality; Metaphor Theory and Biblical Texts; Patristic Interpretation; *and* Theological Interpretation.]

BIBLIOGRAPHY

Boer, Martinus C. de. *Galatians: A Commentary*. Louisville, Ky.: Westminster John Knox, 2011. The most up-to-date critical commentary in English on the biblical book that arguably gives encouragement to Christian allegorizing of the Old Testament.

Boyarin, Daniel. "Origen as Theorist of Allegory: Alexandrian Contexts." In *Cambridge Companion to Allegory*, edited by Rita Copeland and Peter R. Struck, 39–54. Cambridge, UK: Cambridge University Press, 2010. Insightful account of Origen's significance for Christian allegorical interpretation in its infancy.

Buc, Philippe. *' L'Ambiguïté du Livre*. Paris: Beauchesne, 1994. Detailed account of how in the High Middle Ages literal readings of the Bible were used against radical spiritual Franciscan interpretations.

Christman, Angela. *What Did Ezekiel See? Christian Exegesis of Ezekiel's Vision of the Chariot from Irenaeus to Gregory the Great*. Leiden: Brill, 2005. An account of the history of the patristic interpretation of the early chapters of Ezekiel.

Daniel, E. Randolph. *Abbot Joachim of Fiore, Liber de Concordia Novi ac Veteris Testamenti*. Philadelphia: American Philosophical Society, 1983. Text of Joachim's manifesto for biblical interpretation, together with a useful and full introduction.

Dawson, David. *Allegorical Readers and Cultural Revision in Ancient Alexandria*. Berkeley: University of California Press, 1992. A work that considers the tradition of allegorical interpretation among pagans and Jews in ancient Alexandria, culminating with the Christian interpreter, Clement.

Elliott, Mark W. *Engaging Leviticus: Reading Leviticus Theologically with Its Past Interpreters*. Eugene, Ore.: Cascade, 2012. This follows the text of Leviticus commentary-style, but draws on mostly Christian interpreters of significance over the last two millennia.

Goppelt, L. *Typos: The Typological Interpretation of the Old Testament in the New*. Grand Rapids, Mich.: Eerdmans, 1982. English translation of *Die typologische Deutung des Alten Testaments im Neuen*, originally published in 1939. Perhaps the main work that highlighted the importance of the correspondence of types and antitypes between the Testaments.

Heine, Ronald E. "Gregory of Nyssa's Apology for Allegory." *Vigiliae Christianae* 38 (1984): 360–370. A helpful presentation of the rationale for allegorical interpretation from perhaps the most spiritual of the early church writers.

Jacob, Christoph. "Allegorese: Rhetorik, Ästhetik, Theologie." In *Neue Formen der Schriftauslegung?* Edited by Christoph Dohmen, Christoph Jacob, and Thomas Söding, 131–363. Freiburg (im Breisgau, Germany): Herder, 1992. Bold statement of the need for a spiritual-allegorical exegesis of scripture for the sake of the liturgy and Christian theology.

Jenson, Robert. *Song of Songs. Interpretation: A Biblical Commentary for Teaching and Preaching*. Louisville, Ky.: Westminster John Knox, 2005. Rich and thought-provoking account of how human love poetry in the Song is at the same time discourse about divine love, in whose image human love is made.

Klauck, Hans-Josef. *Allegorie und Allegorese in synoptischen Gleichnistexten*. Münster: Aschendorff, 1978. Influential thesis arguing for the Gospel writers' familiarity with allegorical texts and ways of reading.

Kovacs, Judith, and Christopher Rowland, in collaboration with Rebekah Callow. *Revelation: The Apocalypse of Jesus Christ*. Oxford: Blackwell, 2004. Commentary on that most ambiguous and suggestive book of the Bible with insights of visionaries and commentators through the centuries.

Krueger, Derek. "The Old Testament and Monasticism." In *The Old Testament in Byzantium*, edited by Paul Magdalino and Robert Nelson, 199–221. Washington D.C.: Dumbarton Oaks, 2010. An essay that covers some of the much-neglected ground of Byzantine biblical interpretation.

Lubac, Henri de. *Medieval Exegesis*. Grand Rapids: Eerdmans. Vol. 1, 2000; Vol. 2, 2004; Vol. 3, 2009. Magnificent, exhaustive treatment and unapologetic account of the intellectual sophistication of those in the Middle Ages who furthered the spiritualizing interpretation of Origen.

Minnis, A. J. *Medieval Theory of Authorship: Scholastic Literary Attitudes in the Later Middle Ages*. London: Scolar, 1984. Insightful study of the changing views of authorship, divine and human in the later medieval period.

Minnis, A. J., and A. B. Scott, eds. *Medieval Literary Theory and Criticism c. 1100–c .1375: The Commentary Tradition*. Oxford: Clarendon, 1988. Classic account of medieval interpretation from a literary standpoint, although many of the excerpts (and annotations) deal with biblical commentary.

Ocker, Christopher. *Biblical Poetics before Humanism and Reformation*. Cambridge, UK: Cambridge University Press, 2002. Authoritative recent work on the change in medieval biblical interpretation, when the literal sense itself was accorded spiritual meaning.

Pelletier, Anne-Marie. *D'âge en âge les Écritures: La Bible et l'herméneutique contemporaine*. Brussels: Lessius, 2004. A book that suggests how the Bible can speak to "post-modern" spirituality as we understand the biblical text's symbolism and polyvalency.

Pépin, Jean. *Mythe et allégorie: les origines grecques et les contestations judéo-chrétienne*. Paris: Études augustiniennes, 1976. Thorough and influential, though in places idiosyncratic, account of the transformation of allegory in light of its employment by Christian scholars.

Pradié, Pascal, ed. *Bruno de Cologne, Ludolphe le Chartreux, Denys le Chartreux, Le Commentaire des Psaumes des Montées.* Paris: Beauchesne, 2006. A presentation, with introduction, translation of texts, and commentary, which allows the flavor and the details of intense medieval monastic exegesis to be received.

Thiselton, A. C. *The First Epistle to the Corinthians.* Grand Rapids, Mich.: Eerdmans, 2000. A commentary by a scholar informed by hermeneutical theory and the history of the tradition of interpreting Paul's Epistle.

Treier, Daniel. "Typology." In *Dictionary for Theological Interpretation of the Bible*, edited by Kevin J. Vanhoozer, 823–827. Grand Rapids, Mich.: Baker Academic, 2005. Useful account of a way of reading that is older than the term "typology" itself, with a focus on the moral import of biblical texts.

Turner, Denys. "Allegory in Christian Late Antiquity." In *Cambridge Companion to Allegory*, edited by Rita Copeland and Peter R. Struck, 71–82. Cambridge, UK: Cambridge University Press, 2010. A collection of essays on allegory's place through history, from the Ancient Stoics to Walter Benjamin.

Via, Dan Otto. *The Parables: Their Literary and Existential Dimension.* Philadelphia: Fortress, 1967. Clear and insightful account of how New Testament parables are both alike and different from Hellenistic allegories, along with an attempt to bring out their theological meaning.

Watson, Francis. "Allegorie." In *Religion in Geschichte und Gegenwart.* 4. Aufl., Vol. 1, 308–309. Tübingen, Germany: Mohr Siebeck, 1998. Concise and stimulating account of a practice of reading the Bible that goes beyond the obvious sense.

Whitman, Jon, ed. *Interpretation and Allegory: Antiquity to the Modern Period.* Leiden: Brill, 2003. A collection of essays mapping the move from allegory in ancient "pagan" literature through biblical interpretation in early and medieval Christianity and on to its uses in Western Christian and post-Christian literature.

Mark W. Elliott

Anti-Judaism and Anti-Semitism in the New Testament and Its Interpretation

There have been various attempts to define how the terms anti-Judaism and anti-Semitism differ from each other. Many have followed political theorist and philosopher Hannah Arendt who, in her *The Origins of Totalitarianism*, made a sharp distinction between modern and quite often openly atheist and anti-Christian anti-Semitism and "the old religious Jew-hatred" based on traditional forms of Christian anti-Judaism (New York: World Publishing Company, 1951, p. 7). This distinction captures the idea that modern anti-Semitism has to do with racial theories that emerged in late eighteenth- and nineteenth-century Europe, while more traditional Christian forms of anti-Judaism have focused on Judaism as a religion.

However, the distinction between modern, secular, and racial anti-Semitism and Christian, religiously motivated anti-Judaism is not as complete as has been suggested. Uriel Tal has argued that modern anti-Semitism had both religious and anti-religious roots and was able to attract the support of the masses only when racial theories were connected to the classical themes of Christian anti-Judaism ("Religious and Anti-Religious Roots of Modern Anti-Semitism," in *Religion, Politics and Ideology in the Third Reich: Selected Essays*, by Uriel Tal, pp. 171–190; New York: Routledge, 1984). It has become clear that the rise of modern, racial anti-Semitism cannot be aptly explained if we do not take into account earlier forms of religious, racial, economic, and political anti-Semitism (William I. Brustein, *Roots of Hate: Anti-Semitism in Europe before the Holocaust*; Cambridge, UK: Cambridge University Press, 2003).

According to John Gager, anti-Semitism designates hostility against Jews by complete outsiders, while Christian anti-Judaism is a matter of theological and religious disagreement that reflects the strong family ties different early Christian groups had with Judaism (1983, pp. 8–9). Gager also makes a distinction between "intra-Jewish polemic" and anti-Judaism and thus conveys a view that has become much used in recent discussions of the relationship between the New Testament (NT) and anti-Judaism.

The idea that the polemic against Jews in the NT is another variant of intra-Jewish polemic of the time echoes the current scholarly consensus that Jesus and his followers should be placed in the matrix of the manifold Second Temple Judaism. From this perspective, Luke Timothy Johnson has compared the NT's polemic against Jews to the polemic between different Second Temple Jewish groups and concluded that "the NT's slander against fellow Jews is remarkably mild" (1989, p. 441). According to Craig Evans, the NT's polemic continues—even if in a milder form—the prophetic criticism of the Hebrew Bible, while the shift from the in-house criticism to "bludgeoning" of outsiders takes place only after the NT writings (Evans and Hagner 1993, p. 6.)

These comparisons are helpful in putting the NT's polemic against the Jews into a wider socio-rhetorical and historical context. However, even if all the NT writers were Jewish—a debated assumption, for example, in the case of the writers of Mark and Luke-Acts—it does not follow that the NT's polemic could be completely separated from Christian anti-Judaism. The notion that NT writings cannot be anti-Jewish because their writers themselves were Jews overlooks a well-known phenomenon that disagreements between members of the same group quite often lead to growing alienation and even hostility and hate. Proximity does not exclude antagonism but, on the contrary, quite often fuels and escalates it. The much discussed phenomenon of "Jewish anti-Semitism" or "self-hating Jews" is a case in point, how some Jews, rightly or not, have come to be seen as enemies of their own people by other Jews (Levine 2006, p. 105).

Furthermore, the distinction between inside and outside polemic can be maintained only if the meaning of a literary work is seen to be defined solely by the intentions of its authors and its original historical context. The rise of various reader-oriented literary theories in recent decades has suggested, however, that this view is too simplistic and that due weight should be given the reader's input into the interpretation process. The emergence and use of various NT writings and eventually the NT canon in an increasingly Gentile context meant that the same material that originated in a context of inner-Jewish disputes could be interpreted in anti-Jewish ways without any change in wording (Donaldson 2010, p. 150).

Ambivalent Portraits of Jews and Judaism in Some NT Writings. The portraits of Jews and Judaism in NT writings are much more ambivalent than is often acknowledged in the current research that emphasizes the Jewishness of all NT writings. This observation bears directly on the evaluation of the relationship between anti-Judaism and the NT.

Paul. It is well known that Paul's stance toward the law was often ambiguous (Heikki Räisänen, *Paul and the Law*; 2d ed.; Minneapolis: Fortress, 1987). Paul himself quite clearly expresses his continuing identification with the people of Israel in Romans 9:2–5, but his letters were directed to congregations where Gentile Christ believers were prevalent. In this situation, Paul's ambivalent statement about the law (Gal 3:10–14) or his words about the Jews who killed Jesus and persecute Christ believers and thus deserve God's punishment (1 Thess 2:14–16, regarded as an interpolation by some scholars) open the way for the denunciation of Jews and Judaism. As Terence Donaldson remarks, "in his letters, Gentile readers encountered a portrait of Torah religion that no Jews would recognize and that would inevitably produce misapprehension and misunderstanding" (Donaldson, p. 138).

Mark. The remark in Mark 7:3, "For the Pharisees, and all the Jews, do not eat unless they thoroughly wash their hands," suggests that at least some in Mark's audience, if not the writer too, were Gentiles. This perspective is also seen in Mark's treatment of various details of the Jewish law (Wilson 1995, pp. 36–46) Mark's position as an outsider in relation to the law is most clearly seen as the Markan narrator comments on Jesus's words in Mark 7:19. First, Jesus says that what goes into a person does not defile, and, after these words, the narrator adds an explanatory remark, "Thus he declared all foods clean." This comment in practice cancels out Jewish food laws. However, because food regulations continued to be a recurrent topic in various early Christian controversies long after Jesus's death (Acts 10–11; Rom 14:1–4; Gal 2:12), the comment in Mark 7:19 probably does not represent the position of the historical Jesus but is a later development occasioned by the increasing number of Gentile believers in early "Christian" communities. In this kind of context, such texts as the parable of the tenants (Mark 12:1–12), with its closing words, "He will come and destroy the tenants and give the vineyard to others," could easily be read as supporting the replacement of Israel as God's vineyard by the new community of Jesus's followers, even though Mark does not spell this out in his narrative.

Matthew. Matthew's Gospel is often described as the "most Jewish" of all the Gospels, but still Matthew's position in relation to Jewish law is fiercely debated among scholars.

Some scholars agree with Anthony Saldarini who describes the Matthean community as a Law-observant community and interprets Matthew's polemic against the scribes and the Pharisees (Mat 23) as an intra-Jewish debate (Anthony J. Saldarini, *Matthew's Jewish-Christian Community*; Chicago: University of Chicago Press, 1994, pp. 124–164). Other scholars emphasize the newness of Matthew's description of Jesus as the sole authoritative interpreter of the Torah and claim that Matthew signals a break with different strands of first-century Judaism (Douglas R. A. Hare, "How Jewish is the Gospel of Matthew?" *Catholic Biblical Quarterly* 62 [2000]: 264–277). The end of the Gospel (Matt 28:16–20) shows that Jesus's message is meant for all people, including Gentiles, and that baptism is crucial for those who become disciples, whereas circumcision is not mentioned here at all. This indicates that even Matthew is aware of and takes part in the development that led to the gradual partition of most Christian communities from their fellow Jews.

Luke-Acts. Joseph B. Tyson has summarized his review of scholarship on Luke-Acts and Judaism by saying that there is "an impressive if generally unacknowledged agreement" that "there are both pro-Jewish and anti-Jewish materials in Luke-Acts" (1999, p. 140). Those who want to emphasize the continuity of Luke-Acts with Judaism find support for their case in Luke 1–2, where different characters personify righteous Jews who see in Jesus the fulfillment of the scriptures. However, especially the end of the double work in Acts 26:26–27 supports those who urge that NT scholarship should not explain away the anti-Jewish potential in Luke's portrayal but accept this portrayal as "a condemnation of them [the Jews] for rejecting the offer of salvation in Christ (for which God has rejected them) and for being Christ-Killers" (Sanders 1998, p. 311). Tyson evaluates these two opposing trends in Luke-Acts from the point of view of the Gentile implied reader of the work, "who would find in the text much that would confirm a positive view of the Jewish people . . . [but] would finally be persuaded to agree with the negative judgment that Paul expressed through the quotation of Isaiah 6 in Acts 26:26–27" (Tyson, p. 145).

John. The attitude of the Johannine Jesus to the temple, worship, the Sabbath, circumcision, the revelation at Sinai, law, Moses, and Abraham is highly ambivalent, thereby implying a growing separation from Jewish ethos (Hakola 2005, pp. 215–221). In John, the Jewishness of different festivals and customs is underlined (e.g., 2:6; 4:9; 5:1; 6:4), and the Johannine Jesus refers to the law as "your law" (8:17; 10:34; cf. 7:19, 22; 15:25) or to Abraham as "your father" (8:56). This is in line with how John uses mainly the term "the Jews" for Jesus's opponents. The indiscriminate use of the term "the Jews" shows that, even in those instances where "the Jews" could be understood as a specific group of Jewish leaders or Judeans, the conflict between these groups and Jesus is raised to a new and more general level (Hakola, pp. 225–231).

Scholars have quite commonly explained John's harsh portrait of Jews and Judaism by placing John in a context in which the post-70 C.E. rabbinic movement persecuted early Christians and finally expelled them from the synagogue (John 9:22; 12:42; 16:2; John L. Martyn, *History and Theology in the Fourth Gospel*. 3d ed.; Louisville, Ky.: Westminster John Knox, 2003). However, the external evidence for this kind of conflict is meager, and many scholars are now revising their views concerning the influence and power of the early rabbinic movement (Hakola, pp. 41–86). In light of these revisions, it is simply misleading to suppose that the rabbis were the instigators of any kind of systematic oppression of the suspected heretics in general, or early Christians in particular. It is preferable to see in John's ambivalent portrayal of Jews and Judaism a more prolonged and gradual process of separation than a traumatic and one-time expulsion from the synagogue.

The earlier sketches illustrate that the seeds for the development that led groups of Jesus's Jewish followers to turn into more and more Gentile Christian congregations were sown, at least to some extent, in the writings of NT. If this development was well under way, it is all the more complicated to make an exact separation between insider and outsider polemic and locate the shift from the former to the latter in the post-NT period.

The Passion of Jesus and the Jews. The passion narratives of the Gospels provide a framework that has a strong influence on how different individual Gospel passages are read. It is clear that crucifixion was a Roman way to execute in a most brutal and humiliating manner those who were regarded as criminals or political troublemakers. It is probable that the role of the Roman governor, Pontius Pilate, jointly with the Jewish priestly establishment close to him, was great in Jesus's execution. However, scholars have long been aware that one of the major trends in the passion narratives is to emphasize the involvement and responsibility of Jewish leaders or sometimes even Jews in general in Jesus's crucifixion.

Mark's depiction of Jesus's trial before the Jewish council (Mark 14:53–65) is problematic historically but contains a clear apologetic tendency to prove that Jesus was unjustly sentenced to death (Adela Yarbro Collins, *Mark: A Commentary*. Hermeneia. Minneapolis: Fortress, 2007, p. 699). The trial scene narrates that the chief priests had Jesus arrested and handed him to Pilate "out of jealousy" (15:10). A clear tendency is to show that the reasons for Jesus's death were primarily religious, even though it was most probably the political aspects of Jesus's public activity that caught the eye of Roman officials and their priestly allies.

In his account of Jesus's trial before Pilate (15:1–15), Mark illustrates how Pilate believes Jesus to be innocent while the pressure from the chief priests and eventually from the crowd manipulates Pilate to condemn Jesus to death (Collins, p. 713). The amnesty of Barabbas (15:6–15) further underlines the presentation of Jesus's innocence and the culpability of those who desired his death, even though there is no evidence outside the Gospels for a custom to release a prisoner during festivals.

The tendency to present Jewish leaders as culpable for Jesus's death is not restricted to the passion narrative. In the beginning of his Gospel, Mark presents a series of conflict stories (Mark 2:1—3:6), which culminates, after Jesus has healed a man on the Sabbath, in the Pharisees and the Herodians conspiring on how to destroy Jesus (3:6). While the death sentence was not routinely enforced in the case of Sabbath transgressions in Jesus's time (*Damascus Document* 12:3–6. *m. Sabb.* 7:1, *m. Sanh.* 7:8), the willingness of these groups to kill Jesus contributes to an important feature in Mark's narrative plan whereby Jewish religious authorities act as one character in opposing Jesus and finally in handing him over to be crucified (Wilson, pp. 38–39). However, it is noteworthy that the Pharisees do not appear in Mark's passion narrative at all, and in Matthew and John only in passing (Matt 27:62; John 18:3; cf. also John 11:45–52). This probably reflects the Pharisees' limited historical role in the final events leading to Jesus death.

Other evangelists accentuate in various ways the Jewish responsibility for Jesus's death. Matthew adds the scenes of Pilate's wife's dream and begging of her husband not to harm Jesus (Matt 27:19) and of Pilate's washing of his hands (27:24), both of which highlight how unwillingly Pilate takes part in Jesus's execution. In this connection appears a notorious act where "the people as a whole answered, 'His blood be on us and on our children!'" (27:25).

In the Gospel of Luke, Pilate pronounces three times his verdict of Jesus's innocence (Luke 23:4, 13–14, 22). Luke also introduces a scene in which Jesus appears before Herod Antipas who also testifies to Jesus's innocence (23:15). In various speeches in

Acts, the blame for Jesus's crucifixion is repeatedly put on Jews (Acts 3:12–20; 4:10).

In John, the conflict between Jesus and his opponents, who are mostly called "the Jews," is developed in a consistent way already from the beginning of the narrative. It is noteworthy that Jesus's words to his opponents, "You are from your father the devil," are directly connected to the theme of Jesus's death (John 8:44). The devil is called "a murderer," and in the course of the dialogue in John 8:31–59 even the Jews who initially are said to believe in Jesus (8:31) are exposed as seeking to kill him. The Johannine Jesus here lumps the believing Jews together with the Jews who openly seek Jesus's death in such a way that these different groups lose their distinctive characteristics (Hakola, pp. 180–187).

We should not underestimate the power of the passion narratives to direct the reader's interpretation of other Gospel materials. The myth that the Jews are "Christ killers" has had far-reaching and tragic consequences for Jewish-Christian relations (Cohen 2007). In light of the larger narrative framework of the Gospels, individual words and scenes are easily interpreted in an anti-Jewish way. As such, it is defensible that there are, in the background of the Gospel controversy stories, genuine disputes between Jesus and his fellow Jews. However, these disputes were taken out of their original context and systematized as a part of the narrative plot that accentuates Jesus's disagreements with his contemporaries and presents these disagreements as a main reason why Jesus was killed. Through this process, inner-Jewish disputes and polemic were placed into a literary context in which the words, first spoken to Jews, were quite easily understood to be directed against Jews (Levine, p. 111).

Anti-Judaism in the Critical Study of NT.

Beginnings of Critical NT Scholarship. Many recent studies have revealed how anti-Jewish thought models have found their way into the academic study of the NT from its beginnings. Johann Salomo Semler (1725–1791), who has been described as "the founder of the historical study of the New Testament" (Werner Georg Kümmel, *The New Testament: The History of the Investigation of Its Problems*. Nashville: Abingdon, 1972, p. 68; English translation of *Das Neue Testament: Geschichte der Erforschung seiner Probleme*, 1970), in his writings advocated the free investigation of each of the NT writings in their own, distinctive historical contexts. However, Anders Gerdmar has revealed how many anti-Jewish themes that became prominent among later scholars already appeared in Semler's writings (Gerdmar 2009, pp. 39–49). Semler described the Jews and Judaism as the foil for Christianity: The Old Testament has a Jewish-national character, and the Jewish religion is characterized by particularism and outward worship, while Christianity as the true religion supersedes both Jewish and Gentile religions and is, therefore, truly universal. Despite his tendency to denounce the Old Testament and the religion of the Jews, Semler, in the spirit of the Enlightenment, fought for religious tolerance, publicly defended Jews, and argued against anti-Jewish prejudices (Gerdmar, p. 27). This situation shows that there is not always a direct continuation from theological anti-Judaism to political anti-Jewish actions, a paradox that is typical of some other scholars too.

The theology of Johann Gottfried Herder (1744–1803) exemplifies how some forms of Christian theological anti-Judaism may present appreciative statements of Old Testament religion, and, at the same time, provide a distorted and biased portrait of Judaism in Jesus's time. Herder describes the Jews as "the original carriers of divine revelation" and the religion of the patriarchs as "the pure religion of the fathers" that was genuinely universally minded (Gerdmar, p. 53). However, Herder develops the hypothesis that Judaism degenerated after Moses and turned into particularistic, legalistic, and ritualistic religion that only Jesus was able to restore. In subsequent scholarship, the degeneration hypothesis was widely used to preserve the continuity between the Old Testament and Christianity, but there is no place for the positive role of later forms of Judaism in this scheme.

It is now well documented how anti-Jewish themes and structures, presented already at these early stages of critical biblical studies, continued to appear in the works of such leading biblical scholars as Wilhelm M. L. de Wette (1780–1849), Ferdinand Christian Baur (1792–1860), David Friedrich Strauss (1808–1874), and Ernst Renan (1823–1892) (Heschel 1998, pp. 106–161; Gerdmar, pp. 77–131). De Wette developed the degeneration hypothesis by making a distinction between Hebraism and Judaism. Hebraism is characterized by practical monotheism and love for truth and becomes evident in the first books of the Pentateuch and the Prophets, whereas the legalistic and particularistic Judaism started in the Babylonian exile with the compilation of the book of Deuteronomy (Gerdmar, pp. 79–83). These theological ideas were coupled with the philosophically based racial distinction between Oriental and Western cultures when Baur applied the dialectical philosophy of history of Georg W. G. Hegel (1770–1831) to the study of early Christianity. In Baur's grand historical scheme, Judaism becomes the antithesis of Christianity and embodies the Orient with its empty ritualism, external ordinances, inward nationalism, and particularism. In contrast, Christianity is universal, filled with the spirit of freedom, and continues the best Western traditions established by the Greeks (Kelley, pp. 64–88).

Pharisees and the Degenerated Late Judaism. Susannah Heschel has shown how Abraham Geiger (1810–1874) was one of the first who offered a thorough criticism of the anti-Judaism evident in mainstream biblical scholarship. While Geiger's scholarly work has often been dismissed by Christian scholars as apologetic, Heschel proves how Geiger anticipated the major scholarly trend of the last decades of the twentieth century by presenting Jesus consistently as a Jew, and even as a Pharisee, whose message was not unique in his Jewish context and who did not break with Judaism (Heschel 1998, pp. 127–161). Geiger demonstrated that Christian scholarly portraits of first-century Judaism in general and the Pharisees in particular were based to a great extent on uncritical reception of hostile attacks against the Pharisees in the Gospels (e.g., Mt 23) and the selective use of historical sources. Geiger also saw clearly that the Christian religious faith in Jesus's unique status is quite often turned into a historical argument, in which case "the Judaism of his time must be portrayed bleakly so that he rises radiantly above it" (translation quoted from Heschel 1998, p. 196).

Responses to Geiger's challenge reveal how deep seated a traditional portrait of the Pharisees—and consequently all Jews—as dishonest, arrogant, and hypocritical was among Christian scholars. One of the most vehement critics of Geiger was Julius Wellhausen (1844–1918). Wellhausen's rebuttal of Geiger's views on the Pharisees appeared already in 1874, but his quite short book was translated into English only in 2001, with the publisher acclaiming it as "a masterpiece of interpretation" and "a milestone in biblical studies" that "provides a firm foundation for understanding Judaism's influential Pharisees and Sadducees" (Julius Wellhausen, *The Pharisees and the Sadducees: An Examination of Internal Jewish History*; Macon, Ga.: Mercer University Press, 2001; English translation of *Die Pharisäer und die Sadducäer: Eine Untersuchung zur inneren Geschichte*, first published in 1874, 3d ed. 1967).

Wellhausen continues the Christian tradition that presents Judaism in legalistic terms by saying that "the Pharisees killed nature through statute" and thus "left no place for the conscience" (pp. 14–15). In his writings, Wellhausen develops a theory of degenerated "late Judaism," a concept that is indebted to de Wette's distinction between Hebraism and Judaism (cf. above). The Pharisees become the prime examples of late Judaism when Wellhausen colorfully states, "the once young and fermenting wine settled on the lees" (p. 15). Wellhausen rebuts the claims against the authenticity of Jesus's vehement condemnation of the Pharisees in Matthew 23 by saying that "even a Jew will not deny that the wrath in Matthew is justified" (p. 113). This wrath is without doubt based on Wellhausen's description of the Pharisees as the "most outstanding representatives of Jewish educational arrogance" who are "very unattractive as soon as they set themselves up as models for everyone" (p. 16).

Geiger's criticism against biased portraits of the Pharisees and Judaism was advanced by later Jewish scholars who tried to demonstrate that the Pharisees were the very opposite of what Christian scholarship says about them. These Jewish scholars were often quite disillusioned by the reception of their recurrent criticism among Christian scholars. For example, Israel Abrahams wrote in 1924 that Matthew's attack against the Pharisees "belongs to a period later than Jesus . . . [and] is too indiscriminate to be effective. It has been often pointed out how forcibly Pharisaic leaders themselves satirized and denounced hypocrisy. . . . It is disappointing to have again and again to argue this point" (*Studies in Pharisaism and the Gospels*, 2d Series; Cambridge, UK: Cambridge University Press, 1924; repr., Eugene, Ore.: Wipf & Stock, 2004, pp. 30–31).

Transcendent Judaism. George Moore (1921) and later E. P. Sanders (1977, 33–59) have shown that these early Jewish critics of Christian scholarship were right and that Christian theological anti-Judaism continued to flourish in twentieth-century NT research. They have pointed to the influential interpretation by Ferdinand Weber (1836–1879), who shared a common understanding that legalism is the essence of Judaism. For Weber, the logical conclusion from this is that, in Judaism, God's holiness is emphasized to the extent that God becomes absolutely exalted above this world and separated from human beings. Moore and Sanders demonstrate how the idea of the remoteness of God was variously developed in subsequent scholarship by such scholars as Emil Schürer (1844–1910) and Wilhelm Bousset (1865–1920). Bousset, a leading figure in the history of religions school of biblical studies, asserts that the God of Judaism in Jesus's time was withdrawn from the world, which justifies the definition of Judaism as "an abstract, transcendent monotheism" (Moore, p. 242). This idea gained widespread circulation among NT scholars, especially because it was adapted and developed further by Rudolf Bultmann (1884–1976), one of the most influential biblical critics in the twentieth century (Sanders, pp. 42–47). The image of the remote God has become especially useful in later scholarship as scholars have sought to prove the superiority of Christianity to Judaism by maintaining that Jesus's teaching of God as the Father was an innovation that challenged traditional Jewish transcendentalism.

Conservative Christian Anti-Judaism. Theological anti-Judaism did not appear only among liberal-minded, enlightenment theologians but influenced many of their more conservative opponents as well. Anders Gerdmar has shown how many conservative, salvation-historical oriented biblical scholars developed various anti-Jewish themes in their works (Gerdmar, pp. 213–326). Franz Delitzsch (1813–1890), the founder of Institutum Iudaica in the 1870s, was renowned for his study of Hebrew philology and various Hebrew primary sources. He even defended the Jewish community against anti-Semitic attacks but, however paradoxically, fell prey to standard Christian anti-Judaism. Delitzsch gives a specific place for Israel in God's salvation plan and describes Jesus as a Jew but also "talks about the narrow Judaism of the Pharisees and people having become fanaticized (*fanatisiertes Volk*), which led to Jesus's death" (Gerdmar, p. 230). When discussing the role of the Jews in Jesus's crucifixion, Delitzsch bravely says that the time when every Jew is held responsible for it should be over. But he continues that "we cannot evade the conclusion that the handing over of Jesus to the Romans . . . is a national debt that weighs on the Jewish *people*" (as quoted by Gerdmar, p. 227).

Another scholar who was both a vehement critic of liberal biblical studies and highly learned in various Jewish sources was Adolf Schlatter (1853–1838). In a manner similar to Wellhausen (cf. above), Schlatter develops the degeneration hypothesis and the opposition between prophetic and later legalistic Judaism represented by the Pharisees (Gerdmar, 256–260). Schlatter emphatically describes Jesus as a Jew but, by the same token, repeats highly defamatory classic charges by describing Jews as examples of greed, pride, and double standards (Gerdmar, p. 275). Schlatter, like Delitzsch, holds Jews guilty of deicide.

Assessment. The preceding discussion has suggested that it is difficult to maintain a precise distinction between anti-Judaism, anti-Semitism, and intra-Jewish polemic. While these concepts can be separated in theory, the survey of Christian scholarship shows how intra-Jewish polemic is quite easily turned into anti-Judaism, especially because intra-Jewish debates appear already in the NT within the larger canonical context that reflects the increasingly Gentile character of Christianity.

There are obvious risks if NT polemic is identified as intra-Jewish and characterized as harmless and mild. It has been extremely hard for scholars representing various theological positions to avoid anti-Jewish themes in their scholarship if they are not ready to distance themselves from the NT's portraits of Judaism and the most virulent attacks against Jews. If these attacks and the passion narratives in the Gospels are accepted as unbiased and authentic reports, it is difficult if not impossible to fight against Christian anti-Judaism.

Christian, theological anti-Judaism has taken different forms. Some scholars have followed Marcion (second century C.E.), who criticized heavily the Old Testament and saw a clear break between Judaism and Christianity. The attempt to purify Christianity from all that refers to Judaism reached its culmination when some Nazi theologians developed fantastic theories of Jesus's Aryan pedigree and thus dejudaized Christianity (Heschel, 2008).

We should not, however, regard the efforts to untie the bond between Christianity and Judaism as the standard of Christian anti-Judaism. Stephen Wilson has remarked that Marcion, when subjecting the Hebrew Bible to severe criticism and finally rejecting it, "attacked the symbols but left the people alone," while his orthodox opponents "took over the symbols and attacked the people. Judaism was the loser in either case" (Wilson, p. 221). Many later scholars have followed Marcion's opponents when they have attacked either the Jews in Jesus's time or modern Jews but emphasized the continuity between the Old Testament and Christianity. For this form of Christian anti-Judaism, Jesus's Jewishness has never been a real problem. Therefore, while the emphasis on the Jewishness of Jesus and early Christianity in recent scholarship is a genuine advancement, this emphasis is not a sufficient antidote to all forms of theological anti-Judaism.

Christian theological anti-Judaism is not necessarily a thing of the past, even though, since the appearance of E. P. Sanders's *Paul and Palestinian Judaism* (1977), the majority of scholars have become increasingly sensitive to the polemical nature of the traditional Christian picture of first-century Judaism. However, there is always a temptation to present a distorted and biased portrait of first-century Judaism if the defense of the historicity of the NT is coupled with an attempt to give historical reasons for a Christian theological conviction of Jesus's exceptional, divine status.

Amy-Jill Levine has exposed how various recent attempts to elevate Jesus above his historical context have resulted in biased portraits of Judaism (pp. 119–190). When various feminist or postcolonial approaches have been applied to the NT, scholars have repeatedly represented Jesus as the spokesman of the poor, the suppressed, and women while Judaism appears as hierarchical, repressive, and misogynistic. These portraits bring into life and replicate one of the basic assumptions of theological anti-Judaism, an idea that, despite its Jewish origins, Christianity surpasses its predecessor and makes clear its faults.

[*See also* Historical Criticism, *subentry* New Testament; Historical Jesus, Quest for the; Rabbinic Exegesis; *and* Redaction Criticism, *subentry* New Testament.]

BIBLIOGRAPHY

Cohen, Jeremy. *Christ Killers: The Jews and the Passion from the Bible to the Big Screen.* Oxford: Oxford University Press, 2007. Traces the Christ-killer myth from antiquity to the present day and exposes anti-Judaism inherent in Christian renderings of the passion narratives.

Davies, Alan T., ed. *Antisemitism and the Foundations of Christianity.* New York: Paulist, 1979. Essays that respond to and debate with the thesis in Rosemary Radford Ruether's *Faith and Fratricide*; includes a concluding response from Ruether herself.

Donaldson, Terence L. *Jews and Anti-Judaism in the New Testament: Decision Points and Divergent Interpretations.* London and Waco, Tex.: SPCK and Baylor University Press, 2010. A nuanced and perceptive discussion of the ways scholars have interpreted the New Testament in relation to anti-Judaism.

Evans, Craig A., and Donald A. Hagner, eds. *Anti-Semitism and Early Christianity: Issues of Polemic and Faith.* Minneapolis: Fortress. 1993. Essays discussing prophetic critique in the Hebrew Bible and the question of anti-Semitism in relation to Jesus, different NT writings, early Church Fathers, New Testament Apocrypha, and Gnostic writings.

Farmer, William R., ed. *Anti-Judaism and the Gospels.* Harrisburg, Pa.: Trinity, 1999. A collection of essays and responses to them that discuss each of the canonical Gospels, the interpretation of the Gospels in the early Church, and anti-Judaism in the critical study of the Gospels.

Gager, John G. *The Origins of Anti-Semitism: Attitudes toward Judaism in Pagan and Christian Antiquity.* New York and Oxford: Oxford University Press, 1983. Argues that Christian anti-Judaism and Greco-Roman bigotry against Jews evident in some authors (Apion, Tacitus, Seneca) are two different things; claims that Paul's theology is not at all anti-Jewish.

Gerdmar, Anders. *Roots of Theological Anti-Semitism: German Biblical Interpretation and the Jews, from Herder and Semler to Kittel and Bultmann.* Studies in Jewish History and Culture 20. Leiden: Brill, 2009. A thorough survey of how the Jews and Judaism were constructed as the antithesis of Christianity in the salvation-historical and enlightenment-oriented German biblical scholarship from the 1750s to the 1950s.

Hakola, Raimo. *Identity Matters: John, the Jews, and Jewishness.* Novum Testamentum: Supplement 118. Leiden: Brill, 2005. Challenges the hypothesis that John reflects a violent persecution of early Christians and proposes that John's portrayal of Judaism is ambivalent.

Heschel, Susannah. *Abraham Geiger and the Jewish Jesus.* Chicago: University of Chicago Press, 1998. Discusses how Abraham Geiger challenged anti-Jewish currents evident in nineteenth-century Christian biblical studies and boldly presented Jesus as a Jew and a Pharisee.

Heschel, Susannah. *The Aryan Jesus: Christian Theologians and the Bible in Nazi Germany.* Princeton, N.J.: Princeton University Press, 2008. Discusses the emergence and influence of the efforts by some Nazi theologians (most notably Walter Grundmann) to "dejudaize" Jesus by presenting him as an Aryan.

Johnson, Luke Timothy. "The New Testament's Anti-Jewish Slander and the Conventions of Ancient Polemic." *Journal of Biblical Literature* 108 (1989): 419–441. Compares polemic against Jews in the NT to inter-Jewish disputes and the conventions of ancient rhetoric.

Levine, Amy-Jill. *The Misunderstood Jew: The Church and the Scandal of the Jewish Jesus.* San Francisco: HarperSanFrancisco, 2006. Discusses how Jesus should be seen in his Jewish context and exposes how Christian anti-Jewish readings of the NT have presented Judaism in a stark contrast to Christianity.

Kelley, Shawn. *Racializing Jesus: Race, Ideology and the Formation of Modern Biblical Scholarship.* London and New York: Routledge, 2002. Reveals how nineteenth-century Orientalism and Romantic Nationalism were coupled with racial thinking that influenced also modern biblical scholarship.

Moore, George Foot. "Christian Writers on Judaism." *Harvard Theological Review* 14 (1921): 197–254. A classic but often neglected article that betrayed the apologetic, biased disposition of mainstream Christian scholarship toward Judaism.

Parkes, James. *The Conflict of the Church and the Synagogue: A Study in the Origins of Antisemitism.* London: Soncino, 1934. One of the first systematic surveys of Christian anti-Judaism.

Ruether, Rosemary Radford. *Faith and Fratricide: The Theological Roots of Anti-Semitism.* New York: Seabury, 1974. Makes a controversial claim that anti-Judaism is intrinsic to Christian faith by analyzing NT texts and later early Christian literature.

Sanders, E. P. *Paul and Palestinian Judaism.* Minneapolis: Fortress, 1977. Argues against the earlier scholarly consensus that Paul denounces the Judaism of his time because it was filled with rabbinic legalism.

Sanders, Jack T. "Can Anything Bad Come out of Nazareth, or Did Luke Think that History Moved in a Line or in a Circle?" In *Literary Studies in Luke-Acts: Essays in Honor of Joseph B. Tyson*, edited by R. P. Thompson and T. E. Phillips, 297–312. Macon, Ga.: Mercer University Press, 1998.

Tyson, Joseph. P. *Luke, Judaism, and the Scholars: Critical Approaches to Luke-Acts.* Columbia: University of South Carolina Press, 1999. Argues that the Holocaust was a major turning point in NT scholarship and shows how the text's mixed signals have left room for scholars to emphasize either positive or negative aspects of Luke's portrayal of Jews and Judaism.

Wilson, Stephen G. *Related Strangers: Jews and Christians, 70–170 C.E.* Minneapolis: Fortress, 1995. A balanced discussion of Jewish-Christian relations from the NT Gospels to second-century Christian and Jewish evidence.

Raimo Hakola

Asian American Biblical Interpretation

Asian Americans have been readers and interpreters of the Bible for a long time. It is well known, for example, that mission schools played an important role in "Americanizing" the early Chinese populations who landed on US soil in the late nineteenth and early twentieth century by trying to Christianize them, including the use of Bible classes as a vehicle for the teaching and learning of the English language. In 1853, the Presbyterian Board of Foreign Missions helped establish the very first Chinese Christian church in the US in San Francisco. While historical records or traces of such readings are admittedly scarce, they are not entirely absent. For example, the writings of Sui Sin Far—who has the distinction of being called "the grand maternal figure of *all* Asian American letters" (Shih 2005, p. 48)—are full of allusions to and quotations from the Bible. It is even suggested that the Bible was "the single most important model" of Sui Sin Far's own writings, as it accounts for their "short," almost parable-like format and "didactic bent" (Ferens 2002, pp. 95–96).

Contextual Theology, Sociopolitical Contexts, and Racialization in US Society. Following the Second World War, the US economy was reorganized around capital that became increasingly global and globalizing. By the 1960s, new patterns of migration and new laws of immigration also became evident. Most pertinent to our topic is the Immigration Act of 1965, which opened the US door wider for immigrants (even refugees) and with less concern over their national origin. This Act turned out to be the single most important legislation for the current growth and diversity of Asian American communities. Without a quota targeting persons of Asian origins or from an Asian region but with economic and even military engagement by the US in various parts of Asia, large numbers of Asian immigrants began to arrive from East Asia, South Asia, as well as Southeast Asia.

As far as readings by professional scholars within the guild of academic biblical studies are concerned, Asian American biblical interpretation is indebted to the rise of contextual theology in the 1960s in general and the work of African American biblical scholarship in the 1970s in particular. The 1960s was a time of popular or grassroots movements against racism and imperialism within the larger US society. Aiming to construct a sociopolitically relevant and thus contextually specific theology, Christian theologians from within *and* outside of the US, like Gustavo Gutiérrez, James Cone, Choan-Seng Song, and Ahn Byung Mu, developed theologies that were variously located and differently called, from liberation theology and black theology to story theology and *minjung* theology. Since these theological innovations were often undertaken with reference to and grounding in the Bible, African American biblical scholars also began to read and re-read the Bible in ways that became more and more explicitly contextual to their communal histories, lives, and experiences in the US

Asian American biblical interpretation does not bypass material and sociopolitical realities; it also cannot be limited to the discipline of biblical studies. In fact, rigid disciplinary boundaries are built upon assumptions of origin and purity much like those used in national debates over immigration. Such assumptions idealize an "originator" or "owner" of a certain intellectual space that will only be sullied by trespasses or transplants. Those of Asian heritage in the United States, despite their nativity, are often racialized with this logic as perennial border-crossers who do not really belong. Analogous assumptions and arguments are used to patrol not only racial/ethnic borders within a nation but also disciplinary borders within the academy. Asian American biblical interpretation resists this tyranny of purity in both academic *and* racial/ethnic terms. It is therefore about much more than identity formation or cultural heritage; as important as these issues are, Asian American biblical interpretation confronts and challenges the ideology of "purity"—and hence the politics, practices, and realities of exclusion and domination—in academy and society. It is about not only different readers of the Bible (a matter of demographics) but also reading the Bible differently (a matter of disciplinary practice).

The Bible is of particular importance because the exclusion of and discrimination against Asians in the United States have long been enacted in terms of a struggle to protect not only the nation but also Christendom from these racial *and* religious others. Just as society and academy are interconnected, race and religion are also intricately intertwined. Resisting such denials of relations (including the denial or separation signified by the question often asked of Asian Americans, "Where are you from?"), Asian American biblical interpretation not only refuses to let particular readings rule by default by reviewing the Bible and its interpretation, but also requires all readers of the Bible to realize that Asian Americans and the biblical traditions of Christianity are not mutually exclusive. In fact, the "Good Book" has become one generative site for Asian Americans to pursue and push conversation, recognition, and education about various issues, especially, though not exclusively, those related to race and religion, or inclusion and exclusion.

Stage One: Finding Asian American Presence in Biblical Interpretation. When African American biblical interpretation—to which the development of Asian American biblical interpretation is much indebted—gained prominence in the 1970s, one of its major concerns was recognition of black presence in and contribution to *both* biblical narrative *and* biblical interpretation, as Charles Copher (1989, 1991) and Cain Hope Felder (1989, 1991, 1993) argue in reference to the Hebrew Bible and the New Testament, respectively. For instance, Felder argues not only that Mary and hence Jesus are more like "Yemenite, Trinidadian, or African American today" in appearance (1993, pp. 192–94), but also that ancient writers of the Bible acknowledge and admire ancient Africans for having a great and glorious culture (1991).

Following the pioneering work of their African American counterparts, the first generation of Asian American scholars of the Bible also gave attention to Asian presence in the Bible, but were reluctant to claim particular biblical characters as Asians because they are mainly of East Asian heritage and thus geographically far from the "biblical lands" of West Asia and North Africa. Instead, they made their contributions to biblical interpretation by identifying racializing dynamics in biblical texts familiar to Asian Americans, and then by identifying with particular biblical characters in that text who might be important and relevant to Asian American communities. Chan-Hie Kim, for instance, compares the Cornelius story in Acts 10—11 to his own experience as an Asian immigrant to the United States, since both Cornelius and Kim are outsiders interacting with and integrating into a community of another racial/ethnic group (1995). As Kim reads these chapters in terms of both politics of inclusion and practice of integration in a racially/ethnically diverse community, Kim does not specify the race/ethnicity of Cornelius beyond the fact that Cornelius is a non-Jew.

As Asian American biblical interpretation continues to develop, this attempt to find one's presence in the Bible does not disappear. For example, Uriah (Yong-Hwan) Kim, whose scholarly career began a generation after Chan-Hie Kim's, reads the Uriah story in 2 Samuel 11 by focusing on Uriah as a "foreigner" who is readily sacrificed: Uriah is murdered and forgotten by Israelites despite or perhaps because of his attempt to join and even fight for the people of Israel (2002). Without suggesting that the biblical Uriah is an Asian, Uriah Kim simply juxtaposes Uriah the Hittite not only with Vincent Chin as scapegoat victims while their respective killers get away with murder, but also with himself as a "minority" person involved in identity struggles.

Uriah Kim's reference to identity struggle conveniently clarifies two underlying dynamics in the early stage of Asian American biblical interpretation. First, these readings are concerned with the power differential between Asian Americans and the majority white population. Second, they also seem to assume a collective—if not necessarily a stable and known—identity, which all Asian Americans will need to embrace precisely because of their power differential vis-à-vis the white majority. In fact, Uriah Kim makes these two points rather explicitly to conclude his reading of Uriah:

> It could have easily been Uriah Kim, a Korean American, killed instead of Vincent Chin, a Chinese American, because I would have looked like a Japanese male to the perpetrators as much as Vincent or any other Asian male. After all, we all look alike—Japanese, Chinese, Korean, Vietnamese, Filipino, pick your choice, oh Asian, the "others," non-"Americans." (2002, p. 82)

These overlaps between Uriah Kim's work and those of the "first generation" show that an individual scholar's work might develop and span over different stages within the conceptual and heuristic mapping of Asian American biblical interpretation provided here. Similarly, the beginning of a "new" stage does not necessarily mean the end of a previous stage; stages do overlap and run alongside each other.

Stage Two: Foregrounding Asian American Contexts, Interdisciplinarity, and Internal Diversity. Having said that, Uriah Kim's essay does reveal stark differences representative of a new stage in the development of Asian American biblical interpretation. While Chan-Hie Kim starts his reading of the Bible with the Bible and the history surrounding a biblical text (including both the context of the biblical passage as well as how a passage has been read), Uriah Kim starts with his context and experience as a twentieth- and twenty-first-century Asian American. In addition, one finds, on the basis of footnotes and bibliographical entries in his essay, that Uriah Kim's reflection of his context and experience is informed by scholarship in Asian American studies. In contrast, besides biblical and theological scholarship, Chan-Hie Kim's reference is limited to one mention of the 1965 Immigration Act. In what can be called the "second stage," Asian American biblical interpretation becomes more thoroughly informed by scholarship in Asian American studies and hence increasingly interdisciplinary. As Asian American biblical interpretation enters this second stage of development, the interdisciplinary nature of the enterprise involves crossing the boundary not only between theology and biblical studies but also biblical studies and disciplines outside of theological or religious studies.

The combination of these two changes—beginning with a reader's contemporary experience and venturing into the repertoires of other disciplines in general and those of Asian American studies in particular—means that the earlier emphasis on reading the Bible to find and understand race, as far as Asian American biblical interpretation goes, begins to mix with and perhaps even give way to a new priority of reading and understanding race as a lens to read and make sense of the Bible. This is clearly indicated in the title of an essay on the intersection between Asian American racialization and gender by Kah-Jin Jeffrey Kuan and Mai-anh Le Tran: "Reading Race Reading Rahab" (2009). The Bible, in other words, is now explicitly *not* the first entry into an exploration. The concern is now less what the Bible might have to say about Asian American lives and experiences, but more what Asian American lives and experiences have to say about the Bible. Inverting this process is important because biblical studies as a discipline is not unaffected by the infection of racial/ethnic discriminations and colonial impulse. Asian American biblical interpretation at this stage is no longer only about demographics, but a shift of (inter)disciplinary framework. This change in framework leads to a different set of questions and thus the development of alternative understandings.

Another significant change as Asian American biblical interpretation enters this next stage of its development is how the assumptions about struggle and identity mentioned earlier also begin to change, even if that is not visible in the work by Uriah Kim. In this stage, readings begin to manifest a much greater diversity *within* Asian America. As identity struggle involves internal differences, identity becomes multiple, contradictory, no longer singular, and less than stable. Since biblical scholars began to explore, in the first half of the 1990s, how to integrate their racial/ethnic identity as Asian American into, e.g., feminist criticism (see, for instance, Yee 1997), intersections between the racialization of Asian Americans and other identity factors—like gender and sexuality—increasingly emerged in the discussion. Rita Nakashima Brock, a theologian who crosses the disciplinary line and contributed to an anthology of feminist biblical criticism, suggests that an Asian American feminist "hermeneutics of wisdom," through an emphasis on Asian cultures and age-old wisdom but rejection of "innocence," respects the many voices found within the Bible and thus enables Asian American women to reject the Bible's authority without abandoning the Bible (1997). According to Brock, this hermeneutic, or simultaneous adoption of two seemingly contradictory attitudes (like the nonexclusive embrace of two cultures: Asian *and* American), not only shows Asian American women to be resourceful and responsible agents but also helps cultivate and develop multiple perspectives, and hence "a fluid, multilayered self" and "a multifaceted identity" (1997, pp. 65, 68). Of no small significance is how Nakashima Brock both begins and bases her identification of and argument for this hermeneutic of wisdom by way of Asian American literature (1997, pp. 64–66); such literature is, of course, a primary resource for and constant focus of Asian American experiences and studies. Nakashima Brock's (inter)disciplinary crossings are, in other words, also multiple.

Another example that demonstrates the internal diversity of Asian America can be found in the work of Patrick S. Cheng (2002), yet another theologian who has contributed to the development of Asian American biblical interpretation. On the basis of their shared status as "radical outsiders" in terms of both sexuality and geography in general, and their many shared multiplicities in particular ("multiple naming," "multiple silencing," "multiple oppression," and "multiple fragmentation"), Cheng argues that the concubine in Judges 19 can be a "foundational text for understanding the experiences of queer Asian Pacific Americans" (2002, pp. 119, 120). If Cheng's language here seems closer to reading the Bible to find and understand race (in connection with sexuality matters), Cheng's bibliography also shows an interdisciplinary engagement (particularly those of Asian American queer studies) that is characteristic of Asian American biblical interpretation in its second stage of development. Also of significance is Cheng's emphasis that (1) queer Asian Pacific American readings should focus on multiplicity; and (2) such a hermeneutic of multiplicity would look to other Asian cultural and religious traditions of the divine that reflect queer Asian Pacific American identities. If the former emphasis strikes a resonance with Nakashima Brock's Asian American feminist hermeneutics of wisdom, Cheng's later emphasis suggests a priority of queer Asian American experiences over the biblical texts; this latter emphasis also characterizes this second-stage development of Asian American biblical interpretation.

The desire for recognition mentioned in the early stage, while still present, becomes perhaps less desirable once Asian American biblical scholars acknowledge that a recognized identity can become one-dimensional and hence restrictive, with pressure to conform coming from one's own racial/ethnic minority community as well as from the white community. A minoritized people, in resisting racialization, might resort to a rigid identity politics that ends up as monolithic, limiting, and imposing as what they are contesting.

A good example that demonstrates this more complicated identity struggle within Asian American biblical interpretation is an essay by Gale A. Yee, entitled "Yin/Yang Is Not Me" (2006). Yee compares recognition by whites to being an animal in a zoo through what Rey Chow, an Asian American critic in literary/cultural studies, "calls . . . 'coercive mimeticism,' in which racial/ethnic persons are expected to resemble and replicate certain socially endorsed preconceptions about them" (2006, p. 154). At the same time, Yee relates experiences of Chinese Americans in China, including her own, when they are forced to become either Chinese or American but not both, as well as research about Asian American women who self-identify as simply "American"—that is, white—to distance themselves from stereotypical images of Asian women living under patriarchal Asian cultures. Yee's rejection of a single and stable racial/ethnic minority identity leads her to conclude that "an Asian American biblical hermeneutics [is] a hard one to pin down" (2006, p. 163).

In addition to paying tributes to contextual theologians, like Peter Phan and Jung Young Lee, who helped develop Asian American theology and hence inspired Asian American biblical interpretation, Sze-kar Wan (2006) illustrates the methodological divergence, diversity, or fluidity of Asian American biblical interpretation by featuring a "hermeneutics of hyphenation" that can be somewhere or anywhere "betwixt and between"—for lack of better terms—a "historical" or an "ideological" emphasis (2006). This struggle to highlight and clarify the heterogeneity among Asian American readers and readings of the Bible can further be seen in Mary F. Foskett's reading—as an Asian adoptee in the United States—of adoption in Romans 8—9 (2002) and the scholarly search for early Christian origins (2006). One can also see this turn toward Asian America's internal diversity in works that feature generational difference (Yamada 2006), ethnic specificity (Ahn 2006; Liew 2008, pp. 18–33, 57–74), or a mixed racial heritage (Rietz 2002, 2006).

Stage Three: Circularity within Asian American Interpretation and Intercommunal Readings across Minority Groups. As Asian American biblical interpretation moves with the emphases on intersectionality, internal diversity, or intracommunal negotiation into the twenty-first century, there are signs that it is approaching a third stage. The relations between reading the Bible to understand race and reading the Bible through the lenses of race or racialization become, first of all, more and more circular. As one can already see in Cheng's work, beginning with Asian American experiences to read the Bible does not necessarily preclude a reader from seeing a biblical text as also influential or even "foundational" in one's reading of Asian American experiences.

This more circular way of reading is present even more explicitly in a recent essay on Paul by Wan (2012). Focusing on two myths ("perpetual foreigner" and "model minority") that function to racialize Asian Americans in general and have been experienced by Wan personally in his particular context as a professor of the New Testament, Wan spends the first six and a half pages describing and explaining these racial myths and how Asian Americans develop a certain ambivalence (that is, a simultaneous attraction and repulsion) toward "whiteness" and the dominant society. This focus on Asian American experiences as a lens for reading is unmistakable, as Wan only mentions Paul in two short sentences within this opening part of his essay. Wan is also explicit that what he is doing involves "a self-understanding or perhaps a 'pre-understanding' that enables [Asian Americans] to approach the biblical text with boldness and humility" and "inscribe the Asian American experience in the biblical text" (2012, p. 181).

Proceeding then to read Galatians through the dual lens of "perpetual foreigner" and "model minority," Wan argues that Paul's simultaneous attraction to and repulsion by the Roman Empire cause him to be similarly ambivalent toward the Jewish leadership of the Jesus movement. Wan, however, loops back to state that "Paul in turn can help Asian American readers come to terms with the ambivalence of their own social location," as "Asian Americans find in Paul a mirror to understand their own experience of ambivalence" (2012, pp. 176, 187). This "coming to terms" or "understanding" is, for Wan, twofold. First, Paul's "double exclusion" by the Roman Empire and the Jewish leaders is analogous to the marginalization Asian Americans often experience in not only "the white culture of the US" but also "their ancestral cultures in Asia" (Wan 2012, p. 187). Second, the Jewish leaders' "hierarchical" treatment of Paul is a replica of the imperial hierarchy of Rome (ibid.); as such, reading Paul's Galatians serves to remind Asian Americans how Empire institutes a hierarchical "power struggle exclusion" on all levels of a society and provides "the material cause for internal conflicts" (ibid.).

In addition, Asian American Bible scholars in this third stage also begin to work intentionally on intercommunal conversations across minority groups. Aside from an early attempt to establish contact between African American and Asian American Bible scholars in 2002 (Liew and Wimbush 2002), the strongest indication of this inclination is the 2009 volume, *They Were All Together in One Place?*

Toward Minority Biblical Criticism (Bailey, Liew, and Segovia, eds.). While individual essays within this volume do not necessarily demonstrate this crossing, the volume as a whole—by putting three racial/ethnic minority groups together in one volume even if they are not necessarily in one accord—does gesture to a desire not only to seek recognition from each other as racial/ethnic minority communities but also to facilitate communication across color lines for association, affinity, and perhaps even unexpected alliances.

Making scholars of other racial/ethnic minority groups rather than white scholars one's primary conversation partners signals a potential sea change in Asian American biblical scholarhsip. If Asian American biblical interpretation in the second stage shows that racial/ethnic identity is not only constructed but also composite—that is, it involves and is made up of different and multiple elements—the crossings that take place in this third stage hint that the underlying framework has changed from a bipolar ("majority/whites" against "minority/persons of color") to a multipolar or multicentric one. Intercommunal crossings will help Asian American and other racial/ethnic minority readers understand not only the New Testament's role in racialization (both helping and hurting them) but also their role in other people's as well as their own oppression and liberation.

This shift to intercommunal conversations across different racial/ethnic minority communities is hence not only a comparative but also a connective turn: instead of fortifying boundaries to allow for differences within but arrest invaders and interlopers from without, Asian American readers of the Bible now seem to realize that racializations of different minoritized groups are parallel and overlapping processes that contribute to maintaining the dominant structure and power differentials of the US society; these processes, for instance, facilitate the use of divide-and-conquer strategies against minority groups if and when necessary. In other words, racialization of Asian Americans in the United States does not take place in isolation from but in relation to other racial/ethnic minority groups.

Another new direction in Asian American biblical interpretation is being opened up in this third stage of crossings among minoritized communities. Learning about and conversing with other minoritized communities enable not only a shifting of reference but also an opening to better expose race and racialization as social constructions rather than biologically determined. That is to say, as Asian American scholars of the Bible learn more about the racialization of other racial/ethnic minority groups, these scholars may actually have the repertoire to read the Bible with, say, largely African American resources and through African American lenses rather than Asian American ones. This is, for instance, what I attempt to do in reading Jesus's death in the Gospel of John (2008). Reading Jesus's death by the Roman colonizers through the African American experiences of being lynched by white racists, I argue that Jesus's early "knowledge" of his inevitable death in John has to do with the pervasiveness of this death threat among a colonized population. Asian Americans who read and use other minoritized groups' resources and reading lenses to approach the Bible might turn out to be one of the most potent and productive challenges against the ideology of racial/ethnic and academic "purity."

[*See also* African American Interpretation; Chinese Interpretation; Cross-Cultural Exegesis; Cultural Studies; Japanese Interpretation; Korean Interpretation; *and* Race, Ethnicity, and Biblical Criticism.]

BIBLIOGRAPHY

Ahn, John. "A Light to the Nations: The Sociological Approach in Korean American Interpretation." 112–22 in Foskett and Kuan, eds. 2006.

Bailey, Randall C., Tat-siong Benny Liew, and Fernando F. Segovia, eds. *They Were All Together in One Place? Toward Minority Biblical Criticism.* Atlanta, GA: Society of Biblical Literature, 2009.

Cheng, Patrick S. "Multiplicity and Judges 19: Constructing a Queer Asian Pacific American Biblical Hermeneutic." *Semeia* 90/91 (2002): 119–133.

Copher, Charles B. "Three Thousand Years of Biblical Interpretation with Reference to Black Peoples." In *African American Religious Studies: An Interdisciplinary*

Anthology. Edited by Gayraud Wilmore, 105–128. Durham: Duke University Press, 1989.
Copher, Charles B. "The Black Presence in the Old Testament." In Felder, ed., 146–164.
Felder, Cain Hope. "Cultural Ideology, Afrocentrism and Biblical Interpretation." In *Black Theology: A Documentary History. Volume Two: 1980–1992*, edited by James H. Cone and Gayraud Wilmore, 2:184–95. Maryknoll, N.Y.: Orbis, 1993.
Felder, Cain Hope."Race, Racism, and the Biblical Narratives." In *Stony the Road We Trod African American Biblical Interpretation*, ed. Felder, 127–45. Minneapolis, Minn.: Fortress, 1991.
Felder, Cain Hope. *Troubling Biblical Waters: Race, Class, and Family*. Maryknoll: Orbis, 1989.
Ferens, Dominika. *Edith and Winnifred Eaton: Chinatown Missions and Japanese Romances*. Urbana: University of Illinois Press, 2002.
Foskett, Mary F. "The Accidents of Being and the Politics of Identity: Biblical Images of Adoption and Asian Adoptees in America." *Semeia* 90/91 (2002): 135–144.
Foskett, Mary F. "Obscure Beginnings: Lessons from the Study of Christian Origins." In Foskett and Kuan eds., 178–91.
Foskett, Mary F., and Jeffrey Kah-Jin Kuan, eds. *Ways of Being, Ways of Reading: Asian American Biblical Interpretation*. St. Louis: Chalice, 2006.
Kim, Chan-Hie "Reading the Cornelius Story from an Asian Immigrant Perspective." In *Reading from This Place. Volume I: Social Location and Biblical Interpretation in the United States*, edited by Fernando F. Segovia and Mary Ann Tolbert, 165–174. Minneapolis, Minn.: Fortress, 1995.
Kim, Uriah (Yong-Hwan). "Uriah the Hittite: A (Con) Text of Struggle for Identity." *Semeia* 90/91 (2002): 69–85.
Kuan, Kah-Jin Jeffrey and Mai-Anh Le Tran. "Reading Race Reading Rahab: A 'Broad' Asian American Reading of a 'Broad' Other." In *Postcolonial Interventions: Essays in Honor of R. S. Sugirtharajah*, edited by Tat-siong Benny Liew, 27–44. Sheffield: Sheffield Phoenix, 2009.
Liew, Tat-siong Benny. *What Is Asian American Biblical Hermeneutics? Reading the New Testament*. Honolulu: University of Hawaii Press, 2008.
Liew, Tat-siong Benny. "The Word of Bare Life: Workings of Death and Dream in the Fourth Gospel." In *Anatomies of the Fourth Gospel: The Past, Present, and Futures of Narrative Criticism*, edited by Tom Thatcher and Stephen D. Moore, 167–193. Atlanta: Society of Biblical Literature.
Liew, Tat-siong Benny, and Vincent L. Wimbush "Contact Zones and Zoning Contexts: From the Los Angeles 'Riot' to a New York Symposium." *Union Seminary Quarterly Review* 56 (2002): 21–40.
Nakashima Brock, Rita. "Dusting the Bible on the Floor: A Hermeneutics of Wisdom." In *Searching the Scriptures: A Feminist Introduction*, edited by Elisabeth Schüssler Fiorenza, 64–75. New York: Crossroad, 1997.
Rietz, Henry W. "Living Past: A *Hapa* Identifying with the Exodus, the Exile, and the Internment." In Foskett and Kuan, eds., 192–203.
Rietz, Henry W. "My Father Has No Children: Reflections on a *Hapa* Identity toward a Hermeneutic of Particularity." *Semeia* 90/90 (2002): 145–157.
Shih, David "The Seduction of Origins: Sui Sin Far and the Race for Tradition." In *Form and Transformation in Asian American Literature*, eds. Zhou Xiaojing and Samina Najmi, 48–76. Seattle: University of Seattle Press, 2005.
Wan, Sze-kar "Asian American Perspectives: Ambivalence of the Model Minority and Perpetual Foreigner." In *Studying Paul's Letters: Contemporary Perspectives and Methods*, edited by Joseph A. Marchal, 175–190. Minneapolis, Minn.: Fortress, 2012.
Wan, Sze-kar "Betwixt and Between: Toward a Hermeneutics of Hyphenation." in Foskett and Kuan, eds., 137–151.
Yamada, Frank M. "Constructing Hybridity and Heterogeneity: Asian American Biblical Interpretation from a Third-Generation Perspective." In Foskett and Kuan, eds, 164–177.
Yee, Gale A. "Inculturation and Diversity in the Politics of National Identity." *Journal of Asian and Asian American Theology* 2 (1997): 108–112.
Yee, Gale A. "Yin/Yang is Not Me: An Exploration into an Asian American Biblical Hermeneutics." In Foskett and Kuan, eds., 152–163.

Tat-siong Benny Liew

Assyriology and Biblical Interpretation

Assyriology has irreversibly influenced biblical interpretation since the mid-nineteenth century and remains a key discipline for the proper historical contextualization and interpretation of the Hebrew Bible.

Definition. Assyriology is the study of the languages and civilizations of ancient Mesopotamia and the regions surrounding the Upper Euphrates, an area roughly described as present day Iraq, eastern Syria, and southeastern Turkey. Chronologically, Assyriology covers the first half of human history within these geographical limits, beginning with the invention of writing in the late fourth millennium B.C.E. and ending with the demise of cuneiform at the turn of the eras. Sumer, Babylonia, and Assyria are among the most important civilizations studied within the field, but the discovery of several new sites in the twentieth century, especially in Syria (e.g., Mari, Ebla, Alalakh, and Emar), have broadened its horizons substantially. "Assyriology," strictly speaking, is therefore a misnomer, stemming from the fact that the earliest discoveries were made in Assyria.

Assyriologists focus their philological interests on two languages: Sumerian, a language unrelated to all others, and Akkadian, a member of the Semitic language family and thus related to Arabic and Hebrew. Sumerian and Akkadian were written with various forms of cuneiform, a wedge-like script pressed into damp clay with a stylus or carved into stone. For this reason, Assyriology is a member of the broader field of cuneiform studies, which includes Hittitology and Ugaritology, among others. Besides Sumerian and Akkadian, Assyriologists may utilize ancient Elamite, Eblaite, Urartian, Hittite, Hurrian, Ugaritic, Aramaic, Old Persian, biblical Hebrew, and even Hellenistic Greek in their work.

Numerous learned societies support the scholarly goals of the field, including the American Oriental Society and the Canadian Society for Mesopotamian Studies. The International Association for Assyriology sponsors a meeting every summer for Assyriologists to present their research. The leading journals include *Archiv für Orientforschung*, *Journal of Cuneiform Studies*, *Revue d'assyriologie et d'archéologie orientale*, and *Zeitschrift für Assyriologie und vorderasiatische Archäologie*. The incomplete *Reallexikon der Assyriologie und vorderasiatischen Archäologie* (Berlin, 1932–) is the field's most comprehensive encyclopedia.

Early Excavations. Assyriology as a field of study is relatively young, owing its birth to a handful of talented amateurs. Although travelers and explorers had taken notice of the ruins of ancient Babylon and Assyria, projects that could legitimately be called excavations began only in the nineteenth century. Fueled by nationalistic competition for a land route to India, cultural prestige, and political influence, French and English nationals found themselves in the Near East for diplomatic and military reasons. Some of these individuals with antiquarian interests began uncovering the monumental ruins of ancient Near Eastern cities. Spurred on by the excavations of Paul Émile Botta (1802–1870), the French consul in Mosul, at Kuyunjik (later confirmed to be ancient Nineveh) in 1842 and Khorsabad (the ancient site of Sargon II's [721–705 B.C.E.] palace) in 1843, Austen Henry Layard (1817–1894), a secretary to the English ambassador in Constantinople, undertook large-scale excavations at Nimrud (biblical Kalah, though mistaken as Nineveh) from 1845 to 1847. His immediate success ensured funding for a second expedition (1849–1851), which encompassed several other sites, including Kuyunjik (Nineveh). Layard's remarkable discoveries created a sensation in London; the popular, lively account of his explorations and findings, *Nineveh and Its Remains* (1849), was an immediate bestseller. The early archaeological successes gave impetus for digging at many other sites, including Uruk, Larsa, Kish, Ur, Eridu, and Borsippa, in the years immediately following. The Crimean War in 1854 put an end to this first wave of excavations.

The stream of archaeological discovery during the initial period of excavation, communicated via successful commercial books, fed the reading public's enthusiasm. For many, the discoveries vindicated the historicity of the biblical narratives. For example, W. K. Loftus (1821–1858), one of the first excavators of southern Mesopotamia, reports the following from Babylon in the 1850s: "I lay awake for a length of time, recalling to my mind all the wonderful events which had befallen 'the golden city,' and the astounding fulfillment of those prophecies which refer in so remarkable a manner to its present crumbling condition. No one who reflects seriously on such a subject and on such a scene can fail to be impressed with the truth of Scripture"

(*Travels and Researches in Chaldea and Susiana*, New York, 1857, p. 24). Others, however, were not so enthused and worried that the discoveries might be used to question the veracity or authority of scripture. Both kinds of reactions, rooted in religious faith, have clouded the use of Assyriology in biblical interpretation to the present.

Recovering Ancient Texts. Already in the eighteenth century, reports and drawings of wedge-like inscriptions from Persepolis, the ancient Persian capital of Darius I (521–486 B.C.E.), had made their way to Europe. There were also reports about a much longer inscription high on the cliffs of Mount Behistun, located on an ancient road between the Median capital of Ecbatana and Babylon. These inscriptions contained three different languages. One called Old Persian used only forty-four different characters in its cuneiform script, making it the best choice for initial decipherment. The other two, Elamite and Akkadian, utilized a great many more signs; their decipherment would prove much more difficult. By 1802 Georg Friedrich Grotefend (1775–1853), a schoolmaster in Germany, deciphered the short inscriptions available to him in Old Persian. But a longer inscription was needed for a fuller understanding of the language. Beginning in 1835 Henry Creswicke Rawlinson (1810–1895), a soldier for the East India Company, copied the Behistun inscription with much exertion and daring during a decade of intermittent labor. Although other scholars contributed to its decipherment, Rawlinson in 1846 became the first to produce a complete translation of the Old Persian part of the Behistun inscription.

In 1847 Rawlinson, now the British consul in Baghdad, turned his attention to the inscription's Akkadian version, as had a few other scholars, including the Irish clergyman Edward Hincks (1792–1866). The Akkadian text was particularly difficult because its hundreds of signs could represent a syllable, an entire word, or a class of words, and many signs had multiple values. By 1851 Rawlinson, with the insights of others, had a full translation of the Akkadian section of the Behistun inscription. In the following year Hincks and Rawlinson translated a section of Sennacherib's (704–681 B.C.E.) inscriptions that included a description of the Assyrian invasion of Judah in 701 B.C.E. The account is similar to 2 Kings 18:13–16, thus confirming the importance of the Assyrian records for biblical interpretation. But the text was also different enough to cause some uneasiness among Bible readers.

Botta and Layard discovered many cuneiform inscriptions and tablets during their excavations, aiding the deciphering efforts of Rawlinson and Hincks. The most significant find, however, came during Layard's second expedition when he discovered two large rooms filled a foot deep with tablets. A few years later Hormuzd Rassam (1826–1910), who continued excavations at Nineveh for the British Museum, found another great cache of tablets. The thirty thousand tablets that came from these two discoveries comprise the royal archive and library of Ashurbanipal (668–627 B.C.E.). Representing nearly every known genre in Akkadian, these tablets form the foundation of Assyriological philology.

By the mid-1850s reading the myriad cuneiform tablets became a pressing need. But some doubted the reliability of Assyriologists' translations. To put these doubts to rest the Royal Asiatic Society in 1857 challenged Rawlinson, who had returned to London in 1855 to publish tablets, Hincks, and two other scholars, Jules Oppert (1825–1905) and W. H. Fox Talbot (1800–1877), to produce a translation of an unseen cuneiform inscription. Their four translations of an inscription of Tiglath-Pileser I (1114–1076 B.C.E.) were sufficiently similar that judges declared the Akkadian language, or Assyrian, as it was first called, officially deciphered.

Rawlinson and others had already noticed that some of the cuneiform tablets were not written in Assyrian (Akkadian) but in some non-Semitic language they mistakenly called Akkadian. It was not until 1869 that Oppert would correctly identify the language as Sumerian. The lexical lists from Nineveh and elsewhere were fundamental to the process of understanding this obscure language, a process that continues into the present. The French discoveries of Gudea's (ca. 2100 B.C.E.) statues and cylinders at Girsu (modern Telloh) and the American excavation of thousands of school tablets at Nippur in the late nineteenth century would lead to the recovery of Sumerian textual corpora significantly older than most Akkadian texts. Scholars who focus on Sumerian are properly called Sumerologists.

The process of sorting, cataloging, deciphering, and translating the tablets from Nineveh in the British Museum (and elsewhere in Europe) was tedious and time-consuming and remains so even today. During the early days of this work in 1872 George Smith (1840–1876), a young Assyriologist at the British Museum, recognized a tablet that recounted a great flood and a family's survival in a boat. He reported his findings on 3 December 1872 to the newly formed Society of Biblical Archaeology (founded in 1870 by Samuel Birch [1813–1885]) before an audience that included the prime minister. So sensational was the public's reaction to the news that the *Daily Telegraph* offered £1000 for Smith to renew excavations at Kuyunjik to find missing pieces of the flood story. He succeeded in doing so within one week of digging! Although the initial news was received with great excitement, this cuneiform flood account, hundreds of years older than the biblical flood stories, raised many uncomfortable questions about the Bible.

Assyriology to the Present. Archaeological excavations in the Near East began again in earnest in the following decades, with teams from England, France, Germany, and America excavating at sites such as Sippar, Babylon, Ashur, Girsu, and Nippur, among others. Myriads of tablets poured into Western museums. Archaeological excavations of increasing sophistication, diverse national origin (including the Iraqis), and geographical range (including eastern Syria and southeastern Turkey) have continued ever since the late nineteenth century, despite interruptions caused by World Wars I and II and the American-led invasions of Iraq (the latter resulting in the devastation and/or looting of many sites).

The 500,000 tablets so far discovered have greatly exceeded the working capacity of the relatively few professional Assyriologists. Moreover, public interest in and funding for Assyriological work has declined significantly since the days of Layard and Smith. With relatively few university positions available to Assyriologists, this disconnection between materials and resourced researchers will continue into the foreseeable future. This is unfortunate for biblical scholars since Assyriological materials have provided the most important ancient textual data for illuminating the Hebrew Bible.

Biblical Interpretation. The following surveys the use of Assyriology in biblical interpretation thematically and historically, highlighting methodological issues, recurring problems, practical hurdles, and important achievements.

A Privileged Scripture among Tablets. The task of Assyriology is to recover whole civilizations for their own sake. But biblical scholars' interest in the field is generally limited to specific compositions or genres that shed light on the text of their professional focus, the Bible. For many biblicists, therefore, Assyriology is a handmaid to biblical studies. Complicating the intellectual and methodological challenges in using Assyriology for this narrow purpose is, however, another issue. Namely, most of the scholars that have used Assyriology in biblical interpretation have also been personally affiliated with a contemporary religion for which the Bible is scripture. Presuppositions rooted in religious commitments that privilege the Bible have therefore not only motivated interest in Assyriology but also steered comparative results. Ironically, when Assyriologists distanced themselves from biblical studies for these very reasons, the field suffered in terms of public interest and institutional support.

Francis Brown's (1849–1916) address, "Assryiology: Its Use and Abuse in Old Testament Study" delivered in 1884 (published 1885) to his colleagues at Union Theological Seminary in New York (significantly, the first institution in America to teach Akkadian) illustrates the interrelatedness of methodological problems and the privileged position of the Bible in biblical interpreters' use of Assyriology.

The Rush for Relevance. For Brown, apologetics lay at the root of the abuses of Assyriology. Of the three abuses he lists, his first, the hasty use of poorly understood Assyriological texts in biblical interpretation, has been a problem for scholars eager to make the cuneiform record relevant to the Bible—for apologetic reasons or otherwise. In Brown's day several scholars enthusiastically followed Smith's lead in looking for biblical connections to cuneiform tablets. Many fanciful suggestions caused understandable reticence for early translations of cuneiform documents and interpretive claims based thereon. But the same problem occurred repeatedly in the twentieth century, as biblical interpreters hastily misunderstood the texts from Nuzi, Ebla, and elsewhere and then overestimated their biblical implications. For example, some scholars argued for the historicity of features in the patriarchal narratives based on legal practices at Nuzi, but their ideas were based on misreadings of the texts.

Contextual Neglect. Brown also had three positive uses for Assyriology, two of which, ironically, are obviously apologetic. The first use in Brown's list is the rich historical context that Assyriology provides for the Bible. This use has grown in importance in almost unimaginable ways since Brown's day. Unfortunately, with the rise of ahistorical and theological hermeneutical methodologies in the last quarter of the twentieth century (e.g., canonical, reader-centered literary, or ideological approaches), large segments of biblical scholars have neither the training nor the desire to utilize Assyriological material in a substantial, informed manner. A small but growing segment of biblical scholars, however, led by Assyriologist William Hallo (1928–), has attempted to counter these trends in recent decades. Hallo's contextual approach insists on interpreting the Bible within its ancient Near Eastern milieu in a manner that appreciates both its similarities and differences with the texts of neighboring cultures and considers both diachronic development and synchronic comparisons.

Distinctiveness of Israel. Another use of Assyriology, according to Brown, is the opportunity to discern the essential (i.e., uniquely spiritual) distinctiveness of ancient Israel via a contrast with its pagan neighbors. The comparative results of such unabashedly apologetic endeavors are, however, rightfully suspect. Comparative literature, history, and religion are descriptive academic tasks. A theological predisposition to exalt Israel over its neighbors can lead to misunderstandings on both sides of the comparison. Therefore, biblical interpreters should guard against such a tendency, not embrace it. The distinctiveness of ancient Israel as presented in the Hebrew Bible is best approached in a cultural anthropological manner. Cultures may share many similarities with one another, but each is distinctive.

Ammunition against Higher Criticism. According to Brown, Assyriology provides the necessary data to confirm the basic trustworthiness of the historicity of biblical texts. In the late nineteenth century, critical biblical scholarship, a predominantly German endeavor, did not find a sympathetic ear among the majority of English-speaking biblicists. Despite the fact that Julius Wellhausen's synthesis of critical biblical scholarship in 1878 made no use of Assyriology (though he was quite well informed about the field), some hoped Assyriology could ward off the skepticism such scholarship seemed to foster. The title of a book by A. H. Sayce (1845–1933), an Anglican clergyman and Oxford Assyriologist, illustrates this well: *The "Higher Criticism" and the Verdict of the Monuments*, published in 1894 by the Society for the Promotion of Christian Knowledge. Similar books, often resorting to tortuous historical explanations, are published regularly to this day.

A more dispassionate historical approach has reached a different verdict. Although Assyriology provides external verification for some biblical descriptions of events (best judged on a case-by-case basis), it has also given us insights into scribal practices that vindicate and refine source, form, and redaction-critical methodologies.

Babel/Bible Controversy. Between 1902 and 1904 Friedrich Delitzsch (1850–1922), a prominent German Assyriologist, presented three provocative lectures that opened a wound in the relationship between Assyriology and biblical studies that has yet to heal fully. Delitzsch, taking an anti-apologetic stance, argued that the Hebrew Bible and many of its distinctive features (e.g., the Sabbath and the fall of man) were derived from the more advanced and sophisticated Babylonians. Offering numerous examples, he exalted Babylonian ethics over biblical ethics, denied Yahweh's status as a universal deity in the Bible, and questioned the divine inspiration of the Old Testament. With an increasingly anti-Semitic tone, Delitzsch suggested the German church dispense with the Old Testament altogether and purify Christianity of human ideas. A few Assyriologists, such as Hugo Winckler (1863–1913) and Alfred Jeremias (1864–1935), went even farther with an agenda called Pan-Babylonianism, arguing that the Hebrew Bible, the New Testament, and indeed, all ancient religions were based on an astral religious system first expressed clearly in ancient Mesopotamia.

The many sensational and unsupportable claims from these scholars overshadowed Delitzsch's most important point (i.e., Mesopotamian cultures significantly influenced the composers of the Hebrew Bible) and elicited defensive reactions from colleagues. The prominent biblical scholar Hermann Gunkel (1862–1932), for example, conceded in his booklet *Israel und Babylonien* (Göttingen 1903) that Israel had indeed been influenced by Mesopotamia; but influence was not replication. Israel always put its own characteristic imprint on the materials and ideas drawn from its neighbors. This was an important and fundamentally correct evaluation. But Gunkel went on. He asserted, as would many other scholars, that Israel's imprint made the materials and ideas superior to Mesopotamian religion.

With the field's reputation damaged, Assyriologists in the twentieth century relinquished scholarly claims on things biblical and focused their research, with occasional exceptions, on the recovery of cuneiform cultures. Biblical scholars who used Assyriology in biblical interpretation, though suggesting many new insights, by and large remained defensive about biblical literature's ontological distinctiveness.

Availability of Texts. The problem of making Assyriological materials accessible to biblical scholars was recognized already in the nineteenth century. One solution has been the compilation of anthologies that select, introduce, and translate Mesopotamian (and other ancient Near Eastern) texts relevant to the Bible. By gathering a wide selection of relevant documents into a single publication, these anthologies helped biblical scholars contextualize biblical literature more easily and explicate various biblical forms, motifs, metaphors, religious practices, historical perspectives, and more, in light of the Mesopotamian ones. The first anthology was edited by the German Assyriologist Eberhard Schrader (1836–1908) and appeared in 1872. The first English anthology was edited by Samuel Birch; its twelve volumes appeared serially from 1872 to 1881. More than twenty similar anthologies have now appeared in various languages. For English speakers today, the most important anthologies are (the outdated, but useful) *Ancient Near Eastern Texts Relating to the Old Testament* (James B. Pritchard, ed. Princeton, 1950, 1955, 1969) and Hallo and Younger's *The Context of Scripture* (3 vols.; Leiden, 1997–2002). The latter has extensive introductions and suggests biblical cross-references with each translation.

For cuneiform material not appearing in anthologies, the manner in which tablets were published was a significant practical hurdle for Assyriology's use in biblical studies. Tablets were usually published as type-set cuneiform, line drawings, and/or photographs, requiring a scholar to decipher the tablet from cuneiform before using it for research. Transliterations (representations of cuneiform signs in the Roman alphabet) and translations of selected tablets were relegated to scholarly articles, monographs, or text editions, many of which appeared decades after a tablet's publication. But in the last decades of the twentieth century, Assyriological practice changed. Tablets were still drawn and photographed, but transliterations, translations, and often commentary accompanied the images, making the tablets more accessible to non-specialists. With the advent of the Internet, several projects have committed to making all cuneiform tablets available on open-access websites, providing each (eventually) with digital photographs, modern transliterations, and reliable translations. The most important projects are the Cuneiform Digital Library Initiative (http://cdli.ucla.edu/) and the Open Richly Annotated Cuneiform Corpus (http://oracc.museum.upenn.edu/index.html). Availability and accessibility of published materials is no longer as great a problem as it once was for biblical scholars. But, tens of thousands of documents remain unpublished and/or uncataloged.

Interpretive Achievements. Assyriology has opened many new interpretive possibilities for biblical studies, illuminating the biblical text in ways unimaginable before the decipherment of cuneiform.

Language. The discovery of Akkadian enriched comparative Semitics with an early and still growing linguistic corpus. With a vocabulary more than twice that of Biblical Hebrew in a corpus perhaps dozens of times larger than the Bible, biblicists soon realized the benefits of mining Akkadian for lexicographical and idiomatic insights. The first lexicon in English to use Akkadian was the famed *Hebrew and English Lexicon of the Old Testament* (Oxford 1907). Every major lexicographical effort since has followed suit. Exegetes have also scoured the lexicon for help, an activity that will increase now that the *Chicago Assyrian Dictionary* (1956–2010) is complete. Of course, numerous suggestions using Akkadian to explain something in the Bible have been questionable or wrong. For example, Hebrew *šabbāt*, "sabbath," is etymologically related to Akkadian *šapattu*/*šabattu*, "fifteenth day of the month," but there is probably no conceptual connection. Likewise, the name of the garden of Eden is probably not a translation of Sumerian *eden*, "plain, steppe." But Akkadian and Sumerian have proven useful in understanding some things otherwise obscure in Hebrew. Akkadian *diglu*, "vision, look," for example, likely explains the odd statement in Song of Songs 2:4, "*diglô* over/upon me is love." Traditionally *diglô* (from *degel*) is translated "his banner," but a more likely rendering in light of Akkadian is "his look" or "his gaze."

Antediluvian Traditions. Cuneiform sources reveal many close parallels to the biblical narrative in Genesis 1–11, providing important information for contextual interpretation of these chapters. When Smith discovered a Mesopotamian flood story in 1872, the primary question was the extent to which Genesis 6—9 was literarily dependent on cuneiform sources. The same has often been pursued with regard to Genesis 1—2 and the *Enuma elish*. However one answers these questions, there is no doubting that Genesis 1—11 have been influenced by or are reacting to Mesopotamian ideas. For example, creation in Genesis 1:1 and *Enuma elish* both begin with chaotic waters, a great flood in both Mesopotamian and Hebrew traditions divides a former age and present conditions, and the tower of Babel is a Mesopotamian ziggurat, whose description in Genesis 11:4 plays on the name of Marduk's temple in Babylon, É-sag-íl, "house whose top is high." In light of this, the more interesting questions, as Gunkel recognized early on, concern themselves with the distinctiveness of the biblical account, that is, how and why the Israelite scribes incorporated antediluvian stories from the ancient Near Eastern imperial cultures into their own work and what this process accomplished for their ideological concerns. The hermeneutical tools of post-colonialism suggest answers. For example, humankind made in the image of the deity in Genesis 1:27 appropriates Mesopotamian royal rhetoric and applies it to all humans, and the depiction of Babel in Genesis 11 subverts Mesopotamian cultural hegemony via mockery.

Covenant and Law. Cuneiform tablets provide a large corpus of legal and diplomatic documents that opens new avenues for biblical interpretation. Mesopotamian legal material often contains topics and concerns similar to the civil legislation in the Bible. The most striking example is the laws concerning the goring ox (Exod 21:28–32), a topic treated in the Laws of Eshnunna (§§ 53–54, ca. 1770 B.C.E.) and the Code of Hammurabi (§§ 250–251, ca. 1750 B.C.E.). As for diplomatic documents, treaties in Akkadian have refined our understanding of covenantal terminology, literary structure, and social relations of participants. For example, William Moran (1921–2000), drawing on the Amarna correspondence and Neo-Assyrian treaties, demonstrated that the term "love" in Deuteronomy (e.g., Deut 6:4) is in fact a covenantal term that designates a vassal's obligation of loyalty to his sovereign ("The Ancient Near Eastern Background of Love of God in Deuteronomy." *CBQ* 25 [1963], 77–87). In *Deuteronomy and the Deuteronomic School* (Oxford, 1972) Moshe Weinfeld (1925–2009) convincingly argued that Deuteronomy most closely resembles the Neo-Assyrian treaties and loyalty oaths and demonstrated that curses in Deuteronomy 28:26–35 were literarily dependent on curses in Esarhaddon's (680–669 B.C.E.) Succession Treaty (lines 419–430). This insight has put a seventh century date for Deuteronomy's composition on a solid footing, suggesting that Deuteronomy conceived of Yahweh as an alternative to Assyrian hegemony.

History and Historiography. Assyriology offers important resources for reconstructing events in the Levantine states of the mid-second to mid-first millennium. For example, the Amarna Letters, comprising some 350 diplomatic letters mostly exchanged between two Egyptian pharaohs and their Canaanite vassals, have cast remarkable light on the social and political turmoil of mid-fourteenth century Canaan, just a couple of centuries before Israel's emergence. In the period of the divided monarchy (mid-tenth century to 586 B.C.E.), Neo-Assyrian royal annals open an invaluable window on the political and military history of the region, often resulting in a fuller understanding of biblical historical narratives as well as providing background on prophetic pronouncements, rhetorical strategies, and symbolic activities (e.g., Isa 20). The Assyrian royal inscriptions, often extant in multiple copies and editions, also supply excellent material for investigating ancient Near Eastern historiographical practice, that is, the ideological perspectives and compositional/editorial techniques employed by scribes in their textual representations of past events. Understanding these practices provides important analogies for understanding biblical historiography.

Prophecy. The discovery of prophetic cuneiform texts at Mari, Eshnunna, Nineveh, and elsewhere has placed the study of prophecy in the Hebrew Bible on a broader contextual basis. Although there was resistance to seeing the parallel in twentieth century scholarship, it is widely recognized today that this material proves intuitive divination (prophecy) was not unique to the Bible but existed throughout the Near East. Cuneiform sources, most of which come from Old Babylonian Mari and the state archives of the Neo-Assyrian empire in Nineveh, attest oracle reports, delivered as messenger speech ("thus says god so-and-so"), and provide references to prophets or prophecy in various letters and other documents, both official and literary. As in the Hebrew Bible, prophets utilized simile, metaphor, and proverbs in their oracles, and sometimes employed symbolic acts. The oracles are usually directed to the king, unlike the many oracles directed to the people in the Bible, and concern the king's actions, his enemies, or the cult. Unlike much biblical prophecy, which is concerned with judgment, salvation oracles for the king dominate the corpus of Neo-Assyrian prophecies and usually begin with the biblically familiar "fear not!" (e.g., Isa 41:10). The Neo-Assyrian sources include tablets that preserve a single oracle report and tablets that have edited several reports onto one tablet. The latter provide insight into the editorial creation of prophetic literary collections.

Prayers and Laments. The various prayers and laments preserved in Akkadian and Sumerian have also illuminated the Hebrew Bible, especially the Psalms and Lamentations. Despite the many differences in Mesopotamian and Hebrew prayers and laments, a brief perusal of the texts reveals shared religious concepts (e.g., acknowledgment of sin, repentance, trust), ritual gestures (e.g., hands upraised in prayer, prostration), metaphors and idioms (e.g., turning the face), formal structures (e.g., the promise to praise the deity concludes certain Akkadian and Hebrew prayers), and genres (e.g., city laments), considerably broadening our understanding of ancient Israel's religious context.

Early comparative studies, such as Friedrich Stummer's in 1922 and Geo Widengren's in 1937, were marred by poor methodology, lack of attention to genre, and, in Stummer's case, an overt apologetic intent. Later work refined the comparative methodology and applied form criticism more rigorously to the materials with varying success. But one can still see comparative results that betray a theological predisposition. For example, early comparison between Akkadian *shuilla*-prayers and the Hebrew individual psalms of lament revealed that despite several structural similarities there was one outstanding difference: the *shuilla*-prayers begin with a long hymnic introduction that praises the deity's divine attributes; the Hebrew individual laments start with a very simple invocation of the deity. Claus Westermann argued in his influential study *Das Loben Gottes in den Psalmen* (Göttingen, 1954; the fifth edition of 1977 was translated into English as *Praise and Lament in the Psalms* [Atlanta, 1981]) that this formal difference indicates different understandings of divinity. As he sees it, Mesopotamian supplicants begin with descriptive praise of the deity in the context of the pantheon to make the deity favorably disposed to hear petitions, which come later in the prayer. Hebrew supplicants, conversely, boldly begin with petition, reserving declarative praise for the individual thanksgiving psalms, which express gratitude for the deity's intervention on the supplicant's behalf. In Westermann's own words: "[i]n Babylon the psalms primarily praise the . . . god who exists in his world of gods. In Israel they primarily praise the God who acts marvelously by intervening in the history of his people" (p. 42). But Westermann's comparison is ill-conceived, based on a comparison of disparate prayer genres. The *shuilla*-prayers are always directed to high gods by individuals having difficulty with their personal gods, whereas the individual psalms of lament speak to Yahweh in a familial context, addressing personal concerns. Yahweh functions as a personal deity in these prayers. If one looks at Akkadian prayers to personal gods (dingir-šà-dib-ba-prayers), they have very short invocations much like the Hebrew psalms of lament. The basis for Westermann's theological point therefore evaporates. As emphasized by Hallo's contextual approach, proper analysis of genre is an essential component in comparative study.

Topical Studies. Several scholars have written studies that compare some aspect of Mesopotamian (and broadly ancient Near Eastern) culture with the literature of the Hebrew Bible, providing many new insights in the process. Examples include temple building, social justice, creation accounts, concepts of sin and punishment, family religion, women's religion, divine activity in history, scribal practice and textual production/editing, origins and treatment of divine revelation, and the role of the prophet among many others.

Future Prospects. Despite more than a century of comparative scholarship, the study of the Hebrew Bible in its ancient Near Eastern context remains an underworked area of research. Assyriology holds the potential for many new insights into the Bible for those up to the challenge.

[*See also* Form Criticism, *subentry* Hebrew Bible; Hittitology and Biblical Interpretation; Redaction Criticism, *subentry* Hebrew Bible; Source Criticism; *and* Ugaritology and Biblical Interpretation.]

BIBLIOGRAPHY

Chavalas, Mark W. "Assyriology and Biblical Studies: A Century and a Half of Tension." In *Mesopotamia and the Bible: Comparative Explorations*, edited by Mark W. Chavalas and K. Lawson Younger Jr., 21—67. Sheffield, UK: Sheffield Academic Press, 2002. An exploration of the tense relationship between Assyriology and Biblical Studies. A treasure trove of bibliography.

Chavalas, Mark W. "The Comparative Use of Ancient Near Eastern Texts in the Study of the Hebrew Bible." *Religion Compass* 5/5 (2011): 150–165. A wide-ranging summary of materials available for comparative study from Syria, Anatolia, Egypt, and Mesopotamia. The bibliography is very rich with secondary literature.

Clifford, Richard. *Creation Accounts in the Ancient Near East and in the Bible.* Washington, D.C.: The Catholic Biblical Association of America, 1994. A thematic study of creation in the Bible in light of other ancient Near Eastern, and especially Mesopotamian, creation accounts.

Foster, Benjamin R. "Assyriology: 1850–1970." In *Handbook of Ancient Mesopotamia*, edited by Gonzalo Rubio. Berlin: De Gruyter, forthcoming. An authoritative, wide-ranging history of Assyriology by a leading Assyriologist. The author has written several other articles on the history of the field and has produced the premier anthology of Akkadian literature.

Hallo, William W. "Compare and Contrast: The Contextual Approach to Biblical Literature." In *The Bible in the Light of Cuneiform Literature: Scripture in Context III*, edited by William W. Hallo, Bruce William Jones, and Gerald L. Mattingly, 1–30. Lewiston, Me.: Edwin Mellen, 1990. One of several of the author's influential, methodological statements on interpreting the Hebrew Bible within its ancient Near Eastern milieu, emphasizing the importance of proper genre analysis in comparative work. The author has contributed significantly to the renewal of studying the Hebrew Bible within its ancient Near Eastern milieu.

Hays, Christopher B. "Echoes of the Ancient Near East? Intertextuality and the Comparative Study of the Old Testament." In *The Word Leaps the Gap: Essays on Scripture and Theology in Honor of Richard B. Hays*, edited by J. Ross Wagner, Christopher Kavin Rowe, and A. Katherine Grieb, 20–43. Grand Rapids, Mich.: Eerdmans, 2008. Explores the methodological issues surrounding intertextuality and how such a method could prove fruitful in understanding the impact of ancient Near Eastern texts on the Hebrew Bible.

Hendel, Ronald. "Genesis 1–11 and Its Mesopotamian Problem." In *Cultural Borrowings and Ethnic Appropriations in Antiquity*, edited by Erich S. Gruen, 23–36. Stuttgart: Franz Steiner, 2005. A reading of Genesis 1—11 that recognizes significant Mesopotamian influence and interprets the Bible's distinctiveness through Post-colonial theory.

Jong, Matthijs J. de. *Isaiah among the Ancient Near Eastern Prophets: A Comparative Study of the Earliest Stages of the Isaiah Tradition and the Neo-Assyrian Prophecies*. Leiden/Boston: Brill, 2007. A recent comparative study of Isaianic and Neo-Assyrian prophecy that interprets Isaiah in light of eighth century events as a prophet of salvation, much like the Neo-Assyrian prophets.

Lambert, W. G. "Mesopotamian Sources and Pre-exilic Israel." In *In Search of Pre-Exilic Israel: Proceedings of the Oxford Old Testament Seminar*, edited by John Day, 352–365. London: T&T Clark, 2004. A useful survey with bibliographical help of historical sources from Assyria relating to the Hebrew Bible by one of the most respected Assyriologists of the last 50 years.

Larsen, Mogens Trolle. "The 'Babel/Bible' Controversy and Its Aftermath." In *Civilizations of the Ancient Near East*, 4 vols., edited by Jack M. Sasson, 95–106. New York: Charles Scribner's Sons, 1995. Based on the author's previous book on the topic, this is an accessible account of the controversy with a solid bibliography. The encyclopedia in which this work occurs is an indispensible resource.

Lenzi, Alan. *Secrecy and the Gods: Secret Knowledge in Ancient Mesopotamia and Biblical Israel*. Helsinki: The Neo-Assyrian Text Corpus Project, 2008. A recent comparative study of scribal practices and professional mythology relating to the origins and treatment of divine revelation in Mesopotamia and the Bible.

Machinist, Peter. "The Image of Assyria in First Isaiah." *Journal of the American Oriental Society* 103.4 (1983): 719–737. A pioneering and still influential study of how the prophet's oracular rhetoric reflects Assyrian ideology.

Machinist, Peter. "The Question of Distinctiveness in Ancient Israel: An Essay." In *Ah, Assyria—: Studies in Assyrian History and Ancient Near Eastern Historiography Presented to Hayim Tadmor*, edited by Mordechai Cogan, 196–212. Jerusalem: Magnes, 1991. Reprinted in Frederick E. Greenspahn, ed. *Essential Papers on Israel and the Ancient Near East*. New York: New York University Press, 1991, 420–442. An important, nontheological look at the distinctiveness of Israel, whose late, marginal, and precarious political position is considered a fundamental factor for its distinctive national perception and relationship to the deity.

Machinist, Peter. "The Road Not Taken: Wellhausen and Assyriology." In *Homeland and Exile: Biblical and Ancient Near Eastern Studies in Honour of Bustenay Oded*, edited by Gershon Galil, Mark Geller, and Alan Millard, 469–531. Leiden/Boston: Brill, 2009. An insightful intellectual history of Wellhausen's biblical scholarship and its relationship to late nineteenth century Assyriology, which sheds considerable light on the early history of the field.

Saggs, H. W. F. *The Encounter with the Divine in Mesopotamia and Israel*. London: Athlone, 1978. A wide-ranging comparison of Mesopotamian and Israelite religious concepts.

Tawil, Hayim ben Yosef. *An Akkadian Lexical Companion for Biblical Hebrew: Etymological-Semantic and Idiomatic Equivalents with Supplement on Biblical Aramaic*. Jersey City, N.J.: Ktav, 2009. An important compilation of Akkadian etymological, semantic, and idiomatic equivalents to Biblical Hebrew and Aramaic.

Tigay, Jeffrey H. ed. *Empirical Models for Biblical Criticism*. Philadelphia: University of Pennsylvania Press, 1985. An important collection of essays that attempts to show the plausibility of critical methods in biblical studies via scribal practices observed in other early texts, including Mesopotamian ones.

Toorn, Karel van der. *Sin and sanction in Israel and Mesopotamia: A Comparative Study*. Assen: Van

Gorcum, 1985. An important and original comparative study of the concept of sin and punishment in Mesopotamia and Israel by a leading scholar. The author has also written comparative studies on Mesopotamian and Israelite family religion, women's religion, and scribal practices.

Younger, K. Lawson. "The Production of Ancient Near Eastern Text Anthologies from the Earliest to the Latest." In *Orientalism, Assyriology, and the Bible*, edited by Steven W. Holloway, 199–213. Sheffield, UK: Sheffield Phoenix, 2006. A historical overview of the need for and issues surrounding the production of text anthologies. A survey and evaluation of anthologies is included.

Zernecke, Anna. "The Use of Akkadian Prayers in the Study of the Hebrew Bible." In *Reading Akkadian Prayers and Hymns: An Introduction*, edited by Alan Lenzi, 61–68. Atlanta: Society of Biblical Literature, 2011. Freely available here: http://www .sbl-site.org/assets/pdfs/9780199832262.pdf. A history of comparative scholarship in the area of Akkadian and Hebrew prayers with full bibliography. The volume as a whole introduces various genres of Akkadian prayers and provides twenty-nine annotated examples with comparative suggestions for the Hebrew Bible.

Alan Lenzi

Authority of the Bible

Since both Christians and Jews have historically accepted the Bible as authoritative, the primary issue is the nature of biblical authority. How can an ancient text function authoritatively for people today—particularly in a postmodern era? Since the Bible is subject to many interpretations, can one ever claim that the Bible itself is authoritative? How can we understand the authority of the Bible, and in what ways can the Bible operate authoritatively?

The Nature of Authority. The *Concise Oxford English Dictionary* identifies the following senses for the noun "authority": (1) the power or right to give orders and enforce obedience; (2) a person or organization exerting control in a political or administrative sphere; (3) the power to influence others based on recognized knowledge or expertise, as in an authoritative person, book, or other source. In the first and second senses, some people or books may be authoritative by virtue of their position or right, as in a judge, a military officer, monarch, or a law code. Many assert that the Bible exerts the third kind of authority. But recognizing the Bible as authoritative in the first sense is a personal, contextual, and historical matter. The Bible's authority is "personal" in that an individual may choose to follow it or not—just as a patient is free to follow the advice of a physician or not. The Bible's authority is also "contextual" in that its teachings may be embraced and even enforced within a given religious community. And its authority is bound to history, as the role of authority in general has changed historically. (For a helpful historical survey of Jewish and Christian views of the Bible's authority over the millennia, see Goshen-Gottstein et al., 1996)

Why is the Authority of the Bible an Important Matter? Both Jews and Christians make astonishing claims about the nature and origin of the Bible (Jews for the Hebrew scriptures and Christians for both Old and New Testaments). They view the Bible as divine revelation (citing such texts as 2 Pet. 1:21 and 2 Tim 3:16, showing how the early Christians viewed the Hebrew scriptures). If such claims are true, then the Bible's authority assumes paramount importance. If God authored the Bible in some sense (however we might understand the concept of inspiration), then it possesses inherent "authority": the power or right to give orders and enforce obedience (sense 1 above). If the Bible's origin is divine, then it demands preeminence in the lives of God's people—and ultimately of all people.

Can a Human Book Be Authoritative? The Bible presumes that God is the Supreme Being, creator of all. Therefore, God alone possesses authority, though the New Testament sees that authority embodied in Jesus Christ. Even so, given the Bible's point of view, God may delegate authority to angels, to prophets and apostles, and to a document that he authors. Presumably, God could also delegate authority to an institution and its leadership or to other specially appointed individuals. In a Judeo-Christian worldview, God is the source of all authority, and any other claims are valid only to the extent that God has delegated that authority. This raises important issues for assessing religious authorities. To what extent can we view "tradition" as authoritative in governing beliefs and actions? Which claims of certain church bodies or rabbinical councils truly possess divine authority for their positions and pronouncements?

Evangelical scholars think that it is important to affirm that God, rather than the Bible or anything else, possesses ultimate authority. The Bible has authority in a delegated or mediated way. Consequently, as the communication of God, the Bible compels attention and allegiance.

On What Basis Could the Bible be Considered Authoritative? The traditional understanding of the doctrine of inspiration asserts that God guided the writers of scripture to produce precisely what he wanted. Not literally dictated, the scriptures still reveal God's oversight of the writers. God inspired them, shaping their imagination and guiding their actual writing in order to assure the trustworthiness and the efficacy of their witness (Bloesch 1978, p. 55). Divine inspiration has two aspects: the work of the Holy Spirit in directing the writers (2 Pet 1:21) and the documents that resulted from that divine/human concursive activity. If, then, the Bible owes its impetus and content to God, it may be said that the Bible is revelation itself—the divinely inspired medium through which God communicates.

If, however, the claim to divine inspiration is merely unverifiable religious assertion, then the nature of the Bible's authority must be reframed, as many have concluded. Meaningful as it may be, this human production is not necessarily authoritative or even truthful. Certainly it reflects some worldviews and values that people in our era cannot embrace. In this view the Bible's authority comes only as readers affirm or acknowledge the Bible's teaching as useful or true for them. Its ideas are not normative for people today; it can only illuminate or exemplify authority. The Bible's authority is limited to select ideas or teachings, as viewed through the interpreters' grids. For example, a number of feminist cultural critics do not accept as authoritative those biblical texts that marginalize or subordinate certain groups. Consequently, the Bible may contain—but is not—the word of God. In this view the Bible gains its respect and value as an enduring repository of the testimony and experience of God's people in the past. But today's readers must discern that truth for themselves in their contexts and not assume that the Bible's perspective on reality has ongoing validity. From this perspective, interpretation and validity of the Bible are always subject to readers' cultures and worldviews, just as all interpretation is in some ways captive to the pre-understandings of the interpreters.

Thus, the crucial nature of one's presuppositions is evident. On the one hand, if the Bible is regarded as divinely inspired, it assumes authority over its readers as God's Word. They still must interpret what it says, to be sure, and they are always free to believe or disbelieve, to obey, or disobey. On the other hand, if the Bible is the product of human effort alone, then humans stand over the Bible to assess its value and usefulness. Readers proclaim themselves as the authority. Ultimately, people bear the responsibility for choosing to accept the Bible as divinely inspired or not and the consequences that follow.

Is the Authority of the Bible Dependent upon Correct Interpretation? Can it be accurate to say that the Bible is authoritative, or only that "this is an authoritative interpretation?" And if the latter, then who makes the decision? Again, the history of interpretation amply shows that Jews and Christians have invoked various norms to guide interpretation. For the Jews it was the "traditions of the elders" mentioned in the New Testament (e.g., Mark 7:4; cf. Matt 15:2–3, 6; Mark 7:3, 5, 8–9, 13) or the subsequent Mishnah and Talmuds. Christians have devised and adhered to their own church traditions in many and varied forms over the centuries—the early creeds express beliefs; the various formulae for celebrating the Eucharist exemplify traditional practices. Furthermore, interpretations have been weighed against many other criteria: reason, inner experience, cultural fit, the "witness of the Spirit," or agreement within a specific faith-community. Is it possible to have the message right, even if—and especially if—the Bible possesses authority? What is necessary for a plausible interpretation?

Historical Criticism. The human element in the composition of the Bible demands that we assess it with the various critical tactics for understanding ancient artifacts—in this case, literary texts. Exegesis endeavors to clarify to the best of our ability what the authors meant to communicate within the time and culture in which they wrote. The message of the Bible is contained within historically conditioned documents written within a matrix of contexts. Consequently, claims for the Bible's authority are inseparable from a consideration of this matrix. Tactics include investigating the historical and cultural background of the text; examining the literary world in which the documents appear; applying rhetorical criticism or speech-act analysis to assess how the author designed the communication to function; and analyzing grammar as well as studying the words the writers used within their original contexts. Honest, careful, thoughtful, rigorous, critical—the work of exegesis respects the integrity of the text.

Reason. Readers employ reason or logic to qualify interpretations and to exclude what is illogical, arbitrary, or in conflict with human knowledge. A nonsensical interpretation cannot be authoritative, but reason and logic may also be misguided or fallacious (Carson 1996, pp. 87–124). This raises another presuppositional issue: the presence of supernatural phenomena within sacred texts. On the one hand, one who assumes that people cannot walk on water will categorize the Gospel account of Jesus and Peter (Matt 14:25–29) as "myth," and, therefore, removed from any real-world reference. If, on the other hand, one assumes that the supernatural God may enter our space-time continuum, then an axe-head may float (2 Kgs 6:6) or a dead person may be brought back to life (1 Kgs 17:17–24; Luke 7:12–15). (I am not arguing for or against the validity of "myth," only pointing out the role of presuppositions in assessing reasonableness.) Some interpretations are illogical or far-fetched and should be rejected, while other interpretations may violate the normal "rules" of nature or reason, yet still be valid if one assumes that God invades the human space-time continuum. Reason, therefore, aids understanding scripture, but it does not necessarily supplant it.

Tradition. Interpretations of the Bible have molded the more or less formal traditions of many religious communities. Such traditions are inevitable, having both positive and negative consequences. Traditions contribute by preserving memories of the past as well as prescribing how insiders act and what they believe. In the religious realm, traditions catalog and implement the ways biblical texts have been understood over time and form religious communities that see things in a certain way. Such memory works to keep the body—whether church or synagogue—faithful to its origins and mission. Deuteronomy (and other parts of the Hebrew Bible) had this role for Israel. The apostle Paul endorsed the traditions he had received and was determined to preserve and propagate them (e.g., 1 Cor 11:16, 23; 15:3–7). These traditions formed a norm against which to measure Christian life and teaching and became the standard of a developing "orthodoxy."

Experience. Does experience constitute a reliable guide to an authoritative interpretation of scripture? Believers sometimes testify to an "internal witness" or mystical experiences that corroborate for them the reality of their convictions (cf. Rom 8:15). Certainly, words, beliefs, or affirmations ring hollow if they fail to result in behaviors. For example, a test of the biblical affirmation that the fruit of the Spirit is love and joy (Gal 5:22) is whether Christ's followers exhibit love and joy. But as with reason and tradition, experience alone is insufficient as a criterion of validity. While crucial, experience cannot be the sole test of whether an interpretation is valid since its evaluation is too subjective; praxis alone is not sufficient. Even common experiences among a group of "the faithful" are insufficient to assure validity. These may show only that they all have bought into a hoax (apparently a critique of some early Christians that 2 Pet was written to refute).

Those who accept the Bible as authoritative guide for faith and practice deny that experience in itself stands above scripture as a means to assess its validity and authority. How can one distinguish among one's psyche, ego, neurology, and the product of the Holy Spirit? Nor does encounter with the "miraculous" necessarily take precedence over scripture. While Moses performed great miracles through the power of God, so did Pharaoh's magicians (Exod 7:10–11; cf. Matt 7:21–23). While some faith communities may assume that miracles may be evidence of the supernatural, they deny that experience is an autonomous authority to discount or overturn the Bible. The scriptures judge individual experience, not the other way around.

Furthermore, a claim that "the Holy Spirit told me what this text means" does not constitute an authoritative interpretation. Indeed, believers do assert that the Spirit inspired the Bible, as discussed earlier, and so depend upon the Spirit to apprehend its meaning. But that Spirit does not convey the correct (and authoritative) interpretation of a text to someone apart from good exegesis. The interpreter's task is to utilize all means to understand the text—the objective dimension that establishes the basis for the text's authority.

The "GRAND NARRATIVE" of the Bible. The Bible is not merely a collection of disparate writings. Believers interpret the particulars of scripture in light of its larger intent or "story." Even a cursory reading of the New Testament will quickly show that the early Christians—even the Jewish ones—no longer felt obliged to keep all the directives of the Hebrew scriptures. The Apostle Paul could acquiesce to Jewish sensibilities or shelve them when he was with gentiles (e.g., 1 Cor 9:20–23). Christians rejected the need for animal sacrifices to atone for sins because they understood that Jesus paid the penalty for their sins (Heb. 9:26; 10:12). They abandoned Sabbath worship and adopted Sunday because of the significance of Jesus's resurrection on Easter Sunday. Christians and Jews today do not feel obligated to follow all the commands in the Bible. Not all Jews subscribe to kosher regulations, for example; some churches allow women to teach and have positions of leadership.

Key to this phenomenon is one's understanding of the overall purpose or story of the Bible. The Bible points to the *missio Dei*, God's mission of redemption and restoration (see Wright 2006 for an excellent explication of this perspective). When one follows the narrative, as if chapter-by-chapter, elements that feature in earlier parts of the story no longer play the same role or have the same significance in later sections. One outline of the elements of the biblical story might be: Creation/Eden, the Fall, Abraham/Moses/Israel, Jesus, the Church, and Eternal Consummation/Restoration. For Jewish interpreters the Jesus and Church sections would be omitted or assigned different significance.

Demonstrating this principle, Jesus considered the Hebrew scriptures authoritative and not to be set aside (John 10:35), yet he interpreted them in view of his own person and coming. In effect, his mission changed the rules for how to understand and apply the Hebrew scriptures. Conspicuous examples occur in Luke 4:18–19 (using Isa 61:1–2); Matthew 5: 21–22, 27–28, 33–37, 38–39; Mark 7; and Mark 10:2–12. The early Christians' new relationship to the Hebrew scriptures resulted in assigning them a new title: Old Testament (OT). The Hebrew scriptures were not abandoned (as the heretic Marcion attempted to do), but seen as "fulfilled" in Christ (Matt 5:17–20). Matthew's repeated use of fulfillment language highlights his view that a new era has dawned. Jesus represented a new chapter in the grand narrative, and the Christians' role was to write the next chapters. That entailed their new "reading" of the OT, exemplified by Jesus's own instruction of the Emmaus disciples (see Luke 24:27). While affirming the inspiration and authority of the OT (2 Tim 3:16; 2 Pet 2:21), Christians abandoned such practices as circumcision, the Sabbath, and the ritual laws about clean and unclean foods, despite clear biblical commands in the OT (cf. Heb. 8:13; 10:9). Jewish Christians quickly came to embrace the belief that Jesus is Lord, worthy of worship on a par with Yahweh himself (see Hurtado 2005). In light of that monumental shift, they could set aside the authority of many scriptures and the traditions of a thousand years (Dunn 2009, p. 93). A new era had dawned (2 Cor 5:17). The only authoritative interpretation of the OT for Christians was christocentric.

The point of considering the Bible as "grand narrative" is to remind interpreters that various parts of the Bible exist within specific "chapters" of the overall story. One cannot lift out a text from one chapter and expect it to have the same significance or role in another one. It may anticipate a theme developed later. It may insert one that was absent earlier. Paul uses the word *mystērion* (mystery) to capture this phenomenon. He speaks about ". . . my gospel and the proclamation of Jesus Christ, according to the revelation of the mystery that was kept secret for long ages but is now disclosed, and through the prophetic writings is made known to all the Gentiles, according to the command of the eternal God, to bring about the obedience of faith" (Rom 16:25–26). Animal sacrifices had played a role in an earlier part of the story, but became obsolete (for Christians) once Jesus had been sacrificed or (for Jews) when the Temple was destroyed. The OT as given and intended by the OT writers is no longer authoritative for Christians. It belonged to an earlier part of the story that had reached its climax in Jesus (Wright, p. 53).

Religion has become more spiritualized (for both Jews and Christians) in the postbiblical period, even while certain specific prohibitions in the OT remain in force for them all, such as idolatry and immorality (as Paul explains so forcefully in 1 Cor). Christians examine how both the OT and the NT play out in the era of the church—post-OT and post-Jesus. That is to say, Christians feel that Jesus's amendment of the law (and the entire OT) is binding on his followers, summed up in the command to love one's neighbor. In other words, holiness has moved from ceremonial to moral for Jesus's followers and modern Judaism.

The Nature of the Bible's Authority. For believers, the Bible is the repository of God's special, inspired, divine revelation to his people. But in a larger sense, Christians believe in one way or another, that the Bible is the authoritative "story" that God conveys to humanity, with supreme status among other stories. For Christians, the entire Bible, OT and NT together, comprise the authoritative account of reality. It tells the truth about God, God's love for his creation and creatures that endures beyond their rebellion, and his plan for redemption and the restoration of all things through Christ.

Believers also accept the Bible as the inspired story energized by the Holy Spirit in the lives of God's people. What is authoritative about this story? When people choose to enter into the narrative, it transforms them in some way; it affirms that God has taken the initiative in creation and redemption; it suggests that God demonstrates deep concern for people; it portrays God as present in Christ's deeds and teachings; and it demonstrates that God continues his work though his people. What is more, God speaks through scripture, and has done so throughout history (Dunn, p. 103).

How Can the Bible Function as an Authoritative Text in the Lives of People Today? Returning to the definition of "authority" (whether in the realms of government, the military, business, religion, or other spheres), the contributions of influence for good, structure or order, and expertise demonstrate that authorities play an important role in human relationships. The Bible can exert legitimate authority in the world today by several means.

Authorization. Walter Brueggemann prefers the term "authorization" to describe the Bible's authority in the postmodern world. In this view, the Bible does not, or cannot, assert authority; it can only authorize a community to live, act, and hope in a manner that is a witness to the truth of its message. This authorization of a community's obedience and praise becomes recognized in the larger public arena (Brueggemann, "Scriptural Authority," *Anchor Bible Dictionary*, 5, pp. 1050–1052). Other documents may serve such authorizing functions for given communities, but adherents claim that the Bible possesses intrinsic authority over its readers. It speaks the language of truth and command, not simply of authorization (Marshall 2004, 13). In its divine origin, the Bible is trustworthy—an authoritative guide to faith and practice.

As the authority, it has pride of place in all matters to which it speaks.

Empowering. In addition to serving as guide, Christians believe that the Bible works as an enabling or empowering dynamic in the lives of people. Most importantly, it empowers them to live out God's story through the indwelling Holy Spirit. What are the tasks of God's people at this stage of the "grand narrative"? Who are their spiritual ancestors, and what does the life of faith look like today? Specifically, what does this empowerment provide for God's people?

Principal Realities. The Bible deals with the central questions that humans ask. Where did we come from? Is there a God, and what is God like? Why did God bring humans into existence? What is the central human problem (another way of asking, "Why can't we all just get along?")? How has God responded to that problem? How are God's people to live in this world? For Christians: Who is Jesus, and what is the significance of his death? What does it mean to be followers of Jesus? Throughout history many people have dealt with these questions in a variety of ways without invoking biblical teaching. For Christians, however, the Bible provides its own unique account. It has come to be recognized, even by outsiders, as a classic or a monument that makes available what we consider most definitional for human life (Brueggemann, p. 1054).

Establishes the Normative People of God. The Bible mediates God's message through the power of the Holy Spirit enabling people to apprehend its significance. Thus, the Bible has its own self-authenticating power as the word of God within the believing community that it creates. The Bible both constitutes the normative community of God's people and forms (and reforms) them spiritually as they embrace its teachings. The Bible reveals the *missio Dei*, God's story of redemption that provides the foundation and marching orders of an ongoing community. By rehearsing the narrative found within scripture, the community embraces an interpretive framework through which God's people can live out faithfully and purposefully their own part in God's story (Grenz 1994, pp. 508–509). In other words, the Bible is the authoritative constitution for communities of faith enabling its members—both corporately and individually—to exercise their calling in the world.

Energizes the Normative Community. The authority of the Bible is most evident when God's people embrace God's redemptive purposes in the world, working to counter structures of power that perpetuate injustices. Brueggemann observes, "It is staggering evidence of the authority of scripture that even in the face of harsh, systemic brutality there have been and still are communities of faith who have demonstrated this alternative vision in the public arena" (p. 1054). Rather than merely positing "timeless truths" in some a-historical or a-cultural ways, the Bible's story opens God's people up to new opportunities and demands in the life of faith. God's people may recognize canonical trajectories in the Bible that may authorize "moving beyond" the biblical texts themselves. Examples in the history of interpretation include movement beyond the Bible's treatment of slavery and the role of women (see Webb 2001). Vanhoozer suggests cultivating the mind of the canon so that we discern within the Bible itself patterns for correct speaking about God and God's will for people (K. J. Vanhoozer, "Into the Great 'Beyond,'" in Marshall, p. 93).

Embracing the Bible's Authority. The Bible's authority can be addressed from the inside or the outside. From the outside, the topic may be of only passing interest. Outsiders are content to allow those within faith communities to debate any value believers find in ancient texts, but outsiders see limited relevance for themselves. Inside those communities, however, the issue has more gravity. How do the faithful embody the Bible's teaching?

First, believers immerse themselves in the Bible—seeking to grasp the "grand narrative," not merely the specifics (the do's and the don'ts) along the way. Judaism and Christianity have always championed the careful reading of scriptures. The Bible cannot have any life-changing impact on people or their faith communities if they are not nurtured by its teachings. Consequently, there are constraints that govern how believers can embrace the Bible.

Dunn suggests two concepts that are useful in this task: covenant and culture (Dunn, pp. 101–102). As some rulings in the OT no longer applied because of the new era in Christ, or because the world had changed from a Palestinian theocracy to a Greco-Roman province, so we need careful exegesis to assure that we focus on the intent of the text. While most Christians accept divine inspiration in some fashion, they recognize that not all scripture can have the same significance today that it had when it was originally penned. Interpreters must distinguish what in the Bible is descriptive of how matters were (in a different era in the "grand narrative" or in a different cultural context), from what is prescriptive or normative in the lives of believers today. God judged Achan and the Israelites in a specific way (Josh 7; 22:20). In the NT, Ananias and Sapphira also experienced God's judgment (Acts 5:1–11). These texts describe God's responses to these evils, but they do not prescribe how God always operates. Jesus "fulfilled" the OT trajectory (Christ is the "end" of the Law, Rom 10:4). For the early Christians, this meant that they read the OT through the lens of Jesus to decide what in it they embraced, altered, or jettisoned. Theological convictions governed how they treated their sacred Hebrew scriptures. God's people immersed in the Bible attempt to discern how the Spirit continues to speak through these texts—not replacing or rejecting those texts, but clarifying and illuminating their current significance.

[*See also* Cultural Studies; Evangelical Interpretation; Feminist Biblical Interpretation; Historical Criticism, *subentry* Hebrew Bible; Historical Criticism, *subentry* New Testament; Postmodern Interpretation; Rhetorical Criticism; Speech-Act Theory; *and* Theological Interpretation.]

BIBLIOGRAPHY

Barr, James. "The Authority of the Bible." *The Ecumenical Review* 21 (1969): 135–150. Sets out six crucial issues that must be addressed in a discussion of the Bible's authority. This article identifies many of the significant terms in the ongoing debate.

Barr, James. *The Bible in the Modern World.* London: SCM; New York: Harper & Row, 1973. Following up on the previous article, Barr poses questions for the Bible's interpreters: the Bible's relevance to today when our problems differ from the biblical times; its communicability to people today; its limitations—can the Bible really be decisive for people today; its isolation—is the Bible that different from other books; and interpreters' responsibility to convey a valid message for people in this age. A very provocative study that raises questions that all students as well as preachers of the Bible need to answer.

Berkouwer, G. C. *Holy Scripture.* Grand Rapids, Mich.: Eerdmans, 1975. Dutch reformed discussion of a range of topics on the doctrine of scripture, including the testimony of the Spirit, the Bible as canon, inspiration, and the authority and interpretation of scripture. While insisting on the Bible's infallibility, he differs with Warfield in not affirming inerrancy.

Bloesch, Donald. *Essentials of Evangelical Orthodoxy.* Vol. 1, *God, Authority, and Salvation.* San Francisco: Harper & Row, 1978. In a section on the primacy of scripture (pp. 51–78), Bloesch provides a well-balanced discussion of the Bible's divine authority, distinguishes infallibility and inerrancy, and presents the hermeneutical task. He points out some of the misconceptions within evangelicals' views of the Bible.

Carson, D. A. *Exegetical Fallacies.* 2d ed. Grand Rapids, Mich.: Baker, 1996. A handy compendium of all-too-common fallacies committed by scholars and preachers alike, especially focusing on fallacies relating to words, grammar, logic, presuppositions, and history.

Carson, D. A. "Recent Developments in the Doctrine of Scripture." In *Hermeneutics, Authority, and Canon,* edited by D. A. Carson and J. D. Woodbridge, 5–48. Grand Rapids, Mich.: Academie, 1986. A far-ranging critique that seeks to classify and assess recent issues, including rewriting the Bible's history, the phenomena of the Bible, debates over terminology, "proposition" and "literary genre," the new hermeneutic, and the waning of the Bible's authority in the churches.

Dodd, C. H. *The Authority of the Bible.* London: Nisbet, 1928; New York: Harper & Bros., 1962. This volume comprises Dodd's groundbreaking attempt to reestablish biblical authority in the aftermath of modern criticism that had undermined the traditional doctrine of infallibility and its consequent rejection of the Bible's authority. In his view, authority finally resides in the truth alone or, put religiously, in the mind and will of God. The Bible's authority lies not in its inerrancy, but in its persuasiveness, in its appropriation by a community, and in the life of the Jesus it portrays. The Bible presents not "objective truth": it is relative to the minds that receive it. He understands the Bible to be the instrument the Spirit uses to create an experience of divine things.

Dunn, J. D. G. *The Living Word*, 2d ed. Minneapolis: Fortress, 2009. In part I, Dunn supplies very useful discussions of the task of NT interpretation, the nature of gospel oral tradition, pseudonymity in the NT, and a chapter with the intriguing title, "Was Jesus a Liberal? Was Paul a Heretic?" in which he unpacks their respective uses of the OT. While conservative overall, Dunn's treatment in part II of the book rejects the fundamentalist view of inerrancy as erroneous and unhelpful in understanding the Bible's authority and usefulness.

Goshen-Gottstein, Moshe, et al. "Scriptural Authority." In *The Anchor Bible Dictionary*, edited by David Noel Freedman et al. Vol. 5: 1017–1056. New York: Doubleday, 1996. Authored by several leading scholars, this entry contains historical reviews and analyses along with detailed bibliographies of the topic under these subdivisions: Jewish, Eastern Orthodox, Roman Catholic, Early Church, Medieval Church, Protestant Reformation, in the Wake of the Enlightenment, and the Postcritical Period (written by W. Brueggemann).

Grenz, S. J. *Theology for the Community of God*. Nashville: Broadman & Holman, 1994. Grenz locates his discussion of scripture under the broader heading of pneumatology pointing to the Spirit as the instigator and energizer of scripture. Useful rubric of the corporate body of Christ undergirds the entire discussion.

Henry, C. F. H. *God, Revelation and Authority*, Vol. 4, *God Who Speaks and Shows: Fifteen Theses, Part Three*. Waco, Tex.: Word, 1979. Henry pens a polemical defense of the view of scripture as the inerrant word of God. He disagrees with fellow conservatives who are willing to embrace infallibility but not inerrancy.

Hurtado, L. *Lord Jesus Christ: Devotion to Jesus in Earliest Christianity*. Grand Rapids, Mich.: Eerdmans, 2005. This represents a remarkable historical survey tracing the very early Christian movement to apply the category of "deity" to Jesus. In this thoroughly documented and carefully argued work, Hurtado demonstrates that the earliest Christians, within Jewish-Christian monotheism, quickly (within a few decades after Jesus's departure) began to ascribe to Jesus the worship and devotion formerly applied solely to Yahweh. The book traces not only the movement of Christ-devotion into the second century, but he engages all the significant research on the topic in the last century.

Kaufman, G. D. "What Shall We Do with the Bible?" *Interpretation* 25 (1971): 95–112. This work affirms many of the same issues that James Barr underscored. If we are to treat the Bible responsibly in our era, we can't simply go to the Bible itself. The world has changed dramatically; we are vastly different from those who penned the Bible. Kaufman raises the question of "God" for moderns. Since "the Bible does not have special *authority* in this matter as 'God's revelation,'" we can't simply embrace its view of God. In the end, the Bible can't have any pride-of-place role in how modern people construct their worldviews.

Kelsey, D. H. *The Uses of Scripture in Recent Theology*. Philadelphia: Fortress, 1975. As a theologian, Kelsey argues that "authority" refers to the functions that scripture performs in the church, and does so only with God's enablement. He analyzes several key scholars (B. B. Warfield, Hans-Werner Bartsch, G. Ernest Wright, Karl Barth, Lionel Thornton, Paul Tillich, and Rudolf Bultmann), asking diagnostic questions to determine how they view the Bible as authoritative. These various scholars construe the Bible's authority in differing ways: its doctrinal content, its concepts, its narrative, its images, symbols, or myths. Scholars also use these construals to authorize theological conclusions in different ways. These construals also play out differently in their functions within the church.

Marshall, I. H. *Beyond the Bible. Moving from Scripture to Theology*. Grand Rapids, Mich.: Baker, 2004. This short volume written by a leading evangelical New Testament scholar defends a "principled way" of moving from scripture to its contemporary understanding and application by exploring how the biblical writers used the sources at their disposal. Marshall aims to show how we can follow their lead in apprehending scripture today. Two scholars provide insightful responses to his essay: K. J. Vanhoozer, "Into the Great 'Beyond': A Theologian's Response to the Marshall Plan"; and S. E. Porter, "Hermeneutics, Biblical Interpretation, and Theology: Hunch, Holy Spirit, or Hard Work"?

Nineham, D. E. "The Use of the Bible in Modern Theology." *Bulletin of the John Rylands Library* 52 (1969): 178–199. He questions the traditional view that every part of the Bible, when correctly interpreted, can have significance for people today. He doubts that ancient texts, even in the Bible, will necessarily be useful to modern people. He answers "no," to the question: "Am I then committed, as a Christian, to the view that biblical writers can never have been simply wrong for their own times and/or irrelevant for ours?"

Ramm, Bernard. *The Pattern of Religious Authority*. Grand Rapids, Mich.: Eerdmans, 1957. Here is a concise and very useful explanation of the different kinds of authority and why the issue of religious authority is so important. Ramm investigates whether anything has the right (authority) to prescribe religious belief, and, then, what those might be in his estimation. He outlines and defends what he calls "The Protestant Principle" of authority and critiques competing alternatives facing religious conservatives at that time.

Reventlow, H. G. *The Authority of the Bible and the Rise of the Modern World.* Philadelphia: Fortress, 1985. The author explains his purpose in this very substantial (668 pages) volume: "In this study I have set myself the task of looking back at the beginnings of biblical criticism (in which the Old Testament plays an important part) to uncover the motives, the intellectual presuppositions, the philosophical assumptions, and last, but not least, the developments in church politics, which have led to the conclusions at which it arrived" (p. 2). Especially for those interested in historical developments, Reventlow unpacks English theological changes between 1550 and 1750 and shows how those developments impacted modern critical views of the Bible. The foundations for modern biblical criticism were laid in England, not Germany, as if often thought.

Rogers, Jack, ed. *Biblical Authority.* Waco, Tex.: Word, 1977. This collection of six essays within the evangelical camp was written largely in response to the inerrancy versus infallibility debate among conservatives in the 1970s. Collectively, they affirm the Bible's authority, not its inerrancy.

Rogers, J. B., and D. K. McKim. *The Authority and Interpretation of the Bible.* San Francisco: Harper & Row, 1979. The authors contend that the best theology before the Reformation and the best Reformed theology since affirms the infallibility of scriptures in matters of faith and practice without requiring them to be factually accurate in matters of history or scientific details.

Warfield, B. B. *The Inspiration and Authority of the Bible.* Philadelphia: Presbyterian and Reformed, 1948. A Reformed scholar who vigorously defended the authority and inerrancy of scripture in this volume that collects several of his writings on this topic. The book focuses on inspiration, the oracles of God, and canonicity.

Webb, W. J. *Slaves, Women & Homosexuals: Exploring the Hermeneutics of Cultural Analysis.* Downers Grove, Ill.: InterVarsity, 2001. In this study in the practice of interpretation, Webb proffers a "redemptive-movement" hermeneutic theory to understand how to apply the teachings of the Bible in a modern context. Using the three topics as case studies for his approach, Webb seeks to demonstrate the "movement" within the Bible itself as the plan of redemption is worked out—and, therefore, how modern interpreters can venture similar movements today that go beyond the biblical context. So, he shows, using the first topic, how the testaments move from the place of slavery in the Old Testament, to hints of change in the New Testament based on a new understanding of humanity, that rightfully points to the inevitable abolition of slavery as a biblical movement.

Wright, C. J. H. *The Mission of God. Unlocking the Bible's Grand Narrative.* Downers Grove, Ill.: InterVarsity, 2006. In this very important book, Wright, an Old Testament scholar, traces in great detail throughout the pages of the Bible the *missio Dei*, God's plan to redeem and restore all things. In fact he argues that this missional motif explains the entire purpose and story of the Bible, from beginning to end, and that this grand narrative ought to be the hermeneutical lens through which all its parts are viewed.

Wright, N. T. *Scripture and the Authority of God.* New York: HarperOne, 2011. Centering his discussion in the authority of God and the "story" that the Bible portrays, Wright takes a historical approach to showing how the Bible has been used and abused in the past. He seeks to answer three underlying questions: (1) In what sense is the Bible authoritative in the first place? (2) How can the Bible be appropriately understood and interpreted? (3) How can its authority, assuming such appropriate interpretation, be brought to bear on the church itself, let alone on the world?

William W. Klein

Autobiographical and Personal Criticism

Immanuel Kant was one of the first modern-day philosophers who admitted that there is no such thing as an "objective" interpretation and that every interpreter brings a great deal to the text. Until very recently, almost all scholarly writing has been defined by the absence of the "I" or any reference to the personal situation of the writer or to the writing process. This situation has changed drastically with the introduction of autobiographical criticism.

Autobiographical criticism is also known as personal criticism, confessional criticism, autocritography, New Belletrism, New Subjectivism, or even *moi* criticism. It is thus a form of self-disclosure, but the degree of self-disclosure, or self-exposure, varies. Most of the currents in literature theory and criticism in the past thirty years have concentrated on the problematic of readers and reading. The widespread acceptance of responsibility to and for our own reading experiences is one of the major catalysts for the present surge of autobiographical criticism.

Autobiographical biblical criticism entails an explicitly autobiographical performance within the act of criticism. This involves implementing personal criticism as a form of self-disclosure, wittingly, while reading a text as a critical exegete. It requires a willing, knowledgeable, outspoken involvement with the subject matter on the part of the critic. It discloses the fact that the act of reading and interpreting are subjective.

Autobiographical Scholars. The Golden Era for the entrance of autobiographical criticism as genre on the theological academic landscape was in the late 1980s to the mid-1990s. That was the period when the most work on this topic was published. Since then, in certain communities, it has been generally accepted that all theology is in some way autobiographical.

According to Moore (1995, p. 20), four books in particular stand out as exemplifying autobiographical criticism. The first is Nancy K. Miller's *Getting Personal: Feminist Occasions and Other Autobiographical Acts.* The second is *The Intimate Critique: Autobiographical Literary Criticism,* edited by Diane Freedman, Olivia Frey, and Francis Murphy Zauhar. Then there is *Confessions of the Critics,* edited and introduced by H. Aram Veeser. The fourth is the only full-fledged example of confessional criticism to date by a biblical scholar, Jeffrey L. Staley's *Reading with a Passion: Rhetoric, Autobiography, and the American West in the Gospel of John.*

A stream of autobiographical essays has also been issuing from historical Jesus scholars. These have been published either in the Westar Institute's scholarly journal *Forum,* or in its periodical *The Fourth R,* or in independent publications. The scholars publishing these essays include Marcus J. Borg (1993, 1994), John Dominic Crossan, 1985, 2000, M. Eugene Boring (1985), Bruce Chilton (1993), and Walter Wink (1994).

Exploring the Definition. Autobiographical criticism gives scholars a critical forum for exploring the connections between themselves as real readers and their exegesis of biblical texts in a self-conscious and autobiographical manner (Anderson and Staley, 1995, p. 10). The autobiographical mode of criticism can offer itself as a partner in a hermeneutical dialogue with those rhetorical tropes of academic writing that are normally claimed to show scientific objectivity.

Autobiographical criticism helps the reader to assess the collision of the personal and the professional that has resulted from that swerve, along with its consequences or a lack thereof (Moore, p. 20). According to Fowler (1995, p. 232), the current widespread acceptance of responsibility to and for our own reading experiences is one of the major catalysts for the present surge of autobiographical criticism because reading is never disinterested, not even postmodern reading.

Maldonado (1995, p. 91) discerns two levels on which autobiography has an impact on the interpreter. He calls the first the *idio-autobiographical.* This refers to the ordinary, usual meaning of autobiography, namely the particular events, moods, motivations, and agenda that comprise the life story of the individual interpreter. These would, broadly speaking, be the data of a biography or an autobiography. The second level, more elusive and subconscious, he calls the *meta-autobiographical.* This level incorporates the available and recognizable autobiographical plots that the culture of the teller determines. It represents the various metanarrative strands that are available for the production of an (auto)biography.

A single reading can or should never pretend to represent the only way to read a given text. There can never be only one perspective on a text. The inescapability of multiple perspectives only becomes more apparent when both personal experience and social markers are taken into account (Anderson and Staley, p. 11). Autobiographical criticism, by its very nature, underlines multiple perspectives because it highlights the individual as well as some shared experiences that play a role in a reading. Its rhetoric often openly avows the interconnections between the personal and the social. An autobiographical critic does not claim to uncover absolute truth and/or to practice pure science. Instead, the critical text provides an opportunity to introduce the flesh and blood author as a scholar. It makes the point that no writing or academic research takes place in a vacuum.

Autobiographical Exegesis. An autobiographic critical text creates space for contextualization, culture, and experience. However, it can be a dangerous and bewildering enterprise for scholars to explore how their personal experiences and social locations relate to their professional discourse on the Bible. One of the arguments of autobiographical criticism is that these two, scholarship and life, are always connected. In academic language, it is easy to disguise one's person and life with the third person pronoun and with constructions in the passive voice. However, to write about how our personal lives, economic situations, and prejudices affect our interpretation of the Bible is to reveal the tenuousness and interested nature of our exegetical moves. Writing in an openly autobiographical manner exposes our scholarly exegetical enterprises as rooted in "ordinary reading," like all other reading of biblical texts.

One can therefore assume, as Fowler (p. 231) does, that the implied reader in many of our critical texts "was really myself" and that "the meaning that I was finding was the meaning *I* manufactured in the here and now. . . . *I* am responsible to and for what the text says *to me*." Autobiographical biblical criticism allows us to begin to see how and why we sometimes wear tinted glasses, and reading a wide variety of autobiographical criticism allows us to see what we share with others and where the colors of their lenses differ from our own (Anderson and Staley, p. 15).

Autobiographical scholars have discovered (and admitted) that they cannot tell where the text ends and where they, as exegetes, begin. Existential exegesis as "reception aesthetics" yields the admission that the interpreter and interpreted texts are deeply embedded in each other. To say something about yourself in an academic work makes you vulnerable. It is a risk that you take. However, one cannot do biblical criticism without a personal and autobiographical dimension.

Autobiographical biblical criticism is not and should not be or become the only way to do biblical criticism. Nevertheless, it has its place. It represents a discipline that takes seriously the rhetorical question Bultmann asked in an essay: "Is exegesis without presuppositions possible?" According to Bultmann, interpretation can only commence on the basis of a prior understanding of the subject matter. Any text must thus be interpreted in the light of some pre-understanding.

Autobiographical biblical criticism does not mark the end of criticism, but rather points the way toward a more rigorously self-reflective and contextualized biblical criticism. According to Henking (1995, p. 244), it is valuable in the sense that it creates a new tradition of scholarship—one that exposes and enacts the risky business of biblical studies.

Paradigm Shift to Postmodern. The shift to an autobiographical style in doing theology came along with the paradigm shift from a modern to a postmodern exegesis, but it also accompanied a move in many circles away from theological, objective, academic language to personal spirituality.

Postmodernity refers to a style of thought that is suspicious of classical notions of truth, reason, and objectivity. Postmodernism is not so much a method as a stance or posture composed of malleable and conflicting variables. Postmodernism is characterized by three broad and encompassing features: it is antifoundational, antitotalizing, and demystifying (Adam 1995, p. 4). First, it is antifoundational in that it denies any privileged unassailable starting point for the establishment of truth.

Secondly, the stance is antitotalizing in the sense that, according to those who practice it, no theory can provide the full and total answer to questions that are posed. Van Aarde (2002, p. 431) states: "Information contradicting a theory or providing another possible angle can always be found. If a theory claims to be 'total,' it in effect means that the other possibilities that do exist have simply been disregarded or the criteria were designed to eliminate them."

Thirdly, according to Adam (p. 5), postmodernism is also demystifying: "it attends to the claim that certain assumptions are 'natural' and tries to show that these are in fact ideological projections." It questions the presuppositions that certain things are "natural" and others "unnatural" and can therefore be discarded, seen as untrue, or marginalized. Generally accepted values based on the notion that some things have been legitimated, for instance, by God or the Bible, are questioned. These "natural" and "legitimate" values are exposed by postmodernism as concealing underlying ideological motives (Van Aarde, p. 431). Economic or political motives can be camouflaged by claims of universality or necessity. A postmodern version of demystification is therefore a matter of permanent criticism and self-reflective critique.

Postmodernism and Autobiographical Criticism. There are as many varieties of postmodernism as there are people who want to talk about the subject. The name itself suggests that it defines itself as different from "modernity." It is fair to think of it as a movement of resistance. Postmodern thinking evolved as a critique of certain values of modernity.

For a long time, the foundation of philosophical thought was Descartes's *Cogito, ergo sum* (I think, therefore I am). Postmodern thought undermines the assumption that one needs a foundation. Postmodern thinkers argue that no philosophical foundation is foundational enough. Therefore, no foundation is necessary. "They do not do the work one asks of them, and they simply provide one more point to which an opponent can object" (Adam, p. 7). Postmodern thinkers also generally resist totalities. Any reference to totalities raises suspicion. The hermeneutics of suspicion is the only method used by postmodern researchers. Therefore they deconstruct totalities because totalities either include everything altogether or proceed by excluding some possible members. If the totality includes everything, it is intellectually useless. The sort of totality that serves some useful purpose works by differentiating members from nonmembers, human from nonhuman, individual self from not self. However, the process of exclusion requires us to make judgments about what is in and what is out. This is where problems with totalities come in: Who decides what counts and what doesn't?

Totalities are always in flux and a totality in flux simply is not total enough.

Demystification has played a leading role in modern thinking. As Adam (p. 11) comments: "The rationalist criticism of theological doctrine, the Marxist critique of capitalism, the psychoanalytical critique of consciousness, all partake in the demystification of institutions and functions which had been thought 'natural' or divinely ordained." When faith is dismissed as wish fulfillment by an analyst, and when a political agitator points out to what extent the electoral process is restricted by financial issues, he or she displays "the characteristically modern 'hermeneutics of suspicion' which looks in every closet to discover the lurid secrets that are surely concealed there" (Adam, p. 12).

However, modernism has generally restricted the scope of this demystifying suspicion to particular classes of institution and theory. Certain domains have remained above suspicion. Postmodernism is changing this situation. No intellectual discourse is above postmodern criticism.

> Where modern criticism is absolute, postmodern criticism is relative; where modern knowledge is universal, unified and total, postmodern knowledge is local and particular; where modern knowledge rests on a mystified account of intellectual discourse, postmodern knowledge acknowledges that various forces that are ostensibly external to intellectual discourse nonetheless impinge on the entire process of perceiving, thinking, and of reaching and communicating one's conclusions. Nothing is pure; nothing is absolute; nothing is total, unified, or individual. (Adam, p. 16)

An autobiographical manner of doing exegesis and theology is thus a natural consequence of the paradigm shift.

Reading a text in a postmodern way is not to read the text a-historically or even in an antihistorical critical manner. The time, date, place, text-critical notes, grammar, *Sitz im Leben*, and all the other exegetical questions remain important. Postmodern reading remains a critical way of doing biblical exegesis, but, instead of formulating your exegetical results impersonally, or using passive constructions, you are free to formulate them personally, or even autobiographically, if you wish. According to Van Aarde (p. 431), the postmodern way of thinking is interdisciplinary and multidisciplinary, and, from a literary point of view, relevant documents should be read against the background of their chronological periods and respective contexts. When, for example, I do theology, I not only take the context of the texts and their background and chronology into account, I also take myself into account. This *method* can perhaps be called deconstruction.

Deconstruction and Autobiographical Criticism. When deconstruction moves into the discourse of biblical criticism it displaces many of the cardinal characteristics of institutionally legitimated interpretation. First, it underlines antifoundationalism:

> there can be no absolute reference point by which we orient our interpretations: not the text, the author, the meaning, the real historical event, nor any other self-identical authoritative presence. Second, it implies that when an author tries to compose a text that overcomes the limitations . . . she will inevitably fail: there will always be traces of the exclusions and the distinctions that do not make a difference, which a careful reader can locate and use to undermine the rhetorical power of the supposedly authoritative text. (Adam, p. 31)

Second, deconstruction demystifies. It separates history from fiction. Thirdly deconstruction does away with totalities. It does so by deconstructing the identity, the shadowy presence, which they claim to represent. Fourth, deconstruction allows interpreters to interact with texts in ways that they are not accustomed to; according to deconstruction there are no unnatural acts of textual intercourse. Deconstructive biblical interpreters must abandon the illusion that there is something behind the text. No form of exegesis or any research can give you a privileged peek into the composing scene behind the text. There is thus no right or only way to read a text at which you can arrive by means of sufficient research or the right exegetical method. Interpreters should forget the attempt to locate the world behind, or in, or in front of the text and remember that meaning is what we make of texts. Meaning is not an ingredient in texts.

This means that you are autobiographically active with the text. No method can thus claim that it is *the* method. All interpretation is therefore hermeneutical and personal. Doing exegesis autobiographically is thus to join in the search for meaning and to move from the known to the unknown, from what we are familiar with to what may seem strange to us. The faith and the story stay the same, but it is a venture in trying to formulate differently, to address issues, and to come to a new self-understanding in our process of our being busy with and engaging actively with the richness of the texts. Doing postmodern exegesis in an autobiographical style brings with it a shift, in many circles, away from theological objective academic language to a more personal use of language and to a personal spiritual involvement of the critic.

Spirituality and Autobiographical Criticism. All over the world, there is a resurgence of interest in spirituality. This sounds like a contradiction if one compares this statement to the declining numbers of members in institutionalized churches. However, the Bible is no longer only the possession of the church. Many people who do not belong to a church still read the Bible. They decanonize the Bible for themselves when they use it as inspirational literature to guide their meditation and contemplation. In using and studying the Bible, there has been a remarkable shift away from its theological and academic features to its usefulness for personal spirituality.

In the past, theology had become more and more an enterprise of the academy and its professionals and less and less relevant to everyday life. The theological frontier was addressed in learned study and in the library, but ordinary Christians had little knowledge of its usefulness. Today, more people, not only theologians, or even church members, but also ordinary people, some who do not even belong to a church, are talking theology. Even in academic circles, not everyone who is interested in the Bible or theology is a member of a church, or even a Christian. The purpose of theological research is not only to result in the life and preaching of the church anymore. Researchers and theologians have different agendas. For those who do not have the life of the church as their focus when they are doing theology, most of the time, their research and study are either for the sake of the academy itself, or for their own spirituality. This shift facilitates the shift to an autobiographical style.

Autobiographical criticism is thus part of the bigger picture of a paradigm shift toward postmodernity. Writing autobiographically is a shift away from the claim to objectivity. It is a shift away from making authority-bearing statements that claim to consist of eternal truths. It is recognition of the fact that my premise is only another premise. It underlines only *my* point of view. It is also a shift away from theology as an *ivory tower pure science* concept to theology as a spiritual activity between the text and me. Actually, it is also an attempt to take the mythical character of biblical texts seriously. Autobiographical criticism has thus to do with your understanding of, and perspective on, what scripture is for you.

Exposing Myself as Example. Although I believe in God, I have never had a "personal relationship" with Jesus of Nazareth, and I have never *invited* him into my heart because I have never heard him *knocking*. It has just never made any sense to me. I do not understand the concept of a conversion to a relationship with a personal savior that counts as a prerequisite for your life of trust in, and dependency upon God. Since my high school days, when I took Latin and Roman culture and history as a subject, I knew that the miraculous conception, the deifying of a hero savior after his death, and the ascension of a person who died for a good cause were part of a mythological paradigm. For many years, I was just too afraid to ask critical questions. Luckily, time went by, a paradigm shift came, and I discovered that I am not alone. Through reading, I met many people with whom I now can associate. I am no longer afraid to formulate my thoughts.

In my case, then, the Bible is not the word of God, or the only word of God to me, but only a source of testimonies of other people's experiences and understandings of God. I can be autobiographical in my study of the Bible because the Bible only facilitates my spiritual experience. My theology can also be autobiographical because it does not have to result in the life of the church; instead, its results are applicable only to my personal experience of who I think God is. Therefore, Christians outside the church can still read the Bible and do theology—autobiographical theology in fact, because they do not do it for the church or to confirm a dogma. They do it for spirituality, for their own spirituality.

I do not evaluate myths negatively. I evaluate a positivistic interpretation of myths negatively (when myths are interpreted as objective historical data and facts), especially when modern people cling to a mythical worldview (heaven above, earth, and the underworld) of biblicistic fundamentalism. I cannot endorse an anomalous split consciousness allowing people to adhere to premodernism that harmonizes with a fundamentalist interpretation of the Bible because the same people often claim to embrace a modern to postmodern worldview in the remaining aspects of their lives. I take it for granted that one can speak of the transcendent only in a mythical way. Yet it is helpful to distinguish between myth as a vehicle for communication about the otherworldly and myth as referring to a mythological worldview. One does not necessarily need a mythological worldview to use, understand, and appreciate myths. One can appreciate the value of myths even in a postmodern world.

I believe in God, but I do not think that one can regard the Bible as the only word of God. By "Bible" I mean the Old and the New Testaments. One cannot picture Christianity without the Hebrew Bible (Old Testament). To a large extent, the New Testament is the exegetical result of Old Testament theology. For many, the New Testament is the fulfillment of the messianic promises of the Hebrew Bible. The writers of the Gospels picture Jesus as a Moses/Elijah-figure. Paul got a lot of his theology "from the Scriptures." Christians who do not read the Hebrew Bible not only reject much of their heritage but also impoverish their understanding of Jesus and Christianity itself (Borg 2002, p. 58).

Yes, one can find the word of God in the Bible as well. Not every word in the Bible is a word of or from God. Sometimes the word of God is manifested as a meta-narrative beyond the biblical narrative that meets the eye. I therefore decanonize the Bible when I reflect on it for my own existential well-being. I recognize a canon behind or beyond the biblical canon. However, this "canon" is not only behind the biblical canon alone. It is also behind nature, literature, music, conversations, and interactions with other people.

I call myself a Christian, and I am a theologian who has a serious interest in the Bible. I live in a relationship with God within the Christian tradition, even as I affirm the validity of all the enduring religious traditions (cf. Borg 2002, p. x). My academic work and research reflect my own subjectivity. They focus on the issues that trigger my interest. As I investigate these themes, I hope to find a new understanding of my existence, an existence that arises out of the life and death of Jesus as *kerygma*, the *kerygma*, as Bultmann said—based on his understanding of Heidegger—that could lead to a new self-understanding and a total transformation. When I do exegesis or when I produce theology, this is the baggage that I bring to the text, and this is the mode in which my thoughts move.

Conclusion. I can conclude by concurring with Julia O'Brien (1995, p. 119), who said: "I am aware of the problems of self-disclosure, the possibility that biblical studies could collapse into 'what the text means to me,' into an orgy of the ego. And yet, I am uncomfortable with the alternative." All autobiographical criticism asks its practitioners to be more, rather than less, historical-critical. Although one writes as "*I*," one is also a critical scientist, critical not only of the text, but also of the "*I*." Autobiographical critics must critically reconstruct their own historical circumstances and those of the interpretive communities to which they belong, as well as those of other places and times. They must engage in critical self-reflection.

It is one thing to criticize another person's scholarship, but it is quite another thing to comment on another person's life. An autobiographical biblical critic makes himself or herself vulnerable and takes considerable risks, but, on the other hand, biblical criticism was never really without a personal and autobiographical dimension. It is always about what I make of the biblical text.

[*See also* Deconstruction; Postmodern Interpretation; Poststructuralist Interpretation; Reader-Response Criticism; *and* Reception Criticism and Theory.]

BIBLIOGRAPHY

Adam, A. K. M. *What is Postmodern Biblical Criticism?* Minneapolis, Minn.: Fortress, 1995. Explains the interaction with the biblical text from a postmodern perspective.

Anderson, Janice Capel, and Jeffrey L. Staley. "Taking it Personally: Introduction." *Semeia* 72 (1995): 7–18. This introductory article to a collection of essays explores the topic of autobiographical interventions in literary and biblical studies.

Borg, Marcus J. "The Journey Home." *Fourth R* 6 (1993): 3–9. Here Borg writes about his personal interaction with the Jesus of the Gospels.

Borg, Marcus J. *Meeting Jesus Again for the First Time: The Historical Jesus and the Heart of Contemporary Faith.* San Francisco: Harper, 1994. Borg meets Jesus again—this time with post-critical naïveté.

Borg, Marcus, J. *Reading the Bible Again for the First Time: Taking the Bible Seriously but Not Literally.* San Francisco: Harper, 2002. Here Borg asks, if you take the mythological worldview, genre, and text critical studies of the past 30 years into account, how would you read the Bible?

Boring, M. Eugene. "Revolutions in the Jesus Tradition: From Bonnie to Dominic." *Forum* 1 (1985): 56–63. A summary of the results that the Jesus Seminar put on the table during the early 1980s.

Chilton, Bruce. "Finding a Way." *Fourth R* 7 (1993): 9–16. A scientifically sensitive approach to Christian spirituality.

Crossan, John Dominic. "Exile, Stealth, and Cunning." *Forum* 1 (1985): 58–61. An autobiographical profile in which the author discusses his background and the influences that shaped his career.

Crossan, John Dominic. *A Long Way from Tipperary: What a Former Monk Discovered in His Search for the Truth.* New York: HarperCollins, 2000. In this book Crossan summarizes his 30 years dedicated to reconstructing the historical Jesus. He has done so self-consciously and self-critically and has tried to do the same in reconstructing himself.

Fowler, Robert M. "Taking it Personally: A Personal Response." *Semeia* 72 (1995): 231–238. Using reader-response criticism, a pioneering method for reading the Gospel of Mark, Fowler invites contemporary readers to participate actively in making the meaning of the Gospel.

Freedman, Diane P., Olivia Frey, and Frances Murphy Zauhar. *The Intimate Critique: Autobiographical Literary Criticism.* Durham, N.C.: Duke University Press, 1993. With their rich spectrum of personal and passionate voices, the essays in this book challenge and ultimately breach the boundaries between criticism and narrative, experience and expression, literature and life.

Henking, Susan E. "Who Better to Indulge?: (Self) Indulgent Theorizing and the Stuff of Ambivalence." *Semeia* 72 (1995): 239–246. An example of autobiographical feminist theology.

Kitzberger, Ingrid Rosa, ed. *Autobiographical Biblical Interpretation: Between Text and Self.* Leiden: Deo, 2002. An introduction to the autobiographical reading of a biblical text. It provides an excellent encounter with the means and outcomes of autobiographical criticism for beginners and established scholars alike.

Kitzberger, Ingrid Rosa, ed. *The Personal Voice in Biblical Interpretation.* London: Routledge, 1999. An example of personal voice criticism, which takes seriously into account and makes explicit the role of the interpreter's personal voice within the act of interpretation.

Maldonado, Robert D. "Reading Malinche Reading Ruth: Toward a Hermeneutics of Betrayal." *Semeia* 72 (1995): 91–110. This article distinguishes between idio-autobiographical and meta-autobiographical levels in the production of autobiography.

Miller, Nancy K. *Getting Personal: Feminist Occasions and Other Autobiographical Acts.* New York: Routledge, 1991. This book provides a feminist perspective on the interpretation of texts.

Moore, Stephen D. "True Confessions and Weird Obsessions: Autobiographical Interventions in Literary and Biblical Studies." *Semeia* 72 (1995): 19–50. Provides an introduction to the formal beginnings and foundation of autobiographical studies as a discipline.

O'Brien, Julia M. "On Saying 'No' to a Prophet." *Semeia* 72 (1995): 111–124. From a feminist perspective, this essay says "no" to the God that the prophet introduced.

Staley, Jeffrey L. *Reading with a Passion: Rhetoric, Autobiography, and the American West in the Gospel of John.* New York: Continuum, 1995. A pioneering exercise in autobiographical biblical interpretation, offering a critique of New Testament reader-response criticism.

Van Aarde, Andries G. "Methods and Models in the Quest for the Historical Jesus: Historical Criticism and/or Social Criticism." *HTS* Teologiese Studies/Theological Studies 58, 2 (2002): 419–439. In this article a distinction is made between social-scientific criticism and historiography.

Veeser, H. Aram. "Introduction: A Case of Confessional Criticism." In *Confessions of the Critics,* edited by H. Aram Veeser, ix–xxvi. New York: Routledge, 1996. The introduction to a collection of essays about reader-response criticism.

Wink, Walter. "'Write What you See': An Autobiographical Reflection." *Fourth R* 7 (1994): 3–9. An autobiographical essay on Wink's career and life intertwined with his theology.

Zauhar, Frances Murphy. "Creative Voices: Women Reading and Women's Writing." In *The Intimate Critique,* edited by Diane P. Freedman, Olivia Frey, and Frances Murphy Zauhar, 103–116. Durham, N.C.: Duke University Press, 1993. A feminist reader-response critique.

Flip Schutte

C

Canonical Criticism

Canonical criticism, canon criticism, and the canonical approach are terms often used interchangeably, even though the proponents of each discipline have diligently attempted to keep them distinct. What all three disciplines have in common is a general focus on the canonical shaping of the text as a significant locus of meaning. They differ, however, in their motivation, goals, and procedures. While the practitioners of canon and canonical criticism place their work within the scope of modern methods of biblical interpretation, the canonical approach is not presented as a biblical method.

Canonical criticism, most associated with James Sanders, views the formation of the canon as a natural extension of the process of the creation of a text. This method extends the history of the form, traditions, and redactions of a text into the stage of its final placement alongside other texts in a collection viewed as canonical. Canon criticism is an historical method that seeks to trace the processes of canonization in the ancient world; this method is often associated with scholars such as Sundberg and McDonald. Brevard Childs calls his project a "canonical approach," that is, an explicit starting point for a Christian biblical theology. The use of the word "approach" is intended to signify that the notion of canon is a foundational theological construct for Childs. All three disciplines have had a significant impact on the field of biblical studies, particularly within American biblical interpretation.

Canonical Approach (Childs). The canonical approach is a program for the development of a vibrant biblical theology. It seeks to avoid deriving theology either from purely historical reconstructions, or by atomizing individual canonical texts so that their theologies are never placed in conversation with one another. It views the equation of biblical theology with a reconstruction of the religion of Israel as fundamentally flawed. It encourages biblical theologians to take seriously the unity of the Christian Bible, without ignoring the results of historical criticism. In its best form, the canonical approach places the source of that unity, not in a unifying theme nor in anachronistic readings, but in the confessional statement that the Bible as canon is witness to the Christian God throughout its parts.

The work of Brevard Childs has been most influential in a reorientation toward both the final form of texts, as well as their placement within a collection deemed canonical. It is worth keeping in mind that Childs views his approach as an examination of the essential principles for a biblical theology. As a theology, he assumes that those who adopt this approach already view the text as canonical. He does not use the method to assert that it will provide evidence that a given text is sacred, nor does he use the approach to silence other methods. He allows that secular interpretations of biblical texts have a kind of internal legitimacy and often have a role to play in a text's interpretation. Instead, he attempts to flesh out the significance of a very fundamental theological idea: that biblical theology first and foremost assumes that the text is canon. A text's canonical status sets parameters for its theological appropriation by a community of faith.

A canonical approach to the Bible insists that a biblical theology must be built on the final form of the text, and not on some reconstructed earlier form. This tenet of the approach has often been misunderstood by both its critics and its proponents to mean that questions of the history of the text are at least moot, and perhaps even opposed to biblical theology. This is a serious misconstrual of Child's project. He affirms that biblical texts, like the book of Exodus or the texts referring to the Assyrian crisis, are better understood when an interpreter recognizes evidence for the history of their production. What Childs objects to would be giving canonical or normative status to an earlier stage of the text's production, rather than to its final form. For example, building a biblical theology on the Priestly strand in the book of Exodus, rather than the way that this particular strand is shaped and reread by its preservation with other sources would be an incorrect foundation for a biblical theology.

The canonical approach also insists that it is the texts *per se* that are canonical. The texts are not simply windows through which one views a historical event that is then canonical. While some texts do have a relationship to historical events, a canonical approach shifts the focus from the factuality of the text to its role as witness. This is an important distinction, because often the canonical approach has been attractive to those who want to avoid historical methods that appear to question the authenticity of the Bible. In some ways, this assertion is a response to the tendency in American evangelicalism to use the Bible to stress the "truth" of the historical events that it recounts. This type of fundamentalism seems to privilege history over text. For Childs, the historical event, while not irrelevant, is not self-interpreting. In addition, the focus on historical facts distracts the theologian from the text's fundamental function as witness.

Childs prefers the term "witness" to the language of "revelation," yet his description of scripture as witness has much in common with denominational definitions of the role of revelation. For Childs, biblical texts have as their primary function to serve as a witness to the triune God. Because texts that are deemed canon are viewed by communities of faith as being reliable witnesses to the triune God, the texts are read within the confines of these theological parameters.

For Childs, the canon provides limits within which theological interpretation can take place. To give an example, although the portrayal of God is quite different in Nahum than it is in Ruth, the fact that these texts are in the same canon means that it would be incorrect to conclude from these variations that they witness to different gods, that their portrayals are incompatible, or that one text's view of God must be correct and the other false. A canonical approach recognizes, and does not minimize, the differences, but holds them in tension as distinct witnesses to a single divine being.

Childs's view of the triune God is expressed in terms of a christocentric principle, common in both Lutheranism and Calvinism. As with Childs's attitude toward history, this aspect of his work has also been misunderstood by both critics and proponents. Scholars today sometimes claim that a christocentric reading is the same as a christological or allegorical reading of the Old Testament. This criticism of the method is more applicable to some of the work of later canonical theologians than it is to Childs's own work. The principle of christocentrism does not require reading the Old Testament as merely a predictor of Christ. Childs is quite clear that the fully canonical status of the Old Testament is denied when it is reduced to only this predictive role.

If Childs had stressed the fullness of the Godhead revealed in the biblical texts, rather than using christocentric language, perhaps some of the confusion about the approach would have been avoided. Having said that, though, for most Christians, Christ is the fullest form of divine revelation, which is to say, not that Christ adds something to the nature of the divine being, but rather that God is clearest to the believing community in the form of Christ. In this light, a christocentric principle means that whatever is understood about Christ as divine forms limits as well to conclusions about the nature of the Christian God. Given the context of our post-Holocaust world, however, the christocentric principle remains a sensitive issue for biblical theologians, as pointed out by Janowski.

Childs and those influenced by him have struggled with the question of whether there could be a Jewish biblical theology. While Childs maintains that it is possible, it is not his primary concern. One finds a similar attitude toward Catholic and Orthodox communities with their distinct canons. He leaves open the fact that each community of faith will have a canonical approach appropriate for their canon. The reality that different communities of faith have different canons, however, has led to other methods of canonical interpretations.

Canonical Criticism (Sanders). The work of James Sanders bridges the two disciplines of the canonical approach and canon criticism. Sanders presents his method as the natural outgrowth of redaction, tradition, and form criticisms. In his seminal work, *Torah and Canon* (1972), Sanders identifies two events that threatened Jewish identity as the catalyst for the formation of canon: the Babylonian Exile and the fall of the Second Temple. For Sanders, the creation of texts that served a canonical function helped the community to survive these catastrophes by providing a stable expression of group identity.

While the canonical text is the end product of various redactions and reformulations of earlier traditions, reading these texts as "canon" attributes to them a unique form or *Gattung*, a form that does, in fact, shape the reading of that text. Sanders stresses the role of the community in the creation of that new formal element of canon. In *Canon and Community* (1984), Sanders states that the *Sitz im Leben* of the canonical form is the believing community. The canon as a stable list of authoritative books functions as a source of stability for the community. But the fact that these texts must be reread and reinterpreted by each believing community also means that they function as a site for theological adaptation to new circumstances.

Sanders does not describe his project as a biblical theology, in part because he is more interested in describing how the texts function within a community than he is in proposing normative ways that texts should function. While Janowski differentiates between canon as a literary product and canon as a theological criterion, Sanders clearly prefers a focus on the theological function of canons within communities of faith. He notes that the canon allows texts to survive that do not serve a theological function at a given historical period or within a particular community, but that this survival means that they become potential sources for theological appropriations by later or other communities.

In this reconstruction of the canonical process, Sanders notes that the texts themselves cannot be separated from the commentary on religious traditions that led to their canonization. His method operates under the principle that there is a fundamental relationship between the process for a text's production and the process for its canonical status and function. Sanders is quite explicit that what differentiates his work from that of Childs is his insistence that theological interpretation does not begin after the production of the canonical text, *à la* Childs, but rather is always an essential part of the text's production. The result of this process is what Sanders calls a canonical pluralism, meaning that the canon does, in fact, contain conflicting or at least self-correcting points of view.

Barton, in *Reading the Old Testament* (1996), has criticized canonical criticism, arguing that it is not, in fact, a separate method of biblical interpretation. In many ways he is correct; Sanders is not proposing a new set of questions to ask of the text. What Sanders's work does, however, is extend those questions to another stage in the texts' formation. In the traditional applications of redaction criticism, for example, the assumption has been that the meaningful changes in the text occurred before a given text was viewed as canonical. The designation of a text as canonical was viewed as part of the text's postproduction significance that did nothing to the text's inherent meaning. While Sanders is not asserting that there were "canonical redactors" who made further changes to a text as it became canonical, he is pointing out the fact that it does make a difference to a text's interpretation if it is read explicitly as part of a larger canon. This meaning is not foreign to the text. Rather, canonical criticism seeks to exploit that stage in the text's production when it was read in explicit relationship to other canonical texts by a particular believing community.

Canon Criticism. Childs's and Sanders's focus on canon naturally led to renewed efforts to trace the history of the canon's formation. This work by both Jewish and Christian scholars has made clear that a fair amount of the history of the canon remains in shadow. While most scholars agree that the Law and the Prophets functioned as canon by the turn of the era, there are disagreements about such things as whether these two sections were formed together or separately, when and for whom the Writings were ever closed, and whether the Septuagint Old Testament canon reflects the canon of some Jewish communities or was a wholly Christian invention. Similar elements of stability and fluidity are found in the history of the formation of the New Testament.

It is important to note that there is an on-going lively discussion of the terms related to canon. Barton (*Holy Writings, Sacred Text* 1998) points out that the discussion of canon formation is not really about the historical evidence. For him the fluidity of the terms reveals attempts either to project an early stability on to the text or to reconstruct a creative fluidity in scripture. The evidence at this point suggests more stability at an earlier stage for some parts of the Bible and less stability extending into a much later stage of Christian history for other parts of the Bible.

Barton, following Sundberg, distinguishes between "scripture" and "canon." The term "canon" is sometimes used to refer to texts that are widely viewed as authoritative, at other times to a definitive list of books that are considered sacred. McDonald, for example, gathers evidence of these various canonical lists. Those, like Childs, who focus on the final form of a text, on the other hand, often use the term "canon" to mean the fixed final form of a text, that is its "canonical shape." By "shape" he means the creation of distinct collections within the final canon, such as the Torah and the Prophets. Chapman and Seitz (*The Goodly Fellowship of the Prophets* 2009), following Childs, explore how earlier closed sections of the biblical canon, such as the Law and the Prophets, influenced the formation and inclusion of texts in the biblical divisions that remained open.

While McDonald provides ancient evidence of lists of biblical books, others about the purpose of these lists: are they designating books that are canonical in the modern sense of the term, books a community viewed as sacred, books used for worship, or some other category? It is clear that during the Reformation, Christian communities were producing definitive lists of canonical texts. It is also clear that these lists reflected earlier practice. But at what point is it anachronistic to speak of a Christian canon, if by that is meant a closed list of sacred books? Although even Barton places the development of a biblical canon in the third century, the fact that Protestants and Catholics ended up with two different Old Testament canons as late as the sixteenth century suggests that there still remained an element of fluidity at this late date. Ironically, although one cannot find evidence of a Jewish "council" that made a definitive decision about what is in the canon (given that the discussions at Jamnia did not function like a church council), the Jewish canon has remained far more stable since the Roman period than the Christian canon has. This raises the question of whether canon should be understood as a juridical category or a category of praxis.

Canon critics have also not reached consensus on how to incorporate the ancient Greek versions. Some canon critics dismiss the idea that the Septuagint reflects Jewish canonization. Others view the Greek versions as evidence for a longer

Jewish canon. Still others simply do not address the Greek traditions of the Old Testament. Certainly there is evidence of Jewish communities that favored a smaller canon. The canonical lists of Josephus (*Against Apion*) and the Babylonian Talmud (*b. Baba Batra*), for example, reflect this tradition. For some canon critics, this is definitive evidence of the existence of a closed Jewish canon by at least 50 C.E.; what is often unspoken is that scholars also assume this closure reflects the beliefs and practices of global Judaism at the time. The fact remains, however, that early Greek collections of the Bible have more books in their collection. These collections functioned under the presumption of canonicity for most Christians for several centuries. This is also historical evidence of a different sort. The silent acceptance of these books points to less stability in the Old Testament than is sometimes claimed, and these differences still serve to distinguish various Christian communities of faith.

Canon, Normativity, and Postmodernism. Brevard Childs insists that his method is distinct from postmodern approaches to the Bible, and to a certain extent he is correct. However, the postmodern context for the canonical approach cannot be so summarily dismissed. One of the hallmarks of postmodernism is the realization that one's own context is a valid component in one's interpretation of a text. Childs's willingness to entertain a specifically Christian reading of the canon that does not silence the interpretations of other communities of faith reflects this general component of postmodernism. In one way, Childs is simply locating himself as a Protestant Christian biblical interpreter and exploring what it means to read a book like Qoheleth not just as *a text* but as a *canonical* one.

Some of the work of canon and canonical criticisms also pushes in this direction. Canon criticism in particular has ended up focusing on the variety of canons that have circulated throughout Christian history. The current trajectory of the method is moving toward the recognition of a widespread multiplicity of canons extending further into the Christian era than at first recognized. Some scholars have stressed that the theological lesson from the canon is not a rule of faith, but rather a rule of variety, diversity, and flexibility.

Jewish biblical scholars, including those whose work shares some of the foci of Childs and Sanders, avoid calling their work a form of canonical criticism. Jon Levenson avers that there is no such thing as a Jewish biblical theology because of the ways that Christian biblical theology has often revealed an entrenched anti-Semitism, and because Christian theology in the service of systematic theology searches for scripture's "unity." Recently, Marvin Sweeney, whose body of work often shows signs of Sanders's influence, spells out the ways that Jewish biblical theology is distinct from its Christian counterpart. Among these distinctions is the attitude toward normativity. While the text may be normative for Jewish practice, Jewish interpreters do not try to define the nature of God revealed in the text. Instead, Sweeney notes that the Tanak has a dialogical character that defies any attempt to find its center or to unify it under a theological theme or principle. Jewish scholars associate the canonical approach with a claim for normativity and unity that does not resonate with the history of Jewish biblical interpretation.

Although theoretically the canonical approach should allow room for a certain amount of polyvalency, Childs and many of his followers reject the conclusion that the canon is at heart multivalent and pluriform. While Childs states that he is not suggesting that different communities of faith have the same canon, he rejects methods like liberation theology and feminist theology that introduce readings outside of the rule of faith. He states that these methods too completely conflate the ancient text and the modern situation. He laments that feminist theology has not broken free "of its initial identification with liberal Protestant theology" (*Biblical Theology of the Old and New Testaments* 1993, p. 24), and he worries that liberation theology, even when done well, flattens biblical theology to only one focus. Given Childs's insistence that the *res* of biblical theology is the triune God, perhaps what most bothers him in these approaches is their clearer concern for anthropology and sociology over theology. Childs's assessment of these methods, however, misreads much of liberation and feminist theologies, both of which insist that biblical readings that ignore the poor and the marginalized in fact do conflict with the triune God revealed in the canon as a whole.

Lurking within this discussion is the question of what kinds of normative claims are made by application of the canonical approach? Childs tries to avoid this issue in two ways. First, he consistently asserts that he respects the right of other communities of faith to explore the canonical parameters that their canon produces. Second, he concludes that the canon provides limits within which interpretation can take place, thus avoiding the equation of a canonical approach with a specific doctrinal statement. These principles indicate further ways that the canonical approach reflects postmodern principles. In contrast, however, a canonical reading sometimes rejects certain interpretations as outside of those limits. These include readings foreign to the texts' original meaning and interpretations that do not fit the "rule of faith." This normative function, then, distinguishes the canonical approach from other thoroughly postmodern readings of the Bible.

The "rule of faith" is a concept often encountered in the works of those using the canonical approach. The precise meaning of the phrase is not always clear. Childs rejects the more common use of the term to reflect an overarching narrative, akin to salvation history. Both Chapman and Seitz assert that the Law and the Prophets functioned as a kind of "rule of faith" in the formation of the rest of the canon, but they do not define how that specifically plays out. Usually the rule of faith is equated with an assertion of the unity of the Old and New Testaments; the creedal formations of the early Church express the belief that the God encountered in one testament is the same God encountered in the other. In *The Character of Christian Scripture* (2011), Seitz asserts that the "rule of faith," at least for the Anglican tradition, consists in the doxology found in the prayer, "Glory be to the Father, etc." It is unclear how Seitz proceeds from this definition of the rule to a critique of controversies within churches about things like inclusive language and ordination of persons in committed same-sex relationships. Is such a narrowing of the limits of legitimate biblical interpretation a manipulation of the principle of a "rule of faith"? Are feminist interpretations that support the ordination of women or that recognize that gender-based violence is incompatible with the God Christians confess really outside the "rule of faith?" If the "rule" asserts that one encounters the triune God through the canon, then when does that encounter in fact critique the reception history of the text?

The legacy of Childs, Sanders, and others highlights some of the difficulties with the on-going application of canonical questions.

- Do the various canonical disciplines avoid the dichotomy between historical questions (canon formation) and normative ones (canon as threshold for theology), or do they simply exhibit the same fissures between methods that led to Childs's crisis in biblical theology in the first place?
- Can a canonical approach provide the kind of normative function that some of its proponents are looking for? Can the fact that there is a canon adjudicate among competing claims made on the text by various communities of faith? Or does it leave the community with the reality that several competing claims can be made of a canonical text that still fit within the canonical parameters?
- What communities are formed by canon? Are they only the institutional church(es)? Are they only Christian communities? Can there be subgroups within that ecclesial community who are also formed by the canon, communities like Christian women, Latino theologians, or gay pastors?
- Is the canonical approach a method of biblical theology that can be used in various ways by different scholars? Or is it simply a statement about the assumptions on which a biblical theology must be built?
- Finally, although the canonical approach insists that biblical theologies must make

the fact of the canon an essential factor in theological appropriation of the canonical text, does it make any further claims on the reader?

The Future of the Method. It is unclear what the future of these methods will be. First, the question remains whether canon criticism, canonical criticism, or the canonical approach in fact function as methods of biblical interpretation distinct from previous methods. Canon criticism is an extension of historical questions into a later period in the Bible's formation. Canonical criticism furthers redaction, tradition, and form criticism. The canonical approach explores fundamental questions related to biblical theology.

Of the three disciplines, current work within canon criticism continues to grow. Biblical scholars now examine the role of the scribal class and the relevance of textualization as a precursor to canonical thinking. In a culture that was primarily oral, what was the significance of a textual form of a tradition? One approach is to view the writing down of a tradition as secondary to the material's creative production. But other scholars have noted that writing could also take on a kind of quasi-magical practice. To write was to create a reality. The question of what textualization signified about a given tradition has led to an increased focus on the role of scribes in ancient Israel and the rise of a scribal class. Van der Toorn, for instance, argues that the canonical texts come out of a very prescribed social class of temple scribes, which gave the texts a certain normative function especially as they were collected for temple libraries or as part of a curriculum. For him canonization would be an extension of these normative functions.

Those scholars whose work most closely follows that of Brevard Childs have often not avoided the pitfalls of either imposing anachronistic categories on ancient texts or blurring assertions about the texts' history with its canonical function within a contemporary community of faith. There has also arisen a cottage industry of viewing both the final forms of biblical texts and the final collection of biblical divisions as intentionally meaningful. Perhaps the most productive of these attempts have been those that have looked at the final formation of the book of Isaiah, the formation of the Twelve Minor Prophets, and the collection of the Psalms. Scholars have succeeded in uncovering ways that redactors have either bound together disparate parts of these books or how reading a text within the collection as a whole shapes its meaning.

Another influence of Childs's work has been the renewed interest in the history of the interpretation of biblical texts. Childs not only wanted to tie biblical theology more closely to the canonical shape itself, but he also sought to tie contemporary readings of the text more closely to what he called precritical readings of the text. In his wake, there have been many efforts to help recover this history of tradition. Some of these efforts are unrelated to Childs's work; in fact, some biblical scholars pursue this reception history to lay bare either troubling traditions that should be rejected or explanations for contemporary assumptions about the text, some of which should be abandoned. On the other hand, such projects as *The Ancient Christian Commentary Series*, indicate by the sources that are chosen that they attempt to re-create a kind of normative, or at least dominant tradition of biblical interpretation. While this approach more closely mirrors the work of Childs, it remains to be seen whether it will result in a growing body of quasi-normative parameters for biblical interpretation or if the study will collapse under its own weight of heterogeneous evidence.

It remains for biblical scholars to use canon consciousness as a way to explore books whose versions are significantly different in their Greek and Hebrew versions. What would a canonical reading of Jeremiah or Daniel look like? Would it have to privilege one text tradition over another? Eugene Ulrich states that books are canonized, not texts or versions (in *The Canon Debate* 2002). Wouldn't a canonical reading of Daniel have to account for both versions? Or does that decision depend on the version privileged by a given community of faith? For Catholic scholars, where all versions are considered canonical, would a singular canonical approach to Daniel even make sense? These questions expose the extent to which the canonical approach is really about the particular "situatedness" of the biblical interpreter.

In sum, focus on the canonical element of biblical texts has drawn attention to an important aspect of the biblical texts. It has helped scholars extend their discussion of the text's production into the area of its canonization. It has made evident that reading the text as canon does in fact shape or exert influence on the interpretation of that text as canon. It has been less successful in reminding the general faithful readership that the Bible functions, not as a guide for living, nor as a window into historical facts, but as witness to the triune God and a vehicle for divine revelation. It remains to be seen how future biblical theologians build on these insights.

[*See also* Canon of the Bible; Diachronic Interpretation; Form Criticism, *subentry* Apocrypha and Deuterocanonical Books; Form Criticism, *subentry* Hebrew Bible; Form Criticism, *subentry* New Testament; Historical Criticism, *subentry* Hebrew Bible; Historical Criticism, *subentry* New Testament; Postmodern Interpretation; Redaction Criticism, *subentry* Apocrypha and Deuterocanonical Books; Redaction Criticism, *subentry* Hebrew Bible; Redaction Criticism, *subentry* New Testament; *and* Translation Techniques, *subentry* Ancient Versions.]

BIBLIOGRAPHY

Barton, John. *Holy Writings, Sacred Text: The Canon in Early Christianity.* Louisville, Ky.: Westminster John Knox, 1998. Barton's task in this book is to explore why historical reconstructions of the formation of the canon often disagree. He highlights how the use of the same terms, such as canon or scripture, hides the fact that scholars are actually looking at disparate elements of the canonical process. Instead Barton focuses on the function of these texts. This attention to the ways texts were used reveals significant differences between the ancient audience and contemporary canonical critics.

Barton, John. *Reading the Old Testament: Method in Biblical Study.* Rev. ed. Louisville, Ky.: Westminster John Knox, 1996. In this revision of his 1984 book, Barton explores the interconnections between various "final form" methods of biblical interpretation. The monograph focuses on the question of whether a canonical reading of the Bible yields different results from a variety of literary methods, including structuralism, new criticism, form criticism, and redaction criticism. This book describes the presuppositions and goals of each method, guided by the opening question of what difference genre makes to the interpretation of a text.

Beckwith, Roger T. *The Old Testament Canon of the New Testament Church and Its Background in Early Judaism.* Grand Rapids, Mich.: Eerdmans, 1986. Beckwith argues for the formation of the shorter Old Testament canon by the second century, B.C.E. Any subsequent arguments concerning the canonicity of biblical books were actually scholarly arguments about books that were already accepted as canonical. Beckwith also rejects the notion of a longer Alexandrian canon, claiming that inclusion of other books does not necessitate that those books were viewed as canonical.

Chapman, Stephen B. *The Law and the Prophets: A Study in Old Testament Canon Formation.* Forschungen zum Alten Testament 27. Tübingen: Mohr Siebeck, 2000. This book explores the historical relationship between the formation of the canonical sections called the Law and the Prophets. Like Childs, Chapman sees the role of the canon to form limits, or a "grammar," within which theological meaning is formed. By focusing on the role that Deuteronomy and Deuteronomistic theology play in the canon, Chapman concludes that the two sections formed as a canonical collection virtually together, with the prophetic books being perhaps only slightly later. Chapman goes on to suggest that both Judaism's focus on the Torah and Christianity's focus on the Prophets misreads the original foundational connection of these two sections of the canon.

Childs, Brevard S. *Biblical Theology in Crisis.* Philadelphia: Westminster, 1970. This work marks the beginning of Childs's explicit focus on the canonical form of the Bible as significant for biblical theology. The "crisis" is that historical criticism had separated biblical theology from precritical traditions of biblical theology, including the New Testament's use of the Old. Childs sets out to delineate what it might look like to wed contemporary methods of biblical interpretation to precritical methods that focused on the unity of scripture, rather than its atomization.

Childs, Brevard S. *Biblical Theology of the Old and New Testaments: Theological Reflection on the Christian Bible.* Minneapolis: Fortress, 1993. Childs continues his discussion of a proper Christian biblical theology in this monograph that relates the theologies of the Old and New Testaments. He asserts both an ontological and soteriological unity behind the canon, rather than a thematic one. He stresses the need of both the Old and New Testaments as "testimony" to the divine reality. As such, a proper reading of the two testaments moves back and forth between them. Child notes that, while literary readings can achieve similar results, biblical theology ascribes to these readings a normative or at least revelatory function. The bulk of the book examines the theological themes of major sections of the two canons.

Childs, Brevard S. *Introduction to the Old Testament as Scripture*. Philadelphia: Fortress, 1979. In this early work, Childs distinguishes between a canonical approach to the Old Testament and a literary one. First, a canonical approach accepts and explores the historical formation of the final text in order to better understand the final product. But it does not read that final form as an end to itself or as being self-referential. Instead, the final form is the privileged site of interpretation because of its normative role for communities of faith. That normative role provides the community "boundaries" (p. 83) within which theological interpretation occurs. The bulk of the book provides an introduction to each canonical book in canonical order, which discusses historical critical analyses of the texts, moves on to a discussion of each book's canonical shape and ends with a discussion of the theological and hermeneutical implications of these analyses.

Childs, Brevard S. *Old Testament Theology in a Canonical Context*. Philadelphia: Fortress, 1986. This monograph advances a theological appropriation of the Old Testament that is neither subsumed under a New Testament theology nor leaves the meaning of the text in the distant past. Childs attempts to give a fuller explanation of the role that historical criticism plays for a Christian theology. While the book defines the purpose of revelation in explicitly christocentric terms, Childs does not advocate christological readings of Old Testament texts. Instead, a Christian reading is one that confesses continuity between the Old Testament witness and the Christ confessed by contemporary churches.

Janowski, Bernd, ed. *Kanonhermeneutik: vom Lesen und Verstehen der christlichen Bibel*. Theologie Interdisziplinär 1. Neukirchen: Neukirchener, 2007. This collection of essays explores various issues related to canonical questions from German biblical scholars and theologians. Topics include the unity of the two testaments, the canonical hermeneutics of the New Testament and the reception history of the canon. The book includes an extensive bibliography of primarily European scholars.

Levenson, Jon Douglas. *The Hebrew Bible, the Old Testament, and Historical Criticism: Jews and Christians in Biblical Studies*. Louisville, Ky.: Westminster/John Knox, 1993. This collection of essays includes a revision of Levenson's article, "Why Jews Are Not Interested in Biblical Theology." Although much of Levenson's work traces traditions such as creation and law through canonical texts, Levenson notes that Jews are interested in the polyvalence of scriptural texts and not in a single meaning. His article raises questions about the relationship between biblical theology and dogmatics in Christian practice.

McDonald, Lee Martin. *The Formation of the Christian Biblical Canon*, rev. ed. Peabody, Mass.: Hendrickson, 1995. In this revision of an earlier work (1988) of the same title, McDonald surveys the historical evidence for the formation of the canon within both Judaism and Christianity. The book contains extensive appendices with relevant ancient texts that describe or delineate the contents of the various canons.

McDonald, Lee Martin, and James A. Sanders, eds. *The Canon Debate*. Peabody, Mass: Hendrickson, 2002. This is a very well organized set of essays by leading scholars who explore all aspects of canon formation for both the Old and New Testaments. It is a helpful reference work for most issues related to canon formation.

Noble, Paul R. *The Canonical Approach: A Critical Reconstruction of the Hermeneutics of Brevard S. Childs*. Biblical Interpretation Series 16. Leiden: Brill, 1995. This monograph examines the legacy of Childs' canonical approach. In the first part of the book, Noble examines various tensions in Childs's proposals that continue to impact the ways this approach has been both utilized and critiqued. Noble then goes on to propose solutions to some of these tensions, including a stronger role for historical considerations, the explicit use of literary methods to flesh out multiple meanings of texts (especially the dichotomy of what a text meant and how it means for later readers), and a clearer model of inspiration.

Sanders, James A. *Canon and Community: A Guide to Canonical Criticism*. Guides to Biblical Scholarship. Philadelphia: Fortress, 1984. In this monograph, Sanders stresses the role of the community in the canonical process, both in its original formation and in its continued relevance. He stresses that the canonical principle provides theological stability, while the plurality of the text and its own formation through reinterpretation of earlier traditions makes the text adaptable to ever new situations.

Sanders, James A. *Torah and Canon*. Philadelphia: Fortress, 1972. In his seminal work on canonical criticism, Sanders outlines the main elements of the Old Testament canon. He argues that the canon kept Israel "alive" by providing the community with a stable source for their identity during two major national crises: the Babylonian Exile and the destruction of the Second Temple.

Seitz, Christopher R. *The Character of Christian Scripture: The Significance of a Two-Testament Bible*. Grand Rapids, Mich.: Baker Academic, 2011. Seitz examines the "rule of faith" as an essential element in the canonical approach. He argues that the unity of Old and New Testaments is achieved by later texts extending the meaning embedded in the literal sense of earlier texts. He attributes crises in contemporary theology to a breakdown in this rule of faith that leads to a de-valuing of the Old Testament witness.

Seitz, Christopher R. *The Goodly Fellowship of the Prophets: The Achievement of Association in Canon Formation*. Grand Rapids, Mich.: Baker Academic, 2009. Based on a series of lectures, this prolegomena to *The Character of Christian Scripture* looks at the role the fixed collection of the Law and the Prophets played on the formation of both the open canon of "Writings" and the later New Testament canon. Seitz asserts that it is wrong to read texts within the Writings or the New Testament apart from the Law and the Prophets.

Sundberg, Albert C. *The Old Testament of the Early Church*. Harvard Theological Studies 20. Cambridge, Mass.: Harvard University Press, 1964. Sundberg examines whether the Alexandrian canon was in fact the Bible of the early church. He concludes that there was a wide variety of texts circulating as canonical within Judaism at this time.

Sweeney, Marvin A. *Tanak: A Theological and Critical Introduction to the Jewish Bible*. Minneapolis: Fortress, 2012. This book mirrors the outline of Childs's *Introduction to the Old Testament as Scripture*, although methodologically, Sweeney's theological approach owes more to the work Sanders. The introductory chapters outline the current state of Jewish biblical theology. Sweeney then moves through the Tanak in its canonical order introducing the theological themes of the final form of these texts.

Toorn, Karel van der. *Scribal Culture and the Making of the Hebrew Bible*. Cambridge, Mass: Harvard University Press, 2007. Van der Toorn looks at the making of the Hebrew Bible from the perspective of scribal activity. He notes two ancient precursors to a full-blown canonical list. One is the library catalog of a temple and the other a list for curriculum. Both operate under principles of inclusion and exclusion.

Corrine L. Carvalho

Canon of the Bible

Within the realm of biblical interpretation, canon is a term deployed as a key notion in how meaning is made, from ancient writings through the creation of a privileged set of authoritative texts. As such, canon belongs to a larger pattern of human meaning-making, through setting aside sets of objects, practices, or wordings as privileged. According to Jonathan Z. Smith, this identification of a privileged set exists in close coordination with the establishment of a cadre of persons who are called upon to apply the limited set to the infinite variety of human experiences. The tension between the unending field of that which is to be understood and the limited frame of objects, practices, wordings, or texts useful for meaning elicits ingenuity.

In this way, the basic structure of canon as a larger pattern of human meaning-making is, according to Smith, divination. That is, the practice of using a limited number of objects to divine meaning from an endless variety of occasions provides the basic frame for understanding how canon functions for a wide spectrum of religious systems. For instance, the southwestern African diviner with a basket of twenty-four objects uses just those objects in instruction for his clients as they negotiate a large variety of questions and dilemmas about their daily lives. For biblical interpretation, the limited number of interpretive means (i.e., the objects in the basket) are the privileged set of books. Exegetes, hermeneutes, and other castes of interpreters, then, are ingenious agents in the production of meaning from the limited set of texts with reference to an unending variety of human circumstances.

One can note that placing the biblical category in a larger frame of human patterns of behavior does not diminish the canon, but helps identify the particular creative activity inherent in the establishment, management, and practice of privileging a limited set of texts for an ever widening field of human experience.

This also coheres with the etymology of the Greek *kanon* and the Latin *canon.* The basic meaning in these ancient languages is that of a stick or rod used for measuring. It also carries the tangible meaning of charts or lists. By extension it can connote metaphorically standards by which something is judged or the judging itself. In some cases, this extends to the designation of a judging authority. So the ancient (that is, Hellenistic and Greco-Roman) references to *kanon* do not really indicate a collection or even a list of privileged books, but a much larger and more vague category of measurement, with the physical act of measurement dominating over the metaphorical.

For Smith the creativity and meaning provided in the dynamic of canon has almost nothing to do with the quality of the set of "objects" selected. Indeed, that which makes up the list is by and large "arbitrary," although it may in some vague sense represent "preoccupations" of the groups making the selection. The creative ingenuity is in fact heightened by this arbitrary character of the set of, in the case of written canon, books. Nor is the privileged set of objects or texts "closed" or "static." (Smith 1982, p. 44)

This helps make sense of the ways the biblical canons are in fact multiple, have much material that is sloppily repeated, are difficult to decipher in terms of the criteria of the selection of books, and have not been stable throughout history. The power of meaning created by canon does not depend on the privileged set of books remaining the same. Rather, meaning is made primarily through the endless exhibition of different meanings within limited frames.

The Notion of Canon in the Biblical Traditions. Although the notion of "The Bible" itself—whether Hebrew, Protestant, Catholic, Syrian, or Ethiopian—derives from the concept (and/or practice) of canon, it is surprising how late these canons actually developed. The traditions of Israel took more than 750 years even to formulate the most rudimentary set of privileged sets of texts. Similarly, Christianity, with a much stronger built-in legacy of the prestige of that which is written, took at least 400 years for its provisional and regionally-based sets of privileged texts to develop, only to see them remain much less stable than those of Judaism.

David Carr has suggested that the notions of canon for both the traditions of Israel and early Christianity derive primarily from the understanding of Greco-Roman cultures that there was a kind of circumscribed set of classic (mostly) Greek and Roman texts that were required reading for those who were civilized. According to Carr, both initial collections and lists of Israel-related texts and early "Christian" texts need to be considered counter-collections to the classic Greek and Roman texts. This helps understand the relatively relaxed and occasionally loose nature of the protocanons of both spiritual Israel and proto-Christianity in that the notion of classic Greek and Roman texts was only loosely constructed and open to debate.

Inasmuch as Carr's suggestion has merit, such collections within spiritual Israel and proto-Christianity would have been conceived at a somewhat more applied level of resistance than the larger grasp of canonizing tendencies of J. Z. Smith, which includes—but is not limited to—strategies of resistance. In addition, it is important not to perceive the collections/lists of proto-Christianity and spiritual Israel as mutually exclusive. Rather they need—at least from the second to fifth centuries—to be seen as overlapping and based within a larger strategy of countermand and resistance on the part of several kinds of spiritual Israel (and that would include proto-Christianity). The authoritative character of Septuagintal and Hebrew scriptures for a wide range of Christ movements of the first and second centuries would be the primary indication of such overlapping functions and identity.

The Development of the Canon of the Hebrew Bible. There is no real indication of privileged collections—or even lists—of texts within the intertribal or monarchical periods of Israel. There were, of course, libraries and collections of texts: the somewhat legendary accounts of King Solomon in the tenth century B.C.E., King Josiah in the seventh century B.C.E., and Judas Maccabeus in the second century B.C.E. are probably relatively reliable, but little sense of selecting out some of them from others as having primary authority is evident. Even the first designations of privilege for Torah as a specific and guarded collection seem to have occurred in the postmonarchical era. This eventual designation of the authority of a given set of Torah texts, of course, belongs, then, to the more general rise of the importance of texts in the second Temple/colonialized period of Israel, from perhaps the late sixth century B.C.E. through the fifth century C.E. It is difficult to identify exactly when the first privileged collection of Torah texts took place, but the process within colonialized Israel of elaborating and redacting the Torah would not have allowed a designation of such a Torah collection, as it is now known, much before 300 B.C.E.

It is by and large agreed that the first major collection of such privileged texts from Israel actually took place in Egypt with the production of the Septuagint, a collection of the translation of Hebrew texts into Greek accomplished sometime between approximately 300 and 50 B.C.E. by many thinkers within the community of spiritual Israel living in Egypt at that time. The Septuagint contained 45 to 51 books (depending on how one counts the various books as they were included in this collection), the vast majority of which were eventually contained in the later collection of Hebrew scriptures.

The first-century historian Flavius Josephus noted that scriptures of Israel were divided into three types, but did not enumerate what books belonged to each of them. He did say that there were 22 books, 5 of which were the Law, 13 of which were prophetic, and 4 others containing hymns and rules of life.

It is only after the destruction of the second Temple in Jerusalem that rabbinic leaders began to focus on sets of privileged Hebrew texts. By this time, they were also inevitably under the influence of the existing Septuagint. Much of that influence, however, was negative, in that the Septuagint's Greek language had come to represent the Greco-Roman tyranny over Israel. What followed were several hundred years of efforts to establish clearly a privileged collection in the Hebrew language. These efforts were done in the blossoming rabbinic movement, which eventually defined the traditions of Israel for the ensuing years until the present day. The rabbinic collections of Hebrew texts are in interesting tension with similar Hebrew texts collected by the communities at Qumran in the first century B.C.E., in that both the wording and the collections themselves differ from one another. Ben Sirach in the second century B.C.E. and Qumran probably in the first century B.C.E. both seem to have been aware of a privileged status of five books of Torah, Isaiah, Jeremiah, Ezekiel, and a group of twelve other prophets.

In Josephus, Qumran, and the rabbinic foundations, a criterion for giving some texts privilege over others seems to have been a shared notion that nothing after the first destruction of Israel in 587 B.C.E. could have been in such a (vague) privileged circle of texts. This is ironic in that, as noted earlier, the plurality of biblical scholars hold that even the Torah was not completed until well after this date. This most likely resulted in an effort to complete, redact, or compose literature in the colonialized, second-Temple period that had voices meant to approximate those of early Israel.

It is still very difficult to determine when the rabbinic movement completed the task of designating a definitive set of privileged texts one might retrospectively call "canon." It has been held that it occurred at the "council of Jamnia (Yavneh)" in Galilee in the mid-80s C.E., but this opinion no longer holds sway in most scholarly circles. Rather it seems as if this process was brought to closure somewhere between 200 and 400 C.E. In the Mishnah, most likely from the second century C.E., Yadaim 3:5 tells of debates on the status of the Song of Songs and Qoheleth. Unfortunately the documents that to some extent chronicle such choices are not themselves easily dated. These occasional and partial observations present themselves in their current state in a larger collection of Mishnah and Talmud, which hold texts alongside each other without distinction from beginning in the second century B.C.E. through at least the fourth century C.E.

Whenever the rabbinic process was completed, it designated 24 texts as privileged "Tanakh" beyond others. The 24 were 5 books of Torah (Genesis, Exodus, Leviticus, Numbers, and Deuteronomy), 8 books of prophets (Joshua, Judges, Samuel, Kings, Isaiah, Jeremiah, Ezekiel, and the Twelve Prophets, which include Hosea, Joel, Amos, Obadiah, Jonah, Micah, Nahum, Habbakuk, Zephaniah, Haggai, Zechariah, Malachi), and 11 Writings (Psalms, Proverbs, Job, Song of Songs, Ruth, Lamentations, Qohelet, Esther, Daniel, Ezra–Nehemiah, Chronicles). The word Tanakh comes from the first Hebrew letters of each of the three parts of Torah, Prophets, and Writings. The book of II Esdras, dated from the late-first through the mid-second century C.E., is the first book to acknowledge a privileged collection of 24 writings, making clear that at least some rabbinic authorities worked with those 24 privileged texts by the second century C.E. On the other hand, the ongoing awareness in Yadaim of contestation on the status of Qoheleth and Song of Songs in the second century seems to indicate that in some quarters the circle of these 24 texts was still unclear.

Although to some this concludes the development of the privileged "canon" of the traditions of Israel and what came to be called "Judaism," for most contemporary Judaism it is not so simple. Indeed, the privileged collections of Talmud in many ways have a kind of interpretive authority that surpasses that of the "Hebrew Bible." The Talmud is usually considered to have two parts: the Mishnah (perhaps concluded around 200 C.E.) and the Gemara (perhaps concluded around 525 C.E.). The Mishnah reflected on earlier versions of the Torah, prophets, and writings, expanding them and providing limitations on how they might be interpreted. The Mishnah also felt relatively unfettered in adding dimensions of law and meaning, and is in most circles considered to be a part of what is known now as Jewish scriptures. The Gemara worked more to codify the books that eventually came to be the Hebrew Bible and the Mishnah. As one contemplates the various authorities and privileges of Hebrew Bible and Talmud, it becomes clear that the term "Bible" itself does not take seriously enough the complex circles of privileged literature in Judaism.

The Development of the "New Testament." The development of privileged collections of writings for the Christ movements is, at least for the first hundred years, more or less the same as for other traditions of Israel. From the earliest writings of Paul and the earliest gospels in the traditions of Mark and Thomas, there is evidence that the Septuagint was available and considered to have considerable authority as a collection. There seems to be little indication of any privileged collection of Hebrew scriptures in the life of the first century Christ movements, since their literature quotes only the Septuagint.

The collection now known as "The New Testament" did not exist even in an implicit form for at least 330 years after Jesus died. For those first three hundred plus years, the only hints of something that might eventually become the New Testament were various lists from different Christ movement writers and the regional "synods" of the movements. These lists of what early Christ followers should read did not agree with one another. As lists proliferated and Christ groups grew in numbers over the first several centuries, some groups started collecting the actual writings of Paul and others, but none of these collections corresponded to the 27 books that eventually would become the New Testament. In the fourth century, some church officials and groups began to try to propose what the best readings for early Christians were. But no historian—either conservative or liberal—can find even the idea of a collection of books called the New Testament, much less an actual collection of books, before 400 C.E. It was perhaps in the fifth century that the first collection of books actually corresponded to the 27 books of the New Testament. There is no evidence of an actual book called the New

Testament or the (Christian) Bible until at least the eighth or ninth century.

The Lists of Recommended Books. The first person to list what early "Christians" should read seems to have been the theologian Marcion. Around the middle of the second century, Marcion declared that everything written for Christ groups was in error except for the works of Paul and certain parts of the Gospel of Luke. The errors which concerned Marcion had to do with what he perceived as an overdependence on the traditions of Israel in books like the Gospel of Matthew, the Gospel of Mark, and the Gospel and letters of John. It seems relatively certain that Marcion did indeed make such a list, but no writings of Marcion survived the accusations of heresy against him. Nor did the opponents of Marcion produce lists of their own.

Perhaps the most assertive opponent of Marcion was Irenaeus, the bishop of Lyons, France, who wrote in the last several decades of the second century and the first decade of the third century. Irenaeus's critique of Marcion had little to do with Marcion's list of privileged books. Without making his own list of books, Irenaeus seems to be the first thinker to have used the term "The New Testament" as an inexact term for "Christian" documents in distinction from the Hebrew scriptures. Irenaeus also seems to have been aware that there were a number of Gospels. In response to either Marcion's insistence on the one Gospel of Luke or the existence of a number of Gospels, Irenaeus was the first to designate Matthew, Mark, Luke, and John as needing to be considered privileged Gospels. Irenaeus's central point in defense of these Gospels is that one must have four Gospels since there are four corners to the earth and the wind blows from four directions.

Another implicit endorsement of these four Gospels also occurred in the late second century. The Syrian theologian, Tatian, did not so much designate them as privileged as use them as sources for a cut-and-paste story of all four Gospels. This new amalgamation of Matthew, Mark, Luke, and John was probably in response to rising concern among the Christ people about differences among the many gospels. The other "list" of Gospels from the late second century was from Clement of Alexandria. He rejected the full authority for Mark and Luke, and accepted Matthew and John because only those two were at that time thought to be written by apostles.

In the period 190–310 C.E., there seems to have been little interest in establishing a privileged list of books. Nor did the Council of Nicea in the early fourth century produce any such list. However, Constantine's commissioned historian, Eusebius, did produce a list as a part of his writings. Eusebius created three categories of early Christian literature:

1. "recognized" (Matthew, Mark, Luke, John, Acts of the Apostles, 14 letters of Paul, I Peter, I John),
2. "disputed" (James, Jude, II Peter, II John, III John) and,
3. "spurious" (The Acts of Paul, the Apocalypse of Peter, the Teaching of the Twelve Apostles).

The Revelation to John seems to have been both "recognized" and "spurious" in Eusebius's somewhat confusing discussion of it.

This uncertainty in Eusebius's discussion of the Revelation to John highlights the character of Eusebius's lists. Although some twenty-first century writers cite his lists as authoritative, in using the categories of "recognized, disputed, or spurious" it is not clear that Eusebius is making judgments about the value of the different books so much as reporting on how the books were treated.

As it unfolded, the fourth century was eventful, if inconsistent, in regard to the eventual New Testament. Many historians place the Muratorian Fragment in the fourth century, although it can be dated anywhere from 180 to 800 C.E. This document without a known author lists Matthew, Mark, Luke, John, the Acts of the Apostles, 13 letters of Paul, Jude, "two (letters) with the title John," and the Wisdom of Solomon (a book without any mention of Jesus and almost certainly written before Jesus). It does not list either of the letters of Peter, III John, or the Epistle to the Hebrews.

The regional church council of Laodicea in Asia Minor met in 363 and 364. There are no written records of it, but later reports contain two different lists from the council, one recommending the same 27 books as are in today's New Testament, the other recommending 26 books and leaving out the Revelation to John. There was another regional gathering in Hippo, North Africa, but here too there were no records of what was decided. A later council in Carthage reported in 397 that the Hippo "synod" had produced a list of the same 27 books known today as the New Testament.

For most scholars of New Testament canon, the decisive moment for the formation of the New Testament came in the spring of 367 C.E. when Athanasius, a bishop in North Africa, wrote a "festal letter" at Easter, instructing the Christians of North Africa to read 27 books as their authoritative literature. As in Hippo and possibly Laodicea, these 27 books were the same books as eventually came to be the New Testament known today. Athanasius calls this list the "The New Testament" and uses "canon" to refer to his list. This letter was not meant for all of Christianity at the time, but just the Christians of North Africa. Nor did Athanasius provide any of the churches with copies of these 27 books.

The Apostolic Constitutions, most likely written in the early fifth century, listed everything on Athanasius's list except the Revelation to John, but added I Clement, II Clement, and 8 books of the *Constitutions* themselves. This final list discussed here demonstrates, then, some increasing agreement at the beginning of the fifth century on the authoritative status of the 4 Gospels, the Acts of the Apostles, 13 letters of Paul, Hebrews, the 2 letters of Peter, the 3 letters of John, and Jude; but it destabilizes Athanasius's list of 27 with its own list of 36 books.

One complex issue around this discussion of ancient lists that point toward the eventual New Testament is its exclusion of a major nonwestern part of ancient Christianity. While western Christianity grew toward its Catholic and Protestant conceptions of the New Testament, the churches of Syriac and Ethiopian origin treated all of these issues quite differently. These churches developed different and more expansive lists, and even today differ with western Christianity as to what scriptures are authoritative. The Syriac version of the New Testament, known as the Peshitta, does not include II Peter, II and III John, Jude, and the Revelation to John. The Ethiopian New Testament includes books otherwise not a part of other New Testaments: The Sunodos, The Octateuch, The Book of the Covenant, and the Didascalia.

The Collections of Christian Literature. During the first five centuries of Christ communities, there were a number of collections of early Christian literature. In contrast to the various lists, these collections had little relationship to the eventual New Testament. They do demonstrate that for some communities the actual collection of literature became important.

It is likely that by the end of the first century there were at least several collections of the letters attributed to Paul. Since the production of books themselves only began in earnest during the second and third centuries, most of these Pauline collections must have been in scroll form. Who made these collections of Pauline literature is less clear. They could have been from the more established Christ communities in their second and third generations. Or, they could have been collected by some very early Christian schools.

It is quite certain that in the second century a number of "Christian" schools emerged. Some of these schools had at their disposal various written works, both from the "Christian" writers of the first and second centuries and often from important philosophical writers as well. These school collections almost certainly contained works from the eventual New Testament and works outside it. By the fourth century, such school collections could have been relatively large. But there seems to have been little interest in these collections corresponding to the various lists of recommended instructions for "Christians" at large. And, by the fourth century a considerable number of "Christian" communities seem to have collections of literature to read in worship and study settings.

In possibly the third century and certainly the fourth century, monasteries also became centers of considerable study, and they began to have libraries within their building complexes. One of the largest and earliest collections of this sort is the Nag Hammadi "library" found in 1945 in a jar several miles from a fourth-century Pachomian monastery in central Egypt. One of the most interesting aspects of the Nag Hammadi collection is that it is in the form of actual books. From other non-Christian libraries of that time, it seems clear that by the fourth century such a monastic library would have probably contained both books and scrolls.

Relative to the New Testament it is probable that some of these collections included all 27 books of the eventual New Testament. On the other hand, it seems unlikely that any of these collections contained only these 27 or even grouped them together as a "New Testament." Indeed, it seems improbable that there were any separate collections of the 27 books of the New Testament in the first 400 years of Christian tradition.

The Actual Production of New Testaments. Although we have very few actual examples, it is almost certain that some of the collections of "Christian" literature of the fourth century had multiple little "books" in actual leather bound form. For instance, the collections found at Nag Hammadi consist of leather bound books, each of which contains 3–10 separate works.

There are two reasons to doubt that the first 500 years of "Christianity" produced one book called the New Testament that included the specific 27 little "books" that now make up the New Testament. First, the technology of book production was such that putting all 27 "books" into one was most probably impossible. Second, as seen in the above study of the lists of books for "Christians" to read at that time, there was not consensus on what the "mandatory" New Testament content was until at least the fifth century.

Around the year 405, it seems likely that the theologian and translator Jerome had a unified translation of the 27 documents of the eventual New Testament. Later versions of the Vulgate contain an introduction to the translation most likely written by Jerome himself. This introduction both assumes and declares that the Vulgate translation of the 27, and only 27, books has special authority for Latin Christians. So although it was not actually one book, both its unified translation and its introduction come quite close to it being an actual book called the New Testament.

The first New Testaments—as an actual book—were probably produced within two or three centuries of Jerome, as the Jerome's translation of the 27 gained authority in the churches. This production of an actual book of the New Testament somewhere between the seventh and ninth centuries signaled on one level the end of an at least 600 year process of the making of the New Testament as we know it. On another level, this consensus had a number of limits. Perhaps most important is that this "New Testament" was only for those who read Latin. In the seventh through ninth centuries of flourishing Syrian and Ethiopian Christianity the scrolls and codices did not follow the consensus of Latin-speaking North Africa and Western Europe. Rather, in these regions authoritative collections of Christian books were not the same. Even today, the fifth-century decisions of a major part of Syrian Christianity to have a New Testament contain just 22 books (excluding II Peter, II John, III John, Jude, Revelation of John) are still held to be authoritative; and for many centuries Tatian's Diatessaron (described earlier) replaced the four Gospels.

In the ensuing 1,000 or so years (450–1500 C.E.) in both the east and west, many different versions of the New Testament were produced. The vast majority of these New Testaments were in Greek and Latin, languages that no one spoke in most of the areas where Christianity existed.

With the advent of the printing press, the New Testament became available to the broader population beyond those who read it in Latin and Greek. With translations into the common tongues and the mass distribution via the printing press, rather suddenly the New Testament was of direct interest to common folk.

This change in public consciousness produced several responses from church leaders. Martin Luther tried unsuccessfully to have four books—Hebrews, James, Jude, and Revelation—removed from the New Testament as read by the new Protestant public. And, in the sixteenth century, several church-wide bodies (including the Roman Catholic Council of Trent) for the first time declared that 27 specific books officially belonged in the New Testament.

Canonical Criticism. Since the mid-1970s some biblical scholars have participated in what has come to be known as "canonical criticism." The term itself has not been able to focus energy or a collegium of scholars. Nor have people been able to agree on either approaches or conclusions. Nevertheless, it bears noting that even in their disagreement a number of scholars have brought the phenomenon of textual canon to the attention of broader spheres of interest. Together these efforts and disagreements can be characterized as pointing to the way canon as a textual phenomenon convenes particular kinds of meaning. At points this interest in canon in itself as a particular kind of meaning has been as broad as simply acknowledging that closed sets of texts make particular kinds of meaning, while at other junctures this interest in canon has been in the service of an assertion of a particular kind of Christian meaning. Still others have been interested in the ways certain sets of texts have influenced either the course of history or the course of biblical scholarship. More technical aspects of this loose and vague field of canonical criticism have concentrated on how the biblical canon(s) have been formed.

The name most often associated with canonical criticism has been Brevard Childs, although he himself rejected the term. Childs's work has shown great scope, and dealt with technical, philosophical, theological, and—one might say—even apologetic dimensions of canon. The earlier work of James Barr is often seen as a predecessor to that of Childs. James Sanders's more recent scholarship powerfully convened formal and technical interest in what canon meant as both an ancient and modern meaning-maker. In terms not dissimilar, Jacob Neusner and Burton Mack both deconstructed notions of canon formation and reflected on what was at stake in larger cultural investments in canon. Perhaps the most evenhanded and overarching of this work has been done by Lee MacDonald.

Although even the term "canonical criticism" mostly occasions disagreement, this clumsy and charged set of efforts can be credited with two achievements: (1) the unfocused identification of questions about whether "canon" is a naturalized category of meaning within the field of biblical interpretation; and (2) an almost unconscious match between these various assertions of meaning in and for biblical canon with Jonathan Z. Smith's keen observation that the creation of meaning is at the heart of any arbitrary human selection of privileged objects, ideas, or texts.

[*See also* Dead Sea Scrolls; Eastern Orthodox Interpretation; Patristic Interpretation; *and* Translation Techniques, *subentry* Ancient Versions.]

BIBLIOGRAPHY

Brakke, David. "Canon Formation and Social Conflict in Fourth Century Egypt: Athanasius of Alexandria's Thirty-Ninth Festal Letter." *Harvard Theological Review* 87.4 (1994): 395–419.

Childs, Brevard S. *The New Testament as Canon: An Introduction.* Harrisburg, Pa.: Trinity Press International, 1994.

Gunn, David. "What Does the Bible Say?: A Question of Text and Canon." In *Reading Bibles, Reading Bodies: Identity and the Book*, edited by Timothy K. Beal and David M. Gunn, 242–261. New York: Routledge, 1997.

Keefer, Kyle. "A Postscript to the Book: Authenticating the Pseudepigrapha" In *Reading Bibles, Writing Bodies: Identity and The Book*, edited by Timothy K. Beal and David M. Gunn, 232–241. London and New York: Routledge, 1997.

McDonald, Lee M. *The Formation of the Christian Biblical Canon.* Peabody, Mass.: Hendrickson, 1995.

Smith, Jonathan Z. "Canons, Catalogues, and Classics." In *Canonization and Decanonization*, edited by A. van der Kooij and K. van der Toorn, 295–311. Leiden: Brill, 1998.

Smith, Jonathan Z. "Sacred Persistence: Toward a Redescription of Canon." In *Imagining Religion: From Babylon to Jonestown*, edited by Jonathan Z. Smith, 36–52. Chicago: University of Chicago Press, 1982.

Wimbush, Vincent L. "Reading Darkness, Reading Scriptures." In *African Americans and the Bible: Sacred Texts and Social Textures*, edited by Vincent L. Wimbush and Rosamond C. Rodman, 1–22. New York: Continuum, 2000.

Hal Taussig

CATHOLIC BIBLICAL INTERPRETATION

In this day of ecumenical collaboration, one might wonder whether or not there is a specific Roman Catholic approach to biblical interpretation. After all, many biblical exegetes have been trained in other than Roman Catholic universities and schools of theology. Furthermore, most scholars, regardless of their religious affiliation, employ some form of the recognized contemporary critical interpretive methods of examination. A textual difference remains—the fact that the Roman Catholic biblical canon is based on the Septuagint, or Greek version of the ancient Israelite traditions, and includes some biblical books not found in the Masoretic Text (MT), or Hebrew version as adopted by Protestant denominations, but without effect on the methods employed. However, down through the centuries, authorities within the Catholic Church have issued many directives indicating how the biblical tradition is to be understood, which passages are to be read through a particular Roman Catholic lens, and under whose guidance interpretation is to be conducted.

Variations in biblical understanding can be traced back to the very earliest Christian eras. Patristic writers like Justin Martyr (103–165), Athanasius (296–373), and Augustine of Hippo (354–430), to name but a few, all wrote homilies or explanations of the scriptures. Their writings show that they all shaped their distinctive interpretations to meet the needs of the believers of their respective times and places. During the medieval era interpretation was rooted in what came to be known as the "four senses of scripture": the literal or historical sense (a straightforward reading of the passage); the allegorical or christological sense (every important detail of the passage has hidden christological meaning); the tropological or moral sense (every passage contains an underlying moral value); and the anagogical or eschatological sense (everything points to some aspect of the end-time).

It was not until the sixteenth century—with the Protestant Reformation, the Council of Trent, and what came to be known as the Counter Reformation—that diverse understandings significantly separated the Christian community. In fact, the manner in which scripture was interpreted became a distinguishing factor separating the Roman Church from the Protestant Churches. The Romans insisted on the importance of tradition as the lens through which the Bible should be understood. The Protestants argued for *sola scriptura* ("scripture alone") as the supreme authority for interpreting, to which all other authorities (tradition and church leadership) should conform.

An example of how scripture and tradition function within the Catholic Church can be seen in the Bible's own reinterpretation of a particular story. The announcement to the Judean king Ahaz (735–715 B.C.E.) that his wife was with child ("Look, the young woman is with child and shall bear a son, and shall name him Immanuel," Isa 7:14) became, in Matthew's gospel, the announcement of the birth of Jesus ("Look, the virgin shall conceive and bear a son, and they shall name him Emmanuel," Matt 1:23). Since the Roman Catholic Old Testament is derived from the Septuagint, and since the Greek version of the Isaian passage contains the word *parthenos*, which means "virgin," not simply "young woman," that passage has often been understood by Catholics as biblical evidence of the virginity of Mary.

Official documents that provide directives for Roman Catholics for the reading of the Bible can be classified under three headings: conciliar documents issued by an ecumenical council and carrying the heaviest authority; papal documents written by various popes and containing teaching that is often modified at a later time; curial documents published by authoritative congregations or departments within the church usually under the administration of a Vatican official. A brief look at some of these documents will throw light on the history and present character of Catholic biblical interpretation.

Conciliar Documents. Beginning with the Council in Jerusalem (Acts 15:1–35), ecclesiastical leaders and theologians have gathered to discuss and decide upon pertinent matters of church doctrine and practice. The final documents that were published and circulated became the official teaching of the church.

Council of Trent. The Council of Trent (1545–1563) consisted of 25 sessions held in several locales within the Holy Roman Empire. It was precipitated by the defiance of various groups within the church. Over its several sessions, it issued both condemnations of some of the teachings of these dissident groups, teachings which the church viewed as heretical, as well as instructions for those who continued to accept the teachings of the church. Among its various pronouncements were a decision making the Latin version of the Bible official for Roman Catholics, another decision regarding the composition of the biblical canon, and a reinforcement of the importance of tradition as an influencing factor in the faith of the people.

The Latin version of the Bible has a long history. Sometime during the fourth century, St. Jerome was commissioned by Pope Damasus I to produce a revision of Old Latin translations of the Bible. He used the Hebrew version as the basis of his work. He also translated into Latin some biblical material not included in the Hebrew version but found in the Greek and various other manuscripts. By the thirteenth century, this version was considered the *versio vulgata*, which means "commonly used version," hence the name Vulgate. Though Jerome did not consider the latter collection of books that he translated canonical, most of the subsequent Latin versions include them. This second collection consists of: 1—2 Esdras, Tobit, Judith, Additions to Esther, Wisdom of Solomon, Ecclesiasticus, Baruch and the Letter of Jeremiah, and 1—2 Maccabees. Protestant versions regard these books as apocryphal (meaning "hidden," but referring to their unauthorized nature), while the Roman Catholic version considers them deuterocanonical (second canon). There is no dispute regarding the composition of the New Testament canon. The Council of Trent adopted the Latin Vulgate version and the deuterocanonical collection.

The same council decreed that no one may interpret scripture in any way that might contradict what is taught by the church. No examples of this type of interpretation were given. Consequently, this teaching was viewed as granting authority to official church leadership, both those exercising authority at the time this document was issued and those who would follow them down through the ages.

First Vatican Council. The First Vatican Council was convoked by Pope Pius IX in 1868. This gathering of church leaders was convened to address the challenge posed by movements of thought that came to be known as rationalism, liberalism, and materialism. The second chapter of its *Dei Filius* (Dogmatic Constitution on the Catholic Faith; 1870) addresses issues pertaining to revelation. It is there that this council restates the teaching of the Council of Trent, namely that supernatural revelation is contained both in the written books of the Bible and in the unwritten tradition that has been handed down through the apostolic teaching. Furthermore, these books and this tradition, as found in the Latin Vulgate, were believed to have been conceived through the inspiration of the Holy Spirit; they have God as their author; and they have been delivered to the church. This teaching reaffirms the importance of both scripture and tradition as well as the authority of the church in determining the true meaning of the scriptures.

Second Vatican Council. Blessed Pope John XXIII opened the historic Second Vatican Council in 1962. However, he died before it was completed, and Pope Paul VI brought it to a successful conclusion in 1965. Building on the teaching of Leo XII and Pius X as well as the work of the Pontifical Biblical Commission, a curial commission established by Leo XII in 1902, Vatican II issued a document that attested to a notable change in the Catholic Church's method of biblical interpretation. *Dei Verbum* (The Dogmatic Constitution on Divine Revelation; 1965) is considered a principal document of the council. This document clarifies the official Roman Catholic Church's position that both scripture and tradition flow from the same wellspring of divine revelation and constitute a single deposit of faith. The document further states that the bishops' authority to interpret the scriptures belongs to them as successors of the apostles. Thus sacred scripture, sacred tradition, and the teaching office of the church are so linked that one cannot stand without the others.

The document then instructs Catholic interpreters to employ the critical methods that had engaged Protestant scholars for several decades, but which were previously banned in Catholic scholarship. These include both historical-critical and literary approaches. Attention is given to the critical study of both biblical testaments, acknowledging the importance of each in its own right. This directive abolishes any suggestion that the primary value of the Old Testament is as preparation for the New Testament. The document ends with a description of the importance of sacred scripture in the life of the Church. This particular concern lays bare the almost complete reversal of thought that held sway at the beginning of the twentieth century. At that time, most Catholics were ignorant of the Bible and its teachings. In fact, the Bible was considered by many to be a "Protestant book." Now biblical understanding was considered vital for the spiritual life and health of believers. Critical translations of the Bible with informative introductions and footnotes appeared in various languages. Commentaries written by Catholic and Protestants alike became the textbooks in Catholic schools, universities, and seminaries. Ecumenical biblical interpretation was born.

Papal Documents. As the primary teachers of the church, popes issue various forms of instruction. Not all of these instructions carry the same authority. In descending order of formal authority, papal documents include apostolic constitutions, encyclical letters, encyclical epistles, apostolic exhortations, apostolic letters, letters, and messages. To date, one apostolic constitution, five encyclical letters, five apostolic letters, and five messages or addresses pertain to biblical matters.

Pope Leo XIII. Pope Leo XIII (1878–1903) issued two documents that contain instruction regarding the interpretation of scripture. The encyclical letter *Providentissimus Dei* (On the Study of Scripture; 1893) is the first important papal document devoted entirely to this topic. It was meant as a response to two challenges to biblical authority that the church faced during the nineteenth century: scientific discoveries concerning the age of the earth; and the newly advanced theory of evolution. These two issues disputed the literal understanding of the biblical accounts of creation. Moreover, new methods of "higher criticism" (critical approaches to interpretation) threw into question some of the longstanding ways of understanding the biblical writings. The document reacts very strongly against advances in the natural and historical sciences and the critical studies themselves that might contest church teaching, insisting that inspiration from which the Bible flows is incompatible with error.

After restating the church's position regarding the twofold source of revelation, the written scriptures and the unwritten tradition, the document provides instruction for teaching scripture. The Vulgate version is to be the basis of such instruction. Most importantly, no interpretation can be advanced that might be contrary to church teaching. In dealing with difficult passages, interpreters must follow the "analogy of faith." This means that tradition must be consulted and the passage interpreted in such a way that both scripture and tradition, chiefly the patristic writers, are not set in opposition to each other.

An apostolic letter usually deals with a matter of practice rather than of a doctrine or morals as found in encyclicals. in 1902 Leo XIII wrote an apostolic letter *Vigilantiae studiique* (Instituting a Commission for Biblical Studies). The purpose of this commission, known as the Pontifical Biblical Commission and composed more of biblical consultors than of church leaders, was to ensure proper interpretation of the scriptures. It did this by supervising the use of interpretive methods, deciding controversies among biblical scholars, and publishing occasional studies on pertinent biblical topics. This marked a significant step toward recognizing the role of biblical interpretation in the life of the broader church as well as the need to deal professionally with some of the noteworthy currents of thought in the world at large. Though the Pontifical Biblical Commission engaged in scholarly investigation, the church was still in a defensive mode. This was the age of Vatican I with its suspicion, not that of Vatican II with its openness.

Pope Pius X. Pope Pius X (1903–1914) published two apostolic letters, a *motu proprio* (a Latin term meaning "on his own impulse"), and one encyclical that dealt with the interpretation of scripture. Following Leo XIII's concern for proper seminary education in biblical studies, Pius X wrote *Quoniam in re biblica* (On the Study of Scripture in Seminaries; 1906). This study was to include the principles concerning divine inspiration as understood by the church, the Catholic canon of scripture, original texts and early versions, the history of both testaments, and exegetical analyses of the biblical books. It was presumed that all seminary teachers were ordained priests who were bound never to deviate from the general teaching and tradition of the church.

In *Providentissimus Deus* (1893), Leo XIII had denounced divergent ways of thinking that were challenging traditional Catholic thought. By the time of Pius X, these new ways had developed into an intellectual movement known as Modernism. In an encyclical letter entitled *Pascendi dominici gregis* (On the Doctrine of the Modernists; 1907), the pope condemned this movement and the evolutionary principles that governed it. At this time, the struggle facing the church was not with outsiders, but with some influential Catholic theologians who had espoused modernist principles and who were employing interpretive approaches commonly used by Protestant scholars. In his condemnation, the pope made little distinction between the tenets of modernism and biblical methods, condemning everything that was in any way associated with this movement. The influence of this encyclical within the Roman Catholic Church cannot be overestimated. In order to ensure traditional teaching by bishops, priests, and all teachers of theology, a compulsory antimodernist oath of loyalty was issued. This oath remained in force until 1967, when Pope Paul VI abolished it.

The pope defended the statements published by the Pontifical Biblical Commission in a *motu proprio* entitled *Praestentia Scripturae Sacrae* (On the Decisions of the Biblical Commission; 1907). A *motu proprio* is an apostolic letter that is not prompted by any external force or circumstance. The writer simply decides to publish a statement on some issue. In this document the pope both upholds the work of the Pontifical Biblical Commission and severely censures those within the church who do not.

In a final official act of measured support of critical biblical interpretation, Pius X issued the apostolic letter *Vinea electa* (Establishing the Pontifical Biblical Institute; 1909). This institute of higher education became the center of advanced studies of scripture for Roman Catholics. From its inception, it has been under the direction of the Society of Jesus (Jesuits), a religious society known for its rigorous academic demands as well as for its extraordinary commitment to the pope.

Pope Benedict XV. A quarter century after the appearance of *Providentissimus Deus* and in commemoration of the fifteen-hundredth anniversary of the death of the great biblical scholar Jerome, Pope Benedict XV (1914–1922) issued the encyclical letter *Spiritus Paraclitus* (Commemorating the Fifteenth Century of the Death of St. Jerome; 1920). This document was quite negative toward those who questioned the historicity of biblical narratives. It was not only adamant in its support of the church's teaching on biblical inerrancy (the claim that the Bible is free of error), but it also rejected the idea that the Bible should be interpreted according to its literary forms. This directive, along with the antimodernist oath established earlier by Pius X, resulted in the suppression of much Roman Catholic critical biblical interpretation.

Pope Pius XI. The quality of education in biblical studies was taken up again by Pope Pius XI (1922–1939) in the *motu proprio* entitled *Bibliorum* *scientiam* (On Academic Standards for Teachers of Scripture; 1924). Intent on taking full advantage of the actions of his predecessors in establishing the Pontifical Biblical Commission (Leo XIII in 1902) and the founding the Pontifical Biblical Institute (Pius X in 1909), in this apostolic letter Pius XI set down principles for the training of teachers of scripture.

Pope Pius XII. Pope Pius XII (1939–1958) inaugurated the modern Catholic biblical movement with the issuance of the encyclical letter *Divino afflante Spiritu* (On the Most Opportune Way to Promote Biblical Studies; 1943). The document was written to mark the fiftieth anniversary of the issuing of *Providentissimus Deus*, the encyclical that condemned the use of innovative methods of interpretation. Here Pius XII gave permission for a limited use of these modern methods, including archaeology and historical studies as well as literary-critical approaches. This reversal of teaching led to the document's being called the "Magna Carta" of the Catholic biblical movement. Furthermore, the importance of the Latin Vulgate as the only official version of the Bible was diminished by the directive to study the original biblical and cognate or related languages. The document encourages scholars to continue to probe the deep meaning of the scriptures. It closes with an exhortation to bishops and priests to ground their preaching in scripture rather than doctrinal concepts. This document prepared the ground for the teaching of the Second Vatican Council that would follow approximately 20 years later.

Despite the openness expressed in *Divino afflante Spiritu*, Pius XII still struggled with the implications of the use of modern interpretive approaches. This becomes clear in a second encyclical letter that he issued. In *Humani generis* (On Certain False Opinions Threatening to Undermine the Foundations of Catholic Doctrine; 1950), he nuanced the church's position on evolution, but clearly rejected any form of polygenism, the hypothesis that human beings descended from various ancestors rather than from one couple, Adam and Eve, as the Bible claims. The pope believed that the truthfulness of the Bible was under fire, and with the teaching in this document he sought to defend it.

Pope Paul VI. If *Divino afflante Spiritu* gave birth to the Catholic biblical movement, the Second Vatican Council saw it come of age. Though Catholic scholars were not allowed to use modern interpretive methods openly until 1943, by the close of the council Catholic scholarship was on a par with that of Protestant colleagues. Pope Paul VI (1963–1978) had participated in the work of the council, first as a cardinal and then as pope. The council document *Dei Verbum* set the tone for subsequent biblical work. The two documents pertaining to scripture that were issued by this pope are concerned with the Pontifical Biblical Commission.

Paul VI's first document was a *motu proprio* entitled *Sedula cura* (On New Laws Regulating the Pontifical Biblical Commission; 1971). It announces the reorganization of the membership of the commission. It was to be made up of scholars from various schools and nations in order that the diversity present within the church might be acknowledged and employed. The president of the commission was to be the Prefect of the Sacred Congregation of the Doctrine of the Faith (a cardinal), but the vice-president was to be elected from the membership, thus demonstrating the collegiality espoused by the council. Furthermore, the appointments were for a period of five years with the possibility of reappointment. This guaranteed fresh insights on a regular basis. The commission now reflected the change in policy accomplished by the council.

The second document issued by Paul VI was an address delivered to the members of the Pontifical Biblical Commission, "On the Ecclesial Role of Biblical Studies" (1974). In this address the pope reminded the members of the commission that their task was not merely credible scholarship. Their primary duty was to present the meaning of the word of God to the people of God. The pope placed before the members the example of Marie-Joseph Lagrange, O.P., one of the many theologians originally silenced by church authorities, many of whom later became the experts consulted by the bishops and cardinals participating in the Second Vatican Council. Recalling Lagrange demonstrates the radical reversal in thinking brought to the church by that council.

Pope John Paul II. Most of the writings of Pope John Paul II (1978–2005) relating to the Bible are occasional addresses. However, five of them focus on some aspect of biblical interpretation. In an apostolic constitution entitled *Scripturarum thesaurus* (Promulgating the Neo-Vulgate Edition of the Bible; 1979) the pope reaffirmed the status of the Vulgate as the official version of the Bible for Catholics, especially for use in the liturgy. The extent of the implications of this decision would not be realized until well into the twenty-first century. Many within the church considered this decision a move back to pre-Vatican thinking.

In an address to the Pontifical Academy of Science, "Truth Cannot Contradict Truth" (1996), John Paul II assured scientists that there is no necessary opposition between the theory of evolution and the truth about the origin and vocation of human beings as depicted in the biblical accounts of creation. This assurance reflects a remarkable shift in thinking from the opposition to the emerging scientific insights argued by Leo XII in *Providentissimus Deus.* Though John Paul II did not explicitly develop the idea, in this address he acknowledged that the Bible need not be read literally.

In 1990 John Paul II commemorated the twenty-fifth anniversary of the publication of *Dei Verbum* in an address delivered to an audience composed of cardinals, members of the Roman Curia, members of the Catholic Biblical Federation, and guests from other Christian denominations. In it he underscored several of the salient points of that groundbreaking document from Vatican II.

In 1991 The Pontifical Biblical Commission launched a study of methods for the interpretation of the Bible. At the opening of this study John Paul II addressed the commission, encouraging them in this venture and reminding them of the service that their research would provide the church. He addressed them once again in 1993 upon the conclusion of their research and the publication of their findings entitled "The Interpretation of the Bible in the Church."

Curial Documents. The Roman Curia is the central body of official offices in the Roman Catholic Church. These offices are referred to as sacred congregations. On occasion, these congregations or offices issue statements or instructions on topics that fall under the jurisdiction of that congregation, statements or instructions that are relevant to the time.

Sacred Congregation of the Holy Office. The Sacred Congregation of the Holy Office is the oldest of the nine congregations that comprise the Roman Curia. Before 1904 it was known as the Supreme Congregation of the Roman and Universal Inquisition, a name that could strike fear in the hearts of many believers. Today it is known as the Congregation for the Doctrine of the Faith. Its name identifies its responsibility, which is to oversee the authenticity of matters of faith being taught on all levels of the church.

In 1907, this congregation addressed the teachings advanced by the movement of thought that came to be known as modernism. The decree entitled *Lamentabili sane Exitu* (With Truly Lamentable Results) condemned sixty-five propositions of the movement, half of which dealt with matters of biblical interpretation. Later that year, Pius X issued the encyclical letter *Pascendi dominici gregis,* followed by the antimodernist oath in 1910. Catholic biblical study was now carefully controlled by the Holy Office.

As mentioned earlier, Pius XII's encyclical *Divino afflante Spiritu* (1943) opened the door to critical biblical interpretation for Roman Catholics. However, such interpretation did not escape the watchful eye of the Holy Office. in 1961, just before the opening of the Second Vatican Council, that congregation issued "Warning to Those Who Expound the Scriptures." Acknowledging the strides that had been made in the study of the Bible, an affirmation of critical work in general, this statement cautioned against opinions that call into question the genuine historical and objective truth of scripture. The tenor of this statement is markedly different than that of *Lamentabili sane Exitu.* The earlier statement was a stern condemnation; this one was a warning. It appears that the Holy Office was now exercising its responsibility in a very different manner.

Pontifical Biblical Commission. Since its establishment by Leo XII in 1902, the Pontifical Biblical Commission has worked to provide a deeper and clearer understanding of the Bible. Created to safeguard traditional church teachings, it originally acted as a kind of "watchdog of orthodoxy." However, as times changed and the Catholic Church moved from a more defensive stance to one of collaboration, the commission was transformed from being "watchdog" to being "guardian," and the character of its service was revised from correction and condemnation to that of guidance and clarification.

Responses. The earliest statements issued by the Pontifical Biblical Commission were responses to questions posed. Examples include: "On the Mosaic Authorship of the Pentateuch" (1906); "On the Authorship and Historicity of the Fourth Gospel" (1906); "On the Character and Authorship of the Book of Isaiah" (1908); "On the Historicity of Genesis 1–3" (1909); "On the Authorship, Date of Composition, and Historicity of the Gospel of Matthew" (1911); "On the Parousia or the Second Coming of Our Lord in the Letters of Paul the Apostle" (1915). In these responses, questions were formulated in such a way that responses could be either "Negative" or "Affirmative." The very formulations of the questions suggest that insights gained from new interpretive methods appeared to be in opposition to the traditional understanding of the issue. The answers to these early questions show that when such opposition was present, the traditional teaching of the church was reaffirmed.

Instructions. The document that reflects the dramatic change in the commission's character was *Sancta Mater Ecclesia* (Instruction on the Historical Truth of the Gospels; 1964). This was the first official document that accepted form criticism as a valid interpretive approach for Catholic use. Though the phrase "historical truth" appears in the title, the historical character of the Gospels is not directly addressed. Instead, the document explains the three stages which the "Jesus tradition" underwent as it developed into the Gospels that we have today. This instruction shows that the commission was less interested in historical matters than in uncovering the character of the gospel. The legitimacy of the teaching in this document is attested to by Paul VI's signature which concluded the last paragraph.

Encouraged by Vatican II's *Dei Verbum*, Catholic biblical scholars began to engage all of the interpretive methods that had become popular among other scholars. Soon many became expert in these methods and produced cutting-edge monographs and commentaries. They joined and often headed the major learned societies devoted to the study of the Bible and other related fields. Members of the Pontifical Biblical Commission were selected from this pool of experts. Universities and schools of theology began to offer advanced degrees in biblical studies open to lay women and men, unlike the former seminary programs that educated only male candidates for ordination. Vatican II's hope that the Bible would become an integral part of the lives of all believers was becoming a reality.

In an address delivered to the Pontifical Biblical Commission in 1993 upon receiving the commission's document, "The Interpretation of the Bible in the Church," John Paul II summarized the current position on interpretive methods:

> For Catholic exegesis does not have its own exclusive method of interpretation, but starting with the historico-critical basis freed from its philosophical presuppositions or those contrary to the truth of our faith, it makes the most of all the current methods.

This comprehensive document covers four significant areas: current biblical methods; pressing hermeneutical questions; characteristics of Catholic interpretation; and interpretation of the Bible in the life of the church.

At the outset, the document identifies the historical-critical approach as indispensable for a critical study of the Bible. It traces the history of this method from the time of patristic writers such as Origen and Jerome to the time of Protestant scholars such as Hermann Gunkel and Rudolf Bultmann. It then sketches the use of the historical methods beginning with text analysis through genre, tradition, and redaction criticisms. In the assessment of this approach it highlights its value, but also points out its limitations. The same format is used in discussing new methods of literary analysis. There rhetorical, narrative, and semiotic analyses are described. In each case both strengths and weaknesses of the approach are noted.

Modern approaches that are somehow based on the tradition include canonical criticism, Jewish interpretation, and the history of the influence of the text (*Wirkungsgeschichte*). Approaches that use the human sciences include sociological, cultural anthropological, as well psychological and psychoanalytical analyses. Finally, contextual approaches such as liberationist and feminist approaches are identified. Although in the recent past there was criticism of liberationist and feminist thought, the only interpretive approach that is really criticized is the fundamentalist approach—the document actually says that it is "dangerous."

Turning to hermeneutical questions, the document discusses the ways in which the philosophical perspectives of Martin Heidegger, Hans-Georg Gadamer, and Paul Ricoeur have influenced biblical interpretation. Acknowledging the contributions made by philosophical hermeneutics as well as contemporary literary theory, the document addresses the question of inspired scripture. In doing so, it offers a distinction between the literal sense of scripture and its spiritual sense. This discussion ends with an explanation of the "fuller sense" (*sensus plenior*), a way of understanding the inspired character of the text advanced by the Catholic Church in 1925.

According to this document, Roman Catholic interpretation should be marked by certain characteristics. Most importantly, interpreters are warned against attributing to biblical passages a meaning not contained within the text but which is the product of later tradition. This is a very important issue, given the history of Roman Catholic interpretation. Thus, while the interpretation is done within the living tradition of the church, the integrity of the text must be preserved. This has been done by recognizing the inner unity of the entire biblical corpus. For example, later biblical passages are often dependent on earlier ones, resulting in a form of "rereading." Other intertextual links become clear when the relationship between the two biblical testaments is examined. The most obvious characteristic of Catholic biblical interpretation is the attention given to various aspects of tradition. Chief among these are the insights that have come from patristic exegesis and the teaching authority ascribed to various members of the church. While the church maintains that all members have a role in interpretation, the bishops, as successors of the apostles, are seen as the first witnesses and guardians of the scriptures. However, their privileged status does not preclude the importance of the work of biblical scholars, both women and men, in uncovering the meaning of the biblical text and in participating in bringing this message to the broader church.

"The Interpretation of the Bible in the Church," identifies a twofold task for the biblical exegete: research and teaching. To this end, scholars must make the best use of historical-critical methods. However, they must not make it their sole task. Other methods outlined in the document should be employed. In addition, scholars must remember that they are interpreting the "word of God," not merely an ancient document. Therefore, they should be attentive to its spiritual message. The christological importance of a passage, though not always evident, should be made clear whenever possible. Research always precedes good teaching. Therefore, those who exercise leadership within the church should make provisions for such research. They should encourage or select individuals who might become qualified for this service, and they should see that resources are available for this purpose. Finally, both research and teaching are advanced by publishing. This should also be fostered whenever possible.

A final characteristic of Catholic biblical interpretation, as represented in the document, is openness to other theological disciplines. Since scripture provides a privileged foundation for theological studies, exegetes cannot only enhance the study and development of systematic and moral theology, but can themselves be enriched by them. Furthermore, all theological disciplines spring from *fides quaerens intellectum* ("faith seeking understanding"), and they all are somehow at the service of the church. Therefore, mutual influence and development can only be an asset.

The last section of the document outlines how interpretation of the Bible influences the life of the church. "Actualization" is the name given for the process of realizing the force of the message in the lives of people. An added dimension to this actualization is inculturation, an adaptation to specific cultural elements. The document stresses that methods for accomplishing such actualization must be faithful to both the message of the scriptures and the character of the people hearing that message. Actualization takes place in ministerial settings such as the liturgy, prayerful reflection on the scripture through the process known as *lectio divina* ("holy reading"), and catechetical settings. Because the Bible is a treasure that belongs to the entire Christian church, biblical interpretation lends itself to ecumenical activities, as well as certain interfaith initiatives.

The broad scope and genuine openness of this document demonstrate the remarkable change in the church's understanding of the scriptures and of itself as the guardian of that source of revelation.

[*See also* Authority of the Bible; Canon of the Bible; Diachronic Interpretation; Eastern Orthodox Interpretation; Historical Criticism, *subentry* Hebrew Bible; Historical Criticism, *subentry* New Testament; Literary Criticism, Literary Theory, and the Bible; Patristic Interpretation; Synchronic Interpretation; *and* Theological Interpretation.]

BIBLIOGRAPHY

Béchard, Dean P., trans. and ed. *The Scripture Documents: An Anthology of Official Catholic Teachings*, Collegeville, Minn.: Liturgical Press, 2002. A collection of the official Roman Catholic conciliar, papal, and curial documents pertaining to the interpretation of the Bible from the time of the Council of Trent (1546) to the late twentieth century (1993). No commentary is given.

Brown, Raymond E., S.S., and Thomas Aquinas Collins, O.P., "Church Documents." In *The New Jerome Biblical Commentary*, edited by Raymond E. Brown, S.S., Joseph A. Fitzmyer, S.J. and Roland E. Murphy, O. Carm., 1166–1174. Englewood, N.J.: Prentice Hall, 1990. Historical background for and summary of the major church documents pertaining to scripture. Text of documents is not included.

Dianne Bergant

CENTRAL AND SOUTH AMERICAN INTERPRETATION

Each context demands a particular hermeneutical approach to scripture. The theological doctrine in which evangelization took place and the way the Bible was introduced in that context, the cultural background of a people, and the methods and state of the art of biblical knowledge, all decisively influence the outcome of Bible reading for every time and place. In addition, the social location of the reading community and the way the message is communicated influence interpretation. Here we will examine how these contexts have created the particular biblical hermeneutics born out of that part of the American continent that was under Iberian (Spanish and Portuguese) influence, which includes the Spanish-speaking Caribbean, Central and South America (with the exception of the Guyanas, influenced by the colonization of the French, English, or Dutch-Surinam). Although a language difference between the Portuguese-speaking Brazil and the former Spanish colonies exists, there is still a history of parallels and mutual influence, which allows us to make a common approach to the continent as a whole, while recognizing some differences and particularities.

Historical Survey. Since the times of the conquest of the Americas, the Bible has been on the scene in Latin America, partly through its message, but predominantly as a cultural artifact. In fact, for several centuries the Bible was allowed to circulate only in Latin (the *Vulgata*) and exclusively among the priests of the Catholic Church (all other religious expressions were prohibited by the ruling conquerors). So, for most of the population, and especially for the aboriginal people, it was only a symbol of the dominant imposed religion, and never a book to be read. Scriptural texts were scarcely quoted in the catechisms created to instruct the aboriginals and mestizo people. Its message was necessarily mediated through the interpretation of medieval Iberian scholastic theology. History gives us a very early example of how the Bible was presented to the indigenous population: during the invasion of the Incan Empire (today Ecuador, Peru, and Bolivia), the Spanish conqueror Francisco Pizarro meets the Inca Atahualpa, whom he had previously made prisoner, and hands him the Bible, saying "This is the word of God." The Inca puts the book to his ear and exclaims: "Your God does not want to speak to me," and lets the book fall out of his hand. That was the excuse for accusing Atahualpa of sacrilege and justified the following genocide. So the misunderstanding between an oral culture and a religion of the book, the distance between Latin and the aboriginal tongues and the ambiguity included in the expression "the Word" established the polemic place of the Bible during the conquest. While in the lands colonized by protestant empires, the Bible was translated into vernacular tongues and was used in the "evangelization" of the natives, in Roman Catholic regions the Bible was presented as a sacred image among others, closed and in Latin.

Yet, some exceptions occurred. Inspired by a passage in the book of the Wisdom of Jesus ben Sirach (Ecclesiasticus 34:18–22), Friar Bartolome de Las Casas initiated, with some other Dominican friars, their campaign for better treatment of the aboriginals submitted to Spanish rule, claiming freedom and dignity for them. Little more than a century later, Tupac Amaru (José Gabriel Condorcanqui), who was the head of the greatest aboriginal revolt against Spanish rule, also appealed to the Bible. Educated by the Jesuits as an indigenous Inca prince, he was also trained as a lawyer and formed in the Catholic catechism. In his defense in the trial to which he was submitted when he was captured, he called himself "the new Moses who has to deliver his people from serfdom in our own land." He also quoted other scriptural texts in his defense but was nevertheless sentenced to death and dismembered.

Even though several rebel priests participated during the independence wars in Latin America, they did not propose an alternative reading of the Bible. When they argued in favor of the emancipation of the new nations, they defended their perspective more on political, juridical, or even theological bases than through scriptural texts. Protestant churches arrived on the continent in the nineteenth century. In some cases, they consisted of Protestant migrants of European origin, in others, missionaries came mostly from North America. The British and Foreign Bible Society produced and distributed Bibles throughout the continent, using the classical Reformed translation by Casiodoro de Reyna and Cipriano de Valera (RV). Yet, the new communities were still attached to their mother churches, and their reading of the Bible was guided by traditional imported theology. A new interpretation of the biblical text had to await new times.

Latin American Translations of the Bible. The work of Bible translators must also be accounted as hermeneutics. The choice of language, the editorial notes, the titles inserted into the text, and even the type of graphic presentation are part of interpretation, because they too predispose the reader toward particular interpretations. In 1916 the American Bible Society published the *Nuevo Testamento Hispanoamericano* (a short edition containing only the Gospels had been published in 1910). It was the first Spanish edition to use the Nestle version of the NT, and though it was addressed to the Latin American public, its Spanish was harsh and rigid. Church people still preferred the RV. Another pioneering work in the interpretation of the Bible in Latin America was that of Catholic Fr. Guillermo Jünemann Beckschäfer, of Chile, who engaged in translating the Bible into Spanish. He worked with the Greek text, leaving aside the *Vulgata*, and completed his work in 1928. The NT was published that year, but the Old Testament, translated from the *Septuaginta* (LXX), was not printed until 1992. This translation was quite literal and forced the rules of Spanish syntax in order to mirror the Greek text. It did not receive much attention. Both works, in a sense, were insufficient to stimulate a renewal in biblical interpretation in Latin America.

A new impulse for the interpretation of the Bible was initiated in the 1940s. A German Catholic priest, Msgr. Johannes Straubinger, a biblical scholar persecuted in his home country because of his opposition to the Nazi regime, emigrated to Argentina. He formed a group of scholars and began a new translation of the Bible from the original Greek and Hebrew texts into the kind of Spanish used in the South American continent. Their version of the NT, titled *El libro de la Nueva Alianza*, was published in Buenos Aires by Desclée de Brouwer in 1948. This group of scholars produced some of the most influential biblical experts and promoted many of the initiatives of a new local hermeneutics. The complete translation of the Bible was came into being about forty years later (*El libro del Pueblo de Dios*, Buenos Aires, 1990). Straubinger and his group also initiated the first Latin American journal dedicated totally to biblical scholarship, *Revista Bíblica*, which continues to publish the work of some of the most recognized biblical scholars in South and Central America. The group's initiative created an association of Bible scholars, which included some Protestant and Jewish professors (Sociedad Argentina de Profesores de Sagrada Escritura—SAPSE), but it disintegrated in the 1970s because of theological disputes, with some members more open to the new liberationist trend and others closer to Church discipline.

A new translation of the Bible, related to the theological understanding that gained the continent after the 1960s, the so-called liberation theology was produced in 1972 in Chile by the Catholic priests Ramón Ricciardi and Bernardo Hurault. This translation, *Biblia Latinoamericana, edición pastoral*, became very popular (more than thirty editions and one hundred million copies sold) because it used very simple language, and its notes and commentaries related the biblical text to everyday life in Latin America. The translation also knew persecution, and during the dictatorship years in Argentina (1976–1983), it was prohibited and officials publicly burned confiscated copies. Similar situations occurred in other countries. On the Protestant side, the United Biblical Society in Latin America published a dictionary of NT Greek/Spanish, produced by the Mexican Elsa Tamez and Irene Foulkes, a North American missionary with long experience in Latin America, both Bible teachers at the Latin American Bible Seminary (Universidad Bíblica Latinoamericana, in San José de Costa Rica). This was to become an important tool for Bible students who could now rely on a dictionary with local flavor for their work. In 1979 a team formed mostly by Latin American Bible experts produced the New International Version in Spanish.In Brazil the work of the Franciscan Frei João José Pedreira de Castro is important. After studying in Rome de Castro returned to Brazil in 1924 and pioneered a Bible study movement there. Inspired by the encyclical *Divino Afflante Spiritu* in 1946, Father Antônio Charbel called for the *Primeira Semana Bíblica Nacional*, the first national congress for Bible studies, in São Paulo in February 1947. From this association, the *Liga de Estudos Bíblicos* (LEB), was produced to promote the reading of the Bible. A new version in Portuguese, *A Bíblia da Ave Maria*, followed a French translation in 1957; it remains the most popular version of the Bible in Brazilian Catholicism.

Toward a New Biblical Interpretation. These works of Bible translation ran parallel to developments in local hermeneutics, although they were not always theologically consistent. New trends in theology began to emerge in Latin America in the 1950s. In 1955 José Míguez Bonino, who was to become one of the most outstanding Latin American theologians and ecumenical leaders, produced *El Nuevo Mundo de Dios* (Buenos Aires: Editorial Consejo Metodista de Educación Cristiana—God's new world), with a study of the Sermon of the Mount. In a sense it followed the lines of the biblical exegesis of the day, but one can see some hints of what later became crucial tenets of liberation theology. The booklet was distributed by the Latin American section of the Christian Student Federation (CSF). In its publications the CSF, along with other ecumenical youth movements, explored more contextualized approaches to the biblical text. The movement began to grow in the 1960s, inspired by such theologians as the Presbyterian missionary Richard Shaull in Brazil and several then-young theologians, both Protestant and Catholic. Youth movements, ecumenical groups working on issues of church and society, inspired by the Conference of Church and Society of the World Council of Churches (Geneva, 1966), and the nascent base communities, as well as Christian-inspired workers movements, felt the need to relate their faith to their political militancy. Also the growth of the "popular education for liberation," motivated by the practice of the Brazilian teacher Paulo Freire, influenced Christian witness in the lower classes. Little by little they engaged in building a new trajectory in theology and biblical interpretation, a movement that would later be known as Latin American liberation theology. In the early 1970s this theological line was clearly established and took its name from the Peruvian Catholic priest Gustavo Gutiérrez's, *Teología de la Liberación*, which systematized their proposal. This was certainly molded by the political climate after the triumph of the Cuban Revolution (January 1959) that could be considered a "revolutionary situation," as named by Míguez Bonino (*Doing Theology in a Revolutionary Situation*, Fortress, *1975*). The Catholic Episcopal Conference of Medellin (1968), which launched the motto of "the preferential option for the poor," was another decisive influence.

Liberation Biblical Hermeneutics. The Second Vatican Council (1962–1965) was also an important feature in this renewal. The dogmatic Constitution *Dei Verbum*, opened the way to an upsurge in Bible studies in the Catholic Church, which was received with enthusiasm in Latin America. Bible scholars, who had been educated in well-known European and North American universities, started to relate their work in biblical hermeneutics to the contextual situation in Central and South America and its emerging theological lines. Multiple and diverse local bulletins began to show how this new approach to the Bible was gaining ground not only in the para-ecclesiastical organizations, but also within some churches, schools of theology, and seminaries. The Argentinian Catholic scholar José Severino Croatto (1930–2004) pioneered this hermeneutical trend, offering a definitive liberationist interpretation of the book of Exodus. The book, *Liberación y libertad: Pautas hermenéuticas* (*Exodus: A Hermeneutic of Freedom*), became the first fruit of an abundant crop of liberationist biblical studies.

Croatto, probably the most outstanding and influential Bible scholar in Latin America but who was suspended as Catholic priest after his marriage, became a professor at ISEDET, the Protestant School of Theology in Buenos Aires. There he formed a significant school of Bible scholars, with such theologians as René Krüger, Mercedes García Bachmann, Pablo Andiñach, and Néstor Oscar Míguez. ISEDET regularly publishes online the *Journal of Latin American Hermeneutics* (JOLAH), with articles in English, French, and German, and the *Estudios Exegéticos Homiléticos* (EEH), exegetical commentaries and preaching suggestions for the Ecumenical Lectionary.

Together with Croatto, we should also mention Carlos Mesters and José Comblin. Both Mesters and Comblin were Catholic missionaries in Brazil. Mesters, of Dutch origin but living in Brazil since he was 17, studied in Rome (as did Croatto) and specialized in biblical theology. He abandoned teaching in the seminaries in order to dedicate his life to biblical interpretation for the poor and indigenous classes. In 1978 he founded the Centro de Estudos Biblicos (CEBI) in Sao Paulo, Brazil, in order to spread biblical knowledge to a popular, wider audience and in a liberationist vein. He constantly published booklets, commentaries. and other biblical materials in very simple language but with a deep understanding of the meaning of the Christian message for those living in situations of poverty and oppression. Comblin (1923–2012) was educated as a Catholic priest in Belgium. He moved to Brazil in 1958 and was always close to the more progressive wing of the churches in the region. He became a reference for liberation theology and produced several commentaries on different NT books. Together with other scholars he became involved in publishing a series of ecumenical commentaries to the Bible, small books accessible for people who worked in what was then called the "popular reading of the Bible." This vernacular reading led to a biblical renewal that opened the Bible to the poor people of Latin America. The book *El Evangelio en Solentiname*, by the Nicaraguan monk, poet, and political leader of the Sandinista Revolution in 1979 Ernesto Cardenal is but one example. The book registered the interventions of the local people of Solentiname, an island in the Lake of Nicaragua. Instead of preaching in the Sunday Mass, Cardenal read the Gospel of the day and then allowed the participants to contribute their own commentaries, observations, or experiences motivated by the reading. We should not think that interpretation came exclusively in literary form, though. Dramatization, storytelling, drawings, and especially songs and music are popular forms of biblical interpretation dear to the Latin American people. It is amazing how creative some of these can be and how they show new angles and meanings of biblical texts. In this organic process of interpretation, live stories of the poor intertwine with the stories of the Bible.

Alongside Catholic scholars, Milton Schwantes, a Lutheran OT authority, contributed several exegeses in the series of ecumenical commentaries. Schwantes, who taught successively in the Lutheran School of Theology in Sao Leopoldo, Brazil, and then in the Methodist University in Sao Paulo until his death in March 2012, also was one of the founders of the Revista de Interpretación Bíblica Latino Americana (RIBLA—Latin American Biblical Interpretation Review). Initiated in 1988 and still publishing three issues a year. RIBLA reunites the articles of several generations of biblical scholars. Together with Schwantes, Croatto, Mesters, Elsa Tamez, and Pablo Richard, younger scholars submit their interpretations and articles, some of which have been selected and translated into English. Every 18 months the authors gather to plan the upcoming issues and share their studies and experiences. Thematic issues include feminist, indigenous, peasant, and Afro-descendent interpretations. Other issues offer interpretations of biblical books from different angles, always relating to the local context. It is a kind of biblical congress for Latin America and the Spanish-speaking Caribbean. The Brazilian Association of Biblical Research (ABIB) also has a meeting every two years. Once again, we should not think that this occurs only within academic circles. Most of these scholars also partake actively in base communities, popular gatherings, workshops in poorer parishes and those with indigenous peoples, and even in some of the Pentecostal churches that are more open to new approaches to scriptures.

The "Emerging Subjects." The interpretation of the Bible experienced a new turn in the 1990s. Within the liberationist movement appeared the claims of what was labeled as the "emerging subjects," that is, a large part of the Latin American population that did not feel that their identity was completely covered under the label of "popular" or "poor." Feminist movements began to make their voices clear, underlining the fact that their suffering was not caused only because of economic deprivation but also (and mainly) because of cultural and gender-based social oppression. In some ways these new voices were coincident with the claims of feminist movements elsewhere, but Latin American feminists stressed that there were some particularities of Latin American culture, especially regarding social injustice, that had to be expressively addressed. Initiated as protest against male dominance, the movement took a wider approach that covered other gender-related concerns.

In a similar mood, the indigenous people affirmed their identity and their right to read the sacred texts out of their own situation. Of utmost importance was the 1992 commemoration of the five hundred years since the arrival of Christopher Columbus to the American continent. The 1492 date was considered the beginning of a genocide; the memories of the conquest aroused in the original people a need of reparation and a recovering of their dignity. For some, it meant the possibility of reestablishing the ancient religions prior to the Christian imposition. Others felt that they did not need to renounce their present Christian convictions, but that they needed to reformulate Christian faith in a way that did justice to their own traditions and ancestral convictions.

There are, of course, differences among the diverse peoples in Central and South America according to their various cultural backgrounds. There were many different nations before the European invasion, and each of them had their own cultural marks. The Andean plateau in South America is not the same as the Amazonian forest, the plains of the Pampas, or the Mexican peninsula of Yucatan. The inhabitants of each place have organized their lives according to the surrounding world, have established methods of relating to others (some more pacific; others warlike), and retained their own wisdom, stories, and myths. The attempt to homogenize all under the concept of "indigenous" reveals a colonizing arrogance. Part of the recognition of the aboriginal subjects was the conviction that they all had suffered genocide and oppression. Overcoming those things, however, also affirms the diversity to which each nation is entitled. The Bible was then reinterpreted in that light. Parallels were drawn between the biblical narratives—especially those of the OT—and the ancient aboriginal myths. The conviction that God was and is present in all cultures became a guiding principle for their hermeneutics; thus, inculturation became a major word in biblical hermeneutics.

Likewise, African descendants, brought to the Americas in chains as slaves, claimed the right to read the Bible from their own experiences. In some way, the situation was parallel to what happened in North America, but the difference between the evangelization of the slaves in the Protestant North and the Catholic South became decisive. While African Americans of the North were aquainted with the biblical stories, the Africans brought to South America and to the Spanish- or French-speaking Caribbean created their own syncretic religions in the new soil. The recovery of African origins was, then, the central point of the hermeneutics essays of the Christians of Afro-Brazilian, Afro-Caribbean, and other groups of African origin. Biblical interpretation knew a certain dispersion as "peasant reading," "urban reading," "ecological reading," and other "readings" of the Bible began to present a fragmented mosaic of what was previously a homogeneous hermeneutics. The question this fragmented mosaic presents is whether there remains certain common ground in Central and South American interpretation(s) of the Bible, not because of geographical or confessional divergences but because the manifestation of human subjects who were previously silenced and experiences that were previously submerged.

The Question of Method. The search for common ground raises the issue of the hermeneutical method. Notwithstanding the dispersion of viewpoints and themes, a certain agreement exists concerning method. Latin American interpretation of the Bible created its own hermeneutical circle. Bible scholars like Croatto, or theologians like Leonardo and Clodovis Boff, or Juan Luis Segundo, sustained theoretically what was done in practice in popular, native readings of the Bible. This was not just a spontaneous creation; the hermeneutical approach of popular interpretation had also influenced scholars that had reflected on the hermeneutical task through the work of Paul Ricoeur and others.

The starting point of every interpretation is a critical revision of previous interpretations, based on the suspicion that they were formulated in order to justify a given social system, a power structure, ecclesiastical hierarchy, or due to a certain cultural bias. A new hermeneutics "from below" was needed. In order to clarify the way in which oppressive forces had imposed their ideologies and theology, two tools were used: (1) the experience of the oppressed and (2) the social analysis provided by critical social sciences (and later gender theories or anthropological studies). Certainly, the use of historical-critical tools helped clarify the meaning of the texts and that structural analysis was introduced to better understand the fabric of the texts. But nonetheless, many felt that that was not enough. What were the political, cultural, or social projections contained in the text and in previous interpretations? How had those interpretations denied, in many cases, the liberating power of scriptures? How could that concealed strength be recovered? In some circles this was called "to see," the first step of a threefold way that would include "to judge" and "to act."

With that critical understanding in mind, the second step was to consider the reading context, the situation of the readers, their sufferings and hopes, their claims, and how the Bible message related to their particular concerns. A new reading opened the text to respond to those questions, where the faith experience and the everyday struggle for life took a major and decisive role. How do the people relate the Bible stories to our own history? How can we read between the lines of the scriptural texts in the way that the witnesses of God's liberating acts had put forward their own experience? This was called "to judge." But that judgment had to be acknowledged not as an intellectual exercise of understanding the text but also—and primarily—as an impulse to action, as spiritual power in our task of overcoming injustice, of changing society. So the hermeneutical circle can be completed only when the Bible reader is moved to action, experiencing God's message not only in one's own mind, but also in the body, or better, in the community's collective body. The material dimension of hermeneutics, becoming visible in social action, and therefore influencing the context, is part of the hermeneutical circle. The material dimension of hermeneutics in some way or another alters the contexts, brings new experiences, highlights new features, and the hermeneutical task must begin anew.

Once again, the particular ethos of Latin American culture, demanded more. The reading of the Bible needed to include celebration: this is not just an academic exercise in order to fulfill the intellectual curiosity of scholars, nor does it suffice when we are engaged in social struggle. Reading the Bible is part of the vital existence of the community, and that existence, even in situations of distress and grief, is a celebration of life. "To see, judge, act, and celebrate" became a motto for most interpretive circles, and when trained scholars bring in their knowledge to support the popular (aboriginal, Afro-descendent, gender conscious, ecological, etc.) reading of the Bible they take into account that the underlying method will follow these steps and that the celebrative mode is part of it.

Within this larger framework, we need to consider some particularities. In Brazil, for example, Frey Gorgulho and Ana Flora Anderson practiced what they called "reading from the four sides." This presupposes that every text can be analyzed from four different sides: political, ideological, social, and cultural elements, all of which inform faith. Recent interpreters have emphasized a transcultural reading. Without abandoning the three steps of "to see, to judge, to act" and in the spirit of "to celebrate," questions have been raised not only from political suspicion but on how intercultural exchange could illumine other features in the biblical message that remain concealed if examined *only* within the dominant cultural frame.

In short, we can offer a sketch of the method in Latin American Bible reading:

The Hermeneutical Circle in Latin American Bible Studies

- The precondition: a faith commitment:
  - Reading the Bible as sacred text implies assuming partisanship.
  - Biblical interpretation does not come from timeless abstraction but from a certain context (incarnation).
  - Biblical reading in context must engage the Gospel (Good news to the oppressed).
- Three steps and an attitude:
  - To see (to look, to understand, a suspicion on the prevailing interpretations).
  - To judge (analyze and critique, elaborate and propose).
  - To act (praxis as an hermeneutical tool and goal).
  - To celebrate (an attitude of celebrating God's presence that guides and inspires).
- The circularity of hermeneutics:

To see

- We examine previous biblical interpretations, or the existing ideological interpretations, and see their contributions and flaws in our context.
- Then we bring new hermeneutical questions.

To judge

- Out of commitment and partisanship, we see the failures of our context (society, economy, church institutions, etc.).
- Reading in community takes priority over personal, academic, or magisterial interpretation.
- New interpretations are given, guided by the questions and situations of our context.

To act

- We engage in new praxis (social action, political commitment, economic alternatives, community building, ecological care, discursive and ethical renewal, etc.).
- Praxis moves us to reexamine our context.
- This new look obliges us to pose new questions and revise our biblical reading, reinitiating the interpretative task.

To celebrate

- Through worshiping, praying, singing, and working together we enjoy sharing in community and experiencing God's love for and in our brothers and sisters.
- We refresh together our hope and sustain one another in our common task.

Remaining Challenges. The kind of biblical interpretation developed through this method revealed some flaws that should be considered. The main critique presupposes that all biblical texts have a similar origin: that they expose the situation of oppressed people. What are we to do with those texts that show a different class origin, or that are clearly biased by a patriarchal culture? How do we deal with those passages that justify discrimination, that sprout from the upper layers of the Israelite society in Old Testament times, or are sympathetic with a more strict ecclesiastical order? Liberation hermeneutics tends to ignore those texts or force them into something else. Feminist interpretation has been especially aware of this fact, and soon the reading of the aboriginal people could also find these problems in many texts. How does one read the whole Bible while acknowledging the tensions and contradictions found in the text when read as a whole? The need to deal with an entire and complex canon challenges a more superficial affirmation that the entire Bible can indeed be read as a liberationist manifesto.

The use of social analysis poses another problem. To establish a dialogue with secular knowledge requires one to be aware of the underlying premises of that science in order to avoid a naive attitude that "imports" undesired suppositions into biblical interpretation. Social analysis and social theory is indeed far from homogeneous. Different schools and paradigms will expose more clearly some issues and conceal others, and the selection of which approach should be used is not always easy. It is impossible to avoid all subjectivity and establish a neutral viewpoint from which to discern the correct theory or the only valid interpretation. All approaches to reality involve a certain engagement with that reality in one way or another, and hermeneutics is precisely that. Yet, awareness of one's own (or borrowed) ideology ensures epistemological rigor. That is why these methods of interpretation are neither definitive nor correct. At most, they should aspire to be relevant to the context and situation of the reading community while also conscious of their limitations and biases. Liberationist hermeneutics is challenged by the temptation to formulate a new liberationist dogma, as most other biblical interpretations have done. If that happens it will be neither liberationist nor hermeneutics, since it will halt hermeneutical circularity.

That need of permanent renewal poses another challenge. New information, methods, and paradigms appear constantly in biblical exegesis and hermeneutics, whether developed within biblical studies or provided by linguistics, historical studies, archaeology, or other sciences. How willing will the Latin American hermeneutical community be to incorporate these novelties, especially if they come to defy some of its basic assumptions? In some cases these new approaches and emphases are welcome because they help widen the scope of interpretation. For example, the development in narrative analysis has proven valuable. Since aboriginal culture was largely oral and privileged narration was the favorite way of communication, it now becomes compatible with biblical interpretation's narrative studies. The same can be said with postcolonial studies, which helped to uncover the imperial bias and sequels of colonial dominance in biblical reading. But some lines of secularization and postmodern theories, which tend to dissociate the religious validity of discourse or question popular religiosity, can be seen as menaces to the type of engaged hermeneutics practiced by base communities.

Another question is how to deal not only with a complex text but with a complex context. Societies also change, not only because of social praxis but because of technological innovation, foreign influence, economic changes, demographic facts caused by migration, and environmental factors due to global change. It is impossible to ignore the effects of globalization on political issues, as well as the movements of resistance in different societies. How are these going to affect hermeneutics? Some assertions dear to biblical interpretation in Latin America, those which are already part of the hermeneutical tradition of the continent, must be revised in light of these changes.

Not all biblical interpretation in Latin America derives from liberation theology. Although this was the more characteristic and creative trend, and was probably the first hermeneutical approach proper to the context of Central and South America, other lines also exist. In a more evangelical approach but clearly concerned also by the contextual problems of the continent, we should mention Juan Stam, who engaged in a profound work on the book of Revelation. And René Padilla, who completed postgraduate studies in NT under F. F. Bruce in Manchester, England, worked on contextual hermeneutics and published one of the few books on that theme from that particular theological perspective. The growth of Pentecostalism in South and Central America in recent years also promises new approaches to the biblical message. Until now, Pentecostalism has been dominated by the interpretation of the Bible brought by the missionaries and evangelists that support the movement. But there are already some scholars, like Juan Sepúlveda of Chile and Bernardo Campos of Peru, who are introducing a Pentecostalism with a Latin American face, one that proposes its own way of interpreting certain crucial Bible passages. In addition, more traditional Catholic scholars are offering interesting approaches within the framework of established Roman doctrine. The *Comentario Biblico Latinoamericano,* edited by A. Levoratti, published in Spain by Verbo Divino in 2005, is an example. In this case, we can appreciate the contributions at the ecumenical level, with some of the names mentioned earlier. As we can see, Bible interpretation in Latin America has been, and still is, a varied and strong movement. It is broad in its scope and plural in its agents.

[*See also* African American Interpretation; African Biblical Interpretation; Cross-Cultural Exegesis; Cuban Interpretation in the Cuban Diaspora; Feminist Biblical Interpretation; Liberation Hermeneutics; Latina/o Interpretation; Pentecostal Interpretation; Postcolonial Biblical Interpretation; *and* Theological Interpretation.]

BIBLIOGRAPHY

Cardenal, Ernesto. *The Gospel in Solentiname.* Maryknoll, N.Y.: Orbis, 2010.

Croatto, Jose Severino. *Biblical Hermeneutics. Toward a Theory of Reading as the Production of Meaning.* 3d ed. Maryknoll, N.Y.: Orbis, 1995. Also in German: *Die Bibel gehört der Armen. Perspektiven einer befreiungstheologischen Hermeneutik.* Munich: Chr. Kaiser Verlag, 1989.

Croatto, Jose Severino. *Liberación y libertad: Pautas hermenéuticas.* Buenos Aires: Mundo Nuevo, 1973. Translated as *Exodus: A Hermeneutic of Freedom.* Maryknoll, N.Y.: Orbis, 1981.

Kinsler, Ross, and Gloria Kinsler, eds. *God's. Economy: Biblical Studies from Latin America.* Maryknoll, N.Y.: Orbis, 2005. Collection of Latin American essays on Bible and economy.

Mesters, Carlos. *Defenseless Flower: A New Reading of the Bible.* Maryknoll, N.Y.: Orbis, 1989.

Mesters, Carlos. *God, Where Are You?: Meditations on the Old Testament.* Eugene, Ore.: Wipf and Stock, 2003.

Míguez, Néstor. "Latin American Reading of the Bible: Experiences, Challenges and its Practice." *Expository Times* (2006): 118.

Míguez, Néstor. *The Practice of Hope: Ideology and Intention in 1 Thessalonians.* Minneapolis: Fortress, 2012.

Richard, Pabl. *Apocalypse: A People's Commentary on the Book of Revelation.* Eugene, Ore.: Wipf and Stock, 2009.

Tamez, Elsa. *Bible of the Oppressed.* Eugene, Ore.: Wipf and Stock, 2006.
Tamez, Elsa. *The Scandalous Message of James: Faith without Works Is Dead.* New York: Crossroad, 2002.
Vaage, Leif, ed. *Subversive Scriptures. Revolutionary Readings of the Christian Bible in Latin America.* Harrisburg, Penn.: Trinity Press International, 1997.

Néstor Oscar Míguez

Chinese Interpretation

The term *Chinese* is used generally to speak of Han ethnicity and culture (especially its Mandarin language and Chinese script), whether in China, Taiwan, Hong Kong, or other countries (such as Indonesia, the United Kingdom, or the United States). Yet, as a result of ethnic hybridity and cultural mobility, the precise meaning of the term begins to break down as people of non-Han nationalities or non-Chinese interact with Hans. Thus, the broad definition of *Chinese* may refer to cultures in China or to cultures of Chinese living overseas. Even with the narrower definition, the term is too broad to reflect the complex ways in which Han-Chinese language, history, and culture influence biblical interpretation.

A Brief History of Chinese Interpretation. In antiquity, China acquired a beautiful name, *Shenzhou,* which literally means "divine land" or "God's land." The title most likely was used as a political term, suggesting that God had given the elite the divine right to rule. The name of the high God, *Shangdi,* was used very early in Chinese written history, but there is no evidence of biblical interpretation that understands *Shangdi* as equivalent to Yahweh—although the Chinese Bible translates Yahweh as *Shangdi.* It is more meaningful to speak of the introduction of the biblical message to North China (then known as Cathay) in the seventh century by the Syrian Nestorians. Since that time, Chinese biblical interpretation has been unable to disengage from its political context. Over the course of fourteen centuries, intermittent foreign missionaries have contributed to the relatively brief, but intense, history of both Catholic and Protestant biblical interpretations in China and in various regions or territories overseas in which Chinese reside. The following is a brief survey of Chinese biblical interpretations diachronically.

Nestorianism. The Nestorian Tablet/Monument of the Tang dynasty (618–907), found in the city of Xi'an (called Changan then), suggests an attempt by Syrian "missionaries" to contextualize Nestorian Christianity in a Chinese form. The top of the monument shows a carving of two monsters holding a pearl, and a cross that surmounts a lotus (symbol of Buddhism) and a cloud (symbol of Daoism). The integration of Christian faith with indigenous Chinese religious symbols points to an accommodating biblical hermeneutic, probably used as a strategy for self-preservation, a survival tactic of a group seeking identity and security in a largely hostile environment. The Nestorian mission was contained in Xi'an, reaching out only to the official literati, and there was no impact of the gospel outside the city. The non-Chinese names on the monument indicate that church leaders were foreigners. The hermeneutic adopted by Chinese Christians in Xi'an was not cross-cultural and therefore lacked the cultural depth and authenticity to make it a genuinely indigenous biblical interpretation and expanding mission movement.

Franciscan and Dominican Missions. The proselytizing biblical interpretation of Franciscan and Dominican missionaries in the Yuan Dynasty (1280–1367) was committed to converting the world empire of the Khans for the sake of Christ. The Dominican mission had some success, but the Franciscan mission failed to engage Chinese culture in a constructive, dialogical way and therefore never took root in China in forms that could withstand the stress of political and social change. The reasons for the failure of the Franciscan mission in China have to do with cultural proselytizing. First, the Franciscans did not understand or deal constructively with the Chinese veneration of ancestors, the Confucian ethics of family, or the Chinese worldview. Second, the Franciscans failed to work with Chinese converts to devise patterns of Christian faith sensitive to their customs and that could be expressed in indigenous Chinese languages. Instead, Chinese converts were taught Greek and Latin.

Jesuit Missionaries. The first genuine accommodation of biblical interpretation was implemented by the Jesuit Missionaries in the Ming Dynasty (1368–1643). The Jesuits imitated Paul's apostolic style of "becoming all things to all people" (1 Cor 9:19–23) and integrated Christian faith with the Confucian worldview. Matteo Ricci, for example, translated the four books of the Confucian Canon into Latin; he then translated a few Biblical texts into Chinese. Ricci's biblical hermeneutical assumptions could be summarized in two ways. First, he understood history as a progressive movement of promise to fulfillment. He was convinced that the earliest Confucian teaching about *Tian* (heaven) and *Shangdi* (lord above) referred to a personal Supreme Being. Second, Ricci thought it possible to make positive connections between the self-cultivation practices of the Confucius rites and Christian discipleship learned through the spiritual exercises of Ignatius of Loyola. Despite Ricci's positive intention and genuine effort, an unfortunate result of the Catholic mission movement was the infamous Rites (of Chinese ancestor worship) Controversy between the Jesuits, the Dominicans, and the Vatican (1715). The argument offended the Chinese Emperor Kangxi of the Qing Dynasty (1644–1911), and, he banned all missionary activities in 1720.

Protestant Missions. The fourth type of biblical interpretation can be seen in Protestant missionaries (since 1807), who focused on the social needs of Chinese society—such as education (Robert Morrison) and medical services (Peter Parker)—and emphasized the translation, teaching, and preaching of the Bible (the first Chinese Bible was published in 1823). One significant issue that arose was the question of whether the Christian gospel calls for social transformation or is concerned primarily with individual salvation. In Chinese culture, however, cosmology and anthropology, thinking and action, intellect and spirituality are not dualistic, opposing pairs. Instead, they live in healthy tension with one another. As a result, the holistic and dynamic interpretation of the Protestant movement—with its focus on Bible teaching and biblical living to transform individual lives and society—was an interpretive approach of great significance to many Chinese Christians. In fact, it was a matter of life and death. Because gospel preaching and Bible teaching in the past had been conducted primarily by Western missionaries through their cultural lenses, Chinese converts often were accused of betraying their own Chinese culture in favor of a Western religion. The charges were even more serious, however, because the sociopolitical context of nineteenth- to early-twentieth-century China was one of confusion in the eyes of Chinese and Westerners alike—regarding, on one hand, missionary, medical, and educational services of the foreign Christian movement and, on the other hand, opium trade, gunship aggression, and unequal treaty of the foreign powers.

In the modern era, Chinese biblical interpretation has taken a number of forms—from approaches indebted to the West that tend to neglect the task of theological indigenization to forms of accommodation that take seriously the importance of recontextualizing the teaching of scripture in Chinese terms. For example, the Little Flock, founded by Watchman Nee (Ni Duosheng, 1903–1972), appears in certain respects to be an effort at establishing an indigenous Chinese Christian polity and ecclesiology. However, this movement owes much of its theological insight to Western Dispensationalism (John Nelson Darby and the Plymouth Brethren, the Scofield Bible) and Keswick "Victorious Life" teaching. In his book, *The Spiritual Man* (1968), an exposition of Paul's theology, Nee adopts the Western Greek and gnostic view of a body-soul dualism. Saving souls became his focus; helping the poor and victims of war was not part of his prophetic calling. Nee was preoccupied with sanctification concerns such as the "second blessing," "baptism of the Spirit," and "spiritual illumination," and he distinguished the "spiritual" Christian from the "carnal" Christian who spent time in the world.

Accommodation of the Bible and Chinese Culture. Greater sensitivity to the demands of indigenization is found in the fifth movement, including biblical interpretations of Wu Leichuan, T. C. Chao, Y. T. Wu, Jia Yuming, and Bishop Ting Guang-hsun. Wu Leichuan (1870–1944) argued that Chinese theology must address the issue of national salvation of China, in light of the anti-Christian ethos in movements such as the "Non-Christian Alliance" (1922–1924), which protested against the World Student Christian Federation and Christian studies in university education, or the "New Culture Movement" (1917), based on the belief that only science and democracy, not religion, could save and modernize China. Wu argued that the perfect personhood of Jesus, who exemplified unity in word and deed, reveals to humanity a radically new and holistic form of existence. This new way of being truly human is what the "kingdom of God" means—a combination of idealism and materialism, a prototype for a socialist society and communal sharing of property. To Wu, Jesus's kingdom message is the foundation for the "national salvation" of China.

T. C. Chao (Zhao Zichen, 1888–1979) also sought a new accommodation of the Bible and Chinese culture, but adopted a very different approach than Wu did. Chao rejected the idea that Jesus's message is political, much less revolutionary. Although Chao sought to work out a Christian social ethic that was not individualistic, he rejected socialism. He struggled with the question of how to reconcile the Confucian impetus to transform society through a Confucian self-cultivation with a Protestant soteriology based on accepting the free grace of God. Chao's ethic was based on dying and rising with Christ in Romans, a mystical interpretation of the Christ event of death and resurrection, and Chao saw Pauline theology at odds with the Confucian ethic.

In the late 1990s, Bishop Ting proposed the "Reconstruction of Theological Thinking" in his book, *Love Never Ends* (1998). In order to undertake indigenous Chinese theological reconstruction, he considered the context of socialism and emphasized social exegesis, open theology on God's freedom, and self-realization through love. This teaching of love seems to have departed from the traditional Christian doctrine of "justification by faith." Although Ting's theology raises debate among scholars in and outside China, the intent of his call for "reconstruction of theology" is to make Chinese theology more indigenous and practical.

The Current State of Chinese Biblical Interpretations. Recent Chinese biblical interpretations abound in type, method, and purpose. Ideally speaking, Chinese interpretations of the Bible take seriously both scripture and interpreter; they examine both the semantic domain of the biblical texts shaped by Western traditions and, at the same time, the composite horizons of Chinese contexts and presuppositions of interpreters. To miss either of these is to betray the unity of Chinese biblical interpretations. Recent Chinese biblical interpretations can be grouped broadly into two interrelated categories: indigenous interpretations and contextual interpretations.

Indigenous Interpretations. To do justice to the textuality of the Bible, translation is a first step toward indigenous interpretation. Other steps include translating Western Christian classics—such as the works of the Institute of Sino-Christian Studies (Hong Kong), the works of Liu Xiaofeng, and *The Biblical Library* series (edited by K. K. Yeo and Liang Hui, Shanghai: Shanghai VI Horae Publishers, Inc.)—and teaching biblical languages in the native tongues of the people rather than in Latin and English. All translation is interpretation, whether word-for-word, phrase-for-phrase, or concept-for-concept.

Since translation is more than word-for-word—it is more about expressing biblical concepts and narratives in other languages—the use of Chinese texts and resources in indigenous interpretations is prominent in recent Chinese biblical interpretation. Some Chinese scholars explore the intertextual relationship between biblical texts and Asian texts. For example, Timothy Richard identifies, and Andres S. K. Tang rethinks, the affinity between the Christian faith and Mahayana texts; Lai Pan-chiu works on Christology and Yua-yen Buddhism. K. K. Yeo employs Yin-yang cosmology to identify a theological-anthropology of Gen 1:26–27, reads the Analects and Paul's letter to the Galatians intertextually, and engages the wisdom of the Chinese philosopher Zhuangzi ([Chuang Tzu] fourth century B.C.E.) with that of James and Paul—while other scholars engage Zhuangzi with Ecclesiastes (Liang Gong).

Others make use of Asian resources to read the biblical texts. C. S. Song brings together Asian stories and the biblical narratives of Jesus's death and resurrection, for example, in his *The Tears of Lady Meng: a Parable of the People's Political Theology* (1981), highlighting the suffering of the people and how God or heaven's compassion reigns. Archie C. C. Lee works with Psalm 78 and the Chinese Odes; Loh I-To works with Asian images and Christian biblical and liturgical texts; Peter K. H. Lee uses Mencius's *haoan-zhiqi* to reread *ruaḥ* of Yahweh and the Holy Spirit; and several scholars translate the Gospel of John in relation to the Daoist language (He Guanghu, Zhong Zhibang, Zhang Qingxiong, Zhang Xuefu, Xie Wenyi).

An intertextual reading that seeks mutual edification between a Chinese classical text and a biblical text is an interscriptural model that proves promising. When Confucian classics and the Bible are read to complement one another, although they differ radically from each other, holding their incommensurability in tension is a challenging interpretive move that highlights the incompleteness of both texts and yet demonstrates the sacredness of all scriptures. Putting aside even the scriptures' common ground in the areas of genre study, moral and spiritual teaching, redaction criticism, and commentary history, the varied content of the texts allows for multiple points of dialogue and resonance, such as in the following: (1) The Judeo-Christian Bible holds to the cosmogonic belief that the universe is theocentric, that the cosmos is created and sustained by a divine power of goodness. Although Confucian "heaven" (*tian*) as a naturalistic cosmos lacks personal narrative, the transcendent nature of heaven is thought to be *ren* (benevolence) of the moral order; the immanent nature of heaven is expressed in human nature as virtues. A *balanced* worldview that is theocentric *and* anthropo-cosmic is necessary; otherwise, religion becomes divorced from ethics, alienating divine grace from human endeavor; (2) Although Confucian classics assume neither Adam's fall (sin) nor existential estrangement with *tian*, both scriptures seek to overcome social conflicts, moral collapse, and spiritual chaos. The difference between the two scriptures lies in Confucian virtue in self-cultivation and biblical faith in God's grace. However, the Confucian self-cultivation ethic grounded on *ren* (benevolence) and *li* (ritual propriety) can be subsumed under a biblical ethic that is based on the Spirit; together, these two traditions encourage a complete obedience of faith; (3) The cyclical history of Confucian classics and the eschatological view of the Bible can mutually critique each other's "either-space-or-time" interpretive assumption. Such mutual critique can move toward a more holistic and dynamic understanding of a multidimensional, spiral-movement universe; (4) The biblical understanding of cruciform love fulfills the Confucian ideal of *ren* (benevolence); additionally, Confucian ethics on propriety (*li*) and music (*yue*) supplement biblical theology that lacks detailed ethical explication; (5) The relationship between human nature/goodness and divine grace in the Bible and Confucian classics is antithetical; yet, both scriptures agree that only love of neighbor expresses concretely how to be fully human (*Analects* 15:9) or to be holy (Lev 11:44, Mt 5:48, 1 Pet 1:16).

Despite their historical differences, Daoist classics and the Bible share a similar passion for a wisdom outlook of life; thus, an interscriptural reading enables a clearer understanding of Chinese Christian theology. We can look to Paul's christological responses to various problems found in the Corinthian church and view them through Zhuangzi's understanding of love as he responded to vicissitudes of human life and the chaotic world of the Warring States (480–221 B.C.E.). First, to love is selflessness, namely *wangji* (self-forgetting or "letting go and let it happen"; *Zhuangzi*, ch. 2: *wu sang wo* [I have lost my self]). Zhuangzi says that "the perfect person (*zhiren*) has no self (*wuji*), the transcendent person (*shenren*) has no accomplishment (*wugong*), the holy person (*shengren*) has no name (*wuming*)" (*Zhuangzi*, ch. 2). Second, to love is not for the purpose of profit, power, or any self-advantage. Instead, love means befriending all, including other creatures in the universe—such as frogs, birds, fish, and even the robber Chih who sucks on human livers (*Zhuangzi*, ch. 29). Ideally, a leader befriends his followers; Zhuangzi advocates that a rulers' love of the people, a sage-ruler's love, never comes to an end (*Zhuangzi*, ch. 15). However, elsewhere he warns that the moment rulers want to love the people, they will harm them. Unfortunately, this intentional love is bound to become manipulative and turn to biased and self-serving love. Third, to love is not to follow the "cultured" or "civilized" ways of life, but to wander freely despite the tyranny of traditional mores and prevailing ideology. To love is to be creative and spontaneous, maximizing self and social freedom. Thus, "to forget one's physical form" (*wang ji xing*) and "to forget one's heart" (*wang xin*) is different from maintaining one's "constant heart" (*zhang xin*), this last being the ability to attune harmoniously to flux. Fourth, love changes all. In Zhuangzi's language, love transforms (*hua*) all, because we are intricately connected with the manifold, organic, and changing cosmos. Paul's understanding of body as an organic whole can be explained more powerfully by Zhuangzi's understanding of *Dao* as the natural, spontaneous, effortless, emerging, cyclical process of all things (*wanwu*). Because all things are organically related, the way of life is unity, and this process is called *hua*. Zhuangzi writes, "All the ten-thousand things and I are one" (*Zhuangzi*, ch. 1).

Paul's rhetorical theology as a way of counseling those in the church to love one another and to love God is similar to Zhuangzi's admonitions on living with *Dao*, others, and oneself. That is, the Pauline theology of love advocates that one align with the *Dao*/Creator, to love in the way of *wuwei* (effortlessly), and to relate to others as *wangji* (self-forgetting, letting go, letting it happen rather than making it happen). One performs all of this in sincerity (*cheng*) and authentically (*chenren*). Paul wants to bring the Corinthian Christians to a higher spiritual awareness via the "crucified Christ" (1 Cor 1:23, 2:2). Paul preaches only "crucified Christ" to the Corinthian Christians, so that they will deconstruct the civilizational ideals of power (Romans), religion (Jews), and wisdom/philosophy (Greeks). Through such self-deconstruction, they are then able to reconstruct holistic life found only in the "weakness" of God, "miracle-less" faith, and "foolish" understanding (1 Cor 1—2).

The key to attaining *Dao* or entering into heaven is through self-forgetfulness. The attempt to make things happen only manipulates and distorts the true Daoist nature of things: "Forget things, forget Heaven, and be called a forgetter of self. The person who has forgotten self may be said to have entered Heaven" (*Zhuangzi*, ch. 2). The word *forget* (*wang*) in the Chinese pictogram is made up of "losing" and "heart." Our extrapolation reveals a self-centered, narcissistic self as the core problem in the Corinthian churches; Paul admonishes them to be forgetters of self by recalling Christ's selfless love. *Zhuangzi* advocates that "The Perfect Person [*chi-ren*] has no self" (ch. 1). It follows then that the Perfect Community has no self, or in the sense by Paul's account that selflessness means union in Christ's selflessness.

There are too many strong-headed Christians at Corinth. Self-involvement gets in the way of communal unity. They assume they know fully, but Paul has a closer-to-Daoist understanding that *Dao*/Truth (the "All-in-all God") cannot be conceptualized, and we know only partially—like that of frog (limited in a well) and cicada (brief and temporary).

Although of different eras and circumstances, both Zhuangzi and Paul seem to share similar views about the human psyche sick with self-inflation. Their prognosis is conflict and schism, and the prescription is selflessness, namely love. Despite cultural differences between Paul and Zhuangzi, Chinese readers of the Bible understand better both Zhuangzi and Paul as they intertextually read the Pauline theology of love with Zhuangzi's deliberation on *wuwei* (effortlessly), *wangji* (self-forgetting; letting go), and *chenren* (authentically human). The *Zhuangzi's* admonitions on living with *Dao*, others, and oneself enrich the reading of Paul's rhetorical theology as a way of counseling members of the church to love one another and to love God.

Contextual Interpretations. In order to take seriously the composite horizons of the Chinese (whether in China or overseas)—which consist of multiple nationalities, regional groups and dialects, diverse cultures, pluralistic religions, and socio-political realities—Chinese biblical interpretation addresses the various distinctions in the following examples: (1) debating the definition, purpose, goal, and relationship of Sino-Christian theology (Liu Xiaofeng, Zhuo Xinpi, Chin Kenpa) with "Cultural Christians" (Stephen Chan); (2) reinterpreting the biblical understanding of revelation (Chia Yuming) and reason (Chow Lien-hwa), incarnation (Chao Tzuchen), the Christian church of China (Timothy Lew Ting Fang), Christian supra-consanguineous ethics in the Bible (You Xilin), biblical anthropology (Lin Hong-hsin) in light of the socialist context of the New China; (3) coexistence of racial groups in Malaysia (the use of the theology of neighborhood of S. Batumalai by Chinese Christian scholar Hii Kon-ghock, together with Pauline theology in Romans); (4) Christian faith and its interaction with other faiths (Chow Lien-hwa); (5) the mission of the church (Raymond Fung, T. C. Chao, Jonathan Chao Tien-en); (6) response to geopolitical issues of the day such as Hong Kong's relation with China (Lo Lungkwong), Chinese Marxism and end of history (Zhang Xian), secular humanism and Chinese Christianity (Wang Xiaochao), Christian-Confucianism interaction in modern China (Sun Shangyang); and (7) Chinese feminist theology (Gao Shining, Kwok Pui-lan, and K. K. Yeo) in diverse Chinese contexts.

To demonstrate the significance and challenge of contextual biblical interpretation, one may use the question of Chinese ancestor worship (Timothy Richard, Ro Bong-rin), which is rooted in the ethics and spirituality of *hsiao* (filial piety). The Confucian emphasis on filial piety is regarded not merely as human responsibility, but also as a heavenly ordained way of life. The virtue of filial piety, which bears forth the practice of ancestor veneration, is rooted in the cosmic and spiritual value systems of propriety (*li*), *renren* (benevolent persons), community forming, and moral formation. Ancestor veneration is a way of paying respect, reverence, and tribute to one's living parents, and to deceased and even remote ancestors. It also seeks to promote continuity of lineage and family in terms of identity. For the family, it has the value of remembering the past and envisioning the future.

In addition, ancestor veneration includes provision for both an occasion of reunion of the family and for the economical, social, and psychological support of the bereaved family. The meal with the dead is conceived as a common meal with the dead and the living, similar to the idea of the "communion of the saints," and the understanding is that the death and resurrection of Christ makes that possible. All the values of ancestor veneration are compatible with Pauline theologies. However, the cosmological assumptions of Confucianism and ancestor veneration cannot be brushed aside as merely cultural or virtuous. Here, then, is the challenging work of contextual biblical interpretation, that is, how to use the Pauline gospel of the cross to engage and critique the blind spots of Chinese ancestral worship.

The Christ-event presents the most concrete demonstration of the self-critical principle of God in dealing with issues of power (total surrender on the cross), culture (critique of blind obedience to the Jewish Law), race (reconciliation between Jews and Gentiles), gender (male and female), social status (freed, slaves, masters), etc. Many people practice ancestor worship out of superstition and fear. There is a common Chinese belief that gods and ghosts (*kui)* are human beings who passed away into the *yin* (shady) world. Living humans inhabit the *yang* (sunny) world. Ancestors can be mediators between human beings and supernatural beings. If the deceased's soul is not well cared for, the soul could degenerate into *kui*, a ghost, or a demon. The status of the soul can be elevated into a spiritual being, *shen* (god, or a yang soul), if sacrifice and prayers are offered. Thus, in the practice of ancestor worship among common people, although piety is the primary motive, other motives include placating the demons and seeking blessings from the *shen*.

Because the Confucian worldview holds that children and women do not possess full personhood as adult males do, dying infants and single women are never sacrificed to, and seldom remembered, in the rite of ancestral worship. While Paul's language of "adoption as sons" (*huiothesias*) seems not to include females as equals with male believers, I believe that Paul's affirmation of no differentiation between male and female in Christ (Gal 3:28) is basic, as he affirms the worthiness of women and children.

Accepting Paul's understanding of the church as the family of God can help in overcoming a Chinese parochial understanding of family primarily in the sense of lineage. Paul's pessimistic anthropology (human sin as bondage) can temper a Chinese optimism of moral formation. It is the redemption for the new creation in Christ that transforms human beings. Self-actualization is conformed to the image of Christ, rather than extending the image of a family or tribe.

The most challenging task of cross-cultural readings of the Bible is the clashing of worldviews between a culture and the biblical text. In reality, worship and veneration, faithfulness and faithlessness are intertwined in the mind and practice of Chinese pietists. In the process of cross-cultural readings, one begins to discern what is good, permissible, salvific, and honorable—and what is not. The value of this cross-cultural biblical interpretation is precisely this—to allow one's culture and the biblical text to interact, to differentiate, and to be mutually transformed.

Reflective Conclusions. Outside the church and seminary, a new movement of academic interest and research on Christianity as the core of Western civilization has developed in China among scholars, primarily those in humanities and social sciences institutions (e.g., Peking University and People's University in Beijing, Chinese Academy of Social Sciences in Beijing, Fudan University in Shanghai, Sun Yat-sen University in Guangzhou, Zhejiang University in Hangzhou). With more resources and support available, many researchers in conferences and publications are able to produce a greater quantity and quality of work than that of Christian theologians in seminaries. Their works on Christianity range from history and aesthetics to theology and philosophy, but biblical studies continues to be marginalized. Many government researchers are serious about indigenous Chinese Christian theology but not about indigenous or contextual biblical interpretations.

The hope and future of Chinese biblical interpretation depends to a large extent on the development of specifically Chinese approaches to biblical hermeneutics and the working out of contemporary biblical-theological perspectives that do justice to the specific cultural textures of Chinese life. Unfortunately, most Chinese commentaries and other forms of Chinese biblical interpretation today, even outside China, present themselves as "culturally neutral," which tacitly means Western (European and North American). Chinese biblical interpretation today continues to be dominated by and large by Western scholarship—either traditional historical-grammatical exegesis or radical postcolonial interpretation that seeks to deconstruct the Bible and Western culture in the interest of promoting purely Chinese culture. Yet, this raises several questions: What is Chinese culture? And what is Chinese biblical interpretation?

Every culture changes over time. No culture has a homogeneous, unchanging identity. Keeping this in mind, it is important to be clear about basic definitions, what one means by the term *Chinese* and, at the same time, to be cautious and not claim too much for one's definition. In our time, an emerging modern (largely Western) global culture—through trade, travel, technology, etc.—threatens traditional cultural identities and values. Despite that, the perennial Chinese characteristic is found in the Chinese cosmology of *Dao De* (the Way of Morality). Even among those Chinese who intentionally want to reject the Confucianist ideal, the Confucian ethic often still plays a significant role in their thinking and way of life.

The Chinese DNA is not just in the Chinese interpreter, it also is in the Chinese Bible. The nature of the biblical text as written in the original languages and translated into various versions of the Chinese language contributes to the richly textured meaning of the Bible. A Chinese interpreter has both Chinese DNA and Christian DNA, and thus comes to the Bible not as a detached, "objective" observer but as a subjectively engaged and interested interpreter, one who has been shaped by the Bible and by Chinese tradition. A Christian Chinese biblical interpretation is bound up in this tricky, yet exciting, hermeneutical negotiation between the biblical text and Chinese culture.

The holy scripture exerts its sacred life force through the interpretive and communicative process, since scripture assumes that the holy writer of the texts wills the sacred word to speak over time and space—and here we approach the issue of "cross-cultural interpretation"—in both its *descriptive* and *prescriptive* meanings. It is *descriptive* because of the use of cultural resources (such as myths, philosophy, or concepts of the Sumerian, Egyptian, Jewish, or Greco-Roman worlds) by biblical authors to express their understanding of God, and the use of contemporary, cultural resources (such as indigenous texts or cultural frameworks) by biblical interpreters as hermeneutical tools to read the scripture. All theological expression or interpretation is *cross*-cultural to the degree that theology and culture are not identical, although they need each other and share some common tasks. If the cultures of the Bible and those of interpreters are identical, cross-cultural interpretation will not be necessary; if they do not have anything in common, interpretation will not be possible.

It is *prescriptive* because biblical or theological interpretation is a redemptive process, especially for readers. The interpreter reads the text in order to understand the meaning of the text, and the text reads the interpreter in order to inscribe a meaningful narrative and to transform the world of the interpreter. Chinese biblical interpretation is not only geared toward "Chinese biblical interpretation," but also it is committed to "biblical Chinese interpretation." Both terms pay attention to the dynamic relationship between theology/interpretation and Chinese-ness (culture, philosophy, text, ways of life), but the former seeks to express biblical theology *culturally*, while the latter also commits to that task but ultimately reads cultures *biblically*. The prescriptive task of Chinese biblical interpretation is the warrant to read scripture cross-culturally for the sake of "breaking into" Chinese cultures as the scripture is expressed through that cultural medium.

Two issues inform understanding of the reason biblical Chinese theology is the *telos* of Chinese biblical interpretation.

Relationship between Revelation and Language (i.e., the nature and process of sacred texts). Christianity has no sacred language, and the gospel of the church is neither culture- nor language-specific. As Lamin Sanneh writes, Christianity from its beginning until now has been "a translated religion without a revealed language" (2003, p. 97). The biblical message always is proclaimed "in-carnationally," that is, in its own culture "in-linguistically." The Pentecost event demonstrates that the gospel is presented in the local tongues of the people (Acts 2:1–13). Yet, it is precisely this point of the biblical paradigm that warrants Chinese Bible readers to take "local language" seriously, for we have seen in Chinese church history that, when theology is not translated into local tongues, neither is the culture transformed (or fulfilled) nor does scripture maintain its sacred force to transform lives.

Relationship between Local and Global (thus, between contextual and global interpretations of the Bible). Christianity is not a religion bound by borders, confined in buildings, or privileged to any single race. Christian theology "breaks into" cultures, and seeks the process of a homegrown faith. Biblical Chinese interpretation/theology is part of the biblical-theological development that began in the canonical formation of the Bible and will continue until the end times when "every tribe and language and people and nation" glorify God (Rev 5:9; 7:9; 14:6). Biblical Chinese theology is part of the indigenous theology that needs to be shaped globally. Not all interpretations offered by Chinese exegetes are considered "Chinese interpretation." Besides writing in their own languages, many Chinese Bible commentaries are dominated in form and content by Western interpretation, so much so that these

Chinese interpretations have nothing to do with the contexts, experiences, and thinking of the Chinese. A few Chinese biblical scholars even prefer to write exclusively in foreign languages.

The issue is neither whether Western interpretation is inferior nor whether Chinese can read the Bible as critically as any Westerner can. The question concerns incarnational interpretation in a global village. Since reading is always contextual, Chinese interpretations are distinctive in their engagement with Chinese soil, sources, and lived experience. Also, similar to the hellenization process that changed the Jewish world and shaped the Roman culture in antiquity, modern globalization has brought about global interpretations that, on one hand, differentiate contextual readings and, on the other hand, integrate contextual readings into a constructive dialogue. The *Global Bible Commentary* (2004) provides good examples of global interpretations; another helpful resource is *Navigating Romans Through Cultures* (2004). Cross-cultural, intertextual readings of a few Chinese scholars, especially those trained in the West, are moving in the direction of Chinese global interpretation of the Bible.

Both Christians and Chinese treasure scriptures as authoritative rules of life, be they that of the Bible or that of the Chinese. But for Christian Chinese familiar with both texts, Chinese biblical interpretation will seek to fulfill Chinese texts with the Bible, just as Chinese scriptures will amplify the Bible. By grounding our readings scripturally (even for non-Chinese Christians or Christians unfamiliar with Confucian classics), the canonical texts will provide a more stable hermeneutical tool to construct a Chinese biblical interpretation that is helpful not only to itself but also to *global* biblical interpretation. So, the hope is that such Chinese biblical interpretation will benefit both parties: on the one hand, the Chinese culture that awaits its fulfillment from the Bible, and on the other hand, a global theology often dominated by a Eurocentric mindset and thus a "normative" theology in need of critique from contextual biblical interpretations. A truly "biblical Chinese" interpretation will maintain a Chinese *cultural* identity and a *biblical* identity *concomitantly* without capitulating to other cultural interpretations of Christian theologies or the Bible.

As we have seen, Chinese classics and the Bible are fairly close at certain points while differing radically from each other. Holding their incommensurability in tension is a challengingly interpretive move of biblical Chinese interpretation that will fulfill each other's blind spots. Christ will complete or extend what is merely implicit in Chinese culture (theology, transcendence, spirit); without Christ, the Chinese ethic, for example, too quickly (even in early Chinese history) degenerates into a system of ritualistic behavior. But the Chinese ethic amplifies various elements of Christian theologies (e.g., community, virtues) underplayed in western Christianity. The Christ of God (in the Bible) brings Chinese classics and cultures to their fulfillment while protecting the universal church from aberrations of Chinese history, and while protecting China against aberrations of Christian history and interpretation in the West. Chinese biblical interpretation has something to say to the universal church that needs to be heard by all. Chinese biblical interpretation will discover its *global* significance if it can be allowed to find its own biblical interpretation while listening to other contextual biblical interpretations.

[*See also* Asian American Biblical Interpretation; Cross-Cultural Exegesis; Intertextuality; Postcolonial Biblical Interpretation; *and* Theological Interpretation.]

Bibliography

Chiu, Milton M. *The Tao of Chinese Religion.* Lanham, Md.: University Press of America, 1984.

England, John C., and Archie C. C. Lee, eds. *Doing Theology with Asian Resources, Ten Years in the Formation of Living Theology in Asia.* The Programme for Theology and Culture in Asia 1983–1993. Auckland, N.Z.: Pace, 1993.

Nee, Watchman. *The Spiritual Man.* New York: Christian Fellowship, 1968.

Patte, Daniel, et al. eds. *Global Biblical Commentary.* Nashville, Tenn.: Abingdon, 2004.

Russell, Letty, and Kwok Pui-lan, Ada Maria Isasi-Diaz, Katie Geneva Cannon. *Inheriting Our Mothers' Gardens: Feminist Theology in Third World Perspective.* Louisville, Ky.: Westminster, 1988.

Sanneh, Lamin. *Whose Religion is Christianity?: The Gospel beyond the West.* Grand Rapids, Mich.: Eerdmans, 2003.
Sino-Christian Theology Reader, 2 vols. Edited by He Guanghu and Daniel H. N. Yeung. Hong Kong: Institute of Sino-Christian Studies, 2009.
Song, Choan-Seng. *The Tears of Lady Meng: a Parable of the People's Political Theology.* Geneva: The World Council of Churches, 1981.
Song, Choan-Seng. *Theology from the Womb of Asia.* Maryknoll, N.Y.: Orbis, 1986.
Ting, Guang-hsun. *Love Never Ends.* Nanjing: Amity, 1998.
Watson, Burton. *The Complete Works of Chuang Tzu.* New York: Columbia University Press, 1968.
Yeo, K. K. *What Has Jerusalem to Do with Beijing? Biblical Interpretation from a Chinese Perspective.* Harrisburg, Pa.: Trinity Press International, 1998.
Yeo, K. K., ed. *Navigating Romans through Cultures: Challenging Readings by Charting a New Course.* Edinburgh: T.&T. Clark International, 2004.

K. K. (Khiok-khng) Yeo

CLASS CRITICISM

Class may be defined in both objective and subjective terms. Objectively, class designates the difference between those who work to produce goods and those who extract a surplus from those goods but do not produce them. This objective difference is manifested in division of labor, which operates in complex patterns of distinctions between male and female, mind and body, city and country, material and immaterial wealth. The subjective dimension involves a consciousness of belonging to a particular class. That consciousness includes a complex web of cultural assumptions, modes of speech, social codes, world outlook, and religion. Most significantly, class consciousness is determined by a class opponent, the differences with which are marked by opposing assumptions of one's role and importance within production, and by the cultural assumptions each holds. For instance, peasants regard the class that extracts their produce, whether through taxes or direct appropriation (plunder), as exploitative and cruel overlords, while those who extract such surplus regard peasants as ignorant, lazy, earthy, uncultured, and surly.

Anachronism. The problem with modern categories of class, whether Marxist theories of class conflict or Weberian and Lenksian notions of class stratification and status, is that they have developed within the context of capitalism. So the question is: how does one deal with the inevitable anachronism of applying a term such as class to the ancient world? Any discussion of class should at all times be *aware* that it is engaged in an anachronistic task, that such anachronism is a *necessary* feature of any analysis of ancient societies, and that one *structures* the theory in order to include such anachronism in its very workings. In order to do so, the theory used should include a *narrative of difference*; that is, an account, which is continually contested and rewritten, of the vast distance travelled in time between the economy we are investigating and the one from which we undertake such investigation. It thereby stresses the profound sense of the difference between our own social formation and that of the economies (or societies, cultures, texts, and so on) we seek to study.

Technical Terminology. Technical usage usually relies on the work of social theorists, the most common being Weber and Marx. For Weber (1968, pp. 302–305), class initially refers to the layer or group that occupies a common economic situation. It also includes status, which thereby introduces a potential for multiple stratification. This approach is graduational: given the complex overlaps, classes phase into one another and are defined by variables such as income and status. People move more freely between such classes as their circumstances change. A prime instance is Gerhard Lenski (1966), whose work has been used in biblical criticism. For example, Coote and Whitelam (1987) critically deploy Lenski in their reconstruction of the stratifications of Iron Age I society in ancient Israel; Saldarini (1988) argues for the role of Pharisees as "retainers;" while Theissen (1978) attempts to apply Lenski's model to Galilee in the time of Jesus. Fully aware of changes over time and due to different types of social structure, Lenski develops a complex vertical stratification of agrarian societies into twelve "classes," including "governing class," "ruler," "retainer class," and "priestly class." However, Lenski tends to elide categories and groups with classes.

By contrast, a Marxist approach works with sharper distinctions between classes, since objective features are combined with subjective ones of class identity (class consciousness). This is the definition with which this study began, and it is the preferred approach here, due to its richness and complexity. The advantage of such an approach is that it includes a narrative of difference, which makes use of the idea of modes of production: the totality of a social and economic situation is a unique and contradictory conjunction of items which both comes to be and eventually breaks down. What replaces it is an effort to overcome the contradictions that led to the breakdown of the former that is also qualitatively different from what has gone before. Thereby, ancient societies, despite their apparent similarities to ours, are qualitatively different in the way they are organized.

It is important to distinguish between classes, social categories, and groups, although biblical scholars often confuse them (Sneed 1999; Burke 1993). A category designates those who share a common status, such as young people, intellectuals, truck drivers, or—relevant for biblical analysis—scribes. Groups are determined by those who have common interests, ranging from two people (cockroach racers) to large organizations (Hare Krishnas). A class involves ranking, economic resources, subjective identity, and extra-class antagonisms. It is the largest and may include categories or groups.

Finally, we need to be wary of the juridical distinctions appearing in texts, for they do not necessarily match class distinctions (Zel'in 1968; D'iakonoff 1987; Liverani 2005, pp. 17–18). Juridical distinctions between people, such as those in the Hebrew Bible between Israelite and foreigner (Moabite, Ammonite, Canaanite, etc.), women and men, widow and orphan, forced laborer and slave, are not necessarily class distinctions. In fact, such distinctions effectively divide people who are in a similar class position, preventing them from unifying and gaining class-consciousness.

Within Biblical Scholarship. In light of these distinctions, we may assess the proposals made by biblical scholars. Some confuse categories and groups with class, such as McNutt's (1999, pp. 167–169) designation, among others, of scribes, judges, census takers, tax collectors, overseers of forced labor, district governors, noble families, military personnel, agriculturalists, religious professionals, artisans, and dependent laborers; or Dever's (1993) identification of artisans, common laborers, the armed forces, and royalty; or Kovacs's (1973) description of scribes as a "class." Some argue that no classes existed in ancient Israel, since the society was too simple and the data are insufficient, with the vast majority of the population involved in agriculture, a very small percentage acting as rulers, and the absence of a "middle" class (Lemche, 1999; Soggin, 1988). Lemche prefers the patron-client model over against class (Lemche 1999, 1998, p. 102; 2008, pp. 420–421).

Most use class in terms outlined earlier (in contrast to categories or groups). We may distinguish between Marxist-derived or Weberian-influenced approaches by the number of classes differentiated. The greater the number of classes, the more closely they align with a gradualist approach. For example, Handy (1995) distinguishes four classes: royalty, administrators, specialists, and slaves. Many identify three classes, with a ruling class, a class comprised of slaves, peasants, and occasionally artisans, and a class in between variously and (unfortunately) loosely called a "middle class." This last "class" includes royal functionaries, retainers, or warriors (Davies 1999; Snell 1997, pp. 86–87).

Marxist-inspired analysis points out that such a "middle" class was merely an appendage of the ruling class, belonging to the various groups of court functionaries. The basic class formation was an opposition between two, a ruling class (termed variously exploiters, urban creditor, governors, commercial, rich, privileged, powerful, elite) versus those ruled (called exploited, peasants, people of the land, governed, poor, powerless) (Gottwald 1999a, 1992b, 2001, 1992a; 2008, pp. 10–11; Frick 1977, pp. 100–103; Clines 1995, p. 125; Fritz 1995,

p. 188; Sneed 1999, 2004; Mandell 1999; Boer 1996, 2003; Horsley 1996, pp. 118–130; 2007, pp. 58–70; 2008; Carter 2008, p. 120; Belo 1981, pp. 61–4). Chirichigno uses a curious terminology based on categories of "freedom," oscillating between three classes for Mesopotamia (free citizens, semifree citizens, unfree chattel slaves) and two for Israel (free citizens and chattel-slaves, Chirichigno 1993, pp. 49–54, 139–142). This terminology is problematic, since it is over-determined by the rhetoric of freedom within (capitalist) liberal ideology. Noticeably, the terminology here ranges from very loose (rich and poor) to more specific (ruling class, exploited class).

Gottwald's Class Analysis. Two matters deserve fuller attention, one the extensive and systematic treatment of class in the benchmark work of Norman Gottwald, and the other a specific issue, whether the state can be a class (a position assumed by many of those mentioned earlier). In *The Tribes of Yahweh*, Gottwald famously argued that ancient Israel (itself largely Canaanite) arose as a new socioeconomic formation in response to Canaanite oppression, establishing a communitarian mode of production over against a tributary one. In this case, "Israel" is itself a class as a whole, namely the exploited who break away from their exploiters. In opposing Canaanite dominance as well as Egyptian imperial dominance, "Israel" became a distinct entity: "A class in itself, hitherto a congeries of separately struggling segments of the populace, has become a class for itself" (Gottwald 1999b, p. 489). The implication is that as a distinct class for itself, class conflict was not a notable feature of that new society. Thus, he focuses on the slippery terms for tribal organization (a late development in terms of "retribalization"): *šhebet* and *matteh* as tribe, *miš-pāhāh* and, in its armed form, *'eleph*, as a protective association of families, and then at the tertiary level, *bayith* and *bêth-'āv* as an extended family (Gottwald 1999 [1979], pp. 239–292).

In the very different and later situation of the monarchy, class conflict does occur, for it is a return to a tributary mode of production. Class relations change within fundamentally different economic systems. Elsewhere, Gottwald has argued that Lamentations arises from dispossessed peasantry and exploited classes left behind during the Babylonian exile (Gottwald 1962; 1993a, pp. 165–173). By contrast, Deuteronomy comes from a Josianic ruling elite keen to reclaim lost land and power through centralization in Jerusalem, thus denying any status to local religion, social groupings, and economics (Gottwald 1993b, pp. 12–14). In this situation (a return to a "tributary" mode of production), Gottwald argues for the indispensable hermeneutical role of class in biblical interpretation (Gottwald 1993b). He provides a comprehensive statement of class dynamics:

> The key Marxian analytic concepts are *class* as determined by relation of people to the *mode of production* understood as a combination of the *material forces of production* (including human physical and mental powers) and the *social relations of production*, the latter meaning the way that producers (and nonproducers where there is class) organize their work and appropriate the labor product. Class is seen to exist when some people live off the labor product of others. This living off the labor product of others is called *exploitation* in the objective sense that the value of one laborer's production, over and above that laborer's need for subsistence, is appropriated by someone else. This labor product beyond the subsistence need of the laborer is called *surplus product* which is also *surplus value* because the exploiter consumes or exchanges the *good* of the object produced thereby denying the producer the use or exchange of the object that embodies the producer's labor.... Similarly, then, *class conflict* is ... an objective description in that producers and nonproducers struggle to increase, diminish, or arrest the appropriation of labor surplus. (Gottwald 1993a, pp. 147–148; see Gottwald 1999a, p. 10; 2008, pp. 10–11)

Class exists where there are producers and nonproducers (who do not work but live off the result of what the producers make) and where these classes are unequal in terms of power, specifically through exploitation. Thus, producers are denied a portion of their product, which is removed for the consumption of others in positions of power. Given this situation in monarchic Israel, Gottwald argues for two categories of the ruling class: state functionaries obtaining their living through taxes and land rent and latifundiaries who extended their holdings by appropriating land through unpaid debt and then granting credit to peasants by allowing them to continue to work the land now appropriated. He also identifies two categories within the exploited class: free agrarians with land tenure and tenant farmers who, having lost their land through debt closure, work the land of the latifundiaries. Exploitation took place in a twofold cycle of extraction: state taxation in labor and produce and state-induced credit-debt (Gottwald 1992a, pp. 84–85).

The situation is compounded by the two levels at which class operates in much of Israelite history, for not only are there class relations within Israel, but Israel must engage with various imperial forces that exercised differing degrees of control over it. Thus, Israel as a whole becomes the exploited *class* and the external imperial power becomes the ruling class. Even this is deceptively simple, since many different lines of relationship existed between ruling and exploited classes in Israel, their counterparts in other corners of the empire, and ruling and exploited classes in the imperial center. For instance, after the collapse of the monarchy, most of the ruling class went into exile in Babylon and a sizeable portion of a very depressed peasantry remained in Israel. The subsequent restoration of a portion of the ruling class led to their return to influence but also to continual clashes with the peasantry left behind during the exile. The shifting nature of these relationships finally confronted the more efficient Roman practice of using slaves, which became dominant after the defeat of Judah and the destruction of Jerusalem in 70 C.E. Throughout Israelite history the nature of the class relationships varies, depending upon the dominant mode of production at any particular time, whether communitarian, tributary or slave-based (Gottwald 1992b).

Is the State a Class? Most analyses of class in ancient Israel assume that the ruling class is identical with the state, or temple-city complex, and its functionaries. This assumption faces a significant theoretical hurdle, namely that the state is distinct from class and is indeed generated out of class conflict. The way this common conjunction of state and ruling class, assumed by many scholars, emerges is through a narrative of differentiation, by which the despotic state is formed. It goes as follows: under certain conditions (soil fertility, rainfall, trade, or booty) the differentiation of wealth and power sets in and is concentrated in the hands of certain individuals. So class begins when a certain group is disconnected from the production of essential items for survival. This class then relies on those who do produce these essentials and must extract a surplus from them, usually in a mix of coercion and persuasion (technically known as exploitation). With further concentration of wealth and power, chieftains and towns appear. Then, when the extraction of essential items becomes sufficiently complex and requires defense of such wealth, the state and its (usually despotic) ruler emerge. This state is, according to this narrative, identical with the ruling class. Such a narrative is widespread within and without biblical criticism (Lemche 1988, pp. 22–23; Davies 1988, pp. 59–73; Gottwald 2001; Dever 2001; Kautsky 2007 [1908]; Anderson 1974).

A major problem with this narrative is its direction, since it leads inexorably to the conclusion that the concentration of power in a small group is the development of the state; that is, the exploiting class is the same as the state. From here a series of assumptions follow: the state-cum-exploiting class then exploits the village communes, or tribes, and from this point an irresolvable tension is postulated between the state and the village-based tribe (Lemche 1998, pp. 98–100; Simkins 1999; Yee 2003, pp. 60–63; Liverani pp. 75–76; Krader 1975, p. 292). Identifying the problem with this argument begins with the observation from Hindess and Hirst (1975, pp. 192–193) that the identification of the state with the exploiting class is nonsensical in terms of development of the state. The reason is that state and class cannot be identical. We may go a step further: if the state is not the result of the concentration of power and wealth in a small ruling elite, if it is not the same as the city-based ruling class, composed of the chieftain or tyrant and his small group of exploiters, then what is the state? It is the outcome of, and effort to mediate, class conflict. That is, the state emerges between the exploiters and the exploited, between the power and wealth concentrated in a small ruling class and the resilient agricultural basis of the village-commune.

Without Biblical Scholarship. Outside of biblical scholarship, two significant contributions may be identified, one from Karl Kautsky's comprehensive effort to provide the first historical materialist analysis of biblical societies, and the other from Soviet-era Russian contributions to ancient Near Eastern scholarship.

Karl Kautsky. Kautsky (2007 [1908], pp. 33–35, 177–178, 352–359, 384–391) also deploys a narrative of differentiation to account for the rise, not only of the mode of production of biblical societies, but also of class. This narrative moves from an undifferentiated state to one of differentiation, with which comes division of labor, exploitation, and class.

Concerning ancient Israel, Kautsky assumes with the majority of biblical scholars at his time that early Israelites were desert nomads, probably Bedouin. Such a life on the move provided a vital and relatively simple life. However, when these nomads settled in Canaan, they adopted agricultural life on the land. From here differentiation sets in, with some gaining wealth on the land at the expense of others. Wealthy landowners began appropriating ever more land, which they then rented to landless peasants at punitive rates. When these peasants inevitably failed to meet the exorbitant requirements to repay their debts—usually a portion of the produce of the land—they forfeited their rights to the land and were driven to the position of debt-slaves of those same landowners. The move into a slave-based mode of production was inevitable. With this formation, the basic class distinctions are in place: slaves produce the necessary surplus, along with some peasants who are not as central to the production of surplus, and that surplus is appropriated by the ruling class, made up mostly of landowners.

The development in relation to Greece and Rome, the context for the New Testament, is roughly similar, although the result is now chattel-slavery. As differentiation sets in from a prior undifferentiated state, more and more people are removed from production as exploiters, whether wealthy landowners, chieftains, clergy, or a scribal subclass. The outcome is a labor shortage. Not enough manpower is available to till the soil, especially since production is primarily agricultural. The first full mode of production arises from this problem of labor shortage, and the resolution is slavery at the expense of freemen. The Greeks and Romans opted to find slaves primarily by conquest in order to fill the labor shortage. The result was a slave-based mode of production.

Kautsky's basic argument for the Hellenistic world has stood the test of time, but not that concerning ancient Israel (which was not primarily a slave system introduced by nomads). However, beyond the misgivings expressed earlier concerning such narratives, a number of questions may be raised (Boer 2009, pp. 91–119). To begin with, Kautsky's argument has theological echoes from the "fall" narrative of Genesis 2—3. That is, the deeply influential nature of that mythical narrative continues to influence historiography, which requires its own narrative structures in order to make sense (White 1973). Inevitably, those narratives redeploy older narratives despite the claims to "scientific objectivity." Further, the narrative of differentiation in Kautsky's hands assumes a version of primitive communism in the prior undifferentiated agricultural life of early Rome or the nomadic life of the Israelites before they settled down in Canaan. On the contrary, the evidence suggests that no undifferentiated state ever existed. This narrative also assumes a relatively linear path, from undifferentiated to differentiated, without considering ruptures, breaks, multiple paths, and fold-backs. And it leaves unresolved the crucial question of the initial trigger for differentiation. On the last point, Kautsky prefers a naturalist argument, citing soil inequality, climate differences, and the role of natural disasters, such as drought or flood affecting crop yields. The problem of the trigger for differentiation is, however, generated by the narrative itself. That narrative needs a moment of differentiation for the narrative to exist at all. For instance, the narrative structure of Genesis would not exist without the account of disobedience in Genesis 2—3. Imagine a story that remained within the garden, with the first humans meandering about and eating freely from the fruit of the garden, chatting with the deity in the evenings—it would be chronically boring. It therefore needs to be asked what a very different account, without a prior, nondifferentiated state would look like. It would certainly not require differentiation and its trigger.

Soviet-Era Russian Scholarship. The second major contribution from outside biblical criticism comes from neglected Soviet-era Russian scholarship. Deliberations of class took place with the context of debates over the appropriate mode of production for the ancient Near East. Critics variously favored over time the Asiatic mode of production, feudalism, and a slave-based system (Dunn 2011 [1982]; D'iakonoff 1969b; D'iakonoff and Kohl, 1991). In contrast to Western scholarship, where feudalism long held sway (Schloen 2001), it was only briefly considered viable in Russia in the first years of the 1930s. A key moment for the dominance of a slave-based mode of production in that scholarship happened in 1933. In an influential lecture (of four hours!) at the Academy of the History of Material Culture in Leningrad, V. V. Struve sidelined feudalism as a viable term (Struve 1969a). With a broad sweep covering all of the key documents in the histories of Mesopotamia and Egypt, he persuaded most scholars that the evidence pointed toward a slave mode of production. Although slaves were numerically inferior to other classes, such as free laborers or landholders, these slaves were owned collectively by the state and temple complex, worked the whole year and were, therefore, the dominant means for the extraction of surplus value.

After Struve's decisive intervention, scholars took different paths. Some followed and refined his argument (Tyumenev 1969a, 1969b) with debates over the nature of labor and class through detailed exegesis of the available documents (Struve 1969b; Dandamaev 2009 [1974]); others began to distinguish between immature forms of slaveholding society and its mature form in Greece and Rome (Struve himself); yet others argued that the means of coercing large parts of the population into slavery did not exist in the ancient Near East (D'iakonoff 1974), indeed that the bulk of produce was created by free laborers. Gradually, under the weight of further evidence, debate, and myriad qualifications—including a bold effort by Tyumenev (1969b) to argue that apart from the rulers everyone in the whole ancient East was in fact a slave and that Greece and Rome constituted aberrations—Struve's position crumbled (D'iakonoff 1969a, 1974, 1991). As the slave mode of production began to falter, the Asiatic mode of production, now with an impressive array of new data, re-emerged from the wings to reclaim the field (Dunn 2001 [1982], pp. 144–153). Under that mode of production the primary class distinction was that between an exploiting class that sought to extract a minimal "surplus"—although it often cut into the subsistence requirements—of a large class of agricultural producers with its various categories and groups.

Future Directions. Much analysis remains to be done concerning class in biblical societies. The following focuses on two of those questions. A crucial question is that of compulsion, namely, the factors that led to the majority of people in an economic system to play by its unwritten rules. Why did peasants remain so, or slaves, or the ruling class and its various categories? We may distinguish between direct economic compulsion and extra-economic compulsion, although most socioeconomic formations include a mix of the two. For example, under capitalism economic compulsion is primary, taking the form of income differentials and the drive to own capital. Workers are penalized or rewarded with lower or higher wages (the latter more "desired") in order to ensure that they remain within the system. This system is reinforced at an ideological level by the assumption that one must pay higher wages in order to attract the best person to an important job. Conversely, one assumes that a low-skilled position (cleaner or waiter) attracts a lower wage. The list of extra-economic motivations is potentially endless: the status, freedom and security that wealth brings; the potential for all to become wealthy; the need to provide for one's children. However, other economic systems operate with different modes of compulsion. Communist societies find that the economic element of working for the collective is not sufficient, so inevitably resort to extra-economic "cults" of the revolutionary leader in order to provide motivation for working for the cause and collective identity. Feudalism developed a complex pattern of extra-economic justification, both philosophical and theological, for a complex social and economic hierarchy that began with serfs at the wide base, leading all the way up to the singular monarch who was God's appointee on earth.

By contrast, the extra-economic compulsion of the ancient Near East was centered on the sacred. The myriad and overlapped assumptions, customs, daily habits and institutions (kinship structures, judiciary, patron-client relations, the military, government, even taxation in the form of the tithe) sought their models in religious myths of origin that justified the status quo, and provided patterns of divine sanction and punishment to ensure people largely contributed to the system. In this context, class structures were able to be maintained, albeit not without periodic crises which were also built into the pattern of sacred compulsion—as punishment for waywardness. A significant factor, in both the ancient Near East and in the Hellenistic world, was the use of force, usually military. Should a particular group or a vassal state not wish to play by the rules, the local or imperial government had no hesitation is ensuring conformity through the deployment of brute force.

A second issue worthy of further investigation is the nature of class consciousness (the subjective factor of class). In this situation we have mostly the records of those from the ruling class, or at least from the subsection of the scribes. In the biblical texts, the subtleness of that class consciousness may be examined in detail. However, evidence of peasant or slave class consciousness in any systematic fashion is difficult to identity. As Ste. Croix forcefully puts it in relation to the Hellenistic world, "these [the peasants] are the voiceless toilers, the great majority—let us not forget it—of the population of the Greek and Roman world, upon whom was built a great civilization which despised them and did all it could to forget them." (Ste. Croix 1981, p. 210). Archaeological data may provide a good picture of settlement patterns, agricultural practices, and social organization, but the only resource for such a class consciousness comes from the texts written by scribes in the service of the ruling class. In order to identify at least some parts of that comprehensive class consciousness, one must isolate elements of folk stories from ruling class assumptions and attempt to reconstruct a very different sense of class identity. Such a picture will always be fragmentary and speculative, since the complexity of the sense of identity—through stories, beliefs and patterns of daily life—remain outside the zones of historiography.

[*See also* Cross-Cultural Exegesis; Cultural-Historical Criticism; Cultural Studies; Economics and the Bible; Empire Studies and Biblical Interpretation; Ideological Criticism; Materialist Criticism; Postcolonial Biblical Interpretation; Social Sciences, *subentry* Hebrew Bible; *and* Social Sciences, *subentry* New Testament.]

BIBLIOGRAPHY

Belo, Fernando. *A Materialist Reading of the Gospel of Mark*. Translated by M. J. O'Connell. Maryknoll, N.Y.: Orbis, 1981. A groundbreaking analysis deploying complex Marxist theory and detailed economic analysis.

Boer, Roland. *Criticism of Religion: On Marxism and Theology II*. Historical Materialism Book Series 22. Leiden: Brill, 2009. Extensive studies making use of Marxist-inspired approaches.

Boer, Roland. *Jameson and Jeroboam*. Atlanta: Scholars, 1996.

Boer, Roland. *Marxist Criticism of the Bible*. London: Continuum, 2003.

Burke, Peter. *History and Social Theory*. Ithaca, N.Y.: Cornell University Press, 1993. A good survey of social theories in relation to questions of class.

Carter, Warren. "Matthew Negotiates the Roman Empire." In *In the Shadow of Empire: Reclaiming the*

Bible as a History of Faithful Resistance, edited by R. Horsley, 117–136. Louisville, Ky.: Westminster John Knox, 2008. Part of a spate of studies concerning implicit opposition in the New Testament to the Roman Empire.

Chirichigno, Gregory C. *Debt Slavery in Israel and the Ancient Near East.* Journal for the Study of the Old Testament 141. Sheffield, UK: JSOT, 1993. A detailed study of the category of the class fraction of debt slaves.

Clines, David J. A. *Interested Parties: The Ideology of Writers and Readers of the Hebrew Bible.* Sheffield, UK: Sheffield Academic, 1995. A good example that explores ruling class ideology.

Coote, Robert B., and Keith W. Whitelam. *The Emergence of Early Israel in Historical Perspective.* Sheffield, UK: Almond, 1987. A gradualist approach to class using Gerhard Lenski.

Dandamaev, Muhammad. *Slavery in Babylonia: From Nabopolassar to Alexander the Great (626–331 B.C.).* Translated by V. A. Powell. DeKalb: Northern Illinois University Press, 2009 [1974]. A massive and detailed work, part of the collection of Soviet-era Russian work.

Davies, Philip. "Is There a Class in This Text?" In *Concepts of Class in Ancient Israel*, edited by M. Sneed, 37–51. Atlanta: Scholars Press, 1999. A scholar who loosely uses Marxist class analysis, but argues in favor of a "middle" class.

Davies, Philip. *Scribes and Schools: The Canonization of the Hebrew Scriptures.* Louisville, Ky.: Westminster John Knox, 1998.

Dever, William G. "Social Structure in Palestine in the Iron II Period on the Eve of Destruction." In *The Archaeology of Society in the Holy Land*, edited by T. Levy, 416–430. New York: Facts on File, 1993.

Dever, William G. *What Did the Biblical Writers Know and When Did They Know It?: What Archaeology Can Tell Us about the Reality of Ancient Israel.* Grand Rapids, Mich.: Eerdmans, 2001. Prefers a gradualist approach, with many "classes" identified.

D'iakonoff, Igor M. "The Commune in the Ancient East as Treated in the Works of Soviet Researchers." In *Introduction to Soviet Ethnography, Volume II*, edited by S. P. Dunn and E. Dunn, 519–548. Berkeley, Calif.: Highgate Road Social Science Research Station, 1974.

D'iakonoff, Igor M. "General Outline of the First Period of the History of the Ancient World and the Problem of the Ways of Development." In *Early Antiquity*, edited by I. M. D'iakonoff and P. L. Kohl, 27–66. Chicago: University of Chicago Press, 1991.

D'iakonoff, Igor M. "The Rise of the Despotic State in Ancient Mesopotamia." In *Ancient Mesopotamia: Socio-Economic History. A Collection of Studies by Soviet Scholars*, edited by I. M. D'iakonoff, 173–203. Moscow: "Nauka" Publishing House, 1969a.

D'iakonoff, Igor M. "Slave-Labour vs. Non-Slave Labour: The Problem of Definition." In *Labor in the Ancient Near East*, edited by M. A. Powell, 1–3. New Haven, Conn.: American Oriental Society, 1987.

D'iakonoff, Igor M., ed. *Ancient Mesopotamia: Socio-Economic History. A Collection of Studies by Soviet Scholars.* Moscow: "Nauka" Publishing House, 1969b. A major and unfortunately neglected Soviet-era Russian scholar on the ancient Near East.

D'iakonoff, Igor M., and Philip L. Kohl, eds. *Early Antiquity.* Chicago, Ill.: Chicago University Press, 1991. Volume one of three (the other two have not been translated from Russian) of a popular (in the U.S.S.R.) scholarly collection concerning the ancient Near East. Well worth a read.

Dunn, Stephen P. *The Fall and Rise of the Asiatic Mode of Production.* London: Routledge, 2011 [1982]. Recently reprinted, Dunn's work is the best available survey of the whole range of Soviet-era debates concerning economics in the ancient Near East.

Frick, Frank. *The City in Ancient Israel.* Missoula, Mont.: Scholars, 1977. A Marxist-inspired study in the tradition established by Norman Gottwald.

Fritz, Volkmar. *The City in Ancient Israel.* Sheffield, UK: Sheffield Academic, 1995. One of many who use a loose Marxist classification of class.

Gottwald, Norman K. "Early Israel as an Anti-Imperial Community." In *In the Shadow of Empire: Reclaiming the Bible as a History of Faithful Resistance*, edited by R. Horsley, 9–24. Louisville, Ky.: Westminster John Knox, 2008. Classic studies that established the importance of social-scientific analysis of the Hebrew Bible and provided the framework for analyses of class that still operate today.

Gottwald, Norman K. "The Expropriated and the Expropriated in Nehemiah 5." In *Concepts of Class in Ancient Israel*, edited by M. Sneed, 1–20. Atlanta: Scholars, 1999a.

Gottwald, Norman K. *The Hebrew Bible in Its Social World and in Ours.* Atlanta: Scholars, 1993a.

Gottwald, Norman K. *The Politics of Ancient Israel.* Louisville, Ky:. Westminster John Knox, 2001.

Gottwald, Norman K. "Social Class as an Analytic and Hermeneutical Category in Biblical Studies." *Journal of Biblical Literature* 112, no. 1 (1993b): 3–22.

Gottwald, Norman K. "Social Class and Ideology in Isaiah 40–55: An Eagletonian Reading." *Semeia* 59 (1992a): 43–57.

Gottwald, Norman K. "Sociology of Ancient Israel." In *Anchor Bible Dictionary*, Vol. 6, edited by D. N. Freedman, 79–89. New York: Doubleday, 1992b.

Gottwald, Norman K. *Studies in the Book of Lamentations*, revised ed. London: SCM, 1962.

Gottwald, Norman K. *The Tribes of Yahweh: A Sociology of the Religion of Liberated Israel, 1250–1050 BCE*. Sheffield, UK: Sheffield Academic Press, 1999b [1979].

Handy, Lowell. "The Appearance of a Pantheon in Judah." In *The Triumph of Elohim: From Yahwisms to Judaisms*, edited by D. Edelman, 27–43. Grand Rapids, Mich.: Eerdmans, 1995. Offers a gradualist approach to class, with many proposed.

Hindess, Barry, and Paul Q. Hirst. *Precapitalist Modes of Production*. London: Routledge and Kegan Paul, 1975. Rigorous theoretical work that offers some good insights but suffers from lack of consideration of data.

Horsley, Richard. *Archaeology, History and Society in Galilee: The Social Context of Jesus and the Rabbis*. Philadelphia: Trinity Press International, 1996.

Horsley, Richard. "Jesus and Empire." In *In the Shadow of Empire: Reclaiming the Bible as a History of Faithful Resistance*, edited by R. Horsley, 75–96. Louisville, Ky.: Westminster John Knox, 2008. Pioneer analyses of economics and class in the Hellenistic context of the New Testament.

Horsley, Richard. *Scribes, Visionaries, and the Politics of Second Temple Judea*. Louisville, Ky.: Westminster John Knox, 2007.

Kautsky, Karl. *Foundations of Christianity*. Translated by H. F. Mins. London: Socialist Resistance, 2007 [1908]. First detailed Marxist analysis of the economic and class development of both the ancient Near East and Greece and Rome. Not without its flaws, but necessary reading.

Kovacs, Brian. "Is There a Class-Ethic in Proverbs." In *Essays in Old Testament Ethics*, edited by J. Crenshaw and J. Willis, 173–189. New York: Ktav, 1973. Prefers a gradualist approach to class in the Hebrew Bible.

Krader, Lawrence. *The Asiatic Mode of Production: Sources, Development and Critique in the Writings of Karl Marx*. Assen: Van Gorcum, 1975. A comprehensive collection concerning the much-debated Marxist category of the Asiatic mode of production.

Lemche, Niels Peter. *Ancient Israel: A New History of Israelite Society*. Translated by F. Cryer. Sheffield, UK: Sheffield Academic, 1988.

Lemche, Niels Peter. *The Old Testament between Theology and History*. Translated by E. F. Maniscalco. Louisville, Ky.: Westminster John Knox, 2008. Influential historian of the "minimalist" school (which dispenses with biblical material as evidence) who argues against the usefulness of class in analyzing ancient Israel.

Lemche, Niels Peter. *Prelude to Israel's Past: Background and Beginnings of Israelite History and Identity*. Translated by E. F. Maniscalco. Peabody, Mass.: Hendrickson, 1998.

Lemche, Niels Peter. "The Relevance of Working with the Concept of Class in the Study of Israelite Society in the Iron Age." In *Concepts of Class in Ancient Israel*, edited by M. Sneed, 89–98. Atlanta: Scholars, 1999.

Lenski, Gerhard. *Power and Privilege: A Theory of Social Stratification*. New York: McGraw-Hill, 1966. Influential in some areas of biblical studies, Lenski follows a Weberian, gradualist approach concerning class.

Liverani, Mario. *Israel's History and the History of Israel*. Translated by C. Peri and P. Davies. London: Equinox, 2005. Looser Marxist approach to class in a study worthy of careful attention for its other contributions.

Mandell, Sara. "Primary History as a Social Construction of a Privileged Class." In *Concepts of Class in Ancient Israel*, edited by M. Sneed, 21–36. Atlanta: Scholars Press, 1999. Part of a number who use broadly Marxist definitions of class in terms of two opposing classes.

McNutt, Paula M. *Reconstructing the Society of Ancient Israel*. London: SPCK, 1999. One of a number who use a gradualist approach and confuse categories and groups with classes.

Perry, Anderson. *Passages from Antiquity to Feudalism*. London: Verso, 1974. An excellent and clear study that outlines the major features of the Greek and Roman worlds and the key factors of the transition to feudalism in Europe.

Saldarini, Anthony. *Pharisees, Scribes, and Sadducees: A Sociological Approach*. Wilmington, Del.: Galzier, 1988. Another who deploys a gradualist approach and designates the scribes as a class.

Schloen, J. David. *The House of the Father as Fact and Symbol: Patrimonialism in Ugarit and the Ancient Near East*. Winona Lake, Ind.: Eisenbrauns, 2001. Detailed study with a useful survey of class and economic analysis.

Simkins, Ronald A. "Patronage and the Political Economy of Ancient Israel." *Semeia* 87 (1999): 123–144. Argues for a mode of production on the basis of patron-client relations.

Sneed, Mark. "A Middle Class in Ancient Israel?" In *Concepts of Class in Ancient Israel*, edited by M. Sneed, 53–69. Atlanta: Scholars, 1999.

Sneed, Mark. "Qohelet and his 'Vulgar' Critics: A Jamesonian Reading." *Bible and Critical Theory* 1, no. 1

(2004): 1–11. Marxist-informed studies that offer excellent analyses of class and texts.

Snell, Daniel. *Life in the Ancient Near East: 3100–332 BCE.* New Haven, Conn.: Yale University Press, 1997. Argues in favor of a loosely defined "middle" class in ancient Israel.

Soggin, J. A. "Ancient Israel: An Attempt at a Social and Economic Analysis of the Available Data." In *Text and Context*, edited by W. Claassen, 201–208. Sheffield, UK: JSOT, 1988. Like Lemche, Soggin argues against the viability of class as a category in ancient Israel.

Ste. Croix, G. E. M. *The Class Struggle in the Ancient Greek World.* London: Duckworth, 1981. An excellent and comprehensive, Marxist-inspired study of class until 600 C.E. His influence is only just being felt in biblical criticism.

Struve, V. V. "The Problem of the Genesis, Development and Disintegration of the Slave Societies in the Ancient Orient." In *Ancient Mesopotamia: Socio-Economic History. A Collection of Studies by Soviet Scholars*, edited by I. M. D'iakonoff, 17–69. Moscow: "Nauka" Publishing House, 1969a.

Struve, V. V. "Some New Data on the Organization of Labour and on Social Structure in Sumer During the Reign of the IIIrd Dynasty of Ur." In *Ancient Mesopotamia: Socio-Economic History. A Collection of Studies by Soviet Scholars*, edited by I. M. D'iakonoff, 127–172. Moscow: "Nauka" Publishing House, 1969b. The grandfather of Soviet-era Russian studies of the ancient Near East, although he argued for slavery as the major exploited class.

Theissen, Gerd. *Sociology of Early Palestinian Christianity.* Translated by J. Bowden. Philadelphia: Fortress, 1978. An attempt to apply Lenski's gradualist model to ancient Galilee.

Tyumenev, A. I. "The State Economy of Ancient Sumer." In *Ancient Mesopotamia: Socio-Economic History. A Collection of Studies by Soviet Scholars*, edited by I. M. D'iakonoff, 70–87. Moscow: "Nauka" Publishing House, 1969a.

Tyumenev, A. I. "The Working Personnel on the Estate of the Temple of dBa-Ú in Lagas During the Period of Lugalanda and Urukagina (25th–24th cent. B.C.)." In *Ancient Mesopotamia: Socio-Economic History. A Collection of Studies by Soviet Scholars*, edited by I. M. D'iakonoff, 88–126. Moscow: "Nauka" Publishing House, 1969b. A Soviet-era Russian scholar who defended slavery as the major exploited class in the ancient Near East.

Weber, Max. *Economy and Society: An Outline of Interpretive Sociology.* New York: Bedminster, 1968. The classic study that established the gradualist approach to class.

White, Hayden. *Metahistory: The Historical Imagination in Nineteenth Century Europe.* Baltimore: Johns Hopkins University Press, 1975. Influential work on the narrative structures of historiography.

Yee, Gale A. *Poor Banished Children of Eve: Woman as Evil in the Hebrew Bible.* Minneapolis: Fortress, 2003. Excellent Marxist-inspired analysis of the depiction of women in the Hebrew Bible.

Zel'in, K. K. "Principles of Morphological Classification of Forms of Dependence." *Soviet Anthropology and Archaeology* 6, no. 4 (1968): 3–24. A Soviet-era Russian scholar who warns against assuming that juridical distinctions in ancient texts necessarily designate class distinctions.

Roland Boer

Cognitive Linguistics and Biblical Interpretation

Cognitive linguistics is a set of analytic approaches working to build linguistic analyses that are consistent with what we know about cognition. It begins with the recognition that language expresses human thoughts, and linguistic structure therefore both shapes cognitive patterns and is shaped by them. This basic phenomenological observation—the interconnection of language and cognition—has been the subject of an immense range of scientific study in the last several decades. Within cognitive science, the picture of human cognition has become more clearly based in embodied, culture-specific human experience. Obviously, scholars interpreting texts—including biblical scholars—approach those texts with assumptions about language and culture, meaning and epistemology, which in turn shape their understanding of reading, authority, and interpretation. New understandings of some of these key areas thus present opportunities and challenges to biblical scholars.

Cognitive linguistics sees meaning and contextualized usage as central to the study of language, thus standing in contrast to structuralist or generative approaches that study language as a set of abstract syntactic structures and formal rule systems. Further, in contrast with formal semanticists, cognitive linguists do not see meaning as a set of abstract propositions, but as embodied human categories and understandings. The study of syntactic structures in cognitive linguistics is primarily within one of a range of models of construction grammar, which treat grammatical constructions as meaningful forms. There is, however, no unified theory neatly tagged "cognitive linguistics"; it is "a flexible framework rather than a single theory of language" (Geeraerts 2006, p. 2).

Accordingly, among biblical scholars and interpreters employing cognitive linguistics, what we encounter is not a fully articulated or unified theory of hermeneutics or biblical study from a single perspective or using a single method, but rather adoption, adaptation, and application of a variety of practices, techniques, and research aims. These include usage-based grammar as well as semantic models incorporating categorization theory, conceptual metaphor and metonymy, frames and gestalts, and the study of reference via mental space theory and conceptual blending analysis.

Assumptions in Cognitive Linguistics. This section surveys core assumptions and concerns of cognitive linguistics, especially as it is being applied to biblical interpretation.

Meaning, Human Minds, and Embodied Cognition. Writing, reading, and interpretation are acts of human minds. But a cognitive linguist does not understand these as a new critic might. Language use arises from human lived experience, in human bodies and in social environments. Embodiment and the rootedness of all language in primary physical and social experiences are starting points for cognitive approaches to language and literature. Every feature of the process of written communication is anchored in everyday linguistic and conceptual frameworks; this is true for biblical texts as well. Because of this grounding, to the extent that we know a relevant community's cognitive and experiential patterns, we need not pretend we can read an author's individual mind to see cognitive structures in a text. Biblical literature and languages, then, ought to be studied in sociocultural and historical context, and not as sets of formal properties, syntactic structures, and rules.

Forms and Meanings. Cognitive linguists do not deny the patterned, structured qualities of languages, but they insist that the function of linguistic structures is to express meaning. This is what they study: mappings between form and meaning. The relationship between form and meaning is understood as a conventional sign-signifier relationship—as Saussure defined it—but this relationship is present at every level of the linguistic system. From words and affixes, to sentence-level and discourse-level constructions, form conventionally represents meaning. The idea that grammatical constructions are meaningful is radical to some formal linguists, but cognitive linguists working with Construction Grammar present strong arguments for it (Goldberg 2006).

Cognitive linguists say, "The meaning is not in the word." In fact, it could not be. Instead, words are triggers to the human imagination, prompts that activate perception and interpretation. The same verb *open* evokes quite different images in *She opened the book; She opened the door*; and *She opened her eyes*—necessarily so, because of the differences in our experience of books, doors, and eyes. The same name—*Israel*—could refer to (1) the ancient person, (2) the eponymous tribe, (3) the area occupied by the tribe before the Common Era, or (4) a modern state. Meaning resides in human minds; linguistic forms evoke and reflect cognitive connections.

Frame and Schema Semantics. Idealized models and frameworks formed by experience are central to human cognition and language use. *Frames* are "structured understandings of the way aspects of the world function" (Fauconnier and Sweetser 1996, p. 5). These understandings are gestalts in that a whole frame is basic and the parts depend on it. For example, it would be impossible to define "money" without a Commercial Event frame of which money is a part, or "Tuesday" without a calendric system. Framing is central to cognition: not only does it make fast processing possible by bringing up prefabricated structure, but alternative framings can radically change assessments and reasoning about content. An example from biblical scholarship might be labels such as *Old Testament* (invoking the frame of Christian history in its contrast and connections with *New Testament*) as opposed to *Hebrew Bible.*

Verbal communication requires continuous conceptual framing and schematic processing: in the writer before she begins to write; in composition, revision, and editing; in the work of redactors and scribes; and in the receptive practices of reading and interpretation. Since frames are culturally embedded, twenty-first-century readers of ancient texts will experience points of connection and similarity but also of cultural clash. Different ways of reasoning about a situation—or a concept—will result from the way we frame or schematize it.

Linguistic and Reading Communities. Although frames and cognitive models have to exist in individual humans—and indeed a twenty-first-century reader's Family frame would differ from those in biblical texts—shared use of conventional linguistic forms pushes individuals' meanings into relationship with each other. This is why we do not need to mind-read an author to get meaning from a written work if we have learned the relevant conventions. It is also why deep historical and cultural study is critical for work with temporally distant texts: knowledge about the cultural, legal, and social frames associated with a language community, as well as material objects, are crucial for reconstruction of past meaning systems.

Paradigm Shift. Cognitive linguistics is philosophically neither objectivist nor subjectivist but experientialist (Lakoff 1987; Lakoff and Johnson 1999). Most cognitive linguists do believe in the existence of the physical world independent of human understanding, but this question is not essential for the study of language. This is because humans lack access to an independent objective view and can therefore only express their own knowledge and perceptions. Linguistic meanings are human conceptual structures.

History of Cognitive Linguistics. Cognitive linguistics was born in the 1970s and 1980s as linguists became interested in the relationship between mind and language and found structuralist and generative approaches inadequate. The work of psychologists such as Eleanor Rosch and Russell DeValois on object and color categorization helped spark a new understanding of language. Key first-generation figures in cognitive linguistics include Wallace Chafe (cognitive semantics, discourse analysis, psycholinguistics), Charles Fillmore (Frame Semantics, Construction Grammar), Paul Kay (crosslinguistic color categories, Construction Grammar), George Lakoff (Conceptual Metaphor—also called Cognitive Metaphor, categorization theory), Ronald Langacker (Cognitive Grammar), and Leonard Talmy (linguistic imaging systems, cognitive semantics). The International Cognitive Linguistics Association and its journal *Cognitive Linguistics* spawned international development and discussion. *Journal of Pragmatics* has also been an influence, since cognitive linguistics has been informed from the start by pragmatics and Speech Act theory; more recently the International Construction Grammar Conference and the journal *Constructions and Frames* have become prominent.

In the 1980s, Gilles Fauconnier articulated a theory of Mental Spaces, discrete mental models of particular situations structured by concepts in our stock, everyday conceptual systems. The connections established between mental spaces are crucial to linguistic reference. Without knowing that *Israel* is the name of an ancient tribe as well as a modern state, one could not keep track of the distinction between them. In the 1990s Fauconnier collaborated with cognitive scientist and literary scholar Mark Turner to develop the theory of Mental Space Blending (*The Way We Think: Conceptual Blending and the Mind's Hidden Complexities* [New York: Basic Books, 2002]). It is the ability to blend spaces that makes one feel that modern Israel is in some way continuous with ancient Israel though we know that the territory, governance, religious practice, and population are different. Fauconnier and Turner use discourse examples to point out the principles by which conceptual integration occurs—metaphorical mappings from source to target domains, image schemas, force-dynamic schemas, metonymic mappings, frames, and prototypes. Their model overlaps and meshes with both Langacker's Cognitive Grammar and Lakoff and Johnson's theory of metaphor.

Many of these cognitive linguistic models have also appealed to scholars in the areas of stylistics and literary text analysis. Mark Turner's *Death is the Mother of Beauty: Mind, Metaphor, Criticism* (Chicago: University of Chicago Press, 2002) and Lakoff and Turner's *More Than Cool Reason: A Field Guide to Poetic Metaphor* (Chicago: University of Chicago Press, 1989) led a new wave of cognitive literary studies. The Poetics and Linguistics Association (PALA) and its journal *Language and Literature* have been open to cognitive linguistic frameworks and have included work by cognitive linguistics researchers crossing over into literary studies, such as Barbara Dancygier and Eve Sweetser. In North America, cognitive science (Theory of Mind, for example) has been of more interest to literary scholars than cognitive linguistic models of analysis.

Biblical Studies and Cognitive Linguistics. Lakoff and Johnson's 1980 book, *Metaphors We Live By*, appeared concurrently with a surge of interest in metaphor among theologians and biblical scholars, and the book was received enthusiastically. While *Metaphors We Live By* was an engaging account of some pervasive metaphor systems and a persuasive argument for experientialist approaches, later work both integrated metaphor studies into cognitive linguistics and set standards for research methodology. Unfortunately, for many it was both the first and the last book on cognitive linguistics they read. Early appropriations were therefore frequently amateurish and naïve, failing to grasp the paradigm shift entailed in the cognitive approach to metaphor and thought or the larger framework and methods of cognitive linguistics.

Pioneering Appropriations of Cognitive Linguistics in Biblical Studies. Papers employing cognitive linguistic models began to appear in biblical studies journals and at the annual Society of Biblical Literature (SBL) meetings in the 1990s and early 2000s. Most noteworthy are Marc Zvi Brettler's work on metaphors for *God in the Hebrew Bible* (1989) and Ellen van Wolde's applications of *Cognitive Grammar* (1994).

The SBL Consultation and Section. In 2006, the SBL launched a three-year consultation, "The Use of Cognitive Linguistics in Biblical Interpretation," organized by a cluster of scholars connected through the Graduate Theological Union in Berkeley—Mary Therese DesCamp, Joel B. Green, and Bonnie Howe—along with University of California-Berkeley cognitive linguist Eve Sweetser. Howe and DesCamp had studied with Sweetser and George Lakoff, and the consultation's rationale and aims are indicative of the founding scholars' inclinations and hopes: "The emerging field of cognitive science is reshaping longstanding assumptions about self-understanding, epistemology, and metaphor. This Consultation will apply cognitive linguistics to biblical studies with a focus on how language makes meaning, how a text evokes authority, and how contemporary readers interact with ancient texts."

As the consultation developed, three core foci of cognitive linguistics' potential impact on biblical interpretive work emerged: new perspectives on the status of "dead" languages and ancient texts; analytic models for reading texts; and grounding in the embodied nature and social-relational context of languages, cognition, and interpretation. The first consultation session focused on metaphor and cultural framing in biblical texts and interpretation along the lines of those three themes. Sweetser discussed how cognitive linguists approach "dead" languages and ancient texts. DesCamp offered a reading of a psalm using Conceptual Metaphor analysis, frame semantics, and the Conceptual Blending model. Using as a test case the issue of the nature of "conversion" in Luke-Acts, Joel B. Green highlighted the third theme—that cognitive approaches recontextualize readings and ground hermeneutical and theological interpretation.

In its second year, the consultation collaborated with the Rhetoric and the New Testament section to review Gilles Fauconnier and Mark Turner's *The Way We Think*, with Fauconnier responding. An additional collaboration occurred for Lynn R.

Huber's book, *Like a Bride Adorned: Reading Metaphor in John's Apocalypse* (New York and London: T&T Clark, 2007). Both dialogs suggested a potentially productive interface between socio-rhetorical criticism and cognitive approaches to reading and interpretation, especially finer-grained analysis of cultural frames. That same year the consultation also held a session on the construction of authority. In its final year, the consultation worked on embodiment and metaphor. The developer of the Primary Metaphor model, linguist Joseph E. Grady, was present to respond to biblical scholars' appropriations of his model.

Already, the consultation's scholars were displaying facility with a range of cognitive linguistic analytical tools. José Sanders demonstrated corpus analysis methods, focusing on the interpretive impact of the degree of subjectivity in translation. Elizabeth R. Hayes employed Langacker's models in an analysis of divergent understandings of parallelism in Hebrew Bible poetry; and Hugo Lundhaug used Conceptual Blending theory to unpack ritual implications of references to the Eucharist in the Gospel of Philip.

Tackling controversial texts was another focus of the consultation: could cognitive linguistic methods demonstrate distinctive contributions for reading contended texts? In "Pauline Rhetorical Invention: Seeing 1 Corinthians 6:12—7:7 through Conceptual Integration Theory," Robert H. von Thaden Jr., who had done his doctoral work at Emory University with Vernon Robbins, combined Conceptual Blending analysis with socio-rhetorical criticism. S. J. Robinette combined cognitive linguistic and rhetorical critical models to study Jeremiah 17:5–8. Jesper Tang Nielsen used Conceptual Blending and frame analyses in conjunction with narratological methods in "The Cognitive Structures of the Concept of Atonement." David Parris used Cognitive Grammar, Mental Space theory, and Dancygier and Sweetser's work on aspect and viewpoint to study conditionals in "Cognitive Theory, Parables, and Luke 4:23."

By the end of the consultation phase of the program unit in 2008, then, biblical scholars were using an array of cognitive linguistic analytical tools. in 2009, the SBL consultation became a "section" and shortened its name to Cognitive Linguistics in Biblical Interpretation.

The year 2009 marked the publication of *Reframing Biblical Studies: When Language and Text Meet Culture, Cognition, and Context* by Ellen van Wolde (Radboud University of Nijmegen), and a review session of the book, cohosted with the Linguistics and Biblical Hebrew Group, occurred at the 2010 SBL meeting. Also featured in 2010 was a session on cognitive linguistic analyses of performatives, utterances by which a speaker performs a particular act ("I bet," "You are fired!" "Be healed"): Kirsten Marie Hartvigsen, "You Spoke and it Came into Being"; Jin H. Han, "The Peril of Precarious Performativity in Genesis 27"; and Yael Avrahami, "The Performative Nature of Naming in the Hebrew Bible."

In 2011, the Section turned its attention to cognitive linguistic perspectives on translation, with papers by University of California-Berkeley's linguist Richard A. Rhodes, United Bible Societies translation consultant Robert Bascom, and José Sanders. Another session focused on family and power in biblical texts. Papers included Miranda Vroon-van Vugt, "Who is in Charge? Mental Space Analysis and Visualization in a Textual Study, Applied to 1 Sam 28:3–25"; and William Andrews Jr., "Poor Spaces of Power: Mapping Divine and Family Economies in 4Q416." The trend toward method elegance and wider adoption of cognitive linguistic models continued.

Metaphor Theory and Biblical Texts Consultation. A three-year SBL consultation on metaphor theory and Hebrew Bible texts opened in 2010. While this group's exploration was not confined to cognitive linguistic theory, in 2011 they devoted a session to Lakoff's influence and invited him to respond to several papers applying some of his methods.

Cognitive Linguistic Models and Leading Practitioners. This section outlines an array of discrete cognitive linguistics models and names leading practitioners among biblical scholars.

Conceptual Metaphor and Metonymy. Metaphor study has been the gateway cognitive linguistic model for many biblical scholars. Marc Brettler,

Mary Therese DesCamp, Sarah J. Dille, Gregory S. Goering, Pierre J. P. Van Hecke, Bonnie Howe, and Job Y. Jindo are among the pioneers in this area. Dille's *Mixing Metaphors: God as Mother and Father in Deutero-Isaiah* (Journal for the Study of the Old Testament Supplements 398; New York and London: T&T Clark, 2004) applies key components of the Lakoff and Johnson model: metaphor as conceptual, coherent, and structural; the notion that metaphor mappings carry entailments; the concept of metaphoric extension; and the experiential grounding of metaphor. Job Jindo ("Towards a Poetics of the Biblical Mind: Language, Culture and Cognition," *Vetus Testamentum* 59 [2009]: 222–243) demonstrates how metaphor study is inherently about cognition and culture—and therefore opens up the *Weltanschauung* of ancient Israel.

Mental Space Blending and Frame Semantics. We have described the frame semantics model that Charles Fillmore pioneered and the Mental Spaces model that Fauconnier, Sweetser, and Turner have defined and refined. Among biblical scholars' applications of these models, DesCamp's work on *Liber Antiquitatum Biblicarum* (2007) stands out as a clear and refined display of their efficacy for interpretation of a specific text. She uses metaphor analysis in tandem with Mental Space Blending and in conversation with "New" Rhetoric models and Robert Alter's narrative theory. Her blending analyses and diagrams are exemplars of how biblical scholars can appropriate Fauconnier and Turner's model. DesCamp shows how cultural and semantic frames provide structure for the developing conceptual spaces that readers are integrating as they read and interpret; metaphoric mappings and image structures guide connections between elements in the text. The payoff here is not merely methodologically dazzling; DesCamp wields these tools to show how Pseudo-Philo uses women's stories to express ideology and theology.

Another exemplary application is Hugo Lundhaug's work on the Nag Hammadi tractate, "The Exegesis of the Soul." He uses Fauconnier and Turner's conceptual blending model to explicate how in this text *the soul is a woman* and to demonstrate the key roles of interpretive communities' inference capacities and knowledge bases (in Luomanen 2007, pp. 141–160). Lundhaug uses the Fauconnier and Turner model with cognitive literary models: Seanna Coulson on frame shifting, Raymond Gibbs on poetics of mind, and Todd Oakley on narrative and rhetoric.

Category Structure. As mentioned earlier, psychological work on categorization (Rosch) was one of the driving forces in the development of cognitive linguistics, and Lakoff's *Women, Fire, and Dangerous Things: What Categories Reveal about the Mind* (1987) remains one of the most widely-read pieces of cognitive linguistic scholarship. Categorization is the basic process performed by all neural systems, not just by humans. In contrast with classical logical semantic theories (in particular set-membership theories of category structure), cognitive science has shown that linguistic categories can have complex internal structure. This includes *fuzzy boundaries* (classical set theory would predict that one could be "tall" or "not tall" but never "sorta tall"), and *graded membership* defined with respect to a central *prototype* ("fire-engine" red is the central example of *red*, while other reds are genuine but less good examples). So far, nothing about cognitive theories of categorization will seem particularly striking to biblical scholars, few of whom are adherents of set-theoretic logical semantics.

Perhaps more interesting to biblical scholarship are cognitive theories of *polysemy*, the ways in which a single form can develop a network of related but distinct meanings. Some of this categorization is not simply based on similarity, but on frame structure and on figurative meaning links. For an example of a frame-based category, consider camping gear. Tents are not *similar* to sleeping bags, but, as objects used in a shared activity frame, they may well be stored together. Metaphoric extensions are often based on experiential correlations: since people of all cultures experience a correlation between visual experience and new knowledge content (an experiential frame where the two co-occur), it is unsurprising that *knowledge is vision* is a crossculturally pervasive metaphoric construal, and that words meaning "see" often come to refer to abstract knowledge or understanding (Sweetser, 1990). Noticing the ways a word can extend its meaning leads us to expect the possibility of complex networks of meaning attached to a single form; this complexity is well-attested in dictionaries—and examined in detail in *Women, Fire, and Dangerous Things*. Polysemy in biblical texts is equally pervasive and complex.

Construction Grammar. Construction Grammar consists of a number of models (Adele Goldberg, Charles Fillmore, Paul Kay, Ronald Langacker), all of which view grammatical constructions as meaningful forms. Paul Danove applies Fillmore and Kay's Construction Grammar model to exegete a selection of Markan passages, yielding insights into Mark's portrayal of the character of God and how readers are then led to see this displayed in Jesus (Danove, *Linguistics and Exegesis in the Gospel of Mark: Applications of a Case Frame Analysis and Lexicon* [*Journal for the Study of the New Testament Supplement Series* 218; Sheffield, UK: Sheffield Academic, 2001]).

Cognitive Grammar. A number of biblical scholars find cognitive linguist Ronald Langacker's Cognitive Grammar model useful. Langacker speaks of grammar as conceptualization and imagery, and he connects grammar with semantics, reinterpreting traditional formal grammatical descriptive categories. Because in his approach forms directly symbolize meaning, he is a member of the broader community of construction grammarians. Some biblical scholars have applied Langacker's descriptive tools for grammatical "imagery" (profiling, specificity, scope, salience) to analyses of biblical narrative (van Wolde) and poetry (Elizabeth R. Hayes, *The Pragmatics of Perception and Cognition in MT Jeremiah 1:1—6:30* [Berlin, New York: Walter de Gruyter, 2008]).

Van Wolde's *Reframing Biblical Studies* (2009) is a thorough, accessible introduction for biblical scholars to Langacker's model for cognitive grammatical analysis of actual language use in the Hebrew Bible, including a rationale for employing it. She gives detailed examples of nominal profiles (e.g., the nouns "child" and *yeled*), atemporal and temporal relations, and the kinds of mental processing particular words express and evoke. Van Wolde argues that interpreters using Langacker's methods can uncover "the ideological power of cognitive formations" (p. 353)—a radical notion, but one for which she has made a strong case.

David Parris (cited earlier) uses Langacker's model in concert with Mental Space Blending and Conceptual Metaphor models to analyze conditional constructions and hone his interpretation of 1 John 1:6–7 ("If we say that we have fellowship with him while we are walking in darkness."). Parris shows how contrast between conditionals works at grammatical, lexical, and metaphorical levels, and how the mental spaces evoked via grammatical constructions push the reader to participate actively in the author's reasoning process (David Parris, "Conditional Constructions and Meanings in I John 1:5–10" in *Cognitive Linguistic Readings of Biblical Texts*, edited by Bonnie Howe and Joel B. Green [Berlin: De Gruyter, forthcoming]).

Compatible Approaches. Cognitive linguistic methods and interpretive aims cohere with an array of other frameworks. They share and support many of the aims of discourse analysis, especially study of the impact of the social-cultural contexts of biblical writings and readers. The most productive interfaces to date have been in the areas of socio-rhetorical criticism, narrative approaches, and reader-response analyses.

Socio-Rhetorical Criticism. Vernon K. Robbins finds Conceptual Blending and frame analysis fit his socio-rhetorical critical approach and help him "clarify the relation of social places to cultural, ideological and religious spaces" (Robbins, in Luomanen, pp. 161–195). Robert H. Von Thaden Jr. uses Conceptual Blending analysis within a socio-rhetorical framework in his study of 1 Corinthians, *Sex, Christ, and Embodied Cognition: Paul's Wisdom for Corinth* (Emory Studies in Early Christianity 16; Blandford Forum, UK: Deo, 2012). Conceptual integration theory—especially the notions of compression of vital relations, selective projection, and emergent structure—is central to his understanding of Paul's rhetoric.

Narrative Criticism, Reader-Response, and Theological Interpretation. Cognitive linguistic theory and methods fit the aims of narrative approaches to the biblical texts and support reader-response views of reading as communicative encounter and as a dynamic, interactive process. If, as cognitive linguists say, "the meaning is not in the word," but is evoked as readers interact with a text, then readers play a starring role. DesCamp, Jesper T. Nielsen, Joel B. Green, Bonnie Howe, and Hugo Lundhaug are among the many biblical scholars employing cognitive approaches in conjunction with narrative ones. Howe (2006) argues that cognitive linguistic theory and methodology clashes with approaches that treat texts as autonomous objects, as if readers' responses were irrelevant, but cautions that cognitive linguistic theory also describes constraints on the plausible range of meaning a given text can evoke or support, so that it could not endorse radical versions of reader-response theory that assign all of the meaning-making to the reader's imagination.

Joel B. Green's practical theological interpretation model focuses on story and narrative framing, and his hermeneutical practice is anchored in the concept of embodied cognition. Green adopts Eco's "model reader" framework, finding that it coheres with Mark Turner's observation that people use stories to organize thought (Turner 1996). Green adopts this perspective as he sets about the task of reading and interpreting biblical narrative in the sense of the big story that scripture tells. "Embodied human life performs like a cultural, neuro-hermeneutical system, locating (and thus making sense of) current realities in relation to our grasp of the past and expectations of the future; that is, we frame meaning in narrative terms" (Green, *Practicing Theological Interpretation: Engaging Biblical Texts for Faith and Formation* [Grand Rapids, Mich.: Baker Academic, 2011], p. 28).

Critiques of Cognitive Linguistic Approaches. Some biblical scholars and theologians have sampled cognitive linguistic approaches and rejected the cognitive paradigm outright, deeming it useless, unwieldy, or too extreme. At SBL 2010, David Clines responded to Ellen van Wolde's *Reframing Biblical Studies*, with "Why do we need to do that?" Much of the criticism focuses on Conceptual Metaphor Theory, perhaps because metaphor theory has been the most popular piece of the cognitive linguistic toolkit. Theologian Janet Soskice has some awareness of the Conceptual Metaphor model but prefers metaphor's traditional figure of speech status. Peter Macky (*The Centrality of Metaphors to Biblical Thought* [Lewiston, N.Y.: Edwin Mellen, 1990]) deems Lakoff's metaphor theory overreaching and "radical." David H. Aaron (*Biblical Ambiguities: Metaphor, Semantics, and Divine Imagery* [Leiden: Brill, 2002]) joins Macky and Belgian scholar Ralph Bisschops in dismissing experiential "grounding" claims in Conceptual Metaphor Theory and lamenting what they think is Lakoff's undue influence among biblical scholars.

A representative critique of the theory of experiential grounding is Bisschops's claim that some biblical metaphors—"covenant is marriage," "God is groom," and "Israel is bride"—have no such grounding (Ralph Bisschops, "Are Religious Metaphors Rooted in Experience? On Ezekiel's Wedding Metaphors," in *The Bible through Metaphor and Translation*, edited by K. Feyaerts, pp. 113–151 [New York: Peter Lang, 2003]). He makes the erroneous assumption that finding a metaphor lacking direct experiential correlation disproves Lakoff and Johnson's theory. The *covenant as marriage* metaphor is not a Primary Metaphor, although even a fairly young child of that culture would grasp some of the relevant aspects of the marriage frame (in this case, power asymmetry between his/her mother and father and exclusivity of the mother's relationship to the father). Conceptual Metaphor analysis would say that the *covenant as marriage* metaphor is built up in a complex way, not based on direct primary experiential correlation.

Many critiques ignore the fact that, as Conceptual Metaphor Theory has developed, the experiential grounding claims (and empirical observations) have been refined and nuanced. The postscript to the 2003 edition of *Metaphors We Live By* points to some of the more recent iterations of Conceptual

Metaphor Theory, which includes primary and complex or nonprimary metaphors. Claims that conceptual Metaphor Theory is too extreme ("surely not that much of thought and language can be metaphoric") indicate misunderstanding of the theory. Lakoff and Johnson have never argued that all cognition is metaphorical. Such a distorted caricature of Conceptual Metaphor Theory depends on reading only the earliest articulations of the theory and isolating metaphor study from its larger cognitive linguistic framework. Other critics balk at the idea that everyday language can be metaphoric. *Philosophy in the Flesh* and recent neuroscience literature (e.g., Jerome A. Feldman, *From Molecule to Metaphor: A Neural Theory of Language* [Cambridge, Mass.: MIT Press, 2006]) provide extensive evidence for the pervasive presence of metaphor in everyday language and also place metaphor within a larger cognitive framework involving prototypes, frames, and mental spaces.

Friendly disputes arise between practitioners who prefer particular cognitive linguistic models. Ellen van Wolde sees Langacker's model as having the firmest theoretical foundations and yielding the most fruitful results; she finds the Conceptual Metaphor and Mental Space Blending models too fuzzy, less convincing. But other scholars (DesCamp, Howe) bemoan the inability of the Langacker-based studies to provide a reading or interpretation at the level of discourse.

Prospects for Future Research and Development of the Topic. While many biblical scholars are just now encountering this area of study, a few have already achieved an impressive level of method elegance. Some dissertations have been published and others are in the pipeline, and major publishers are expressing interest in making the SBL Cognitive Linguistics in Biblical Interpretation unit's work available in book form and launching a book series. But considering the multitude of descriptive and analytical models offered by cognitive linguistics, biblical scholarly adoption of the wider range of tools is still tentative and inexpert. We dabble, wade in the shallows, hug the shore. Conceptual Metaphor study has been the favorite cognitive linguistic tool taken up by biblical scholars. But serious engagement must draw one into deeper waters. Metaphor theory belongs within the broader cognitive linguistics array; since metaphor theory is about mapping frames, one needs the tools of frame semantics for thorough study. Metaphor and metonymy need to be studied together—and at this point, Mental Space Blending analyses become helpful. The SBL Cognitive Linguistics Section session on performatives demonstrated potentially fruitful new fields of study. So also, if biblical scholars can grasp and apply the semantics-grammar connections of Langackerian Cognitive Grammar, the results may be profound.

Cognitive linguists argue that embodied experience grounds language use and language meaning. Thus, it matters *which* words, and in *what* context, we are reading. They also argue that the reading audience matters because imaginations are formed, informed, and excited by particular experience in everyday life. These two realities—embodied experience and social-relational experience, both of which are completely embedded in cultural life—shape our imagination, shape our understanding, and shape our interpretation. If cognitive linguistic tools only offered another pretty reading, that would be a good reason to disregard them. But as we learn more about how brains work and how language truly functions in human beings, cognitive linguistic methods have the potential to reshape our understanding of language so that our methods are congruent with the best current research outside of biblical studies.

[*See also* Cultural Anthropology, *subentry* Hebrew Bible; Cultural Anthropology, *subentry* New Testament; Genre Criticism; Metaphor Theory and Biblical Texts; Narrative Criticism and Narrative Hermeneutics; Reader-response Criticism; Reception Criticism and Theory; Rhetorical Criticism; Semiotics, Socio-rhetorical Criticism; Speech-Act Theory; *and* Theological Interpretation.]

BIBLIOGRAPHY

Brettler, Marc Zvi. *God is King: Understanding an Israelite Metaphor.* Journal for the Study of the Old

Testament: Supplement Series 76. Sheffield, UK: Sheffield Academic, 1989, 2009. A revised dissertation employing a tensive view of metaphor, this book represents an early attempt to employ Lakoff and Johnson's metaphor theory, metaphor mapping, and the notion of entailments.

Dancygier, Barbara. *The Language of Stories: A Cognitive Approach.* Cambridge, UK: Cambridge University Press, 2011. Uses Mental Space Blending theory and Construction Grammar to analyze the processes giving rise to the emergence of literary meaning in narrative.

Dancygier, Barbara, and Eve Sweetser. *Mental Spaces in Grammar: Conditional Constructions.* Cambridge Studies in Linguistics. Cambridge, UK: Cambridge University Press, 2005. Uses a Mental Space model of semantics to analyze syntax and semantics of a wide range of English conditional constructions.

DesCamp, Mary Therese. *Metaphor and Ideology:* Liber Antiquitatum Biblicarum *and Literary Methods through a Cognitive Lens.* Biblical Interpretation Series 87. Leiden: Brill, 2007. DesCamp demonstrates metaphor and Mental Space Blending analysis and includes exemplary blend diagrams.

Fauconnier, Gilles, and Eve Sweetser, eds. *Spaces, Worlds, and Grammar.* Chicago and London: University of Chicago Press, 1996. Twelve essays displaying the utility of the Mental Spaces framework for working on a range of linguistic issues, including analogical counterfactuals, the metaphor system for conceptualizing the self, deictic expressions, and conditional constructions. Contributors include Claudia Brugman, Gilles Fauconnier, George Lakoff, José Sanders, and Eve Sweetser.

Fillmore, Charles. "Frames and the Semantics of Understanding." *Quaderni di Semantica* 6, no. 2 (1985): 222–253. Foundational and seminal explication of frame semantic theory and method.

Geeraerts, Dirk, ed. *Cognitive Linguistics: Basic Readings.* Berlin: de Gruyter, 2006. Introduces the landscape of Cognitive Linguistics and provides exemplary pieces from an array of methods.

Goldberg, Adele. *Constructions at Work: The Nature of Generalization in Language.* New York: Oxford University Press, 2006. Analyzes language acquisition in children and adults, the links between forms and functions, and how cross-linguistic and language-internal generalizations arise.

Hecke, Pierre J. P. Van. *From Linguistics to Hermeneutics: A Functional and Cognitive Approach to Job 12—14.* Studia Semitica Neerlandica. Leiden: Brill, 2010. Using functional grammar and cognitive semantics models, Van Hecke gives a detailed linguistic analysis and exegesis of Job 12–14.

Howe, Bonnie. *Because You Bear This Name: Conceptual Metaphor and the Moral Meaning of 1 Peter.* Biblical Interpretation Series 81. Leiden: Brill, 2006. SBL paperback reprint, 2008. A rationale for the Conceptual Metaphor model applied with frame semantic and Mental Space Blending analyses to reading 1 Peter as moral discourse.

Lakoff, George. *Women, Fire, and Dangerous Things: What Categories Reveal about the Mind.* Chicago: University of Chicago Press, 1987, 1997. Argues that how people categorize both objects and concepts displays the embodied grounding and imaginative quality of human thought. This is a benchmark piece for both cognitive linguistic theory and its empirical, analytical methods.

Lakoff, George, and Mark Johnson. *Metaphors We Live By.* Chicago: University of Chicago Press, 1980, 2003. Groundbreaking exposition of Conceptual Metaphor theory and early metaphor mapping methods. The 2003 edition includes a must-read postscript explaining developments in metaphor theory and cognitive linguistics since the 1980s.

Lakoff, George, and Mark Johnson. *Philosophy in the Flesh: The Embodied Mind and its Challenge to Western Thought.* New York: Basic Books, 1999. Argues for a paradigm shift to experiential realism while locating that position on the philosophical family tree. The topically arranged bibliography provides gateways to exploration of empirical literature in cognitive science and linguistics.

Langacker, Ronald W. *Cognitive Grammar: A Basic Introduction.* New York: Oxford University Press, 2008. Introduces usage-based cognitive grammatical theory and covers conceptual semantics, grammatical classes and constructions, and form-meaning pairings at all linguistic levels. Examples cover nominal structure, clause structure, and complex sentences.

Luomanen, Petri, Ilkka Pyysiäinen, and Risto Uro, eds. *Explaining Christian Origins and Early Judaism: Contributions from Cognitive and Social Science.* Biblical Interpretation Series 89. Leiden: Brill, 2007. See especially Hugo Lundhaug, "Conceptual Blending in the 'Exegesis of the Soul'" (141–160), and Vernon K. Robbins, "Conceptual Blending and Early Christian Imagination" (161–195).

Robbins, Vernon K. "Socio-Rhetorical Interpretation." In *The Blackwell Companion to the New Testament,* edited by David E. Aune, 192–219. West Sussex, UK: Blackwell, 2010. See the discussion of Conceptual Blending and rhetography (199–208).

Sweetser, Eve. *From Etymology to Pragmatics: Metaphorical and Cultural Aspects of Semantic Structure.* Cambridge Studies in Linguistics. Cambridge, UK: Cambridge University Press, 1990. In a study of semantic change, Sweetser demonstrates how systematicity in lexical polysemy and pragmatic ambiguity displays both metaphorical and cultural aspects of human cognitive structure.

Turner, Mark. *The Literary Mind: The Origins of Thought and Language.* Oxford: Oxford University Press, 1996. Turner argues for the narrative structure of human thought, with *story* the organizing principle of everyday experience and knowledge.

Wolde, E. J. van. *Reframing Biblical Studies: When Language and Text Meet Culture, Cognition, and Context.* Winona Lake, Ind.: Eisenbrauns, 2009. Masterful introduction of Langacker's Cognitive Grammar and application to specific Hebrew Bible texts.

Wolde, E. J. van. "A Text-Semantic Study of the Hebrew Bible, Illustrated with Noah and Job." *Journal of Biblical Literature* 113 (1994): 19–35.

Bonnie Howe and Eve Sweetser

Conservative Jewish Interpretation

Conservative Jewish biblical interpretation (hereafter, CJBI) is essentially a hologram. That is to say, what one may perceive or observe as CBJI is largely a constructed reflection of disparate elements, not all of which necessarily appear together in every case. This entry will consider whether there are hermeneutic principles or analytical methods that, taken together, comprise what should be considered "Conservative Jewish biblical interpretation" and, if so, what those elements are and what they represent. However, to imitate one element of biblical style, this article will begin with a short version of its main point, followed thereafter by recounting that theme in greater detail.

Conservative Jewish biblical interpretation makes use of all available exegetical and analytical tools, exploring contextual understandings of the Hebrew Bible (*peshat*) as well as drawing upon a range of classical noncontextual interpretations (*derash*), intending to derive religious value and humanistic meaning from both approaches. Thus, while for CBJI "how to read" (and, therefore, how to interpret) the biblical text has numerous facets, it is no less anchored by one approach of "how not to read" (or how not to interpret) the biblical text: the interpretive approach that is eschewed is a "literalist" or "fundamentalist" reading of the Hebrew Bible.

Conservative Jewish Biblical Interpretation and Conservative Judaism. First, as has often been noted, it is not always easy to delineate Conservative Judaism (CJ) itself, and it is harder still, if not impossible, to confirm CJ in action solely by observing demonstrable behaviors or visible clues. The frequently heard negative definitions—"Conservative Judaism is neither Orthodoxy nor Reform Judaism" or "Conservative Judaism is the movement between Reform and Orthodoxy"—are unhelpful at best and inaccurate at worst. The Conservative Movement or, better, Conservative Jewish approaches, are delineated by a broad matrix of views on sources of religious (and communal) authority, theologies, and practices. As such, Conservative Judaism is wide-ranging, sometimes appearing to meld into other "movements" or Jewish denominations to its left or right. That is because denominational differences may blur at the edges between the main Jewish "movements" if one looks only at religious observance. However, when observance is overlaid with "belief systems" (including views of revelation and sources of authority, as well as their ramifications) patterns emerge that generally enable one to sculpt what may be a Conservative exegetical approach and what, by comparison, would not fall within the parameters of CJBI. This essay attempts to articulate the categories useful in determining CJBI, or at least what can be subsumed within CJBI and what cannot. No single criterion alone is determinative, but taken together the criteria forge an outline for what one may rightfully call CJBI. What are those criteria or, to return to the opening metaphor of a hologram, what elements contribute to the reflected image of Conservative Jewish biblical interpretation"?

Assumptions. The twofold primary assumption of Conservative Jewish biblical interpretation is that the Hebrew Bible has been and remains a sacred and authoritative text of the Jewish people, and that it must be interpreted to offer religious guidance to contemporary communities and congregants affiliated with the Conservative Movement of Judaism as well as to those who, while without a formal denominational affiliation, subscribe to the basic premises or approaches of Conservative Judaism. Another foundational assumption of CJBI is that "the implicit ideology of the (Conservative) Movement viewed Torah, whatever its divine source, as a cultural document that has always responded to changing historical conditions and that can therefore be studied with all of the resources available for the study of any human creation" (Gillman 1993, p. 157). Thus, CJBI often compels the exegete to exercise intellectual acumen in the service of the search for religious or existential meaning.

Revelation. An exegete's perspective on revelation is a core factor in his or her hermeneutical approach. However, CJ encompasses an exceedingly broad spectrum of views about revelation, as shown in just several brief statements excerpted from *Emet Ve-Emunah: Statement of Principles of Conservative Judaism* (pp. 19–20), one of a very few joint publications of its major constituent organizations. It is not only one of the few Movement-wide publications, but "it took over a century for the Movement to produce its own ideological platform" (Gillman, p. 150). The section of *Emet Ve-Emunah* titled "Revelation" declares at the outset that "The Conservative Movement affirms its belief in revelation, the uncovering of an external source of truth emanating from God." Nonetheless, it is significant that the very same statement of principles endorses the pluralistic notion that "the nature of revelation and its meaning for the Jewish people, [sic] have been understood in various ways within the Conservative community." Further expanding the breadth of legitimate views, within the space of several paragraphs the statement of principles explains that "the single greatest event in the history of God's revelation took place at Sinai, but was not limited to it" and also that revelation is "seen as an ongoing process rather than as a specific event" (pp. 19–20). This is not the context in which to refute what detractors of CJ proclaim to be internal contradictions, other than to say CJ is founded upon a profound pluralism in the areas of philosophy and action. That pluralistic approach sometimes makes defining Conservative Judaism difficult, but it is the keystone to an appreciation of CJ. Accepting the principle and practice of pluralism also confounds an easy definition of CJBI, but it is equally critical to understanding the multivocality reflected in CJBI.

Interpretive Techniques and Tools. CJBI is distinguished from most, but possibly not from all, other exegetical approaches by the dual sets of tools it employs in the process of trying to establish the manifold meanings of biblical material, known by the terms *peshat* and *derash*.

Peshat. On one hand, CJBI seeks to understand the biblical text based on what is known as *peshat*, that is, the "contextual" understandings—including historical, linguistic, literary, and geographic contexts—of a biblical passage. *Peshat* is usually, but incorrectly, translated as the "simple" or "literal" meaning of the text. However, it is neither simple (given the need to explore the various multiple contexts just noted) nor literal (since *peshat* recognizes and appreciates the use of both idioms and metaphorical language). To observe the difference, one need only consider an obvious English example, the difference between the literal meaning and the contextual (or *peshat*) meaning of "It's raining cats and dogs." Literally, the phrase means that cats and dogs are falling from the sky. By contrast, its meaning according to the *peshat*, which understands and values the use of idiomatic language, means that "it is raining very heavily."

Language. The target of interpretation is the Hebrew Bible, even if the exegete draws upon material from other canonical collections or the sacred literatures of many other faith traditions. Since CJBI interprets the Hebrew Bible, by definition the interpreter must be able to work competently with the Hebrew (and, as appropriate, Aramaic) texts of the original. Therefore, one indispensable tool, or series of tools, for serious CJBI is the proficiency to navigate and draw upon numerous linguistic skills necessary for the analysis of an ancient Semitic language. Interpreters clarify biblical language by its location within the Northwest sub-family of Semitic languages (in both Canaanite and Aramaic stocks, according to the classic definition of H. L. Ginsberg [1970]) and, in different ways, by comparison with other Semitic subfamilies, notably (West), Central, South, and East (according to a more recent delineation by Gary Rendsburg [2003]). The CJ interpreter must consider as many aspects of biblical Hebrew as possible. For instance, the exegete must consider morphology, grammar, and syntax of the material, appropriate to its historical era, to the degree that one can determine or presume the historical timeframe of the material under study.

Ancient Near Eastern Context. Another essential aspect of *peshat* contextualization is exploring how biblical material is similar to and, even more important, different from its companion literatures of the Ancient Near East. (Of course, archaeology has been an essential tool in this enterprise, helping to bring the ancient literatures to light as it also uncovers many facets of the realia of relevant ancient cultures.) CJBI focuses on ways in which biblical myth, narrative, poetry, law, custom, institutions, or structures may parallel extrabiblical writings from Mesopotamia, the Levant, and Egypt, and how the Hebrew Bible may reflect those other works, how it may have incorporated them, modified them, been influenced by them, or influenced them. On occasion, a distinctive message conveyed by the Hebrew Bible is brought into sharper focus through the comparative process. At other times, as Peter Machinist (1991) explains, one needs to consider the overarching sweep of the biblical corpus to see what may stand out as the distinctiveness of the Hebrew Bible.

Lower Criticism. CJBI also uses the many components that, together, comprise "text" (or "textual," or "lower") criticism. Thus, commentators may compare the biblical text with other manuscripts, for example, the two great Tiberian manuscripts, the Aleppo Codex and the Leningrad Codex, as well as other versions of the ancient text including those in Hebrew (e.g., the Dead Sea Scrolls texts or the Samaritan Pentateuch), those in other Semitic languages (e.g., various Aramaic Targumim, or the Syriac Peshitta); as well as a variety of ancient translations in non-Semitic languages (e.g., the Greek Septuagint versions or the Latin translations). While some exegetes may use the ancient versions or translations in the elusive attempt to establish (or create) an "original *Urtext*," decades ago Moshe Greenberg (1977) demonstrated an exegetically more sophisticated benefit to the comparative exercise. The variant readings and traditions enable the exegete to understand each version—including the so-called "Masoretic Text(s)"—on its own terms, reflecting the particular concerns and nuances of each version.

History of Interpretation. CJBI seeks insights into the biblical text and looks for suggestions to deal with textual difficulties from every imaginable resource. No source is considered off limits, as long as its assumptions, concerns, and methods are recognized and used to evaluate how to apply that source. This allows the CJ exegete to explore the seemingly endless history of interpretation of the Bible, starting with internal biblical exegesis and with the appearance of biblical terms, phrases, or metaphors used in more than one location within the Bible itself. The search for guidance may easily continue by mining interpretive suggestions posited in early rabbinic interpretive traditions and literatures, in patristic commentaries, and in early medieval traditions, including masoretic notations which may be a useful, if often obscure, exegetical tool. So, too, the exegete consults medieval lexicographers and commentators such as Saadiah Gaon (tenth century Egypt), Jonah ibn Janah, Menahem ibn Saruq, and Dunash ben Labrat (all three tenth century Spain), Rashi (eleventh century France), Rashbam (eleventh century France), Abraham ibn Ezra (twelfth century Spain), Bechor Shor (twelfth century France), David Kimchi (twelfth and thirteenth centuries France), Nahmanides (thirteenth century Spain), Gersonides (fourteenth century France), Don Isaac Abravanel (fifteenth century Spain), or countless others reflecting different points of view, diverse geographic, linguistic, and religious orientations, and divergent techniques and exegetical goals. Further, the search for elucidation continues to the modern day, tapping every conceivable spring; every fountain is an eligible resource for CJBI, regardless of its religious or secular origin. The key is to recognize both the derivation and the predisposition of an interpretive insight, and to take those into consideration when making use of it.

Higher Criticism. Another component of *peshat* has to do with the historical contexts, and even the historical development, of the Hebrew Bible. Higher criticism (part of which is also known as "source criticism" or the "documentary hypothesis") seeks to determine what sources (or, according to some formulations of the hypothesis, what traditions) were edited together to form the Torah. This aspect of *peshat* interpretation was not originally part of CJBI; it was certainly not part of the curriculum of the Jewish Theological Seminary in its early years. (Founded in 1886 and reorganized by Solomon Schechter in 1902, JTS was the first educational institution to train rabbis and cantors, as well as teachers and laity, for the Conservative Movement.) In one of his more notorious statements, Schechter, then president of JTS and founder of United Synagogue of America, the organization of Conservative synagogues, proclaimed that "The genesis of this Higher anti-Semitism is partly . . . contemporaneous with the genesis of the so-called Higher criticism of the Bible" (Schechter 1915, p. 36). While historical-critical study of the Bible did become part of the JTS curriculum, it was not until Moshe Greenberg taught a course on Exodus in the mid-1960s that a book of the Pentateuch was included in that part of the curriculum. Thereafter, however, source critical study not only became a commonly accepted part of CJBI, in some circles it was so common as to be considered passé or religiously irrelevant, until less emphasis was placed on the presumed disparate sources and greater emphasis was placed on the role of the editorial process of weaving them together.

Derash. An entirely separate tool chest may be found in an expansive collection of works often incorporated under the rubric of *midrash.* Though the works of *midrash* also vary by date, extending over more than a millennium, provenance, and techniques used, midrashic literature generally shares several assumptions that enable us to classify the works collectively and also to differentiate them from the commentaries and assumptions of works of *peshat.* Whereas *peshat* is always concerned with the contexts of the biblical material, *midrash* is defiantly not. (Ironically, *derash*—not *peshat*—can be literal, or even "hyper-literal," as in the riotous rabbinic notation to Exodus 8:2 that the plague of frogs entailed one huge frog, since the singular noun and verb form were used, in contrast to the plural noun and verb forms appearing in the very next verse. *Peshat,* in capturing the linguistic context, would see the singular as a collective noun. Impressively, Everett Fox [1995] captured both senses in his inspired translation "frog-horde.")

The most salient feature of *derash,* in fact, is its willful lack of contextual concern; *midrash* is entirely acontextual interpretation. Grammatical, historical, geographic, linguistic, and literary contexts are unimportant for the approach of *midrash.* The two methods of exegesis don't really map onto the diachronic and synchronic analyses, either, since *peshat* itself may focus on both whereas *derash* avoids the diachronic. The reason *midrash* chooses to reject the contexts for its interpretations and is, therefore, often atomistic, is that it proceeds from a particular assumption about the language of the *Tanakh.* While the language of the Hebrew Bible is (or at least "looks like") Hebrew, *midrash* doesn't treat this Hebrew of the Bible as part of the Semitic language families. *Derash* functions as if this language is unique—a special "God language"—and is, therefore, to be analyzed by interpretive rules different from rules used to interpret any other (human) language. Without reviewing those special hermeneutic rules, what is relevant to the current discussion is that the goal of *midrash* is to interpret (or even to "decipher") an embedded meaning or message in the biblical text. The message derived by *derash* is often a moral, homiletical, or "religious" message, inherent, if sometimes hidden, in the biblical text and often not apparent to the person reading the biblical material in context.

Peshat Together with Derash. While CJBI adamantly values the insights derived by *peshat* exegesis, it also values the teachings and lessons discovered by *midrash*. A passage from the Babylonian Talmud (*Shabbat* 31a) in which a non-Jew asked Shammai (first century C.E.) "How many Torahs do you have?" echoes that dual need. (The wording of the narrative makes clear that the question was about how many "kinds" of Torah, that is to say, how many fundamental approaches to interpretation of Torah were in existence, not how many Torah scrolls.) Although the point of the talmudic narrative is to point out how another scholar, Hillel, gave a more compassionate response to the non-Jew, both Shammai and Hillel answered that there were two kinds of Torah, the "written Torah" and the "oral Torah." Those two "Torahs," though not identical to *peshat* and *derash* interpretations, overlap significantly with them. Thus, CJBI has an important ancient antecedent in that model from the Talmud. At the end of the nineteenth century, Schechter wrote, "It is not the mere revealed Bible that is of first importance to the Jew, but the Bible as it repeats itself in history, in other words, as it is interpreted by Tradition" (1896, pp. xvii–xviii). Since Schechter first articulated that viewpoint stressing the virtually exclusive role for meaning determined by tradition, however, CJBI has been developing and transforming.

Development. If there were disagreements about the curriculum and orientation of biblical studies during the earliest stages of Conservative Jewish institutions such as the Jewish Theological Seminary when "positive-historical Judaism" and *Wissenschaft des Judentums* (the so-called "science of Judaism") carried the day in at least theoretical ways, the affinity to engage with both *peshat* and *derash* has a long history. In fact, one might posit that an important intellectual forebear of CJBI is Samuel David Luzzatto (1800–1865), known by the acronym of his name as Shadal. He was a prolific nineteenth-century Italian scholar—philosopher, philologist, and Bible commentator—who taught in Padua (at the rabbinical college there and, it appears, at the University of Padua). As part of the Hebrew introduction to his Italian *Commentary to the Book of Isaiah*, Luzzatto offers principles of exegesis (or, better, principles for exegetes) that combine "traditional" and "modern" approaches and reflect the combined use of *peshat* and *derash*. What follows are excerpts from the ten exegetical principles in the "Introduction":

> This commentary which I now provide for you (and the rest of the commentaries I have published over the past thirty years and others I have written but which have not yet been published) are all based upon these ten principles:
>
> The first principle: the reality of the Creator. That is to say, heaven and earth and all their "host" are not (anciently) eternal, but rather their existence had a beginning, and they were created by the intention and will of the Creator who is beyond and distinct from them. He alone is eternal and rules over all.
>
> The second principle: [the belief in] divine providence and reward and punishment in this world.
>
> The third principle: miracles (e.g., God's providing manna for the Israelites in the desert) are beyond nature and prophecy.
>
> The fourth principle: the love of truth, the goal of which is to understand the truth of the Bible's intention . . . even if their [Rashi's and Rashbam's] explanations went against Jewish law (as, for example, Rashi on Exod 23:2 or Rashbam on Lev 7:18).
>
> The fifth principle: to leave one's own location and time period and to bring ourselves into the time and place of the Bible, although we cannot do so entirely.
>
> The sixth principle: habituation to ancient Israel's texts and to the writings of the holy language.
>
> The seventh principle: to deepen one's focus on the cantillation marks [trope], because they are the traditionally accepted reading, from mouth to mouth, [down] to the Sages of the Second Temple. . . . For example, see the meaning of . . . Genesis 1:11.
>
> The eighth principle: in sacred [biblical] poetry and in prophetic rhetoric, the exegete must, no less, have a poetic soul (and that, in particular, for biblical poetic style, not for the style of Greek or Latin).
>
> The ninth principle: the interpretive explanations of the Rabbis (of blessed memory), and also the

(Aramaic) translation [*Targum*], and vocalization [vowels], and the cantillation [trope] aren't always the proof of what their (the Rabbinic Sages') opinion was about the meaning of the texts.

The tenth principle: although the sacred texts were always preserved in the midst of Israel as a precious and noble treasure, and no hand was ever set upon them in order to falsify them, or to add to or diminish from them, nonetheless, it is impossible that one wouldn't discern in them, here and there, at least small textual variants of which one is correct and derived from the "author" of the book, and the other of which is nothing other than an error of the scribal copyist.

(Padova [Padua], end of Tammuz, ca. 1854)

This is not the place to stand in awe of Luzzatto's ability to "hop on the two boughs" (1 Kgs 18:21) or even to marvel at his apparent desire to incorporate several "critical" principles at the time he wrote his introduction approximately a century and a half ago. For all of his nineteenth-century audacity, he was able to apply his tenth principle to only the Prophets and Writings, but not to the Torah itself. For that he was later chided by Arnold Ehrlich, an important biblical scholar of the latter nineteenth and early twentieth century. In addition to the exegetical development in method from Luzzatto to Ehrlich, the chain of tradition continued for several more scholarly generations. Ehrlich's methods were influential on H. L. Ginsberg, the mid-twentieth century biblicist and doyen of the JTS Bible faculty for roughly half a century. Significantly, Ginsberg was teacher and mentor of many of the current generation of JTS Bible faculty.

Settings. Some methods, such as the use of textual criticism or certain other components appropriated by *peshat* exegetes, make it relatively easy to differentiate CJBI from Orthodox Jewish biblical interpretation (even though Orthodox interpretation is not entirely monolithic). Other methods, such as the use of Jewish *midrashic* material make it relatively easy to differentiate CJBI from Christian biblical interpretation (although Christian interpretation is also far from monolithic). Yet, are there criteria or markers that differentiate CJBI from Reform Jewish biblical interpretation or Reconstructionist Jewish biblical interpretation? In other words, is CJBI simply a cipher for a more inclusive category to be labeled "liberal Jewish interpretation," as several current biblical scholars in Conservative Jewish institutions aver, or might there be additional factors that enable distinguishing CJBI from other forms of liberal Jewish interpretation?

Barry Holtz stresses that the teaching contexts or "milieus" (citing Schwab), particularly narrower or more localized contexts, play a significant role in determining much about curricular matters and didactic orientation (2003, especially chapter 1). In practice, it seems that the setting and the audience may actually be the main factors enabling one to differentiate between "liberal Jewish interpretation" and "Conservative Jewish biblical interpretation." The audience and setting not only facilitate the differentiation from other forms of liberal interpretation, but they foster and even compel such a differentiated CJBI. The approaches described here as being "liberal Jewish" interpretive modes *become* Conservative Jewish biblical interpretation when they are offered in and tailored to Conservative Jewish audiences, in Conservative seminaries and seminars, congregations, schools, conferences, and similar study settings. Whether in classes, lectures, sermons, or publications, the specific needs, concerns, practices, interests, and questions of the Conservative Jewish listeners and participants add the final element that compels the instructional approach to be, and to become, CJBI. This is immediately apparent in the following excerpt from the Introduction to the one-volume Torah commentary now used in countless Conservative synagogues throughout North America:

Etz Hayim: Torah and Commentary is a product of the Conservative (*Masorti*) Movement. As such, it incorporates the very best of modern Bible scholarship.... The first commentary on the page under the Bible text is the *p'shat*... illuminated by the finest contemporary scientific scholarship on the Torah. The second commentary on the page is the midrashic commentary (*d'rash*). . . . Also included at the bottom of many pages is a section on Conservative halakhic practice (*halakhah l'ma'aseh*), indicating how contemporary Conservative *halakhah* is linked to the biblical laws (pp. xvii–xviii).

CJBI is both a scholarly activity *and* a religious endeavor. Although it cannot lack an intellectual foundation, it cannot be purely an academic exercise. CJBI is an exploration that uses the insights of a long history of hermeneutic traditions actively enriched by an ever-expanding series of new interpretive tools and foci. CJBI assumes that the use of all potential human capacities is warranted, even obligatory, in the study of the Hebrew Bible. A special text, the Hebrew Bible, necessitates special study—not for reasons that classical *midrash* applied special interpretive methods to it (as explained earlier)—but because of the central, albeit indirect, role assigned to the *Tanakh* in the life of the Conservative Jewish community. CJBI proceeds from the basis that the Hebrew Bible can withstand any forms of analysis and scrutiny applied judiciously not because it is a uniquely divine document written in a unique language, but because it has garnered a public sanctity over the centuries that affirms its richness and vitality.

In the dynamic interplay of text and community, as James Sanders clarified (1984), the biblical canon helps form the community which accepts it, and the community accepting it helps confirm that text's canonicity. Moreover, the explanation of Conservative Jewish biblical interpretation goes a step further. It is not merely the acceptance of a canon that determines the communal nature of its faithful, but the *manner in which* a community interprets its canonical writings—that is, the assumptions, techniques, and goals of its interpretation—differentiates that community (or subcommunity) from other communities (or subcommunities) interpreting even the same canonical document. Ismar Schorsch, a recent Chancellor of JTS asserted, "We are Conservative, rather than Orthodox, because our historical knowledge teaches us that Jews in every generation have interpreted, modified and applied God's Torah in an effort to enhance Jewish life. . . . We are Conservative because we regard the Torah *she 'b' al peh* [ongoing interpretation that was originally 'oral,' e.g., the Talmud, in contrast to the 'written' Torah] as evolutionary; and we are traditional because that is the language in which we communicate with God" (Schorsch 2004, p. 68; reprinted from *Women's League Outlook*, Winter, 1994).

Summary. Conservative Jewish biblical interpretation is a complex analysis of the *Tanakh*, the Hebrew Bible, using both *peshat* methods and *derash* commentaries (contextual study and non-contextual interpretations). It remains cognizant of the different assumptions, techniques, and goals of each method while seeking to derive meaning for a modern community of faith whose tradition and temperament claim to be based upon the Hebrew Bible as interpreted, "not just out of obligation, but out of love" (Eisen 2000, p. xv) over the generations. That task is seldom easy, revealing both interpretive art and science, but meeting the challenge is fundamental to the integrity of Conservative Judaism's institutions of higher education as they convey its complex message, in an intelligible way, to its congregations, schools, camps, study groups, and individual devotees. The tripartite exegetical form described here—using the methods of *peshat*, the employment of *derash*, and the particular study setting, whether communal or private—is what distinguishes Conservative Jewish biblical interpretation from other interpretive paradigms and, therefore, what differentiates Conservative Judaism from other religions and from other Jewish denominations. Perhaps unconsciously, the Conservative Movement's exegetical stance embodies the observation expressed in Ecclesiastes 4:12: "A three-ply cord is not quickly severed."

[*See also* Midrash; Orthodox Jewish Interpretation; Rabbinic Exegesis; Reconstructionist Interpretation; *and* Reform Jewish Interpretation.]

By way of thanks and acknowledgment, the general thesis described in this entry has benefited from the insights of virtually every full-time member of the

Bible faculties at all institutions of higher education of Conservative Judaism (The Jewish Theological Seminary, New York; American Jewish University, Los Angeles; Schechter Institutes/Machon Schechter, Jerusalem; and Seminario Rabínico Latinoamericano, Buenos Aries). Of course, only the author is responsible for the formulation expressed herein.

BIBLIOGRAPHY

Cohen, Martin, and Michael Katz, eds. *The Observant Life: The Wisdom of Conservative Judaism for Contemporary Jews.* New York: The Rabbinical Assembly, 2012.

Dorff, Elliot. *Conservative Judaism: Our Ancestors to Our Descendants.* New York: United Synagogue Youth, 1977.

Ehrlich, Arnold B. *Mikrâ Ki-pheschutô: The Bible According to its Literal Meaning,* 3 vols. New York: Ktav Publishing House, 1969 reprint [Berlin, 1899–1901]. Prolegomenon by Harry M. Orlinsky.

Eisen, Arnold M. *Taking Hold of Torah: Jewish Commitment and Community in America.* Bloomington: Indiana University Press, 2000.

Emet Ve-Emunah: Statement of Principles of Conservative Judaism. New York: Jewish Theological Seminary of America, The Rabbinical Assembly, United Synagogue of America, Women's League for Conservative Judaism, Federation of Jewish Men's Clubs, 1988.

Fox, Everett. *The Five Books of Moses.* The Schocken Bible 1. New York: Schocken, 1995.

Garfinkel, Stephen. "Applied *Peshat*: Historical-Critical Method and Religious Meaning." *Journal of the Ancient Near Eastern Society* 22 (1993): 19–28.

Garfinkel, Stephen. "Clearing *Peshat* and *Derash.*" In *Hebrew Bible/Old Testament: The History of Its Interpretation,* edited by Magne Sæbø, vol. I, part 2, 129–134. Gőttingen: Vandenhoeck & Ruprecht, 2000.

Gillman, Neil. *Conservative Judaism: The New Century.* New York: Behrman House, 1993.

Ginsberg, H. L. "The Northwest Semitic Languages." In *The World History of the Jewish People.* Vol. 2. Edited by Benjamin Mazar, 102–124. New Brunswick, N. J.: Rutgers University Press, 1970.

Greenberg, Moshe. "The Use of the Ancient Versions for Interpreting the Hebrew Text: A Sampling from Ezekiel ii 1—iii 11." *Vetus Testamentum Supplements* 29, Congress Volume. (1977): 131–148.

Greenstein, Edward L. "Medieval Bible Commentaries." In *Back to the Sources: Reading the Classic Jewish Texts,* edited by Barry W. Holtz, 213–259. New York: Summit, 1984.

Holtz, Barry W. *Textual Knowledge: Teaching the Bible in Theory and in Practice.* New York: Jewish Theological Seminary, 2003.

Lieber, David, ed., *Etz Hayim: Torah and Commentary.* New York: The Rabbinical Assembly; The United Synagogue of Conservative Judaism, 2001. (See various articles at the end of the volume, including "Biblical Archaeology"; "Ancient Near Eastern Mythology"; articles about Revelation; and articles about Methods of Bible Study.)

Luzzatto, Samuel David. *Commentary on the Book of Isaiah.* Tel Aviv: Devir, 1970 reprint [Padua, Italy, 1855].

Machinist, Peter. "The Question of Distinctiveness in Ancient Israel." In *Essential Papers on Israel and the Ancient Near East,* edited by Frederick E. Greenspahn, 420–442. New York: New York University Press, 1991.

Rendsburg, Gary A. "Semitic Languages (with Special Reference to the Levant)." In *Near Eastern Archaeology: A Reader,* edited by Suzanne Richard, 71–73. Winona Lake, Ind.: Eisenbrauns, 2003.

Sanders, James A. *Canon and Community: A Guide to Canonical Criticism.* Philadelphia: Fortress, 1984.

Schechter, Solomon. *Seminary Addresses and Other Papers.* Cincinnati: Ark, 1915.

Schechter, Solomon. *Studies in Judaism.* New York: Macmillan, 1896. [Reprinted as *Studies in Judaism: First Series.* Philadelphia: Jewish Publication Society, 1945.]

Schorsch, Ismar. *Polarities in Balance.* New York: The Jewish Theological Seminary, 2004.

Wertheimer, Jack. *Tradition Renewed: A History of the Jewish Theological Seminary.* 2 vols. New York: Jewish Theological Seminary, 1997.

Stephen Garfinkel

CROSS-CULTURAL EXEGESIS

Cross-cultural exegesis refers to biblical analysis that intentionally draws from the cultural background and experiences of the scholar him/herself in order to suggest analogies to historical phenomena in biblical history, propose alternative views on the context of a biblical passage, or otherwise nuance an interpretation of a text and/or artifact.

The Contours of "Cross-Cultural Exegesis." There is some debate about differentiating between cultural perspectives that may be considered relevant for historical or textual analysis itself (i.e., what the text is understood to be referring to historically: "what it meant then"), or cultural perspectives that influence the assessment of the wider significance of a given text or historical event (what the possible interpretations or significances of the text may be: "what it means now"). There are important methodological differences between those two endeavors, but many scholars working in cross-cultural exegesis often raise questions about whether the classic difference between the historical-critical and the theological significance can really be so cleanly separated. Furthermore, it is also true that cross-cultural exegesis in many cultural/national traditions is not easily separated into the discrete fields of theology and biblical studies, which is a long established European distinction in theological studies departments generally. Finally, particularly in the twentieth and twenty-first centuries, many "cultural" traditions have found it difficult if not impossible to consider "cultural" apart from political contexts, and thus in the twenty-first century, "cross-cultural" exegesis is often present in the same studies with conscious applications of postcolonial categories of analysis. One of the most influential early collections of essays, for example, *Voices from the Margin*, continued to mix approaches in its various updated editions (Sugirtharajah 1995, 2006).

The most common practice for cross-cultural exegesis, however, has been to draw on one's own tradition and/or experiences in reference to a proposed biblical analysis. However, particular scholars may also draw on information from other cultural traditions (anthropological studies, cultural studies, or the work of biblical scholars in other traditions/cultures). In addition, there is a clear tendency to cross traditional disciplinary boundaries *within* their own defined cultural tradition. For example, an African American biblical scholar may draw from significant work by African American historians or novelists, but also historical sources such as slave narratives, lyrics of spirituals or blues, or texts of sermons, because the other approach (i.e., drawing on more than one tradition or culture) is typically not exclusive of economic, social, or political perspectives that are also cited for suggestive perspectives in dealing with particular biblical texts.

In addition, "cross-cultural exegesis" is virtually synonymous with such terms as "cultural interpretation" (Blount 1995); "cultural exegesis" (Smith-Christopher 1995), and arguably quite similar to perspectives such as: "global" commentaries (Patte 2004); "Intercultural reading" (de Wit 2004); some aspects of "Readings from a Social Location" (Segovia and Tolbert 1995); and "heritagist readings" (Sugirtharajah 2002); as well as certain aspects of "liberationist" readings where there is a more consciously cultural rather than economic/Marxist emphasis (Mesters 1989; Romero 1992) or some entries featured in "*The People's Companion to the Bible*" (DeYoung et. al. 2010). Having said this, however, "cross-cultural" perspectives rarely are the exclusive style of arguments, comparative examples, or analogies that biblical scholars draw upon in constructing their culturally informed analysis of texts. As such, cross-cultural exegesis is rarely an exclusive methodological approach in any given study, especially in twenty-first century published work.

As with many (if not most) "methods" or "approaches" to biblical analysis developed in the twentieth century, there are clear lines of influence on biblical scholarship that can be traced back to other disciplines (postmodernist literary analysis, Marxist economic analysis, psychotherapeutic interpretations, etc.). It is notable, however, in the case of cross-cultural analysis of the Bible, that there is no single or even predominant disciplinary influence from outside theological studies that led directly to cross-cultural approaches to biblical analysis in the way that, for example "reader response" approaches to literary work led directly to a "reader response" approach to biblical analysis.

Finally, an emerging "school" largely found in recent studies of mission history and historical cases of conversion is also identifying ways in which converted peoples assert their own interpretations and readings of the Bible in direct contrast (and often opposition) to the readings/meanings that European missionaries attempted to impose upon them. Where these cases can document particular readings of scripture, they are beginning to be highlighted as important examples of cross-cultural exegesis worthy of renewed modern attention (McNally 2000).

What Isn't a Cultural Reading? One celebrated way to define an intellectual "school" that is typically considered subsidiary to a larger defined discipline (e.g., "surrealist" art, "liberationist" theology, "cladist" approaches to zoological taxonomy, and therefore also *cross-cultural* biblical analysis) would be to simply provide an annotated bibliography of significant works that have collectively contributed to the suggested "school," "movement," or "category." Such an approach presumes that reading a significant number of these suggested works allows one to become more aware of the parameters of the topic (and perhaps also become more aware of the difficulties of being too narrow in defining terms!). In the case of cross-cultural analysis of scripture, however, there is arguably an inherent danger with this kind of approach—namely that the determination of items that are considered appropriate to the list often already hides dubious presumptions.

It is important that a variety of examples are highlighted, even if it is impossible to be comprehensive in such an introductory overview. However, at the outset, it is critical to highlight the observation that *all* exegesis of the Bible is "cultural" (Donaldson 1998). Virtually all scholars whose work can be called "cross-cultural exegesis" insist that there can be no such thing as "noncultural" (and thus a purely "objective") approaches to the interpretation of ancient texts any more than there is purely objective analysis of artifacts, whether ancient or modern. There ought to be little tolerance, therefore, with any temptation to label "cross-cultural" approaches to the Bible as virtually synonymous with "non-European" (or worse: "other than mainline") approaches. Indeed, recent studies of European bias in the analysis of ancient texts (Holloway 2002), archaeological analysis (Dietler 2005), and cultural studies (Said 1979) clearly point to European (and European Diaspora) biblical studies as themselves also examples of analysis in a "cultural context" that is typically unexamined because of the false claims of noncultural "objectivity."

Locating Cross-Cultural Exegesis in Hermeneutical Methodology. An important conceptual foundation for cross-cultural exegesis of the Bible is to establish some of the epistemological presumptions of this method. Here we return to the problem of separating questions about analyzing the historical texts (what the text actually said at the stages of writing and final editing) and contemporary assessments (how people read and understood the finished text over time). While most scholars would agree that cultural perspectives are obviously relevant to the second question (assessment, evaluation, theological development, etc.)—is it possible that cultural perspectives can actually also enhance the understanding and historical-critical analysis of a text even on the level of grammatical, philological, and lexical issues? There are a variety of arguments that would strongly suggest an affirmative answer to this provocative question—provocative because it is at this level of textual analysis that one normally encounters the most vehement insistence that such detailed historical-critical work can be, and indeed must be, "objective" based on a scientific and rational model. The analogy with scientific method, however, encounters interesting difficulties at this point, because subjective perspectives are now widely acknowledged even in this intellectual paragon of modernist objectivity (so Kuhn 1962; Feyerabend 1975). Taking this more open approach to models of scientific investigation (open, that is, to what was previously thought to be "inappropriately subjective" elements in determining scientific method or hypotheses for investigation) would be to suggest that opening up the analysis of ancient texts to cross-cultural perspectives is not only an issue of moral virtue (e.g., a more virtuous practice, a foundation that may not be universally convincing) but is rather to suggest alternative approaches that may or may not yield significant, verifiable results or probabilities in historical-critical analysis. New forays (however they may be inspired by a cultural "cue" or insights) can thus redefine a new "obvious," a more nuanced sense of "normal," or to put it bluntly, a "redefined objectivity." In short, "cross-cultural" exegesis could well be defined as a presumed baseline for all contemporary biblical studies.

Perhaps the most straightforward way to further establish the rationality of this argument in a morally neutral way (and thus further establish the intellectual need for encouraging cross-cultural analysis) is to consider important work in the psychology of cross-cultural perception (which is, itself, not a recent study). In sum, scholars in this field have clearly established that there are genuinely significant differences across cultures in the perception of phenomena, most particularly visual phenomena (Deregowski 1980; McPherson 1965; Lee 1950), but also cross-cultural differences in the perception of photographs (Wendl 1996) and music (Balkwill and Thompson 1999). Lee, in her work with what she called Native American cultural "codes" (e.g., modes of perception and appropriation) already in the mid-twentieth century provocatively concluded that interacting with culturally different perspectives of the same phenomenon (as in a kind of cross-culturally "synoptic" view) may actually "lead us to aspects of reality from which our own . . . [cultural] . . . code excludes us" (Lee 1950).

A second approach, less interested in a rational/empirically analogous defense, would be to simply affirm the methodological validity of "interested" perspectives. Citing the earliest work by feminist scholars of the Bible, for example, Fiorenza points out that "interested" perspectives are methods of study that are willing to be open about the academic questions they bring to the study of texts and history (Fiorenza 2009). These questions are explicitly generated by the "interests" or commitments of the scholars themselves, (e.g., female academics who investigate the role of women in novels, plays, or biblical texts). Therefore, other "interests" could follow, such as the role of minorities, the presence and role of class conflict in ancient texts, or the evidence for phenomena that today are identified under quite different terms, (e.g., spirit possession vs. contemporary psychological analysis vs. post-traumatic stress disorder, etc). Cross-cultural analysis, then, would simply be grouped with "interested" approaches to biblical analysis.

Examples of Cross-Cultural Exegesis. To illustrate how this may work, one may cite the provocative suggestions of C. Gilbert Romero. In his 1992 essay, "Tradition and Symbol as Biblical Keys for a U. S. Hispanic Theology," Romero proposed that contemporary Mexican-American cultural practices (e.g., home altars; only one of his examples) may provide significant clues to fully understanding the ritual experience of ancient Israel as it is described in the biblical text in a way that those from less ritualized cultural experiences could easily miss. It was thus not the contemporary significance of biblical texts that Romero was exclusively interested in—but also the historical comprehension of the Israelite traditions themselves.

Similarly, Hisao Kayama proposed that Japanese cultural perspectives in relation to the status of the Burakumin minority in Japan may enhance an understanding of the relation between ancient Hebrew categories of clean and unclean as they may have applied in the Cornelius Story of Acts 10 (Kayama 1995). Note that there is a methodological similarity here with an analysis of a biblical text that applies, for example, Freudian categories of analysis to clarifying the text of Ezekiel (e.g., Halperin 1993), or Marxist economic analysis for possibly achieving a clearer understanding of ancient peasant economies of Iron Age Israel as represented in the Hebrew texts (Premnath 2003).

Finally, the work of David Sanchez (2008) illustrates what he calls a "dialogue" with the text of Revelation. By surveying the ubiquity and meaning of the image of the Virgin of Guadalupe in the Mexican-American context of Los Angeles, he then offers new insights into the potential Roman period significance of the "Virgin versus the Dragon" themes in the book of Revelation.

What differentiates these arguments from the more widely practiced "contextual based reading of texts" approach is that the emphasis of the former is on making contributions *to a historical-critical goal of clarifying the actual text,* rather than a focus on assessing various interpretations, applications, or theological development performed on the *basis of* the biblical texts. "Cross-cultural exegesis" works on both questions, and even though some biblical scholars seriously question the possibility of separating these kinds of studies, there is a conceptual difference that is important to maintain. In sum, virtually every historical and even (at times) lexical analysis progresses by analogy, hypothesis, and evaluation of data. The promise of cross-cultural exegesis is that it enriches the repertoire of analogous possibilities, grammatical or societal possibilities, and even the assessment of what can, and should, be considered as "data."

Clearly, however, there are also many important examples of the other primary approach identified here—namely a culturally based "appreciation" or commentary on the significance of a given text, apart from critical reconstructions of the text (and its historical context). To better engage these aspects of cross-cultural exegesis, however, it is important to turn to a cursory survey in order to illustrate something of the depth, and range, of studies that contribute to the notable accomplishments of this approach to biblical analysis. The summaries provided here are not intended to be comprehensive in any sense, but simply to point readers in general directions so that they can follow up on particular writers, cultural traditions, or particular studies. Finally, however, these summaries intend to clearly communicate that cross-cultural exegesis is a global undertaking, promising a new level of dialogue across virtually all contemporary social and cultural contexts.

Africa. Work by the late Ferdinand Deist (1994) and modern work by Gerald West (e.g., 2007) illustrates an interesting awareness of the South African context for both European and African populations. A historically important contribution was Mosala's monograph of 1989, and but important work also continues in the Black South African contexts with the continued work of Masenya (1995, 1997, 1998). African scholars, along with African American and other "Diaspora" African scholars contributed to the important "Africana Bible" project (Page et al. 2009), and in this regard, the more evangelical-based work, the *Africa Bible Commentary* (Tokunboh 2010) is also significant for wide variety of continental African participation. Aliou Niang (2009), a Senegalese-American scholar teaching in the United States, produced a detailed monograph examining Galatians in its historical critical context, but consciously drawing on his own (Senegalese) African cultural context to inform his New Testament analysis. Interesting work is also being done drawing on older African Christian traditions, such as those of Ethiopia, in the context of thinking about African culturally based contemporary readings (Cowley 1989). The amount of work coming from Nigeria is particularly noteworthy (Dada 2010) and Nigerian scholars continue to develop themes of comparing African tribal/social/cultural practices and traditions with biblical examples that are illuminated by the comparison (e.g., chieftaincy; see Asaju 2005).

Australia. The work of Norman Habel (1993) arguably laid the groundwork in Australia for reading biblical texts from a uniquely Australian perspective, although he has since moved toward environmental issues (which represent a major concern for the churches in Australia and New Zealand). Other Euro-Australian scholars have taken steps toward thinking about doing biblical analysis in the context of a frightening history of the abuse of the indigenous people of Australia. Again, many of these studies cross the disciplinary lines that often separate theology and biblical studies. The work of Brett (2009), Boer (2008), and Budden (2009) have pointed in notable directions. There are significant beginnings of Aboriginal Christian engagement with academic biblical studies in the works of Pattel-Gray (1996), and Djiniyini Gondarra (1996). Some of the newsletters of the Aboriginal Australian training school for ministry, Nungalinya College in Darwin, also include thoughtful considerations of Aboriginal appropriation of scripture, and there is growing interest in examining Aboriginal song traditions, including the lyrics of Aboriginal Christian songs (similar to interest in African American "spirituals" in the American experience) for sources of Aboriginal reflection on scripture (Magowan 2007).

Canada. The work of Canadian scholars unfortunately too often falls under the shadow of American scholarship, but there are notable developments among Canadian biblical scholars, many of whom work in the United States as well as in Canadian universities. Some Canadian biblical scholars are thinking seriously about the unique contextual challenges and cultural perspectives in the particularities of the Canadian context. Barbara Lai's essay, "Engaging Daniel Ethno-Culturally: A Chinese-Canadian Reading," for example, pursues questions of immigrant communities' interaction with scripture in the Canadian context. Her essay is scheduled to appear in an important new book with chapters featuring Korean, Latino, Indian, First Nation, Chinese, Jamaican, and Ghanaian perspectives rooted in the Canadian experience (*Reading in Between: Biblical Interpretation in Canada*, 2012). Medina has engaged in a critical review of *mestizaje* theological proposals, which includes serious thinking about the biblical analysis involved in that movement (Medina 2009). Important "First Nation" reflections are part of innovative programs such as the indigenous emphasis at Vancouver School of Theology, but publications are not yet available.

India. For an introduction to biblical studies in India, note Premnath's important overview (Premnath 2006). There are significant biblical studies journals in India, including two from Catholic seminaries (*Bible Bhashyam*; see, e.g., Soares-Prabhu 1978; and *Jeevadhara*; see, e.g., Kuzhuvelil 1982) and biblical essays often appear in the *Indian Journal of Theology*. ISPCK (New Delhi) has been a helpful publisher of Indian theology, especially of materials related to Christian theology and the Dalits (low-caste and tribal groups) in India. A significant amount of Indian cross-cultural analysis has tended to deal with themes suggested from the struggles of low-caste and tribal peoples in India (for studies of the legacy of the significant rate of conversion to Christianity that occurred among these subordinated peoples in the Indian context, see Rayan 1978; Clarke 2002). The Centre for Dalit/Subaltern Studies has been working on a commentary series reflecting these significant social issues in the Indian context (ten volumes of New Testament studies were published from 2006 through 2009, and five of an anticipated twenty volumes of Old Testament commentaries appeared in 2011). Massey, one of the general editors, states that these commentaries are "not reader-response . . . but a challenge-response to the caste context of rejection, subjugation and violence" (Massey 2010).

Earlier cross-cultural experiments with Indian textual traditions and exegetical methods applied to biblical studies were suggestive (note attempts to use "Dhvani" methods derived from the analysis of Sanskrit poetics; see Vellanickal 1995, and Soares-Prabhu 1978). Soares-Prabhu was particularly important among Indian New Testament scholars interested in cross-cultural readings, and he was especially interested in developing New Testament themes (1980a, 1980b), and more recently, Monica Melanchthon is among the current generation of Indian scholars consciously working on cross-cultural approaches to Old Testament analysis while also creatively incorporating work in feminist analysis (2007, 2010a, 2010b).

New Zealand. Similar to the Australian context, New Zealand has begun to emerge as a center for South Pacific thinking on biblical analysis. While traditional academic biblical studies have been a mainstay of institutions such as Victoria (Wellington) and Otago Universities, and more recently also University of Auckland, there are significant moves in the direction of cultural interests in biblical analysis.

The publication, "Out of Place: Doing Theology on the Crosscultural Brink" represents an important step toward a maturing of Oceania perspectives in biblical analysis. Notable in this regard is the work of Dr. Jione Havea (Havea is Tongan, currently teaching in Australia; see Havea, (2004, 2011) and Nasili Vaka'uta (Vaka'uta 2011), who both approach Old Testament themes from a consciously South Pacific perspective and analytical framework. Vaka'uta's work, for example, is an important rereading of the mixed marriage crisis in Ezra 9—10 from the perspective of South Pacific cultural and familial structures (Vaka'uta is also Tongan, based at the University of Auckland, New Zealand). The establishment of the Oceania Biblical Scholars Association is promising and publication efforts are under way. The recent presentation at the Annual Meetings of the Society of Biblical Literature (2011, San Francisco) by Rev. Donald Tamihere, which featured the "reading" of an actual Maori carved rendering of Micah 4:1–5, points toward important developments in thinking about Maori approaches to biblical analysis based in Gisborne, New Zealand.

China. Any overview of contemporary Chinese work on the Bible (as opposed to "Chinese American" or "Asian American") from a specifically national Chinese perspective is advanced by Yieh's important survey (2006). Liang Gong edits the only biblical studies journal in China, *Biblical Literature Studies*, and is chair of the only program in China allowed to use the term "biblical" (the Biblical Literature Studies program) at Henan University. In Hong Kong, however, Archie C. C. Lee, has been quite active at the Chinese University of Hong Kong for many years and publishes in cross-cultural approaches to Old Testament texts—especially comparative analysis that he has called "cross textual analysis" (Lee 1994, 1999).

Debates in the United States. Although the United States shares its predominant multicultural reality with other historically immigrant/forced migration countries such as Canada, Australia, and New Zealand, it is arguably the case that discussions in biblical studies—fostered especially by a very active American disciplinary academic organization, the Society of Biblical Literature—have been especially voluminous in the United States, and particularly among Hispanic/Latino/a scholars, African American scholars, and Asian American scholars. There are notable beginnings among Native Americans, but this still needs to be nurtured within the discipline at this writing, particularly given the critically difficult circumstances still faced by the Native American population as a whole, including higher education opportunities (see Charleston 1996).

Hispanic/Latino/a Cultures. In a 2011 article in Princeton's journal, *Theology Today*, Aguiles Ernesto Martinez writes that although Hispanic/Latino/a theology has "reached maturity. . . . Sadly, we cannot make the same enthusiastic claim about the work of our 'biblistas' in helping us articulate our Latino/a biblical interpretation." (Martinez 2011, p. 134). To be self-critical is usually a good trait for scholars, but in this case, the sweeping generalization may overly detract from important work that has certainly taken place in the Hispanic/Latino/a contexts at the time of this writing. Here, attention can be drawn to three important contributors to the maturing of Hispanic/Latino/a biblical analysis in the US context (but including a trans-national perspective from those whose identification is more than one geographical territory).

As a starting point, González's *Santa Biblia* (1996) set out to make some preliminary discussions for reading the Bible "Through Hispanic Eyes." After firmly establishing a central plank of the "cross-cultural exegesis" platform, namely the inescapable reality of a reader's context and perspective, González named his brief chapters for themes that he thought contributed to a Hispanic perspective and context for interpreting scripture: marginality, poverty, *mestizaje* and *mulatez* (the "mixed" racial and cultural identities of many Hispanic national contexts), exiles and aliens, and solidarity.

One of the most voluminous and articulate contributions has been made by the many writings of Cuban American New Testament scholar Fernando Segovia. To date, his fullest exposition of his methodological suggestions for biblical analysis is his work, *Decolonizing Biblical Studies* (2000) with the interesting subtitle, *A View from the Margins.* Segovia, however, ranges far wider than a "cross-cultural" approach, and has moved toward a "diasporic" perspective more in dialogue with post-colonial criticism of the Bible, although always rooted in his perspectives as a Cuban American biblical scholar.

Along these lines, it is significant to take note of the work of Jean-Pierre Ruiz. Ruiz's 2011 work, *Readings from the Edges: The Bible and People on the Move* is notable for a number of reasons. First, in the acknowledgments, one is struck by the number of formal organizations of Hispanic/Latino/a scholars that Ruiz names, acknowledges, and thanks. Clearly, there has been an impressive growth of formal academic associations. Secondly, however, Ruiz's work, somewhat similar to González's earlier work, also focusses on particular contexts and settings for reading the text in a Hispanic/Latino/a perspective—although some important new themes are identified by Ruiz, clearly having become important in the years subsequent to González's listing of contexts. Ruiz includes immigration reform and borders as important themes, but also urbanization, exile, and relations with other Hispanic countries and populations. Further, Ruiz's reading is a more sophisticated analysis than González's intentionally popular approach, and is in dialogue with a wide range of critical literature with which he is in dialogue.

Finally, one must acknowledge the critical work of Miguel De La Torre, who has published monographs and commentaries on Old Testament themes (and was not even mentioned by Martinez in his critical review) as well as the groundbreaking work of Gregory Lee Cuellar, whose work comparing passages of Isaiah to Mexican *Corridos* lyrics represents striking examples of culturally grounded analysis of scripture (Cuellar 2008).

De La Torre, however, has taken a somewhat pessimistic attitude as to whether cross-cultural analysis of the text will impact the general discipline. De La Torre is clear—Euro-Americans are largely not trusted for a credible analysis, because "Euroamerican Christians, either from the fundamentalist right or the far liberal left, probably have more in common with each other and understand each other better than they do Christians on the other side of the racial and ethnic divide" (De La Torre 2007, p. 125).

African American and "African Diaspora" Cultures. In the African American tradition, there is a tremendously rich literature. As in the cases of Latino/a scholarship and Asian American scholarship, the interaction between those who do "theology" and those who focus on "scripture" is often very close. "African American History" and "Cultural Studies" is also influential. Scholars such as Vincent Wimbush, Charles Copher, and Cain Hope Felder have noted the long-term engagement of African Americans with the Bible in North America. Wimbush helpfully outlined roughly identifiable "stages" of African American engagement with scripture, beginning with a kind of mystification of the book that slave holders held in such esteem in seventeenth and eighteenth century experiences, and moving through periods of increasing familiarity, toward stronger emphases on exodus and exile (evident in the lyrics of spirituals and content of sermons; see Raboteau [2004]; and Brooks 2003), toward a modern situation of some conflict between fundamentalist appropriation of conservative Protestant attitudes toward the Bible that discourages historical critical study, to the beginnings of an African American critical engagement that grew into a significant literature by the beginning of the twenty-first century.

As with other cultural groups, a strong emphasis has emerged on African Americans reading scripture from a context of oppression and marginalization in the North American contexts. However, there have been some notable works that significantly contributed to biblical scholarship. Among many, two are especially important. Renita Weems's work, *Battered Love* (1995), represented a feminist/womanist perspective that raised serious questions about the violence toward women that is evident in imagery used especially by the prophets Hosea and Ezekiel (a concern shared by other scholars such as Randall Bailey). Secondly, the work of African American scholars largely within the Society of Biblical Literature resulted in the publication of *Stony the Road We Trod* (1991), a summary and "state of the art" compendium of essays by significant scholars in the field, past and present.

Asian American Cultures. While there have been important works from Asian American biblical scholars in the late twentieth century that consciously draw on Asian themes and identity (Yeo 1997, 1998; Wan 1995), a significant milestone was the publication in 2006 of the collected volume *Ways of Being, Ways of Reading* (2006, comparable in many ways to the impact of *Stony the Road we Trod* in the African American scholarly context), which included retrospective and survey essays, personal reflections on academic work (Yee 2006; Lee 2006; Yamada 2006; cf. Liew 2008), as well as examples of contemporary work of some of the most prominent American scholars working in cross-cultural approaches. In some cases, scholars initially drawing on reflections of personal or national experience (reflections on the Korean context, so Ahn 2006, Kim 2006) then led to major monographs in historical-critical analysis that develop these insights in great detail (thus Ahn 2010; Kim 2005). Further development of methodology and hermeneutical theory for Asian American biblical analysis is evident in Tat-Siong Benny Liew's detailed monograph outlining implications for New Testament work (Liew 2008), which suggests that future Asian American analysis will need to be in deeper dialogue with other emerging trends in biblical analysis such as post-colonialism.

Finally, in terms of the American context, it is notable that Segovia, Liew, and Bailey have initiated a dialogue between these three representatives of Latino/a American, Asian-American, and African American scholarship in hopes of finding common ground in "minority" analysis of the Bible (Bailey, Liew, and Segovia 2009).

Europe. At an early gathering to explore the meaning of "Cultural Exegesis" held at Loyola Marymount University in Los Angeles (Smith-Christopher 1995), Finnish scholar Roger Syren reflected on the cultural context of Scandinavian biblical analysis, one of the most striking examples of profound (and historically productive) cultural influences on biblical analysis (Syren 1995), and John Barton explored how a cultural approach to the work of Julius Wellhausen might also be fruitful (Barton, 1995, cf. Pasto, 1998). The continued work of John Rogerson (1984, 2009), particularly on the history of English and German biblical scholarship, provides a foundation for reflecting on the cultural contexts for the rise of the historical-critical method itself. Finally, Anthony Reddie (2006, 2008) writes from a consciously African-British (Caribbean) identity, illustrating a move toward reflections of minorities within the European cultural contexts as well.

Caribbean Contexts. With the move in African American cultural studies more generally toward concepts of the "African Diaspora," there is thus a widening dialogue that includes biblical analysis from North-American, but also Afro-Hispanic and Afro-Caribbean perspectives on Scripture (Jennings, 2007; Davidson 2011).

South America. South American biblical analysis from a cultural perspective is almost entirely a joint product with the prodigious production of writings associated with liberation theology. Beginning with the classic of liberation theology, Gustavo Gutierrez's 1974 work *A Theology of Liberation*, biblical analysis—especially of the exodus narrative—was arguably much more central to this theological school than biblical studies has been in other similarly influential theological schools of thought. Not surprisingly, then, when the "cultural move" seemed to indicate a unique direction in South American biblical analysis, it was led by many scholars who also had roots in liberationist concerns. The late Argentinian Old Testament scholar J. Severino Croatto also worked on the "Popular Reading" of the Bible in addition to his own academic work (1981), and another early work that focused specifically on "peasant readings" of the Bible was Carlos Mesters *Defenseless Flower* (1989). Pablo Richard's work on Revelation (2009) also crosses between a politically concerned "liberationist reading" and "cross-cultural exegesis," and, indeed, the South American context is perhaps one of the most difficult geographical locations for attempting a clear differentiation between liberationist and cultural approaches to the text. Ruiz now refers to the wider "cross-border" work being done in Latin American countries, and among Latin American scholars in the United States. The dialogue across the border is especially noteworthy in the biblical work of Mexican-born liberation theologian Elsa Tamez (2002, 2006).

Readings outside Christianity. What should be called "cross-cultural" readings of the Bible are not limited to Christian scholars, of course. Although usually not identified as "cultural," some Jewish approaches to reading scripture arguably qualify as such, applying historical approaches identified, for example, from Rabbinic and later Jewish traditions of textual analysis. Certainly Daniel Boyarin's critique of Paul (1997) is a Jewish cultural perspective on Paul (but including historical analysis) and reflects contemporary as well as historical cultural concerns. Reynolds's analysis of the Quʿran (2010) in the light of Jewish and Christian scriptures is mainly historical, but with Khalidi's gathering of Islamic sayings of Jesus (2003; Khalidi often points out New Testament parallels) presents the beginnings of Islamic analysis of biblical literature and traditions that should also be noted.

[*See also* Asian American Biblical Interpretation; Central and South American Interpretation; Chinese Interpretation; Class Criticism; Cuban Interpretation in the Cuban Diaspora; Cultural Studies; Feminist Biblical Interpretation; Ideological Criticism; Japanese Interpretation; Korean Interpretation; Latina/o Interpretation; Postcolonial Biblical Interpretation; Race, Ethnicity, and Biblical Criticism; *and* Reader-Response Criticism.]

BIBLIOGRAPHY

Agosto, Efrain. "Social Analysis of the New Testament and Hispanic Theology: A Case Study." *Journal of Hispanic/Latino Theology* 5, no. 4 (1998): 6–29.

Ahn, John. *Exile as Forced Migrations: A Sociological, Literary, and Theological Approach on the Displacement and Resettlement of the Southern Kingdom of Judah.* New York: deGruyter, 2010.

Ahn, John. "A Light to the Nations: The Sociological Approach in Korean American Interpretation." In *Ways of Being, Ways of Reading,* edited by J. Kuan and M. Foskett, 112–122. St. Louis, Mo.: Chalice, 2006.

Asaju, Dapo. "Africentric Biblical Hermeneutics Enroute: A Contextual Study of Chieftaincy Institution in Post-colonial Nigeria," *Asia Journal of Theology* (2005): 143–165.

Bailey, Randall, T. S. Benny Liew, and F. F. Segovia, eds. *They Were All Together in One Place?: Toward Minority Biblical Criticism.* Semeia Studies 57. Atlanta: Society of Biblical Literature, 2009.

Balkwill, Laura Lee, and William Forde Thompson. "A Cross-Cultural Investigation of the Perception of Emotion in Music." *Music Perception,* 17 (1999): 43–64.

Barton, John. "Wellhausen's Prolegomena to the History of Israel: Influences and Effects." In *Text and Experience: Towards a Cultural Exegesis of the Bible,* edited by Daniel Smith-Christopher, 316–329. Sheffield, UK: Sheffield Academic, 1995.

Blount, Brian K. *Can I Get a Witness? Reading Revelation through African American Culture.* Louisville, Ky.: Westminster John Knox, 2005.

Blount, Brian K. *Cultural Interpretation: Reorienting New Testament Criticism.* Minneapolis: Fortress, 1995.

Boer, Roland. *Last Stop before Antarctica: The Bible and Postcolonialism in Australia.* Atlanta: Society of Biblical Literature, 2008.

Boyarin, Daniel. *A Radical Jew: Paul and the Politics of Identity.* Berkeley: University of California Press, 1997.

Brett, Mark. *Decolonizing God: The Bible in the Tides of Empire.* Sheffield, UK: Sheffield Phoenix, 2009.

Brooks, Joanna. *American Lazarus: Religion and the Rise of African-American and Native American Literatures.* New York: Oxford University Press, 2003.

Brown, Michael J. *Blackening the Bible: The Aims of African-American Biblical Scholarship.* Harrisburg, Pa.: Trinity Press International, 2004.

Budden, Chris. *Following Jesus in Invaded Space: Doing Theology on Aboriginal Land.* Princeton Theological Monograph Series. Eugene, Ore.: Pickwick, 2009.

Charleston, Steve. "The Old Testament of Native America." In *Native and Christian,* edited by James Treat, 68–81. New York: Routledge, 1996.

Cheon, Samuel. "Biblical Interpretation in Korea: History and Issues." In *Ways of Being, Ways of Reading,* edited by J. Kuan and M. Foskett, 31–44. St. Louis, Mo.: Chalice, 2006.

Clarke, Sathianathan. "Viewing the Bible through the Eyes and Ears of Subalterns in India." *Biblical Interpretation* 10, no. 3 (2002): 245–266.

Cowley, Roger. *Ethiopian Biblical Interpretation: A Study in Exegetical Tradition and Hermeneutics* (University of Cambridge Oriental Publications) Cambridge, UK: Cambridge University Press, 1989.

Croatto, Severino J. *Exodus: A Hermeneutics of Freedom.* Translated by Salvator Attanasio. Maryknoll, N.Y.: Orbis, 1981.

Cuellar, Gregory L. *Voices of Marginality: Exile and Return in Second Isaiah 40–55 and the Mexican Immigrant Experience.* New York: Peter Lang, 2008.

Dada, Adekunle. "Repositioning Contextual Biblical Hermeneutics in Africa: Towards Holistic Empowerment." *Black Theology: An International Journal,* 8 (2010): 160–174.

Davidson, Steed. *Empire and Exile: Postcolonial Readings of the Book of Jeremiah.* Library Hebrew Bible/Old Testament Studies. New York: T.&T. Clark, 2011.

Deist, Ferdinand. "The Dangers of Deuteronomy: A Page from the Reception History of the Book." In *Studies in Deuteronomy: In Honour of C. J. LaBuschagne*, edited by, F. G. Martinez, A. Hilhorst, J. van Ruiten, and A. v.d. Woude. Leiden: Brill, 1994.

De La Torre, Miguel. *Liberating Jonah: Forming an Ethic of Reconciliation.* Maryknoll, N.Y.: Orbis, 2007.

De La Torre, Miguel. *Reading the Bible from the Margins.* Maryknoll, N.Y.: Orbis, 2002.

Deregowski, J. B. *Illusions, Patterns, and Pictures: A Cross-Cultural Perspective.* New York: Academic, 1980.

De Wit, Hans, Louis Jonker, Marleen Kool, and Daniel Schipani, eds., *Through the Eyes of Another: Intercultural Reading of the Bible.* Elkhart: Institute of Mennonite Studies, 2004.

DeYoung, C. P., et al. *The Peoples' Companion to the Bible.* Minneapolis: Fortress, 2010.

Dietler, Michael. "The Archaeology of Colonization and the Colonization of Archaeology: Theoretical Challenges from an Ancient Mediterranean Colonial Encounter." In *The Archaeology of Colonial Encounters: Comparative Perspectives*, edited by Gil Stein, 33–68. Santa Fe, N.M.: School of American Research Press, 2005.

Donaldson, Laura. "Are We All Multiculturalists Now? Biblical Reading as Cultural Contact." In *In Search of the Present: the Bible through Cultural Studies*, edited by S. Moore: 79–97. Atlanta: Society of Biblical Literature, 1998.

Felder, C. H., ed. *Stony The Road We Trod: African American Biblical Interpretation.* Minneapolis: Fortress, 1991.

Feyerabend, Paul. *Against Method*, 4th ed. New York: Verso, 2010.

Fiorenza, Elizabeth. *Democratizing Biblical Studies.* Louisville, Ky.: Westminster John Knox, 2009.

Foskett, Mary, Jeffrey Kah-Jin Kuan, and John Ahn, eds., *Ways of Being, Ways of Reading: Asian American Biblical Interpretation.* St. Louis, Mo.: Chalice, 2006.

Garcia-Treto, Francisco. "Reading the Hyphens: An Emerging Biblical Hermeneutics for Patino/Hispanic U.S. Protestants." In *Protestants/Protestantes: Hispanic Christianity with Mainline Traditions*, edited by D. Maldonado. Nashville, Tenn.: Abingdon, 1999.

Gondarra, Djiniyini, "Aboriginal Spirituality and the Gospel," in Pattel-Gray, *Aboriginal Spirituality.* 1996: 41–53.

González, Justo L. *Santa Biblia: The Bible through Hispanic Eyes.* Nashville, Tenn.: Abingdon, 1996.

Habel, Norman. *The Land is Mine: Six Biblical Land Ideologies.* Overtures to Biblical Theology. Minneapolis: Fortress, 1993.

Halperin, David. *Seeking Ezekiel: Text and Psychology.* University Park: Pennsylvania State University Press, 1993.

Havea, Jione. *Elusions of Control: Biblical Law on the Words of Women.* Society of Biblical Literature Semeia Studies 41. Atlanta: Society of Biblical Literature, 2004.

Havea, Jione. "Return, Medium of Endor." In *Out of Place: Doing Theology on the Cross-cultural Brink*, 255–256. Oakville, Conn.: Equinox, 2011.

Holloway, Steven W. *Assur is King! Assur is King!: Religion in the Exercise of Power in the Neo-Assyrian Empire* (Culture and History of the Ancient Near East, 10). Leiden: Brill, 2002.

Jennings, Stephen. "'Ordinary' Reading in 'Extraordinary' Times: A Jamaican Love Story." In *Reading Other-Wise*, edited by Gerald O. West, 29–48. Atlanta: Society of Bible Literature, 2007.

Kayama, Hisao, "The Cornelius Story in the Japanese Cultural Context." In *Text and Experience*, edited by Smith-Christopher, 180–194. Sheffield: Sheffield Academic Press, 1995.

Khalidi, Tarif. *The Muslim Jesus: Sayings and Stories in Islamic Literature.* Cambridge, Mass.: Harvard University Press, 2003.

Kim, Uriah. *Decolonizing Josiah.* Sheffield, UK: Sheffield Phoenix, 2005.

Kim, Uriah. "The Realpolitick of Liminality in Josiah's Kingdom and Asian America." In *Ways of Being, Ways of Reading*, edited by J. Kuan and M. Foskett, 84–98. St. Louis, Mo.: Chalice, 2006.

Kuhn, Thomas. *The Structure of Scientific Revolutions.* Chicago: University of Chicago Press, 1996.

Kuzhuvelil, Mathew V. "No Pooja but Prema, No Yajna but Iswara Jnana: An Indian Hermeneutics on the Book of Hosea." *Jeevadhara* 12 (1982): 105–110.

Lai, Barbara. "Engaging Daniel Ethno-Culturally: A Chinese-Canadian Reading." In *Reading in Between: Biblical Interpretation in Canada*, edited by Nestor Medina and Alison Singh. Biblical Interpretation Series. Leiden: Brill, 2012.

Lee, Archie C. C. "The Chinese creation myth of Nu Kua and the biblical narrative in Genesis 1–11." *Biblical Interpretation* 2, no. 3 (1994): 312–324.

Lee, Archie C. C. "Returning to China: Biblical Interpretation in Postcolonial Hong Kong." *Biblical Interpretation* 7, no. 2 (1999): 156–173.

Lee, Dorothy. "Lineal and Nonlineal Codifications of Reality." *Psychosomatic Medicine*, 12 (1950): 89–97.

Liew, Tat-Siong Benny. *What is Asian American Biblical Hermeneutics?: Reading the New Testament.* Honolulu: University of Hawai'i Press, 2008.

Magowan, Fiona. *Melodies of Mourning: Music & Emotion in Northern Australia.* Santa Fe, N.M.: School for Advance Research Press, 2007.

Martin, Joel, and M. Nicholas, eds. *Native Americans, Christianity, and the Reshaping of the American Religious Landscape.* Chapel Hill: University of North Carolina Press, 2010.

Martinez, Aquiles E. "U.S. Hispanic/Latino Biblical Interpretation: A Critique from Within." In *Theology Today*, 68, no. 2, 134–148, 2011.

Masenya, Madipoane. "The Bible and Women: Black Feminist Hermeneutics." *Scriptura* 54 (1995): 189–201.

Masenya, Madipoane. "A Bosadi (Womanhood) Reading of Genesis 16." *Old Testament Essays* 11, no. 2 (1998): 271–287.

Masenya, Madipoane. "'. . . but you shall let every girl live': Reading Exodus 1:1—2:10 the Bosadi (Womanhood) Way." *Old Testament Essays,* 15, no. 1 (2002): 99–112.

Masenya, Madipoane. "Proverbs 31:10–31 in a South African Context: A Reading for the Liberation of African (Northern Sotho) Women." *Semeia* 78 (1997): 55–68.

Masenya, Madipoane. "What Differences do African Contexts Make for English Bible Translations?" *Old Testament Essays* 14, no. 2 (2001): 281–296.

Massey, James, and T. K. John, eds. *One Volume Dalit Bible Commentary: New Testament.* New Delhi: Centre for Dalit/Subaltern Studies, 2010.

McNally, Michael. *Ojibwe Singers: Hymns, Grief, and a Native Culture in Motion.* New York: Oxford University Press, 2000.

McPherson, Angus D. "A Study of Susceptibility to Geometric Illusion among Cultural Subgroups of Australian Aborigines." *Psychologia Africana,* 11 (1965): 1–13.

Medina, Nestor. "Mestizaje: Remapping Race, Culture, and Faith in Latina/o Catholicism." *Studies in Latino/a Catholicism.* New York: Orbis, 2009.

Melanchthon, Monica. "Akkamahadevi and the Samaritan Woman: Paradigms of Spirituality and Resistance." In *Border Crossings: Cross-cultural Hermeneutics*, edited by D. M. Premnath, and R. S. Sugirtharajah, 35–54. Maryknoll, N.Y.: Orbis, 2007.

Melanchthon, Monica. "Dalit Women and the Bible: Hermeneutical and Methodological Reflections Hope Abundant: Third World and Indigenous Woman's Theology." In *Hope Abundant: Third World and Indigenous Women's Theology*, edited by Kwok Pui Lan, 103–122. New York: Orbis, 2010.

Melanchthon, Monica. "The Servant in the Book of Judith: Interpreting her Silence, Telling her Story." In *Dalit Theology in the Twenty-first Century: Discordant Voices, Discerning Pathways,* edited by S. Clark, D. Manchala, and P. Peacock, 231–251. New Delhi: Oxford University Press, 2010.

Mesters, Carlos. *Defenseless Flower: A New Reading of the Bible.* Maryknoll, N.Y.: Orbis, 1989.

Mosala, Itumeleng. *Biblical Hermeneutics and Black Theology in South Africa.* Grand Rapids, Mich.: Eerdmans, 1989.

Niang, Aliou. *Faith and Freedom in Galatia and Senegal.* Leiden: Brill, 2009.

Page, Hugh R. et al., eds. *The Africana Bible: Reading Israel's Scriptures from Africa and the African Diaspora.* Minneapolis: Fortress, 2009.

Pasto, James. "Islam's 'Strange Secret Sharer': Orientalism, Judaism, and the Jewish Question." *Comparative Studies in Society and History*, 40 (1998): 437–474.

Patte, Daniel, ed. *Global Bible Commentary.* Nashville, Tenn.: Abingdon, 2004.

Pattel-Gray, Anne, ed. *Aboriginal Spirituality: Past, Present, Future.* Blackburn, Victoria: Harper Collins, 1996.

Premnath, D. N. *Eighth Century Prophets: A Social Analysis.* St. Louis: Mo.: Chalice, 2003.

Premnath, Devadasan N. "Biblical Interpretation in India: History and Issues." In *Ways of Being, Ways of Reading,* edited by J. Kuan and M. Foskett, 1–16. St. Louis, Mo.: Chalice, 2006.

Raboteau, Albert. *Slave Religion: The "Invisible Institution" in the Antebellum South.* Oxford: Oxford University Press, 2004.

Rayan, Samuel, S.J. "Jesus and the Poor in the Fourth Gospel." *Bible Bhashyam* 4, no. 3 (1978): 213–228.

Reddie, Anthony. *Black Theology in Transatlantic Dialogue.* New York: Palgrave Macmillan, 2006.

Reddie, Anthony. "Re-Imagining Black Biblical Hermeneutics in Britain—A Participative Approach." *Journal of Adult Theological Education,* (2008): 158–177.

Reynolds, Gabriel. *The Qur'an and Its Biblical Subtext.* New York: Routledge, 2010.

Richard, Pablo. *Apocalypse: A People's Commentary on the Book of Revelation.* Maryknoll, N.Y.: Orbis, 2009.

Rogerson, John. *Bible and Criticism in Victorian Britain: Profiles of F. D. Maurice and William Robertson Smith.* Sheffield, UK: Sheffield Academic, 2009.

Rogerson, John. *Old Testament Criticism in the Nineteenth Century: England and Germany.* London: SPCK, 1984.

Romero, C. Gilbert. "Tradition and Symbol as Biblical Keys for a U.S. Hispanic Theology." In *Frontiers of Hispanic Theology in the United States,* edited by A. Deck, 41–61. Maryknoll, N.Y.: Orbis, 1992.

Ruiz, Jean-Pierre. *Readings from the Edges: The Bible and People on the Move.* Maryknoll, N.Y.: Orbis, 2011.

Said, Edward. *Orientalism.* New York: Vintage, 1979.

Sanchez, David A. *From Patmos to the Barrio: Subverting Imperial Myths.* Minneapolis: Fortress, 2008.

Segovia, Fernando, and Mary Ann Tolbert, eds. *Reading from This Place.* 2 vols. Minneapolis: Fortress, 1995.

Segovia, Fernando. "The Text as Other: Towards a Hispanic American Hermeneutic." In *Text and Experience*, edited by Daniel Smith-Christopher, 276–298. Sheffield, UK: Sheffield Academic, 1995.

Segovia, Fernando. *Decolonizing Biblical Studies: A View from the Margins.* Maryknoll, N.Y.: Orbis, 2000.

Smith-Christopher, Daniel, ed. *Text and Experience: Towards a Cultural Exegesis of the Bible.* Sheffield, UK: Sheffield Academic, 1995.

Soares-Prabhu, George. "The Dharma of Jesus: An Interpretation of the Sermon on the Mount." *Bible Bhashyam* 6, no. 4 (1980): 358–381.

Soares-Prabhu, George. "Good News to the Poor: The Social Implications of the Message of Jesus." *Bible Bhashyam* 4, no. 3 (1978): 193–212.

Soares-Prabhu, George. "And There Was a Great Calm: A 'Dhvani' Reading of the Stilling of the Storm (Mk 4, 35–41)." *Bible Bhashyam* 5, (1979): 295–308.

Soares-Prabhu, George. "Towards an Indian Interpretation of the Bible." *Bible Bhashyam* 6 (1980): 151–170. A longer version is published in *Theologizing in India.*

Sugirtharajah, R. S. *Postcolonial Criticism and Biblical Interpretation.* Oxford: Oxford University Press, 2002.

Sugirtharajah, R. S. *Voices from the Margin: Interpreting the Bible in the Third World.* Maryknoll, N.Y.: Orbis, rev. ed., 1995; 3d ed., 2006.

Syren, Roger. "Before the Text and After: The Scandinavian School and the Formation of Scripture." In *Text and Experience*, edited by Daniel Smith-Christopher, 225–237. Sheffield, UK: Sheffield Academic, 1995.

Tamez, Elsa. *The Bible of the Oppressed.* Eugene: Ore.: Wipf & Stock, 2006.

Tamez, Elsa. *The Scandalous Message of James: Faith without Works is Dead.* Rev. ed. New York: Crossroad, 2002.

Thomas, Oral. *Biblical Resistance Hermeneutics within a Caribbean Context.* Sheffield, UK: Equinox, 2010.

Tokunboh, Adeyemo. *Africa Bible Commentary: A One-Volume Commentary Written by 70 African Scholars.* Grand Rapids, Mich.: Zondervan: 2010.

Vaka'uta, Nasili. *Reading Ezra 9–10 Tu'a-wise: Rethinking Biblical Interpretation in Oceania.* Atlanta: Society of Biblical Literature, 2011.

Vellanickal, Matthew. "A Dhvani Interpretation of the Bible: According to Indian Tradition." In *Text and Experience: Toward a Cultural Exegesis of the Bible*, edited by Daniel Smith-Christopher, 195–209. Sheffield UK: Sheffield Academic, 1995.

Wan, Sze-Kar. "Allegorical Interpretation East and West: A Methodological Enquiry into Comparative Hermeneutics." In *Text and Experience: Toward a Cultural Exegesis of the Bible*, edited by Daniel Smith-Christopher, 154–179. Sheffield UK: Sheffield Academic, 1995.

Weems, Renita J. *Battered Love: Marriage, Sex, and Violence in the Hebrew Prophets.* Minneapolis: Fortress, 1995.

Wendl, Tobias. *Warum sie nicht sehen, was sie sehen Kônnten: Zur Perzeption von Fotografien im Kulturvergleich.* Anthropos 91 (1996): 169–181.

West, Gerald. "(Ac)claiming the (Extra)ordinary African 'Reader' of the Bible" In *Reading Other-Wise*, edited by Gerald West, 29–48. Atlanta: Society of Biblical Literature, 2007.

West, Gerald. *Biblical Hermeneutics of Liberation: Modes of Reading the Bible in the South African Context.* Maryknoll, N.Y.: Orbis, 1995.

West, Gerald, ed. *Reading Other-wise: Socially Engaged Biblical Scholars Reading with Their Local Communities*, Atlanta: Society of Biblical Literature, 2007.

Wimbush, Vincent. *African-Americans and the Bible: Sacred Texts and Social Textures.* New York: Continuum, 2000.

Yeo, Khiok-khng. *Rhetorical Interaction in 1 Corinthians 8 and 10: A Formal Analysis with Preliminary Suggestions for a Chinese, Cross-Cultural Hermeneutic.* Biblical Interpretation 9. Leiden: Brill, 1997.

Yeo, Khiok-khng. *What Has Jerusalem to Do with Beijing? Biblical Interpretation from a Chinese Perspective.* Harrisburg, Pa.: Trinity Press International, 1998.

Yeo, Khiok-khng. "The "yin and yang" of God (Exod 3:14) and humanity (Gen 1:26–27)." *Zeitschrift für Religions- und Geistesgeschichte* 46, no. 4 (1994): 319–332.

Yieh, John Yueh-Han. "Chinese Biblical Interpretation: History and Issues." In *Ways of Being, Ways of Reading*, edited by J. Kuan and M. Foskett, 17–30. St. Louis, Mo.: Chalice, 2006.

Daniel Smith-Christopher

CUBAN INTERPRETATION IN THE CUBAN DIASPORA

The title of this article is a somewhat awkward way of referring to its subject matter, but it will serve as an expedient marker for its content, as long as that content becomes more clearly defined. "Cuban

Interpretation" alone would require an attempt at a presentation of the history of biblical interpretation in Cuba and by Cuban authors since the sixteenth century—clearly not what is intended here. A companion article to this one would deal with biblical interpretation in Cuba since the Revolution and, along with this one's subtitle "Cuban Diaspora," begin to define more precisely its subject matter. Given Cuba's colonial history, there have been Cubans dispersed from the island and settled in the United States since before the nineteenth century. This article will deal with tendencies in biblical interpretation as done by Cuban Americans of the latest Diaspora: the one that began in the 1950s with the Revolution. It will also focus on interpretation that consciously adopts a perspective shaped by the experience of Cubans in the Diaspora. In the interest of accuracy, it should be said that Cuban American biblical interpreters, like most exilic Cubans—at least those of the first generation—do not usually refer to themselves as "Cuban Americans," but prefer to call themselves simply Cuban. Not really contradicting that fact, the biblical interpreters discussed in this article prefer to subsume that identification under terms such as "Hispanic" or "Latino(a)," indicating a characteristic solidarity with other ethnic groups that US society at large so identifies. There are strong political and hermeneutical consequences deriving from that identification. A related characteristic of Cuban American biblical interpretation is the ecumenical manner in which it is practiced. Hispanic /Latino(a) Catholics and Protestants tend to set aside their denominational differences to a much larger degree than would have been the case in prerevolutionary Cuba, or before Vatican Council II, in order to cooperate in ecclesiastical and academic projects in unprecedented ways (see García-Treto 1999, p. 164).

A rough approach to the issue of identifying Cuban American biblical interpreters might be to take a comprehensive recent biblical commentary and compendium of biblical interpretation written by a good number of members of the biblical studies academic guild, and search the list of contributors for the names of Cuban American scholars. In fact, the *New Interpreter's Bible* (Nashville, Tenn.: Abingdon Press, 1994) lists ninety-six contributors, four of whom are Cuban Americans. In the order in which they are listed, with their denominational affiliation and the title of their contribution, they are: Francisco O. García-Treto, the author of this article (Presbyterian Church [United States], *Nahum*), Justo L. González (The United Methodist Church, *How the Bible Has Been Interpreted in Christian Tradition*), Fernando F. Segovia (The Roman Catholic Church, *Reading the Bible as Hispanic Americans*) and Moisés Silva (The Orthodox Presbyterian Church, *Contemporary Theories of Biblical Interpretation*). Of course there are others who did not contribute to the *NIB*, but the intended goal here is to deal with the distinctive contribution that Cuban American interpreters—some with academic credentials in biblical studies, some grounded in other, related disciplines—have brought to biblical interpretation *from their perspective* in the Cuban Diaspora, or as several of them say, adopting a phrase coined by Cuban literary critic Gustavo Perez-Firmat in his 1994 book *Life on the Hyphen: The Cuban-American Way*, from their life "on the hyphen." That is to say, a life lived between two cultures, being at the same time both/and, and neither/nor, Cuban and American: the experience of living in exile. In a very general way it can be said that the Hispanic /Latino(a) hermeneutical project, and the work of most of its Cuban exponents, has roots in Liberation Theology, which originated among Catholics in Latin America, as well as in intercultural studies and in postcolonialism. (See De La Torre 2002, pp. 112f.; González 2010, pp. 31f.; Segovia 1994, pp. 168–171; 2000, pp. 87–177) Three of the four scholars just mentioned (García-Treto, González, and Segovia) fit that general description, while the fourth (Silva) espouses a traditional position rooted in classical Reformed Theology, as his critique of contemporary hermeneutical theories in the abovementioned article shows. Finally, there is what may be called a "metadisciplinary" character to the work of many of these interpreters, who, fully qualified in one or another disciplinary field by virtue of their academic credentials, nevertheless supply the needs of the community of faith by labors beyond their "discipline." What follows will focus mainly on the work of two scholars, Justo González and Fernando Segovia, perhaps the most influential among Cuban American interpreters to date.

González: Reading in Exile. Justo L. González can be considered the dean of Cuban American biblical interpreters, while his academic field, strictly speaking, is the history of Christian thought (Yale Ph.D.), and indeed his teaching and publication record reflects this. On the other hand, he is also the author of biblical commentaries, notably on the Gospel of Luke (González, 2010), the Acts of the Apostles (2001) and the Book of Revelation (1999), and has been the general editor and facilitator of two multi-volume series of biblical commentaries in Spanish (*Comentario Bíblico Hispanoamericano*, Editorial Caribe, and *Conozca su Biblia*, Fortress). Among his many publications are two books of special interest to the subject at hand: *Mañana: Christian Theology from a Hispanic Perspective* (1990) and *Santa Biblia: The Bible through Hispanic Eyes* (1996).

In *Mañana*, González introduces the notion of "Reading the Bible in Spanish," widely adopted in the development of US Hispanic/Latino(a) hermeneutical perspectives. In the chapter he devotes to this concept (pp. 75–87), he defines it as a result of the point of view that all Hispanics can derive from a "noninnocent" view of their history. Contrasting with the tendency on the part of many in Anglo American culture to idealize and retroactively sanitize their history—producing what González calls an "innocent" reading—Hispanics "know that we are born out of an act of violence of cosmic proportions in which our Spanish forefathers raped our Indian foremothers. We have no skeletons in our closet. Our skeletons are at the very heart of our history and our reality as a people" (González 1990, pp. 77–78). An "innocent" reading of the Bible functions in the same way as, and goes along with, an innocent reading of national history: it encourages, for example, an unrealistic hagiographic view of Old Testament characters that the Bible actually presents as tricksters or oppressors, at least at times (Jacob, David, and others) and worse, it views the history of God's people—the model for the church—with a "selective forgetfulness used precisely to avoid the consequences of a more realistic memory" (González 1990, p. 79). On the contrary, reading and interpreting the Bible should promote "responsible remembrance," which leads to "responsible action," particularly in the social and political realm. González challenges Hispanics to read the Bible in such a way as "constantly to remind [the dominant] group of their immigrant beginnings, of the Indian massacres, of the rape of the land, of the war with Mexico, of riches drawn from slave labor, of neocolonial exploitation, and of any other guilty items that one may be inclined to forget in an innocent reading of history" (González 1990, p. 80). He insists on a reading of the "Older Testament" that neither assumes that it is unrelated to the Newer, or that is superseded by it, and that remembers that "the scope of God's action and revelation includes much more than life after death," reminding us "that God's salvation is not purely 'spiritual'... but is also political and social" (González 1990, p. 83). Reading the Bible in Spanish, in the social situation of US Hispanics, is reading the Bible as a political book, "in the vernacular," from the perspective of the people and not from that of those who hold power. Accordingly, he says that in the Andes, "the equivalent of our reading in Spanish would be a reading in Quechua, and from the perspective of the Quechua-speaking people oppressed by the Spanish-speaking" (González 1990, p. 85). In his earlier mentioned article in the *Interpreter's Bible*, Fernando Segovia lists four principles of the "very specific grammar" which González proposes for a reading of the Bible "in Spanish": "(1) It must focus throughout on the question of power and powerlessness in the Bible. (2) It must see the Bible as addressing the community of faith. (3) It must be particularly attuned to what the poor and the simple find in the Bible. (4) It must let itself be interpreted by the Bible in terms of its own historical pilgrimage" (Segovia 1994, p. 171). González' nuanced portrayal of current reading of the Bible in Hispanic churches describes a hermeneutical approach that transcends fundamentalist or liberal readings—although both tendencies are present there—one that "in our better moments" seeks to read the Bible "in the vocative," that is, to see it addressing the community that expects "to learn something significant, not only about Moses or about Christian doctrine, but about ourselves and our world" (González 1990, p. 87).

In *Santa Biblia*, González devotes chapters to each of five major themes or perspectives that constitute his paradigmatic vision of the reading of the Bible being carried out and developed among US Hispanics, using examples drawn from both church and academic sources. These themes mark the social, economic, ethnic/cultural, political and communitarian dimensions of the life of US Hispanics, and together they shape a platform for reading and interpretation of the Bible, in which Hispanic interpreters see reflections of their own lives, or as González says, they read the Bible with "Hispanic eyes . . . the perspective of those who claim their Hispanic identity as part of their hermeneutical baggage, and who also read the Scripture within the context of a commitment to the Latino struggle to become all that God wants us and all of the world to be . . . the struggle for salvation/liberation" (González 1996, pp. 28f.). The themes of this kind of reading are: (1) marginality, (2) poverty, (3) *mestizaje* and *mulatez*, (4) exiles and aliens, and (5) solidarity. Briefly, marginality has to do with power relations, specifically with the experience of being excluded from the cultural and political center, a familiar experience to US Latinos. González refines that observation in two ways: one, that we live in a "polycentric society," and thus stand in a complex web of power relations, in varied locations relative to different centers, and two, that marginality is under some circumstances sought by Hispanics and by other groups in order to maintain a culture (language, religious practices, etc.) that would otherwise be threatened with extinction. Poverty is associated in most cases with marginality, and González is quick to make the connection, while insisting that the application of poverty as a hermeneutical key does not lead to asking "what can we discover in the Bible about the proper attitude of the church to the poor?" but instead, "what do the poor find in the Bible that is an important message to the entire church?" (González 1996, p. 58). *Mestizaje* and *mulatez* are concepts derived from the Spanish words *mestizo* and *mulato*, pejorative terms that designated the mixed-race populations of Spanish America, but which have become, for Hispanic/Latino(a) biblical interpreters, positive symbols of the cultural hybridity they recognize in themselves and in the Bible. González recognizes that Cuban Americans, as all Hispanic/Latino(a)s in the United States, partake of a double cultural hybridity: they bring, and seek to maintain, a *mestizaje* or *mulatez* that shapes them, and at the same time their life situation in the United States adds another level of hybridization for all involved, Latino(a)s of all national backgrounds as well as Anglo Americans. Places where two cultures meet, González asserts, can be defined as frontiers—unidirectional, growing by conquest, attempting to be hard and impermeable "like medieval armor"—or as borders—places that grow by encounter, permeable "like skin," and "if we ever close up our skin, we die" (González 1996, p. 87). One of the examples of Hispanic—in this case Cuban American—interpretation that he brings forward to show how an awareness of the culture of *mestizaje/mulatez* helps us to read a biblical story (Josh 9:1–27) is González' (1996, p. 87–89) sensitive reading of my article on Joshua 9:1–27 (García-Treto, 1996). There, by the use of the (illegal!) wiles of the trickster, the Gibeonites subvert the "frontier" conquest/extermination agenda of the deuteronomistic story, to turn it into a "border" situation in which they encounter the people of Israel in terms that force both sides to change for mutual benefit. Exiles and aliens is another category with obvious relevance for Cuban Americans. It is well-known that much of the Liberation Theology written in Latin America gives the Exodus priority as the central paradigmatic biblical narrative, but González prefers to say that "for many of us in the United States that function belongs to the Babylonian exile . . . we find ourselves in a land not our own. . . . In that land, we must find a way to live, to survive, and to be faithful" (González 1996, p. 91).

Given that much of the Old Testament is either exilic or postexilic in composition—and the importance of conceptions of exile, survival, and return in so much of biblical literature—it is not surprising to find Cuban American authors using that literature to interpret their own life experience, and vice versa (see for example Isasi-Díaz 1995 and De La Torre 2003, pp. 52–80 on Ps 137, and García-Treto 2000 on Joseph as an exile). González is also careful to note that the category of exile applies to people whose ancestors were the historical exiles, but who, several generations later, still have to deal with being considered aliens in the country of their birth. Solidarity, finally, reflects the fact that in general, Hispanics are more aware, because of being more traditionally connected, of the importance of community structures, beginning with the extended family and community. The feeling of solidarity extends to the church—the family of God—and influences readings of biblical texts that preserve it in ways that tend to be lost in the more individualistic societal context of the United States today.

Segovia's Hermeneutics of Diaspora. Fernando F. Segovia has done the most significant theoretical work among Cuban American biblical scholars in terms of proposing a "hermeneutics of the diaspora," which he defines as "a hermeneutic of otherness and engagement" (Segovia 1995, pp. 57–73). Segovia rejects the traditional academic construct of the "universal and informed" reader of the Bible, that is to say, the "neutral and disinterested" academic expert reader, equipped with "sophisticated training in criticism and theory of whatever sort" as the only one worthy of attention (Segovia, 1995, pp. 12f., pp. 18f.). That construct, with variations, belongs in the three broad, competing paradigms that Segovia identifies as having dominated biblical interpretation in modern times, that is to say, Historical Criticism, Literary Criticism, and Cultural Criticism. After a reasoned and generally appreciative discussion of the methodologies used and the contributions made by each (Segovia 1995, pp. 9–28), Segovia turns to a fourth paradigm, which in his programmatic essay he calls "Cultural Studies" (pp. 28–32). In the first three paradigms the text is foregrounded—Segovia's subtitles for his discussion of them make this clear: "Historical Criticism: the Text as Means" (p. 9), "Literary Criticism: The Text as Medium" (p. 15) and "Cultural Criticism: The Text as Means and Medium" (p. 20). The fourth paradigm subtitle reveals a different focus: "Cultural Studies: The Text as Construction" (p. 28). If the text is construction, with all that the term implies, the weight of interpretation shifts to the reader, who can no longer be the "universal and informed reader" of the first three paradigms. In its place, Segovia puts forward the alternative construct of "a flesh-and-blood reader (a real reader who is always situated and engaged, socially and historically conditioned, reading and interpreting from a variety of different and complex social locations)" (Segovia 1995, p. 59). This construct is the center of a "paradigm or umbrella model of interpretation within biblical criticism," which Segovia, honoring the multiplicity of readers and the resultant plurality of their readings, also identifies as intercultural criticism. The paradigm includes "engagement in a joint critical study of texts and readers of texts, for analysis of textual as well as interpretive perspectives and ideologies," for seeing all models of interpretation, all reading strategies, all retrievals of meaning from texts and all reconstructions of history behind texts as "constructions, formulated and advanced by flesh-and-blood readers." It is important, Segovia insists, that the text itself be considered as a "socially and culturally conditioned other" (Segovia 1995, p. 68). The hermeneutics he proposes begins "by recognizing that the biblical text comes from a very different historical situation and cultural matrix, a very different experience and culture . . . all texts, including the biblical texts, are contextual products . . . no text—not even the biblical text—is atemporal, asocial, ahistorical, speaking uniformly across time and culture" (Segovia 1995, p. 68). Not only are the biblical texts to be considered as socially and culturally conditioned in their production, but readers, the "flesh and blood readers" of Segovia's hermeneutical paradigm, are irreducibly so. The bicultural experience of Hispanic Americans allows them facility in understanding "that all reality, as construction, has its own way of seeing and acting, and that such vision and behavior have in turn their own historical and cultural roots." At the same time, the same experience "shows us that it is possible to live and function with relative ease in more than one reality" (Segovia 1995, p. 70), and that the "theology of otherness and mixture" fosters "a commitment to acknowledge and allow for the voice of otherness in a world of incredible diversity," while the "hermeneutics of otherness and engagement" promotes "a commitment to see readers, all readers and readings, as distinct and autonomous voices within such a rich diversity" (Segovia 1995, p. 70. For an expansion of the principle of "engagement" into the biblical text itself see García-Treto 1998). Segovia places his proposed paradigm within "a much larger process of liberation and decolonization taking place in the discipline since the mid-1970s," and sees it working to break down the "traditional and fundamental Eurocentric moorings and boundaries of the discipline in favor of a multidimensional and decentered mode of discourse." The proposed mode of discourse will be global, one in which "all readers have a voice and engage one another out of their own respective social locations, out of their own otherness." While Segovia puts on the foreground of his study the Diaspora, specifically the Hispanic American Diaspora in the United States as the place for his own perspective as a Cuban American, he cautions that his strategy of intercultural criticism is by no means the only possible or valid one. In the hermeneutics of engagement and otherness that he proposes, there must be openness to all voices, from whatever social location: global, diasporic, colonized, marginalized—and a resistance to absolutizing any reading of the Bible into totalizing "master narratives."

***Ajiaco* and *Mujerista* Hermeneutics.** Two other voices that must be mentioned are those of Miguel A. De La Torre, Cuban American social ethicist and theologian, and of Ada María Isasi-Díaz, *mujerista* theologian and ethicist, both of whom also contribute to Cuban American biblical interpretation. De La Torre, whose personal experience includes growing up with parents who practiced *santería*, which he calls "the African-based religion of resistance and survival" (De La Torre 2002, p. 78), is a Baptist minister and college and seminary professor of Christian Ethics and Latino(a) Studies. De La Torre has adopted the term *ajiaco*, first used by Cuban anthropologist Fernando Ortiz to characterize Cuban culture, as his preferred term for *mestizaje/mulatez*. *Ajiaco* is a traditional Cuban soup—or better, stew—that typically consists of a variety of vegetables and meats cooked in their own rich broth. It serves well as an image for a culture based on a rich hybridity where varied components, while remaining identifiable and distinct, nevertheless contribute to the flavor of a dish that is more than simply the sum of its parts. De La Torre is critical of attempts, on the part of scholars of religion, to overlook the religious distinctiveness of Exilic Cubans—his term for the Cuban community in the United States, which he contrasts to Resident Cubans, that is, the Cubans in Cuba—by attempting to blend it into a general Hispanic/Latino(a) pot. Critical as he is of many of the political and social attitudes of "Exilic Cubans" in Miami and elsewhere in the United States, (see De La Torre 2003, pp. 13–25 and *passim*), he chooses, as an example of the multiplicity of readers and reading communities which Segovia adumbrates, to formulate an *ajiaco* Christianity: a theology of the Diaspora "deeply rooted in the theoretical contexts of postmodernism, postcolonialism and liberation theology" which, "at its core... becomes a theology of flesh-and-blood exile (De La Torre 2003, p. 22). Not only does he quote Segovia, he also uses, as an epigraph for the book, a famous line of Cuba's venerated nineteenth-century poet and revolutionary, José Martí: "*El vino, de plátano; y si sale agrio, ¡es nuestro vino!*" [Our] wine, [made] from bananas; and if it turns out sour, it's [still] our wine! Not surprisingly, De La Torre ends his commentary on *Genesis* in the series *Belief: A Theological Commentary on the Bible*, with these words: "For Genesis to come alive, to have meaning, to be transformative, requires those of us from marginalized communities to read the text with our own eyes, situated within our own social location, surrounded by our own community of faith" (De La Torre 2011, p. 348).

Ada María Isasi-Díaz, a Christian ethics professor and a leader in Latina feminist (*mujerista*) theology, has also made significant contributions to biblical hermeneutics, such as her reading of Psalm 137 from her standpoint as a Cuban in exile (Isasi-Díaz 1995). She has formulated a *mujerista* hermeneutics that she puts forward in her article "A *Mujerista* Hermeneutics of Justice and Human Flourishing" (Isasi-Díaz 2009). Her *Mujerista* hermeneutics is centered on the concept of *lo cotidiano* (daily life, or better, the daily struggle, *la lucha*), as she names the everyday existence of poor Latinas. Her sensitive reading of the Parable of the Day Workers in Matthew 20:1–16 illustrates her method admirably, and it gives an example of the kind of reading that Segovia and De La Torre promote. In Jesus's parable, interpreters begin by reading the landowner as a figure of God—even some Hispanic interpreters with whom Isasi-Díaz chooses to disagree (p. 185). In fact, she blames the (mis)reading of the landowner as God on Matthew, who sought to alter—or who misread—Jesus's parable as referring to the coming of the Kingdom (Isasi-Díaz prefers to use "Kin-dom," but that is another matter), and to cast the *patrón* as God. Isasi-Díaz makes use of the findings of the Jesus Seminar to separate the Matthean frame that has those effects from the original parable, thus making it possible to read the parable in the context of *lo cotidiano,* in this case the daily struggle of the day-workers for justice and for dignity as they search for their meager wage, against a landowner who is the epitome of arrogant unconcern. He plays an arbitrary game that is not only unjust, but that insults their dignity, and the workers have no other recourse but to complain, bitterly, against him. The landowner has the economic and political power to do as he wishes, but at least the workers have saved their dignity by calling for justice, and some day their just cause will prevail.

In the work of these scholars, Cuban American readings of the Bible, flavored by the perspectives of exile and by a "non innocent" view of history, and by the openness to hybridity which has long characterized Cuban culture, have begun to have an impact, not only within the Latino(a) community, but also in the broad contexts of the academy and of the church in the United States.

[*See also* Central and South American Interpretation; Latina/o Interpretation; Liberation Hermeneutics; *and* Postcolonial Biblical Interpretation.]

BIBLIOGRAPHY

De La Torre, Miguel A. *La Lucha for Cuba: Religion and Politics on the Streets of Miami.* Berkeley: University of California Press, 2003.

De La Torre, Miguel A. *Genesis.* Louisville, Ky.: Westminster John Knox, 2011.

De La Torre, Miguel A. *The Quest for the Cuban Christ: A Historical Search.* Gainesville: University Press of Florida, 2002.

García-Treto, Francisco O. "Crossing the Line: Three Scenes of Divine-Human Engagement in the Hebrew Bible." In *Teaching the Bible: The Discourses and Politics of Biblical Pedagogy,* edited by Fernando F. Segovia and Mary Ann Tolbert, 105–116. Maryknoll, N.Y.: Orbis, 1998.

García-Treto, Francisco O. "Exile in the Hebrew Bible: A Postcolonial Look from the Cuban Diaspora." In *They Were All Together In One Place?: Toward Minority Biblical Criticism,* edited by Randall C. Bailey, Tat-Siong Benny Liew, and Fernando F. Segovia, 65–78. Semeia Studies Number 57. Atlanta: Society of Biblical Literature, 2009.

García-Treto, Francisco O. "Hyphenating Joseph: A View of Genesis 39—41 from the Cuban Diaspora." In *Interpreting beyond Borders,* edited by Fernando F. Segovia, 134–145. The Bible and Postcolonialism 3. Sheffield, UK: Sheffield Academic, 2000.

García-Treto, Francisco O. "The Lesson of the Gibeonites: A Proposal for Dialogic Attention as a Strategy for Reading the Bible." In *Hispanic/Latino Theology: Challenge and Promise,* edited by Ada María Isasi-Díaz and Fernando F. Segovia, 73–85. Minneapolis: Fortress, 1996.

García-Treto, Francisco O. "Reading the Hyphens: An Emerging Biblical Hermeneutics for Latino/Hispanic U.S. Protestants." In *Protestantes/Protestants: Hispanic Christianity within Mainline Traditions,* edited by David Maldonado Jr., 160–173. Nashville, Tenn.: Abingdon, 1999.

González, Justo L. *Acts: The Gospel of the Spirit.* Maryknoll, N.Y.: Orbis, 2001.

González, Justo L. *For the Healing of the Nations: The Book of Revelation in an Age of Cultural Conflict.* Maryknoll, N.Y.: Orbis, 1999.

González, Justo L. *Luke.* Louisville, Ky.: Westminster John Knox, 2010.

González, Justo L. *Mañana: Christian Theology from a Hispanic Perspective.* Nashville, Tenn.: Abingdon, 1990.

González, Justo L. "Reading from My Bicultural Place: Acts 6:1–7." In *Reading from this Place, Vol. 1: Social Location and Biblical Interpretation in the United States,* edited by Fernando F. Segovia and Mary Ann Tolbert, 139–147. Minneapolis: Fortress, 1995.

González, Justo L. "*Revelation*: Clarity and Ambivalence, A Hispanic/Cuban American Perspective." In *From Every People and Nation: The Book of Revelation in Intercultural Perspective,* edited by David Rhoads, 47–61. Minneapolis: Fortress, 2005.

González, Justo L. *Santa Biblia: The Bible through Hispanic Eyes.* Nashville, Tenn.: Abingdon, 1996.

Segovia, Fernando F. "And They Began to Speak in Other Tongues" and "Toward a Hermeneutics of the Diaspora: A Hermeneutics of Otherness and Engagement." In *Reading from this Place, Vol. 1: Social Location and Biblical Interpretation in the United States,* edited by Fernando F. Segovia and Mary Ann Tolbert, 1–32, 57–73. Minneapolis: Fortress, 1995.

Isasi-Díaz, Ada María "'By the Rivers of Babylon': Exile as a Way of Life." In *Reading from this Place, Vol. 1: Social Location and Biblical Interpretation in the United States,* edited by Fernando F. Segovia and Mary Ann Tolbert, 149–163. Minneapolis: Fortress, 1995.

Segovia, Fernando F. "Introduction: Pedagogical Discourse and Practices in Contemporary Biblical Criticism" and "Pedagogical Discourse and Practices in Cultural Studies: Toward a Contextual Biblical Pedagogy." In *Teaching the Bible: The Discourses and Politics of Biblical Pedagogy,* edited by Fernando F. Segovia and Mary Ann Tolbert, 1–28 and 137–167. Maryknoll, N.Y.: Orbis, 1998.

Isasi-Díaz, Ada María "A *Mujerista* Hermeneutics of Justice and Human Flourishing." In *The Bible and the Hermeneutics of Liberation,* edited by Alejandro F. Botta and Pablo R. Andiñach, 181–195. Semeia Studies 59. Atlanta: Society of Biblical Literature, 2009.

Segovia, Fernando F. "Reading the Bible as Hispanic Americans." In *The New Interpreter's Bible* Vol. 1, edited by Leander E. Keck et al., 167–173. Nashville, Tenn.: Abingdon, 1994.

Segovia, Fernando F. "Toward Latino/a American Biblical Criticism: Latin(o/a)ness as a Problematic." In *They Were All Together In One Place?: Toward Minority Biblical Criticism,* edited by Randall C. Bailey, Tat-Siong Benny Liew, and Fernando F. Segovia, 193–223. Semeia Studies 57. Atlanta: Society of Biblical Literature, 2009.

Francisco O. García-Treto

Cultural Anthropology

[*This entry contains two subentries,* Hebrew Bible *and* New Testament]

Hebrew Bible

The fields of cultural anthropology and biblical studies have been intertwined from their beginnings as modern academic disciplines in the late nineteenth century. This relationship was initially beneficial and even foundational for both areas, and anthropology has continued to have an extremely positive influence on biblical studies to the present day. This article will briefly review the history of interaction between the two fields before discussing at greater length the most important uses of anthropology within the study of the Hebrew Bible in the last three decades. During this recent period, the interaction between anthropology and biblical studies has gone primarily in one direction, with some biblical scholars making use of anthropological research, theories, or models, but with biblicists making much less of an impact on the discipline of anthropology. The article will close, then, by reflecting upon how a mutually beneficial relationship between anthropology and biblical studies might be restored.

Anthropology and Biblical Studies: The First Few Decades. Anthropology is the study of human cultures and societies. In the past, lines were drawn between social and cultural anthropology, with the former dealing more with social organization and institutions and the latter having a more holistic approach, "oriented to the ways in which culture affects individual experience" (Wood 1997, p. 17). However, many anthropologists feel these divisions no longer hold up today, and one frequently sees the nomenclature "sociocultural anthropology." Following this trend, this entry will not differentiate between social and cultural strands of anthropology in tracing the use of anthropological ideas in the study of the Hebrew Bible. The disciplinary division between anthropology and sociology has also broken down in recent decades. In the past, anthropologists focused their research on simpler societies while sociologists dealt primarily with complex, and especially western cultures, but this distinction, too, no longer holds water as anthropologists have in a sense "encroached" on the study of western societies. Today, distinctions between the two fields are often methodologically grounded—sociology has become quite quantitative in method, while anthropology is still very much centered on ethnography and fieldwork. Sociology is often concerned with macro-level social issues, such as crime or patterns of social inequality in a whole society, while anthropology tends to begin by examining more localized settings, for example, a village or a neighborhood, and then to proceed to broader theoretical questions.

The earlier history of interaction between the social sciences and the modern, critical study of the Hebrew Bible is already well documented (see, for example, Rogerson 1978; Lang 1985; Esler and Hagedorn 2006; focusing on sociology, but still relevant are Gottwald 1992; Wilson 1984, 2010). A cursory review will thus suffice here, beginning with the work of William Robertson Smith. While not following the methods that would later become the norm in the burgeoning discipline of anthropology, Robertson Smith was a nineteenth-century orientalist whose work addressed many matters of interest to anthropologists, including kinship, marriage, and sacrificial rituals. Robertson Smith both drew upon and further developed the cultural evolutionism so typical of his time that saw human societies as progressing in stages from a base primitivism to the advanced levels of culture he thought were exemplified by European societies. Robertson Smith applied such ideas not only to the study of early Arabia but also to the Israelites. In fact, Robertson Smith had been trained as a biblical scholar, and his work influenced both anthropology and biblical studies.

The same is true of Sir James G. Frazer, who, like Robertson Smith, was a Scot and a proponent of evolutionistic thinking. Some consider Frazer to be the father of anthropology, though he did not perform fieldwork and is in some ways the "armchair anthropologist" *par excellence*. Nonetheless, his book *The Golden Bough*, a 12-volume compendium of religious and "magical" ideas from both ancient and modern societies, was quite popular and influential at the time it was written. Published soon after was his extensive *Folklore in the Old Testament*. Though it cannot be said that Frazer's influence has stood the test of time, his work is an interesting example of the early confluence of anthropology and biblical studies.

A contemporary of Frazer's who is quite worthy of mention is Marcel Mauss, the nephew of Emile Durkheim, the French thinker often considered to be the founder of sociology and whose work continues to be incredibly important today. While Mauss, like Frazer and many others at this time, did not perform fieldwork, his essays are still very much worth reading. His long essay on sacrifice, written with Henri Hubert, was an important early attempt to understand the nature of sacrifice across cultures. It is noteworthy for our purposes because it discusses Israelite sacrifice at length.

Turning to biblical scholars, there were several biblicists of the nineteenth and early twentieth centuries who displayed anthropological interests. Robertson Smith had trained as a biblicist himself, but the other early biblical scholars interested in anthropology include such major figures as Julius Wellhausen, who was not only a biblical scholar but an Arabist; Albrecht Alt, who traveled extensively in Palestine and drew upon his knowledge of the Bedouin customs of that area in his work on the emergence of the Israelites; and Hermann Gunkel, who made use of early folklore studies.

Anthropology and Biblical Studies: The "Second Wave" to the Present. Certain anthropologists continued to show interest in the Bible in the decades to come. For example, the functionalist anthropologist Bronislaw Malinowski cited examples from biblical texts in his book *Sex, Culture, and Myth*. In general, however, there was a major lull in interest in the Hebrew Bible on the part of anthropologists and in anthropology on the part of biblicists as biblicists turned to source criticism and anthropologists to research based on ethnographic fieldwork. The mutual interests of these fields began to revive, however, in the 1960s and 1970s. In 1966, the anthropologist Mary Douglas published the seminal work, *Purity and Danger: An Analysis of the Concepts of Pollution and Taboo.* This book treats the purity ideas of many cultures and notably contains an entire chapter on the Hebrew Bible entitled "The Abominations of Leviticus." The chapter, as well as the book as a whole, proved influential not only in anthropology but among biblicists, transforming the study of biblical purity laws. Mary Douglas continued to write on the Hebrew Bible and Israelite religion, among other topics, until the time of her death in 2007. The anthropologist Marvin Harris, proponent of an approach called cultural materialism, also addressed biblical dietary laws in his work. The structuralist anthropologist Edmund R. Leach displayed much interest in biblical texts, discussing sacrifice in *Culture and Communication: The Logic by which Symbols are Connected* and a host of biblical topics in *Structuralist Interpretations of Biblical Myth.* While the number of anthropologists interested in biblical studies was not large, the anthropologists who did analyze biblical texts in their work were scholars of note.

During roughly the same period, the interest of biblical scholars in social scientific approaches, both anthropological and sociological, revived in what is called the "second wave" of social-scientific biblical criticism. Since this revival of interest, there has been no subsequent lull in the production of anthropologically-informed biblical scholarship as there had been after the "first wave" of such scholarship. While scholars interested in applying anthropological ideas to the study of the Hebrew Bible and ancient Israel have continued to comprise only a small minority of biblicists, since the 1970s this group has nonetheless produced an impressive amount of scholarship. Considering the intimate involvement of Mary Douglas in biblical studies, it is unsurprising that scholars who work on purity issues have engaged with her work, and sometimes with the work of other anthropologists. In the area of folklore, also, there have been various works of biblical scholarship that have engaged with anthropology. The work of Susan Niditch stands out in this area, and she has been particularly prolific in applying anthropological research in other areas such as warfare, the relationship between orality and writing in Israelite literature, and the body and identity. Other scholars have made use of anthropological research in the study of writing and literacy (see particularly Sanders 2009), and in the study of the body (see, e.g., Olyan 2000, 2008; Berquist 2002).

It would be impossible to treat or even mention here every piece of biblical scholarship that has made use of anthropology, or even every area of biblical studies in which anthropology has been applied. The focus here instead will be upon certain areas of study in which anthropologically interested biblicists have produced a great deal of scholarship and/or very influential scholarship, namely, the study of early Israel, kinship and marriage, prophecy and apocalypticism, and honor and shame.

Early Israelite Society. Because written evidence from the earliest period of Israelite history—that is, the Iron I period spanning roughly from 1200 B.C.E. to 1000 B.C.E.—is lacking, historians of ancient Israel have had no choice but to turn to other sources in order to reconstruct the realities of this era. Both archaeology and anthropology have proven pivotal in this endeavor, though sociology, too, has been as important. George Mendenhall was one of the first biblical scholars of the "second wave." As the first proponent of the peasant revolt theory of Israelite origins, Mendenhall drew upon sociological and anthropological evidence on state formation and tribalism. Norman Gottwald, in his lengthy work *The Tribes of Yahweh: A Sociology of the Religion of Liberated Israel,* expanded upon Mendenhall's ideas while making use of a much wider range of sources. Gottwald's approach was self-consciously Marxist and materialist in orientation; he also made use of functionalist anthropological research on a type of social organization centered on kinship that anthropologists call a segmentary lineage system. (The term "functionalist" is used here as a synonym of "structural-functionalist.") Gottwald's work did not use social-scientific research as an ornament, merely gussying up what was at best more traditional biblical scholarship. To the contrary, it was permeated by sociological and anthropological ideas. While critiqued on many scores, Gottwald's book has proven enormously influential in biblical studies, and many scholars have followed him in using social-scientific research in reconstructing the early Israelite period.

One of Gottwald's critics was Niels Peter Lemche. While Lemche critiqued many of Gottwald's arguments, he agreed with Mendenhall and Gottwald that the Israelites were not outsiders to Canaan but rather emerged from within Canaanite society, building as Gottwald did upon anthropological research on segmentary societies to make his case. Lemche also utilized research on pastoral nomadism to nuance the rather simplistic understanding of nomadism held by biblical scholars, Gottwald included, to that point. (C. H. J. de Geus had also made efforts in this area.) One of Lemche's critiques of Gottwald and also of Mendenhall is especially worth noting here. He states: "The revolution hypotheses of Mendenhall and Gottwald are based . . . on an entirely too limited circle of American social anthropologists" (1985, p. 209). Lemche is right in pointing to this as a methodological flaw. It is, nonetheless, a trait that has continued to affect even to the present anthropologically informed biblical scholarship, some of which even now relies on outdated anthropological research or on the work of too few anthropologists. Because it is difficult to stay up-to-date on two academic fields, biblical scholars are understandably not always aware of wider or even conflicting trends in anthropology.

The "peaceful transition" or "symbiosis" models of Israelite emergence that succeeded Gottwald's "peasant revolt" model, and which have been accepted by most scholars in the past 20 years, rejected certain aspects of Gottwald's reconstruction while accepting others. Various scholars have developed these models, including Robert Coote, Keith Whitelam, Israel Finkelstein, and others. While these scholars' works have been informed by anthropological research, one could argue that other methods dominated their analysis, especially in the case of Coote and Whitelam. But eclecticism in method was and is typical of the work of biblical scholars who make use of social-scientific evidence, with researchers often utilizing historical, archaeological, sociological, anthropological, and other methods. This eclectic approach has been used quite fruitfully to explicate various features of early Israelite society, not only tribalism and pastoralism, but women's roles (Meyers 1988), centralization and the transition to monarchy (e.g., Flanagan 1988; Frick 1985), ethnicity (Killebrew 2005), and other features.

Kinship and Marriage. In some ways related to these studies of early Israelite society and culture are various works examining Israelite kinship and marriage from an anthropological perspective. Certainly, many of the scholars mentioned earlier were interested in matters of kinship, and so research on Iron I often intersects in subject matter with works that examine Israelite kinship and/or marriage in later periods or over a longer span of Israelite history. Abraham Malamat was the first to apply anthropological ideas to the study of Israelite genealogies (1973). Robert R. Wilson was soon to follow suit in his *Genealogy and History in the Biblical World* (1977). Wilson has demonstrated in this and other works an awareness of the methodological issues involved in utilizing anthropological and sociological research, and he has even suggested guidelines for the use of cross-cultural evidence.

Lemche deals at some length with issues of kinship in his work on early Israel. Both Lemche and J. W. Rogerson (1986) have expressed some skepticism about the applicability of kinship models from anthropology, which were generally based on segmentary societies in Africa, to the study of the Israelites. Lemche circumvents this problem in his own work by also examining evidence from Middle Eastern groups. There is a certain geographical determinism assumed by such critiques, however. That is, some scholars assume that the Israelites would as a matter of course be more similar to modern groups who live in the same region where they once lived than to those who live elsewhere. Often enough, this assumption is not borne out by comparative evidence. Still, Lemche's and Rogerson's critiques have held some weight among scholars.

Another scholar who has been critical of previous approaches to the study of early Israel is J. David Schloen. Schloen argues for the rejection of functionalist anthropological methods, which are ultimately based in the ideas of Emile Durkheim, in favor of an approach deriving from Max Weber. Thus, Schloen presents a different model for understanding Israelite kinship structures and ideologies in his work (2001) than have other biblicists.

Two recent works discuss kinship and marriage in ancient Israel. Naomi Steinberg, in *Kinship and Marriage in Genesis*, assesses the marital practices discussed in the first book of the Bible, utilizing anthropological ideas in her analysis. T. M. Lemos, in *Marriage Gifts and Social Change in Ancient Palestine: 1200 BCE to 200 CE*, examines the interrelationship between marital practices and various features of social structure in a broad range of sources, both biblical and extrabiblical, providing a lengthy examination of anthropological research on marriage gifts.

On the whole, one can only conclude that anthropological approaches have been of extreme importance to research performed on early Israel over not only the last three decades, but over the last century.

Prophecy and Apocalyptic. Anthropological research has proven as pivotal to the study of Israelite prophecy in the past 30 years as it has to the study of Israelite kinship. Beginning in the 1970s and proceeding into the 1980s, Thomas Overholt examined Israelite prophecy together with a very wide range of cross-cultural ethnographic evidence on what are generally termed "intermediaries," that is, persons who are thought to communicate with and for deities, enter into ecstatic states in ritual settings, or exhibit other behaviors similar to those of Israelite prophets. Robert R. Wilson published what many consider a landmark study of Israelite prophecy called *Prophecy and Society in Ancient Israel* (1980), in which he also makes heavy use of social-scientific research in order to understand the relationship between Israelite prophets and their social contexts. David Petersen (1981) and Robert Carroll (1979) also produced important studies of Israelite prophecy that were informed by social-scientific approaches and models.

The rise of apocalyptic literature and apocalypticism has also been examined utilizing social-scientific research, though perhaps leaning more in the direction of the sociological. Paul Hanson produced an important work on apocalyptic literature called *The Dawn of Apocalyptic* (1975), arguing that this literature and the social movements that produced it were the result of social conflicts between priests and prophets. While Stephen L. Cook has challenged aspects of Hanson's argument, he follows Hanson in using sociological and anthropological evidence to study apocalyptic (1995). More recently, Anathea Portier-Young, in *Apocalypse against Empire*, has drawn upon the anthropologist James C. Scott's work on resistance to examine how apocalyptic literature responded to the hegemony of foreign powers over the Judeans (2011). Overall, the use of social-scientific research and models in the study of both prophecy and apocalyptic literature has been pivotal in advancing our knowledge of these phenomena.

Honor and Shame. One of the more interesting test cases for how biblical scholars have made use of anthropological research and models may be found in the study of honor and shame. This research will be discussed at some length because it is in some ways exemplary of how biblical scholars have engaged with anthropology. The study of the "values" of honor and shame in the Hebrew Bible intensified in the 1990s. (The word "values" is placed in quotation marks because these are at base emotions and only secondarily cultural values.) This work on the Hebrew Bible followed the application of anthropological research on honor and shame to the New Testament by such figures as Bruce Malina. Examinations of honor and shame have drawn upon the field of Mediterranean anthropology and particularly upon the work of Julian Pitt-Rivers and J. G. Peristiany, both of whom argued that the whole of the Mediterranean constituted one culture area sharing certain cultural values and features.

Dozens of works have applied the ideas of Mediterranean anthropologists to the Hebrew Bible and New Testament in the past 20 to 30 years. (See, in particular, Malina 1981; Matthews and Benjamin 1996; Stiebert 2002; Lemos 2006.) Before examining how they have done so, the work of the Mediterraneanists themselves must first be considered. Julian Pitt-Rivers, who discussed the Bible in his landmark work on the Mediterranean titled *The Fate of Shechem, or the Politics of Sex: Essays in the Anthropology of the Mediterranean*, and J. G. Peristiany produced a certain model of "Mediterranean personality" in their works. Model-making by necessity involves painting with broad strokes; it requires "boiling down" specificities to find certain general principles or observations. Already in the 1980s, Michael Herzfeld and others took exception to this reduction of the Mediterranean to one seamless culture area, arguing that the approach of Mediterraneanists did not account enough for differences between Mediterranean cultures and that this approach was not nuanced enough. Some scholars felt gender ideals were distorted by Mediterraneanists and that what they were doing at times approached the level of stereotyping Mediterranean peoples.

This discussion has been lost on some biblicists. While it is typical for biblical scholars writing today to refer to these critiques, they often neglect to incorporate the substance of the critiques into their analyses. Many uses of Mediterranean anthropology by biblical scholars only summarize or distill the main arguments of the classic works of anthropologists such as Pitt-Rivers and Peristiany. Yet, as was just stated, the models provided by these latter scholars themselves "boil down" social and cultural patterns to their most salient features for the purposes of cross-cultural comparison. If one further distills the social-scientific model of these Mediterraneanists, what one is left with is often too formalistic to be convincing or even more akin to cultural stereotyping than what one finds in Pitt-Rivers's and Peristiany's work. As a whole, work in biblical studies has drawn from, rather than contributed to, wider discussions of honor and shame in the social sciences. While this research has been very fruitful for biblical studies, it has at times been the case that biblicists have not always made the best use of anthropology in the study of these important features of Israelite and Judean culture. (See Schwartz 2010 for a serious critique of this research, though his work, too, has certain shortcomings in its treatment of biblical material.)

Anthropology and the Hebrew Bible: Where We Stand and Where to Go from Here. The recognition that some biblical scholars' use of anthropological research has been flawed, combined with the postmodern turn away from comparativism toward a constructivist specificity, has had the result of "scaring off" some biblical scholars from anthropology. While there has been a resurgence among biblicists of traditional methods such as source- and redaction-criticism, even though these approaches present just as many methodological problems as do social-scientific approaches, nonetheless there are biblicists who continue to draw upon anthropology in their work, and some are doing so in very sophisticated ways.

A few problems should be addressed before considering the question of where the relationship between anthropology and biblical studies should go in the future. One issue is that anthropologists and biblical scholars rarely speak to each other. Even though many anthropologists, because of the flourishing of postcolonialism, have retreated from the avowed antihistoricism of functionalist anthropology, anthropology is still very much a field ensconced in the present. A continued and justified emphasis on ethnographic methods has led to a certain incommensurability between anthropology and historical fields such as biblical studies. Yet, some anthropologists, most notably Mary Douglas and Jack Goody, have attempted to bridge the divide. Biblical scholars, on the other hand, almost never engage with anthropologists directly. They might utilize anthropological and other types of theories, but they do very little theorizing of their own. The result of this is that scholars in other disciplines have little reason to read the work of biblical scholars. The extreme caution with which biblical scholars approach theorizing and comparative research seems unwarranted. It would be beneficial for both fields if biblicists worked harder to create a true dialogue between biblical studies and anthropology.

Another impedance to performing good anthropologically-informed research on the Hebrew Bible is the fact that anthropology is a discipline concerned only marginally with literary interpretation. While some anthropologists—mainly structuralists such as Claude Lévi-Strauss or Leach—were in the past interested in the interpretation of texts, this is not where anthropology stands at the present. Many biblicists, on the other hand, are concerned overwhelmingly with texts. Their prime interest is in understanding the Bible, with an interest in understanding the Israelites being only secondary. At times, biblical scholars will utilize anthropological research and ideas, but rather than doing so to come to conclusions about ancient Israelite society and culture, they instead choose to limit their analysis to biblical literature. By doing this, they avoid the (admittedly thorny) question of how texts relate to the cultures that produce them, as well as recent queries about whether it is really possible to reconstruct the history of ancient Israel with the limited evidence we have. This textual focus places the work of these scholars methodologically at odds with the anthropological work they are using. As Bernhard Lang puts it, "Anthropologists study living people, not books" (p. 3). The analysis of texts, when it does happen in anthropological circles, occurs only in service of understanding people and places—it is not an end in itself. For many biblicists, understanding the Bible *is* an end in itself. In this way, biblical studies and anthropology can be a rather unhappy marriage, particularly for those scholars who are primarily literary critics or theologians.

There are many approaches available in biblical studies, but scholars in this field are not always self-conscious about method, or even about what overarching questions they seek to answer in their research. One of the major effects of postmodernism has been a greater self-consciousness about presuppositions, social location, and methods throughout the humanities and social sciences. This has been felt in biblical studies, as well, but rather unevenly. The field seems more conflicted and confused than ever. And so, one must ask, where do we go from here? For those biblicists who see themselves as primarily social historians, there is a clear way forward. A productive future for biblical scholars with anthropological interests lies in greater engagement with those in the social sciences, a more engaged spirit in the task of theorizing, and an insistence on more varied training at the doctoral level.

[*See also* Cross-Cultural Exegesis; Folklore and Biblical Interpretation; *and* Social Sciences, *subentry* Hebrew Bible.]

Bibliography

Alt, Albrecht. *Essays on Old Testament History and Religion.* Translated by R. A. Wilson. Oxford: Blackwell, 1966.

Berquist, Jon. *Controlling Corporeality: The Body and the Household in Ancient Israel.* New Brunswick, N.J: Rutgers University Press, 2002.

Carroll, Robert P. *When Prophecy Failed: Cognitive Dissonance in the Prophetic Traditions of the Old Testament.* New York: Seabury, 1979.

Cook, Stephen L. *Prophecy and Apocalypticism: The Postexilic Social Setting.* Minneapolis: Fortress, 1995.

Coote, Robert B., and Keith W. Whitelam. *The Emergence of Early Israel in Historical Perspective.* Sheffield, UK: Almond, 1987.

Douglas, Mary. *Purity and Danger: An Analysis of the Concepts of Pollution and Taboo.* London: Routledge and K. Paul, 1966.

Esler, Philip F., and Anselm Hagedorn. "Social-Scientific Analysis of the Old Testament: A Brief History and Overview." In *Ancient Israel: The Old Testament in its Social Context,* edited by Philip F. Esler, 15–34. Minneapolis: Fortress, 2006.

Finkelstein, Israel. *The Archaeology of the Israelite Settlement.* Jerusalem: Israel Exploration Society, 1988.

Flanagan, James W. *David's Social Drama: A Hologram of Israel's Early Iron Age.* Sheffield, UK: Almond, 1988.

Frazer, James G. *Folk-lore in the Old Testament: Studies in Comparative Religion, Legend, and Law.* London: Macmillan, 1918.

Frazer, James G. *The Golden Bough.* 3d ed. London: Macmillan, 1906–1915.

Frick, Frank S. *The Formation of the State in Ancient Israel: A Survey of Models and Theories.* Sheffield, UK: Almond, 1985.

Geus, C. H. J. de. *The Tribes of Israel: An Investigation into Some of the Presuppositions of Martin Noth's Amphictyony Hypothesis.* Assen: Van Gorcum, 1976.

Gottwald, Norman. "Sociology (Ancient Israel)." *Anchor Bible Dictionary.* VI: 79–89. New York: Doubleday, 1992.

Gottwald, Norman. *The Tribes of Yahweh: A Sociology of the Religion of Liberated Israel, 1250–1050 B.C.E.* Maryknoll, N.Y.: Orbis Books, 1979.

Hanson, Paul. *The Dawn of Apocalyptic.* Philadelphia: Fortress, 1975.

Harris, Marvin. *Cows, Pigs, Wars, and Witches: The Riddles of Culture.* New York: Vintage, 1974.

Herzfeld, Michael. *Anthropology through the Looking Glass: Critical Ethnography in the Margins of Europe.* Cambridge, UK: Cambridge University Press, 1987.

Herzfeld, Michael. "Honour and Shame: Problems in the Comparative Analysis of Moral Systems." *Man* 15 (1980): 339–351.

Hubert, Henri, and Marcel Mauss. *Sacrifice: Its Nature and Functions.* Translated W. D. Halls. Foreword E. E. Evans-Pritchard. Chicago: University of Chicago Press, 1964.

Killebrew, Ann. *Biblical Peoples and Ethnicity: An Archaeological Study of Egyptians, Canaanites, Philistines, and Early Israel, 1300–1100 B.C.E.* Atlanta: Society of Biblical Literature, 2005.

Lang, Bernhard. "Introduction: Anthropology as a New Model for Biblical Studies." In *Anthropological Approaches to the Old Testament,* edited by B. Lang, 1–20. Philadelphia: Fortress, 1985.

Leach, Edmund R. *Culture and Communication: The Logic by which Symbols are Connected.* Cambridge, UK: Cambridge University Press 1976.

Leach, Edmund R., and D. Alan Aycock. *Structuralist Interpretations of Biblical Myth.* Cambridge, UK: Cambridge University Press, 1983.

Lemche, Niels Peter. *Early Israel: Anthropological and Historical Studies on the Israelite Society before the Monarchy.* Leiden: Brill, 1985.

Lemos, T. M. *Marriage Gifts and Social Change in Ancient Palestine: 1200 BCE to 200 CE.* Cambridge: Cambridge University Press, 2010.

Lemos, T. M. "Shame and Mutilation of Enemies in the Hebrew Bible." *Journal of Biblical Literature* 125.2 (2006): 225–241.

Malamat, Abraham. "Tribal Societies: Biblical Genealogies and African Lineage Systems." *Archives européenes de sociologie* 14 (1973): 126–136.

Malina, Bruce J. *The New Testament World: Insights from Cultural Anthropology.* Atlanta: John Knox, 1981.

Matthews, Victor H. and Don C. Benjamin, eds. *Honor and Shame in the World of the Bible.* Atlanta: Scholars, 1996.

McNutt, Paula. *Reconstructing the Society of Ancient Israel.* Louisville, Ky.: Westminster John Knox, 1999.

Mendenhall, George. "The Hebrew Conquest of Palestine." *Biblical Archaeologist* 25 (1962): 66–87.

Meyers, Carol. *Discovering Eve: Ancient Israelite Women in Context.* New York: Oxford University Press, 1988.

Niditch, Susan. *"My Brother Esau is a Hairy Man": Hair and Identity in Ancient Israel.* Oxford: Oxford University Press, 2008.

Niditch, Susan. *Oral World and Written Word.* Louisville, Ky.: Westminster, 1996.

Niditch, Susan. *Underdogs and Tricksters: A Prelude to Biblical Folklore.* New York: Harper and Row, 1987.

Niditch, Susan. *War in the Hebrew Bible: A Study in the Ethics of Violence.* Oxford: Oxford University Press, 1993.

Olyan, Saul M. *Disability in the Hebrew Bible: Interpreting Mental and Physical Differences.* Cambridge, UK: Cambridge University Press, 2008.

Olyan, Saul M. *Rites and Rank: Hierarchy in Biblical Representations of Cult.* Princeton, N.J.: Princeton University Press, 2000.

Overholt, Thomas W. *Channels of Prophecy: The Social Dynamics of Prophetic Activity.* Minneapolis: Fortress, 1989.

Overholt, Thomas W. *Prophecy in Cross-Cultural Perspective: A Sourcebook for Biblical Reseachers.* Atlanta: Scholars, 1986.

Peristiany, J. G., ed. *Honour and Shame: The Values of Mediterranean Society.* London: Weidenfeld & Nicolson, 1965.

Petersen, David L. *The Roles of Israel's Prophets.* Sheffield, UK: JSOT, 1981.

Pitt-Rivers, Julian. *The Fate of Shechem, or the Politics of Sex: Essays in the Anthropology of the Mediterranean.* Cambridge, UK: Cambridge University Press, 1977.

Portier-Young, Anathea. *Apocalypse against Empire: Theologies of Resistance in Early Judaism.* Grand Rapids, Mich: Eerdmans, 2011.

Rogerson, J. W. *Anthropology and the Old Testament.* Atlanta: John Knox, 1978.

Rogerson, J. W. "Was Early Israel a Segmentary Society?" *Journal for the Study of the Old Testament* 36 (1986): 17–26.

Sanders, Seth L. *The Invention of Hebrew.* Urbana: University of Illinois, 2009.
Schloen, J. David. *The House of the Father as Fact and Symbol: Patrimonialism in Ugarit and the Ancient Near East.* Winona Lake, Ind: Eisenbrauns, 2001.
Schwartz, Seth. *Were the Jews a Mediterranean Society?: Reciprocity and Solidarity in Ancient Judaism.* Princeton, N.J.: Princeton University Press, 2010.
Smith, William Robertson. *Lectures on the Religion of the Semites.* New York: Appleton, 1889.
Steinberg, Naomi. *Kinship and Marriage in Genesis: A Household Economics Perspective.* Minneapolis: Fortress, 1993.
Stiebert, Johanna. *The Construction of Shame in the Hebrew Bible: The Prophetic Contribution.* Sheffield, UK: Sheffield Academic, 2002.
Wilson, Robert R. *Genealogy and History in the Biblical World.* New Haven, Conn.: Yale University Press, 1977.
Wilson, Robert R. *Prophecy and Society in Ancient Israel.* Philadelphia: Fortress, 1980.
Wilson, Robert R. *Sociological Approaches to the Old Testament.* Philadelphia: Fortress, 1984.
Wilson, Robert R. "Reflections on Social-Scientific Criticism." In *Method Matters: Essays on the Interpretation of the Hebrew Bible in Honor of David L. Petersen.* Edited by Joel M. LeMon and K. H. Richards, 505–522. Leiden: Brill, 2010.
Wood, Peter Wyatt. "Anthropology, Cultural and Social." In *The Dictionary of Anthropology.* Edited by Thomas Barfield, 17–21. Malden, Mass.: Blackwell, 1997.

T. M. Lemos

New Testament

Brief Synopsis. New Testament studies have become a richly interdisciplinary endeavor and that confluence now includes insights both from cultural anthropology and the cognitive science of religion. Cultural anthropology provides the suitable models required for a social-scientific interpretation of the New Testament documents. In 1979 Bruce J. Malina's seminal book, *The New Testament World. Insights from Cultural Anthropology*, was published. It was to have a profound impact on the translation and interpretation of the New Testament texts (2001). The book was written to equip readers of the New Testament with the tools needed to become considerate readers of it. Considerate readers are those showing prudent awareness of the differences in the social and cultural circumstances of the world of Jesus and Paul from their own. Malina's overriding concern was to address the propensity of modern readers to impose their religious sensibilities, political views, ways of reading and understanding, cognitive habits, cultural and social values, and lived experiences on the biblical texts without regard for their original social and cultural context.

A brief example of this tendency will illustrate the point. Mark 2:1–12 records the story of a paralytic being transported on a mattress by four carriers to Jesus's home. Unable to enter the house because of the large crowd gathered around it, they clambered up on the roof, scooped a hole in it, and lowered the man on the mattress to Jesus presumably to seek his healing. Noting the loyalty and persistence of the carriers, Jesus announced that the sins of the paralytic had been excused or forgiven (2:5). Confronted with the word "forgiven" contemporary readers automatically fill it with meaning. Their theological sensibilities interpret the announcement of forgiveness as Jesus releasing the man from his innate, sinful depravity—a forgiveness Jesus was able to offer because as son of God he died to save humankind from their sins. But would the people gathered around Jesus, the religious authorities, and paralytic have inferred this meaning from the words of Jesus? Armed with insights from cultural anthropology, Neufeld (2008) argued that such a notion of forgiveness was foreign to them. They, instead, heard what Jesus said about sins and forgiveness in the key of honor and shame and from the perspective of the social structures of patronage and clientage—vital cultural values in antiquity.

Malina desired that the texts of the New Testament be interpreted fairly, i.e., that they be understood on their own terms even when the ideas, values, social patterns, and meanings in them expose modern readers to culture shock. He proposed that taking into account the findings of cultural anthropology and other social sciences mitigated the tendency for ethnocentric (assuming that our values are superior to ancient values) and anachronistic (that our cultural values and perspectives are the same as that of ancient Roman society) readings of the texts of the New Testament. To counter ethnocentrism and anachronism, Malina proposed a series of certainties that define the value orientations and behaviors of persons in the ancient Mediterranean world. I include a number of them but by no means all of them. First, that these persons were enculturated and socialized in specific social systems, during given times and places. Second, that these persons shared meaning with others in their social groups expressed in language, gesture, and custom. Third, that these persons were enculturated in collectivist societies and therefore they were collectivist personalities not individualistic. Fourth, that these persons were concerned with their group and group integrity—their families and fellow villagers. Fifth, that these persons assessed other people and groups in terms of in-group and out-group boundaries drawn on general group patterns such as family, village, region, and ethnic group.

Models in Cultural Anthropology and New Testament Interpretation. Cultural anthropological studies contribute to New Testament interpretation by developing models that help with understanding the symbolic universe of the Greco-Roman culture in which the authors of the New Testament lived. The models operate at high levels of abstraction because they seek the culturally common and generic in persons and groups rather than seeking to determine what makes them unique. For example, the pivotal values of honor and shame were common to all groups and persons regardless of their social location on the status map—men and women competed for it; children sought for it; elites desired it; slaves strove for it. Of course, account must be taken of local variations in expressions of honor and shame in the respective courts of reputation in which what counted for honor and shame were deliberated and distributed at their whim.

Models in cultural anthropology help modern readers to understand the values that were operative in the social world of the New Testament. Culturally sensitive appreciation of values such as honor/shame, ways of viewing the world/cosmos (healing and health care), social institutions (kinship, politics, economics, religion), psychological nature of persons (monadic/dyadic), collateral relationships over individualism (collectivist/individualist), patronage and clientage (brokerage), time orientation (present/past), and views of how humans relate to nature (subordination/mastery) open up the New Testament for a culturally appropriate understanding of its social milieu. Pilch and Malina have helpfully collected a large number of social values and provided their social meanings in a handbook using insights from cultural anthropology (2009). Malina's book (2001) covers the models of honor and shame (pivotal values of the first-century Mediterranean world), the first-century personality (individual and group), the perception of limited good (maintaining one's social status), kinship and marriage (fusing families together), and categories of clean and unclean (rules of purity, sacred and profane).

Since the publication of Malina's book, interpretative models developed by anthropologists, refined and applied to the New Testament, have advanced remarkably (Lawrence & Aguilar 2004). Models of phenomena such as social identity (Esler 2003), ethnicity (Duling 2010), gender (Osiek & Pouya 2010), conversion (Crook 2004), ritual (DeMaris 2008), illness, sickness and disease (John J. Pilch 2000), money, debt, and taxes (Oakman 2008), landscape and spatiality (Stewart 2009), collective memory (Kirk 2010), and altered states of consciousness (J. J. Pilch 2002) have been advanced and successfully applied to the textual data.

Moreover, models from the cognitive science of religion have been deployed to understand the variety of resurrection beliefs, notions of the afterlife, out-of-body experiences, visionary experiences, and spirit possession operative across a broad spectrum of texts in the New Testament (Craffert 2009) and social networking in early Christianity using social networking theory (Luomanen, Pyysiainen, and Uro 2007). While we see and understand descriptions of spirit possession and out-of-body experiences in ancient discourses as anomalous, abnormal, and reflective of a nonrational, nonscientific primitive mentality, for ancients they were perfectly normal, everyday incidences experienced by professional and nonprofessional alike. Insights gained from neuroanthropology, neurobiology, cultural neuroscience, and evolutionary psychology help us to normalize these experiences rather than falling into the tiresome debates about whether the resurrection of Jesus was a bodily raising from the dead in time-space and verifiable historically or whether Paul really had an out-of-body journey to the third heaven (2 Cor 12:2–4). These were cultural realities that arose from alternative notions of how the world worked and were confirmed by tradition and experience in the meaning cycle of everyday life. One of the basic elements in a cognitive science of religion approach is that thoughts and ideas regarding resurrection and out-of-body experiences are made possible by the evolved cognitive capacities of the human mind. Such an approach helps to explain the repeated patterns and endless variations of postmortem representation in the corpus of the New Testament and in the early developing church.

Economic Anthropology. Our exposition will of necessity be selective but illustrative of the importance of cultural anthropological models in helping us to decipher the social world inhabited by Jesus and Paul. Our selection will discuss issues of money, taxes, and debt in the New Testament from the viewpoint of economic anthropology. Under the broad rubric of the cognitive science of religion our exposition will encompass some of the most recent work on Jesus's resurrection and Paul's ecstatic states by taking into account neuroanthropology and neurobiology.

> So he said, "A nobleman went to a distant country to get royal power for himself and then return. He summoned ten of his slaves, and gave them ten pounds, and said to them, 'Do business with these until I come back.' But the citizens of his country hated him and sent a delegation after him, saying, 'We do not want this man to rule over us.' When he returned, having received royal power, he ordered these slaves, to whom he had given the money, to be summoned so that he might find out what they had gained by trading. The first came forward and said, 'Lord, your pound has made ten more pounds.' He said to him, 'Well done, good slave! Because you have been trustworthy in a very small thing, take charge of ten cities.' Then the second came, saying, 'Lord, your pound has made five pounds.' He said to him, 'And you, rule over five cities.' Then the other came, saying, 'Lord, here is your pound. I wrapped it up in a piece of cloth, for I was afraid of you, because you are a harsh man; you take what you did not deposit, and reap what you did not sow.' He said to him, 'I will judge you by your own words, you wicked slave! You knew, did you, that I was a harsh man, taking what I did not deposit and reaping what I did not sow?'" (Q 19:12–13, 15–24, 26/Luke 19:12–27)

From the sample text in the preceding paragraph, sound investment strategies and acquisition of wealth appear to drive ancient economies in the same manners as modern ones. Yet, ancient economies were not industry based or capitalist oriented. They did not promote individualistic acquisition of wealth, nor were they stock market driven, or global in perspective. Rather they were preindustrial, agrarian and trade based, driven by peasants and tenants suffering under the burden of exploitative taxation and rents, and centered on land that was distributed, owned, and supervised by the elite. As such these agrarian economies were founded mainly on food production through subsistence farming by the peasants.

Rents and taxes were extracted from the peasants to garner the favor and support the wealth of the aristocrats—who consisted of no more than 3 percent of the population. The elites were comprised of royal families, aristocrats, religious leaders, and some priests. They drew income from rural estates and temple structures and were supported by a small class of retainers consisting of government, bureaucratic, and religious functionaries—they could be slaves and freedmen/women—who profited socially and economically by their status. Their status depended directly on the good will and favorable regard of the elite. Peasants made up 90 percent of the population. They supported the continued asymmetrical distribution of wealth and special advantage to the elite. Taxes, tithes, and rent generated by the labor of the peasantry flowed to the urban centers such as Rome and the temple in Jerusalem. Wealth was redistributed to reflect the needs and desires of the wealthy and not the peasantry, the primary producers. Both David A. Fiensy (2010) and Douglas Oakman (2008) confirm that the economic system reflected in the New Testament was agrarian and not industrial and was based on the essential division of society into peasants and aristocrats with profound implications for how we understand Jesus's parables of fields, birds, sowers and seeds, harvest, growth of weeds, coins, and wealthy noblemen entrusting money to slaves.

The parable in Q 19:12–13, 15–24, 26/Luke 19:11–2 illustrates well the rather large gap that exists between modern capitalist economies promoting industry and venturesome investment and ancient agrarian economies promoting the redistribution of wealth in a limited good society where an absentee landlord stands to gain at the expense of his slaves. We should note that it is a difficult parable to reconstruct and thus has caused much interpretative consternation among commentators. The details of reconstructing the parable notwithstanding, we come away with a sense of how ancient economic systems functioned. What is important for us to understand is that Western interpreters enculturated in the capitalist West have found it virtually impossible to imagine the social dynamics of an agrarian-based economy and the labor of peasants to which this parable would have appealed. For modern readers, Jesus appears to be extolling the virtues of capitalism and the amassing of personal wealth. Hence, generally, the third slave who failed to meet his master's demands has been portrayed as weak, timid, and less than adventuresome in his investment strategies. He hoards the money entrusted to him and is overly cautious with his master's money—fearful of his overlord he, in the Lukan version, wraps the coins up in a cloth rather than banking them for a reasonable rate of return. The other two servants are portrayed positively because they contribute to the master's wealth through wise investment schemes. They are rewarded for their efforts. The parable appears to support the capitalist exhortations of a hard work ethic and the acquisition of personal wealth.

But if we take into account that peasant economies were subsistence economies in which the purpose of labor was primarily for the preservation of one's family and the well-being of one's village a different picture emerges. And, if this is a parable of the kingdom of God, it holds bad news indeed for peasants. To them it appeared that not much had changed and confirmed that God and Jesus operated rapaciously in the same way as the system in which they were embedded. Even though a kingdom story, Richard L. Rohrbaugh emphasizes the realism of the parable in contradistinction to the allegorizing version of it in Matthew (25:14–30) and labels the parable in Luke a "text of terror" (1993).

In the version of the parable under consideration, ten slaves are entrusted with silver coins and instructed by the landlord that they are to invest them while he is out fetching for himself a royal kingdom. Two of them invest the silver coins entrusted to them and reported what gain they achieved during the landlord's absence. One, however, failed in his assignment and garnered the harsh anger of his master who condemned him as an evil slave (19:22). Not surprisingly, in the ears of the slaves and peasants, the nobleman was marked negatively as one who had power and was seeking more of it, as holding expectations of return from his slaves that were impossible to realize, and exhibiting conduct that was contemptible. This characterization was reinforced when the noble person says to his slave that he was inexcusably aware "that he harvests where he sows not and gathers from places in which he has not scattered seed" (19:22). His ruthless character is highlighted earlier in the story when the kingdom inhabitants he wishes to expropriate for himself send a delegation with the news that they did not wish him to rule over them (19:14). Indeed, the news triggers anger in him with the response that his enemies be brought to him and slaughtered before him (19:27). He is hard and unbending in his demands and leaves the last slave in a deeply compromised position without legal recourse or protection—it is s legal system unfavorable to the interests of slaves. In the ears of the elite, of course, his anger with the third servant was justified as was his extortionist plan with its outrageous demands.

How then do we make sense of this parable? Basically it means for us to adopt a peasant's mindset. Peasants would have been mindful that in a limited-good society, seeking gain was morally wrong—their gain meant someone else's loss. Persons with a sense of honor and appropriate shame meant seeking neither loss nor gain but meant maintaining what they already had. In the view of peasants the two servants who had fallen prey to the master's extortionist scheme were no more than thieves. The third slave, however, had maintained an honorable position by refusing to become involved in the plan—it earned him the condemnation of the overlord whereas the other two were rewarded for their acquiescence to his demands. In the world of the peasants, life went on as usual. What then is the point of the story? Basically it condemned the conduct of the wealthy and those coopted by the prosperous to enact their arrangements—of robbing the poor and rewarding those who cooperated with their powers to obtain property, funds, or patronage. And as a kingdom of God parable, it was a reminder to the auditors that the current injustices and social inequities would eventually be transcended when adherence to the teaching of Jesus to serve God rather than mammon triumphed (Luke 16:13–14).

Cognitive Science of Religion. Humans universally have evolved with the cognitive propensities to imagine varieties of postmortem experiences for saints and sinners, have visions and dreams reflecting alternate realities, experience other-worldly journeys either in-body or out-of-body, develop variations in resurrection beliefs and enshrine them in tradition, envisage physical bodies after death with persistence of mind still expressing some level of desire, emotionality, and epistemic process, believe that bodies come back from the dead are no longer constrained by walls and locked doors, and see the cosmos populated with spirits, demons, ghosts, and gods (John 20:25–27). A cognitive science of religion approach gives us the tools necessary to understanding how and why humans have these propensities and why some of their beliefs simply fade into obscurity and others survive to become dogma. The cognitive sciences are made up of a coalescence of approaches that include evolutionary psychology, neuroanthropology, neurobiology, and others. These approaches represent the latest advances to make sense of the variety and dissimilarity of accounts about death, resurrection, ecstatic states, and postmortem existence in the New Testament.

> I know a person in Christ who fourteen years ago was caught up to the third heaven—whether in the body or out of the body I do not know; God knows. And I know that such a person—whether in the body or out of the body I do not know; God knows—was caught up into Paradise and heard things that are not to be told, that no mortal is permitted to repeat. (1 Cor 15:2–4)

> While they were talking about this, Jesus himself suddenly stood among them and said to them, "Peace be with you." They were startled and terrified, and thought that they were seeing a ghost. He said to them, "Why are you frightened, and why do doubts arise in your hearts? Look at my hands and my feet; see that it is I myself. Touch me and see; for a ghost does not have flesh and bones as you see that I have." (Luke 24:36–39)

Clear from these examples is that ancients had the propensity of mind to imagine and construct after-life realities that were counterintuitive to the mundane reality of human experience. Death and the rot of physical bodies were undeniably a part of the cycle of life. They appeared to defy and nullify the notions of the rise to life of newly reconstituted physical bodies, yet such ideas nevertheless flourished in astonishing variety. The resurrected Jesus was portrayed with a body of flesh and bones that was scarred, famished (he ate broiled fish in their sight), and fingered, yet appeared out of nowhere in the midst of a conversation on the road to Emmaus and passed through walls and locked doors with ease (John 20:26; Luke 24:13–36, 42–43). The disciples, preoccupied by the events they just witnessed, were so startled and fear-stricken by Jesus's sudden appearance on the road to Emmaus that they thought him to be a ghost (Luke 24:39).

A diversity of beliefs and practices about death, resurrection, bodies, souls, and the afterlife existed side-by-side in earliest Christianity. Each of these views was equally real for different groups of people living in dissimilarly constructed worldviews and perceptions of reality. The Acts of the Apostles records the rather divisive differences in perception that existed between the Pharisees and Sadducees about the resurrection of the dead, angels, and spirits (Acts 23:6–8). Modern readers under the influence of scientific discoveries pushing back the mysteries of the universe, postenlightenment rationalism, genome research, and advances in medical research tend to dismiss the stories of resurrected bodies with skepticism or they get bogged down in debates about whether Jesus was really raised bodily from the dead.

How does one account for the rise and persistence of some afterlife beliefs and the demise of others? What are the fundamentals of the cognitive science of religion that help us to explain why humans developed the mindset of imagining and constructing afterlife notions of existence? Cognitive scientists argue that cognition, like other human characteristic habits, was shaped by evolutionary selection. Evolution, as we know, affects not only genetics but also behaviors and ideas. The human brain, in particular, evolved the cognitive ability to keep track of the thoughts and feelings not only of oneself but also of others and to posit intentionality upon the thoughts and feelings observed. Human minds developed the capability to interpret and predict other people's words, conduct, emotions, desires, and bodily demeanor and understand them to be different from one's own. We observe, for example, someone sitting in a chair with fidgeting feet and a tense body, suddenly jumping out of the chair and running from the room. Based on the circumstantial evidence provided by a dentist's office, we automatically project meaningful intentions on the person. The response was not governed by the physical properties of the dentist's office but by this person's state of mind—we infer that the flight was driven by fright and the desire to get away as quickly as possible.

This finely honed ability is often referred to as Theory of Mind. In its simplest form, essential to Theory of Mind is our tendency to project intentionality onto the actions of other agents. Moreover, this tendency to project intentionality also comes into play when we predict the mental states of people who are physically absent. A parent might exhort a child to good behavior because it will make grandpa happy even though he has long been dead. The parent has attributed meaningful intentions to the mind of the grandfather hoping, perhaps, to exert control on the child's behavior. Indeed, cultures the world over represent the minds of the deceased to be active—in particular, as noted earlier, the active continuance of states of mind such as emotion, desire, and thinking processes. Research shows that generally humans are not inclined to attribute psychobiological (hunger/thirst) and perceptual states (smell/vision) to the dead, though exceptions are made in the fearful descriptions of the fate of the dead. Luke records the story of Lazarus's and the rich man's death and their respective fates—Lazarus ends up by the side of Abraham in a state of bliss and the rich man in Hades in a state of torment. Not only are the flames agonizing but they trigger intense thirst. He begs for water to cool his tongue (Luke 16:24). Most of us accept the idea that the capacity to attribute these states of mind to the living does not turn off after the death of someone but continues on. Happiness, bliss, joy, no more tears, pain, and sorrow, and the absence of thirst and hunger are but a few of the many intuitions humans have about the state of mind of the dead.

Humans globally have an extraordinary capacity for thinking up and adhering to thoughts, ideas, and beliefs that are moderately counterintuitive. Indeed, counter-intuitivism plays a significant role in the formation, memorization, and transmission of beliefs related to human idealization and construction of post-mortem experiences. Studies show that the minds of humans favor counterintuitive constructions of a moderate sort that do not violate too many ontological categories (Boyer 2001). The story of Jesus walking on water retains some of the physical features we attach to a body in locomotion on land but it also violates basic intuitive physics when it does so on water (Matt 14:25). It represents an example of borrowing intuitive properties from another category—a heavy ship floating on water and attaching it to humans in such way it does not violate too many intuitive categories. Thus, had Jesus been depicted summersaulting across the water holding a floatation device in the middle of a storm it intuitively would have violated too many properties effectively to promote long-term interest or recollection. The Apocryphal Gospels, in the course of their cultural transmission and circulation, presented countless excessively counterintuitive variants of the extraordinary birth of Jesus, his precociousness shortly after birth, and his exploits as a child. The selection process was such that many of them survived and became attached to Jesus but did not find consensual reality in the same way as, e.g., the Synoptic Gospels.

We have periodically referred to a series of well-attested, innate ontological categories that when violated in some limited way account for why postmortem ideas take foot and become wide spread in human religious imagination. The ontological categories that are widely accepted are person, plant, animal, natural object, and artefact. On the basis of these ontological categories we make inferences that aid us in the quick and easy identification and placement of objects. Unstated assumptions about these categories place constraints on human behavior and direct a wealth of mundane events and thoughts. In other words, intuitive ontology organizes human experiences in order to make sense of them. Imaginations of a human body in a post-mortem state intuitively violate certain features of these categories while at the same time retaining others.

Take as an example, Odysseus. While in Hades, he tried to embrace his mother's ghost but each time she flitted from his embrace as if it were a dream or phantom. When he queries her why she does not stay still when he attempts to embrace her she responds by saying that all people are like this when they are dead—the sinews no longer hold the flesh and bones together (Odyssey xi). In the New Testament, ghosts are mentioned several times in connection with Jesus. Without question, the disciples' believed Jesus to be a ghost when they saw him walking on the sea (Matt 14:26; Mark 6:49; Luke 24:37, 39). Similarly, Jesus implicitly accepted the existence of ghosts without question when he responded to the disciples, "Why are you frightened... Look at my hands and my feet; see that it is I myself. Touch me and see; for a ghost does not have flesh and bones as you see that I have" (Luke 24:39). The existence of ghosts is tacitly admitted in the response. A ghost preserves some of the features we attach to the category of human bodies but also transgresses intuitive physics by positing bodies that do not have flesh and bones. It is a body unlimited in its movement from place to place and a body buoyant enough to transverse a sea without sinking beneath its stormy waves. Boyer argues that these modest counterintuitive violations increase the likelihood of these beliefs being remembered and transmitted.

Similarly, the persistence of minds after death and the positing of resurrected bodies are counterintuitive phenomena of a sort that are memorable in the long run. Sometimes, however, ideas that are excessively counterintuitive run into resistance and eventually disappear or are reformulated to make an appearance in other forms. For instance, take the case of Paul explaining the resurrection to the community that he established in Corinth. Communal consensus about the nature of the resurrection appears to have disintegrated in his absence. Insights gained from a cognitive science of religion approach suggest that what Paul initially proposed about the body, death, and resurrection may have run up against the innate cognitive tendencies of the group in Corinth. On the basis of 1 Corinthians 15 and other texts in the epistles of Paul, Paul saw his visionary experiences of the resurrected Jesus as constituting legitimate evidence for Jesus's resurrection (Shantz 2009). Using insights offered from the perspectives of neuroanthropology, Craffert argues that Paul's visions were reality creating events and for him constituted the basis of his belief that Jesus was resurrected from the dead (2011). Moreover, he hoped that his community would accept the implications that the resurrection of Jesus had for the life-after-death body—it would be a spiritual body discontinuous from the physical body of flesh, albeit still a body (1 Cor 15:18).

He, however, does not bother to describe what properties these bodies of flesh might take on as spiritual bodies, as, for example, the Gospel writers long after Paul's death do in their portrayal of Jesus's postresurrection body. It appeared suddenly out-of-nowhere and then disappeared just as quickly, it moved through closed doors, and it ingested food. Lacking clarity on the matter, Paul's claims that Jesus's bodily resurrection had implications for all human bodies individually ran up against the innate cognitive tendencies of his community in Corinth and found rejection.

Conclusion. The New Testament documents speak from particular social worlds. Knowledge of the social institutions and values and attitudes of the ancient Mediterranean world are thus essential to translating and interpreting the New Testament. The ability to penetrate the ordinary and everyday meaning systems of the original composers and their audiences requires an intimate awareness of the connection between language and the social values that made up their social worlds. Cultural anthropology and the cognitive sciences provide modern readers with the appropriate social and cultural lenses with which to interrogate the texts of the New Testament.

[*See also* Disability Criticism; Economics and the Bible; *and* Social Sciences, *subentry* New Testament.]

BIBLIOGRAPHY

Boyer, P. *Religion Explained: The Evolutionary Origins of Religious Thought.* New York: Basic Books, 2001. This fascinating volume, explains the human propensity universally for counterintuitive thinking when formulating after-life beliefs.

Craffert, P. F. "I 'witnessed' the raising of the dead": Resurrection Accounts in a Neuroanthropological Perspective." *Neotestamentica* 45 (2011): 1–28. This is a fascinating study of the resurrection of the dead from the perspective of neuroanthropology. Visionary experience is surveyed as a potential source for understanding the postresurrection appearances of Jesus before his disciples and Paul.

Craffert, P. F. "Jesus' Resurrection in a Social-Scientific Perspective: Is there Anything New to be Said?" *Journal for the Study of the Historical Jesus* 1 (2009): 126–151. Examines the scholarly debate centered on the question of whether Jesus's resurrection was an actual event in history and proposes an alternate view from the perspective of the social sciences.

Crook, Z. A. *Reconceptualising Conversion: Patronage, Loyalty, and Conversion in the Religions of the Ancient Mediterranean.* Berlin and New York: W. de Gruyter, 2004. Placing Paul's conversion experience within the culture of patronage, clientage, and benefaction help Westerners to overcome psychologized and individualized models of conversion.

DeMaris, R. E. *The New Testament in its Ritual World.* New York: Routledge, 2008. Recognizes the importance of ritual activity in all of human life and explores the New Testament from the perspective of ritual.

Duling, D. C. "Ethnicity and Paul's Letter to the Romans." In *Understanding the Social World of the New Testament,* edited by D. Neufeld and R. E. DeMaris, 68–89. New York: Routledge, 2010. The contrast that Paul makes between Greeks, Israelites, and Judeans from the language and theory of ethnicity is addressed in this study.

Esler, P. F. *Conflict and Identity in Romans: The Social Setting of Paul's Letter.* Minneapolis, Minn.: Fortress, 2003. This study provides an illuminating reading of Romans from the perspective of group formation and the conflict invariably generated when Pauline communities sought to define their identities.

Fiensy, D. A. "Ancient Economy and the New Testament." In *Understanding the Social World of the New Testament,* edited by D. Neufeld and R. E. DeMaris, 194–206. New York: Routledge, 2010. The agrarian nature of ancient economies is explored from the standpoint of land ownership and farm production.

Kirk, A. K. "Memory Theory: Cultural and Cognitive Approaches to the Gospel Tradition." In *Undertsanding the Social World of the New Testament,* edited by D. Neufeld and R. E. DeMaris, 57–67. New York: Routledge, 2010. Memory, what is remembered, memory recall, and the social dimensions of memory formation are discussed in terms of the latest theories of memory and then applied to the gospels traditions about Jesus.

Lawrence, L. J., and M. I. Aguilar. *Anthropology and Biblical Studies: Avenues of Approach.* Leiden, The Netherlands: Deo, 2004. A helpful and exhaustive study that chronicles the rise of anthropological and social scientific studies of the biblical text.

Luomanen, P., I. Pyysiainen et al., eds. *Explaining Christian Origins and Early Judaism. Contributions from Cognitive and Social Science.* Leiden, Netherlands: Brill, 2007. This volume is an exhaustive introduction to the cognitive sciences and their application to ritual, social identity theory, the sociology of knowledge, and a number of other significant topics for the study of Christian origins.

Malina, B. J. *The New Testament World: Insights from Cultural Anthropology.* Louisville, KY: Westminster/John Knox, 2001. This seminal work introduced models of cultural anthropology and applied them to understanding the social world of the New Testament.

Neufeld, D. "Sins and Forgiveness: Release and Status Reinstatement of the Paralytic in Mark 2:1–12." In *The Social Sciences and Biblical Translation,* edited by D. Neufeld, 51–64. Leiden, Netherlands: Brill, 2008. This article explores the idea that forgiveness should be understood not so much as an internal transformation in attitude but as an external one with profound social implications.

Oakman, D. E. "Jesus and Agrarian Palestine: The Factor of Debt." In *The Social World of the New Testament,* edited by J. H. Neyrey and E. C. Stewart, 63–84. Peabody, Mass.: Hendrickson, 2008. Debt in perpetuity, landless peasants, and Jesus are the focus of this excellent study.

Osiek, C., and J. Pouya. "Constructions of Gender in the Roman Imperial World." In *Understanding the Social World of the New Testament,* edited by D. Neufeld and R. E. DeMaris, 44–56. New York: Routledge, 2010. Body, sexuality, and how ancients constructed notions of masculinity and femininity help to understand Paul's preoccupation with gender issues.

Pilch, J. J. "Altered States of Consciousness in the Synoptics." In *The Social Setting of Jesus and The Gospels,* edited by W. Stegemann, B. J. Malina and G. Theissen, 103–116. Minneapolis, Minn.: Fortress, 2002. Visions, dream-like states, other worldly journeys, and the transfiguration of Jesus are the focus of this study.

Pilch, J. J. *Healing in the New Testament: Insights from Medical and Mediterranean Anthropology.* Minneapolis, Minn.: Fortress, 2000. Eschewing a medical-centric approach of the western world, this article insightfully discusses issues of healing, illness, sickness, and disease in the world of the New Testament.

Pilch, J. J., and B. J. Malina. *Handbook of Biblical Social Values.* Grand Rapids, Mich.: Baker Academic, 2009. Values and their meaning such as nudity, parenting, limited good, evil eye, shame, and a host of others are covered in this handbook.

Shantz, C. *Paul in Ecstasy: The Neurobiology of the Apostle's Life and Thought.* Cambridge, UK: Cambridge University Press, 2009. Paul describes an experience of having ascended to the third heaven, whether in body or out-of-body he does not know, which this study insightfully investigates from the viewpoint of neurobiological studies of human brain function.

Stewart, E. C. *Gathered Around Jesus: An Alternative Spatial Practice in the Gospel of Mark.* Eugene, OR: Wipf & Stock, 2009. This study uses spatial theory to argue that Jesus founds his movement in the borderland territories of the wilderness/desert, the sea, and the mountain to create a unique space of the kingdom of God.

Dietmar Neufeld

Cultural-Historical Criticism

In the field of biblical studies, cultural-historical criticism explores how biblical words, images, things, and ideas of "the Bible" take particular meaningful forms in particular cultural contexts. It is not about interpreting biblical texts so much as it is about interpreting biblical interpretations, paying particular attention to how such interpretations reveal historically particular cultural meanings of the biblical texts. The larger goal of this approach is to understand the biblical cultures in which such productions of biblical meaning operate. Its goal, then, is not to understand the Bible but to understand the cultures in which the Bible takes on particular meanings, and to examine how those meanings are produced, reproduced, and transformed over time.

Cultural History in General. In academic discourse, cultural history refers generally to historical research that explores the ways meaning takes form within culture, often but not exclusively popular culture. Often drawing on anthropological approaches (some cultural historians prefer to be called historical anthropologists), it presumes that meaning is a matter of cultural production; it is produced and reproduced through our words, our actions, the things we make and use, and the media technologies by which we extend ourselves into our world. These words, actions, things, and media technologies are the ways a society expresses itself, revealing its more or less conscious desires, anxieties, sensations, memories, and so on. Cultural historians examine various cultural phenomena, be they "high" or "low," as signs, or symptoms, by which we may diagnose cultural meanings, which are not always, indeed not often, explicit or conscious.

Cultural history has emerged over the past few decades out of, and sometimes over against, Marxist base-superstructure approaches (e.g., the French *Annales* school and British and American social history), which understood a society's economic mode of production as the base, or cause, of all other aspects of social organization and culture. Such social-historical approaches treated cultural meanings as superstructural effects of the base economic system. Cultural history, on the other hand, takes such phenomena more seriously, on their own terms, as means of exploring how human beings, as cultural subjects, are both producers and products of culture.

There are many different theoretical and methodological influences that have helped shape the field of cultural history. In fact, several of the most influential anthropological approaches, moreover, are familiar to students of religion, including Mary Douglas's study of purity, pollution, and taboo in Leviticus; Edward Evans-Pritchard's work on magic and witchcraft; and Clifford Geertz's work on religion as a cultural system. Beyond these, two nonreligionist scholars are particularly helpful in developing a cultural-historical approach to Bible: Raymond Williams on culture and the structure of feeling, and Michel Foucault on discursive practices and the archaeology of knowledge (for fuller treatments of these two figures, see Deal and Beal 2004; Burke 2008).

Influence of Raymond Williams. Rejecting the elitist idea of culture as "high culture," the special possession of "cultivated people," Raymond Williams developed a theory of culture that incorporated two key aspects: on the one hand, the ordinary, that is, the commonly held meanings of a society's "whole way of life"; and on the other hand, the individual, innovative meanings that derive from arts and learning, and that can challenge the common and ordinary aspects of a culture (Williams 2001, pp. 10–13). Whereas the former aspect of culture is what makes it common and familiar, the latter is what explains individual difference and allows for cultural transformation.

Another key concept in Williams's understanding of culture that is especially provocative vis-à-vis religion and biblical studies is what he calls the "structure of feeling," that is, the character and quality of common lived experience within a culture. This lived experience involves complex interactions between, on the one hand, "official" aspects of culture such as laws, doctrines, and other formal regulations that control behaviors, feelings, and values in obvious ways, and, on the other hand, subtle, unofficial "structures" that order people's shared feelings and "common sense." The phrase "structure of feeling" seems contradictory: "structure" implies something solid that orders and determines culture, whereas "feeling" suggests something unstructured and highly personal. Yet, within any given culture, people's feelings tend to follow common patterns and adhere to a shared "sense of life," even when there are no explicit, official regulations in place to structure such common experiences. The primary evidence for unofficial structures of feeling, then, is found in the fact that different individuals and groups within a culture so often share feelings and commonsense perspectives that are not determined by official rules and regulations.

Of course, different people fit more or less comfortably within a culture's dominant structures of feeling. This fact raises an important question: How do power and dominance work within culture, and what dynamic relations make change and even revolution possible? Williams identifies three aspects or dynamics of any historical period within a culture: (1) *dominant* aspects of a culture, that is, the structures of feeling and common meaning that try to dictate and authorize certain behaviors and thoughts while discouraging or punishing others; (2) *residual* aspects, that is, older values and meanings from previously dominant cultural formations that have survived into new cultural contexts; and (3) *emergent* aspects, that is, new values and meanings that put pressure on dominant aspects of culture and indicate potential cultural shifts and changes. Culture, then, is never a monolithic whole but a system of dynamic relations in which different kinds of individual and collective power and knowledge are forming and reforming.

Influence of Michel Foucault. The French philosopher and historian Michel Foucault has been especially influential in drawing attention to how such formations and reformations of knowledge and power take place within a culture. He was especially interested in how our particular, individual thoughts, beliefs, and behaviors—indeed, our very selves and worlds—are constructed by our discursive practices, that is, systems or "grids" of thought and meaning comprising shared worldviews, beliefs, values, ideas, and morals. This process of *subjection* to discourse is, paradoxically, the way we become thinking, acting *subjects* within society. The ways we think and the truths we hold to be self-evident are cultural constructions, produced and perpetuated within discursive practices that are as familiar to us as the air we breathe.

The task of the cultural historian, then, is a sort of "archaeology of knowledge": to uncover these discursive practices, determine the structures and rules embedded within them that make them functional, and, in the process, bring to light the fact that the various ideas, values, and practices that a culture takes for granted as self-evident and timeless have been produced and concretized through the "long baking process of history" (Foucault 1977, p. 144). The things we take for granted as common sense (e.g., medicine, religion, the state) are not historical givens but are, rather, "discursive objects" that take form within the systems or grids of thought and meaning within which we exist. They are "truth-effects" produced within those systems through concrete, everyday human practices.

How, then, does change happen? Where do new ideas and courses of action come from? What are the mechanisms by which the thinkable within a culture alters? How are new truth-effects produced? What particular, individual, concrete practices effectively disrupt established grids of knowledge and power and produce new ways of thinking and acting? Addressing these questions calls for an approach that biblical scholars might describe as *exegetical*: eschewing generalizations and universal claims, one must attend very closely to the specific details of particular texts, objects, and practices within a cultural archive, treating them as individual discursive practices that produce or reproduce unique forms of knowledge within particular cultural-historical contexts.

Cultural History of *Bible*. Just as cultural history in general explores the ways meaning takes form within culture, the cultural history of Bible, then, explores the ways the meanings of biblical texts, images, and "the Bible" itself take form within culture. It too presumes that such meanings are matters of cultural production; they are produced and reproduced not only through spoken or written words but also through popular media, material objects, and embodied actions. These words, things, actions, and media technologies are the ways a culture expresses its conceptions of the Bible and the biblical. The cultural historian of Bible, therefore, treats these data as meaning-bearing symptoms of biblical culture.

The absence of a definite article, "the," in "cultural history of Bible" is intentional. The proper focus of cultural-historical criticism in biblical studies is not *the* Bible, but *Bible*. From the perspective of cultural history, "Bible" is indefinite. It is not a singular thing or a self-evident object of analysis; it is not timeless or fixed; its form, content, and meaning change within different cultural networks of knowledge and power. Particular concepts of "the Bible" are produced through particular cultural practices, including collective and individual ritual, education, publishing, media technology, and so on. Such practices generate a sense of "Bibleness," a discursive formation of the Bible and the biblical that is both an explicit ideological object and a structure of feeling.

A cultural-historical approach to Bible, therefore, presupposes that any instance of "the Bible" is not a thing but an idea that is culturally produced and reproduced. What Foucault said of other subjects of historical research, such as medicine and the state, may also be said of the Bible and the biblical: they are not given or self-evident intellectual objects to be particularized or incarnated in various interpretations through time; they are, rather, formulations of discourse, constantly changing as they are made and remade in different cultural productions of meaning. "The Bible" that predominates American evangelical culture today, for example, is the product of a network of loosely related cultural products and practices, from teaching and preaching in churches, to group Bible studies for adults and youth, to personal devotionals, to Bibles and biblical curricula produced and marketed by large evangelical publishing houses, to name a few. All these, moreover, are embedded within larger cultural networks of power and knowledge, and all are susceptible to larger processes of cultural transformation. How, for example, will the current media revolution affect "the Bible" as discursive formulation in evangelical Christian culture? To what extent is its general concept of the biblical tied to print culture, especially to the idea of the print book, and how might it change vis-à-vis the rise of digital network media culture?

It follows, then, that a cultural-historical approach in biblical studies does not separate literary content from material form. There is no such thing as a disembodied Bible or biblical text. Bible is always material as well as symbolic, sensual as well as semantic. The cultural history of Bible is about things as much as ideas, forms as much as contents, performances as much as interpretations, media as much as message. One cannot separate contents, words, or message from material form and media technology. The first verse of Genesis in a handwritten Hebrew Torah scroll chanted aloud in a Shabbat service is not the same as the first verse of Genesis in a contemporary English version. *Biblezine* read alone during quiet time at a Baptist Bible camp retreat is not the same as a production of *Jesus Christ Superstar* at the local public high school.

Cultural History's Relation to Reception History. The main precursor to cultural history of Bible is biblical reception history, which explores the history of the reception of biblical texts, images, stories, and characters through the centuries in the form of citation, interpretation, reading, revision, adaptation, and influence. Rooted in literary theorist Hans Robert Jauss's "aesthetics of reception" (Jauss 1970 [German 1967]) and, behind Jauss, the philosophical hermeneutics of Hans-Georg Gadamer (1989 [German 1960]), biblical reception history finds the meaning of a text neither in the text itself nor in the experience of the reader, but in the relationship between the two. With Jauss, biblical reception history insists that biblical texts do not exist independent of the history of their reception by readers; their meaning is, rather, a dynamic, historically situated *relationship* between production and reception—in Gadamer's terms, a "fusion of horizons" of the text and readers (Gadamer; see Luz 2006, pp. 124–125; Deal and Beal, pp. 77–78). As such, biblical reception history moves beyond earlier research into the history of biblical interpretation, insofar as it embraces a much broader definition of "interpretation," including not only academic and theological readings but also biblical appearances in visual art, literature, music, politics, and other cultural works.

Yet, whereas reception history focuses on the impact or influence of biblical texts, the cultural history of Bible focuses more sharply on the cultural meaning of them, as well as of "the biblical" and "the Bible" itself, insofar as those too are cultural constructs whose meaning and value are culturally contextual. Indeed, a cultural historical approach begins with the fact that there is no singular, fixed, original "the Bible" or "the biblical" to be received across history; rather, there are multiple, often competing, symbolic and material productions of them that are generated and generative in different scriptural cultures. In this light, the cultural history of Bible inverts traditional biblical interpretation, including reception history: it is less about interpreting the Bible via culture than it is about interpreting culture via Bible.

Cultural History of Bible in Practice: Three Approaches. The cultural history of Bible is a field, not a method. There is no single prescribed disciplinary procedure, but rather a range of approaches, drawing on different disciplines, all aimed at understanding how meanings of biblical texts, images, and values in particular, as well as meanings of the Bible and the biblical in general, are generated within particular cultural contexts through particular discursive practices. Within this range of cultural-historical biblical research and analysis, we may identify three general approaches.

First, ethnographic and anthropological approaches that analyze particular biblical practices, such as group Bible studies, worship services, and individual devotionals. These approaches usually involve extensive ethnographic fieldwork, including close observation of such practices and interviews with participants. Examples include anthropologist James S. Bielo's *Words upon the Word: An Ethnography of Evangelical Group Bible Study* (2009), an exploration of evangelical Bible study practices based on close observation and qualitative analysis of hundreds of Bible study meetings involving nineteen groups over more than a year and a half (see the pioneering work of Malley 2004), and Dorina Miller Parmenter's analysis of the public display among American evangelicals of heavily worn Bibles and the phenomenon of "duct-tape Bibles," including not only Bibles whose worn-out covers and binders were repaired with duct tape, but also brand-new duct-tape Bibles sold by large evangelical publishers who understand that there is sacred capital in that well-used look (Parmenter 2010).

A second approach focuses on close reading and analysis of particular biblical media, that is, particular Bibles and related products, which may be studied either as a whole or with regard to their presentations of particular biblical texts, images, or stories. Understanding that the medium is the message, such an approach attends not only to the translation of the text but also to material form, the media technologies employed, the visual appearance and layout of the text, as well as the value-adding, and often values-adding, supplemental notes, and commentary. An excellent book-length example of this approach is David Dault's *The Accessorized Bible* (2012), which delves deeply into the theological interests and diversions of many popular evangelical Bibles on the market today by reading their biblical texts in close relation with other "supplementary" material, including notes, comments, page layout, and illustrations.

The third and most common cultural-historical approach in biblical studies focuses on the critical examination of particular cultural productions in which interpretation or representation of biblical texts, stories, images, or even of the Bible itself figures prominently. Often such an approach focuses on mainstream works of popular culture in which Bible is a prominent dimension. Consider, for example, studies of movies or television shows that tell biblical stories, such as the Gospel narrative of Mel Gibson's 2004 film, *The Passion of the Christ*, or of Pier Paolo Pasolini's 1964 film, *Il vangelo secondo Matteo* (*The Gospel According to Matthew*), or the Joban tale of the South Park episode, "Cartmanland," in which Kyle believes he is reliving the biblical story of Job, asking why the wicked prosper and questioning God's justice, when he is smitten with the ultimate hemorrhoid after Cartman inherits $1 million and opens a lucrative amusement park. Such cultural productions help produce and reproduce the discursive network of meaning that generates a specific understanding of Bible and biblical values and motivates radical militant social identity and action.

Assessment. While representing a diverse range of disciplinary backgrounds and interests, all three of these approaches to cultural-historical criticism in biblical studies share certain interests and priorities that distinguish them from other approaches in the field. First and foremost, they all assume that the

Bible and the biblical are not self-evident things, handed down through religious history in the same essential form with the same essential contents; rather, they are cultural concepts. What Foucault said about medicine and the state are equally true about the Bible. It is a discursive object that is produced, reproduced, and deconstructed within particular cultural contexts.

The second commonality follows logically from the first. If the Bible and the biblical are not changeless things that are received and interpreted within different cultural contexts but are discursive objects that are produced in different biblical cultures, then the aim of the cultural historian of Bible is to understand those particular biblical cultures, past and present, as systems of meaning that produce particular, historically contingent conceptions of the Bible, biblical values, and biblical practices. The cultural historian of Bible therefore must pay close, almost exegetical attention to the ways particular biblical practices and things (a Bible study, duct-tape Bible lore, a teen study Bible, a white supremacist interpretation of Numbers) produce, reproduce, or undermine those meanings. In any case, the goal is not to evaluate the validity or truth-value of a particular biblical culture as right or wrong, good or bad interpretation, but rather to understand how the meaning it produces works, how it makes sense, for those who are part of that culture.

Third, these different approaches to the cultural history of Bible are all centrally concerned with the intimate relationship between knowledge and power, how power produces knowledge and knowledge produces power. When we talk about one, we are talking about the other—power/knowledge. One becomes a thinking, speaking, acting subject within a cultural system in the process of becoming subjected to it. Subjectivity and subjection go hand in hand, and therefore so do knowledge and power. That is the paradox of subjection: one gains power as a subject in the process of being subjected to the system in which one's power is realized. Power cannot be completely consolidated or controlled by any one position within culture. Within any network of power/knowledge, there are forces of discipline and oppression as well as forces of resistance and change. Power does not simply come down from on high; it circulates through the entire social body.

Clearly, cultural-historical approaches to Bible do not replace other, more familiar approaches and methods in biblical studies, especially those that focus on close textual analysis of biblical texts, including textual criticism, form and source criticism, redaction criticism, rhetorical criticism, structural and post-structural approaches, and other literary-critical approaches. Such approaches, which are staples of traditional theological studies curricula, are centrally concerned with either the historical reconstruction of the early literary and religious history of the text or with the structures, meanings, and dynamics within the texts themselves.

The central concern of biblical cultural history, by contrast, is to understand the cultures that produce the meanings of those biblical stories and texts, as well as the meaning of the Bible itself. As such this approach is perhaps less at home in the field of biblical theology within a seminary or divinity school and more at home in the field of academic religious studies in a college or university. Indeed, although cultural histories of Bible "won't preach" in most cases, we may recognize in them new and exciting potential contributions that biblical scholars can offer in academic religious studies and in the academic humanities and social sciences more generally.

[*See also* Cross-Cultural Exegesis; Cultural Studies; Intertextuality; Literary Criticism, Literary Theory, and the Bible; Materialist Criticism; Pop Culture and the Bible; Postcolonial Biblical Interpretation; Postmodern Interpretation; Reception Criticism and Theory; *and* Theological Interpretation.]

BIBLIOGRAPHY

Beal, Timothy. "Reception History and Beyond: Toward a Cultural History of Scriptures," *Biblical Interpretation* 19 (2011): 357–372.

Bielo, James S. *Words upon the Word: An Ethnography of Evangelical Group Bible Study*. New York: New York University Press, 2009.

Burke, Peter. *What is Cultural History?* 2d ed. Cambridge, UK: Polity, 2008.
Dault, David. *The Accessorized Bible*. New Haven, Conn.: Yale University Press, 2012.
Deal, William E., and Timothy K. Beal. *Theory for Religious Studies*. New York: Routledge, 2004.
Foucault, Michel. "Nietzsche, Genealogy, History." In *Language, Counter-memory, Practice: Selected Essays and Interviews*, edited by Donald F. Bourchard. Ithaca, N.Y.: Cornell University Press, 1977. English translation of "Nietzsche, la généalogie, l'histoire," first published in 1971.
Garber, Marjorie. *Symptoms of Culture*. New York: Routledge, 1998.
Hans-Georg Gadamer, *Truth and Method*, translated by Joel Weinsheimer and Donald G. Marshall. New York: Continuum, 1989. English translation of *Wahrheit und Methode*, first published in 1960.
Hunt, Lynn. *The New Cultural History*. Ithaca, N.Y.: Cornell University Press, 1989.
Jauss, Hans Robert. "Literary History as a Challenge to Literary Theory," *New Literary History* 1 (1970): 7–37. English translation of chapters V–XII of *Literaturgeschichte als Provokation der Literaturwissenschaft*, first published in 1967.
Luz, Ulrich. "The Contribution of Reception History to a Theology of the New Testament." In *The Nature of New Testament Theology: Essays in Honour of Robert Morgan*, edited by Christopher Rowland, Christopher Mark Tuckett, and Robert Morgan. Oxford: Blackwell, 2006.
Malley, Brian. *How the Bible Works: An Anthropological Study of Evangelical Biblicism*. Walnut Creek, Calif.: AltaMira, 2004.
Parmenter, Dorina Miller. "Iconic Books from Below: The Christian Bible and the Discourse of Duct Tape." *Postscripts* 6:1–3 (2010): 185–200.
Williams, Raymond. "Culture is Ordinary." In *The Raymond Williams Reader*, edited by John Higgins. Oxford: Blackwell, 2001.

Timothy Beal

Cultural Studies

Although cultural studies is neither homogenously formed nor consensually defined, it may be seen as an interdisciplinary "theoretical-political project" (Beverly 2004, p. 17) that is, an engaged academic and political movement that seeks to democratize culture (those "persistent forms or patterns of thought" [Chaney 1994, p. 2] shared by a given group's members) and to interrogate all cultural productions (that is, cultural practices, operations, and formations). At its best, the movement deploys a convergence of research methodologies (not a single or unified methodological prism) to interrogate the valorization of culture, to demystify the politics of representation, to foster practices of self-reflexive inquiry, and to promote actively a radical progressive cultural politics. In interrogating the valorization of culture, the movement considers all cultures as important, though it especially seeks to give attention to a given society's everyday and ordinary cultural practices (like the practices of eating or offering hospitality), cultural operations (like the varying types of kinship systems that operate in different societies), and cultural formations (like the technological innovations of urban hip-hop youth or the sophisticated acrobatics of the Brazilian martial arts dance-form known as Capoeira). That is, the cultural studies movement does not support the high-low culture valorization once advocated by Matthew Arnold but exposes the discursive processes of valorization that control what counts as culture. Thus, cultural studies would be as observant of the appliqué quiltmaking of the unlettered Harriet Powers in the nineteenth century as it would be of the art deco style of the Harlem Renaissance artist Aaron Douglas. In demystifiying the politics of representation, the movement asks: "who has the power to produce authorised representations of the world?" (Söderström 2005, p. 13). In fostering practices of self-reflexive inquiry, the movement examines the wider cultural currents in which all engagement with cultures takes place, including cultural studies' own practices. Thus, serious attention is given to the role of contextuality in informing one's *gaze* on a given culture. How one reads or understands a culture is not a *natural* or universal operation (as if all persons would view that culture in the same way) but largely controlled by one's own contextual factors, including one's conception of knowledge, which often may go unnoticed or unexposed until attention is placed on the ideological commitments, discursive construals, and power dynamics of that conception. In actively promoting a radical progressive cultural politics, moreover, this movement takes an ethical stance beyond simply analyzing culture. That is, the movement also intervenes through the ongoing production of countercultural discourses that challenge each new instantiation of a given culture's domination and power over all others.

Cultural Studies in the Anglophone World. In the Anglophone world, cultural studies began as a populist movement that "grew out of curricular innovations introduced into post-secondary educational programs for non-elite students taking degree courses outside Britain's ancient . . . regional universities" in the late 1940s (Sprinkler 1997, p. 385). In that iteration, cultural studies commenced as a type of "oppositional politics" among the British working-class, with a greater focus on the resistance potential of vernacular cultures as opposed to traditionally defined elite culture, with a greater concern for culture in and of itself (as with the New Left of Western Marxism) than with a mechanistic view of culture as simply a reflection of the material forces of production (as with the vulgar Marxism of the Soviet Marxists), and with a greater interest in the examination of the ideological production of texts or genres or other artifacts within a concrete political economy than in formalist (stylistic or aesthetic) analysis of those texts (Sprinkler, pp. 386–390). That beginning was arguably cultural studies' *culturalist* or *sociology of culture phase*—because its leaders (Raymond Williams, Edward P. Thompson, and Richard Hoggart) all drew upon Weber, Marx, and Mannheim, among others (Wolff 1999, p. 501), to show that working class persons should be considered as culture producers or agents and not simply mass culture consumers. This was soon followed by its *French theory phase*—when cultural studies' Birmingham Centre turned to antihumanistic French thinkers like Althusser among others to show the wider ideological forces (like educational and ecclesiastical systems as opposed to economic conditions) that *a priori* both regulate the conditions of possibility for human cultural operations and shape the conditions of possibility for human subjectivity. The second phase was later followed by a third one, cultural studies' *radical plurality and internationalization phase*—when cultural studies (a la Antonio Gramsci) once more acknowledged that self-determining human subjects could challenge a seemingly common-sensical and prevalent set of conditions and, relatedly, when cultural studies began to consider the great diversity of human identities along racial/ethnic, gender, and geopolitical lines as sites for the examination of cultures.

In truth, though, it is now generally acknowledged that "the Brits don't own cultural studies" (Mellor 1992, p. 664). That is, each variation of cultural studies in the Anglophone world has to be weighed in the light of specific historical and contemporary material conditions operating for each, whether one considers within the United States, for example, the black feminist cultural criticism of bell hooks, the Chicano cultural studies of José David Saldívar, or the media cultural criticism of Douglas Kellner. Still, whether in Britain, the United States, or elsewhere in the Anglophone world, cultural studies has developed into a burgeoning field. It has produced mega-anthologies and enjoyed institutional (and therefore, even disciplinary) success, though, admittedly, such success at times, especially in parts of the United States, seems to have resulted in a loss of the movement's initial interests in diffusing traditional disciplinary boundaries and in developing "alternative cultural productions" (Sprinkler, pp. 393–394).

Cultural Studies in "Latin America." Outside of the Anglophone world, for example, in what is (often uncritically) called "Latin America," the evolution of cultural studies had a different genealogy (one that actually *predates* the Birmingham and US varieties) and a different set of material conditions altogether.

First, what may be called the democratic project of cultural studies existed there initially free of the label "Latin America" (which, as Walter D. Mignolo has noted, is a geopolitical vestige of Europe's colonization of lands now subsumed in that spatial designation) and again initially free of any connection with the Birmingham School of cultural studies (Mignolo 2005, pp. x–xx; Trigo 2004, p. 5). From the conquest on, "there never was any question that culture *mattered*," as questions in this region were often raised about the West's failure to value indigenous cultures, about the impact of cultural imperialism and colonial languages, and about the relationship between culture and resistance to Western hegemony (McClennen 2011a, pp. 191–192). Accordingly, when cultural studies began to develop theoretically in this region, it did so primarily by focusing on the work of its own intellectuals (McClennen 2011a, p. 191), for example:

- the writing of José Carlos Mariátegui, who formed the Socialist Party in Peru and gave shape to the "sociopolitical essayistic tradition of Peru" (Ríos 2004, p. 23);
- the transculturation theory of Fernando Ortiz, the Cuban essayist who argued that cultural contact, however violent, always results in both loss and gain and never simply in a unilateral or unidirectional imposition of the dominant culture on the dominated one (Ríos p. 24; Weinberg 2012, p. 331);
- the work of Roberto Fernández Retamar, another Cuban essayist whose countercultural and ironic inversion of Shakespeare's Caliban, an enslaved character in *The Tempest*, makes the character a positive literary symbol for the region, not a vilified figure who perpetuates a colonialist "hierarchy of values" (Retamar 1989; Ríos p. 25; Matibag 1991, p. 5);
- and the writings of Antonio Cornejo Polar, a Peruvian cultural critic whose theory of heterogeneity proposes that the different form or system in which literature is produced (with its technology of alphabetic writing) compared to oral cultures already perpetuates falsely the view that the former is better than the latter because the former is historically tied to the conquest, with letters being the "sign of the difference between the colonizer and the colonized." (Tarica 2012, p. 175)

During the 1960s and 1970s, moreover, the region also offered to the wider world its own cultural studies critical practices through, for example:

- the critique of the "banking" concept of teaching (the view that teachers deposit knowledge into students) in Brazilian Paulo Freire's *Pedagogia do oprimido* (*Pedagogy of the Oppressed*) (Freire 1973; McClennen 2011a, p. 191; Trigo p. 7);
- the "theology of liberation" of Rubem Alves, Gustavo Gutiérrez, José Míguez Bonino, and the Boff brothers (Ríos, p. 27);
- the critique of the cultural imperialism implicit in Disney comic representations as argued by Chilean Ariel Dorfman in *Para leer al Pato Donald (How to Read Donald Duck*);
- the political critique of *nueva canción*, or the new song movement, which was led by Violeta Para, Víctor Jara, and Mercedes Sosa and which featured a type of underground music that stood at odds with fascist militias such as the one led by Augusto Pinochet of Chile (McClennen 2011b, p. 139);
- the literary boom that included Gabriel García Márquez's *Cien años de soledad* (*One Hundred-Years of Solitude*) (Irwin and Szurmuk 2012, p. 3);
- or the representation of history through the witness narratives known as *testimonios* (as in, for example, Miguel Barnet's *Biografía de un cimarrón* [*Autobiography of a Runaway Slave*]; Poblete 2012, pp. 199–200).

Second, even if cultural studies in the region today (as illustrated by the proliferation of cultural studies journals and anthologies along with several cultural studies graduate programs in Ecuador, Costa Rica, Peru, Chile, Argentina, Mexico, and Colombia) is cross-fertilized by a type of pan-cultural cultural studies, postnational cultural studies in the region is likely an effect of the rise of the ideology of neoliberalism (or global capitalism), which gives little or no attention to the distinctive interests of national states and "civic subjects" within those states in the interests of promoting global markets (McClennen 2011a, pp. 192–194; Irwin and Szurmuk, pp. 4–8).

Cultural Studies and Other Theoretical Perspectives. Still, whether in the Anglophone world or elsewhere, cultural studies intellectual workers—like those in gender studies, subaltern studies, postcolonial studies, and intersectionality theory—are concerned with operations of power, that is, with the ways in which a critique of culture exposes unequal relations of power. Like *gender studies*, cultural studies argues that gender is neither a natural nor fixed identification category. Nor is it "linked to the biological differences that [typically] distinguish men from women" (Ricalde 2012, p. 153). Rather, gender is a culturally constructed script, role, or set of regulatory practices that helps to identify a given society's hegemonic norms about material bodies (Ricalde, p. 153). Examining gender in cultures then exposes the submerged histories of those who do not fit such norms.

Like *subaltern studies*, cultural studies also takes stock in Gramscian concepts such as "hegemony" (or "ideological dominance" [Kellner 1995, p. 31]) and the "subaltern class" ("a name for the general attribute of subordination . . . whether this is expressed in terms of class, caste, age, gender and office, or in any other way" [Guha 1988, p. 35]) to show the relationship between power and representation. The disciplinary protocols of professional societies, hegemonic traditions of historiography, institutional curricular constraints, lines of logic (for example, linear binary logic as opposed to relational logic), and modes of representation (whether history is presented as written or oral, for example) can all foster a climate in which submerged voices are ignored, silenced, or negated.

Like *postcolonial studies*, cultural studies critiques the on-going legacies of coloniality ("the logic of domination") but without viewing the encounter between cultures simplistically as the imposition of the dominant culture onto another (Mignolo, p. 7; Rabasa 2012, p. 254). The production of knowledge for cultural studies, then, is never separated from wider historical legacies that foster domination, exploitation, and cultural flow (that is, cultural interconnections).

Like *intersectionality theory*, cultural studies provides an optic or prism for understanding the complexity of social identity or identification and the power differentials (or structures of inequality) associated with subject formations (McCall 2005, p. 1771). Cultural studies does not advocate a simplistic liberal-pluralist (additive-linear) model of social identity (or identification), as if social identity were determined solely by a single subject formation variable such as race, class, or gender, all of which are themselves "socially constructed categories of social experience" in association with embodied experiences (Adams et al. 2000, p. 2). In fact, considerations of a person's social identity in terms of only one of these analytical factors entails the homogenization of social identity, as if a person's humanity were limited to only one so-called essentialist subject formation. Such considerations also lock social identity into simplistic dichotomies that deny either heterogeneity or variation within an aggregate human grouping and obscure the power differentials that exist within a human grouping. Two African Americans, one classified as *dis/abled* and the other as *abled*, for example, are both similar yet different because the "ideology of ability" negatively targets the one classified as *dis/abled* (Siebers 2008, p. 7). Two women, one identified as an Anglo-American and another as an Asian American from a Southeast Asian lineage, are both similar yet different because the ideology of "whiteness" privileges the Anglo-American woman. Cultural studies, then, provides a prism for seeing more clearly the ways in which the members of a specific target group (a group affected by oppression) may be affected differently because its members are also differently aligned to multiple other subject formations that place the members in dominant or targeted positions with respect to power and access (Adams et al., pp. 2–3).

The Conjunction between Cultural Studies and Biblical Studies. Given these general indices of cultural studies, the conjunction between cultural studies and Western biblical studies may be seen both in the light of the history of that conjunction and in the light of some of the key emphases of that conjunction with respect to the cultural studies goal of exposing operations of power. In the West, the conjunction between cultural studies and biblical studies occurred only after other methodological prisms had gained prominence in biblical studies. That is, historical criticism, veritably a "family of [historical] approaches," was the first major methodological optic used in Western biblical studies from its postenlightenment emergence until the mid-1970s (Meeks 2005, p. 159). Later, both literary criticism and sociocultural criticism gained prominence in biblical studies from the mid-1970s to the 1990s. From the 1990s to the present, however, cultural studies has come into prominence within the biblical studies field largely because the field has witnessed the influx of a wide variety of voices, including non-Western, nonmale, and nonheterogendered voices, and the explosion and acceptance of a bewildering collection of methodological optics from wider contemporary currents (Segovia 2008, pp. 25–28). At its best, however, the conjunction is not controlled by those who are otherwise labeled as biblical studies professionals. Instead, works under this conjunction defy disciplinary boundaries, with the common affinity being the desire to name the ideological commitments and power dynamics that "underwrite and legitimate the social life of scripture" (Bielo 2006a, p. 7).

Locating Operations of Power in Texts and Interpreters. Given such a conjunction, intellectual workers who share the aforementioned affinity deploy a cultural studies perspective to expose or engage operations of power in three key areas (Liew 2011, p. 7). First, cultural studies locates operations of power in the cultural contexts of biblical traditions and of biblical interpreters. In part, a focus on contextualization highlights how biblical writers, many of whom were colonized by empires, struggled against hegemony. Examinations of a biblical tradition's counterdiscursive (or alternative) myths, syntax, or cosmologies, for example, reveal the struggles of colonized groups against imperial and patriarchal forces as well as the negotiated use of imperial strategies and a patriarchal political economy by the colonized themselves (Portier-Young 2011, p. 13; Bailey et al. 2009, p. 25).

In part, though, a focus on contextualization also highlights the power plays of interpreters who assume their values to be biblical or their methodological prisms to be disinterested (Bailey et al., p. 25). Accordingly, even if US "family values" organizations assert that their values are drawn from the Bible, in truth, such organizations may actually presuppose a modern or postmodern nuclear family, which stands strikingly at odds with a wide variety of family/marriage constitutions in the biblical literature (Petersen 2005, pp. 5–23). That is, in Genesis alone, notions of family are expansive, ranging from "patrilineal endogamy" (marriage between near relatives) to polycoity (male "sexual access to more than one female") to "sororal polygyny" (marriage between one person and two siblings), and hardly ideal and acceptable for most of those espousing the notion of biblical family values (Petersen, pp. 16–17). To say that an organization reflects biblical family values, then, could simply be a *rhetorical practice* designed to sanction a particular construal of "family values." In the United States, for example, adherents of traditional "family values" ideologically construct a *family rhetoric* (ideas about a family) in pursuit of their own political agendas without demystifying their assumptions of what constitutes a family (Collins 1998, pp. 62–82). Inherent in their constructions, thus, is a belief that their construals of this "imagined community" are just *natural*, not actually construals at all (Collins, pp. 62–82; Anderson 2006). As Elizabeth Bounds (1996, pp. 111–126) has noted, though, "family" is "a highly contested ideological concept."

Likewise, even if some interpreters view their methodological prisms as free from wider cultural currents, they are not. There is no "Holy Grail" of methodological inquiry free of culture (Kellner, p. 24). All methods are "culturally contextualized" (Segovia 2008, p. 24). Form criticism depends heavily on Hermann Gunkel's importation of the Brothers Grimm German folk collection. Narrative criticism is firmly rooted in humanistic thinking and in moral psychology (Frow 1986, p. 228). Reader-response criticism in the United States draws heavily on the ideas of (US) American individualism (Mailloux 1989, pp. 51–52). Wolfgang Iser's reader-response theory, in association with the

Constance School of Aesthetic Reception, depends heavily on phenomenology (Iser 1974). Sociocultural criticism, which arose hard on the heels of the civil rights era and other liberation movements that emphasized social structures of oppression and enhanced a more self-reflective consciousness, draws heavily from the social sciences and anthropology (Horsley 1994, p. 2). Thus, all "rituals of reception" regarding the Bible—from traditions of what the Bible is (and thus the authority it has) to traditions of hermeneutical strategies for reading the Bible to deployments of the Bible as "cultural capital" in arguments—are already grounded in "culturally ordered" contexts (Bielo 2006a, pp. 5–7).

Interrogating Operations of Power in the Cultural Products of Biblical Discourse. Second, cultural studies interrogates operations of power in the cultural productions of biblical discourse such as canons, manuscript traditions, translations, biblical maps, family Bibles, or niche Bibles. Ascendant Christian canons are not simply lists of authoritative texts. Wrought in the fires of political contestation, they reveal—as do the biblical manuscript traditions—the norms and values of the political winners in the struggles between the early proto-orthodox Christians and their opponents (Ehrman 2005, pp. 170–173). The same ascendant canons, when subsequently imposed on non-Christian traditions, also are instruments of cultural imperialism. Likewise, translations are not innocent representations of some original truth. As Musa Dube has shown, power dynamics are involved. For example, in the Setswana translation, the word *Badimo* (originally a *neuter* word for ancestral intermediaries) is used to translate the Greek word for "demons," thus both changing the gender of the expression and viewing *Badimo* in a pejorative manner (Dube 2011, p. 226). Biblical maps are not mirrors. They confer importance through what they include or exclude. Ideological commitments are revealed, for example, when biblical atlases omit the "region south of Palestine and Egypt" or when they designate *biblical lands* as "the Near East" or "the Middle East," a spatiality reflecting a European bias" (Martin 1989, pp. 105–135; Sadler 2007, p. 25). The "Family Bibles" published by the British and Foreign Bible Society in the early nineteenth century were not simply reproductions of the King James Bible. Rather, in bracketing certain parts of that version as suitable only for the assumed "Masters of the family," that is, apart from women, children, and servants, such Bibles exposed its editors' patriarchal and patently paternalistic ideological commitments (Carpenter 2003, pp. 33–47). Niche Bibles—from the American Bible's Society's *Good News Bible* and Taylor's *The Living Bible* (actually a paraphrase) to the current proliferation of Biblezines (*Becoming, Explore, Refuel, Blossom, Revolve, Magnify, Align,* and *Redefine*), moreover, do not simply include biblical material (Beal 2011, pp. 14–16, 41–42). Driven by market research, new formatting and print technology, conservative evangelical ideology, and a visual canon of physical beauty that favors mostly white teenage girls, the supplemental material of *Revolve*, for example, shapes thought and constructs ideals of a cultural norm (Beal, p. 50; Harding 2009, pp. 176, 178; Gutjahr 2008, p. 342).

Engaging the Powers through Interventions in and beyond Biblical Studies. Third, cultural studies engages operations of power through multiple interventions, from theoretical and pedagogical/curricular interventions in academia to social/public policy activism in the larger world. For example, in addition to contextualizing all biblical studies research methodologies for their historical situatedness and—in some instances—their complicity with structures of oppression (Meeks, p. 160), cultural studies' theoretical intervention also interrogates the continuing influence of any research optic's "museum curator's view of history" (Fabisiak 2010, p. 190), a view that, in effect, supports those approaches that "lock the history of interpretation in the past and evade the contemporary issues such as racism and intercultural dialogue" (Myers 1991, p. 41).

Cultural studies' pedagogical intervention also interrogates the top-down "banking system" formats (for example, the "master-disciple" model [Mata 2010, p. 250]) and "individualized" learning strategies that prevail in many Western biblical studies classrooms despite a growing body of evidence that reveals the "socially embedded" nature of all reading or actualization practices (Bielo 2006b, p. 161). More positively, cultural studies acknowledges multiple learning strategies (communal and "individualized") and assumes a variety of *learning intelligences* (from kinesthetic to musical to visual/spatial and so forth [Gardner 2006]).

Cultural studies curricular interventionists not only interrogate the typical institutional norms and disciplinary protocols that police what counts as scholarship or knowledge but they also question the assignment of a "monotextual status" to the Bible (Lee 2010, pp. 35–45) as if it is the only foundational narrative, charter story, or scripture around. Such interventionists thus advocate cross-textual study or contrapuntal reading approaches that seek to recognize "the reality of the plurality of scriptures" (Lee 2010, p. 36; Liew 2008, p. 217) in many countries and the varying notions of scriptural authority associated with such plurality. Furthermore, cultural studies suggests that the dominant view of scriptural authority in the West (that the Bible is an absolute authority) is itself historically conditioned, that is, it is a tradition rooted in the European Reformation (Bielo 2006a, p. 5).

Freed from the bankrupt notion of intellectual disinterestedness, proponents of cultural studies (or those with shared affinities) also actively involve themselves in the demystification of the politics behind those public discourses and institutional powers that deploy scripture to limit human inclusion or flourishing. Cultural studies intellectual workers thus recognize the cultural capital of the Bible, that is, that many faith communities draw on it not only as a lexical storehouse but also as a basis for shaping views of themselves and others. In the long history of biblical discourse, this has meant that the Bible has often been used as a tool for "clobbering" or "textual harassment," that is, as a weapon to sanction the marginalization of women, to justify the exploitation of the lands of others (from Africans to the indigenous of the Americas to Pacific Islanders), and to demean gays, lesbians, bisexuals, and transgendered persons (Tolbert 2000, pp. vii–xi). Thus, to counter such negative depictions and the exploitation of human groupings, cultural studies intellectual workers engage wider publics through news editorials, documentaries, public conferences, and various intellectual centers (like the Center for Lesbian and Gay Studies in Religion and Ministry among other radically progressive centers) that demystify how and why the Bible has been used historically in such demeaning ways.

[*See also* Central and South American Interpretation; Class Criticism; Cultural-Historical Criticism; Pop Culture and the Bible; Postcolonial Biblical Interpretation; Race, Ethnicity, and Biblical Criticism; Reader-Response Criticism; *and* Reception Criticism and Theory.]

BIBLIOGRAPHY

Abbas, Ackbar, and John Nguyet Erni et al., eds. *Internationalizing Cultural Studies.* Malden, Mass.: Blackwell, 2005.

Adams, Maurianne, et al., "Readings for Diversity and Social Justice: A General Introduction." In *Reading for Diversity and Social Justice: An Anthology on Racism, Antisemitism, Sexism, Heterosexism, Ableism, and Classism,* edited by Maurianne Adams et al., 1–4. New York: Routledge, 2000.

Anderson, Benedict. *Imagined Communities: Reflections on the Origin and Spread of Nationalism.* London: Verso, 2006.

Bailey, Randall C., Benny Tat-Siong Liew, and Fernando F. Segovia. "Introduction: Toward Minority Biblical Criticism: Framework, Contours, Dynamics." In *They were All Together in One Place?: Toward Minority Biblical Criticism,* edited by Randall C. Bailey, Benny Tat-Siong Liew, and Fernando F. Segovia, 3–43. Atlanta: Society of Biblical Literature, 2009.

Beal, Timothy. *The Rise and Fall of the Bible: The Unexpected History of an Accidental Book.* New York: Houghton Mifflin Harcourt, 2011.

Beverly, John. *Subalternity and Representation: Arguments in Cultural Theory.* Durham, N.C.: Duke University Press, 2004.

Bielo, James S. "Introduction: Encountering Biblicism." In *The Social Life of Scriptures: Cross-Cultural Perspectives on Biblicism,* edited by James S. Bielo, 1–9. New Brunswick, N.J.: Rutgers University, 2006a.

Bielo, James S. "Textual Ideology, Textual Practice: Evangelical Bible Reading in Group Study." In *The Social Life of Scriptures: Cross-Cultural Perspectives on Biblicism*, edited by James S. Bielo, 157–175. New Brunswick, N.J.: Rutgers University, 2006b.

Blount, Brian K. *Can I Get a Witness?: Reading Revelation through African American Culture*. Louisville, Ky.: Westminster John Knox, 2005.

Boer, Roland. *Knockin' on Heaven's Door: The Bible and Popular Culture*. London: Routledge, 1999.

Bounds, Elizabeth, "Between the Devil and the Deep Blue Sea: Feminism, Family Values, and the Division Public and Private." *Journal of Feminist Studies in Religion* 12 (1996): 111–126.

Carpenter, Mary Wilson. *Imperial Bibles, Domestic Bodies: Women, Sexuality, and Religion in the Victorian Market*. Athens: Ohio University Press, 2003.

Chaney, David. *The Cultural Turn: Scene-Setting Essays on Contemporary Cultural History*. London: Routledge, 1994.

Collins, Patricia. "It's All in the Family: Intersections of Gender, Race, and Nation." *Hypatia* 13 (1998): 62–82.

del Sarto, Ana, Alicia Ríos, and Abril Trigo, eds. *The Latin American Cultural Studies Reader*. Durham, N.C.: Duke University Press, 2004.

DeYoung, Curtiss P., et al., eds. *The Peoples' Bible*. New Revised Standard Version. Minneapolis: Augsburg Fortress, 2008.

Dube, Musa. "Towards Postcolonial Feminist Translations of the Bible." In *Reading Ideologies: Essays on the Bible and Interpretation in Honor of Mary Ann Tolbert*, edited by Tat-siong Benny Liew, 215–239. Sheffield, UK: Sheffield Phoenix, 2011.

Ehrman, Bart. *Misquoting Jesus: The Story Behind Who Changed the Bible and Why*. San Francisco: Harper-SanFrancisco, 2005.

Exum, Cheryl J., and Stephen D. Moore, eds. *Biblical Studies/Cultural Studies*. Sheffield, UK: Sheffield Academic, 1998.

Fabisiak, Thomas. "On the Fringes of the 'Big Tent' of Graduate New Testament Studies." In *Transforming Graduate Biblical Education: Ethos and Discipline*, edited by Elisabeth Schüssler Fiorenza and Kent Harold Richards, 183–197. Atlanta: Society of Biblical Literature, 2010.

Freire, Paulo. *Pedagogy of the Oppressed*. 9th ed. Translated by Myra Bergman Ramos. New York: Seabury, 1973.

Frow, John. "Spectacle Binding: On Character." *Poetics Today* 7 (1986): 227–250.

Gardner, Howard. *Multiple Intelligences: New Horizons*. New York: BasicBooks, 2006.

Grossberg, Lawrence, Cary Nelson, and Paula Treichler, eds. *Cultural Studies*. New York: Routledge, 1992.

Guha, Ranajit. "Preface." In *Selected Subaltern Studies*, edited by R. Guha and Gayatri Spivak, 35–37. New York: Oxford University, 1988.

Gutjahr, Paul C. "The Bible-zine Revolve and the Evolution of the Culturally Relevant Bible in America." In *Religion and the Culture of Print in Modern America*, edited by Charles L. Cohen and Paul S. Boyer, 326–348. Madison: University of Wisconsin Press, 2008.

Harding, Susan. "*Revolve*, The Biblezine: A Transevangelical Text." In *The Social Life of Scriptures: Cross-cultural Perspectives on Biblicism*, edited by James S. Bielo, 176–193. New Brunswick, N.J.: Rutgers University Press, 2009.

hooks, bell. *Yearning: Race, Gender, and Cultural Politics*. Boston: South End, 1990.

Horsley, Richard. *Sociology and the Jesus Movement*. New York: Continuum, 1994.

Irwin, Robert McKee, and Mónica Szurmuk, "Introduction." In *Dictionary of Latin American Cultural Studies*, edited by Robert McKee Irwin and Mónica Szurmuk, 1–11. Gainesville: University Press of Florida, 2012.

Iser, Wolfgang. *The Act of Reading: A Theory of Aesthetic Response*. Baltimore: The Johns Hopkins University, 1974.

Kellner, Douglas. *Media Culture: Cultural Studies, Identity and Politics between the Modern and the Postmodern*. New York: Routledge, 1995.

Lee, Archie C. C. "Cross-Textual Biblical Studies in Multiscriptural Contexts." In *Transforming Graduate Biblical Education: Ethos and Discipline*, edited by Elisabeth Schüssler Fiorenza and Kent Harold Richards, 35–45. Atlanta: Society of Biblical Literature, 2010.

Lee, Richard E. *Life and Times of Cultural Studies: The Politics and Transformation of the Structures of Knowledge*. Durham, N.C.: Duke University Press, 2003.

Liew, Benny Tat-siong. "Introduction: Reading Ideologies and Ideologies of Reading." In *Reading Ideologies: Essays in Honor of Mary Ann Tolbert*, edited by Benny Tat-Siong Liew, 1–28. Sheffield, UK: Sheffield Phoenix, 2011.

Liew, Benny Tat-siong. "Postcolonial Criticism: Echoes of a Subaltern's Contribution and Exclusion." In *Mark & Method: New Approaches in Biblical Studies*, 2d ed., edited by Janice Capel Anderson and Stephen D. Moore, 211–231. Minneapolis: Fortress, 2008.

Mailloux, Stephen. *Rhetorical Power*. Ithaca, N.Y.: Cornell University Press, 1989.

Martin, Clarice. "A Chamberlain's Journey and the Challenge of Interpretation for Liberation," *Semeia* 47 (1989): 105–135.

Mata, Roberto. "Beyond Socialization and Attrition: Border Pedagogy in Biblical Studies." In *Transforming Graduate Biblical Education: Ethos and Discipline*, edited by Elisabeth Schüssler Fiorenza and Kent Harold Richards, 247–266. Atlanta: Society of Biblical Literature, 2010.

Matibag, Eugenio D. "Self-Consuming Fictions: The Dialectics of Cannibalism in Modern Caribbean Narratives." *Postmodern Culture* 1 (1991): 1–22.

McCall, Leslie. "The Complexity of Intersectionality." *Journal of Women in Culture and Society* 30 (2005): 1771-1800.

McClennen, Sophia A. "Cultural Studies and 'Latin America'." In *The Renewal of Cultural Studies*, edited by Paul Smith, 188–195. Philadelphia: Temple University Press, 2011a.

McClennen, Sophia A. "What's Left of Latin American Cultural Studies." *Minnesota Review* 76 (2011b): 127–140.

Meeks, Wayne. "Why Study the New Testament?" *New Testament Studies* 51 (2005): 155–170.

Mellor, Adrian. "Discipline and Punish: Cultural Studies at the Crossroads." *Media, Culture and Society* 14 (1992): 663–670.

Mignolo, Walter D. *The Idea of Latin America*. Malden, Mass.: Blackwell, 2005.

Miller, Toby, ed. *A Companion to Cultural Studies*. Malden, Mass.: Blackwell, 2006.

Moore, Stephen D., ed. "In Search of the Present: The Bible Through Cultural Studies." *Semeia* 82 (1998).

Myers, Williams H. "The Hermeneutical Dilemma of the African American Biblical Student." In *Stony The Road We Trod: African American Biblical Interpretation*, edited by Cain Hope Felder, 40–56. Minneapolis: Fortress, 1991.

Petersen, David. "Genesis and Family Values." *Journal of Biblical Literature* 124 (2005): 5–23.

Poblete, Juan. "Latin/o Americanism/o." In *Dictionary of Latin American Cultural Studies*, edited by Robert McKee Irwin and Mónica Szurmuk, 197–204. Gainesville: University Press of Florida, 2012.

Portier-Young, Anathea E. *Apocalypse against Empire: Theologies of Resistance in Early Judaism*. Grand Rapids, Mich.: Eerdmans, 2011.

Rabasa, José. "Postcolonialism." In *Dictionary of Latin American Cultural Studies*, edited by Robert McKee Irwin and Mónica Szurmuk, 252–258. Gainesville: University Press of Florida, 2012.

Retamar, Roberto Fernández. *Caliban and Other Essays*. Minneapolis: University of Minnesota Press, 1989.

Ricalde, Maricruz Castro. "Gender." In *Dictionary of Latin American Cultural Studies*, edited by Robert McKee Irwin and Mónica Szurmuk, 153–160. Gainesville: University Press of Florida, 2012.

Ríos, Alicia. "Forerunners." In *The Latin American Cultural Studies Reader*, edited by Ana del Sarto et al., 15–34. Durham, N.C.: Duke University Press, 2004.

Sadler, Rodney S., Jr. "The Place and Role of Africa and African Imagery in the Bible." In *True to Our Native Land: An African American Commentary on the New Testament*, edited by Brian K. Blount, Clarice Martin, Cain Felder, and Emerson Powery, x–xx. Minneapolis, Minnesota: Fortress, 2007.

Saldívar, José David. *Border Matters: Remapping American Cultural Studies*. Berkeley: University of California Press, 1997.

Segovia, Fernando F. *Decolonizing Biblical Studies: A View from the Margins*. Maryknoll, New York: Orbis, 2000.

Segovia, Fernando F. "The Bible as a Text in Cultures: An Introduction." In *The Peoples' Bible*, edited by Curtiss P. DeYoung et al., 23–30. Minneapolis: Augsburg Fortress, 2008.

Siebers, Tobin. *Disability Theory*. Ann Arbor: University of Michigan Press, 2008.

Smith, Abraham. "Cultural Studies: Making Mark." In *Mark & Method: New Approaches in Biblical Studies*, 2d ed., edited by Janice Capel Anderson and Stephen D. Moore, 181–209. Minneapolis: Fortress, 2008.

Smith, Abraham."'I Saw the Book Talk': A Cultural Studies Approach to the Ethics of an African American Biblical Hermeneutics." *Semeia* 77 (1997): 115–138.

Söderström, Ola. "Representation." In *Cultural Geography: A Critical Dictionary of Key Concepts*, edited by David Atkinson, et al., 11–15. London: Tauris, 2005.

Sprinkler, Michael. "We Lost it at the Movies." *Modern Language Notes* 112 (1997): 385–399.

Tarica, Estelle. "Heterogeneity." In *Dictionary of Latin American Cultural Studies*, edited by Robert McKee Irwin and Mónica Szurmuk, 174–179. Gainesville: University Press of Florida, 2012.

Tolbert, Mary Ann. "What Word Shall We Take Back?" In *Take Back the Word: A Queer Reading of the Bible*, edited by Robert E. Goss and Mona West, vii–xii. Cleveland, Ohio: Pilgrim, 2000.

Trigo, Abril. "General Introduction." In *The Latin American Cultural Studies Reader*, edited by Ana Del Sarto, Alicia Ríos, and Abril Trigo, 1–14. Durham, N.C.: Duke University Press, 2004.

Weinberg, Liliana. "Transculturation." In *Dictionary of Latin American Cultural Studies*, edited by Robert McKee Irwin and Mónica Szurmuk, 331–337. Gainesville: University Press of Florida, 2012.

Wolff, Janet. "Cultural Studies and the Sociology of Culture." *Contemporary Sociology* 28 (1999): 499–507.

Abraham Smith

D

Dead Sea Scrolls

The ancient Jewish manuscripts known collectively as the Dead Sea Scrolls, often called the greatest archaeological discovery of the twentieth century, were accidentally discovered in caves along the western shore of the Dead Sea, beginning in 1947. The find locations, from north to south, are the caves of the Wadi Daliyeh, the 11 caves in the vicinity of Khirbet Qumran, the caves of Wadi Murabbaʿat, the caves of Naḥal ever, and the Herodian fortress of Masada. The manuscripts range in paleographic age from the fourth century B.C.E. (Wadi Daliyeh) to the second century C.E. (Wadi Murabbaʿ at and Naḥal Ḥever). All of these sites, with the exception of Wadi Daliyeh, which did not include religious documents, contained manuscripts of the books of the Hebrew Bible, as well as religious works that referenced, in various ways, the biblical books. The Qumran caves yielded by far the largest collection, producing more than eight hundred manuscripts. Therefore this article will concentrate on the Qumran collection, referring to the other collections when appropriate.

The Dead Sea Scrolls give us a window into Jewish biblical interpretation in the late Second Temple period (ca. 332 B.C.E.–70 C.E.) by the sheer number and diversity of the manuscripts in the collection. The methods of biblical interpretation found among the Qumran scrolls are diverse, but what emerges from the collection is the insight that biblical interpretation was absolutely central to the practice, theology, and worldview of the Jews who collected them. The scrolls contain many different types of exegesis, from straightforward interpretation that attempts to explain a scriptural passage to complicated eisegesis that reads a particular sectarian ideology back into the scriptural text.

Biblical Texts and the Canon of Scripture. The term “biblical” is anachronistic in any discussion of the Dead Sea Scrolls, since the Hebrew Bible in its present form did not exist in the last centuries B.C.E. and the first centuries C.E However, it serves as a convenient label to distinguish those books that later became part of the Jewish Bible from those that did not. Thus it will be used in this article. The term “canon” is likewise anachronistic, since the present Jewish canon of scripture did not reach its final form until the fourth century C.E. The Jewish canon in the late second Temple period was a work-in-progress, with different Jewish groups according authoritative status to different groups of books.

All of the books of the Hebrew Bible, with the exception of Esther, were found in the eleven Qumran caves; approximately 25 percent of the Qumran manuscripts are biblical. That simple statement, however, does not convey the complexity of the picture presented by the Qumran collection. It is clear from the details of the collection that all biblical books did not enjoy equal authority, and some of those books may not even have been considered scriptural. The absence of the book of Esther, and the lack of mention of Purim in the Qumran calendars, indicates that that book was not considered scripture, at least by the group that stored the manuscripts in the Qumran caves. The number of copies of other books in the collection indicates their importance to the Qumran community.

Deuteronomy (32), Psalms (36), and Isaiah (21) were found in the greatest number of copies. As this essay will demonstrate, they, along with the other books of the Pentateuch, are also the most frequently quoted or otherwise interpreted in the other Qumran manuscripts. It is worth noting that these three books are the most frequently quoted books in the New Testament as well. The number of copies of these three books attests to their importance in the Qumran collection. On the other hand, four or fewer copies were preserved of Joshua, Judges, 1–2 Samuel, 1–2 Kings, Job, Proverbs, Ruth, Song of Songs, Ecclesiastes, Lamentations, Ezra–Nehemiah, and 1–2 Chronicles. The paucity of copies of these books, all either from the historical books or the Writings, raises the question of their authoritative status for the Qumran community. This is especially the case when one considers that books that did not become part of the later Jewish canon, such as *Enoch* (20 copies, including the *Book of Giants*) and *Jubilees* (14 or 15 manuscripts), existed in many more copies, and, as will be demonstrated, were quoted or interpreted extensively.

These findings indicate that the roster of authoritative or scriptural books for the Qumran community (and possibly wider Judaism as well) was different from the present Jewish canon. During the last century B.C.E. and the first century C.E., the canon was still in a nascent state, undergoing a process of development. The Pentateuch or Torah (Gen, Exod, Lev, Numbers, and Deut) was authoritative for all Jews everywhere no later than the fourth century B.C.E. The Prophets (Isaiah, Jeremiah, Ezekiel, and the Twelve Minor Prophets) and Psalms had probably acquired authoritative status for all Jews by the late third or early second century B.C.E., followed by Daniel in the latter half of the second century B.C.E. However, the evidence from Qumran indicates that the status of the other books is open to question. For example, it is likely that Joshua was considered authoritative at Qumran, since it is quoted in other works found there (e.g., *Apocryphon of Joshua*). However, Chronicles, which is never quoted or otherwise used in another composition, most likely was not. Further, *Enoch* and *Jubilees*, quoted and alluded to throughout the Qumran collection, most likely had authoritative status in the Qumran community, and possibly other Jewish groups as well (*1 Enoch* is also quoted in the New Testament Epistle of Jude as an authoritative text). The *Damascus Document* cites the book of *Jubilees* as an authoritative text (parallel to the Torah) at the end of its admonition: "Therefore, a man shall take upon himself (an oath) to return to the Torah of Moses, for in it everything is specified. And the explication of their times, when Israel was blind to all these; behold, it is specified in the Book of the Divisions of the Times in their Jubilees and in their Weeks" (CD 16:1–4). It alludes to *Enoch* as an authoritative text in its recitation of history: "Walking after the wantonness of their heart(s), the Watchers of heaven fell" (CD 2:17–18). These examples demonstrate that the final Jewish canon was not in effect during the time the Dead Sea Scrolls were copied and collected.

The text, or words, of the biblical books was also not fixed. Rather, the text of these books was fluid, undergoing changes that were part of a process of interpretation that began almost as soon as a book reached a recognizable shape. The manuscripts of the biblical books found at Qumran are filled with variants (a variant is a difference in a word or words in a particular verse, between manuscripts of a particular biblical book). These variants can be minor, such as the presence or absence of the definite article, or significant, so that the meaning of the text changes depending upon the variant. An example of a significant variant is found in Deuteronomy 32:8. The Masoretic Text (the canonical text in

Judaism) and the Samaritan Pentateuch (the canonical text of the Samaritan community) read: "When the Most High apportioned the nations, when he divided humankind, he fixed the boundaries of the peoples according to the number of the *sons of Israel*." The septuagint (the Greek translation of the Hebrew scriptures) and the Qumran manuscript 4QDeut[j] read: "When the Most High apportioned the nations, when he divided humankind, he fixed the boundaries of the peoples according to the number of the *sons of God*." The variant, "sons of Israel" versus "sons of God," changes the theological meaning of the text. It is likely that the reading "sons of God" is original, the "sons of Israel" variant being introduced to cleanse the text of any hint of polytheism.

Although all the manuscripts of the biblical books contain variants, in some cases the number of variants is so numerous and systematic that the book can be said to exist in two or more separate editions. Examples of this phenomenon include the books of Exodus, Numbers, Jeremiah, Psalms, and Daniel. In the case of Jeremiah, the manuscripts 4QJer[b,d] and the Septuagint Jeremiah preserve one textual edition. 4QJer[a,c,e] and the Masoretic Text preserve a second edition, which is one eighth longer than the first edition and has a different order of chapters. What is fascinating about these different editions is that they resided side-by-side in Cave 4, and the community did not differentiate between them; all forms of a scriptural book seem to have been equally authoritative.

These different editions of biblical books point to the activity of scribes, whose task was to pass on the written tradition of Israel to future generations. Scribes did this by copying earlier manuscripts, but also by reworking and updating the text to interpret it for their contemporaries. Thus the task of the scribe was an interpretive one. The evidence of the Qumran caves shows that the scriptural texts existed on a spectrum, with the text expanding and changing as interpretation took place. The shape of the biblical book remained the same; Exodus, for example, began with the Israelites in Egypt, moved through the call of Moses, the plague and Passover narratives, and the exodus itself, and ended with the journey to Sinai and the giving of the law. But the text within that shape could vary, and did, according to the interpretive scheme of the scribe. The text version of the book that became canonical in each religious community varied; in the Jewish canon a shorter version of Exodus became canonical, but the longer version of Jeremiah was chosen.

As texts moved along the spectrum further away from the parent text, at a certain point a dividing line was crossed and a new composition came into being. Those compositions will be explored in the next section.

Rewritten Bible or Scriptures. This term was first coined by Geza Vermes in 1961 (*Scripture and Tradition in Judaism*, Leiden) to describe a group of Jewish compositions that took a biblical book or books as a base text and proceeded to rework it or them into a new composition. A good working definition of Rewritten Scriptures is "a category or group of texts which are characterized by a close adherence to a recognizable and already authoritative base text (narrative or legal) and a recognizable degree of scribal intervention into that base text for the purpose of exegesis" (Crawford 2008, pp. 12–13). Thus the Rewritten Scripture compositions are exegetical or interpretive in nature.

The Qumran caves yielded many manuscripts that fit into the category Rewritten Scripture, including the Reworked Pentateuch group, the *Genesis Apocryphon*, and Pseudo-Ezekiel; we will consider two of the largest, *Jubilees* and the *Temple Scroll*.

Jubilees. The book of *Jubilees* was discovered in fourteen or fifteen manuscripts in five of the eleven Qumran caves, in its original Hebrew. The oldest manuscript dates to approximately 50 B.C.E. *Jubilees* itself was composed in the mid-second century B.C.E.

The base text for *Jubilees* is the book of Genesis and the first fifteen chapters of Exodus. It is presented as a divine revelation from God through an Angel of the Presence to Moses on Mount Sinai, parallel to the Torah itself. Although the author often simply reproduces his base text, he also freely reworks it to emphasize his exegetical concerns.

One of these concerns is chronological. *Jubilees* follows a 364-day solar calendar, and divides time into jubilee periods of 49 years, within which are seven "weeks" of years. This calendar is divinely ordained (*Jub.* 6:35). Every event in the base text is dated according to this calendar. For example, the Israelites escape from Egypt in "the second year in the fiftieth jubilee" (*Jub.* 48:1), and they enter the promised land at the end of that jubilee period (*Jub.* 50:4).

A second major concern in *Jubilees* is to present the ancestors in Genesis as morally and ethically upright, and as obeying the laws of the Sinai covenant even before they were given. Thus when Noah exits the ark and plants a vineyard, he celebrates the feast of *Shevu'ot* (*Jub.* 6:17–18). When Abram and Sarai enter Egypt, *Jubilees* merely reports that Pharaoh took Sarai into his harem (*Jub.* 13:13); no mention is made that Abram tried to pass Sarai off as his sister (Gen 12:11–13).

Two other concerns of the composer are the priesthood and the last days, the *eschaton*. According to *Jubilees*, the priestly line begins not with Levi but with Adam, and passes through such patriarchs as Enoch, Noah, Abraham, and Jacob before culminating in Levi. Thus the priesthood existed from the beginning of time, and is divinely ordained. Finally, *Jubilees* has an eschatological flavor missing from its Genesis-Exodus base text; it looks forward to a time when, after punishment, God will purify and restore his chosen people (chs. 1 and 23).

Temple Scroll. The *Temple Scroll*, a Hebrew composition found only at Qumran, was preserved in four copies. Three copies, dating to the first century C.E., were found in Cave 11, while a fragmentary copy, dating to the mid-second century B.C.E., was found in Cave 4. The following comments are based on the most complete manuscript, 11QTemple[a].

The base texts for the *Temple Scroll* are sections of Exodus, Leviticus, Numbers, and Deuteronomy, although the composer also utilizes large blocks of nonbiblical sources. While the *Temple Scroll* follows the basic order of Exodus-Deuteronomy, it is not a narrative, but a revelation of laws concerning certain specific topics: the temple and its courts; purity regulations; a festival calendar; and laws concerning life in the promised land. It is also a pseudepigraph of the most audacious sort: the revelation is presented directly by God to Moses, with God speaking in the first person throughout. The *Temple Scroll* uses various techniques to accomplish its purpose. It gathers texts on the same subject from different books together in one place (thematic association); for example, col. 52:4 quotes Deuteronomy 17:1 prohibiting the sacrifice of a blemished animal, followed by prohibitions on another type of profane sacrifice taken from Leviticus 22:28. It also harmonizes duplicate commands, clarifies obscure passages, and, finally, adds whole new blocks of material (such as the specifications for the ideal temple found in cols. 2–13 and 30–47).

The *Temple Scroll* uses its base text as a springboard to promote its vision of the Israelites in the land: as a worshipping community surrounding a gigantic temple complex, for which purity regulations leading to holiness (which become more stringent as they move closer to the temple at the center of the land) take precedence over secular concerns. So, for example, sexual intercourse, even between married persons, is completely banned in the temple city (col. 45:11–12), a regulation that would not have been in effect in contemporary Jerusalem. This ideal, perhaps even eschatological, vision takes its cues from its Pentateuchal base narrative, but is the creation of its composer, who uses his sources, both biblical and nonbiblical, to produce a unique new work.

Parabiblical Texts. Now we will leave the spectrum of biblical and related texts, and turn to another category of interpretive texts found among the Dead Sea Scrolls, the parabiblical texts. These compositions "use a passage, event, or character from a scriptural work as a 'jumping-off' point to create a new narrative or work" (Crawford, p. 14). They are interpretive in the sense that they begin with a biblical passage as a base for what may become an entire literature in its own right. Often the connection to the original biblical text becomes very tenuous.

An example of a parabiblical composition found at Qumran is the books of *Enoch*. *Enoch*, an Aramaic work, was preserved in twenty copies from four caves. This extensive eschatological and apocalyptic work, which may have carried scriptural authority for the Qumran community, is based on the intriguing figure of Enoch in Genesis 5: 21–24: "When Enoch had lived sixty-five years, he became the father of Methuselah. Enoch walked with God after the birth of Methuselah three hundred years, and had other sons and daughters. Thus all the days of Enoch were three hundred sixty-five years. Enoch walked with God; then he was no more, because God took him." From this mysterious quote an expansive and theologically important literature grew. Other examples of parabiblical texts among the Qumran scrolls include the *Aramaic Levi Document*, the *Visions of Amram*, and the *Testament of Qahat*.

Lemma Interpretation. The second half of this essay will discuss a more familiar (to contemporary readers) form of interpretation: the interpretation of individual lemmas (verses or groups of verses) from the scriptural text. This type of interpretation is frequent in the Qumran scrolls, especially in commentaries and rule books.

Pesher Commentaries. Pesher commentaries, which take their name from the Hebrew word *pishrô*, "its interpretation is," are the oldest examples of the lemma + commentary form of interpretation in early Jewish literature. In this particular example of the form, found only among the Qumran scrolls, the scriptural text is applied to the contemporary sectarian setting. The structure of these pesher (Heb. pl. *pesharim*) comprises the lemma + an interpretive formula (*pishrô*) + the comment. An example from the *Pesher Habakkuk* demonstrates this structure:

> *For I am now about to raise up the Chaldeans, that brutal and reckless people* (Hab 1:61). Its interpretation [*pishrô*] concerns the Kittim, w[ho ar]e swift and mighty in war, annihilating many." (1QpHab col. ii, 10–13)

A pesher commentary seeks to reveal the true, hidden meaning in the ancient scriptural texts by inspired exegesis, which is available to the community (and especially to its leader, the Teacher of Righteousness) through divine revelation. This true meaning is narrowly sectarian and pertains to contemporary events. *Pesher Habakkuk* makes this plain in its interpretation of Habakkuk 2:1–2:

> *So I will stand on watch and station myself on my watchtower and wait for what he will say to me, and [what I will reply t]o my rebuke. Then the LORD answered me [and said, 'Write down the vision pl] ainly on tablets, so that with ease [someone can read it.'* (2:1–2) Thi]s[refers]t[o . . . Then God told Habakkuk to write down what is going to happen to the generation to come; but when that period would be complete he did not make known to him. When it says, '*so that with ease someone can read it,*' this refers to the Teacher of Righteousness to whom God made known all the mysterious revelations of his servants the prophets. (1QpHab 6:12—7:5)

There are three subtypes of pesharim, continuous, thematic, and single or isolated.

Continuous Pesharim. A continuous pesher selects one biblical book and systematically subjects it to a pesher interpretation according to a contemporary sectarian understanding, which is often eschatological. Pesharim on the following biblical books were discovered in the Qumran caves: Isaiah, Hosea, Micah, Nahum, Habakkuk, Zephaniah, and Psalms. All of these books are prophetic (Psalms was treated as a prophetic book by the Qumran community, as it was in the New Testament). As such, the prophets do not speak to their own time, but to events far in the future (again, this resembles New Testament exegesis). The sectarians, through their own inspired exegesis, are able to reveal the true meaning hidden in the prophetic book. The continuous pesharim contain veiled references (usually by using allegorical names, or titles instead of proper names) to historical characters and events, such as the Kittim encountered earlier (usually understood to refer to the Romans), the Teacher of Righteousness, the Wicked Priest, etc. Unfortunately, the identities of these veiled references and sobriquets remain elusive, thus making the details of the pesharim difficult to determine definitively.

Thematic Pesharim. This type of pesher takes one concept (always eschatological) as a structuring theme and weaves together quotations from separate scriptural books that are applied to that concept as proof texts. The same interpretive structure, often including the word *pesher*, is applied to each quotation. Examples of this subtype include *4QFlorilegium*, *4QCatena*^{a,b}, *4QAges of Creation A and B*, *11QMelchizedek*, and *4QTestimonia* (which does not, however, contain the word *pesher*). As an example let us consider *4QFlorilegium*.

4QFlorilegium takes as its unifying theme "the last days," and utilizes passages from Exodus 15, Deuteronomy 33, 2 Samuel 7, and Psalms 1 and 2 as its main lemmas, with verses from Deuteronomy 23, Amos 9, Isaiah 8, Ezekiel 37, and Daniel 12 adduced as proof texts. The variety of passages indicates that almost any scriptural lemma could be the subject of pesher exegesis. These passages are all interpreted as pertaining to the end of days and especially the role of the sectarian community therein. The lemma from Psalm 2 and its interpretation serves as a good illustration (note that the passage is very fragmentary).

> *[Why do] the nations [rag]e and the peoples imag[ine a vain thing? The kings of the earth set] themselves, [and the ru]lers take counsel together against the Lord and against [his anointed.* (Ps 2:1–2). The in]terpretation of the passage [. . . na]tions and the Elect of Israel in the last days: That is the time of trial that is co[ming.

Single or Isolated Pesharim. The final subtype of the pesher is the isolated pesher, which appears in various sectarian documents. As its name implies, it is a single scriptural lemma given a pesher exegesis, which appears in another type of work altogether. An example occurs in the *Damascus Document*, one of the rule books from Qumran. The passage is Numbers 21:18.

> And they dug the well. *The well was dug by the princes and excavated by the nobles of the people, with a ruler* (Numbers 21:18). The *well* is the Torah and those who *dig* it are the penitents of Israel who depart from the land of Judah and dwell in the land of Damascus. God called them all *princes*, for they sought him and their honor was not rejected by anyone's mouth. And the *ruler* is the Interpreter of the Torah, of whom Isaiah said, *He takes out a tool for his work* (Isa 54:16). And the *nobles of the people* are those who come to excavate the *well* with the statutes which were ordained by the *ruler* to walk in them in the entire time of evil, and who will obtain no others until the rise of the one who will teach righteousness in the end of days. (CD 6:3–11)

The complex, atomized exegesis demonstrated here (which brings in another scriptural text from Isaiah as a proof text) concerns the last days and the inspired scriptural exegesis of the leader(s) of the sectarian community.

Non-Pesher Interpretation. The most common form of interpretation, found throughout the Qumran corpus, is straightforward exegesis of scriptural texts. Legal exegesis, or the interpretation of the laws of the Torah for the community's life, permeates the rule books and other nonexegetical texts from the Qumran collection. The goal of this exegesis was to create a way of life strictly in accord with the commandments of the Torah as the sect understood them. The primacy of the Torah and its exegesis for the sect is illustrated by these passages from the *Community Rule*:

> They (the members of the Community) are not to deviate in the smallest detail from any of God's words as these apply to their own time. . . . They shall turn aside from his unerring laws neither to the right nor the left. (1QS col. 1, 13–15)
>
> In any place where is gathered the ten-man quorum, someone must always be engaged in study of the law, day and night, continually, each one taking his turn. (1QS col. 6, 6–7)

The community appeared to have had a strict understanding of the commandments of the Torah, which manifests itself in different ways in their legal interpretation. For certain commandments a "strict sense" interpretation is given. So, for example, Qumran legal interpretation does not except the concept of *tevul yom*, but insists that the entire period of purification must be observed before the impure person becomes ritually pure (11QTemple^{a} 45:9–10 et al.).

Most often, however, Qumran legal interpretation expands the application of the commandment, making its reach broader. This is most often done by analogy, as is the case for uncle-niece marriage:

> And each man takes as a wife the daughter of his brother and the daughter of his sister. But Moses said, 'Do not approach your mother's sister, she is a blood relation of your mother.' The law of incest, written for males, applies equally to females, and therefore to the daughter of a brother who uncovers the nakedness of the brother of her father, for he is a blood relation. (CD 5:7–11; see 11QTemple[a] 66:16–17)

The commandment ("But Moses said") is Leviticus 18:12–14, which forbids a nephew to marry his aunt. The *Damascus Document* extends the commandment to prohibit a niece from marrying her uncle as well (it is interesting to note that the Pharisees did not prohibit uncle-niece marriage, and even encouraged it, since it was not expressly forbidden in the Torah).

All Qumran legal exegesis is based on the Torah. The passage to be interpreted can be referred to explicitly with a citation formula (e.g., "as Moses said") or merely alluded to, as in the *Damascus Document*'s long list of Sabbath prohibitions (CD 10:14–11:18), which is introduced by the statement, "Concerning the Sabbath to guard it according to its precept" (10:14), an allusion to, but not a quotation of, Exodus 20:8–11/Deuteronomy 5:12–15.

Since the correct practice of the commandments of the Torah was central to the community's self-definition, its legal interpretation is usually transparent, that is, it is quite clear what passage is being interpreted and why. However, nonlegal texts are also full of scriptural citations and allusions; scripture simply is the language in which the community expresses itself, regardless of genre. The hymns of the *Hodayot* (*Thanksgiving Hymns*), for example, abound in scriptural language, even though very few direct quotations of scripture appear in them. Take, for example, *1QHodayot[a]*, col. 8, 17–18:

> Blessed are you, O Lord, Creator of [a]ll things and gr[eat] in deed because all things are your works. Behold, you have determined to b[e] merciful [with me] and be gracious to me by the spirit of your compassion and [ ] your glory. You alone possess righteousness, for you have done al[l these things.]

Although none of these lines contains direct quotations of scripture, the spirit of scripture, especially the Psalms, is clear throughout.

We can thus conclude that the interpretation of scripture, in myriad forms, was an ongoing concern of the Jewish community that preserved and at times may have composed the Qumran scrolls. Some of the forms of interpretation found among the Dead Sea Scrolls disappeared from use in later Judaism and Christianity (e.g., Rewritten Scripture), others were unique to the Qumran community (e.g., the *pesher* form), but the lemma + commentary form, and the use of scriptural passages as proof texts for particular legal or theological arguments, persisted in later Judaism and early Christianity.

[*See also* Masora and Masoretic Interpretation; Midrash; Textual Criticism, *subentry* Apocrypha and Deuterocanonical Books; Textual Criticism, *subentry* Hebrew Bible.; *and* Translation Techniques, *subentry* Ancient Versions.]

Bibliography

Primary Texts

Discoveries in the Judean Desert. Various authors. Vols. 1–40. Oxford: Clarendon Press, 1955–2010. This series is the vehicle for the publication of the majority of the manuscripts of the Dead Sea Scrolls. The reader will find photographs, transcriptions, translations when appropriate, and commentary by members of the official editorial team.

Parry, Donald W., and Emanuel Tov, eds. *The Dead Sea Scrolls Reader*, 6 vols. Leiden/Boston: Brill, 2005. A convenient multivolume set of translations of the Dead Sea Scrolls; a Hebrew transcription is given on the left-hand page, while an English translation is provided on the right.

Yadin, Yigael. *The Temple Scroll.* rev. Eng. ed. 3 vols. Jerusalem: Israel Exploration Society, 1983. The definitive edition of *11QTemple[a]*.

Reference Works

Schiffman, Lawrence H., and James C. VanderKam, eds. *Encyclopedia of the Dead Sea Scrolls.* 2 vols. New York: Oxford University Press, 2000. As its name implies, a collection of articles on various aspects of the Scrolls by leading scholars in the field.

Monographs on Specific Topics

Crawford, Sidnie White. *Rewriting Scripture in Second Temple Times.* Grand Rapids, Mich.: Eerdmans, 2008. An accessible introduction to and discussion of the phenomenon of Rewritten Scripture, concentrating on the books of the Pentateuch.

Hempel, Charlotte. *The Damascus Texts.* Companion to the Qumran Scrolls. Sheffield, UK: Sheffield Academic, 2000. A guide to the *Damascus Document* and its interpretation.

Lim, Timothy H. *Pesharim.* Companion to the Qumran Scrolls. London/New York: Sheffield Academic, 2002. A guide to the phenomenon of the pesher form in the Qumran scrolls.

Articles

Lim, Timothy H. "Authoritative Scriptures and the Dead Sea Scrolls." In *The Oxford Handbook of the Dead Sea Scrolls,* edited by Timothy H. Lim and John Collins, 303–322. Oxford: Oxford University Press, 2010. Focuses on issues of canon and authority in the Qumran collection.

Nitzan, Bilhah. "The Continuity of Biblical Interpretation in the Qumran Scrolls and Rabbinic Literature." In *The Oxford Handbook of the Dead Sea Scrolls,* edited by Timothy H. Lim and John Collins, 337–350. Oxford: Oxford University Press, 2010. Concentrates on the pesharim.

Zahn, Molly M. "Rewritten Scripture." In *The Oxford Handbook of the Dead Sea Scrolls,* edited by Timothy H. Lim and John Collins, 323–336. Oxford: Oxford University Press, 2010.

Sidnie White Crawford

DECONSTRUCTION

The term, coined by French philosopher and critic Jacques Derrida (1930–2004), refers to an amalgam of techniques and philosophical assertions regarding the relationship of language to meaning. Deconstruction consists of a collection of strategies for reading texts that expose their underlying tensions. These tensions come from inherent fissures within, and contradictions between, its surface meaning and other voices. Deconstruction represents a grabbag of devices that expose the inner workings of written communication, the process of reading, and the production of meaning. Although few biblical scholars would name themselves deconstructionists, it continues to have a great impact upon many newer methods in biblical interpretation. This article considers the following topics: (1) In the Beginning was Derrida; (2) deconstruction and the Bible; (3) chief characteristics; (4) techniques for reading texts; and (5) theological and hermeneutical considerations.

In the Beginning was Derrida. To deconstruct is to take apart something that had previously been constructed by somebody for some purpose. The deconstructed thing is necessarily complex, having many parts. It is thereby dismantled, separated into its components, to expose the hidden forces that produced it and make it work. There is violence in deconstruction. The one who constructed the object to be so examined would have wanted the structure to remain intact and undisturbed. When the object to be deconstructed is the Bible, the stakes become much higher.

Why "deconstruct" the Bible? The motivation is not, as some claim, cynical nihilism, destruction for its own sake, a foundationless hatred of all forms. Rather, deconstruction originates as an intellectual curiosity, an attempt to come to an understanding of how things work by taking them apart and exposing their "components."

Although Jacques Derrida was not the only theoretician of deconstruction, this article will use his writing to stand for the whole. At the same time, this is not an essay on Derrida, but on deconstruction and its influence on biblical studies. Derrida wrote in dialogue with many nineteenth- and twentieth-century philosophers, but always with his own playful twist on their ideas. He questioned their efforts to ground language in some unmediated reality. For Descartes, it was the human as a thinking consciousness, on which he predicated sure knowledge. For Hegel, it was "being." Derrida examined these assertions and declared that they could not function as the basis of meaning. All human experience, perception, and communication are heavily mediated. There is therefore no "transcendental signified," by which he meant the ultimate essence to which all signs pointed. It would be, as Stephen Moore observes, "an order of meaning that would be originary, self-identical, and self-evident" (1989, p. 182). It does not point beyond itself and is regarded as the final term to which all other terms refer. Derrida introduced the word "logocentrism" to describe the belief that the word, the logos, provides an unerring connection to the transcendental signified.

So, although the Western philosophers of the Enlightenment and afterwards had rejected the theocentric universe of the medieval philosophers, they still labored under the same basic metaphysical assumptions. For the medieval philosophers the transcendental signified was God. For post-Enlightenment philosophers it could be something else. Nietzsche, enormously influential on Derrida, challenged the viability of any transcendental signified at all.

There is, however, a serious problem with speaking about deconstruction in this manner, as if it were a "thing" that can be isolated and described. To speak thus is to ignore the central premise of Derrida and act as if none of his ideas mattered. On the one hand, deconstruction has certain characteristics that one can recognize and various techniques that one may teach. On the other, for deconstruction there is no thing behind the sign (the sign in this case being the word "deconstruction") that presumably points to the object for analysis, "deconstruction." And yet, to write about deconstruction, one must use words, and describe it as if it were a thing to be examined, as if the writer were an objective observer describing a discrete object.

Deconstruction asserts that there is only language, signs pointing to other signs. This appears to be counterintuitive. Of course there are things. This outrageous claim may be understood in the following manner: Humans experience reality only in mediation—there is no place of pure perception without prior interpretation. Therefore, that which we regard as an object to be contemplated, explored and analyzed, is already a text, an interpretation of something else. In the Bible, for instance, historical Israel, or the historical Jesus, are not objects to be discovered and described, but already complex, heavily interpreted signs. Therefore, they are already texts that come with considerable baggage.

If there is no "thing" called deconstruction, the alternatives are few. One might be silent, but Derrida was not silent. He struggled heartedly to address this difficulty. He created unusual linguistic devices that acknowledged the problem and sought to compensate. He coined the word *différance*. He claimed it is neither a word, nor a concept. In French it resembles the words "difference" and "defer." Because it is not a word, however, it serves to temper his metaphysical claims. He uses a non-word to describe an absence. Language creates meaning, not by pointing to things in the real world, but by differing with other signs. *Différance*, not being a word, and not pointing to anything non-linguistic (he supposes), manages to avoid the pitfalls one faces whenever one tries to say anything meaningful using language or writing.

The second unusual linguistic device he called "under erasure." Derrida acknowledged the necessity of borrowing words that assume a nonverbal reality behind them. He fashioned this artifice (which Heidegger had used in a different context) whereby he made statements "under erasure." He would instruct his printer to overtype an X upon words that he spoke under erasure ("~~thing~~," "~~is~~," "~~being~~"). He recognized the impossibility of saying anything without using words from discredited philosophical world views. He visually overlaid with an X these metaphysical words that assume a transcendental signified. By using the X, he recognized that he had no right to speak. He must speak anyway. He does under erasure. Much of what follows in this essay also must be said "under erasure," if Derrida's ideas are taken seriously.

Derrida is difficult to read. First, he assumes an intimate knowledge of the major Western philosophers. Second, his ideas undermine key assumptions about the reliability of language and the basic structures of reality, many unconsciously held. Therefore, his analysis is counterintuitive to most readers' sensibilities. Third, he self-consciously makes his style of discourse the embodiment of his ideas. He claims that writing never yields a clear and unambiguous meaning, so he deliberately writes in a manner difficult to pin down as well. Fourth, he engages in a kind of verbal play, using puns, neologisms, and deliberate misreadings of other writers. Fifth, he is sometimes a poor and careless writer, creating unnecessary layers of obscure language.

A study of deconstruction should not begin by reading Derrida. But if one must, there are two good places to start. "Des Tours de Babel" ("About the Tower of Babel") appeared first in French, but the journal *Semeia* printed an English translation in 1991. It is one of the few essays where Derrida actually deconstructs a biblical text. His *Of Grammatology*, with Spivak's preface as a guide, provides a good introduction to his thought.

Deconstruction and the Bible. God undergirds the reality claims of the Bible. Many biblical voices proclaim the presence of the transcendental signified, God, and that words may give access to the divine. There is then a dramatic disconnect between Derrida's claim that the transcendental signified is unavailable and these biblical claims of divine presence.

Derrida began writing in the 1960s, and his ideas became popular in North America, particularly among literary critics and scholars of English literature. That became the link to the biblical academic field. In the 1970s and 1980s many biblical scholars began to explore literary theory to fashion an alternative method of interpretation that differed from historical criticism. These individuals read literary theory at the very time when Derrida had become a celebrity among the literary theorists. They presented this new paradigm to the biblical scholarly community. Discussions of deconstruction took place most frequently in three academic forums: one journal and two scholarly societies. *Semeia*, a journal published by the Society of Biblical Literature, called itself, "an experimental journal for biblical criticism," and devoted at least two issues exclusively to the writings of Derrida and their impact on biblical studies. In the Society of Biblical Literature, the groups "Semiotics and Exegesis," "Ideological Criticism," and "Literary Theory," and, in the Catholic Biblical Association, the "Theory Group," which functioned under various names, all dealt seriously and sympathetically at one time or another with deconstruction.

Deconstruction moved into biblical scholarship by means of literary criticism. Groups such as the Modern Language Association, which was made up of English professors, comparative literature specialists, and scholars of literature, popularized Derrida at just the time when many biblical critics had begun reading literary theory. Traditional historical criticism dissatisfied them, and so they searched for new ways to approach and understand the biblical text. However, the first works where deconstructive ideas begin to address the biblical text were by those who wrote in systematic theology, not biblical theology or biblical interpretation. For example, Thomas Altizer was one of the chief spokespersons for the Death of God movement in the mid 1960s. In the 1980s he began to bring together Derrida and Christian theology, giving great attention to the difficulties of God language in the current philosophical climate. His discussions of the Bible, though a bit peripheral to his overall argument, brought the two (Derrida and the Bible) together. Another theologian who greatly influenced the first biblical critics to incorporate deconstruction was Louis Mackey. He wrote an notable article in *The Anglican Theological Review* in 1983, whose title describes its content: "Slouching toward Bethlehem: Deconstructive Strategies in Theology." The deconstructive critics in the late 1980s and early 1990s frequently cite him.

Peter Miscall was an early user of Derrida in the interpretation of biblical texts. Miscall's writing provides a strong indication of how pervasively the ideas of deconstruction have infused the biblical field. After 30 years, many of his assertions about the Bible no longer seem so radical but have become almost commonplace. Jewish biblical and Rabbinic scholar Edward L. Greenstein's work on Genesis 11 (the Tower of Babel) and Leviticus 10 (two priests burned by Yahweh) are some of the best examples of deconstruction in biblical interpretation. When coupled with his encyclopedic knowledge of the Jewish interpretive tradition, this essay makes an invaluable contribution. New Testament critic Gary Phillips too is one of the pioneer scholars who brought Derrida to very hostile audiences.

Some of the earlier interpreters of Derrida's ideas of de-centering were feminist critics. Deconstructive ideas are intrinsic to contemporary feminist biblical scholarship. It consciously seeks to demonstrate that the presumed objective biblical interpretation (the previous religious and scholarly conventional wisdom) is in fact interested and represents the concerns of white males. Feminists seek actively to overturn male reading and read instead for the ones on the margin. Phyllis Trible's *Texts of Terror* (1984) is an early example of this feminist deconstructive writing. She examines five biblical narratives where a woman is robbed of her voice and abused. She highlights this absence of voice and challenges the gender binary that puts women in this position.

Two early adopters of Derridean ideas were New Testament scholars Stephen Moore and Fred Burnett, both of whom wrote about Derrida beginning in the early 1980s. They have continued to explore notions of absence and traces in the literature of primitive Christianity. Burnett provided some of the earliest explanations of Derrida and the other deconstructive philosophers of Europe. Moore continues to bring absorbing and original interpretations of the New Testament to his writings.

Australian Hebrew Bible scholar Roland Boer speaks more commonly of the "Frankfurt School" of interpretation. They were a group of European Marxists writing in the middle years of the twentieth century. However, Boer is both conversant with deconstruction and one of the few biblical scholars (other than Stephen Moore) who can manage the Derridean style of playfully deconstructing his own argument while he gives it. Canadian David Jobling, along with Boer, employs deconstruction politically, using Marxist concepts of "means of production" and "Asiatic mode of production" to describe Israelite society and subsequent consumption of the biblical text. Jobling has organized many sessions and overseen many ambitious editorial projects that use deconstruction, as well as writing his own elegant biblical interpretations.

Danna Fewell and her frequent writing partner David Gunn are literary critics, and their efforts in gender studies particularly use deconstructive techniques. Their book *Gender, Power, and Promise* considers the gender binaries in Genesis through 2 Kings and overturns them.

Chief Characteristics. The short definition given earlier was: "Deconstruction consists of a collection of strategies for reading texts that expose their underlying tensions." This section expands that definition and describes (under erasure) the chief characteristics of these strategies and their underlying assumptions.

The Text as a Site of Conflict. Most traditional critics see the text as a discrete object that must be examined by an objective observer who will then determine the true interpretation. Deconstruction interprets texts (whether philosophical, literary, or classical/sacred) as sites where conflicts between warring narratives take place. These conflicts are, first, inner contradictions within the text, contradictions of detail. Why does the flood narrative in Genesis say both 40 and 120 days of rain? Why two animals instead of seven? Second, there are conflicts between the passage and adjoining portions. For example, there are two versions of creation that differ in detail, vocabulary, and theology. By uncovering the fault lines in a text, one may locate and examine the warring narratives. The task of the interpreter, then, is not to reconcile these differences, to show which narrative is "right," but rather to highlight and illuminate these dissonant features.

This is particularly apt when one considers the Bible, for its books have been written by many over a long period of time. The scrolls passed through numerous communities before the books became fixed, and each community left its imprint, its traces. Therefore, profound ruptures abound in scripture, which for a deconstructionist are the sites of conflicts, signs of struggle between at least two different strategies. Each attempts to render meaning in the text. As a result, linguistic discourse (communication through language) is inherently slippery and full of contradictions. Because of the unstable text, the reader plays a significant role in the process of inscribing meaning. The writing is an ambiguous, unstable vehicle. Therefore, no single, monolithic interpretation ever gains total control. The text is not unified, but rather divided against itself. The interpretation is not, as Gary Phillips says, "univocal, natural, or self evident" (1990, p. 11).

The Bible already contains its own deconstruction. The interpreter, using deconstructive techniques, only exposes the fault lines already in the text (under erasure). So if an interpreter points out, for instance, that the pronouncement of the Serpent, "you shall not die," actually was correct, that fault line was in the text itself. In Genesis 2 and 3, the master narrative regards Yahweh as stern and fair, whether monarch, parent, or friend. The serpent challenges Yahweh's authority. He says in contradiction to Yahweh that the first humans will not die after eating forbidden fruit. Indeed, they do not die, and that result conflicts with the notion that Yahweh is stern and fair. This conflict is embedded in the text, not imposed from outside. This is where the action is, in the interplay and dialogue between multiple narratives and interpretations. The discourse never reaches the transcendental signified. Layers of language block one's access to a transcendental signified, and this occlusion is insurmountable in any way that would produce a clear and unambiguous message from the other side.

There is No Signified. The French structuralist Ferdinand Saussure (1857–1913) explained meaning as the relationship between the signified and the signifier. The signifier (or sign) points to something in the external world, the signified. For Saussure, language is a matter of difference. Meaning is differentiation between signs. However, Derrida, although heavily dependent on Saussure's terminology, asserted that there is no signified, only an endless procession of signs, each one pointing to the next one. Derrida noted, therefore, that neither writing nor speech might produce unconflicted, clear meaning. Meaning is always up for grabs because the signified remains unavailable. All the signifiers point to other signifiers, ad infinitum.

The Bible too addresses in its own way the tension between signified and signifier. Edward Greenstein points to two different biblical passages where he finds this signifier tension. First, in Genesis 1 the signifier (the word "light") existed in speech before the signified (light) actually came into existence. The sign preceded the signified and brought it into existence. Although that does not exactly reproduce Derrida's notion of an endless procession of signs, it does at least suggest that signs have a reality and importance that go beyond what they point toward. The second has to do with Genesis 11, the Tower of Babel. (Derrida also addressed this in an article in *Semeia.*) It concerns the relationship of signs to their appointed objects. The people of Shinar, by wanting to make a name for themselves, claim the right to generate meaning with their own words. They declared independence from God, their transcendental signified. Yahweh, in response, confounded their language, creating an impenetrable barrier between the words and their meaning. Greenstein used this as an etiology and allegory, not for the profusion of languages, but rather for the gulf between word and meaning, between sign and signified.

There is Nothing behind the Text. If signs only point to other signs, language is always and only about itself. This claim causes some to allege that deconstruction speaks nonsense. Of course there is something behind the words. There are actual human beings who wrote them. And they wrote from within their own experiences. That these facts, activities, and personages existed behind writing and were responsible for its production is so obvious as to be irrefutable. And yet the deconstructionist claims there is no text. What do they mean by that?

Contemporary readers find unavailable the origin of ancient writing, whether the author, the world in which it was produced, or the circumstances of its production. The Bible and other corporately produced sacred texts operate in this manner. No one can determine what moment in the Bible's production would constitute "authorship." In fact, there is no one moment of authorship, nor one author. The whole notion of a work owned and defined by a single person turns out to be an imaginary construct and a contemporary one. So, therefore, to speak as if the Bible had individual authors is anachronistic and not useful.

There is No Center. Biblical theologians long have sought to find a center, a ruling metaphor by which all the disparate parts of the Bible may be held together. For Martin Luther it was "law and gospel," and for Walther Eichrodt it was "covenant." Gerhard von Rad regarded tradition as the defining concept, and for many others it was salvation history. Deconstruction says either that there is no center, or that claims to a center function as a means of concealment, so that a particular interpreter might shape and control the production of meaning. Anyone who identifies the Bible's center steers interpretation that way, magnifies the importance of certain passages, and suppresses or forcibly harmonizes the parts that do not fit. Interpretation of the Bible then becomes an exercise in power and domination, one group over another.

The Bible, however, is made up of disparate parts that cannot be successfully and decisively put together in any sort of single coherent picture, however complex. Biblical scholars have always known that the Bible is full of these fissures. The most common response, however, has been to harmonize—to change the meaning of the miscreant texts so that they fit in with a larger schema. Deconstruction would rather highlight the miscreant and elevate it as the most important voice.

Overturn and Reconfigure Binaries. Western metaphysics arranges experience in binaries, unequal pairings that define and organize the world, for example, soul and body, content and form, or depth and surface. Humans gravitate to binaries or concept pairs. They seem completely natural and intrinsic to human experience. Even in Genesis, God creates by dividing in two: heaven and earth, day and night, light and darkness, sea and dry land, male and female.

Deconstruction overturns binaries. One of the pair is usually considered the outlier, the opposition, the other. Arranging the world in binaries controls the field and gains a monopoly on the production of meaning. Derrida takes the underling of the pair and elevates it to central place, thus overturning the hierarchy. Subsequently, the hierarchy itself must yield to a new structure of understanding. In the Bible, the gender binary of male-female elevates the male in the hierarchy. If one counter-reads a story by placing the woman in the center, the hierarchy reverses. For example, Phyllis Trible wrote *Texts of Terror* (1984) in which each chapter addressed a woman from a biblical narrative (Hagar, Jephthah's daughter, Tamar, and the unnamed woman in Judges 19) who, by virtue of being a woman, was terrorized. Trible centered these women, giving them voice. She thus reversed the hierarchy. However, she then overturned the hierarchy itself. By her interpretation of these biblical figures, she brings into question the whole notion of gender hierarchy.

One cannot avoid the political implications of such an activity as deconstruction. It exposes the weaknesses of the dominant reading. It challenges that reading and elevates the weak and marginalized. The entrenched powers, the patriarchy, the gatekeepers of society, the wealthy are the ones who feel threatened when someone disturbs the divinely sanctioned order. Although deconstruction has not always produced political ferment, it always has the potential.

Techniques for Reading Texts. Deconstruction does not try in any traditional sense to offer a single method of interpretation or viewpoint. It looks for what Jonathan Culler (1982) calls "metaphysical oppositions in their arguments." To review, deconstruction is based on the following assumptions:

1. The text is a site of conflict.
2. These conflicts are the result of warring narratives embedded in the text.
3. Meaning is not a process by which one employs the words and sentences to uncover a truth hidden behind the pages. Rather, interpretation seeks to explore conflicts between texts.
4. Rather than a core meaning, texts contain traces, marks of absence, festering sores that are the keys to meaning.

5. Texts are signs that point to other signs and not to a transcendental signified.
6. Totalizing claims conceal power.

It now remains to consider how these assumptions translate into specific interpretive strategies.

Read Suspiciously. A deconstructionist reads against the grain. Every text has a master narrative, a particular point of view that tends to dominate and thus steer the reading in a certain direction. Deconstruction suspects methods that promise a complete understanding. It identifies that master narrative and works to undermine it. When institutions explain and justify themselves, their witness is self-serving. So, in the Book of Joshua, deconstruction would elevate the Canaanites. In Judges, it speaks for Delilah, and in 1 and 2 Kings for Jezebel. In the Garden of Eden (Genesis 2—3), the master narrative portrays God as righteous and kind. The deconstructionist highlights the truth-telling serpent.

Unexamined assumptions are always suspect. Many assumptions about the Bible are unconscious and assumed without reflection. Whenever things seem so obvious as to be beyond argument, those very assumptions should be most suspect and subject to rigorous critical examination.

Look for the Cracks and Fault Lines in the Master Narrative. Fault lines in the Bible are obvious. There are differing details, varieties of characterization, and moral lapses (such as a command to genocide, slavery, or the mistreatment of women). There are also literary seams and ambiguous language that resists clarification. Most commonly, when readers come to such places of textual rupture, they seek to smooth them over. Some do this through harmonization, making all the parts of the Bible into a single harmonic voice. Others fit the biblical text into a new and different master narrative, such as a historical one. In deconstruction, these lapses are highlighted and worried over. They become the source for meaning.

Note the Binaries and Overturn Them. Look for pairs of things. Usually one in the pair represents presence and links to the transcendental signified. The other, the counterpart, is held off or silenced. Home in on the submerged member of the binary. Elevate it. Fill in the gaps left by its silencing. Reverse the hierarchy. Finally, engage in metacriticism. Examine the process by which this binary has produced meaning.

The Book of Proverbs divides humankind into the wise and the foolish. The sages meant for their readers to embrace the habits of the wise and to avoid foolish behavior. The deconstructionist asks: How does behavior divide into these two categories and who gets to decide? And then: Does the division wise and foolish mean anything more than a grab for power? Both wisdom and her definition remain elusive and multivocal. Differing understandings of wisdom are the site for the production of meaning. In this is uncovered a rupture in the biblical text. Proverbs suggests that wisdom resides in following the traditions of the sages who came before. Job and Ecclesiastes reject hallowed tradition. This rupture is not a problem but an opportunity. It is a site of conflict and ambiguity that compels the reader to enter in and participate in the process. The opening chapters of the Book of Job present a binary between Yahweh and the Satan. A deconstructive interpretation reads sympathetically for the Satan and then uses that to draw into question the whole Israelite concept of God. By examining these ruptures, one uncovers lines of control and efforts to conceal.

Look for the Marginal. Because the conflict of the text is suppressed, one must focus on the seemingly unimportant point. Therefore, deconstructive readings are characteristically very close, attending to the loose detail, the puzzle piece that does not fit. Deconstruction does not harmonize or depend upon a historical explanation. There are always figures on the margins of the narrative, often unnamed, or if named, demonized. Attending carefully to these figures reverses the hierarchy.

Theological and Hermeneutical Considerations: Objections to Deconstruction. Deconstruction has not entered easily into biblical studies. The objections are strong and nearly overpowering, although they often stem from dramatic misunderstandings and caricatures of this approach.

Nihilism believes there is nothing to believe in. From where does one get the idea that deconstruction is nihilistic? First, from the insistence that there is no center, no one ruling metaphor that explains the whole. Deconstruction claims no transcendental signified. However, this argument so framed is a bifurcation. Either one believes in a present and available transcendental signified, or one believes in nothing. Derrida's flair for grand, sweeping statements and oracular pronouncements might give that impression. Deconstruction rather problematizes the process by which humans create meaning (rather than discover it). It is possible to deny a center and still be able to act with integrity and courage. Things matter in deconstruction, although reasons why they should matter hang in air, or reside under erasure. Deconstruction claims that all philosophies similarly hang in air, that is, they are signs pointing to other signs. Monotheistic theologians and philosophers must appeal to a text (Bible or Qurʾan), which is not self-authenticating. Or else they point to natural law, which is always subject to interpretation.

On occasion, Derrida identifies God as the transcendental signified. So, therefore, to claim that the transcendental signified is a figment, and that one's cherished ideas hang in air, sounds like atheism. Nietzsche in *Thus Spake Zarathustra* had his protagonist declare to the crowds that God was dead. However, where Nietzsche says "God is dead," another claims, "God is impenetrable mystery." Both are compatible with deconstruction. The second coheres as a negative theology, one that insists that no words adequately describe the divine. One may only say what God is not. That sounds a good deal like Derrida's notion of absence and traces.

The assertion that there is nothing but texts has often been misunderstood. Derrida meant that there is no unmediated reality. What most people regard as nontextual human experience is already an interpreted event. It is, therefore, in his terminology, a text. All human experience is interpreted at the outset.

If the techniques of textual deconstruction are practiced in interpreting the Bible, are there controls or checks upon interpretation, or can the Bible mean anything at all? Does the interpreter have sole prerogative to create any meaning out of the Bible? If a written work can mean absolutely anything, then it does not have any meaning at all. Texts are indeed open and unstable, and there are a great many interpretations that differ, and there is no obvious limit to them. However, constraints exist that keep a biblical passage from meaning anything at all. First, there are the words themselves. The interpretation must have some connection with the actual words on the page. Second, there is the audience—there must be some group willing to listen and consider. Third, there are moral considerations—inhumane interpretations (using the Bible as a justification for slavery or the mistreatment of women) are rejected out-of-hand.

Even though Derrida speaks against divine presence, there is much in the Bible that suggests a similar absence of God. Gideon bemoaned the mislocation of the God who had appeared in the stories he heard: "And where are all his wonderful deeds that our ancestors recounted to us, saying, 'Did not the Lord bring us up from Egypt?' But now the Lord has cast us off, and given us into the hand of Midian" (Judg 6:13). Portions of the Psalms and the overall concerns of the books of Job and Ecclesiastes question divine presence in agonizing terms. Prophets too had their moments of doubt and pain in the soul's dark night. And as Gideon pointed out, even the dramatic stories of divine presence, with Adam and Eve, with Abraham and Moses, were ancient stories at the time they were told, not part of the writers' everyday experience. Divine absence characterized their daily life. Because many of the biblical writers address divine presence and absence, the Bible is a uniquely suitable subject for deconstructive examination.

If God does not serve as transcendental signified but rather as a word that highlights an absence, why speak of God at all? The answer is that God, even in many biblical and theological traditions, remains a mystery. By mystery is meant that God's apparent actions make no sense, or else they conflict with what the traditional teachings say about God. Many have recognized the inadequacy of any human language to encompass the divine. Derrida never claims that there is no ultimate reality out there. Rather he claims that access to that reality is occluded by the difficulties of language and text. He further asserts that claims of access to ultimate reality are smokescreens to conceal efforts to assert power.

Does deconstruction let in the cold? Should we protect our children from it? Does it bring chaos? First one must question the division hot and cold. One person's soul-paralyzing cold is another's fresh air. Deconstruction, not always under that name, has been a source of fresh and exciting interpretation of the Bible. It is not a matter of letting it in. Under many names other than deconstruction, it has already arrived.

[*See also* Formalist Interpretation; Poststructuralist Interpretation; Reader-Response Criticism; Semiotics; Structuralist Interpretation; *and* Synchronic Interpretation.]

BIBLIOGRAPHY

Adam, A. K. M. *What is Postmodern Biblical Criticism?* Minneapolis: Fortress, 1995. An engaging introduction from a first-rate New Testament critic; includes a good basic chapter on deconstruction and an excellent bibliography.

Boer, Roland. *Novel Histories: The Fiction of Biblical Criticism.* Sheffield, UK: Sheffield Academic, 1997. This clever and original book combines first-rate biblical analysis with a playful fictional representation of a major Old Testament critic and thus breaks down many assumed boundaries in scholarly writing.

Burnett, Fred. "Postmodern Exegesis: The Eve of Historical Criticism." *Semeia* 51 (1990): 51–80.

Burnett, Fred. "The Undecidibility of the Proper Name 'Jesus' in Matthew." *Semeia* 54 (1991): 123–144. These two articles provide some of the earliest attempts to address Derrida and deconstruction in relationship to biblical criticism.

Caws, Mary Ann. "French Theory and Criticism: 4. Early Twentieth Century." In *The Johns Hopkins Guide to Literary Theory and Criticism,* edited by Michael Groden and Martin Kreiswirth, 296–298. Baltimore: The Johns Hopkins University Press, 1994. This, and three additional articles listed later, come from this very excellent reference produced by the American literary critical establishment in the 1980s and 1990s. Together these articles provide a basic perspective on Derrida and deconstruction.

Culler, Jonathan. *On Deconstruction: Theory and Criticism after Structuralism.* New York: Cornell University Press, 1982. Edition with a new preface, 2007. This important book is one of the first significant efforts to explain Derrida to an American audience. It was a must-read for many biblical critics in the 1980s and 1990s.

Derrida, Jacques. "Des Tours de Babel." *Semeia* 54 (1991) 3–34.

Derrida, Jacques. *Of Grammatology.* Translated by Gayatri Chakravorty Spivak. Baltimore: Johns Hopkins Press, 1976. The article in *Semeia* is one of the few places where Derrida focuses on deconstructing a biblical text. *Of Grammatology* might be a good introduction to his theoretical writings; the preface by Spivak is especially helpful.

Fewell, Danna Nolan, and David M. Gunn. *Gender, Power, and Promise: The Subject of the Bible's First Story.* Nashville, Tenn.: Abingdon, 1993. A good example of feminist, literary deconstructive analysis. Fewell and Gunn examine the "first biblical story," by which they mean Genesis through 1 Kings, and consider issues of gender and binaries.

Greenstein, Edward L. "Deconstruction and Biblical Narrative." *Prooftexts* 9:1 (January 1989): 42–71. This is the first place to go to see creative deconstructive analysis of the Bible and the insights it brings. Greenstein's extensive knowledge of rabbinic writings greatly enriches his interpretations.

Jobling, David. "Writing the Wrongs of the World: The Deconstruction of the Biblical Text in the Context of Liberation Theology." *Semeia* 51 (1990): 81–118. Jobling here ably demonstrates the political implications of a deconstructive methodology.

Kneale, J. Douglas. "Deconstruction." In *The Johns Hopkins Guide to Literary Theory and Criticism,* edited by Michael Groden and Martin Kreiswirth, 185–192. Baltimore: Johns Hopkins University Press, 1994. A good overview, although a bit technical.

Mackey, Louis. "Slouching Toward Bethlehem: Deconstructive Strategies in Theology." *Anglican Theological Review* 65:3 (July 1983): 255–272. One of the earliest introductions to deconstruction for theology. Many of the biblical critics in the 1980s and early 1990s cite this clearly written and epochal essay. Aside from being an excellent introduction to the theological implications of deconstruction, this essay also addresses the Gospels from a deconstructive standpoint.

McGowan, John. "Postmodernism." In *The Johns Hopkins Guide to Literary Theory and Criticism*, edited by Michael Groden and Martin Kreiswirth, 585–587. Baltimore: Johns Hopkins University Press, 1994. Postmodernism overlaps deconstruction in many ways; helpful sections of this article refer directly to deconstruction.

Miscall, Peter D. *The Workings of Old Testament Narrative.* Philadelphia: Fortress, 1983. One of the first serious efforts to address an Old Testament narrative from the perspective of deconstruction.

Moore, Stephen D. *The Bible in Theory: Critical and Postcritical Essays.* Atlanta: Society of Biblical Literature, 2010. In this collection of essays, Moore demonstrates wide reading in literary theory and its application to biblical studies. It represents the fruit of 20 years of writing on the subject.

Moore, Stephen D. *Literary Criticism and the Gospels: The Theoretical Challenge.* New Haven, Conn.: Yale University Press, 1989. A pioneering work that applies continental philosophy, including Derrida, to New Testament research.

Penchansky, David. *The Politics of Biblical Theology: A Post-Modern Reading.* Studies in American Biblical Hermeneutics 10. Macon, Georgia: Mercer University Press, 1995. This book examines a group of Old Testament critics from the 1950s and 1960s, the Biblical Theology Movement, and deconstructs the conflict that arose in the academy over the bifurcation of Hebraic and Greek approaches to knowledge.

Penchansky, David. "Up for Grabs: A Tentative Proposal for Ideological Criticism." *Semeia* 59 (1992): 35–41. This article appeared in the Ideological Criticism issue of *Semeia*. It provides my fullest explanation of the text as a site of conflict and focuses on an obscure passage in the beginning of the Book of Judges.

Phillips, Gary A. "Exegesis as Critical Praxis: Reclaiming History and Text from a Postmodern Perspective." *Semeia* 51 (1990): 7–50. An early manifesto of how deconstruction will affect biblical studies.

Rabaté, Jean-Michel. "Derrida, Jacques." In *The Johns Hopkins Guide to Literary Theory and Criticism*, edited by Michael Groden and Martin Kreiswirth, 197–201. Baltimore: Johns Hopkins University Press, 1994. Especially good for tracing Derrida's intellectual output and his relationship to other philosophers.

Raschke, Carl A., ed. *Deconstruction and Theology.* New York: Crossroads, 1982. A collection of essays from theologians about the intersection of the two fields. The introduction to this book of essays, written by Carl A. Raschke, is particularly helpful; see "History as Apocalypse" by Thomas J. J. Altizer.

Spivak, Gayatri Chakravorty. In *Other Worlds: Essays in Cultural Politics.* New York: Routledge, 1988.

Spivak, Gayatri Chakravorty. Preface to *Of Grammatology* by Jacque Derrida. Translated by Gayatri Chakravorty Spivak. Baltimore: Johns Hopkins Press, 1976. Spivak is one of the best interpreters of Derrida. The first entry is a lengthy preface to one of Derrida's seminal works; the second is a collection of her essays. Both are calculated to give the reader a "feel" for Derrida.

Trible, Phyllis. *Texts of Terror:* Literary-Feminist Readings of Biblical Narratives. Philadelphia: Fortress, 1984. An excellent example of deconstructive feminist criticism.

David Penchansky

Diachronic Interpretation

Diachronic interpretation is a general designation for methods that seek to determine the stages and processes by which biblical texts developed into their present forms. Part of the broader "historical-critical method," diachronic (lit., "through time") interpretation focuses on the traditions, sources, and strata that may underlie the text, as well as the different phases of composition and editing through which it emerged. In recent years, diachronic interpretation has included renewed interest in the final form of biblical books as whole literary compositions.

The major methods that have constituted diachronic interpretation are source criticism, form criticism, tradition criticism, and redaction criticism. The perspective represented by these methods should be distinguished from synchronic interpretation, which foregrounds elements of the text's final form and concerns of readers and the reading process. Even so, recent scholarship increasingly recognizes that the distinction between diachronic and synchronic approaches has often been overdrawn (see Assessment and Contribution later). John Barton (2007, p. 44) contends that diachronic interpreters throughout the twentieth century were often interested in the text's final literary shape and have been driven by an essentially literary goal—to find the level at which a text has literary coherence when such coherence is not present on the surface of the text's final form. Additionally, the diachronic methods considered here should be distinguished from other historically oriented modes of study that nonetheless do not focus extensively on questions of the text's origins and development through time. These include historical criticism generally, which has sought to use the biblical texts as evidence to reconstruct historical events and to locate the texts within particular historical settings. Likewise, the "history of religions" approach, which studies comparative ancient Near Eastern religious texts; the "social-scientific interpretation" approach, which seeks to locate texts within particular social settings and dynamics; and the "new historicism" approach, which blends social and ideological considerations in the examination of the writing and reading of history, all foreground historical dimensions but not primarily those related to the text's prehistory. Historical philology, which examines grammar and lexicography to trace the growth of languages, and textual criticism (traditionally called "lower criticism"), which attempts to retrace textual transmission through studying the available manuscripts (see McCarter 1986; Metzger 2005), come the closest to the diachronic methods under consideration here (traditionally called "higher criticism"). Recent text criticism in particular has begun to examine the various manuscript traditions as indicators of different social, theological, and hermeneutical contexts within the history of Jewish and Christian tradition (see Epp 2005; Ehrman 2006). Still, these methods lack a sustained concentration on the text's prehistory of sources, traditions, authors, and editors.

History and Development. Diachronic interpretation of the Bible began in earnest in the Enlightenment of the seventeenth and eighteenth centuries, as new developments in science and other disciplines led to new ways of approaching scripture (see Hayes 2003; Rogerson 1985). The impulses that gave rise to such perspectives, however, initially emerged in conjunction with the European Renaissance's interest in returning to the earliest sources for literary study and the Protestant Reformation's emphasis on the ability of individuals to investigate scripture apart from ecclesiastical tradition (see Barton 2007; Freiday 1979; Scholder 1990). Diachronic methods flourished within early critical work on the origins and composition of the Pentateuch and the Synoptic Gospels. At one level, early diachronic investigations often served efforts at historical reconstruction, as many interpreters sought the literary prehistory of the Pentateuch or the Synoptic Gospels as a means of reconstructing the religious and political history of ancient Israel or the earliest sayings and stories of the historical Jesus (e.g., Wellhausen 1994 [orig. 1878]). At another level, the diachronic interpretation in these early studies was an essentially literary investigation. Interpreters sought to read biblical texts such as the Pentateuch as coherent wholes, but found elements in the text's final form (doublets, contradictions, etc.) that worked against literary coherence. In response, diachronic interpreters posited that one could find literary coherence in the sources and traditions that stood behind the text's now composite form (Barton 2007).

Early pioneers of the diachronic study of the Pentateuch included Isaac de la Peyrère (1596–1676), Thomas Hobbes (1588–1679), and Baruch Spinoza (1632–1677), who highlighted literary features such as anachronisms in order to propose that the Pentateuch was a composite work from the period after Moses. These initial impulses developed into detailed theories of the Pentateuch's literary sources throughout the latter seventeenth and mid-eighteenth centuries. The French Catholic priest Richard Simon (1638–1712), in an attempt to show the necessity of church tradition and discredit the Protestant notion of *sola scriptura*, posited a literary prehistory for the Pentateuch in which scribes created documents that recorded various events and were used as sources by biblical authors. The French physician Jean Astruc's *Conjectures sur les Mémoires* (1753) offered the more developed theory that Moses had used four written sources that could be distinguished on the basis of the different Hebrew names for God. Throughout this period, much diachronic interpretation also came from Protestant scholars with apologetic aims. Far from attempting to undermine the Bible or Christianity, many diachronic interpreters sought to offer a reasonable explanation of the character and complexity of the biblical text, albeit in nontraditional ways.

By the nineteenth century, diachronic interpretation largely centered in German Protestantism and the development of source theories for the Pentateuch had gained the primary place (see Rogerson; Hayes 2003). The notion of sources that could be identified on the basis of internal literary criteria and related to developments within Israelite history gradually displaced other theories of the Pentateuch's composition that posited multiple unconnected fragments or only a single primary source. These currents led to the emergence of full-blown "source criticism," represented most significantly by the work of W. M. L. de Wette (1780–1849) and Julius Wellhausen (1844–1918) (see Source Criticism later). De Wette argued for a late dating of Deuteronomy in conjunction with the reforms of King Josiah of Judah in the seventh century B.C.E. (2 Kgs 22–23), and Wellhausen's *Prolegomena to the History of Israel* (first published in German in 1878) attempted a full articulation of four Pentateuchal sources (J, E, D, P) and their relationship to various periods of Israelite political and religious history. Wellhausen's work set the agenda for the next century of study of the composition of the Pentateuch, solidifying the conviction that texts reveal historical information only about the periods in which their sources were composed and not necessarily about the time of the events they describe.

In this same period, diachronic interpretation gained prominence outside of the Pentateuch through the work of scholars such as Bernard Duhm, whose 1892 commentary on Isaiah developed earlier ideas into the theory of a three-part composite nature of the book's origins and composition (Duhm 1892). Similar source-critical work took place on other books such as 1 and 2 Samuel and Jeremiah, accompanied by the increasing discovery and decipherment of comparative ancient Near Eastern texts that added to biblical scholarship's focus on historical contexts and compositional processes. Within New Testament studies, diachronic interpretation played its most important early role in the study of the so-called "Synoptic Problem"—the effort to establish the literary and historical relationships and common sources among the Synoptic Gospels (see Source Criticism later). The historical interests of scholars such as G. E. Lessing (1729–1781) and David Friedrich Strauss (1808–1874) and the analyses of F. C. Baur (1792–1860), G. G. Wilke (1786–1854), and H. J. Holtzmann (1832–1910) eventually led to the prominent nineteenth century two-source theory for the Gospels. This theory identified Mark as the earliest Gospel, used in different ways as a source by Matthew and Luke, who also used a shared sayings source (*Q* or *Quelle*, "source") (see Streeter 1961 [orig. 1924]; Longstaff and Thomas 1988).

In the first half of the twentieth century, diachronic interpretation's focus on literary sources broadened into the methodologies of form criticism, tradition criticism, and redaction criticism (see Techniques and Practices later). This movement produced new interest in the significance of tradition (both oral and written) and community for understanding the origins and character of both the Hebrew Bible/Old Testament and New Testament (HB/OT, and NT) (Hayes 2003, p. 49). Hermann Gunkel (1862–1932) introduced a new emphasis on the identification of the form/genre of biblical texts, the relationship of genres to various social situations in which they originated, and the development of texts from their earliest oral phase to their final literary form. Subsequent scholars such as Martin Dibelius (1883–1947), Rudolph Bultmann (1884–1976), and Hans Conzelmann (1915–1989) within NT and Albrecht Alt (1883–1956), Martin Noth (1902–1968), and Gerhard von Rad (1901–1971) within HB/OT developed these emphases into new methods for investigating how the traditions underlying the biblical texts emerged through various historical phases and what theological significance they carried in those different stages. In the following decades, investigations sought to identify the editing process by which various traditions were included in the final form of biblical texts and what that process reveals about the theological interests of the Bible's writers and editors.

From the 1970s to the present, each of the major diachronic approaches has continued to function but has been reexamined and reformulated, resulting in an altered landscape of diachronic study today (see Assessment and Contribution later). In some cases, such as the quest for sources that underlie the Pentateuch, many scholars have worked within the paradigm popularized by Wellhausen, often postulating increasingly refined theories of sources and literary growth, while others have suggested moving outside the notion of discreet literary sources altogether (see Rendtorff 1990; Blum 1990). Likewise, the methods of form and redaction criticism have acquired new emphases on the connections between oral and written material and the importance of the biblical books as whole literary works in their final form, with increasing attention being paid to the formative role of the Persian period (538–333 B.C.E.) in the production of the HB/OT texts in particular (see Buss 1999; Sweeney and Ben Zvi 2003). Alongside these developments, however, both philosophical and methodological critiques, as well as the rise of synchronic methods of biblical study, have questioned the established assumptions, procedures, and, for some scholars, plausibility of diachronic interpretation.

Techniques and Practices. Several methods of diachronic interpretation emphasize different aspects of the development of biblical texts through time. The methods encompass various attempts to identify potential sources (oral or written) used by biblical writers, particular forms (oral or written) employed in texts, theological traditions that influenced the work of writers and editors, the elements and character of the editing process, and the dynamics of the final literary compositions produced. In spite of the impression given by the methodological sophistication of these approaches, the criticisms used in diachronic study are best seen not as pseudoscientific methods whose procedures yield predictable outcomes, but in a more humanistic vein, as means of seeking the literary coherence and character of biblical texts whose present form does not immediately yield such coherence (Barton 2007, p. 62).

Source Criticism. The earliest of the major diachronic methods was source criticism, known until the mid-twentieth century as "higher criticism" or "literary criticism." It attempts to identify the literary sources used by biblical writers to construct a text and the ways in which those sources have been combined in the text's present form. The starting point is the recognition of elements in the final form of the text that suggest a composite nature for the text at hand (doublets and other repetitions, inconsistencies in thought, style, and terminology, disjointed transitions, etc.). Beginning from the assumption that the biblical writers would aim to be consistent in style, terminology, and perspective, source criticism interprets inconsistencies in these matters as evidence of the combination of different sources. The method then attempts to isolate each prior independent source, describe its defining characteristics, identify its date and provenance, and explore how it has been combined with other sources in the text's final form.

Source criticism emerged in earnest within the study of the Pentateuch in the nineteenth century (see History and Development earlier), receiving particular popularization through Wellhausen's *Prolegomena to the History of Israel* (orig. German 1878). Prior to Wellhausen, scholars had identified multiple sources (commonly four) that had been combined in the Pentateuch, typically concluding that the priestly source, with its legislation concerning sacred rituals and priestly practice, reflected the oldest period of Israelite history. Wellhausen's "documentary hypothesis," however, posited that the priestly source was a late reflection of postexilic Israelite religion, and thus offered a new explanation of the order and characteristics of the Pentateuch's four sources. With various modifications, the general tenets of Wellhausen's source analysis remained the accepted view of the Pentateuch's composition until the 1970s. More recently, a number of proposals have moved away from the traditional documentary hypothesis, proposing new dates and configurations of the standard sources (Van Seters 1975) or altogether new explanations that posit the gradual development of individual traditions into increasingly larger accounts (Rendtorff; Blum). Source criticism of other HB/OT texts has built upon clues such as the explicit references to sources in the historical books (e.g., "the book of the annals of the kings of Judah" 2 Kgs 23:28) to propose that books such as 1 and 2 Samuel may also consist of originally independent narrative sources (e.g., the ark narrative in 1 Sam 4:1—7:2).

Within NT studies, source criticism primarily developed through the interpretation of the Gospels (see History and Development earlier). The question of the composition and relationship among the Synoptic Gospels ("Synoptic Problem") produced numerous proposals for the books' order and interdependence, as well as the possibility of other prior sources utilized by the Gospel writers. Source criticism led to the common scholarly explanation that Mark was the earliest Gospel written and Matthew and Luke used Mark as a source. Commonalities between Matthew and Luke outside of their use of Mark's material also led to the hypothesis of the so-called "Q" (*Quelle*) source, typically understood as a collection of sayings compiled between 50 and 70 C.E. (for an early articulation, see Streeter). Likewise, some scholars have proposed potential sources for the Gospel of John, including an independent "signs source" that may explain John's inclusion of Jesus's seven miracle stories, while others have suggested possible sources underlying such texts as the accounts of Paul's church visits and the "we" memoir passages in Acts (see Gillingham 1998, p. 12).

Form Criticism. Traditionally, form criticism has paralleled the search for potential written sources used by the biblical writers, but has been focused on the nature of the material within the smaller units of the text and the possible connections of that material to social settings within the contexts of ancient Israel and early Christianity (see McKnight 1969; Tucker 1971). The working assumption is that there are identifiable units within the text that can be distinguished from their larger literary context and had an independent, often oral, existence related to the social life of the community prior to their inclusion in the final composition. Form criticism attempts to classify those units into specific genres and set forth the potential settings and processes within human life and society in which those genres may have functioned. At the most basic level, the method searches for patterns of language within the text, identifying the typical structure, content, and setting associated with each pattern.

In form-critical terminology (see Sweeney 1999, p. 59), "genre" (German, *Gattung*) designates a conventional type or pattern of material that has a typical structure and content. Commonly identified genres within the biblical literature include etiological narrative, proverb, law, parable, controversy story, and miracle story (see Barton 2007, p. 64). The phrase "setting in life" (German, *Sitz im Leben*) designates the earlier social settings with which form critics have associated these genres. These settings are recurring, communal, often institutional occasions of human experience, rather than specific historical situations. Interpreters seek to identify the discreet genres within the text and then posit that those units had been earlier oral traditions from social settings within shared human experience. In this way, the method reconstructs the hypothetical oral prehistory of a biblical text.

The primary work on form criticism began with Hermann Gunkel's studies of Genesis and Psalms in the late nineteenth and early twentieth century (see History and Development earlier). Gunkel drew upon an emerging interest in oral literature and folklore studies to classify the genres of material in these books and posit that the earliest stages of the genres were simple, oral forms that became more developed over time. His work (Gunkel 1998 [orig. 1926]), for instance, identified five major psalm types, including various kinds of hymns, laments, and royal psalms. More significantly, he argued that one could penetrate behind the earliest written sources of the Pentateuch to recover the oral stage in which the material originated and was transmitted. He proposed that many of the Bible's traditions originated as oral etiologies, especially for religious institutions and social practices. Gunkel's approach, then, addresses a dilemma created by Wellhausen's documentary hypothesis (Di Vito 1999, p. 95). In its classic form, the documentary hypothesis concludes that sources such as J, E, D, and P can provide historical information pertaining only to the times in which they were written (e.g., the monarchical period or the postexilic period). By contrast, Gunkel proposed that form criticism could recover earlier oral sources and that the literary sources were the product of reliable oral tradition. Hence, one can gain access to earlier historical realities prior to the time of the written sources.

In the years following Gunkel, HB/OT form criticism ran parallel to the study of the history of religions and its interest in the origins and development of particular religious ideas and practices, as scholars analyzed such genres as HB/OT law and wisdom in comparison to similar forms in ancient Near Eastern texts. Within NT studies, form criticism remained more focused on the reconstruction of the oral forms and stages of development behind the Synoptic Gospels. The initial work of Martin Dibelius, a student of Gunkel, identified six kinds of materials in the Gospels (sermons, parables, tales, legends, passion story, myth; see Dibelius 1971 [orig. 1919]; Gillingham, p. 163), and Rudolph Bultmann divided the Gospel materials into the broad categories of "sayings" and "narratives," seeking to identify the sociological setting of each passage and the ways that various forms have been taken up by the Gospel writers (Bultmann 1976 [orig. 1931]). In recent years, ongoing reexamination and critique have resulted in a variety of formulations of the method, the newest of which move away from strictly diachronic concerns (see Sweeney and Ben Zvi). Under the umbrella of form criticism, one finds some approaches that simply provide genre analysis, others that trace the history of a particular genre or reconstruct the history of a tradition using genre considerations, and others that focus on the present structure of a whole text (see Buss). Significant critiques have questioned the hypothetical nature of the original oral forms that supposedly stand behind the present texts, as well as the older assumptions that such forms were initially simple and associated with specific cultic and institutional settings. Interpreters have moved away from a strict distinction between oral and written forms and employed form criticism in both diachronic and synchronic ways, as well as from aesthetic and socio-rhetorical perspectives (Wilder 1964; Robbins 1996; Sweeney, p. 58). Recent work has been particularly literary-oriented, focusing on the ways that certain genres contribute to the function of the present form of the text (rather than its origin) and examining the overall literary structure and character of larger compositions such as entire biblical books (see Sweeney and Ben Zvi).

Tradition Criticism. The method of tradition criticism attempts to reconstruct the transmission history of specific traditions that appear within biblical texts and articulate the import of those traditions for the present literary compositions of which they are a part (Di Vito, p. 91). Tradition criticism shares the assumption of form criticism that the present biblical texts are the end-products of a dynamic process of the growth and adaptation of older materials. The method's primary goal is to trace the full range of a given tradition's development by recovering the meaning that the tradition ("*traditum*") may have had at each stage of its evolution ("*traditio*") and thereby to reconstruct the growth of particular biblical texts or themes that draw upon or further develop that tradition (see Knight 2006). This full history of transmission includes possible oral and written stages, as well as the meaning attached to a tradition by its present literary context in larger compositions (e.g., the Deuteronomistic History, Gospel of Mark) and specific texts. Interpreters have sought to identify the ways that persons and communities adapted the traditions at each stage of their development and how those adapted meanings became part of the tradition itself as it was passed on to new tradents and settings.

The origins of tradition criticism go back to Gunkel's form criticism and the notion that earlier oral materials could be recovered behind the Pentateuch's written sources (see Jeppesen and Otzen 1984). Form criticism provides the means to identify older units of tradition within a text and the potential settings in life from which they emerged, yet Gunkel focused on identifying the smallest, earliest forms that began the process of transmission. Subsequent scholars developed these ideas by seeking the full sweep of the traditioning process that produced the larger literary themes and structures within the biblical texts (Di Vito, p. 96). The work of Gerhard von Rad and Martin Noth in the mid-twentieth century sought the origins of the eventual literary sources of the Pentateuch in the development of individual traditions at different times and places in ancient Israel. Von Rad (1938), for instance, identified brief confessions of faith within the pentateuchal texts (e.g., Deut 26:5–9; 6:20–24) that he believed originated within Israelite worship and gave rise over time to the Pentateuch's major traditions. Similarly, Noth (1981 [orig. 1948]) proposed that the Pentateuch's literary sources developed through the gradual unification of originally independent themes (e.g., guidance out of Egypt, guidance in the wilderness) that emerged from various contexts within Israel's premonarchic period. Throughout the twentieth century, scholars continued to search for the origins and development of HB/OT traditions such as the exodus from Egypt, creation, and Zion, often seeking their origins in oral performance within ancient Israel's social or cultic institutions. While most interpreters pointed to the development of these traditions into written forms, an important group of Scandinavian scholars (e.g., Sigmund Mowinckel, Ivan Engnell) maintained the vitality of the purely oral transmission of HB/OT traditions until the latest stages of the Bible's development. Although the length of time available for the transmission of traditions was significantly shorter for the materials of the NT, tradition criticism has found a place in NT studies, especially within the redaction criticism of the Synoptic Gospels. The focus has been on the extended process of oral preaching and teaching that preserved the materials from which the Gospels were created, although the extent to which the traditioning process altered those materials remains debated. Other NT materials that have received tradition-critical analysis include possible hymns (e.g., Phil 2:6–11; Col 1:15–20), summaries of Christian preaching (1 Cor 15:3–5), and portions of creedal statements (e.g., Rom 3:21–26; 1 Cor 8:4–6) that may predate the text's final form.

After using source and form criticism to identify potentially older units of material within a text, tradition criticism seeks to define the tradition, reconstruct its oral prehistory within the context of other early traditions and ancient settings, search for comparable ancient Near Eastern or Greco-Roman traditions, and posit how the particular tradition developed into its present written form. The interests of tradition criticism also go further to investigate how individual texts came to be connected with larger literary collections such as the Pentateuch or Deuteronomistic History, and even the canon as a whole. Since the 1970s, however, critiques of the classic tradition-critical approach have emerged, especially of the method's assumption that extensive oral traditions lie behind the biblical texts and can be accurately reconstructed (see Thompson 2002 [orig. 1974]; Van Seters 1975). Significant debate continues on these issues, even as scholarly interest in the orality of ancient Israelite culture remains high (see Niditch, 1996).

Redaction Criticism. The approach designated as redaction criticism has traditionally studied the ways by which an editor ("redactor") has shaped and supplemented older materials into a new composition and what the apparent editorial features reveal about the concerns and interests of the editor and final literary product. The method's primary concern is to identify evidence of editing within a text in the form of interpretive additions, compositional arrangement, and so on. While sharing some affinities with tradition criticism, redaction criticism in its classical sense returns the focus of analysis to the individual writer or editor rather than the communal traditioning process, concentrating on the creative role and special concerns of the editor but also highlighting the literary and editorial features of the text's final form. The method presupposes the diachronic results of source and form criticism concerning the existence of earlier materials, yet it offers a corrective to the tendency of these methods to focus only on smaller units of the text and to deemphasize as merely secondary the later editorial elements that produced the text's present form. Redaction criticism's interest in these elements is particularly theological in nature, operating with the conviction that the editing, arrangement, and addition of materials in a given text reveal the theological intentions of the writer or editor (Perrin 1969).

Source criticism already implied that a redactor combined the literary sources that constituted biblical texts. Prior to the mid-1900s, however, scholars viewed these redactors as merely collectors and compilers who played no significant role in the shaping of their materials. A new approach emerged with the work of Gerhard von Rad and Martin Noth mentioned earlier, as these scholars identified the so-called Yahwist editor responsible for the J source of the Pentateuch (von Rad 1972) and the Deuteronomistic Historian responsible for Joshua through 2 Kings (Noth 1991) as creative writers and theologians who shaped new compositions with their own significance (see Rendtorff; Blum). Redaction criticism's most important developments, however, occurred in the 1950s and 1960s within the study of the Synoptic Gospels. While earlier scholars had emphasized the redactional work of the Gospel writers in the study of source hypotheses (e.g., Streeter) or particular themes (e.g., Wrede 1901), the aim was to strip away the redactional elements to recover the earliest, original material. By contrast, pioneering work in redaction criticism appeared in the studies of Hans Conzelmann on Luke, Willi Marxsen on Mark, and Günther Bornkamm on Matthew. These works emphasized the Gospel writers as creative theologians who shaped their source material into new compositions with unique theological perspectives on matters such as eschatology and salvation history (Conzelmann 1982 [orig. 1954]; Marxsen 1969 [orig. 1956]; Bornkamm, Barth, and Held 1963).

Since the mid-1900s, redaction criticism has taken diverse forms that use the method's insights in various ways, including some critiques that challenge the very notion of editors and editorial composition (Van Seters 2006). Some approaches continue older interests in recovering the most original material (e.g., Funk, Hoover et al. 1993), while others extend the older investigations of the interests and activity of the redactors themselves. Within HB/OT studies in particular, redaction criticism has been especially prominent among German scholars and has tended toward increasingly complex proposals of numerous redactional layers for specific biblical compositions. In the last few decades, however, newer trends have challenged this fragmentation and concentrated on the holistic analysis of the literary and theological dynamics of the final form of biblical books and larger compositions. Particular interest has focused on the HB/OT prophetic books (e.g., Ben Zvi 2005), exploring, for instance, the holistic dimensions of the book of Isaiah as an intentionally unified composition (Williamson 1994) or considering the unifying connections across the Book of the Twelve (Nogalski 1993).

Assessment and Contribution. Since its inception, most diachronic interpretation has focused on reconstructing the processes that produced the biblical texts rather than exploring the possible dimensions related to their present forms and their interactions with various readers, communities, and contexts. Given their origins and background, diachronic approaches are subject to the longstanding critiques of historical criticism in general. Their conclusions remain predominantly hypothetical and many observers sense their reliance upon Enlightenment notions of objective historical reconstruction. Postmodernist perspectives have raised significant questions about the ability to recover an author's or editor's intentions and the extent to which such intentions are important for a text's meaning. Rather than abandoning diachronic interpretation as an outmoded Enlightenment-based method, Barton (1998; 2007) has shown that diachronic interpretation throughout the modern period did not exclude other interpretive concerns, such as an interest in a holistic engagement with the final form of the wisdom literature or Pauline letters, and the advancement of scholarship in general does not demand that previous approaches be completely forsaken. Diachronic methods continue to aid contemporary interpreters in closing the historical and cultural distance that separates them from the biblical texts.

In present scholarship, diachronic, particularly redaction-critical, interpretation continues to flourish especially in German-language scholarship on the Pentateuch and prophetic literature. Recent works offer increasingly intricate and sophisticated proposals of redactors and redactional layers from different historical contexts (e.g., Levin 1993; Vielhauer 2007; see Baden 2009; Dozeman and Schmid 2006). Such study has produced comprehensive attempts to reconstruct the literary history of the HB/OT or NT as a whole (e.g., Schmid, 2008; Theissen 2011; Carr 2011). These works highlight diachronic interpretation's ongoing contribution of paying careful attention to the details of the text as pieces of evidence for the text's origin and character. Developments in the diachronic methods within the last two decades, however, allow their contribution to go beyond the study of particular details to provide new insights into the literary dynamics and theological functions of even the final forms of biblical compositions. These broader developments suggest that the distinction between diachronic and synchronic approaches has been too rigidly drawn (see Barton 2007, p. 32), and several diachronic and synchronic methods overlap in their interests and procedures (Gillingham, p. 173). For instance, both source criticism and deconstructionist criticism begin from the same perceived inconsistencies and literary seams within the text's final form, diverging thereafter as source criticism seeks the causes of those elements in the text's compositional history. Other interpretive methods, such as rhetorical criticism, blend a literary interest in the text's stylistic elements and formal features with a diachronic interest in the text as an act of persuasion crafted within a specific context (see Kelle 2005).

Diachronic interpretation today, then, can properly include approaches that study various dimensions of the Bible's historical dynamics, even if these approaches have not traditionally been considered diachronic methods. Alongside the classic interests in sources, forms, traditions, and redactors, approaches such as sociological and feminist explorations of the realities of women's lives in the ancient world or sociopsychological analyses of the impact of trauma and its effects on the biblical literature may likewise be considered diachronic. In both the classic and newer forms, diachronic interpretation provides an ongoing reminder of the Bible's dynamic nature, as it leads readers to a recognition of the creative, human processes that produced these historically situated texts and traditions. The methods provide a sense of the complex and cross-generational interactions by which sacred texts were formulated, interpreted, and transmitted.

[*See also* Form Criticism, *subentry* Apocrypha and Deuterocanonical Books; Form Criticism, *subentry* Hebrew Bible; Form Criticism, *subentry* New Testament; Historical Criticism, *subentry* Hebrew Bible; Historical Criticism, *subentry* New Testament; Redaction Criticism, *subentry* Apocrypha and Deuterocanonical Books; Redaction Criticism, *subentry* Hebrew Bible; Redaction Criticism, *subentry* New Testament; Socio-rhetorical Criticism; Synchronic Interpretation; Textual Criticism, *subentry* Apocrypha and Deuterocanonical Books; Textual Criticism, *subentry* Hebrew Bible.; Textual Criticism, *subentry* New Testament; *and* Tradition-Historical Criticism.]

BIBLIOGRAPHY

Astruc, Jean. *Conjectures sur les Mémoires Originaux don't il Paraît que Moïse S'est Servi pour Composer le Livre de la Genèse, avec des Remarques qui Appuient ou qui Eclaircissent ces Conjectures.* Brussels: Chez Fricx, 1753.

Baden, Joel S. *J, E, and the Redaction of the Pentateuch.* Forschungen zum Alten Testament 68. Winona Lake, Ind.: Eisenbrauns, 2009. New study of the J and E documents of the Pentateuch that moves away from classic source-critical conclusions.

Barton, John. "Historical-Critical Approaches." In *The Cambridge Companion to Biblical Interpretation*, edited by John Barton, 9–20. Cambridge Companions to Religion. Cambridge, UK: Cambridge University Press, 1998. A highly nuanced discussion of historically oriented methods within past and present biblical interpretation.

Barton, John. *The Nature of Biblical Criticism.* Louisville, Ky.: Westminster John Knox, 2007. An insightful reconsideration of the definition, character, and practices of biblical interpretation.

Ben Zvi, Ehud. *Hosea.* Forms of Old Testament Literature 21a. Grand Rapids, Mich.: Eerdmans, 2005. Form-critical commentary on Hosea that emphasizes the context of the book as a whole literary composition.

Blum, Erhard. *Studien zur Komposition des Pentateuch.* Beihefte zur Zeitschrift für die Alttestamentliche Wissenschaft 189. Berlin: Walter de Gruyter, 1990.

Bornkamm, Günther, Gerhard Barth, and Heinz Joachim Held. *Tradition and Interpretation in Matthew.* Philadelphia: Westminster, 1963.

Bultmann, Rudolph. The History of the Synoptic Tradition. Translated by John Marsh. New York: Harper and Row, 1976. English translation of *Die Geschichte der synoptischen Tradition,* first published in 1931.

Buss, Martin J. *Biblical Form Criticism in Its Context.* Journal for the Study of the Old Testament: Supplement Series 274. Sheffield. UK: Sheffield Academic, 1999. A philosophical analysis of the notion of form and its use within biblical form criticism.

Carr, David M. *The Formation of the Hebrew Bible: A New Reconstruction.* New York: Oxford University Press, 2011. A new consideration of the methods for reconstructing the growth of the HB/OT and the reconstruction of the pre-stages of the texts.

Conzelmann, Hans. *The Theology of St. Luke.* Translated by Geoffrey Buswell. Philadelphia: Fortress, 1982. English translation of *Die Mitte der Zeit,* first published in 1954.

Dibelius, Martin. *From Tradition to Gospel.* Library of Theological Translations. Cambridge, UK: James Clarke, 1971. English translation of *Die Formgeschichte des Evangeliums,* first published in 1919.

Di Vito, Robert A. "Tradition-Historical Criticism." In *To Each Its Own Meaning: An Introduction to Biblical Criticisms and Their Application,* edited by Steven L. McKenzie and Stephen R. Haynes, 90–104. Rev. ed. Louisville, Ky.: Westminster John Knox, 1999. Introductory survey of the history and practice of tradition criticism within biblical studies.

Dozeman, Thomas B., and Konrad Schmid, eds. *A Farewell to the Yahwist?: The Composition of the Pentateuch in Recent European Interpretation.* Society of Biblical Literature Symposium Series 34. Atlanta: Society of Biblical Literature, 2006. Survey of newer European scholars who are advancing an alternate view of the compositional history of the Pentateuch focusing on larger, independent blocks of material.

Duhm, Bernhard. *Das Buch Jesaia: übersetzt und erklärt.* Handkommentar zum Alten Testament 3/1. Göttingen: Vandenhoeck & Ruprecht, 1892.

Ehrman, Bart D. *Studies in the Textual Criticism of the New Testament.* New Testament Tools and Studies 33. Leiden: Brill, 2006. A collection of studies that exemplify elements of the development of textual criticism within NT studies.

Epp, Eldon Jay. *Perspectives on New Testament Textual Criticism: Collected Essays, 1962–2004.* Supplements to Novum Testamentum 116. Leiden: Brill, 2005. A collection of frequently cited essays over four decades dealing with the history and development of NT textual criticism.

Epp, Eldon Jay, and George W. MacRae, eds. *The New Testament and Its Modern Interpreters.* The Bible and Its Modern Interpreters. Philadelphia: Fortress, 1989. Survey of major approaches to NT study written by practitioners in various methods.

Freiday, Dean. *The Bible: Its Criticism, Interpretation and Use in 16th and 17th Century England.* Catholic and Quaker Studies 4. Manasquan, N.J.: Catholic and Quaker Studies, 1979. Survey of the development and characteristics of biblical interpretation within pre-Enlightenment England.

Funk, Robert W., Roy W. Hoover, and the Jesus Seminar. *The Five Gospels: The Search for the Authentic Words of Jesus.* San Francisco: Harper, 1993. An evaluation of material related to the historical Jesus and the authenticity of sayings associated with Jesus that reflects the procedures and theories of the Jesus Seminar.

Gillingham, Susan E. *One Bible, Many Voices: Different Approaches to Biblical Studies.* London: SPCK, 1998. A highly nuanced survey of the methodological diversity within contemporary approaches to biblical study.

Gunkel, Hermann. *Introduction to Psalms: The Genres of the Religious Lyric of Israel.* Translated by James D. Nogalski. Mercer Library of Biblical Studies. Macon, Ga.: Mercer University Press, 1998. English translation of *Einleitung in die Psalmen,* first published in 1926.

Hayes, John H. "A History of Interpretation." In *Mercer Commentary on the New Testament,* edited by Watson E. Mills and Richard F. Wilson, 23–53. Macon. Ga.: Mercer University Press, 2003. A detailed and comprehensive account of the history of biblical interpretation from the biblical period through the twentieth century.

Hayes, John H., ed. *Dictionary of Biblical Interpretation.* 2 vols. Nashville, Tenn.: Abingdon, 1999.

Comprehensive collection of essays on major methods and interpreters within the history of biblical interpretation.

Jeppesen, Knud. and Benedikt Otzen, eds. *The Productions of Time: Tradition History in Biblical Scholarship.* Sheffield, UK: Almond, 1984. A collection of papers on tradition criticism, with special emphasis on the Scandinavian emphasis on oral tradition.

Kelle, Brad E. *Hosea 2: Metaphor and Rhetoric in Historical Perspective.* Society of Biblical Literature Academia Biblica 20. Atlanta: Society of Biblical Literature, 2005. An exegetical study of Hosea 2 emphasizing rhetorical criticism with a historical focus.

Knight, Douglas A. *Rediscovering the Traditions of Israel.* 3d ed. Society of Biblical Literature Studies in Biblical Literature. Atlanta: Society of Biblical Literature, 2006. Classic treatment of the development and practice of tradition criticism within OT studies.

Knight Douglas A., and Gene M. Tucker, eds. *The Hebrew Bible and Its Modern Interpreters.* The Bible and Its Modern Interpreters. Atlanta: Scholars, 1985. Survey of major approaches to HB/OT study written by practitioners in various methods.

Levin, Christoph. *Der Yahwist.* Forschungen zur Religion und Literatur des Alten und Neuen Testaments 157. Göttingen: Vandenhoeck & Ruprecht, 1993. A redactional treatment of the Yahwist source of the Pentateuch.

Longstaff, Thomas Richmond Willis, and Page A. Thomas, eds. *The Synoptic Problem: A Bibliography, 1716–1988.* New Gospel Studies 4. Macon, Ga.: Mercer University Press, 1988. A survey of scholarship related to the Synoptic problem specifically and the question of sources for the Gospels generally.

Marxsen, Willi. *Mark the Evangelist: Studies on the Redaction History of the Gospel.* Translated by James Boyce. Nashville, Tenn.: Abingdon, 1969. English translation of *Der Evangelist Markus,* first published in 1956.

McCarter, P. Kyle. *Textual Criticism: Recovering the Text of the Hebrew Bible.* Guides to Biblical Scholarship. Philadelphia: Fortress, 1986. A general survey of the history and method of textual criticism on the OT.

McKenzie, Steven L., and Stephen R. Haynes, eds. *To Each Its Own Meaning: An Introduction to Biblical Criticisms and Their Application.* Rev. ed. Louisville, Ky.: Westminster John Knox, 1999. A collection of essays treating the major modern and postmodern methods of biblical interpretation written by practitioners of the various methods.

McKnight, Edgar V. *What Is Form Criticism?* Guides to Biblical Scholarship. Philadelphia: Fortress, 1969. An introductory survey of the history and practice of form criticism.

Metzger, Bruce M. *The Text of the New Testament: Its Transmission, Corruption, and Restoration.* 4th ed. New York: Oxford University Press, 2005. An in-depth study of NT textual criticism and the corresponding manuscript evidence.

Niditch, Susan. *Oral World and Written Word: Ancient Israelite Literature.* Library of Ancient Israel. Louisville: Westminster John Knox, 1996. An examination of literacy and oral culture within the ancient world and their significance for the biblical texts.

Nogalski, James. *Literary Precursors to the Book of the Twelve.* Beihefte zur Zeitschrift für die Alttestamentliche Wissenschaft 217. Berlin: Walter de Gruyter, 1993. An early, trendsetting examination of literary links among the Book of the Twelve as a unified composition.

Noth, Martin. *The Deuteronomistic History.* Journal for the Study of the Old Testament: Supplement Series 15. Sheffield: JSOT Press, 1991. English translation of *Überlieferungsgeschichtliche Studien,* 1–110 in the 2d ed., first published in 1943.

Noth, Martin. *A History of Pentateuchal Traditions.* Translated by Bernhard W. Anderson. Chico, Calif.: Scholars, 1981. English translation of *Überlieferungsgeschichte des Pentateuch,* first published in 1948.

Perrin, Norman. *What Is Redaction Criticism?* Guides to Biblical Scholarship. Philadelphia: Fortress, 1969. An introductory survey of the development and practice of redaction criticism through its formative period in the 1960s.

Rad, Gerhard von. *Das formgeschichtliche Problem des Hexateuchs.* Beiträge zur Wissenschaft vom Alten und Neuen Testament 6. Stuttgart: Kohlhammer, 1938.

Rad, Gerhard von. *Genesis: A Commentary.* Old Testament Library. Philadelphia: Westminster, 1972. English translation of *Erste Buch Mose: Genesis,* first published in 1953.

Rast, Walter E. *Tradition History and the Old Testament.* Guides to Biblical Scholarship. Philadelphia: Fortress, 1972. An introductory survey of the development and practice of tradition criticism within OT studies up to the 1970s.

Rendtorff, Rolf. *The Problem of the Process of Transmission in the Pentateuch.* Translated by J. J. Scullion. Journal for the Study of the Old Testament: Supplement Series 89. Sheffield, UK: JSOT Press, 1990. English translation of *Das überlieferungsgeschichtliche Problem des Pentateuch,* first published in 1977.

Reventlow, Henning Graf. *History of Biblical Interpretation Volume 4: From the Enlightenment to the Twentieth Century.* Translated by Leo G. Perdue. Society of Biblical Literature Resources for Biblical Study 63. Atlanta: Society of Biblical Literature, 2010. English translation of *Epochen der Bibelauslegung*, first published in 2001. A comprehensive overview of major figures and trends in the history of biblical interpretation within the modern period since the Enlightenment.

Robbins, Vernon K. *Exploring the Texture of Texts: A Guide to Socio-Rhetorical Interpretation.* Harrisburg, Pa.: Trinity Press International, 1996. A defining work that outlines a socio-rhetorical approach to NT texts within a form-critical perspective.

Rogerson, John. *Old Testament Criticism in the Nineteenth Century: England and Germany.* Minneapolis: Fortress, 1985. A survey of the major figures and trends within HB/OT studies in nineteenth-century England and Germany.

Schmid, Konrad. *The Old Testament: A Literary History.* Minneapolis: Fortress, 2012. English translation of *Literaturgeschichte des Alten Testaments: eine Einführung*, first published in 2008. A comprehensive discussion of the task, history, and conditions of the composition of the HB/OT literature.

Scholder, Klaus. *The Birth of Modern Critical Theology: Origins and Problems of Biblical Criticism in the Seventeenth Century.* Translated by John Bowden. London: SCM, 1990. A discussion of the origins of elements of modern biblical criticism within the theological developments of the 1600s in Europe.

Streeter, Burnett H. *The Four Gospels: A Study of Origins, Treating of the Manuscript Tradition, Sources, Authorship, and Dates.* Rev. ed. London: The Macmillan Company, 1961, first published in 1924.

Sweeney, Marvin A. "Form Criticism." In *To Each Its Own Meaning: An Introduction to Biblical Criticisms and Their Application*, edited by Steven L. McKenzie and Stephen R. Haynes, 58–89. Rev. ed. Louisville, Ky.: Westminster John Knox, 1999. A thorough survey of the history and practice of form criticism in the modern period.

Sweeney, Marvin A., and Ehud Ben Zvi, eds. *The Changing Face of Form Criticism for the Twenty-first Century.* Grand Rapids, Mich.: Eerdmans, 2003. Insightful collection of essays exploring the past, present, and future prospects of form criticism and its related perspectives.

Theissen, Gerd. *The New Testament: A Literary History.* Translated by Linda M. Maloney. Minneapolis: Fortress, 2011. A comprehensive discussion of the history and conditions of the composition of the NT literature.

Thompson, Thomas L. *The Historicity of the Patriarchal Narratives: The Quest for the Historical Abraham.* Rev ed. Harrisburg, Pa.: Trinity Press International, 2002, first published in 1974. Groundbreaking study that challenged older assumptions concerning the historicity of the patriarchal stories and the source and traditional critical assumptions that supported older views.

Tucker, Gene M. *Form Criticism of the Old Testament.* Guides to Biblical Scholarship. Philadelphia: Fortress, 1971. A general survey of the history and practice of form criticism within HB/OT studies.

Van Seters, John. *Abraham in History and Tradition.* New Haven, Conn.: Yale University Press, 1975. Groundbreaking study that challenged older assumptions concerning the historicity of the patriarchal stories and the source and traditional critical assumptions that supported older views.

Van Seters, John. *The Edited Bible: The Curious History of the "Editor" in Biblical Criticism.* Winona Lake, Ind.: Eisenbrauns, 2006. A challenge to the commonly held assumptions concerning the editing process and the role of editors within the formation of the biblical literature.

Vielhauer, Roman. *Das Werden des Buches Hosea: Eine Redaktiongeschichtliche Untersuchung.* Beihefte zur Zeitschrift für die Alttestamentliche Wissenschaft 349. Berlin: Walter de Gruyter, 2007. A new redactional study of Hosea that identifies several redactional layers from different historical periods within the book.

Wellhausen, Julius. *Prolegomena to the History of Israel.* Scholars Press Reprints and Translation Series. Atlanta: Scholars Press, 1994. An English translation of *Geschichte Israels I*, first published in 1878.

Wilder, Amos N. *The Language of the Gospel: Early Christian Rhetoric.* New York: Harper and Row, 1964. An early example of aesthetic and rhetorical perspectives within NT form criticism.

Williamson, H. G. M. *The Book Called Isaiah: Deutero-Isaiah's Role in Composition and Redaction.* Oxford: Clarendon, 1994. An example of newer approaches to Isaiah that emphasize the interconnected development and unity across various portions of the book.

Wrede, Wiliam. *The Messianic Secret.* Translated by J. C. G. Greig. Library of Theological Translations. Cambridge, UK: J. Clarke, 1971. English translation of *Das Messiasgeheimnis in den Evangelien*, first published in 1901. A redaction-critical study that identified the so-called "messianic secret" in Mark as a later redactional element not drawn from earlier traditions.

Brad E. Kelle

Diaspora Studies

Diaspora comes from the Greek verb meaning "to sow over" (*speiro* + *dia*). Implemented during the Greco-Roman period to repopulate war-torn cities or uninhabitable poleis by starting over, the practice can be traced back to the Neo-Assyrians and Neo-Babylonians. With two levels of assistance, individual and collective, land was distributed for retired military with roads, buildings, and infrastructure financed by the empire. In due course, the hope was for each polis to become a social, economic, and geopolitical contributor of the empire. This concept is not incompatible with the exile *golah*/*galut* (Hebrew, singular/plural). The key difference, however, is in the *telos*, that is, the Diaspora becomes home but in exile—there is a longing to return to the homeland. In the deep structure, *golah*/*galut* is understood as national punishment for sin. Without an end to the forced migration, living in exile was understood as living in condemnation. This precept changed across three generations in Babylon. Regions in which Judeans either involuntarily or voluntarily migrated—whether on the other side of the Jordan River, in Mesopotamia, on the coastlands or Egypt, or across the vast terrains of the Mediterranean basin—would also become home.

Modern scholarship of the exile consists of three major historical periods and one transitional phase (first, transitional, second, and currently third [see Ahn, *Exile as Forced Migrations*, 2011]). In the second major period, a group of minimalist European biblical scholars revived C. C. Torrey's theory on the Exile and postexilic periods. They misrepresented his view on the exile, however, erroneously claiming that Torrey suggested that the exile never occurred. They then coupled this precept with Hans Barstad's "myth of the empty land" (1996) that placed Second Isaiah in Judah, not in the Babylonian exile, adding that the exile clearly was a mythopoeic, a historical construct since there was no narrative on the period. Only a minority in the upper and skilled classes of the people was actually "deported" to Babylon, and life continued without any serious disruption since the majority of the people were farmers. Thus, it was a myth to think that the land was empty when in fact, it was still populated. This insight on the land being populated is an important progressive contribution. Even a cursory reading, however, suggests that a nation that loses its economists, politicians, scribes, educators, skilled workers, and artisans will not be undisrupted. Furthermore, the problem rests in reframing exile, which has been heavily theological, as "deportation." The term was debated without full uniformity before launching and impacting the field. The application of the term to the Judeans of the sixth century B.C.E. was ill thought. "Deport" or "deportation" in political, social, legal debates, and other media denote "deporting illegal immigrants." The construct then suggests that the Judeans were in their land "illegally." Being "deported" to Babylon carries an undesirable double meaning. Some scholars have desperately tried to justify the usage of the term by going back to the *Oxford English Dictionary*. Going backward is not the solution. The term should no longer refer to the experience of forced migration or exile. The proper nomenclature is "to displace" or "to dislocate." In 2008, in the Society of Biblical Literature (SBL), the Exile-Forced Migrations in Biblical Literature Consultation (now Group) was created to address these and other issues. In 2011 the same scholars formed the International (SBL) counterpart, Forced-Return Migrations in Biblical Literature. As a first correction, "forced migration," a term accepted and advanced by social scientists and migration studies experts, replaces "deportation" when referring to the Exile or the sixth century B.C.E. Second, the al-Yahdu text, an extrabiblical artifact that attests to a Judean ethnic enclave in Babylon, shows the displacement and resettlement of people from the Southern Kingdom of Judah. Even without this discovery, however, the sociological approach uncovers new data to help reconstruct the historical generations in the sixth to the fifth centuries B.C.E. Forced migration studies, which take into account theories of migration, reasons for such force, and analyses of displaced peoples, seek to identify factors or forces that cause involuntary movements of peoples. Forced migration produces a host of structural problems: urban redevelopment, population structure, redistribution policies, and regional redevelopment as well as challenges to identity and ethnicity. With identifiable typologies in Diaspora studies—such as victim Diaspora, labor diaspora, trade Diaspora, imperial Diaspora, and cultural Diaspora, to name a few—forced migration studies and Diaspora studies become the future on most aspects of exile in the Hebrew Bible, Intertestamental literature, the Dead Sea Scrolls, and New Testament studies.

Diaspora Consciousness. A salient feature of Diaspora or forced migration consciousness—that dislocation and identity play a complex and significant relationship—rests in preserving and passing down the unapologetic individual and collective human experiences of displacement and resettlement for future generations. Diaspora studies is truly global in nature, bridging and cutting across scores of major and minor issues and concerns, which are often hidden or veiled in communities that have experienced involuntary or voluntary forced migration. The examination of geopolitics, hybridity, nomadism, creolization, and symbols—including the interpreting of sacred texts—are involved. There is much complexity since phenomenology is involved. From searching for a home in a state of homelessness to seeking out welcome and acceptance in new habitual place of residence, the chief questions are: Will "we" be fully accepted? And one day, can we also become hosts?

Experience. Life in the Diaspora is markedly different because of two primary agents: age and socioeconomics. Specifically, dispersal from and the degree of longing for home, collective myth and memory about past heroes and how they lived and survived in similar circumstances, the development of a return migration plan, ethnocentrism, sympathy for other displaced and resettled communities, and the acceptance of pluralism due to experience of exclusionism are all broadly sociological and anthropological in nature. Inasmuch as history repeats, so do social structures. The Chinese Diaspora in Colombia, the Indian Diaspora in Kenya, Caribbeans in New York, the British Sikh Diaspora, Iraqi Kurdish Diaspora, Estonian Diaspora, Armenian Diaspora, Iranian immigrants in Sweden, or the comparative study of Korean, German, and Polish forced migrant communities in the Russian Far East, among other empirically driven studies, provide relevant parallels to help clarify and reconstruct the dislocated Judeans in Babylon, Egypt, or the coastlands, the Essenes by the Dead Sea, or first-century Jews scattered across the Mediterranean basin and beyond. In fact, as advanced and technologically sophisticated as society has become, human emotions and responses to displacement and resettlement have not changed all that much, if any. Pain remains pain. Experiencing discrimination is discrimination. The simple joys and happiness of one community—birth of a child, marriage, and achievements—are causes for celebration in ancient and contemporary communities. Yet, a displaced and resettled community's coping mechanism for combating hardship is none other than hard work that we witness in immigrant families coupled with prayer (see Jer 29).

Culture. The web of influences that truly matter, in the constitution of the old and new merging together as new culture (Geertz 1973) occurred as a direct consequence of the geopolitical shift from Jerusalem to Babylon. The first-generation Judeo-Babylonians experienced "there" and "here." In the social construction of reality (Berger and Luckmann 1966), the "dramaturgical" (Goffman 1959) was found in the solidarity of the community living outside national time and space in order to live within it (Clifford 1997).

Several studies that integrate cultural studies, biblical studies, and the Diaspora or forced migration studies have since been in circulation. They are John Collins's *Between Athens and Jerusalem* (1999), John Barclay's *Negotiating Diaspora* (2004), and John Ahn's *Exile as Forced Migrations* (2011). These works deal with issues of assimilation-acculturation, generation-unit, and integrative-oppositional as cultural and countercultural. Interestingly, most contemporary Diaspora studies begin by descriptively pointing to the historical memory of the Judean exile to Babylon in the sixth century B.C.E. However, the consciousness that gave rise to the Diaspora is said to be 587 B.C.E., the destruction of the Temple, and the loss of Judah as a nation. This is an error. In the first place, the sovereignty of Judah was relinquished by Jehoiachin in 597 B.C.E., not 587. The balance of the "Davidic Covenant" and Zion theology in complete jeopardy, the decision to give up the throne for the sake of saving lives, and the difficult choice between colonialism or elimination of a nation all create a completely different picture and a starting point of Diaspora consciousness. In addition, the destruction of the Temple as the genesis of Diaspora consciousness must fade into the shadow of the pathos of losing innocent infants and children—dashed and violently killed against the rock or the wall of Jerusalem—the symbol that was supposed to protect was reversed and used as a weapon of destruction. As the synecdoche for the loss of an entire generation (Ps 137:8–9), these needed historical references help contemporary Diaspora scholars to focus on the people, not an edifice, transcending Cliffordian "there" and "here," the spatial and temporal makers create a new third space, between the nation-state and "traveling cultures."

Textual Witnesses. The memory of Diaspora consciousness is found in Genesis 3 and 4. Adam and Eve are displaced from the garden of Eden as punishment. In the ensuing generation, after fratricide of his brother Abel, Cain is marked and forced to migrate. The primeval history ascends to Babel/Babylon (Gen 11) only to be scattered. And from there, a new generational narrative sequence begins, cast in three generations—Abraham, Isaac, and Jacob, with the fourth-generation Joseph Diaspora novella added later on (Gen 12—50). Exodus is precisely about a new generation, a new leader in Moses, whose Sargonlike birth is redeemed from the waters; then he too experiences forced migration until he is called to return to the land and lead his people out of Egypt. The first-generation Israelites' wandering in the wilderness is seen as a punishment for disobedience and refusing to enter the Promised Land. The same potential misappropriation lies before the second-generation Israelites. The key episode is sparked by the second-generation Gadites and Reubenites requesting land, permanent residence on the Transjordan. Moses's interpretation for their request on the other side of the Jordan is seen as a serious threat to the promise. He rejects the initial proposal. With conflict and tension rising, the Gadites and Reubenites make a counterproposal, namely, that they will in fact traverse and help all Israel claim land in the Cisjordan. When each tribe has settled down, then, they would return home, to the other side, to their wives, children, and material goods. Moses agrees and blesses them (Num 32). This chapter is one of the most important yet least understood chapters in the book of Numbers. This narrative may be a retrospection, from the period of third- or fourth-generation Judeo-Babylonians seriously questioning and justifying to turn to Yehud (Judah) in order to return home.

The prophets (Isaiah, Ezekiel, Jeremiah) predict (*vaticinium ex eventu*) or warn of forced migration for sin and return migration as God's purpose. The Wisdom Tradition, Job, and Qoheleth reading through the lenses of Judah's experience of forced migration in sixth century B.C.E. finds echoes in the Apocrypha: Tobit, 1 Esdras, Prayer of Azariah, Bel and the Dragon, Song of the Three Children, Susanna, Judith, and the Letter of Aristeas, all pertaining to coping with hardships and challenges of life and rebuilding lives in the Diaspora. The Damascus Document (CD) opens with a reference to the 390 years since Nebuchadnezzar, which is immediately followed by a marker to one generation, meaning "twenty years." The context behind this community's document is voluntary displacement rather than forced migration to Babylon. This group neither sought refuge in Egypt nor experienced forced migration to Babylon but escaped to the coastlands or Damascus. Today we would call such people "refugees." If this is an earlier form of the disciple's manual that was fully developed and extended in the Qumran Rule of the Community (1QS), this group may have been the forerunner to the Essenes who voluntarily lived in displacement and resettlement in Qumran. Echoed in 1 and 2 Peter, the sojourners or foreigners are considered second- or third-, or fourth-generation Christians. They experience marginalization from society but are nevertheless encouraged to live in the hope of their priesthood and calling until the Lord's return. Indeed, identity is shaped and reformed in, through, and by the experience of the Diaspora.

Identity in the Diaspora. Diaspora identity is marked by a historical memory and generational consciousness. The root of uprootedness and dispersal occurred in 597 B.C.E. with the first wave of forced migrants. King Jehoiachin, his royal family, his officials, the upper class and skilled laborers, the warriors or military class, priests, prophets, and scribes experienced Derivative Forced Migrations (DFM), a geopolitical, cartographical realignment when the Neo-Babylonian Empire conquered Judah to increase its border. The first wave of Judeans is identified as development-induced displaced persons (DIDPs) for Babylonian economic gain. Displaced and resettled in "ethnic enclaves" (contrast to ghettos with no economic output), the Judeans re-established war-torn and dilapidated cities through corvée labor on primary, secondary, and tertiary irrigation canals of Babylon. Through "chain migration" (same ethnic group from the same location) in 587 and 582, these Judeans experienced "Purposive Forced Migration" (PFM). The purpose of PFM could be profit driven (Uganda, 1972), culture oriented (Cambodia, 1975–1979), religious persecution, (North Ireland, 1969), security of a dominating nation (the Kurds, 1980), for punishment (the Chechens after World War II), and revenge (Rwanda-Burundi, 1962). Internally displaced persons (IDPs), everyday common "people of the land," were also forced to move from the periphery of the empire to the center. Interestingly, the Hebrew Bible is silent on the 582 B.C.E. group. Perhaps this was due to their unaccepted hybridity as Samaritan-Judeans. Intermarriage likely began as early as post-587 B.C.E. for individual and communal survival. Under Gedaliah's leadership at Mizpah, the people of the land continued to sustain and generate some form of economic viability by contributing to Babylon, producing an abundance of summer fruits, wine, and balsam. When Ishmael, the son of Nethaniah and grandson of Elishama, led a small but well organized anti-Babylonian group of ten men to murder Gedaliah, this economic and political colonialism ended. For whatever reason, the Judeo-Babylonian tradents—ironically, given their own hybridity—rejected and did not record the experience of this particular displaced and resettled group in Babylon. On the contrary, their 582 counterpart—the group that voluntarily fled to Egypt with Johanan and other leaders, including Jeremiah—experienced "Responsive Forced Migration" (RFM), a voluntary forced migration as a response to natural or human threats. Then, there were others that likely sought refuge in the north, in particular the coastlands or Damascus (CD), but more research is needed on this important group.

The total of "seventy-years" in Babylon represents three and a half generations, marked as three or four generations. These basic factors must now be accounted for when examining Diaspora studies. Once resettled in the Babylon, generational consciousness fully developed. In fact, the threefold generation of Abraham, Isaac, and Jacob is no accident. To this paradigm, the fourth generation, in the form of a continuing Diaspora novella, Joseph, like Esther, who succeeds through assimilation and eventually benefits all of society, was added. The book of Daniel also stresses issues of assimilation and acculturation, education and food, music and culture, traditions and customs, arriving at individual and communal success through intermarriage (Joseph and Esther) or possibly living as eunuchs (Daniel and his three friends). Identity formation, addressing the polarities of home/homelessness, insider/outsider, power/powerless, success/failure, and center/periphery are pertinent literary themes but also sociological issues in everyday life for displaced persons. The final form in the four-generation framework is clearly a generational consciousness that eventually split between those who remained in Babylon as home from those who returned to Yehud/Judah to start over.

Each generation responds to its experience of forced migration without dismissing the previous generation. There is layering of those experiences. The first generation experienced complex lament (Ps 137). The transitional 1.5 generation (i.e., those who were teenagers or preteens when taken to

Babylon, like Daniel and his three friends or Ezekiel; in the New Testament, between the first-generation apostles and the second-generation Christians or the Gospel authors, Paul functions as a transitional 1.5 generation) discovered *golah* hope through proactive hard work and prayer (Jer 29). It is this important transitional generation that functions as a bridge to the future. The second generation become the beneficiaries as new creation, crystallizing monotheism (Isa 43)—though there were significant differences between those who were born to the patricians of the 597 B.C.E. group from those who were born to the plebeians of 587/582 B.C.E. group. There was a further distinctiveness between those who were born to the 1.5 generation, who joined the patricians but with a stronger sense of their religious and ethnic identity. By the third generation, those who made it in Babylon would come to define home on the other side of the Jordan, like the Gadites and Rubenites (Num 32), in Babylon. However, for the underclass that never experienced hope or new creation, they welcomed, envisioned, and embraced Second Isaiah's grand utopian vision for turn to Yehud/Judah. This suffering community was represented by their suffering servant. The fourth generation would establish itself, finally finding by dreaming in Persia, eventually becoming investors and landholders as some are recorded in the Murashu documents.

In contrast, from the perspective of the Judeans or Judahites who also experienced Derivative Forced Migrations (DFM) because of cartographical realignment, an exile-less exile, their situation remained static and pessimistic. Their experience lacks any progress, deemed and codified as "punishment down to the third or fourth generation" (Exod 20:5; Deut 5:9).

Through the Diaspora. Studies on assimilation theory as it pertains to second-generation communities show three lines of trajectory. The first is a "straight-line" (or the bumpy-line assimilation) that leads to the majority. The second is "downward" that leads to the underclass. The third theory also leads upward to the majority but with a greater awareness of one's ethnicity and cultural ethos. In our second-generation Judeo-Babylonian context, the children born to the upper class of the 597 group were the ones who assimilated into the mainstream majority. They are identified as "Israel." The second generation born to the parents of the 587 and the 582 groups, more commonly known as the "people of the land," assimilated into the underclass as "Jacob." And last, the second generation born to the considerably younger 1.5 generation, also assimilated upward but with deeper consciousness of their ethnicity and religious zeal. They are called or identified as "I belong to the LORD" group (Isa 48:1.5; see Isa 44:5).

In Isaiah 43:1 Jacob and Israel are immediately noticed. Isaiah 44:5 identifies the third aforementioned group. Each of the three groups' distinctive voice is unmistakably marked by the proximal demonstrative *zh*. Indeed, one group says "*I am the LORD's*," one group (this one) calls itself by the *name of Jacob* (41:21; 45:19; 48:20; 49:26 [60:16]; 58:1, 14; 59:20), and yet another group (this one) says that it will write on his hand the LORD's and take the *name Israel* (45:17, 25; 46:13; 49:3; 56:8; 63:7, 16; 66:20). The problem of "Israel-Jacob" in the book of Isaiah has been critically examined since 1989. This study has now extended into the book of Chronicles. And although a recent study by Reinhard Kratz suggests that "Israel" is more a theological nuance than a historical one, Kratz did not demarcate sociologically whether Jacob-Israel is one monolithic community or two distinctive and separate groups.

Consistently in Second Isaiah (Isa 40–55), where both Jacob and Israel appear together, there are subtle but noticeable differences. For example, "Fear not, you *worm* Jacob, you men of Israel," (41:14); "he who *created* you, O Jacob, he who *formed* you, O Israel" (43:1); "*did not call* upon me, O Jacob; but you *have been weary* of me, O Israel" (43:22); "Therefore I profaned the princes of the sanctuary, and have given Jacob *to the curse* and Israel *to reproaches*" (43:28); "But hear, O Jacob *my servant*, Israel *my chosen*!" (44:1); "the LORD has *redeemed* Jacob, and will be *glorified in* Israel" (44:23); "Jacob *my servant*, Israel *my chosen* (45:4); "O house of Jacob, who are *called by the name of Israel*, and who came . . . from the loins of Judah" (48:1); "And now the LORD says, who formed me from the womb to be his servant, *to bring Jacob back to him*, and that

Israel *might be gathered to him*" (49:5); and "*raise up the tribes* of Jacob and to *restore the survivors preserved* of Israel" (49:6). In Second Isaiah, the verbs attributed to Jacob are inferior to those that predicate Israel. Jacob needs to be brought back to God; he is part of Israel but Israel is never a part of Jacob. Jacob must be redeemed and transformed, whereas Israel is consistently chosen. Jacob will then be glorified in Israel. Jacob will leave Babylon with shouts of joy (48:20).

Within the second-generation Judeo-Babylonian community, as preserved in Isaiah 48:1, we have three distinctive groups: "Hear this, O house of *Jacob*, the ones who call themselves *Israel*, and they (that) come forth from the waters of Judah, and *the ones who adjure by the name of the Lord*." To substantiate this, in Isaiah 43:1, we also notice "Jacob," "Israel," and the "I have called you by name" groups. Then, in v. 7, we unmistakably see the three different verbs of creation to distinguish and demarcate each group that forms the collective second generation Judeo-Babylonian community: I *created* him [Jacob], I *formed* him [Israel], and surely, I *made* him [Name of Yahweh group].

What is most interesting about the third group is that although they are acknowledged and identified as "I belong to the Lord," in contrast to Jacob and Israel, in Isaiah 40:27; 41:8, 14; 42:24; and 49:5, this group eventually drops out, leaving a Jacob-Israel dichotomy.

By the Diaspora. The Jeremianic vision for a prosperous community (Jer 29) saw fruition in "Israel." This likely became the model for return migrations to recreate Yehud/Judah through "Jacob," who needs to integrate with those in the land. Clearly, a punctuated, singular mass movement of peoples would create a host of social and distribution problems. The first return migration is said to have occurred under Sheshbazzar in 538 B.C.E., the second return migration under Joshua and Zerubbabel in 520 B.C.E., and the third return migration, under Nehemiah in ca. 445–420 B.C.E. Nehemiah ushers in a new period of reform by rebuilding the walls of Jerusalem—how symbolic. Through *synocecism*, the binding together of forced resettlement of peoples, and *seisachtheia*, a one-time debt forgiveness program, socioeconomic reform would take place inside the city wall, possibly creating a new class-boundary. But the more pressing issue and question has been: where does Ezra fit in? Traditionally, two Persian governors in one location are not possible. Scholarly debate on Nehemiah arriving before Ezra was prominent until recent times, where now, some suggest that Ezra precedes Nehemiah, arriving in Yehud/Judah with a significant number of return migrants. Some scholars have even suggested that Ezra arrived between 433 and 432 B.C.E. when Nehemiah provisionally returned to Persia. A possible reconstruction may be as follows:

First Return Migration: Sheshbazzar in 538 B.C.E.

- Edict of Cyrus, re-establish Yehud
- Ezra 1:5–11; 5:13–15
- Begins to build the temple, but abandons the project (economic)

Second Return Migration: Joshua (Jeshua) and Zerubbabel in 520 B.C.E.

- Darius the Great
- 515 Temple is rebuilt
- Ezra 2:2b–70 // Neh 7:7b–73
- Hag 1:1; Hag 2:20–23; Zech 3:8; 4:6–7; 6:12

Third Return Migration: Ezra 458 B.C.E.

- Artaxerxes I 465–424/3
- Torah was fixed and became the law of the land
- Intermarriage forbidden
- Segregation exclusivist theology—ethnic cleansing

Fourth Return Migration: Nehemiah in 445–430 B.C.E.

- Artaxerxes I
- Nehemiah as full governor
- *Synoecism* "binding together"—forced resettlement of peoples and *seisachtheia* σεισάχθεια "one time cancellation of all debt" (sixth century B.C.E. Athens—Solon)
- Walls of Jerusalem refortified
- Strict Sabbath observance
- Economic division established by the wall

Another important question is why Cyrus would proclaim an edict of emancipation. To a list of possibilities, my suggestion is overpopulation, or more specifically, that of the underclass probably outnumbering the upper and skilled merchant classes. Cyrus inherited from Nabonidus the economic downfall and overpopulation from forced migrations left unattended. Cyrus's edict would reestablish the Babylonian-Persian economy by displacing and resettling unwanted and unskilled laborers cloaked in humanitarian gesture. However, what would motivate successful Judeo-Babylonians/ Persian to make the trip back? What would make them finance the expensive and arduous trip? The construction of the temple and religiosity are not sufficient. The likelihood of reclaiming ancestral land, possibly cultivating and leasing it, and finally returning home to Babylon is a working hypothesis. And so, through gradual repeated return migrations for all displaced and resettled peoples in Babylon to Yehud/Judah, a return to former economic prosperity would be achieved for all parties involved.

The return migration from 538 to 520 B.C.E. may be seen as a period of "temporary return migration" as opposed to the "permanent return migrations" of 520, 458, and 445 B.C.E. In other words, those who arrived with Sheshbazzar may have simply turned to claim their ancestral land in order to return home, to Babylon, mirroring the preference of the Gadites and Reubenites in Numbers 32. Without leadership and infrastructure in contrast to the experience of leaders of the 597 group of exiles, this "early" postexilic or return migrations period saw socioeconomic and theopolitical disarray, causing high inflation and unwanted socioreligious problems. Yehud was a mess and this period may be a time of high complaint, a time of the wilderness-wandering period, with masses calling for return to Egypt (Babylon).

Clearly, the most troublesome return migration is Ezra's. Under his leadership, the call to remove all marriages to foreign wives and children borders ethnic cleansing. There is no redemptive value in such an act. To frame his initiative as a "covenant" according to the law is a reminder of injustice and extremism, though justified in some circles. In my opinion, this is the "sin of exile" in the Hebrew Bible. Ezra is no Moses. The voices of opposition, Jonathan son of Asahel and Jahzeiah son of Tikvah found support from just two Levites, Meshullam and Shabbethai. Their opposition is preserved. The book of Ruth is also a powerful rejoinder. The chiastic structure of Genesis 12—25, where the center of the Abrahamic cycle is the expulsion of Hagar and Ishmael, reflecting Ezra 9—10 is another witness preserved, codified in the very law that Ezra spoke of, and passed down as a protest and what not to do for future generations.

A. Genealogical framework (11:10–32)
- B. Migration from Haran: separation from Nahor ([12:1–3] 12:4–5a)
  - C. Building of Altars; land promised (12:5b–9 [13:14–18])
    - D. "Sister-Wife" episode (12:10–20)
      - E. Border/Land dispute with Lot (13:1–13)
        - F. The King of Sodom—Lot is rescued (14:1–24)
          - G. God's Covenant with Abram (15:1–21) [15:6—key verse])
            - X. Expulsion and Rescue of Hagar and Ishmael (16:1–16) // Expulsion of wives and children in the post-exilic community (Ezra 9–10)
          - G'. God's Covenant with Abram Circumcision (17:1–27)
        - F'. Sodom episode and rescue of Lot (18:1–19:38)
      - E'. Water-well dispute with Abimelech (21:22–34) [21:1–20 Isaac/Ishmael]
    - D'. Sister-wife episode (20:1–18)
  - C'. Building of altar (22:6–9); land promised (23:1–20)
- B'. Migration to Haran; reunification with Nahor's lineage (24:1–67; [22:20–24])

A'. Genealogical framework (25:1–18)

Assessment. From the perspective of those who lived in the new center, Babylon (Persia), the return of migrants to Yehud/Judah is starting anew. They would come to experience what they missed out on in Babylon: hope, new creation, and home. Developed in, through, and by the Diaspora, the lasting expressions of forced migrations and Diaspora are found in scripture and prayer. The authority of the king (597 B.C.E.) dramatically shifted to the authority of the text, giving rise to canonical consciousness or scripturalization. The loss of that generation against the wall, further symbolized by the destruction of the temple (587 B.C.E.) took external sacrifice and transformed it inwardly, to prayer, for healing, outcry, and personal expressions of faith and doubt—facing Jerusalem three times a day, remembering those dates 597, 587, and 582 B.C.E., as Daniel observed and practiced. Shifting to Second Temple Judaism, Jesus too, would teach his disciples how to pray. With this Davidic king's displacement in ca. 33 C.E., and his early followers scattered, with Damascus entering the scene again, the loss of lives and the destruction of the Temple (70 C.E.) precipitates a new canonical consciousness—the Gospels, letters, and apocalypse—with John in forced migration on Patmos. Biblical literature received final form (Masoretic Text Babylon; LXX Egypt; Samaritan Pentateuch) by the experience of the Diaspora. Additional diasporic consciousness progressed in the Midrash and Talmud—between the Palestinian and Babylonian. Interestingly, the latter became authoritative. In closing, Tractate Berachot 7a says that God also prays. It asks, what does God pray? "May it be that My will that My mercy may suppress My anger, and that My mercy prevail over My [other] attributes, so that I may deal with My children in the attribute of mercy and on their behalf, stop short of the limit of justice."

[*See also* Cross-Cultural Exegesis; Cuban Interpretation in the Cuban Diaspora; Cultural Anthropology, *subentry* Hebrew Bible; Cultural Anthropology, *subentry* New Testament; Cultural Studies; Empire Studies and Biblical Interpretation; Historical Criticism, *subentry* Hebrew Bible; Historical Criticism, *subentry* New Testament; Postcolonial Biblical Interpretation; Social Sciences, *subentry* Hebrew Bible; Social Sciences, *subentry* New Testament; *and* Trauma Theory.]

BIBLIOGRAPHY

Ahn, John J. *Exile as Forced Migrations: A Sociological, Literary, and Theological Approach on the Displacement and Resettlement of the South Kingdom of Judah.* Beihefte zur Zeitschrift für die Alttestamentliche Wissenschaft 417. Berlin and New York: De Gruyter, 2011.

Ahn, John J., and J. Middlemas, eds., *By the Irrigation Canals of Babylon: Approaches to the Study of the Exile.* Library of Hebrew Bible/Old Testament Studies 526; New York: T&T Clark, 2012.

Alan, James. "Questioning the Terminology and Definitions of Forced Migrations." In *The Politics of Forced Migrations: A Conceptual, Operational, and Legal Analysis*, edited by Nitza Nachmas with Rami Goldstein, 39–61. Baltimore: Publish America, 2004.

Barclay, John M. G., ed. *Negotiating Diaspora: Jewish Strategies in the Roman Empire.* Library of Second Temple Studies. *Journal for the Study of Pseudepigrapha: Supplement Series* 45. London: T&T Clark, 2004.

Barstad, Hans. *The Myth of the Empty Land: A Study in the History and Archeology of Judah during the "Exilic" Period.* Symbolae Osloenses Fasc. Suppl. 28. Oslo: Scandinavian University Press, 1996.

Berger, Peter, and Thomas Luckmann. *The Social Construction of Reality.* New York: Anchor, 1966.

Boras, George J., ed. *Issues in the Economics of Immigration.* Chicago: University of Chicago Press, 2000.

Clifford, James. *Routes: Travel and Translation in the Late Twentieth Century.* Cambridge, Mass.: Harvard University Press, 1997.

Cohen, Robin. *Global Diasporas: An Introduction.* New York: Routledge, 2008.

Collins, John J. *Between Athens and Jerusalem: Jewish Identities in the Hellenistic Diaspora.* 2d ed. Grand Rapids, Mich.: Eerdmans, 1999.

Davies, Philip R. "Exile? What Exile? Whose Exile?" In *Leading Captivity Captive: "The Exile" as History and Ideology*, edited by Lester L. Grabbe, 128–138. Journal for the Study of the Old Testament: Supplement Series 278/European Seminar in Historical Methodology 2. Sheffield: Sheffield Academic Press, 1998.

Geertz, Clifford. *Interpretation of Cultures.* New York: Basic Books, 1973.

Goffman, Erving. *The Presentation of Self in Everyday Life.* Garden City, N.Y.: Doubleday, 1959.

Mannheim, Karl. "The Problem of Generations." In *Essays on the Sociology of Knowledge*, edited by Paul Kecskemeti. New York: Oxford University Press, 1928.

Millar, Fergus. "A Rural Jewish Community in Late Roman Mesopotamia, and the Question of a 'Split' Jewish Diaspora." *Journal for the Study of Judaism* 42 (2011): 351–374.

Pearce, L. "New Evidence for Judeans in Babylonia." In *Judah and the Judeans in the Persian Period*, edited by O. Lipschits and M. Oeming, 399–411. Winona Lake, Ind: Eisenbrauns, 2006.

Suleiman, Susan Rubin Suleiman. "The 1.5 Generation: Thinking about Child Survivors and the Holocaust." *American Imago* 59 3 (2002): 277–295.

Torrey, Charles C. *The Composition and Historical Value of Ezra-Nehemiah. Beihefte zur Zeitschrift für die Alttestamentliche Wissenschaft* 2. Giessen: J. Ricker, 1896.

Wettstein, Howard, ed. *Diasporas and Exiles: Varieties of Jewish Identity*. Berkeley: University of California Press, 2002.

Wilson, Robert R. "Forced Migration and the Formation of the Prophetic Literature." In Ahn and Middlemas, *By the Irrigation Canals of Babylon*.

John Ahn

Disability Criticism

Disability criticism is the study of impairment from the perspective that there is nothing intrinsically negative about those conditions or forms of embodiment that have traditionally been evaluated as disabilities. It is a form of identity criticism that takes as its starting point the idea that disability is not a stable biological phenomenon but, rather, a social construct of individual societies that changes over time and according to context. In this way, a particular impairment might be evaluated negatively in one social situation and positively in another. The classic example of this is the evaluation of wheelchair use in various situations. In the context of a marathon, wheelchair use is a considerable advantage: wheelchair users consistently outpace runners by a considerable amount. Faced with a set of stairs, however, the use of a wheelchair becomes a disability. In some instances, a biological phenomenon might, over time and with changing social norms, cease to be considered a disability at all. For example, many people in the ancient world considered being female to be a negative physiological shortcoming or disability. Aristotle, for instance, compares the formation of women in the womb to underbaked bread (Hippocrates, *Regimen* 1.34). Women are literally the product of inadequate cooking. In the modern world gender is considered natural and neutral and, thus, if prejudice against women continues to exist, it is not grounded in the idea that being female is a biological defect. These constructions of disability are often tied to medical standards and to related understandings of gender, race, ethnicity, and class. Like other forms of identity criticism, disability criticism of the Bible describes the ways in which these valuations of impairments are made and function both for the original authors and audiences of the Bible and for modern readers.

History of Scholarship. Disability criticism emerged in both the United States and the United Kingdom in the 1980s. In the United Kingdom, disability criticism grew out of Marxist concerns for an oppressed underclass and heavily emphasized society as the root of disability. For a discussion of the historical and political underpinnings of UK research (see Oliver 1990, pp. 1–10). In the United States, disability criticism is an offshoot of feminist criticism. American disability critics see disability as a facet of identity akin to gender and race.

Regardless of their critical pedigree, all disability critics have divided historical treatments of disability into three chronologically successive models: a religious model, a medical model, and a social or cultural model, each of which has a different view of the nature, cause, and proper response to bodily differences. The religious model, which critics assume was predominant until the Enlightenment, posits that disability is a form of punishment caused by sin against God or in a demonic interference, which is removed using religious measures and divine intervention. In this model, both the disability and the disabled person are, therefore, aligned with sin and evil. The medical model, which gained prominence with the "rise of science" in the Enlightenment, viewed disability as a medical condition caused by external agents (e.g., disease) or some inherent deficiency (e.g., genetic predisposition).

As with any disease, the proper response to disability was to attempt to cure or eradicate it using medical measures.

The final period, precipitated by the rise of disability criticism, is referred to either as the social model or the cultural model of disability. The social model emphasizes the social constructedness of "disability" in contradistinction to "impairment." According to this view, the impairment that leads an individual to use a wheelchair becomes a disability only when this individual encounters discrimination in society. Consequently, it is only prejudice that actually disables a person. The cultural model, advocated by Lennard Davis, Sharon Snyder, David Mitchell, and Rosemary Garland Thompson, blurs the boundaries between impairment and disability, positing that the experience of disability includes a larger complex of social structures. The cultural model sees disability not just as a medical condition or issue of discrimination, but as an embodied experience that encompasses both human variation and socially mediated difference (Mitchell and Snyder 2006). With respect to the distinction between the "social model" and the "cultural model," a certain ideological cleft can be traced between scholars in the United Kingdom and those in the United States. This can be attributed to the varying underlying commitments of their work. The cultural model as advocated by Lennard Davis, David Mitchell, and Sharon Snyder dominates in North American scholarship and has come to form the theoretical underpinnings of American biblical scholarship on disability in, for example, the work of Jeremy Schipper and Rebecca Raphael. For a succinct summary of the history of disability studies see Schipper (2006, pp. 15–24).

Study of Disability in the Bible to 1985. Prior to the advent of disability criticism as a discrete and theorized area of study in the humanities in the 1980s, scholarly approaches to cases of disability in the Bible assumed that the authors of the Bible were working with a religious model of disability. Scholarly analyses followed the medical model of disability and consisted, as Hector Avalos (1999) has argued, almost exclusively of medical diagnoses. These kinds of analyses of disability concerned themselves with diagnosing, using modern medical terminology, those conditions that impressed the modern scholar as particularly troublesome. Famous examples of this include scholarly efforts to identify Paul's "thorn in the flesh" (2 Cor 12:7) and the translation of the ambiguous yet ubiquitous "skin abnormality" (*ṣāraʿat*) of Leviticus 13–14. In both of these cases, scholars have played amateur physician. In his magnificent commentary on Leviticus, for example, Jacob Milgrom (1991) writes both that the symptoms of the condition resemble psoriasis and that he consulted a respected dermatologist about the condition. Discussions about the nature of Paul's condition in 2 Corinthians were similarly modernist. Until recently, this kind of modern diagnostic translation constituted the dominant approach to disability.

Metaphorical interpretations of disability in the Bible, by contrast, approached stories and language of disability as symbols. All references to disability were treated as imagery for more serious moral, religious, and ethical failings. To a certain extent, this approach mirrored the linguistic tendency of society as a whole, in which terms such as "lame," "dumb," or "turn a deaf ear/blind eye" are used as colloquial terms and phrases for stupidity and willful ignorance. Where scholars engaged with metaphors of disability for practical theology or pastoral care, they reinforced the idea that disability was always negative, even as they sought to avoid the dangerous ethical implications of this assessment. These efforts followed one of two lines of argumentation. The first was that the presence in the text of individuals with disabilities—for example the reproductively challenged matriarchs in Genesis or impaired individuals in the Gospels—demonstrates that God selects or cares for individuals with disabilities. The fact that God "works through" the apparently barren matriarchs and that Jesus spends so much time with the disabled is seen as evidence of God's care for everyone. The difficulty with this line of argument is that the matriarchs do not remain infertile and those who encounter Jesus with faith are healed. The idea that God chooses the disabled is overshadowed by the idea that God's favor is evident only in their healing.

The second approach to disability in the Bible, advocated primarily by biblical theologians, focused on the *eschaton* and the resurrection of the body. In the kingdom of heaven, they argue, the disabled would be vindicated because they would be healed. Both this and the caring approach to disability in the Bible assumed that disability was always secondary, inferior, and negative, reproducing the biases that they sought to avoid.

Biblical Studies and Disability 1985 to the Present. The advent of critical disability theory and the recognition that the category of disability is both constructed and representative of social experiences and culture has had a profound impact on historical studies. This impact, in turn, has led to a renaissance in the study of diseases and disabilities in the Hebrew Bible and the application of the "religious model of disability" to scriptural texts. The construction of categories of disability, especially in the priestly literature of the Hebrew Bible, has been the subject of renewed interest. Much of this work has taken up the methodological finesse of disability studies as a redress to the unreflected diagnostic approach of prior historical criticism to great effect.

Additional interest in the subject emerged out of social-anthropological study of the Bible and the work of social scientists, in particular Hector Avalos, whose two books *Illness and Health Care in the Ancient Near East* (1995) and *Healthcare and the Rise of Christianity* (1999) reconsidered illness and disability in terms of their social and economic capital and function. Avalos's arguments about the centrality of healthcare and access to healthcare in the ancient world offered a fresh and radically new take on the ways in which religion worked in ancient societies and the reasons for the success of the Jesus Movement. Avalos's work, while not self-consciously tied to critical disability theory, prefigured much of the subsequent work in the field since. In a similar vein, John Pilch examined the New Testament and Jesus's role as healer using medical anthropological models (2000). His work, begun in the 1980s, utilized anthropological distinctions between disease and illness and explored the way that Jesus functions as a healer in the New Testament. He argued that Jesus responds to purity concerns and illness as a holy person and on behalf of his father. Healing, Pilch demonstrated, involved social rehabilitation and reassimilation. Healing was not merely physical, but also social. Persons of disability were cast out by society and, in healing them, Jesus reintegrated the disabled into the mainstream. Pilch's work gestures toward the general principle that disability is a social construct. In the case of the story of the healing of woman with the flow of blood in Mark 5:24b–34, for instance, her condition is seen as disabling in the sense that she is alienated and distanced from society.

Disability studies first entered biblical scholarship in the work of constructive theologians and especially in the work of Nancy Eiesland, whose 1994 book, *The Disabled God*, made the first inroads into theological engagement with disability criticism. Eiesland's study included an influential analysis of Gospel stories about the resurrection of Jesus and the nature of Jesus's resurrected body, in which she proposed that the retention of the wounds of crucifixion in the body of Jesus offered a positive perspective that subverted traditional theological understandings of disability.

In the late 1990s, under the influence of disability theory and theologians like Eiesland, biblical scholars began to alter the ways in which they approached passages about disability. Rather than assuming that there is an essential quality to disability in the Bible, they began to look at the ways in which disability serves to order biblical society. Explicit interest in disability studies was often tied to political activism on behalf of persons with disabilities and the efforts of constructive theologians like Eiesland, whose writings were intended to serve pastoral functions. The relative newness of disability studies meant that these scholars, like feminist critics before them, had to justify both the intrinsic value and the scholarly credentials of their work. The volume of essays, *This Abled Body*, edited by Avalos, Schipper, and Sarah Melcher in 2007, offered the first effort to bring scholars together to do work that was both biblical and engaged constructively with disability and theology.

The first major monograph on disability, Jeremy Schipper's pioneering work on Mephibosheth, published in 2006, drew attention to a number of important ways in which disability had been misrepresented. Schipper's work was the first monograph in biblical studies to present disability as a facet of human identity akin to gender or race and to argue that disability is grounded in real lived experience. Schipper made the observation that disability was more common and extended in antiquity than in the modern world. The limitations of ancient medicine were such that a much higher proportion of ancient audiences had disabilities and received passages concerning disability differently. Disability was not an incidental detail in the biblical text, but instances of disability were rather sites of interpretation.

Even apart from the methodological difficulties that ancient texts present to trained medics (e.g., brief descriptions of conditions, the absence of important medical data such as blood tests, the incomplete nature of the medical history, etc.), diagnosis ignores the different cultural value ascribed to these conditions. Even if the terms "sacred disease" and "epilepsy" do refer to the same condition, equating the sacred disease with epilepsy obscures the specific cultural value attached to the sacred disease in the ancient world. Diagnostic biblical scholarship persists, however, in the historically grounded work of JoAnn Scurlock and Burton R. Andersen (2005) and the pastorally minded contributions of Donald Capps (2008).

An alternative perspective on disability has been pursued by scholars like Saul Olyan and Tracy Lemos, whose work on the Hebrew Bible analyzes the way that categories of disability and the violence associated with disability serve to organize society, to deny access to religious locations, and to inscribe hierarchy in the communities for which these texts were written. Olyan's *Disability in the Hebrew Bible: Interpreting Mental and Physical Differences* (2008) examines the ways in which textual representations of disability express patterns of social inequality. The book is grounded in historical and philological analysis of the Hebrew Bible and, while taking a sensitive approach to disability, insists upon using ancient categories of analysis.

Prospectus. The ethics and politics of disability still have great currency among modern biblical scholars. For a large number of theological interpreters—Hans Reinders, Amos Yong (2011), and Thomas Reynolds among them—interest in disability stems from pastoral concerns or issues of relevance and applicability in the modern world. In the work of these authors, biblical scholarship remains, or should remain, constrained by the interests of the disabled.

At the same time, however, even as pastoral or theological interpretations of biblical disability continue to play a prominent role among systematic and practical theologians, biblical scholarship has focused on contextualizing disability in the ancient world. These new approaches focus on differentiating between different lines of thought in ancient literature, using ancient medical literature and practices to reappraise the presentation of disability in the Bible, and revisiting the topic of disabled imagery and rhetoric in the writings of individual authors.

The uncritical adoption of the religious model of disability meant that in the past scholars rarely distinguished between different lines of thought, perspective, and argumentation among biblical authors. Many scholars generally assumed that, when it comes to disability, biblical authors are united in a way unparalleled by their varied approaches to any other theological question. Recent scholarship by Joel Baden and Candida Moss (2011) on the presentation of skin disease in the Hebrew Bible has contrasted the perspectives of the biblical authors with one another. Rather than assuming that all authors subscribed to the religious model of disability, Baden and Moss have demonstrated the ways in which the etiologies of disease and valuations of various conditions differ from one author to another.

The work of Rebecca Raphael (2009) explicitly adapts various methodologies from disability studies in her rereading of disability in narrative and poetry. Raphael adapts Mitchell and Snyder's idea of narrative prosthesis—the way in which the disabled serve to initiate and propel the plot of a work only for the disability to disappear in the resolution of the tale to remarkable effect. Additionally, Raphael explores the use of the senses in various biblical texts by tracing images and metaphors of audition throughout the Hebrew Bible to contrast the ways in which different senses were privileged by individual sources. The interest in the ways that the senses and imagery of sensory impairment are identified, grouped, and assessed is paralleled in the work of Louise Lawrence (2011). Sensory criticism, which is informed by cross-cultural anthropology of the senses, pays particular attention to the ways in which biblical authors used and privileged the senses in biblical texts. In her work on Mark, Lawrence identifies the account as an "audio-centric" text, which she sees as a deliberate strategy to resist the dominance of sightedness in contemporary imperial propaganda.

Recent New Testament scholarship that engages disability has sought to resituate miracle stories and descriptions of disability within the rich landscape of ancient Greco-Roman medicine, aesthetics, and culture. Influenced by the work of Robert Garland and Martha Rose, New Testament scholars have begun to see the ways in which imagery of disability in the Bible and early church is influenced by contemporary culture. This interest, exemplified in the work of Avalos, Parsons (2006), Moss, and Lawrence, is also found in treatments of noncanonical texts. The work of Nicole Kelley (2009) on disability in early Christian literature exemplifies this approach. Kristi Upson-Saia's work on scarred bodies in the resurrection in the thinking of Augustine offers a reappraisal of the ways that scars are treated in early Christian texts about the *eschaton* that reflects ancient aesthetics and discourse about scarring. This study, with its focus on the idealism of resurrected bodies, parallels Schipper's and Moss's more recent works on eschatological imagery of healing in Isaiah and in the early church.

"Second wave" biblical scholarship on disability has challenged assumptions about the ways that disability functions positively in certain narratives. Rather than attempting to diagnose unambiguous examples of disability, these scholars focus on the rhetorical function of disability for ancient authors and on the intersection of disability and other hermeneutical approaches. The 2012 collection, *Disability Studies and Biblical Studies*, focuses on integrating disability criticism with feminist, historical-critical, queer, reception-historical, and postmodern approaches to scripture. While disability critics were initially interested in producing readings that spoke to persons with disabilities in distinction to historical-critical readings, recent scholarship has seen disability criticism as a helpful supplement not only to theology but also to historical-critical, rhetorical, and other identity-based criticisms.

[*See also* Class Criticism; Cultural Anthropology, *subentry* Hebrew Bible; Cultural Anthropology, *subentry* New Testament; Cultural-Historical Criticism; Feminist Biblical Interpretation; Lesbian, Gay, Bisexual, and Transgender Interpretation; Queer Criticism and Queer Theory; Race, Ethnicity, and Biblical Criticism; Social Sciences, *subentry* Hebrew Bible; *and* Social Sciences, *subentry* New Testament.]

Bibliography

Avalos, Hector. *Health Care and the Rise of Christianity.* Peabody, Mass.: Hendrickson, 1999. Here Avalos offers an alternative vision of the spread of Christianity predicated on the free healthcare that it offered to the poor.

Avalos, Hector. *Illness and Health Care in the Ancient Near East: The Role of the Temple in Greece, Mesopotamia, and Israel.* Atlanta: Scholars, 1995. This was the first work to look at the different venues in which healthcare took place in terms of social function. Rather than assuming modern medical practices, Avalos looked at the role of healing centers in the ancient world as an entrée into the Biblical text.

Avalos, Hector, Jeremy Schipper, and Sarah Melcher, eds. *This Abled Body: Rethinking Disabilities in Biblical Studies.* Semeia Studies 55. Leiden: Brill, 2007. The first collection of essays on disability in the Bible, this volume focuses more on the Old Testament than the New.

Baden, Joel S., and Candida R. Moss. "The Origin and Interpretation of *ṣāra'at* in Leviticus 13–14." *Journal of Biblical Literature* 130:4 (2011): 643–661.

Capps, Donald. *Jesus the Village Psychiatrist.* Louisville: Westminster John Knox Press, 2008.

Dorman, Johanna. *The Blemished Body: Deformity and Disability in the Qumran Scrolls.* Groningen: Rijksuniversiteit, 2007. Dorman's is the first study of disability in the Dead Sea Scrolls.

Eiesland, Nancy. *The Disabled God: Toward a Liberatory Theology of Disability.* Nashville, Tenn.: Abingdon, 1994. This groundbreaking and innovative study of disability in theology includes discussions of the resurrection appearances of Jesus.

Garland, Robert. *The Eye of the Beholder: Deformity and Disability in the Graeco-Roman World.* 2d ed. London: Bristol Classical, 2010.

Kelley, Nicole. "The Deformed Child in Ancient Christianity." In *Children in Late Ancient Christianity*, edited by Cornelia B. Horn and Robert R. Phenix. Studien und Texte zu Antike und Christentum 58. Mohr Siebeck: Tübingen, 2009.

Lawrence, Louise, "Exploring the Sense-scape of the Gospel of Mark." *Journal for the Study of New Testament* 33:4 (2011): 387–397. This article is a sensory-critical analysis of Mark, which argues that the focus on audition is a deliberate effort to reject imperial values.

Milgrom, Jacob. *Leviticus 1–16.* Anchor Bible 3. New York, Doubleday, 1991.

Moss, Candida R. "Heavenly Healing: Eschatological Cleansing and the Resurrection of the Dead in the Early Church." *Journal of the American Academy of Religion* 79:3 (2011): 1–27. Moss discusses the eradication of disability in early Christian constructions of resurrected bodies.

Moss, Candida R. "The Man with the Flow of Power: Porous Bodies in Mark 5:25–34." *Journal of Biblical Literature* 129:3 (2010): 507–519. Moss uses ancient medical theories of disease to argue that the body of Jesus is fundamentally weak.

Moss, Candida R., and Jeremy Schipper. *Disability Studies and Biblical Studies.* New York: Palgrave MacMillan, 2011. This collection of essays is a dialogue between disability studies and feminism, queer theory, Foucault, reception history, source criticism and ancient medicine.

Oliver, Michael. *The Politics of Disablement: A Sociological Approach.* New York: St. Martin's, 1990.

Olyan, Saul M. *Disability in the Hebrew Bible: Interpreting Mental and Physical Differences.* New York: Cambridge University Press, 2008. Olyan examines hierarchy and social structures in, especially, priestly material in the Bible.

Parsons, Mikeal. *Body and Character in Luke and Acts: The Subversion of Physiognomy in Early Christianity.* Grand Rapids, Mich.: Baker, 2006. Parsons uses Greek physiognomical treatises to analyze the healing miracles in the Luke-Acts.

Pilch, John J. *Healing in the New Testament: Insights from Mediterranean and Medical Anthropology.* Minneapolis: Fortress, 2000. As a social scientific analysis of the New Testament healing stories, this work incorporates anthropological analysis and models to discuss the New Testament.

Raphael, Rebecca. *Biblical Corpora: Representations of Disability in Hebrew Biblical Literature.* Library of Hebrew Bible/Old Testament Studies 445; New York: T.&T. Clark, 2009. Raphael uses Disability Studies, especially the notion of "narrative prosthesis" to analyze a wide variety of texts about impairment in the Hebrew Bible.

Schipper, Jeremy. *Disability and Isaiah's Suffering Servant.* Oxford: Oxford University Press, 2011. Schipper offers a piercing analysis of the history of scholarship and the ways in which scholars have neglected the fact that the suffering servant is disabled.

Schipper, Jeremy. *Disability Studies and the Hebrew Bible: Figuring Mephibosheth in the David Story.* Library of Hebrew Bible/Old Testament Studies 441; New York: T.&T. Clark, 2006. In this first major monograph on disability in the Hebrew Bible, Schipper takes Mephibosheth as his starting point for discussing the ways in which disability is central to understanding the Old Testament.

Scurlock, JoAnn, and Burton R. Andersen. *Diagnoses in Assyrian and Babylonian Medicine: Ancient Sources, Translations, and Modern Medical Analyses.* Chicago: University of Illinois Press, 2005. This work is an excellent treatment of Assyrian and Babylonian medical texts and the ways in which they diagnose and treat disease.

Snyder, Sharon L., and David T. *Cultural Locations of Disability.* Chicago: University of Chicago Press, 2006.

Thomson, Rosemarie Garland. *Extraordinary Bodies: Figuring Physical Disability in American Culture and Literature.* New York: Columbia University Press, 1997.

Yong, Amos. *The Bible, Disability, and the Church.* Grand Rapids, Mich.: Eerdmans, 2011. A recent theological study of disability in the Bible and Christian theology, this book is concerned with theology and practicality, not necessarily history.

Candida R. Moss

Dispensationalist Interpretation

Dispensationalism is a conservative evangelical approach to Christian biblical interpretation and theology whose author-centered hermeneutic leads to the conclusion that Israel's status as the covenant people of God has not been superseded by the rise and gradual separation of the church from its Jewish roots. Dispensationalism interprets biblical prophecy to be primarily about Israel and its future, and understands the church as benefiting from God's promises to Israel, although distinct in some ways from Israel. Historically the hermeneutic of dispensationalism has been styled as consistently literal, although this has been challenged by covenant theologians and given greater nuancing by progressive dispensationalists.

Historical Background. A brief sketch of dispensationalism's history is necessary for an understanding of its approach to biblical interpretation (see further Bateman in Bateman 1999, pp. 21–60). Dispensationalism has certain features in common with the chiliasm of the early church, and certain of its tenets arguably found voice in earlier theologians. Nevertheless, it is clear that the life and writings of John Nelson Darby (1800–1882) spawned dispensationalism as a distinct system of biblical interpretation and theology. Darby studied at Trinity College, Dublin, where he graduated as classical gold medalist in 1819. After ordination as a priest and success in ministry in the Church of Ireland, he became dissatisfied with the state of piety of his church and of institutional Christianity as a whole. Reacting against what he viewed as clerical hierarchicalism and religious nominalism, Darby began an itinerant ministry in England, Europe, Canada, the United States, and New Zealand. The low-church movement which resulted from his ministry became known as the "Plymouth Brethren" due to its place of origin. It featured independent assemblies, lay elders, simplicity in worship, spontaneous Bible teaching, and weekly observance of the Lord's Supper.

Darby's dispensational views were in varying degrees accepted by others outside the "brethren" movement, aided to a great extent by summer Bible conferences in North America. James H. Brookes (1830–1897) was a Presbyterian pastor in St. Louis, Missouri and a prominent figure in the Niagara Bible Conference, held at Niagara on the Lake, Ontario from the 1870s into the 1890s. Around 1880 Brookes met and mentored a recently converted lawyer, Cyrus Ingersoll Scofield (1843–1921), and introduced Scofield to Darby's views. Scofield entered the ministry as a Congregationalist and wrote *Rightly Dividing the Word of Truth*, a treatise on dispensational interpretation of the Bible, in 1888. But the contribution that made "Scofieldism" a pejorative synonym for dispensationalism was a King James Version Bible, which Scofield annotated with introductions to the biblical books, cross references, paragraph headings, and explanatory notes placed at the bottom of the page. The immensely popular *Scofield Reference Bible* was published by Oxford University Press (1909; New and Improved Edition, 1917; revised *New Scofield Reference Bible*, ed. E. Schuyler English et al. 1967).

In the United States, the founding of such schools as Moody Bible Institute (1886, Chicago), the Bible Institute of Los Angeles (now Biola University, 1908), Philadelphia Bible College (now Philadelphia Biblical University, 1913), Dallas Theological Seminary (1924), Grace Theological Seminary (1937, Winona Lake, Ind.), and Grand Rapids Baptist Seminary (1941, now Grand Rapids Theological Seminary of Cornerstone University, Mich.), promoted dispensationalism to thousands of students who in turn taught dispensationalism after graduation. Many people today are aware of dispensationalism due to popularizing "dispensensational" perspectives on the end of time found in such books as Hal Lindsey's *The Late Great Planet Earth* (Grand Rapids, Mich.: Zondervan, 1970) and the *Left Behind* series of sixteen novels coauthored by Tim LaHaye and Jerry B. Jenkins (Carol Stream, Ill.: Tyndale House, 1995–2007).

Forms of Dispensationalism. While Blaising (Blaising and Bock 1992, pp. 21–56) identifies three forms of dispensationalism, a study of the history of dispensationalism shows developments leading to at least four distinct approaches.

Classical Dispensationalism. Held by Darby, Scofield, and others such as C. H. Macintosh (1820–1896, an Irish author and preacher) and Lewis Sperry Chafer (1871–1952, the founder of Dallas Seminary), classical dispensationalism stressed a dualistic scheme in which Israel was an earthly people redeemed by keeping the law, while the church was a heavenly people saved by grace alone.

Revised Dispensationalism. This form of dispensationalism removed the dualistic earthly and heavenly people scheme of classical dispensationalism and softened the law and grace dichotomy somewhat while maintaining an eternal distinction between Israel and the church. Influential revised dispensationalists included John F. Walvoord (1910–2002, president of Dallas Seminary from 1952–1986), Alva J. McClain (1888–1968, president of Grace Theological Seminary, Winona Lake, Ind., 1937–1968) Charles C. Ryrie (1925–, former president of Philadelphia Bible College and professor of theology at Dallas Theological Seminary).

Progressive Dispensationalism. This brand is a relatively recent development stemming from an informal gathering of dispensational scholars at the annual meeting of the Evangelical Theological Society in 1985. While maintaining certain dispensational emphases, such as the future of national Israel and the imminence of Christ's return, progressive dispensationalists stress the cohesive progress of revelation throughout the Old and New Testaments (OT, NT), the unity of God's saving plan, and the continuity of the church with Israel. Notable progressive dispensationalists include Craig A. Blaising (1949–, Provost and Professor of Theology, Southwestern Baptist Theological Seminary, Fort Worth, Tex.), Darrell Bock (1954–, Research Professor of New Testament, Dallas Theological Seminary), and Robert L. Saucy (1930–, Distinguished Professor of Systematic Theology, Talbot School of Theology).

Ultra-dispensationalism. Dispensationalism (e.g., Baker 1971; DeWitt 2002) of this fourth form, which is also known as hyperdispensationalism, tends to contrast Israel and the church and law and grace to a degree greater than even classical dispensationalism. The beginning of the church is tied to a point in Paul's ministry (Acts 9—28), rather than to the outpouring of the Holy Spirit on the Day of Pentecost (Acts 2), which is understood only as the origin of a short-lived Jewish-Christian community. Prominent adherents to this sort of approach include E. W. Bullinger, a Church of England clergyman (1837–1913), Cornelius R. Stam, an American pastor and founder of the Berean Bible Society (1908–2003), and Charles F. Baker, president of Grace Bible College, Grand Rapids, Mich. (1905–1994).

The Dispensations Summarized. Although differing on some particulars, dispensationalists were concerned to present a "panoramic view of the Bible" (Scofield 1917, pp. v–vi) in seven periods of time, each involving a distinct way in which God administered the plan of redemption. It is clear, then, that dispensationalists are motivated by an interpretive agenda to make sense of the Bible as a whole. In common with historic Christianity, dispensationalists believed that God was uniquely working through the individual biblical authors' historic situations and writings to provide an overall, unified, comprehensive account of the divine plan for humanity and for the world that God created for humans. It must be noted that the term "dispensation" has been used by nondispensationalists prior to and after the rise of "dispensationalism" to describe the flow of biblical history and the biblical covenants (Blaising and Bock, pp. 116–119).

Flowing from their interpretive agenda, dispensationalists concluded that a pattern emerged when biblical history was surveyed: a series of distinct divine administrations, each involving a unique test for humanity, a failure of the test, and a divine judgment leading to transition into the next dispensation. Although the dispensations admittedly emphasized the differences that emerge as biblical history is studied, there was also an affirmation of an overall continuity and progression, and a denial that the dispensations were separate ways of salvation. To the contrary, in each dispensation humans were accountable to obey God's new revelation as a stewardship of faith (English, p. 3, note 3; Ryrie, *Dispensationalism*, 110–31).

Below is a typical presentation of the traditional dispensations:

1. Innocence (Gen 1:1—3:6): God created Adam and Eve, placed them in a perfect environment, and required them to obey his command. They disobeyed when tempted by the serpent and were judged by being put out of the garden.
2. Conscience/moral responsibility (Gen 3:7—8:14): Adam and Eve and their descendants became accountable to do what they knew was right as prompted by their conscience. They failed to do so, and were judged by Noah's flood.
3. Human Government (Gen 8:15—11:32): After the flood Noah's family became corporately accountable to protect human life and to punish those who took human life (Gen 9:6). The building of Babel indicates that humans failed in this stewardship, and God judged them by scattering them and confusing their language (Gen 11:1–9).
4. Promise (Gen 12:1—Exod 18:27): God promised to bless Abraham and his descendants in their own land if only they would respond to his call to go to that land. Yet the Israelites abandoned the promised land for Egypt and rashly exchanged the promise for the law.
5. Law (Exod 19:1—Acts 1:26): God gave the law to Israel through Moses as a temporary measure to show them the superiority of the promise to Abraham. Israel repeatedly violated their covenantal obligations and eventually suffered the exile.
6. Grace/Church (Acts 2:1—rapture of the church): At the coming of the Holy Spirit at Pentecost, the church is empowered to disciple the nations, who are accountable to believe in Jesus. The unbelief of humanity brings on the judgment of the tribulation after the church has been taken to heaven in the rapture (1 Thess 4:13–18).
7. Kingdom (Rev 20:1–16): Satan is bound, and humanity is accountable to Jesus, who reigns with his resurrected people for one thousand years. Satan's release (Rev 20:7–10) signals the final human rebellion, and history ends with the judgment of the great white throne (Rev 20:11–15), leading to the eternal new heavens and new earth. (Rev 21—22)

Dispensationalists themselves, not to mention their critics, have noted difficulties with certain details of the preceding scheme. Discerning a clear pattern of stewardship, failure, and judgment in each dispensation is difficult. Features of previous dispensations continue into the next dispensation, calling into question the notion of each dispensation's uniqueness. The transition between promise and law seems especially tenuous. Perhaps the most serious issue is that the New Testament makes very little of certain dispensations (Conscience, Human Government) and makes much of others (Innocence, Promise) as background for redemption in Christ. Accordingly, progressive dispensationalism places greater emphasis on the continuity of biblical history and the interrelationships of biblical covenants. One such approach has four dispensations, (1) Patriarchal, encompassing biblical history until Sinai; (2) Mosaic, from Sinai to Christ's ascension; (3) Ecclesial, from the ascension to Christ's return; and (4) Zionic, the millennium and the new heavens and earth (Blaising and Bock, pp. 120–127).

Dispensational Distinctives. Dispensationalism is far more than a premillennial eschatology with a distinctive view of Israel's future. Blaising (Blaising and Bock, pp. 13–21) identified eight features: (1) the authority of scripture, (2) scriptural "dispensations" as historically sequential ways in which God relates to humans and humans relate to God, (3) the distinctive newness of the church due to the outpouring of the Holy Spirit at Pentecost (Acts 2), (4) the universal church and cooperative ministries versus a narrow denominationalism, (5) biblical prophecy and the future implications of salvation in Christ, (6) premillennialism (Christ will return after an end-time tribulation to rule the earth) and the pretribulational rapture (believers will be removed from the earth before the end-time tribulation), (7) expectation of Christ's imminent (any moment) return, and (8) the future turning of Israel as a nation to faith in Jesus as Messiah to fulfill Old Testament prophecies.

Taken together, these eight features broadly characterize all dispensationalists, yet many of the individual features are true of other Christians. For example, belief in the authority of scripture is common to all evangelical Christians. Some nondispensational theologians hold to a future national turning of Israel to faith in Jesus as Messiah. Nondispensational students of the Bible have also used the term "dispensation" to describe biblical epochs, yet they have not utilized the term in the specialized sense of a specific area of accountability which humans fail to obey, leading to divine judgment and a new dispensation. The pretribulational rapture view is probably the most unique and debatable of these features.

What some dispensationalists insist is its most essential and crucial feature is not included in the preceding list: the consistent use of literal (grammatical-historical) hermeneutics in the study of scripture. This is the second of three concepts proposed by Charles C. Ryrie (*Dispensationalism Today*, pp. 44–47; *Dispensationalism*, pp. 39–41) as the *sine qua non* of dispensationalism. Ryrie's first concept is the distinction between Israel and the church, which is alleged to result from the consistent use of literal hermeneutics. Yet nondispensationalists also make distinctions between Israel and the church, and one may note varying degrees of distinctiveness even among dispensationalists themselves. Ryrie's third concept, that the purpose of God in the Bible is to bring glory to himself, is in the view of many even less unique, and is actually commonplace in Christian theology. Accordingly, attention must be given to the matter of dispensationalism's "literal" hermeneutics.

Dispensational Hermeneutics. Traditional dispensationalists commonly affirm that their hermeneutic, especially their view of Israel and the church, is simply the result of consistently interpreting the Bible literally. If pressed, dispensationalists tend to describe literal interpretation as taking the Bible normally, as its authors meant it to be understood, through grammatical and historical exegesis, with awareness of and allowance for figures of speech (Ryrie, *Dispensationalism Today*, pp. 86–109; *Dispensationalism*, pp. 79–104; Ice in Willis and Master, *Issues in Dispensationalism*, pp. 29–49; Thomas in Pate, *Four Views*, pp. 180–182). Nondispensationalists (e.g., Bass, *Backgrounds to Dispensationalism*, pp. 21–24; Gerstner, *Wrongly Dividing the Word of Truth*, pp. 83–101) have alleged the inadequacies of this approach, arguing that it does not allow for metaphorical language at all. Yet this charge is overstated if not mistaken (DeWitt, *Dispensational Theology*, pp. 77–131; Johnson, *Expository Hermeneutics*, pp. 44–50; Tan, *The Interpretation of Prophecy*, pp. 29–39).

More to the point is the argument of Poythress (pp. 78–117) that dispensationalists who take into account only the obvious figurative language are still left with a "flat" interpretation which does not reckon seriously with the divine authorship, prevalent intertextuality, and canonical richness of the Bible. Poythress's approach in some ways anticipated what has recently come to be known as "theological interpretation," an approach that exposes the inadequacy of purely grammatical-historical-critical exegesis and insists on the value of a divinely-intended intertextual biblical unity, traditionally known as the "analogy of faith," and of the church's history of reflection on this theological richness (see further Daniel J. Treier, *Introducing Theological Interpretation of Scripture: Recovering a Christian Practice*. Grand Rapids, Mich.: Baker, 2008).

Progressive dispensationalists tend to advocate a more nuanced hermeneutic, one that augments grammatical-historical insights with emphasis on how biblical genres communicate meaning, the implications of biblical intertextuality, and the resulting biblical theology of Israel and the church (e.g., Bock in Blaising and Bock, pp. 57–105; Saucy, *The Case for Progressive Dispensationalism*, pp. 19–21). This approach is sometimes described as a "complementary" hermeneutic in which the NT interpretation of the OT brings out nuances not fully understood during OT times (Bock in Bateman, pp. 85–119). Traditional dispensational opponents of this approach construe it as adding further meanings to the literal meaning (Johnson in Bateman, pp. 63–84), sometimes styling these as spiritual or allegorical. Yet any such meanings are arguably not the result of atomizing or allegorizing interpretation, but are derived from historical exegesis, which develops implications that flow naturally from the literal meaning of the text seen in its canonical context. This approach is consistent to some extent with the tenor of the famous saying of St. Augustine, "*novum testamentum in vetere latet; vetus in novo patet*" (*Quaestiones in Heptateuchum*, 2.73), which teaches that the NT is latent or hidden in the OT, while the OT is patent or made clear in the NT.

On reflection, it is doubtful whether consistent literal hermeneutics has ever been the sole domain of dispensationalists. Older dispensationalists commonly insisted against covenant theologians that biblical prophecy must not be spiritualized, yet they affirmed typological or spiritual meanings of legal and narrative biblical texts, viewing them not only as historical but also as anticipatory of Christ and the church. Accordingly, differences in exegetical conclusions in debates between dispensationalists and nondispensationalists, not to mention in intramural debates between dispensationalists themselves, are often not due to disparate hermeneutical theory in the broad sense but to different individual variables in the application of a common exegetical methodology. Each exegete inevitably interprets individual texts from a previous overall theological understanding. Additional variables such as exegetical competence, rigor in exegetical effort, and human foibles and finiteness lead to the conclusion that disparate exegetical conclusions may be reached when the same exegetical method is applied by different exegetes. Accordingly, the common dispensationalist resort to claims about consistent literal hermeneutics is usually counterproductive.

Ongoing hermeneutical discussion among dispensationalists will likely focus on the relationship of this sort of grammatical-historical exegesis to literary, intertextual, and canonical dimensions of meaning. Traditional dispensationalists tend to view these with suspicion, fearing that the literal meaning of the biblical text will be eclipsed, if not outright allegorized. Progressive dispensationalists tend to welcome the expanded insights that come from these approaches, believing not only that they are complementary to the literal meaning of the text but are indeed the result of literal hermeneutics rightly understood.

Issues in Dispensational Hermeneutics. Certain areas of NT exegesis are key as dispensationalists continue discussion of the viability of the literary, intertextual, and canonical aspects of hermeneutics.

Synoptic Gospels. Traditional dispensationalists commonly have had doubts about the direct normative bearing of the teaching of Jesus for the church. This is due to the perception that Jesus's teachings are the culmination of biblical law, which is for Israel, not for the church, according to the dispensational reading of such Pauline texts as Gal 2:15–19; 3:10–14; Rom 3:19–31; 6:14–15. This affinity for Pauline texts on grace and faith leads some traditional dispensationalists to prefer the Gospel of John over the Synoptics. Another reason for this view is that dispensationalists note the prominence of the kingdom of God in Jesus's Synoptic teaching, and in their view the kingdom is the future time of prophetic blessing on Israel (the millennium), not the present rule of God over Christians. The dispensational approach to the teaching of Jesus as law comes to a head in the traditional dispensational understanding of the "Sermon on the Mount" (Matt 5–7) and of the "Great Commission" (Matt 28:18–20; cf. Mark 16:15–16; Luke 24:46–48).

In traditional dispensationalism the Sermon on the Mount is viewed as pure law, culminated by Jesus's life and teaching. As law, it has no primary or direct authority over Christians (who are under grace), yet it contains truths that are morally applicable to Christians, just like the ritual purity laws of the Old Testament (Scofield, pp. 999–1000, note 2; English, 997, note 4; Ryrie, *Dispensationalism Today*, pp. 105–109). However, even the secondary application to Christians of lessons or principles is problematic in the case of the Lord's Prayer (Matt 6:9–15; Luke 11:1–4), because the prayer seems to condition one's forgiveness on one's willingness to forgive.

Instead of viewing the relationship of being forgiven by God and being forgiving toward others as cause and effect (Christians forgive because they have been forgiven; cf. Matt 18:21–35; Eph 4:32–5:1), many traditional dispensationalists view the prayer as "legal ground" (Scofield, pp. 1002, note 1) where forgiveness is conditioned upon forgiving others. Progressive dispensationalists take a different view of these matters due to their understanding of continuity between law and grace and their view of the kingdom as both present and future (Martin in Blaising and Bock, pp. 248–263). Accordingly, in progressive dispensational understanding, the Sermon on the Mount is not merely a source of occasional applicational lessons and principles for the church but is directly mandatory for followers of Jesus at any time and place (Turner, pp. 703–705).

Another issue in dispensationalism's interpretation of the Synoptic Gospels is its understanding of the "Great Commission." Since dispensationalism views the church as distinct from Israel, beginning in Acts 2 (or even later in the case of ultra-dispensationalism), some dispensationalists have minimized Jesus's mandate that his disciples make disciples from all the nations. Matthew's version of the commission (28:18–20) causes special tension because in it Jesus commands the disciples to teach the nations to obey all he has taught them. For some dispensationalists, this smacks of a legalism which is in tension with and is superseded by Paul's teaching about grace motivating Christian obedience. Progressive dispensationalism has no issue here because it takes a more continuous view of Israel and the church and a more gracious view of the law in the Old Testament (Turner, pp. 712–714).

The Fourth Gospel. The Johannine Gospel's emphasis on individual faith and its relative lack of emphasis on the kingdom of God and the law of Moses endear it to traditional dispensationalists. One text that looms large in this regard is John 1:17, which by traditional dispensationalists is read to indicate a bifurcation between the Mosaic dispensation of obedience to law and the Christian dispensation of faith in God's grace (Scofield, p. 1115, note 1). However, there is no adversative conjunction ("but") between the two clauses in the Greek text of John 1:17, which simply juxtaposes the giving of the law through Moses and the coming of grace and truth through Jesus. The contextual relationship of Moses and Jesus is arguably more along the lines of progress and continuity than bifurcation and contrast. Also, it is apparent that the Johannine prologue's intertextual background prominently features Exodus 33—34, especially 34:6. Moses' indirect experience of God's grace and truth pales when compared with the revelation of grace and truth by the Word incarnate (John 1:14–18). Although the *New Scofield Reference Bible* (English 1967, p. 1124) repeats much of Scofield's note on John 1:17, it moderates the contrast between law and grace to some degree by acknowledging the presence of grace before Christ came.

Acts 2—3. In Acts 2:25–36 (cf. Ps 16:8–11; 110:1; 132:11) and 3:18–26 (cf. Deut 18:15–19; Gen 12:3), several OT citations support Peter's arguments about the significance of Christ's resurrection and ascension. For progressive dispensationalists (e.g. Bock in Blaising and Bock, pp. 47–61) these texts speak of the fulfillment of the Davidic Covenant (2 Sam 7:8–16) by the inauguration and consummation of God's kingdom, accomplished respectively by Christ's exaltation to God's right hand (Acts 2:30–35) and Christ's return to accomplish all that the prophets promised (Acts 3:20). Traditional dispensationalists resist the linkage of Acts 2 to OT Davidic promises, arguing that the throne of Acts 2:30 is God's heavenly throne, not a Davidic throne in any sense, and that Christ's kingdom is strictly future (Hodges in Willis and Master, pp. 172–178). This disagreement points to the need for dispensationalists to continue discussion of the nature of God's kingdom and of the fulfillment of the biblical covenants (Johnson and Bock in Bateman, pp. 121–225).

Paul, the Mystery, and the People of God. Paul repeatedly describes the distinctive nature of his message and mission as a "mystery" which was not previously revealed or understood (e.g., Rom 16:25–27; Eph 3:3–12; Col 1:24–27). This mystery apparently centers on the inclusion of the gentiles in the people of God simply through faith in Jesus. On its face, this teaching poses discontinuity between Israel and the church since it portrays the equal participation of gentiles with Jews in the church as something not revealed through the OT prophets. Ultradispensationalists make much of this teaching, positing the church as a strictly Pauline entity, entirely separate not only from OT prophecy but even from the teaching of the other apostles of Christ. Traditional dispensationalists have a less rigorous yet clearly discontinuous view in which the church as a Pauline mystery temporarily intervenes in God's prophetic program for Israel. Progressive dispensationalists take an even more moderate view of this discontinuity, arguing that the mystery encompasses only the means of gentile salvation. That gentiles could be saved is not foreign to the OT. That gentiles could be saved through faith in Christ alone, without Torah observance, and be incorporated through the Spirit into a new community with Christian Jews is a new revelation (see further Saucy, *The Case for Progressive Dispensationalism*, pp. 143–173).

Other Pauline texts appear to speak of Paul's teaching about the church as continuous with OT promises about Israel's ultimate redemption. Such texts caution against a simplistic reading of Paul's mystery texts. Paul states that his gospel was previously promised by the OT prophets (Rom 1:2). Paul portrays the salvation of the gentiles with a horticultural metaphor of wild olive branches being grafted into a cultivated olive tree, referring to God's promises to the patriarchs (Rom 11:13–25). Paul teaches that gentiles, formerly bereft of God's mercy, have through Christ in the Spirit become sharers in God's promises to Israel and members of a new messianic community with Jewish believers in Jesus (Eph 2:11–22). In light of their historic emphasis on the distinctiveness of Israel and the church, dispensationalists of all varieties must reflect on the ecclesial unity of Jews and Gentiles portrayed here (see further Hoch in Blaising and Bock, pp. 98–126).

1 Peter. In the general or catholic epistles, the church's current problems are commonly addressed from the standpoint of Israel's past problems (e.g., Heb 3:7—4:16; Jas 2:21–26; 2 Pet 2:1–22; Jude 5—19). This implicit continuity is augmented at times with explicit intertextual connections of the church's identity to Israel's identity as the people of God. (e.g., 1 Pet 2:9–10; Glenny in Blaising and Bock, pp. 156–187). This prevalent implicit and explicit connection of the church and Israel poses a problem for traditional dispensationalism, which posits a great degree of discontinuity between the two. But the continuity that is evident in this text poses a problem for progressive dispensationalism as well: has the church replaced Israel?

Traditional dispensationalism's view that the church is an intercalation that interrupts God's plan for Israel is difficult to maintain in the face of the NT connections of Israel and the church. Progressive dispensationalism's view that the church is an unexpected expansion of God's plan for Israel also has difficulties due to its similarity to various forms of covenant theology that posit the church as the new recipient of God's promises originally made to Israel. It is incumbent upon progressive dispensationalists to explain the difference between their views and those of covenant theologians (see further Hoch, pp. 255–262).

The Apocalypse. Well-known pop-dispensational approaches to the apocalypse ("dispensensationalism") generally involve attempts to interpret the book of Revelation through current events. Traditional dispensationalists take a strictly futurist approach to the Apocalypse, viewing Revelation 4:1 as the beginning of a portrayal of things to come. Some ultradispensationalists go even further in holding that the Lord's day in Revelation 1:10 refers to the OT day of the Lord, the time of final judgment and blessing. In this view the seven churches of Asia (1:4, 11, 20 2:1—3:22; 22:16) are understood as Jewish congregations that will exist during the tribulation period. Traditional dispensationalists have frequently held a literal-historicist view that the churches are not only first century congregations but also portray prophetically the general course of church history in seven periods of time. Progressive dispensationalists take a more eclectic view of the apocalypse and attempt to incorporate what they view to be legitimate insights of the preterist and idealist views into a moderately futurist view of the book.

It appears that further dispensational discussions of the Apocalypse should focus on the genre of the book, its historical setting, and its prevalent symbolism. Some traditional dispensationalists have advocated the prophetic genre of the book, apparently because they think that this buttresses a literalist, futurist approach and lessens the importance of the book's prevalent symbolism. This advocacy of Revelation as nonapocalyptic prophecy is problematic in terms of the Apocalypse itself but also betrays a lack of understanding of biblical prophecy as a poetic genre that speaks of the future only as a means of addressing its immediate audience at a covenantal and ethical level. Progressive dispensationalism's "already not yet" view of the kingdom and its willingness to consider preterism's stress on the original setting of the Apocalypse may enable it to bring together the original and ultimate implications of the Apocalypse (see further Thomas and Pate in Pate, pp 133–229).

A Way Forward. It is apparent from the complexity of canonical scripture, from recent developments in hermeneutical theory, and from their own current debates that dispensationalists of all varieties should give further thought to interpretive theory and practice. Additional discussion over the propriety of grammatical-historical exegesis alone (traditional dispensationalism), versus grammatical-historical *and* literary-theological exegesis (progressive dispensationalism), might be facilitated by reviewing two resources. The work of E. D. Hirsch is relatively familiar to credible dispensational scholars. Hirsch's theory of meaning and implication and his notion of typology of meaning should be pondered as a way forward from what Poythress called flat interpretation (E. D. Hirsch, *Validity in Interpretation.* New Haven: Yale, 1967, pp. 44–51, 61–67, 126 note 37, 265–274). More recently Kevin Vanhoozer has attempted to articulate an approach that is both author-centered and conversant with recent hermeneutical developments such as speech-act theory and theological interpretation. Vanhoozer's informed discussion of author-centered and ethically directed interpretation could be a helpful starting point for fruitful discussions among dispensationalists (Kevin J. Vanhoozer, *Is There a Meaning in this Text?* Grand Rapids, Mich.: Zondervan, 1998, pp. 197–452).

Dispensational discussions of the pervasive phenomenon of biblical intertextuality must reckon with the implications of the divine origin of scripture. Dispensationalists agree that grammatical-historical exegesis of individual biblical texts is the starting point for theology. Dispensationalists do not agree that such exegesis if done rightly leads inevitably to literary and canonical aspects of the texts. Yet biblical intertextuality necessitates a canonical approach to exegesis, one that does justice to the continuity underlying the intertextuality. One canonical issue looms large, not only in provincial dispensational discussions but also in the overall history of Christian biblical interpretation. This is the relationship of Israel and the church, perhaps the greatest test case for any theology which purports to be biblical and Christian. Dispensationalism's insistence that God's action in Christ does not eventuate in the abandonment of Israel positions it for a unique approach to the supersessionism question. Perhaps the ongoing intramural dispensational discussions of the relationship between Israel and the church will help facilitate a way forward for the entire church.

[*See also* Canonical Criticism; Evangelical Interpretation; Historical Criticism, *subentry* Hebrew Bible; Historical Criticism, *subentry* New Testament; Intertextuality; Narrative Criticism and Narrative Hermeneutics; Pentecostal Interpretation; *and* Theological Interpretation.]

BIBLIOGRAPHY

Archer, Gleason L., et al. *The Rapture: Pre-, Mid-, or Post-Tribulational?* Grand Rapids, Mich.: Zondervan, 1984. Interactive presentations and responses on an issue frequently viewed as essential for dispensationalism.

Baker, Charles F. *A Dispensational Theology.* Grand Rapids, Mich.: Grace Bible College, 1971. An evangelical theology with an "ultradispensational" views of Israel, the Church and eschatology.

Bass, Clarence B. *Backgrounds to Dispensationalism: Its Historical Genesis and Ecclesiastical Implications.* Grand Rapids, Mich.: Baker, 1960. Reprinted by Wipf and Stock, 2005. A former dispensationalist's critique of classic dispensationalism's novelty and hermeneutics.

Bateman, Herbert W. ed. *Three Central Issues in Contemporary Dispensationalism: A Comparison of Traditional and Progressive Views.* Grand Rapids, Mich.: Kregel, 1999. A helpful and accessible source for understanding the different types of dispensationalism.

Blaising, Craig A., and Darrell L. Bock, eds. *Dispensationalism, Israel and the Church: The Search for Definition.* Grand Rapids, Mich.: Zondervan, 1992. A collection of essays that present seminal progressive dispensational thinking.

Blaising, Craig A., and Darrell L. Bock. *Progressive Dispensationalism.* Wheaton, Ill.: Bridgepoint, 1993. Comprehensive biblical theology from a progressive dispensational perspective.

Darby, John N. *The Collected Writings of J. N. Darby.* 34 vols. William Kelly, ed. London: G. Morrish, 1867–1883. Seminal writings for the so-called "Plymouth Brethren" movement and for dispensationalism in particular.

DeWitt, D. S. *Dispensational Theology in America during the Twentieth Century.* Grand Rapids, Mich.: Grace Bible College, 2002. A well-informed, nuanced, irenic discussion by a moderate ultradispensationalist.

English, E. Schuyler, et al., eds. *New Scofield Reference Bible.* New York: Oxford, 1967. A revision of the 1917 Scofield Reference Bible. The editorial committee included Frank E. Gaebelein, William Culbertson, Charles L. Feinberg, Allan A. Mac Rae, Clarence E Mason, Alva J. McClain, Wilbur M. Smith, and John F. Walvoord.

Feinberg, John S., ed. *Continuity and Discontinuity: Perspectives on the Relationship between the Old and New Testaments. Essays in Honor of S. Lewis Johnson Jr.* Westchester, Ill.: Crossway, 1988. Several authors' comments on foundational issues from a variety of theological positions.

Fuller, Daniel P. *Gospel and Law: Contrast or Continuum? The Hermeneutics of Dispensationalism and Covenant Theology.* Grand Rapids, Mich.: Eerdmans, 1980. Detailed analysis of the two systems by a nondispensationalist.

Gerstner, J. H. *Wrongly Dividing the Word of Truth: A Critique of Dispensationalism.* Brentwood, Tenn.: Wolgemuth and Hyatt, 1991. A heavy-handed polemic by a reformed theologian.

Hoch, C. B., Jr. *All Things New: The Significance of Newness for Biblical Theology.* Grand Rapids, Mich.: Baker, 1995. A progressive dispensational approach to NT Biblical Theology. Helpful appendices (253–318) discuss the relationship of the Church to Israel.

Johnson, Elliott E. *Expository Hermeneutics.* Grand Rapids, Mich.: Zondervan, 1990. The most detailed and informed discussion of hermeneutics from a dispensational perspective.

McClain, Alva J. *The Greatness of the Kingdom.* Chicago: Moody, 1968. An inductive study of the kingdom of God in the Bible. Provides a dispensational biblical theology without much emphasis on the dispensations.

Pate, C. Marvin, ed. *Four Views on the Book of Revelation.* Grand Rapids, Mich.: Zondervan, 1998. A collection of statements of preterist, idealist, and futurist views of Revelation, the latter supplied by both progressive (Marvin Pate) and classical (Robert Thomas) dispensationalists.

Poythress, Vern S. *Understanding Dispensationalists.* Grand Rapids, Mich.: Zondervan, 1987. An irenic volume by a covenant theologian, which facilitates dialogue between dispensationalists and nondispensationalists.

Ryrie, Charles C. *Dispensationalism.* Chicago: Moody, 1995. A virtual reprint of the 1965 volume, with updates on issues raised by progressive dispensationalism.

Ryrie, Charles C. *Dispensationalism Today.* Chicago: Moody, 1965. A classic and irenic exposition of revised dispensationalism by a longtime professor at Dallas Theological Seminary.

Saucy, Robert L. *The Case for Progressive Dispensationalism.* Grand Rapids, Mich.: Zondervan, 1993. A careful exegetical and theological work, conversant with both dispensational and non-dispensational scholarship.

Saucy, Robert L. "The Crucial Issue between Dispensational and Nondispensational Systems." *Criswell Theological Review* 1 (1986): 149–165. An article that argues that the relationship between Israel and the church is the crucial issue, not hermeneutics.

Scofield, C. I., ed. *The Scofield Reference Bible.* New York: Oxford, 1917. The edition of the Bible originally published in 1909, but the 1917 edition has been the basis of subsequent reprints.

Tan, Paul Lee. *The Interpretation of Prophecy*. Winona Lake, Ind.: BMH, 1974. A detailed but somewhat provincial and dated dispensational defense of literal interpretation of prophecy.

Turner, David L. "Matthew Among the Dispensationalists." *Journal of the Evangelical Theological Society* 53 (2010): 697–716. A contrast of traditional and progressive dispensational understandings of key texts and themes in Matthew.

Willis, Wesley R., and John R. Master, eds. *Issues in Dispensationalism*. Chicago: Moody Press, 1994. A collection of essays from a classical dispensational perspective responding to issues raised by progressive dispensationalists.

David L. Turner

E

Eastern Orthodox Interpretation

Eastern Orthodox churches have long remained fervently committed to the organic interrelationship between scripture and ecclesial tradition (Florovsky 1972; Bulgakov 1988, pp. 9–26; Staniloae 1994, pp. 37–78; Vassiliadis 2005; Stylianopoulos 2008). From its inception, they believe, the church relied both on a canon of Holy Scripture (taken over from Judaism and eventually expanded with a "New" Testament) and on a "canon of truth" or rule of faith based at once in scripture itself and in the sanctified intuition of the church (Irenaeus, *Against Heresies* 1.9.4; 1.10.1–3). The Christian biblical canon and the theological canons of its legitimate interpretation developed in tandem, in a necessary but fruitful circularity. Theology, for the Orthodox, *is* the interpretation of scripture because scripture, though diversified in its contents, is intrinsically theological, giving the church access to the sacred mysteries of the Trinity, the person of Jesus Christ, and the means to salvation and deification.

Biblical interpretation in the Orthodox traditions has its formative roots in five principal sources: (1) the hermeneutical and exegetical legacies of the Greek and Byzantine church fathers; (2) the major doctrinal controversies of the age of the ecumenical councils (300–800 C.E.), in which theological interpretation of scripture played a vital role; (3) the religious use of the Bible in the context of liturgy and devotion; (4) the monastic engagement of scripture, especially as represented in the *Philokalia*; and (5) the response of contemporary Orthodox theologians to the challenges posed by biblical higher criticism.

Legacies of Greek and Byzantine Patristic Interpretation. Rather than a mere directory to methods of interpretation, the Orthodox tradition assumed from its patristic authorities a broad theological and christocentric vision of the economy (*oikonomia*) or "strategy" of divine revelation. Irenaeus's doctrine of "recapitulation" (cf. Eph 1:10), whereby all of cosmic history had its focus and climax in the divine incarnation in Jesus Christ (*Against Heresies*, Books 4—5), was extended by Byzantine theologians (e.g., Athanasius, *On the Incarnation*; Gregory of Nyssa, *Catechetical Oration*; Cyril of Alexandria, *Commentary on John*; Maximus the Confessor, *To Thalassius* 60) and became a mainstay of Orthodox hermeneutics. While certain of his theological speculations had been condemned by an ecumenical council in 553, elements of Origen's teaching on the economy of scripture (see Daley 1998) also endured in Eastern Christianity. His notion of the "embodiment" of the Word in the scriptural text paralleling the Word's gracious accommodation to humanity in the incarnation, and his assertion that the Holy Spirit had providentially crafted and even problematized the biblical text in order to spur readers to greater spiritual maturity (*On First Principles*, Book 4), found fresh expressions in the Cappadocian fathers, in Eastern monastic writers, in Dionysius the Areopagite, and in Maximus the Confessor. From Origen, too, stemmed the principle of the inexhaustibility and polyvalence of the Word, which Greek and Byzantine patristic interpreters largely took for granted. Christ himself was the embedded "author" of scripture and so also constituted its "fuller sense" (*sensus plenior*), its ever richer spiritual meaning for the church. As one modern Orthodox theologian puts it, "for the Fathers the Bible *is* Christ, because his every word brings us into the presence of the one who spoke it" (Evdokimov 2011, p. 194).

Eastern Orthodoxy has thoroughly embraced the patristic distinction between "literal" and "spiritual" interpretation, but less as a science of fixed "senses" of scripture than as dynamic "reading strategies" (Young 1997, pp. 117, 212, 247, 299) for discerning the trinitarian and christocentric "scope" of biblical texts—what Athanasius called the "*skopos* of faith" (*Orations against the Arians* 3.35). Largely through the Cappadocian fathers, Gregory of Nyssa in particular, Orthodoxy learned to trust theologically disciplined use of spiritual (figurative, allegorical, etc.) interpretation in relation to the literal meaning (*historia*) of texts. Gregory demonstrated in his *Life of Moses*, for example, how spiritual interpretation could amplify rather than subvert the literal. An event like the Sinai theophany (Exod 19—34), he proposed, was already "literally" less about Israel's reception of the Torah than about God's people being initiated in the ineffable mystery of the triune God, with Moses as a mediator. The "spiritual" or "visionary" interpretation, or *theôria*, in turn explored the deeper nuances of this sublime mystagogical adventure in ways edifying to the church in the present.

From the so-called "Antiochene school" of patristic exegesis (Diodore of Tarsus, John Chrysostom, Theodore of Mopsuestia, Theodoret of Cyrus et al.), Orthodoxy inherited a healthy skepticism toward unconstrained allegorism and respect for a mode of figural exegesis that enhanced typologies and symbolism already warranted in biblical *historia*. Antiochene *theôria* sought to recover the "spiritual" horizon of the biblical authors themselves and their overarching perception of sacred revelation. John Breck, reclaiming *theôria* for contemporary Orthodox hermeneutics, calls it "an inspired vision or contemplation of divinely revealed Truth, granted both to the [prophetic and] apostolic writer *and to future interpreters* by the Holy Spirit," thus aligning it with the *sensus plenior* (Breck, pp. 36–37). Maximus the Confessor called this "the power of the literal meaning (*historia*) in the Spirit, which is constantly being realized and abounding into its fullness" (*To Thalassius*, 17).

Through influential Byzantine interpreters like Cyril of Alexandria, Dionysius the Areopagite, and Maximus, the "anagogical" *theôria* of the Alexandrians, aiming at sublime contemplation of all things in God, and the tempered *theôria* of the Antiochene heritage effectively converged. The "fullness" of scripture to be envisioned was the height, depth, and breadth of the incarnational mystery of Jesus Christ, who mediated to humanity both knowledge of the Trinity and deifying grace. Cyril opens his *Glaphyra* on Genesis: "We will explain what happened historically, such that, transposing the narrative through figure (*typos*) and shadow (*skia*), we will render a clear account, our explanation disposing us toward the mystery of Christ, with Christ himself as the projected goal, since it is true that Christ himself is the end (*telos*) of the Law and Prophets" (cf. Rom 10:11). Cyril holds true to form in his New Testament exegesis as well. His *Commentary on John* explores the individual pericopae of Jesus's ministry each as a montage of intimations of the mystery of divine incarnation.

Dionysius, in his treatise *On the Divine Names*, imagines all of scripture as a magnificent hierarchy of figures and symbols that serve paradoxically to conceal the incomprehensible Trinity from the faithful, and, through appropriate anagogical interpretation, graciously to disclose God's truth, beauty, and goodness according to creatures' receptive capacity. Maximus, in his hermeneutical synthesis, uses many forms of spiritual and anagogical interpretation to unearth the deeper christocentric riches of scripture (Blowers 1991, pp. 196–228). His exegesis, often directed toward ambiguities or "difficulties" (*aporiae*) in the biblical text, puts into practice his conviction that the divine Logos is always working through the *logoi* (semantically pregnant "words") of scripture to educate and transform the Christian and the church. Overall, Byzantine patristic hermeneutics bequeathed on later Orthodoxy a careful distinction between—but also interweaving of—*theologia* and *oikonomia*, the mystery of the triune God and the "economy" of his self-revelation in sacred history and in the ongoing life of the church.

The legacy of the great patristic commentators enshrined itself in Orthodox tradition through various media, not only through the transmitted commentaries and homilies themselves but also the compilation of *catena* ("chain") commentaries stringing together the comments of respected authorities on biblical books, and florilegia, or anthologies of statements from the fathers on exegetical and theological issues. In Russia, Maximus the Greek (1470–1555) played an important, albeit controversial, role in referencing patristic interpretation while also introducing proto-critical hermeneutical principles for the study of the Bible in the church (Negrov 2008, pp. 51–54).

The Refiner's Fire of Doctrinal Controversy. The biblical commentaries and homilies of the Greek fathers frequently had a polemical as well as didactic and pastoral orientation, since many were composed amid doctrinal debates where precise interpretations of scripture were decisive. Very early, for example, Greek patristic commentary on Genesis targeted pagan cosmology as well as those gnostic and Marcionite interpretations that forced a wedge between the Hebrew scriptures and the emerging New Testament. From Theophilus of Antioch (*To Autolycus*) in the second century to the Cappadocians Basil of Caesarea (*Homilies on the Hexaemeron*) and Gregory of Nyssa (*Apologia on the Hexaemeron*) in the fourth, Greek patristic exegetes elaborated sophisticated theological interpretations of the Genesis creation account that claimed that Jesus Christ was the true "beginning" (Gen 1:1; John 1:1) of the world, and that the whole history of salvation was already latent in the six-day creation narrative. In doing so they relied not on pure allegorization but on something more akin to Augustine's theologically "literal" interpretation in his commentaries on Genesis, which actually admitted multiple exegetical approaches to the creation story so as to expose its metaphysical and theological complexities. Such is exactly what freed later Orthodox hermeneutics from polarizing spiritual and literal exegeses, in the interest of holistic interpretations that aspired first and foremost to doctrinal coherence, or what Gregory of Nyssa called the "*logos* of truth."

The interrelation between *theologia* and *oikonomia* so crucial to Eastern Orthodox hermeneutics was sharpened in the fourth-century trinitarian controversy. Defending the full divinity of the Son of God against Arian opponents who used the Gospels' depictions of Jesus's weakness and ignorance to prove he was a creature, Athanasius's famous "double account" of the incarnation ascribed the miracles and supernatural deeds to the divine Son and the frailties to Jesus's human constitution. This exegetical axiom in turn funded the doctrine of the *communicatio idiomatum*, the mutual communication of divine and human attributes in Christ, and ultimately also the Chalcedonian Definition (451) of Christ as "one person in two (unconfused) natures." Gregory of Nazianzus, in his *Theological Orations*, mastered the art of rhetorically interweaving *theologia* and *oikonomia*, drawing together a wide array of biblical texts and allusions to convey the union in Christ of the eternally-generated Son of God and the created human nature of Jesus the child of Mary (*Orations* 29–30; see McGuckin 2005).

Also amid controversy over the Trinity, Gregory of Nyssa modeled a form of theological and mystical exegesis based on painstaking analysis of the nature of biblical language itself. Against Arian rationalists who allegedly settled for theologically superficial and baldly literalistic readings of sensitive biblical texts to support their unitarian teaching, Gregory ruled that "following the suggestions of scripture,

[we] have learned that the [divine] nature is unnamable and unspeakable, and we say that every term either invented by human custom or handed down to us by the scriptures is indeed explanatory of our conceptions of the divine nature but does not include the signification of that nature itself" (*To Ablabius*). Trinitarian orthodoxy relied at once on the apophatic denial of any pretention to capture God's mystery through scripture's own language and on assiduous exegesis of its testimonies to the relations between Father, Son, and Holy Spirit in the economy of creation and redemption. Eastern Orthodox trinitarian dogma has never moved beyond this rule of theological interpretation.

The extended Eastern christological controversies of the fifth, sixth, and seventh centuries also proved to be an important testing ground for the theologically reasoned "literal" interpretation of scripture. There are many examples, but an especially extraordinary one is Maximus the Confessor's exegesis of Jesus's prayer in Gethsemane (Matt 26:39 and parallels). Maximus's seventh-century Monothelite opponents insisted that, lest there be an opposition of divine and human wills in Christ, his singular divine will must have already preempted any human volition. Integrating careful exegesis of Jesus's prayer with the precedential logic of the Chalcedonian Definition, Maximus argued (*Opusculum* 6) that the *literal* meaning of the Gethsemane prayer was Jesus's handing over of his human will to the will of the Father. The two wills were different but not intrinsically opposed. The agony of Gethsemane demonstrated precisely the consonance of divine and human wills for the sake of human salvation. This teaching was vindicated at the Council of Constantinople of 681 and became standard in Orthodox (Chalcedonian) Christology.

The Bible in Orthodox Liturgy and Devotion. Christian liturgy, from its inception, has been an instrumental mode of "performative" interpretation, an embodied participation in the living Word. A presupposition of liturgy in the Eastern Orthodox tradition is that the worshipping congregation here and now, in the long wake of Christ's incarnation, already stands at the threshold of the eschatological age, and that it sacramentally rehearses, through ritual action and anamnesis, the drama of sacred history (the economy of salvation) that continues to play out to its consummation. In the Divine Liturgy, Orthodox Christians hear scripture read, chanted, prayed, and preached (Lash 2008; Theokritoff 2005). Visually, they behold the Gospel Book in procession through the congregation, the so-called Little Entrance. The Eucharistic Prayer (anaphora) and the liturgy as a whole—its prayers, litanies, hymns, etc.—are saturated with scriptural language and allusions, in an ambiance intended to convey the spatial convergence of heaven and earth. Icons of Christ, the Theotokos (Virgin Mother), biblical saints and events, and the historic saints of the Christian East, are venerated in liturgy and in private devotion, drawing the faithful into a perduring communion of saints. As in the West, biblical readings in the liturgies are regulated according to the major feasts of the liturgical calendar, providing rhythms and sequences that frame Christian identification with—*and in*—scripture's salvific narrative. Baptismal and eucharistic practices are shot through with biblical typologies. As in the ancient Greek church (see Daniélou 1956, pp. 70–113), baptism simulates not only new creation, a saving deluge, a new exodus through water, a reentry into paradise, but also, most importantly, death, burial, and resurrection with Christ (Rom 6:3–5). The Eucharist abounds in Paschal symbols that bridge the ancient Passover with the new Pascha of Christ in the church's defining sacred meal (Daniélou, pp. 127–176).

Already the early Byzantine commentators on the Divine Liturgy like Dionysius the Areopagite and Maximus the Confessor reflected less on the biblical meaning disclosed in the liturgy than on the significance of the very action of reading scripture publicly in the assembly (*synaxis*). Promulgating sacred history and scriptural admonitions prepared believers morally to be worthy of sacramental grace (Dionysius, *Ecclesiastical Hierarchy* 3; Maximus, *Mystagogia* 10), while the reading of the Gospel text was a virtual epiphany of the Logos as High Priest descending from the heavenly sanctuary to lead the faithful to "the vision of spiritual principles and realities" (Maximus, *Mystagogia* 13).

And yet the broader liturgy, notably the hymns coming into use in the Divine Office, did indeed carry typological and allegorical interpretations of biblical texts to help the faithful to identify with the texts morally and spiritually (Theokritoff). The *kontakia*, or sermonic hymns, of Romanos the Melodist (ca. 485–ca. 560), the most celebrated Byzantine hymn writer (see Lash 1995), exhibited an imaginative interpretive poetics designed to engross audiences in the biblical story. Like an ancient counterpart to "reader-response," they prompted audiences to appropriate the meaning of the narrative existentially, sometimes using the reinforcing refrains between a *kontakion*'s strophes. The Syrian-born Romanos, who provided a living link to the richly poetic hermeneutics of Ephrem the Syrian and the Syriac Christian exegetical tradition, implemented a number of consistent interpretive techniques (see Trigg 2001). Like Ephrem, he favored collapsing together biblical types, as in his first *kontakion On the Nativity*, in which he parallels the "unwatered root" (cf. Isa 11:1), the "undug well" from which David desired to drink (cf. 2 Sam 23:15–17), and the Virgin's womb destined to satisfy the thirst of Adam and David alike. Romanos also used amplified paraphrase of biblical stories, inventing exchanges between characters to evoke the full spiritual force of a narrative, as when he stages intimate conversation between Mary and Christ on his way to crucifixion (*On the Lament of the Theotokos*), and a dialogue between Christ, just before his ascension, and the apostles struggling with separation anxiety at his imminent departure (*On the Ascension*). Generally, Romanos seeks to elicit all the latent dramatic elements (irony, suspense, etc.) in biblical stories to enhance the audience's identification in them.

Also noteworthy in this hymnological tradition is the Great Canon composed by Andrew of Crete (seventh century) and used in Great Lent, which employs the model of closely identifying its audience directly with individual biblical personages to solicit earnest penitential response: "Having rivaled the first-created Adam by my transgression, I realize that I am stripped naked of God and of the everlasting kingdom and bliss through my sins." "Like Cain, we too, O wretched soul, have likewise offered, to the Creator of all, foul deeds, defective sacrifice, and a useless life. Therefore, we too are condemned."

On the whole, Orthodox liturgy, iconography, and music communicate and interpret scripture narratively, rhetorically, didactically, symbolically, and not least aesthetically and dramatically, shaping the identity of Orthodox Christians over and beyond a merely cerebral reception of the sacred texts. As God's own Word, scripture is understood to be *sacramental* in its nature and power, and in its use in connection with worship, preaching, and the sacraments its *pastoral* significance is also made manifest (Bathrellos 2005).

Biblical Interpretation in the Eastern Christian Monastic Tradition. Interpretation of the Bible in the monastic context cannot be segregated from the larger developmental streams of Eastern Orthodox hermeneutics. Historically, many of the prolific Orthodox theologians and biblical interpreters have been ascetics, monks, or monk-bishops, and monastic influence has permeated the liturgical and devotional use of the Bible in Orthodox churches. The strongly pragmatic orientation of early Eastern monastic interpretation took shape in the primarily oral culture of desert anchoritism in the fourth and fifth centuries, well documented in the collections of *Apophthegmata patrum [et matrum]* (*Sayings of the Desert Fathers and Mothers*) that eventually took written form (see Burton-Christie 1993). These traditions tell the stories of "conferences" between younger monks and their sage elders, who discouraged formal questions about the theological meaning of scripture and pointed their disciples toward the urgent ascetical and ethical exigencies of obedience to the Word. Discouraging the private reading of scripture, since it could render monks too curious, they encouraged the memorization of scriptures heard in worship and in teaching, which could help fortify the soul against demonic assault and keep monks focused. The *Apophthegmata* also contain abundant instructions using biblical *exempla*, the profiles of biblical saints who modeled for monks (and for all Christian faithful) the virtues integral to godly living.

The most pronounced influence of monastic biblical interpretation, however, obtained through the writings of great monastic sages of the fourth to fifteenth centuries compiled in the eighteenth-century *Philokalia*, now the spiritual handbook of the Eastern churches translated into a number of languages. Among its many constituent authors are venerable figures in Orthodox tradition like John Cassian, Maximus the Confessor, John of Damascus, Symeon the New Theologian, and Gregory Palamas. Maximus and Symeon are especially exemplary, as both of them bridged the hermeneutical pragmatism of the desert tradition with the contemplative and anagogical approach to scripture inherited from Origen. Maximus composed a treatise on *The Ascetic Life* that mimicked the pattern of the "conference" in the *Apophthegmata*, with an elder monk instructing a younger monk on fulfilling the evangelical commandments of Christ. Some of Maximus's ascetical *Chapters* (*Capita*), which included not only practical teaching from scripture but figural and allegorical interpretations to encourage spiritual growth, were included in the *Philokalia* and thus reached a wider public.

Much later, Symeon the New Theologian (949–1022), an eminent monk of Constantinople, emulated Maximus's hermeneutics, proposing that all of scripture teemed with spiritual verities waiting to be mined. Literal, allegorical, and mystical interpretations all appear in Symeon's ascetical and catechetical writings as means to advance the soul toward greater intimacy with God (Alfeyev 2000, pp. 43–72). This deeper understanding, however, was available only to the worthy, and granted incrementally. In one of his dicta included in the *Philokalia*, Symeon warns: "Many read the Holy Scriptures and hear them read. But few can grasp their meaning and import. For some what is said in the Scriptures is impossible, for others it is altogether beyond belief. Some again interpret them wrongly: they apply things said about the present to the future, and things said about the future to the past or else to what happens daily. In this way they reveal a lack of true judgment and discernment in things both human and divine" (*Practical and Theological Texts* 60; Palmer 1995, p. 36). Symeon's disciple and eventual biographer, Nicetas Stethatos, doubtless echoes his teacher when he claims that "the reading of the scriptures means one thing for those who have but recently embraced the life of holiness, another for those who have attained the middle state, and another for those who are moving rapidly toward perfection" (*On the Inner Nature of Things, and on the Perfection of the Intellect*; Palmer 1995, pp. 133–134). Symeon and other *Philokalia* authors cherished John 5:39 ("Search the scriptures"), considering it Christ's injunction to penetrate the inexhaustible depths of the Bible. For the twelfth-century writer Peter of Damascus, it was an invitation to the diligent to pursue the *sensus plenior*, since the texts continuously conveyed fresh meanings to those growing in grace and truth. Remarkably, within this context of spiritual reading (i.e., *lectio divina* in Western monastic tradition), Peter affirms the relative utility of "secular knowledge" in aiding understanding of the biblical texts, but only on condition that it "acts as a vehicle for the higher wisdom of the Spirit" (*Discourses* 28; Palmer 1984, pp. 263–268). For these and other witnesses in the *Philokalia*, the *process* of searching the scriptures, and not alone the discernment of its spiritual riches, is saving and deifying (see Burton-Christie 2012).

Again, largely because of the *Philokalia*, this tradition is not restricted exclusively to monastic settings, and at least one contemporary Orthodox biblical scholar, John Breck, has commended the cultivation of such a *lectio divina* for Orthodox laity (Breck, pp. 67–86).

Contemporary Orthodox Interpretation and the "Neo-Patristic" Synthesis. Among Orthodox churches, the rise of biblical higher criticism did not ignite the same profound sensation experienced in Roman Catholic and Protestant contexts, and thus, not surprisingly, far fewer critical biblical exegetes and higher-critical studies of scripture have emerged from Orthodox circles. In the twentieth century, certain prominent Orthodox theologians, like the late Romanian theologian Dumitru Staniloae, issued strong censures of the "demythologizing" tendencies of Protestant biblical criticism (Staniloae 1980, pp. 109–154). Staniloae and the Russian émigré theologian Georges Florovsky both challenged radical historicism and called for an approach to the Bible that attended to its character as sacred or covenantal history, a history "thick" with internal typologies, images, and symbolisms, as well as narratives (Staniloae 1980, pp. 109–180; Staniloae 1994, 15–36; Florovsky, pp. 17–36). But they also rejected the Protestant fundamentalism that treated the Bible as a virtual scientific textbook. "The Bible is no authority on social science, as it is no authority on astronomy" (Florovsky, p. 34). Meanwhile some Orthodox theologians recognized real utility in the new methods of biblical criticism. Sergius Bulgakov, another eminent Russian émigré theologian, affirmed the relative value of tradition-historical and literary approaches to the Bible, suggesting that they were already being incorporated into dogmatic and religious interpretation and could operate constructively within the organic stream of ecclesial tradition (Bulgakov, pp. 16–25).

Protestantism in the twentieth century witnessed the emergence of neoorthodoxy, which provided a vitally important constructive criticism of the scientific study of the Bible and helped renew theological interpretation. Roman Catholicism saw the rise of "La Nouvelle Théologie" in France, attempting critically and constructively to deal with the effects of modernism and secularism and to generate a *ressourcement* that would bring patristic theology and hermeneutics to bear on contemporary concerns of the church's faith. Meanwhile, Orthodox thinkers undertook their own "Neo-Patristic Synthesis" to revitalize theology and biblical interpretation. In some respects this is a misnomer, for the vital patristic element in Orthodox hermeneutics had never been lost. What was new was the proactive application of patristic insights to a situation where, especially for Orthodoxy in the West, the churches encountered an intellectual culture in which biblical studies was increasingly being secularized. Theologians like Staniloae, Florovsky, and Paul Evdokimov recurred to the patristic consensus, wherein the church was the primary matrix of biblical interpretation because only in the church was available a time-tested rule or *skopos* of faith to understand scripture in its christocentric wholeness (Florovsky, pp. 72–120; Williams 1993; Evdokimov, pp. 194–199). Their point was rather simple. Interpreting the Bible, for the church fathers, was not ultimately about rendering sacred revelation transparent to the conditions of history and culture; it was about achieving communion with Christ the Word. As Staniloae puts it, "The words of scripture are the inevitable occasion for us to enter through the work of the Spirit into relation with the authentic person of Christ who transcends them. . . ." (1994, p. 44).

Orthodox biblical scholars have taken this "Neo-Patristic Synthesis" to heart in defining the science of exegesis in an Orthodox context. Breck's appeal to contemplative interpretation (*theôria*) is but one example. Theodore Stylianopoulos has reclaimed nine operative interpretive principles from patristic tradition: (1) respect for the authority, primacy, and unity of scripture under divine inspiration; (2) the mystery of Jesus Christ as preeminent interpretive criterion; (3) interdependence between scripture and ecclesial tradition; (4) coherence between theology and spirituality; (5) deference to the "rule of faith" and theological tradition; (6) use of various available methods with a focus on "spiritual" interpretation; (7) interpretation in the light of the context, *skopos*, and "narrative coherence" (*akolouthia*) of scripture; and (8) accessibility of scripture to all Christians for their pastoral benefit; and (9) the role of "ongoing living tradition as normative interpretive agent" (Stylianopoulos 2008, pp. 30–31). For the Orthodox, this represents not antiquarianism but a deep trust in the integrity of the church's patristic heritage and its capacity for being translated across times and cultures.

[*See also* Patristic Interpretation.]

Bibliography

Alfeyev, Hilarion. *St. Symeon the New Theologian and Orthodox Tradition.* Oxford: Oxford University Press, 2000.

Babawi, George. "The Bible in the Eastern Churches." In *The Oxford Illustrated History of the Bible*, edited by John Rogerson, 242–255. Oxford: Oxford University Press, 2001.

Bathrellos, Demetrios. "The Eastern Orthodox Tradition for Today." In *The Bible in Pastoral Practice: Readings in the Place and Function of Scripture in the Church*, edited by Paul Ballard and Stephen Holmes, 42–58. Grand Rapids, Mich.: Eerdmans, 2006.

Blowers, Paul M. "The Anagogical Imagination: Maximus the Confessor and the Legacy of Origenian Hermeneutics." In *Origeniana Sexta: Origène et la Bible/ Origen and the Bible: Actes du Colloquium Origenianum Sextum, Chantilly, 30 août-3 septembre 1993*, edited by Gilles Dorival and Alain le Boulluec, 639–654. Leuven: Peeters, 1995.

Blowers, Paul M. "Eastern Orthodox Biblical Interpretation." In *A History of Biblical Interpretation*, Vol. 2: *The Medieval through the Reformation Periods*, edited by Alan Hauser and Duane Watson, 172–200. Grand Rapids, Mich.: Eerdmans, 2009.

Blowers, Paul M. *Exegesis and Spiritual Pedagogy in Maximus the Confessor: An Investigation of the* Quaestiones ad Thalassium. Notre Dame, Ind.: University of Notre Dame Press, 1991.

Breck, John. *Scripture in Tradition: The Bible and Its Interpretation in the Orthodox Church*. Crestwood, N.Y.: St. Vladimir's Seminary, 2001.

Bulgakov, Sergius. *The Orthodox Church*. Translated by Lydia Kesich. Crestwood, N.Y.: St. Vladimir's Seminary, 1988.

Burton-Christie, Douglas. "The Luminous Word: Scripture in the *Philokalia*." In *The Philokalia: Exploring the Classic Text of Orthodox Spirituality*, edited by Brock Bingaman and Bradley Nassif, 73–86. New York: Oxford University Press, 2012.

Burton-Christie, Douglas. *The Word in the Desert: Scripture and the Quest for Holiness in Early Christian Monasticism*. New York: Oxford University Press, 1993.

Daley, Brian. "Origen's *De Principiis*: A Guide to the Principles of Christian Scriptural Interpretation." In *Nova et Vetera: Patristic Studies in Honor of Thomas Patrick Halton*, edited by John Petruccione, 3–21. Washington, D.C.: Catholic University of America Press, 1998.

Daniélou, Jean. *The Bible and the Liturgy*. Notre Dame, Ind.: University of Notre Dame Press, 1956.

Evdokimov, Paul. *Orthodoxy*. Translated by Jeremy Hummerstone. Hyde Park, N.Y.: New City Press, 2011.

Florovsky, Georges. *Bible, Church, Tradition: An Eastern Orthodox View*. Belmont, Mass.: Nordland, 1972.

Lash, Ephrem. "Biblical Interpretation in Worship." In *The Cambridge Companion to Orthodox Christian Theology*, edited by Mary Cunningham and Elizabeth Theokritoff, 35–48. Cambridge, UK: Cambridge University Press, 2008.

Lash, Ephrem, ed. and trans. *Kontakia on the Life of Christ: St. Romanos the Melodist*. San Francisco: HarperCollins, 1995.

McGuckin, John. "Patterns of Biblical Exegesis in the Cappadocian Fathers: Basil the Great, Gregory the Theologian, and Gregory of Nyssa." In *Orthodox and Wesleyan Scriptural Understanding and Practice*, edited by S. T. Kimbrough, 37–54. Crestwood, N.Y.: St. Vladimir's Seminary Press, 2005.

Negrov, Alexander. *Biblical Interpretation in the Russian Orthodox Church*. Tübingen: Mohr Siebeck, 2008.

Palmer, G. E. H., Philip Sherrard, and Kallistos Ware, eds. and trans. *The Philokalia: The Complete Text Compiled by St. Nikodimos of the Holy Mountain and St. Makarios of Corinth*, Vol. 3. London: Faber and Faber, 1984.

Palmer, G. E. H., Philip Sherrard, and Kallistos Ware, eds. and trans. *The Philokalia: The Complete Text Compiled by St. Nikodimos of the Holy Mountain and St. Makarios of Corinth*, Vol. 4. London: Faber and Faber, 1995.

Staniloae, Dumitru. *The Experience of God: Orthodox Dogmatic Theology*, Vol. 1. Translated by Ioan Ionita and Robert Barringer. Brookline, Mass.: Holy Cross Orthodox, 1994.

Staniloae, Dumitru. *Theology and the Church*, trans. Robert Barringer. Crestwood, NY: St. Vladimir's Seminary, 1980.

Stylianopoulos, Theodore. *The New Testament: An Orthodox Perspective*. Brookline, Mass.: Holy Cross Orthodox, 1997.

Stylianopoulos, Theodore. "Scripture and Tradition in the Church." In *The Cambridge Companion to Orthodox Christian Theology*, edited by Mary Cunningham and Elizabeth Theokritoff, 21–34. Cambridge, UK: Cambridge University Press, 2008.

Theokritoff, Elizabeth. "Praying the Scriptures in Orthodox Worship." In *Orthodox and Wesleyan Scriptural Understanding and Practice*, edited by S. T. Kimbrough, 73–87. Crestwood, N.Y.: St. Vladimir's Seminary, 2005.

Trigg, Joseph. "Romanos's Biblical Interpretation: Drama, Imagery, and Attention to the Text." In *In Dominico Eloquio/In Lordly Eloquence: Essays on Patristic Exegesis in Honor of Robert Louis Wilken*, edited by Paul Blowers, Angela Christman, David Hunter, and Robin Darling Young, 380–394. Grand Rapids, Mich.: Eerdmans, 2001.

Vassiliadis, Petros. "Canon and Authority of Scripture: An Orthodox Hermeneutical Perspective." In *Orthodox and Wesleyan Scriptural Understanding and Practice*, edited by S. T. Kimbrough, 21–35. Crestwood, N. Y.: St. Vladimir's Seminary Press, 2005.

Williams, George H. "The Neo-Patristic Synthesis of Georges Florovsky." In *Georges Florovsky: Russian Intellectual, Orthodox Churchman*, edited by Andrew Blane, 287–340. Crestwood, N.Y.: St. Vladimir's Seminary Press, 1993.

Young, Frances. *Biblical Exegesis and the Formation of Christian Culture*. Cambridge, UK: Cambridge University Press, 1997.

Paul M. Blowers

ECOLOGICAL BIBLICAL CRITICISM

Ecological biblical criticism is the analysis of the Bible and biblical interpretation in relation to ecological science and principles of ecojustice. The philosophy of interpretation on which it is based is commonly called ecological hermeneutics. Ecological biblical criticism is most directly influenced by feminist and postcolonial biblical interpretation and has similarities to ecocriticism in literary studies. Ecological criticism shares with feminist criticism hermeneutical approaches that can be described as suspicion and retrieval—suspicion that the Bible and its interpretation may support ecological exploitation, and retrieval of interpretations that support ecojustice. Individual scholars may place more emphasis on suspicion than retrieval, or vice versa, but most share a desire to address the ethical questions raised by the threats to life posed by widespread human destruction of the biosphere.

Ecological hermeneutics is founded on an analysis of the thinking in western culture that has facilitated the ecological crisis. As a result, ecological biblical criticism tends to ask certain key questions of biblical passages and the ways they have been interpreted. Are they anthropocentric? Is there a dualism between humanity and nature? Are all parts of the biosphere viewed as interrelated, interdependent, and having intrinsic worth? In brief, ecological biblical critics seek to analyze how the interpretation of a passage may have provided or could be used to provide ideological support for ecological exploitation and to recover interpretations that are more ecological.

Historical Development. The history of ecological biblical criticism has paralleled the development of the environmental movement. During the 1960s, as the modern environmental movement was beginning, Lynn White Jr. provoked the ire of many Christians when he published an article in *Science* arguing that western Christianity had legitimated environmental destruction. The article did, however, identify many of the issues that continue to be debated in environmental ethics and ecological biblical criticism. Initially, biblical scholars responded to White either by arguing that "dominion" did not mean exploitation or by discussing nature in the Bible. At the same time, ecofeminist theologians were recognizing the interrelationship between feminism and ecology and pointing to biblical passages that supported ecojustice. There were also a few biblical scholars, like Theodore Hiebert and Terence Fretheim, who produced pioneering works that moved beyond the discussions of nature in the Bible and the meaning of dominion.

Around the beginning of the third millennium, ecological issues began to move into the mainstream of public concern, media attention, and political discourse. In biblical studies, Norman Habel initiated the Earth Bible project and formed the Ecological Hermeneutics section of the Society of Biblical Literature, the largest, international gathering of biblical scholars. This was a watershed moment for ecological hermeneutics because it created a community of scholars developing and working with an ecojustice methodology. As the third millennium begins, the number of articles and books has been steadily increasing along with the depth and breadth of the analysis of the Bible. This includes book-length ecological critical treatments of bodies of literature (such as those by Ellen Davis, Arthur Walker-Jones, and Richard Bauckham); the Exeter Project, led by David Horrell, Cherryl Hunt, and Christopher Southgate; and the appearance of the multivolume Earth Bible commentary edited by Norman Habel.

Lynn White. No article is more often cited in ecological hermeneutics than Lynn White Jr.'s 1967 article in *Science* magazine. Sometimes lost in the furor of all the responses to his article is that he was actually arguing for a reinterpretation of Christianity modeled on the theology of St. Francis. Whether or not one agrees with White, he did identify in concise and eloquent form many of the issues that continue to generate discussion in the field. White argued that western Christianity served to legitimate ecological exploitation, because it was an extremely anthropocentric religion. It has historically claimed that humans were created in the image of God and everything else had been created solely for their use. Nature had value only as it was useful to humans. In addition to this dualism between humanity and nature, Christianity created a dualism between spirit and matter. In many pre-Christian religions, rocks, trees, and streams were inhabited by the spirits of ancestors, totems, and divine and semidivine creatures, who had to be consulted and placated in order to dig a well, dam a river, cut timber, or dig a mine. In contrast, Christianity removed spirit from the land and made it an inanimate object that could easily be exploited. These issues—anthropocentrism, the value of nature, and dualism—continue to be debated and inform critical principles in ecological readings of the Bible.

Anthropocentrism. In western culture, anthropocentrism has involved a sense of superiority over, and separation from, the rest of creation. In the great chain of being, humans are below God and angels and above animals and minerals. Anthropocentrism is, thus, a focus on human beings to the exclusion of all other species, which then facilitates the use and abuse of other species and the planet.

Biblical stories are anthropocentric inasmuch as human beings are the focus, and other species appear only as resources for human beings, background scenery, or poetic metaphors. The biblical story is often understood as being about the salvation of human beings from an evil world that will be destroyed when humans are taken to heaven. Ecological criticism, therefore, asks: Are the biblical stories only about human beings? Are human beings separate from and superior to nature? Or are humans an interrelated and interdependent part of the biosphere?

Intrinsic Worth or Value. Related to the question of anthropocentrism is the question of value. The view of humans as separate from, and superior to, the rest gives them supreme value, and other parts of Earth community are devalued. The parts of the biosphere have often been valued in western culture according to their usefulness to human beings, or their utilitarian value. Ecological hermeneutics, however, asks whether other species and the planet are treated as having intrinsic value, apart from any usefulness they may have for humans.

Dualism. Lynn White suggested that dualisms between humanity and nature, and spirit and matter, facilitated environmental exploitation. Carol Merchant and other ecofeminists have pointed out that these are just two of a whole series of interrelated dualisms in western culture that legitimate the exploitation of women, indigenous people, and the environment. Dualistic thinking involves a whole series of binary oppositions:

Heaven / Earth
God / Human
Male / Female
Rational / Emotional
History / Nature
Human / Nature
European / Indigenous
Civilized / Uncivilized
Spirit / Matter

This list could be expanded considerably, but these dualisms are sufficient as an illustration. The problem is that western language and culture tend to associate the items on each side together, and consider those on the left superior to those on the right.

One example of these dualisms in western culture is Gaughin's paintings of Maohi Nui (French Polynesia). Gaughin includes few Maohi men in his best-known paintings and the women often appear scantily clad or naked in lush, paradisiacal settings.

Indigenous culture is portrayed to the Europeans who bought Gaughin's paintings as a feminine, earthy, paradise. Maohi Nui remains a colony of France to this day and was the location of French nuclear tests that have left many Maohi Nui suffering the aftereffects of exposure to radiation. This is but one example of the way that those on one side of the dualisms—women, indigenous people, and nature—are associated together in a way that has facilitated the degradation of all three.

The importance of environmental issues is sometimes minimized by the charge that the environment is an upper-middle class concern and poor peoples and countries have more pressing concerns. But Gaughin's paintings and the colonization of the Maohi Nui are an example of the way that social and ecological justice issues are interrelated and interdependent. Whether it is the disproportionate number of toxic waste dumps located in African American communities, Uranium mines and clearcut logging on indigenous lands, or the famines, wars, and disease that follow ecological disasters in Africa, ecological justice is interrelated with other justice issues.

Methodological Development. Ecocriticism of the Bible is, therefore, based on analysis of the dualisms that legitimate exploitation. On the one hand, it asks whether the interpretation of a passage is dualistic, and on the other hand, it seeks interpretations of passages that will help blur or overcome such dualisms. Thus, Norman Habel noted in the second volume of the Earth Bible series, that the Hebrew word translated "heavens" could be translated "skies," and in *Exploring Ecological Hermeneutics*, Theodore Hiebert noted that "spirit" and "wind" are the same word in Hebrew. These observations blur the western dualism of heaven and earth, spirit and matter, by understanding "skies" as part of Earth, rather than a separate divine realm and by identifying God's spirit with Earth's winds.

Apocalyptic Eschatology. An issue that was not identified by White, but may be even more significant for ethics, is Christian apocalyptic eschatology and belief in the end of the world. If the world is going to be destroyed and Christians taken to heaven, then there is little motivation to care for this world. In fact, this kind of theology has considerable political influence in North America and has been used by some to argue against Christian involvement in care for creation.

Recently, a number of theologians and biblical scholars have argued that the writers of the Christian New Testament did not look forward to going to heaven and Earth being destroyed, but a transformation of this world. For instance, Jesus tells his disciples to pray, not that they will go to heaven, but that God's "will be done, on earth as it is in heaven" (Matt 6:10). Paul speaks of creation longing for redemption (Rom 8:19–23) and the Apocalpyse of John pictures the New Jerusalem coming to Earth (Rev 21:2–3). This New Testament vision of the transformation of this world could provide support for social and ecological justice work.

Language. Language is an issue for ecological hermeneutics. The word *environment*, for instance, is often understood as simply referring to that which is around (*environs*) humans, rather than as conveying an understanding, as ecological science does, that humans are interrelated and interdependent parts of ecosystems. Similarly, the word, *nature*, tends to be understood as that which is separate from humans. Nature is socially constructed in western culture as either something restorative and healing or something dangerous that has to be conquered. Since these understandings of nature are carried by language and reinforced by other aspects of culture, such as Gaughin's paintings mentioned earlier, they tend to be hardwired into the consciousness of interpreters. Hence, a change in language and consciousness becomes necessary for the development of an ecological hermeneutics. But developing an Earth conscious language and consciousness is a long process.

Dominion, Stewardship, and Creation Care. Many early works by biblical scholars written in response to Lynn White were about the interpretation of God's creation of humanity in the image of God to "have dominion" and "subdue" Earth (Gen 1:26–28). They often argued that "dominion" refers, in its historical and literary context, to benevolent stewardship or, more recently, to creation care. In essence, this is an argument that the anthropocentrism of Genesis 1:26–28 was benevolent and not exploitative. Others, however, think stewardship and creation care continue to be less than ideal, because they maintain a separation between Homo sapiens and other species.

Whether anthropocentrism is the problem or whether there are different kinds of anthropocentrism, continues to be a source of debate. On the one hand, some have argued that science and technology give humans tremendous power and a responsibility to use this "dominion" benevolently to preserve and protect the biosphere. On the other hand, just as it is difficult to imagine many feminists arguing that men can continue to have a special, patriarchal role as long as they are more humble, many environmentalists will probably continue to be suspicious of anthropocentrism, even a more humble anthropocentrism.

The Earth Bible series, which will be discussed later, attempts to develop a more ecological anthropology inspired by the worldview of Australian aborigines. The Earth Bible's principle of mutual custodianship understands humans as custodians, but this is a custodianship they share with other species and Earth.

Ecofeminism. Ecofeminist theologians led the way in the 1990s by pointing toward ecojustice interpretations of the Bible. Anne Primavesi was critical of apocalyptic visions of the destruction of Earth, as the title of her book *Apocalypse to Genesis* implies, and presented an ecofeminist reversal of traditional interpretation of the Bible that emphasized the goodness of creation. Rosemary Radford Ruether was also critical of apocalyptic traditions in her book *Gaia and God.* She argued that Christian tradition could be reinterpreted to support ecotheology. The dualism of Greek philosophy had been imposed on the Bible, but the ancient Israelites understood God as present in nature, and the covenant protected the rights of other species and the land through laws like the Jubilee legislation (Lev 25). She highlighted the ecological humility of Job 38–42, in which humans are just one of the species cared for by God. In fact, many of the species are of no use, or are even dangerous, to humans. Jesus's ministry was understood as the announcement of Jubilee (Luke 4:18–19) and could be understood as an announcement of good news for all creatures.

Pioneers. Several biblical scholars produced pioneering work in this era. Biblical scholars had read the western dualism between nature and history into ancient Israelite religion and had claimed that creation was secondary to history in Israelite religion so that Israelite historical religion was contrasted to Canaanite nature religion. Claus Westermann argued for the importance of creation in Israelite religion, and Theodore Hiebert and Terence Fretheim illustrated that the western dualism between nature and history had been read into the Bible. Hiebert showed that the oldest source in the Bible was very much concerned with nature and agrarian values in *The Yahwist's Landscape.* In his article, "The Plagues as Ecological Signs of Historical Disaster," Fretheim showed that the Exodus event, which had been considered one of the premier examples of the mighty acts of God in history, was, in fact, an example of God's work in and through creation.

Sometimes activists pointed the way for biblical scholars. For example, Ellen Bernstein, founder of the first Jewish environmental organization, wrote *The Splendor of Creation,* and Bill McKibben, who wrote the first book for the general public about climate change, *The End of Nature,* also wrote *Comforting Whirlwind* highlighting the ecological humility of the God Speeches in Job (38–41).

Earth Bible. The appearance of the Earth Bible Series was a watershed in ecological biblical criticism. Norman Habel gathered a team of biblical scholars, theologians, and ecologists to develop ecojustice principles for interpreting the Bible and then assembled an international group of biblical scholars to write articles on various parts of the Bible. The first volume, *Readings from the Perspective of Earth,* appeared in 2000. It began with a couple of chapters explaining the Earth Bible hermeneutical and ecojustice principles, followed by chapters illustrating the method in various bodies of biblical literature. The method and ecojustice principles were discussed briefly at the beginning of each of the subsequent volumes: *The Earth Story in Genesis* (2000), *The Earth Story in the Psalms and the Prophets* (2001), *The Earth Story in Wisdom Traditions* (2001), and *The Earth Story in the New Testament* (2002). Habel also produced worship materials for churches in *Seven Songs of Creation*. Norman Habel and Peter Trudinger, another member of the Earth Bible Team, founded the Ecological Hermeneutics Section of the Society of Biblical Literature and collected some of the resulting papers in *Exploring Ecological Hermeneutics*.

Content and Praxis of Ecological Biblical Criticism. An ecological hermeneutic recognizes that both readers and texts have biases that have generated and continue to generate misunderstandings of nonhuman entities as objects, thus creating a sense of distance from these nonhuman entities because they are other and alien. An ecocritical hermeneutic challenges these biases by redefining earth and its nonhuman entities as subjects with inherent value, as ends in themselves, and not as means to human ends and objects for human research, analysis, and exploitation. Following is a description of the most important elements in ecological biblical criticism.

Suspicion, Identification, and Retrieval. The Earth Bible adopted from feminist criticism a hermeneutic of suspicion and retrieval. It approached the interpretation of a passage with the suspicion that it devalued Earth because the Bible has often been used to justify exploitation of Earth, and the Bible was written by humans for humans. Suspicion is necessary to identify and defuse the power of interpretations that could devalue Earth. Only once their power is defused can the recovery or retrieval of an ecojustice interpretation begin.

The Earth Bible added *identification* to suspicion and retrieval. A reader or hearer identifies with a character or characters in a story and identification with different characters can produce different interpretations. The Earth Bible sought not just to talk about Earth in the Bible, but to identify with Earth as a character in the story. By this emphasis on identification with Earth as a subject in the story, the Earth Bible is distinguished from most previous studies, and many subsequent studies.

Ecojustice Principles. The questions ecocriticism asks come out of an analysis of what has been wrong with the dominant forms of western thinking and what more ecological thinking might look like. There are, of course, minority voices in western culture that are important to recover, but the dominant forms of thought have legitimated exploitation and destruction. So, for instance, if the dominant forms of western thought have treated humanity as separate from, and superior to, the rest of creation, then is there evidence in the Bible that humanity is one of many interrelated and interdependent species? If western thought has only considered creation of utilitarian value, then is there evidence in the Bible of the intrinsic value of other species and the planet? If western thought has treated Earth as an inanimate object, then is there evidence that Earth is a subject, alive and capable of communicating and acting?

Six ecojustice principles appear at the beginning of each volume of the Earth Bible series and are reproduced verbatim here:

- **The Principle of Intrinsic Worth.** The universe, Earth, and all its components have intrinsic value/worth.
- **The Principle of Interconnectedness.** Earth is a community of interconnected living things that are mutually dependent on each other for life and survival.
- **The Principles of Voice.** Earth is a subject capable of raising its voice in celebration and against injustice.
- **The Principle of Purpose.** The universe, Earth, and all its components are part of a dynamic cosmic design within which each piece has a place in the overall goal of that design.
- **The Principle of Mutual Custodianship.** Earth is a balanced and diverse domain in which responsible custodians can function as partners, rather than rulers, to sustain a balanced and diverse Earth community.

- **Principle of Resistance.** Earth and its components not only suffer from injustices at the hands of humans, but actively resist them in the struggle for justice.

Scholars who contributed to the Earth Bible Series were asked to interact with one or more of these principles. While some principles received more attention than others, individual interpreters used a variety of historical and literary critical methods, depending on the text being interpreted, and their own preferences. The ecojustice principles were debated within the series with questions about whether some principles should be included, how they should be understood, and whether other principles should be added. Some have suggested that these principles were imposed on the biblical text, but every critical method brings critical principles and questions to the text, and the Earth Bible is commendable for making clear those principles, so that they could be debated. The principles also had a visionary function, challenging biblical scholars to think beyond the confines of nineteenth and twentieth century western rationality and to explore more Earth-conscious approaches to interpretation.

Earth as Subject. An important contribution of the Earth Bible was the treatment of Earth as a subject. Astrophysicist and environmentalist, James Lovelock, had argued in his book, *Gaia: A New Look at Life on Earth*, that Earth functioned more like an organism than an inanimate object when viewed from space. Ecotheologians like Jay McDaniel and Sallie McFague have also suggested understanding Earth as a living organism. The Earth Bible principles treat Earth as a subject with a voice, purpose, and ability to resist injustice. Rather than speaking of *the earth* as an object, the Earth Bible adopted the practice, also followed by this article, of using *Earth* as the name of a subject.

Recent Works. Since the publication of the Earth Bible, individual scholars have produced book-length works that have extended the discussion. Ellen Davis wrote *Scripture, Culture, and Agriculture: An Agrarian Reading of the Bible* (2008). She used the agrarianism of Wendell Berry as a lens through which to view the Hebrew Bible and demonstrated that ancient Israelite religion was far more intimately concerned with the well-being of the land than modern, urban, biblical scholars had previously imagined. Arthur Walker-Jones's book *The Green Psalter* showed that the book of Psalms had an understanding of ecojustice and the story of the Psalter climaxed in all creation's praise of the Creator (Ps 148), so that humanity was just one part of a choir in which all parts had intrinsic worth. Hilary Marlow argued that the interrelationship of God and the human and nonhuman worlds in Amos, Hosea, and First Isaiah was relevant to issues in contemporary environmental ethics. Recent contributions to ecological criticism of the Bible are not always identifiable from their title. Terence Fretheim's magnum opus *God and World in the Old Testament: A Relational Theology of Creation* (2005) shows that a biblical theology of creation can be ecological.

Religion and Science. Cosmologies and the relation of religion and science are important issues for ecocriticism. How does ecological biblical criticism avoid the perils of either a rejection of science or an uncritical acceptance? William Brown's learned *Seven Pillars of Creation* is particularly important, because it models how ecologically concerned biblical scholarship can engage in dialogue with science. Of course, Brown finds disjunctions, but he also finds correlations between biblical creation stories and contemporary science, such as the theme of emergence and chaos theory. Brown demonstrates how dialogue with contemporary science can extend and transform the meaning of the Bible in ways that have implications for an ecological theology and ethics.

Exeter Project. The formation of a second major research project is evidence of growing interest in ecological biblical criticism. The Exeter Project began with David Horrell, Cherryl Hunt, and Christopher Southgate in their attempt to assess the use of the Bible in ecological ethics and has resulted in several books. *Ecological Hermeneutics* is an edited volume similar to those produced by the Earth Bible, with a methodological introduction and a series of articles by an international team of scholars, some of whom had also contributed to the Earth Bible.

The Exeter project made a contribution by raising several issues related to the social function or ethics of interpretation. First, members of the project argued that interpretation needed to be recognizable as in continuity with Christian tradition in order to inform Christian ethics. There are, of course, many Christian traditions, and diverse communities, but they are rightly concerned with what interpretations might be widely accepted among Christians so as to motivate action on behalf of Earth community.

Second, they noted that popular interpretations of the Bible, which have not usually been considered worthy of discussion by biblical scholars, need to be discussed in ecological criticism. Thus *Ecological Hermeneutics* contains an article by Harry Maier on the Book of Revelation with a discussion of its interpretation by evangelicals.

Third, they propose the use of narrative criticism based on the work of the literary critic, Northrop Frye, in order to make connections between Paul and contemporary narrative theology and ethics, like that of Stanley Hauerwas. Since ecological biblical criticism has its roots in a concern for the ecological crisis, it is by its nature interested in the social function of biblical interpretation. Narrative criticism holds promise for ecocriticism because Frye's method seeks to analyze not only the way story shapes Christian practice, but the social power of narratives and metaphors in the broader society.

Paul. Three leaders of the Exeter Project, David Horrell, Cherryl Hunt, and Christopher Southgate, produced *Greening Paul*, the first book-length argument that Paul's theology and ethics could be understood as supporting ecological ethics. They examine the Pauline texts traditionally cited as supportive of ecotheology (Rom 8:19–23; Col 1:15–20) but question the argument already mentioned that New Testament and Pauline apocalyptic can support an ecotheology because it envisions, not the destruction, but transformation of Earth. Even though a transformation of this world is in view, the transformation is so radical it can hardly motivate essential but mundane ecological initiatives like recycling. Nevertheless, they show that these and other texts do assume the redemption of creation. The redemption of all creatures can then be used as a hermeneutical lens to read two central aspects of Paul's ethics. The model of Christ's sacrifice for others can be extended to all creatures, and the corporate solidarity of the body of Christ can be understood as encompassing the community of all creatures. The hermeneutical lens of the redemption of all creatures, therefore, allows central aspects of Paul's ethics to be interpreted in support of Christian ecological ethics.

Jesus. Equally important was the appearance of a book-length treatment of Jesus. There was a time not too long ago when Jesus was considered a problem for ecotheology, but Richard Bauckham's *Living with Other Creatures* makes a convincing case that the Synoptic Gospels can be read ecologically. Just as biblical scholars have used the historical and social context of the Gospels to interpret them, they could use the ecological context to interpret the Gospels. Far more research needs to be done on the many references to animals and agriculture in the Gospels, but the number of concrete references to plants, animals, and agricultural methods, especially compared to Paul and Rabbinic literature, indicates that Jesus's teachings were shaped by his ecological location. Bauckham also shows that Jesus's teaching assumes the Hebrew Bible's creation theology. Jesus's teaching assumes that God has created the world and cares for all its creatures. The note in Mark 1:13 that "he was with wild beasts" refers to Jewish beliefs that the righteous would not be harmed by dangerous animals and that Jesus's ministry anticipated the new age of peace between species (Isa 11).

Prospects. While the number of ecocritical biblical interpretations has accelerated, much work remains to be done. First, work needs to be done on the ecological contexts of biblical writers and their audiences. The references to flora, fauna, geography, weather, and agricultural practices have received little study. This basic ecological information is essential to ask deeper questions about how ecosystems have influenced writers and their audiences, and whether the references devalue or value, conceal or reveal Earth's story. Not only is much work needed to investigate the facts, but a shift in consciousness is also necessary so that interpreters can move away from a preoccupation with humanity's story to begin telling Earth's story.

Second, ecojustice principles for interpretation will continue to be discussed. This will include whether existing principles should be reassessed or others added. For instance, The Earth Bible Series functioned with a largely unstated principle that indigenous voices should be included in the conversation because they might offer constructive alternatives to a western worldview. Thus the principle of mutual custodianship was inspired by the understanding of Australian Aborigines, and the volumes included articles by indigenous authors from various parts of the globe. Another reason that indigenous perspectives might receive preference is that the marginalization and exploitation of indigenous people and Earth are often interrelated. In addition to developing new principles, scholars will continue to analyze and refine the existing ecojustice principles. In the last volume of the Earth Bible series, Norman Habel noted that many authors used the principle of interdependence but may have understood it differently than ecologists would. Also the principle of purpose was widely neglected, and he challenged researchers to write an *Erdsgeschichte* (Earth story), which would balance *Heilsgeschichte* (holy history).

Third, ecological hermeneutics will have an inherent interest in the social function of biblical interpretation and how biblical interpretation is used to legitimate exploitation, as well as how it can be used to encourage Earth consciousness. This will require that biblical scholars develop critical and analytical tools to understand the social function of interpretation. Marxist, feminist, and postcolonial criticisms will continue to provide critical tools for ecocriticism. In addition, narrative criticism may provide tools for understanding the social and political power of biblical images and narratives. The importance of this kind of analysis for ecological ethics should be evident in a culture where marketing companies and the media have become highly sophisticated in their use of images and associated stories to influence behavior.

Last, but by no means least, ecological biblical criticism needs to develop an analysis of the ecological locations of readers. Just as other liberation hermeneutics have emphasized the social and political locations of interpreters, ecological hermeneutics will find it necessary to develop a critical analysis of ecological location. The choice of Earth as a name for the planet, for instance, reflects a particular ecological location. Viewed from space, most of Earth's surface is water, and soil is only a thin layer on the land masses. The choice of Earth reflects cultures that were historically based on agriculture, though the relationship to soil is largely a historical memory in urbanized cultures. Because ecological location shapes language and culture, it also shapes politics. An interpreter from a particular ecological location may not be able to speak for other ecosystems. Ecological hermeneutics, therefore, will need to focus on who speaks for an ecosystem and how green the politics of an interpretation are.

The challenges are great, since the continued development of ecological biblical criticism requires nothing less than a major shift of consciousness. The development of greater Earth consciousness may seem radical because the devaluing of Earth has been hardwired into western languages and culture. The need, however, is urgent because the threats to life on Earth are great and the time left to change behaviors short.

[*See also* Allegory and Allegorical Interpretation; Geography and Topography in Biblical Interpretation; Feminist Biblical Interpretation; Ideological Criticism; Materialist Criticism; *and* Postcolonial Biblical Interpretation.]

BIBLIOGRAPHY

Bauckham, Richard. *Bible and Ecology: Rediscovering the Community of Creation.* Waco, Tex.: Baylor University Press, 2010. This book is an ecological interpretation of the Bible by a prominent New Testament scholar. Bauckham examines texts such as Job 38—48, Psalms 104, 148, Jeremiah, Hosea, and Joel in order to argue that the Hebrew Bible understands humanity as an interdependent part of the "community of creation" dependent on the Creator. This understanding could support greater ecological humility and responsibility for the care of creation. The New Testament shares the Hebrew Bible's theology of creation and looks forward to the renewal of creation.

Bauckham, Richard. *Living with Other Creatures: Green Exegesis and Theology.* Waco, Tex.: Baylor University Press, 2011. This book continues the argument of Bauckham's previous book and includes a detailed discussion of "dominion," but places more emphasis on the New Testament. It is the first sustained argument that Jesus's teaching is influenced by its rural, agrarian, ecological context and shares with the Hebrew Bible an understanding of God's care for all creatures. The note in Mark 3:1 that Jesus was "with the wild animals" is an anticipation of the transformation of creation (Isa 11) and the presence of four beasts praising God around the throne (Rev 4) is the eschatological culmination of the Hebrew Bible's theme of all creation's praise of God.

Bernstein, Ellen. *The Splendor of Creation: A Biblical Ecology.* Cleveland, Ohio: Pilgrim, 2005. The founder of the first national Jewish environmental organization weaves together commentary, midrash, autobiography, and the writings of naturalists into a poetic and impassioned interpretation of Genesis 1.

Brown, William P. *The Seven Pillars of Creation: The Bible, Science and the Ecology of Wonder.* New York: Oxford University Press, 2010. Brown brings biblical scholarship on seven biblical cosmogonies into dialogue with science and draws out implications for ecological interpretation of the Hebrew Bible.

Davis, Ellen F. *Scripture, Culture, and Agriculture: An Agrarian Reading of the Bible.* Cambridge, UK: Cambridge University Press, 2008. Davis makes a powerful and prophetic argument that biblical writers had agrarian values similar to those of Wendell Berry and that the recovery of agrarian values could help address the ecological crisis that has been created by contemporary agriculture. She emphasizes the Priestly writers, the concept of hereditary property, the prophets Amos and Hosea, and Wisdom literature.

Fretheim, Terence. *God and World in the Old Testament: A Relational Theology of Creation.* Nashville, Tenn.: Abingdon, 2005. This volume is the culmination of a lifetime of work on a biblical theology of creation and ecology. Fretheim shows that God is relational and shares the ongoing work of creation, so that Creator, creation, and creatures are interrelated and interdependent. Fretheim's careful exegetical work and extensive documentation show that this relational theology of creation undergirds major themes and bodies of literature in the Hebrew Bible.

Fretheim, Terence. "The Plagues as Ecological Signs of Historical Disaster." *Journal of Biblical Literature* 110 (1991): 385–396. With this article, Fretheim became one of the first prominent biblical scholars to argue that the Hebrew Bible understood God not only as active in history but as working in and through nature.

Gray, Elizabeth Dodson. *Green Paradise Lost.* Wellesley, Mass.: Roundtable, 1981. This wide-ranging work by an early ecofeminist theologian working at Harvard Divinity School used "responsible stewardship" as an example of patriarchal thinking and practices that were inadequate for a contemporary environmental ethic. She argued for a spirituality that understood humanity not as different and superior but as embodied and interconnected with the web of creation.

Habel, Norman C., *The Birth, the Curse, and the Greening of Earth: An Ecological Reading of Genesis 1—11.* Earth Bible Commentary, Vol. 1; London and New York: Sheffield Academic, 2011. This is the first volume of a groundbreaking multivolume, ecocritical commentary on the Bible. Habel shows that Genesis 1—11 can be interpreted, not just as God's, or humanity's story, but as Earth's story.

Habel, Norman C., ed. *The Earth Story in the Psalms and the Prophets.* Earth Bible, 4. Sheffield, UK: Sheffield Academic; Cleveland, Ohio: Pilgrim, 2001.

Habel, Norman C., ed. *The Earth Story in Wisdom Traditions.* Earth Bible, 3. Sheffield, UK: Sheffield Academic; Cleveland, Ohio: Pilgrim, 2001.

Habel, Norman C., ed. *Readings from the Perspective of Earth.* Earth Bible, 1. Sheffield, UK: Sheffield Academic; Cleveland, Ohio: Pilgrim, 2000. This is the inaugural volume of the series that established ecological biblical criticism as a method of criticism within the field of biblical studies. It begins with a history of literature and discussions of ecological hermeneutics, ecojustice principles, and ecofeminist contributions to ecological hermeneutics. This is followed by examples of ecological criticism of biblical passages by a variety of scholars.

Habel, Norman C., ed. *Seven Songs of Creation: Liturgies for Celebrating and Healing Earth.* Cleveland, Ohio: Pilgrim, 2004. This is a collection of liturgies, prayers, and hymns based on the ecojustice principles of the Earth Bible and intended to introduce and promote ecojustice in churches.

Habel, Norman C., and Vicky Balabanski, eds. *The Earth Story in the New Testament.* Earth Bible Series, 5. London & New York: Sheffield Academic; Cleveland, Ohio: Pilgrim, 2002.

Habel, Norman C., and Peter Trudinger, eds. *Exploring Ecological Hermeneutics.* Society of Biblical Literature Symposium Series, 46. Atlanta: Society of Biblical Literature, 2008. This is a collection of 15 articles applying ecological criticism to a variety of biblical passages. The articles were originally read in an ecological hermeneutics consultation at the Society of Biblical Literature Annual Meetings in the years following the publication of the Earth Bible. The volume has a brief introduction to ecological hermeneutics by Norman Habel and indications of the refinement and development of the method.

Habel, Norman C., and Shirley Wurst, eds. *The Earth Story in Genesis.* Earth Bible, 2. Sheffield, UK: Sheffield Academic; Cleveland, Ohio: Pilgrim, 2000. In this and subsequent volumes (also listed here), scholars apply the ecojustice principles of the Earth Bible Series to passages from particular books and genres of biblical literature.

Hessel, Dieter, ed. *Theology for Earth Community: A Field Guide.* Maryknoll, N.Y.: Orbis, 1996. This was a significant contribution to ecotheology and influenced the development of ecological hermeneutics because it brought together prominent scholars from various theological disciplines—George Tinker, Mary Evelyn Tucker, Kosuke Koyama, Catherine Keller, and Theodore Hiebert—to address the ecological crisis.

Hiebert, Theodore. *The Yahwist's Landscape: Nature and Religion in Early Israel.* New York: Oxford University Press, 1996. Hiebert showed that the earliest source of the Hebrew Bible had agrarian values and understood God as present not just in history, as had been widely argued, but also and inextricably in nature.

Horrell, David G., Cherryl Hunt, and Christopher Southgate. *Greening Paul: Rereading the Apostle Paul in a Time of Ecological Crisis.* Waco, Tex.: Baylor University Press, 2010. A product of the Exeter project, this book is significant for biblical studies and Christianity, because it is the first book-length ecological treatment of the works of Paul. Although the Pauline texts often cited in support of ecotheology (Rom 8:19–23; Col 1:15–20) portray transformation rather than destruction of Earth, the authors argue the understanding of transformation is too radical to support an environmental ethic. But they argue that Christian interpreters such as Augustine and Luther have always read Paul through a hermeneutical lens, and the redemption of creation can provide such a hermeneutical lens to develop an interpretation of Paul that would support a Christian environmental ethics of sacrifice for, and solidarity with, all creatures.

Horrell, David G., Cherryl Hunt, Christopher Southgate, and Francesca Stavrakopoulou, eds. *Ecological Hermeneutics: Biblical, Historical and Theological Perspectives.* New York: T.&T. Clark International, 2010. These essays are the result of a collaborative research project on the Bible and environmental ethics at the University of Exeter. It includes articles by twenty scholars, predominantly located in Britain, with three from Australia, one each from Canada, South Africa, and the United States. The introduction indicates a slightly more conservative approach to the authority of the Bible and Christian tradition, and includes more historians and theologians than the Earth Bible, but the hermeneutical approach and critical principles are similar.

Lovelock, J. E. *The Ages of Gaia: A Biography of Our Living Earth.* New York: Norton, 1988. In his 1970 classic *Gaia: A New Look at Life on Earth,* the astrophysicist James Lovelock put forth the hypothesis that Earth functions, not as an inanimate object, but as an organism. The initial book sparked both controversy and new research. This second treatment benefits from additional research and wider acceptance of the hypothesis. It provides a scientific analogue to the Earth Bible's treatment of Earth as a subject that is capable of resistance.

Marlow, Hilary. *Biblical Prophets and Contemporary Environmental Ethics: Rereading Amos, Hosea, and First Isaiah.* Oxford: Oxford University Press, 2009. This wide-ranging and readable book discusses the history of the Christian doctrine of Creation and environmental ethics in order to develop an ecological hermeneutic and show that the prophets Amos, Hosea, and First Isaiah understood the divine, human, and nonhuman as intimately interrelated.

McKibben, Bill. *The Comforting Whirlwind: God, Job, and the Scale of Creation.* Grand Rapids, Mich.: Eerdmans, 1994. Republished Cambridge, Mass.: Cowley, 2005. McKibben is an accomplished writer and environmentalist. He has written an eloquent and insightful argument that Job's suffering and God's response can provide a lens for understanding the suffering

humanity is experiencing because of the environmental crisis and how humanity can respond.
Merchant, Carolyn. *The Death of Nature: Women, Ecology, and the Scientific Revolution.* San Francisco: Harper & Row, 1980. In this classic work in environmental history and ecofeminism, Merchant argued that the mechanistic worldview of the scientific revolution facilitated the exploitation of women and nature.
Plumwood, Val. *Feminism and the Mastery of Nature.* New York & London: Routledge, 1993. Plumwood's classic work on the philosophical connections between feminism, environmentalism, and postcolonialism includes an explanation of the dualisms that legitimate oppression in western culture.
Primavesi, Anne. *From Apocalypse to Genesis.* Minneapolis: Fortress, 1991. This early work by an ecofeminist theologian argues for an ecological reinterpretation of the Bible and Christianity.
Ruether, Rosemary Radford. *Gaia and God: An Ecofeminist Theology of Earth Healing.* San Francisco: HarperSanFranciso, 1994. This is a significant work by one of the leading ecofeminist theologians. It outlines ways Christian theology and the Bible could provide foundations for an ecotheology.
Santmire, H. Paul. *The Travail of Nature: The Ambiguous Ecological Promise of Christian Theology.* Minneapolis: Fortress, 1985. Santmire provides a historical study of the problems and promise of Christian theology in addressing the ecological crisis. He concludes with an assessment of three biblical root metaphors—mountain, fertility, and promised land—for their relevance to an ecotheology.
Walker-Jones, Arthur. *The Green Psalter: Resources for an Ecological Spirituality.* Minneapolis: Fortress, 2009. Walker-Jones argues that the biblical Book of Psalms could support a contemporary ecotheology, because it includes a concept of ecojustice, and moves the reader toward integration into all creation's praise of God.
Westermann, Claus. "Biblical Reflection on Creator-Creation." In *Creation in the Old Testament*, edited by Bernhard Anderson, 90–101. Minneapolis: Fortress, 1971. This is an early argument by a prominent, German biblical scholar that creation theology was an important part of Israelite religion.
White, Lynn, Jr. "The Historical Roots of Our Ecological Crisis." *Science* 155 (1967): 1203–1207. This article has been republished many times and is cited in almost every discussion of ecological biblical criticism. White argued that western Christianity had been used to justify the exploitation of the environment, because it removed spirit and sacredness from nature, and understood everything as being created for the use of humans.

Arthur Walker-Jones

Economics and the Bible

At its essence, economics is the study of how societies make decisions on the allocation of limited resources. Whether subsistence, capitalist, socialist, or totalitarian, each society faces complex choices regarding the distribution of goods and utilities. In making such choices, economics involves the study of the various allocation processes such as production, consumption, exchange, forecasting, scarcity, and risk. But in all of these activities, economics is observable only through human behavior. Consequently, efforts to isolate economic behavior from social spheres are heuristic at best, misleading at worst. Economic decisions reflect deeper ideological values, hierarchies, and positions of power, often revealed in the dominant social institutions such as the royal court or the temple. A proper understanding of ancient economics can enhance understanding of the social worlds and moral visions of the Bible.

Despite the pervasive influence of economics, biblical interpretation rarely focuses on such matters as outlined within the Hebrew Bible and New Testament. Economic activities form such a vital and intrinsic component of life that one rarely sees outside of native paradigms. For example, most people cannot conceive of an economic life without currency, even though it was completely absent in most of ancient Israel during the HB period and limited as a marker of value in the Greco-Roman culture of the NT. The majority of peoples in biblical times lived a primarily agrarian lifestyle centered on subsistence. In addition, the wealthiest elites dominated all economic decisions of the biblical worlds. Economies served political purpose, and most peoples had to adjust their own subsistence strategies around elite coercion, whether politically through imperial taxation or socially through vehicles such as local temple tribute.

A single verse can illustrate the important role of economics in biblical interpretation. In Matt 6:24 (cf. Luke 16:13) Jesus declares, "No one can serve two masters; for a slave will either hate the one and love the other, or be devoted to the one and despise the other. You cannot serve God and wealth." The verse assumes implicit knowledge of the economic background. What is the status between a household slave and a master? Does wealth/*mammon* refer to stored wealth or purchasing power? Does such a verse counter temple ideology or reinforce imperial allegiance? How can an individual understand such a statement in a world where economic choices are so limited? In order to assess the economic issues of biblical interpretation, this article briefly outlines the intellectual history of economic study of the Bible, then summarizes some of the social theories of economies that help to contextualize biblical interpretation. This leads to a brief investigation of the possible sources for reconstruction. Finally, three specific examples illuminate some of the issues of economics and biblical interpretation.

History of Research. For much of the modern scholarship period, biblical studies have neglected intentional research on the economic aspects of the text. One of the first HB monographs to focus on economics was Moshe Elat's *Economic Relations in the Lands of the Bible* (1000–539 B.C.E.), published in 1977. Elat used the Neo-Assyrian tribute lists to understand the dynamics of exchange in the southern Levant. The decade of the 1980s witnessed a major development of social scientific approaches to the Bible and significant interaction with broader debates on the nature of the ancient economy. From this period, major works appeared that focused on the economics of biblical and ancient law, wisdom literature, and most prolifically, the historical contexts of preexilic prophetic literature. Most recently, southern Levantine archaeology has integrated social scientific theories with biblical texts to draw conclusions concerning the economics of ancient Israel.

New Testament scholarship shares a similar intellectual history. Before the 1980s, most studies—with rare exceptions such as Constantin Brunner (*Our Christ: The Revolt of the Mystical Genius*, 1921)—did not focus on economic systems. Biblical scholars built on the economic research in related fields such as classics and sociology, but it was not until the emergence of the NT Context Group that economic aspects of the NT world took a place of prominence. Bruce Malina's first edition of *The New Testament World: Insights from Cultural Anthropology* (1981) was particularly influential in his emphasis on the relationship between meaning and the social system of that particular language. For Malina, terms like "wealth" in the Greco-Roman world carry little semantic value to the modern reader. Malina's studies inspired many significant works focusing on the social world of Jesus, while drawing on stock phrases in anthropology such as honor-shame or limited good. Naturally, these studies made their way into the epistles and apocalyptic portions of the NT as well as Qumran literature.

With the growing recognition of the importance of reader context, coupled with interest in social settings of the biblical texts, the study of economics in the Bible enters a period of great fecundity. In order to properly engage in these studies, biblical interpreters of both testaments must begin by considering the nature of the ancient economies of the biblical world.

Ancient Economies. Although ancient economics is a fairly recent arena of study for biblical scholars, ancient historians and anthropologists have long debated the nature of such economies. A brief overview of these discussions is crucial for an informed understanding of biblical economics.

Formalism. The majority of scholarship on economics and the Bible tends to assume formalism, that is, a world in which the principles of supply and demand govern allocation decisions. The pervasiveness of this viewpoint symbolically begins with Adam Smith (*An Inquiry into the Nature and Causes of the Wealth of Nations*, 1776), who famously argued that if left to itself, an "invisible hand" will signal market forces to make collective decisions on allocations, which will ultimately serve the greater good. Smith wanted to separate political decisions and leave economic control in the hands of the general population. Despite certain objections, Smith understood his capitalist theories as universal and timeless, and its essence remained unchallenged in the Western world until the twentieth century. The fundamental assumption of free markets on supply and demand is so intrinsic to Western thought that most ancient Near Eastern scholars make these assumptions without explicit explanation. In fact, outward defense of formalist economics arose only as a response to the counter theory of economic substantivism.

Substantivism. In response to the classical political economy of Smith's *Wealth of Nations*, a growing number of anthropologists challenged the basic assumptions of supply-and-demand capitalism by drawing on direct ethnological observations. These anthropologists observed the efficiency of complex economic systems without the usage of currencies. Rather than rely on supply and demand, substantivist economies revolved around a different set of traditional forces: duties and obligations, beliefs and magic, social ambition and vanities. The works of early twentieth-century anthropologists influenced scholars of the ancient world, most notably Karl Polanyi, who in turn brought the conversations to biblical studies. Unlike Smith, Polanyi considered economic transaction as socially embedded at its core. Polanyi understood all economic exchange before the Industrial Revolution to fall under two general categories: reciprocity and redistribution. *Reciprocity* occurred as socially embedded exchange between equals under the obligation of an established relationship over any perceived profit. In contrast, *redistribution* refers to an asymmetrical exchange, with a central authority collecting goods, storing, then re-allocating them. Neither reciprocity nor redistribution depended on any supply and demand, but rather the enforcement and maintenance of these exchange patterns depended on social norms.

While Polanyi was arguing for the substantivist economy of the HB world, the classicist Moses Finley made similar arguments for the Greco-Roman society in his monumental publication, *The Ancient Economy* (1985). Although by the NT times the Greeks had developed markets, improved exchange networks, and left an abundance of archaeological and numismatic evidence for trade, Finley argued that such infrastructure did not necessitate formalist exchange and that the coinage was symbolic more than functional. He also maintained that the interworking of the ancient economy depended on status, which restricted the options for commercial trade.

Marxism. Much of the debate over the Bible and economics occurs because of the polarization of formalism-substantivism, though other important interpretive frames emerged, primarily as alternatives to formalism. Among them, those of Karl Marx had an enormous influence on both biblical studies and the economies of the ancient Near East. Marx saw a grand progression of struggle among capitalists along a dialogical continuum. Marx's primary contribution lies in the emphasis on the relations of production and its inevitable result in class-consciousness. Marxism fueled multiple trajectories that have been very influential in interpreting the ancient economic world. Karl Wittfogel (1957) argued that the Marxist concept of the Asiatic Mode of Production could explain the ancient Near East, with its restricted access to crucial resources resulting in an economic stagnation. The Leningrad School, comprised of scholars from both the East (Muhammad Dandamaev) and the West (Roland Boer), support some version of a two-sector model of the ancient Near East: a free sector alongside a nonfree sector. Immanuel Wallenstein's expression of Marxism in the world-system theory argues that resources freely move from periphery to center under coercion in a way analogous to the Marxian dichotomy of the exploited proletariat an the capitalist bourgeoisie. Marxism continues to be significant in biblical studies outside of ancient economic history. Indeed, Marxism was the theoretical basis for the influential peasant-revolt interpretations of Israelite state formation. In addition, Marxist hermeneutics continue to serve as a theoretical platform for postcolonial readings of both testaments.

Patrimonialism. Unlike laissez-faire capitalism and Marxism, Max Weber never envisioned a universal paradigm of economic systems. Instead, Weber argued that each economy reflected a particular set of social norms. Formalist economic principles of Smith may govern modern Western economic behavior, but Weber acknowledged the noncapitalist motivations of other economies. For much of the ancient world, Weber argued that the system of patrimonialism served as an ideal type (*Verstehen*) for biblical economies. In patrimonialism, the larger governing structures, such as the court and the temple, patterned themselves after family households. Patriarchy also drove the governance of the smaller units such as the chiefdom, clan, or even the single household. In *Ancient Judaism* (1952), Weber identified biblical law as the single most powerful indicator of such patriarchal economic life in accord with the absence of any collective ownership and the assumption of the family as the dominant economic unit. He argued that Israel's religious commitment to covenant regulated an economic life centered on an egalitarian ethos. With the diversified topography of Israel and Judah, despotic centralized control was impossible. Weber thus argued that the social obligations of patrimonialism could manage the economies more effectively than political coercion.

Kinship. Related to the idea of patrimonialism, the aspect of kinship finds expression in the economies of the NT. Malina argued that kinship connects political, religious, and economic spheres. Kinship was particularly important in allocation issues as it determined occupations, dowry, inheritance, and land tenure. As an illustration of the ties of kinship to economics, one can consider that Herod the Great did not propose to the Hasmonean princess Mariamme out of amorous desire, but rather initially made a marriage contract with her family. Financial stipulations for the long process of marriage are listed in Josephus, the Mishnah, and early Jewish literature. Similarly, ancient Near Eastern literature contains several textual examples on the conditions of inheritance, prioritizing the claims of sons (Num 27:3–4).

Patronage. The anthropological model of patron-client relationships has served as a powerful paradigm for understanding the economic world of the NT. During the time of Jesus, Jerusalem was under the authority of Roman client-rulers, running an extractive, hierarchal economy. The patron would provide a variety of services to the clients (legal support, provisions, citizenship, tax release, etc.) in return for the client's loyalty and honor. The Roman emperor was the primary patron and set a network of clients by which to oversee the empire. Such dominance on patronage creates gross economic disparities as the patrons continue to extract agrarian surplus, while rewarding the clients and not the peasants. It is within this patron-client setting that one can understand the instructions of Jesus reversing such patterns during his meal at the home of a prominent Pharisee. Jesus acknowledged that such banquets intended to give a patron (Pharisee) a chance to reinforce partnerships with guests (clients), though Jesus turned over this patron-client system by insisting, "But when you give a banquet, invite the poor, the crippled, the lame, and the blind" (Luke 14:13).

Sources. In studying the economics of the Bible, one must understand and actively engage in the major extrabiblical sources in reconstructing the social institutions of the ancient world. An informed understanding of these sources allows one to control hermeneutics and reveal new insights within biblical texts about economic life.

Archaeology. In the last few decades, Levantine archaeology has revealed a greater sophistication in understanding economic systems as the advent of the "new archaeology" of the 1970s has forced new questions regarding the ancient social world. Archaeology no longer merely produces raw data, but the discipline now attempts to identify proper social theories and use them judiciously to interpret and articulate this data. In interpreting the ancient economy of the Bible, such data afford a unique opportunity to rethink economic systems. The study of archaeology is vast and overwhelming with its own multivalent theoretical approaches, but the limited space requires a focus on only two minor subdivisions of archaeology that are particularly important for illuminating ancient economies: installations and numismatics.

Installations. The presence of any sort of production installation is tremendously valuable for reconstructing the ancient economy. Large productive installations, such as rock-cut oil presses, have significant fixed costs. They require the procurement of supplies and recruitment of dedicated labor; thus they presuppose some sort of central agency with the political and economic support for dedicated construction. The presence of a large-scale production facility, such as the Iron Age olive oil presses at seventh century B.C.E. Tel Miqne (Ekron) reveals that the society made a conscious decision to produce olive oil efficiently and at capacities far beyond local consumption. Such an investment requires the presence of a powerful and coercive central authority to manage the industry. With so much productive capacity, the olive oil must have traveled beyond the local vicinity whether as a tax, a gift, or an exported commodity. The olive oil installations at Tel Miqne contrast with the oil production facilities at Mansur al-ʿAqab. These presses are large but not as numerous, and they existed alongside *miqvaot* or "ritual baths." This juxtaposition of oil presses and baths suggest that the production of oil at Mansur al-ʿAqab required purity and that such oil was not useful for commodity trade but for ritual usage in the temple.

Numismatics. Coins begin to appear in the ancient Near East in the sixth century B.C.E., but they become much more common with Hellenization of the fourth and third centuries. Archaeological studies of coinage and dies can reveal their social functions. They were markers of value and tokens of symbolic payment. To a degree, they facilitated trade, although the NT rarely refers to coinage in this sense. Numismatics often combined local and imperial cultural elements. For example, a coin may be struck at Gaza according to the actual die inscription yet still contain the Athenian owl, known throughout the Hellenistic empire. The limited distribution of locally made coinage demonstrates that they were primarily intended for local usage. In addition, coinage with its symbolic properties shows the inseparability between political hegemony and economic systems. For example, the Bar Kokhba rebellion devoted enormous resources to mint their own coins, despite the short-lived nature of their regime. Undoubtedly, the development of such coinage was an attempt at self-legitimization of their reign. This shows that political desires deeply imbedded within economic systems.

Textual Evidence. Epigraphic records provide one of the most valuable sources for reconstructing the economic world of the Bible. The genres of written sources are much too exhaustive to cover. Besides the obvious economic archives, scholars turn to court records, epistolary letters, royal inscriptions, mathematic exercises, tribute lists, as well as ancient historiography, narrative, graffiti, treatises, seals, and seal impressions. Not all relevant textual evidence originates from biblical lands. For example, the Persepolis Fortification archives provide a rich resource for understanding the distributive organization of the Persian Empire. This discussion of textual evidence will be limited to two examples to illustrate the valuable usage of epigraphic texts for economics and the Bible: the Samaria Ostraca and the writings of Josephus.

Samaria Ostraca. The Samaria Ostraca are a collection of pottery shards with ink, which document a distribution of oil and wine among various individuals surrounding the capital of Samaria during the eighth century B.C.E. Although seemingly mundane, this archive provides a rare direct window into the prophetic invectives of Amos and Hosea. Significantly, the archive does not refer to mere wine and oil but consistently modifies the commodities as "aged wine" and "fine oil," signifying luxury goods over subsistence commodity. Also, the units of the product are not particularly voluminous but are instead a mere *nebel*, (roughly one liter), which negates any significant movement of commodity. Consequently, the archive does not reveal a mercantile setting but more of an elite movement of luxury goods around a capital city in small quantities. This elite economy centered on acts of prestation to gain political loyalties.

Josephus. Nonarchival literary texts can provide a valuable window to the economic world. For example, Josephus writes as a historian under the control of Roman propaganda, yet his writings reveal many aspects of the NT economy. He famously declared that despite industrial developments under the Roman Empire, "Judeans in Palestine were primarily agricultural" (*Ag. Ap.* 1.60), a figure confirmed by studies that estimate 80–90 percent of the workforce involved in agrarian work. Josephus also confirms the patron-client role of Herod (*J.W.* 1.408–15), the presence of a harbor for expanding sea trade (*J.W.* 1.409–14), and a variety of other economic indicators during the NT. Although historical documents contain biases and they do not intend to articulate descriptions of economic systems, their assumptions within the text allow for scholars to glean valuable insight to aid in economic concerns of biblical interpretation.

Limitations. Although the biblical interpreter has a broad range of sources to aid in discovering the economic issues of the Bible, these sources are highly limited and require judicious caution for multiple reasons. First, much of the HB period has a relative dearth of epigraphic archival documents, particularly in comparison to other chronological periods such as the Late Bronze Age Levant or Ptolemaic Egypt. Second, even with impressive advances in archaeological technology, the limited evidence cannot solve certain fundamental economic questions. For example, archaeological science can now identify the Judaean Hills origins of wheat according to the residue of ceramics of Ashkelon. But this cannot determine whether the wheat traveled to the port of Ashkelon for usage as a gift, tax, tribute, or commercial product. Third, one must beware of any economic reductionism in any of these sources, including biblical texts. When asking economic questions, one gets economic answers, which may not adequately cover the scope of the evidence.

Illustrations. The discipline of biblical studies is interested in economic systems because these systems reflect human behavior. The economic oppression in Egypt catalyzes the events of the Pentateuch and the concomitant law codes designed to counter future injustices ("Remember that you were a slave in the land of Egypt," Deut 15:15). The possession of land, the most valuable economic resource of antiquity, drives the entire conquest narrative and the ensuing division of that land. Economic issues play a central role throughout historical narratives of the Israelite and Judean monarchies (1 Kings 5:10–12; 10:1–9). Prophets often critique the economic plans of nations with a greater call to justice (Isa 58). Reference to economic blessing and the curse of financial destitution are frequent in the liturgy of the Psalms (12, 72, 82) and the teachings of wisdom literature (Prov 22:1–16).

The NT world addresses similar economic concerns but within the Greco-Roman client rule. The parables of Jesus regularly include tax collectors, estate managers, and slaves. Because of the enormous disparities in wealth, many of the teaching of Jesus combat this disparity, as well as the concomitant oppressive measures of debt and taxation. An economic reading of the Lord's Prayer (Matt 6:9; Luke 11:2) shows remarkable congruence with the social condition of most of the would-be hearers, making referring to hunger and provision, as well as issues of debt. This teaching is often explicitly coupled under the rubric of the kingdom of God, which countered the present oppressive economic realities of the day. The Pauline corpus also highlights the economic inequities (1 Cor 11:22), but also encourages the wealthy to sponsor communities of fictive kinships through the assembly or church (1 Cor 16:15). Acts implies a more favorable attitude toward Roman powers as the empire helps the Christian movement and the text takes a neutral view of commerce. (Acts 26:31–32) In contrast, Revelation boldly protests against the present economic practices, condemning Roman commercial practices (Rev 13:16–17).

A few brief examples can demonstrate a more specific analysis of the importance of economics in biblical interpretation.

The Law of Jubilee. The importance of kinship necessitates the inalienability of land to the proper holder as determined by kinship ties. Several biblical passages reinforce this value (Gen 23, 1 Kings 21). The land of Canaan was God's gift to people, both in covenantal promise, conquest, and subsequent allocation among the tribes. But due to the vagaries of agrarian economies in ancient Israel, farmers were vulnerable to economic downturns through drought, pestilence, or war. In such situations farmers had little choice but to go into debt, and the inevitable default on such debt resulted in seizure of their only asset, the family plot of land. In this context, the law of Jubilee protects the families from permanent loss of their ancestral land, "And you shall hallow the fiftieth year and you shall proclaim liberty throughout the land to all its inhabitants. It shall be a jubilee for you: you shall return, every one of you to your own property and every one of you to your family" (Lev 25:10).

The law of Jubilee has a lengthy history of precedent in other ancient law corpora, most prominently the Laws of Eshnunna. Ancient Near Eastern kings would proclaim such Jubilee as a symbol of their reign of justice. The essence of the Jubilee is the return of land to the original possessors.

Not only does one return the land, but the law of Jubilee allows for a release of Israelite slaves to their clans. "Then they and their children with them shall be free from your authority; they shall go back to their own family and return to their ancestral property" (Lev 25:41). Again, this law attempts to correct the results of economic circumstances that may lead an Israelite to be a bonded servant. Debt crises also resulted in indentured service along with the forfeiture of land to the lender. The release of Israelite slaves is thus tied to the release of the land—the emphasis of the field lying fallow for the Jubilee year connects the law to the holiness of the sabbath. Therefore, while the law is economic, the motivation to follow this biblical law is not economic but moral and religious. Few scholars contend that ancient Israel actually instituted such measures, as the Jubilee law is utopian and idealistic in character. But the codification of the Jubilee into biblical law reveals specific aspects of the ancient Israel economy. Land was theoretically inalienable, but certain economic circumstances must have resulted in the loss of land plots from their original holders. The Jubilee law intended to level such a social inequities. The motivation is not economic gain but rather recognition of the holiness of the land.

Amos's Condemnation of the Wealthy. Both the patristic interpreters and early Jewish writings recognized the explicit economic content of Amos. An economic reading of Amos 6:1–7 brings new insight to the background of a particularly derisive invective. In this passage, the prophet explicitly condemns the "notables of the first of the nations," a term in parallel with those "at ease in Zion" and "secure on Mount Samaria."

A few observations emerge in an economic reading. First, the inhabitants of Samaria and Judah likely found much solace in their economic strength rather than devotion to Yahweh. The inhabitants saw their prosperity as a reflex of God's blessing, a natural understanding of much Old Testament ethic. A brief survey of the eighth-century strata of Samaria, in fact, confirms much of this prosperity in a thriving city and significant luxury items such as ivories in the material remains. But for Amos, such material blessing does not equate spiritual well-being. The prophet compares them to other polities, specifically the Hittite city Calneh, the Aramaic stronghold Hamath, and the Philistia metropolis, Gath. All three city-states had thriving economies but eventually experienced major military defeat. In this sense, Amos points out that economic oppression may bring financial gain, but it is temporary and subservient to the providence of God's justice. Significantly, the prophet does not condemn the entire populations but only the "choicest," implying a significant division between the elite and the peasants who fed and provided for the elite. The former certainly read the words of Amos with fear and scorn, while the latter saw Amos as a hopeful message of blessing.

Second, Amos further condemns the material blessing of the elite by pointing out many of the trappings of their wealth. Amos condemns:

(1) ostentatious furniture: "beds of ivory" (v. 4), "couches" (v. 4); (2) luxurious meals: "lambs from the flock" (v. 4), "calves from the stall" (v. 4), "wine from bowls" (v. 6), "finest oils" (v. 6); (3) excessive leisure: "sound of the harp" (v. 5), "instruments of music" (v. 5). All of these terms are consumption goods beyond the level of mere subsistence. Amos contrasts these items with the Israelites' own spiritual heritage and obligation. As a result, the prophet portends disastrous consequences, "Therefore they now be the first to go into exile, and the revelry of the loungers shall pass away" (v. 7). The prophetic condemnation is not against the wealthy but against the accumulation of wealth via unjust means.

The Parable of the Pounds. Luke 19:11–27 (cf. Matt 25:14–30) presents a particularly puzzling condemnation of an economic situation through parable. A master compliments several of his stewards for taking an initial investment and increasing the total gain. But when one steward confesses to merely hiding the financial investment at no profit, he is sharply criticized, "Why then did you not put my money into the bank? Then when I returned, I could have collected it with interest" (Luke 19:23). The king then revokes the initial investment and hands it over to a faithful steward. Most interpretations of this parable center on two themes: (1) eschatology through admonition to act responsibly in preparation for Jesus's second coming, or (2) stewardship to exhort faithfulness and responsibility of one's resources given by God.

An economic reading of the parable of the pounds allows for a different understanding. Within a political economy of oppression, and an unmitigated cycle of elites extracting goods from the majority peasants, a social scientific approach shows that Jesus's parable attempts to expose these inequities. The returns of tenfold and fivefold from the initial investment are not revealed as anomalous but, in fact, line up with debt practices of the Greco-Roman peasants. Because peasants practiced subsistence strategies, the ideas of amassing wealth was incongruous to their own lifestyles, particularly in light of the anthropological notion of limited goods. Although the nobles who heard the story may have discerned a parable on honor and responsibility to the patron-client relationship, the peasants likely saw this parable as a protest against an economic system that allows such disparity. The protest becomes explicit when Jesus condemns the inequality by stating, "I tell you, to all those who have, more will be given; but from those who have nothing, even what they have will be taken away" (Luke 19:26). On a secondary exegetical level, interpretation must distinguish between the social context of the illiterate Galilean peasants who heard this message during the life of Jesus of Nazareth and the elite scribes who wrote this message.

An Assessment of Economics and the Bible. Biblical interpretation must continue to pursue an informed understanding of the economics of the text as they relate to the foreground and the background of the biblical message. Dialogue between the spheres of philology, anthropology, and archaeology provides a solid foundation for these matters. Continued advancements in each of these fields, as well as the growing technological prowess in archaeology, portend optimism in the field of economics and biblical interpretation.

[*See also* Class Criticism; Empire Studies and Biblical Interpretation; Historical Criticism, *subentry* Hebrew Bible; Historical Criticism, *subentry* New Testament; Materialist Criticism; Postcolonial Biblical Interpretation; Social Sciences, *subentry* Hebrew Bible; *and* Social Sciences, *subentry* New Testament.]

BIBLIOGRAPHY

Boer, Roland. "The Sacred Economy of Ancient 'Israel.'" *Scandinavian Journal of the Old Testament* 21 (2007): 29–48.

Chaney, Marvin L. "Bitter Bounty: The Dynamics of Political Economy Critiqued by the Eighth-Century Prophets." In *Reformed Faith and Economics*, edited by R. L. Stivers, 15–30. Lanham, Md.: University Press of America, 1989.

Dandamaev, Muhammad A. *Slavery in Babylonia: From Nabopolassar to Alexander the Great (626–331 B.C.)*. Translated by Victoria Powell, Marvin Powell, and David B. Weisberg. Dekalb: Northern Illinois University Press, 1984. English translation of *Rabstvo v vavilonii*, first published in 1974.

Elat, Moshe. *Economic Relations in the Land of the Bible (1000–539 B.C.E.).* Jerusalem: Mosad Bialik, 1977.

Faust, Avraham, and Ehud Weiss. "Judah, Philistia, and the Mediterranean World: Reconstructing the Economic System of the Seventh Century B.C.E." *Bulletin of the American Schools of Oriental Research* 338 (2005): 71–92.

Finley, Moses. *The Ancient Economy.* 2d ed. London: Hogarth, 1985.

Friesen, Steven. "Poverty in Pauline Studies: Beyond the So-Called New Consensus." *Journal for the Study of the New Testament* 26 (2004): 323–361.

Gottwald, Norman. *The Tribes of Yahweh: A Sociology of the Religion of Liberated Israel, 1250–1050 BCE.* Maryknoll, N.Y.: Orbis, 1979.

Hanson, K. C., and Douglas Oakman, eds. *Palestine in the Time of Jesus: Social Structures and Social Conflicts.* Minneapolis: Fortress, 1998.

Katz, Hayah. *A Land of Grain and Wine... A Land of Olive Oil and Honey: The Economy of the Kingdom of Judah.* Jerusalem: Yad Ben-Zvi Press, 2008.

Longenecker, Bruce W., and Kelly D. Liebengood, eds. *Engaging Economics: New Testament Scenarios and Early Christian Reception.* Grand Rapids: Eerdmans, 2009.

Malina, Bruce. *The New Testament World: Insights from Cultural Anthropology.* Rev. ed. Louisville: Westminster/John Knox, 1993.

Murphy, Catherine M. *Wealth in the Dead Sea Scrolls and in the Qumran Community.* Leiden: Brill, 2002.

Nam, Roger. *Portrayals of Economic Exchange in the Book of Kings.* Leiden: Brill, 2012.

Neyrey, Jerome, ed. *The Social World of Luke-Acts: Models for Interpretation.* Peabody, Mass.: Hendrickson, 1991.

Oakes, Peter. *Reading Romans in Pompeii: Paul's Letter at Ground Level.* Minneapolis: Fortress, 2009.

Polanyi, Karl. *The Great Transformation: The Political and Economic Origins of Our Time.* Boston: Beacon Press, 1944.

Scheidel, Walter, Ian Morris, and Richard Saller. *The Cambridge Economic History of the Greco-Roman World.* Cambridge: Cambridge University Press, 2008.

Wallerstein, Immanuel. *World-System Analysis: An Introduction.* Durham: Duke University Press, 2004.

Weber, Max. *Ancient Judaism.* Translated by H. H. Gerth and D. Martindale. New York: Free Press, 1952. English translation of *Das Antike Judentum*, 1917–1919.

Wittfogel, Karl. *Oriental Despotism: A Comparative Study of Total Power.* New Haven, 1957.

Roger S. Nam

Egyptology and Biblical Interpretation

Egypt was a vital and vibrant player on the ancient Mediterranean and Near Eastern world stages where biblical histories, narratives, and faiths were born and nurtured. For biblical literature, Egypt is particularly fundamental as the setting of foundational faith accounts such as the exodus, the Joseph story, and the flight of the holy family from Herod's wrath. Historically, Late Bronze Age Egypt administered an empire that stretched from Nubia (Kush) in the south to the Orontes River of Syria in the north and that created a cosmopolitan context which lasted throughout the first millennium B.C.E., in which different biblical peoples mingled in various circumstances (e.g., "Asiatics" in Egyptian tomb and temple depictions and inscriptions; a mercenary Jewish colony in Elephantine with its unorthodox and unsanctioned temple to Yahweh; the vibrant and creative Jewish community in Alexandria, the largest outside of Israel). Egypt also played a key historical role in the Hellenistic transformation and transmission of particular biblical writings (e.g., the Septuagint was created, according to legend, when Ptolemy II commissioned 72 Jewish scholars to translate the Torah from Hebrew into Greek for inclusion in the library of Alexandria; the Jewish philosopher Philo of Alexandria was greatly influenced by the doctrine of the Logos, also popular in early Christian understandings of Jesus, and interpreted the Septuagint by applying the Greek allegorical method, whereby he construed Moses as a philosopher who was the source of all later philosophy; Origen's Hexapla, the first major Christian recension of the Septuagint, was compiled in Alexandria). Furthermore, Gnosticism and Christian monasticism originated in Egypt, and Egypt was the place where key players in early Christianity lived and where important events and developments of early Christianity played out.

Egypt in the Bible. Egypt is referenced in numerous places in the biblical text. Sometimes it serves as the setting for a prolonged narrative (for example, the Joseph story in Gen 37—50; the beginning of the exodus narrative in Exod 1—15); sometimes for a brief account (for example, Pharaoh taking Sarah into his household in Gen 12:10–20); and sometimes it is mentioned or referenced only in passing (in genealogies and lists of nations as in Gen 10:6, 13; as a physical boundary or geographical designation such as the Wadi or Brook of Egypt as in Num 34:5; 1 Kgs 4:21; 2 Chr 7:8, 26:8; Isa 19:19, 27:12; Ezek 47:19; as the sister–wife analog in Gen 20:1–2 where Abraham tells Abimelech king of Gerar that Sarah is his sister). Most often Egypt occurs as a brief invocation of the collective memory—or retelling—of the exodus experience ("out of Egypt"); here Egypt is the ultimate, overweening tyrannical oppressor. Only occasionally and in scattered locations is the information about or reference to Egypt explicit, as in the following examples: individual pharaohs (e.g., in 2 Kgs 17:4; Shishak in 1 Kgs 11:40, 14:25 and 2 Chr 12:2, 5, 7, 9; Necho in 2 Kgs 23:29; 2 Chr 35:20 and Jer 46:2; Hophra in Jer 44:30) and specific Egyptians (e.g., Hagar in Gen 16:1; Bithiah daughter of pharaoh in 1 Chr 4:17); identifiable Egyptian cities (e.g., Memphis in Isa 19:13, Jer 2:16, 44:1, 46: 14, 19; Ezek 30: 13, 16 and Hos 9:6; Thebes in Ezek 30:15; Pelusium in Ezek 20:15); Egyptian gods (e.g., Amon of Thebes, Jer 46:25) and magicians (Gen 41:8, Exod 7:11, 22); and specific Egyptian commodities (e.g., horses in 1 Kgs 10:8; colored linens in Prov 7:16; cucumbers, melons, leeks, onions and garlic in Num 11:5).

Most commonly, however, Egyptian references in the Bible are nonspecific and even generic: the pharaoh/king of Egypt, fortresses of Egypt, cities of Egypt, riches of Egypt, "an Egyptian," and so forth. Neither the pharaoh nor the pharaoh's daughter that Solomon supposedly wed is identified by name in 1 Kgs 3:1. Ironically, Egypt is depicted in the biblical narrative not only as a place of oppression, but also as a place of refuge, especially for those seeking respite from famine and displacement, or fleeing politics or the law (e.g., Abraham in Gen 12:10; Hadad in 1 Kgs 11:17; Jeroboam in 1 Kgs 11:40; the flight into Egypt of the holy family in Matt 2:13–23) and even as a place of nostalgia for the Israelites wandering in the wilderness after Moses led them out of Egypt (Num 11:5).

Such references to Egypt may function on different levels in different contexts. They may be interpreted as literal or metaphorical, historical or literary. Their exact form and usage may reflect varying formative eras and processes within the textual history and poetics of the Hebrew Bible. Sorting out original from redacted and historical from fictional, and deciphering layers and nuances of meaning and reference are at best complex undertakings and at worst impossible ones. Egyptology can offer significant assistance with some—but not all—of these issues for passages invoking Egypt by providing independent assessments in two main areas: the reliability or extra-textual factuality of the Egyptian references within a given biblical text; and a reconstruction of the historical world and the forces shaping it at particular times. Questions of biblical interpretation most often asked of Egyptology thus focus around historical and chronological issues: the historicity and date of the Israelite slavery in and exodus from Egypt; the earliest mention of Israel as a people or "nation"; or the general historicity, or "reliability," of a particular biblical account. Redford, for example, undertook a thorough Egyptological study of the background setting of the Joseph story and came to two conclusions: first, that the Hebrew authors had only limited knowledge of Egypt; and second, that the genuine Egyptian elements in the story fixed its date between the seventh century B.C.E. and the third quarter of the fifth century B.C.E. (the Saite and early Persian periods in Egyptian history).

Further investigations have assessed possible Egyptian prototypes for specific literary genres, conventions, or passages: the relationship between Egyptian wisdom literature and the Book of Psalms; shared folkloric motifs such as the Egyptian "Tale of Two Brothers" and the biblical story of Joseph and Potiphar's wife; possible influences or intertextual relationships between Egyptian love poetry and Akhenaten's Hymn to the Aten on the one hand and the Song of Songs and Psalm 104 on the other. Similarly, Egyptology has helped illuminate the historical, religious and political background, and development of early Christianity in Egypt in ways that are beyond the scope of this article.

The Discipline of Egyptology. Egyptology may be defined as the modern academic study of ancient Egypt. Egyptologists, those who are trained in and practice Egyptology, sometimes discriminate further. For some, Egyptology proper includes only the study of pharaonic Egypt (Dynasties 1—30; until quite recently Dynasties 21—30 were often considered of marginal interest). For others it incorporates, in addition to pharaonic times, some or all of Egyptian prehistory (anything prior to Dynasty 1) and/or some or all of the period between the end of Dynasty 30 and the Islamic conquest of Egypt by ʻAmr Ibn Ben As in 641 C.E. (mainly Ptolemaic, Roman, and Late Antique Egypt). Egyptology has a number of subspecialties, including but not limited to: philology, epigraphy, archaeology, history (social history, economic history, political history, etc.), art history, religion, literature, papyrology, and Coptology (the study of Coptic language and literature). Sometimes scholars specializing in language-based study are designated "Egyptologists" in distinction from those studying material culture that lacks or has minimal language components, who are termed "Egyptian archaeologists."

Egyptologists go through years of training and typically spend their lives studying ancient Egypt. They function, to the extent possible, as modern interpreters of ancient Egyptian language, society, and culture. Egyptological training is critical for understanding nuances of language and for decoding and interpreting the visual culture of ancient Egypt, whether found in Egypt or elsewhere in the ancient Near East. In ancient Egypt, art, language, and cultural practice were symbiotically intertwined and highly formalized (although not unchanging), and knowledge of the language and culture is needed to understand art and text. Two examples will suffice to illustrate the point. First, seemingly discrete, historical battle accounts and reliefs in sacred settings (e.g., temples), belong to a symbolic rather than a literal historic world. While they may sometimes represent specific military events, more or less accurately portrayed, they also, and to the Egyptians more importantly, functioned as a nonhistorical representation of the semidivine power and status of the Egyptian king, who was responsible for vanquishing the enemies of Egypt and keeping chaos at bay. Kings, sometimes separated by thousands of years and sometimes far less, could and did simply copy earlier relief and battle campaign lists and thereby subsumed their precursor's achievements as a reflection of their own power and authority (just as a king could and did usurp a statue of his predecessor simply by erasing the name of the former owner and substituting his own). For example, a tribute scene belonging to the Fifth Dynasty King Sahure (approximately 2435–2429 B.C.E.) was copied with minimal changes by the Nubian king Taharqa (690–664 B.C.E.) in his Dynasty 25 Kawa Temple. The symbolic *functioning* of the scene was identical in both cases; historical accuracy was irrelevant.

Similarly, lists of conquered territories and towns (e.g., of Canaanite cities and locales found at Karnak Temple) are sometimes partial or whole copies of each other, rather than independent attestations of different historical campaigns. Thus, the reliability of what may appear to us initially to be historical Egyptian texts and relief cannot be assumed, but must be carefully investigated.

Second, Egyptian gods and goddesses do not have individually unique sets of attributes and titles; rather, they often share visual characteristics and epithets. A lioness goddess could represent Mut, Sekhmet, Pakhet, or any number of lesser-known deities. Many deities could be depicted with solar discs and horns. Only an accompanying text can identify with certainty the specific god or goddess depicted. Just as an intimate knowledge of Hebrew and the material culture of Israel and Palestine are required to truly appreciate the artistry and nuance of the biblical text and the cultural settings of the biblical narrative, so an extensive background in Egyptology is necessary to truly evaluate and appreciate Egyptian influence on and in the biblical narrative, or the intertextual dialogue between the two cultures. The late Miriam Lichtheim, an accomplished Israeli Egyptologist, once commented in a book review: "[C]an a Bible scholar who is not also a full-fledged Egyptologist deal adequately with the interrelations of Israelite and Egyptian wisdom literatures? I think the answer is, No."

"Ancient Egypt," the primary focus of Egyptologists' research, may be defined as the territory comprising the Egyptian delta (Lower Egypt), the Faiyum, and the Nile Valley (Middle and Upper Egypt). This territory extends from the Mediterranean Sea to the first cataract at Aswan. Egyptologists also often study related areas with extensive ancient Egyptian remains, such as the five western desert oases, Sinai, and Nubia.

Conventionally, the origins of modern Egyptology as a scholarly discipline are traced back to Napoleon's military and cultural invasion of Egypt from 1798 to 1801. This "French Expedition" was the first major imperialist incursion into the Middle East in modern times. In addition to soldiers, Bonaparte's forces included "savants," scholars who were charged with studying and recording both the surviving remnants of ancient Egyptian civilization and current Egyptian life ways. The results of their work were published between 1809 and 1829 in the monumental, multivolume *Description de l'Égypte*. Publication of the *Description* both marked a climax of European antiquarianism in the Middle East and inaugurated a new, professional stage in the study of Egypt which was given further impetus and authority by the decipherment of the three-script dual language Rosetta Stone (unearthed by Napoleon's troops and seized by the British as a spoil of war) by Champollion in 1822–1824. Europeans would dominate all aspects of Egyptology for approximately the next century, and they maintained a jealous, colonial control over ancient Egyptian antiquities throughout this time, excluding, with rare exception, Egyptians from the study of their own past. In the 1880s, Petrie did for Egyptian (and Palestinian/Biblical) archaeology what Champollion had done for Egyptian language, placing it on a sound scientific basis (within a positivist notion of science).

Prior to Bonaparte's invasion, Western interest in ancient Egypt had been dominantly antiquarian, and filtered through the twin Renaissance lenses of classical civilization and biblical text. Both lenses fostered cultural dichotomies, implicit and explicit, whereby ancient Egypt was the "other": an alien, exotic and despotic land and culture to be seen in opposition to "civilized" classical or "sacred" biblical society, history and culture. Egypt was especially essential to the creation of what has been dubbed the Judeo-Christian tradition, a conceptual construct that elides historical, theological and cultural differences and has recently come under much criticism. It was in Egypt that Joseph and the Israelites sojourned; it was in Egypt that the Israelite captivity occurred; and it was from Egyptian tyranny that the Israelites fled under the liberating leadership of Moses during the exodus. Egypt was also presented as the childhood home of Christ and the birthplace of monasticism. With increasing travel to and familiarity with Egypt both before but especially after the French Expedition, an ongoing conflation of the ancient Egyptian and modern Islamic worlds took place in the minds of Western visitors, and a progressive, self-reinforcing and disaffecting "orientalism" was set in motion that continued into the nineteenth and twentieth centuries and still colors popular opinion about and some scholarship on Egypt even today.

Egyptology and Biblical Studies. Egyptology and biblical criticism thus came of age at approximately the same time. Both fields, along with biblical and Ancient Near Eastern studies more generally, achieved major linguistic, archaeological, and methodological breakthroughs during the nineteenth and through the mid-twentieth centuries, with new discoveries continually and sometimes spectacularly expanding frontiers of knowledge. For example, the unearthing, around 1887, of the Amarna letters detailing relations between fourteenth century B.C.E. pharaohs and their vassals in Syria-Palestine as well as with contemporaries in the eastern Mediterranean and Near East was followed by the identification and investigation—still ongoing—of Amarna/Akhet-Aten, the capital city of the "heretic" pharaoh Akhenaten. Both these discoveries were of major importance for illuminating the broader biblical world of the fourteenth century B.C.E. Another major find of this era was Carter's discovery in 1922 of the almost intact tomb of the pharaoh Tutankhamon in the Valley of the Kings.

During this time disciplinary divisions remained more fluid, specializations less exacting, consensus views more easily achieved (doubtless at least partially because there were comparatively fewer scholars in any given field), and the sheer quantities of available knowledge less overwhelming than is the case today. Consequently, a number of scholars were able to pursue training in multiple related fields both within and across cultural areas. Early pioneering linguists such as de Sacy and Champollion were polyglots; early archaeologists such as Petrie worked in both Egypt and Palestine. Most of the earlier Egyptologists concerned themselves not only with pharaonic Egypt, but also equally with Graeco-Roman and Coptic Egypt. Many Egyptologists of the nineteenth and earlier twentieth centuries studied classical and Semitic languages and undertook archaeological work in Egypt as well. Similarly, early biblical scholars, such as Albright, were proficient in numerous Semitic languages, as well as Egyptian, and often also practiced what was then known as biblical archaeology.

Although Egyptology and biblical studies were distinct, separate fields, there was a cross fertilization between the two that was founded on and often reinforced by the perceived common Judeo-Christian heritage of the practitioners of both disciplines that crossed national boundaries. This perceived common heritage invoked a shared, faith-based interest in the history and development of the Bible and the world in which it purported to take place that also underpinned and reinforced the imperialism and colonialist endeavors of the time. Thus, in 1882 the British Society for the Promotion of Excavation in the Delta of the Nile was founded and funded specifically to recover "a lost period of biblical history" by locating and investigating sites associated with the Joseph and Exodus narratives. And throughout the disciplinary advances of the next approximately one hundred years, a shared belief in and acceptance of the basic historicity and "reliability" of the biblical narrative dominated biblical research.

Critical methodologies concentrated on applying different tools to tracing the origins and historical development of what was seen as a predominantly historical biblical narrative. This consensus view was accepted, reflected, and supported by scholars investigating the intersections of biblical studies and Egyptology. Accordingly, in 1959, the eminent French Egyptologist Montet published a slim volume entitled *L'Égypte et la Bible* (published in English in 1968, after Montet's death, as *Egypt and the Bible*) that examined Egyptian references in the Hebrew Bible by accepting the basic historicity, reliability, and primacy of the Hebrew text as the starting point of his investigation. Montet perfectly captured the then-consensus view that accepted the apparently historical portions of the Hebrew Bible largely at face value. The biblical text was to be understood literally and factually, and Egyptological insights were to be applied as relevant to flesh out or clothe the biblical body.

As the later twentieth century has progressed and turned into the twenty-first, scholarship and scholars have become ever more specialized and the mass of relevant available knowledge ever more copious and weighty. Different, more highly nuanced and sophisticated interpretive and theoretical paradigms have come into favor, drawn, *inter alia*, from related fields such as sociology, anthropology, psychology, history, and literary criticism. The prior consensus on the basic historical reliability and recoverability of different stages of the biblical narrative has long since vanished, initially replaced gradually and then abruptly in a burst of publicity in the 1990s, by the highly contentious and often political debates between the so-called "minimalists" (who believe that the biblical text is too untrustworthy to be used even selectively for historical purposes, and that the concept of what they term "biblical Israel" is hopelessly problematic) and the so-called "maximalists" (those who defend the historical reliability of the Bible).

Neither group is monolithic and both have extremes eschewed by the vast majority of biblical scholars. Minimalist Philip Davies, for example, believes that the bulk of the Bible was composed during the Persian Period in the fifth century B.C.E., whereas fellow minimalist Niels Peter Lemche dates the composition of the Bible to Hellenistic times (third to second centuries B.C.E.). Some maximalists, such as archaeologist William Dever, are continuing proponents of a modified version of the earlier consensus view of the basic historical reliability of the Hebrew Bible; others, such as Iain Provan and Egyptolotists Kenneth Kitchen and James Hoffmeier are conservative evangelical Christians. Practitioners on each side, however, share a basic approach to and attitude about the historicity of the Hebrew Bible and "biblical Israel."

Much of biblical scholarship has now moved beyond this so-called minimalist-maximalist dichotomy. Some of the minimalist arguments have been rejected; others have been adapted and adopted into mainstream biblical scholarship. In particular, a growing number of biblical scholars see major discrepancies and contradictions between the biblical account of history and the history that has been and is being uncovered, *inter alia*, by the application of new archaeological and literary methodologies and theories and differing sociological, historical, and psychological models. Even some of those who continue to see the biblical narrative as offering a reliable historical framework view that reliability as diminishing with increasing levels of detail. Attention is now more often turned inwards and focused on issues such as collective memory and self-understanding, the processes of redaction and collective authorship and transmission of individual biblical books, intertextual biblical conversations, and the explication or interpretation of particular biblical passages.

The pace of new archaeological and historical discoveries has slowed, although not stopped, and the sheer mass of accumulated data and knowledge and theoretical approaches in diverse disciplines has long since precluded the once comparatively easy movement of scholars across disciplinary boundaries. No longer can one scholar control all the material available in even one discipline, let alone several, and few scholars today undertake serious training in more than one field. This is unfortunate, as proper assessment of Egyptian references in and possible influence on the biblical text really requires training in both fields. The few Egyptologists who also have training in biblical studies and who today still venture into biblical studies on a regular basis include Donald Redford, Jan Assmann (also a distinguished scholar of the history of religions), Stefan Jakob Wimmer, James Hoffmeier, and Kenneth Kitchen. Biblical scholars with Egyptological training include Manfred Görg, Nili Shupak, and Michael V. Fox.

Understanding the direction and focus of biblical research and how biblical scholars evaluate and have evaluated the historical worth of the biblical text are critical to understanding past, present, and possible future contributions of Egyptology to biblical studies. Egyptology and Egyptologists can help illuminate the biblical text, but only within strict parameters. Occasionally and indirectly, references to Egyptian material can illuminate a redaction or date of composition, as demonstrated by Redford's analysis of the Joseph narrative. Literary parallels of genre and motif, such as Wisdom Literature, the narrative of the sister-wife, and the man seduced by another man's wife, can be identified by those with general knowledge of the literary output of both Egyptian and biblical culture. However, only those scholars fluent in both biblical languages and Egyptian can speak with authority about potential Egyptian linguistic influence on the nuances and turns of phrase in the biblical text.

Where Egyptology has made, and likely will continue to make, its greatest contribution to biblical studies is in its provision of an independent, outside (non-Israelite) witness to the broader historical currents and international players that provided the framework within which biblical society operated and biblical events played out. This testimony is particularly important for those eras prior to the Saite Period (Dynasty 26, 664–525 B.C.E.), during and after which a combination of cross-cultural and internal synchronisms provide, with only rare exception, very secure dates across the Eastern Mediterranean and Near Eastern worlds. Thus, for example, the Merenptah Stela, also known as the Israel Stela, discovered in Merenptah's mortuary temple at Thebes by Petrie in 1896, provides the earliest generally accepted reference to "Israel." Israel is spelled with the determinative (grammatical marker) for peoples, although exactly what entity "Israel" designates in this context remains unclear.

In the 1970s, the late Egyptologist Frank Yurco examined reliefs at Karnak traditionally dated to Ramesses II (1279–1213 B.C.E.) and redated them to Merenptah (1213–1203 B.C.E.), son of Ramesses II. These reliefs include four battle scenes, three of which illustrate the capture of cities. Only one vignette preserves the name of the city depicted: Ashkelon. Yurco hypothesized, in parallel with the Merenptah Stela, that the other two cities shown were Gezer and Yanoam. The fourth scene, of which only the bottom is preserved, depicts a battle in open hilly terrain against an enemy clothed in Canaanite garb; Yurco identified this enemy as the Israelites. Although Yurco's interpretation is intriguing, it nevertheless deals with probabilities rather than certainties. Since only one relief caption survives, that identifying Ashkelon, Yurco's equation of the remaining three scenes with the passage in the Merenptah Stela referencing Israel, as well as the identification of the scene depicting Israelites, can be done by inference only—and assumes to begin with that Yurco's redating of the relief scenes to Merenptah, which is not accepted by all Egyptologists, is correct.

A similar situation pertains to the exodus. Despite years of active searching, and the spilling of gallons of scholarly ink, absolute proof of the historicity of the exodus remains elusive. Scholars still must rely on probability and inference when invoking Egyptian evidence to support a historical exodus. Religiously conservative scholars and others who affirm the primary historicity of the Bible argue that there is nothing in the Egyptian evidence that contradicts a historical exodus, and much that supports the biblical account.

How one evaluates the importance of Egyptology's independent Egyptian witness to biblical events and the wider biblical world therefore depends entirely on how one assesses the general historical reliability of the Bible. Only occasionally are there comparatively clear and straightforward biblical accounts that provide helpful cross-cultural synchronisms with Egypt. One such example is Shishak's invasion of Judah in the fifth year of King Rehoboam (1 Kgs 14:25; 2 Chr 12:2). Shishak may be identified with Sheshonq I (943–923 B.C.E.), the first king of Egypt's Libyan Twenty-second Dynasty (Kitchen uses biblical chronology to date Sheshonq I). Sheshonq I had inscribed on the walls of Karnak Temple a detailed account of his campaign into Judah, and here there is a discrepancy with the biblical testimony. The biblical narrative explicitly states that Shishak conquered Jerusalem; however, Jerusalem is not found among the cities and territories that Sheshonq proclaimed to the world at Karnak that he vanquished during his military campaign to Judah. Another example of an event recounted in the Bible that connects Egyptian and biblical history is the killing of Josiah, king of Judah, by the Egyptian Pharaoh Necho at Megiddo (1 Kgs 23:29; 2 Ch35:20–22).

Egyptology cannot and should not be used to interpret metaphorical uses of Egypt in biblical poetry or its role as a foil for the construction of an Israelite collective identity and the self-understanding that underlies it within the world of biblical narrative. Egyptology is irrelevant to that self-understanding and to the construction of Israelite identity vis-à-vis a constructed, often metaphorical Egyptian "other," especially when Egypt merely represents that which is not the biblical collective self. Egyptology cannot nor should it comment on Israelite memories of Egypt or anything else. Postbiblical rabbinic exegesis increasingly refers to such a metaphorical Egypt, simply because of its historical distance from ancient Egypt. Egyptology is therefore also irrelevant for rabbinic references to Egypt in their biblical exegesis, except when such references are to late antique Talmudic contemporaries of Egyptian culture and history.

Thus, Egyptology can help and has helped shine important historical, cultural, and literary light on particular historical eras, practices, events, and individuals in the biblical narrative as well as on literary topoi at those points where the Egyptian and Israelite historical and literary worlds intersect. Here Egyptology has much to offer biblical interpretation. In cases where biblical scholarship chooses to focus on Israelite collective memory and self-understanding, however, Egyptology can offer precious little.

[*See also* Diachronic Interpretation; Historical Criticism, *subentry* Hebrew Bible; *and* Translation Techniques, *subentry* Ancient Versions.]

BIBLIOGRAPHY

Baines, John, and Jaromir Malek. *Cultural Atlas of Ancient Egypt*. Rev. ed. New York: Checkmark Books, 2000. Still the best single-volume introduction to and overview of ancient Egypt.

Fox, Michael V. *The Song of Songs and the Ancient Egyptian Love Songs*. Madison: University of Wisconsin Press, 1985.

Frerichs, Ernest S., and Leonard H. Lesko, eds. *Exodus: The Egyptian Evidence*. Winona Lake, Ind.: Eisenbrauns, 1997. This slim volume presents a collection of six papers by well-known scholars that provides an overview of recent scholarship on the Exodus and Israelite settlement, with extensive bibliographies.

Hoffmeier, James K. *Israel in Egypt: The Evidence for the Authenticity of the Exodus Tradition*. Oxford: Oxford University Press, 1996. Hoffmeier provides a detailed examination of the biblical Exodus account that incorporates recent textual, historical archaeological scholarship. He concludes by affirming the plausibility and inherent likelihood of the historicity of that account. Hoffmeier dedicated this volume to K.A. Kitchen.

Kitchen, K.A. *On the Reliability of the Old Testament*. Grand Rapids, Mich.: Eerdmans, 2003. Kitchen is a prolific, erudite and very eminent emeritus professor of Egyptology who for many years was almost the only major Egyptologist with a serious interest in Egypt of the first millennium B.C.E. In this 684 page book, Kitchen marshals his extensive learning and conservative religious beliefs in defense of the basic historicity of the biblical narrative and to make the strongest case possible for minimizing the minimalists.

Montet, Pierre. *Egypt and the Bible*. Philadelphia, Fortress, 1968. This slight volume by one of the most eminent Egyptologists of his time (who passed away while the English translation of the book was in preparation) is divided into two parts, both of which privilege the biblical narrative. The first deals with "historical facts and geographic settings;" the second sets out information provided "explicitly or implicitly" by the Bible about "the customs, religion, and ethics of the ancient Egyptians." The book is mostly of interest as an example of unsophisticated and unquestioning acceptance of the biblical historical account.

Redford, Donald B. *A Study of the Biblical Story of Joseph (Genesis 37–50)*. Leiden, Netherlands: Brill, 1970. Redford undertakes a thorough study of the story of Joseph, assessing it from a literary and biblical perspective and also evaluating it from the point of view of an Egyptologist seeking to determine how much knowledge of Egypt was actually reflected in the narrative. He concludes that the story reflects surprisingly little real knowledge of Egypt and Egyptian customs, and that the Egyptian background portrayed in the narrative may be dated between the seventh century B.C.E. and the third quarter of the fifth century B.C.E.

Reid, Donald Malcolm. *Whose Pharaohs? Archaeology, Museums and Egyptian National Identity from Napoleon to World War I*. Berkeley, Calif.: University of California Press, 2002. Reid examines the evolution of Egyptology in the context of Western imperialism and incipient Egyptian nationalism. Reid writes pioneering Egyptians back into the history of Egyptology and discusses Western and Egyptian perceptions of the various stages of Egypt—pharaonic, Greco-Roman, Coptic, and Islamic.

Russell, Stephen C. *Images of Egypt in Early Biblical Literature: Cisjordan-Israelite, Transjordan-Israelite, and Judahite Portrayals*. New York: Walter de Gruyter, 2009. Russell's book is a revised version of his NYU doctoral dissertation. Building on recent scholarship, Russell argues that the memory of Egypt (by which he essentially means the exodus from Egypt) in early biblical traditions was not monolithic, but instead differed in different regions, reflecting a diversity of the memory of Egypt. He examines biblical texts he identifies as early, and differentiates temporal and geographical differences in biblical memories of Egypt in those texts.

Ulmer, Rivka. *Egyptian Cultural Icons in Midrash*. New York: Walter De Gruyter, 2009. Rivka addresses the significance of Egypt in Rabbinic texts, concentrating on rabbinic use of Egyptian images and concepts in midrash. She notes that one of the major objectives of rabbinic portrayals of Egypt was to present rabbinic Judaism in opposition to Egyptian culture, thereby establishing and reinforcing boundaries of Jewish identity.

Whitehouse, Helen. "Egypt in European Thought." In *Civilizations of the Ancient Near East*, Vol. 1, edited by Jack M. Sasson, 15–31. New York: Simon & Schuster Macmillan, 1995. Whitehouse provides a brief overview of Western attitudes to and knowledge of ancient Egypt from Late Antique times to approximately the mid-twentieth century.

Yurco, Frank J. "Merenptah's Canaanite Campaign," *Journal of the American Research Center in Egypt* 23 (1986): 189–215. Yurco's article lays out his discovery and interpretation of reliefs at Karnak that he redates from the time of Ramesses II to that of Merenptah and that he believes include a battle vignette depicting Israelites.

Carol A. Redmount

EMPIRE STUDIES AND BIBLICAL INTERPRETATION

Empire studies, also known as empire-critical or imperial-critical approaches, are a recent development in biblical scholarship. Though some contemporary Hebrew Bible work has increasingly foregrounded engagement with empires (Horsley 2008; Carr and Conway 2010; Portier-Young 2011; Perdue 2012), Empire studies have largely examined New Testament (NT) texts. Because of space limits, the NT scholarship will be the focus of this article.

NT Empire studies developed in the 1990s. While a few previous NT works took the Roman Empire seriously as the context for the emergence of the early Jesus movement and its writings—for example, Adolf Deissmann's groundbreaking *Light from the Ancient East* (1910)—twentieth-century New Testament scholarship has largely ignored the imperial world. Since the early 1990s, Empire studies have been redressing this neglect through journal articles (*Union Seminary Quarterly Review* 2005), edited volumes (Horsley 2008) and monographs (Carter 2006). Scholarship has examined interactions with the Roman Empire involving the historical Jesus, Paul and the Pauline tradition, the Gospels and Gospel communities, and other NT writings including Revelation.

Definition. Empire studies understand and engage the NT writings and early Jesus movement as products of the Roman Empire, namely the extensive area, people, and resources over which the central city of Rome exercised its power and extended its control by various political, economic, military, and religious means. Empire studies (hereafter ES) focus on the interactions between Jesus-followers and the Roman Empire. The approach recognizes that the early New Testament texts emerge from, are enmeshed in, and engage this world of empire in which power was located in the hands of a small wealthy, high status elite. ES thus investigate, make visible, and evaluate the represented interactions between this pervasive context of empire and the New Testament texts and early Jesus communities.

The task of "making visible" is fundamental because frequently contemporary readers of the NT writings, living in social contexts that differ significantly from those of the Roman Empire and socialized into reading strategies not attuned to imperial realities, are not familiar with the structures of imperial rule that pervade the texts and with which the texts are engaged in various ways. The plural language of multiple forms of engagements and interactions indicates that such engagements between Jesus-followers and the empire were not monolithic. New Testament texts are neither wholly opposed to the imperial world nor wholly in support of it. Rather, they negotiate it with diverse, simultaneous interactions.

Empire studies, then, investigate such matters as strategies by which Jesus-followers negotiated the Roman imperial order on a daily basis, how the NT texts represent and engage the vision of human existence and societal organization enacted by Rome, how the writers of the NT texts conceive of life in the empire for those committed to the purposes/empire of God manifested in Jesus, and how NT texts validate, cooperate with, imitate, reinscribe, contest, compete with, counter, or attack (and combinations thereof) the ways in which life and society are organized under Roman rule.

Empire studies also address two further matters. Much NT scholarship has not considered questions of imperial engagement, and so has interpreted NT texts without taking into account imperial dynamics. ES evaluate, critique, and expose the neglect of imperial dynamics in existing scholarship. In doing so, their readings frequently contest the nonpolitical, spiritualized, religious reading strategies that much biblical interpretation has employed. In addition, with a focus on matters of power and societal visions, ES are well placed to consider the implications of imperial-critical readings for contemporary ecclesial and neo-imperial contexts.

Emergence of Empire Studies. At least seven factors account for the emergence of ES in the late twentieth century, partly as a reaction against the limited purview of existing methods, and partly as an embracing of new questions and approaches.

One factor reacts against the long history of depoliticized and spiritualized interpretations or readings of NT texts. Such readings have, more often than not, focused on ideas and concepts ("doctrine"), avoiding sociopolitical factors. They have constructed early Jesus-followers as minds without bodies, relationships, and societal interaction. Since the 1970s, social-scientific criticism, employing sociological and cross-cultural anthropological models, has emphasized the embodied, communal, and cultural practices of the early Christian movement. Such a focus inevitably requires consideration of the Roman imperial world.

Also contributing to the neglect of imperial realities in NT scholarship has been a widespread (mis) understanding of religion as a private matter of individual choice. In the Roman world, religion was much more civic and communal than private and individual. Likewise, contemporary emphases on the (imagined) separation of church and state have blinded scholars to the ways in which religion was embedded in political, household, civic, economic, and societal institutions and practices in the Roman world. To speak of religion in the Roman Empire is to speak of these dimensions. Engaging the NT texts must lead into, not away from, sociopolitical dimensions.

A third factor involves the irony of recognizing the nonhistorical manner in which historical studies have often misrepresented first-century Jesus and Jewish communities. Commonly the early Jesus movement and its texts have been examined as distinct from and against first-century "Judaism." That approach is problematic for several reasons, not the least of which is that it artificially and anachronistically separates the early Jesus movement from Judaism. But it also constructs Jewish communities and Jesus-believers as "religion-only" communities, isolating them from the sociopolitical and economic realities of the invisible Roman imperial world. The construction fails to recognize, for example, the numerous ways that Diaspora synagogues were societally engaged, with multiple ways of negotiating imperial power (Carter 2011). Moreover, this pervasive emphasis on ethnicity in NT studies (Gentiles versus Jews) neglects other factors of power including gender and societal status.

Fourth, since the second half of the twentieth century, scholars have paid much attention to the diversity and vibrancy of first-century Jewish life and traditions. While the discovery of the Dead Sea Scrolls and renewed attention to other collections of Jewish literatures have helpfully revised negative stereotypes, less attention has been paid to the Greco-Roman world. Empire studies trouble this exclusive Jewish focus by recognizing that Jewish and Jesus communities interacted with a complex world that comprised larger political (Roman imperial) and cultural (Hellenistic) forces all too often neglected by a monolithic focus.

Fifth, when scholarly attention has been paid to the Roman Empire, it has often misrepresented its structures and reach. To depict the empire as a "New Testament background," for example, significantly diminishes the imperial foreground of sociopolitical, economic, cultural, and religious structures that the Jesus-movement engaged. The language of "background" distances Jesus-believers from the empire, thereby rendering invisible the numerous ways by which Jesus-followers negotiated that imperial world. Some "Church-and-State" approaches have, ironically, paid little attention to Roman imperial structures and practices (Pilgrim 1999). Others, including popular sentiments, have foregrounded persecution as the dominant dynamic despite the lack of evidence for first-century Jesus-followers being subjected to daily, empire-wide, life-and-death persecution. More adequate formulations are needed.

Sixth, postcolonial perspectives have foregrounded previously silenced, neglected, and marginal voices and groups, and focused attention on the means, impact, and legacy of imperial power over colonized peoples. Numerous studies of the experiences of colonized peoples, pioneered for instance in the work of Edward Said (1993), have provided NT scholars with a body of theoretical and lived knowledge that provides insights for investigating the NT writings and communities that also originate among colonized peoples. These studies have shown that such relationships are much more complex than a restricted focus on persecution, or a simplistic "fight or flight" alternative, or an opposition-accommodation dualism employed by early Empire studies.

And seventh, as often happens in NT studies, impetus for exploring questions concerning imperial power has come from contemporary situations. These situations include international discourse over the roles of superpowers such as the United States in the global village, as well as studies of empires in disciplines such as literary and international relations studies, and especially various and multidisciplinary forms of postcolonial studies. These situations of impetus also involve increasing numbers of scholars from former colonies of European powers with first-hand experience of colonial power.

Pioneering Studies and Practitioners. While Empire studies have engaged most NT writings, space limits permit only a selective account here. Attention will focus briefly on work on the historical Jesus, Pauline and Gospel writings, and Revelation.

Jesus. Within NT studies, the resurgence of work in historical Jesus studies in the 1980s provided initial openings. The axiom, articulated for example by E. P. Sanders (1985, p. 55), that accounts of Jesus's life and teaching must account for Jesus's crucifixion, required scholars to take seriously Jesus's crucifixion as a distinctively Roman form of execution. Attention to this question meant locating Jesus in relation to imperial dynamics. Books such as Richard Horsley's, *Jesus and the Spiral of Violence: Popular Jewish Resistance in Roman Palestine* (San Francisco, 1987) and John Dominic Crossan's, *The Historical Jesus: The Life of a Mediterranean Jewish Peasant* (San Francisco, 1991) sought to understand Jesus's interaction with his imperial context, as did William Herzog's *Parables as Subversive Speech: Jesus as Pedagogue of the Oppressed* (Louisville, Ky., 1994). More recent discussions include Richard Horsley, *Jesus and Empire: the Kingdom of God and the New World Disorder* (Minneapolis, 2003), and John Dominic Crossan, *God and Empire: Jesus Against Rome, Then and Now* (San Francisco, 2007).

Paul. Work on Paul's negotiation of the Roman Empire gained initial momentum from several sources. Neil Elliott's *Liberating Paul: The Justice of God and the Politics of the Apostle* (Maryknoll, N.Y., 1994), spurred by contemporary geopolitical events such as the first Iraq war, employed a liberation hermeneutic to wrestle with Paul and his often oppressive legacy in order to construct a Paul who speaks a liberating word in the midst of oppressive empires past and present. Elliott's goal was to find an ecclesially useful Paul, one that could shape liberative visions and acts of justice.

Further attention emerged from the Society of Biblical Literature's Paul and Politics Group chaired initially by Richard Horsley and Cynthia Kittredge. Between 1997 and 2003, this section published three books exploring interaction between Paul and the Roman Empire, comprising some seven hundred pages and at least thirty-six chapters, the work of about thirty scholars (Horsley 1997, 2000, 2003).

The clearest methodological statements appear in the introductory essays to several of these volumes. In his introductory essay to *Paul and Empire,* Horsley observes the irony that before Christianity became the Empire's established religion, it "was an anti-imperial movement" (Horsley 1997, p. 1). Horsley rejects a Lutheran theological Paul but sees Paul as one who, while expecting the end of this imperially-dominated age, was establishing assemblies that were alternative to the "assemblies" of the empire's provincial cities.

Horsley finds these emphases anticipated in Krister Stendahl's significant essay (1963) that challenged the predominantly theological and individualized interpretation of Paul (Horsley 2000, pp. 5–15). Stendahl moved the emphasis from individual sin, salvation, and justification by faith to salvation history that included both Israel and Gentiles, and to social-human relations in the messianic communities Paul addressed. In turn, these emphases were developed by participants in social movements for liberation such as African American, feminist, non-European and/or "two-thirds World," and Jewish interpreters, as well as by dis-eased western male scholars. These scholars shared a common concern with diverse and interrelated forms of domination such as race, gender, ethnicity, social status, etc. They exposed, for instance, the use of Paul by colonizing western missionaries to enforce submission of women and local peoples, and by Christian scholars to perpetuate anti-Judaism.

Horsley highlights the limits of Western privatized and depoliticized interpretations of biblical texts. He points especially to the imperialistic nature of scholarly inquiry that assumed and asserted European/American elite male interests to be universal and that silenced the interests, experiences, identities, and voices of all others. He also notes the silence of biblical scholars on major sociopolitical issues, the inability of the "new perspective on Paul" to move outside the traditional opposition of Paul to Judaism, and the continuing neglect of imperial and power dynamics in various other new methods (social-scientific; postmodernist; cultural studies).

In this context, the SBL "Paul and Politics" group emerged to investigate four interrelated areas: Paul and the politics of the Roman Empire, of Paul's churches, of Israel, and of interpretation of Paul (Horsley 2000, p. 11). Horsley outlines four principles that guide political interpretations of Paul. (1) Texts and interpretations are sites of struggle among various voices. (2) The production and interpretation of texts do not just involve ideas but power relations, interests, values, and visions. (3) Both texts and interpreters occupy particular social locations and contexts requiring systemic analysis of wider political-economic-religious structures and power relations as well as of local assemblies. There is a special interest in "readings from below," in the marginalized and oppressed with demystification and liberation in view. (4) Interpreters' identity and social location are hybrid and complex, embracing multiple positions and perspectives involving various interrelationships of class, gender, race, and ethnicity. Horsley summarizes the approach by saying: "The aims and agenda of the Paul and Politics group are, broadly, to problematize, interrogate, and re-vision Pauline texts and interpretations, to identify oppressive formulations as well as potentially liberative visions and values in order to recover their unfulfilled historical possibilities, all in critical mutual engagement among diverse participants" (Horsley 2000, p. 15).

Beyond the Paul and Politics group, John Dominic Crossan and Jonathan Reed's 2004 book, *In Search of Paul* (San Francisco, 2004), presents Paul in a somewhat limited, monolithic, oppositional relationship to Rome's Empire ("the normalcy of civilization") with God's kingdom embodied in alternative communities. Pursuing an analysis based on this oppositional dynamic, they see clashes between two visions of peace (the empire's based on military victory and God's based in justice), between Rome's golden age and Paul's eschatology (1 Thess), between the blessings of Romanization and gospel blessings (Gal), between contrasting visions of divinity (Phil), between hierarchical patronage and equality (1 Cor), between global imperial distinctions and global unity and justice (Rom). Moving beyond many of the discussions in the Paul and Politics volumes, Crossan and Reed explicitly engage implications for contemporary followers of Jesus living in the American empire.

Other contributions have continued to expand or nuance the discussion, particularly in moving beyond a monolithic antithetical interaction. Peter Oakes (2005) sought to move away from an exclusively oppositional model of interaction between Jesus-assemblies and the empire in 1 Thessalonians and Philippians. In relation to these Pauline letters, Oakes considers four possible interactions: Rome and Jesus-believers follow common patterns from the past; Jesus-believers follow or imitate Rome; Rome conflicts with and pressures Jesus-believers; Jesus-believers conflict with Rome. He finds option four in 1 Thessalonians and options three and four in Philippians. Ironically, his attempt to delineate more complex interactions, while well directed, emphasizes conflict and opposition, and fails to recognize imitation and self-protection in Paul's eschatological formulations.

Davina Lopez's *Apostle to the Conquered: Reimagining Paul's Mission* (Minneapolis, 2008) develops issues of both gender and ethnicity in Paul's negotiation of empire. Rome commonly constructed conquered nations as women subjugated by manly power. Lopez argues that Paul abandons his imperially imitative, violent, masculine "power over" persecution of Jesus-believers to become their mother (Gal 4:19) in solidarity with the conquered. Lopez insists on the liberationist and transformational quality of Paul's ministry and communities. Neil Elliott's *Arrogance of Nations: Reading Romans in the Shadow of Empire* (Minneapolis, 2008) examines the interplay between this letter to the churches in Rome and aspects of Roman imperial theology, notably rule by force, justice, mercy, duty, and courage. Significantly, Elliott recognizes that while aspects of Paul's rhetoric subvert some imperial propaganda claims, Paul was a creature of his times who reinscribed imperial thinking and practices. Brigitte Kahl (*Galatians Re-Imagined: Reading with the Eyes of the Vanquished*, Minneapolis, 2010) develops the analysis in relation to Galatians. A volume edited by Christopher Stanley (*The Colonized Apostle: Paul Through Postcolonial Eyes*, Minneapolis, 2011) extensively engages issues of gender, ethnicity, and colonialism.

This more recent work on Paul has generally recognized increasingly multivalent and complex interactions with the empire. It has become less confessional and "protective" of Paul, and more willing to identify a Paul who imitates or reinscribes imperial ways rather than always offers liberative visions and practices.

Gospels. Scholarship on the Gospels has proceeded along similar lines. Initial empire-critical studies of Mark, Matthew, and John extended sociopolitical analyses of the historical Jesus, thereby countering conventional spiritualized readings of the Gospel narratives. This work exposed ways in which the Gospels constructed and negotiated imperial structures, matters ignored in previous scholarship. This initial work also commonly posited resistance as the dominant form of engagement. Discussions of interactions with Roman power in Luke's Gospel and Acts, which had been ongoing through the twentieth century (Walton, 2002), received renewed attention (Rhoads et al, 2011).

Ched Myers's *Binding the Strong Man: A Political Reading of Mark's Story of Jesus* (Maryknoll, 1988) was a pioneering work in setting the Gospels in conversation with the Roman Empire. Myers sees Mark's Gospel emerging from Rome's reoccupation of Galilee in the late 60s C.E. It offers a strategy of engagement that was both subversive and constructive, but which rejected options such as collaboration, withdrawal, rebellion, and Pharisaic activism (Myers, 86–87). Richard Horsley's *Hearing the Whole Story: The Politics of Plot in Mark's Gospel* (Louisville, 2001) reads Mark as the story of Jesus's renewal movement for Israelite villages in opposition to the subjugating Roman rulers and their provincial allies. Warren Carter's *Matthew and the Margins: A Sociopolitical and Religious Reading* (Maryknoll, 2000) and *Matthew and Empire: Initial Explorations* (Harrisburg, Pa., 2001) extended the discussion to Matthew's Gospel. In *Matthew and Empire*, Carter discusses Matthean christology, soteriology, eschatology, salvation history, and ecclesiology, along with various Gospel texts, to show Matthew's pervasive engagement with imperial realities. While this initial work largely emphasized opposition to the Roman Empire, Carter's subsequent work, such as his discussion of Matthew in the *Postcolonial Commentary on the New Testament Writings* (2007, pp. 69–104), presents a much more multivalent and ambiguous interaction involving contesting, imitating, and reinscribing imperial structures. Carter also argues that the struggles between Matthew's community and a synagogue community that Matthean scholars have seen only in religious terms reflect the vertical pressure of imperial power (2011). Work on John's Gospel has also developed with Lance Richey's *Roman Imperial Ideology and the Gospel of John* (Washington, D.C., 2007), Warren Carter's *John and Empire Initial Explorations* (New York, 2008), and Tom Thatcher's *Greater than Caesar: Christology and Empire in the Fourth Gospel* (Minneapolis, 2009). Other scholarship has explored dimensions such as gender constructions (Moore and Anderson 2003; Conway 2008).

Revelation. The book of Revelation has received much attention since Leonard Thompson argued convincingly that accommodation with the imperial world, not persecution, was the book's pervasive context (1990). Wes Howard-Brook and Anthony Gwyther developed this analysis for Revelation in relation to imperial politics, economics, culture, and myths. They moved beyond the book itself to draw connections with contemporary Global Capital (1999). In a series of studies, Stephen Moore has demonstrated that Revelation both mimics and replicates basic aspects of Roman imperial ideology and structures even while it resists and erodes them (2006, 2007). Particularly, Moore has attended to the intersection of gender representations and empire in Revelation, both the performance of masculinity, especially in relation to the recurring feature of war (1999), and of femininity in, for example, the presentation of Rome as a woman and prostitute (2009).

In summary, ES or imperial-critical approaches examine and evaluate the interaction between New Testament communities and texts and the Roman imperial world. ES examine these texts and communities through eyes interested particularly in multivalent negotiations of Roman imperial power.

Methods. Empire studies do not employ a formulaic or monolithic method, but are eclectic, interdisciplinary, and intertextual. The approach finds one starting point in historical-critical, particularly classical and archaeological, studies that investigate first-century conditions within the Roman Empire experienced by Jesus-followers (Huskinson, 2000; Morley 2010). Such investigation will, though, enact an agenda marked by a focus on power disparities and the circumstances of non-elites.

There are, however, numerous obstacles to such investigation. Sources, often from winners and elites, do not mention the Jesus movement. They are interested in the powerful and the exercise of power in politics, wars, and the lives and roles of "great men." Conventional history pursues the establishing of when, what, and how something happened. The Jesus movement, though, was not a powerful and elite movement exercising political or military power. It was not under the patronage of great men. It was a subculture that has to be viewed from below, not from above, located in larger imperial structures, and understood as a collective movement marked by powerlessness.

Historical inquiry known as "People's History" helpfully foregrounds such perspectives (Horsley 2005). Central for this inquiry are common folks and their everyday socioeconomic conditions within the larger imperial world. Crucial matters pertain to the distribution and exercise of power and resources, along with the complex negotiated interactions between dominant and subordinated groups. Dynamics of power, gender, ethnicity, and social status constitute vital dimensions. Historical and classical studies, viewed through the eye of People's History, provide a starting point for identifying some of these dynamics such as the role of military power, vast economic disparities and exploitation including taxes and tribute, slavery, extensive poverty and food insecurity, the concentration of political power in the hands of a small elite, alliances between Rome and provincial, urban elites, the significance of the imperial cult especially in the east and promoted by agonistic provincial elites, and the foundational claims of the ruling ideology.

Yet the limited and partial nature of the surviving data, their bias toward elites, public political events and military actions, and the relative invisibility of non-elites and their discreet and self-protective actions means these sources cannot provide an adequate picture of the vast range of human and communal experience within the empire. Not only does the partial nature of the material or artifactual remains present one problem, so also does the challenge of relating the various existing pieces to each other. Importantly, material or artifactual remains gain significance in the context of a larger, complex, imperial structure of power relations which the archaeological record itself cannot reconstitute.

Social-science models of empires usefully provide a wholistic framework, a heuristic view or map of the imperial structure that allows dots to be joined and the significance of individual pieces of existing data to be seen in relation to the whole. Dennis Duling discusses numerous models of empires (2005). Gerhard Lenski's model of agrarian-aristocratic empires (1984), modified by John Kautsky's inclusion of commerce and trade (1982), has been helpful for empire studies. Lenski focuses on the exercise of power, posing the question, "who gets what and why?" and emphasizing the significant verticality in its social stratification. A small but powerful elite controlled resources, land, and populations. For the elite, life was quite comfortable; for most, living around subsistence levels to varying degrees, daily existence was a struggle.

Such a model of the larger structure of Rome's empire, nuanced and elaborated by classical and archaeological studies, allows the function and significance of specific dynamics to be seen in relation to the whole. The model focuses on power and so broadens a conventional historical concern with politics, war, religion, or "great men" to the overall structure, to the interrelatedness of parts, to collective movements, and to non-elites so often ignored in historical studies but crucial for the early Christian movement.

Necessary, though, is access to how non-elites negotiate massive differentials of power. Several approaches provide access. The work of cultural anthropologist James Scott (1985, 1990) recognizes that whenever power and control are asserted in societies like Rome's empire, opposition and resistance are inevitable. Scott identifies three means or spheres whereby elites extend domination and exploitation (1990, p. 198): material (appropriation of grain, taxes, etc.), status (acts of humiliation and assaults on dignity), and ideological (justifications for practices: coins, inscriptions, buildings, texts, ceremonies, personnel, speeches, etc.). These spheres of domination constitute a public transcript or "official" versions of reality that enhance elite power.

They also create both compliance and numerous forms of resistance. Open, violent and direct challenges to power such as boycotts, nonpayment of taxes, attacks on ruling personnel and their property and resources are relatively infrequent. But Scott deconstructs a false alternative of violent protest or ready compliance. Scott's work exposes the inadequacies of the view that since Jesus did not advocate open revolt, the Gospels are "apolitical" or "politically indifferent" or "spiritual" (Horsley 2004).

Scott argues that more often in peasant societies, resistance is expressed not through violence but in more covert, self-protective, and calculated ways, taking the form of disguised and low profile resistance. Disguised forms of resistance to material domination may involve pilfering, foot dragging, poaching, and cheating on taxes. Disguised forms of resistance to status domination comprise non-expressions of honor (a sneer, no greeting), anger, subversive songs or stories, rumors, and disarming acts of seizing initiative from the powerful like carrying a soldier's pack farther than the stipulated mile, or handing over one's garments to expose the harshness of the powerful one's demand (Matt 5:38–42). Disguised forms of resistance to ideological domination involve the development of a dissident subculture such as millennial religions (the eschatological expectations in Paul and the Gospels), social banditry, or world-upside-down imagery. Scott argues that where there is autonomous space away from the always-controlling eyes of the elite, non-elites nurture alternative versions of reality or hidden transcripts. These hidden transcripts of counter-ideology contest and negate the elite's dominant public version, assert the honor and dignity of the powerless, keep alive hopes and visions of different forms of societal interaction, imagine another world, and legitimize self-protective (and occasionally publicly rupturing) forms of dissent.

In Scott's terms, the Gospel stories of Jesus crucified by Rome, raised by God, and returning in power, can be seen as alternative transcripts that expose the limits of Roman power and contest (even while they also imitate) the public transcript, or elite, "official," normalizing view of reality. Jesus articulates and enacts a transcript of the empire of God that condemns imperial domination, repairs its damage through Jesus's healings, exorcisms, and feedings, and imitatively anticipates the establishment of God's justice. Jesus exemplifies the politics of disguise and anonymity, notably through his proclamation and demonstrations of the rumor of God's imminent removal of Rome's world and establishment of God's empire. The Gospels also recognize that Jesus occasionally ruptures the political order with direct challenges to the ruling powers (the temple attack) who respond by executing him.

The disputed and diverse multidisciplinary discipline of postcolonial studies also focuses on the exercise and effects of imperial power in relation to race, ethnicity, hybridity, marginality, and diaspora. According to R. S. Sugirtharajah (1998, p. 17), postcolonial studies unmask and resist the complex assertions and reassertions of imperial power, while also imagining and structuring an alternative world. Edward Said has emphasized a "contrapuntal reading" of imperial sources that engages both official and resistant discourse, especially the interactions between the two (1993, p. xxv). To do so means a refusal to accept colonialist readings as the definitive depiction of the past and present, and an embracing of hitherto silenced voices of subordinated groups with their experiences of marginalization, hybridity, and new identity.

Empire Studies and Contemporary Readers. Empire studies or imperial-critical work employ such approaches to recognize that the NT texts and the early Christian movement emerge from a world of Roman imperial control. Neither the texts nor the movement were narrowly religious, isolated from sociopolitical, economic, and cultural life, but were embedded in and engaged with the imperial world. This approach brings the imperial context and content to the fore in order to identify the interaction with the pervasive Roman imperial world portrayed in the NT texts and practiced in daily lives by Jesus-followers. To address this issue, ES employ historical, classical, and archeological studies of the Roman imperial world, as well as cross-cultural anthropological models of empires. They also employ other approaches such as people's history, anthropological, and postcolonial studies to elaborate the experience of powerless non-elites.

Such exploration is both historical and contemporary work. The attempt to determine the texts' and movement's interactions with the Roman world enables the evaluation of the influence of these texts on the interactions of subsequent readers with imperial and ruling powers. This work raises questions for contemporary readers, especially those of Christian communities, about the neocolonial structures, visions, and interactions of our own world. Some have criticized ES for not engaging these contemporary issues enough (Fiorenza 2007, pp. 2–7). Others have seen a focus on the ancient world and a neglect of contemporary social structures as a point of differentiation between ES and postcolonial studies. Moore elevates the latter while castigating Empire studies for (supposedly) evading difficult contemporary disparities of power by its focus on the past (Moore 2011, p. 22). Moore, though, does concede that ES are "not without teeth" in wrestling with the question as to whether biblical texts can be said to resist empire. Others have seen postcolonial studies as an umbrella entity engaging imperial power across a vast spectrum of human history involving the ancient world, reception histories, and the contemporary world (Segovia 2005, pp. 64–76). This vast spectrum necessitates selective attention, with ES more often examining the negotiation of imperial structures in the text's originating circumstances rather than in contemporary reception. This focus, however, does not mean indifference to contemporary issues. It is undeniable that ES have pioneered investigations of NT texts in ways that have been accessible to contemporary readers. In doing so, ES have raised important questions about the origins and interpretations of these important texts, as well as posing for contemporary audiences, especially ecclesial and seminary communities, important questions about the challenges, benefits, and victims of contemporary imperial power. Unencumbered by some types of theoretical discussions that have often obfuscated postcolonial work, and marked by a constant attention on biblical texts, ES have created space for contemporary audiences to be aware of, engage, and evaluate contemporary neo-imperial realities. Empire studies have fostered readings of the biblical writings in relation to the worlds from which they have emerged and in which they are engaged, focusing attention on interactions between the NT texts and the power dynamics and societal structures of empires, ancient and contemporary.

[*See also* Class Criticism; Dead Sea Scrolls; Greco-Roman Context; Historical Criticism, *subentry* New Testament; Postcolonial Biblical Interpretation; *and* Social Sciences, *subentry* New Testament.]

BIBLIOGRAPHY

Carr, David M., and Colleen M. Conway, *An Introduction to the Bible: Sacred Texts and Imperial Contexts*. Malden, Mass.: Wiley, 2010. An introductory exploration of the interaction between the Biblical writings and contexts of empire.

Carter, Warren. "The Gospel of Matthew." In *A Postcolonial Commentary on the New Testament*, edited by Fernando Segovia and R. Sugirtharajah, 69–104. Louisville, Ky.: Westminster John Knox, 2007.

Carter, Warren. "Matthew: Empire, Synagogues, and Horizontal Violence." In *Mark and Matthew 1: Comparative Readings: Understanding the Earliest Gospels in their First-Century Settings*, edited by Eve-Marie Becker and Anders Runesson, 285–308. Wissenschaftliche Untersuchungen zum Neuen Testament 271; Tübingen: Mohr Siebeck, 2011. Argues that conflicts between/within synagogues and Jesus-believers are examples of horizontal violence precipitated by vertical imperial pressure.

Carter, Warren. *The Roman Empire and the New Testament*. Nashville, Tenn.: Abingdon, 2006. Introductory discussion of structures of Rome's empire and ways in which NT writings negotiate them.

Conway, Colleen. *Behold the Man: Jesus and Greco-Roman Masculinity*. Oxford: Oxford University Press, 2008. Examines presentation of Jesus in relation to (elite) constructions of masculinity in the Roman Empire.

Deissmann, Adolf. *Light from the Ancient East. The New Testament Illustrated by Recently Discovered Texts of the Graeco-Roman World*. London and New York: Hodder and Stoughton, 1910.

Duling, Dennis. "Empire: Theories, Methods, Models." In *The Gospel of Matthew in Its Roman Imperial Context*, edited by John Riches and David Sim, 49–74. *Journal for the Study of the New Testament: Supplement Series* 276. London: T.&T. Clark, 2005. Important discussion of social-science theories and models of empires.

Horsley, Richard A, ed. *Paul and Empire: Religion and Power in Roman Imperial Society*. Harrisburg, Pa.: Trinity Press International, 1997.

Horsley, Richard A., ed. *Paul and Politics: Ekklesia, Israel, Imperium, Interpretation: Essays in Honor of Krister Stendahl*. Harrisburg, Pa.: Trinity Press International, 2000.

Horsley, Richard A., ed. *Paul and the Roman Imperial Order*. Harrisburg, Pa.: Trinity Press International, 2003.

Horsley, Richard A., ed. *Hidden Transcripts and the Arts of Resistance: Applying the Work of James C. Scott to Jesus and Paul. Semeia* 48. Atlanta: Society of Biblical Literature, 2004.

Horsley, Richard A., ed. *Christian Origins. A People's History of Christianity*. Vol. 1. Minneapolis: Fortress, 2005.

Horsley, Richard A., ed. *In the Shadow of Empire: Reclaiming the Bible as a History of Faithful Resistance*. Louisville, Ky.: Westminster John Knox, 2008. Series of articles examining interactions with empires across the biblical writings.

Howard-Brooks, Wes, and A. Gwyther. *Unveiling Empire: Reading Revelation Then and Now*. Maryknoll, N.Y.: Orbis Books, 1999. Important study of the Book of Revelation and the Roman Empire.

Huskinson, Janet, ed. *Experiencing Rome: Culture, Identity, and Power in the Roman Empire*. London: Routledge/Open University, 2000. Excellent collection of articles about Roman culture, identity, and power.

Kautsky, John H. *The Politics of Aristocratic Empires*. Chapel Hill: University of North Carolina Press, 1982. Important analysis of imperial systems.

Lenski, Gerhard. *Power and Privilege: A Theory of Social Stratification*. Chapel Hill: University of North

Carolina Press, 1984. Provides an influential social-scientific model of empires, and engages the central question of "who gets what and how?"

Moore, Stephen D. *Empire and Apocalypse: Postcolonial Studies and New Testament Studies.* The Bible in the Modern World Series. Sheffield, UK: Sheffield Phoenix Press, 2006.

Moore, Stephen D. "Metonymies of Empire: Sexual Humiliation and Gender Masquerade in the Book of Revelation." In *Postcolonial Interventions*, edited by Tat-siong Benny Liew, 71–97. The Bible in the Modern World, 23. Sheffield, UK: Sheffield Phoenix Press, 2009. Explores the presentation of Rome as a woman in Revelation in relation to the cult of the goddess Roma.

Moore, Stephen D. "Paul after Empire." In *The Colonized Apostle: Paul through Postcolonial Eyes*, edited by Christopher D. Stanley, 9–23. Minneapolis: Fortress, 2011.

Moore, Stephen D. "Revelation." In *A Postcolonial Commentary on the New Testament Writings*, edited by Fernando F. Segovia and R. S. Sugirtharajah, 436–454. The Bible and Postcolonialism Series. New York: T.&T. Clark International, 2007.

Moore, Stephen D. "War Making Men Making War: The Performance of Masculinity in the Revelation to John." In *The Apocalyptic Imagination: Aesthetics and Ethics at the End of the World*, edited by S. Brent Plate, 84–94. Glasgow: Trinity St. Mungo Press, 1999.

Moore, Stephen D. and Janice Capel Anderson, editors. *New Testament Masculinities.* Semeia Studies 45; Atlanta: Society of Biblical Literature, 2003. Important study on presentations of masculinity in the Roman Empire and NT texts.

Morley, Neville. *The Roman Empire: Roots of Imperialism.* London: PlutoPress, 2010. Analysis of Roman power, especially attentive to its impact and victims.

"New Testament and Roman Empire." *Union Seminary Quarterly Review* 59 (2005) Nos. 3–4.

Oakes, Peter. "Re-mapping the Universe: Paul and the Emperor in 1 Thessalonians and Philippians," *Journal for the Study of the New Testament* 27 (2005): 301–22.

Perdue, Leo. *Israel and Empire: A Postcolonial History of Israel and Early Judaism.* London: Continuum, 2012. Employs postcolonial perspectives and insights in an analysis of Israel's interactions with a succession of empires.

Pilgrim, Walter E. *Uneasy Neighbors: Church and State in the New Testament.* Minneapolis: Fortress, 1999.

Portier-Young, Anathea. *Apocalypse against Empire: Theologies of Resistance in Early Judaism.* Grand Rapids, Mich.: Eerdmans, 2011. Focuses on the Seleucid domination of Judea and apocalyptic theologies of resistance.

Rhoads, David, David Esterline, and Jae Won Lee, eds. *Luke-Acts and Empire: Essays in Honor of Robert L. Brawley.* Eugene, Ore.: Wipf and Stock, 2011. Important set of essays focusing on Luke-Acts.

Said, Edward. *Culture and Imperialism.* New York: Random House, 1993. Very influential contribution from a leading postcolonial and cultural critic.

Sanders, Ernest P. *Jesus and Judaism.* Philadelphia: Fortress, 1985.

Schüssler Fiorenza, Elisabeth. *The Power of the Word: Scripture and the Rhetoric of Empire.* Minneapolis: Fortress, 2007.

Scott, James. *Domination and the Arts of Resistance: Hidden Transcripts.* New Haven, Conn.: Yale University Press, 1990. Influential work on the many ways the powerless dissent from and resist oppressive power.

Scott, James. *Weapons of the Weak: Everyday Forms of Peasant Resistance.* New Haven, Conn.: Yale University Press, 1985.

Segovia, Fernando. "Mapping the Postcolonial Optic in Biblical Criticism: Meaning and Scope." In *Postcolonial Biblical Criticism: Interdisciplinary Intersections*, edited by Stephen Moore and Fernando Segovia, 23–78. London: T.&T. Clark, 2005.

Stendahl, Krister. "The Apostle Paul and the Introspective Conscience of the West." *Harvard Theological Review* 56 (1963): 199–215.

Sugirtharajah, R. S. *Asian Biblical Hermeneutics and Postcolonialism: Contesting the Interpretations.* Maryknoll, N.Y.: Orbis Books, 1998.

Thompson, Leonard. *The Book of Revelation: Apocalypse and Empire.* New York: Oxford University Press, 1990.

Walton, Steve. "The State They Were In: Luke's View of the Roman Empire." In *Rome in the Bible and the Early Church*, edited by Peter Oakes, 1–41. Grand Rapids, Mich.: Baker Academic, 2002. Helpful classification of diverse views on Luke-Acts' engagement with Roman power.

Warren Carter

EVANGELICAL INTERPRETATION

While the label "evangelical" has a wide range of meanings, for the purposes of this article, it will refer to someone in the conservative Christian movement, which originated in the nineteenth and twentieth centuries, mainly out of reaction to the higher-critical conclusions about the biblical text and some of the patterns of Enlightenment thinking. Historically, evangelicalism finds its roots in the doctrines of the Reformation, especially in *sola scriptura* and *sola gracia*. However, it does not have a unified voice on an overall doctrinal platform, nor is it monolithic in its stances, for it is represented widely among people throughout most of Christian denominations and theological traditions, exhibiting a spectrum of practices and emphases that range from moderate evangelicals to those who argue that some secondary issues are just as important as the basic items in the gospel (i.e., the Greek word, *euaggelion*), as announced by the Apostle Paul in 1 Corinthians 15:1–4.

The Three Levels of Interpretation. The discipline of interpretation, whether it is evangelical interpretation or not, is usually discussed under three levels: general hermeneutics, exegetical methodology, and application.

General Hermeneutics. At the level of general hermeneutics, the most basic question is this: Do the biblical texts have a meaning that is objectively there, or is that meaning created afresh through an interaction between the reader and the text, so that the texts have no fixed or determinate meaning in themselves? Along with this key question, is a second one, which of late some are asking: How does language "work," and what is the implication of this for understanding what is going on in a biblical text?

Exegetical Methodology. The second level of interpretive theory is that of exegesis, which focuses on the various methods and tools of interpretation readers employ to get at the meaning or sense of a text. Do they begin with the "final text" of scripture before them, or should they try to establish what sources lie *behind* the text and how various new approaches to the text yield nuanced insights into its meanings?

Application. The third hermeneutical level is application, where the questions are: How does this ancient text have something to say to contemporary readers? Must the reader go beyond the sacred text in making trajectories from the text in order to get answers to the modern questions that were not directly anticipated in that ancient culture and text?

These three levels broadly trace what is involved in the interpretive challenge, and all three need to be addressed in any single system for a complete answer to the problem of interpretation. Moreover, all three areas involve particular challenges for all interpreters, wherein some questions pose certain difficult issues for evangelicals while others often offer a different set of issues. The procedure for obtaining the answers, however, remains essentially the same in principle and practice.

General Hermeneutics and the Text. Hermeneutics is the discipline that is both a science and an art of sorting out the principles of interpretation. It derives its name from the Greek god Hermes, who also was the deity for interpretation and communication. Despite the formal tone of this definition, however, interpretation is an essential part of communication, which is needed for such mundane tasks as reading a newspaper, even though most people have never taken a formal course on "How to read a Newspaper," or even a course in "The Hermeneutics of Conversation." For most of these tasks, readers act almost instinctively, for in the interpretive tasks with their peers on contemporary matters, they share much the same vocabulary, culture, historical background, and contexts. But in the act of interpreting the scriptures, which are removed from the present day by several millennia, much of the common ground is lost and additional tasks are called for as the interpreter must attempt to bridge the linguistic, cultural, historical, and literary distances.

Perhaps the best place to begin an examination of these issues is with the view of William Ames (1576–1633), whose book served as the standard text at Harvard for decades—from the founding of that institution in the seventeenth century. He contended that:

> [T]here is one meaning for every place in Scripture. Otherwise the meaning of Scripture would not only be unclear and uncertain, but there would be no meaning at all—for anything which does not mean

> one thing surely means nothing. (Ames, *The Marrow of Theology*, 1968, p. 188)

Bishop J. C. Ryle (1816–1900), the conservative Bishop of Liverpool, expressed the same sentiment:

> I hold it to be a most dangerous mode of interpreting Scripture, to regard everything which its words may be tortured into meaning as a lawful interpretation of the words. I hold undoubtedly that there is a mighty depth in all Scripture, and that in this respect it stands alone. But I also hold that the words of Scripture were intended to have one definite sense, and that our first object should be to discover that sense, and adhere rigidly to it. I believe that, as a general rule, the words of Scripture are intended to have, like all other language, one plain definite meaning, and that to say words *do* mean a thing, merely because they *can* be tortured into meaning it, is a most dishonourable and dangerous way of handling Scripture. (Ryle, *Expository Thoughts on the Gospels*, Grand Rapids, Mich., 1953, 2:383)

The problem of meaning, however, changed dramatically about 1946, following the end of World War II. The literary shot that was heard around the world came from two literary critics, W. K. Wimsatt and Monroe Beardsley. While Wimsatt and Beardsley carefully developed three types of internal evidence for discovering meaning, their distinctions were generally swallowed up in the popular version of their article that focused on the issue of "The Intentional Fallacy" (1946, pp. 3–18). In the estimate of the "New Criticism," as it was later to be called, the main fault evident in an interpretation was to be found in the "intentional fallacy," that is, the fallacy of depending on what an author meant to say for an understanding of that text. This seemed to call for interpreters to get inside the mind of the author. Most evangelicals, however, firmly denied the claim arguing that the author must be allowed to have his say first before readers agreed or disagreed with his truth-intentions or assertions.

The great decade for contributions to hermeneutical theory came undoubtedly in the 1960s. Evangelicals were especially attracted, at least at first, to the writings of an (non-evangelical) English Professor at the University of Virginia, E. D. Hirsch, Jr. In 1967, Yale University Press produced his *Validity in Interpretation*, which affirmed, partially under the influence of a 1955 work by the Italian historian of law, Emilio Betti, that the meaning of a literary work is to be determined by a return to the author's intention, which sense was fixed and unchanging as it stood in its written form. Some of his key concepts were:

1. Verbal meaning is whatever someone (usually the author) has willed to convey by a particular sequence of words and that can be shared by means of linguistic signs.
2. The author's truth-intention provides the only genuinely discriminating norm for ascertaining valid or true interpretations from invalid and false ones.
3. The primary objective in the interpretive process is to make clear the text's meaning, not its significance. *Meaning* is represented by the linguistic signs in the text, for that is what the author meant to say. On the other hand, *significance* names a relationship that the meaning, once it is established, has with another person, situation, or a number of possible associations.
4. Meaning is fixed and cannot change once it is written, but the significance of a text may change depending on the times, culture, or historical circumstances of readers. If an author changes her mind on what is meant, then that author must either retract what was said, or oppose it in another explanation.

Evangelicals, by and large, quickly accepted Hirsch's views as being in accord with many of their own views and a continuation of the views of those in the older Reformed and Puritan traditions.

However, at about the same period in history, a reaction developed to the perceived deadness of the historical-critical method of exegeting scripture. Some conservative interpreters, attempting to preserve partially what they had learned in their university doctoral studies, attempted to use historical criticism as a preliminary step in exegeting a text, but then went on to declare in addition what they heard the text was saying to them as readers.

Even more evangelicals found the concept of *sensus plenior* to be the answer to what a number of conservatives were searching for in their hermeneutical quests to accommodate both the human author and the divine author of the Bible. In this view, the human writer and the divine author could be combined to give a proper interpretation of the biblical text. This new hermeneutical move was made possible mainly by the work of Raymond E. Brown. In 1955, Brown published his dissertation on *sensus plenior*, a term that had actually been introduced by F. Andre Fernandez as early as 1927 (1927, p. 306). According to Brown,

> The *sensus plenior* is that additional, deeper meaning, intended by God, but not clearly intended by the human author, which is seen to exist in the words of a biblical text (or group of texts, or even a whole book) when they are studied in light of further revelation or development in the understanding of revelation.

Later, he clarified matters by candidly instructing interpreters:

> Let us apply the term *sensus plenior* ["fuller sense"] to that meaning of his [author's] text which by the normal rules of exegesis would not have been within his clear awareness of intention, but which by other criteria we can determine as having been intended by God. (1963, pp. 268–269)

The problem with this view, as it turned out, was trying to identify the criteria for discerning this "deeper meaning" in the text. Brown and others denied it was to be found precisely in the words, the grammar, or the syntax of the text, for then it would have been part of the author's intentionality. If it was not in any of these places, then it must be between the lines of the text, or perhaps even in a larger message or the bigger picture of the whole book, but whatever and wherever that sense was located, evangelicals began to realize that it was not part of *graphe*, the "written" form of the text, which the Apostle Paul had declared was the only portion that was inspired (2 Tim 3:16). This problem of the locus of meaning was a serious blow to the evangelical source of authority. Nevertheless, the concept of *sensus plenior* persisted in evangelical hermeneutical thinking.

Exegesis of the Text. Meanwhile, another issue had been stirring in evangelical exegesis involving the New Testament writers' use of the Old Testament. Do the New Testament writers accurately reflect the context and meaning of the Old Testament texts when they cite them in the New Testament, or do they present a new meaning for the Old Testament? If they present a new meaning, does that freedom also extend to contemporary interpreters? May interpreters also posit meanings that go beyond what the authors had intended in their original meanings?

In the view of some, the New Testament writers who cited the Old Testament texts, used what these scholars labeled as "Second Temple Jewish Exegetical Methods." In the view of these scholars, instead of reading the Old Testament in a straightforward, natural, or plain sense of the words used by the writers of the Old Testament, these scholars argued for a new interpretive method that they allege came from the Second Temple period, namely, the "Midrashic" or "Pesher" method of interpretating a text.

The midrashic method was a more involved approach to getting at the meaning of a text. The word itself comes from the Hebrew word, *darash*, meaning "to seek, expound or interpret." Although this method begins with scripture, it seeks to explain any hidden or embedded meanings supported by the general spirit of the text, which may yield meanings not immediately obvious to the reader. In order to accomplish this result, the interpreter had to follow interpretive rules, also known as *middoth*. Originally, there were only seven rules, attributed to Rabbi Hillel, who lived in the generation that preceded the Christian era, but these seven were expanded much later into thirty-two rules by Ishmael ben Elisha and Eliezar ben Jose. These rules ranged from fairly obvious general remarks to more imaginative ones. By that time additional techniques were being included such as *gematria*, the computation of the numerical values of letters to get a deeper meaning, and *notrikon*, the breaking up of one word into two or more or reconstructing a word by using the initials of many words.

With the discovery of the Dead Sea Scrolls, which included commentary on some of the biblical books, the pesher interpretation also became a new factor in the *exegesis* of biblical texts. The word pesher means "solution" or "interpretation," but instead of offering a straightforward explanation of the text, these interpreters using this method assumed that their "Teacher of Righteousness" realized the meanings of these veiled eschatological references in the ancient words so that he would declare: "This [eschatological event in these last days] is [what] that [text] is saying!" So strong was their belief that this text referred to events of their times that they never imagined that this same text had an earlier reference to people or events in their past.

This issue of the New Testament writers' use of the Old Testament triggered a whole new genre of evangelical scholarship as this topic became a favorite theme for evangelical doctrinal dissertations, including E. Earle Ellis's 1957 publication of his dissertation on "Paul's Use of the Old Testament"; E. D. Freed's release of his "Old Testament Quotations in the Gospel of John" in 1965; Robert H. Gundry's Brill publication of his dissertation topic in 1967, "The Use of the Old Testament in St. Matthew's Gospel"; and Douglas J. Moo's "The Old Testament in the Gospel Passion Narratives" in 1983. These works were followed up by Darrell L. Bock's extensive article in *Bibliotheca Sacra* in 1985 on "Evangelicals and the Use of the Old Testament in the New," as well as Bruce K. Waltke's straightforward question in his 1983 article, "Is it Right to Read the New Testament into the Old?"(1983, p. 77).

The appendix in Nestle's Greek New Testament lists some 950 quotations and allusions to the Old Testament in the New (1952, 658–671). But these constituted only about 300 direct quotations from the Old Testament. While these 300 texts have been the occasion for a huge amount of evangelical discussion, many evangelical scholars feel that the New Testament writers sensed very little disparity between the meaning of the Testaments. There seemed to be little need to search for a so-called "hidden meaning" in the Old Testament that had somehow been mysteriously embedded into the text. Nevertheless, not all evangelical writers would agree with this summary, for some found "thicker" meanings in the older text, as seen through the eyes of the new, but rarely did they present agreed-upon criteria by which these embedded items could be identified, much less provide additional hermeneutical advantages to those who wished to imitate this method in their own reading of the older texts.

Application of the Text. In today's world, perhaps the most important aspect in the evangelical system of exegeting is the *application* of the text. Few have pointed out this fact better than J. I. Packer in his essay, "Understanding the Bible: Evangelical Hermeneutics," in which he stressed the distinctive character of evangelical hermeneutics:

> [E]vangelicals say that they should listen to Holy Scripture, and finally let its teaching guide them, however much reordering of their prior ideas and intentions this involves, and however sharply it may set them at odds with the mind-set of their peers and their times. (1999, p. 150)

According to Packer, after the interpreter has inferred what the human authors were consciously expressing, all the biblical teaching on the topic raised in the text must be brought together as a working hypothesis, involving the tasks of coherence, harmony, and veracity. Accordingly, application involves the synthesizing of what the various biblical passages teach, with each item finding its proper place and significance in the organism of revelation as a whole. Consequently, the concept of progressive revelation is not an evolutionary process—that is, one in which cruder concepts are left behind or exchanged for a replacement of that concept—but a progress in which the earlier revelation becomes the foundation for the later revelation. Packer went on to identify what happens in this process of applying the biblical text as part of the interpretive procedure:

> So, just as it is possible to identify in all the books of Scripture universal and abiding truths about the will, work and ways of God, it is equally possible to find in every one of them universal and abiding principles of loyalty and devotion to the holy and gracious Creator; and then to detach these from the particular situations to which, and the cultural frames within which, the books apply them, and to reapply them to ourselves in the places, circumstances, and conditions of our own lives today.
>
> Rational application of this kind, acknowledging but transcending cultural differences between Bible worlds and ours, is the stock-in-trade of the evangelical pulpit and the recognized goal of the evangelical discipline of personal meditation on the written text. . . . Evangelicals do not find their models of interpretation in the "critical" commentaries of the last century and a half, which stop short at offering historical explanations of the text and have no applicatory angle at all; they find them, rather, in the from-faith-to-faith expository styles of . . . older writers. (p. 157)

Therefore, to apply a biblical text, the evangelical interpreter may choose either of two routes: (1) When the biblical command or situation is identical or comparable to our own situation, then she can apply the biblical text directly; or (2) If the contemporary situation is different from the biblical setting, then evangelicals need to discover the principle that underlies and is behind the command and then apply that principle to the comparable one the present.

Even though these rules and principles for applying the text have received a fairly wide assent among evangelicals, the practice has not always resulted in agreed upon results. As illustrated in the Apostle Peter's complaint about Paul's writings, "His letters contain some things that are hard to understand, which ignorant and unstable people distort, as they do the other Scriptures, to their own destruction" (2 Pet 3:16), not everything is immediately knowable or immediately accessible.

This disagreement among evangelicals in praxis is evident in the various answers given to the question of the ordination of women or in earlier days, in support of the practice of apartheid in that part of evangelicalism known as the "Reformed" tradition. It is also evident in the current evangelical debate over the final judgment of unbelievers and whether that final judgment involves conscious, eternal torment, or the annihilation of the wicked. It is further evident in the controversy with evangelical charismatics: Is there a second work or a separate baptism by the Holy Spirit that grants the special gifts of tongues, healing, or prophesying? All of these questions and more present special issues within evangelical scholarship and are areas of continuing discussion and research.

The task of applying the text, however, is even more difficult when dealing with contemporary issues for which there exists no analogous one in scripture or in the ancient world. Issues that are frequently raised in this area involve searches for guidance on matters such as *in vitro* fertilization, genetic modification, euthanasia, and the like. How are evangelicals to apply scripture when it does not even recognize these questions and issues? As Richard Longenecker phrased the question, "[How] are the ideas and solutions of the writers of the New Testament [much less of the whole Bible relevant] for contemporary social issues when society has changed so dramatically and situations are not at all the same?" (*New Testament Social Ethics for Today*, p. ix).

Longenecker called his answer to this problem a "Developmental Hermeneutic," wherein the New Testament pointed to new ethical patterns (e.g., as Gal 3:28 gave new patterns for slaves and gender issues); no longer should the Bible be regarded as a static book of codes, but one that calls each successive generation to answer in an organic, dynamic methodology, which develops responses to these new cultural challenges.

Further discussion was stimulated by the 2004 publication of I. Howard Marshall's *Beyond the Bible: Moving from Scripture to Theology*. Some critics, however, pointed out that the critical problem with going "beyond scripture" is that it is difficult to hold in one and the same breath that scripture is the sole authority for evangelical ethics and theology and then to announce that in some way interpreters must "go beyond" scripture in a trajectory set by an alleged apostolic example or some other direction.

In addition to the models for application of scripture offered by Packer, Longenecker, and Marshall, William Webb proposed an unusual trajectory to lead the interpreter beyond the text of the Bible. Webb began by taking note of and utilizing the "Ladder of Abstraction," which Kaiser had proposed for moving hermeneutically from the abstract ethical statement to its contemporary particularization in our day (Kaiser 1987, pp. 164–166). He, too, began by observing the *abstract* meaning in the text as the starting point and then moving to a *concrete* application in the present. But there was a difference, as Webb noted, for Kaiser viewed the Ladder of Abstraction and principalized method of treating the words of scripture as having a static meaning from which the particular applications emerged. In contrast, the trajectory movement model advocated by Webb pointed to a "logical and theological extension of the redemptive spirit that comes out of the text" (in Gundry and Meadors, *Four Views*, pp. 142–145). Since no answer was forthcoming as to the manner in which that redemptive spirit reveals itself outside the text, the issue of application was still problematic. For the most part, the views of Packer, Longenecker, Marshall, and Webb on application of scripture offered variations on the same theme. Consequently, there remained issues that still needed to be resolved in the evangelical understanding of application of scripture.

Theological Interpretation of Scripture. More recently, beginning in the 1990s, another new evangelical quest was inaugurated by the works of Francis Watson, Stephen Fowl, Kevin Vanhoozer, Daniel Treier, and Joel Green. The impulse of the development of this quest was the recognition that the theological interpretation of scripture has tended to decline in scholarship under the impact of the rise of the "historical-critical" view of the Bible. However, this trend was suddenly reversed, it would appear, in 1921 when Karl Barth published the second edition of his famous commentary on the book of Romans, which historians insist on labeling as a "bombshell dropped on the playground of the theologians." Subsequently Barth's work was seen as a work in theology rather than merely a biblical commentary.

Barth's influence continued to extend in several significant ways. One line of influence went to Brevard S. Childs of Yale University (1997, pp. 16–26), whose "canonical approach" to scripture argued that priority should be given to the "final form" of the biblical text, even though he still paid his dues and began with the critical approach to scripture, which he generally aborted as he explained the final form of the text. Many evangelicals were looking for an approach that would explain the text in front of them rather than give them a discussion of what was behind that text and its sources, and Childs was determined to help.

A second line of influence was David Kelsey, also from Yale, whose revised 1999 book, *Proving Doctrine*, focused on doctrine in the biblical narratives. One must also mention Hans Frei (1991), who complained of the modern obsession with the "historical truthfulness" of the biblical narratives resulting in the loss of their meaning. Though he was not from the Yale School, some include Stanley Hauerwas in this category, who did, nevertheless, earn his PhD from Yale and reflected Barthian influence (1993). Though none of these four men claimed to be part of the evangelical movement, they had a profound impact on it.

By time of the early 1990s, theological hermeneutics was developing its own history and agenda. Two projects appeared to set the pace for research: (1) The development of a textual interaction with Christian doctrine and (2) The development of concern about how biblical interpretation should shape or be shaped by Christian theology.

Some would conclude, then, that Hirsch's author-centered approach was no longer hermeneutically dominant for evangelicals. Instead, more recent defenses of authorial discourse interpretation seemed to be open to contributions from later texts or contexts to aid in the understanding of biblical texts. In other words, there has been a shift in the last decade or two for evangelicals, leading some to conclude that the authorial intention in the original context does not exhaust the textual meaning. Such an admission, however, does not violate the original text's meaning so long as it is related to other canonical passages. Still, it does raise the issue of whether interpreters should read New Testament meanings into the Old Testament. Ordinarily, when this is done, it is known as *eisegesis*. Therefore, a final assessment of evangelical hermeneutics must await another day, for it is presently in a period of transition.

[*See also* Authority of the Bible; Canonical Criticism; Exegesis; Historical Criticism, *subentry* Hebrew Bible; Historical Criticism, *subentry* New Testament; Literary Criticism, Literary Theory, and the Bible; Lutheran Interpretation; Midrash; Pentecostal Interpretation; Rabbinic Exegesis; Reformed Christian Interpretation; Theological Interpretation; *and* Wesleyan Biblical Interpretation.]

BIBLIOGRAPHY

Ames, William. *The Marrow of Theology*. Edited and translated by John D. Eusden, Boston: Pilgrim, 1968. A classic text used for some 150 years in Ivy League schools of New England.

Beale, Greg K., and D. A. Carson. *Commentary on the New Testament Use of the Old Testament.* Grand Rapids, Mich.: Baker Academic, 2007. An encyclopedia of all uses of the Old Testament quotations in the New Testament.

Childs, Brevard S. "Toward Recovering Theological Exegesis," *Pro Ecclesia* 6.1 (1997): 16–26. Argued for a theological understanding of the Bible based on reading the Bible as a whole canon.

Ellis, Earle E. *Paul's Use of the Old Testament in the New.* Grand Rapids, Mich.: Baker Academic, 1957. One of the first contributions on the Use of the Old Testament quotes in the Pauline corpus of the New Testament.

Fernandez, F. Andre. "Hermeneutica," *Institutiones Biblicae Scholis Accomodata.* 2d ed. Rome: Biblical Institute, 1927. This text is from the pioneer in *sensus plenior* theory and application.

Fowl, Stephen E. *Theological Interpretation of Scripture.* Eugene, Ore.: Cascade Books, 2009. An important work, which makes the case for interpreting scripture theologically.

Freed, E. D. *Old Testament Quotations in the Gospel of John.* Novum Testamentum Supplements 2. Leiden: Brill, 1965. One of the key studies of John's use of the Old Testament quotes in his Gospel.

Frei, Hans W. *The Eclipse of Biblical Narrative: A Study in Eighteenth and Nineteenth Century Hermeneutics.* Grand Rapids, Mich.: Eerdmans, 1991. A critique of previous readers of scripture for being motivated by apologetic readings instead of narrative readings of the Bible.

Green, Joel B. *Practicing Theological Interpretation.* Grand Rapids, Mich.: Baker Academic, 2011. An evangelical case of approaching the Bible theologically.

Gundry, Robert H. *The Use of the Old Testament in St. Matthew's Gospel. Novum Testamentum Supplements 18.* Brill, 1967. The classic statement of Matthew's use of quotations from the Old Testament from an evangelical perspective.

Gundry, Stanley N., and Gary T. Meadors, eds. *Four Views on Moving Beyond the Bible to Theology.* Grand Rapids, Mich.: Zondervan, 2009. Four different answers as to how we can derive guidance from the Bible to modern questions not anticipated in the times and culture of the Bible.

Hauerwas, Stanley. *Unleashing the Scripture: Freeing the Bible from Captivity to America.* Nashville, Tenn.: Abingdon, 1993. Another strong argument for reading the Bible theologically.

Kaiser, Walter C., Jr. *Toward Rediscovering the Old Testament.* Grand Rapids, Mich.: Zondervan, 1987. A topical approach to issues of interpreting the Old Testament.

Kaiser, Walter C., Jr. *The Uses of the Old Testament in the New.* Chicago: Moody Press, 1985. Reprinted by Eugene, Ore.: Wipf and Stock, 2002. An early attempt to group the uses of the Old Testament quotes in the New by categories.

Kelsey, David H. *Proving Doctrine: The Uses of Scripture in Modern Theology.* Harrisburg, Penn.: Trinity Press International, 1999. An argument that doctrine and theology were legitimate gains from understanding the Bible.

Longenecker, Richard N. *New Testament Social Ethics for Today.* Grand Rapids, Mich.: Eerdmans, 1984. One of the evangelical approaches to issues of social ethics as treated in the New Testament.

Longenecker, Richard N. *New Wine into Fresh Wineskins.* Peabody, Mass.: Hendrickson, 1999. An updated version on his 1984 book.

Marshall, I. Howard with Kevin Vanhoozer and Stanley Porter. *Beyond the Bible: Moving from Scripture to Theology.* Grand Rapids, Mich.: Baker Academic, 2004. An early evangelical discussion between three leading scholars on treating modern issues not directly taken up in the Bible.

Moo, Douglas J. *The Old Testament in the Gospel Passion Narrative.* Sheffield, UK: Almond, 1983. A discussion of the quotations of the Old Testament in the passion narratives of the New Testament.

Packer, J. I. *Honouring the Written Word God: The Collected Shorter Writings of J. I. Packer.* Vol 3. Carlisle: Paternoster Press, 1999, 174–160. Essays that have become classics in their own day for evangelicals in Bible interpretation in all its aspects.

Trier, Daniel J. *Introducing Theological Interpretation of Scripture.* Grand Rapids, Mich.: Baker Academic, 2008. The best statement for an evangelical, theological understanding of the Bible.

Vanhoozer, Kevin J. "Body-Piercing, the Natural Sense, and the Task of Theological Interpretation," *Ex Auditu* 16(2000): 1–29. Another evangelical statement of theological understanding of the Bible in non-traditional forms.

Waltke, Bruce K, "Is It Right to Read the New Testament into the Old?" *Christianity Today* 27(1983): 77. A surprisingly bold positive answer arguing for an eisegesis of the Old Testament through reading the New Testament into it.

Wimsatt, William K. *The Verbal Icon: Studies in the Meaning of Poetry.* New York: Farrar, Straus, 1958. This is an important work for anyone looking for a refinement of the earlier thesis on the "intentional fallacy."

Wimsatt, William K. and Monroe Beardsley, "The Intentional Fallacy," *Sewanee Review* 54(1946): 3–18. This article is the work of two scholars responsible for inaugurating the important discussion of the "intentional fallacy."

Walter C. Kaiser Jr.

EXEGESIS

In classical Antiquity, the term ἐξήγησις (from the Greek verb ἐξηγέομαι "to lead out," and by extension "lay out," "interpret" or "narrate") was the term for methods and praxes related to the reception and transmission of texts that developed in schools for grammarians, rhetors, jurists, or philosophers. Common to these methods and praxes was the conception that texts form a system of "signs," through which a text's meaning is communicated and from which such meaning can be extracted. Today, the term is commonly used to refer to the commentary of a text, especially in the case of religious scriptures. Within biblical studies and related fields, "exegesis" can therefore be used to refer to virtually any form of commentary, ancient or modern, of the Jewish and Christian canons, such as midrashic exegesis or patristic exegesis. However, there also exists a more specialized use of this term, according to which "exegesis" refers to the academic study of the Bible that has developed in modern times. In this restricted understanding, exegesis designates a form of commentary that seeks to explain and interpret the contents of a given text by resorting to rational, scientific methods rather than to a community's tradition of interpretation. As in the case of other classical disciplines, such as the study of ancient Greek literature or Assyriology, the academic study of the Bible has long privileged philological methods, especially in the form of so-called "historical-critical exegesis." However, since the second half of the twentieth century several other academic approaches to the biblical texts have gradually emerged, which have significantly renewed scholarly engagement with these texts. The following entry is primarily devoted to exegesis as an academic discipline, including its origins, methods, purposes, as well as current challenges. Prior to that, however, some general comments regarding the relationship between "canon" and "exegesis" in Antiquity should be made.

Canon and Exegesis in Antiquity. Although exegesis is sometimes considered essentially a post-canonical phenomenon, we know in fact that the composition of the texts that would later comprise the Jewish canon already involved a considerable degree of exegetical activity. The ancient scribes who produced and transmitted these texts from the Neo-Assyrian to the Hellenistic periods sought to clarify passages that had become obscure or were no longer adapted to the present historical context; in the course of that process, new texts were formed, which supplemented, revised or even sometimes replaced older texts while reusing their language. Such exegetical activity, which is usually referred to as "inner-biblical exegesis" (although "inner-scriptural" might be a better term, as there was yet no "Bible"), ranges from minor glosses offering explanatory comments—e.g., 1 Sam 9:9 where it is explained that the "prophet" (*nābîʾ*) was formerly called "seer" (*roʾeh*)—to sophisticated reformulations of earlier texts in new ones, as in the case of the revision of the Covenant Code in Deuteronomy (cf. Levinson, 1997) or the rewriting of older prophecies in so-called "Second" Zechariah (Zech 9–14; for this phenomenon in general, see Fishbane 1995).

As a result of the gradual stabilization of the Jewish scriptures that began around the second century B.C.E., and culminated in the eventual fixation in the first century C.E. of one textual form to the exclusion of all others, exegesis gradually moved to commentaries distinct from the scriptural text. The transition from "inner-scriptural exegesis" to commentaries distinct from the scriptural text must be viewed as the result of a complex process spanning several centuries; throughout the Second Temple period, the relationship between the Jewish scriptures and their commentary appears to have been relatively fluid, as can be seen from the phenomenon of "Rewritten Scripture" (such as Jubilees, the Temple Scroll, or 4QReworked Pentateuch), the last example of which—the *Liber Antiquitatum Biblicarum* of Pseudo-Philo—dates from the late first century C.E. (see Crawford 2008). Gradually, however, the genre of Rewritten Scripture entirely disappeared, replaced by a form of interpretation—typically exemplified in the *pesher* exegesis—in which the citation of a scriptural passage and its comment are clearly distinguished one from the other.

Despite the considerable variety of forms they could take—such as anthologies of selected scriptural passages (4QFlorilegium), commentaries on specific passages (the *pesher* exegesis) and entire books (Philo's *Questions on Genesis*), translation cum commentary (the Targums), and so forth—ancient commentaries on Jewish scripture reflect a similar attempt to clarify the meaning of authoritative texts that had become obscure and to interpret these scriptures from the perspective of the group for which that commentary was intended. Philo (a typical representative of Alexandrian Judaism) elaborated an allegorical exegesis largely influenced by Greek philosophy in order to convince his Hellenistic audience of the cultural superiority of Judaism; the *pesher*-type of exegesis at Qumran explained passages of scripture from the twofold perspective of the community's past history and its eschatological expectations; the emerging Christian communities read these same scriptures from the perspective of their conviction that Jesus was the messiah, and that they themselves represented the true "Israel"; and so on.

During Late Antiquity and the Middle Ages, both Jews and Christians developed distinct traditions of commentary pertaining to their respective scriptures. They codified what they considered to be the relevant techniques and principles for exegeting scripture, such as the rabbinic *midrashim*—themselves divided into *Midrash halaka* (legal material laying out rules of conduct in keeping with legal requirements) and *Midrash haggada* (narrative material with an edifying and instructive purpose). Similarly, early Christian exegetes usually advocated a reading of scripture that was both literal and allegorical, but their own approach was more significantly influenced by Greek/Hellenistic exegetical techniques; eventually, it culminated in the theory of the four meanings of scripture (literal/historical, allegorical, tropological, and anagogical), which was apparently formulated for the first time by John Cassian (ca. 360–435 C.E.) in his Conferences (14:8) and later developed by medieval commentators. In addition, in both Jewish and Christian traditions the opinions of earlier commentators were recorded and considered to be authoritative alongside scripture. Around 200 C.E., R. Judah ha-Nasi produced a compilation of oral doctrine—the Mishnah, or "Interpretation"—collecting the views of sages on disputed halakhic issues. Further exegetical discussions, especially on halakhic issues, were recorded and compiled in the two Talmuds (Talmud Yerushalmi and Talmud Babli), from around the sixth century C.E.; and in one *baraita*, the Mishnah and the Talmud are defined as subjects of study alongside the "Mikra" (Bible). Somewhat similarly, Western Christians created *catenae*, or "chains" of tradition that compiled, summarized, laid out and harmonized patristic exegesis of Christian scripture; manuscripts containing the texts of scriptures were glossed with exegetical material drawn from the Church Fathers; and so on. In general, as in the case of Judaism, exegesis of the Bible played a considerable role in forming the Christian culture in late Antiquity and the Middle Ages (see, e.g., Young 1997).

The Origins of Historical-Critical Exegesis. Throughout the Middle Ages, the recourse to traditional authorities for scriptural interpretation did not remain unchallenged—as is shown by the Karaites, or "scripturalists," a Jewish sect advocating reading scripture without the lens of rabbinic authorities—but it remained marginal. The development in Western Europe of an exegetical approach to scripture that was (at least in principle) free from the influence of traditional authorities, which started with the Renaissance and went on in the following centuries, must be linked to a number of factors. Among such factors were especially, albeit not exclusively, the desire, characteristic of the Renaissance, to return to the "sources" (*ad fontes*) of Western culture, which led in particular to the collation of the Latin text of the Bible used by the church with Hebrew, Aramaic, and Greek versions of that same Bible; conflicts and controversies between Catholics and Protestants, the latter explicitly disputing the church's claim to control interpretation of scripture and emphasizing its priority over tradition (*sola scriptura*) and the right of individuals to engage personally with scripture without the mediation of the church; lastly, the profound transformation in the image of the world, especially as a result of world exploration, scientific discoveries, and the general development of rationalism and critical thinking, which logically led to a growing questioning of traditional authorities on many matters, including the Bible.

During the sixteenth and seventeenth centuries, several authors—such as Thomas Hobbes (1588–1679) or Baruch Spinoza (1632–1677)—subjected biblical texts to critical examination, based on the general assumption that the Bible was written by human authors who were influenced by their own social-historical contexts (Spinoza, for instance, considered the story in Genesis-Kings to have been written by Ezra). During the eighteenth century, the quest for the historical meaning of the texts (*sensus historicus*) was gradually systematized, and gave birth to the so-called historical-critical method. The latter then came to be taught in the universities of various European countries during the late eighteenth and nineteenth centuries, predominantly those countries with a strong Protestant tradition such as Germany and the Netherlands. The development of historical-critical exegesis by Protestant scholars as a distinct discipline, with its own set of methods, has classically been viewed as the continuation, and even the culmination, of the historical-philological criticism that started with the Renaissance and gradually sought to separate the study of the Bible from the authority of the church and the tradition. That picture is partly correct, but also somewhat simplistic. In the context of the late eighteenth and early nineteenth centuries, historical-critical exegesis was a way of adapting the study of the Bible to the new standards of Enlightenment rationality, and thus of legitimizing the continuation of Bible study as an academic discipline. In addition, historical-critical exegesis sought to rationalize the apparent inconsistencies contained in the Bible, and thus served simultaneously as a response to the various conceptions emerging in the eighteenth century that ridiculed the Bible as being nothing but a collection of superstitions full of contradictions. As such, historical-critical exegesis always had an important apologetic function within the Protestant circles where it was developed.

The historical-critical approach to the biblical texts that was elaborated in the late eighteenth and nineteenth centuries was mostly based on a form of internal criticism of the biblical texts, although some effort was also made to integrate the comparative evidence that was available at that time. Features such as apparent contradictions, variations in language, or the presence of parallel traditions within a given book, or broader collections (e.g., the Pentateuch) were used to reconstruct the literary genesis of such collections. Differences between the textual witnesses that were known at the time for the Hebrew Bible/Old Testament and the New Testament could also be used in such reconstructions, although textual criticism, at that time, was an emergent discipline. Despite the variety of reconstructions offered, general conclusions were gradually developed, all of which had a long-term impact on the field and have continued dominating the scholarly discussion in many ways.

Although all the books of the Christian Bible (as noted earlier, historical-critical exegesis was essentially a Christian enterprise at that time) were analyzed and scrutinized in this light, special attention was devoted to the Pentateuch and the Gospels. The Pentateuch was considered to consist of different written traditions, or "documents," which came from different periods, were characterized—among other things—by their different uses of the divine name, and were initially transmitted separately before being combined together by a "redactor," who was himself often identified with Ezra on the basis of the account in Nehemiah 8. This model was designated as the "documentary hypothesis" (in German, *Urkundenhypothese*); it received its classical formulation in the second half of the nineteenth century, in the so-called "New Documentary Hypothesis" associated with the names of Julius Wellhausen and Abraham Kuenen. Building on the work of earlier scholars in the first half of the nineteenth century (Eduard Reuss, Wilhelm Vatke, and Johann Friedrich Leopold George), Wellhausen and Kuenen identified four discrete documents: the Yahwist (J), the Elohist (E)—both of which, according to Wellhausen, were already merged in the Neo-Assyrian period to form the "Jehovist" (JE)—the "D" source or document (consisting of an earlier form of the book of Deuteronomy), and the Priestly (P) document, from the Persian period. Both the identification of these four documents and their relative chronology would remain canonical for at least one century, and are still considered as valid by some scholars today.

In the case of the Gospels, by the beginning of the nineteenth century several significant conclusions had been achieved. A distinction was made between the three "synoptic" Gospels and the Gospel of John, and the attribution of the Gospel of John to the disciple of Jesus of that name was already questioned by Edward Evanson in 1792. Mark rapidly came to be regarded as the earliest of the three synoptic Gospels, as argued by Gottlob C. Storr in 1786. Finally, the idea that the writers of the synoptic Gospels had access to a discrete source, no longer extant and designated as "Q" (for German *Quelle*), was proposed for the first time by Herbert Marsh in 1801. Along these developments, several attempts were made throughout the nineteenth century to reconstruct the "historical Jesus" by subjecting the material found in the Gospels to critical analysis, using the biblical traditions to produce a portrait of Jesus that significantly differed from the images found in those traditions themselves. This so-called "quest" for the historical Jesus, associated with the names of scholars such as David Friedrich Strauss or Ernest Renan, was very much in line with the historicism of the nineteenth century; it had a considerable intellectual impact, even beyond the sole academic circles, and was continued throughout the twentieth century.

Apart from the Pentateuch and the Gospels, other books, as noted earlier, were also subjected to similar investigations. In the case of the prophetic books of the Hebrew Bible, more and more attention was given to the separation between allegedly "authentic" material (i.e., material likely to go back to the prophetic figure associated with that book) and later additions. Especially in the case of books like Isaiah or Jeremiah, this approach gradually led to the view that the material collected in those books was the product of several centuries of compilation and revision, with only a limited amount of the texts reflecting utterances made by the prophets themselves (an extreme example can be seen in the commentary on Jeremiah by Bernhard Duhm from 1901). Similarly, the distinction between "authentic" and "inauthentic" material in the Pauline epistles rapidly became a major area of investigation during the nineteenth century, and the notion that the so-called "pastoral epistles" were not from Paul himself but reflected later developments within the first Christian communities was already argued at length by Ferdinand Christian Baur in 1835.

Developments and Challenges of Historical-Critical Exegesis. During much of the twentieth century, so-called "historical-critical" exegesis remained the dominant approach to the Bible. Still today, it comprises the main—and sometimes even the sole—approach taught in many Western universities, especially in "Continental" Europe. Although they have become significantly more refined and sophisticated, the aims and methods of historical-critical exegesis have remained much in keeping with those that were gradually elaborated during the eighteenth and nineteenth centuries. The general purpose of historical-critical exegesis is still the analysis and interpretation of a given text by reconstructing its underlying traditions, by retracing its process of composition, and—finally—by placing it in its presumed historical context. This is achieved by using various philological methods, such as especially textual criticism, which compares existing witnesses for a given text or passage and seeks to determine which one is likely to preserve the earliest reading when these witnesses disagree; form and genre criticism, an approach associated with the name of Hermann Gunkel (1862–1932), which initially sought to identify the genre of a text (such as, e.g., instruction, lamentation, prophecy, and so on) as well as its social-institutional context (temple, palace, school, etc.), and which became increasingly concerned during the twentieth century with the reconstruction of earlier, possibly preliterate "forms" of a given text; or source and redaction criticism, which is concerned with the identification of the written documents ("sources") and/or the literate stages in the composition of biblical material based on the evidence found in that material such as, the presence of doublets, reformulations, or internal contradictions, for example.

Since the nineteenth century, however, our knowledge not only of the Hebrew Bible and the New Testament, but also of the cultures that produced these texts, has been profoundly transformed by a series of discoveries: new textual traditions, previously unknown (e.g., the Dead Sea scrolls found at Khirbet Qumran); new archaeological and epigraphic finds, documenting the administration, economy, politics, religion, and everyday life of the ancient societies in which the Hebrew Bible and the New Testament were composed and transmitted; and considerable comparative evidence from other ancient Western Asian societies, such as Mesopotamia, Ugarit, Phoenicia, Greece, or Rome, which were not or only partly accessible to earlier scholars.

To such developments may be added the considerable progress made in the knowledge of the ancient languages in which the Hebrew Bible and the New Testament were written, that is, Hebrew, Aramaic, and Greek. In general, these various developments have been slow to impact the methods of historical-critical exegesis, for a variety of reasons. In faculties of theology, for instance, students trained in biblical exegesis did not necessarily study other ancient languages beyond Hebrew and Greek, such as Akkadian, Sumerian, Ugaritic, or Hittite, making access to sources written in such languages difficult or impossible for them. In addition, the tendency to regard ancient Israel as a culture distinct from the surrounding social groups, which was already present in nineteenth century liberal Protestant circles, became considerably radicalized in the twentieth century as part of a reaction against liberal theology after World War I, which significantly hindered the development of comparative studies for several decades. By contrast, in Jewish academic circles where historical-critical exegesis was studied, an approach was developed that tends to emphasize the continuity between ancient Israel and its Western Asian environment in areas such as law, royal ideology, or the temple. Although this approach did much to foster the development of the comparative approach in biblical exegesis, especially in the case of the Hebrew Bible, it has also been sometimes criticized for lacking a proper theoretical framework, and for tending to overemphasize the continuity between Mesopotamian and Israelite traditions.

Gradually, however, the evidence mentioned earlier left a profound impact on historical-critical exegesis. Combined with partial integration of new, especially literary, methods, and with a critical discourse on its own traditional methodology, this trend led to some significant transformations in the discipline. Even though, as noted earlier, many of the methods of historical-critical exegesis—and even some of the basic hypotheses, such as the existence of "Q" used by the authors of the synoptic Gospels, or the notion that the Pentateuch is composed of a "Priestly" document combined with other traditions—are derived from the nineteenth century, the ways in which these methods are applied and the results achieved by this approach have undergone major changes in recent decades. To name only some of the most obvious examples, the Qumran finds, coupled with the discovery or rediscovery of various ancient Jewish apocryphal and pseudepigraphic writings that were previously unknown (e.g., the Temple Scroll) or little studied (1 and 2 Enoch, Jubilees, 4 Ezra) have renewed the study of several texts from the New Testament, such as Hebrews (in the case of Qumran and the New Testament, see for example Brooke 2005). Similarly, much effort has been made in the past two decades to understand and situate the emerging Jesus movement(s) responsible for the production of New Testament literature against the social and cultural background of the multiple forms of Judaism that characterized the end of the period of the Second Temple, an approach that has also profoundly impacted the so-called "quest" for the historical Jesus. In the case of the Pentateuch, better appreciation of the material culture and of the political-economic history of Judah in the monarchic period led to questioning several classical hypotheses like the existence of a "Yahwistic" source or document from the time of Solomon or the antiquity of the traditions on Abraham. In turn, these developments have gradually led to the formulation of new models that either date "J" in the Neo-Babylonian or even Early Persian period, or that even deny the existence of J and envisage instead the creation of the Pentateuch as resulting from the combination in the Persian period of different sets of traditions (such as, e.g., the patriarchs and the exodus; see, e.g., Schmid 2010; and, for a general overview, Ska 2009). Today, the only result of Pentateuchal scholarship that remains the subject of a broad consensus is the distinction between "priestly" and "nonpriestly" material within that collection.

At the same time, the gradual integration of the sort of evidence provided by archaeology, epigraphy, and numismatics on the one hand, and by new manuscripts (or fragments thereof) on the other, has also raised a number of issues and challenges for the methods of historical-critical exegesis. In the case of several books of the Hebrew Bible—the most obvious (but not the only) example being the short and the long forms of the book of Jeremiah preserved in the Septuagint (LXX) and the Masoretic Text respectively—the neat distinction between redaction and text criticism, and correspondingly between the history of the text's composition and its transmission, has proved impossible to maintain. Even more significantly perhaps, the Qumran finds, combined with in-depth work on ancient versions such as the LXX, have emphasized the considerable complexity and fluidity of the textual history of most of the books of the Hebrew Bible, thus raising in turn important questions regarding the possibility and the relevance of reconstructing the "original" Hebrew base of these books. (In the case of the New Testament, the existence of an eclectic edition [Nestle-Aland] is viewed by most scholars as a usefully heuristic device, but only some would regard this today as representing "the" original text of the New Testament.) The deciphering of literary works from Ugarit, Mesopotamia, and elsewhere has considerably enriched our understanding of literary genres in Antiquity; but this development has also shown many of the assumptions made by nineteenth century philologists in this respect—for example, the existence of fixed forms, or the simple correlation between a given genre and its "Sitz im Leben" (social setting)—to be false or unwarranted. Somewhat similarly, comparative work on ancient writings whose textual genesis is materially documented by the existence of multiple successive versions—as in the case of the Gilgamesh epic—casts some significant doubt on the possibility of retrieving the complete literary prehistory of these texts on the basis of their sole final, "canonical" shape, because these texts have usually been too significantly overwritten in the course of their transmission (Tigay 1982, 1985; and cf. also Carr 2011).

Exegesis in a Context of Methodological Plurality. During the second half of the twentieth century, the academic monopoly of the historical-critical exegesis was gradually challenged, as a number of new methods and approaches to the Bible emerged. Several factors influenced that development, prime among which was the growing impact in the field of social sciences and literary theories at a time when scholars were becoming more and more aware of the limitations of the historical-critical methodology. In many academic contexts, including several European universities, the historical-critical method was perceived as Euro-centric and hegemonic, and scholars felt the need to develop more "pluralistic" approaches to the Bible. In this way exegesis of the Bible has followed the path of many other disciplines concerned with ancient texts after World War II (e.g., the study of ancient Greek literature), which likewise developed alternative models and approaches completing, revising, and sometimes even replacing the classical philological approach. In the case of the Hebrew Bible and the New Testament, however, the fact that these writings are still considered to be of contemporary relevance by many Jewish and Christian communities in the world has logically given to this phenomenon an additional dimension.

The methods that have developed are so diverse that any attempt to draw an exhaustive list is problematic, all the more because many are actually "hybrids" that take up and adapt a variety of approaches and influences. Some approaches have mostly or exclusively developed in academic contexts, whereas others are more closely related to the concerns of a specific group (e.g., feminist or African American exegesis); some are focused on, or compatible with, an approach that centers on the production and transmission of biblical texts in their ancient contexts, whereas others—especially those approaches strongly influenced by cultural and/or postmodern studies—are mostly concerned with the discourse(s) generated by the Bible in contemporary societies (including, of course, academic courses), and the ways in which those discourses are informed by power struggles and contribute to them.

One typology that has often been proposed, although it is certainly not the only possible one, considers different methods and approaches from the perspective of the relation between "text" and "world," differentiating between methods that focus on the world behind, within, and in front of the text (cf., e.g., Tate 2006; compare also Oeming 2006). The first category includes methods and approaches that are concerned with reconstructing the social-historical context in which a given text was composed, as well as the cultural repertoire that is presupposed by that text (e.g., tradition criticism, comparative methods, social-scientific approaches); the second comprises methods that focus on the world "encoded" within the text, and on the various features and strategies with the help of which that world is communicated to the reader (rhetorical criticism, genre analysis, text pragmatics, etc.); finally, the third corresponds to those methods that emphasize the world "beyond" the text, such as especially the role of the reader, of social structures, or ideological constraints—or a combination of these factors—in constructing and defining the meaning of a text (e.g., new historicism, postcolonial criticism, various forms of deconstructionist or feminists analyses, etc.).

It needs to be observed, however, that for all three categories it is possible to find examples that cross the lines, so that here again generalizations are problematic. For instance, classic source and redaction criticism—insofar as it seeks to reconstruct on the basis of internal criteria an earlier, precanonical form of a given text and to situate that precanonical text within the broader collection of which it was a part (such as when a Jesus saying is considered to be part of the "Q" source)—may be viewed as addressing the first and second categories jointly, since it scrutinizes selective aspects of the world of the text in order to reconstruct the historical and literary context in which that text was composed. Moreover, in recent decades, many historical approaches to the Hebrew Bible and the New Testament have adopted and adapted aspects of approaches that are typically interested in the world "beyond" or in front of the text: for instance, certain concepts of postcolonial criticism such as the notions of "hybridity" and "hybridation" have been used by historical studies that sought to understand how the emergence of genres or collections of Jewish and Christian writings—such as, e.g., apocalypses—could be explained in the light of the strategies characteristically developed by minority cultures in imperial contexts. Conversely, some of the approaches focusing on the role of the reader and of social or ideological structures, such as certain forms of feminist criticism, have highlighted the need to interpret biblical texts in their ancient context in order to critically address the way in which these texts are deeply informed by the patriarchal structures of their time (e.g., Schüssler Fiorenza). At the same time, several diachronically oriented analyses have been working with biblical books, questioning the possibility of reconstructing earlier stages in the production of those writings, which has also led them to make use of tools developed in the context of methods that are more focused on the final forms of the biblical books such as narrative analysis or rhetorical criticism.

In this respect, several of the methodological distinctions that have become almost canonical within the field, such as the distinction between "diachronic" and "synchronic," or between "modern" and "postmodern" approaches, should not be regarded as absolute; in practice, the line between those methods is frequently more difficult to draw. This does not mean, however, that it is possible, or even desirable, to develop large-scale syntheses combining as many of these methods as possible, even if that sort of approach is sometimes encouraged in introductory manuals and other methodological writings.

Perspectives for Biblical Exegesis. In the 1980s and 1990s, it was not uncommon to find the assertion that the classical historical-critical approach to the Bible was being rapidly replaced with new methods and models developed in the fields of social theory and literary criticism, and would soon largely if not entirely disappear. This prediction has not been realized; on the contrary, diachronic approaches to the biblical texts have remained relatively well established in the field, although many other approaches are now available. This situation has presumably several grounds. It may point, in particular, to the fact that biblical texts remain in many ways deeply rooted in their ancient contexts, and that they do not necessarily "read" or "translate" more easily in the context of postmodern societies than of modern ones. Approaches that do not take seriously the complex process of transmission through which these texts have reached us, as well as the specific codes—linguistic, economic, iconographic, religious, etc.—that inform them, seriously run the risk of being unable to objectivize their readings of these texts in the way that is expected in academic contexts. Moreover, in other academic fields, such as linguistics or sociology, the former opposition between "diachronic" and "synchronic" approaches has generally come to be regarded as too simplistic, and has gradually been replaced by models favoring a combination of the two.

On the other hand, it must be emphasized that historical approaches to biblical texts in recent decades have been moving more and more in a direction that, in many ways, departs significantly from the methods and models inherited from nineteenth century philology. As noted earlier, some methods have virtually disappeared (form criticism), others have become significantly marginalized (redaction criticism), and still others have undergone profound changes in their own self-definition (text criticism). By contrast, presumably the most fruitful approaches that have developed in the last decades are those that have crossed long-standing traditional boundaries in the field: between the texts and the material culture of the societies in which the Hebrew Bible and the New Testament were composed (archaeology, epigraphy, iconography, and numismatics); between the biblical texts themselves and the whole "parabiblical" literature (apocrypha and pseudepigraphs) that was transmitted alongside them and which, in Antiquity, was often regarded as having comparable authority; and finally, between the production of the texts and their reception in Antiquity. In spite of their differences, all these approaches share a common concern to relate more carefully the history of the texts with the social, cultural, and intellectual history of the ancient societies in which they were transmitted. In this light, the aim of exegesis should not be to reconstruct the original "meaning" of a text (and especially not something like its "religious" or "theological message"!), but to recreate the social discourse of which that text was a part in different periods (e.g., the dynastic promise to David in 2 Sam 7 as part of the general discourse on kingship in ancient Judah), and to understand the function(s) this text served as part of that discourse, its relation to other parts of the same discourse, and its impact on the discursive and nondiscursive praxes of the group in which that text was composed and transmitted.

[*See also*: Dead Sea Scrolls; Diachronic Interpretation; Form Criticism, *subentry* Hebrew Bible; Form Criticism, *subentry* New Testament; Historical Criticism, *subentry* Hebrew Bible; Historical Criticism, *subentry* New Testament; Historical Jesus, Quest for the; Literary Criticism, Literary Theory, and the Bible; Midrash; New Historicism; Patristic Interpretation; Postcolonial Biblical Interpretation; Postmodern Interpretation; Rabbinic Exegesis; Redaction Criticism, *subentry* Hebrew Bible; Redaction Criticism, *subentry* New Testament; Rhetorical Criticism; Source Criticism; Synchronic Interpretation; Textual Criticism, *subentry* Hebrew Bible; *and* Textual Criticism, *subentry* New Testament.]

BIBLIOGRAPHY

Brooke, G. J. *The Dead Sea Scrolls and the New Testament: Essays in Mutual Illumination.* London: SPCK, 2005.

Carr, D. M. *The Formation of the Hebrew Bible: A New Reconstruction.* New York: Oxford University Press, 2011.

Crawford, S. W. *Rewriting Scripture in Second Temple Times.* Grand Rapids, Mich.: Eerdmans, 2008.

Fishbane, M. *Biblical Interpretation in Ancient Israel.* Oxford: Clarendon, 1985.

Hauser, A. J., and D. F. Watson, eds. *A History of Biblical Interpretation.* 2 vols. Grand Rapids, Mich.: Eerdmans, 2003–2009.

Levinson, B. M. *Deuteronomy and the Hermeneutics of Legal Innovation.* New York: Oxford University Press, 1997.

Mulder, M. J., ed. *Mikra: Text, Translation, Reading and Interpretation of the Hebrew Bible in Ancient Judaism and Early Christianity.* Philadelphia: Fortress, 1988.

Naissance de la méthode critique. Colloque du centenaire de l'Ecole biblique et archéologique française de Jérusalem. Patrimoines. Christianisme. Paris: Cerf, 1992.

Oeming, M. *Contemporary Biblical Hermeneutics: An Introduction.* Translated by J. F. Vette. Aldershot, UK: Ashgate, 2006.

Reventlow, H. *History of Biblical Interpretation.* Atlanta: Society of Biblical Literature, 2009–2010.

Rogerson, J. W. *The History of Christian Theology. Vol. 2: The Study and Use of the Bible.* Grands Rapids, Mich.: Eerdmans, 1988.

Rogerson, J. W. *Old Testament Criticism in the Nineteenth Century: England and Germany.* London: SPCK, 1984.

Saebø, M. *Hebrew Bible, Old Testament: The History of Its Interpretation.* 3 vols. Göttingen: Vandenhoeck & Ruprecht, 1996–.

Schmid, K. *Genesis and the Moses Story: Israel's Dual Origins in the Hebrew Bible.* Siphrut: Literature and Theology of the Hebrew Scriptures 3. Winona Lake, Ind.: Eisenbrauns, 2010.

Schüssler Fiorenza. E. *In memory of Her: A Feminist Theological Reconstruction of Christian Origins.* London: SCM, 1986 [1983].

Schüssler Fiorenza. *But She Said: Feminist Practices of Biblical Interpretation.* Boston: Beacon, 1992.

Ska, J.-L. *The Exegesis of the Pentateuch: Exegetical Studies and Basic Questions.* Forschungen zum Alten Testament 66. Tübingen: Mohr Siebeck, 2009.

Tate, W. R. *Interpreting the Bible: A Handbook of Terms and Methods.* 3d ed. Peabody, Mass.: Hendrickson, 2006.

Tigay, J. H., ed. *Empirical Models for Biblical Criticism.* Philadelphia: University of Pennsylvania Press, 1985.

Tigay, J. H. *The Evolution of the Gilgamesh Epic.* Philadelphia: University of Pennsylvania Press, 1982.

Tov, E. "The Significance of the Texts from the Judean Desert for the History of the Text of the Hebrew Bible: A New Synthesis." In *Qumran between the Old and*

New Testaments, edited by F. H. Cryer and T. L. Thompson, 277–309. Journal for the Study of the Old Testament: Supplement Series 290. Sheffield UK: Sheffield Academic, 1998.

Tov, E. "La nature du texte massorétique à la lumière des découvertes du désert de Juda et de la littérature rabbinique," In *L'enfance de la Bible hébraïque. L'histoire du texte de l'Ancien Testament à la lumière des recherches récentes*, edited by A. Schenker and P. Hugo, 105–131. Le Monde de la Bible 52. Genève: Labor et Fides, 2005.

Young, F. M. *Biblical Exegesis and the Formation of Christian Culture.* Cambridge, UK: Cambridge University Press, 1997.

Christophe Nihan

f

Feminist Biblical Interpretation

As an academic discipline, feminist biblical interpretation was inspired and nurtured by the politics of the second feminist movement in the early 1970s. It was then that feminist exegetes began exploring the reconstruction of biblical history centered on women and gender, the recovery of feminist meanings in biblical texts, and the deconstruction and resistance to androcentric biblical historiographies, literary meanings, and cultural appropriations. Since the emergence of the field, feminist exegetes have used various methods to interpret biblical literatures. They have taken seriously the notion of interlocking patterns of domination and studied gender together with race, class, sexuality, disability, nationality, and geopolitical conditions. They have also adhered to different hermeneutical stances, preferring various disciplinary alliances based on individual preferences and epistemological assumptions.

Although many feminist biblical interpreters focused on the historical and literary recovery of women in the Hebrew Bible and the early Christian movements during the pioneering phase of the 1970s, the emergence of womanist, mujerista, queer, postcolonial, and postmodern interpretations in subsequent decades is intimately linked with the early phase in the 1970s and cannot be understood apart from it. Today's feminist biblical exegesis foregrounds the vast diversity of approaches to studying women and gender. Feminist biblical interpretation has come to challenge modernist notions of objectivity, disinterestedness, and the possibility of extracting an original meaning inherent in the text. It understands its project as the critical analysis of multiaxial power relations in which gender, sexuality, race, ethnicity, nationality, age, physical abilities, and other ideological-theological stances play central roles. In other words, the notion of "social location," also prominent in other fields in the humanities, has gained considerable traction in feminist biblical interpretation since its inception.

More recently, some feminist biblical interpreters have expressed concern about the future and viability of the field. There are few degree programs with a specialization in feminist biblical interpretations, few if any endowed professorships in feminist biblical hermeneutics, and a decreasing number of explicitly feminist publications in the field. There are also co-opting tendencies among some women exegetes, as the field continues to face considerable hurdles in recognition and valuation. For instance, sometimes women exegetes avoid the term "feminist" in their work and adapt to the "malestream" status quo by avoiding explicitly feminist research topics. Institutional support for and cultural attention to feminist biblical hermeneutics are minor in contrast to the worldwide abundance of androcentric exegesis from Christian conservative literalist, modernist historical, and linguistic viewpoints. Thus, as an alternative hermeneutical enterprise, feminist biblical interpretation resides on the institutional and cultural margins despite its enormous exegetical accomplishments during the past 40 years.

Historical Development of Feminist Biblical Interpretation. Since women have been Christians and Jews for as long as these religious traditions have existed, they have always participated in the reading of the Bible. While women were mostly recipients of biblical meanings as transmitted by androcentric institutions such as church and synagogue, and also faced considerable dangers in speaking before public audiences, some of them were nevertheless active and resistant readers of the text. Although most records of ordinary women's resistance to androcentric biblical interpretation are lost to us, a few sources still exist that depict women in religious orders and the upper classes as biblical exegetes of high intellect and strong convictions. Their interpretations challenged male political and religious leaders, and they demanded women's equality not only before God but also in society.

One of these was the fourteenth-century Christian writer, Christine de Pisan, who defended women's equality on the basis of Genesis 1—2. She maintained that woman, like man, was not only created in God's image but also consisted of much better material than man. Woman was taken from human flesh whereas man was only made from soil. Moreover, de Pisan observed that the location of woman's creation was better than man's. She was created in paradise, and so her noble nature was guaranteed by God. To de Pisan, woman was God's masterpiece, the culmination of the creation.

Another courageous woman interpreter was Elizabeth Cady Stanton, a renowned nineteenth-century US-American suffragist and abolitionist. Stanton gathered a team of like-minded white women to interpret the Bible against the status quo of patriarchal order and social hierarchies. Stanton considered the Bible as the original cause of women's oppression. She was convinced that only a systematic study of oppressive biblical passages would dismantle sexist forces in society and lead to women's equality. Stanton also wanted to dispel women's attraction to religion by showing its deep complicity with androcentric domination. Her landmark anthology, *The Woman's Bible* (1895 and 1898), exposed the negative influence of the Bible on women's status throughout Western history. To be sure, Stanton's vision was impaired with respect to questions of race, class oppression, and anti-Judaism; here she wore the same androcentric and patriarchal lenses as her male contemporaries. Yet, for the time in which she lived, Stanton was a courageous visionary in her insistence that the Bible itself was an androcentric product, and that women's social and political equality could not be achieved without confronting the androcentric nature of the scriptures.

In the first half of the twentieth-century, many of the arguments of the nineteenth-century debate on women's rights and the Bible were forgotten. Although women continued to publish books and articles on "women in the Bible," including journalists such as Edith Deen, none of these works had the proto-feminist and early-feminist impetus of the earlier writings. In addition, few women were admitted to the ranks of academia and even fewer made it as biblical scholars. Those who did, such as Hedwig Jahnow (1879–1944) in Germany or Mary Ely Lyman (1887–1975) at Union Theological Seminary in New York City, enjoyed little academic support and fellowship. Moreover, they did not identify as feminist scholars during this era of sociopolitical, economic, and cultural retrenchment. Others, writing from feminist perspectives such as the philosopher Simone de Beauvoir, did not concern themselves with the Bible and its history of interpretation.

The situation changed only in the 1960s, sometimes earmarked with Betty Friedan's 1963 publication, *The Feminine Mystique*. After several decades of renewed compliance to patriarchal conditions, some women discovered their feminist voices and began questioning androcentric practices and traditions. In religious and theological studies Mary

Daly's books, *The Church and the Second Sex* (1968) and *Beyond God the Father: Toward a Philosophy of Women's Liberation* (1973), confronted male-dominated church power and society with a theo-historical analysis that provoked feminist Bible scholars to examine feminist concerns in biblical history and literature. For the first time, feminist Bible scholars located primarily in the United States, credentialed with doctoral degrees and teaching at colleges, universities, and seminaries, began examining the Bible and its history of interpretation with a feminist hermeneutic. They reissued the challenge that the Bible is gendered literature with a gendered history of interpretation.

In this early phase of academic feminist biblical interpretation, two publications shaped the feminist exegetical research agenda, and they were read by feminist Christians and Jews alike. They defined mainstream feminist biblical studies in North American religious and theological institutions of higher learning. By reframing epistemological, hermeneutical, and methodological priorities, they brought scholarly legitimacy to research on women and gender in the field of biblical studies. One of these pioneering books is Elisabeth Schüssler Fiorenza's *In Memory of Her* (1983). As Schüssler Fiorenza explained in the introduction to the tenth anniversary edition of her work, she "set out to explore the problem of women's historical agency in ancient Christianity in light of the theological and historical questions raised by the feminist movements in society and church and to do so in terms of critical biblical studies" (1993, p. xiv). Schüssler Fiorenza showed that women and men of the first Christian century attempted to practice "the call to coequal discipleship," but with various degrees and levels of success. At the time Schüssler Fiorenza worried whether feminists would dismiss the book as "male scholarship," while mainstream colleagues would not take it seriously. She was also concerned that her book would be dismissed for eschewing value-neutrality and embracing an explicitly partisan perspective. Her worries were unfounded. Colleagues, such as feminist ethicist Beverly W. Harrison, immediately recognized the book as a milestone accomplishment, stating: "In *Memory of Her* is, I believe, the most fulsome proposal we yet possess for a feminist hermeneutics that addresses the full circle of human interpretation" (*Horizons* 11, no. 1 [Spring 1984], p. 150).

The other book that galvanized feminist biblical studies into today's field is Phyllis Trible's *God and the Rhetoric of Sexuality* (1978). Equipped with the literary method of rhetorical criticism and a feminist hermeneutics, Trible examined biblical narratives and poetry that feature women and female metaphors. She defined feminism as a critique of culture in light of misogyny, applied this notion to her interpretation of the selected biblical literature, and demonstrated that in the process text and world gain renewed meaning. In her companion book, *Texts of Terror* (1984), Trible chose four "ancient tales of terror" because, as she explained, they "speak all too frighteningly of the present" (p. xiii). She read the narratives of Hagar, Tamar, an unnamed woman in the book of Judges, and the daughter of Jephthah as "stories of outrage on behalf of their female victims in order to recover a neglected history, to remember a past that the present embodies, and to pray that these terrors shall not come to pass again" (p. 3). Trible acknowledged that her study was possible only because of her earlier and more joyous work. Both volumes, but especially *Texts of Terror*, unearthed stories about women and gender in the Hebrew Bible that Christian and Jewish exegesis had previously neglected. Trible's recovery project jolted scholars and lay readers alike into a newfound awareness that these biblical texts carry tremendous significance for discussions on women and gender.

Alongside the landmark works of Schüssler Fiorenza and Trible stand numerous other feminist publications of continuing significance that were produced in the 1980s and 1990s. Together they constitute a veritable explosion of feminist knowledge concerning biblical literature and related disciplines. In Hebrew Bible studies they include the publications of Phyllis Bird, Peggy L. Day, Tikva Frymer-Kensky, Esther Fuchs, Alice L. Laffey, Carol Meyers, Katharine Doob Sakenfeld, Elisabeth

Schüngel-Straumann, and Renita J. Weems. In New Testament and Early Christian studies, they include the works of Bernadette Brooten, Mary Rose D'Angelo, Jane Schaberg, Sandra M. Schneiders, Luise Schottroff, Mary Ann Tolbert, and Antoinette Wire. Furthermore, feminist scholars from related fields, such as Judith Plaskow, Letty Russell, Ross Kraemer, Karen King, and Kwok Pui-lan, also enriched and strengthened explorations into the gendered nature of the Bible and the history of interpretation.

Current Trends in Feminist Biblical Interpretation. During the past few decades, feminist biblical scholars have expanded and deepened their work, especially in two areas. First, feminist exegetes have produced an increasingly differentiated vocabulary on the interlocking structures of domination, owing in no small part to the contributions of women of color, both from North America and across the globe. Second, feminist exegetes, in contact with developments related to women's studies, have engaged in discussions on the nature of gender. Like feminist scholars in other academic disciplines, feminist biblical exegetes learned to acknowledge that the study of gender does not pertain only to sexed bodies. Rather, it also requires the conceptualization of gender as a discourse of power in society, and within this discourse, sex itself must be understood as a social construct.

Increased Attention to the Multiaxial Nature of Structures of Domination. Although it was not the central focus for all, some white feminists of the 1970s and 1980s understood the need for a broader analysis of the interlocking nature of systems of oppression. For instance, Katherine Doob Sakenfeld, in an article published in 1982, acknowledged the cultural and functional inseparability of racism, sexism, and classism, and encouraged feminist biblical scholars to pay more attention to these intersections. Also Phyllis Trible's work showed sensitivity to the interlocking systems of gender with class and nationality. Similarly, the first volume of Schüssler Fiorenza's *Searching the Scriptures* (1993) was dedicated to nineteenth-century African American feminist thinker, Anna Julia Cooper, and so signaled the "as yet unrealized possibilities of the diverse locations and divergent traditions of feminist biblical interpretation" (p. ix). Yet at the time, it was quite possible—as it still is in some quarters today—for white feminist Bible scholars to focus on gender oppression alone.

This cannot be said for womanist Bible interpreters who have always had a complex view of the interlocking nature of oppression. For instance, Renita Weems (1988) explored women of the Hebrew Bible with a focus on race, class, and gender, and systematic theologian Delores Williams (1986) posed piercing questions about the connection of race, gender, nationality, and class in her reading of Hagar. In 1987, ethicist and womanist scholar Toinette M. Eugene classified the examination of intersecting forms of oppression as central to womanist biblical hermeneutics. She explained that due to the doubly and triply oppressed status of women of color in patriarchal society, the analysis of sexism must be intrinsically linked to the study of other oppressive ideologies. She called for a feminist biblical hermeneutics, built upon both women's struggles against oppression and women's experiences of survival, envisioning a liberating praxis for *all* oppressed people.

In subsequent years, Eugene's call has resonated in feminist exegesis, particularly with scholars embracing postcolonial and intersectional hermeneutical perspectives. They include a growing number of African American women interpreters, along with exegetes from African countries. All of them have challenged white feminist biblical discourse for the neglect of race. Many of them prefer the term "womanism" for Christian Black women's scholarship, based on Alice Walker's famous definition. Womanist theologians repeatedly state that racism is at least as urgent as sexism, and they propose that feminist biblical scholarship investigate both gender and race (e.g., Koala Jones-Warsaw 1993).

It is also important to note that postcolonial feminist interpreters from African, Asian, and Latin American countries have developed exegetical approaches that analyze biblical literature with political and social convictions at the forefront of their work. Hence, feminist postcolonial interpreters are less interested in historically reconstructed meanings and find textual alignments between biblical women and women of their societies significant. They recognize that ordinary readers, especially ordinary two-third world women, have much to contribute to the meaning-making process of biblical literature. They also place exegetical discussions within (post)colonial histories, as demonstrated in the work of Judith E. McKinlay (2004), and examine these histories in light of the Bible, its interpretation histories, and gender. Attention to the interlocking structures of domination is thus firmly established in feminist biblical interpretation today.

Theorizing Gender and Sex. Another area in which the scope of feminist biblical interpretation has expanded in recent decades relates to the increasingly complex notion of what the study of gender entails. In the 1970s and 1980s, feminist scholars in biblical studies, as in the humanities in general, focused much energy on retrieving and restoring women to history and history to women. Theoretical discussions sharply influenced by historian Joan Wallach Scott's essay, "Gender: A Useful Category of Historical Analysis" (pp. 28–50 of *Gender and the Politics of History*, New York: Columbia University Press, 1988), ensured that the early focus on "woman" expanded to "women," gender, and eventually also to sexuality. A growing number of feminist exegetes began to view gender not just as the analysis of sexed bodies, but as part of the broad discourse on power, as it organizes social relationships. Results of this work in Hebrew Bible and New Testament Studies have included publications—sometimes, but not always, explicitly aligned with feminist perspectives—that demonstrate the socially constructed nature of masculinity, and the varying ways biblical texts either conform to or defy hegemonic notions of masculinity (e.g., Conway, 2008; Moore and Anderson 2004).

Finally, and similar to the academic shifts that morphed "Women's Studies" into "Women's and Gender Studies" and then into "Women's, Gender, and Sexuality Studies," the field of feminist biblical interpretation has also opened up to sexuality studies. Although not all biblical scholars in sexuality studies work from an explicitly feminist perspective, often they do. Sometimes they employ traditional historical criticism (e.g., Brooten 1996), and sometimes a queer hermeneutics (e.g., Guest 2011). They aim to disrupt hegemonic heteronormative assumptions and argue for the socially constructed nature of gender and sex either in the societies that produced the biblical literatures, or in the literary meanings of the biblical texts, or in the world of the readers of the Bible.

Beyond the Canon and Toward the Readers: Illustrating Feminist Biblical Interpretation in Action. Procedures and benefits of feminist biblical interpretation are far too numerous to describe comprehensively, so this section illustrates them only in regard to the discussions on the expanded canonical boundaries and the move toward a reader-centered hermeneutics. In the field of New Testament and early Christianity, one impetus for an expanded notion of canonical boundaries was the discovery of the so-called Gnostic texts from Nag Hammadi, Egypt, in the 1950s. These texts, dating to the early centuries of Christianity, contain numerous images of the divine as feminine, and otherwise push against conventional gender boundaries (see, for example, *Thunder, the Perfect Mind, or the Hypostasis of the Archons*). In addition, several of these texts privilege Mary Magdalene as a spiritual leader within the Jesus movement, thus reinforcing the strong image of Mary Magdalene already known from the extracanonical Gospel of Mary. Feminists have embraced these texts that challenge prevailing orthodox Christian assumptions on gender, including the fact that women have been unjustly silenced in dominant Christian theological settings. The newly discovered literature has also drawn attention to the gendered power dynamics in operation when Christian authorities classified persons and ideas as orthodox or heretical (King 1988; Schaberg 2004). Another impetus for the push beyond canonical boundaries has been renewed attention to the centrality of women in the Apocryphal Acts. The *Acts of Thecla* in particular, with its strikingly aggressive female protagonist, has garnered interest as a text probably produced by a community that rejected the stern patriarchal admonitions of the canonical Pastoral Epistles. Thus, feminists, working with extracanonical texts such as the Gnostic literature and the Apocryphal Acts, have shown that these texts preserve signs of early Christian struggles between orthodox and so-called heretical factions about the place of women in Christian communities.

In feminist biblical interpretation the question of how far the limits of canonical boundaries should be expanded is ongoing. Those equipped with a postcolonial critique of Western hegemony and wanting to include the world's population in the conversation on the meaning of sacred literature have called for biblical scholars to embrace a much broader textual base for their inquiries than customary in (feminist) biblical studies. These exegetes have raised questions about what constitutes a religious text. For instance, Musa Dube (2000) criticizes *Searching the Scriptures: A Feminist Commentary* (1993), edited by Elisabeth Schüssler Fiorenza, for its exclusive focus on Jewish and Christian biblical texts. Dube charges that the volume, privileging Western voices, ignores indigenous voices of the Two-Thirds World. She proposes a vast expansion of what is meant by the "Bible" and suggests including religious sites, texts, and traditions of all the peoples of the world. Dube's criticism of the Western focus in feminist biblical interpretation resonates with calls from scholars who emphasize race and postcolonialism in their efforts to decenter Western Christian scholarship. For example, postcolonial critic R. S. Sugirtharajah argues for an emphasis on the role of India in early Christianity, and New Testament exegete Gay Byron calls for more research on the Axumite Empire in Africa that produced many religious texts during the early centuries of Christianity.

An effort of expanding canonical boundaries and an increased concern for readers in the meaning-making process are also advanced in feminist Hebrew Bible Studies. Influenced by cultural studies, feminist Hebrew Bible scholars began transgressing the canonical configurations of traditional source materials, as they examined representations of women and gender in art, film, and music (e.g., Exum 1996; Leneman 2007). The notion of linking feminist biblical interpretation with texts, concerns, and worldviews from contemporary societies has also been productively applied to sexual violence and rape. One such work is *Sacred Witness: Rape in the Hebrew Bible* by Susanne Scholz (2010). This study relates contemporary feminist debates on rape to the interpretation of biblical prose, poetry, and legal codes. Taking a thematic approach, the volume organizes the selected literature according to contemporary categories of rape, such as acquaintance, marital, gang, or male rape, and analyzes numerous biblical texts as rape texts that other interpreters ignored or considered as literature about marriage, consensual sex, or even love. Scholz's interpretation demonstrates that contemporary categories of rape, as developed in feminist theory, can productively be applied to the field of biblical interpretation. Accordingly, the story of Tamar in 2 Sam 13 is a tale of incestuous acquaintance rape, the fate of Hagar in Genesis 16 and 21 as well as the experiences of Bilhah and Zilpah in Genesis 29—30 turn into rape stories of enslaved women, and the encounter between Ehud, the judge, and the Moabite king, Eglon, depicts a murderous male rape (Judges 3) (see especially Guest, Deryn, Robert E. Goss, Mona West, Thomas Bohache, eds. *The Queer Bible Commentary*. London: SCM Press, 2006).

Another publication in feminist Hebrew Bible studies expands the notion of the biblical canon, while remaining connected to its rabbinical Jewish tradition. It also emphasizes the hermeneutical significance of readers. *The Torah: A Women's Commentary* (ed., Tamara Cohn Eskenazi and Andrea L. Weiss) makes a historic contribution to the feminist study of the Pentateuch from across the spectrum of mainly US-American Reform, Conservative, Reconstructionist, and Orthodox Judaism. The commentary's effectiveness is easily illustrated with interpretations of Exod 19:15. In this verse Moses changes the divine command by adding that the male Israelites shall not go near a woman. Jewish feminist interpreter, Diane M. Sharon, states that the verse has been particularly painful for Jewish feminists because it reports of Moses modifying

God's command and it raises the problem of who is the final authority over divine revelation. To Sharon, this problem is only solved when the entire section of Exod 19:10–15 is interpreted from a reader-driven perspective that questions an omniscient external authority and empowers women readers to define biblical meaning. Another commentator, Judith Plaskow, also stresses the need to reject external voices of authority, such as from Moses, and to develop women's understandings of revelation throughout Jewish history.

In short, feminist biblical interpreters are often much less bound to androcentric doctrines about the nature of the canon and sacred scripture. They propose biblical meanings that foster liberation, empowerment, and healing in a world filled with structures of domination and injustice, and they are willing to expand the notion of "bible" in the service of this liberation. The goal is to make the Bible relevant in its multivalent and plurivocal form as a resource for feminist analysis and practice. The notion of the biblical canon and its function in feminist biblical interpretation has been vastly expanded, and the significance of readers in the meaning-making process has been greatly emphasized both in feminist Hebrew Bible and New Testament studies.

Central Issues in Feminist Biblical Interpretation Today. Feminist biblical interpretation is not monolithic and its practitioners do not proceed in lockstep when it comes to methods, approaches, and the proper scope of the field. Without being exhaustive, this section presents a sampling of ongoing concerns and debates animating current feminist biblical work.

Christian Anti-Judaism. The historically intractable problem of Christianity's repeated assertions of supersessionism, formulated against the foil of an inferior Judaism has also spilled over into Christian feminist biblical interpretation. One indication of the pervasiveness of the problem is that feminist exegetes often reproduce anti-Jewish formulations even when they are aware of the issue and attempt to avoid it. The problem of Christian (feminist) anti-Judaism becomes even more complex when it is viewed through the prism of global Christianity and postcolonial biblical interpretations.

The history of Christian anti-Judaism is tied specifically to the West, and redressing the problem has become acute in the post-Holocaust European and North American contexts. Yet the extent of Christian anti-Judaism is global, also due to earlier missionary movements from the West to Africa, Asia, and Latin America. Sometimes interpreters attempt to redress anti-Judaism by avoiding dualistic assertions of Christian "goodness" over Jewish "badness." For liberationist Christians from Asia, Africa, and Latin America, however, problems of more immediate urgency than anti-Judaism prevail. In these contexts, interpreters often utilize the New Testament as an emancipatory resource, sometimes highlighting Jesus's goodness as a means to criticize oppressive Christian leaders and practices, while assimilating the Gospel's "Jewish Other" with their own enemies. Interestingly, the issue of anti-Judaism in feminist Hebrew Bible studies is only marginally examined. The topic flared up in the late 1980s when the goddess movement tried to recover a prepatriarchal and pre-Israelite matriarchal era (Frymer-Kensky 1992). However, a broad-based discussion does not yet exist in feminist Hebrew Bible studies.

The Challenge of Competing Epistemological Paradigms. Feminist biblical interpreters have always acknowledged the political and social impetus of their work, aiming for gender justice in religious traditions that have forsaken women for centuries. Initially and even today, feminist exegetes have relied on the dominant methods in the field, such as historical criticism. They also employed literary methods not widely recognized as mainstream exegetical tools in the 1970s and early 1980s. Since then, this situation has changed and nowadays a plethora of methodologies prevails. Still, an ongoing challenge relates to the divergent epistemological paradigms in the field. Elisabeth Schüssler Fiorenza (2007) has contributed to this discussion perhaps unlike any other feminist biblical scholar. She recognizes that biblical texts are sites of struggle over power, norms, and influence in society and religion, and she proposes to redesign the methodologies in biblical studies according to what she calls the rhetorical-political paradigm. This paradigm fosters explicitly ethical-political interests in opposition to the prevalent scriptural-theological and philological-historical paradigms. She thus criticizes sharply the empiricist-scientific epistemology, dominant since the emergence of the modern worldview in the sixteenth century C.E., and suggests that feminist biblical scholars examine the rhetorical function of biblical and other ancient texts in past and present historical and literary contexts.

The epistemological challenge is increasingly recognized in biblical studies. For instance, Todd Penner and Davina C. Lopez (2011) suggest that every interpretation of the Bible, whether historically or otherwise conceptualized, is never merely about a historical or literary account. Rather, such work is about (post)modern scholars using the ancient world to reconstruct biblical meanings for and in the present time. Thus, in their view, it is the task of contemporary exegetes to give an account of these usages and to expose the sociopolitical, economic, and religious interests that stand behind them.

The presentation of such accounts is, of course, exactly what feminist exegetes have done when they highlighted women's roles in the text or in the worlds behind the texts. Thus, historically, feminist biblical interpreters were never only focused on antiquarian or literary biblical meanings, but worked to make the Bible relevant for contemporary feminist purposes. Indeed, much of the feminist biblical scholarship of the 1970s and 1980s was published within the context of heated ecclesiastical debates over women's ordination. Many of these women, opting not to follow Mary Daly's call to exit the church as hopelessly patriarchal, maintained ties, however loose, to Christian and Jewish theological institutions and faith communities, as numerous feminist Bible scholars still do. They continue to acknowledge the perspectival nature of all scholarship and repudiate the pervasive assumption that "real scholarship" aims for neutrality, universality, and objectivity. An advantage of the feminist epistemological premise is that it facilitates connections with grassroots groups interested in the Bible, who are most often affiliated with religious institutions. However, the epistemological challenge is ongoing because the empiricist-scientific paradigm is still dominant in biblical studies.

The Connections to Sexuality, Queer, and Masculinity Studies. Although some feminist exegetes still focus exclusively on "women" and gender, recent developments in feminist scholarship have made the analysis of sexuality, queer, and masculinity studies central. In other words, the academic study of "women" is now embedded in a discourse on gender that includes matters of sexuality, the dominance of heteronormativity, the discourse of queerness as resistance to any kind of normativity, and also the study of masculinity. In biblical studies, historical critical investigations on lesbian life in early Christianity led the way to challenge and to reinvigorate feminist exegesis limited to "women." For instance, Bernadette Brooten's *Love between Women: Early Christian Responses to Female Homoeroticism* (University of Chicago: 1996) demonstrates that lesbians existed in the early Christian centuries. Similarly, but hermeneutically far less bound by historical criticism, Deryn Guest (2005) calls for a lesbian identified hermeneutic that breaks with heteronormative standards prevalent in biblical studies and in society at large. Furthermore, queer biblical theorists remind biblical scholars that no categories are stable and any notion of homosexuality merely reinforces heteronormativity (Punt 2011). The emergence of masculinity studies does not resolve this dilemma, but the critical analysis of maleness in biblical texts and scholarship nevertheless has further illuminated the discourse of power (Creanga 2010; Moore and Anderson 2004). In short, the emergence of a complex and differentiated discourse on women, men, sexuality, and queer studies constitutes an important development in feminist biblical interpretation.

The Challenges from the Christian Right. The Christian Right's discourse on gender and the Bible has proliferated since the 1990s. While located in the United States, its missionary zeal has spread far beyond the North American continent. The Christian Right considers the Bible as inerrant, and the movement communicates its biblical views on gender in widely distributed publications, as well as in visual materials, such as DVDs for children, and in an overwhelming online presence. Christian Right interpreters have taken three major positions. There is, first, the "complementarian" position, sometimes also identified as "hierarchicalism" or "traditionalism." Second, there is the "egalitarian" stance that in evangelical circles is considered to be a feminist position. Third, there is a moderate evangelical conviction that consists mainly of evangelical Christian theologians who do not explicitly affiliate with either the complementarian or the egalitarian position. All three positions are deeply engaged in defining contemporary practices related to gender, family, and sexuality with the Bible, grounding their readings in a literalist methodology with historical claims.

Because of their remarkable expertise in communicating with today's media tools, the Christian Right maintains a high profile on the North American continent and elsewhere. Although they participate in the conversation on feminism, religion, and the Bible, they do not usually engage feminist biblical interpretations directly, because they reject its politically progressive stance. The challenge for feminist biblical scholars is to identify and to develop academically sound procedures that investigate the Christian Right's success in communicating theologically, hermeneutically, and socially conservative positions that are popularized far beyond the Christian Right context.

Moving toward an Interfaith Feminist Biblical Hermeneutics. In recent years, at least two forces have encouraged feminist biblical interpreters to an increased collaboration across religious traditions. First, those working in feminist postcolonial interpretation have highlighted the damage done to indigenous traditions by zealous Christian missionary efforts. They want representatives of those indigenous traditions to have a rightful place in exegetical and theological discourse. Second, in the aftermath of the destruction of the Twin Towers in New York City on September 11, 2001, interest in interfaith relations among Jewish, Christian, and Muslim feminists has significantly increased. Feminist biblical scholars have also begun rereading biblical passages on religious exclusivism, and they have identified "minority" readings in the effort to create openness toward peoples of other faiths. An anthology, edited by Letty Russell and Phyllis Trible (2006), exemplifies this impetus. The various essays engage the stories of Sarah and Hagar from Jewish, Christian, and Muslim perspectives. However, these efforts are still in an incipient phase. A helpful institutional resource toward multireligious feminist dialogue is the *Journal of Feminist Studies in Religion (JFSR)*, which frequently publishes articles and discussions from multireligious perspectives and locations.

In conclusion, the field of feminist biblical interpretation has produced innovative and important scholarship that shapes historical, literary, and cultural explorations of the Bible and the Bible's place in the world, it aims to eliminate structures of domination, and it nurtures religious, societal, political, and economic forces toward justice and peace.

[*See also* Gnosticism and Gnostic Interpretation; Lesbian, Gay, Bisexual, and Transgender Interpretation; Masculinity Studies; Queer Criticism and Queer Theory; Race, Ethnicity, and Biblical Criticism; *and* Womanist Interpretation.]

BIBLIOGRAPHY

For comprehensive bibliographies on feminist biblical studies, visit online:

Penner, Todd, and Davina C. Lopez. "Feminist Scholarship on the New Testament." *Oxford Bibliographies*: http://www.oxfordbibliographies.com.

Scholz, Susanne. "Feminist Scholarship on the Old Testament." *Oxford Bibliographies*: http://www.oxfordbibliographies.com.

Publications referenced in this article:

Brooten, Bernadette. *Love Between Women: Early Christian Responses to Female Homoeroticism.* Chicago: University of Chicago Press, 1996. Expert analysis on the history of lesbian existence in the early Christian period, as evidenced in both well-known and rarely consulted ancient texts, manuscripts, and artifacts.

Conway, Colleen. *Behold the Man: Jesus and Greco-Roman Masculinity*. Oxford: Oxford University Press, 2008. An exploration of how New Testament authors engaged the gender ideology of the Roman Empire in their depictions of the masculinity of Jesus.

Creanga, Ovidiu, ed. *Men and Masculinity in the Hebrew Bible and Beyond*. Sheffield: Sheffield Phoenix Press, 2010. Pioneering anthology that interrogates biblical texts, ancient Near Eastern sources, and the history of interpretation on men and masculinity.

Dube, Muse, *Postcolonial Feminist Interpretation of the Bible*. St. Louis, MO: Chalice, 2000. Landmark volume in postcolonial feminist biblical interpretation, considering biblical literature alongside other literature of colonization, in view of the perspective of women in the two-thirds world.

Eskenazi, Tamara Cohn, and Andrea L. Weiss, eds. *The Torah: A Women's Commentary*. New York: WRJ, 2008. A historic contribution to the feminist study of the Pentateuch from across the spectrum of mainly US-American Reform, Conservative, Reconstructionist, and Orthodox Judaism.

Eugene, Toinette M. "A Hermeneutical Challenge for Womanists: The Interrelation between the Text and Our Experience." In *Perspectives on Feminist Hermeneutics*, edited by Gayle G. Koontz and Willard Swartley, 20–28. Elkhart, IN: Institute for Mennonite Studies, 1987. Groundbreaking essay on the significance of a womanist heremeneutic in biblical studies.

Exum, J. Cheryl. *Plotted, Shot, and Painted: Cultural Representations of Biblical Women*. Sheffield: Sheffield Academic Press, 1996. Innovative feminist study on female characters of the Hebrew Bible in Western art, writing, and film that exposes the insistence of masculine superiority in Western culture.

Frymer-Kensky, Tikva. *In the Wake of the Goddess: Women, Culture, and the Biblical Transformation of a Pagan Myth*. New York: Free Press, 1992. Leading feminist-historical study on women and goddesses in biblical and ancient Near Eastern texts.

Guest, Deryn. *When Deborah Met Jael: Lesbian Feminist Hermeneutics*. London: SCM Press, 2011. Innovative hermeneutical study exploring the differing social locations of lesbian-identified hermeneutics in biblical studies.

Jones-Warsaw, Koala. "Toward a Feminist Hermeneutic: Reading of Judges 19–21." In *Feminist Companion to Judges*, ed. Athalya Brenner, 172–186. Sheffield: JSOT Press, 1993. Important investigation on the horrific story in Judges taking into account the power dynamics of men over women as well as over men, especially when difference in race and ethnicity is taken into account.

King, Karen, ed. *Images of the Feminine in Gnosticism*. Philadelphia: Fortress, 1988. A collection of essays centered on understanding gnostic perspectives on gender, and the question of the relationship of gendered mythology to social description.

Leneman, Helen. *The Performed Bible: The Story of Ruth in Opera and Oratorio*. Sheffield: Sheffield Phoenix, Press, 2007. Significant feminist scholarly contribution on the book of Ruth as appropriated in the selected Western musical genres.

McKinlay, Judith E. *Reframing Her: Biblical Women in Postcolonial Focus*. Sheffield: Sheffield Phoenix Press, 2004. Important investigation of selected biblical texts and issues from a postcolonial feminist hermeneutical stance.

Moore, Stephen and Janice Cape Anderson, eds. *New Testament Masculinities*. Atlanta, GA: SBL, 2004. A collection of essays on the New Testament and related literature, exploring the construction and performance of masculinity.

Penner, Todd and Davina C. Lopez. "Homelessness as a Way Home: A Methodological Reflection and Proposal." In *Holy Land as Homeland? Models for Constructing the Historic Landscape of Jesus*, edited by Keith W. Whitelam, 151–178. Sheffield: Sheffield Phoenix Press, 2011. Innovative proposal for a refocused investigation of the use of exegetical methodologies in biblical studies in general and early Christian studies in particular.

Plaskow, Judith. *Standing Again at Sinai: Judaism from a Feminist Perspective*. New York: Harper Collins, 1990. Highly influential work on feminist Jewish theology making many important references to the Hebrew Bible.

Punt, Jeremy. "Queer Theory, Postcolonial Theory, and Biblical Interpretation: A Preliminary Exploration of Some Intersections." In *Bible Troubles: Queer Reading at the Boundaries of Biblical Scholarship*, edited by Teresa J. Hornsby and Ken Stone, 321–341. Atlanta, GA: SBL, 2011. Theoretical essay elaborating on the crucial links between queer and postcolonial theories for biblical hermeneutics.

Sakenfeld, Katherine Doob. "Old Testament Perspectives: Methodological Issues." *Journal for the Study of the Old Testament* 22 (1982): 13–20. Important early discussion on methods in feminist biblical interpretation.

Schaberg, Jane. *The Resurrection of Mary Magdalene: Legends, Apocrypha, and the Christian Testament*. New York: Continuum, 2004. With Virginia Woolf as her companion, Schaberg employs a hermeneutics of suspicion in examining depictions of Mary Magdalene in ancient sources and up to the present. Credits Mary Magdalene with the invention of Christianity, and exposes the patriarchal forces that have distorted her legacy.

Scholz, Susanne. *Sacred Witness: Rape in the Hebrew Bible*. Minneapolis, Minn.: Fortress, 2010. Comprehensive investigation on rape in biblical prose and poetry, as well as in selected ancient Near Eastern texts, interpreted within today's global rape culture.

Schüssler Fiorenza, Elisabeth. *The Power of the Word: Scripture and the Rhetoric of Empire*. Minneapolis, Minn.: Fortress, 2007. An examination of the power exercised by scripture, and a call for a feminist decolonizing reading that identifies both the destructive powers and the radical visions of justice and wholeness contained in scripture.

Schüssler Fiorenza, Elisabeth. *In Memory of Her: A Feminist Theological Reconstruction of Christian Origins*. 10th Anniversary Ed. New York: Crossroad, 1983. 2002. A landmark volume in feminist biblical interpretation reconstructs Christian beginnings with women at the center of the story, while challenging androcentric and patriarchal methodologies that have excluded women from historical narratives.

Schüssler Fiorenza, Elisabeth, ed. *Searching the Scriptures*, Volume 1: *A Feminist Introduction*. New York: Crossroad, 1993. The first of two volumes of feminist commentary on the New Testament and related literature, focused on methodological issues related to gender and other axes of domination, including race and nationality.

Trible, Phyllis. *God and the Rhetoric of Sexuality*. Philadelphia: Fortress, 1978. Pioneering feminist exegetical monograph on selected texts and characters in the Hebrew Bible.

Trible, Phyllis. *Texts of Terror: Literary-Feminist Readings of Biblical Narratives*. Philadelphia: Fortress, 1984. Groundbreaking literary-feminist study on biblical stories about sexual violence, rape, and child murder previously ignored in Christian and Jewish exegesis.

Trible, Phyllis and Russell, Letty M., eds. *Hagar, Sarah, and Their Children: Jewish, Christian, and Muslim Perspective*. Louisville, KY: Westminster John Knox, 2006. Collection of biblical, historical, theological, and ethical explorations on Hagar and Sarah in the three religious traditions.

Weems, Renita J. *Just a Sister Away: A Womanist Vision of Women's Relationships in the Bible*. New York: Grand Central Publishing, 1988. Influential study on selected biblical women and texts from a womanist exegetical perspective.

Williams, Delores S. "The Color of Feminism: Or Speaking the Black Woman's Tongue." *Journal of Religious Thought* 43, no. 1 (Spring–Summer 1986): 42–58. Influential essay on the nexus of womanist Christian theology and Hagar in Gen. 16; 21 in African American interpretation of the Bible.

Susanne Scholz and Shelly A. Matthews

FOLKLORE AND BIBLICAL INTERPRETATION

Folklore, the interdisciplinary academic field and the corpus of material studied, has been variously defined by folklorists. This scholarly conversation about folklore intertwines and intersects with the history and practice of biblical interpretation in complex and thought-provoking ways.

Folklorists on Folklore. Folklorists of the nineteenth and early twentieth centuries engaged in the collection of verbal and nonverbal popular antiquities, often without regard for the creators or original settings of the material. The contemporary field has developed into a complex variety of cultural studies. Folklore is a living phenomenon, including various forms of stylized cultural communication. Pieces of folklore are ever changing and adapting, reflecting and affecting folk groups who produce and receive these media. Folk media point to and address critical cultural concerns and tensions, and are characterized by recurring conventions in language and content that signal key meanings and messages within social groups.

Folklorists grapple with the challenges of doing ethnographic research as participant observers, aware of the implications of inserting themselves into the activities of those they study, and honest about their own subjectivities. Such work with living subjects is nevertheless relevant to questions posed concerning ancient Israelite culture, as scholars try to imagine actual composers and contexts and the ways in which the traditional literature of the Bible operated in ancient Israel. Folklorists' engagement in ethnography is also relevant to contemporary work in the reception history of the Bible, a boundary where the fields might fruitfully intersect.

Early folklorists suggested that proverbs, folktales, myths, riddles, jokes, and other forms were universal genres. While such European or Western designations remain useful, scholars have become much more sophisticated in describing "ethnic genres," a term coined by Dan Ben-Amos, who points out that cultural and linguistic groups define and recognize genres of folklore in particular ways. For example, the *māšāl* in ancient Israel not only was a saying or proverb, but also could refer to a kind of oracle, to a parable, and to other forms associated with the term *māšāl* in biblical literature. Folklorists have always placed emphasis on material culture, items produced or arranged that communicate culture much as do verbal creations. The material aspect of folklore is relevant to thinking about folklore and the Bible in relation to the role of archaeology in the study of ancient Israel.

Some contemporary folklorists emphasize that true folklore only operates in performance and experiential, communicative cultural settings. For such scholars, written accounts of performances or folklore-style materials that exist only in writing—for example, traditional stories found within the Hebrew Bible—do not count as true folklore. Others point to the presence of contemporary folklore in written forms, for example, the vast amount of stylized cultural communication that is now a part of social networking, and consider folklore relevant to an appreciation of an ancient written corpus such as the Hebrew Bible and the Israelite cultures behind it.

Text, Texture, and Context. Key concepts that describe pieces of folklore, oral, written, and nonverbal, fall under the headings offered by folklorist Alan Dundes: "texture," that is, the style of a work, how words are employed or visual motifs repeated; "text," content, for example the plot and characters in a folk narrative; and "context," the setting in which a work is produced, received, or preserved. We have already implicitly alluded to these categories in mentioning stylization, genres containing certain kinds of content, and communicative settings. Thinking in terms of texture, text, and context helps to present major approaches and interests of folklorists, to draw comparisons between folkloristics and biblical studies, and to explore the benefits of thinking of the Bible as folklore.

Structuralism: Ways of Viewing Texture and Text. The concern with structure is a critical component in various areas of folklore study and touches upon texture and text. Students of oral literature, influenced by the seminal work of Albert Lord and his teacher Milman Parry, explore the formulaic patterns of language in works of folklore created extemporaneously in performance settings. Studying epic traditions about war, absence, and return, Lord concluded that the Iliad and the Odyssey share with Balkan epic material certain key markers of oral composition, in particular a high degree of formulicity, "a formula being a group of words which is employed under the same metrical conditions to express a given essential idea" (1960, p. 30). Style thus reveals repetition, an economy of language in the words chosen to portray images and ideas. The very content or plot or structure of folk narratives is also highly formulaic, composed of recurring themes as in the musical "themes" of an opera or other musical genre. John Miles Foley has built on Lord's work, pointing to the ways in which key phrases or images or terms encode culture, so that an epithet or a color or a brief description can invoke the larger cultural and narrative tradition that is shared by the creator and receivers of the work of folklore.

Considerations of text inform the historical-geographic school of folklore, originating in Finland and associated with an American folklorist of the twentieth century, Stith Thompson. Defining motifs as small, reducible pieces of content, for instance a magic instrument, an action, or a character, these scholars collect both international versions of motifs found in traditional narratives and the patterns in which they are combined to produce tale "types." They then catalog the motifs and types according to systems of letters and numbers. Type 510, for example, includes versions of the Cinderella story, a set of tales about unlikely heroes who rise from lowly status to high status. The original reason for massing these collections was to trace the development of tales. Scholars would look for the most common denominator versions of particular tale types, their location and frequency, and try to ascertain where and when the tale had begun and how it had changed over time, across which geographic areas. These expressly chronological and geographic goals are no longer shared by many folklorists, but the indices of motifs and types and their systems of reference remain enormously useful to all students of traditional narrative, providing a comparative fund of variants that allows one to explore what is unique and what is transcultural in the traditional stories that human beings tell.

Overtly structuralist in orientation is the formalism of Vladimir Propp. Propp sought to show that there was one essential "text," in Dundes's sense, shared by one hundred Russian "wonder tales." All of the tales in Propp's classic study are treated as variants on the same morphology of key action events, tracing a plot from *Lack* to *Liquidation.* Scholars have explored whether all cultures have similar overriding morphologies that characterize folk forms, and indeed whether the relevance of Propp's pattern of content extends beyond the hundred tales of his study. Propp himself realized that the delineation of a pattern of content was just a first necessary step in exploring the meanings and messages of variations upon that essential morphology within particular settings, and this brings us to the category of context.

Implications for Context. Much of the structuralist work described earlier has implications for matters of context. Lord and Parry's work was overtly ethnographic. They collected and recorded tales in the Balkans in the 1930s from illiterate bards, taking stock of performance settings, modes of composition and transmission, and cultural ideas reinforced by the tales. They were interested not only in how language and content operated to create narratives but also in the reception and cultural implications of the stories and the process of producing folklore. Practitioners of the historic-geographic method and formalism have been accused of taking the folk out of folklore, but the indices produced by Thompson and others and the morphology developed by Propp can serve as entry points to questions of context. This sort of work allows for the appreciation of multiplicity and variation among folk traditions and for the emphasis on comparison that can reveal much about particular settings for one or another piece of folklore.

Folklore, the Social Sciences, and Context. As an interdiscipline, the field of folklore draws upon sociology, psychology, anthropology, ethnolinguistics, gender studies, and other social sciences to approach questions about context. Scholars explore ways in which folk genres function in a variety of relationships and settings, addressing and revealing cultural and ethnic concerns, tensions within families and other social groups, or personal sources of self-awareness and self-doubt. A classic study in this vein, relevant to biblical material, is Barbara Kirshenblatt-Gimblett's analysis of a *māšāl* or parable in context (1974).

Folklore and Biblical Scholarship: Previous Work. Presenting folklore in terms of texture, text, and context leads to an intellectual border shared with the biblical methodology of form criticism and the seminal work of late nineteenth and early twentieth century scholar Hermann Gunkel. Gunkel was fully aware of folklore as studied in his time. His introduction to the commentary on Genesis, later published as *Legends of Genesis,* evidences the direct influence of Axel Olrik who pointed to key features of traditional-style narration such as single-strandedness of plot and the presence of no more than two characters to a scene. Gunkel's attention to stylistic features, shared, for example, by Genesis 20 and tales of Joseph, his comparative work with a variety of ancient Near Eastern texts and inner-biblical variants, and his constant attention to *Sitz im Leben,* or life setting, mark him as an early practitioner of folklore and biblical interpretation.

It is perhaps somewhat surprising in the light of these folkloristic dimensions of his work, that Gunkel insisted that the Bible in its inherited form does not contain folklore as such. He shared contemporaries' views that folklore media are primitive and popular. Thus "folklore" is not sufficiently sophisticated and theologically self-conscious to be deemed biblical or to have been produced by biblical writers. Rather the authors behind the writings of the Hebrew Bible transformed more primitive materials into biblical literature, be it prophetic or narrative or sapiential. This point of view, which for Gunkel was no doubt rooted normatively, is shared by Robert Alter who paradoxically, like Gunkel, is exquisitely attuned to recurring biblical patterns he calls "type scenes" and to the repetitive, conventionalized quality of biblical language—to those qualities that, in short, exemplify folklore. Others espouse a more overtly positive attitude to the relevance of folklore to biblical interpretation. Dorothy Irvin explores variants of tales of the life of the hero to appreciate biblical stories of Joseph and Moses. Gregory Mobley presents tales of the charismatic biblical warriors called judges in comparison with international epic heroes. David Gunn analyzes recurring language, content, and structures in biblical battle reports. Susan Niditch applies an eclectic assortment of folkloristic methodologies and ideas to deepen the study of a range of biblical works. The interest in oral-traditional literature has of late become particularly influential in the discussion of biblical literature and its social context. The benefits of these various approaches rooted in the study of folklore are many. There have been, however, a number of missteps by biblical scholars particularly in relation to Lord's work.

Lord's work initially led to a host of useful, but less than satisfying searches for "oral roots" of biblical works. The degree of formulicity was not high enough to "prove" oral composition. But the search for oral-traditional roots in biblical literature was very valuable in revealing the traditional-style aesthetic of Israelite literature. This aesthetic is related to matters of worldview and cultural context. It turns out that the emphasis on provable oral composition is misdirected, as is the sharp divide often imagined between oral worlds and literate worlds, oral composition and works crated in writing. Biblicists sometimes have held to a rigid view of the evolution from oral to written works. The form-critical approach is grounded in the notion that early, oral, simpler works are eventually written down and complicated by literate, sophisticated writers.

The Interplay between Oral and Written. In fact, orally composed works can be long or short, created by people who can read and write or by those who can read but not write. Written traditional-style literature can be meant to be read aloud while orally composed works are set in writing by means of dictation or recreated in writing through memory. Writers can imitate oral style. Written works, their plots and characters enter the oral end of the spectrum and vice versa. Once writing and reading are around a culture or even nearby, even if only practiced by elites, the two ways of imagining and creating literature influence one another and belong on a sliding scale or continuum as Ruth Finnegan has shown. Nor does oral style serve as a certain marker of relative chronology. That is, a more oral-style work—in terms of Lord's criteria—may have been composed later than a work that varies its language, speaks in lengthy subordinate clauses, and so on. It is a matter of register. Oral works and oral-style works are created and recreated even when writing is common. It is, moreover, no simple matter to distinguish between the orally composed work and the written work imitating orally composed works. Indeed in the Hebrew Bible it is impossible to do so. Increasingly, one sees an emphasis on the role of memory in the oral-literate interplay as it affects the composition, preservation, and reception of traditional-style literatures. The work of biblical scholar David M. Carr is a good example of this attention to the way in which memory relates to the border where oral and written meet.

Where Folklore Can Lead the Biblicist. Attention to these matters of oral-traditional texture, text, and context relate to biblical studies in critical and potentially innovative ways. First, the student of scripture pays special attention to recurring patterns of language in biblical material, in particular to ways in which the same phrase is used in comparable situations or to convey similar content. The presence of a similar phrase, for example the way in which Pharaoh of Genesis 40 and Nebuchadnezzar of Daniel 2 call for aid from their magicians and wisemen in the interpretation of a dream, does not necessarily imply intertextuality or borrowing of one source from another, but may be evidence of a culturally recognized and shared medium of expression. Awareness of oral-traditional aesthetics attunes us to the significance of epithets and key terms. An Israelite example of such an "aesthetic of traditional referentiality" to use a phrase of Foley's is provided by the epithet for Yahweh, "the bull of Jacob." It brings to bear on a psalm or a legal text the full range of notions of Yahweh as virile, macho, fecund creator. The victory-enthronement pattern is implicit in the phrase with all that implies.

Emphasizing the qualities of repetition and variation in traditional-style works may also lead to a different sort of text-critical work. In contrast to much of biblical exegesis in which the scholar seeks to establish a best text or even an urtext from available manuscripts, one might treat readings from various manuscript traditions as variants, thereby offering a richer sense of the versions received by and produced in communities rather than an artificial scholarly construct or the "original" text. The notion of an original text is contrary to a culture in which literary works exist in multiplicity, whether in written or oral form. Finally, as in Everett Fox's translation of the Pentateuch, biblical texts in translation can be formatted to emphasize the self-contained thought phrases, often begun with "and," that reflect what Lord and Parry called "an adding style." Attention to Lord's work thus affects exegetical emphases, text-critical-approach, and ideas about formatting in translation.

Case Study 1: Genesis 2—3 as the Emergence of Culture. Approaches drawn from the field of folklore affect interpretations of meaning and message in significant ways. Due to the lengthy history of Christian interpretation, the tale of Genesis 2—3 is still usually presented in terms of sin and punishment, obscuring both universal and culturally specific aspects of the biblical narrative. Approaching Genesis 2—3 as a folklorist allows us to recognize the presence a key narrative pattern that unifies the primeval history of Genesis 1—11 and emphasizes critical themes in Israelite thought. A folklorist who seeks out international variants of certain kinds of tales, perhaps with help from Thompson's Indices, and who takes stock of inner-biblical variations on the same narrative pattern, sees that Genesis 2—3 is not about sin but about the onset of culture, with its hierarchies, challenges, and realities. This is a story told around the world, specified within particular groups, and repeated with variations three times in Genesis 1—11.

An imagined ideal early world lacks social structure and classification; all live happily in peace, often without the need for work. Food, for example, is often provided by benevolent forces. Then some prohibition, implicit or explicit, is broken, and reality descends with its clearly differentiated socio-structural roles, with the presence of enmity and competition, with the need for hard work and other life challenges. This essential story pattern is found in creation tales all over the world, perhaps giving witness to a universal desire to find some reason for the difficulties of life, including death itself. The narrative suggests the capacity to imagine, perhaps wistfully, the existence of a paradise. The Israelite version in Genesis 2—3 shows a particular attitude toward gender, a particular agrarian orientation, and a particular set of beliefs about snakes. The essential morphology that traces a pattern from ideal to reality is also found in Genesis 6:1–4, the story about the sons of God who choose wives from the daughters of men, and in Genesis 11:1–9, the tale of the Tower of Babel that describes the differentiation of languages, the creation of ethnicities, and the scattering of groups over the earth. Ideal community, sometimes with nuances of unlimited life, is followed by a breaching of divine territoriality (by eating in Gen 2—3, by sex in Gen 6:1—4, or by a spatial dimension in Gen 11:1–9), a limitation on life, and the emergence of differentiated reality. These tales are Israelite contemplations on mortality, the desire for community, the distance between divine and earthly, and the burdens of human existence. Awareness of internal and external variants thus deeply enriches our understanding of Genesis

2—3 as literature and as an expression of worldview, revealing quintessentially human concerns made Israelite-specific. This sort of study releases us from normative, theological approaches to the material.

Case Study 2: Proverbs and Riddles in Context. A second set of biblical texts that reveal the benefits of folklore, especially for issues of genre and sociological context, involves biblical writers' use of proverbs and riddles. The book of Judges is particularly rich in examples. The riddling contest with its verbal jousting is supposed to safely play out animosities between opposing, in-marrying groups. In the tales of Samson, no such amicable resolution occurs, but it is awareness of the form and function of the traditional medium of the riddle that makes the scene come alive.

The proverb in Judges 8:2 is another good example that captures performance context. The author beautifully understands and portrays the occasion for a *māšāl*. The Ephraimites are angry with Gideon for having gone to battle without them, thereby denying them a chance for additional honor and glory. He responds, "What have I done now in comparison with you? Is not the gleaning of the grapes of Ephraim better than the vintage of Abiezer. God has given into your hands the captains of Midian, Oreb and Zeeb; what have I been able to do in comparison with you?" The form of the proverb has the typical pattern "better x than y" as found in Proverbs 22:1 and Ecclesiastes 7:1. The saying is set in the syntax of a rhetorical question. The author portrays a typical setting for the deploying of a proverb or *māšāl*, in Hebrew. This brief speech act draws a comparison between a present situation or event and some metaphorically relevant motif, scene, or story that reduces tension or resentment in an interaction between groups or individuals who are protective of their status. Gideon graciously compliments the Ephraimites stating obliquely through the saying and then overtly in its interpretation that the Ephraimites have, after all, captured the greatest prizes of battle—enemy leaders—making his own conquests pale by comparison. Hearing what they want to hear about themselves, they depart, anger abated, and the disagreement does not lead to blows. The context has to do with status, the deflection of anger, and peaceful resolution; it is attention to the traditional style, form, and setting of the proverb that underscores these important shadings. Another example is offered by Jotham's *māšāl* in Judges 9:8–20, in which a traditional form provides a means of social critique for the powerless. If one were not attuned to oral-traditional contexts of such material, one would not appreciate the full meanings, messages, and cultural settings of this material.

Case Study 3: Formula Patterns in Judges 5 and Genesis 16 and Describing Heroes. A final case study in folklore and the Bible relates formulas in Judges 5 and Genesis 16 to matters of texture, text, and context and exemplifies the ways in which awareness of patterns in folklore assists in translation and in appreciation of the message of the ancient composers. Judges 5, a victory song, most clearly displays qualities of an Israelite oral-traditional register. Lord's emphasis on formula patterns and compositional technique attune us to the limited vocabulary in this beautiful ancient piece, the role of refrains, and more specifically to the catalog in 5:16–17, which has been misunderstood. Judges 5 has a chiastic thematic structure that juxtaposes the activities of the divine warrior and his minions with the activities of human heroes. At the center of the piece is a description—indeed a traditional catalogue of Israelite warriors—that might be compared with *Iliad* 3:160–244. This example is one of a number of biblical passages in which translators have often ignored the traditional nature and forms of the material and provided forced translations that suit the scholars' own interpretation.

The problem begins with a word of three letters, *lmh*. Most modern biblicists translate *lmh*, "why," for the opening of verse 16. This translation admittedly is typical in the Hebrew Bible but leads translators to use forced translations of all the verbs in order to describe various tribes as cowardly and unwilling to fight. In the NRSV translation, for example, the singer asks Reuben, the tribe referenced in verse

15, "Why did you tarry among the sheepfolds to hear the piping for flocks?" In turn this leads the translator to translate verse 17 "Gilead stayed beyond the Jordan; and Dan, why did he abide with the ships? Asher sat still at the coast of the sea, settling down by his landings." The verbs in verses 16 and 17, however, most commonly refer not to delaying or tarrying or sitting still but to residing, dwelling, and literally plying one's tent. The NRSV translation ill suits the final entry in the description of warriors at verse 18 in which Zebulun and Naphtali's bravery is described and is jarring in light of the structure of the song, in which a condemnation of those who do not participate in the battle comes at a later point in the passage (v. 23).

Frank Moore Cross, however, suggests that *lmh* is best read not as "why," as is most common in biblical Hebrew, but as an example of the "emphatic lamed extended by -ma known from Ugaritic" (1973, p. 235n) and so translates "verily." The many discussions seeking to explain why Reuben, Gilead, Dan, and Asher supposedly hold back from the fighting and the somewhat forced translations that accompany them thus become unnecessary.

The catalog listing the members of this confederation is a traditional topos found several times in ancient Hebrew literature in genealogies, testaments, or other forms. Constituted by brief notices about heroes or groups, which sometimes appear singly—in the annunciation form, for example—the catalog serves a critical cultural function in asserting group identity. It says essentially, this is how we are constituted, who our ancestor heroes are; here is a slice of our history as we understand it. In Judges 5, various groups are described—where they dwell, what their occupations are, and how brave they are. These parts map the whole, the people Israel with its disparate parts, characteristics, and geographic origins.

> Verily you dwell between the settlements
> to hear the whistling for the flocks.
> Concerning the divisions in Reuben,
> great are the stout of heart.
> Gilead in the Transjordan plies his tent,
> and Dan, verily, he resides in ships.
> Asher dwells on the shore of the sea
> and on its promontories, he plies his tent.
> Zebulun is a people whose soul taunts Death
> and Naphtali on the heights of the open country
>
> (Judg 5:16–18; see Niditch 2008, p. 74)

A traditional catalog formula—"tribe + location + tenting/residing"—characterizes the references from Genesis and those concerning Gilead, Dan, and Asher in Judges 5:17. These descriptive formulas are building blocks of tradition. Comparisons might be drawn with Genesis 49:13 and 16:12.

A folklorist's approach to Genesis 16:12 suggests that typical treatments of the verse have misled on the levels of content, meaning, and message. The language in Genesis 16:12 concerns Ishmael, brother of Isaac, son of Abraham, and ancestor hero of the Ishmaelites. Hagar, Ishmael's mother-to-be, has fled from her oppressive mistress Sarah. Sarah resents the concubine who gains new status, having conceived her husband Abraham's child in an ancient form of maternal surrogacy. The deity intervenes with the woman, who is marginalized and alone, declaring in traditional biblical-style content that the son of such a woman will indeed be a hero, a typical motif in the biographies of heroes. She need not fear.

> He will be a wild ass of a man,
> his hand will be in everything
> and everyone's hand will be in his,
> and next to his kin he will ply his tent.

Genesis 16:12 has generally been mistranslated to create a forced and negative portrait of Ishmael, but the verse really refers to his whereabouts and occupation, as is usual in a particular recurring biblical formula pattern that we might describe as comparison to virile animal/occupation/place of dwelling. NRSV is typical of less than satisfying translations: "He shall be a wild ass of a man, with his hand against everyone, and everyone's hand against him; and he shall live at odds with his kin." Implied is that being like a "wild ass" is bad, that Ishmael and his kin are violent aggressors and troublemakers who disrupt society. The modern translators expect the Israelite writers to condemn Ishmaelites, to draw differences between themselves as good citizens and their neighbors as anti-social marauding wild-men, the dangerous ethnic "Other." Biblical heroes, however, are regularly compared to fecund, wild, macho animals such as bulls, strong donkeys (Gen 49:14), and ravenous wolves (49:27). It is a positive thing to use such metaphors.

The word "wild ass" connotes fertility, sexual liveliness, and machismo. In an admittedly negative context, Jeremiah uses the female wild ass to develop the metaphor of Israel as loose woman on the prowl who deserts her husband, Yahweh, to seek lovers, that is, other gods. She never tires (Jer 2:24). I would suggest, however, that what is bad for the goose is good for the gander. The deity himself is known by the epithet, "the bull of Jacob" which in English Bibles is frequently translated "the Mighty One of Jacob." As P. D. Miller has shown, however, Yahweh as divine warrior, like his Canaanite counterpart Baal, is a horned, fertile, randy bull. In Deuteronomy 33:17, Joseph is positively compared to first-born bull/a horned wild ox in images of warrior prowess. Similarly, in the Blessing of Jacob, the tribe/hero Issachar is called a strong or boney donkey (Gen 49: 14–15). The catalog concerning Issachar is similar in content and structure to Genesis 16:12, describing his manly quality via an animal metaphor, the location where he dwells, and the kind of work he does.

The virile Ishamael and hence future Ishmaelites are traders, those who literally have their hand in everything while everyone deals with them. They make their dwelling place close to Israel. In biblical material, the Ishmaelites are known as traders par excellence—we recall for example their presence in the tale of Joseph (Gen 37:25–27); the imagery of Genesis 16:12 thus comports with the larger tradition or mythology about Ishmaelites. This material is of a kind with the descriptions of heroes/tribes in Judges 5:16–17 with the component parts of hero's name/ethnic identity, location, and occupation. This sort of formula can be a part of a catalog in a victory song as in Judges 5, an annunciation of a hero to be born as in Genesis 16, or a prophetic testament, as the patriarch Jacob is said to bless his sons before his death and thereby predict and describe the future roles of the groups descended from them. Such works have significance for the political outlook and worldview of their authors, of those who deploy these formula patterns, saying something about their own views of Israelite identity, even while they conform to the shared conventions of pan-Israelite traditional literature.

Folklore and Biblical Interpretation: Final Reflections. It might be suggested that Bible scholars generally engage in many of the approaches typical of the field of folklore: close philological work with attention to style; work with structure or form; efforts to understand the life settings of writings. The field of folklore, however, leads to emphases on multiplicity, variation, formulicity, performance, and referentiality that allow for a deeper appreciation of biblical literature as traditional literature. Such a literature is composed, received, and preserved by members of cultures in which the written reflects and interplays with the oral. In such cultures, literature is, in a sense, lived. Continuities with the past are important, even while innovation and fresh variation within the contours of shared, recognizable conventions is characteristic. Approaching the Bible as folklore allows the scholar to reconsider ways of treating text-criticism, translation, and intertextuality. It sensitizes the reader to the place of biblical compositions in a wide fund of international folklore and encourages the scholar to explore universal, culture-specific, and composer-specific possibilities for meaning, message, and context in biblical literature.

[*See also* Orality Studies and Oral Tradition, *subentry* Hebrew Bible.]

BIBLIOGRAPHY

Alter, Robert. "Samson without Folklore." In *Text and Tradition: The Hebrew Bible and Folklore*," edited by Susan Niditch, 47–56. Semeia Studies. Atlanta: Scholars, 1990. A psychoanalytically informed study critical of "folkloristic" approaches to tales of Samson.

Ben Amos, Dan. "Analytical Categories and Ethnic Genres." In *Folklore Genres*, edited by Dan Ben-Amos, 214–242. Austin: University of Texas Press, 1976. An influential study of genre in cultural context.

Carr, David M. *Writing on the Tablet of the Heart. Origins of Scripture and Literature.* New York: Oxford, 2005. An important contribution to the study of oral and written in the formation and preservation of ancient Near Eastern literature, with particular interest in the role of memory.

Cross, Frank Moore. *Canaanite Myth and Hebrew Epic: Essays in the History of the Religion of Israel.* Cambridge, Mass.: Harvard University Press, 1973.

Dundes, Alan. *Interpreting Folklore.* Bloomington: Indiana University Press, 1980. A collection of this important folklorist's groundbreaking articles.

Finnegan, Ruth. *Literacy and Orality.* Oxford: Blackwell, 1988. A major study of the relationships between oral and written literatures.

Foley, John Miles. *Immanent Art: From Structure to Meaning in Traditional Oral Epic.* Bloomington, Ind.: Indiana University Press, 1991.

Fox, Everett. *The Five Books of Moses: Genesis, Exodus, Leviticus, Numbers Deuteronomy: A New Translation with Introductions, Commentary, and Notes*, New York: Schocken, 1995.

Gunkel, Hermann. *The Legends of Genesis.* New York: Schocken, 1964.

Gunn, David. "The Battle Report: Oral or Scribal Convention?" *Journal of Biblical Literature* 93 (1974): 513–518. An exploration of biblical literature as orally composed literature.

Irvin, Dorothy. "The Joseph and Moses Stories as Narrative in the Light of Ancient Near Eastern Narrative." In *Israelite and Judaean History*, edited by John H. Hayes and J. Maxwell Miller, 180–209. Philadelphia: Westminster, 1977.

Kirshenblatt-Gimblett, Barbara. "The Concept and Varieties of Narrative Performance in East European Jewish Culture." In *Explorations in the Ethnography of Speaking*, edited by Richard Bauman and Joel Sherzer, 283–308. Cambridge, UK: Cambridge University Press, 1974.

Lord, Albert Bates. *The Singer of Tales.* New York, Atheneum, 1960. The presentation of Lord and Parry's groundbreaking theory of oral composition.

Miller, Patrick D. "Animal Names as Designations in Ugaritic and Hebrew." *Ugarit-Forschungen* 2 (1970): 177–186. An important study of the role of animal names as cultural symbols in ancient Near Eastern myth.

Mobley, Gregory. *The Empty Men: The Heroic Tradition of Ancient Israel.* The Anchor Yale Bible Reference Library. New Haven, Conn.: Yale University Press, 2007. A study of the biblical judges as epic heroes.

Niditch, Susan. *Folklore and the Hebrew Bible.* Minneapolis: Fortress Press, 1993. An overview of the field of folklore as it enriches the study of biblical literature.

Niditch, Susan. *Judges. A Commentary.* Old Testament Library. Louisville: Ky.: Westminster John Knox, 2008. A commentary informed by the field of folklore providing additional bibliography by Niditch and others.

Niditch, Susan. *Underdogs and Tricksters: A Prelude to Biblical Folklore.* San Francisco: Harper and Row, 1987. A study of recurring traditional narrative patterns dealing with unlikely heroes, a favorite biblical theme.

Olrik, Axel. "Epic Laws of Folk Narrative." In *The Study of Folklore*, edited by Alan Dundes, 129–141. Englewood Cliffs, N.J.: Prentice-Hall, 1965. An influential study of content and style in typical traditional narratives.

Propp, Vladimir. *The Morphology of the Folktale.* Austin: University of Texas Press, 1968. The classical statement of the Russian formalist's methodology.

Thompson, Stith, ed. and trans. *The Types of the Folktale.* FF Communications 75: 184. Helsinki: Suomalainen Tiedeakatemia, 1964. Expanded edition of Antii Aarne's *Verzeichnis der Märchentypen.*

Susan Niditch

FORMALIST INTERPRETATION

The various forms of narrative analysis of biblical texts that emerged in North America in the last decades of the twentieth century represent a development, at least in part, out of New Criticism. New Criticism was an outgrowth of an earlier movement known as Formalism, which in turn was grounded in Saussurian linguistics.

New Criticism as a Discipline. New Criticism, which emerged within English-speaking scholarship after World War I, approached a piece of art or literature as a self-standing work that generates its own interpretive frame of reference. Its primary tool was described as *close reading*, which meant careful analysis of the values and functions of words within the interpretive world established by the piece of art or literature. Taking its name from a work by John Crowe Ransom (*The New Criticism*, 1941), New Criticism focused primarily on poetry, seeking to name and characterize the unique nature of poetic language. Any meaning drawn from such poetry was to be found in the experience of reading the text. New Critics sought to block out from the interpretive process concerns for biography, history, the intent of an author, or the effect upon a reader—sometimes describing these approaches as fallacies—and to read the text in its own terms.

These approaches were developed in the works of I. A. Richards (*The Principles of Literary Criticism*, 1924; *Practical Criticism*, 1929); William Empson (*Seven Types of Ambiguity*, 1930); John Crowe Ransom (*The New Criticism*, 1941); Cleanth Brooks and Robert Penn Warren (*Understanding Poetry*, 1938; *Understanding Fiction*, 1943); W. K. Wimsatt Jr. (*Explication as Criticism*, 1963); Allen Tate; R. P. Blackmur; T. S. Eliot, and others. New Criticism dominated American literary studies from the 1930s through the 1960s—largely through the influence of *Theory of Literature* by René Wellek and Austin Warren—and it influenced many subsequent modes of interpretation.

Neither the theory nor the strategy of New Criticism was new. Aristotle offered a functional description of literary pieces and devices, giving priority to the role of actions over agents. The close reading employed by New Critics has antecedents in the *Explication de texte* employed in French literary studies. More importantly, New Criticism is rooted in Saussurian linguistics and in Formalism.

Saussurian Linguistics. Formalism drew upon the work of the Swiss linguist Ferdinand de Saussure, whose ideas became known after his death when his students published his lectures in 1916. Saussure argued that synchronic linguistics is concerned with "the logical and psychological relations that bind together coexisting terms and form a system in the collective mind of speakers" (1959, pp. 99–100). He approached linguistics as a language-state with a delimited framework within which change is minimal (p. 122), and he insisted that "language is a form and not a substance" (pp. 101–102).

Saussure set his work over against the historically oriented philology of the nineteenth century through four oppositions: *langue/parole*; signified/signifier; synchronic/diachronic; syntagmatic/associative. Saussure used *langue* to refer to the entire language system to which a speaker has access, while *parole* refers to the parts of that system actually employed by the speaker. Saussure maintained the distinction between what is signified and the element that signifies. Synchronic linguistics treats elements within the same time frame, while diachronic linguistics considers elements across temporal spans. Syntagmatic relations are linear, while associative relations treat connections made between a term and some element outside its linear plane.

Formalism as a Discipline. Russian Formalists were among the first to extend this type of linguistics into literary concerns. Arising in part as a revolt against romantic and symbolist standards of interpretation, Russian Formalism sought a practical, even scientific, way to describe and analyze the text (primarily poetry). A key—and often contested—component was their insistence that literature is a distinct and peculiar type of writing that intentionally distances itself from ordinary forms of discourse, an "organized violence committed on everyday speech" (Roman Jakobson). This makes literature subject to its own mode of analysis in which form takes priority over content or, in some cases, form is content. The interest of Formalists was not literature, but *literariness*—the estrangement that separated this language from others. Their attention to literary devices that sustain this literariness was soon developed into a focus on the larger literary system in which such devices operate.

Russian Formalism had its origins in the Moscow Linguistic Circle (1915) and in the Society for the Study of Poetic Language in St. Petersburg (1916). Leading proponents were Victor Shklovsky, Boris Eichenbaum, Osip Brik, Yury Tynianov, Boris Tomashevsky, and Roman Jakobson. The movement was suppressed by Stalinists in the 1930s, but it continued in Prague, with Jakobson providing the connection. There linguists studied the role of phonology—

particularly the phoneme—in structural linguistics. In addition to the influence of Saussure and Russian Formalists, the Linguistic Circle of Prague included Dutch, German, Yugoslavian, English, and French scholars. This circle complemented synchronic analysis with diachronic and comparative analysis and sought to describe larger phonological systems. In a similar way, the Copenhagen School under the influence of Louis Hjelmslev sought a deductive system of formal logic that could be used to describe both a given text and the larger language system upon which the text was founded.

Roman Jakobson linked the Russian, Czechoslovakian, and French schools. While he worked as a linguist and was foundational in Formalism, Jakobson turned his attention to literature. Retaining his emphasis on the poetic nature of language, he studied the means of production of a work. It was Jakobson's concern for the literary function of linguistics that provided a basis for structural analysis of narrative material. Both Roman Jakobson and René Wellek left the Prague Circle to become influential at universities in North America, with Wellek shaping New Criticism and Jakobson prodding the development of narratology.

In 1928, Vladimir Propp moved the focus of Formalism from poetry to folktales. He criticized folklorists for categorizing tales by their origins and called for a thorough description of what the tale itself represents. Propp gathered a limited group of folktales and constructed a morphology: "a description of the tale according to its component parts and the relationship of these components to each other and to the whole" (1968, p. 19). Propp's morphology, based on both compositional elements of the text and the dynamics of their interaction, moved Formalism into the field of narrative studies.

After meeting Jakobson in 1941, anthropologist Claude Lévi-Strauss applied the principles of structural linguistics to myths. Lévi-Strauss looked beyond the sequential structure of the narrative to the underlying structures that sustain the creation of myth. He believed these foundational structures were rooted in binary oppositions and shed light on the activity of the human mind in articulating meaning. Noam Chomsky followed this trajectory toward a generative grammar—the grammar that lies behind a language and serves as the generative base for all grammatical expressions of that language. A few scholars (Jerrold Katz, Jerry Fodor, Tuen van Dijk) attempted to extend Chomsky's work directly into the field of literature. Thus, clear lines of influence can be seen from the structural linguistics of Saussure through the Formalists to the New Critics to modern narrative criticism.

Formalism as an Approach to Biblical Interpretation. Various individuals connected these literary movements to the reading of biblical narratives. Hermann Gunkel applied Form Criticism to categorize the components and the dynamics of the Psalms. Rudolf Bultmann, Karl Schmidt, Martin Dibelius, and others developed a Form Criticism for New Testament materials, with a particular focus on the Synoptic Gospels.

Bultmann categorized Gospel stories by their form and function and developed a type of grammar for the way such stories are told. For Bultmann these stories were important because they evolved under fixed standards of transmission of tradition and provided evidence of the various historical and sociological stages in the development of primitive Christianity. For Bultmann, such stories developed through three types of *Sitz im Leben* (life setting): the historical Jesus, primitive church traditions, and the redactional stages of the Gospels. Thus, Bultmann used literary analysis to pursue sociological and theological settings. Though aware of the aesthetic or literary implications of his work, he made a conscious choice to devalue these in light of his concern for the history and theology of primitive Christianity. Thus, the initial application of formalistic methods to New Testament studies was a preliminary step that enabled the interpreter to shift the focus from the literary event to history, sociology, and theology.

In his 1973 *Habilitationschrift*, Gerd Theissen consciously advanced form criticism by applying it to the synoptic miracle stories (1983). Theissen roots his work in the linguistic theory of Saussure and addresses three levels of the text—synchronic, diachronic, functional. His use of a synchronic approach is based on his recognition that Form Criticism "analyses literary forms or genres, which is to say that it classifies similarities and connections between texts whose contemporaneity in a cultural area makes possible a methodological (not a fundamental) bracketing of their historical succession" (1983, p. 1). Theissen then takes Saussurian linguistics beyond the walls of Formalism, giving attention to the social setting of such stories, but he moves beyond Bultmann's focus on general situations to the broader significance and function within social groups. Theissen thus intends to "examine miracle stories synchronically as structured forms, diachronically as reproduced narratives, and from a functional point of view as symbolic actions" (p. 2). For his synchronic approach, Theissen develops a catalog of thirty-three motifs, describes their compositional structure, and establishes a motif field. He catalogs six themes, describes their compositional structure, and establishes a theme field. He then considers the larger category of the miracle story genre.

Theissen has thus employed a fully formalistic approach to the miracle stories that is rooted in Saussure's linguistics, but also in the work of Propp, Greimas, Jakobson, Lévi-Strauss, Welleck, Warren, Greverus, and a large field of German scholarship on narrative forms. Theissen believes that structural linguistic methods are not directly applicable to literary forms, so literary studies must be inspired by these models to develop their own structural methods (p. 16). Theissen follows Bultmann in moving beyond aesthetics to seek the developmental history of such texts and their function within particular social settings:

> We do not understand traditions until we understand them in terms of their life-context. Neither can their development be derived from structures specific to a genre, nor are these structures taken from the historical life-context. Genres are much more the expressions of historical life-worlds; their variations go back to changes in historical and social life. The synchronic and diachronic approaches thus lead with inner necessity to the functionalist approach. This treats texts as elements in a wider life-context of conditions, intentions and effects. (pp. 24–25)

While the analysis of Theissen represents a more nuanced and complex development of Form Criticism, he ultimately follows Bultmann in the judgment that texts are shaped by rather determined processes and unveil the social dynamics that created them. For Theissen, the ultimate function of these stories is existential: "Primitive Christian miracle stories are symbolic actions in which a new understanding of existence is opened up" (p. 287). Theissen concludes that "Primitive Christian miracle stories are symbolic actions in which the experienced negativity of human existence is overcome by an appeal to a revelation of the sacred" (p. 300). While Theissen makes an explicit connection to Formalism, he agrees with Bultmann that formal analysis is a step toward the ultimate goal of interpretation, which is sociological, theological, and existential in nature.

Erhardt Güttgemanns presented an extended critique of Form Criticism and of Redaction Criticism, both in their approaches and in their interpretive goals (1979). Güttgemanns then used *Gestalt* theory to call for a generative grammar of biblical texts. Theissen raised questions about the difficulty of defining and articulating a generative base that accounts for all variations of a text, and he expressed doubts about the possibility of a generative grammar for literary forms. Despite Güttgemanns's call, Theissen's more functional treatment of the synoptic miracle tradition would be as close as any New Testament scholar would come to a comprehensive system of how such stories are composed.

By the time biblical scholars turned intentionally to literary techniques, Formalism and New Criticism no longer controlled the field of interpretation in literary studies in general. Meir Sternberg, in *The Poetics of Biblical Narrative* (1985), gathered his work on the Hebrew Bible as an ideological narrative. He sought to push beyond the framework of form and typology to the communicative—historical, ideological, aesthetic—function of narratives. He was particularly concerned to move beyond the focus on limited narrative elements to "the business of biblical poetics" (1985, p. xiii). For Sternberg, this poetic required a systematic theory, and it was intricately linked to the history of narrative. Sternberg saw this focus on the poetics of the Bible as an ideological text as the way forward:

> Gaps, ambiguity, redundancy, exposition, temporal ordering, omniscient viewpoint, reading process, patterns of analogy, alternative forms of reference, indirect characterization and rhetoric: such concepts (among the most productive so far) show signs of generating a powerful discourse about the Bible, which traditional scholarship must come to terms with. I for one am now more convinced than ever that here lies the future of biblical studies as a whole. (1985, p. xii)

In New Testament studies, structural and anatomical models were drawn in an eclectic way, primarily from French, British, and North American departments of literature, then retooled for application to specific biblical texts. Seminal works were written on the Fourth Gospel (Culpepper 1983); the Gospel of Mark (Kelber 1974; Rhoads and Michie 1982); the Gospel of Luke (Charles H. Talbert 1982); and the Gospel of Matthew (Jack Dean Kingsbury 1986). These studies provided both application and development of literary methods, and they were followed by a wide range of studies of the narrative functions of biblical material.

Formalistic Studies in the Gospel of Mark. Formalism and the subsequent New Criticism seemed to have been left behind in this wave of narrative studies, with many scholars exhibiting no awareness of earlier methods. One line of research, however, drew consciously from Formalism and sought to develop a method tooled distinctly for New Testament texts.

Miracles Stories and Christology. In a dissertation published in 1992 (*Teaching with Authority: Miracles and Christology in the Gospel of Mark*), Edwin Broadhead revisited the relation of miracle stories and Christology in the Gospel of Mark. He noted an impasse over the Markan strategy: Was Jesus presented as the Divine Man who worked miracles or was there a conscious critique of Divine Man Christology? Broadhead sought to move beyond this impasse by a critical focus on the narrative world created by this Gospel. He made conscious use of Formalism to construct an interpretive approach tooled specifically for Markan miracle stories. His goal was to "outline a narrative grammar that is descriptive, not generative" (1992, p. 33).

Using inductive textual analysis, *linguistic* grammar provided a model for construction of a descriptive *narrative* grammar of the Markan miracle stories. Just as linguistic analysis identifies various components around which language operates, Broadhead described narrative elements such as *actions*, *agents* (both *roles* and *characters*), *motifs*, *thematic genres*, and *narrative systems*. Limiting analysis to the narrative world of the Gospel of Mark, these categories were used to describe the *Narrative Morphology* of the Markan miracles. This description of compositional elements was supplemented by a focus on patterns of distribution and interaction, which he called the *Narrative Syntax*. The end product is a *Narrative Analysis* focused on three distinctions: between *significance* (signification within the narrative world) and *meaning* (the use of external factors to assign meaning to narrative signs); between patterns of *morphosis* (narrative construction) and *metamorphosis* (narrative reconstruction of existing elements); between local and extended analysis.

For Broadhead, "The narrative syntax operates upon the morphological elements of the miracle stories to generate a distinct narrative significance" (1992, p. 207). In the Gospel of Mark, the key role of the miracles stories is characterization of Jesus; thus the stories serve primarily as christological signifiers. What emerges is not a bare Divine Man image, but a more balanced and multifaceted characterization whose central focus is the teaching ministry of Jesus. The characterization of Jesus as one who teaches with authority is closely linked to two corollary issues: "Jesus's teaching establishes the ideal and the demand for disciples" and at the same time it "instigates the opposition and conspiracy which lead to his death" (1992, p. 209). In this way, "the Gospel of Mark avoids the Christological dichotomy between the Jesus of the miracles and the Jesus of the cross. Instead, the narrative grammar constructs an integrated portrait: Jesus is the powerful proclaimer whose wondrous teachings lead to his death" (1992, p. 213).

Passion Story and Gospel Story. In a second dissertation, completed at the University of Zürich and published in 1994 (*Prophet, Son, Messiah: Narrative Form and Function in Mark 14—16*), Broadhead turned to the passion story in Mark 14—16 and its relationship to the rest of the Gospel. He noted how the history of research perceives the Gospel of Mark in one of three ways: as an extended passion account to which other materials have been appended, as a dialectical narrative in which the passion story dominates all other elements, or as a unified narrative marked by a complex interaction of various concerns. To revisit this question, Broadhead now constructs his Formalistic analysis within a larger literary framework: "Employing a formalistic analysis set within a *traditionsgeschichtliche* context, the analysis which follows will describe the dynamic strategy which guides Mark 14—16" (1994, p. 27). This methodology shows refinement and extension beyond his previous work and now operates around three poles: synchronic analysis, comparative analysis, narrative analysis. New to the method is a revised form of diachronic analysis that seeks to differentiate itself from the archeological or genealogical models of the evolution of a tradition. Here diachronic analysis means comparative analysis of various forms of a story in order to highlight commonalities and distinctions in how a story operates within the narrative world of the Gospel of Mark: "diachronic analysis can be used to define a precise literary context within which to interpret the present text, highlighting both its similarities and its uniqueness" (1994, p. 19). The primary stock for such comparison is found in the canonical Gospels, but also in other parts of the New Testament, in a range of noncanonical Christian texts, and in Jewish and Roman materials. It is noteworthy that such comparisons are not used to discuss history, social setting, or identity formation: this comparative, diachronic analysis frames a clearer narrative analysis of the way the death story in Mark 14—16 interacts with the larger gospel story in Mark 1—16.

Broadhead concludes that:

> Formalistic analysis provides an orderly description of the narrative components and moves at work in Mark 14—16. Various regions of narrative structure and narrative strategy may be identified. Various agents and actions combine to provide a wide range of narrative motifs. Selected motifs are configured into an unusual collection of pronouncement reports which provide the stock of the passion account. These elements serve as components in an effective narrative strategy. This syntactical strategy focuses the image of Jesus and confronts the reader with a continuum of faith and failure. Most significantly, patterns of plotting and characterization merge in a decisive Christological strategy which unites prophetic Christology with passion Christology. Consequently the characterization of Jesus provides the key element in the passion narrative and in its strategy of presentation. (1994, p. 267)

After considering both the content and the process of this characterization, Broadhead returns to the key question: How do passion story and gospel story relate in the Gospel of Mark, and what does this say about the nature and purpose of this Gospel?

Narrative analysis demonstrates two literary traits that challenge efforts to see in the passion narrative the sole image of Jesus or the exclusive corrective of all other images. First, varied and contrasting images of Jesus circulate throughout the story. Secondly, these images engage in a mutual interpretive exchange, which ultimately corrects and realigns all images of Jesus. Consequently, the intricate and paradoxical characterization of Jesus in the Gospel of Mark emerges from a complex narrative strategy of reciprocity. Through a process of mutual interaction the passion story partakes of the wider interpretive world of the narrative. Through this intratextual process the passion account both shapes and is shaped by the larger portrait of Jesus. All lines of characterization remain effective, with none consumed and none unchanged (1994, pp. 280–281).

Only then are the implications of this reciprocal strategy for the nature and purpose of the Gospel of Mark considered:

> Formally the Gospel presents itself as a unified narrative text which must be interpreted in the context of its own distinct *gestalt*. Materially the content of this narrative is Christological, centering on the identity and mission of Jesus as the messiah. Functionally the narrative defines proclamation as the central, comprehensive task. Thus, narrative analysis shows that the Gospel of Mark is a narrative account of Jesus's messianic life, death, and resurrection shaped by and for the task of proclamation. (1994, p. 284)

As a final step, these findings are applied to historical, sociological, and theological questions. In light of the inherent unity of passion story and gospel story, Broadhead calls for "renewed attention to the question of authorship and sources, to the nature and purpose of the Gospel of Mark, to the question of Gospel genre, and, indeed, to the history of development of the Gospel traditions" (1994, p. 28).

Titles for Jesus. Broadhead constructed a Formalistic approach to the titles of Jesus in *Naming Jesus: Titular Christology in the Gospel of Mark* (1999). He notes that the history of research reflects an ongoing dialectical quest between history and dogma. The thesis that all titles originate in Jesus's own consciousness and proclamation was countered by the antithesis that the church was responsible for all christological titles and dogma applied to Jesus. The New Quest offered a type of synthesis in which the christological titles are church formulations based on faith, but this faith is rooted in the history of Jesus.

Broadhead calls for a step beyond this dialectic. He argues that no titles for Jesus are inherently christological and that they are "best understood not simply as historical or editorial markers, but as formal elements that operate within a cohesive narrative world" (1999, p. 27). Reflecting earlier concerns for the larger framework of literary studies, he notes that "This formalistic approach to the titles does not preclude their use in the history of religions, on the lips of Jesus, in the life of the early Church or in the minds of the Evangelists, but narrative form and function are taken as the *first* key to understanding christological elements of the Gospel of Mark" (1999, p. 27). Because of this, he shifts from the essentialist term *Christological titles* to the more dynamic and functional concept of *Titular Christology*: the narrative manipulation of titles is thus one strategy for doing Christology.

Broadhead's method returns to the language of Formalism, but also to the question of context:

> This analysis will provide a formalist description of the narrative titles set against a *traditionsgeschichtliche* (history of traditions) context. Through this approach the uniqueness of the title or its dependence upon prior tradition will come into view. Each investigation will provide a broad sketch of the historical background of the title. Attention will then be given to the foreground of the title as it operates within the Gospel of Mark. This formalist analysis will note the distribution of the term through the Gospel and the patterns of association established around the title. The level of confirmation offered by the narrative will be analyzed. Attention will then be given to the development of the term within the larger literary strategy and to the effect of this strategy upon the christological presentation. A concluding statement will focus the formal operation of the title within the characterization of Jesus, particularly in light of other uses of this tradition. (1999, p. 30)

After investigating the form and function of sixteen names or titles, he concludes that:

> It becomes evident, following a controlled analysis, that the Gospel of Mark does not simply import a few prepackaged titles which are inherently messianic to articulate its view of Jesus. On the contrary, the Gospel of Mark shapes and reshapes numerous images into a stream of titular Christology. This construction of names for Jesus is one element in a larger, more

> complex strategy of characterization. The processes through which the Gospel of Mark gives names to Jesus provide one key to its presentation of the Christian kerygma. (1999, p. 159)

For the final analysis, Broadhead seeks to link narrative strategy to issues of history, sociology, and theology. He considers Titular Christology in terms of content, process, hermeneutics, the history of the titles' use with Jesus and early Christianity, and the development of the Christian kerygma or proclamation.

A Commentary Rooted in Formalism. Broadhead's Formalism within a history of traditions context reappears in his commentary on the Gospel of Mark (2001, p. 2009). Because of the commentary format and the focus on the entire Gospel, he now links formalistic analysis to the concerns of reader-response theory:

> several elements are imperative for a narrative commentary on the Gospel of Mark. The first of these is a clear analysis, stated in palatable language, of what goes on in the text. What is the story told? Where is it told, when is it told and who is telling it? What narrative components are used and how are they developed? What information is conveyed? What claims are made? The second requirement for a narrative commentary is some awareness of who is reading the text and what is happening in the process of reading. (2009, p. 2)

Broadhead now attends to the process of reading, and even to the reader. He compares the Gospel of Mark to a musical score—"a script with a long and complex history of composition and transmission" (2009, p. 14). While close analysis can bring to light the complexity of development and arrangement, the script cannot perform itself: "Like good music and good theatre, good reading is an event; it is guided by the script, but performed by the reader" (2009, p. 3).

Necessary for any performance of the Gospel of Mark is recognition of the status of sacred text, the presence of an engaged reader, and a defined strategy for reading. Broadhead's strategy for reading the entire Gospel reflects his early grounding in Formalism and tradition history, but also his renewed concern for the reading process. He posits a historical context in which the text was first read, then speaks to the context of modern readers. He notes questions raised by the text itself and by ancient or modern readers. Only then does Broadhead return to the standards of Formalism, where he pursues four levels of analysis: morphology (what the text contains); syntax (how the components of the story are arranged and how they relate to one another); signification (what signs, claims, worldview are generated); meaning (what the reader does with the text).

Broadhead argues that the Gospel of Mark asks for a reading that is primarily reflective: the significance of one unit is informed by reflection upon other units and upon the whole of the narrative. His conclusion reflects upon the whole of the Gospel in Formalistic categories: structure, strategy, significance, and meaning. The *structure* is defined by a sequential account of Jesus's ministry and death, but this account is given in episodes. These episodes are key to the narrative *strategy* because they provide for manageable units, representation, repetition, cycles, recollection, variation. Through these episodes, particular focus is given to the characterization of Jesus and to the role of discipleship. This episodic strategy also supports a reciprocity that links varying aspects of Jesus's story into a coherent account. Through this structure and strategy, the Gospel of Mark offers a complex of *signification.* Four major signs emerge: the coming of the Kingdom of God; the portrait of Jesus as the key to the Kingdom; the crossing of boundaries engendered by the Kingdom; and the failure of both the religious leadership of Israel and of Jesus's own followers. Only in the aftermath of this Formalistic analysis does Broadhead look beyond the narrative world to ask what such stories and signs might *mean* for the first readers of this Gospel and for modern readers.

Summation. Formalism provides a key stage in the development of critical methods of interpretation, but it also exercises an enduring impact on modern literary theory. This is true in general, but particularly so in relation to interpretation of biblical texts. Form Critics and modern literary critics all stand in the shadow of Saussurian linguistics and Russian Formalism, though these connections are seldom recognized or consciously developed.

The role of Formalism, however, goes beyond that of formative influence. For a range of studies, Formalism provides the hermeneutical key by which to exclude, at least in theory, the noise of external influences and to attend to the inner workings of the text. Indeed, one could make the case that any analysis should begin with a descriptive narrative grammar—with a clear and systematic account of what the text contains, how it functions, and what it produces.

Moreover, Formalistic analysis has served for various scholars as a bridge to other realms of inquiry, including historical questions, sociological context, the transmission of texts and traditions, and the emergence of Christian theology. As Rudolf Bultmann and Gerd Theissen demonstrated, attention to the framing and the dynamics of biblical traditions can be a part of locating them within a larger stream of literature and human experience. When Broadhead later applied Formalism to the Gospel of Mark, he too connected the workings of the text to issues such as setting, genre, community, and kerygma.

It is clear that Formalism played an important, if largely unnoticed, role in the development of interpretive approaches to the Bible. It is also clear that much potential remains, both in the strategic use of Formalism and in its potential connections to other areas of inquiry.

[*See also* Form Criticism, *subentry* New Testament; Historical Jesus, Quest for the; Literary Criticism, Literary Theory, and the Bible; Narrative Criticism and Narrative Hermeneutics; Reader-Response Criticism; Redaction Criticism, *subentry* New Testament; *and* Synchronic Interpretation.]

BIBLIOGRAPHY

Aristotle. *De Poetica*. Translated by I. Bywater. In *Introduction to Aristotle*, edited by R. McKeon, 665–712. New York: The Modern Library, 1947. Aristotle's attempt to categorize the forms and functions of literary texts. He identified actions as the key structural element, with agents as a necessary corollary.

Broadhead, Edwin K. *The Gospel of Mark*. 2d ed. The Readings Commentary Series. Sheffield, UK: Sheffield Academic, 2009 (2001). A formalistic, narrative reading of the entire Gospel with an eye to its impact on ancient and modern readers.

Broadhead, Edwin K. *Naming Jesus: Titular Christology in the Gospel of Mark*. Sheffield, UK: Sheffield Academic, 1999. An effort to shift the focus from Christological titles to the dynamic process of constructing a Titular Christology within the Gospel of Mark.

Broadhead, Edwin K. *Prophet, Son, Messiah: Narrative Form and Function in Mark 14—16*. Sheffield, UK: Sheffield Academic, 1994. A refinement of Broadhead's formalistic approach in order to reconsider the relationship of passion story to gospel story in the Gospel of Mark.

Broadhead, Edwin K. *Teaching with Authority: Miracles and Christology in the Gospel of Mark*. Sheffield, UK: Sheffield Academic, 1992. An attempt to articulate a formalistic approach designed to advance the debate over the role of the miracle stories in the development of Christology in the Gospel of Mark.

Bultmann, Rudolf. *The History of the Synoptic Tradition*, revised edition. Translated by J. Marsh. New York: Harper & Row, 1963. English translation of *Die Geschichte der synoptischen Tradition*, first published in 1921. The classic form-critical analysis of various traditions within the first three canonical Gospels.

Culpepper, R. Alan. *Anatomy of the Fourth Gospel*. Philadelphia: Fortress, 1983. A foundational text for the application of narrative studies to a Gospel text, indirectly demonstrating both the connection to and the distance from Formalism.

Dibelius, Martin. *From Tradition to Gospel*. Translated by B. Woolf. Cambridge, UK: James Clark, 1971. English translation of *Die Formgeschichte des Evangeliums*, first published in 1919. A classic text in the use of Form Criticism to trace the history of the Gospel traditions.

Gunkel, Hermann. *Einleitung in die Psalmen: Die Gattungen der religiösen Lyrik Israels (Introduction to the Psalms: The Genres of Israel's Religious Lyrics)*. Göttingen: Vandenhoeck and Ruprecht, 1933. A classic in the development of Form Criticism for biblical texts, applied here particularly to the Hebrew psalms.

Güttgemanns, Erhardt. *Candid Questions Concerning Gospel Form Criticism*. Translated by W. Doty. Pittsburgh: Pickwick, 1979. English translation of *Offene Fragen zur Formgeschichte des Evangeliums*, first published in 1970. A call to move beyond Form Critical categories to articulate a generative grammar of New Testament materials.

Kelber, Werner. *The Kingdom in Mark: A New Place and a New Time.* Philadelphia: Fortress, 1974. A foundational statement of how narrative analysis can be used to interpret the design and intent of a Gospel.

Kingsbury, Jack. *Matthew as Story.* 2d ed. Philadelphia: Fortress Press, 1988 (1986). A foundational attempt to apply narrative studies to the text of the Gospel of Matthew.

McKnight, Edgar V. *Meaning in Texts: The Historical Shaping of a Narrative Hermeneutics.* Philadelphia: Fortress, 1978. A useful resource for tracing the development of traditions of interpretation.

Propp, Vladimir. *Morphology of the Folktale*, 2d ed. Edited by L. A. Wagner. Austin: University of Texas Press, 1968. English translation of *Morfologija skazki*, first published in 1928. A foundational work for applying formalistic analysis to a piece of narrative. Propp's work appeared in Russian in 1928 and first appeared in English in 1958.

Rhoads, David, and Donald Michie. *Mark as Story: An Introduction to the Narrative of a Gospel.* Philadelphia: Fortress, 1982. An early attempt to read the Gospel of Mark in light of its narrative traits and strategies. A revised edition (1999) is now available.

Saussure, Ferdinand de. *Course in General Linguistics.* Edited by C. Bally and A. Sechehaye in collaboration with A. Reidlinger. Translated by W. Baskin. New York: Philosophical Library, 1959. English translation of *Cours de linguistique générale*, first published in 1916. The classic text on how language operates within its own environments. Saussurian linguistics are foundational to Formalism, New Criticism, structuralism, and modern narrative criticism. Saussure's notes were published by his students.

Sternberg, Meir. *The Poetics of Biblical Narrative: Ideological Literature and the Drama of Reading.* Bloomington: Indiana University Press, 1985. Here Sternberg gathers his work from the 1960s forward. He emphasizes the distinctiveness of narrative in relation to other genres, but his primary concern is with the principles involved in a poetics of the Hebrew Bible.

Talbert, Charles H., *Reading Luke: A Literary and Theological Commentary on the Third Gospel.* New York: Crossroads, 1982, 2002. A foundational attempt to apply the techniques of narrative analysis to the text of the Gospel of Luke.

Theissen, Gerd. *The Miracle Stories of the Early Christian Tradition.* Edited by J. Riches. Translated by F. McDonagh. Philadelphia: Fortress, 1983. English translation of *Urchristliche Wundergeschichten: Ein Beitrag zur formgeschichtlichen Erforschung der synoptischen Evangelien*, first published in 1974. An attempt to develop Form Criticism in a more nuanced way and to apply it to the larger sociological framework of early Christianity.

Edwin K. Broadhead

FORM CRITICISM

[*This entry contains three subentries,* Hebrew Bible, Apocrypha and Deuterocanonical Books, *and* New Testament]

Hebrew Bible

"Form Criticism" (FC) is an English rendering of the German term *Formgeschichte*, literally "history of the form," a critical research methodology that seeks to understand ancient texts—especially the Bible—by giving careful attention to their "forms," that is, the typical genres of verbal and written discourse. At its heart, the method is one of comparison, in which texts (or parts of texts) are better understood when we read them alongside other texts that are similar. This article will consider FC's origins and general contours in terms of theory and practice.

Origin of Form Criticism. Prior to the Enlightenment (ca. eighteenth century), the Bible's genre was primarily understood as "divine word." This does not mean that pre-Enlightenment scholars failed to notice that different types of literature were in the Bible; rather, whatever these others genres were, they were considered secondary to the Bible's status as divine discourse. And because the Bible was a divine book, both Jews and Christians interpreted it differently from other books. They anticipated that their respective Bibles would provide a single, coherent understanding of God and theology. As a result, when two biblical laws seemed to contradict each other, the Jewish rabbis would resolve the contradiction by employing one of their interpretive rules, such as *kelal upherat* ("the general and the particular"), or by interpreting one or both conflicting texts as allegories. Early Christians also used allegories for this purpose. The details of these interpretive strategies are not important; the important point is that the traditional understanding of the Bible's genre as "divine word" significantly affected the secondary generic judgments made by Jews and Christians about its human genre. Equally important for our understanding of early interpretation is the fact that for much of Western history, biblical interpreters underestimated the historical distance that separated them from the world of the biblical text. Traditional interpreters, whether they lived in the fifth, tenth, or fifteenth centuries, usually assumed that a seamless fabric connected their world with the biblical world. So the Bible was a divine book, and its cultural world was our world.

During the late medieval period, and especially during the subsequent Renaissance period, this understanding of the biblical world was gradually shattered by the rise of historical consciousness. Scholars studying Latin and Greek texts, and the classical historical contexts described in them and assumed by them, began to realize that human languages and traditions change radically over the course of time. At first this observation was not rigorously applied to the Church and the Bible, but eventually scholars turned their critical eye on these religious institutions. Just as the Reformation uncovered the historically contingent nature of Church tradition and doctrine, so the Enlightenment revealed that the Bible was a product of many different historical and cultural perspectives. These developments laid the groundwork for the first critical engagements with the Bible's genres.

Scholars of the Enlightenment and early post-Enlightenment eras attended closely to the historically and socially conditioned nature of the Bible's "forms" and genres. One thinks immediately of the Jewish scholar, Baruch Spinoza, or of the Christian scholar David Strauss. But the father of FC was undoubtedly Hermann Gunkel (1862–1932). To understand his work, we must note two key elements in his agenda: (1) his reservations about the limitations of Julius Wellhausen's "Source Criticism," and (2) his desire to apply the insights of Folklore Studies to the Bible.

By the nineteenth century, scholars had long recognized that the Pentateuch was composed of diverse materials that reflected differing sources and viewpoints. Wellhausen's great accomplishment was to clearly explain this diversity by isolating four hypothetical literary sources in the Pentateuch, each the product of a different author working in a distinct historical context (known respectively by the sigla) J, E, D, and P. While Gunkel found some merit in this approach, he concluded that Wellhausen's four-source thesis was only half of the answer. Because Israel had originated as a primitive oral society, it followed (said Gunkel) that any effort to recover the Pentateuch's composition history would need to peer behind the literary sources to the smaller oral traditions from which the literature was eventually composed. It was this observation that spawned Gunkel's interest in Folklore Studies.

During the nineteenth century, the Brothers Grimm assembled and cataloged their famous corpus of oral German folktales. Gunkel surmised that the forms of these tales were comparable to stories in the biblical narrative and so concluded that the Grimm tales, and similar traditions, could be used as the basis for positing the original oral contexts of tales in the Pentateuch (see Gunkel 1921; also J. G. Frazer). Moreover, at about the same time, there was a strong belief emerging among folklorists that oral traditions followed very specific "laws" (e.g., Olrik) and that it was possible to trace the development of traditions from their "primitive" oral origins to their more advanced literary forms (Jolles). For Gunkel, the chief end of this exercise was not merely to recover the history of Israel's oral and literary traditions. Rather, the goal was more ambitious: to reconstruct the social history of ancient Israel.

Essential to Gunkel's project was to identify the form of each individual tradition unit so that its genre might be correctly identified and then attached to an historical situation. This process of generic classification employed three key indices:

mood, *form*, and *Sitz im Leben*, where "mood" referred to the affective dispositions that inspired the tradition, form to the structure of its discourse, and *Sitz im Leben* to the "life setting" or context that produced the genre (*Gattung*). In actual practice, however, it was *Sitz im Leben* that eventually took center stage in this analysis because history was the chief interest of the early form critics. Like other scholars during his age, Gunkel's view of genre presumed the neoclassical view that each form or genre reflected a single unique *Sitz im Leben*. While this inflexible equation made it easy to determine the context of a particular biblical pericope (one only needed to identify the form and the context followed), later theorists recognized that FC's rigidity on this point was actually an "Achilles heel." We will return to this problem later.

Gunkel rigorously applied his method to both Genesis and Psalms and, although few scholars would now accept his conclusions at face value, it is fair to say that Gunkel's work produced lasting results. Modern scholars routinely accept his conclusion that Genesis contains etiological legends about the origins of Israel's institutions and that a fivefold classification of the Psalms (hymns, communal laments, individual laments, individual thanksgiving songs, and royal psalms) provides a useful rubric for studying that Hebrew collection. In sum, Gunkel succeeded in his effort to demonstrate that Genesis and Psalms reflect a broad range of genres stemming from varied historical contexts.

Form Criticism and the Hebrew Bible. European scholars were quick to apply Gunkel's new method to the Hebrew Bible, producing landmark studies of Hebrew law (Alt), the Pentateuch (Noth; Von Rad), the Deuteronomistic History/Chronicler (Noth), the prophetic books (Hölscher; Gunkel; Lindblom; Westermann), and the Psalms (Mowinckel). Gunkel's emphasis on the priority of orality in the Bible was subsequently taken up with gusto by the so-called "Scandinavian school" (represented by of H. Birkeland, I. Engnell, E. Nielsen, H.S. Nyberg, S. Mowinckel et al.), which attributed nearly all of the Hebrew Bible to oral modes of composition (see Knight).

Scholars following these forebears continue to acknowledge the role of orality in biblical tradition, but it is no longer in vogue to imagine that most of the Bible can or should be traced back to oral composition. It is now more common to attribute the biblical materials to literary rather than oral processes, with signs of orality increasingly attributed to the influences of oral patterns upon literary texts (Kirkpatrick). One result of these developments is that FC's purview has expanded gradually to include not only the Bible's smallest oral traditions but also its genres on a larger literary scale, so that, for example, one may speak not only about the "casuistic form" of a single law in Deuteronomy 15:12 but also of the "treaty form" that characterizes the book of Deuteronomy as a whole (German *Gattungsgeschichte*). This expansion of FC's purview from the parts to the whole was a natural development. The limitation of FC to smaller units was in fact an accident, which resulted from an artificial distinction between Source Criticism, which focused on the longer written sources used to compose the Bible, and FC, which sought to discern the nature and character of the smaller tradition units. All units of verbal discourse—whether large or small, oral or written—have a generic character that can be considered in terms of "form."

One reason that the purview of FC broadened to include larger text types was the emergence of comparative evidence from the Bible's ancient world. During the nineteenth and early twentieth centuries, archaeologists began to recover the lost societies of the ancient Near East from Egypt, Mesopotamia, Syria, Anatolia, Persia, and the Levant. Many texts were unearthed in these digs, but at first the languages were unknown and the texts could not be read. Scholars managed to decipher the ancient scripts in a relatively short time thanks to linguistic brilliance and the discovery of two multilanguage texts, the Behistun Inscription of Darius (which permitted scholars to decipher the Akkadian script of Mesopotamia) and the Rosetta stone (which permitted them to decipher Egyptian hieroglyphs). The feat of decipherment was so great that some of the world's best scholars at first doubted its accomplishment.

The texts from Mesopotamia had the most sensational effects in Europe and America. During the 1870s scholars published Akkadian literature that was closely connected to the Bible. Some of these texts, which referred to Israel, Judah, and their kings, were heralded as proof of the Bible's historicity and accuracy, but other texts created certain problems. Notable in this regard were *Enuma Elish*, the Gilgamesh Epic, and the Sargon Birth Legend, which were respectively similar (for many, uncomfortably similar) to the creation story in Genesis, the biblical flood story, and the story of Moses's birth. These texts appeared to undermine the supposed uniqueness of the Bible as the divine word. Some influential scholars began to think of Israel and its Bible as merely one small part of ancient Babylonian culture. A strong tension soon emerged between the new field of Assyriology, which was discovering and publishing these new texts, and Biblical studies, largely influenced by conservative Judaism and Christianity. The tension persists to this day in some quarters of scholarship.

The "pan-Babylonian" and "parallelomania" approaches tended to assume that every similarity between Israelite and Mesopotamian literature was a result of borrowing from Mesopotamia. For some this meant that the writers of the Bible were reading and copying Mesopotamian texts, while others thought that the Bible reflected a degraded memory of the more ancient and impressive Mesopotamian tradition. Scholars soon realized, however, that these theories offered deficient accounts of the matter. They doubted that Israelite scribes living in Palestine, hundreds of miles from Mesopotamia, read and imitated cuneiform texts, and there were also clear differences between Israelite and Mesopotamian cultures. As a result, during the twentieth century scholars increasingly attributed these similarities to the general diffusion of religious and cultural ideas throughout the Near East. The Israelite scribes did not copy Mesopotamian texts—they merely reflect common religious and cultural patterns that permeated the ancient world.

In the last few decades, however, the pendulum against Mesopotamian influence has swung modestly the other way. Biblical texts that were once believed to come from early in Israel's history are now dated to the exilic and postexilic periods, at a point when the biblical writers really did live in Mesopotamia or under its cultural influence. One result has been a renewed interest in the Near East and its literature among scholars and students of the Hebrew Bible.

The Hebrew Bible in Its Near Eastern Context. Notions of "form" and "genre" reflect our natural human tendency to understand texts (and verbal discourse in general) through a process of comparison and contrast. Form criticism makes this implicit process more explicit by seeking out comparative exemplars that aid our reading and understanding of the literature in the Hebrew Bible. Here we will briefly outline some of the enduring results of this comparative effort, using as our rubric the threefold division of the Hebrew Canon (the Law, Prophets, and Writings. [For specific details on the following cited examples, see Sparks 2005]).

The Pentateuch (or Law) contains a dizzying array of generic types, many with parallels in the Near Eastern literature. The creation stories in Genesis share many motifs with myths from both Mesopotamia and Egypt. Among these motifs are the creation of humanity from earth's dust or by divine decree, the food and drink of life (or death), trees and plants that rejuvenate life, serpents that block human access to life, the loss of eternal life by deception, and the requirement that human beings tend the earth's gardens and fields. The similarities are so close in one case (*Enuma Elish*) that many scholars believe the author of Genesis knew the myth itself. Also, in addition to these motifs, the general structure of the so-called "Primeval History" in Genesis 1—11 follows Near Eastern forms. The four-movement narrative in Genesis, which includes (1) Creation, (2) Genealogy, (3) Flood, and (4) Genealogy, was probably influenced by a similar rubric found in the *Sumerian King List*, *Eridu Genesis*, and *Atraḫasis Epic*, where the pattern is (1) Creation, (2) King List, (3) Flood, and (4) King List.

Elsewhere in Genesis, the stories and genealogies of the Hebrew patriarchs have been fruitfully compared to Near Eastern narratives and genealogies.

Specifically, the Abraham, Isaac, and Jacob stories include motifs and patterns found in the Ugaritic Epics (*Kirtu* and *Danel*) and Greek histories (Hesiod's *Catalogue of Women* and the *Histories* of Herodotus), while the Joseph Story, being more "novelistic," is reminiscent of the Egyptian *Tale of Sinuhe*; the author of Joseph also drew upon other Egyptian tales and tropes, such as the *Tale of Two Brothers* (cf. Joseph and Potiphar) and the tradition about seven years of plenty and famine. Near Eastern influence appears in what immediately follows in the book of Exodus, where Moses is depicted, like the Sumerian King Sargon, as a child exposed at the river bank but rescued to become the savior of his people (see the *Sargon Birth Legend*). In sum, the Pentateuchal narrative is permeated with Near Eastern traditions.

As for laws and rituals, here too the Pentateuch is rich with Near Eastern patterns and motifs. A parade example is the law code of Exodus and its imitation of Hammurabi's Babylonian law code in both organization and individual laws. Less well-known in popular circles is that the Bible's ritual laws are also similar to (and in some cases influenced by) Near Eastern exemplars. Foremost we can cite the Punic Sacrificial Tariffs (cf. Lev 1—7) and several Mesopotamian texts, including the priestly ordinations (cf. Lev 8), *Kuppuru* rituals (cf. Lev 16), and temple topographies and construction narratives (cf. Exod 25—42).

Of the books of the Pentateuch, none is so Near Eastern in its overall structure as the book of Deuteronomy. The author composed his book as a "covenant" between Israel and Yahweh, using as his model the form and content of then-current Neo-Assyrian treaty texts and loyalty oaths. This was one way of saying that Yahweh, rather than Assyria's king, was Israel's true overlord and master.

These examples only scratch the surface of the many instances in which Near Eastern texts help us read the Pentateuch.

The second portion of the Hebrew Canon, "the Prophets," includes both historical literature and books that are more conventionally "prophetic" in nature. Both types of texts have close parallels in the Ancient Near East. The historical books of Samuel and Kings are very similar to Mesopotamian chronicles and annals. Among other things, we learn from this comparison that the biblical and Near Eastern historians were more interested in serving theological and political agendas than in reconstructing history "as it actually happened." Moreover, we can deduce that these "historians" sometimes wished to preserve ancient traditions or tell a good story rather than to write "history" in the modern sense. It follows that we must use these sources with care if we wish to consult them as grist for our modern historical work.

As for the Bible's prophetic books (Isaiah, Jeremiah, Ezekiel and the Twelve), we have recovered from the Near East both individual prophetic oracles (see the Mari Prophecies) and larger texts that gather up these oracles into "books" of prophecy (the Neo-Assyrian prophecies). The Mari texts are particularly instructive inasmuch as they show how natural it was for a single prophetic oracle to be edited and reinterpreted by those who heard and repeated it. If we may judge from the Neo-Assyrian prophetic collections, this process of reinterpretation continued as the oracles were gathered and edited to create small oracle collections. From this we may deduce that the biblical prophecies are neither wholly foreign to the prophets who uttered them nor verbatim reports of their words. Rather, to some extent or other, the editors and tradents who passed on the oracles also had their say in the prophetic message.

The "Writings" is the most diverse of the three parts of the Hebrew canon. It includes collections of songs and proverbial wisdom (Psalms, Lamentations, Song of Songs, and Proverbs), works of theological "skepticism" (Job and Qohelet), apocalyptic prophecies (Dan 7—12), short novelistic stories (Ruth; Esther; Dan 1—6), and historical and biographical narratives (1—2 Chronicles; Ezra; Nehemiah). All of these "forms" have striking parallels in the Near Eastern literature, particularly if we include as "Near Eastern" those Hebrew texts (like Judith and Tobit), which were not accepted into the Jewish canon.

To compare with the Psalms we have numerous songs, prayers, and laments as well as complete song collections, such as the *Sumerian Temple Hymns* and collections of laments and prayers. We learn by comparison that the biblical Psalm collection is far more diverse and less generically homogeneous than these other collections. Thus, in what foreshadows a point to be made later, the biblical Psalms are far more than an effort to compile similar songs and prayers; rather, it seems that the editors sought to collect almost every kind of cultic song that they could find. The laments in the book of Lamentations were never folded into this collection, undoubtedly because they stood as a coherent witness to the fall of Jerusalem in 586 B.C.E. The book has many parallels in Mesopotamian literature, but most of these city laments are Sumerian and hence much older than Lamentations. Whether and how they might have influenced the biblical book is hard to say.

To compare with Job and Qohelet we have several texts that question the conventional wisdom that good behavior leads to divine blessing. Foremost among them are the *Babylonian Theodicy* (cf. Job) and the *Gilgamesh Epic* (cf. Ecclesiastes). The Theodicy describes an instance of unjust suffering and the victim's struggle to understand his suffering in light of theology and piety. The author of Job was not alone in asking these kinds of questions. As for the *Epic*, its author accentuated the inevitability of death and the futility of human efforts to secure life and immortality. Qohelet seems to have quoted the *Epic* in 4:12, thus suggesting that he was familiar with and to some extent inspired by this ancient piece of skeptical wisdom.

To compare with Proverbs we have the Sumerian Proverbs and the Aramaic *Proverbs of Ahiqar*. The latter includes an introductory tale whose purpose was to stimulate interest in the proverbs themselves. This confirms that the authors of Proverbs, who wrote their own introduction in chs. 1—10, were not the only ancient sages who labored to inspire an interest in their wise maxims.

The apocalyptic collection in Daniel 7—12 reflects Jewish resistance to the Seleucid Greeks. While it is unique in the Hebrew Bible, the collection turns out to be one of many when viewed in light of the comparative evidence. Babylonian and Egyptian exemplars (the *Dynastic Prophecy* and *Demotic Chronicle*) attest to the fact that the Jews were not alone in their resistance to Greek oppression. Among other things, all three texts present history as a cycle of rising and falling kingdoms, use esoteric or symbolic language, practice *vaticinia ex eventu* ("prophecies" after the fact), and follow their pseudoprophecies with genuine predictions that Greek tyranny will end. The same patterns appear in many other Jewish apocalyptic texts. Thus we know that the book of Daniel is better understood as a book of political and religious resistance than as a book of future predictions.

Thus far, most of the cited parallels have been of Mesopotamian origin. But the closest parallels to the biblical Song of Songs are undoubtedly the Egyptian love songs, whose tone and content reveal that the Song is likewise a text about the joys and perils of young love. Also Egyptian are the funerary autobiographies, which spoke well of the deceased and thus hoped to secure a blessed afterlife. We cannot say whether this was the author's goal when writing Nehemiah, but the book was undoubtedly penned to present Nehemiah in very favorable light. Parts of the book were indeed written using the first-person address of an autobiography, prompting many scholars to conclude that the book's author consulted an autobiographical source for his history (the so-called "Memoir of Nehemiah").

The biblical stories of Ruth, Esther, and Daniel and his friends (Dan 1—6) also have ready parallels from the ancient world. The Egyptian *Tale of Sinuhe* is an example, but better comparative exemplars are shorter stories from Mesopotamia and the Jewish tradition. Among these texts are the *Tale of Ahiqar* (which introduces the *Proverbs of Ahiqar*) and the Jewish stories of Tobit and Judith. We learn by comparing these texts that ancient Jewish authors sometimes used egregious errors to signal that their literature was fictional. The author of Judith thus introduced us to "Nebuchadnezzar, King of *Assyria*" (every good Jew knew that he was the king of Babylon), and the author of Esther thus introduced us to

"Mordecai of Kish" and "Haman the Agagite" (when every good Jew knew full well that both families, "Saul of Kish" and "Agag, King of Amalek," had been executed already in the book of 1 Kings).

Thanks to modern translations, anyone can read the Bible and get a sense of ancient Hebrew literature and history without the benefit of FC. But as these examples show, FC enhances our ability to comprehend the literature and its import for our understanding of religion, history, and the human situation.

Our comparative survey of Israel's canonical literature reveals that the Hebrew canon is itself a "form" of sorts. Given the diversity of form and perspectives represented in the literature, the editorial interest in constructing this canon cannot have been to serve the needs of a monolithic theological and ideological agenda. Rather, we must presume that the scribes and tradents embraced as their first priority to collect and preserve the best of Jewish literature, regardless of its theological profile or genre. That is, tradition and diversity were deemed more valuable and important than ideological uniformity and homogeneity.

Form Criticism: Retrospect and Prospect. In spite of its obvious and undeniable utility for biblical interpretation, as practiced FC has also displayed certain weaknesses. James Muilenburg was among the first biblical scholars to put his finger on the problem. He noted that when the form critics classify texts into generic categories on the threefold basis of mood, form, and setting, their tendency is to focus only or mainly on the similarities of the texts and to overlook or underappreciate the differences. In order to compensate for this oversight, Muilenburg proposed that biblical scholars add *Rhetorical Criticism* to their theoretical chest of research tools. Rhetorical Criticism begins where FC ends by closely examining texts of the same genre to determine what distinguishes them from each other. So while a form critic might point out that Psalms 8 and 22 are "individual lament psalms," the rhetorical critic will go on carefully attending to the differences between these laments.

The importance of FC has been eclipsed in the last few decades by two new developments in biblical studies, postmodern Reader-Response Criticism and Redaction Criticism. Reader-Response Criticism is interested primarily in the role of the text's final form in evoking responses in its readers. In such cases the critic has no interest in either the ostensible intentions of the text's author or in the oral and literary sources he or she may have used. The interpretive posture of Reader-Response Criticism precludes its value for answering the sociological and historical questions posed by many biblical scholars. As for Redaction Criticism, this was a natural response to the limitations of FC. Form critics were so preoccupied with the Bible's preliterary traditions that they often failed to consider how the traditions were finally combined by authors and editors to produce extended literary works like the Pentateuch. Redaction Criticism focuses on the process of collecting, arranging, and organizing the text and hence has become, along with FC, an indispensable element in critical readings of the Bible.

In recent years FC has undergone extensive reevaluation by scholars of the Hebrew Bible (see Buss; Koch; Sweeney/Ben Zvi), but it is not clear that their critiques have generally appreciated the theoretical problems inherent in FC (for two exceptions, see Longman; Van Leeuwen). If we base our critique on the observations of modern generic theory (e.g., Hempfer; Todorov), it becomes clear that the primary problem with FC is its tendency to reify genres, to imagine that generic categories reflect hard, fixed realities rather than comparative taxonomies created by readers. For instance, traditional FC wanted to draw a sharp distinction between individual lament psalms and corporate laments, each a unique genre sporting its own distinctive *Sitz im Leben*. However, it is clear that on one level the two psalm types are of the same genre (both are "lament psalms"), while on another level they are of entirely different genres (one composed for individual use and the other not so). This reality is not a philosophical sleight of hand but reflects the nature of "analytical genre" as a classification system based on flexible criteria for identifying similarities and differences between texts. A related weakness of FC is its struggle to account for the generic flexibility inherent in verbal discourse. For instance, how can the label "individual lament" be permanently affixed to a psalm that will later be used in a corporate context? FC's traditionally rigid conceptual link between genre and *Sitz im Leben* does not adequately explain variations like this, in which a text's "intrinsic genre" (or, actual genre) changes as it passes through the successive hands of new readers. In sum, traditional FC has generally failed to appreciate the nature of both analytical and intrinsic genres, and it has multiplied the problems by inadvertently blending together these two conceptually distinct aspects of generic study.

By focusing attention on the importance of genre in interpretation, FC has made a lasting contribution to the study of the Hebrew Bible. If biblical scholars will hear the critiques of FC offered by modern generic theory, then the prospects of FC are bright indeed. The reason is that, according to most modern generic theories, all interpretation is based on acts of generic comparison, so that, in the end, there is no aspect of interpretation that cannot be subsumed under the rubric of "Form Criticism." However, in order to avoid expected confusion, it is perhaps helpful to refer to this new, more broadly conceived version of FC with fresh labels, such as "Genre Criticism" or "Literary Competence."

[*See also* Diachronic Interpretation; Form Criticism, *subentry* Apocrypha and Deuterocanonical Books; Form Criticism, *subentry* New Testament; Genre Criticism; Historical Criticism, *subentry* Hebrew Bible; Redaction Criticism, *subentry* Hebrew Bible; Reader-Response Criticism; *and* Source Criticism.]

BIBLIOGRAPHY

Blum, E. "Formgeschichte—A Misleading Category? Some Critical Remarks." In *The Changing Face of Form Criticism for the Twenty-First Century*, edited by M. A. Sweeney and E. Ben Zvi, 32–45. Grand Rapids; Mich: Eerdmans, 2003.

Buss, M.J. *Biblical Form Criticism in Its Context.* Journal for the Study of the Old Testament: Supplement Series 274. Sheffield: Sheffield Academic, 1999.

Gunkel, H. *Das Märchen im Alten Testament.* Tübingen: J.C.B. Mohr, 1921 [ET, *The Folktale in the Old Testament*].

Frazer, J. G. *Folktale in the Old Testament.* New York: Macmillan, 1923.

Hallo, W.W. "Compare and Contrast: The Contextual Approach to Biblical Literature." In *The Bible in the Light of Cuneiform Literature*, ed. W. W. Hallo et al., 1–30. Lewiston, NY: Mellen, 1990.

Hayes, J. H., ed. *Old Testament Form Criticism.* San Antonio, TX: Trinity University Press, 1974.

Hempfer, K. *Gattungstheorie.* Munich: Funk, 1973.

Jolles, A. *Einfache Formen.* Halle: Niemeyer, 1929.

Knight, D.A. *Rediscovering the Traditions of Israel.* Rev. ed. SBLDS 9. Missoula, Mont.: Scholars Press, 1975.

Kirkpatrick, P. G, *The Old Testament and Folklore Study.* Journal for the Study of the Old Testament: Supplement Series 62. Sheffield: Sheffield Academic Press, 1988.

Koch, K. *The Growth of the Biblical Tradition: The Form-Critical Method.* New York: Scribner's, 1969.

Knierim, R. "Old Testament Form Criticism Reconsidered," *Interp* 27 (1973): 435–48.

Longman, T. III., "Israelite Genres in Their Ancient Near Eastern Context." In *The Changing Face of Form Criticism for the Twenty-First Century*, edited by M. A. Sweeney and E. Ben Zvi, 177–195. Grand Rapids; Cambridge: Eerdmans, 2003.

Olrik, A. *Principles for Oral Narrative Research.* Trans. K. Wolf and J. Jensen. Folklore Studies in Translation. Bloomington: Indiana University Press, 1992 [*Nogle Grundsaetninger for Sagnforskning*, 1921].

Russell, D. S. *The Method & Message of Jewish Apocalyptic.* Philadelphia: Westminster, 1964.

Sparks, K. L. *Ancient Texts for the Study of the Hebrew Bible.* Peabody, MA: Hendrickson, 2005.

Sweeney, M. A., and E. Ben Zvi, eds., *The Changing Face of Form Criticism for the Twenty-First Century.* Grand Rapids, Cambridge: Eerdmans, 2003.

Todorov, T. *Genres in Discourse.* Cambridge, N.Y.: Cambridge University Press, 1978.

Tucker, G. M. *Form Criticism of the Old Testament.* Philadelphia: Fortress, 1971.

Van Leeuwen, R. "Form Criticism, Wisdom, and Psalms 111–112." In *The Changing Face of Form Criticism for the Twenty-First Century*, edited by M. A. Sweeney and E. Ben Zvi, 65–84. Grand Rapids; Cambridge: Eerdmans, 2003.

Westermann, C. *Basic Forms of Prophetic Speech.* Louisville, KY: Westminster John Knox, 1991.

Kenton Sparks

Apocrypha and Deuterocanonical Books

Form criticism serves the study of the Apocrypha and the deuterocanonical books by identifying and analyzing the genres to which these texts belong. Genre, or *Gattung* in German scholarship, may be defined as a constellation of literary elements:

typical mood, typical setting/function, and typical—even formulaic—expression. The modifier "typical" recurs because form criticism as a method focuses on typical or generic aspects of literature. Genre thus comprises mood, setting, and expression in the classical definition of form criticism set forth by Hermann Gunkel (1933, pp. 22–24) and his school. Others working in this discipline have substituted elements such as plot or theme to conceive of genre somewhat differently, an indication that the method is not static and has developed historically. In general, however, genre indicates a complex set of literary elements that are typical and that correspond to aspects of human life as it is experienced in a society. Form criticism attempts to capture this social dimension, which is referred to as the setting-in-life, or *Sitz im Leben*. Understood to be both textual and social, the generic aspects or elements of literature are the subject of form criticism as it is applied to the study of the Apocrypha and the deuterocanonical books.

Although the Apocrypha and deuterocanonical books have long been defined in contrast to the books included in the Hebrew Bible/Old Testament, increasingly scholars are critical of such a canonically driven approach. Lest one imply inferior status for the Apocrypha and deuterocanonical books, the texts in question are identified as significant literary witnesses to Second Temple Judaism. That is, in the circles of popular religion and to some degree at the levels of higher authority, these documents had a prominent place and influenced the thought and religious practices of the communities responsible for them. They are important windows on prerabbinic Judaism and early Christianity. There are dozens of titles involved, too many to list individually. Among the most prominent examples of Apocrypha are 1–2–3 Enoch, the Sibylline Oracles, 2 Baruch, 4 Ezra, the Testaments of the Twelve Patriarchs, Jubilees, and the Prayer of Manasseh. The deuterocanonical books, so called because they are found in the Catholic and Orthodox Bibles as part of the canon, are a distinct collection in each church. For example, the Roman Catholic church defines the deuterocanonical books as: Tobit, Judith, 1 and 2 Maccabees, Wisdom, Sirach/Ecclesiasticus, and Baruch. Together, the Apocrypha and deuterocanonical books represent a wide range of genres, including apocalyptic literature, testaments, so-called rewritten Bible, prayers and psalms, and historical accounts along with fictionalized accounts of history and fiction per se (novels and novellas). This article's point of departure is the intersection of the genres noted here and the practice of form criticism as it has developed in modern scholarship.

The apocalyptic literature provides examples of apocryphal works that are profitably studied in terms of their genre. The genre of apocalyptic literature has recurring characteristics that, analysis shows, are eminently typical. That is, the language is imbued with imagistic oracles that may be heavily symbolic. The mood communicates concern for an underlying problem, often rooted in an individual or a collective misdeed. The setting comprises an earthly plane intersecting the heavenly world of the angels and other noncorporeal beings. A test case for the form-critical study of the apocalyptic literature is found in 1 Enoch. One Enoch is not a single work but rather a collection of writings that scholars describe as five books: the Book of the Watchers (chs. 1—36), the Similitudes (chs. 37—71), the Astronomical Books (chs. 72—82), the Book of Dreams (chs. 83—90), and the Epistle of Enoch (chs. 91—108). The Book of the Watchers incorporates several of the generic elements of apocalyptic literature. For example, 1 Enoch 6—11 indicates a crisis experienced by the group responsible for the text and perhaps shared more widely in its society. The crisis, suggestive of lawlessness and violence, is not articulated in historical terms, however, and instead the crisis is played out on a celestial plane, where parts of this particular scenario fit into patterns that extend across generations. The crisis, and moreover its resolution, is thus transcendent in terms of both space and time. The crisis is described in language that is symbolic in that it vilifies certain of the fallen angels such as Semihazah. Language, setting, and mood combine to indicate the genre of apocalyptic literature as it forms and informs the Book of the Watchers. In the words of John J. Collins (1998,

p. 59), "Whatever crisis generated this text, it is viewed from a distinctive apocalyptic perspective." Indeed, the crisis in 1 Enoch is not presented in terms of historical elements; the writer's expression is primarily through literary aspects that indicate the apocalypse's structure and suggest something of the setting in life that gave rise to the text.

Beyond Form Criticism. A generation ago, in an influential article entitled "Form Criticism and Beyond," James Muilenburg (1969, p. 5) indicated a number of issues that had arisen with studying ancient texts primarily through genre. For example, he noted that texts may imitate a given genre by incorporating select literary elements but not all of the elements thought to be constitutive of the genre. In these cases, modern interpreters sometimes critique the text as imitative and flawed form-critically. Muilenburg, however, challenged such critique and took a different approach to the ancient text; he spoke of the creativity and consummate skill that the authors of the "imitations" demonstrated in their writing. Moreover, he encouraged his colleagues to think beyond the defined genres of ancient religious literature because there are significant texts that range across form-critical categories to suggest the development of mixed genres. Muilenberg did not call for an end to form-critical study, but he asked its practitioners to apply the method judiciously when working with a text in which genres are mixed and the form-critical determination requires nuance.

Decades after Muilenburg attempted to redirect the practice of form criticism, there remains concern about this method of studying ancient texts. Rolf Knierim (2000, pp. 42–43) writes: "We are preoccupied at this juncture with a number of fundamental problems that are built into the very system of the form-critical method." In general, Knierim's assessment echoes that of Muilenburg; as the former writes: "individual texts are more flexible than form criticism has been prepared to assume." Not surprisingly, Knierim calls for form critics to be less ideological in their focus and to be more flexible in using the method's various tools. He suggests that the major traditional categories of form criticism should function as "heuristic tools" that allow scholars to discover the typicality or typicalities governing a text. In general, Knierim advocates abandoning the notion that genre is immutable and wedded to certain settings in life, in favor of the view that there are distinct typicalities that govern texts. Studying the interrelationships of the typicalities, moreover, allows for discussions of genre that will, on the whole, be more measured than those of generations past, but no less fruitful.

Although form criticism as a methodology is waning, form-critical reading strategies are an important tool of scholarship today, as the present study will demonstrate. Informed by Muilenberg and Knierim, this study will explore certain of the Apocrypha and Deuterocanonical books from a form-critical perspective by focusing on three distinct genres: fictional prose, poetry, and history writing. There are other genres that would be incorporated into a longer treatment of the subject, but the three genres studied here constitute a literary triad that provides a representative overview of the Apocrypha and the deuterocanonical books.

Judith and Tobit as "Jewish Novellas." The deuterocanonical books Judith and Tobit represent a distinct genre within ancient Jewish literature, the Jewish novella. The Jewish novella, in turn, forms part of a broader category of novelistic literature that is exemplified by the Greek and Roman novels of the second and first centuries B.C.E. To speak of these ancient works as novels is not anachronistic, as some might charge. The ancient novels are long fictional prose narratives that are highly similar in sentiment and plot structure (Stephens and Winkler 1995, p. 3). Examples of this category or genre include Chariton's *Chaereas and Callirhoe* and Patronius's *Satyricon.* With these non-Jewish works, Judith and Tobit share a number of quintessential features: settings that are idealized and whimsically designed, lively plots punctuated with peril, pleasing resolutions of plot, and women characters who exude chastity. In the story of Judith, a God-fearing widow sets aside the sackcloth and makes herself beautiful only so that she might destroy the enemies of Israel by beheading their leader Holofernes.

In Tobit the righteous protagonist suffers indignation and penury but triumphs in the end when the angel Raphael assists Tobit's son Tobias in securing a fortune as well as a worthy bride and a cure for his father's ailment. Both novellas are highly entertaining, and the recent literature on Tobit and Judith often focuses on their comic qualities (McCracken 1995, p. 403; Portier-Young 2001, p. 53). The comic dimension, in turn, aligns Judith and Tobit form-critically with the Greek and Roman texts that typify the genre of the novel in this period.

The comic aspects of Tobit and Judith, however, have led some scholars to draw different conclusions, with implications for genre designation of the texts as Jewish novellas. On the one hand, there is the claim that despite Tobit's humorous touches, the work is no comedy as it underscores rather the serious theme of divine providence (Schellenberg 2011, p. 315). Schellenberg relates divine providence in Tobit to the concept of simultaneity as it is found in the writings of Herodotus and Polybius, to imply that Tobit's genre coincides more with the ancient histories rather than the novels. On the other hand, certain studies deny Jewish novellas such as Judith a place alongside their Greek counterparts because of the former's lack of literary sophistication (Zeitlin 2008, p. 107). These studies conclude that Judith's picaresque tone and the overarching playfulness of its storyline leave the Jewish novella too prosaic to inhere in a genre of high literature; by virtue of its comedy, Judith departs from the Greek and Roman novels. There is not, therefore, perfect consensus that Judith and Tobit belong to the generic category of the ancient novel, although many scholars make this association on the basis of the comic elements that are common to the Jewish and non-Jewish novelistic works.

Pleasure as a Defining Element. Other studies of Judith and Tobit develop a related perspective, that of pleasure, that serves to align the Jewish and non-Jewish novelistic works. The notion of pleasure is derived from the reading experience as it is combined with the structure of the text. In the words of L. M. Wills (2011, pp. 155–156):

> In terms of kinship of genre, however, the question is really whether there is a common structure and reading experience—a common pleasure—that is found in all the different sizes and subtypes of Greek, Roman, Egyptian, Christian, Jewish and other indigenous novelistic literature. This question is now often, but not always, answered in the affirmative.

The reference to pleasure forms the crux of Wills's argument and it informs other scholarly work. Simon Goldhill (2008, p. 187), for example, defines and describes genre in terms of the pleasure that it summons from author and audience alike. Goldhill relates comedy to the pleasure of laughter, lyric poetry to the pleasure of sublime emotion, and the novel to the pleasure of enchantment as it is derived from narrative. By narrative he likely means the turn of plot whereby protagonists such as Judith and Tobias, the son of Tobit, brush up against peril time and again before their fate is resolved positively. Who does not relish a happy ending, especially after it seemed unattainable for much of the story? The pleasing denouement in the Jewish novellas is complex as the accomplishment of God's purpose is both surprising and not surprising. It is not surprising because success for Judith and Tobias has been virtually guaranteed on the narrative level. Yet certain characters are genuinely unknowing, and reading through their eyes helps one feel, for example, that the life of young Tobias hangs in the balance on the night of his marriage. The reader ultimately knows that Tobias is not in mortal danger, and having knowledge that some of the characters (e.g., Raguel) do not have makes the story that much more enjoyable. The narration, in technical terms, creates dramatic irony, a perspectival pleasure that is indicative of the novelistic genre in ancient literature.

The Application of Newer Theoretical Perspectives. A relatively new vein of scholarship construes Judith and Tobit as forming a response to empire, specifically the empire that Hellenistic rulers brought to the East. Such postcolonial readings credit eastern authors such as those responsible for the Jewish novellas with critiquing the dominant order and the power that resides at its center. In this critique, new ideas and collective thinking no longer travel from center to periphery exclusively and may advance from the periphery to the center. L. M. Wills refers to this dynamic as "colonized and colonizers mutually energized at a charged boundary" (p. 152).

The application of postcolonial theory to Tobit and especially Judith has implications for the study of genre. The exaggerated comedy that led Zeitlin to discount Judith as novelistic literature leads in these circumstances to a somewhat different analysis of genre. From a postcolonial perspective, the exaggerated comedy of Judith and Tobit points to a conscious reversal of generic literary conventions. The reversal subverts a range of readerly expectations that would otherwise keep separate the real and unreal, the traditional and new, the respectable and the entertaining. In sum, the reversal distorts proportions and, in the case of Judith, creates a scenario in which localized and limited details of history become associated with a larger sphere that is global and all-inclusive.

A telling example is Nebuchadnezzar, who represents the hostile force that Judith overcomes. He is presumably the historical Nebuchadnezzar, who as Babylonian emperor from 605 to 562 B.C.E oversaw three sieges of Jerusalem in the first half of the sixth century. The book of Judith, however, associates Nebuchadnezzar with Assyria, making him as well an eighth-century enemy of the Israelites. The transhistorical profile of Nebuchadnezzar recasts him as a composite enemy who reflects many (indeed all) empires, and whose true adversary, in turn, is God as well as God's people. The insight of Ernst Haag (1963, p. 78), that Judith's Nebuchadnezzar is tantamount to the "the eschatological enemy of God," has influenced many scholars, and informs, at least indirectly, certain postcolonial readings of the ancient Jewish novel. The beheading of Holofernes and the defeat of Nebuchadnezzar, in such readings, subverts hegemonic structures that have been encoded into the literary structures of the text. The characterization of Nebuchadnezzar exemplifies the relationship between eastern, colonized, nationalistic prose fiction, and the literary ideal as found in Greek novels. In the words of L. M. Wills (p. 162), "Authors of both groups . . . reflect opposite poles of a colonizer/colonized interface. Just as the Greek novel expresses a desire to reimpose a distinction with the barbarian, the Jewish barbarian [sic] wants to reestablish the superior position of a God's eye view of dignity and virtue. . . . Both are responding to Hellenization from opposite sides of the porous membrane we call colonial relations."

Baruch's Prayer of Complaint (Bar 1:15—3:8). The apocryphal Book of Baruch is attributed to Baruch, the son of Neriah and secretary to Jeremiah, although most scholars think the book was written not in the purported time of the Babylonian exile but sometime during the second century B.C.E. The book nonetheless explores the theme of exile, defined as the consequence of disobeying God's law (4:12) and clearly elaborated in the book's four parts. An introduction (1:1–14) is followed by a public prayer of penitence (1:15—3:8). After the prayer concludes by highlighting Mosaic law and the obedience it elicits, the third section (3:9—4:4) follows in the form of a poem that compares the Mosaic law to wisdom, an association not uncommon in the period of the Second Temple (Ps 1:1–2; Sir 24:23–29). The fourth section (4:5—5:9) is a prophetic address signaling the restoration of exiles to Jerusalem as a result of their repentance. Exile is both the theme of the book and the historical occasion to implore God's grace and mercy.

There are important form-critical issues in Baruch, especially in the book's second section, a public prayer of penitence (1:15—3:8). The prayer approximates one genre in particular, the psalms of communal lament as found in the biblical psalter. The prayer's phrasing and wording approximates that of the communal laments, and most importantly Baruch in these verses incorporates all the literary elements that collectively define the lament genre. That is, Baruch begins with an invocation to God and follows with a description of the current difficulty, a petition for deliverance, a motivation for God to act, an admission of guilt, an affirmation of trust, and finally a promise of praise complete with a vow to offer thanksgiving sacrifice. The form-critical likeness between Baruch's prayer of penitence and the psalms of communal lament is striking; all the basic elements of the psalm genre recur in Baruch's extended petition for God's forgiveness. Moreover, Baruch's prayer aligns thematically with communal laments such as Psalm 79, in which the petitions "deliver us" and "forgive our sins" are conjoined (Ps 79:8–9). The deuterocanonical text in this case builds upon the two themes, forgiveness and deliverance from exile, as they are linked inextricably at the center of Psalm 79 (Floyd 2007, p. 71).

A Newfound Penitential Dimension. Comparing Baruch's prayer to Psalm 79 and other communal laments also sheds light on the main difference between the two texts, namely the degree to which the penitential dimension in Baruch's prayer is developed and articulated. First, there is added emphasis on sin as well as on the confession of sin. Baruch defines sin historically as the people's turning from God's word in age after age, with the major periods of Israel's history indicated. The periodization of sin, however, is linked to the notion of repentance, which Baruch describes as heartfelt sorrow resulting in human deeds of rectification. By depicting the current generation of pray-ers as likely recipients of God's forgiveness, Baruch contrasts them with the ancestors, who did not repent. Those associated with the prayer of Baruch, however, *have* turned back to God, repented of their sin, and await both divine forgiveness and release from exile. Because their prayer of petition is to be met with God's favor, their experience is theologically different from that portrayed in the communal laments, where the pray-ers appear to be abandoned.

Studying Baruch's penitential prayer from a form-critical perspective clarifies larger issues related to the text and its genre. First, scholars debate whether penitential prayers such as Baruch 1:15—3:8 are an extension of an existing genre (i.e., the psalms of communal lament) or whether they constitute a new genre that has emerged in the postexilic period. The so-called new genre would comprise prayer texts such Nehemiah 9:6–37 and Daniel 9:4–19. Does Baruch belong on this list? Its penitential theology notwithstanding, Baruch's prayer does not depart significantly from the generic form of the lament psalms. The prayer incorporates the elements of the lament psalms, and the elements tend to function in conventional ways. In light of these facts, scholars are disinclined to invoke a new genre of penitential prayer when describing this text form-critically, and they are judicious in suggesting where and how the prayer in Baruch reaches beyond the design of the lament psalms. For example, Richard Bautch (2003, p. 145) observes that in Baruch, a confession of sin motivates the petition of mercy in 3:2, a development that typifies the postexilic prayers of penitence. He notes, however, that the petition for deliverance in 2:3–14 is motivated by a psalmic trope, the appeal to God's honor in 2:15–18, and not by the confession of sin in 2:12. Bautch suggests that only when the confession of sin functions uniquely as the motivation of the petition are there grounds for speaking of Baruch 1:15—3:8 as materially different from the lament psalms.

Second, Claus Westermann (1981, pp. 165–213) argued that the advent of penitential prayers in the Second Temple period eclipsed the practice of lament and effectively silenced the raw complaint against God that punctuates parts of the psalter. Numerous scholars have followed Westermann and maintain that religious texts after the exile reflect a different theology than that expressed in the psalms of lament. The theological difference is essentially Deuteronomistic in that it views human misfortune as the effect of a prior misdeed, which prompts the penitential reflex in the prayer text. Close readings of the texts in question, including this study of Baruch, affirm their Deuteronomistic character but militate against the notion that penitential prayer displaced lament. As Michael Floyd observes (p. 77):

> Since rituals of penitence were communal, there might have been some functional overlap between those celebrated periodically at the temple and the communal complaint rituals occasionally celebrated there. This could conceivably have led to the demise of communal complaint rituals, but we have no direct

> evidence on this score, and indirect evidence suggests that communal complaints continued.

It rather appears that a symbiotic relationship prevailed between the lament and the penitential prayer, as indicated by other Second Temple period texts such as Isaiah 63:7—64:11, a postexilic prayer whose expressions of penitence draw upon the language of lament and share lament's focus on culpability (Bautch 2006, p. 98).

2 Maccabees: A Deity Defending its City or Temple. The deuterocanonical book 2 Maccabees cites as its basis the five-volume history of Jason of Cyrene (2 Macc 2:19–32), a work no longer extant. The loss of this source complicates the form-critical study of 2 Maccabees, but only to a degree. The narrative of 2 Maccabees conforms to a classic Greek structure, the story of a city facing civil strife and troubles from without but saved by an exceptional event, such as the death of a heroic figure or the intervention of a deity partial to the city. Commentators (Schwartz 2008, p. 65) compare 2 Maccabees, written in standard Greek, to works such as Euripides's *Phoenician Women.* The latter features a city not unlike Jerusalem where the struggle of two brothers threatens the commonweal, and a resolution comes through the suicide of a leading citizen who is like Razis, the noble elder who kills himself in spectacular fashion near the conclusion of 2 Maccabees (2 Macc 14:37–46). Commentators consider the relationship between 2 Maccabees and *Phoenician Women* to be especially relevant. In addition to the form-critical alignment of 2 Maccabees with the Greek literary genre depicting a city defended and saved, discrete sections of the Jewish text are illuminated through a comparison to non-Jewish texts with the same literary structure. An example is 2 Maccabees 3:1–40, the repulse of Heliodorus.

Heliodorus is an agent of Seleucus IV, the Seleucid ruler whom the text identifies as the king of Asia. Heliodorus attempts to plunder the Jerusalem temple but fails. Inside the temple structure and ready to breach the treasury, Heliodorus is met by a manifestation of God, in the form of a horse with a frightful rider wearing golden armor (2 Macc 3:25). After the rider strikes down Heliodorus, two other young men arrive and flog him until he lies on the ground senseless. When Heliodorus subsequently recovers, the two young men exhort him to proclaim the majesty of God's power (2 Macc 3:34). As Heliodorus does so, he directs his words to King Seleucus. The episode represents a great reversal of fortune for the city of Jerusalem, whose inhabitants respond with joy and gladness (2 Macc 3:30).

The account of Heliodorus in 2 Maccabees 3:1–40 parallels stories of a deity defending his or her city or temple. The form of the story comprises the following elements: the attackers approach the city, the city's defenders ask the deity for help, the deity responds, the attackers are repulsed, and the defenders rejoice. The pattern is established in non-Jewish writings such as the Cos inscription, which tells of Apollo turning back the Gauls from Delphi in 279 B.C.E. Another inscription from Panamaros describes Zeus Panamaros defending his city from attack. Finally, the Lindos Chronicle recounts how Athene turned back the Persian forces from that city. These and other annals from the Greek tradition situate 2 Maccabees 3:1–40 in a fresh light; the Heliodorus episode is a distinctively Jewish instance of the deity defending his city from foreign invaders.

Correlating Form to Setting in Life. Form criticism provides the appropriate designation for the Heliodorus episode, in terms of the type or genre of literature that it represents. In this instance, a term other than the generic "form" is in order. Doran (1981, p. 47) does not refer to the inscriptions from Cos and Panamaros as examples of the same literary form "because the ways in which the deities defend their temples are so various that no tight, recurring order of content emerges." To appreciate Doran's point, one may recall that a rather exact comparison emerges when the psalms of communal lament are placed alongside postexilic penitential prayers such as Baruch 1:15—3:8. The patterned repetition of literary elements is much less evident when the above inscriptions are compared to 2 Maccabees 3:1–40, although the Heliodorus episode exhibits some level of genetic connection to the accounts of a deity defending his city. The question becomes: How best to articulate the formal connection? Doran (p. 47) speaks of a general shared pattern that constitutes a "*topos*." The term *topos* indicates a complex of ideas (Fischel 1973, pp. 60–61), and in this case it suggests a literary connection between the classical genre and the Jewish traditions included in 2 Maccabees. Doran remarks that, as terminology, "*topos*" has looser connotations than the designation "form" but is not as controversial as "motif" or "theme." Doran's work typifies scholarship that is focused on form-critical issues and exacting in its comparison and contrast of a deuterocanonical book such as 2 Maccabees with classic Greek literary structures.

Doran's highlighting of the literary significance of the Heliodorus passage, however, has led some scholars to ask whether his approach understates the text's historical aspect. Portier-Young (2001, p. 80) argues that the episode in 2 Maccabees 3 reveals the politics in play during the years before Seleucus's death in 175 B.C.E. As the Seleucid king came increasingly under Rome's aegis, he in turn exerted greater fiscal control over the Jerusalem temple and the worship conducted there. His strategy is typified in the mission of Heliodorus, which has a historical basis. By authorizing such missions Seleucus violated a prior agreement protecting the local administration of the temple and he heightened tensions within and among the Jerusalem elite. The historical picture that Portier-Young provides adds much to the form-critical study of 2 Maccabees 3 as the account of a besieged city embroiled in civil strife but saved by the intervention of its deity. A typical story has been joined to a setting in life that is decidedly political, with an imperial government seeking to extract more revenue from the boundaries of its empire. At first glance the political world of Seleucus IV is not a traditional setting in life; form critics have tended to employ the concept of *Sitz im Leben* to identify cultic locales and the ritual practices therein. With the infusion of postcolonial theory into biblical studies, however, the temple-based Jerusalem cult may be viewed as a crucial setting in the political life of a preeminent Jewish community. Generations of scholars have known that the Jerusalem temple serves as a political locus, but there is new emphasis on this fact. That is to say, the fundamental correlation in form criticism between genre and setting may be evolving with the study of texts and their contexts.

Conclusion: Form-critical Reading Strategies. The earlier discussion of Muilenburg and Knierim implied a crisis of confidence in form criticism. The method associated with Gunkel and his school no longer appears capable of identifying a text's genre, and risks misreading literature that does not fit neatly into form-critical categories. Misguided as well are the attempts to connect text and world, in the hopes of identifying a setting in life for the content that inheres in the literary form. It is little wonder that today few studies engage the form-critical method in a sustained and detailed manner. This review of select deuterocanonical and apocryphal books, however, shows that the demise of form-critical study is not yet at hand. The evidence is to the contrary.

First, the plain fact is that scholars continue to focus on literary form in their evaluation of texts such as Judith, Tobit, and 2 Maccabees. These works are not *sui generis*. In each case the writer was influenced by a classic Greek form, and he adopted and adapted the form to express views current in the Jewish community that stands behind the text. The prayer in Baruch is similarly patterned after a time-honored Jewish form, the communal lament. "Form is meaning" to quote the literary critic Cleanth Brooks (1951, p. 45), whose dictum could as easily be attributed to our ancient writers. Present day scholars explore the shades of difference between Judith and the Greek novel, between Baruch's prayer and the psalms of communal lament, between 2 Maccabees and the classic story of a deity saving a city under siege. Adducing differences and divergences in form, scholars bring forth new meaning. True, the form critic is a vanishing breed, but the reflexes of reading long associated with this creature are still in evidence. Indeed, the form-critical reading strategies continue to yield insights.

Second, postcolonial theory is breathing new life into form-critical reading strategies by heightening readers' awareness of a text's setting in life. The settings in question reflect the politics of imperial forces pursuing colonization. As such, the setting reflects light back on the text in its formal design and illumines the text anew. To recall the cogent example of Judith as read by L. M. Wills, the Jewish novella violates certain conventions of Greek writing to challenge the norms imposed upon the East by Hellenistic rulers from the West. In writing Jewish novels that break free of formal conventions, the Eastern authors critique the dominant order and the power at its center. The work of Portier-Young similarly examines the interplay of literary form and historical *realia*, with emphasis on the latter.

Third, form-critical reading strategies bring into sharp relief social questions well beyond those raised by postcolonial theory. Study of the Jewish novellas has sparked a discussion about the role of pleasure in reading these and other texts. The pleasure in reading Tobit is not simply dramatic irony but what Wolfgang Iser (1980, p. 63) calls "the interplay of illusion-forming and illusion-breaking." If pleasure is an intrinsic part of the reading experience, there are implications for our understanding of the process of reading. Study of Baruch's prayer provides new impetus to the debate on whether penitential theology silenced the practice of lament in Second Temple Judaism. The so-called silencing of lament has been a fraught issue in contemporary theology. A host of relevant questions come to the fore when form-critical reading strategies are employed.

In sum, the practice of identifying and analyzing the genres to which texts belong, that is, form criticism, has become the first move in a hermeneutical process. That process revolves around the application of form-critical reading strategies in coordination with social concern and, in many cases, political critique. The critic of tomorrow will be tasked with explaining anew the meaning to be found in a text that exhibits literary form and has an impact on the world.

[*See also* Diachronic Interpretation; Empire Studies and Biblical Interpretation; Form Criticism, *subentry* Hebrew Bible; Form Criticism, *subentry* New Testament; Genre Criticism; Postcolonial Biblical Interpretation; *and* Rhetorical Criticism.]

BIBLIOGRAPHY

Bautch, Richard J. *Developments in Genre between Post-Exilic Penitential Prayers and the Psalms of Communal Lament.* Society of Biblical Literature Academia Biblica 7. Atlanta: Society of Biblical Literature, 2003.

Bautch, Richard J. "Lament Regained in Trito-Isaiah's Penitential Prayer." In *Seeking the Favor of God, Vol. 1, The Origins of Penitential Prayer in Second Temple Judaism*, edited by Mark J. Boda, Daniel K. Falk, and Rodney A. Werline, 83–99. Early Judaism and its Literature 21. Atlanta: Society of Biblical Literature, 2006.

Brooks, Cleanth. "The Formalist Critics." *Kenyon Review* 13, no. 1 (1951): 72–81.

Collins, John J. *The Apocalyptic Imagination: An Introduction to Jewish Apocalyptic Literature.* 2d ed. Grand Rapids, Mich.: Eerdmans, 1998.

Doran, Robert. *Temple Propaganda: The Purpose and Character of 2 Maccabees.* Catholic Biblical Quarterly Monograph Series 12. Washington, D.C.: The Catholic Biblical Association of America, 1981.

Floyd, Michael H. "Penitential Prayer in the Second Temple Period from the Perspective of Baruch." In *Seeking the Favor of God, Vol. 2, The Development of Penitential Prayer in Second Temple Judaism*, edited by Mark J. Boda, Daniel K. Falk, and Rodney A. Werline, 51–81. Early Judaism and its Literature 22. Atlanta: Society of Biblical Literature, 2007.

Goldhill, Simon. "Genre." In *The Cambridge Companion to the Greek and Roman Novel*, edited by Tim Whitmarsh, 184–200. Cambridge, UK: Cambridge University Press, 2008.

Gunkel, Hermann. *Einleitung in die Psalmen: Die Gattungen der religiösen Lyrik Israels*, edited by Joachim Begrich. Göttingen, Germany: Vandenhoeck & Ruprecht, 1933.

Haag, Ernst. *Studien zum Buche Judith: Seine theologische Bedeutung und literarische Eigenart.* Trierer theologisches Studien 16; Trier, Germany: Paulinus, 1963.

Iser, Wolfgang. "The Reading Process: A Phenomenological Approach." In *Reader-Response Criticism: From Formalism to Post-Structuralism*, edited by Jane P. Tompkins, 50–69. Baltimore, Md.: Johns Hopkins University Press, 1980.

Knierim, Rolf. "Old Testament Form Criticism Reconsidered." In *Reading the Hebrew Bible for a New Millennium: Form, Concept and Theological Perspective*, edited by Wonil Kim et al., 42–71. Harrisburg, Pa.: Trinity Press International, 2000.

McCracken, David. "Narration and Comedy in the Book of Tobit." *Journal of Biblical Literature* 114, no. 3 (1995): 401–418.
Muilenburg, James. "Form Criticism and Beyond." *Journal of Biblical Literature* 88, no. 1 (1969): 1–18.
Portier-Young, Anathea. "Alleviation of Suffering in the Book of Tobit: Comedy, Community, and Happy Endings." *Catholic Biblical Quarterly* 63, no. 1 (2001): 35–54.
Portier-Young, Anathea E. *Apocalypse against Empire: Theologies of Resistance in Early Judaism.* Grand Rapids, Mich.: Eerdmans, 2011.
Schellenberg, Ryan S. "Suspense, Simultaneity and Divine Providence in the Book of Tobit." *Journal of Biblical Literature* 130, no. 2 (2011): 313–327.
Schwartz, Daniel R. *2 Maccabees.* Commentaries on Early Jewish Literature. New York: de Gruyter, 2008.
Stephens, Susan A., and John J. Winkler. *Ancient Greek Novels: the Fragments: Introduction, Text, Translation, and Commentary.* Princeton, N.J.: Princeton University Press, 1995.
Westermann, Claus. *Praise and Lament in the Psalms.* Translated by Keith R. Crim and Richard N. Soulen. Atlanta: John Knox, 1981.
Wills, L. M. "Jewish Novellas in a Greek and Roman Age: Fiction and Identity." *Journal for the Study of Judaism* 43 (2011): 141–165.
Zeitlin, Froma. "Religion." In *The Cambridge Companion to the Greek and Roman Novel*, edited by Tim Whitmarsh, 91–108. Cambridge UK: Cambridge University Press, 2008.

Richard J. Bautch

New Testament

[The first sections of this essay are in part revisions of material from McKnight 1969, repr. 1997. Used by permission of Wipf and Stock Publishers. www.wipfandstock.com.]

New Testament form criticism describes what happened to the Jesus tradition as it was handed on before being written down in the Gospels. Form criticism has shown that the church's vital life exerted a creative influence in terms of content and "form" allowing criticism to classify individual units in the Synoptic Gospels according to literary form (or *Gattung*).

Background for New Testament Form Criticism. The form-critical approach to the New Testament was influenced by Hermann Gunkel's study of the stories in Genesis as originally oral stories developed and modified in the life of Israel. Also important was the identification of four sources behind the Synoptic Gospels (Mark, M, and L standing for the sources peculiar to Mark, Matthew, and Luke; Q, from German *Quelle*, designating a source postulated to explain material common to Matthew and Luke but absent from Mark) and the need to pry back historically into the period before the composition of the Gospels. More directly influential was Karl Ludwig Schmidt's suggestion that the lack of relationship between the units in the Gospel of Mark (the oldest Gospel) shows that the oldest tradition of Jesus is an abundance of individual stories. Only occasionally from the inner character of the story can these individual stories be fixed in respect to time and place.

An exception to the rule that there were no connected narratives of the life of Jesus in the earliest tradition is the passion narrative. Schmidt saw in the Marcan passion narrative a unified construction answering the question as to how Jesus could have been brought to the cross by those who were blessed by his signs and wonders.

Pioneers in New Testament Form Criticism. The definition of the task of form criticism and the early application of this tool were the work of Martin Dibelius and Rudolf Bultmann. The term "form criticism" came to be used in biblical studies because the title of Martin Dibelius's 1919 volume was *Die Formgeschichte des Evangeliums.* Dibelius's purpose was to explain the origin of the Jesus tradition, and therefore to penetrate back into the period before the one in which the written sources of the Gospels were recorded.

Bultmann's volume on the history of the synoptic tradition appeared two years after that of Dibelius, but his name and method of analysis have been more closely associated with form criticism that has the name of Dibelius. Bultmann's purpose was the discovery of what the original units of the Synoptics were—both sayings and stories—to try to establish what their historical setting was, whether they belonged to a primary or secondary tradition, or whether they were the product of editorial activity.

The major presuppositions and procedures in a form-critical analysis may be delineated using the works of Bultmann and Dibelius. The fundamental assumption making form criticism both necessary and possible is that the tradition basically consists of individual sayings and narratives united in the Gospels by the editorial work of the Gospel writers.

The determination of the earliest written form of the unit is important in analysis. When the unit is found in all three Synoptic Gospels, it may be assumed that the earliest written form is that of Mark. If the passage is found in Matthew and Luke but not in Mark, Matthew and Luke must be compared and the earliest written form of Q serve as the basis for analysis.

The assumption that the tradition served the needs and purposes of the church is central for the early form critics. Dibelius follows a constructive method and Bultmann follows an analytical method. That is, Dibelius reconstructs the history of the synoptic tradition from a study of the earliest Christian community while Bultmann begins with the text instead of the church. Dibelius sees the origins of the Christian movement occurring in the Aramaic-speaking Palestinian circle of Jesus. Next comes a pre-Pauline Hellenistic Christianity in close proximity to Judaism. Finally comes the Pauline church, much less closely related to Judaism. Dibelius declares that the synoptic tradition acquired its form in the pre-Pauline Hellenistic church closely associated with Judaism.

Bultmann's analytical approach does not demand as detailed a picture of the church as does the constructive approach of Dibelius. Bultmann begins with a division of early Christianity into Palestinian Christianity and Hellenistic Christianity.

Both Dibelius and Bultmann affirm that the form enables students to reconstruct the history of the tradition. When Dibelius says that a critical reading of the Gospels shows that the Gospel writers took over units of material that already possessed a form of their own, he is speaking of a "style" that has been created by its use among early Christians. The forms developed out of primitive Christian life itself. The units, therefore, have a form that is related to their place in the life of the church.

Bultmann is in accord with this assumption. "The proper understanding of form criticism rests upon the judgment that the literature . . . springs out of quite definite conditions and wants of life from which grows up a quite definite style and quite specific forms and categories" (1921, p. 4). Every literary category then will have its own "life situation" (*Sitz im Leben*), which is a typical situation in the life of the early Christian community.

Narrative Forms in Dibelius and Bultmann. The main concern of Dibelius is with the narrative material of the Gospels, and so in addition to the passion narrative, Dibelius deals extensively with paradigms, tales, and legends.

Paradigms. According to Dibelius the sermons of the early Christians did not contain simply the basic message of the gospel "but rather the message as explained, illustrated, and supported with references and otherwise developed" (1919, p. 25). Narratives of the deeds of Jesus were introduced as examples to illustrate and support the message. These examples constitute the oldest Christian narrative style, and Dibelius suggests the name "paradigm" for this narrative form.

The tribute money (Mark 12:13–17) is an example of a pure paradigm with the five characteristics Dibelius sees as essential in such a form: (1) independence from the literary context; (2) brevity and simplicity for use as examples in the sermon; (3) religious rather than artistic coloring; (4) didactic style causing the closing words of Jesus to stand out clearly; and (5) an ending in a thought useful for preaching.

Bultmann's category "apophthegm" is basically the same as Dibelius's paradigm. But Bultmann does not agree that the form arose in preaching in every case. Rather than "paradigm," he uses the term "apophthegm," a category from Greek literature denoting merely a short, pithy, and instructive saying. The term "apophthegm" does not prejudge the matter of origin. Bultmann sees three different types of apophthegms characterized by the different settings or causes for the sayings: controversy apophthegms, scholastic apophthegms, and biographical apophthegms. In Bultmann's opinion the three types of apophthegms are "ideal" constructions of the church. It is true that Jesus engaged in disputations and was asked questions about such things as the way to life and the greatest commandment. It is also true that a particular apophthegm could easily contain a historical reminiscence; that is, a decisive saying of an apophthegm may go back to Jesus himself. But the apophthegms as they stand are church constructions. Bultmann judges that they are Palestinian church constructions, as may be seen by comparison with similar rabbinical stories.

Tales. The tales in the Gospels are stories of Jesus's miracles that originated in their present form, according to Dibelius, not with preachers but with storytellers and teachers who related the stories from the life of Jesus "broadly, with colour and not without art" (1919, p. 70). Indeed, "literary style in reporting miracles . . . appears in the Tales with a certain regularity" (1919, p. 82). The style of the tale compares with the style of similar stories from ancient to modern times: first comes the history of the illness, then the technique of the miracle, and finally the success of the miraculous act. Tales belong to a higher grade of literature than paradigms.

The first tale in Mark is the healing of a leper (Mark 1:40–45). (The recounting of the miracle in Mark 1:23–27 is a paradigm, not a tale.) The characteristics of tales are clearly seen here: (1) the tales are individual stories complete in themselves; (2) tales are longer than paradigms; (3) they contain a greater breath of description; (4) devotional motifs are lacking and there is a gradual retreat of any words of Jesus of general interest; (5) the conclusions do not contain material helpful for preaching.

Dibelius explains the origin of tales through the extension of paradigms and through the introduction and use of motifs and materials strange to the original paradigm. The story of Jesus walking on the water, for example (Mark 6:45–52), may have resulted from the introduction of an epiphany motif into a primitive story of Jesus's intervention in a difficulty caused by winds and waves.

Bultmann's category "miracle stories" is what Dibelius means by "tales," namely stories of healing, and nature miracles in which the miracle constitutes the main theme and is described with considerable detail. Miracles occur among the apophthegms, but there the miracle is subordinated to the point of the apophthegm.

Bultmann compares the synoptic miracle stories with the miracle stories of Jewish and Hellenistic origin and discovers that the Gospel stories have exactly the same style as the Hellenistic miracle stories. The condition of the sick person is described, the healing is recounted, then the consequences of the miracle are unfolded. Bultmann asks at what stage the tradition was enriched by the addition of miracle stories and concludes that a Palestinian origin is probable for several miracle stories—the stilling of the storm (judged by its content), the feeding stories, and the healing of the leper. But "for the rest, the *Hellenistic* origin . . . is overwhelmingly the more probable" (1921, p. 240).

Legends and Myths. According to Dibelius, legends, "religious narratives of a saintly man in whose works and fate interest is taken" (1919, p. 104) arose in the church to satisfy a double desire: the desire to know something of the human virtues and lot of the holy men and women in the story of Jesus and the desire that gradually developed to know Jesus himself in this way. The story of Jesus when he is 12 years old (Luke 2:41–49) shows most clearly the qualities of legend. As far as history is concerned, Dibelius says that a narrator of legends is not interested in historical confirmation, and opposition to increasing the material by analogies is not offered.

Dibelius is convinced that the story of Jesus is not of mythological origin. The oldest witness of the process of formation of the traditions (the paradigms) does not tell of a mythological event. Dibelius lists the baptismal miracle, the temptation of Jesus, and the transfiguration as the only narratives describing a mythological event ("a many-sided interaction between mythological but not human persons," 1919, p. 271).

Following Bultmann's thought, legends are religiously edifying narratives, which are not properly miracle stories—although they may include something miraculous. And they are not basically historical—although they may be based on historical happenings. Historical stories and legends must be treated together because of the impossibility of separating the two. Some passages are purely legendary, an example being the narrative of the temptation of Jesus. But even the stories with a historical basis "are so much dominated by the legends that they can only be treated along with them" (1921, p. 245). For example, the historicity of Jesus's baptism by John is not to be disputed, according to Bultmann. But as the story is told in the Synoptic Gospels (Mark 1:9–11) it must be classified as a legend whose purpose is not history but religious edification. It tells of Jesus's consecration as Messiah; it is a faith legend. When the context is the faith and worship of the community, the result is a faith legend; when the context is the life of some religious hero, the result is a biographical legend.

Bultmann observes that the legendary motifs in the narratives are of diverse origin. Some materials show the influence of the Old Testament and Judaism, others show Hellenistic elements, still others have motifs that have developed within the Christian tradition itself.

Dibelius's Confident Approach to the Sayings of Jesus. Although Dibelius emphasized the narrative material of the Synoptic Gospels, he dealt with the sayings of Jesus and he finds preaching (especially catechetical instruction) as the place of formulation of such teachings. Dibelius presupposed a law at work with the sayings of Jesus that was different from the law concerning narrative material. The Jews of Jesus's day took the rules of life and worship more seriously than they took historical and theological tradition. Just so, the Christians treated the sayings of Jesus more seriously than they did the narratives. Modifications took place as the sayings of Jesus were transmitted. The hortatory character of the words of Jesus was strengthened. There was also a tendency to include Christological sayings, so as to gain from the words of Jesus not only solutions to problems or rules for one's own life but also indications about the nature of the one uttering such words.

Dibelius's study of Jesus maintained that a distinction must be made between the historical reliability of units of the tradition on the basis of their form. The passion story is unique and the general outline of the passion story is trustworthy. Paradigms are the most historical of the three forms of narrative material because they arose among the eyewitnesses. These eyewitnesses could control and correct the tradition. They arose in connection with preaching and "the nearer a narrative stands to the sermon the less is it questionable, or likely to have been changed by romantic, legendary, or literary influences" (1919, p. 61).

The tales and legends are less historical than paradigms. Tales, however, are not all on the same level historically. They arose in three different ways—extension of paradigms, the introduction of foreign motifs, and by borrowing foreign material. The historical judgment upon the tale is related to its origin. A historical basis is to be presupposed when the tale developed from a paradigm. Even legends must not be ruled out as possible vehicles of history.

In general, Dibelius is confident of the trustworthiness of the sayings. He says that we can observe that the Jesus's sayings were handed down with great fidelity thanks to the unencumbered memory of his unspoiled followers and their reverence for Jesus's words. He suggests that it is proper to speak of nongenuine sayings only where the later circumstances of the church are clearly presupposed.

Bultmann's Skeptical Analysis of Discourse Material. Bultmann provides a detailed analysis of the dominical sayings (proverbs, prophetic and apocalyptic sayings, and law and community regulations). He also gives a separate treatment of parables and I sayings (sayings attributed to Jesus in which he speaks of himself, his work, and his destiny), although by content both belong to the dominical sayings.

Proverbs. The proverb shows Jesus as the teacher of wisdom comparable with wisdom teachers throughout the Orient. Three basic "constitutive" forms exist in all proverbial literature—including that of the Synoptic Gospels. The proverb in a declarative form sets forth a principle or a declaration: "The laborer deserves his wages" (Luke 10:7). Exhortations take an imperative form: "Physician, heal yourself" (Luke 4:23). Proverbs also take the form of questions: "And which of you by being anxious can add one cubit to his span of life?" (Matt 6:27).

In regard to the relationship of the proverbs of the Synoptics to Jesus, Bultmann sees several possibilities: Jesus himself is responsible for some of the proverbs; Jesus occasionally made use of popular proverbs; and the primitive church placed in Jesus's mouth wisdom sayings that really go back to Jewish proverbial lore. Bultmann's judgment is that the wisdom sayings are "least guaranteed to be authentic words of Jesus and they are likewise the least characteristic and significant for historical interpretation" (1925, p. 55).

Prophetic and Apocalyptic Sayings. Prophetic and apocalyptic sayings are those in which Jesus proclaimed the arrival of the reign of God and preached the call to repentance. Bultmann sees proof in the little apocalypse of Mark 13:5–27 that Jewish material has been ascribed to Jesus by the church. Bultmann asks to what extent the rest of the material must go back to the church. In some sayings Jesus must be the origin; the immediacy of eschatological consciousness indicates that Jesus himself must have been the origin (Luke 10:23–24). Not all sayings that are judged unlikely to have originated in Judaism come from Jesus, however, for the early church formulated some passages. A church origin is more likely the more there is a relationship of the saying to the person of Jesus.

Statements Regarding the Law and Jewish Piety and Regulations of the Early Community. The third group of sayings treated by Bultmann is made up of statements regarding the law and Jewish piety and regulations of the early community. Bultmann declares that the history of the sayings can be seen with desirable clarity in this legal material. The church possessed a stock of genuine sayings of Jesus—especially important and genuine are the brief conflict sayings expressing Jesus's attitude to Jewish piety (Mark 7:15; 3:4; Matt 23:16–19, 23–24, 25–26). Concerning these sayings Bultmann says that "this is the first time that we have the right to talk of sayings of Jesus both as to form and content" (1921, p. 147). The tradition gathered these genuine sayings, giving them a new form, enlarging them by additions, and developing them further. Other Jewish sayings were collected and fitted for reception into the treasury of Christian instruction. New sayings were produced from the church's consciousness of a new possession, sayings that were ingeniously put into the mouth of Jesus. Bultmann especially attributes to the church the Old Testament citations, which are frequently found in combination with debating sayings, as well as the sayings with rules for the discipline of the community and for its mission, and the sayings in which the church expresses its faith in Jesus.

I Sayings. Bultmann acknowledges that it is impossible to prove that Jesus could not have spoken in the first person about himself. But such serious considerations are raised up against so many of the sayings that "one can have but little confidence even in regard to those which do not come under positive suspicion" (1921, p. 155). The sayings as a whole express the retrospective point of view of the church and were predominantly the work of the Hellenistic churches.

The Parable. The parable is a concise and simple story—much like a popular story in its concrete language, use of dialectical language and soliloquy, and repetition. The story is told to call forth a judgment on the part of the hearer—a judgment regarding the story of everyday human affairs and relations—and then judgment is applied in the realm of the spiritual life. Jesus spoke in parables, and the church transmitted the parables and used them for its own purpose. Here and there the form has been changed and applications added to make them more relevant to the later church. Alterations are even seen in Matthew's and Luke's use of the written sources. But Bultmann sees more radical alteration by the church: the placement of the parables into particular contexts and the giving of introductions that affect the meaning of the stories; the placement of a new parable alongside an older independent story; the providing of allegorical additions and explanations; and the augmentation of the store of parables from the Jewish tradition.

The history of the parables in the tradition makes it clear that some of the parabolic material does not go back to Jesus but to the church. Bultmann concludes his treatment of parables with a rule that enables us to discover the genuine parables of Jesus: "We can only count on possessing a genuine similitude of Jesus where, on the one hand, expression is given to the contrast between Jewish morality and piety and the distinctive eschatological temper that characterized the preaching of Jesus; and where on the other hand we find no specifically Christian features" (1921, p. 205).

Bultmann's analysis of the gospel tradition results in a skeptical attitude to the possibility of historical research into the life of Jesus. He is skeptical of the historicity of the narrative tradition. He does not doubt that Jesus lived and did many of the sorts of things reported in the tradition. But he doubts that any specific activity is a historical report. And he is certain that the narratives in the tradition cannot give us knowledge of the life and personality of Jesus.

Bultmann is less skeptical about the sayings. We know enough to construct a consistent picture. Yet the sayings as well as the narratives go back to the church, which not only passed on actual sayings of Jesus but also placed its own teachings on the lips of Jesus. How can we distinguish between authentic and inauthentic sayings? Helpful is knowledge that the Synoptic Gospels were written in Greek in the Hellenistic community, while Jesus and the primitive church lived in Palestine and spoke Aramaic. Everything that could have originated only in Hellenistic Christianity must be excluded. But not everything thus retained goes back to Jesus, for there was an Aramaic-speaking Palestinian church after the time of Jesus. Different layers within the Palestinian material must be distinguished. Whatever materials show characteristics of related development or specific interests of the church must be rejected as secondary. Even here one must be cautious if not skeptical. "Naturally we have no absolute assurance that the exact words of this oldest layer were really spoken by Jesus. There is a possibility that the contents of this oldest layout are also the result of a complicated historical process which we can no longer trace" (1926, p. 13).

Bultmann's work on Jesus, therefore, is the treatment of the message that can be recovered from the oldest layer of the synoptic tradition. By the tradition, Bultmann admits, Jesus is named as the bearer of the message. According to probability Jesus was the messenger, but Bultmann allows the name "Jesus" to be placed in quotation marks and understood as an abbreviation for the historical phenomenon that can be uncovered with the help of form criticism.

Early Scholarly Evaluation and Use of Form Criticism. New Testament scholars differed widely in their reaction to form criticism. Some continued to emphasize source criticism and virtually ignored the new discipline. Others defended the basic historicity of Mark and the other sources of the Synoptic Gospels but were increasingly affected by form criticism.

Continued Use of Source Analysis Alone. B. H. Streeter and Arthur C. Headlam represent scholars who continued to emphasize source analysis alone. B. H. Streeter summed up the results of the scientific study of the Gospels to his day in the great book, *The Four Gospels: A Study of Origins.* Streeter first published his work in 1924 and took no account of the work of form criticism. The year before Streeter's book appeared, A. C. Headlam published his work, *The Life and Teachings of Jesus the Christ,* which utilized the results of the analysis of the sources of the Gospels. Headlam sees himself as a defender of the "general credibility of the traditional account of the life and work of our Lord" against a school of critics that, while accepting Jesus as a real person and founder of Christianity, holds that "the greater part of the contents of the Gospel tells us not what He taught, but what the Christian Church which grew up after His death thought" (p. ix).

Challenges to Form Criticism. C. H. Dodd, T. W. Manson, Harald Riesenfeld, and Birger Gehardsson challenged basic presuppositions of form criticism. In 1932 Dodd challenged the assumptions of form criticism regarding the framework of the gospel narrative. Dodd denied that the order of the units of Mark is arbitrary and that the framework is only an artificial construction. The conclusion Dodd drew is that "we need not be so scornful of the Marcan order as has recently become the fashion." He admitted, however, that "we shall not place in it the implicit confidence it once enjoyed" (1952, p. 11). T. W. Manson, a noted English New Testament scholar and teacher, whose career continued until his death in 1958, remained throughout his lifetime much more confident of the historicity of the gospel tradition than did the form critics. In light of Manson's general defense of the authenticity of the Marcan framework, it is important to note his grudging concession to the form critics. He admitted that "it is no longer possible to regard the Marcan framework, in all its details, as a rigid and nonalterable scaffolding, into which everything must somehow be fitted. . . . Many concessions may have to be made to the disruptive criticism of Mark" (1962, p. 26).

Two Scandinavian scholars, Harald Riesenfeld and Birger Gehardsson, attempted to prove false the postulate upon which the discipline of form criticism most depends, that the formation of the material took place in the later Christian community. Riesenfeld stated the basic arguments in an address delivered at the opening session of the congress on "The Four Gospels in 1957" in Oxford. Riesenfeld held that "the beginning of the gospel tradition lies with Jesus himself" (1957, p. 23). Riesenfeld attempted to establish this by identifying the origin and transmission of the Christian tradition with the origin and transmission of Jewish tradition. A pupil of Riesenfeld, Birger Gerhardsson, in his book *Memory and Manuscript*, carried forward Riesenfeld's work by presenting in great detail the evidence from Judaism and early Christianity that supports the case.

Cautious Use of Form Criticism. Burton Scott Easton, Vincent Taylor, and R. H. Lightfoot represent the cautious acceptance and use characteristic of the attitude and practice of most New Testament scholars. Burton Scott Easton was one of the earliest American scholars to evaluate form criticism. In December, 1927, he gave a series of lectures at the General Theological Seminary, New York, in which he dealt with form criticism. Some of the tradition may be classified in terms of form, according to Easton. This is true of the form known to Dibelius as paradigm and to Bultmann as apophthegm, the tale, and the parable. But attempts to classify other narratives and teaching material have not proved helpful, and form critics violate the rules when they classify in any way other than by form. Although Easton denies that form criticism as such is historical criticism, he does not deny the validity of the historical criticism engaged by the form critics. Indeed "form criticism may prepare the way for historical criticism" (1928, p. 81). Easton's own evaluation is that the synoptic narratives and sayings go back not to the early church but to the earthly Jesus.

Vincent Taylor very cautiously evaluated form criticism as a legitimate tool in lectures given at the University of Leeds in 1932. He does not see the discipline as totally negative at all. In fact, he declared, "Form criticism seems to me to furnish constructive suggestions which in many ways confirm the historical trustworthiness of the Gospel tradition" (1933, p. vi). Taylor is responsible for the use of "pronouncement story" for the form called paradigm by Dibelius and apophthegm by Bultmann. The term does justice to the dual nature of the form.

Form criticism received a champion in England in R. H. Lightfoot at the University of Oxford. Although Lightfoot disclaims the title of "champion" of the claims of form criticism, in the Bampton lectures of 1934 he introduced the insights of form critics to his compatriots, and in this series of lectures and later works he applied the method to the Gospel of Mark. The most valuable aspect of form criticism is the way it seeks to relate the individual stories to the life of the church that preserved them and used them to give its message to the world. "In this way the Gospels can be to us . . . within limits which need to be carefully guarded, a mirror of the hopes and aspirations, the problems and the difficulties, of the early church" (1950, p. 102). Lightfoot's interest in the total purpose of the evangelists led him to apply form criticism to the Gospels in a different way than the earlier scholars. Lightfoot became a pioneer, then, in yet another method of Gospel study, redaction criticism.

The Challenge of Structuralism. "Structuralism" refers to a theory concerning the composition of literary texts and other human productions and the technique of analysis of those productions. In basic terms, the text is to be analyzed primarily in terms of principles of internal organization not in terms of the historical process that produced it. And the organization on the level of "deep structure" not "surface structure" is of greatest interest.

The most radical structural-linguistic approach to New Testament texts was offered by Erhardt Güttgemanns of the University of Bonn. His 1970 book was a declaration that the whole tradition of New Testament scholarship has to be shelved. Historical criticism must be replaced by a linguistic exegesis based on the principle of structural linguistics. Form criticism was the first opponent to be demolished in Güttgemanns's work. For Güttgemanns, history and the sociological situation of the early church had nothing to do with the *essence* of the forms of the Synoptic Gospels. The forms grow out of nonhistorical anthropological and linguistic factors.

In his application of structural analysis, Güttgemanns concludes that whoever wants to learn the production of Gospel narratives does not need to learn the "performance" or surface level phenomena but simply the abstract categories (character types and types of action) and the possibilities of the combinations of the abstract categories as determined by logic. Humankind is capable in the present day and in modern verbalization of narrating stories of God through which they carry on the synoptic stories from the perspective of *genre* so that the present proclamation represents a generative expansion of the canonical Synoptic Gospels. (1976, pp. 168–169).

Güttgemanns was influenced by French narratology to stress the "profound" or "deep" or "generative" level of the literary structure. Historical positivism was replaced by a linguistic positivism. "Jesus and the kerygma belong to the *pragmatic* basis of narrative proclamation. This basis motivates the proclamation, but at the same time makes use of an *a priori* linguistic basis. Jesus and the kerygma are therefore, to be sure, a necessary, but not a sufficient condition for Gospel narrative. Rather, the sufficient condition is exclusively narrative competence of humankind. Consequently, in each case grammar ontologically and logically precedes history" (1976, p. 169).

The radical nonhistorical or antihistorical perspective was not inevitable in French narratology or the work of Güttgemanns. Daniel Patte provided for English-speaking scholars an introduction to structural methodology and specific procedures in *What Is Structural Exegesis?* Patte sees that attention can be given to structures closer to the surface of the text and is aware that the methods he introduces complement traditional historical critical methods.

Through the structuralist interlude of the 1970s and 1980s a number of important contributions other than those of Patte were made by New Testament scholars. Elizabeth Struthers Malbon's 1986 work on the "geographical code" in Mark showed how the structural organization of spaces provides a major key to what is going on in the Gospel.

Aesthetic and Rhetorical Examination of Forms. Contemporary form and redaction criticism attempt to integrate traditional historical approaches with nonhistorical linguistic and literary methods of study. The expansion of the concept of *Sitz im Leben* ("life-setting") allows conventional criticism to embrace newer approaches. Individual units and completed Gospels are seen not only in the light of institutional settings but also in the light of linguistic, literary, and other cultural settings. The tradition and the completed Gospels will be explained by a plurality of historical and nonhistorical settings.

Concern with genuine literary matters began to surface in the 1960s and 1970s and became commonplace in the 1980s. The lack of interaction with genuine literary criticism in the early Bultmann tradition hindered the task among students of Bultmann, but in his 1964 publication, *The Language of the Gospel*, Amos Wilder advocated a move that takes advantage of literary insights. He expounds the New Testament "language event" in terms of literary form. There is reference in the text but the reference is not the same as that in conventional study of the Gospels. Students of the New Testament can learn about its literary language and reference from students of poetry: "this kind of report of reality—as in a work of art—is more subtle and complex and concrete than in the case of a discursive statement, and therefore more adequate to the matter in hand and to things of importance" (p. 133).

A comprehensive New Testament study will be open to all sorts of questions—different kinds and levels of literary, historical, and theological structures. The conventional historically-oriented form-critical approach to reading the New Testament text has been supplemented but not effectively displaced by the formalist-structuralist and other literary approaches.

[*See also* Literary Criticism, Literary Theory, and the Bible; Redaction Criticism, *subentry* New Testament; *and* Structuralist Interpretation.]

BIBLIOGRAPHY

Bultmann, Rudolf. *Form Criticism: Two Essays on New Testament Research*. Edited and translated by Fredrick Clifton Grant. New York: Willett, Clark and Co., 1934. English translation of *Die Erforschung der synoptischen Tradition*, first published in 1925. This is a popular exposition of the method elaborated much more fully in the *History of the Synoptic Tradition*.

Bultmann, Rudolf. *History of the Synoptic Tradition*. Translated by John Marsh. New York: Harper & Row, 1963. English translation of the third edition of *Die Geschichte der synoptischen Tradition*, first published in 1921. This was the first study of the entire synoptic tradition from the perspective of form criticism. Bultmann attempted to write the history of the tradition and to show the forces at work on the tradition as it was formed and transmitted. This book is basic to modern-day form criticism.

Bultmann, Rudolf. *Jesus and the Word*. Translated by Louise Pettibone Smith and Erminie Huntress Lantero. New York: Charles Scribner's Sons, 1934. English translation of *Jesus*, first published in 1926. A treatment of the message of Jesus based on Bultmann's understanding of the history of the synoptic tradition.

Dibelius, Martin. *From Tradition to Gospel*. Translated by Bertram Lee Woolf. New York: Charles Scribner's Sons, 1934. English translation of *Die Formgeschichte des Evangeliums*, first published in 1919. The third German edition (1959) contains an essay by G. Iber on form criticism since Dibelius. Dibelius applied Gunkel's principles for the study of the narrative material of the synoptic tradition. In retrospect he is seen as a conservative form critic.

Dibelius, Martin. *Jesus*. Translated by Charles B. Hendrick and Fredrick C. Grant. Philadelphia: Westminster, 1949. English translation of *Jesus*, first published in 1939. An application of Dibelius's form critical method to a study of the life and teachings of Jesus.

Dodd, Charles Harold. "The Framework of the Gospel Narrative." *Expository Times* 43 (1932): 396–400; reprinted in *New Testament Studies*. New York: Scribner's, 1952: 1–11. Dodd attempted to show that the arrangement of the units in Mark is based at least in part upon the traditional framework of the history of Jesus.

Easton, Burton Scott. *The Gospel before the Gospels*. New York: Charles Scribner's Sons, 1928. A cautious American introduction to form criticism. He stressed the limitations of form criticism as a historical tool.

Fascher, Eric. *Die formgeschichtliche Method*. Giessen: Töpelmann, 1924. Fascher stressed the limitations of form criticism, declaring that the discipline itself does not establish the authenticity or lack of authenticity of units of the tradition.

Gerhardsson, Birger. *Memory and Manuscript: Oral Tradition and Written Transmission in Rabbinic Judaism and Early Christianity*. Translated by Eric J Sharp. Lund: Gleerup, 1961. An attempt to support the thesis of Riesenfeld by careful study of the transmission of the tradition in Judaism and of Christian sources that tell of the delivery of the gospel tradition.

Gunkel, Hermann. *The Legends of Genesis: The Biblical Saga and History*. Translated by W. H. Carruth. New York: Schocken, 1964. English translation of the introduction to *Genesis*, first published in 1901. Gunkel applied form criticism to the units of Genesis and provided a critical procedure for a study of the units of the Synoptic Gospels.

Güttgemanns, Erhardt. *Candid Questions Concerning Gospel Form Criticism*. Translated by William G. Doty. Pittsburgh Theological Monograph Series 26.

Pittsburgh: Pickwick, 1979. English translation of *Offene Fragen zur Formgeschichte des Evangeliums: Eine methodologische Skizze der Grundlagenproblematic der Form- und Redaktionsgeschichte*, first published in 1970. Challenged the basic assumptions of form criticism.

Güttgemanns, Erhardt. "Narrative Analysis of Synoptic Texts." *Semeia* 6 (1976): 127–179. Translated by William G. Doty from "Analyse synoptischer Texte." *Linguistica Biblica* 25/26 (1973): 50–73.

Headlam, C. Arthur. *The Life and Teaching of Jesus the Christ*. 2d ed. London: John Murray, 1927. Headlam assumed that the life of Jesus could be constructed from the four independent sources identified by source critics.

Lightfoot, Robert Henry. *The Gospel Message of St. Mark*. Oxford: Clarendon Press, 1950. In this and the previous work, Lightfoot both introduced form criticism to the English-speaking academic world and began to use the discipline to discover the theological message of the Gospel writers. This aspect of the discipline of form criticism has become known as "redaction criticism."

Lightfoot, Robert Henry. *History and Interpretation in the Gospels*. London: Hodder and Stoughton, 1935.

Malbon, Elizabeth Struthers. *Narrative Space and Mythic Meaning in Mark*. New York and San Francisco: Harper & Row, 1986.

Manson, Thomas Walter. *Studies in the Gospels and Epistles*. Philadelphia: Westminster, 1962. A collection of Manson's lectures given between 1939 and 1953. In these lectures Manson affirmed his belief in the historicity of the Gospels.

Manson, Thomas Walter. *The Teaching of Jesus: Studies of its Form and Content*. Cambridge, UK: Cambridge University Press, 1931. The study of Jesus's teachings based on the view that the earliest written sources are basically historical.

McKnight, Edgar V. *Meaning in Texts: The Historical Shaping of a Narrative Hermeneutics*. Philadelphia: Fortress, 1978.

McKnight, Edgar V. *What Is Form Criticism?* Philadelphia: Fortress, 1969, repr. Eugene, Ore.: Wipf & Stock, 1997.

Patte, Daniel. *What Is Structural Exegesis?* Philadelphia: Fortress, 1976.

Riesenfeld, Harald. *The Gospel Tradition and its Beginnings: A Study in the Limits of "Formgeschichte."* London: Mowbray, 1957. Riesenfeld attempted to show that the gospel tradition was derived from Jesus himself and that the tradition was passed down carefully as was the rabbinic tradition.

Schmidt, Karl Ludwig. *Der Rahmen der Geschichte Jesu. Literarkritische Untersuchungen zür ältesten Jesusüberlieferung*. Berlin: Trowitzsch und Sohn, 1919. This book gave the final blow to faith in the Marcan framework. Schmidt isolated individual units from the framework and prepared the way for other scholars to classify and study the individual units and the contribution of the editor or author of the Gospel.

Streeter, Burnett Hillman. *The Four Gospels: A Study of Origins*. London: Macmillan, 1924. Revised edition, 1930. Streeter's comprehensive summary of the results of the study of the Gospels to his day. His original contribution is the "four document" theory of Gospel origins.

Taylor, Vincent. *The Formation of the Gospel Tradition*. London: Macmillan, 1933. Second edition, 1935. A cautious introduction to form criticism that acknowledges its usefulness as a limited tool.

Wilder, Amos N. *The Language of the Gospel: Early Christian Rhetoric*. New York: Harper & Row, 1964. Wilder was the literary critic and New Testament scholar who opened the door for correlation of genuine historical and literary study at a time when Rudolf Bultmann's existential approach cast a shadow on historical study and was out of tune with literary imagination.

Edgar V. McKnight

G

Genre Criticism

Genre refers to the type of literature to which a writing or an oral tradition belongs. Appreciating genre alerts the reader or hearer to the trajectory that is to be followed by a communication, its purpose, and the emotional tone to be struck. It makes a great difference, for example, to know from the outset whether one is about to join the story of the origin of one's people, to celebrate their victories in battle, to lament their defeats, to explore the joys of love, to mourn the passing of a once vigorous collective and personal life, or to investigate how divine wisdom can be accessed in the midst of life's seeming chaos.

These genres—and many more—are developed within the Bible. Sometimes, in the case of literate authors such as Paul of Tarsus, a template of the literary form in question (in his case, the epistle or letter) is in mind, and it helps to know what authors decided to do with their forms, and how readers and hearers would have assessed the work in terms of their expectations. A fallacy, however, commonly afflicts the assessment of genre. Because any work of literature by its definition can be appreciated as a whole, every book in the Bible—no matter how large or small—belongs to some genre or another (and sometimes to a combination of genres). But that observation does not warrant the conclusion that every biblical author attempted to fit a given composition into an established genre. In many cases, biblical compositions pioneered their genres, interacting with precedents from their culture and other cultures, yet framing fresh forms of literature that arose from the unique experience of unusual communities. Even when applying an apparent genre, a writer's purpose might be to introduce twists that underline a surprising message, as in the case of the book of Jonah.

For this reason, genre should not be approached as an abstract category, as if forms of literature existed prior to biblical compositions, and the authors always attempted to write to those preexisting templates. Rather, genre unfolds with a literature over time, sometimes self-consciously, but for the most part as an organic expression of the kind of communication that is concerned. This article traces that development by following and describing some prominent genres of literature in the Bible that emerged over time, following the order of chronology rather than the order of the canon.

Epic. The literary basis of the Bible was laid long after 1800 B.C.E., the putative time of Abraham, the wandering Aramaean who is revered as the primordial patriarch of Israel. Even the exodus from Egypt (ca. 1300 B.C.E.) was a distant memory for the clans of people who settled in the land of the Canaanites and claimed common descent from Abraham, Isaac, and Jacob. But such early events and characters, portrayed in heroic terms, became the basis and the background of an epic presentation: the story of a people's survival told in often poetic form on the basis of the triumphs and failures of ancestors. What Israel remembered directly, in the earliest sources of the Bible, was the place in which it first grew up: the land they called Israel and its earlier inhabitants called Canaanites. The story of how the war god Yahweh helped his twelve clans (or "tribes") of people conquer the land he promised them, and inflicted punishment on anyone who abrogated the basics of his agreement with them (the covenant) is the opening phase in the story of the Bible. Judges 2–3, 4–5, 6–9, 11, 13–16, 17–18, 19–21; Joshua 1–8, 9–11, 18, 20, 24; and 1 Samuel 1–15 represent this epic genre.

Joshua 10:1–14 speaks of the sun standing still to allow Israel to destroy its enemies; the source of the statement that Yahweh fought for his people in this way is given as "the book of Jasher." The initial community that produced these texts in Hebrew was a loose confederation of clans that gathered to make war. Stories from the earliest sources in the Bible (detectable in their style of Hebrew, their patterns of thought, and their historical allusions) depict a decentralized social structure. Central leadership was lacking, and clans allied for purposes of war under charismatic military adventurers called "judges" supported by Yahweh, often by miraculous means and signs. Their policies could be ruthless and frequently set one clan at war against another. Some judges were also prophets, or at least consulted with prophets: by means of sacrifice, music, and trance, they claimed to speak for Yahweh, the god who linked the clans. But priestly sacrifice was also undertaken by many people from the clan of Levi. They settled in what we mostly now call the highlands of territorial Israel. Principally an oral culture, this phase of Israel's existence nonetheless produced the beginnings of a literature, some of which may have been consigned to writing near the point of origin.

Scribal Narrative and Myth. Kingship emerged as a necessary military, and eventually juridical, institution, an innovation that brought with it a revised understanding of the divine covenant (see 2 Sam 7 in relation to David's dynasty), and a powerful scribal class. Scribes became not only the privileged group that happened to be able to write, but also the intellectual branch of the royal propaganda machine: Israel's first historians.

Kings legitimated their reigns by means of regular consultation with the prophets who had once been oracles, judges, and warlords. They were still in many ways comparable to the mantic sages of Canaan, using their prophetic trance and ecstatic sacrifice to divine the future. Divination became one means by which Israel's foreign, domestic, and sacrificial policy was set.

The prophets with their oracular powers emerged literally as kingmakers (and breakers) during this period, but the influence of monarchy was irresistible even for them. The reigns of David (1010–970 B.C.E.) and Solomon (970–922 B.C.E.) saw a period of equilibrium among king, priests, prophets, and scribes. Their alliance produced a narrative line within the Pentateuch (the first five books of the Bible later attributed to Moses), which tells the story of Israel from the creation of the first human couple to Israel's inheritance of the land.

This narrative includes political theology, poetry, history, and myth as reflected in many parts of the Pentateuch, an intellectual monument to the extent of the influence of David and Solomon over Israel. Examples of this work include 1 Samuel 15–31; 2 Samuel 1, 3, 6–7, 11–20, 24; 1 Kings 2–3, 5–11; Genesis 2:4b–4; 11:1–9, 12. The narrative succeeds in extending the epic of Israel from the creation of human beings, through the call of the Patriarchs and the liberation from Egypt, and on to the rise of the Davidic dynasty. The extension of the epic of Israel both back in time, to the creation of humanity, and forward in time, to the establishment of the monarchy and the challenges it posed, developed new genres. The primordial past was related by myth, in which features of human life are explained on the basis of their interaction with the divine. Recent (in some cases nearly contemporary) events became the domain of historiographic interests. Once myth and history were developed, they could be mixed with one another, as well as with epic, poetry, and prophecy, to produce interesting combinations within the Pentateuch and throughout the story of Israel's experience.

At times, the result is coherent composition, in which—for example—Adam's attempt to deflect blame from himself in the Garden of Eden (Gen 3:12) is echoed in Saul's alibi at Gilgal for not completing the slaughter of the Amelekites (1 Sam 15:15). Considerable scribal independence (and an accurate awareness of events) is reflected in stories such as David's adultery with Bathsheba (2 Sam 11:1—12:25). Scenes of this kind pose the question of the intended audience of the narrative. Kings valued scribes for their propaganda, but their work evidently trumped that genre, and broke into history and theological reflection. Prophets were a clear influence in that development, and they then emerged with their own voices.

Prophecy. The power of the Davidic dynasty resulted in the exploitation of peoples of the other Israelite clans by the Judeans (David's own clan), leading the former to secede under Solomon's son Rehoboam in ca. 922 B.C.E. (1 Kgs 11—12; 14—16; 17—2 Kgs 11). The name "Israel" went to the north, because all that was left to the house of David was the territory of Judah itself.

Bereft of the support and wealth of the northern clans, Jerusalem proved an easy target for Pharaoh Sheshonq (Shishak) who pillaged the city. Meanwhile, Israel prospered under powerful monarchs who encouraged trade and alliances with surrounding peoples (see 1 Kgs 14—16). Because these alliances were perceived as introducing foreign gods into their country, the prophets increasingly opposed them, and their fundamental message was put into writing for the first time: only complete loyalty to Yahweh could ensure Israel's survival. Any other course, they claimed, would inevitably and swiftly bring disaster.

The perceived abuses of the Israelite monarchy in the north, then, set in motion the forces that would elevate prophecy into an influential institution with a distinctive literary voice. During the period of the judges, it had been one of the few centripetal powers in Israel. To some extent domesticated during David's successful legitimation of his reign, it came to independent prominence again after the secession of the north from the south, especially during the reign of Ahab. The prophetic activities of Elijah and Elisha became emblematic of prophecy forever after, involving a dedication to vision and access to the "chariot" of God's presence, an often strident demand for social justice, overt resistance to the political rule of the house of Ahab and its successors, a violent opposition to idolatry, and a cogent expression of Yahweh's objection to Israelite practice. The cycle of stories included in 1 Kings 17—2 Kings 11, with the story of Elijah's miraculous sign on Mount Carmel in his dispute with the prophets of Baal (1 Kgs 18) perhaps provides the best single example. The elevated character of the prophet also influenced the telling of stories of Moses (Exod 3:13–15) and Joseph (Gen 37—50) in the Pentateuch.

During the eighth century in the north, prophetic works emerged as a literary genre, where the prophet's words—and increasingly, as the genre emerged, his deeds—were presented as communications from Yahweh to his people as a whole. One hallmark of this evolving prophetic message was that of the impending doom of the north, taken to be a soon-to-be-exacted vengeance for the prophets as well as just satisfaction for Yahweh's justice. Amos is the closest to the oral origins of prophecy, and its oracles are a good index of how prophets spoke in ancient Israel (see Amos 1—2). But within the same century, Hosea (also in the north) pioneered a literary arc for the prophetic genre, developing the narrative comparison between Israel and a faithless wife (compare Hos 1–2, 8). For works to be copied, and especially for them to be crafted into structured wholes, assumes the cooperation of some scribes with prophets, and this collaboration is confirmed by the development of prophecy in the south, where the book of Isaiah heightens classic motifs of vision (Isa 6—8) and connects them to the Temple: the theme of God's miraculous protection of Jerusalem is developed in a miraculous history of deliverance from Sennacherib (Isa 36—39). The story of that protection is also narrated in 2 Kings 18:13—19:37, which shows the close relationship that developed between scribes and prophets. Still, the book of Micah from the south in the eighth century retains an earlier style (comparable to the book of Amos), while Nahum and Zephaniah from the seventh century show the continuing vigor of that style, albeit with further development.

Aggregation and Apocalypse. While Israel prospered, Yahweh's prophets could be dismissed as annoyances and monarchs could seek friendlier counsel. But in 722 B.C.E., the powerful northern kingdom was broken by the invasion of the Assyrians and their policy of cultural genocide: moving conquered peoples from their own lands, and settling strangers in their place. Northern Israel, along with "Galilee of the nations," became a foreign province. In the south, Judah escaped Israel's fate, through a combination of good fortune (the preoccupation of Assyria with greater powers) and its own relative insignificance in Assyrian eyes. That enabled Yahweh's prophets in Judah (some of whom had actually fled from the north) to draw together the writings of their great predecessors in the north as well as the south and to rewrite history according to the principle that Yahweh rewarded loyalty to him with prosperity and punished rebellion with exile.

Ironically, just as that work was completed—signally represented by the book of Deuteronomy and the initial edition of the Deuteronomistic History—and was embraced by King Josiah as a matter of state policy, surrounding powers closed in on Judah. Josiah himself was killed in 609 B.C.E. at Megiddo (which gave its name to ultimate disaster in the word Armageddon, see Rev 16:16), and then the new empire of Babylonia besieged and destroyed Jerusalem itself in 587 B.C.E. The close of the second book of Kings (2 Kgs 24—25) articulates a tragic vision of history, according to which the sins of previous kings made even the reforms of Josiah inadequate to please God and avert disaster.

The Babylonians pursued the same policy of dispersing conquered enemies that the Assyrians had devised. Prominent prophets and priests found themselves with the royal family in exile in Babylon. Desperation made them cooperate in a way they never had in territorial Israel. The result of that cooperation was the Bible much as we know it: the Pentateuch was completed in exile, and the prophetic works were compiled with the Pentateuch into a canon. Israel had been lost on the ground, but it had been rediscovered in writing, understood as the Word of Yahweh himself.

The Pentateuch, or Torah, was compiled by editing previous narratives, reaching back to the Davidic court and to the prophetic movement in the north. These sources provide stories of the patriarchs and the exodus, but they sometimes locate cognate traditions in different places, according to the geographical bias of each. In addition, the Pentateuch includes a great prophetic addendum attributed to the Deuteronomist (named after the book of Deuteronomy) and the Priestly work ("P"). This complex collection, together with the emerging Prophetic canon, gave landless Israel a charter for its existence that survived the exile in Babylon.

Even with a written Bible, how many generations could Israel have lasted in exile? Had the Assyrian/Babylonian policy been pursued to its intended end, the most we would have known of the Torah and the Prophets would probably have been a few papyrus fragments from scrolls. Jerusalem's name and buildings would have been buried beneath the settlement of whatever peoples came to inhabit the rubble the Babylonians had left behind. But Babylon itself did not last, and Cyrus the Persian developed a radical new policy: toleration. In 539 B.C.E. he permitted his subject peoples to return to their own lands and worship their own gods. This event was momentous to the extent that an addition was written to the book of Isaiah (chs. 40—55), hailing Cyrus as God's anointed, or messiah (Isa 45:1–4).

The prophetic books that stem from after 587 B.C.E. show an intense degree of scribal engagement.

Sometimes additions to prophetic books reveal this activity, but the book of Jeremiah was composed with the active help of named personnel (see the reference to Bar in Jer 36), which was necessary for Jeremiah to communicate to people as far away as Babylon, to whom his letter is quoted (Jer 29). He died before the return from end of the exile that he had forecast, which happened more quickly than the 70 years he specified (Jer 29:10). Specifics for the restoration of the Temple are delivered in the book of Ezekiel. Here scribal assistance is also apparent, but also a new focus on the visionary world entered on the moving throne of God, the chariot (Ezek 1). The specifics of vision become imperatives in Ezekiel, where a plan for the restored temple is set out in detail (Ezek 40—48). In this, and in the development of elaborate visions such as valley of dry bones and its interpretation (Ezek 37) Ezekiel anticipates the development of apocalyptic literature.

When some Israelites did return to Jerusalem, many covenanted themselves to the prophetic promise and eventually set about rebuilding the temple (from 520 B.C.E.). Haggai, Zechariah, and Malachi, the latest of the prophetic books, articulate incentives for that program. But others were quite happy to accept the customs and in some cases the women of foreigners. The result was deep conflict between scribes like Ezra (see and Ezra and Nehemiah) and large numbers of assimilationists.

Ezra's program is said in the book of Ezra (fourth century B.C.E.) to extend to the command that Israelites should separate from foreign wives and children (Ezra 10). Although not as separatist as Ezra's program, support for a triumphalist point of view was offered from a feminine perspective in the book of Esther and (later) the book of Judith. Those who opposed the separationists especially relied on traditions that centered on the divine feminine, Wisdom, the consort of Yahweh. The literature of Wisdom includes several genres, including aphorism, poetry, philosophical questioning, and theodicy, but the underlying assumption is that Wisdom leads—whether in confidence or in despair—to a clearer understanding of God. Wisdom was usually represented as consistent with the prophetic tradition, and also as manifest in the patterns of nature and in the best of all human cultures. Wisdom is praised in the book of Proverbs, a collection of earlier aphorisms and poems that is given a central core by this praise (Prov 8). Much of the material in Proverbs may be compared with Egyptian and Babylonian sources, as is also case in other Wisdom works, the books of Job, Ecclesiastes, and later (from the second and first centuries B.C.E., respectively) Ecclesiasticus and the Wisdom of Solomon.

Pseudonymity is characteristic of this postexilic period, a convention that permitted the work of aggregation to go on, sometimes with creative mixtures of genres. The secular poetry of the Song of Songs could be attributed to Solomon and the cultic poetry of Psalms (as a whole) to David, and in that way the biblical inheritance of Hebrew poetry was incalculably deepened.

One of the most fascinating aspects of Israelite literary history during this period is the absence of prophecy. The resettlement of the land brought no respite from internal conflict, and the lure of assimilation only grew after Alexander the Great claimed territorial Israel in 332 B.C.E. Yet neither the assimilationists nor the separationists claimed to speak directly in the name of the God of Israel. A principal reason for this was that the power of the scribes on both sides of the argument had fixed the prophetic voice in writing. Further guidance for Israel was to come from interpretation, rather than directly from inspiration. But that apparent dominance of the scribal mode cannot completely conceal what is evident in the writings that record the folk literatures of Israel (such as Tobit in the Apocrypha and the *Genesis Apocryphon* in the scrolls from Qumran): the prophetic voice continued, but in a different key. Instead of using the language of direct inspiration, vision became the principal guide into the divine world. A growing dedication to the guidance of seers was about to reshape the literary theological terrain of Israel, producing a new genre.

Apocalyptic literature anticipates a final apocalypse ("disclosure"), when God himself will bring justice to Israel and all the nations in an ultimate judgment that will include them all. The final chapter of Zechariah (Zech 14) as well as additional material in the book of Isaiah (Isa 56—66) illustrate this development. The full emergence of apocalyptic literature occurred in an environment of persecution and resistance. One of Alexander's successors, Antiochus IV Epiphanes, claimed the temple for Hellenism in 167 B.C.E. by offering swine (a delicacy as far as Zeus was concerned) on the altar. The response to that act and the severe repression that accompanied it was the Maccabean revolt, the most militarily successful movement in the history of Israel (see 1 Macc and 2 Macc).

The book of Daniel characterizes apocalyptic, in its attribution to a sage from the past, interpretation of dreams, visions, and omens, an emphasis on supernatural beings such as angels, a tendency toward dualism between good and evil, and the dividing up of time into epochs or periods. This literature is also concerned with the future, as well as describing the past and present with the help of imagery and symbolism drawn from mythological literature. Daniel 7 presents a vision seen by Daniel in which there is a battle between beasts whose description draws upon the mythic images of the chaos that preceded creation. Its climax is the coming of "one like a son of man," to whom dominion, glory, and kingship are given. Daniel is unusual in the Hebrew Bible in being composed in two languages (Ezra also containing some letters written in Aramaic). Daniel begins in Hebrew (1:1—2:4a) but soon has a long section in Aramaic (2:4b—7:28), which includes the well-known stories and the strikingly different chapter 7. The remainder of the book is in Hebrew again. Aramaic had become the lingua franca of the Near East with the rise of the Persian Empire; Daniel's partial composition in that language probably reflects its popular appeal.

Although the revolt of the Maccabees enjoyed apocalyptically motivated support, the members of the Maccabean dynasty proved no less ambitious than their Davidic predecessors. They attempted to arrogate the powers of kingship and priesthood to themselves and earned the contempt of many apocalyptists, priests, scribes, and Wisdom teachers. So the victory that might have brought unity in fact resulted in further factionalism. The Essenes of Qumran combined the interests of priests and apocalyptists, while other apocalyptic movements were more purely literary. The Pharisees maintained a loyalty to the Mosaic traditions of Yahweh, but in an oral form (to steer clear of the control of scribes). Meanwhile, diehard zealots yearned for the days of the Maccabees, and the Wisdom school thrived in the Greek speaking Diaspora. In the midst of such conflict, it was easy for the Romans to assert their control over Jerusalem (in 63 B.C.E.) and the entire kingdom of the Maccabees, handing it over to Herod the Great and his family.

The New Testament: Letters, Gospels, and Catholic Writings. Paul was the single most important figure in spreading the movement that began with Jesus and came to be known as Christianity to the wider Roman world. His influence was largely literary (and postmortem). During antiquity, definite types of letters emerged as literary forms, including the argumentative, the deliberative (or advisory), and the commendatory. Although Paul's genuine letters (1 Thess, Gal, 1 Cor, 2 Cor, Rom, Philm) are predominantly deliberative, they skillfully weave in the other types, as well. Near the end of Paul's life, the influence of his disciple Timothy became increasingly obvious, and the letters more commendatory (in Phil, Col, Eph). Later imitations of Paul's work aim to make a dogmatic impact (the Pastoral Epistle [1 Tim, 2 Tim, Titus], 2 Thess, Heb.).

In the Book of Acts Paul also features as a central figure, although there are crucial difference between what he says or implies in his letters and what is said about him in Acts. Yet Acts does preserve valuable information about Paul's career and the strategy of other apostles and leaders to bring Jesus's message to the Mediterranean basin.

Although Paul's primary concern is Jesus's redefining of the covenant people, the Hellenistic influence on him is apparent in both the literary structure of his writing and in several characteristic aspects of his thought. When Paul describes what the Spirit produces in the moral life of the believer (Gal 5:22), he begins with qualities that are based in the biblical tradition: love, joy, and peace. But he then shifts to terms that come out of Stoic ethics: patience, kindness, goodness, faithfulness, gentleness, and self-control. The argument of the letter to the Romans builds on the assumption that, just as Jews have the law of Moses given to them by God, so the gentiles have the law within (Rom 2:14–16), what Stoics would call the law of nature, which provides them with norms by which they should live. He goes on to show that both Jews and gentiles disobey the law they have received in a manner consonant with Stoicism. Far from finding any conflict between his convictions as a devout Jew and the insights he has gained from pagan culture, Paul draws on both to make his arguments.

Similarly, Paul's style in his letters shows affinities with Jewish modes of interpretation of scripture, while at the same time he also utilizes the rhetorical style of his Greco-Roman contemporaries. He poses, for example, questions that would be raised by his opponents and then goes on to answer them—a method of argument characteristic of Hellenistic culture. Paul's cultural mix in background and outlook helps explain his effectiveness in reaching out to a wide gentile audience. As is evident from his letters, he was articulate—even eloquent—in Greek, although he always eschewed the kind of classical allusions of a writer (such as Philo) who had more thoroughly embraced Hellenistic culture.

After periodic revolts, the national Jewish war against Rome was too much for the patience of the Empire, and Titus burned Jerusalem and the temple in 70 C.E. In a single act, he destroyed the power base of the priests, just as he exterminated the Essenes. Jews in the Diaspora continued to cherish Wisdom, but increasingly they found their loyalties divided between the traditionalism of the Pharisees and the apocalyptic fervor of groups such as the sect called the Christians. Jesus's followers developed—like the Pharisees, their principal competitors in the Diaspora as well as in Israel—their own oral traditions to meet the crisis of the Temple's destruction with the promise of a messiah who would at long last bring the final Israel to earth.

Just as the Pentateuch can only be appreciated by means of a familiarity with its sources, so the different cycles of tradition within the Gospels need to be recognized. They were developed by the most important teachers within earliest Christianity: Peter, James (Jesus's brother), the select group of twelve apostles who appear to have compiled Jesus's sayings (as a rabbi's teaching would be collected in a Mishnah), Mary Magdalene, and Barnabas (a Levite from Cyprus and Paul's sometime companion). Paul's relationship to this considerable establishment of power is also important to assess. Yet all the while those developments were unfolding (until their climax in the Revelation of John), all these Christian teachers were shadow boxing with their Pharisaic contemporaries, who were shaping Rabbinic Judaism during just the period when the New Testament took shape.

The Gospels are a unique form of literature, which emerged as a result of Jesus's own teaching and the movement that he inspired. The word in Greek, *euanggelion*, traditionally rendered "gospel" in English, literally means "good news," but that translation is too generic to do justice to how this term was used originally. The Greek version of the scriptures of Israel shows that, contextually, the issue was good news in the context of battle, so the word refers to a message or announcement of victory. In the Aramaic of Jesus's time, *besorta'*—which corresponds to *euanggelion*—referred to such a message of victory. In the book of Isaiah in its Aramaic version (the Targum), for example, the verbal form *basar* is used to speak of the tidings of God's final triumph (Isa 52:7), while the noun refers to the message of the prophet who speaks that promise (Isa 53:1).

No Gospel is simply a copy of another; rather, each represents the choices among varying traditions, written and/or oral, and the development of those traditions that had taken place in a given locality. Although a consensus is emerging in regard to the cities in which each Gospel arose, their origins are a matter of inference, based upon clues in the texts themselves and later traditions of the Church. Similarly, the actual authors of each Gospel are unknown. Who they were, where they worked, and what the purpose of their writing was, are all matters that must be inferred from the texts themselves.

These writings are so distinctive that the term "gospel," originally an Aramaic term for a prophetic announcement of God's victory, came to be applied to them as an appropriate title—and a new genre of literature. In the case of the Synoptic Gospels, the purpose appears to have been to prepare converts for baptism, while John develops a homiletic approach, on the basis of established familiarity with the new faith.

The second-century teacher Justin Martyr referred to the Gospels today included in the New Testament as "memoirs of the apostles" (*Apology* 66.3). By his time, a powerful new concept had become current among the followers of Jesus: they believed that God directly addressed the church at large, not only individual congregations, by means of what the apostles said in their writings, and that the apostolic message concerned the ultimate fate of all humanity and the end of the world as we know it.

This conviction insisted that the words of the apostles were universal, or "catholic" (*katholikos*) in the language of the time, and that they included apocalyptic truth. In this literature the community of God's people is typically called upon to accept suffering and even martyrdom during the present period of cosmic struggle, but they are given assurance that they will be vindicated and will enjoy new life in the age to come. The eschatological expectations of Christianity varied, but a commitment to eschatology, and to the conviction that the apostolic message addressed the Church as a whole, not merely particular localities, remained constant factors.

The dating of the individual documents that voice this consensus is still open to discussion, and several of them found their way among the books accepted in the New Testament only late and with difficulty. Seven of them (Jas, 1 Pet, 2 Pet, 1 John, 2 John, 3 John, and Jude) are known as the Catholic Epistles, since they address Christians beyond particular communities. Because they are not communications with specific communities, and are for the most part pseudonymous, these writings stretch the genre of letter into that of epistolary instruction. In addition, other works produced after the destruction of the Temple in 70 C.E. (Mark 13; Matt 24–25; Luke 21; 2 Thess; Acts; and Rev) show how a catholic consensus emerged out of apocalyptic convictions.

The first apocalypse written in Jesus's name appears in Mark 13, Matthew 24—25, and Luke 21. Unlike his other teachings in the Synoptic Gospels, this "Little Apocalypse" (as it is called) is arranged as a continuous discourse, a carefully crafted speech. It comes complete with notes to the reader, in the form of a reference to the book of Daniel; the "abomination of desolation" in the Little Apocalypse alludes to the destruction of the temple (Mark 13:14; Matt 24:15; Luke 21:20; cf. Dan 11:31; 12:11). The literary structure of the discourse is so unlike the usual form of Jesus's teaching, it is generally regarded as a speech synthesized from elements of Jesus's sayings together with references to Daniel. Jesus's teaching could be collected under various genres of statement, for example, the parable, the aphorism, the prophetic announcement, and the command. Groupings of these collections are evident in the Gospels, but the Little Apocalypse is unusual for its extent and cohesion. Unlike the book of Daniel, however, the Little Apocalypse steps back from calculating a calendar of the end time. It seems to move confidently in that direction, with its account of disaster and war, and the coming of the Son of Man. But then comes the warning, "But concerning that day and hour no one knows, neither the angels in heaven nor the son, except the Father" (Mark 13:32; cf. Matt 24:36; Acts 1:7).

The Acts of the Apostles is composed as a companion volume to the Gospel according to Luke. Its presentation precisely explains its purpose, and its difference in genre from the Gospel. Although the author is the same in Luke and in Acts, the genres differ. Where Gospel aims to instruct in the basics of Christianity (Luke 1:4), Acts is composed in the genre of an exemplary history (such as 2 Macc) for believers. The risen Jesus here says to his apostles:

"It is not for you to know the periods or times that the Father set by his authority, but you shall receive power when the Holy Spirit comes upon you and you shall be my witnesses both in Jerusalem and in Judaea, and in Samaria and until the end of the earth" (Acts 1:7–8). Both in what it negates and in what it asserts, this statement represents an overture to the entire program of Acts. The power of apocalypse is here calibrated, away from knowing the end and toward witnessing by the power of the Spirit until the end.

The Revelation of John is a trenchantly visionary work that takes the genre of apocalypse to a new level. It presents itself as a communication of precise visions and a guide to explain how they can be understood. Such features also appear, of course, in works such as Ezekiel, Zechariah, Daniel, and the Little Apocalypse. In the case of the Revelation, however, visions become the staple content of the whole, mediated through various means. The initial "letters" to the seven churches are so general as to be catholic, and are presented as messages from heaven. The book introduces its core with the opening of a gate or door in heaven (Rev 4:1), which invites the seer to be shown the mysteries that surround the throne of God in the following chapters. The divine throne had long featured in prophetic literature before John wrote his apocalypse. Visionary narratives include those of Moses (Exod 24:9–11), Isaiah (6:1–4), Ezekiel (1:4–28) Zechariah (3:1–9), and Daniel (7:9–14), all of which find citations or allusions in the Revelation to John. Detailed though those visions often are, in its extent and depth, the Revelation represents a conscious synthesis and extension of their imagery.

[*See also* Canon of the Bible; Dead Sea Scrolls; Folklore and Biblical Interpretation; *and* Mythology and Biblical Interpretation.]

BIBLIOGRAPHY

Akenson, Donald Harman. *Saint Saul: A Skeleton Key to the Historical Jesus.* Oxford: Oxford University Press, 2000.

Alter, Robert. *The Art of Biblical Poetry.* New York: Basic Books, 1985.

Anderson, Bernard W. *Understanding the Old Testament,* 5th ed. Englewood Cliffs, N.J.: Prentice-Hall, 2007.

Brown, Raymond E. *An Introduction to the New Testament:* The Anchor Bible Reference Library. New York: Doubleday, 1997.

Chilton, Bruce, general ed. *The Cambridge Companion to the Bible.* 2d ed., with contributions from Howard Clark Kee, Eric M. Meyers, John Rogerson, Amy-Jill Levine, and Anthony J. Saldarini. Cambridge, UK: Cambridge University Press, 2008.

Clements, R. E., ed. *The World of Ancient Israel: Sociological, Anthropological and Political Perspectives.* Cambridge, UK: Cambridge University Press, 1989.

Collins, Adela Yarbro. *Is Mark's Gospel a Life of Jesus? The Question of Genre.* Milwaukee: Marquette University Press, 1990.

Coogan, M. D. *The Old Testament: A Historical and Literary Introduction to the Hebrew Scriptures.* New York: Oxford University Press, 2006.

Gottwald, Norman K. *The Hebrew Bible: A Socio-literary Introduction.* Philadelphia: Fortress, 1985.

Hallo, William W. ed., *The Context of Scripture.* 3 vols. Leiden: Brill, 1997–2002.

Lang, Bernhard. *The Hebrew God: Portrait of an Ancient Deity.* New Haven, Conn.: Yale University Press, 2002.

Metzger, Bruce M. *The Canon of the New Testament: Its Origin, Development, and Significance.* Oxford: Clarendon Press, 1987.

Nicholas, William C., Jr., *I Saw the World End: An Introduction to the Bible's Apocalyptic Literature.* New York: Paulist Press, 2007.

Puig i Tàrrech, Armand. *Jesus: A Biography.* Waco, Tex.: Baylor University Press, 2011.

Riesner, Rainer. *Paul's Early Period: Chronology, Mission Strategy, Theology.* Translated by D. Stott. Grand Rapids, Mich.: Eerdmans, 1998.

Smith, Mark. *The Early History of God: Yahweh and the Other Deities in Ancient Israel.* 2d. ed. Grand Rapids, Mich.: Eerdmans, 2002.

Stowers, Stanley K. *Letter Writing in Greco-Roman Antiquity.* Philadelphia: Westminster, 1986.

Talbert, Charles H. *What is a Gospel? The Genre of the Canonical Gospels.* Philadelphia: Fortress, 1977.

VanderKam, James C. and William Adler, eds. *The Jewish Apocalyptic Heritage in Early Christianity.* Compendia rerum Iudaicarum ad Novum Testamentum, Section 3, Jewish Traditions in Early Christian Literature 4. Assen: Van Gorcum; Minneapolis: Fortress, 1996.

Bruce Chilton

GEOGRAPHY AND TOPOGRAPHY IN BIBLICAL INTERPRETATION

"Students of the Bible desire to see a background and to feel an atmosphere; to discover from 'the lie of the land' why the history took certain lines and the prophecy and gospel were expressed in certain styles." So says the preface to the first edition of George Adam Smith's *The Historical Geography of the Holy Land* (see later). These and other aspects of geography and topography, and some issues relating to their significance for biblical interpretation, will be the focus of this article. Matters such as climate and flora and fauna are, of course, important, but for reasons of space what follows will concentrate on the physical geography. Only brief mention can be made of the significance of the availability of water; settlement was possible close to water sources or in areas where water storage and irrigation were possible. Travel routes were governed by the contours of the land and the presence of valleys. Towns might develop where there was good access to roads, or to guard strategic points such as crossroads or passes; for example the significance of Megiddo owed much to its location (2 Kgs 23:29; Rev 16:16).

The attempt to understand the Bible better by relating its contents to their geographical setting in the southern Levant in particular, and in the wider ancient Near Eastern and East Mediterranean milieu, is no recent phenomenon. It was for this reason that Jerome, at the end of the fourth or early fifth century C.E., translated into Latin (under the title *Liber de situ et nominibus locorum hebraicorum*) the Greek *Onomasticon*, compiled by the historian Eusebius early in the fourth century C.E. The rather different needs of early pilgrims, wishing to walk "in the footsteps of Jesus," and Crusaders, wishing to free holy places, kept alive an interest in such locations, and accounts of their travels have been preserved.

The nineteenth century witnessed a notable expansion of interest. A significant contribution was made by Edward Robinson's publication of the accounts of his travels in Palestine and neighboring regions in 1838 and in 1852. The establishment of the Palestine Exploration Fund in 1865 enabled a major development in the study of the topography of the southern Levant. In 1871, under its auspices, Captains Kitchener and Conder of the Royal Engineers were sent to survey the land, and gather geographical, archaeological, and natural-historical data relevant to the Bible. They surveyed the region to the west of the Jordan and recorded the names of many ancient sites, describing such physical remains as were visible, and attempting to identify them with sites mentioned in the Bible. Then, in 1894, came the landmark (in more senses than one) publication of George Adam Smith's classic *The Historical Geography of the Holy Land.* In subsequent years other works on geography, and numerous atlases of the Bible have appeared, and it has become commonplace for Bibles to include a set of maps to aid the reader.

The Settings of Stories, Songs, and Speeches. Stories are often set in a particular location. In some works of fiction, where the setting too is entirely imaginary, a map is provided to help the readers to follow the story. Those who write "historical" novels conduct research in order to provide an accurate geographical setting, again perhaps with a map, even if the actual contents are primarily fictional. Many legends are given geographical settings, although their precise locations are the subject of argument: Robin Hood in Sherwood Forest, King Arthur at Camelot. Historiographers who recount the stories of those they understand as real people, and the events associated with them, often do so with reference to the geographical settings of the activities described. Therefore it is important for the readers of stories to have an awareness of their geographical setting. Even in the context of myth, where the term "geographical" may not be strictly accurate, gods live on mountains, in the sea, in the underworld, and so forth, and their activities take them from place to place. If this is true of stories in general, it is certainly true of those in the Bible, and it is important to stress that the provision of a geographical setting, or even a map, is not in itself an indication of historicity. But they provide a context in which a story is to be read, and it is likely that the writers provided such information to help the reader or hearer to understand. The point also needs to be made that not all sites can be identified with certainty, as the number of question marks on the maps in some atlases indicates, for example in charting the supposed route of the Exodus.

The setting of stories in particular locations is not simply to enable the reader to follow the movement of the characters, though this can certainly aid interpretation. However, it can also be fraught with difficulties. Any attempt to follow the route of the Exodus soon runs into problems, such as where Moses and his followers were envisaged as having crossed the "sea," and which sea it was (the "Red Sea" as was traditionally understood, or the "Reed Sea," a more accurate translation of the Hebrew phrase), and the fact that most of the places mentioned on their journey (including Mount Sinai) cannot be located with certainty. (The identification of biblical Mount Sinai with Jebel Musa, in the southern part of what is now known as the Sinai Peninsula, can only be traced back with certainty to the fourth century C.E. Some have suggested alternative locations, for example on the basis of the assumption that the phenomena described in Exodus 19:16–19 imply that the mountain was a volcano and so must have been in a region of volcanic activity. But it is more likely that the phenomena are those related to a theophany and hence need not be associated with an active volcano. Perhaps those who passed on the story of the Exodus and the journey through the wilderness were not so much concerned to provide an itinerary as to underline the length and tortuous nature of the wanderings and the importance for later generations of an encounter with God in such circumstances. It may be more straightforward (though not entirely without problems) to trace the approximate routes of Paul's missionary journeys on the basis of information in Acts and the Epistles, and thereby gain a better understanding of aspects of the early spread of Christianity.

It is not simply a matter of routes. A frequently cited instance is the parable of the Good Samaritan (Luke 10:29–37), where knowledge of the terrain through which the road from Jerusalem to Jericho passes adds significantly to the appreciation of the story. And this does not only apply to narratives. The beginning of the Book of Amos (Amos 1—2) becomes much more meaningful when read with an awareness of the geographical locations of the places mentioned. The prophet's declaration of God's judgment begins with places some distance away—Damascus, Gaza, and Tyre—moves closer with its references to the Transjordanian kingdoms of Edom, Ammon, and Moab, and then closer still to the southern neighbor Judah. Eventually, and inexorably, the judgment reaches Israel itself. To stay with the Book of Amos, the question, "Do two walk together unless they have made an appointment?" (Amos 3:2) implies the perspective of someone used to the countryside; in towns, people would often meet without appointment. And Amos's encounter with the priest Amaziah at Bethel takes on additional meaning when it is remembered that a southerner from Judah has crossed the border into the northern kingdom, Israel, and this Judahite sheep-breeder is daring to challenge the Israelite royal court and royal sanctuary.

Moving to poetry, to the person who knows Jerusalem with its temple, royal buildings, and fortifications, the psalmists' songs of Zion become a vehicle of praise to the God who dwells there. No wonder those geographically removed, "by the rivers of Babylon" (Ps 137:1), wept when required to sing such a song. Understanding their setting helps the reader to appreciate their grief. One of the interpretative issues arising from Psalms 42—43 is the nature of the psalmist's distress and how the apparent geographical allusions are to be understood. Does Psalm 42:6 refer to the region of Mount Hermon and the sources of the Jordan, suggesting that the psalmist is physically far removed from Jerusalem and its longed-for temple worship and great festivals? Or is it perhaps that the impossibility of attendance at worship (perhaps because of uncleanness through sickness or some crime having been committed) is being likened to being geographically cut off? Either way, a geographical awareness aids interpretation.

Scriptural Settings. It is not necessary to read many pages of the Bible before geography is encountered. After the great opening account of God's creative activity at the very beginning of Genesis there is a rather more down-to-earth creation story that is provided with what can appropriately be called a geographical setting. The writer locates the story in a type of place (a garden), in a region that has a name (Eden), and which, from the perspective of the storyteller, is in the east (Gen 2:8). Nowadays very few would seek to locate Eden on a world map, but it is clear that the story does reflect a geographical interest, even if that is not its main concern, though it has been suggested that the writer may be indicating an awareness of the development of civilization further to the east. There is also a geographical interest in the description of the river that flowed out of Eden, its four "branches," and where they flowed (Gen 2:10–14). To this day, commentators on Genesis will use the clues provided to try to identify the actual rivers they believe the writer has in mind. At the other end of the Christian Bible, the Book of Revelation, after a brief introduction, witnesses a geographical interest in addressing the seven churches of Asia, with their named locations (Ephesus, Smyrna, Pergamum, Thyatira, Sardis, Philadelphia, and Laodicea). This helps the reader to appreciate the extent of the area being addressed and so also the spread of the church in Asia Minor. But details are also potentially important. The description of the church at Laodicea as being lukewarm, and neither cold not hot (Rev 3:15–16) is thought to allude to the fact that neighboring cities had hot springs (Hierapolis to the north) and cold springs (Colossae to the south). Later there is a description of the New Jerusalem (Rev 21:10—22:5)—a place which could not be located on a map, but an awareness of what Jerusalem was actually like would enhance the realization of how different the New Jerusalem would be.

In between these biblical "bookends" is material of a great variety of genres and types of setting. Soon after the account of the garden of Eden, the stories are given a geographical setting, which can more easily be related to what is known of the ancient world, for example Abraham's epic journey from Ur to Canaan. That those who passed on the story of Abraham saw geography as relevant to their purpose is indicated in a number of ways. Abraham's home, and the starting point of his journey, is identified as Ur "of the Chaldeans" (Gen 11:31), an anachronistic designation, which was probably intended to convey geographical rather than ethnic information, making it clear to later readers that this city of Ur was located in southern Mesopotamia. The passing reference to the fact that the journey was via Haran, where they settled for a while, tells the reader with a knowledge of geography that they followed the River Euphrates in a north-westerly direction before heading south, as would have been necessary for those with flocks and herds, travelling round much of what was to become known as the Fertile Crescent. But when the story becomes more focussed on Abraham's travels within Canaan, the writer is at pains to tell the reader that Abraham "journeyed on by stages towards the Negeb" (Gen 3:9) and to mention several of the stopping places where he built altars.

This prompts the question of the extent to which stories such as this are in any sense "historical" in that they describe actual events and real people. The issue has been and continues to be much debated. Of course the answer will vary depending on the particular story. But it may be less important or appropriate to ask whether something happened, than to consider whether a story is given a real geographical setting and, if so, whether it is possible to use a knowledge of geography and topography to illuminate the story and understand more about why it was told. The detailing of Abraham's altar-building activities may be important for bringing certain sites into the ambit of Israel and its sanctuaries (see later on Aetiology and Etymology). The story of Abraham's apparent willingness to sacrifice Isaac (Gen 22:1–14) is often held up as an example of obedience. But what greater example of obedience could there be than that of an Abraham who was willing to travel the length of the known world in response to God's call! Here we are perhaps beginning to think of theological geography, something to be further considered later.

It has been suggested that, if a story has preserved accurate information about the geographical context in which it is set, surely it may have preserved accurately the details of the people about whom and the events about which the stories are told. Given that that is sometimes the case, then surely the Bible can be seen as a reliable historical source. This is to overlook the fact that different types of material can be given geographical settings. Nevertheless it can be helpful for the reader to have an awareness of the world in which the biblical narratives are set—the context against which the text is to be read.

Ancient Mapping. A number of factors need to be taken into account when considering apparently geographical statements in the Bible, not least that of the geographical awareness of those who made the statements and the extent to which the intention was to pass on information which was purely geographical. So it will be appropriate to look for evidence of geographical awareness and to note some issues which arise from such evidence as there is.

Unlike some modern story tellers, the biblical writers did not supply maps to accompany or illustrate the stories they told. But two extra-biblical examples can appropriately be noted. There is in the British Museum an intriguing little clay tablet, dating from about 600 B.C.E., which contains a diagram which might be termed a "map," purporting to depict the world as then known. At the center is the city of Babylon on the River Euphrates; the Persian Gulf is shown as a river encircling the land, and beyond it are mysterious places far distant from Babylon. The "map" was intended to illustrate an account of the military campaigns of king Sargon of Akkad in the latter half of the third millennium B.C.E. Dating from significantly later, but still relatively early, is the Madaba Map, so called because it was discovered toward the end of the nineteenth century, in a Byzantine Church at Madaba in Transjordan, probably dating from the sixth century C.E. The mosaic floor of this church represents a relatively early attempt to map the lands of the Bible. Of particular interest is the fact that the map includes a representation of the city of Jerusalem, and shows several details of the city as it was at the time, including the Church of the Holy Sepulchre and other churches, streets lined with columns, and the city's walls and gates. The "map" includes a number of biblical quotations, and it has made a significant contribution to our knowledge of the topography of the region. Such early maps are a rarity, but they do point to a geographical awareness that perhaps goes beyond a concern merely to locate places, in that they indicate the special status of Babylon and Jerusalem.

The Madaba Map also alerts us to the issue of the geographical perspective of ancient sources, in that it has an east-west orientation. It is all too easy for the modern reader to assume the customary north-south perspective. The significance of this can be illustrated with reference to discussions as to whether Qumran, the site associated with the Dead Sea Scrolls, was an Essene community. Pliny the Elder (23/24–79 C.E.), in Book V of his work *Natural History*, says that "below the Essenes was the town of Engedi." A modern reader, assuming a north-south orientation, might naturally read this statement as implying that Engedi, on the shore of the Dead Sea, lay to the south of the Essene settlement. This would be true if the reference is to Qumran. But Pliny's words *could* be understood as locating the Essene settlement in the hills above Engedi.

Maps in Words. Although the biblical writers have not left us maps in the sense of plans or diagrams, there are a number of passages which might be said to present verbal maps. The so-called "Table of the Nations" in Genesis 10 purports to be a list of the descendants of the sons of Noah after the flood. But what soon emerges is that many of the individuals named are actually nations or peoples, for example the immediate descendants of Ham are listed as Cush, Egypt, Put, and Canaan (Gen 10:6). There is sometimes an indication of where they lived (for example in vv. 19 and 30), and the chapter ends with the statement: "These are the families of Noah's sons, according to their genealogies, in their nations; and from these the nations spread abroad on the earth after the flood" (Gen 10:32). The whole chapter represents an attempt to "map" the ancient world, thereby providing the context in which the stories of Abraham and his descendants are about to be set.

A rather different type of verbal map is to be found in the book of Joshua, whose opening chapters recount stories such as that of the battle of Jericho but much of whose latter part, prior to Joshua's farewell discourses, comprises lists, particularly of towns and of boundaries. These are presented as the allocations of land to the various tribes after the land had been captured. The origins of these lists are uncertain, but it is likely that they reflect some ancient attempt to define boundaries and territorial possessions. They also show that the biblical narrators, or those responsible for the sources upon which they may have been drawing, were aware of how parts of the land related to others geographically. But here again the significance goes beyond the delineation of territories and the location of towns. Above all, in their canonical context, they now serve a theological function in that they show how God's promise to Abraham and his descendants (that they would have a land in which to dwell) was fulfilled. Here were the details of the land whose original possession proved that God's promises had been fulfilled. And perhaps they served as a word of hope to later generations who had lost the land; this was what they might regain if only they were obedient like Abraham (and Joshua).

Very different again is the verbal map presented at the end of the book of Ezekiel. Chapter 48 envisages a future land of Israel, restored to its maximum extent after the successive destructions of the northern kingdom (Israel) by the Assyrians and the southern kingdom (Judah) by the Babylonians, and the subsequent exile in Babylon. The sections of the land are arranged in a highly schematic fashion. The tribes are allocated successive latitudinal ("from the east side to the west") swathes of land, from Dan in the north to Gad in the south. Between the territories allotted to Judah and Benjamin there is to be a "sacred" or "holy" portion, set apart from the rest of the land. And at the very heart of this would lie the Temple. The previous chapter has made a remarkable claim about the future Temple (Ezek 47:1–12). From its threshold there would flow a river whose waters would gradually get deeper and deeper as they flowed eastwards until they reached the Dead Sea, where they would give life to its waters, enabling fish to live there and plant life to flourish around its shores. An awareness of the actual geography, in particular the nature of the Dead Sea, enables the reader to understand the significance of the bold theological claim being made in these chapters. God's temple in Jerusalem will be at the heart of God's land and be a source of life in the most remarkable way, made possible by the sort of God who can bring to life a whole valley of dry bones (Ezek 37:1–14).

Theological Geography. The clear theological significance of Ezekiel's presentation of a restored Israel raises the fact that there are many biblical statements and descriptions that purport to be geographical or topographical but whose primary purpose is in fact theological. Mention has already been made of God's promise to Abraham. The wording of that promise, which included the statement that to his descendants would be given territory stretching from the Nile to the Euphrates (Gen 15:18) should be read as a piece of hyperbole, an expression of the idea of a "Promised Land" akin to the type of picture presented by Ezekiel.

In the shaping of the accounts of the life of Jesus in the Gospel narratives, some apparently geographical indications may have a greater theological significance. In Mark, all of Jesus's early ministry is set in Galilee. The pivotal point, halfway through Mark's account, is Peter's declaration that Jesus is the Messiah (Mark 8:27–30). This incident is located in Caesarea Philippi, in the far northernmost part of the land. Thereafter Jesus begins his journey from the remotest point to the religious heart of the land, Jerusalem, and to his death. Luke's Gospel too presents the life of Jesus as a journey on which the disciples follow their master, an idea, which accords with the Lucan description of Christianity as "the Way," mentioned a number of times in the Acts of the Apostles (Acts 9:2; 19:9, 23; 24:14, 22).

An awareness of the actual geography and topography enables some apparently geographical statements about Jerusalem, and Mount Zion in particular, to be appreciated as theological. Although Psalm 46 does not actually name Jerusalem, it is probably implied by "city of God" in verse 4. Here the city is associated with a river with streams. The small stream emerging from the Gihon spring hardly fits this description. This raises the possibility that the depiction may owe something to the tradition of the river, which flowed out of the Garden of Eden and split into four branches, one of which is actually named as Gihon (Gen 2:10–14). Jerusalem is perhaps being likened in some way to Eden. In Psalm 48:1–3, reference is made to Zion, but appears to suggest (though translations vary) that Zion was located "in the far north" (so NRSV). But this does not make sense geographically. The Hebrew word for "north" (*ṣāpôn*) may derive from the name of Mount Zaphon (modern Jebel el-Aqra in Syria) which, according the texts from Ras Shamra, (ancient Ugarit, a city on the coast of modern Syria, whose Late Bronze Age texts provide perhaps the best source of evidence we have of the religious beliefs of the Canaanites), was the dwelling place of the gods and where Baal had his palace. The psalmist is probably not giving us geographical information about the location of Mount Zion, but claiming it as, or likening it to, the divine abode. The oracle preserved in Isaiah 2:2 and Micah 4:1, albeit speaking about the future, envisages "the mountain of the LORD's house" (i.e., Zion) as becoming "the highest of the mountains" and "raised above the hills." Those familiar with the topography of Jerusalem will realize that Zion is in fact overlooked by higher hills such as Mount Scopus and the Mount of Olives. But what is envisaged is not a geographical upheaval but a theological transformation.

Another possible, though rather more speculative, example of a type of theological geography is perhaps to be found in the way some of the Gospel writers, Matthew in particular, tell the story of the life of Jesus in such a way as to demonstrate that what had come to be regarded as messianic prophecies had been fulfilled. So Jesus's birth had to be presented as, or else stressed as being, in Bethlehem (rather than Nazareth) so that the prophecy of Micah could be seen to have been fulfilled (Mic 5:2; compare Matt 2:6). It was necessary for Matthew to present Jesus as having been taken to Egypt. "This was to fulfill what had been spoken by the Lord through the prophet, 'Out of Egypt I have called my son'" (Matt 2:15; compare Hos 11:1 where the allusion is reasonably certainly to Israel and the Exodus tradition). Such statements become claims about Jesus's messiahship.

The Navel of the Earth? In the context of theological geography, mention should also be made of the possibility that, within the Bible, there are a few hints at a belief that Israel, or some location in Israel—perhaps Jerusalem—was the "navel" or very center of the world. In the Book of Ezekiel, the Israelites are described as those "who live at the center of the earth" (Ezek 38:12). The Hebrew word translated "center" here is *ṭabbûr*, and in the Greek translation, the Septuagint, the word used is *omphalos*, i.e., "navel." Elsewhere in the book of Ezekiel, Jerusalem is claimed to have been placed "in the center of the nations" (Ezek 5:5), and this idea is preserved in some later sources (for example, in the book of *Jubilees* 8:19). The Jewish historian Josephus (first century C.E.) says of Jerusalem in his *Jewish War* Book III, that "some have quite appropriately called her the navel of the country." (It is noteworthy that the placing of Jerusalem at the center persisted in later mapmaking; see for example the famous medieval *Mappa Mundi* in Hereford Cathedral, thought to date from about 1300 C.E.)

Geographical Aetiology and Etymology. Reference was made earlier to the fact that, in the account of Abraham's travels in Genesis 12, the text notes several of the stopping places where he built altars, including Shechem. Archaeology suggests that the sanctuary at Shechem dates back to the Middle Bronze Age and that it was a feature of the Late Bronze Age city. But Genesis 12:6–7 relates that God appeared there to Abraham, who marked the theophany by erecting an altar. This raises another probable feature of a number of biblical stories, not unrelated to the idea of theological geography. They seem to have been preserved principally to explain why a particular place was a holy place, and (in some instances) why it was given its particular name. A good example of a story, which combines both of those elements, and perhaps adds another, is that of Jacob at Bethel (Gen 28:10–22). It accounts for why Bethel was an Israelite holy place, by explaining that God had revealed himself there to the ancestor Jacob/Israel. It explains the place's name as originating from Jacob's realization that it was "none other than the house of God;" in Hebrew, Bethel means "house of God," but it is likely that the name actually reflects the fact that originally it was a temple of El, the head of the Canaanite pantheon. The story may also explain a feature of the sanctuary at Bethel, a standing stone—Jacob's so-called pillow. So the example of Bethel suggests that in part the purpose may be to bring much older sanctuaries into the sphere of Israelite worship. But above all the place was holy because God had appeared there. Such stories come into the category of aetiology.

Aetiologies are stories that explain how something came to be as it was, or (in the case of etymological aetiologies) why someone, somewhere, or something was given a particular name. There are many such in the Bible, though not all have any geographical or topographical association. However a number do relate to places or features. It used to be argued that the presence of an aetiological element almost automatically rendered a story unhistorical, but this not a necessary corollary. The story of how there came to be a temple in Jerusalem is of a somewhat different order from that of how there came to be a tower in Babel. But with many such stories the interpretation will see them primarily as attempts to provide an explanation for a feature of the landscape or a structure, and/or its name, and relate it to an incident or person of the sacred (or not-so-sacred) past.

The first half of the book of Joshua contains several such stories and it is not always clear whether they refer to some natural feature of the landscape or to a human-made structure. Joshua is said to have set up twelve stones at Gilgal, to mark the crossing of the Jordan (Josh 4:1–9). Here the story seems to be intended to explain two things: the presence of a stone circle, and why the place was so-called (Gilgal may mean "circle;" though there is a different explanation of the name in Joshua 5:9, connecting it with a verb meaning "to roll.") But what about the "great heap of stones" mentioned in Joshua 7:25—6, purporting to be those with which Achan was stoned? Are these natural or the result of human activity? Both accounts end with the type of phrase found in many aetiological stories, that the feature remains "to this day"—presumably an invitation to the reader to check the veracity of what has been claimed. In Joshua 5:2–7, the place name Gibeath-haaraloth ("hill of the foreskins") is explained by recalling how there Joshua had circumcised the sons of the generation that had come out of Egypt. A significant example of a double explanation of a place name is to be found in the story of the digging of the wells at Beersheba (Gen 21:22–34). To mark an agreement between Abraham and Abimelech confirming that Abraham had dug the wells, Abraham set aside *seven* lambs, and they swore an *oath*. The name Beersheba could mean "well of seven" or "well of an oath." The preservation of this story may have had another important aetiological function—that of establishing the ownership rights over an important oasis on the edge of the wilderness. A geographical awareness of the location of Beersheba helps to underline the significance of these traditions.

Geographical Perspectives. Much of the material in the Bible purports to give accounts of past events, of people, of what things they had said or what deeds they had done, and very often *where* they had said or done these things. This is particularly true of narrative material, but many other types of literature, such as prophetic oracles against foreign nations, or epistles written to new churches, may actually allude to or presuppose geographical settings and topographical knowledge. To appreciate the geographical and topographical perspectives of the ancient authors and the settings into which they placed their material is to give the interpreter a deeper understanding of the message these writers and thinkers sought to convey.

[*See also* Dead Sea Scrolls; Diachronic Interpretation; Greco-Roman Context; Historical Criticism, *subentry* Hebrew Bible; *and* Historical Criticism, *subentry* New Testament.]

BIBLIOGRAPHY

Aharoni, Yohanan. *The Land of the Bible: a Historical Geography*. London: Burns and Oates, 1967. Translated by A. F. Rainey from the Hebrew original, published 1962.

Baly, Denis. *Geography of the Bible*. Rev. ed. New York: Harper and Row, 1974 (first edition published in 1957). A compact version, *Basic Biblical Geography*, Philadelphia: Fortress was published in 1987.

Borowski, Oded. *Daily Life in Biblical Times*. Atlanta: Society of Biblical Literature, 2003.

Braybrooke, Marcus (Old Testament author) and James Harpur (New Testament author). *The Essential Atlas of the Bible*. London: SPCK, 1999.

Curtis, Adrian. *Oxford Bible Atlas*. 4th ed. Oxford: Oxford University Press, 2007 (hardback); 2009 (slightly revised paperback edition).

King, Philip J., and Lawrence E. Stager. *Life in Biblical Israel*. Louisville, Ky., and London: Westminster John Knox, 2001.

Pritchard, James B., ed. *The Times Atlas of the Bible*. London: Times Books, 1987.

Rogerson, John. *Atlas of the Bible*. Oxford: Phaidon, 1989.

Smith, George Adam. *The Historical Geography of the Holy Land*. London: Hodder and Stoughton, first published in 1891. This work was subsequently provided with supplementary notes, revised, and reprinted in numerous editions.

Stanley, Arthur Penrhyn. *Sinai and Palestine in Connection with their History*. London: John Murray, 1883. George Adam Smith makes a number of references to this earlier work.

Tishby, Ariel, ed. *Holy Land in Maps*. Jerusalem: Israel Museum, 2001. A fascinating collection of maps through the ages, from the Madaba Map to satellite images.

Adrian Curtis

GNOSTICISM AND GNOSTIC INTERPRETATION

Around the year 180 C.E., a Christian bishop, Irenaeus of Lyons, launched the following scathing attack against the interpretive practices of some fellow readers of scripture:

> As people would say, they attempt to braid ropes of sand. They try to adapt to their own sayings in a manner worthy of credence, either the Lord's parables, or the prophets' sayings, or the apostles' words, so that their fabrication might not appear to be without witness. They disregard the order and the connection of the Scriptures and . . . they disjoint the members of the Truth. They transfer passages and rearrange them; and, making one thing out of another, they deceive many by the badly composed phantasy of the Lord's words that they adapt. (*Against Heresies* 1.8.1, Unger and Dillon)

Who were these scriptural interpreters whose readings of the sacred texts amounted—in the bishop's view—to so many futile yet insidious attempts to braid ropes out of sand? Irenaeus is careful to distinguish the group he speaks about here (whom he dubs "Valentinians") from other sects, including the so-called "Gnostics" (*Against Heresies* 1.11.1). Yet he also grouped this diversity under a single category of error, "what is falsely called knowledge" (see 1 Tim 6:20). And until very recently, both modern Christian tradition and critical scholarship followed his lead, conjuring a single historical entity out of these and other groups of this period that were deemed heretical with historical hindsight—hence, "Gnosticism." In the process, there has often been a tendency to elide, ignore, or otherwise fail to analyze with sufficient precision a rich, variegated, and not easily reducible set of hermeneutical strategies that produced the kind of biblical interpretation Irenaeus so trenchantly dismissed.

Was There Such a Thing as "Gnosticism"? The term "Gnosticism" is not an ancient one. While early Christian writers made repeated reference to the Greek term for "knowledge" in various forms—the adjective *gnōstikos*, the noun *gnōsis*, and people who call themselves *gnōstikoi*—the birth of the term as an "-ism" is an early modern invention, coined by Henry More in the seventeenth century as part of a Protestant diatribe directed against Roman Catholics (Layton 1995). In this context, it was used as roughly equivalent to the phrase "the gnostic heresy" (*gnōstikē hairesis*), a formulation that can be found in early Christian texts (see *Against Heresies* 1.11.1; Pearson in Marjanen 2005). But does this mean that there actually *was* such a thing as a "Gnostic religion" in the ancient world, and if so, what sort of religious phenomenon was it? Was it a Christian sect, either one of the many varieties that existed in the tradition's earliest moments, or a later (and derivative) heresy? A pre-Christian or non-Christian entity, perhaps growing out of Hellenistic Judaism, concurrent (and in competition) with Christianity? A totally independent movement?

While these different possibilities have been increasingly debated by scholars during the nineteenth and twentieth centuries, the traditional definition of "Gnosticism" as a diffuse and internally diverse early Christian heresy has proven hard to shake. Along these lines, many modern historians have tended to delineate the movement typologically in terms of a common set of characteristics. These characteristics could vary, but often included belief in the power of esoteric knowledge (or *gnōsis*), a devaluation of the material world, a vigorous body-soul dualism, a deterministic soteriology, the idea of a divine element within (some) human beings, a docetic Christology, a tendency toward either radical asceticism or libertinism, and—perhaps most importantly for the subject matter at hand—the use of "subversive" exegetical techniques (Jonas 1963; Rudolph 1983).

Yet recent scholarship has increasingly questioned the adequacy of this sort of broad, typological definition. Whereas the characteristics described earlier had generally been gleaned from the writings of Irenaeus, Clement of Alexandria, Tertullian of Carthage, Hippolytus of Rome, and other early Christian heresiologists, the discovery of the Nag Hammadi codices in 1945 allowed scholars to read a wide swath of so-called "Gnostic" literature for themselves. What they discovered did not conform neatly to any discernible typology. Rather, the Nag Hammadi texts offered a window into a bewildering landscape of early Christian theological, philosophical, and exegetical diversity. In light of this diversity, some scholars have called into question the basic viability of "Gnosticism" as an analytical category. Michael Williams's work dismantles many of the standard classifications used to define the term through a careful examination of the extant primary sources. He argues instead for classifying Nag Hammadi and related early Christian texts through the use of more precise typological identifiers—such as, for example, the presence of an inferior "demiurgical" creator god in interpretations of the Genesis narrative (Williams 1996). Karen King attacks the usefulness of "Gnosticism" from a different angle, showing the degree to which historically it has been—and continues to be—a production of normative Christian discourses of orthodoxy and heresy. The term is thus rendered incoherent once it has been ostensibly removed from these discourses to function as a stand-alone category (King 2003).

Other scholars continue to see a usefulness to the term. While few if any experts in the literature would still argue for "Gnosticism" as an all-inclusive category covering the entire Nag Hammadi corpus and the full range of "heresies" described by early Christian heresiologists, some have mounted a spirited defense for a more historically careful and circumscribed use of the term or one of its variants (i.e., "Gnosis," "Gnostic religion," "the Gnostics")—often either partially overlapping with, or in contradistinction from, other early Christian movements such as Valentinianism. Certain versions of this argument remain typologically oriented, positing not a discrete religious formation in antiquity that ought to be characterized as "Gnostic," but rather a set of characteristics that can serve as a useful heuristic device for analyzing theological concepts, myths, and/or references to rituals found in multiple ancient texts—even if the authors and movements behind those texts had little or no direct historical contact (Markschies 2003; Meyer 2005).

Another position, represented most forcefully by Birger Pearson, contends on phenomenological grounds that there actually was an independent Gnostic religion. This religion, he maintains, was distinct from Christianity or Judaism, placed its primary emphasis on *gnôsis* (as opposed to either faith or Torah), and is epitomized most clearly by one particular text, the *Secret Book of John* (Pearson 2004, 2005). Finally, a third position maintains that historically, a group of ancient Christians designated themselves as "Gnostics," and were bound together (albeit not rigidly) not only by this self-designation, but also by a shared set of myths and ritual practices (Layton; Brakke 2010). Here again the *Secret Book of John* is of paramount importance, along with other texts and polemical descriptions that share a similar cosmological myth. This myth has been often characterized as "Sethian" in other scholarship because of an emphasis, at least in some texts, on the biblical figure of Seth and his progeny (Schenke 1974; Turner 1986).

While the scholarly debate around the utility of the category "Gnosticism" is far from settled, it has pushed scholars on all sides to pay closer attention to the specificities of texts previously lumped under a blanket category. And with respect to biblical interpretation, it has become increasingly clear that there is no unitary Gnostic hermeneutic or exegetical approach (Williams, p. 78). Although only sometimes considered a "Gnostic"—and increasingly less so—in critical scholarship, the second-century thinker Marcion of Sinope represents one unambiguous approach to biblical hermeneutics: the rejection of Jewish scriptures and the expunging of the traces of those scriptures from Christian sacred texts. Yet when it comes to the literature of Nag Hammadi and related texts, the hermeneutical situation proves far more complicated. While these texts may revise, supplement, allegorize, correct, parody, and/or read scriptural traditions against the grain, as King rightly points out, this interpretive complexity cannot be reduced to "the simplistic and misleading stereotype that 'Gnostics rejected Jewish scripture.' Some did, some didn't; those who did, did so differently" (2008, p. 79). It is to this convoluted but fascinating exegetical diversity—encompassing not only the Jewish scriptures but also the texts of a still nascent New Testament—that we now turn.

Biblical Interpretation in Nag Hammadi Texts. Scholarly generalizations about Gnostic biblical interpretation have often portrayed it as a kind of "tendentious rewriting" (Jonas, p. 95) or "protest exegesis" (Rudolph, p. 54). While these characterizations may arguably apply to specific exegetical moves within individual texts, such sweeping generalizations with respect to the entire Nag Hammadi corpus are no longer tenable. Rather, we need to look closely at specific texts, the hermeneutical moves that they make, and the intertextual maneuvers that they perform, as they read scriptural passages together with one another and with other philosophical and cultural resources available in the ancient world. What follows will delve into these questions—without attempting comprehensiveness—through an examination of three representative examples from the Nag Hammadi corpus: the *Secret Book of John*, the *Tripartite Tractate*, and *On the Origin of the World*.

Each of these examples interprets the scriptural story that perhaps loomed largest in the theological imaginations of (at least some of) the anonymous authors who penned this literature: the narrative of cosmic and human creation found in Genesis 1—3. While an excellent broad overview of "Gnostic" interpretations of Genesis has recently been published (Dunderberg 2011), the ensuing exploration will focus more narrowly on specific exegetical motifs and interpretive connections deployed by the texts in comparison to one another. Of the three texts to be examined, the first has typically been categorized as Sethian (or Gnostic in the more delimited sense favored by Layton and Brakke), the second as Valentinian, and the third as not quite either—though most likely related to both. As such, the three texts' hermeneutical common ground (both undeniable but also difficult to pin down with precision) and their divergences in specific explications of the Genesis text showcase both the benefits and the limitations of classificatory schemes with respect to the question of Gnostic interpretation.

The Secret Book of John. As noted earlier, the *Secret Book of John* (second century C.E.) has been treated by many scholars as the epitome of classic "Gnostic" scripture—a group that also includes such texts as the *Revelation of Adam*, and the *Hypostasis of the*

Archons, among numerous others. In its interpretation of creation, the *Secret Book of John* engages not only the Genesis narrative, but also numerous other ancient cultural resources including Platonizing philosophy and mythological speculations, Jewish wisdom literature, and Christian (especially Johannine) traditions—to name only its most prominent interlocutors. Yet this kaleidoscopic interpretive performance cannot be reduced to simple descriptors such as "reversal," "caricature," or "parody" with respect to the biblical text (though all these terms remain relevant). Rather, as King notes, the *Secret Book* deftly navigates apparent gaps within, and differences between, such texts as Genesis, the Gospel of John, and Plato's *Timaeus* by means of a range of hermeneutical techniques and devices: retelling of the various narratives, recontextualization of smaller pieces of stories into a different plot structure, narrative elaboration, allegory, and identifications between otherwise unrelated characters from different texts (King 2006, pp. 185–188).

The *Secret Book* frames its revelatory narrative in terms of a dialogue, an imparting of secret knowledge by Christ to his disciple John. Here Platonizing speculations about the nature of ultimate deity are resituated in terms of the Genesis narrative. Negotiating the classic Platonic conundrum of "the One and the many," the text explains the unfolding of a complex divine hierarchy out of a single first principle—an invisible spirit superior to deity, transcendent, and ultimately indescribable except in apophatic terms. From this first principle emanates a realm of divine beings or *aeons*, proceeding down a well-ordered hierarchy and together constituting a perfect unity. One of these *aeons*, Sophia (Wisdom), rashly decides to act out of her own self-determining thought, bringing forth a being who is divine, but who is not part of the approved hierarchy of divine emanation. This being, known as Ialdabaoth, and the rulers (or "archons") he engenders, represent a distortion—one that introduces rupture, deformity, and problematic difference into the previously unblemished cosmos.

With respect to the Genesis narrative, all of this can be considered a kind of divine backstory, an explanation of cosmological happenings prior to—or more precisely, outside of or apart from—Genesis 1:1 (Brakke, p. 63). Ialdabaoth, then, functions in the *Secret Book* as the creator God of Genesis, but also as a kind of craftsman or "deimurge" modeled on Plato's *Timaeus*. The move to harmonize selective aspects of Genesis and Plato in interpretations of creation was not new, being at least as old as Philo of Alexandria (c. 30 B.C.E.–50 C.E.). Yet the goodness of Plato's craftsman, creating the best possible world on the model of the eternal Forms, had always begged the question of the origins of evil. The *Secret Book* navigates this thorny question by demoting Ialdabaoth to a position of ignorance, hubris, and even malice—though not radical evil in any absolute sense. Rather, the relationship between Ialdabaoth and his mother Sophia (as well as the rest of the divine realm) enacts a kind of broken mimesis. While Ialdabaoth retains a genealogical connection (and thus some continuity) to Sophia's divinity, he is at one and the same time not like her. The mimesis fails, and the continuity between Ialdabaoth and the divine realm, such as it is, is therefore marked by deception and brokenness—and as a result, not to be trusted. So too this deep ambivalence will mark the created world order that Ialdabaoth brings about (King 2006, p. 200).

Exegesis of the Genesis text, explicitly marked as such, begins as the *Secret Book* turns to an account of Sophia's repentance. According to Genesis 1:2, "a wind [or spirit] from God swept over the face of the waters." Here Christ informs John that "Moses" is not to be trusted: the movement in question refers not to the creator god or to literal waters, but rather to Sophia moving back and forth out of shame at her transgression, a first step toward her eventual repentance. Meanwhile Ialdabaoth and the rulers get to work establishing the created order—and most especially fashioning Adam, the first human being. Reading Genesis 1:26 ("Let us make humankind in our image, according to our likeness") disjunctively so that "image" and "likeness" apply to two different referents—a common exegetical move among Jews and Christians in this period—the *Secret Book* asserts that Adam is created according to an *image* derived from the higher divine realm and according to the flawed and distorted *likeness* of Ialdabaoth and the rulers. In a critical revision of Genesis 2:7 (in which Adam is formed from the dust), the rulers mold the first human's body out of soul (i.e., psychic) substance. The result is an inanimate and inert creature, a concrete manifestation of the rulers' true impotence. Only when the higher divine powers trick Ialdabaoth into blowing his mother Sophia's power into Adam's inert psychic body does he spring powerfully to life.

Through a retooling of Eve's creation in Genesis 2:18–25, the text then recounts how the true deity implants a "helper" within Adam (cf. Gen 2:18), a luminous thought or principle who instructs Adam, but whose glowing presence within him causes his soul-substance body to shine. After encasing Adam in the "tomb" of a terrestrial body, Ialdabaoth attempts to retrieve this luminous thought from within Adam, putting him into a kind of trance in order to extract the desired power. The text figures this episode as a corrective gloss on Genesis 2:21 ("So the LORD God caused a deep sleep to fall upon the man, and he slept; then he took one of his ribs and closed up its place with flesh"), clarifying that Moses was wrong to characterize Adam's state as "sleep" or to designate the power being retrieved "a rib." Here the basic narrative arc of Genesis remains intact, but with a twist: Eve emerges in this moment, yet she is not stigmatized as the original wrongdoer. Rather, as the luminous thought originally hidden within Adam, she is the source of true enlightenment. Ialdabaoth and the rulers make various attempts to control these human rivals (including a violent rape of Eve; cf. also the *Hypostasis of the Archons*), but all of these end in frustration or failure. The result is a rereading of Genesis 4 that presents the second generation of human beings in terms of the *Secret Book*'s specific soteriological vision. Cain and Abel are the misbegotten consequence of Eve's brutal rape, while Seth, begotten legitimately by the human couple, is the "other seed" referenced in Genesis 4:25. It is his offspring who will partake in the divine image and the power of Sophia, and will therefore ultimately share in salvation.

Throughout this intricate mythological account, the interpretation of Genesis is regularly informed by the creative rereading of other scriptural intertexts—such as the description of Wisdom as cocreator in Proverbs 8, or the account of divine light illuminating the creation in the Johannine prologue. But as King has shown, the text's Platonic commitments also shape its exegesis of Genesis in a very specific way through interpreting aspects of the story twice (King 2006, pp. 222–223). That is to say, the *Secret Book* renders visible in its exegetical technique the Platonic distinction between heavenly and earthly realms (or Being and becoming) by reading portions of the Genesis story in terms of both spheres. For example, the text invokes the trope of paradigmatic female figures who trigger major turning points in the story at both divine and human levels (i.e., Sophia and Eve), and it appeals to the notion of "image and likeness" twice, not only in the creation of the first human being, as discussed earlier, but also with respect to the emergence of Forethought, a particularly prominent divine aeon. In this way, Platonic philosophical ideals impact not only the content but the actual structure of the *Secret Book*'s biblical exegesis.

Valentinianism and The Tripartite Tractate. Around 140 C.E., an Egyptian Christian named Valentinus came to Rome and began to gather a following. While we have only limited evidence for Valentinus's individual views, his followers in the succeeding generations—commonly referred to as "the school of Valentinus"—went on to develop their own theological systems and hermeneutical techniques, not always entirely in keeping with the views of their founder. Thus it proves challenging to demarcate the precise limits of what early Christian literature ought to be considered "Valentinian." In addition to quotations and summaries preserved in the writings of the heresiologists, Ismo Dunderberg identifies the following texts from Nag Hammadi: *The Prayer of the Apostle Paul, The Gospel of Truth, The Tripartite Tractate, The Treatise on the Resurrection, The Gospel of Philip, The (First) Apocalypse of James, The Interpretation of Knowledge,* and *A Valentinian Exposition* (Dunderberg 2008).

When taken together, this evidence does not constitute a uniform theological position or interpretive stance, but instead emerges as a loosely related patchwork of viewpoints, claims, and exegetical approaches.

Still, it remains possible to draw some broad generalizations regarding Valentinian theology and exegesis. Participating (like the *Secret Book of John*) in a larger conversation regarding the relationship between "the One and the many" that animated much of ancient thought, Valentinian texts generally conceptualize the universe and the place of human beings within it in terms of a single-minded desire for cosmological oneness. An original state of union had given way to multiplicity, separation, and division, but would one day be restored—the chaotic plurality of the created world finding reconciliation in a return to perfect unity. Thus Valentinians looked forward to the eradication of difference and otherness, conceptualized as a recapitulation of primordial beginnings in the realm of divine fullness.

We see one example of this cosmological narrative playing out in *The Tripartite Tractate* (third century c.e.)—arguably the most thorough and complete account of Valentinian theology still extant. As in the *Secret Book of John*, the text's creation account begins with a single unified principle. This principle, characterized here as "the Father," produces the Son out of his own self-thinking activity, and then together the Father and Son generate an array of spiritual powers or aeons. One of these, the Logos (approximately equivalent to Sophia in other similarly structured accounts), attempts to grasp the incomprehensibility of the father, thereby generating a fissure in the divine unity. This introduction of division and deficiency ultimately results in the multiplicity that characterizes the created world. Like Sophia in the *Secret Book*, the Logos eventually turns back toward the true divine fullness in an act of conversion, an important byproduct of which is the generation of the Savior.

One noteworthy aspect of the *Tripartite Tractate*'s interpretation of Genesis (which it shares with other Valentinian literature) is the way in which the text reads the Genesis narrative together with Pauline anthropological categories. In 1 Corinthians 15:42–49, Paul makes reference to a number of bodily states including the choic (earthy), the psychic ("soulish" or animate), and the pneumatic (spiritual). And while Paul himself never triangulated these three categories, Valentinian Christians read the Pauline categories together with Platonic notions of the tripartite human being, constituted—most commonly—in terms of body, soul, and mind. The result, among certain Valentinians, was to assert that there are actually three different kinds of human beings: choic (or a synonym—hylic, often translated "material"), psychic, and pneumatic. In the *Tripartite Tractate*, all three of these categories are treated not as figures of speech, but rather as actual substances (Thomassen 2009). Thus we should not allow the tendency to translate *hyle* as "matter" to obscure the fact that from the standpoint of ancient physics—and informed especially by Stoic notions of matter and materialism—all three categories have "materialistic, concrete, and tangible" dimensions (Engberg-Pedersen 2010, p. 19). The text's creation narrative explains the origins of the three substances: the Logos's deficient begetting and his ensuing conversion bring about the hylic and psychic substances respectively, whereas the pneumatic substance comes about due to the joy that the Logos experiences at the Savior's appearing.

These three substances, then, figure heavily in the tractate's account of human creation. While the basic plotline bears notable similarities to the *Secret Book of John*, here a specific emphasis is placed on providing an origin story for the emergence of the three kinds of humans. In this reinterpretation of Genesis, the Logos, the demiurge-creator figure, and the rulers each contribute one of the substances—pneumatic, psychic, and hylic respectively—to the first human's creation. The pneumatic substance is characterized in terms of singularity (thereby evoking the original—and longed for—primordial oneness), the psychic substance in terms of doubleness, and the hylic substance in terms of multiplicity. All three of these together make up Adam, who is a kind of "mixed modeling." He is heterogeneous—and thus adulterated—from the moment of his formation. This originally compound human eventually gives way to a world populated by hylics/choics, psychics, and pneumatics, though exactly how this transition takes place is never clearly explained. Furthermore, Eve does not figure explicitly in the tractate's creation account (though femaleness is associated with weakness, illness, and division). Rather, the text places its primary focus on the interplay, distribution, and eventual eschatological destiny of these primal substances in its account of human creation. And while the tractate's assertions regarding the fate of the three substances have led to accusations of eschatological determinism, numerous scholars have shown that this conclusion is unwarranted, at least in its most extreme forms (Buell 2005; Dunderberg 2008). In a necessarily ambiguous and perhaps paradoxical way, there remains space for human fluidity, education, and transformation within this mythological universe—a vision of the cosmos that a Valentinian author produced by reworking the Genesis narrative with an eye to appropriating Pauline anthropological categories (read simultaneously through Platonic tripartite divisions of the human and Stoic materialism) as the fundamental building blocks of creation.

On the Origin of the World. Our final case is an unnamed treatise from Nag Hammadi, commonly referred to as *On the Origin of the World* (second to early fourth century C.E.). With respect to the question of so-called Gnostic biblical interpretation, what makes this case particularly interesting is that it is so difficult to classify. The text has narrative similarities to Sethian or "classic Gnostic" texts including the *Secret Book of John* and the *Hypostasis of the Archons* (for example, the presence of Ialdabaoth as an ignorant demiurge figure), but it differs from these texts in important ways and cannot be considered straightforwardly Sethian. Neither is it Valentinian, although the tripartite anthropology discussed earlier figures significantly in its mythology. Scholars have approached this problem of classification in various ways, such as placing the text in a supplemental category dubbed "Ophite" (Rasimus 2009) or positing a primitive tradition redacted first by a Valentinian and later by a Sethian (Painchaud 1991). What is important for our purposes, however, is to note how *On the Origin of the World* cites and reinterprets not only the Genesis narrative but also various Pauline, Platonic, Sethian, and Valentinian concepts, tropes, and exegetical motifs to its own specific ends. In so doing, it unsettles rigid definitional boundaries and underscores just how richly diverse were the hermeneutical possibilities that fall under the broad umbrella of Gnostic interpretation.

Two short examples will suffice to illustrate this point. First to consider is the creation of Adam and Eve. Similar to the *Secret Book of John*, *On the Origin of the World* reads Genesis 1:26 in terms of a disjunction between image and likeness. And it too envisions Adam's creation according to a fusion of both—in this case, the image of Ialdabaoth and the rulers on the one hand and the likeness of a luminous, paradigmatic "Adam" figure from the divine realm on the other (note the inversion of the trope as it appears in the *Secret Book*). But the text then goes on to offer a kind of counternarrative of human creation, one in which the Sophia character draws on a different image (her own, in the form of a drop of light) and a different likeness (that of her divine mother) to create a second human being: Eve. In this way, Eve emerges as the luminous woman who derives from an entirely different genealogy of image and likeness than does Adam. As such, she embodies for the rulers an unrecognizable and inassimilable difference. This serves as an affront and a threat to their aspirations to dominate the created order. And as in the *Secret Book* and the *Hypostasis of the Archons*, the rulers respond with violence (i.e., Eve's rape), though arguably for different reasons. As for Genesis 2:21 (Adam's sleep and the removal of his rib), it is no longer needed to justify Eve's creation, given her alternate origins. However, rather than discarding or ignoring the verse, the text resituates it so that no creation actually happens in this moment. Rather, "the rib" is only the rulers' subterfuge, a false story told to Adam so that he will remain ignorant of Eve's true divine origins (Dunning 2009).

Secondly, *On the Origin of the World* also makes use of the Valentinian tripartite anthropological categories discussed earlier. Accordingly, its creation narrative is peopled with characters described variably and at different moments as choic, psychic, and pneumatic. Yet rather than straightforwardly assenting to these categories' (at least partially) Pauline roots—and thus implicitly to the authority of Paul—the text actually uses the tripartite categories to polemicize against a different Pauline theological construct: the typology of Adam and Christ as first and second Adams (Rom 5, 1 Cor 15). Rather than acknowledge Christ as second (and final) Adam, it argues—in a direct riposte to Paul in 1 Corinthians 15—for *three* paradigmatic Adam figures, the first being pneumatic, the second psychic, and the third choic (Painchaud). Consequently, the Pauline typology is both inverted and subverted: the "first Adam" is not the Adam of Genesis 1–3, but instead a figure from the divine realm; the "third Adam" is the rulers' earthly creation and without salvific value; and the "second Adam" is not Christ, but none other than Eve. While gender is an important aspect of numerous Nag Hammadi texts (King 2000), here Pauline concepts and categories are both relied upon and undercut in a rereading of Genesis that offers a remarkably distinctive take on the origins and meaning of human sexual difference. *On the Origin of the World* portrays the sexual binary as a primary rather than secondary aspect of created humanity (a deeply unusual move for a text so indebted to Platonic ways of thinking), grounded in two separate processes of creation, both of which remain central to the text's mythology (Dunning).

Assessment. The texts of the Nag Hammadi corpus and others traditionally categorized as Gnostic display a dazzling array of exegetical techniques and hermeneutical postures in their varied approaches to Jewish and Christian scriptures. These include not only interpreting scriptural texts against the grain (itself a multifarious undertaking), but also reading a range of texts intertextually to generate innovative and hybrid lenses for understanding. Through such lenses, both scripture and other cultural authorities such as Plato's *Timaeus* and Stoic physics took on new meanings for ancient readers, thereby shaping their perceptions and their practices in relation to the divine, the human, and the place of both in the larger cosmos. While these complex realities have often led to accusations of "syncretism" or analyses of the texts' various departures from some imagined normative Christian stance (a clear anachronism in the second and third centuries), such lines of inquiry are less helpful for the task of understanding the dynamics that animate Gnostic biblical interpretation. Rather, the ongoing scholarly task is to investigate with rigor and precision the specific ways in which this literature, like all early Christian literature, interprets multiple texts and traditions—scriptural and otherwise—in light of one another in order to fill gaps, iron out ambiguities (often creating new ambiguities along the way), and navigate theological and exegetical problems.

[*See also* Greco-Roman Context.]

BIBLIOGRAPHY

Brakke, David. *The Gnostics: Myth, Ritual, and Diversity in Early Christianity*. Cambridge, Mass.: Harvard University Press, 2010. An important new study arguing for the "Gnostics" as a self-identified group within early Christianity.

Buell, Denise Kimber. *Why This New Race: Ethnic Reasoning in Early Christianity*. New York: Columbia University Press, 2005.

Dunderberg, Ismo. *Beyond Gnosticism: Myth, Lifestyle, and Society in the School of Valentinus*. New York: Columbia University Press, 2008. An excellent recent analysis of a variety of issues in Valentinian myth and practice.

Dunderberg, Ismo. "Gnostic Interpretations of Genesis." In *The Oxford Handbook of the Reception History of the Bible*, edited by Michael Lieb, Emma Mason, and Jonathan Roberts, 383–396. Oxford and New York: Oxford University Press, 2011.

Dunning, Benjamin H. "What Sort of Thing Is This Luminous Woman?: Thinking Sexual Difference." In *On the Origin of the World. Journal of Early Christian Studies* 17, no. 1 (2009): 55–84.

Engberg-Pedersen, Troels. *Cosmology and Self in the Apostle Paul: The Material Spirit*. Oxford and New York: Oxford University Press, 2010.

Irenaeus of Lyons. *Against the Heresies Book I*. Translated and annotated by Dominic J. Unger and John J. Dillon. New York: Paulist, 1992.

Jonas, Hans. *The Gnostic Religion: The Message of the Alien God and the Beginnings of Christianity.* 2d rev. ed. Boston: Beacon, 1963. The classic typological exposition of Gnosticism in terms of existential alienation.

King, Karen L., ed. *Images of the Feminine in Gnosticism.* Harrisburg, Pa.: Trinity Press International, 2000.

King, Karen L. *The Secret Revelation of John.* Cambridge, Mass.: Harvard University Press, 2006. A thorough study of this major text with a focus on biblical interpretation and intertextuality. Includes a new translation.

King, Karen L. *What Is Gnosticism?* Cambridge, Mass.: Harvard University Press, 2003. An influential critique of "Gnosticism" from the standpoint of its role in Christian discourses of orthodoxy and heresy.

King, Karen L. "Which Early Christianity?" In *The Oxford Handbook of Early Christian Studies,* edited by Susan Ashbrook Harvey and David G. Hunter, 66–84. Oxford and New York: Oxford University Press, 2008.

Layton, Bentley. "Prolegomena to the Study of Ancient Gnosticism." In *The Social World of the First Christians: Essays in Honor of Wayne A. Meeks,* edited by L. Michael White and O. Larry Yarborough, 334–350. Minneapolis: Fortress, 1995. An important article arguing for "Gnostic" as an early Christian term of self-designation and group identity, roughly akin to "Sethian."

Marjanen, Antti, ed. *Was There a Gnostic Religion?* Helsinki: Finnish Exegetical Society/Göttingen: Vandenhoeck & Ruprecht, 2005. An excellent overview of the scholarly conversation around the term "Gnosticism," but not easily available.

Markschies, Christoph. *Gnosis: An Introduction.* Translated by John Bowden. London: T.&T. Clark, 2003. English translation of *Die Gnosis,* first published in 2001.

Meyer, Marvin. *The Gnostic Discoveries: The Impact of the Nag Hammadi Library.* New York: HarperCollins, 2005.

Pagels, Elaine. *The Gnostic Gospels.* New York: Vintage Books, 1989. A classic and still valuable introduction to the so-called Gnostic Gospels.

Painchaud, Louis. "The Redactions of the Writing without Title (CG II.5)." *Second Century* 8, no. 4 (1991): 217–234.

Pearson, Birger A. *Gnosticism and Christianity in Roman and Coptic Egypt.* New York: T.&T. Clark, 2004.

Rasimus, Tuomas. *Paradise Reconsidered in Gnostic Mythmaking: Rethinking Sethianism in Light of the Ophite Evidence.* Leiden: Brill, 2009.

Robinson, James, ed. *The Nag Hammadi Library in English.* 3d ed. New York: HarperCollins, 1990.

Rudolph, Kurt. *Gnosis: The Nature and History of Gnosticism.* Translated by Robert MacLachlan Wilson. San Francisco, Harper & Row, 1983. English translation of *Die Gnosis: Wesen und Geschichte einer spätantiken Religion,* 2d ed., first published in 1980.

Schenke, Hans-Martin. "Das sethianische System nach Nag-Hammadi-Handschriften." In *Studia Coptica,* edited by Peter Nagel, 165–174. Berlin: Akademie Verlag, 1974. A pioneering article that argued for the category of "Sethianism."

Thomassen, Einar. *The Spiritual Seed: The Church of the "Valentinians."* Leiden: Brill, 2006. A masterful and comprehensive study of Valentinianism; useful for advanced research.

Thomassen, Einar. "Valentinian Ideas about Salvation as Transformation." In *Metamorphoses: Resurrection, Body and Transformative Practices in Early Christianity,* edited by Turid Karlsen Seim and Jorunn Økland, 169–186. Berlin: de Gruyter, 2009.

Turner, John. D. "Sethian Gnosticism: A Literary History." In *Nag Hammadi, Gnosticism, and Early Christianity,* edited by Charles W. Hedrick and Robert Hodgson Jr., 55–86. Peabody, Mass.: Hendricksen, 1986.

Williams, Michael Allen. *Rethinking "Gnosticism": An Argument for Dismantling a Dubious Category.* Princeton, N.J.: Princeton University Press, 1996. One of the seminal critiques of the term "Gnosticism." Argued on typological grounds.

Benjamin H. Dunning

GRECO-ROMAN CONTEXT

Definition. The Greco-Roman context of the Bible refers to the temporal period when the Greeks, followed by the Romans, were the dominant powers in the ancient Mediterranean world. By convention, this period begins with the victory of Alexander the Great (356–323) over the Persians at Gaugamela (in modern Iraq) in 331 B.C.E. and ends with Constantine the Great (272–337), who in 313 C.E. co-issued the Edict of Milan, which restored to Christians their confiscated property and granted them religious freedom. Although the last books of the Bible were written long before the time of Constantine, and the Roman Empire in the West continued long after his death, his reign marked a fundamental change in the history of the early church, and thus it provides a convenient terminus for this period, which was to be of monumental importance for both Jews and Christians.

Biblical History and the Greco-Roman World. The necessity of giving attention to the Greco-Roman world arises from Jewish and Christian history. A year before Alexander defeated the Persians, he had already secured control of Judah (332 B.C.E.). Following his death in 323 B.C.E., his generals and their descendants began jockeying among themselves for power. Three major Hellenistic kingdoms emerged from these power struggles; since their founders traced their origins to Alexander, they became known as his *Diadochoi* or "Successors." Of these three Greek kingdoms, two proved to be of crucial significance for the history of early Judaism during the Second Temple period. These were the Ptolemaic dynasty, centered in Alexandria, and the Seleucid dynasty, centered in Antioch. The area of Coele-Syria (lower Syria, including Judea) lay between these two competing powers, which fought six Syrian Wars during the third and second centuries in an effort to secure control of the region. Chapter 11 of the book of Daniel traces some of the major outlines of this struggle between the successors of Alexander, "the warrior king" (Dan 11:3), with different Ptolemaic rulers designated "the king of the south" (Dan 11:5–6, 9, 11, 14–15) and various Seleucid monarchs called "the king of the north" (Dan 11:6–8, 11, 13, 15).

From 301 to 198 B.C.E., the Ptolemies were in effective control of Palestine, and it was during this same time period that the city of Alexandria emerged as a major center of Diaspora Judaism. Furthermore, it was here during the third century that the Hebrew Bible began to be translated into Greek. The Jewish pseudepigraphical work known as the *Letter of Aristeas* purports to give the circumstances under which this translation, known as the Septuagint, was undertaken. Whatever the true history of this translation project, the final result was a Greek version of the Torah, and eventually of the entire Hebrew Bible, as well as some other writings. The Septuagint was used by Jews throughout the Greco-Roman world, and it was read and quoted by the early Greek-speaking Christians as well. For that reason alone, all biblical scholars agree that cognizance must be taken of the Greek text of the Septuagint, and how its translators rendered the Hebrew into Greek. Another book purporting to give information about the Jewish experience during Ptolemaic times is 3 Maccabees, which Eastern Orthodox Churches regard as deuterocanonical. It narrates three episodes that supposedly occurred during the reign of Ptolemy IV Philopator (221–204 B.C.E.).

During the Fifth Syrian War (202–195 B.C.E.) the Seleucid king Antiochus III (the Great) wrested control of Coele-Syria away from the Ptolemies. Although pro-Ptolemaic Jews were disappointed by this political shift, the Jews of Jerusalem welcomed Antiochus III with open arms and even helped him dislodge the garrison of Ptolemaic soldiers occupying the citadel. Antiochus rewarded the Jerusalemites by granting them various rights and privileges, but these were subsequently revoked by his son, Antiochus IV Epiphanes. The revocation of these rights and other indignities, including the desecration of the altar at the Jerusalem temple, prompted a revolt, led by Judas the Maccabee and his brothers, that culminated in the establishment of an independent Jewish state led by the descendants of Judas's family (167–63 B.C.E.). The deuterocanonical books of 1 and 2 Maccabees deal with the struggles and interactions of the Jewish people with the Seleucids both before and after the revolt, down to 134 B.C.E. In addition, 1 Maccabees refers to various Maccabean interactions with Rome, doing so in laudatory terms (8:1–16) and describing the making and renewal of a Jewish alliance with Rome (8:17–32; 12:1–4). Another work that deals with this Jewish-Seleucid conflict is 4 Maccabees; though not canonical, it does appear as an appendix in some manuscripts of the Septuagint.

Toward the end of this period of Jewish political independence, Rome once again appears on the scene, but this time as an even more formidable military power than it had been when it checked the advance of Antiochus III the Great at Magnesia in 190 and at the beginning of the Maccabean period (167–63 B.C.E.). By this point in time, Rome had expanded far beyond the small city-state that it was when Alexander had become king of Macedon (336). Over the course of more than two and a half centuries, it conquered the Italian peninsula; secured control of the western Mediterranean by defeating Carthage in three Punic Wars; culminated four Macedonian Wars by establishing Macedonia as a Roman province in 148 B.C.E.; razed Corinth in 146 B.C.E. during the Achaean War; solidified control of Asia Minor; completed three wars against Mithridates, the Hellenistic king of Pontus; and brought the Seleucid kingdom to an end with the establishment of Syria as a Roman province. The end of the Maccabean kingdom came in 63 B.C.E., when Pompey the Great intervened in a Jewish civil war between two Maccabean princes and inaugurated the Roman period in Jewish history. A generation later, in 40 B.C.E., the Roman Senate declared Herod the Great, an Idumean ally of the Romans, "King of the Jews." Herod secured his kingdom by 37 B.C.E. and reigned as a Roman client king until his death in 4 B.C.E. Jesus was born toward the end of Herod's reign and resided in Galilee, where Herod Antipas, one of Herod the Great's sons, was the ruler. Antipas was responsible for the execution of John the Baptist, and Jesus was publicly crucified just outside the city of Jerusalem of Judea, on the orders of Pontius Pilate, a Roman prefect. Agrippa I, a Herodian whose political power derived from his friendship with two Roman emperors, martyred one of Jesus's apostles, James the brother of John. In short, the ministries of John and Jesus as well as the early years of the church took place within the context of Rome's occupation of Syria-Palestine and the rule of the Herodians as clients of Rome.

In a similar way, the expansion of early Christianity into the larger Greco-Roman world occurred first and foremost within the provinces of the Roman Empire. Those provinces were not populated exclusively by Romans and other Gentiles, for many, if not most of them contained major Jewish settlements, attesting the wide expanse of the Jewish Diaspora by the first century C.E. Consistent with this geographical reality, 1 Peter makes use of Diaspora language in addressing the recipients of the letter (1:1). The apostle Paul was one of those Diaspora Jews; not only was he born in the Roman province of Cilicia, but Acts 22:39 depicts him as a proud citizen of his native city of Tarsus. Wherever Paul went on his missionary journeys, whether to Syria, Cilicia, Cyprus, Pisidia, Galatia, Macedon, Achaia, Asia Minor, or Rome itself, he went to Roman territory. Both his oral proclamation of the gospel and his letters were aimed at inhabitants of the Roman Empire. Furthermore, Acts depicts Paul as a Roman citizen (22:25–29) who exercised one of his rights of citizenship by requesting a judicial change of venue (25:11). According to reliable early church tradition, both Paul and Peter were martyred in Rome, the capital of the Empire, which is the object of fierce polemic by the seer John, the author of Revelation.

As this brief and selective survey is meant to illustrate, the Greco-Roman world provides the overarching context for the biblical story and the postbiblical history of early Christianity in the period from Alexander to Constantine. The political shift from Greek to Roman power did not entail any significant cultural change for the peoples of the eastern Mediterranean, as many of the social issues remained the same. Some Jews were attracted to Greek culture and Roman power, whereas others were repulsed by both, and Jews revolted three times against Rome during the period of 66–135 C.E. The first revolt led to the destruction of the Jerusalem temple in 70 C.E; the second took place from 115 to 117 C.E. in Jewish communities located in Cyrene, Egypt, and Cyprus; and the third, the famous Bar Kokhba revolt (132–135 C.E.), resulted in the devastation of Judah and caused the center of Jewish life to shift from Judea to Galilee, where the Mishnah was formed.

As far as early Christianity is concerned, there was a remarkable demographic shift as time elapsed. At the beginning, Jesus and all his followers were Jewish, but already by the end of the first century the vast majority of Christians were Gentiles whose cultural background was the Greco-Roman world. No other religion has undergone such a dramatic demographic shift in such a short period of time. Like their Jewish counterparts, these Gentile Christians had various attitudes toward the larger Greco-Roman world, some positive and some negative, depending on the particular aspect of that world that was in view.

One reflection of this demographic shift is the language of the New Testament. Even though Jesus and his apostles spoke Aramaic, all four of the canonical Gospels were written in Greek. All of Paul's letters, including his letter to the Romans, were written in Greek, as were all of the other documents that comprise the New Testament. Greek was the lingua franca of the eastern Mediterranean world, and the language of the New Testament is in keeping with that cultural and linguistic reality.

The Greco-Roman Context in Treatments of Second Temple and Hellenistic Judaism. Interaction between Greece and the Levant began long before the military campaigns of Alexander the Great. As the finds at Lefkandi in Euboea prove, the Greeks had contacts with Cyprus and the Levant at an early pre-colonial stage, with Syria-Palestine a vital part of the Mediterranean exchange network in the late Protogeometric period of ca. 950–900 B.C.E. In the Levant itself, Mycenaean pottery was found at Sabouni, a hill town closely associated with the Iron Age port city of Al Mina. The latter, located in the delta of the Orontes, is usually viewed as the site of the first Greek presence in Syria, perhaps as early as 825 B.C.E., though the preponderance of Greek pottery found there dates to ca. 750. Scholarly tradition regards Al Mina as an important trading post where Greeks resided and perhaps constituted a small colony, but some scholars perceive it as devoid of any true cultural significance. Two other coastal sites in North Syria, located to the south of Al Mina, are also generally viewed as showing signs of a Greek presence from a slightly later period: Ras el Bassit ("Poseidon") and Tell Sukas (for bibliography on these various sites, see Fitzgerald 2004, pp. 349—350 n. 28). These early contacts between Greece and the Levant played a key role in fostering the so-called "orientalizing revolution" in archaic Greece that significantly affected early Greek culture, myth, and philosophy.

Alexander's campaigns set the stage for the much greater cultural interaction that occurred between East and West during subsequent centuries. The cities that he founded were his greatest cultural legacy, and it was primarily in and through these cities as well as those founded by his successors that "Hellenization" occurred. "Hellenization" refers to the "interactive process by which Greek customs, ideas, institutions, practices, and terms spread into non-Greek regions and, to varying degrees, were not only appropriated by some indigenous individuals and groups but also resisted and rejected by others" (Fitzgerald 2010, p. 984). As indicated, Alexander did not initiate this interactive process but rather accelerated it.

Diaspora Judaism was everywhere affected by its Greco-Roman context, and all studies of Hellenistic Jewish authors (such as Philo and Josephus) and texts typically seek to situate them in regard to both that context and their Jewish heritage. Numerous scholars have contributed to the study of these authors and texts, as well as to the impact of Hellenization in Syria-Palestine, including such early luminaries as E. J. Bickerman, E. R. Goodenough, M. Hengel, A. Momigliano, E. M. Smallwood, and V. Tcherikover. Among more recent contributors, the work of J. M. G. Barclay, M. Goodman, and T. Rajak has been highly influential.

Debate on the impact of the Greco-Roman world, both positive and negative, on Judaism in the land of Israel has centered on the difficult task of properly assessing the time and degree of that influence. It is generally agreed that it begins slowly during the Ptolemaic period, increases during the Seleucid and Maccabean periods, receives a strong impetus with the Herodian dynasty, and reaches an unprecedented apex with Hadrian's trip to the Roman East in 129–131 C.E. Suffice it to say that the degree of impact varied according to the place, the individuals involved, and the time period.

For example, Caesarea Maritima was far more directly impacted by Greco-Roman culture than were the villages and towns of Galilee. Caesarea Maritima was a port city constructed by Herod the Great, who, in keeping with a policy designed to placate both his Roman patrons and his Jewish constituents, erected here a pagan temple of Roma and Augustus; it served as a complement to his expansion and beautification of the temple at Jerusalem, which was pleasing to many but not all of his Jewish constituents. It was also at Caesarea Maritima that the Roman prefects (procurators) resided who administered Judea and Samaria. Pilate, one of those prefects, dedicated here a monumental Latin inscription to the emperor Tiberius, and it was here that the apostle Paul appeared before Felix and Festus (Acts 24–25) as well as Agrippa II, a Herodian who functioned as an advisor to the Romans (Acts 26). Yet, while Caesarea Maritima was undoubtedly more Romanized than the villages of Galilee, that does not mean that the latter were not impacted by Greco-Roman culture. Excavations at Yodefat (Jotapata), a hilltop town that served as the Jewish administrative center for central Galilee until it was destroyed by Rome during the First Roman-Jewish War, have uncovered a house with frescoed walls done in the Second Pompeian style of ancient Roman mural painting, and with a "floor decorated with frescoes of red and black pavers," which thus far have been found in Israel only in the orchestra of the Herodian theater at Caesarea Maritima (Aviam 2011, p. 31). As this finding indicates, people of affluence lived in Galilean towns during the first century c.e., and Hellenization/Romanization is attested there, though not to the degree that it is elsewhere.

The Greco-Roman Context in Ancient Church History and Modern Scholarship. Already in antiquity it was recognized that the perspectives of certain pagan authors were often similar to those of NT authors. This was especially true of the Stoic philosopher Seneca, whose sentiments so frequently coincided with Christian ideas that Tertullian (*De anima* 20) referred to him as "often *our* Seneca." Some in later generations even regarded Seneca as a convert to Christianity (Jerome, *De vir. ill.* 12, and Augustine, *Ep.* 153.14), and the perception of a close affinity between the thought of Seneca and Paul led to the creation of a pseudonymous correspondence between the two thinkers.

The Renaissance witnessed a burgeoning of new interests in the classical tradition, and this led to a renewed discovery of certain similarities in thought and expression between early Christian literature and classical literature. One of the byproducts of this revitalized interest in the relationship of early Christianity and classical culture was the search for parallels between the language and formulations of the New Testament and those of pagan authors who wrote in Greek or Latin (White and Fitzgerald, 2003). Greek-Latin glossaries of the NT began to be published, with the first such glossary appearing in volume five of the Complutensian Polyglot, which also contained the first printed Greek NT (printed in 1514, published in 1522). Commentators such as J. Camerarius (1500–1574) began to cite classical authors in support of their interpretations of the NT text, and various collections of "notes" (*annotationes*) on individual words and phrases of the Bible were also published, with the most important of those by Hugo Grotius (1583–1645), who gave copious citations of classical authors to support his interpretative decisions. This proliferation of linguistic and comparative studies culminated in the publication in 1751–1752 of an extensive collection of parallels by J. J. Wettstein, who included them in his critical edition of the New Testament text.

By the nineteenth century, the practice of citing non-Jewish authors in NT lexica and commentaries became routine. Compilations of parallels also continued, with that of E. Spiess in 1871 being the best known, but the significance of these parallels now began to be vigorously debated, with some scholars claiming a direct literary relationship between a NT document and a pagan text. These extravagant claims prompted more judicious treatments and the first systematic attempts to explore the relationships of Greco-Roman authors to the New Testament and other early Christian writers.

Especially pivotal was the work of C. F. G. Heinrici, particularly in his commentaries on the Corinthian correspondence. He argued that "there is such an accumulation of analogies with Polybius, . . . with Epictetus, with Plutarch, with Dionysius of Halicarnassus, and others that it can only be explained by a common spiritual sphere of life" (1887, p. 594). Although criticized by some contemporaries for exaggerating the Greek element over the Semitic in Paul's letters, Heinrici made it impossible for future New Testament scholars to ignore the Hellenistic character of Paul's letters. With copious examples he made a compelling case that Paul thought and spoke under the influence of Hellenistic culture. Heinrici influenced others, notably J. Weiss and his student R. Bultmann, and through them a whole new generation of scholars. Bultmann's 1910 dissertation took up the topic of the diatribe following Heinrici's observations on stylistic similarities, and his early work on form criticism exploited Greco-Roman materials to understand the transmission of the Synoptic tradition.

During this same period of time Heinrici began to organize a group of younger scholars for the purpose of producing a "new Wettstein," that is, a new collection of relevant parallels to the New Testament. As co-editors he enlisted the services of A. Deissmann (whose years of work on a NT lexicon illustrated primarily from the Greco-Roman papyri never materialized), E. von Dobschütz, H. Lietzmann, and H. Windisch, all of whom made extensive use of materials from the Greco-Roman context of early Christianity. When Heinrici died in 1915, his place on the team was taken by J. Leipoldt, and the chief responsibility for overseeing the project shifted to von Dobschütz, who apparently bestowed on it the name by which it was subsequently known, "Corpus Hellenisticum Novi Testamenti." The project subsequently moved to Uppsala under the leadership of A. Fridrichsen but, unfortunately, never succeeded in producing the intended "new Wettstein."

Fortunately, the use of Greco-Roman materials to illuminate the New Testament was not dependent on the Corpus Hellenisticum Novi Testamenti project. While that project languished during the first half of the twentieth century, other scholars were actively exploiting Greco-Roman materials for interpretive purposes. They included F. Cumont, F. J. Dölger, T. Klauser, A. D. Nock, R. Reitzenstein, and M. Vermaseren. Among lexicographers, W. Bauer was unsurpassed in collecting Greco-Roman materials to illuminate NT vocabulary. Eventually, however, the Corpus Hellenisticum Novi Testamenti project was revitalized, first under the leadership of W. van Unnik, and then of H. D. Betz; it ultimately produced six volumes on individual authors and texts, including Aelius Aristides, Apollonius of Tyana, the Corpus Hermeticum, Dio Chrysostom, and Plutarch. More recently, a multivolume collection, initiated under the direction of G. Strecker and continuing under U. Schnelle, has begun to appear, carrying the title *Neuer Wettstein: Texte zum Neuen Testament aus Griechentum und Hellenismus.* A much smaller collection of Greco-Roman materials, titled *Hellenistic Commentary to the New Testament,* was produced by M. E. Boring, doing so on the basis of a German edition by K. Berger and C. Colpe.

Such collections and studies of individual authors comprise only a portion of biblical scholarship that seeks to interpret the NT in light of its Greco-Roman context. Those collections simply provide a convenient synopsis of the results of research by many scholars, and even the best of them are far from being complete. For reasons of space, only the work of selected contemporary scholars can be mentioned here, and only a few of their works cited in the bibliography. Among scholars who are now retired but still active and productive, three names stand out: David E. Aune, Hans Dieter Betz, and Abraham J. Malherbe. Of the three, Aune has been the most comprehensive in regard to the NT as a whole, writing one book on NT literature in its Greco-Roman literary context (1987) and editing another such volume, as well as co-editing a related volume on Greco-Roman culture and the NT. He has been particularly interested in apocalypticism and prophecy (1983) and fully exploited his knowledge of the Greco-Roman context to illuminate the book of Revelation in a massive three-volume commentary (1997–1998).

In addition to editing two volumes on Plutarch for the Corpus Hellenisticum Novi Testamenti project, Betz has made important contributions to the study of the Greco-Roman context in its own right, especially in regard to Lucian of Samosata, the Greek magical papyri, and the Mithras liturgy. He has brought his knowledge of the Greco-Roman world to bear in his various commentaries and studies, especially on the Sermon on the Mount (1995), 2 Corinthians 8–9 (1985), and Galatians (1979). His use of Greco-Roman rhetoric to read Paul's letters has been highly influential, helping to transform the way in which the apostle's letters and other NT documents are understood.

Whereas Betz promoted the use of rhetoric, Malherbe emphasizes epistolography, giving particular attention to ancient epistolary theory and various epistolary collections, such as the pseudonymous Cynic epistles, and inspiring similar studies by his students and others (Klauck 2006). Although he has used his knowledge of Greco-Roman culture and society to identify salient social aspects of early Christianity, his real métier is Hellenistic moral philosophy. From the beginning of his academic career he has demonstrated again and again the hermeneutical relevance of the Greco-Roman moralists, such as Dio Chrysostom and Seneca, for early Christian literature, especially in regard to paraenesis and psychagogy (the guidance of souls). Within the NT, he has focused on Paul (1989), especially his correspondence with the Thessalonians (1987; 2000).

Of younger scholars, the work of two Europeans stands out: Troels Engberg-Pedersen and Hans-Josef Klauck (now at Chicago). Like Malherbe, Engberg-Pedersen focuses on Greco-Roman philosophy and Paul, but he is particularly interested in Stoicism and its relation to the thought of the apostle (2000). He is also adamant that it is methodologically wrong to make a sharp division between Judaism and Hellenism in approaching authors such as Paul, and he sees his work and that of others as overcoming this longstanding divide in scholarly approaches to the apostle. Whereas Malherbe and Engberg-Pedersen have focused on Hellenistic philosophy, Klauck, an expert on Hellenistic religions and magic, has employed a new history-of-religions approach in interpreting the New Testament in light of its religious environment (2000).

As this brief survey has indicated, the Greco-Roman context has been used to interpret the entire NT, including Jesus and the Gospels. Its application to research on the Gospels stands in contrast to a general tendency for many years to claim that the canonical Gospels were unique literary documents completely unlike Hellenistic biographies and the memoirs and lives of the philosophers, and a related tendency to use only Jewish "backgrounds" to interpret the words and works of Jesus. Current research indicates that the Gospels are not utterly unique in form and content, but rather constitute a new subtype of the biography (*bios*) genre of Greco-Roman literature. Furthermore, some scholars have made use of Cynic materials and depicted Jesus and the early Jesus movement in that light, whereas other scholars have used that same Cynic material to stress that the differences outweigh the similarities.

Advocates of using the Greco-Roman context to interpret the NT rarely, if ever, argue that it should be used exclusively. On the contrary, they insist that it should be used in combination with other hermeneutical approaches (e.g., archaeology) and in recognition of the undeniable fact that the NT has a strongly Jewish component. Therefore, scholars typically endeavor to interpret Paul in light of both his Jewish heritage and the larger Greco-Roman world in which he carried out his apostolic work. A similar tendency to utilize both Jewish and non-Jewish materials is also typical in discussing other NT documents. When the NT document makes reference to some person, event, or passage found in the Hebrew Bible, attention naturally focuses on the biblical referent and the treatment of that person, passage, or event in Jewish materials (midrashim, targums, and so forth). When the NT reference is to some nonbiblical person, practice, or site, the Greco-Roman context is often invoked to provide information or an explanation. For instance, Revelation's letters to seven Christian communities in Asia Minor (Rev 2–3) typically evoke the use of both Jewish and Greco-Roman materials to elucidate particular references, with Jewish materials used to clarify such references as the one to Balaam and

Balak (Rev 2:14), and Greco-Roman materials to explicate the enigmatic reference to Pergamum as the site of "Satan's throne" (Rev 2:13). At times this dual use of Jewish and Greco-Roman materials blends together, as in Revelation's use of "Babylon" (14:8; 16:19; 17:5, 18; 18:2, 10, 21) as a code name for Rome, which is further identified by the allusion to its famous "seven hills" (17:9). Use of Greco-Roman materials with other NT documents varies according to the topic under consideration. Discussions of NT passages dealing with slavery, for example, typically entail use of Greco-Roman materials on slaves.

The overarching context of the early Christians was the Greco-Roman world, and it is natural that the NT should reflect its cultural, economic, philosophical, political, rhetorical, and social context. To acknowledge the early Christians' genuine indebtedness to Hellenistic terms, techniques, and traditions does not undermine their theological integrity. Theological significance pertains to what they did with these derived concepts and customary practices, not the sources themselves. Yet determining those Greco-Roman sources and contexts is important for at least four reasons. First, they alert us to the intellectual, cultural, and social matrix in which various ideas and themes appear in the world of the first Christians. Second, they help us to identify the nexus of ideas within a given matrix, that is, the so-called "linkage group" to which they belong. Third, they aid us in recognizing how NT authors selectively adopt and adapt those ideas and practices in service to their theology. Fourth, attention to both the NT text and the Greco-Roman context enables us to recognize similarities as well as differences between them, and thereby to appreciate the distinctiveness of each (Fitzgerald 2001).

Future Directions. In looking to the future use of the Greco-Roman context to interpret the Bible, it will be important not to isolate that context from antiquity as a whole. To be sure, the Greco-Roman period was a distinct epoch in the ancient world, and that distinctiveness allows historians to distinguish it from the periods immediately before and after it. At the same time, it must be remembered that, while there was much that was new in the Greco-Roman period, there were also elements of continuity with what preceded and what followed. Historically, that is usually the case with different temporal periods, and the Greco-Roman period is not an exception to the general rule. More important for the purposes of this article, the Greco-Roman period may be profitably treated as part of what many scholars refer to as the "axial age" (*Achsenzeit*) of world history. This term, which originated in the nineteenth century, was made famous by the German psychiatrist and philosopher Karl Jaspers (1883–1969), who used it to refer to an unprecedented period of philosophical and religious development. Jaspers himself dated the "axis of history" to approximately 500 B.C.E. and the axial age to the period 800–200 B.C.E., but many subsequent scholars have correctly extended the temporal limits of the axial age to include Second Temple Judaism, early Christianity, and the beginnings of rabbinic Judaism. One of the distinguishing features of the axial age was the idea of transcendence, that is, "a kind of critical, reflective questioning of the actual and a new vision of what lies beyond" (Schwartz 1975, p. 3). The result was "the perception of a sharp disjunction between the mundane and transmundane worlds" and "a concomitant stress on the existence of a higher transcendental moral or metaphysical order which is beyond any given this- or other-worldly reality" (Eisenstadt 1982, p. 296). The idea of separation from the mundane world and attachment to a higher, transcendental reality became culturally widespread. "The religious goal of salvation (or enlightenment, release and so forth) is for the first time the central religious preoccupation" (Bellah 2005, p. 366) and that entailed a fundamental rejection of this world and its values. As is readily apparent, such concepts are found also in writings from the biblical tradition. Consequently, the axial age thesis is important in placing various developments within Judaism and early Christianity not merely within the immediate context of the Greco-Roman world but also within their larger global context, of which the Greco-Roman world itself was merely a part (Fitzgerald 2011).

[*See also*: Diachronic Interpretation; Historical Criticism, *subentry* New Testament; *and* Historical Jesus, Quest for the.]

BIBLIOGRAPHY

Aune, David E. *The New Testament in its Literary Environment.* Library of Early Christianity 8. Philadelphia: Westminster, 1987. Treats the genre of the Gospels, including the issue of the Gospels as ancient biographies, Luke-Acts as ancient historiography, early Christian letters within the context of ancient letters, and Revelation in light of ancient revelatory literature.

Aune, David E. *Prophecy in Early Christianity and the Ancient Mediterranean World.* Grand Rapids: Eerdmans, 1983. A judicious discussion of prophecy in the ancient Mediterranean world as a whole, giving significant attention to oracles and related phenomena in Greek and Roman religious and civic life. Also includes ancient Israelite prophecy, Jesus as prophet, and early Christian prophecy.

Aune, David E. *Revelation.* 3 vols. Word Biblical Commentary 52A, 52B, 52C. Dallas: Word, 1997–1998. Aune's *magnum opus* is the preeminent, most exhaustive commentary on Revelation, discussing the biblical text in light of all the various contexts that it reflects and the multiple Jewish and Greco-Roman myths and traditions that the author employs.

Aviam, Mordechai. "Socio-economic Hierarchy and its Economic Foundations in First Century Galilee: The Evidence from Yodefat and Gamla." In *Flavius Josephus: Interpretation and History*, edited by Jack Pastor, Pnina Stern, and Menahem Mor, 29–38. Supplements to the *Journal for the Study of Judaism* 146. Leiden: Brill, 2011. An important recent contribution to the discussion of the economy of first-century Galilee by a first-rate Israeli archaeologist, who demonstrates the presence of various social and economic levels in Yodefat, located not far from Nazareth.

Bellah, Robert. "What Is Axial about the Axial Age?" *European Journal of Sociology* 46 (2005): 69–89. A helpful discussion by an eminent sociologist of religion regarding key features of the Axial Age.

Betz, Hans Dieter. *Galatians: A Commentary on Paul's Letter to the Churches of Galatia.* Hermeneia. Philadelphia: Fortress, 1979. The first major commentary to discuss a NT letter in light of ancient rhetorical theory and practice.

Betz, Hans Dieter. *The Sermon on the Mount: A Commentary on the Sermon on the Mount, including the Sermon on the Plain (Matthew 5:3—7:27 and Luke 6:20–49).* Hermeneia. Minneapolis, Minn.: Fortress, 1995. Illustrates the use of both Greco-Roman and Jewish materials to interpret Matthew's Sermon on the Mount and Luke's similar Sermon on the Plain.

Betz, Hans Dieter. *2 Corinthians 8 and 9: A Commentary on Two Administrative Letters of the Apostle Paul.* Hermeneia. Philadelphia: Fortress, 1985. Treats 2 Cor 8 and 9 as originally two separate letters written by Paul that dealt with the collection for the Jerusalem church.

Eisenstadt, Shmuel N. "The Axial Age: The Emergence of Transcendental Visions and the Rise of Clerics." *European Journal of Sociology* 23 (1982): 294–314. An Israeli sociologist, student of Martin Buber, and major advocate of the Axial Age hypothesis, Eisenstadt's research focused on broad social changes and on major dynamics within civilizations. This article discusses the social implications of the emergence of transcendental visions during the Axial Age.

Engberg-Pedersen, Troels. *Paul and the Stoics.* Louisville, KY: Westminster John Knox, 2000. A reading of portions of Romans, Galatians, and Philippians in light of Stoic ethics.

Fitzgerald, John T. "Cultures of the Greco-Roman World." In *The New Interpreter's Bible One Volume-Commentary*, edited by Beverly Roberts Gaventa and David Petersen, 983–987. Nashville: Abingdon, 2010. A succinct discussion of the Hellenistic context of Second Temple and Hellenistic Judaism as well as early Christianity, with a focus on the political history of the Greco-Roman world, its cultural interactions, religions, education, rhetoric, and philosophy.

Fitzgerald, John T. "Gadara: Philodemus' Native City." In *Philodemus and the New Testament World*, edited by J. T. Fitzgerald, D. Obbink. and G. S. Holland, 343–397. Supplements to Novum Testamentum 111. Leiden: Brill, 2004. A discussion of the Hellenistic town of Gadara, one of the cities of the Decapolis, and its surrounding area, where Matt 8:28–34 locates one of Jesus's most famous exorcisms.

Fitzgerald, John T. "Paul and Paradigm Shifts: Reconciliation and Its Linkage Group." In *Paul Beyond the Judaism/Hellenism Divide*, edited by T. Engberg-Pedersen, 241–262. Louisville, KY: Westminster John Knox, 2001. A discussion of the standard paradigm of reconciliation within the Greco-Roman world, showing how Paul's understanding of reconciliation involves a shift in certain key aspects of the paradigm.

Fitzgerald, John T. with William Scott Green. "How Does Religion Imagine Society?" In *Judaic and Christian Visions of the Social Order: Describing, Analyzing, and Comparing Systems of the Formative Age*, edited by Jacob Neusner, Bruce D. Chilton, and Alan J. Avery-Peck, 1–29. Studies in Religion and the Social Order. Lanham: University Press of America, 2011. Focuses on the emergence of utopian visions of society as one of the characteristic features of the Axial Age.

Heinrici, Carl Friedrich Georg. *Das zweite Sendschreiben des Apostels Paulus an die Korinther.* Berlin: Hertz, 1887. A commentary on 2 Corinthians written with the conviction that Paul's language, style, and thought was significantly influenced by Hellenistic culture.

Klauck, Hans-Josef. *Ancient Letters and the New Testament: A Guide to Context and Exegesis.* Waco: Baylor University Press, 2006. Treats nonliterary and diplomatic correspondence, literary letters, epistolary theory, Jewish letters, and NT letters.

Klauck, Hans-Josef. *The Religious Context of Early Christianity: A Guide to Graeco-Roman Religions.* Studies of the New Testament and its World. Edinburgh: T.&T. Clark, 2000. Contains carefully nuanced discussions of civic and domestic religion (including the sacrificial cult, the associations, and the cult of the dead), the mystery cults, astrology, soothsaying, healing cults, magic, ruler cults, religion and philosophy, and Gnosticism.

Malherbe, Abraham J. *The Letters to the Thessalonians: A New Translation with Introduction and Commentary.* Anchor Bible 32B. New York: Doubleday, 2000. The preeminent commentary on 1 and 2 Thessalonians in light of its Greco-Roman context.

Malherbe, Abraham J. *Paul and the Popular Philosophers.* Minneapolis, Minn.: Fortress, 1989. A collection of eleven of Malherbe's most important essays from the earlier part of his academic career.

Malherbe, Abraham J. *Paul and the Thessalonians: The Philosophic Tradition of Pastoral Care.* Philadelphia: Fortress, 1987. An enlightening discussion of 1 Thessalonians as a paraenetic letter, comparing and contrasting Paul's pastoral approach with the method of psychagogy employed by ancient philosophers with their students.

Schwartz, Benjamin L. "The Age of Transcendence." *Daedalus* 104/2 (1975): 1–6. Focuses on transcendence as the most salient feature of the Axial Age.

White, L. Michael, and John T. Fitzgerald. "*Quod est comparandum:* The Problems of Parallels." In *Early Christianity and Classical Culture: Comparative Studies in Honor of Abraham J. Malherbe,* edited by J. T. Fitzgerald, T. H. Olbricht, and L. M. White, 13–39. Supplements to Novum Testamentum 110. Leiden: Brill, 2003. Discusses the history and contemporary practice of using materials from the Greco-Roman world to interpret early Christian literature.

John T. Fitzgerald

H

Historical Criticism

[*This entry contains two subentries,* Hebrew Bible *and* New Testament.]

Hebrew Bible

Historical Criticism analyzes the biblical text as both an artifact of the past and a record of the past. Thus, historical criticism traditionally has sought to use the Hebrew Bible as evidence for historical events and conditions that are key to the text's stories or that influenced the text.

"Historical criticism" is also sometimes applied as an umbrella designation for various types of readings that use historical circumstances or ideas about the past as keys to biblical interpretation. Thus, form criticism, source criticism, redaction criticism, and tradition history are all historically-premised or diachronic methods sometimes considered types of historical criticism. However, the present entry will primarily focus on historical criticism's use of the Hebrew Bible as a source of historical information and on its understanding of the Hebrew Bible as a product of specific historical contexts.

The Beginnings of Historical Criticism. The intellectual and philosophical underpinnings of historical criticism were made possible by developments in thought in the seventeenth and eighteenth centuries C.E. The Ages of Reason and Enlightenment introduced systematic critical thinking as a preferred mode of thought over and against superstition, and offered rational explanations for natural phenomena and past events that had traditionally been explained by supernatural forces and divine intervention.

Rational and critical examinations of the natural world led to the scientific method. These principles applied to the biblical text led to historical criticism, whereby the text was understood as a product of humans who were influenced by historical circumstances, and as a document that gave evidence of its own historical development. Advancing alongside these ideas and lending them support were critical readings of the text that acknowledged contradictions and disjunctions in it and that began to question the historical accuracy of the Hebrew Bible's account, including traditional assumptions about its authorship and history.

A few early, influential historical critics include Benedict Spinoza (1632–1677) and Richard Simon (1637–1712), who were skeptical that Moses had written the Pentateuch. Predictably, many saw such insights as detrimental to faith. Thus, other scholars combined their developing historical-critical theories with attempts to explain that although humans in particular historical circumstances had produced the biblical books, traditional theology and beliefs were not fatally challenged. For instance, Jean Astruc (1684–1766) affirmed that Moses was one author of the Pentateuch, along with others, but claimed that later writers had corrupted the text. Johann Gottfried Eichhorn (1742–1827) saw in the text myths that, stripped of their primitive trappings, preserved authentic accounts of the past.

By the nineteenth century, especially in Germany, historical-critical questions about the Hebrew Bible defined the discipline. In particular, the development of the religion evidenced in the text became a focus of much investigation. Julius Wellhausen published the most famous and influential study of this topic in 1883, *Prolegomena zur Geschichte Israels* (*Prolegomena to the History of Israel*). Wellhausen's argument, which built on hypotheses of Wilhelm Martin Leberecht de Wette (1780–1849), Karl Heinrich Graf (1815–1869), and others, wove theories about Pentateuchal sources and their composition (the documentary hypothesis) into a particular understanding of the development of Judaism from Yahwism. Put simply, Wellhausen believed that early texts in the Pentateuch reflected an anthropomorphic, Yahwistic religion that had its roots in pre-monarchic, tribal Israel. Later texts, Wellhausen argued, showed an increase in the priestly and legalistic ideas that he believed defined Judaism.

Wellhausen's arrangement of the documents that were believed to make up the Pentateuch and the theory of the development of Israelite religion he proposed have functioned as springboards for every subsequent discussion of the history of the biblical text and Israelite religion. Now, the documentary hypothesis has several variants and competes with many other theories about the composition of the Pentateuch. Some of these radically upend Wellhausen's chronology, and others reject rigid partitioning and dating of the text. Furthermore, substantially more is known today about religion in the time period the Bible describes. Nevertheless, Wellhausen's theories helped solidify many classic tenets of historical criticism.

Historical Criticism in the Early and Mid-Twentieth Century. Well into the twentieth century, historical criticism, or higher criticism as it was sometimes called, remained the primary pursuit of scholars of the Hebrew Bible. Though most of its practitioners were religious, usually protestant Christians, and were often trained in theology, higher criticism remained controversial. Its claims that the text was composed under the influence of historical circumstances and did not always report the past completely or accurately challenged notions of divine inspiration and began to put a noticeable wedge between the academy and Christian believers. Nevertheless, most historical criticism did not seek to overturn the validity of the Bible, but rather to promote the view that proper understanding of the Hebrew Bible gave evidence of God's actions in the past. Furthermore, by understanding the layers of textual development and the progression of religious ideas over time, the adept historical critic believed he or she could strip away later, less pure forms of religious practice and understanding and expose an original, pristine form of biblical religion.

Scholars advancing historical criticism in the early twentieth century included Hermann Gunkel (1862–1932), who sought to illuminate the historical life settings (*Sitz im Leben*) out of which texts arose by positing different genres that had predictable origins. Gerhard von Rad (1901–1971) is also noteworthy for his contributions to redaction criticism, which seeks to understand how and why the biblical text was edited over time.

As historical criticism of the Hebrew Bible advanced in the early and mid-twentieth century, so did archaeological investigation of the ancient Near East. In Palestine, the sites of many biblical events were found and excavated. Egypt and Mesopotamia provided texts with tantalizing possibilities for comparison with the Hebrew Bible. The history of ancient Israel became deeper and broader, and more about Israel's past could be known in greater detail.

By the mid-twentieth century, methods for investigating the biblical past and the conclusions scholars drew about it were segregating themselves along continental lines. In Germany, Albrecht Alt (1883–1956) and Martin Noth (1902–1968) applied tradition-historical understandings of the biblical text and sociological notions to topics such as the religion of the patriarchs, the formation of a tribal Israelite coalition, the rise of the monarchies and states of Israel and Judah, and the composition of the Deuteronomistic history (Josh–2 Kgs). Noth's *Geschichte Israels* (*History of Israel*, 1950) was an outworking of the Altians' theories and a groundbreaking comprehensive study of the topic in light of current evidence.

In the United States, William F. Albright (1891–1971) and his students relied heavily on archaeology and the study of ancient Near Eastern cultures in their reconstructions. Albrightians paid special attention to the patriarchs and conquest and other aspects of early Israel. John Bright's (1908–1995) *A History of Israel* (1st ed., 1959) put the Albrightian paradigm to work on the entire span of Israelite history, from Abraham to Judaism just prior to New Testament times.

Despite the differences in the Altian and Albrightian "schools" of biblical history, in retrospect, the historical-critical judgments they made about the Bible appear more similar than different. Their historical reconstructions helped solidify the idea that much of the Hebrew Bible contained accurate historical information, but that this information might not be self-evident. The methods of historians, with help from the social sciences such as anthropology and archaeology, were needed to ferret out that information.

Common Historical-Critical Conclusions in the Mid-Twentieth Century. Despite the differences in the Altian and Albrightian approaches in the mid-twentieth century, the scholarly consensus was that the stories beginning in Genesis 12 contained actual memories of a patriarchal age. The details of when this age occurred and how historians sifted through the storytelling devices of Genesis to get accurate details about it varied. Nevertheless, the stories of Abraham, Isaac, Jacob, and Joseph were mined for details about pre-Israelite population movements, religion, neighboring peoples, customs and laws, and other aspects of the distant past. Occasionally, recently discovered ancient Near Eastern texts referred to past events and circumstances that appeared similar to ones in the Hebrew Bible, and often when biblical scholars compared the two sources they concluded that the ancient documents substantiated the authenticity of the Bible.

Many of the conclusions about this patriarchal age, especially the connection the ancestors of Israel appeared to have with Mesopotamia (such as Abraham coming from Ur, Gen 11:31), also played into the interpretation of the "Primeval History" (Gen 1—11). Science since the nineteenth century had challenged creationism and the idea of a worldwide flood, but, building on the work of scholars such as Gunkel and using the increasing number of mythological texts found in Mesopotamian sites, historical critics were able to explain the biblical creation accounts and flood story, as well as mythological imagery for God elsewhere (such as in Ps 74), as Israelite instances of common ancient Near Eastern myths.

Mid-twentieth century biblical history also found plenty of apparently accurate historical details and allusions in Exodus through 2 Kings. The biblical accounts of the exodus, the conquest of Canaan, and the makeup of pre-monarchical Israel were all used liberally in historical reconstructions of the past. Many historical-critical investigations of these books assumed that poetic accounts (such as the Song of Miriam, Exod 15:21, and the Song of Deborah, Judg 5) were older and more accurate, but that the narratives reflected actual events and circumstances, too. The Albrightians were famously fond of the conquest model of Israel's emergence due to archaeological evidence that they claimed supported it, and Noth put forward a reconstruction of an early Israelite tribal coalition (the amphictony) that held sway for a while.

In the mid-twentieth century, the availability of an increasing number of annals, chronicles, and king lists from the ancient Near East added to the historical critic's tools for interpreting the biblical stories of the monarchical period. Mentions of events such as the siege of Samaria (on the Assyrian king Sennacherib's prism and in 2 Kgs 18), and details such as Israelite and Judean kings' names in ancient Near Eastern records, confirmed for most that the Hebrew Bible was a reliable and important historical source.

In short, up until the early 1970s, biblical criticism and historical criticism were practically synonymous. Historical criticism was able to draw on the results of archaeology, both texts and other artifacts, as well as on insights from other disciplines, to defend its basic premises—the biblical text and overall biblical storyline reflected real circumstances and events, and careful investigation could uncover them. Though the occasional voice of dissent to historical criticism's supremacy in biblical studies and historical criticism's generally positive assessment of historicity in the Bible had arisen, it was not until Noth and Albright died that scholars began to seriously challenge both notions. Over the decades since then, new evidence and especially new interpretations of evidence have transformed the way scholars approach the Bible for historical information.

Current Historical-Critical Approaches and Conclusions. The remainder of this entry will review major developments in historical criticism of the Hebrew Bible, understood primarily as the search for historical information in or relevant to the text, since the shifts that began in the 1970s. The overarching story is one of increased skepticism that the biblical account is primarily historical or representative of the time it describes. Serious questioning of these ideas began in the study of patriarchal and matriarchal period (beginning in the 1970s), moved through examinations of early Israel and the monarchy (especially in the 1980s and 1990s), and has now reached the latest horizons of the "Old Testament Period," namely, the historical reconstruction of postexilic Judah. Furthermore, historical-critical investigation of the Hebrew Bible along these lines (not related to diachronic analysis of the text's composition and editing) is now almost nonexistent for many of the biblical books, apart from the work of a few religiously conservative scholars.

Historical Criticism of the Pentateuch (Genesis through Deuteronomy). At first glance, the Pentateuch appears to present a smooth story of the patriarchal and matriarchal ancestors of Israel, the exodus, and the wilderness wanderings. As discussed earlier, scholars well into the twentieth century took these as historical in some sense. However, they did have trouble locating these stories in a specific time period. Extrabiblical texts seemed to help some with this problem by elucidating customs, practices, and even population movements that appeared to locate the patriarchs and matriarchs in the Middle Bronze Age (ca. 2000–1550 B.C.E.). As inhabitants of that era, then, the patriarchs' and matriarchs' religion and lifestyle were considered indicative of Palestine at that time and formative for Israelite religion and memories later.

Two books, *The Historicity of the Patriarchal Traditions* by Thomas Thompson (1974), and *Abraham in History and Tradition* (1975) by John Van Seters put to rest the idea that the patriarchal and matriarchal stories were uniquely datable to the Middle Bronze Age, and further showed that these stories could not be definitively located at any time in the past. In short, Thompson and Van Seters showed that names and customs in extrabiblical texts used to date the biblical stories were too widespread in time and space to form meaningful comparisons to the biblical stories, and that the biblical stories of the patriarchs and matriarchs addressed concerns (such as land ownership) that would have been important to a settled, organized society, rather than to a nomadic one. In other words, the stories about the patriarchs and matriarchs spoke to a society very different from the one described in the stories.

Thus, for the most part, historical-critical investigation of the patriarchs and matriarchs has ended, and their stories are seen as undateable, unconfirmable, and as likely written in and built on experiences in the Iron Age (ca. 1200–586 B.C.E.) or later. In 2005, for instance, Mario Liverani proposed a new reading of the patriarchal stories in light of postexilic (i.e., sixth century B.C.E. and later) concerns, as support for his argument that the significant composition and/or editing of these traditions occurred in the Persian period (539–333 B.C.E.). However, a conservative, somewhat positive assessment of the historicity of the patriarchs and matriarchs—and many of the other biblical stories no longer considered reliable as historical evidence by most historians of ancient Israel—that constitutes a minority opinion in scholarship can be found in Iain Provan, V. Philips Long, and Tremper Longman's *A Biblical History of Israel* (2003).

The historicity of the Egyptian sojourn that began with Joseph and ended with the Exodus and the wilderness wanderings was also once largely taken for granted. Located by earlier scholarship sometime in the late Middle Bronze Age or the early Late Bronze Age (ca. 1550–1200 B.C.E.), the Exodus and wilderness wanderings were considered accounts of actual events that had been perhaps exaggerated, but that were real nonetheless. The generic nature of the stories (e.g., the Pharaoh of the Exodus is not named), and the lack of archaeological evidence for a connection between Egypt and the central Palestinian villages that appear to have given rise to Israel and Judah are two of the challenges to historicity more recently offered by historical-critical scholarship.

Now, historical-critical scholarship on the Egyptian sojourn, Exodus, and wilderness wandering stories has effectively ceased. Current critical interpretation of these narratives is accomplished with methods for which a historical reality behind the text is not necessary for interpretation.

Historical Criticism of the Historical Books or Former Prophets (Joshua through 2 Kings). Historical-critical investigation of the biblical stories of Israel's emergence in the land and the eventual monarchies and kingdoms of Israel and Judah has followed a similar trajectory to historical-critical study of the Pentateuch. Traditionally, and in most biblical scholarship into the mid-twentieth century, these books were seen as largely objective records of actual events. These conclusions held despite growing interest in the composition of these books, including de Wette's early claim that the book found by Josiah in 2 Kings 22 was Deuteronomy, and Noth's theory of the Deuteronomistic history, which tied the composition of Deuteronomy to that of Joshua–2 Kings and suggested a date of the books' final form just after the exile.

In other words, even though historical investigation of the formation of the historical books pointed to a date in the seventh or sixth centuries B.C.E. or later, historians still considered them largely historically accurate when describing events that occurred centuries earlier. Bolstering this opinion were finds from the ancient Near East that confirmed that Israelite and Judean kings reported in the Hebrew Bible were known to the Assyrians and Babylonians, and that the Bible appeared to accurately report leaders, wars, and conditions of other ancient Near Eastern kingdoms.

Close reading of these books, combined with increased knowledge of the conditions in ancient Palestine and surrounding areas in the late eleventh through sixth centuries B.C.E. (the rough setting for their stories), showed that the historical picture was more complicated than traditional historical retellings allowed. For instance, the book of Joshua emphasizes the military unity of early Israel and its conquest of Canaan, while Judges presupposes a fractured tribal system whose military unity arose only occasionally, when Israel was threatened by other groups living in Canaan. Thanks to archaeology the conquest theory was eventually discredited, but Judges' picture of a village-based society that had few outward signs of unity did seem similar to the past it uncovered. Furthermore, the locations of the most important tribes of Israel in Judges coincide loosely with places where new villages sprang up in the hills of Palestine in the early Iron Age. Yet, historical criticism also recognizes the formulaic and often legendary elements of the stories in Judges, and has thus provided history with only the possibility that some of Israel's authentic memories are preserved there, and that these may be no more specific than the memory of unorganized, rural origins.

The books of 1—2 Samuel and 1—2 Kings describe the first attempts at permanent organization among the tribes and the subsequent monarchies and kingdoms of Israel and Judah. Though it is clear that the memory of historical events in these stories is colored by the eventuality of the demise of both kingdoms, historical-critical scholarship long assumed the historical veracity of many details in these books. This assumption was largely premised on the idea that certain sections, such as the succession narrative (2 Sam 9—1 Kgs 2), were recorded close to the time of the events they describe and were thus accurate.

Certainly, some of the memories in Samuel and Kings appear to be historically accurate or possible. That the Philistine threat prompted the central hill country tribes to consider a permanent monarchy is, for instance, plausible. However, close readings combined with archaeological knowledge revealed that the story of the kingdoms is not as simple as a rise to greatness and unity, a split, and then a fall from greatness due largely to apostasy.

Recent historical-critical readings of the Hebrew Bible's stories of the early monarchy and kings have noted, for instance, that Saul and David operated in different territories (Saul in the north, David in the south), raising the question of whether David folded Saul's kingdom into his rather than succeeded him. They have also shown that David's kingship is not described as a traditional monarchy. David did not have a seat of power, a complex bureaucracy, and a military, but rather is portrayed as gaining power from the loyalty of his kin and close associates, and from others by using tactics of intimidation and domination. These observations have combined with serious questions about whether the evidence from central Palestine in the early tenth century B.C.E. points to any kind of unified government there, and have resulted in a picture of David as a transitional figure between local leadership and central leadership about whom almost nothing specific can be known. Some would even doubt the soundness of claiming that David existed, given the lack of direct extrabiblical evidence for him.

Solomon, too, has received a historical-critical makeover. The Hebrew Bible has usually been interpreted as describing Solomon as a traditional, impressive king, but that portrayal has fallen out of favor. Most of the evidence marshaled against the historical veracity of such a picture comes from knowledge of conditions in Palestine and the wider ancient Near East, which in most historians' minds show that a great Solomonic empire was very unlikely. Readings of the Solomon stories now recognize that they served a cultural-literary purpose—many ancient Near Eastern cultures had stories of their ancient, great, wise king—and that documents and lists attributed to his reign could have been invented or borrowed from another time period, since there is scant evidence for sophisticated literary activity in tenth century B.C.E. Judah.

Historical-critical readings of the stories of the subsequent kings have also shown that the reality of the kingdoms of Israel and Judah and their monarchs was more complex that the biblical portrait suggests. For instance, the perspective of the book of Kings is that Israel was an apostate kingdom because it committed the sin of breaking away from the Davidic dynasty and routinely tolerated the worship of gods other than Yahweh. Its monarchs were evil and the kingdom fared badly, resulting in its destruction by the Assyrians in 722 B.C.E. On the other hand, Kings reports that Judah, under Yahweh's anointed Davidic dynasty, fared better on the whole, until an evil king, Manasseh, provoked Yahweh's anger and thus the destruction of Jerusalem and the temple by the Babylonians in 586 B.C.E.

According to the Bible, then, the land experienced many years of full-fledged, independent monarchies. Knowledge of the wider ancient Near East, however, puts the biblical picture in a very different perspective. From the ninth to the sixth centuries B.C.E., the activities of the empires of Assyria and Babylonia, and to a lesser extent, Egypt, controlled what went on in Palestine. Who ruled there, and how they behaved, depended on conditions and politics in these empires. When read with this in mind, the biblical accounts of the years of the monarchies show themselves to be a selective interpretation of at least some verifiable events.

The presence of Assyria is clear in the Bible, especially in some prophetic texts (see later). Also, the existence of at least the kingdom of Israel (usually referred to in ancient texts as the House of Omri or by reference to another of its kings) is confirmed in Assyrian sources. Israel—the apostate, inferior kingdom, according to the Bible—not Judah, was a kingdom of which Assyria took notice. At times, Israel functioned well in the Assyrian-controlled ancient Near East, but, eventually, Israel teamed up with former nearby rivals such as Aram-Damascus to resist Assyria. They ultimately failed, and thus Samaria, the Israelite capital, was destroyed by the Assyrians in 722 B.C.E. Furthermore, Judah appears to have been dependent on Israel, largely following it politically. However, Judah did not revolt against Assyria, and thus was spared, but Assyrian pressure on Judah did not let up until the Babylonians took over the Assyrian Empire in 609 B.C.E.

The Assyrian destruction of Samaria is the end of the biblical story of the kingdom of Israel. Biblical scholars now know that what happened in Samaria and greater Israel was typical of what happened after an Assyrian takeover of a region: some of the population was deported (especially elites), some people from elsewhere were resettled there, but life went on. In fact, Yahwistic religion persisted in the area—its followers, the Samaritans, are mentioned in the New Testament. In other words, history continued, even if the biblical story did not.

Though Judah survived the Assyrians, its relations with the next empire, Babylonia, deteriorated to the point where Babylonia invaded and destroyed Jerusalem, including the temple, and took prominent Judeans into exile. (There was one exile in 598 B.C.E., and a second exile and the destruction of Jerusalem occurred in 586 B.C.E.) From the Jerusalem-centric perspective of the Bible, these events constituted the end of an era and a major break in history. Again, however, historical investigation has shown that the Bible ignores the fact that a substantial portion of the population remained where it was, and that Yahwistic religion carried on in the area.

In short, historical-critical assessments of the overarching story lines and major foci of the biblical texts pertaining to the monarchy show that the biblical writers had perspectives and aims that greatly affected how they described past events. In addition, in some cases not only does the Bible's overall story line need contextualizing in light of ancient Near Eastern evidence, its reports of specific events must also be considered very carefully before assuming they are accurate.

These are just some examples of the conclusions of recent historical-critical readings of the books of Joshua–2 Kings. In short, such readings pay attention to the historical contexts and perspectives of the texts and also utilize knowledge of the ancient Near East in the Iron Age. They show that the historical setting of some of these narratives can be determined, especially when the time frame is the ninth century onward thanks to overlap with Assyrian and Babylonian records. However, the most obvious conclusion of historical-critical scholarship on these books is that the biblical stories of the monarchies and kingdoms of Israel and Judah cannot be taken as complete, reliable reports. The Bible's aims and perspectives, combined with the likelihood that many of the stories were written centuries after the events they describe, mean that the stories must be read as selective interpretations of past events.

Historical Criticism of Ezra, Nehemiah, and Chronicles. Ezra and Nehemiah are set in the Persian period, and historical-critical examination of Chronicles has determined that it was a product of the Persian period. Thus, historical-critical examination of all three books seeks to understand what information about the Persian period is reflected in them, how the Persian period milieu affected the events in them, and how the Persian period context affected the formation of their stories. The books of Ezra and Nehemiah pose challenges upfront for historical critics, as the dates for the activity of Ezra are not clear, nor is the chronological relationship between the two men. Furthermore, none of the Persian sources cited in the books are known from elsewhere, and there is some debate about whether they faithfully preserve Persian royal correspondence in word or in spirit. The description of Jerusalem's population, its relationships with its near neighbors, and how the city was rebuilt (including Nehemiah's wall), are all historical questions of interest to biblical scholars. Just as scholarship in the past 40 years has challenged simplistic historical readings of the Pentateuch and historical books, so, recently, the historical veracity of Ezra and Nehemiah's accounts have come under increased scrutiny. Also limiting the books' usefulness for historical questions is their narrow geographical and chronological perspective—Ezra and Nehemiah cover only a few decades of the Persian period, and focus almost exclusively on happenings in Jerusalem.

Chronicles, read historically-critically as a product of the Persian period, provides insight into many Judean attitudes, such as how some Jews attempted to broaden the group of people considered God's people. In addition, Chronicles is interesting to historical critics because it is essentially a retelling of the books of Samuel and Kings. In many cases, Chronicles' new slant consistently indicates a bias, such as its pro-David spin on some events, and as a secondary source is not considered a reliable account. Nevertheless, in some cases, Chronicles' new or different information has prompted scholars to ask whether, in fact, better historical information may occasionally be found there than in Samuel–Kings. For instance, the story of Manasseh being taken captive to Babylon in 2 Chronicles 33 (which does not appear in Kings) has been considered a possibly accurate story.

Historical Criticism of the Prophetic Books. The study of the prophetic literature has long had a historical component. From the superscriptions of the books, to the wars and other events mentioned in them, the prophets seem to provide first-hand evidence of past events. For instance, Isaiah's account of the Assyrian threat, Jeremiah's experiences in the years of Babylonian domination of Judah, and Ezekiel's activities while in Babylonian exile continue to inform historians' portrayals of these eras. However, for better or for worse, the study of the historical background of the prophetic books and of the historical information they may impart has generally not been a large part of historical-critical study aimed at telling a comprehensive story of Israel's past. For that endeavor, historical criticism of the historical books has been paramount. Rather, the historical-critical study of the prophets has been a subset of research into the prophetic literature.

Historical Criticism of Other Books in the Hebrew Bible. Historical criticism initially touched on almost every book of the Hebrew Bible. Some books, such as Ruth and Esther, despite their historical settings, were determined to fit better in the realm of story than history, and are not used as evidence for reconstructing events in Israel's past. Wisdom books, such as Proverbs and Ecclesiastes, are understood as relics of historically contextualized modes of thought, but, again, not as potential evidence for past events. Psalms has long been the object of a type of historical-critical study. Yet, form criticism of the Psalms is a subdiscipline of Psalms studies and is not normally used by historians to reconstruct ancient Israel.

Current Approaches to the Hebrew Bible and History. Historical criticism was once the primary academic method applied to the Hebrew Bible. Over time, evidence that the biblical story is incomplete, sometimes impossible to examine in the framework of a known historical context, and even, at times, historically inaccurate, led to a reduction of historical criticism's prominence in biblical studies. Nevertheless, the discussion of what kind of historical information the Bible can provide is still active. Traditional historical criticism concerned itself with the accuracy of events, conditions, and people reported in the text, and with locating extrabiblical evidence that could help contextualize the biblical story. Now, historical interest in the Bible is more focused on understanding the historical development of the overarching ideas that influenced how Israel remembered its past. Thus, studies of ideas such as monotheism, and of topics such as the impact that the Babylonian exile had on religious and personal life, are common historical-critical topics. Scholars writing the history of ancient Israel also now rely less on ongoing historical-critical analyses of the texts and more on archaeology, sociology, and wider ancient Near Eastern study for their evidence for Israel's past.

[*See also* Diachronic Interpretation; Form Criticism, *subentry* Hebrew Bible; Redaction Criticism, *subentry* Hebrew Bible; Source Criticism; *and* Tradition-Historical Criticism.]

BIBLIOGRAPHY

Albertz, Rainer. *Israel in Exile: The History and Literature of the Sixth Century* B.C.E. Society of Biblical Literature Studies in Biblical Literature 3. Atlanta: Society of

Biblical Literature, 2003. A comprehensive historical-critical study.

Albright, William F. "Abram the Hebrew: A New Archaeological Interpretation." *Bulletin of the American Schools of Oriental Research* 163 (1961): 36–54. A now discredited argument for Abraham's historicity based on archaeology and biblical evidence.

Alt, Albrecht. *Der Gott der Väter: Ein Beitrage zur Vorgeschichte der Israelitischen Religion.* Beiträge zur Wissenschaft vom Alten und Neuen Testament 3. Stuttgart: W. Kohlhammer, 1929. English translation: "The God of the Fathers." In Albrecht Alt, *Essays on Old Testament History and Religion*, 3–66. Oxford: Basil Blackwell, 1966. A reconstruction of early Israelite religion based on historical-critical readings of the patriarchal and matriarchal stories.

Ben Zvi, Ehud. "Total Exile, Empty Land and the General Intellectual Discourse in Yehud." In *Concept of Exile in Ancient Israel and Its Contexts*, edited by Christoph Levin and Ehud Ben Zvi. Beihefte zur Zeitschrift für die Alttestamentliche Wissenschaft 404. Berlin: de Gruyter, 2010. An example of modern historical-critical study's shift to investigating the historical contexts and development of ideas.

Brettler, Marc Zvi. "Method in the Application of Biblical Source Material to Historical Writing (with Particular Reference to the Ninth Century BCE)." In *Understanding the History of Ancient Israel*, edited by H. G. M. Williamson, 305–336. Proceedings of the British Academy 143. Oxford: Oxford University Press, 2007. Pays particular attention to the use of prophetic literature for historical reconstruction.

Bright, John. *A History of Israel.* 4th ed. Philadelphia: Westminster, 1959. Louisville, Ky.: Westminster John Knox, 2000. The classic articulation of the Albrightian assessment of the Bible as a historical source and Israel's history based on it.

Davies, Philip R. *In Search of "Ancient Israel."* Journal for the Study of the Old Testament: Supplement Series 148. Sheffield, UK: Sheffield Academic Press, 1992. Questions many assumptions of historical criticism and histories based on it, and challenges the predominance of the Hebrew Bible as a historical source for the past.

Finkelstein, Israel, and Neil Asher Silberman. *The Bible Unearthed: Archaeology's New Vision of Ancient Israel and the Origin of Its Sacred Texts.* New York: Free Press, 2001. An archaeological perspective on the Bible's historicity.

Grabbe, Lester L., ed. *Can a "History of Israel" Be Written?* Journal for the Study of the Old Testament: Supplement Series 245. European Seminar in Historical Methodology 1. Sheffield, UK: Sheffield Academic Press, 1997. Scholars from several perspectives tackle the growing realization that the Hebrew Bible is a problematic historical source.

Graham, M. Patrick, Kenneth G. Hoglund, and Steven L. McKenzie, eds. *The Chronicler as Historian.* Journal for the Study of the Old Testament: Supplement Series 238. Sheffield, UK: Sheffield Academic Press, 1997. A collection of opinions about Chronicles' value for history writing, and the historical context from which it came.

Handy, Lowell K., ed. *The Age of Solomon: Scholarship at the Turn of the Millennium.* Studies in the History and Culture of the Ancient Near East 11. Leiden: Brill, 1997. Scholars discuss what can be said about Solomon given increasing doubt about the historicity of the biblical stories about him.

Hayes, John H., and J. Maxwell Miller, eds. *Israelite and Judaean History.* Philadelphia: Westminster, 1977. A snapshot of historical-critical scholarship and its implications for history, just as questions about the historicity of the patriarchs and conquest were beginning to be taken seriously.

Henige, David. "In Good Company: Problematic Sources and Biblical Historicity." *Journal for the Study of the Old Testament* 30 (2005): 29–47. A comparison of the Hebrew Bible with other ancient historical texts that argues that neither should be uncritically trusted.

Kelle, Brad E., and Megan Bishop Moore. *Israel's Prophets and Israel's Past: Essays on the Relationship of Prophetic Texts and Israelite History in Honor of John H. Hayes.* Library of Hebrew Bible/Old Testament Studies 446. New York: T.&T. Clark, 2006. A collection of perspectives on the relationship of the prophetic books to history writing and history's role in understanding the prophets.

Lemche, Neils Peter. *The Old Testament between Theology and History: A Critical Survey.* Louisville, Ky.: Westminster John Knox, 2008. Seeks a new understanding of the Hebrew Bible after what Lemche calls "the crisis of historical-critical scholarship."

Liverani, Mario. *Israel's History and the History of Israel.* Bible World. London: Equinox, 2005. A recent, creative, history of Israel that finds some authentic information in the Hebrew Bible, but also late, Persian period ideas reflected in the text.

Miller, J. Maxwell, and John H. Hayes. *A History of Ancient Israel and Judah.* 2d ed. Philadelphia: Westminster, 1986. Louisville, Ky.: Westminster John Knox, 2006. A history of Israel that begins its discussion of every period with a historical-critical examination of the relevant Hebrew Bible texts.

Moore, Megan Bishop, and Brad E. Kelle. *Biblical History and Israel's Past: The Changing Study of the Bible and History*. Grand Rapids. Mich.: Eerdmans, 2011. A comprehensive overview of historical criticism's assessment of the Hebrew Bible as a historical source.

Na'aman, Nadav. "In Search of Reality behind the Account of David's Wars with Israel's Neighbors." *Israel Exploration Journal* 52 (2002): 200–224. A historical-critical assessment of some of the stories of David.

Noth, Martin. *Geschichte Israels*. Göttingen: Vandenhoeck & Ruprecht, 1950. English translation: *The History of Israel*. New York: Harper, 1958. The classic history written from the perspective of the German "Altians."

Provan, Iain, V. Philips Long, and Tremper Longman III. *A Biblical History of Israel*. Louisville, Ky.: Westminster John Knox, 2003. A conservative history, which argues that the historian's first impulse should be to trust the historicity of the biblical account.

Thompson, Thomas L. *The Historicity of the Patriarchal Narratives: The Quest for the Historical Abraham*. Beihefte zur Zeitschrift für die Alttestamentliche Wissenschaft 133. Berlin: de Gruyter, 1974. Repr., Harrisburg, Pa.: Trinity Press International, 2002. Helped discredit the historicity of the patriarchs and matriarchs, in part by showing faulty methodology in comparisons with extrabiblical sources.

Van Seters, John. *Abraham in History and Tradition*. New Haven, Conn.: Yale University Press, 1975. Helped discredit the historicity of the patriarchs and matriarchs, in part by showing that the concerns of the text were the concerns of a settled society.

Williamson, H. G. M. *Ezra/Nehemiah*. Word Biblical Commentary 16. Waco, Tex.: Word, 1985. A biblical commentary with a historical-critical focus that has been extremely important for historical reconstruction of the Persian period.

Megan Bishop Moore

New Testament

Since the nineteenth century, scholars have approached the New Testament (NT) with methodological tools that help to reconstruct the original settings and meanings of the texts, as well as to evaluate the historicity of the events and characters that are mentioned in these ancient writings. Although historical critics realize that a text may have many different meanings, they are particularly interested in recovering the original authorial intent and the earliest audiences for the texts that were collected into the Christian canon. This methodology is more concerned with determining the history of individual texts and authors than in reconstructing a biblical theology that assumes the Bible speaks univocally. The historical-critical method argues that the NT is best understood when readers attempt to place the texts within their original, specific Jewish, Hellenistic, and Roman cultural contexts.

This methodological approach to the NT also tries to determine what actually happened in the first and early second centuries during the rise of earliest Christianity. As such, historical critics seek to reconstruct a more complete history of Christian origins, into which the individual texts of the NT can be placed. Scholars have increasingly recognized that the canonical texts provide us with an incomplete and subjective picture of early Christian history. Increasingly, the goal of this method has been to move beyond the individual texts and write a historical account that acknowledges the limitations of the canonical books; a legitimate history of early Christianity cannot be written if the canonical books are used as our only sources. In light of this concern, the discoveries of many noncanonical Christian texts in the Oxyrhynchus papyri and the Papyrus Berolinensis 8502 (both sets of texts were discovered in the late nineteenth century) and the Nag Hammadi Library (discovered in 1945) have provided new resources for historical reconstructions of early Christianity. The immense collection of material in the Dead Sea Scrolls (discovered from 1946 to 1956) has also provided new insights into the Jewish context of the first century. While still limited by the incomplete nature of the ancient sources, these textual discoveries have led to a significant increase in the ability to provide a more complete picture of how, when, and why Christianity began.

For the past two centuries, this methodology has often led to conflicts between readers who use the method to defend a theological or ecclesiastical understanding of the NT (apologetic and dogmatic history), and those who seek to reconstruct a secular history that focuses on placing the writings in their earliest literary and cultural settings. Historical critics have increasingly begun with the premise that all NT texts were human products; that starting point differs substantially from ecclesiastical and devotional approaches that believe the texts were divinely inspired and that the texts must be understood within a theological context. Nevertheless, in modern practice, this method is used equally by secular and theologically minded scholars. Historical criticism recognizes the long tradition history of textual interpretations and attempts to peel back the interpretative layers in order to reconstruct an original author, sources, audience, cultural context, social setting (*Sitz im Leben*), and provenance for each NT text.

To accomplish the goals of historical criticism, after the Enlightenment biblical scholars began using and developing a wide variety of literary and social-historical methods, many of which were first employed by literary scholars and historians in other fields. In the nineteenth and early twentieth century, text criticism, philology, form criticism, and early forms of redaction criticism were further developed as tools of historical critics who desired to better understand the original wording, meaning, and compositional history of NT texts. Since the mid-twentieth century, comparative literary criticism, archaeological analysis, social-scientific analysis, and an interest in the socioeconomic history of the Roman world have also been widely used to reconstruct earliest Christianity and the wider cultural contexts in which the NT texts were written. Thus historical criticism is now used as a category that encompasses a variety of subdisciplines, all with the common goal of understanding the ancient texts within their earliest cultural and literary contexts. Historical critics are usually trained in ancient languages (Hebrew, Greek, Latin, and possibly Coptic, Aramaic, and Syriac), which allows them to make arguments about the original wording and meaning of the narrative and conduct comparative studies with other literature and cultural traditions from the Roman world, late Hellenistic and early Roman Judaisms, and the ancient Near East.

For example, when applying this method to the Gospels, historical critics are interested in who wrote the narratives, what ancient genre category best fits their style, when they were written, what sources were used, and the original wording of the texts. At the same time critics are also concerned to differentiate between the theology of the author and the actual events in the story that can be plausibly traced back to the life of the historical Jesus and his first followers. If one argues that due to the reference to the destruction of the Jerusalem Temple (Mark 13), Mark was written during or just after the Jewish War with Rome (ca. 72 C.E.), then the question is not simply what does the Gospel of Mark tell us about the historical Jesus; it also asks what can be known about the late first century author and audiences who produced and interacted with the story. In other words, historical critics of the Gospels are interested both in the historicity of the stories about Jesus and in the historical settings of the authors of the texts. This includes a desire to know the author's original wording and the meaning of the text (text criticism and philology), the sources used and compositional tendencies of the author (form and redaction criticism), as well as an interest in cultural and literary contexts and analogies (archaeology, and social-scientific analysis).

Nineteenth-Century Applications of the Method. Although the roots of historical criticism of the Bible can be traced back to the periods of the Reformation and Renaissance in Europe, the rise of the Tübingen School in the early nineteenth century provides the clearest line of descent for modern historical critics of the NT. Two major areas of interest dominated the debates (as they still do): the historical Jesus, and the historicity of the stories in the Acts of the Apostles.

Ferdinand Christian Baur (1792–1860) began the modern deliberations about the usefulness of the Acts of the Apostles as a reliable history of earliest Christianity. If the stories in the canonical Acts were historically reliable (as they had been understood by pre-Enlightenment thinkers), then much of the historical-critical enterprise related to the NT would be unnecessary. Since the time of Irenaeus in the late second century, Acts had provided the basic framework of historical events, into which many of the other books of the NT (most notably, the letters attributed to Paul) were chronologically arranged. In contrast to the ecclesiastical tradition that accepted the Acts narrative as historical fact, Baur argued in his 1845 publication of *Paul, the Apostle of Jesus Christ* that the narrative was intentionally written by a follower of Paul in order to reconcile the differences between Peter and Paul. Rather than presenting a reconstruction of earliest Christianity that stressed unified origins from Jerusalem, Baur highlighted the oppositional nature of the earliest Christian leaders. Since the author of Acts was interested in a synthesis between originally disparate positions (thesis and antithesis), he was not interested in presenting a historically accurate picture of the past. Instead, he framed the story of Christian origins in a way that was favorable to his early second-century setting.

Influenced by G. W. F. Hegel's philosophy of history, in which two opposing historical forces create a tension that resolves through synthesis, Baur posited that Luke-Acts was written in order to unite Jew and gentile factions in earliest Christianity thereby presenting a unified picture of Christian origins and setting the stage for Catholicism. According to Baur, Acts explained the mission of Paul to the gentiles of the church in Rome in the early second century. Baur's contention that there was diversity in earliest Christianity rather than consistent accord has exacted a wide range of responses. While the traditional understanding of Christianity deriving from unified origins—based on a literal reading of Acts—was seriously challenged, Baur's opponents (those who refused to question the historicity of the NT) were both numerous and powerful. They held significant professorships on the theological faculties of most European universities and refused for most of the nineteenth century to allow Baur's historical-critical methodology to infiltrate too deeply into the educational system.

At about the same time that the reliability of the Acts narrative was first seriously called into question by Baur, David Friedrich Strauss (1808–1874) began the modern debate about the historical Jesus. In *The Life of Jesus, Critically Examined* (German, 1835–1836; English translation by Georg Elliot in 1846), he questioned whether the miracles of Jesus in the Gospels were historically verifiable, and whether scholars could actually reconstruct the life of Jesus. His answers were negative: we can neither accept that the miracles were authentic nor reconstruct the historical Jesus. Strauss declared that the Gospels were not historically reliable; their mythological nature made them ineffectual as historical sources.

The publications of F. C. Baur and D. F. Strauss serve as two of our earliest examples of historical-critical scholarship on the NT. By drawing on the Hegelian philosophy that was increasingly popular in the nineteenth century, they provided a new reconstruction of first- and early-second-century Christianity. For the first time, Baur and Strauss made available an alternative view of early Christian history that was not based primarily on a theological model of sacred history, in which the Bible should be interpreted only within the light of a divine plan of salvation.

In the mid-nineteenth century, several notable scholars defended and expanded on Baur's ideas. While they helped spread the influence of the Tübingen School, their exuberance for the recently formulated historical methodology was also met with stiff resistance. For example, Albert Schwegler agreed with Baur's thesis and applied the same Hegelian methodology to his study of early Christianity (*Nachapostolischen Zeitalters* [Postapostolic Age], 1845). Although he claimed that the audience was the Jewish-Christian community in Rome, ca. 110–150, rather than the gentiles, Schwegler's entire project was based on the model of the Hegelian dialectic. Similarly, Edward Zeller agreed with Baur's thesis but argued that the real story of Paul was changed in order to appease the Roman Jewish-Christians. Zeller questioned the reliability of the stories and speeches in Acts, and determined that they were mostly the mythical creation of the author. He also argued that the author of Acts intended his story to be a defense of Christianity before the Roman authorities. Because of their strict adherence to Hegel's philosophy of history, and Baur's model of how it could be applied to historical research on the NT, Schwegler and Zeller were staunchly opposed by scholars who rejected this historical-critical approach and defended a theologically based model of historical inquiry.

Despite the extensive rejection of their historical reconstructions, The Tübingen School's early example of historical-critical scholarship had a lasting impact on the field. Rather than assuming that the books of the NT were written under divine inspiration by individuals in unknowable settings, the new scholarly challenge was to attempt to locate a social situation where these texts made sense within a larger historical framework of Christian origins. Although the dialectic approach of the Tübingen School has long been rejected as the most useful philosophy of history, many of our relevant historical-critical questions related to the NT were formulated in these early nineteenth-century debates. Until the last quarter of the twentieth century, these questions set the basic parameters for the historical-critical debate. Throughout the twentieth century, Baur's interest in the relationship between Jewish and gentile Christianity, and the purpose and social setting of the Gospels and Acts, continued to be considered central to our modern reconstructions of Christian origins. The historical relationship between the Pauline epistles and Acts also has been a significant interest, with many modern scholars in general agreement with Baur's contention that Acts was written at the end of the first or beginning of the second century, when the issue of the relationship between Jewish and gentile Christianities was in need of resolution.

Early Twentieth-Century Applications. The best way to examine this methodology is to examine several of the key scholarly developments during the twentieth century. By the beginning of the twentieth century, several shifts in the historical-critical method can be observed. The interest in the sources for the Gospels and Acts became a central focus (Redaction and Form Criticisms). The study of NT texts as literary achievements, which continues to be the focus of many recent studies, also began in earnest at the beginning of this period. Finally, the comparison of early Christian texts with other literature from the Greco-Roman period became more prevalent.

Ernst Troeltsch provided a model of historical analysis for biblical scholars, which differed from the Hegelian dialectic. Most importantly for the historical-critical method, his notion of history was based on a late-nineteenth-century scientific model that insisted on the similarity of past and current human behavior (the principle of analogy). If the virgin birth and the resurrection of the dead are currently impossible, they should not be considered valid in the ancient historical record. Troeltsch held that the history of Christianity should not be based on dogmatic belief; rather, historical reconstruction must be a scientific pursuit based on probabilities and open to modification over time. Troeltsch provided considerable impetus to twentieth-century historical-critical inquiry on the Bible, even while apologetic, nonsecular historiography retained its dominant position in most theology departments.

Regarding the general goal of reconstructing a history of earliest Christianity, the usefulness of the narrative of Acts continued to be a topic taken up by many historical critics. Acts is a type of ancient historiographical literature, and, as such, it provides our earliest story of Christian origins. However, by the beginning of the twentieth century, many questions had already been raised about the usefulness of Acts in modern historiography. This ancient story of Christianity, which had been revered for eighteen hundred centuries, was found to be lacking the essential qualities of historical analysis that would make it a reliable source. Attention to the scholarship on Acts in the past century provides a useful overview of how the methodology developed and grew to prominence in the field of biblical studies.

With several major publications on the book of Acts, Henry J. Cadbury became one of the most influential scholars of the first half of the twentieth century. Cadbury shifted the focus from attempting to discern the historical setting of Luke-Acts, which had consumed the Tübingen School, to an interest in the style and literary skill of the author. For example, based on his assessment of the writing style in Acts, Cadbury is well known for refuting the claim that the author of Acts was Luke the physician, which is briefly referred to in Colossians 4:14. Regarding the authorship and setting of Luke-Acts, Cadbury doubted the uncritical attribution of the text to a companion of Paul or more generally to an eyewitness of the events. He developed the thesis that the author was quite at home in an urban rather than a rural setting. He also made a persuasive argument in favor of viewing the author as quite familiar with a variety of cultures and traditions: Greek, Roman, Jewish, and Christianity. Cadbury also made a variety of contributions to the major historical-critical publication project of the early twentieth century, *The Beginnings of Christianity.* Cadbury argued negatively against taking the speeches of Acts as the actual speeches of the historical characters. Based on the fact that they were written in Lukan style and on his comparison of these speeches with other Greco-Roman authors who employed speeches as a literary convention, Cadbury found that there was no reason to assume the historicity of the speeches.

The influential five-volume collection to which Cadbury contributed, *The Beginnings of Christianity* is illustrative of NT historical-critical scholarship in the early twentieth century. Many of the essays in the collection reveal a concern to place the study of the NT generally within the context of the Greek and Jewish traditions of historiography. The authors sought to understand Acts as history in the same way we understand the Chronicler of the Hebrew Bible, Tacitus, or Josephus. They were also concerned to show that Acts was written by someone who was dependent upon sources (particularly the "we" sections in Acts). The editors of *The Beginnings of Christianity* made a reasonable argument for understanding Luke-Acts as an apologetic historian whose purpose was to give religious instruction. After reviewing the basic theological perspective of Luke-Acts, they reviewed the primary evidence for establishing the provenance of Acts. They concluded that Luke-Acts was clearly not acceptable to all Christian communities. Since the Gospels of Mark and Matthew, and the Pauline epistles do not agree with Luke-Acts, they found it difficult to imagine these texts arising in the same type of early Christian communities.

In contrast to the more progressive historical critical studies in this collection, C. W. Emmet took up the apologetic task of defending Luke, the physician and companion of Paul, as the author of Acts. His arguments, organized as a point-by-point refutation of all who denied an early date and Luke (Paul's companion according to Colossians) as the author, are typical of the traditional way of reasoning. His basic argument was that Paul's autobiographical chronology in Galatians 1—2 is consistent with the story of Acts. Thus there is reason to suppose that a companion of Paul wrote Acts. He argued that there was no friction between Peter and Paul that would have occasioned the writing of Acts, therefore Acts is historically accurate and should be used as the modern history of Christian origins.

Hans Windisch argued for the exact opposite position, with a line of argumentation that was in many respects in line with the Tübingen School: Galatians and Acts have quite distinct pictures of the relationship between Paul and Jerusalem, and they are chronologically dissimilar. Windisch suggested a date of composition prior to the end of the first century, when he thought that the Pauline epistles would not yet have been collected or well known. This date is also supported on the grounds that Acts appears to have been written before the persecutions of Christians began, before the Gnostic influences on Christianity needed a detailed refutation, and at a time when apocalyptic expectations appeared in a weakened form in comparison to Paul's epistles.

Writing just after Windisch, B. H. Streeter is typical of a more theologically acceptable, historical-critical attempt to solve the problem of the relationship between the author of Luke-Acts and Paul. He argued that the author was Luke, a man from Antioch who moved to Rome and became a companion of Paul. He concluded that one reason Luke did not reveal a clear knowledge of Paul's letters and ideas in the stories in Acts was that his Roman audience would have already been familiar with Paul's theology from the Letter to the Romans; he did not want to repeat what the audience already knew. In general, Windisch—as a representative of the larger project of *The Beginnings of Christianity*—and Streeter's response—from a slightly more conservative perspective—summarized the positions of much of the historical-critical scholarship prior to the Second World War.

By the time of his death in 1947, Martin Dibelius was one of the most well-known practitioners of the historical-critical method in NT studies. He outlined and developed a basic thesis that dealt mainly with Acts as a literary achievement comparable to other literature of ancient historiography. He was interested in the sources of Acts and provided a detailed analysis of the purpose of the speeches in Acts. Dibelius's application of style-criticism (*Stilkritik*) brought renewed interest in Acts as a literary achievement: the narrative was written by an author who was more interested in a meaningful story than he was in (modern) historiography. Dibelius found the author to have had greater freedom with his limited source material, in contrast to the Gospels—where he understood the work to be much more that of an editor: compiling and arranging earlier sources with less freedom of expression. For Dibelius, the purpose of Luke was not to provide a scientific history of these events but to compose, as a literary artist or Christian preacher, a narrative that was meaningful for his audience. Thus Luke combined traditional travel narratives and stylized sermons with more historical details known from his own experience or from brief reports. Dibelius considered Luke's use of speeches to be typical of ancient historiographic literature, in which the author introduced speeches into the story when they were relevant to his purpose. The speeches were meant as sermons and practical examples for his audience. Dibelius argued that Luke's purpose was more that of a preacher than a historian.

Second Half of the Twentieth Century. After World War II, relations between German, English, and American NT scholars were mended fairly rapidly. German scholarship continued to dominate historical-critical studies, as many notable American scholars received their advanced degrees in Germany, and German scholars moved to the United States to teach in theological seminaries and secular universities. From the 1950s through the 1970s, the critical method was dominant in biblical studies on both sides of the Atlantic. Increasingly, the historical-critical method asked questions about authorial settings and the social purpose of NT texts. There was a growing acknowledgment that noncanonical books needed to be given more prominence in the reconstructions of the origins of Christianity. There was also wider acceptance of the realization that the NT books are widely divergent, in terms of their theologies and Christologies, social-historical settings, and purpose.

In the 1950s, Ernst Haenchen (1894–1975) sought to further understand the theological purpose of the author of Acts. His commentary is a thorough evaluation of the Lukan purpose, rather than a traditional analysis of Acts as history. For Haenchen the question was not: Did Acts represent Paul correctly and, if so, how should we understand the differences between the epistles and Acts? Rather, the question was: How does the picture of Paul in Acts make sense in the setting of a Christian community removed by one or two generations from the time of Paul? One of the most evident ways that the author of Acts brought out this significance was through telling a story that presented the uniformity and simplicity of the origins of Christianity. The author was not writing history for history's sake; the intention was to develop ideals for his present community. As such, Haenchen preferred to call Acts a historical novel rather than a work of history.

Hans Conzelmann was also interested in understanding Luke's reason for writing this story. Conzelmann's study was the most influential historical critical monograph on Luke-Acts in the mid-twentieth century. While few recent critics of Luke-Acts agree completely with Conzelmann's ideas, his work, in combination with Haenchen's commentary, established the set of questions that scholars would bring to the study of Luke-Acts for the next 30 years. Conzelmann maintained that the author intended to develop a tripartite scheme of history in order to lessen anxiety among Luke's readers regarding the second coming. In Luke-Acts the story of Jesus became a middle stage, between the prophetic age (ending with John the Baptist) and the age of the church. The author provided his readers with a salvation history, with a blatant tendency to de-eschatologize the vocabulary of Jesus and present the Kingdom of God as an existing heavenly realm, rather than a near *parousia*.

Late Twentieth-Century Developments. By the last quarter of the twentieth century many of the key topics for historical critics of the NT were well established. Literally hundreds of studies based on this method were produced on an annual basis, tracing the origins, socioeconomic settings, functions, and specific historical meanings of the texts.

Archaeology became a more prominent feature of historical reconstructions, as scholars saw the value in integrating scientifically excavated material culture into their work. This was especially the case with historical studies of the lives of Paul and Jesus. In Pauline studies, archaeology in Turkey, Greece and Rome has been used to fill out the details of the social and political world of the Roman Empire. Increasingly, scholars have been interested in clarifying the relationship between Paul and the empire. They have accomplished this not only through a careful analysis of Paul's language and imagery but also through a more thorough development of the specific cultural settings where Paul and the earliest Christian communities were established (Antioch, Eph, Cor, Rom, etc.).

As the twentieth century came to a close, work on the historical Jesus also rose in prominence for historical critics. Since the work of Strauss in the mid-nineteenth century, many scholars had taken up the goal of placing Jesus into a first-century historical context. Nevertheless, the results of historical Jesus research for the past century and a half often tells us as much about the scholar's affinities as it potentially does about Jesus's original setting and purpose (remaking the past in our own image). Many scholars have used the historical-critical method in order to make the character of Jesus represent modern ideas and interests.

In what has been called the "Third Quest" (referring especially to scholarship since the 1980s), historical critics have been guided by three major principles: (1) scholars must place Jesus within his early first-century Jewish context; (2) the canonical Gospels must be supplemented by other early Christian writings that provide diverse stories and sayings (*Gospel of Thomas*, *Gospel of Peter*, *Gospel of Mary*, etc.); and (3) studies should avoid theological discourse and aim to understand Jesus within the human context of the Roman province of Galilee (Theissen and Winter 2002). Since the late 1980s, these studies have been greatly enhanced by the archaeological work in Galilee, including significant excavations in the Roman-period strata of the Jewish city of Sepphoris (Zippori).

In recent scholarship on Acts, partially in response to Conzelmann, early Christian eschatological ideas gained more attention. Even though many scholars rejected his idea that Luke was moving away from high eschatological expectation, the issue has remained a major topic of debate. Another topic of increasing interest is the role of Paul in Acts. Many recent scholars have followed the pattern set by previous historical-critical analysis, observing that the Paul of Acts is quite distinct from the Paul of the epistles. With regard to the setting and date of Luke, the picture of Paul in Acts has typically caused scholars to separate Luke from close temporal proximity to Paul or his followers. In the past two decades there has also been a move away from the strict dichotomy of "Jewish Christians" versus "gentile Christians" that was proposed and debated in the nineteenth and early twentieth century. Scholars now recognize that distinctions between Jewish and gentile followers of Jesus were much more complicated than Baur's early work implied. Literary analysis, with important implications about the genre, purpose, and social setting of Acts, also became a widely practiced field of inquiry. Although many scholars have moved away from uncritical acceptance of the story of Acts as the actual history of earliest Christianity, assessing the historicity of every element in the story has remained an extremely popular topic for historical-critical examination.

Prospectus for Future Research and Questions about the Methodology. In order for historical criticism to develop and stay relevant in the coming century, scholars need to continue to adjust their practices in light of several valid critiques of the method. Besides the ongoing conflict between biblical scholars who use this method and ecclesiastical and devotional readers who are more inclined to read the NT through theological lenses, historical criticism of the NT since the late twentieth century has been increasingly criticized on at least two other grounds.

First, detractors of traditional historical criticism have noted the long-standing domination of Western and colonial biblical interpretation that resulted in the relative lack of attention to issues related to women and minority readers. Historical criticism, they observe, has been used in many modern settings to justify the resistance to and oppression of women and minorities in ecclesiastical and other settings. Traditional historical criticism has also been used to support Western imperialistic practices. Since the late twentieth century, feminist and gender scholarship on the Bible and scholars interested in reception history have begun the process of reformulating historical and interpretive questions in order to avoid propagating dangerous worldviews in our present interpretive context. Similarly, historical criticism of the NT has increasingly been negatively assessed for paying so much attention to first- and second-century authors and audiences that there is little interest in understanding readers in other times and places. Reader-response criticism, literary criticism, and cultural studies approaches are much more interested in the active role that the reader has in deciding the meaning of the text, in ancient and modern settings. Although literary critics and historical critics often approach a text with different questions, the future success of both methods will require cooperation and mutual interest between the practitioners of these methods; they are not mutually exclusive scholarly enterprises.

Second, scholars have regarded the historical positivism and objectivism of this method to be romantic and overly optimistic. Historical critics have been judged to be too often uncritical of their own biases, which cloud and influence their historical reconstructions. With the espoused goal of writing objective history, scholars have, in fact, often been unaware of their own assumptions and theories. Especially prior to the rise of postmodernism in the second half of the twentieth century, Leopold von Ranke's famous dictum, that historians should primarily tell how things actually (or essentially) were (*wie es eigentlich gewesen*), was held by many to be a reasonable and worthy goal. With the rise of postmodern critique, scholars using this method must be aware of the serious pitfalls of historiography and thus make every effort to fully explore their own assumptions and biases, which inevitably influence their historical reconstructions.

[*See also* Cultural Anthropology, *subentry* New Testament; Form Criticism, *subentry* New Testament; Greco-Roman Context, Redaction Criticism, *subentry* New Testament; *and* Social Sciences, *subentry* New Testament.]

BIBLIOGRAPHY

Methodological Studies and History of Scholarship

Baird, William. *History of New Testament Research, I: From Deism to Tübingen.* Minneapolis: Fortress, 1992.

Blanton, Ward. *Displacing Christian Origins: Philosophy, Secularity, and the New Testament.* Chicago: University of Chicago Press, 2007.

Epp, Eldon Jay, and George W. MacRae, eds. *The New Testament and Its Modern Interpreters.* Atlanta: Scholars Press, 1989.

Kümmel, Werner Georg. *The New Testament: The History of the Investigation of Its Problems.* Translated by S. M. Gilmour and H. C. Kee. Nashville: Abingdon, 1972.

McKenzie, Steven L., and Stephen R. Haynes, eds. *To Each Its Own Meaning: An Introduction to Biblical Criticisms and Their Applications.* Rev. ed. Louisville: Westminster/John Knox, 1999.

Penner, Todd, and Caroline Vander Stichele, eds. *Her Master's Tools?: Feminist And Postcolonial Engagements of Historical-critical Discourse.* Global Perspectives on Biblical Scholarship 9. Leiden: Brill, 2005.

Theissen, Gerd, and Dagmar Winter. *The Quest for the Plausible Jesus: The Question of Criteria.* Translated by M. E. Boring. Louisville: Westminster/John Knox, 2002.

Nineteenth to Mid-Twentieth-Century Examples of the Method

Baur, Ferdinand Christian. *Paul the Apostle of Jesus Christ: His Life and Works, His Epistles and Teachings; A Contribution to a Critical History of Primitive Christianity.* 2 vols. London: Williams and Norgate, 1873–1875. English Translation of *Paulus, der Apostel Jesu Christ: Sein Leben und Wirken, seine Briefe und seine Lehre.* Stuttgart, 1845.

Cadbury, Henry J. *The Book of Acts in History.* New York: Harper, 1955.

Conzelmann, Hans. *The Theology of Saint Luke.* Translated by G. Buswell. New York: Harper and Row, 1960. English Translation of *Die Mitte der Zeit.* Mohr, 1954.

Easton, Burton S. *The Purpose of Acts.* London: S.P.C.K., 1936.

Foakes-Jackson, Frederick, and Kirsopp Lake, eds. *The Beginnings of Christianity.* 5 vols. London: Macmillan, 1920–1933.

Haenchen, Ernst. *The Acts of the Apostles: A Commentary.* Translated by B. Noble, G. Shinn, and R. McL. Wilson. Philadelphia: Westminster, 1971. English Translation of *Die Apostelgeschichte,* 14th ed. Göttingen: Vandenhoeck und Ruprecht, 1965.

Schwegler, Albert. *Das nachapostolische Zeitalter in den Hauptmomenten seiner Entwicklung.* 2 vols. Tübingen: J. C. B. Mohr, 1846.

Streeter, Burnett H. *The Four Gospels: A Study of Origin.* London: Macmillan and Co., 1924.

Windisch, Hans. "The Case Against the Tradition." In Foakes-Jackson and Lake, *The Beginnings of Christianity,* 2:265–297.

Zeller, Edward. *The Contents and Origin of the Acts of the Apostles, Critically Investigated.* 2 vols. Translated by Joseph Dare. London: Williams and Norgate, 1875–1876. English translation of *Die Apostelgeschichte nach ihrem Inhalt und Ursprung kritisch untersucht.* Stuttgart, 1854.

Recent Examples of the Method

Koester, Helmut, and James M. Robinson. *Trajectories through Early Christianity.* Philadelphia: Fortress, 1971.

Kraemer, Ross Shepard, and Mary Rose D'Angelo. *Women and Christian Origins.* New York: Oxford University Press, 1999.

Levine, Amy-Jill, Dale C. Allison Jr., and John Dominic Crossan, eds. *The Historical Jesus in Context.* Princeton, N.J.: Princeton University Press, 2006.

Mack, Burton L. *Who Wrote the New Testament?: The Making of the Christian Myth.* San Francisco: HarperOne, 1996.

Milton C. Moreland

HISTORICAL JESUS, QUEST FOR THE

The "Quest for the Historical Jesus" is a phrase that commonly refers to scholarship devoted to determining what may be said about Jesus of Nazareth from a purely historical standpoint. It began with the Enlightenment and scholars' realization that the depiction of Jesus in the Christian Gospels as a divine human being was inconsistent with the newly emerging view of the world as governed by natural laws and understandable through reason. The quest subjects the Gospels and other sources to historical critical analysis in an attempt to arrive at a more historically defensible portrait of Jesus.

Beginnings. The quest was launched in the private notebooks of an otherwise obscure professor of Oriental languages in the German city of Hamburg. Hermann Samuel Reimarus (1694–1768) believed that the supernatural portrait of Jesus in the Gospels was created by his disciples. It was they who invented the virgin birth, the nature miracles, the resurrection, and the idea of the second coming of Jesus. The *historical* Jesus was a Jewish messianic figure, who preached the arrival of the kingdom of God, but failed to win a following and so was eventually captured and executed. Reimarus was a Deist, who saw in the Gospels the beginnings of a church characterized by superstition and presided over by a parasitic clergy—a church he believed had plagued the world of Christendom to his day. Deism inspired many early proponents of the rationalist historical approach to Jesus, including America's third president, Thomas Jefferson, who created the so-called Jefferson Bible, a collection of Jesus's moral teachings cut and pasted (literally) into a notebook of his own. The Deist-inspired works of Jefferson and Reimarus were published only posthumously. Reimarus's notes on Jesus were issued anonymously by the German philosopher G. E. Lessing in 1778 under the title, *Von den Zwecke Jesu und seiner Jünger. Noch ein Fragment des Wolfenbüttelschen Ungenannten* (*Concerning the Aims of Jesus and His Disciples. Another Fragment of the Anonymous Wolfenbüttel Author*).

In nineteenth century Germany the critical study of the Bible took root in an academic system steeped in the Enlightenment ethos of rigorous investigation of every question. In the great centers of learning, like Berlin, Jena, and Leipzig, a new liberal theology emerged that sought to free the church from traditional dogma and reground it in historically revealed moral truths. Much of this work proceeded along strictly rationalistic lines. The miracles, the resurrection, and twists and turns in the Gospel narratives themselves, were explained as rationally as possible. Jesus did not walk on water, but on the nearby shore, obscured by fog or dark of night. He did not actually multiply loaves and fishes, but inspired people to share out of their secreted abundance. These things were, in any event, extraneous to the real point of Jesus's life: the way he embodied the love of God and neighbor.

Among the most prominent early proponents of the quest was Friedrich Schleiermacher (1768–1834), whose Berlin lectures on Jesus in the 1820s and 1830s enjoyed wide popularity. Schleiermacher, like most critical theologians of his day, had come to assume that the Bible could not be taken as historical without qualification. His interest, however, was not simply in sketching out Jesus's life in more rational strokes. Nor was it to replace Christian dogma with Christlike moral teaching. His interest was in a theologically relevant historical Jesus. The heart of Christianity, for Schleiermacher, was the experience of an immediate relation to the divine, the infinite, God. Jesus's importance lay in his own embodiment of that experience. Jesus is the heart of Christianity because in him the Christian experience of absolute dependence on God finds its fullest expression. The historical Jesus, he thought, need not unseat the Christ of Christian faith. He was, in a sense, the first Christian.

As influential as Schleiermacher was among theologians, in the wider culture his ideas were overshadowed by those of his younger, more radical contemporary, David Friedrich Strauss (1808–1874). Strauss also favored the quest, but less for what it revealed about Jesus than for what it said about the sources, the Gospels. In contrast to Schleiermacher, Strauss took the position that the Gospels are not to be construed as history in any way. In his two-volume massive, fifteen-hundred-page *Das Leben Jesu, kritisch bearbeitet* (*The Life of Jesus Critically Examined*), published in 1835–1836, Strauss argued that the Gospels are to be understood as myth, not history. By myth he did not mean a fairy story or tall tale, but the narrative embodiment of an eternal idea. The idea conveyed in the Gospels, he believed, was one then championed by Hegel, that God is incarnate in humanity.

Strauss's work met with strong resistance from conservative church leaders and politicians in Germany who had grown wary of what they regarded as the radical element in the universities. This prevented Strauss from ever holding an academic position, and he was forced to live off his considerable celebrity. But opposition to Strauss also came from critical scholars influenced by Schleiermacher, who began in earnest to subject the Gospels to more rigorous critical analysis in the hope of recovering a historically defensible account of Jesus's life and teachings. The search for the earliest Gospel account led to the theory of Markan Priority and the discovery of Q, the lost source thought to have been used by Matthew and Luke. The result was a number of historical treatments of the life of Jesus, like that of Heinrich Julius Holzmann (1832–1910), which made use of the latest insights in the burgeoning new method of studying scripture historically and critically.

Albert Schweitzer. Perhaps the most famous of the early questers was Albert Schweitzer (1875–1965). His 1906 book, *Von Reimarus zu Wrede*, was translated in 1910 under the popular title, *The Quest* *of the Historical Jesus.* In it, Schweitzer chronicled the quest through the eighteenth and nineteenth centuries. Its high point, in his view, came near the end of the nineteenth century with the work of Johannes Weiss and William Wrede. Weiss argued that Jesus's preaching was utterly grounded in the early Jewish conviction of an approaching apocalyptic reckoning. The kingdom of God was not simply a way of speaking about the moral life, as many Liberal theologians had thought, but a thoroughly eschatological concept rooted in contemporary Jewish apocalypticism. If Weiss was right, said Schweitzer, the nineteenth-century quest had completely misunderstood the heart of Jesus's preaching. For his part, Wrede showed that the earliest Gospel, Mark, upon which virtually all of the questers were now relying for their reconstructions, was governed not by historical interests, but a theological interest in projecting back into the life of Jesus a developing messianic consciousness. If this is true, then even the most rigorous historical critical methods could not hope to reveal any more than a faint shadow of the historical figure standing behind the Gospels.

It is often said that Schweitzer's work brought the quest to a halt. He had shown that a century's work had revealed only that when scholars gaze into the well of history they are capable only of seeing their own reflection staring back. But this is mistaken. True, the twenty-six-year-old Schweitzer had concluded that the whole collective effort of the nineteenth century had all been for naught. But he was himself in no way discouraged about the possibility of recovering something of the life and teachings of Jesus. As much as Schweitzer admired Wrede's historical skepticism, he did not in fact buy it. He preferred instead to assume that the Gospels present a cogent historical view of Jesus if one interprets them in light of Weiss's thoroughgoing eschatology. In the final chapter of his book, Schweitzer offers his own critical reading of Mark, supplemented with material from Matthew's Sermon on the Mount, to reconstruct a portrait of Jesus as an eschatological prophet, who believed himself to be the Messiah. When Jesus's own expectations of the coming apocalypse failed to materialize, he decided to sacrifice himself in the hope that by his own resolve and dedication he could bend the will of God to his own. But he was wrong. Christians, however, have at least the by-product of his great personality: his passionate contempt for the conventional life and a utopian urgency that demanded a response. For his part, Schweitzer accepted the challenge of his Jesus, took up medicine, moved to Africa, and made his mark on history as a humanitarian.

The Quest in the Twentieth Century. Although the quest would soon come to an end in Germany, it did not end in Great Britain or the United States, where, it was just getting started. Among the British questers in the early twentieth century, one may count the great Cambridge Classical scholar and historian T. R. Glover (1869–1943), whose book, *The Jesus of History,* went through sixty-eight editions between 1916 and 2004. Glover accepted the results of critical scholarship—Markan priority, the existence of a second, lost source (Q), the fundamentally unhistorical nature of John, and the problematic historicity of the Synoptics. Still, if the Gospels do not permit a biography of Jesus, they do nonetheless communicate much about the ways and words of Jesus. He was clever, compassionate, and charismatic. He proclaimed a new kingdom of God that was, in a sense, a new way of understanding God. Jesus's God was tender and loving, especially to women and children, and called all to lives of meaning and worth. He condemned sin and wasted living but did not share John the Baptist's apocalyptic message. It is easy to see why Glover's book was popular among progressives and young people (a special Student Christian Movement edition was published in 1917).

Through the first half of the twentieth century British scholarship continued to work at the Jesus question within the constraints imposed by a critical understanding of the sources. Among them one might count the works of F. C. Burkitt, T. W. Manson, and C. J. Cadoux. All of these scholars embraced more or less the higher criticism of the Germans, but with moderation. The Synoptic Gospels, while not biographies, could nonetheless offer a reliable picture of Jesus proclaiming the kingdom of God manifest in his exorcisms, healings, and teaching. Cadoux (1883–1947), in his 1943 book *The Historic Mission of Jesus*, stressed Jesus's personal moral and religious qualities, especially the command to love even enemies and to accept sinners. He was not an apocalyptic seer, as Schweitzer had thought. But he believed himself to be the Jewish Messiah, through whom God's kingdom would be established on earth.

The American Quest. In the United States biblical scholarship was, at the beginning of the twentieth century, still in its infancy. The First and Second Great Awakenings had already by then given American Christianity its characteristic evangelical flavor, and Scottish fundamentalism had found its academic home in Princeton Seminary. But higher criticism had taken root at Harvard, Yale, Union Seminary in New York, and the Divinity School at the University of Chicago. Historical Jesus scholarship flourished in these places.

At Yale, the German tradition of rigorous criticism found an advocate in Benjamin Bacon (1860–1932). He, too, understood that the Gospels are not history but a mix of history and interpretation. But unlike the nineteenth-century German questers, he did not elevate history over interpretation. The task, he thought, was to show historically how the gospel *of* Jesus could have lead to the gospel *about* Jesus. His *The Story of Jesus and the Beginnings of the Church* (1927) was an attempt to do this. Methodologically, Bacon anticipated the so-called New Quest on American soil, which asked not about the break between Jesus and the church, but about the continuity. His theory that Jesus aimed at the restoration of Israel is more or less consistent with the more contemporary American view associated with E. P. Sanders and others today.

The most distinctive American contribution to the quest in this period came from the Chicago School—the ideas associated with the University of Chicago Divinity School from the turn of the century to the 1930s. Shirley Jackson Case (1872–1947) was a student of Bacon at Yale and had studied in Germany. But at Chicago he transformed the historical critical method of the Germans into the sociohistorical method that would become the hallmark of the Chicago school. It was important, Case believed, to establish as precisely as possible the social context for Jesus and his followers in Galilee, as well as the various social contexts that have left their mark on each of the Gospels. The influence of form criticism and the History of Religions School is apparent, as is the newly emerging discipline of Sociology. Shailer Mathews (1863–1941), Case's colleague in Chicago, was a founding figure in the discipline of Sociology and also wrote his own treatment of Jesus, *The Social Teaching of Jesus* (1897), long a staple of the Social Gospel movement in the United States. In *Jesus: A New Biography* (1927), Case offered what was then a state of the art description of the social and political conditions prevailing in the world that gave birth to Christianity. He believed that consistency with known Galilean social conditions was as reliable an indicator of authenticity as any literary judgment about the texts. But while his methods were distinctive, his results were not. The Jesus who came from that world was a prophet, not a messiah (Jesus rejected the title), who believed that God's rule would soon commence.

German Scholarship without the Quest. Meanwhile in Germany, the home of higher criticism, the quest for the historical Jesus was reaching as impasse. Alongside the work of Wrede, that of Carl Ludwig Schmidt (*Der Rahmen der Geschichte Jesu* [*The Framework of the Story of Jesus*] [1919]), served to further the conviction that Mark's narrative is not historical. It reads not like a modern biography but like so many oral stories joined together like beads on a string. In the 1920s Julius Wellhausen, Rudolf Bultmann, and Martin Dibelius introduced form criticism—the study of oral tradition. Their discovery that oral tradition tends to adapt itself to the ever changing life setting in which it is cultivated further undermined the confidence of historians in the biblical narrative. Bultmann (1884–1976), however, was himself less skeptical on this point than he is often thought to have been. In 1926 he wrote a very popular book titled *Jesus*, later rendered for English-speaking audiences as *Jesus and the*

Word (1934), in which he embraced the view of Johannes Weiss—that Jesus belonged fundamentally to the world of Jewish apocalypticism. He therefore famously remarked that Jesus is to be regarded as one of the precursors to Christian theology, not its first and most important voice.

Perhaps the most important figure in the turn away from the historical Jesus was Martin Kähler (1835–1912). In his 1896 book, *Der sogenannte historische Jesus und der geschichtliche, biblische Christus* (*The So-Called Historical Jesus and the Historic, Biblical Christ*), Kähler argued that the subjective work of the historian can never offer a reliable foundation for Christian theology. What the church possesses is the Bible and its witness to the significance of Jesus. This is what the church needs: witness, not history. This would pave the way for Karl Barth's return to the Bible as the Word of God and the foundation for neoorthodox dogmatics.

The New Quest. The German hiatus in the quest was lifted, at least for a season, in the 1950s among the students of Bultmann. In 1953 Ernst Käsemann (1906–1998) offered a paper to an annual gathering of Bultmann's former students in Jugenheim, West Germany, titled "Das Problem der historischen Jesus" ("The Problem of the Historical Jesus"). Käsemann argued that the gospel, properly understood, is always involved in a war on two fronts: Jesus cannot be understood apart from the early Christian preaching about him; but that preaching cannot be understood apart from the Jesus of history, if it is not to become a kind of new, biblical Docetism. Christian theology cannot simply be *biblical* theology; it must also have a place for Jesus. In this essay Käsemann had opened what would become known as the New Quest. It was a post-Bultmannian enterprise, which would presuppose the results of form criticism and the literary studies of Wrede and Schmidt—there would be no naïve rationalistic historicizing of the Gospel narratives. Methods and criteria would have to be developed by which to identify authentic materials embedded in the texts. These Käsemann derived from the earlier work of Bultmann, his teacher. From form criticism Käsemann drew one negative criterion: one should question the historicity of traditions for which there is a clear life setting within the early Christian community. From Bultmann's *Jesus and the Word* Käsemann drew his second, positive criterion: dissimilarity—one may credit those things that could not be imagined as deriving from the common stock of ancient Jewish or Hellenistic religious lore, or from the dogmatic interests of the early church. Käsemann was especially interested in sayings where the church seems to have modified the received tradition, "having found it too bold for its taste" ("The Problem of the Historical Jesus," p. 37).

The New Quest thrived in Germany in the 1950s and 1960s, along with a renewed interest in critical biblical scholarship. Its best-known proponent was the Heidelberg scholar, Günther Bornkamm (1905–1990), whose 1956 book, *Jesus of Nazareth*, was translated into English and remained a staple of German and American seminary classrooms for many years. Willi Marxsen (1919–1993) produced a series of provocative essays around the concept of the *Sache Jesu* (the Jesus business), meaning the substance of Jesus's preaching and how it was carried into the New Testament. His critical treatment of the resurrection—which would not have raised an eyebrow 100 years earlier—landed him in hot water in 1960s Germany, where in 1966 a mock trial was convened in Dortmund to condemn him and his fellow Bultmannians of heresy.

In the United States the New Quest was translated and interpreted by James M. Robinson, whose 1959 book, *A New Quest of the Historical Jesus*, chronicled what had been happening in Germany but also added a theoretical framework to the quest. Robinson argued that a new philosophy of history made it possible to approach the Gospels historically, problematic though they may be. History, after all, asks not about the past as it really was, but the past in its significance for human self-understanding. This is what the Gospels convey—not the *historical* Jesus, but the *historic* Jesus. This at least creates the possibility of a new quest, where form criticism seemed to have closed the door.

One of the questions raised by the New Quest was the old question of eschatology. Schweitzer had insisted on an apocalyptic reading of Jesus, but not everyone had embraced his view. Bultmann had assumed it in *Jesus and the Word*, but many of the American and British scholars of the early twentieth century had not been convinced. Now, several of the leading post-Bultmannians doubted it: Philipp Vielhauer, Hans Conzelmann, and Käsemann himself. Käsemann argued that while Jesus certainly began as a follower of John the Baptist, "his own preaching was not stamped by apocalyptic but proclaimed the immediate nearness of God" ("The Beginnings of Christian Theology," *Journal for Theology and the Church* 6 [1969]: 40). This aspect of the New Quest was planted in American soil by Norman Perrin (1920–1976). In *Rediscovering the Teaching of Jesus* (1967) he argued that Jesus used the term "kingdom of God" as a "tensive symbol," referring to no particular apocalyptic scenario but to the activity of God present more subtly in the midst of human life. Important in Perrin's assessment was the saying found in Luke 17:20–21: "The kingdom of God is not coming with things that can be observed; nor will they say, 'Look, here it is! Or 'There it is!' For, in fact, the kingdom of God is among you." In Luke the saying is followed, paradoxically, by an apocalyptic scenario complete with "things that can be observed." Little wonder that scholars have been divided so severely over this issue. Is the kingdom of God an apocalyptic concept or present reality? The tradition itself is profoundly divided about it, and scholarship remains so today.

One result of the New Quest was a fresh focus on the question of historical criteria. In the wake of German higher criticism and Bultmann's form criticism, scholars now had to approach the texts very differently from their nineteenth-century predecessors. In the first quest, scholars had assumed that the Gospels were more or less historical, but written by ancients who were unable to tell rational fact from superstitious fairy tale. So they concentrated on finding rational explanations for the irrational things they were reading in the Gospels. This was true of German scholarship up through Schweitzer, as well as much early twentieth-century British and American scholarship. But after Wrede demonstrated the fictive nature of the Gospels and Bultmann the malleability of oral tradition, this could no longer be assumed. Scholars of the New Quest began rather with the opposite view: the Gospels are not historical. They may contain historical material, but this must be demonstrated in the case of individual traditions, never assumed. But what arguments, what critieria might one use to establish the historicity of individual sayings of or stories about Jesus? I have already mentioned Käsemann's criteria for attempting to disentangle historical material from the Gospels: a certain distinctiveness over against Judaism on the one hand and primitive Christianity on the other. But Käsemann himself acknowledged the real drawback of this approach: "we shall not, from this angle of vision, gain any clear view of the connecting link between Jesus, his Palestinian environment and his later community." He simply believed that it is more important "to gain some insight into what separated him from friends and foes alike" (Käsemann, p. 37).

The Continuing Quest. The New Quest did not last long among the German post-Bultmannians, but it set the stage for the resurgence of interest in historical Jesus research in English-speaking lands. But unlike the New Quest, which emphasized Jesus's distinctiveness, much of this new work emphasized his more typical Jewishness. Among the most important of these new studies were Gesa Vermes's *Jesus the Jew* (1973), E. P. Sanders's *Jesus and Judaism* (1985), and Sean Freyne's *Galilee, Jesus, and the Gospels* (1988). These scholars were less interested in solving the historical problems posed by Gospel criticism and more in reaching a more accurate view of first-century Judaism, Jesus's cultural home. If one's historical Jesus did not make sense in a first-century Jewish—or Galilean—context, then he was probably not very historical. This new generation of scholars also found it necessary to expand the conversation about Jesus to more than just the Synoptic Gospels. Paula Fredrikson (*From Jesus to Christ*, 1988) offered a view of Jesus predicated as much on the Gospel of John as the Synoptics. John Dominic Crossan (*The Historical Jesus*, 1991) made use of the noncanonical Gospel of Thomas to establish a set of early, multiply attested (primarily synoptic) sayings upon which to build his portrait of Jesus, that of "a Mediterranean Jewish Peasant." In addition to Jewish history under Roman rule, Crossan also drew upon anthropological modeling to understand the lives of peasants living in ancient agrarian empires like that of the Romans.

In 1985 Robert Funk convened the Jesus Seminar and invited John Dominic Crossan to co-chair it with him. Funk and Crossan had met two decades earlier in a seminar headed by Perrin's Chicago colleague Amos Wilder, which revolutionized the study of parables. Parables were not, as Joachim Jeremias (1900–1979) thought, metaphors for the coming judgment, but Jesus's attempt to bring narrative life to an immediate experience of the kingdom of God unfolding among his followers. When Funk and Crossan convened the Jesus Seminar to examine systematically everything attributed to Jesus in the literature of the first three centuries c.e., among the first topics they took up were the parables and the nature of the kingdom of God. If the parables were not to be seen as allegories for the coming judgment, but narrative metaphors for life in the (present) kingdom, then Jesus must not have been the apocalyptic seer he appears to be in the Synoptic Gospels. Within the Jesus Seminar, which met from 1985 to the late 1990s, the focus soon fell on the countercultural parables and aphorisms of Jesus, many of which were found not only in the Synoptic Gospels but also in the Gospel of Thomas. Among the more than one hundred or so scholars who participated in the Jesus Seminar, Crossan and Burton Mack urged an understanding of Jesus on analogy to first-century Cynic philosophy. Stephen Patterson argued for a Jesus rooted in a countercultural version of Jewish wisdom theology. Marcus Borg added the category of "holy man" to that of sage. Borg may also be credited with raising new doubts about the apocalyptic interpretation of Jesus, a position for which the Jesus Seminar became well known, even though participants actually remained quite divided about the issue. What was perhaps most characteristic of the Jesus Seminar was its tendency to favor those sayings, parables, and acts of a transgressive and provocative nature. Funk himself summarizes the gist of this line of thought in his 1996 book, *Honest to Jesus*: "God has a preference for the lowly, the poor and undeserving, the sinner, the social misfits, the marginalized, the humble. I doubt if there is any typification, any generalization, about the words and acts of Jesus in which we can have more confidence" (p. 196).

This newer period of research was characterized by much greater attention to method and the criteria by which one might identify historically relevant material in the Gospels. First, the New Quest's criterion of dissimilarity is no longer decisive. These scholars simply have not valued as much the things that made Jesus distinctive. They are more interested, for example, in how Jesus reflects his Jewish culture rather than how he stands out from it. Second, critical scholars generally remain skeptical of the historicity of the Gospels, but there is limited agreement on how to glean historically relevant information from them. Many (Crossan and the Jesus Seminar, for example) have embraced the advantage of multiple independent attestation for the leverage it affords in both isolating a saying from its secondary narrative context and in establishing a plausible tradition history for a saying, including its earliest verifiable form. For these scholars, new texts like the Gospel of Thomas have become very important. Others, however, have been skeptical of multiple attestation and tradition history (Sanders and Dale Allison, for example), and prefer to work in broad strokes with points of general historical agreement. Third, scholars of this generation have generally embraced the view that religion is complexly embedded in culture and that Jesus cannot be understood apart from a thorough and nuanced description of his culture. Never before have scholars known so much about ancient history, the social and political world of the Galilee, Second Temple Judaism, and the daily lives of peasants. Archaeology is prominent in this work, and culture has become an important tool.

The Evangelical Quest. The provocative work of the Jesus Seminar emerged just as American evangelical scholarship was coming to maturity in countless seminaries and Bible colleges throughout North America. The Jesus Seminar had aimed its sights at 1980s fundamentalist televangelists, for whom scholarship was as foreign as the European soil from which it had come. But what fired back was a very different opposition. Learned evangelical scholars, skilled in the ancient languages and arcane methods of biblical scholarship and well educated in the finest European academies, began to produce their own scholarship on Jesus, much of it intended to counter that of the Jesus Seminar. For leadership they looked to prominent British scholars, like N. T. Wright, whose three-volume study is perhaps the most extensive work ever undertaken on Jesus. Wright makes an elaborate case for the basic historicity of the Gospels, including the bodily resurrection of Jesus. Whether such things can happen, he argues, depends upon the worldview one chooses to embrace. This appealed to evangelical scholars who could now turn the methods of historical Jesus research onto topics that were seldom discussed among critical scholars: the nature miracles, healings, the virgin birth, and especially the resurrection. Among the British they also found in James Dunn a learned advocate for a greater degree of historicity in the canonical Gospels, built, in his view, upon reliable memories encoded in oral tradition. Richard Bauckham has even argued in a new way for the traditional view that the Gospels offer eyewitness testimony to the events they purport to describe. Since the 1980s, hundreds of books and thousands of essays have been published in this tradition, each arguing for the historicity of this or that aspect of the biblical account. In the twenty-first century, the emergence of American evangelical scholarship is by far the most important development in the quest. It has challenged the very nature and assumptions of modern biblical scholarship.

A Catholic Quest? For most of its history the quest has been the province of Protestant biblical scholarship. Roman Catholic scholars played a smaller role, due in part to the differing structure of Roman Catholic thought, which places greater stress on the teachings of the *magisterium* than the findings of historians, and in part to greater restrictions on the extent to which critical biblical scholarship was sanctioned by the Church. That changed in 1943 with Pope Pius XII's historic encyclical, *Divino Afflante Spiritu*, which effectively opened the doors of critical biblical scholarship to Catholic scholars. Vatican II embraced the idea that the Gospels are interpretive works, not reports of what Jesus actually said and did. Among the first to pursue the quest for the historical Jesus were Roman Catholic Latin American Liberation theologians, like Leonardo Boff and Jon Sobrino, who saw in Jesus a model for the human struggle for liberation from structures of oppression. In South Asia, Tissa Balasuriya made a similar appeal during the war-ravaged 1970s in Sri Lanka. All three, however, have run afoul of the *magisterium*. So has Elisabeth Schüssler Fiorenza, a leading feminist critic of the quest, as well as a participant. She has criticized the quest for its failure to account for its own social location among elite, white men in Europe and North America. Among current Catholic scholars in good standing with the Pontifical Biblical Commission, John Meier has written the most comprehensive study of Jesus perhaps in the history of Catholic scholarship, a four-volume work titled *A Marginal Jew* (1991–2009). More recently Pope Benedict XVI took the unusual step of laying aside his papal identity to add his own voice and scholarship to the discussion as Joseph Raztinger (*Jesus of Nazareth*, 2007).

The State of the Quest Today. Today the quest is as vigorous a scholarly enterprise as it ever has been. It continues to drive discussion about the methods and assumptions of biblical scholarship and to expose the fissures present in a vast and expanding field of study. Among critical scholars there is broad agreement that Jesus can be understood historically only when his time and place—first-century Galilee—has first been understood. He was Jewish, a handworker in an eastern province of the Roman Empire, which was undergoing colonial transformation, including the urbanization of the landscape, the commercialization of agriculture, and the monetizing of the economy. In this process, many local villagers, like Jesus, found themselves to be expendable. Jesus's words and deeds—however one might identify them—reveal a careful observer of local life, one who criticized the rich and powerful and favored the poor and marginal. Many would also agree that he engaged in activities that drew to himself negative attention, including exorcism, keeping company with questionable figures like prostitutes and tax collectors, and speaking openly about a new empire of God. But critical scholars still do not agree about Jesus's central theme, the kingdom of God. Did he have in mind a future moment of apocalyptic judgment, or was this a way of living to be embraced by people already in the present time, or something else entirely? Critical scholars generally agree that the Gospels do not offer a biography of Jesus, but not on how much detail they reveal or how to identify the historical memory behind or embedded in the texts.

Over against this centuries-long critical conversation there now stands an evangelical conversation that begins and ends in a very different place. It begins with the proposition that the Gospel texts are reports that more or less get the history right. It ends with a description of Jesus that is consistent with the biblical portrait: he was a divine human being, who performed miracles, spoke of his own messianic calling, and was raised from the dead after his execution at the hands Pilate and a Jewish mob.

The historical Jesus, then, still lies at the center of the most critical and contentious fault lines of modern biblical scholarship. Is the Bible reliable, historically speaking? And if it is not, what would this mean? Through the more than two centuries of its unfolding, the quest for the historical Jesus has become more than the pursuit of a simple historical question. Whether to quest, how to quest, and what might lie at the end of the quest have become questions through which the very meaning of the Christian tradition is contested. Because of this, at the beginning of the twenty-first century, the quest is flourishing.

[*See also* Cultural Anthropology, *subentry* New Testament; Historical Criticism, *subentry* New Testament; Social Sciences, *subentry* New Testament, *and* Synoptic Problem.]

BIBLIOGRAPHY

Allison, Dale. *Jesus of Nazareth: Millenarian Prophet.* Minneapolis: Fortress, 1998. Rejects the tradition-historical approach to the quest and works with broad areas of historical agreement to argue for a more apocalyptic understanding of the historical Jesus.

Balasurya, Tissa. *Jesus Christ and Human Liberation.* Quest Series 48. Colombo, Sri Lanka: Centre for Society and Religion, 1976. An important contribution to historical Jesus studies from South Asia and global Liberation Theology.

Bock, Darrell, and Webb, Robert L. *Key Events in the Life of the Historical Jesus. Wissenschaftliche Untersuchengen zum Neuen Testament* 247. Tübingen: Mohr/Siebeck, 2009. A collection of studies by prominent American and British scholars representative of the recent wave of evangelical scholarship on the historical Jesus and a measure of the extent to which this scholarship has become mainstream.

Borg, Marcus. "A Temperate Case for a Non-Eschatological Jesus." *Foundations and Facets Forum* 2 (1986): 81–102. This essay effectively launched a new phase in the debate about Jesus and apocalyptic.

Bultmann, Rudolf. *Jesus and the Word.* Translated by Louise Pettibone Smith and Erminie Huntress. New York: Scribner/London: Collins, 1934. Translation of the German original, *Jesus,* first published in 1926. Bultmann's historic work on Jesus.

Case, Shirley Jackson. *Jesus: A New Biography.* Chicago: University of Chicago Press, 1927. An important example of American historical Jesus scholarship in the early twentieth century and representative of the Chicago School and the sociohistorical method.

Crossan, John Dominic. *The Historical Jesus: The Life of a Mediterranean Jewish Peasant.* New York: HarperCollins (HarperSanFrancisco), 1991. The most innovative approach to the historical Jesus in more than a century, both for its method and its results, and the most important constructive statement to emerge from out of the Jesus Seminar.

Dunn, James D. G. *Jesus Remembered.* Vol. 1, *Christianity in the Making.* Grand Rapids, Mich. and Cambridge, UK: Eerdmans, 2003. An important recent British contribution arguing that the Synoptic Gospels preserve a reliable historical memory of Jesus.

Fredrikson, Paula. *From Jesus to Christ: The Origins of the New Testament Images of Jesus.* New Haven: Yale University Press, 1988. A novel treatment of Jesus and his relationship to the Jewish authorities that draws more upon the Gospel of John than is conventional.

Funk, Robert W. *Honest to Jesus: Jesus for a New Millenium.* San Francisco: Harper Collins, 1996.

Funk, Robert W., Roy Hoover, and the Jesus Seminar. *The Five Gospels: The Search for the Authentic Words of Jesus.* New York: Macmillan, 1993. The first report of the Jesus Seminar, which sparked much public controversy in the United States and gave the quest new impetus among American scholars.

Glover, T. R. *The Jesus of History.* London: Student Christian Movement, 1917. An important representative of British historical Jesus research in the early twentieth century.

Käsemann, Ernst. "The Problem of the Historical Jesus." In *Essays on New Testament Themes,* 15–47. Translated by W. J. Montague. Studies in Biblical Theology 41. London: SCM, 1964. Translation of the German original, "Das Problem des historishen Jesus," published originally in *Zeitschrift für Theologie und Kirche* 51 (1954): 125–153. Käsemann's historic essay that launched the so-called New Quest.

Meier, John P. *A Marginal Jew: Rethinking the Historical Jesus.* 4 vols. Anchor Bible Reference Library. New Haven: Yale University Press, 1991–2009. The most important recent Roman Catholic treatment bearing the Papal Imprimatur and representative of the state of Catholic historical criticism at the end of the twentieth century.

Perrin, Norman. *Rediscovering the Teaching of Jesus.* New York: Harper and Row/London: SCM, 1967. An important translation of the New Quest onto North American soil when interest in the historical Jesus was low.

Reimarus, Hermann Samuel. *Fragments.* Translated by Ralph Fraser. Edited by Charles Talbert. Life of Jesus Series, Leander Keck, General Editor. Philadelphia: Fortress, 1970. English translation of a portion of Reimarus's unpublished *Apologie oder Schutzschrift für die vernünftigen Verherer Gottes,* "Von dem Zwecke Jesu und seiner Junger" ("The Aims of Jesus and His Disciples"), published anonymously and posthumously by G. E. Lessing in 1778. Reimarus's historic notes on Jesus.

Robinson, James M. *A New Quest of the Historical Jesus.* Studies in Biblical Theology 25. Naperville: Allenson/London: SCM, 1959. Robinson's historic work chronicling the New Quest.

Sanders, E. P. *Jesus and Judaism.* Philadelphia: Fortress, 1985. A study that begins with several broad areas of historical agreement and argues that Jesus was a Jewish prophet who proclaimed the restoration of Israel.

Schleiermacher, David Freidrich. *The Life of Jesus.* Translated by S. MacLean Gilmour. Edited by Jack Verheyden. Life of Jesus Series, Leander Keck, General Editor. Philadelphia: Fortress, 1975. English translation of *Das Leben Jesu: Vorlesungen an der Universität Berlin im Jahr 1832,* published posthumously by K. A. Rutenik in 1864. Schleiermacher's historic lectures, reconstructed and edited by his student Rutenik.

Schuessler Fiorenza, Elizabeth. *Jesus and the Politics of Interpretation.* New York: Continuum, 2000. An important feminist critique of a discussion that has taken place for two centuries almost entirely among men.

Schweitzer, Albert. *The Quest of the Historical Jesus: A Critical Study of Its Progress from Reimarus to Wrede.* Translated by W. Montgomery. London: Adam and Charles Black, 1910. English translation of *Von Reimarus zu Wrede,* first published in 1906. Still one of the best and most readily available accounts of historical Jesus scholarship from Reimarus (late eighteenth century) to Wrede (end of the nineteenth century).

Strauss, David Friedrich. *The Life of Jesus, Critically Examined.* 3 vols. Translated by George Eliot. Continuum Classic Texts. London and New York: Continuum, 2005. Reprint of the 1846 edition. English translation of *Das Leben Jesu, kritisch bearbeitet,* first published in 1835–1836. Strauss's historic work on Jesus.

Vermes, Gesa. *Jesus the Jew: An Historian's reading of the Gospels.* Philadelphia: Fortress, 1973. A pioneering effort to locate Jesus within the words of first-century Judaism.

Wright, N. T. *Christian Origins and the Question of God.* Vol. 1, *The New Testament and the People of God* (1992); Vol. 2, *Jesus and the Victory of God* (1996); and Vol. 3, *The Resurrection and the Son of God* (2003). 4 vols. London: SPCK/Minneapolis: Fortress, 1992–2003. Perhaps the most extensive work ever undertaken to establish the historical reliability of the Gospels as a witness to the historical Jesus.

Stephen J. Patterson

HITTITOLOGY AND BIBLICAL INTERPRETATION

Prior to the restoration of the Hittites to their proper place in world history, a process begun in the nineteenth century, they were known only through scattered biblical references, which mostly identified them as a people living in Palestine. Unraveling the puzzle of who these Iron Age "Hittites" were and how they might be related, if at all, to the Hittites who ruled a Late Bronze Age empire, has been an ongoing process that has had as a side benefit the illumination of the biblical text itself. Hittitology moreover, has offered—and continues to offer—a rich repository of data that enrich our understanding of the origins of the Bible as a book and the Israelites as a people.

Definition. Hittitology is the study of the ancient civilization of the Hittites, their languages, scripts, history, religion, and culture, through their texts and material remains. The Hittites established hegemony over much of the peninsula of Anatolia (currently occupied by the Republic of Turkey) sometime in the seventeenth century B.C.E. (the Middle Bronze Age), and during their heyday in the Late Bronze Age, ca. 1400–1180 B.C.E., they ruled a network of vassal states in the west and southeast that together formed the Hittite Empire. Thus, Hittitology as a field of study also encompasses those cultures and languages with which the Hittites were in intimate contact, including Hattians, Palaians, Hurrians, and Luwians, as well as the study of Sumerian and Akkadian, languages that feature prominently in the Hittite textual corpus.

The collapse of the Hittite Empire at the end of the Bronze Age initiated a new era in which small independent kingdoms were formed out of the territories once controlled by the Hittite ruling house. In some cases, the rulers of these kingdoms were a part of the Hittite royal line. This coterie of states has been labeled in modern parlance the Neo-Hittite kingdoms (mid-twelfth through early-seventh centuries B.C.E.). Though politically distinct entities, they shared cultural and historical ties. In terms of biblical interpretation they are especially significant because they were contemporary with, and geographically adjacent to, Israel in the monarchic period.

History of Hittitology. With the dissolution of the Neo-Hittite states at the hands of the Assyrians, the Hittites faded from historical memory, and the process of rediscovering them would not begin for another 2,500 years.

Rediscovery. The Hittites finally achieved an identity independent of the biblical text with a lecture delivered by Assyriologist Archibald Henry Sayce in 1880 to the Society for Biblical Archaeology in London declaring that the monumental carvings and hieroglyphic inscriptions that had been discovered throughout Anatolia and northern Syria in recent decades should be attributed to the Hittites. This was soon followed by the publication of *The Empire of the Hittites* (1884) by the missionary William Wright (1837–1899), which introduced the Hittites to the broader public and in which he asserted that the Hittites had ruled an Empire. The first Hittite cuneiform tablets to come to light were two letters from the king of Arzawa that were among the cache of Amarna tablets found in 1887. J. A. Knudtzon was able to identify the language of these two letters as Indo-European in 1902, but his discovery seemed too far-fetched and failed to find acceptance. In the meantime, tablets written in the same language had been found during test diggings at the village of Boghazköy in north-central Anatolia, and excavations began at the site in 1906 under the auspices of the German Oriental Society and the direction of the Assyriologist Hugo Winckler (1863–1913). More than ten thousand cuneiform tablets were discovered in the first year of excavation, and it quickly became clear to Winckler that this site was the capital of the Hittite Empire (ancient Hattusa). With the conclusive decipherment of the language of the cuneiform tablets by the Czech scholar Biedrich Hrozný in 1915, Hittitology became its own distinct field of study.

The Twentieth Century and Today. The Boghazköy archives have now produced more than thirty thousand cuneiform tablet fragments, and the enormous task of publishing copies of these documents is finally coming to a conclusion at the time of this writing. Copies of the tablets discovered in the initial excavations of Theodor Makridi and Hugo Winckler were published in the first six volumes of the series *Keilschrifttexte aus Boghazköi* (*KBo*). The modern excavation of the site began in 1931 under the direction of Kurt Bittel, only to be discontinued in 1939. The tablets recovered in these years were published in the series *Keilschrifturkunden aus Boghazköi* (*KUB*; complete at 60 volumes).

Excavations were picked up again in 1952 and have continued ever since. To accommodate the tablets found in the postwar excavations, the old series *KBo* was revived and as of 2012 contained 65 volumes. Additional volumes contain miscellaneous collections of text copies, and only a small number of the tablets from Boghazköy remain unpublished.

Most of the published cuneiform texts have been translated and analyzed in one form or another, although only a small percentage are published in a form or venue that is accessible to a nonspecialist audience. The entire Iron Age hieroglyphic corpus, on the other hand, is now available, thanks to the massive three-volume undertaking, *The Corpus of Hieroglyphic Luwian Inscriptions*, by J. David Hawkins of the School of Oriental and African Studies, University of London.

A field once dominated by German scholars (Hans Ehelolf, Emil Forrer, Johannes Friedrich, Albrecht Goetze, and Ferdinand Sommer), Hittitology today is truly international. Scholars not only in Germany, England, and the United States but also in the Netherlands, Italy, France, Israel, Japan, and, of course, Turkey are contributing significantly to reconstructing the language, culture, and history of the Hittites. Our knowledge of the Hittites is no longer limited to the capital city and the early excavations at Karkamis, Alaca, and other cities. Modern excavations conducted at Hittite sites like Ortaköy-Šapinuwa, Maşat-Tapikka, and Kuşaklı-Šarissa, among others, are not only enlarging the corpus of Hittite cuneiform texts, but are also providing data about life on the plateau inaccessible to us prior to the application of modern excavation techniques. Among the many resources being made available through the open-access initiative, Hethitologie Portal Mainz, are digital photographs and modern transliterations and translations of the texts.

Biblical Interpretation. Scholarship was slow to recognize the potential of Hittitology for biblical interpretation, but once the door was opened, the flow of comparative studies continued steadily. The question of the identity of the "Hittites" named in the Bible does not necessarily have a bearing on Hittitology's importance for biblical interpretation; however, this could not be assumed at first, and discussions of connections have rarely been undertaken without some consideration given to the biblical Hittites.

Hittites in Palestine? Sayce himself was among the first to address the question of the Hittites in the Old Testament in an article in 1928 that attempted to align the Hittite evidence to the biblical text (see Hoffner, 2002, p. xxix). Like his contemporaries, he assumed that the Hittites of the Hebrew Bible were the same as the Hittites of Anatolia. Only in the 1930s did the work of the Hittitologists Emil Forrer (1936 and 1937) and Louis Delaporte (1936–1938) advance the discussion. Both pointed out that the label "Hittite" had multiple applications historically; it did not apply only to the Anatolian Bronze Age empire. Thus, not all of the biblical references to "Hittites" were necessarily to the same group. Both also suggested a migration to explain the presence of Hittites in Iron Age Palestine. Forrer was the first to put forward historical evidence, in the form of a historically attested migration of people from Anatolia to Palestine in the reign of Mursili II (1321–1295 B.C.E.). This ingenious theory continues to receive the attention of scholars (see, e.g., Singer 2006, pp. 730–732), although it is pure conjecture.

From the biblical side, F. F. Bruce, in a published lecture (*The Hittites and the Old Testament*. London: Tyndale, 1947), assessed possible theories to explain Hittites living in Palestine, based on a literal understanding of biblical chronology. He also advocated, following Franz Böhl (1916 and 1930) for the identification of King Tidal of Goiim (Gen 14) with one of the Hittite kings bearing the name Tudhaliya. Up to this point, the search for parallels was not a priority on the agenda of scholars from either side. Although certain shared *Kulturwörter* had in fact been acknowledged since the beginning of the century, and Forrer saw in the Hittite custom of "drinking the deity" a forerunner of the Christian Eucharist (1940), it was not until 1954, when biblical scholar George Mendenhall put forward a compelling case for the dependence of the biblical covenant on the Hittite treaty form, that the potential of the Hittite material for elucidating the world of the Bible was recognized. Since then, several biblical scholars, among them, Milgrom, Weinfield, and Moyer, have drawn attention to significant parallels, especially in the religious sphere.

Among Hittitologists, the pursuit of parallels at this time was limited primarily to the work of Harry A. Hoffner Jr. (summarized in his 1969 and 1973 articles, and most recently 2002). Having argued against a direct connection between the Palestinian and Anatolian Hittites, Hoffner also downplayed the importance of the question for appreciating the significance of Hittitology for biblical studies.

Tackling the question from the perspective of archaeology, Aharon Kempinski returned to the idea of a migration as a way to account for Hittites in Palestine, this time focusing on the possibility that refugees from Anatolia could have penetrated deep into Palestine following the collapse of the Hittite Empire. He assessed architectural, artistic, and funerary evidence that documents the presence not only of trade but of influence on Syria-Palestine in the period prior to the collapse. Following on the work of Kempinski, Itamar Singer has focused attention on the various seals and *objets d'art* of Anatolian provenance or style that have been unearthed in Palestine, all or most bearing testimony to intensified contact in the period of the Egypto-Hittite Peace. Singer also theorized as to the identity of the Hittites in the Bible (2006), offering two possible explanations: the first allows for the possibility that Hittites from Anatolia migrated into Palestine following the Empire's collapse, adapting to the local culture so thoroughly that the biblical writers disregarded their Anatolian origins. His second proposal is that the biblical writers inherited the use of the term "Hittite" from Neo-Assyrian and Neo-Babylonian usage, wherein it served as a synonym for "Canaanite" and "Amorite," and thus the biblical Hittites have nothing to do with the Anatolian Hittites.

Most recently, Collins has argued that the biblical Hittites are connected to the second-millennium Hittites by means of the merging of threads of literary tradition, and rejects the notion that a group of Hittites might have lived in Palestine in the biblical period. Beyond those references to Hittites that are generally agreed to correspond to the Neo-Hittite states of the early-first millennium (1 Kgs 10:29 || 2 Chr 1:17; 2 Kgs 7:6; 1 Kgs 11:1; Josh 1:4; Judg 1:26), two threads of tradition can be traced. First is the lists of nations, which includes the Hittites with the Canaanites, Jebusites (an Amorite tribe?), Hivites (Cilicians), Amorites, Perizzites, and Girgashites (see, e.g., Deut 20:16–17). Although incorporated into the biblical text only later, these lists retain a historical memory of the earlier period, which was preserved in the Canaanite traditions upon which the Israelites were later heavily to depend.

The rhetorical and ideological use of "Hittites" that appears in Ezekiel 16:3 ("your mother was a Hittite") and elsewhere, on the other hand, draws on the Assyrian rhetoric of Sargon II against the Neo-Hittite cities of northern Syria (he calls them "evil Hittites" repeatedly in his inscriptions). When the Assyrians destroyed Samaria, Israelite refugees moved to Judah. These northerners—who had presumably been exposed both to Canaanite historical memory of Hittites and other groups who had inhabited the territories to their north and also to the more contemporary anti-Hittite Assyrian rhetoric—may have carried both of these traditions with them. The two threads merged and the Hittites became, along with the Jebusites, Hivites, Amorites, and so on, a convenient "Other" imagined as living in the Hill Country for the "newly arrived" Israelites to conquer. In other words, the Jerusalem-based biblical authors of the late-eighth century incorporated the Hittites and other groups into their foundational story of Israelite origins. The presence of the Hittites in the narratives of Israelite beginnings is thus rhetorical and ideological rather than historical. At the same time, however, a kernel of historical memory is reflected in the lists of nations, so that the Hittites of Palestine, although a literary construct, can nevertheless be connected to the Hittite Empire of the Late Bronze Age.

Despite the absence of corroborating evidence—archaeological or otherwise—to support a literal interpretation of the biblical references to Hittites living in the hill country of Judah, some biblical scholars continue to take these references at face value.

Influences: Key Issues and Assumptions. Compared with Assyriology, the pursuit of biblical parallels in Hittite texts has not been a quest for relevance. Considered a subfield within Assyriology, Hittitology has largely flown under the radar of the Babel-Bible controversy. Discoveries in Anatolia—unlike Mesopotamia—did not impact the veracity of the Bible. Indeed, if anything, Hittite studies suffered a backlash from the pan-Babylonian movement of the early-twentieth century. In his initial publication describing the Hittite origins of the Sinai covenant form, George Mendenhall wrote: "The writer has no intention of beginning a "pan-Hittite" school of biblical interpretation: he would maintain that in most if not all cases, the Hittite materials simply happen to be the source from which we know customs which were to a large extent common property to many cultures of Palestine, Syria, and Asia Minor, many of which are also attested or indicated in the Amarna Letters" (1954, p. 54, n. 11). The geographical, chronological, and cultural remoteness of the Hittites from Israel have been taken as insurmountable barriers to any direct influence between the Hittites and Israelites.

Although early practitioners like Sayce and Wright had a clear religious orientation, Hittitology as a distinct field was pursued from a secular perspective. The work of Forrer and Delaporte notwithstanding, the Bible was not a focal point for the field. The great controversy of the early years (and indeed still today), was the so-called Ahhiyawa Question, which focused the attention of Hittitologists on the West. To this day, few Hittitologists have an interest in biblical connections and fewer still are familiar enough with the biblical material and languages to pursue such connections (see Hoffner, 2002, p. xxix). By the same token, biblical scholars are not always aware of the work of Hittitologists. As Hoffner laments, this is in large measure a failure on the part of Hittitologists, who have been slow in making the texts available to non-specialists. This is changing slowly with the publication of several anthologies, most notably, *The Context of Scripture* (Brill) and the Writings from the Ancient World series (Society of Biblical Literature) and its counterpart *Texte aus der Umwelt des alten Testaments* (Gütersloher Verlagshaus).

Methods and Payoff. Within biblical studies, there has been a shift away from a diachronic focus on origins and development in favor of a synchronic approach that seeks to understand the meaning of phenomena within their immediate biblical context, or, alternatively, to understand ancient phenomena through the application of modern theory. Some argue that the quest for the origins of the biblical text is missing the point; what is significant is not a ritual's (for example) original intent—what it might have meant or how it might have been introduced originally—but what it means in its present context. Hittitologists are perhaps more likely than biblical scholars to focus on origins, as a means of adding value to a field of study whose significance is often overlooked.

Despite changing scholarly fashions, many compelling parallels and similarities have been put forward over the past six decades, especially in the legal, literary, and religious spheres.

International Law and Legal Procedures. The most celebrated and discussed parallel was put forth in 1954 by the biblical scholar George E. Mendenhall, who noted that the biblical covenant between Yahweh and Israel followed the model of the Hittite vassal treaties, including (in order) a historical prologue that reviews past relations between the parties to the agreement, stipulations of the obligations of both parties, instructions for the deposition of the agreement, a list of witnesses, and the issuance of blessings and curses. In addition, both the biblical covenant and the Hittite treaties presuppose the willing participation of the subordinate partner. A further corollary is the detailed descriptions of the borders allotted to the subordinate party, which were used as a means of reward and punishment and which only the suzerain had the right to alter. Although some biblical scholars prefer to connect the biblical covenant with the Assyrian Iron Age treaties, in form these lack many elements of the Hittite Bronze Age treaties, including the historical prologue, the provision for deposition of the agreement, and the blessings. Moreover, the Iron Age treaties are rooted in the ideology of brute subjugation by military force whereas the Hittite treaties were based upon the principal, however fictional and propagandistic, of reciprocity and voluntary submission, bringing them much closer ideologically to the biblical concept of covenant.

Several stipulations in the Hittite Laws have parallels in biblical law, for example, a case of murder by an unknown assailant (HL §6 and Deut 21:1–2), compensation for an incapacitated person as the result of assault (HL §10 and Exod 21:18–19), levirate marriage (HL §§192–193 and Deut 25:5–10), the determination of rape or adultery (HL §197 and Deut 22:23–27), and sexual relations with animals (HL §§187, 199 and Lev 18:23–24). Unlike the treaty form, these parallels are likely to be a manifestation of a common Near Eastern legal tradition.

Literature. Herbert M. Wolf in a 1967 Brandeis dissertation directed by Harry A. Hoffner Jr. was the first to suggest direct literary influence of the Apology of Hattusili III on the story of David's rise to power (1 Sam 16—2 Sam 6), a theme that Hoffner himself pursues in "Propaganda and Political Justification in Hittite Historiography" (1975). The two accounts share several significant themes, among them the king's utter blamelessness in his dealings with his predecessor as his path to the kingship is ineluctably smoothed for him by popular support, the trust of the royal family, and the favor of the deity. Both stories also incorporate a contest of champions. Hoffner shies away from suggesting a direct link, preferring to attribute the similarities to the sharing of "a certain loose literary form." His caution is applauded by McCarter in his analysis of the story of David's rise, which he too places in the genre of political self-justifications, a genre that for him was a part of the "general cultural milieu" at the time that the story of David's rise was composed. Still, given the interest that Hattusili III had in advertising his legitimacy and that of his line, and the close ties that his administration enjoyed with the Levantine coast during the peace with Egypt, we cannot rule out the possibility that copies of this text were circulating in Palestine at the end of the thirteenth century, where they could have been absorbed into the local literary tradition. This text also belies the distinction that some have made between the *historia sacra* of Judeo-Christian tradition, which encompasses the idea of a divine plan in history, and polytheistic systems, in which history was allegedly just a field of possible interventions by the gods, favorable or punitive. However, the role of the goddess Shaushga in shaping the events in Hattusili's life suggests that a divine plan was at work in Hittite history.

There are also Hittite analogues to biblical stories. The Zalpa legend about the queen who gives birth to thirty daughters and thirty sons has echoes in Judges 10:3–4 and Judges 12:8–9. The Appu myth recalls the patriarchal narratives with the childless couple, the appearance of the deity as a human, and the feud between two brothers (cf. Appu [Abu] and Abraham). And the topos of the potter and his clay creation (Isa 29:16, 45:9; Jer 18:6; Rom 9:20–21) has an antecedent in the parable of the coppersmith and the cup that curses its maker in the Hittite-Hurrian Song of Release. Note also the theme of the divine destruction of the city of Ebla for failure to manumit its slaves, which has been compared to Yahweh's destruction of Judah for failure to observe the sabbatical years (2 Chr 36:17–21).

Official Religion. Numerous correspondences in the realm of official religion have been noted. Jacob Milgrom has compared the division of roles within the Hittite guard (temple servants and keepers) with that between the priests and Levites as described in the Priestly Code. David Wright has pointed to the similarity of the placement of the hand(s) on the sacrificial animal in Hittite and Israelite sacrificial ritual, as either conferring authorization on another to act on behalf of the one making the gesture or to attribute the offering to the one making the gesture. Although the idea of kingship was borrowed from Mesopotamia and Egypt, the practice of anointing kings may have come from the Hittite world, perhaps via the Hurrians in the second millennium or the Neo-Hittite states in the first. Finally, the biblical notion of guilt passing from one generation to the next has analogues in Hittite prayers and treaties.

Hoffner suggests a connection between the biblical term *kōmer* referring to pagan priests and Hittite *kumra-*, which he suggests is the Hittite reading of GUDU12, one of the main classes of priest in the Hittite priesthood. He further suggests this class of priest, originating in Anatolia, was active in Syria-Palestine, and thus offers a possible conduit for cult influences. On the other hand, his attempts to find correspondences in the area of divination—specifically the proposed connections between Hurrian *api-*, a ritual pit used to communicate with the deities of the underworld, with Hebrew *'ôb* (in, e.g., 1 Sam 28; Isa 29:4) and Hittite *tarpi-* with Hebrew *teraphim*—have met with strong criticism from biblical scholars.

Personal Religion. In the area of ritual power, the best-known parallel is that between the Hittite rituals attributed to Ashella and Uhhamuwa and the biblical scapegoat rite described in Leviticus 16. Both the Hittite and biblical rites have as their goal the elimination of pollution from the community by means of a scapegoat sent into the wilderness or the enemy camp; in the case of Ashella's ritual, several scapegoats (rams) are used, along with a woman. Just as the Azazel rite is balanced with sin offerings to Yahweh (Lev 16:11–19), Ashella's ritual complements the scapegoat rite with sacrifices performed for the god who caused the plague on the third day of the four-day ritual (§7). This ritual has its roots in a north Syrian tradition.

The episode of the Philistines and the ark of the covenant described in 1 Samuel 5—6 draws comparison to two separate Hittite rituals. The ritual attributed to Ambazzi uses two mice, one a "scapegoat," the other an offering, and may explain the mice sent along with tumors as a guilt offering when the Philistines returned the ark to the Israelites. The Ritual of Samuha affected the removal of curses by sending a model boat laden with gold and silver images of the oaths and curses down the river to the sea as propitiatory gifts for the offended deity. The shaping of the offerings in the form of the calamities is a striking parallel to the mice and tumors of the Philistine ritual. Thus 1 Samuel 5—6 may reflect Anatolian practices introduced by the Philistines whose origins, some assert, were in Anatolia.

The Hittite texts attest to the use of blood as a means of expiation, purification, and consecration, a rite (called *zurki-*, after the Hurrian word for blood) that parallels the biblical sin offering in both its procedure and goals (e.g., KUB 9.22+ and Lev 14). Feder argues that, just as with the scapegoat rite, this practice stems from a common tradition with its roots in Syria (whether of Hurrian or Semitic origin). Also a part of this common tradition was the double ritual, comprising both burnt and well-being offerings, which appears in Hurro-Hittite and Syrian ritual texts and the Bible.

Among the various means of disposing of impurity, the Hittite rituals attest to the placing of evils and contaminated materials in containers sealed with lids of lead that were then symbolically deposited in the underworld or beneath the sea. This theme reemerges in Zechariah 5:5–11 and in the Greek myth of Pandora.

Finally, it is worth pointing out that the Hittite evidence can be used to illuminate the Bible even when no specific parallel is at issue. The prohibited acts in Isaiah 66:3 are best understood as oblique references to ritual traditions that were widespread in the eastern Mediterranean, including the sacrifice of dogs and pigs, to which discussion the Hittite texts contribute a great deal.

Channels of Influence. There are many routes by which the Hittite world might have influenced the biblical. Some correspondences may be a real phenomenon, others a function of the fact that the Hittites and Israelites are both a part of the greater cuneiform culture of Mesopotamia. But others no doubt have a more direct connection. In the Iron Age, the Neo-Hittite cities and the Sea Peoples Diaspora may both account for the conveyance of some Anatolian ideas and practices to Palestine.

For the Bronze Age, Singer has persuasively advocated for the period of the Egypto-Hittite Peace at the end of the thirteenth century as a fertile ground for contacts between Hittite officials and functionaries who were among the diplomatic core operating in the region and the inhabitants of Palestine. Further, Collins has argued, building on the recent work of biblical scholars, that the time span between the Hittite collapse to the composition of the relevant sections of the biblical text is bridged by historical memory and scribal continuity over the centuries. Syria undoubtedly provided the context for the exchange of ritual traditions, while the biblical covenant form and the story of David's rise to power were almost certainly borrowed directly from the Hittite imperial records.

Impact and Relevance. While scholars do not hesitate to see direct borrowing from Neo-Assyrian treaties in Deuteronomy, most have been hesitant to draw such connections with the Hittite treaties, to which the covenant form bears a closer resemblance, preferring to understand the Hittite treaties as a cross-cultural phenomenon, representative of a form of political discourse that was de rigueuer throughout the Near East. (The discussion of covenant by Mendenhall and Herion in the Anchor Bible Dictionary refers to "Late Bronze Age treaties" even though the evidence it adduces is all Hittite.) A similar reluctance to consider the possibility of direct influence has dominated the discussion of literary parallels, as noted earlier. The distance in time is compounded by the date of the biblical text itself, and the Priestly document (P) in particular, which many maintain is quite late. This presumption, however, is not uncontested.

The reluctance to see the Hittite data as anything other than phenomenological ignores the political and cultural impact of the Hittite Empire on the Near East, and especially on Syria, which was an integral part of that empire. By the same token, privileging Mesopotamian evidence however ill-fitting as preferable to a Hittite origin serves to trivialize the contribution of the Hittite sources. Until scholarly consensus moves forward to remove these methodological obstacles, the full impact and relevance of Hittitology for biblical interpretation will remain unacknowledged and underexplored.

Future Prospects. Despite the challenges, the potential of Hittitology for biblical interpretation has not diminished. Recent contributions by a new generation of scholars, some of whom are trained both in Hittite and in Biblical Hebrew, indicate that much more remains to be discovered.

[*See also*: Assyriology and Biblical Interpretation; Diachronic Interpretation; *and* Historical Criticism, *subentry* Hebrew Bible.]

BIBLIOGRAPHY

Berman, Joshua A. "God's Alliance with Man." *Azure* 25 (2006): 79–113. Seeks to resituate the modern discussion of covenant in its proper ancient Near Eastern (specifically Hittite) context to answer the question what is the original, biblical meaning of covenant.

Cancik, Hubert. *Grundzüge der hethitischen und alttestamentlichen Geschichtsschreibung.* Weisbaden: Harrassowitz, 1976. A systematic attempt to demonstrate important similarities between Israelite and Hittite historiography.

Collins, Billie Jean. *The Hittites and Their World.* Atlanta: Society of Biblical Literature, 2007. A comprehensive survey of the contributions of Hittite studies to biblical interpretation. It represents the first attempt to collect in one place all of the parallels that have been proposed over decades of research. The chapter "Hittites in the Bible," details the author's theory as to how "Hittites" came to appear in the Bible and an epilogue discusses the various possible channels of influence.

Feder, Itzhaq. *Blood Expiation in Hittite and Biblical Ritual: Origins, Context, and Meaning.* Writings from the Ancient World Supplement Series 1. Atlanta: Society of Biblical Literature, 2011. Demonstrates the shared tradition of biblical and Hittite blood rites.

Forrer, Emil. "The Hittites in Palestine, I." *Palestine Exploration Quarterly* 68 (1936): 190–203; "The Hittites in Palestine, II." *Palestine Exploration Quarterly* 69 (1937): 100–115. The first and most influential attempt to address the question of the identity of the Hitties in the Bible. Part I investigates the identity of the Hittites in Palestine. Part II offers a theory as to how they might have arrived there.

Hoffner, Harry A., Jr.,"The Hittites and Hurrians." In *Peoples of Old Testament Times*, edited by D. J. Wiseman, 197–228. Oxford, 1973.

Hoffner, Harry A., Jr. "Hittite-Israelite Cultural Parallels." In *The Context of Scripture.* Vol. 3: *Archival Documents*, edited by William H. Hallo and K. Lawson Younger Jr., xxix–xxxiv. Leiden: Brill, 2002. A brief and current overview of the history of investigation into the subject with a review of the most significant parallels drawn to date.

Hoffner, Harry A., Jr. "Some Contributions of Hittitology to Old Testament Study." *Tyndale Bulletin* 20 (1969): 27–55. A summary of what was known to date about the Hittites in Palestine and Hittite materials that could elucidate the Hebrew Bible.

Janowski, Bernd, Klaus Koch, and Gernot Wilhelm, eds. *Religionsgeschichtliche Beziehungen zwischen Kleinasien, Nordsyrien und dem Alten Testament.* Orbis Biblicus et Orientalis 129. Göttingen: Vandenhoeck & Ruprecht, 1993. A collection of essays by both biblical scholars and Hittitologists investigating specific points of correspondence, including the scapegoat tradition (Janowski and Wilhelm); the Hurrian ritual KUB 9.22+ and Lev 14 (Haas); and cult steles and baityloi (Hutter); among others.

Kempinski, Aharon. "Hittites in the Bible: What Does Archaeology Say?" *Biblical Archaeology Review* 5, no. 4 (1979): 21–44. Approaches the question of the identity of the Hittites in the Bible from the perspective of the archaeological and iconographic evidence.

McCarter, P. Kyle, "The Apology of David." *Journal of Biblical Literature* 99 (1980): 489–504. Building on the work of Wolf and Hoffner, an analysis of the narrative of David's rise to power in light of the Apology of Hattusili III.

Mendenhall, George E. "Covenant Forms in Israelite Tradition." *Biblical Archaeologist* 17 (1954): 50–76. The seminal discussion of the dependence of the Israelite covenant tradition on the Hittite treaty formula.

Mendenhall, George E., and Gary A. Herion, "Covenant." *Anchor Bible Dictionary* 1:1179–1202. Detailed and current examination of the nature of the biblical covenant and its connection to ancient Near Eastern (specifically Hittite) covenant traditions.

Milgrom, Jacob, "The Shared Custody of the Tabernacle and a Hittite Analogy." *Journal of the American Oriental Society* 40 (1970): 204–209. A topical study of one of the more important parallels that has come to light and which has withstood scrutiny.

Moyer, James C., "Hittite and Israelite Cultic Practices: A Selected Comparison." In *Scripture in Context*, Vol. 2, edited by William W. Hallo, James C. Moyer, and Leo G. Perdue, 19–38. Winona Lake, Ind.: Eisenbrauns, 1983. A summary and evaluation of proposed parallels to date.

Singer, Itamar. "The Hittites and the Bible Revisited." In *"I Will Speak the Riddle of Ancient Times": Archaeological and Historical Studies in Honor of Amihai Mazar on the Occasion of His Sixtieth Birthday*, edited by Aren M. Maeir and Pierre de Miroschedji, 723–756. Winona Lake, Ind.: Eisenbrauns, 2006. A comprehensive presentation of the question of the identity of the biblical Hittites, with a detailed discussion of the historical, archaeological, and philological evidence for a Hittite presence in and influence on Palestine, as well as a brief survey of the most significant parallels.

Wazana, Nili. "Border Descriptions and Cultural Barriers." In *Akten des IV. Internationalen Kongresses*, edited by Gernot Wilhelm, 696–710. Wiesbaden: Harrassowitz, 2001. With Feder and Yakubovitch, this article offers a recent addition to the growing list of parallels, testifying to the continuing contribution of Hittitology to biblical interpretation. Wazana deftly demonstrates the conceptual and literary similarities between the Syro-Anatolian steles and biblical sources to Late Bronze Age Hittite border descriptions, providing further evidence of continuity and transformation.

Yakubovitch, Ilya. "Were Hittite Kings Divinely Anointed? A Palaic Invocation to the Sun-God and Its Significance for Hittite Religion." *Journal of Ancient Near Eastern Religions* 5 (2005): 122–137. An intriguing discussion of the evidence for the anointment of Hittite kings, offering a response to Ernst Kutsch (*Salbung als Rechtsakt im Alten Testament und im alten Orient.* Berlin, 1963), and a possible context for the importation of the anointment ritual by the Israelites.

Billie Jean Collins

HOMILETICS

Homiletics is the study and practice of preaching in sacred spaces. It is done in churches, in synagogues, in mosques, and in any space where a religious leader presumes to speak to humans on behalf of the Divine. This chapter traces a history of Christian preaching and its styles; looks at a major shift in preaching in the mid-twentieth century that set the tone for preaching into the twenty-first century; then it addresses the impact that women preachers and woman-identified liberationist thought and practices have begun to have on the field of homiletics, as it relates to interpreting Bible for the work of preaching, beginning in the late twentieth century until now.

Homiletical studies reside at the intersection of interpretation of ancient texts and the lives of peoples and cultural places many years removed from those texts. This field requires a careful study of and use of rhetorical devices as it mines these texts. In the case of Christian preaching, these texts are either sixty-six books (majority of Protestant bibles) or seventy-three books in the Anglican or Roman Catholic Bibles. From these loci, preaching occurs.

Assumptions. It is a foolish thing we do to stand up and dare to speak a word of salvation, of hope, of grace, of God's absurd vision of *shalom* (really, a wolf and a lamb together?). And yet preachers do it every week, some several times a week, as they proclaim the mystery of faith. Paul meant "foolish" as over against the world's wisdom, and he meant "mystery" as over against other mystery cults. The gospel is never preached in a vacuum and without conversation partners. As a preacher, one looks to turn up the volume on God's foolish, lavish, inscrutable vision for *shalom*. It becomes the preacher's interpretive task to continually seek to make sense of the Bible, or as Craddock notes, "It is the task of the pastor to put the book and the church together" (Craddock 2011). There are no "disinterested" interpretations of the biblical texts for preaching. Certainly Rudolf Bultmann, in trying to answer the question that became his lifelong quest "is exegesis without presuppositions possible?" came to two conclusions:

> The question whether exegesis without presuppositions is possible must be answered affirmatively if "without presuppositions" means "without presupposing the results of the exegesis." In this sense, exegesis without presuppositions is not only possible but demanded. In another sense, however, *no* exegesis is without presuppositions, inasmuch as the exegete is not a *tabula rasa*, but on the contrary, approaches the text with specific questions or with a specific way of raising questions and thus had a certain idea of the subject matter with which the text is concerned. (Bultmann, p. 197)

Brief History of Biblical Interpretative Homiletics. From Moses standing at Sinai and declaring the law, to Jesus delivering the Sermon on the Mount to Peter standing in the streets of Jerusalem to explain the outbreak of languages by people who had not learned them on the Day of Pentecost, preaching has been the currency of Christian declaration. The apostle Paul would declare that God chose "the foolishness of preaching" to save the believing (1 Cor 1:21, King James Version). Of course, there was no end of preaching between the church's inception and the eighteenth century. By the time the evangelical fervor that engulfed the colonies in the eighteenth century produced Jonathan Edwards and George Whitfield, certain styles of preaching were established, such as the university sermon that included three points, jokes, and a poem. Another form, the expository, line-by-line of scripture dominated the preaching style in North America (O. Allen 2010, p. 3).

While these men were preaching, Jarena Lee became the first woman in the nascent African Methodist Episcopal church to preach the gospel in the colonies in 1811 (Simmons and Thomas, p. 160). The famed testimony about her call to preach demonstrates an astute interpretation of biblical texts in which her experience and her success as a preacher is lifted as evidence that "nothing is impossible with God" (Simmons and Thomas, p. 164). She declares that Mary Magdalene was the first to proclaim the risen Christ: "Did not Mary *first* preach the risen Saviour and is not the doctrine of the resurrection the very climax of Christianity—hangs not all our hope on this, as argued by St. Paul?" (Simmons and Thomas, p. 164).

Lee, like other African American women preachers such as Zilpha Law and Julia Foote, add their astute handling of biblical texts for proclamation to the history of the First and Second Great Awakenings in North America. They were especially pietistic, calling for holiness like their male counterparts and concerned about the freedom of people enslaved in the North American context. For such preachers, the Bible was the source for freedom, spiritually and socially, for those in bondage. Martha Simmons and Frank A. Thomas would say that these black women preachers display "profound sermonic insights" because of "the cultural habit of the close observation of life, which yields a rich storehouse of interesting, true stories illustrative of biblical precepts with which the hearer may identify" (Simmons and Thomas, pp. 7–8), or what they term "existential exegesis."

In the early twentieth century, Harry Emerson Fosdick, the storied preacher at New York's Riverside Church and a theology professor at Union Theological Seminary, set the tone and shaped the future for "liberal theology." In an article published in 1928 in *Harper's Magazine*, he asked and answered the question, "What's the matter with preaching?" His answer was, bitingly, that most sermons were boring and did not speak to the needs and concerns of the people, that the sermon itself was irrelevant. He argued that too many preachers "take a passage from Scripture and, proceeding on the assumption that the people attending church that morning are deeply concerned about what the passage means, they spend their half hour or more on historical exposition of the verse or chapter, ending with some appended application to the auditors. What could be more sure predestined to dullness and futility?" (Fosdick, *Preaching Today*, 9). For Fosdick, such an approach to the text is "grossly misusing the Bible." In the article, he argued that people care most about what concerns them personally, because that is at the core what the biblical writers themselves care about. The point is not what these texts possibly "meant" but how they participate in meaning-making in the present. Fosdick maintained that preaching is pastoral care at its best and that the starting point for the preaching task is the lives of people. This shift from text to people was not subtle and it took hold, even in more conservative circles.

This turn toward decentering the biblical text as the starting point for biblical interpretation is reflected in some ways in the most biblically centric homileticians of the mid- to late-twentieth century, as described in O. Wesley Allen Jr.'s *The Renewed Homiletic*. Allen argues that Fosdick, alongside R. E. C. Brown and H. Grady Davis, foreshadowed the work of these "pillars of the new homiletic." The hermeneutic at work for the school of thought would be:

> Instead of approaching Scripture as history or as a collection of eternal truths, or even as myths to be demythologized, they viewed Scripture as *word event*. Language does not simply refer; it acts, it does, it is an event that creates meaning and meaningfulness. Over against the approach of earlier historical critics who tried to study Scripture in a scientific, objective, distant manner, the New Hermeneutic argues that proper interpretation of Scripture requires that one be existentially invested to allow the Word to act upon you. (Allen 2010, p. 6)

What these homileticians share is the move toward this hermeneutic, which also led them into the literary critics' circles where understanding scripture and the move from text to preaching include taking seriously the role and power of storytelling. It would be wrong to collapse the work of these five men into one, but it is fair to say that although they come to it in different ways, each calls for an appeal to emotion, to story, to plot, to narrative, and to culture as a way to get from the ancient pages to the contemporary context (Allen, 2010, passim).

Each essayist also is keenly aware of being in a stream of history. None speaks as if working in a vacuum. They are aware of the upheavals of culture around them, all of them working in the midst of civil rights unrest, the questioning of authority and authoritative voices, and thus each seeking a way to address how and whether preaching remains "relevant" as a mode of communication. Each would affirm that preaching remains powerful and relevant, but only with this turn toward narrative and deliberate attempts to engage people in the pew in the preaching event. In Allen's book, each homiletician reflects on his initial work many years later. In addition, at least two homileticians on whom their work has had an impact, reflect on the "pillars" work and offer their own assessments in the contemporary milieu. These secondary offerings push into what preaching looks like in a world of Facebook, Twitter, video cameras, and the like. Thus, this small volume will be a gift of history and interpretative and homiletic theories and methods for years to come.

Hermeneutics. Preaching takes the very artistic text of the biblical world and lyrically speaks into a contemporary community to "shape and lead it with words" (Lischer, p. xiii). The preacher is charged with using words to persuade humans and to connect them to a particular worldview that is teased from a foreign land, that is, the biblical landscape. Thus, the work of hermeneutics is a first and primary task because the church claims the Bible as a source and resource. Depending on the denomination, the degree to which this claim is made varies—for interpreting the Bible is a cornerstone to preaching. At the point in which preaching claims to unpack the biblical story and the biblical claims on those who follow it, preaching becomes Hermes's or Mercury's vehicle.

Preaching requires hermeneutics, translating the ancient and foreign texts into the present, making sense of the texts as sacred, and thus speaking on behalf of God. The term "hermeneutics" comes from the Greek pantheon of gods, referring to Hermes, the Greek god who was the intercessor between mortals and the gods—an emissary and messenger. Thus, preachers claim that same duty of messenger and emissary. Hermes also was a god of transitions and boundaries who knew how to move freely between divine and mortal worlds. Following this characteristic, the preacher learns this trait of traveling between worlds—the world of the text and the world of the listeners—and becomes an apt translator and with that becomes a great storyteller.

Hermes often is depicted as a traveler, as well as shepherd or worker. Here, too, it is apparent why preaching is connected with this Greek god. Preachers, as interpreters of texts, journey with their listeners to new terrain, new understanding. This traveling is work as the preacher also shepherds the listeners into a shared field of meaning, and the shepherding is localized and particular. Each shepherd leads to the pastures one knows, what Lenora Tubbs Tisdale calls "local theology." It is the reason that on Sunday mornings, with many Protestant churches using the Revised Common Lectionary (RCL), different preachers in different locations throughout the world will preach wildly different sermons from the same texts. How is that possible? One way that accounts for these differences is that biblical texts are not as fixed as "objectivity" might suppose. Certainly one must also account for the differences among the preachers themselves. It is true that preachers might be guilty of eisegesis, that is, reading into the text one's own biases, premises, and presuppositions. It is more often the case that the texts, unfixed in Jacques Derrida's sense of unfixed, lend themselves to multivalent meaning. Or, as Renita Weems so aptly notes in her article, "Reading *Her* Way through the Struggle," "You can only see from where you stand" (Weems 1991, p. 62).

Biblical interpretation starts always with the social location of the interpreter, whether she is aware of her positionality or not. It is paramount that interpreters do locate themselves, or exegete themselves. It allows the preacher to be transparent and honest with the listening conversation about what she is doing. What questions has the preacher brought to the biblical text? What tools has she used to unearthed possible meanings that must still be translated or mediated into a different theological time zone? How has she accounted for her biases and her myopia?

In the early twentieth century, historical-critical methods held absolute sway, promising that it would be unnecessary, to the trained exegete, to think beyond the texts as a source for understanding God and the Christian life. Students were seduced into believing that one might truly know what the text meant in its original context—that archeology, linguistic studies, redaction criticism, and other methodologies could unearth the "real" meaning and eliminate most, if not all, ambivalence. Biblical preaching, then, would be mere reporting from the field of what the preacher saw and heard in the manageable texts. These promises proved elusive. Certainty refused to be still, as Weems and Derrida would find themselves in the same camp as they proclaimed that perspective mattered.

Another fallacy of interpreting for preaching is that one may know the meaning of a word and thus get the meaning of a text. Word searches and free association of word search carry an inherent danger, which is that one word does not a phrase, sentence, or paragraph make. We may know what the individual words "once," "upon," "a," and "time" mean, but unless we get to know and understand the idiom "once upon a time," we may never understand fairy tales and the way they convey stories. The same is true in biblical interpretation in general, but certainly in interpretation for preaching. In other words, genre matters, and genre ought to affect interpretation as well as proclamation. A sermon from Genesis 12 ought not take the same shape as a sermon from Psalm 19. Indeed, biblical scholarship is the kissing kin to interpretation. New understanding and information, new archeological digs, new insights from ancient worlds beyond the biblical texts, and new understanding about what it means to be human in our times, all affect interpretation for preaching.

Finally, it would be an oversight to miss that Christianity's reading of biblical texts for preaching has a peculiar problem, or as Ricoeur noted:

> There has always been a hermeneutic problem in Christianity because Christianity proceeds from a proclamation. It begins with a fundamental preaching that maintains that in Jesus Christ the kingdom has approached us in decisive fashion. But this fundamental preaching, this word, comes to us through writings, through the Scriptures, and these must constantly be restored as the living word if the primitive word that witnessed to the fundamental and founding event is to remain contemporary. (Ricoeur, p. 212)

Christians try to make sense of radically different texts with radically different claims, as one finds in the Old and New Testaments and the intertestamental texts for some Christians. Interpreters seek to find either conversation between the testaments or continuity, and it is not easily done. Over the interpretative span, interpreters have relied on the "four senses of scripture: historical, tropological, allegorical, and anagogical." By way of example, John Cassian offered that Zion/Jerusalem is historically the city of the Jews; allegorically, the Church; anagogically, the heavenly city of God, and tropologically, the soul of a human being. The fourfold method makes plain Ricoeur's concern for hermeneutics where Cassian forces upon Zion/Jerusalem interpretations that are nowhere near apparent in the text. But certainly we see that the Bible may be creatively engaged, even if we might reject some earlier ways of doing so.

The Twenty-first Century Turn to Ideological Homiletics. Womanist preaching finds its home in an explosion of liberationist preaching as found in womanist, feminist, mujerista, black theology, and queer readings. Liberationist interpreters reflect a natural progression from the work of the new homiletic in the way such interpretations not only tell the story but also excavate the story for its ideological claims. It begs the question that the Hebrew Bible scholar Renita Weems asked that has begun to guide the work of womanist biblical interpreters who also preach: what difference will it make that women were in the pulpits at the turn of the twenty-first century (Weems 2006, 27)? This question, from Weems's point of view, is that if women sound exactly like the men around them, then they have not brought their concerns and their fully embodied selves to the interpretative work and the preaching task. If women do not raise different questions, then they have been co-opted by a male-centric set of concerns, as if such concerns genuinely represent the concerns of full humanity.

For womanists, interpreting the Bible for preaching is fraught with danger. One may not simply follow a trope often used among black evangelical preachers, "and the Bible says," as if one may simply quote what one has read and the work is done. For one thing, the Bible itself is foreign to many contemporary contexts. It is, as Fernando Segovia has taught us, a stranger, an "Other," that deserves to be met on its own terms. Indeed, "Womanist preaching requires an unswerving stare into texts that teach and speak death, risk the well-being of people, and choosing to resist or to reject them" (Bridgeman, p. 7).

The homiletician Donna E. Allen uncovers the hermeneutical work of the civil rights activist and self-identified womanist preacher, the Reverend Doctor Prathia Hall, an American Baptist preacher who worked closely beside the Reverend Martin Luther King Jr. Allen examines several sermons that Hall preached to see whether she employed specific womanist homiletical and hermeneutical strategies. Allen notes that the womanist preacher has the diligent task of uncovering "stereotypical images" of black women and "linguistic violence," following Katie Cannon (Allen 2005, p. 113).

Allen quotes Hall as saying that womanist interpretation identifies background information and asks whether the scripture was written in a context of sexism, classism, or racism, and whether or how a text attempts to address the life of the community (Allen 2005, p. 58). Womanist interpretative work is "an interrogatory conversation," Hall insists. This interrogatory conversation is a highly imaginative and exploratory conversation. Good hermeneutics, and by extension good preaching, requires an active and vivid imagination. It becomes easy merely to repeat examples heard over and over rather than to ask the kinds of questions that make texts come alive, to uncover interlocking privileges or oppressions in the text in order to discover what has shaped both the text and the interpreter.

The Bible is dangerous to handle—like dynamite—but it is the church's book and deserves for its full breadth to be taken into account. How does one weigh what one reads? Is it possible or even desirable to give every text the same weight? Where are such decisions located within interpretive communities?

For those who put their ideological claims in view (e.g., womanists, feminists, mujeristas, black liberationists, queer), interpretation for proclamation allows for resistance to any part of the canon that does not advocate for freedom and life for all people. This resistance does not mean that one ignores the canon—quite the contrary. Instead, when one approaches the texts—RCL or personally chosen—one reads with an eye toward liberation and responsibility, always being willing to walk away if necessary. Womanist interpretations must take into account race, class, and gender in the rubric of lived experience. As such womanists embrace an ethic of resistance to oppression, to counter "the negative real-world consequences of sexist wording that brothers and sisters propagate in the guise of Christian piety and virtue" (Allen 2005, p. 119). The hermeneutic at work uncovers the ethical consequences and political functions of interpretation, thereby allowing the interpreter to identify the scaffolding of sexist-racist social constructions buried in sacred rhetoric so that interpreters may make life-giving decisions about the proclamation.

Whose voices are absent in these texts? Where is life here? What is death dealing? Whose interests are being served? How is God present or absent in the text? With the will to choose or reject, may we say no to this text, given what we now know about humanity, about creation, and about God? Is the ancient witness still our witness, or may we say, "that was then, this is now?" This particular kind of interrogating might be described as "listening in." The preacher leans into the text to hear faint sounds not always distinct, but if one continues to ask, the text will yield a counter and liberating voice to death, and when it does not, the womanist preacher is obligated to argue back. But when the text yields a peaceable harvest, and the preacher finds herself overhearing an eternal and transformative word, she bears witness by way of crafting a sermon that translates those sounds into a call to salvific freedom, to justice, and to reconciliation. And while womanists often address texts with women in them, this kind of interrogatory conversation and listening in may be applied to any text.

A Model of Womanist Homiletics. The story of Ananias and Sapphira in Acts has been used in some settings for stewardship drives. In the story, both Ananias and Sapphira in separate moments drop dead for lying to the Spirit, according to the text. The story ends when "great fear seized the whole church" after people heard what happened (Acts 5:11). The last sentence in this story ought to be instructive for interpretation for preaching: Why would we want to live in a community where the thing that "keeps us in line" is fear? In what world does a man drop dead and is buried without his wife knowing that he has died and been buried? That piece of information alone disrupts the story as plausible. And if it's not plausible that a man would die and his wife not know (at the very least as she walks into the room with the disciples, would not someone warn her not to lie?), how else might this story be functioning?

I once preached a sermon from this text titled "Ghost Stories and Other Scare Tactics" and argued that the story is like sitting around the campfire in the woods being told ghost stories (complete with dead people and scary apostles who should not be crossed lest it cost you your life). We are supposed to be terrified into "unity." But, as a homiletic turn, is fear a reason to give financially or to serve the church? Do we want leaders who threaten us with death and call down divine wrath? I note that Ananias and Sapphira are under the peer pressure of the generosity from Joseph from Cyprus (also known as Barnabas), who sold a field and gave the proceeds (Acts 4:36–37). But maybe peer pressure isn't a reason to give either.

In other words, I resisted the usual reading of this text, as I resist the flattening and demonizing of the couple, and lay some of the struggle in the larger church and a leadership trying to portray a unity, which a scratching of church history would reveal just was not so. In addition, I lift up a historically coded use of the name "Sapphira" and how black women have often been called Sapphira, much like they were named Jezebel or Delilah, other "bad women" of the Bible. This subtext is not minor, precisely because it is subliminal. The repositioning of women as human and not as targets for ridicule or sin carriers in sermons is a part of the work Weems called womanist preachers to engage.

I do not deconstruct and reconstruct a world just for the sake of doing so. That would amount to Bible somersaults and high-wire walking for the "oohs" and "aahs." Rather, I suggest that the interpretation demands a different worldview of the church and of the God of the church. It also demands a different view of the woman and the man who are unwitting antagonists in the text. It is the place of meaning, where meaning occurs in the clash between two worlds and among several possibilities. The possibilities that text-bound characters might be round, not flat, gives the interpreter other options for making the quantum leap from text to contemporary worlds. Rather than fear as motivator and a spirit ready to pounce, I push back and suggest that we *not* use this text to promote giving or unity. I argue for an alternative reality: Why not ignore the ghost story and decide to give as we are able—out of joy and relationship with God and God's people. Why not, I suggest, choose *not* to succumb to peer pressure and to do as Paul suggests in another place in the text and give as one purposes to do so, out of a cheerful heart (2 Cor 9:7)?

The Future of Liberationist Homiletics. Using womanist hermeneutics as an example, I have argued that deliberately liberationist interpretative strategies will lead the way in this century. If I am right, by default I also am arguing for a shift in the narrative put forth by the New Homiletic paradigm of the late twentieth century and suggesting a prophetic shift, or at least the possibility of a prophetic shift. The very act of preaching is revolutionary, using womanist hermeneutics. Turning over the soil of scripture with questioning tools designed to unearth the texts' interests and ideologies can be dicey. It is possible that the interpreter sees only what she wants to see; but if she questions herself as she questions the ancient texts, then she is being a faithful exegete.

The goal, then, becomes to look over into divine imaginings and see a different landscape, a different commonwealth where sexism, racism, classism, and other death-dealing oppressive structures are laid bare. And the good news includes skills of resistance as well as tools for constructing a new reality, a God reality. For Christians, such resistance must include an appeal to the role of Spirit to enliven and to empower the revolution. Although this essay does not explore the role of the Spirit, it would be a good next step for womanist interpretation for preaching.

An increasingly post-Christian world will and should demand a more rigorous accounting for ways in which Christians tell our own stories in the context of larger religious, human stories. Liberationist hermeneutics tap into a longing for freedom that is persistent in the human heart and consistent with the mission and ministry of Jesus of Nazareth.

It is not that womanist interpretative tools are the only ones, but rather they sit in the circle of conversation with many others who have the shared goal of God's grace spoken into the world in such a way that individual lives are changed and creation is made new. It is a liberating meaning-making venture. But meaning is "not inherent to texts or readers, but is discovered somewhere on the meeting grounds between them," or more clearly on the margins surrounding each. The womanist interpreter/preacher makes the margins visible—a task that requires "an unswerving stare into texts that teach and speak death"—and chooses to resist or reject them. Womanist interpreters remind the community that their task is prophetic, "continuous from the ancient Hebrew texts we claim as Christian texts into these witness-bound words of disciples. We bear witness to a God peeking from these pages but not bound by or to them" (Bridgeman 2008, p. 7). At the center of all this work is the ancient book that belongs to the believing Christian community. Womanist interpreters honor the book without worshiping it by taking seriously the implications of its impact as interpreted and proclaimed in the community. It is necessary work. It is revolutionary work. It is prophetic work.

[*See also* African American Interpretation; Class Criticism; Feminist Biblical Interpretation; Ideological Criticism; Narrative Criticism and Narrative Hermeneutics; Race, Ethnicity, and Biblical Criticism; Theological Interpretation; *and* Womanist Interpretation.]

BIBLIOGRAPHY

Allen, Donna E. *Toward a Womanist Homiletic: Katie Cannon, Alice Walker, and Emancipatory Proclamation.* PhD diss., Vanderbilt University Graduate School of Religion. Nashville, 2005.

Allen, O. Wesley Jr., ed. *The Renewed Homiletic.* Minneapolis: Fortress, 2010. A volume of essays reflecting on the contribution to the field of homiletics, with contributions by David Buttrick, Fred B. Craddock, Eugene L. Lowry, Henry H. Mitchell, Charles L. Rice, and others.

Bridgeman, Valerie. "'It Ain't Necessarily So': Resistance Preaching and Womanist Thought." Contextual Hermeneutics Section of the Society of Biblical Literature, 22 November 2008. This article is scheduled to be published in a volume of essays, J. Dwayne Howell, ed., *Preaching and the Personal: Prophecy, Witness and Testimony*, Eugene, OR: Pickwick Publications, 2013.

Bultmann, Rudolf. "Is Exegesis Without Presuppositions Possible?" In *Existence and Faith: Shorter Writings of Rudolf Bultmann*, 289–296. New York: Meridian, 1960. Reprinted in *The Company of Preachers: Wisdom on Preaching, Augustine to the Present*, edited by Richard Lischer, 196–203. Grand Rapids: Eerdmans Publishing Co., 2002.

Craddock, Fred B. *Craddock on the Craft of Preaching.* Edited by Lee Sparks and Kathryn Hayes Sparks. St. Louis: Chalice, 2011.

Craddock, Fred B. *Preaching.* Nashville: Abingdon, 1985.

Doob Sakenfeld, Katharine. "Feminist Uses of Biblical Materials." In *Feminist Interpretation of the Bible*, edited by Letty M. Russell, 55–64. Philadelphia: Westminster, 1985.

Fosdick, Harry Emerson. "What is the Matter with Preaching?" reprinted from *Harper's Magazine* (July 1928), 7–19. In *What's the Matter with Preaching Today?* edited by Mike Graves, 133–141. Louisville: Westminster/John Knox, 2004.

Leadbetter, Ron. "Hermes." *Encyclopedia Mythica.* Last modified 8 February 2007. http://www.pantheon.org/articles/h/hermes.html.

Lischer, Richard, ed. *In the Company of Preachers: Wisdom on Preaching, Augustine to the Present.* Grand Rapids: Eerdmans, 2002.

McMickle, Marvin A. *Where Have All the Prophets Gone? Reclaiming Prophetic Preaching in America.* Cleveland: Pilgrim, 2006.

Ricoeur, Paul. "The Hermeneutic Question," In *The Conflict of Interpretation*, edited by Don Ihde, 381–388. Evanston: Northwestern University Press, 1974. Reprinted in *The Company of Preachers: Wisdom on Preaching, Augustine to the Present*, edited by Richard Lischer, 211–217. Grand Rapids: Eerdmans, 2002.

Simmons, Martha J., and Frank A. Thomas, "Introduction." In *Preaching with Sacred Fire: An Anthology of African American Sermons, 1750 to the Present*, edited by Martha J. Simmons and Frank A. Thomas, 1–11. New York: W. W. Norton, 2010.

Tubbs Tisdale, Lenora. *Preaching as Local Theology and Folk Art.* Minneapolis: Augsburg Fortress, 1997.

Weems, Renita J. "How Will our Preaching be Remembered? A Challenge to See the Bible from a Woman's Perspective." *African American Pulpit* (Summer 2006): 26–29.

Weems, Renita J. "Reading *Her* Way Through the Struggle." In *Stony the Road We Trod: African American Biblical Interpretation*, edited by Cain Hope Felder, 62. Minneapolis: Augsburg Fortress, 1991.

Valerie Bridgeman

I

Ideological Criticism

Ideology is one of those words that has accrued a variety of uses (Larrain 1979; Eagleton 2007). It can vary from the neutral description of a system of ideas such as an institution to a system of ideas, held by society, that underlie the power and values of a certain class. Hence, theology could be the ideology of Christianity and thus the ideology be virtually synonymous with theology. Of greatest interest, however, is the use of term within the Marxist tradition, succinctly put in Karl Marx's "The German Ideology" (Marx 1998), to indicate the way in which ideas are intimately related to the struggle for power and hegemony and particularly the ways in which ruling elites promote their values by recourse to "ideologies" that are deemed to be natural or normal but, in fact, serve their interests. Thus, by subscribing to such ideas in their culture and everyday lives, the majority of people are unaware that they are supporting the interests of their rulers and other powerful groups. This lack of awareness is what Marxists call false consciousness. While the Bible contains numerous examples of false consciousness, a glaring one is when the oppressed Hebrew slaves, who are on the verge of a degree of freedom, find themselves looking back to the ideology of Egypt and its culture: "If only we had died by the hand of the Lord in the land of Egypt, when we sat by the fleshpots and ate our fill of bread; for you have brought us out into this wilderness to kill this whole assembly with hunger" (Exod 16:3a).

Ideology and Texts. All texts are ideological in some sense and have a relationship to vested interest in relation to social formations (Jameson 1981; Williams 1987). The text is an individual representative of the struggles between social classes and the contradictions of human existence. Texts' relationships to the world are never straightforward, as they both reflect and refract social reality. Through them the tensions of wider society are expressed, for example, offering a resolution of the contradictions and frustrations of the world. A text may be interpreted as part of a struggle between different class interests in which a ruling class ideology seeks to offer itself as "common sense" or "normality" and all else as deviant, abnormal, and irrational. A ruling class ideology will offer strategies of legitimation, while an oppositional culture or ideology will often, in covert ways, seek to contest and to undermine the dominant value system. But there is also an attempt by the powerful to pick the best ideas of the opposition and use those to minimize their potency and the strength of the opposing groups who use them. However loud the note of protest in a text, it is going to be shot through with the ambiguities of being part and parcel of a world that is itself full of contradiction and pain. Any text's relation to that struggle will not necessarily stand firmly on one side or another. Sometimes it will manifest the voice of the oppressor and his ideology in the process of seeking to articulate that subversive memory. Part of the task of interpretation is to lay bare the ambiguities and contradictions that are inherent in all texts. A critical examination of the Bible suggests that texts that have had a radical impact in the subsequent history of religion—such as Second Isaiah—were in their original production a means of reinforcing the ideas of the ruling elite who were transported into exile and then sought to establish their God-given right to lead on their return. So, even what may appear to us to be the most reactionary texts, produced by the elite's representatives, may surprise us by offering what Jameson calls a "utopian impulse."

Ideological Criticism. Ideological criticism is rooted in historicism, but its social and political edge pushes it much further into the actualities of history as compared to much of the results of historical criticism that are frankly usually ideological in nature, whether in the neutral or more political sense. Hegel discusses the detachment that is typical of historical study of the Bible, which, whatever its other virtues, can miss the political character of its own discourse and the extent to which its exponents are themselves implicated in maintaining the citadels of power in their own day or unaware of the extent to which there may have been similar struggles going on within and behind the biblical text:

> It is to be noted that there is a type of theology that wants to adopt *only a historical attitude* towards religion; it even has an abundance of cognition, though only of a historical kind. This cognition is no concern of ours, for if the cognition of religion were merely historical, we would have to compare such theologians with counting-house clerks, who keep the ledgers and accounts of other people's wealth, a wealth that passes through their hands without their retaining any of it, clerks who act only for others without acquiring any assets of their own. They do of course receive a salary, but their merit lies only in keeping records of the assets of other people. In philosophy and religion, however, the essential thing is that one's own spirit itself should recognise a possession and content, deem itself worthy of cognition, and not keep itself humbly outside. (Hegel 1984, p. 128, quoted in Bennett, 1997–1998)

Detachment, according to Hegel, is an impoverished form of knowledge, for it ignores our part in maintaining certain ideas and values. Standing at a distance is impoverished knowledge and it risks ignoring the deeper truths of why certain ideas are deemed more important than others. For Hegel true knowledge and the knower are inseparable, as also the knower is inseparable from that which is known, be it nature, the human community, or God. As the title of the book *Knowledge and Human Interests* by one of the most distinguished modern critical theorists writing in the Marxist tradition, Jürgen Habermas, suggests, knowledge and human interest are inextricably interwoven (Habermas 1978). That applies as much to the biblical authors as their modern interpreters. "Theologians do not live in the clouds" (Boff 1978, p. 265; Freire 1985), however much they might like to think they do.

Ideological criticism suggests the imposition of modern concerns onto the text of the Bible. Such imposition is true even if we think that we search the pages of the Bible to find reference to either ideology or criticism. It is the case that in an intellectual world in which the Marxist tradition has played such a significant role, it was only a matter of time before discussions of class, ideology, and praxis caught up with biblical studies. But it is appropriate that it has done so. Ideological criticism may not be referred to explicitly in the Bible, but the underlying characteristics of what we know as the criticism of ideology are. Thus, particularly in the New Testament, we have texts, that emerge not from the center of power but from a marginal group, which was not just religious but political. We need think only of the terms that it used about itself—even *church* is a term rooted in the Hebrew word (*qahal*, which is widely believed to lie behind the Greek, *ekklesia*) for a community. Church gives entirely the wrong impression. Elsewhere, languages about commonwealth, cities, even the body of Christ have a political ring to them. People became Christians in antiquity for a variety of reasons, but they soon came to realize that they were signing up to a different kind of political culture and values. It may be difficult at times to live out those ideas in the world of Roman domination, but that difficulty did not stop them from exploring exactly that. Theirs was not some retreat into a holy huddle but the exploration of a different kind of politics, which for two centuries was rather marginal from the power politics of the Roman Empire. Here was a group from the margins, who through their intellectuals, gave a different picture of the kingdoms of this world, which challenged the center of power in the *Realpolitik* of empire from the angle of the down trodden and nobodies. This is not to say that the early Christian texts were revolutionary tracts (de Ste. Croix 1983). Far from it, but their focus on the story of a man executed for blasphemy in a Roman colony is symptomatic of the critical perspective that is typical of much early Christian literature and has remained true down the centuries even when Christianity became a central part of the kingdoms of this world after Constantine.

In *The German Ideology*, Marx and Engels start from "real human beings," who must produce their means of subsistence in order to satisfy their material needs. So, material life conditions social life. The political and legal institutions of society are explained by the nature of the economic structure. The nature of a society's ideology—its religious, artistic, moral, and philosophical belief—is determined by its economic structure and the wielders of economic power. Marx's understanding of the critique of ideology was more on the basis of a conventional academic analysis of economics and the power relations, which such an analysis laid bare. The effect of that approach is essentially the same as a long standing critique of what has come to be called ideology, the series of ideas that are part and parcel of a society's culture, many of which are taken for granted as representations of normality when, in fact, they exhibit patterns of deference and subordination whose wide acceptance guarantees the imbalance of power and injustices in society. The challenge to ideology goes back deep into the memories of Jewish origins in the critique of Pharaoh and of idolatry that is imbedded in the Bible but most particularly in the apocalyptic tradition represented by the book of Revelation.

Ideological Criticism of the Bible. In the Hebrew Bible, apologists for priests and kings and other elites may have their say but the pages of this remarkable collection, as two centuries of biblical scholarship have shown, evince different kinds of power struggles between priest and prophet, between true and false prophet, between one holy place, Jerusalem in particular, and the rest, and between those who supported the institution of kingship and those who did not. To describe this as an ideological struggle is entirely appropriate. To embark on ideological criticism of the Bible is not to impose alien categories on it.

The poverty of our historical sources prevents any certainty in the practice of ideological criticism even to the story as we have it, let alone to whatever historical circumstances may lie behind the text. But the latter may be less important than the impression that the author wishes to communicate. Thus, the way in which the situation of the Hebrews in Egypt is presented in Exodus gives a clear impression of a group who, at the very bottom of the pile sociologically, were exploited and vulnerable to the whims of an autocratic political system. Their Lenin-like leader Moses, however, was, to use Gramsci's terms, "an organic intellectual," the one who enabled the peasants' revolt to become something more than a mass revolt against the oppression of the Egyptian Pharaoh and to turn into the emergence of a different kind of society as exemplified in Deuteronomy or the laws of Exodus (Gottwald 1999; Gramsci 1982, p. 9). The ideological infection is nowhere better demonstrated than in the words "the fleshpots of Egypt" illustrating the deprivations of political struggle: "If only we had died by the hand of the Lord in the land of Egypt, when we sat by the fleshpots and ate our fill of bread" (Exod 16:3a).

Ideological struggles can be found in the Hebrew Bible: the building of the Temple (2 Sam 7, a point picked up in Stephen's speech in Acts. 7:47: "*But* it was Solomon who built a house for God") and especially over its rebuilding after the exile. Then the returning exiles, themselves a humbled and deprived elite, found themselves, in the collective memory, at the whims of another autocrat, as the opening chapters of the book of Daniel indicate. But it would appear that the returning exiles had little time for the ordinary people who were left behind but fell out among themselves about the rebuilding of the Temple. The advocacy for the latter project exemplified in Haggai and Ezekiel contrasts with another, perhaps more utopian, vision in the later chapters of Isaiah, which culminates in a recognition of the failure of the visionaries and a pessimism that any change can come about except through divine intervention (Isa 59, especially 15–21; Hanson 1975).

In the New Testament Gospels, a provincial prophet conflicts with contemporaries and is executed on the basis of his sense of vocation. Ideological criticism will set Jesus in the context of contemporary movements for change (*Jewish War* vi. 281ff and 301ff; *Antiquitics* p. xx. p. 97ff; 167ff; 185ff). Jesus is presented as an *agent* of the Kingdom of God rather than waiting for some kind of divine intervention. Like John the Baptist and Jesus, son of Ananias, mentioned in Josephus's *Jewish War* Book VI, a prophet of doom could end up on the wrong side of authorities and be seen as a political threat. Jesus's journey to Jerusalem was a politically provocative act. The entry into the city (according to the Synoptic Gospels) and the "cleansing" of the Temple could be seen as threats to public order that demanded a response (so Mark 11.18; John 11:49). As a result, there was a conflict between Jesus and the semiautonomous hierarchy in Jerusalem backed by Roman colonial power. Historically, the Jesus movement was a failure as he was crushed by the political desire of the priestly elite that "one should die for the people," so that the Romans would not take away the Holy Place or the nation. But both of those things happened within half a century of his death. The story that the first Christians told about him was of one who not only fractured the power of the Temple, this central economic motor and ideological symbol of Jewish society, but also was himself identified with it so that holy space was now Jesus's space (1 Cor 3:9; 6:19). That daring move was not an unqualified blessing for Christianity gradually inheriting language of restriction and exclusion, but it indicates that the story they told of Jesus was a challenge to an ideology that unmasked the power and pretensions of those who maintained it (Belo 1981). But emerging Christianity before the fourth century C.E. was characterized by such a countercultural ethos. An alternative political commitment was supported by practical and administrative arrangements manifested in networks of communication and mutual support. The latter in particular embodied an alternative polity that could be seen at the local level (Justin *Apology I* 65—67) and internationally (Paul's collection for the poor in Jerusalem being the earliest and most remarkable example of this; e.g., Rom. 15: 25; 2 Cor 8–9). What is so striking about the New Testament texts is that they were written by people who had little or no political power and with a vision of the world that was at odds with the prevailing culture. Christians were a different sort of people, committed to a different kind of life and culture, more often than not (until the time of Constantine) at odds with the wisdom and politics of the age. Once it became the religion of the rulers (Bloch 2009; de Ste. Croix), its inclusive rhetoric could easily be used to serve rather different ends. The radical slogan of Galatians, 3:28, "There is neither Jew nor Greek, slave nor free, male nor female," has a rather different ring when uttered to serve as the "social glue" of an inclusive, cosmopolitan, and eventually fragmenting empire.

Theology and Ideology. Marxist philosophers like Ernst Bloch (Bloch 1986, 2009) have noted the ideological critique in early Christian discourse. He provides suggestive insights into the character of Christian doctrine and its mutation into an ideology of the powerful. In this, he contrasts Jesus, the Son of Man coming on the clouds of heaven to establish justice for the poor, with the Lord Christ enthroned in heaven in a glorious state similar to the imperial oppressors of the poor. He contrasts the expectation of the Son of Man as liberator and vindicator who would come to transform the lot of the lowly with the figure of the Kyrios, buttress of church and authorities. He shows how the former expectation has moved to the margins of the Christian tradition, ostracized by the exponents of the dominant ideology. Gradually, this Son of Man belief was displaced by the divine Kyrios, a title "which," as he puts it, "admirably suited the purposes of those who would reduce the Christian community to a sort of military service of their cultic hero" (p. 36). The language of Kyrios with all the panoply of the Divine Pantocrator took the place of the apocalyptic maverick, who died on a Roman gallows. He rightly points to the eclipse of the expectation of the messiah who would subjugate the earthly principalities and powers and to the transformation of heaven by the Son of Man's ascension, a promise that divinity will be manifest on earth in an age of perfection in the future. According to Bloch, the Second Coming reveals the real point of the Ascension, as transformation of heaven as the preserve of God into heaven as the city of humanity, the New Jerusalem, which is to come down to earth. Bloch's utopian horizon, illuminating forgotten paths and sensitive to the growth of ideology, goes alongside his repeated emphasis on the present need to live *as if* the new age were here. This is similar to what New Testament theologians have often stressed about the ethical priorities of the New Testament: the tension between the now and the not yet, living in the present age but seeking to live as if the reign of God were here. Bloch considers that the utopian is not something far off in the future but is at the heart of human experience; it is already at hand in an anticipatory and fragmentary way. These fragments are themselves an encouragement to human action in the present. Since utopia is not fully possible within the limitations of the present order of things, Bloch looks for its fulfillment beyond the limitations of the present world. Consequently, he disputes Engels's belief that utopianism is merely a retreat into a fantasy world, for the vision of a better world is the other side of the coin of the unmasking of political and economic power. Living "as if" may mean opposition, but it more often requires discovering the cracks in history to survive and inhabit in the face of the seemingly impregnable cliff face of the dominant power and its ideology. In the face of this compromise, an accommodation is necessary: "the powers that be are ordained of God" (Rom 13:1). Living "as if" may mean that change in conformity with the New Jerusalem has to be put on hold. Engels saw radical Christian movements as "the anticipation of communism by fantasy" (1972, p. 112; quoted in Turner 1983, p. 167).

From a strict Marxist point of view, communism could only come after the bourgeois revolution to which they were opposed, and such anticipatory politics could not succeed. All that the political analysts could do was interpret the world. Indeed, Marx's view of the utopian movements in 1848 was distinctly suspicious (Avineri 1968), more akin to Romans 13 than any kind of revolutionary politics. But Bloch rightly indicates that there is more, and life "as if," even with all its failings, is crucial for the ideologically critically aware. As Marx himself wrote, "the philosophers have only interpreted the world, in various ways. The point, however, is to change it" (Marx 1992, p. 11). That means going wrong and even, as in the case of the Jesus movement, ending in death.

The death of Jesus in the Gospel of Mark, for example, is a sign of the revolutionary potential of martyrdom, as the ideological system based on the Temple is challenged when the veil of the Temple is torn in two from top to bottom, but what Fernando Belo terms "the cross narrative" is at odds with the "Kingdom narrative." That tension represents the contradiction confronting the revolutionary this side of the new age (Belo; Clévenot 1985; Myers 2008). The appeal to follow the example of the suffering Christ can have the effect of leaving the world very much as it is. A very different understanding of the example of Christ emerges in the way in which the cross is seen as an act of rebellion, whereby the interests of the powerful are challenged. So, when Jesus told his followers to take up the cross, he was advocating the path of rebellion and capitulation to the hierarchy and monarchy and, more importantly, its practice from surrounding culture. Thus, in the evolution of its theology (what might be termed ideology) and its adoption of the language of the authority and power from the contemporary culture, we see in the church the gradual infiltration The words of the Johannine Jesus, "my kingdom is not from this world. If my kingdom were from this world, my followers would be fighting to keep me from being handed over" (John 18:36) are not a recipe for otherworldliness but a challenge to the pity of this world by the emissary from that world in the name of nonviolence and one "commandment" you shall love one another. It is a theme that runs throughout all the Gospels. It is a king who is meek and lowly who rides into Jerusalem (Matt 22:5). Also, Jesus advises his disciples: "You know that those who are supposed to rule over the Gentiles lord it over them, and their great men exercise authority over them. But it shall not be so among you; but whoever would be great among you must be your servant" (Mark 10:42–44; Wengst 1985).

The Apocalypse: Unmasking Empire as Ideological Criticism. The visions of Revelation do not provide the currency of our everyday exchange of ideas and patterns of existence. Yet, in the ancient world visions and dreams were regarded as having great theological importance. They proved to be a potent force for understanding the divine and the human, not to mention the pretensions of economic and political power. What passed as normal is criticized in the unmasking of the effects of evil, as a millennial dream of what things may be like, and offers an alternative horizon of hope. Revelation is the least "churchy" text in the New Testament. Christ stands outside the door of the church never to be coopted to the values of those in the comfort of the ecclesiastical, or indeed any other, ghetto. The political and economic challenge Revelation presents includes the church members. They are not exempt from the judgment meted out on those taken in by the political and economic injustice of the imperial beast and its Babylonian culture. There is no escape from having one's nose rubbed in the brutality of imperial power and the harsh realities of the nature of the injustice of the political system of John's day, which is imagined and evoked in awesome graphic word painting. Like the most pungent political cartoon, John's imagery challenges and may probe the defenses of human complacency.

Dietrich Bonhoeffer seems to have glimpsed something of the interpretative potential of the book of Revelation in its ability to challenge the Laodicean culture by unmasking the character of Christian compromise and the beast of nationalism and oppression when he exhorted fellow church men and women to be "a community which hears the Apocalypse . . . to testify to its alien nature and to resist the false principle of inner-worldliness" and so to be at the service of "those who suffer violence and injustice." In his view, "the Church takes to itself all the sufferers, (all) the forsaken of every party and status. 'Open your mouth for the dumb'" (Prov 31:8; Bonhoeffer 1965, pp. 324–325). Witness and countercultural character are well exemplified by the Apocalypse. In the Germany of the 1930s, Revelation, so often suspected in the Lutheran tradition, offered a resource for theology that enabled another perspective on the terrible events through which Bonhoeffer and his contemporaries were living.

In his striking messianic tract written at the very end of his life as he contemplated persecution and death, Walter Benjamin wrote of "utopian hopes and critical energies" as "a necessary corrective to the repetition of the 'ever- the same' in the guise of the new, the return of the seemingly repressed even amidst apparent enlightenment" (Benjamin 1992, p. 247). The subversive, apocalyptic memory witnesses to those affirmations of utopia "that seem so out of place against the more frequent hopes of bleak despair." The "unmasking of Babylon" may show that "the cultural monuments celebrated by official, establishment history could not be understood outside the context of their origins, a context of oppression and exploitation. Apocalypse offers a fleeting glimpse of an alternative, the 'involuntary memory of a redeemed humanity' that contrasts with convention and false tradition. That means that it is necessary to rescue tradition from the conventional and conformity and to wrest tradition away from a conformism that is about to overpower it" (Benjamin, p. 247). No more eloquent description of the ideological criticism and the hermeneutics of the Apocalypse could be offered.

The book of Revelation, and the apocalyptic tradition generally, has often been linked to the projects of agents of social change, yet just as often it can be found buttressing the projects of those whose quest for utopia is firmly rooted in conventional values and the nostalgic yearning for a golden age of moral perfection based on hierarchy and subservience. In this nostalgic quest, apocalyptic symbolism serves to undergird a view of the world that supports the conviction of a comfortable elect that they will ultimately be saved. On the one hand, this outlook, with its alternative horizon beckoning toward a different future, enables a group to maintain clearly defined lines between the godly and the godless. On the other hand, apocalyptic symbolism can serve to enable the oppressed to find and maintain a critical distance from an unjust world from the prospect of the hope of a reign of justice. There is little new in this struggle over the language of apocalypse. The apocalyptic symbolism has never been the sole preserve of the oppressed and poor. Even in postexilic Israel, in the very years when eschatological hope was being formed, there was a common stock of images that two sides in a struggle for power used to achieve preeminence for their own positions.

A Later Ideological Unmasking: Gerrard Winstanley (c. 1625–1676). Ideological criticism based on the Bible did not start with Marxism. Gerrard Winstanley was a seventeenth century practitioner of ideological criticism and in many ways took up the baton of his apocalyptic predecessors. Winstanley shot to prominence in 1649, and then almost completely disappeared from the annals of history for the rest of his life (he died in 1676). He grasped a moment of the king's execution as an opportunity to establish a different kind of society and interpreted that moment in the light of the Bible as a word for his time. Like many of his radical predecessors, Winstanley engaged dynamically with the imagery of the books of Daniel and Revelation—particularly the references to the beasts arising from the sea—as a means to comprehend the oppressive political powers that kept the common people in thrall. Perhaps his most daring interpretation was of Genesis 2—3, the story of "the Fall." For Winstanley, the Fall meant that humans had turned toward a life of "covetousness" and the maintenance of self-centeredness, institutionalized in private property and the social inequalities that arise from it and justified by a theology that is ideological, when the earth was to have been originally a "common treasury" for all to share. Winstanley's theological hope is that this situation may be overcome through "consciousness raising" that might, thereby, lead to a restoration of humankind to a very different vision of the world grounded in justice and equality.

To support his version of ideological criticism, he offers a reading of the Bible in which social and political combine with the exegetical to enable an engagement with the Bible and to read it "relative to life," as the liberation exegete Carlos Mesters puts it (Mesters 1993, 1989); so there is an unmasking of the reality of the power relations. Winstanley brilliantly relates Daniel 7 to the oppressive behavior of the wielders of political and economic power of his day. According to Winstanley, the first of the four beasts in Daniel was royal power, which by force makes a way for the economically powerful to rule over others, "making the conquered a slave; giving the earth to some, denying the Earth to others" ("Fire in the Bush" In Corns et al. 2009, vol. 2, p. 190). The second beast he saw as the power of laws, which maintain power and privilege in the hands of the few, by the threat of imprisonment and punishment. The third beast is what Winstanley calls "the thieving Art of buying and selling, the Earth with the fruits one to another" (p. 191). And the fourth beast is the power of the clergy that is used to give a religious or (in something like Marx's sense) an ideological gloss to the privileges of the few. According to Winstanley, the Creation will never be at peace until these four beasts are overthrown, and only then will there be the coming of Christ's kingdom (pp. 190–196). Here the apocalyptic imagery of the Bible enables one to discern the way in which religion, the opium of the people sensitized the populace to the injustices that were being perpetrated.

A Cautionary Conclusion. The tone thus far has been positive about the ideological critique within the Bible itself, but in one respect, the liberationist hermeneutics that has been crucial in promoting ideological criticism (Segundo 1976; Rowland and Corner 1989) was at least initially not attentive to the issue of gender. A major feature of ideological criticism has been the way in which feminist criticism has laid bare the androcentrism that pervades the whole of the Bible (de Boer and Økland 2008). An ideological criticism must have this as a central focus. The Bible presents a more difficult interpretive problem than other liberation approaches. For example, women's experiences and voices are not evident in its pages, and when they are found, the women are usually portrayed as the problem. The Bible has been a tool of the oppression of women and a source to legitimate the dominance of men. It is not only a question of the way in which women are portrayed, or even the acceptance of patriarchally constructed relationships between men and women; it is at a much deeper level an issue of the kind of God portrayed in the Bible and the nature of the God who endorses and authorizes the Bible. The images and language for God, as well as the actions ascribed to God, are predominantly male in character. The male and stereotypically masculine attitudes, capacities, and actions, are thus more highly valued and regarded as "god-like." It is this God whose omnipotence authorizes and guarantees the sacred text, and "He" whose authorized interpreters are so often male, the justification for which is both biblical and also based on the very nature of God in Christ. Liberation theology privileges the voices of those who are not being heard, of the oppressed, but women's experience raises radical question marks over that story itself.

[*See also* Class Criticism; Diaspora Studies; Disability Criticism; Empire Studies and Biblical Interpretation; Feminist Biblical Interpretation; Liberation Hermeneutics; Materialist Criticism; New Historicism; Postcolonial Biblical Interpretation; Race, Ethnicity, and Biblical Criticism; Reception Criticism and Theory; Social Sciences, *subentry* Hebrew Bible; Social Sciences, *subentry* New Testament; *and* Synchronic Interpretation.]

BIBLIOGRAPHY

Aichele, G., et al. *The Postmodern Bible.* New Haven, Conn.: Yale University Press, 1995. This work includes an essay on ideological criticism in a survey of modern interpretative strategies.

Avineri, S. *The Social and Political Thought of Karl Marx.* Cambridge, UK: Cambridge University Press, 1968. This is a treatment of Marx's thought that traces the essential continuities and his ambivalence about support for the revolutionary movements of his own day.

Belo, F. *A Materialist Reading of the Gospel of Mark.* New York: Orbis, 1981. Belo's work is an application of Roland Barthes's structuralist analysis of Balzac's Sarrasine in *S/Z* and a Marxist approach to ideology that is applied to the Gospel of Mark.

Benjamin, W. *Illuminations: Essays and Reflections.* Edited and with an introduction by Hannah Arendt. London: Fontana, 1992. This book includes Benjamin's "Theses on the Philosophy of History," which was written in the last months of his life as he fled Nazi captivity and before his tragic death. Its pessimistic tone reflects the more sober Marxism of the Frankfurt School.

Bennett, Z. "On Copy Clerks, Transformers and Spiders: Teachers and Learners in Adult Theological Education," *British Journal of Theological Education.* 9, no. 3, (1997–1998). A leading expert on adult theological education relates the Hegelian tradition and the contribution of Paulo Freire to understanding the practice of education.

Bloch, E. *Atheism in Christianity: The Religion of the Exodus and the Kingdom,* with an introduction by Peter Thompson. London: Verso, 2009. Bloch explores the ideological character of theological ideas and the radical alternatives.

Bloch, E. *The Principle of Hope.* Oxford: Basil Blackwell, 1986. This work is an exploration of hope in human life and culture from a Marxist perspective.

Boer, R. *Marxist Criticism of the Bible.* London: T.&T. Clark, 2003. This work consists of discussions of various Marxist theorists (e.g., Gramsci, Althusser, Bloch, Lukács, and Benjamin, and more recent critics, like Jameson and Eagleton) followed by the application of their theories to various a biblical texts.

Boer, R., and J. Økland. *Marxist Feminist Criticism of the Bible.* Sheffield, UK: Sheffield Phoenix Press, 2008. The authors describe the ways in which the ideological critique of Marxism complement the challenges of feminism.

Boff, L. *Jesus Christ Liberator: A Critical Christology of our Time.* New York: Orbis, 1978. A leading Brazilian liberation theologian, who was "silenced" by the Vatican for the views expressed in his book *Church, Charism and Power*, reflects on a classic theological theme from the perspective of liberation theology.

Bonhoeffer, D. *No Rusty Swords.* London: Collins, 1965. This collection of Bonhoeffer's lectures and letters is an excellent introduction to his thought.

Botta A. F., Andiñach, P. R. *The Bible and the Hermeneutics of Liberation.* Leiden: Brill, 2009. This is a collection of essays from authors from different contexts in which various biblical texts are explored from a liberationist perspective.

Clévenot, M. *Materialist Approaches to the Bible.* New York: Orbis, 1985. This work offers a simplified version of the kind of thesis exemplified by Fernando Belo's book.

Corns, T. N., A Hughes, and D. Loewenstein. *The Complete Works of Gerrard Winstanley.* 2 vols. Oxford: Oxford University Press, 2009. This is the first edition of the complete works of Gerrard Winstanley (1609–1676), the foremost radical English thinker and activist of the English Revolution.

De Ste. Croix, G. E. M. *The Class Struggle in the Ancient Greek World.* London: Duckworth, 1983. This pioneering study offers an account of forms of exploitation in the ancient world and demonstrates the rich possibilities of a Marxist perspective on the texts from antiquity, including Christianity.

Eagleton, T. *Ideology: An Introduction.* London: Verso, 2007. This work is a doyen of literary of British and Irish criticism whose work was influenced by Raymond Williams and left-wing Roman Catholicism.

Freire, P. *The Pedagogy of the Oppressed.* Harmondsworth: Penguin, 1985. This is the classic text of modern liberationist pedagogy in which the experience of ordinary people is valued and the dominant ideologies and power relations challenged in the context of enabling "literacy" for life.

Gottwald, N. *The Tribes of Yahweh: A Sociology of the Religion of Liberated Israel.* 1250–1050 B.C.E., Sheffield, UK: Sheffield Academic Press, 1999. This classic study explores the Jewish origins and the emergence of a rival liberationist ideology in the circumstances of revolt.

Gottwald, N., and R. Horsley. *The Bible and Liberation: Political and Social Hermeneutics.* New York: Orbis 1993. A collection of essays on the influence of liberationist interpretation on biblical exegesis including a classic essay by Carlos Mesters on reading the Bible in Basic Ecclesial Communities.

Gramsci, A. *Selections from the Prison Books*, Lawrence and Wishart: London, 1982.

Habermas, J. *Knowledge and Human Interests.* 2d ed. London: Heinemann, 1978. Habermas's work is a seminal study from arguably the most influential member of the Frankfurt School of Marxist philosophers.

Hanson, P. D. *The Dawn of Apocalyptic.* Philadelphia: Fortress, 1975. Hanson presents a study of the later chapters of Isaiah as a power struggle between hierarchy and visionaries in post-exilic Judaism.

Hegel, G. W. F. *Lectures on the Philosophy of Religion of 1824, Vol. 1. Introduction and Concept.* Edited by P. Hodgson. Berkeley, University of California Press, 1984. This work is a presentation of Hegel's final and most decisive contents of his philosophy.

Horsley, R. A. *Hidden Transcripts and the Arts of Resistance: Applying the Work of James C. Scott to Jesus and Paul.* Atlanta: Society of Biblical Literature, 2004. This work introduces a new quest for a contextually historical Jesus. The work will engage both biblical scholars and others who are interested in teasing the out of the biblical texts the historical Jesus through an examination of the words and actions of Jesus.

Jameson, F. *The Political Unconscious.* London: Methuen, 1981. Jameson presents an outstanding application of Marxist theory to literature that demonstrates the ways in which literary texts betray the tensions and contradictions of their authors' place within specific social contexts.

Larrain, J. *The Concept of Ideology.* London: Hutchinson, 1979. Larrain gives a thorough examination of the value of some of the most important conceptions of ideology, from Mannheim to the modern structuralist.

Marx, Karl, with Friedrich Engels. *The German Ideology: Including Theses on Feuerbach and Introduction to the Critique of Political Economy.* Amherst, N.Y. Prometheus, 1998. This is considered by many to be Marx's first fully matured statement about his thinking.

Marx, Karl, and Friedrich Engels. *Marx and Engels on Religion.* Moscow: Foreign Language Publishing House, 1972. The collection includes works in which Karl Marx and Frederick Engels present their views on the essence and origin of religion and its role in class society; these works lay the theoretical foundations of proletarian, Marxist atheism.

McLellan, D. *Marxism and Religion: A Description and Assessment of the Marxist Critique of Christianity.* Basingstoke: Macmillan, 1987. This important work offers a consideration of the different forms of Marxist thought and the possibilities of their relationship with religion.

Mesters, C. *Defenseless Flower: A New Reading of the Bible.* Maryknoll, N.Y.: Orbis, 1989. This volume is a concise summary of the nature of grassroots education and biblical study in Basic Ecclesial Communities in Brazil written by someone immersed in popular education for decades.

Mesters, C., 'The Use of the Bible in Christian Communities of the Common People.' *In The Bible and Liberation: political and Social Hermeneutics,* edited by N. Gottwald and R. Horsley, 119–133. New York: Orbis, 1993.

Mosala, I. J. *Biblical Hermeneutics and Black Theology in South Africa.* Grand Rapids, Mich.: Eerdmans, 1989. Mosala engages in a detailed investigation of competing ideological discourses in the prophecy of Micah.

Myers, C. *Binding the Strong Man: A Political Reading of Mark's Story of Jesus.* 2d ed. Maryknoll, N.Y.: Orbis, 2008. This work is an approach to Mark that follows the method of modern literary and historical study of the gospel more closely yet with a clear grasp of the text's counter-cultural agenda and ideological critique.

Pippin, T., ed. *Ideological Criticism of Biblical Texts. Semeia* 59, 1992. This volume of *Semeia* is a collection of essays by different authors on different biblical and related texts that take ideology and the issue of the mode of production seriously.

Rowland, C. *The Cambridge Companion to Liberation Theology.* Rev. ed. Cambridge, UK: Cambridge University Press, 2007. A selection of essays, this work examines the emergence and character of liberation theology, including Gerald West's *The Academy of the Poor: Towards a Dialogical Reading of the Bible,* on the biblical interpretation.

Rowland, C. "The Theology of Liberation and its Gift to Exegesis." *New Blackfriars,* 66 (1985): 157–172. Rowland examines Fernando Belo's book, *A Materialist Reading of the Gospel of Mark,* and its relationship with the theology of liberation.

Rowland, C., and M. Corner. *Liberating Exegesis: The Challenge of Liberation Theology to Biblical Studies.* London: SPCK, 1989. The author gives a discussion of the interpretation of the Bible in the theology of liberation, including popular education material and an application of Frederic Jameson's method to the Book of Revelation.

Scott, J. C. *Domination and the Arts of Resistance: Hidden Transcripts.* New Haven, Conn.: Yale University Press, 1990. This work is an influential examination of the ways in which a subaltern culture finds way of exercising power to resist in the face of dominant ideologies and power structures.

Segundo, J. L. *The Liberation of Theology.* Maryknoll, N.Y.: Orbis, 1976. This is an influential essay from one of the seminal figures in liberation theology on the ways in which liberation theology offers a critique "from below" of the dominant ideology embodied in mainstream Christianity.

Turner, D. *Marxism and Christianity.* Oxford: Blackwell, 1983. This work is an important contribution to the ongoing Christian-Marxist dialogue in which Turner approaches the problem of the relation between Marxism and Christianity.

Wengst, K. *"Pax Romana" and the Peace of Jesus Christ.* London: SCM, 1985. Wengst explores the ways in which different New Testament texts manifest contrasting compromises with the dominant ideology of their day.

West, G. *The Academy of the Poor: Towards a Dialogical Reading of the Bible.* Sheffield, UK: Sheffield Academic, 1999. West argues that recent trends in biblical exegesis create opportunities for serious dialogue between biblical scholars and readers living in poor and marginalized communities.

Williams, R. *Marxism and Literature.* Oxford: Oxford University Press, 1977. This volume is a classic discussion of the relationship between Marxism and literature from the foremost British Marxist literary scholar of his day.

Christopher Rowland

Inner-Biblical Interpretation

Inner-biblical interpretation is the study of biblical texts that appear to interpret or otherwise intentionally evoke other biblical texts. Concerned with the apparent intent of a literary work to interpret or evoke specific prior literary works, inner-biblical interpretation is distinct from the more reader-oriented, synchronic discipline of "intertextuality," which designates rather "[a work's] participation in the discursive space of a culture" (Culler 1981, p. 103). There have been two related but distinct movements in biblical studies, both diachronic in orientation but using identical terms differently and proceeding toward goals only partly shared. Because confusion about basic terms has been almost the defining characteristic of the study of "inner-biblical interpretation," I will first isolate the phenomenon from "intertextuality" and "influence" and also distinguish within inner-biblical interpretation between nonfigurative "interpretive" texts and figurative "allusive" texts. We will then be in a better position to summarize the history of the study of inner-biblical interpretation, a history that, again, is marked by an only slowly emerging consensus regarding terminology and method.

Inner-biblical Interpretation and Intertextuality. In hindsight, it is clear that "intertextuality," as coined by Kristeva (1969), is different enough from the diachronic study of inner-biblical interpretation that the use of "intertextuality" as an umbrella term for literary dependence has only bred confusion. Intertextuality seeks to discover how a text depends on and participates in the linguistic culture out of which it arises, exploring the unpredictable patterns of meaning that might unfold for a given "modern," real reader between two or more texts, without regard for diachrony or author's intent. Inner-biblical interpretation, by contrast, seeks to determine whether a given text interprets or evokes an earlier text, by the design of an author, in anticipation of that interpretation's or evocation's recognition by a competent reader who is contemporary to the author. Despite these clear differences in goals and presuppositions, scholars undertaking "inner-biblical interpretation" have too commonly described their project as "intertextuality," even while often (but not always) offering a disclaimer that they do not mean "that" intertextuality. Miller's review of this academic history in Hebrew Bible studies is excellent (Miller 2011; cf. too Elam 1994; Fewell 1992).

Inner-biblical Interpretation and Influence. Inner-biblical interpretation is also distinct from "influence." In literary terms, "influence" involves the study of how an artist labors, consciously or unconsciously, simultaneously by the inspiration and in the shadow of her predecessors (Bloom, *The Anxiety of Influence*; Elam, "Influence"). Less technically, "influence" simply refers to the effects that earlier works can have, directly or indirectly, on later works. Regarding "influence," the critic does not assume that an author consciously cites or evokes preceding works. Contrastingly, inner-biblical interpretation describes a conscious choice on the part of an author to engage a specific prior text, such that the engagement is apparent to the competent reader.

So, inner-biblical interpretation differs from "intertextuality," and also from "influence." The way is clear, then, to describe what varying kinds of literary dependence can be included within the term, "inner-biblical interpretation."

Inner-biblical Exegesis and Inner-biblical Allusion. Sometimes, a biblical text appears to undertake an explanation or solution of the meaning of an earlier text. Depending on genre and the habits of a biblical scholar, instances may be called "inner-biblical exegesis," "inner-biblical midrash," or "pesher," or something similar. The later text interprets the earlier text, referring to it directly or indirectly. Especially in studies on "the Old Testament in the New," this continuum between indirect (covert, tacit) and direct (overt) reference is an important object of study, with the term "allusion" often understood to define the indirect or "covert" end of that spectrum (with "citation," or "quotation," often at the other end; e.g., Porter, "The Use of the Old Testament in the New Testament," pp. 81, 91). As far back as the 1970s, however, literary critics have challenged this use of "allusion" as a mere indirect reference (as when we introduce a speaker by saying to an audience, "Help me welcome our illustrious guest") and preferred a more technical use of the term to denote rather a figurative trope, akin to metaphor, for the simultaneous, imaginative activation of two literary texts for the benefit of a reader competent to discern the trope (Ben-Porat 1976, pp. 107–108). The basic distinction between "inner-biblical exegesis" (the later text exists to explain the earlier text) and "inner-biblical allusion" (the later text appropriates the older text in the crafting of a figurative trope) has been well marked in biblical studies (e.g., Collins 1984, pp. 9–10, 42–43, 56, 113; Fishbane

1985, pp. 321, 415–417; Kugel 1987, p. 208; Sommer 1996, p. 23). Nonetheless, critics of inner-biblical interpretation have not achieved the clarity regarding terms like "allusion" that their literary critical counterparts have striven for.

Recent History of Inner-biblical Interpretation. The study of biblical texts believed to lie in a diachronic, dependent relationship has progressed, beginning in the 1980s, along two trajectories, largely independent until recently. One scholarly trajectory privileges the text as a locus of meaning and includes (but is not limited to) the Tel Aviv "school" of literary poetics and its conversation partners. First, for this school, allusion is not simply an "indirect reference," but a text-intended figurative trope functioning in a way akin to metonymy. (Here, "intent of the text" essentially means the intent of the author as apparent in textual details; cf. Hatina 2002, p. 56.) This figurative meaning is crafted for the benefit of a competent reader in the text's historical context, as judged again on the basis of warrants in the alluding text. And second, terms such as "intertextuality," "allusion," and "echo" should, as much as possible, be agreed upon and used scientifically. The other trajectory, not less diachronic in its orientation than the first, works from different assumptions. First, "allusion" is as apt to mean "indirect reference" (as opposed, e.g., to citation) as it is to refer to a figurative trope. Second, this tradition is less concerned about whether meanings are located with a competent original reader or with a given, real reader in her modern reading community. And third, terms are used more freely, as ultimate literary judgments arise less from method than from an informed sensitivity. With its flexibility about "the reader," the latter trajectory often bears a resemblance to synchronic "intertextuality," and the critic is as apt to cite that tradition as an influence as he is the more text-oriented literary criticism.

Before these trajectories diverged, there was Fishbane's *Biblical Interpretation in Ancient Israel.* Fishbane did not discover inner-biblical interpretation, but his watershed work marks a first attempt at a comprehensive portrait of inner-biblical interpretation and puts its study on a methodological footing. (Kugel, in his criticism of Fishbane's work, briefly describes how questions of inner-biblical interpretation arose before Fishbane). The sheer scope and detail of Fishbane's work accelerated scholarly interest in the phenomenon of inner-biblical interpretation. At the same time, central aspects of *Biblical Interpretation in Ancient Israel* did not gain traction among many readers otherwise impressed and influenced by the work. Especially, the categorization of examples into "scribal, legal, aggadic, and mantological exegesis" was quickly deemed to be anachronistic and overly speculative regarding the identities of the interpreting biblical authors (Kugel, pp. 274–276). Interestingly, while Kugel's counter-proposal for a more narrative "*history* of biblical interpretation in ancient Israel" (emphasis his) has not yet been realized, a recent critic independently describes something like this as a hopeful and logical "prospect for the future" (Miller, p. 303). The delay can best be explained by the fact that, in the relative vacuum left by the field's general rejection of Fishbane's categories, continuing scholarship in inner-biblical interpretation has drawn instead on two largely incommensurable inspirations from literary criticism, called here "the Ben-Porat trajectory" and "the Hollander trajectory."

History: The "Ben-Porat Trajectory." Encouragingly, it would be in the responses to Fishbane's work that "inner-biblical interpretation" would begin to assume such shared terminology and engagement with nonbiblical allusion criticism it can boast of today. Kugel was quick to point out that most of Fishbane's examples of "inner-biblical exegesis" are not so much "exegetical" as allusive in the figurative sense (Kugel, p. 208; so also Sommer 1996, p. 488 n. 23). The alluding texts do not exist primarily to elucidate the older text, but rather employ the trope of allusion in order to simultaneously activate the two texts and generate intertextual patterns of meaning in the reader competent to discern the figure. In a later essay, Eslinger (1992) similarly proposed that "inner-biblical allusion" would provide a clearer and more accurate rubric than "exegesis" for most relevant biblical literary phenomena. However, Eslinger's use of the word "allusion" does not derive from the nonbiblical scholarship on allusion as an intentional diachronic trope, and the program he calls for is much closer to the synchronic, reader-oriented field of "intertextuality" (so Sommer 1996; 1998, p. 207 n. 11). Sommer himself would seek to further clarify the field by explicitly appropriating the nonbiblical literary-critical work in "allusion" by Conte (1986), Ben-Porat (1976), Perri (1978), Kronfeld (1985), and Garner (1990).

The classicist Conte, with his reviewer Johnson, had already closely investigated the ways in which "allusion" may function as a figurative trope akin to metaphor. In metaphor, one speaks of one thing in terms reminiscent of another; in allusion, a text says something in terms reminiscent of another text. In a metaphor, the "vehicle" (the thing named) points both to itself and to its "tenor" (the thing being evoked; for "vehicle" and "tenor," see Richards 1936, p. 93). Just so in allusion, a textual "marker" points both to itself and to the "marked" in an evoked text. In allusion as in metaphor, the vehicle or alluding text will by some means seek to activate certain connotations in the tenor or evoked text, while suppressing others. Ben-Porat further argued that the mundane sense of "allusion" as an "indirect reference" needed to be set aside (compare to Miner 1965). For Ben-Porat, the word "allusion" is better used only to denote a figurative "device for the simultaneous activation of two texts" (pp. 107–108; so Perri, p. 292). In this figure, a "marker" in the alluding text recalls a "marked" in the evoked text ("marker" and "marked" being a special case of the familiar "sign" and "signified" of prior literary theory; Ben-Porat, pp. 108–111; Perri, p. 295; Kronfeld). Perri and Kronfeld, along with Garner, would incorporate Ben-Porat's insights into continuing examination of "allusion" as a figurative trope, and the influence of this trajectory is still seen in literary criticism (e.g., Pucci 1998; Irwin 2001; and Lennon 2004).

For this "school," the competent reader undergoes four stages in the performance of a literary allusion: first, *recognizing* the textual marker in the alluding text; second, *identifying* the evoked text; third (and necessarily to speak of "allusion"), *modifying* her interpretation of the marker in light of imaginative interplay between the marker and the marked; and fourth (potentially, in some, but by no means in all, instances), *activating the larger context* of the evoked text, forming unpredictable "maximum intertextual patterns" (Ben-Porat, pp. 110–111). Work in this trajectory of literary criticism has sought, in part, continually to improve our understanding of allusion-as-metaphor. Finding that allusion is best understood as a kind of metonymy, Conte had explored how knowledge of simile might shed light on interliterary devices close to, but not achieving, allusion (Conte, pp. 67–69; cf. Perri, p. 304). In addition, Conte has closely studied the way in which the alluding text, having one coherent meaning in its own literary context while evoking another, must have some jarring element of "irrelevance" or "non-pertinance" (Conte, p. 55, cf. pp. 45–47). Perri, then, explored how this necessary element of "insufficiency of sense" relates to Ben-Porat's "stage one," in which the reader recognizes the presence of an allusive trope (Perri, p. 300). Finally and importantly, Perri demonstrates that figurative allusion can be entirely overt rather than covert, making conclusive Ben-Porat's initial case that "allusion" can no longer be usefully defined as a "covert or tacit reference" (Perri, *passim*).

Adopting Ben-Porat's "four stages" and engaging her interlocutors, Sommer offered a further clarification of terminology by defining "echo" as the phenomenon by which the first two of four stages are met, but in which figurative troping is not apparently invited by the "echoing" text (e.g., as when the only aim is to draw authority from the source text or to appear erudite; Sommer 1998, pp. 15–17, 104). Sommer's explicit engagement with these text-centered, literary-poetics scholars inaugurated something almost resembling a school in its own right in inner-biblical allusion. A degree of influence might be discerned in those who similarly refer, including Hatina on allusion in Mark's narrative, with his commitment to a narrative poetic) to the "intent of the text" and allusive readings "rooted in the ideological and socio-historical context" of the alluding text (Hatina, pp. 49, 56); Hylen, whose work on allusion in John 6 is in conversation with nearly all those in literary poetics cited earlier (Hylen 2005); Vassar on the Psalter and the Pentateuch (2007); Hutton on possible allusion to Ugaritic hymnody in Isaiah (2007); and Lyons on "Ezekiel's Use of the Holiness Code" (Lyons 2009).

History: The "Hollander Trajectory." Richard Hays's *Echoes of Scripture* (1989) represents a trajectory parallel to and separate from that represented earlier by Conte, Johnson, Ben-Porat, Perri, Kronfeld, Garner, and Sommer. For Hays's use of the terms "allusion" and "echo," his methodological muse is Hollander. Where Hollander uses the term "allusion," it is frequently in what Ben-Porat and others would describe as its mundane sense—an indirect reference, often not to a literary work, and not figurative, although potentially delightful. For example, Hollander writes, "In . . . Miranda's [utterance] 'O brave new world . . . ,' the audience recognizes an allusion to a literal hemisphere" (Hollander 1981, p. 50). "Allusion" here is *not* a simultaneous activation of two literary texts, but a mere "indirect reference" to Galileo's discoveries. Hollander's "allusion" of indirect reference sits on a continuum between overt and covert, with his interest in the latter because, in his view, this covertness is what makes it poetic rather than expository (Hollander, p. ix). Hollander is free in his use of terms: a covert, indirect reference is variously called "echo," "allusive echo," "figurative echo," "poetic echo" (p. ix). While his approach is diachronic, he nears a more reader-response "intertextuality" in that he is not overly concerned to distinguish between text-intended allusion and connections originating in the mind of any given reader (p. ix).

Hollander's influence on Hays is clear and frequently acknowledged by the latter (1989, pp. 18–21; 2005, 3 n. 5, 34–35, 43, 166, 173). Writing as he does of Paul's use of the Hebrew Bible, Hays shares Hollander's interest in diachrony, seeking to distinguish between the "five loci" of meaning—the author's mind, his hearers, the text, "my" reading, and readings of a community (pp. 26–28). The goal is to determine what might unfold for the author's "contemporary community of competent readers" (pp. 31–32; cf. pp. 24, 28). At the same time, in practice, Hays shows Hollander's open-endedness about locus, adding an effective "sixth locus" in Paul's unconscious or "bones" (p. 43; cf. p. 70: "whether he intended it or not," it is still "an allusive connotation"). For Hays as for Hollander, "allusion" still often denotes any covert reference, over against an overt citation (e.g., a given text "is allusive rather than overt in its communication strategies" [p. 155]). Additionally, Hays's flexible use of terms recalls Hollander's. For example, Hays uses the word "echo" as a synonym of what Ben-Porat would call "allusion" (e.g., echo is "an intertextual fusion that generates new meaning"), sometimes conjoining the two into "allusive echo" as does Hollander. At the same time, he uses "echo" to denote intertextual events generally, as distinguished from "pure echo" (or sometimes, "recollection") as a synonym for "allusive echo" (pp. 20–21, 26). Elsewhere, "echo" is what sits further along the spectrum opposite "citation" with "allusion" in the middle (p. 23). Finally, "echo" seems sometimes to mean intertextual connections unintended by the author yet made by a given reader (p. 29). As Hays notes, "I make no systematic distinction between the terms" (p. 29).

Hays is similarly flexible in his use of Hollander's term, *metalepsis*, originally a classical term referring to a particular auditory trope, adapted and extended by Fletcher (p. 241 n. 33) and in turn by Hollander (pp. 113–149) and finally by Hays (1989). In Hollander's usage, *metalepsis* describes a specific literary usage in which a poetic figure in one text recalls a poetic figure in a prior text, evoking as a "middle term" some set of shared connotations, producing a third figurative trope of "allusion" (in Ben-Porat's sense); it is "a figure of linkage between figures" (pp. 113–114). For example, Marlowe's "the face that launched a thousand ships" is *metalepsis* only insofar as "face" can be seen as synechdoche for Helen, and the "launching" can be seen as a metaphor for causing the war. A connecting trope (a face launching) connects two other tropes (Hollander, pp. 135–136). To propose a possible biblical example, if Mark 1:17 ("I will make you fish for people") intends to evoke Jeremiah 16:16 ("I am now sending for many fishermen"), as proposed by Knowles (p. 66), then this would be an example of Hollander's *metalepsis*. Each text is already a figurative trope (with their image of a fisher as a vehicle for one gathering up people), and their simultaneous activation in the figurative device of allusion creates a "trope between the tropes." (Miscall understands Hollander's *metalepsis* in similar, but not identical, terms [Miscall, pp. 46–47]). However, while Hays's use of *metalepsis* is dependent "directly on Hollander" (2005, p. 173), he comes to use the term in a broader and even different way: *metalepsis*, or allusive echo, "functions to suggest to the reader that text B should be understood in light of *a broad interplay* with text A, encompassing aspects of A *beyond those explicitly echoed*" (2005, p. 20, emphasis mine). Again, "[m]etalepsis" is a rhetorical and poetic device in which one text alludes to an earlier text in a way that evokes resonances of the earlier text *beyond those explicitly cited* (2005, p. 2, emphasis original). For Hays, *metalepsis* has ceased to mean a figure that connects two *figures*, and has come to mean a figure between any two *texts* in which the literary context of the evoked text beyond the "marked" is brought into play. In other words, it has become identical to Ben-Porat's optional fourth stage of allusion.

Hays shares Hollander's comfort with ambiguity in other ways. For Hays, Hollander's approach is "less a matter of method than of sensibility;" it is not to be "applied," but should help today's reader "tune [her] ears" (1989, p. 21). An inadequately "sensitive" critic will flounder, regardless of methodological helps (cf. Moyise on Hays 2008, p. 140). The goal is to generate, not a theory of "intertextuality," but "good readings" (Hays 1989, p. 32) teaching us how we should read the texts read by the alluding authors (Hays 2005, p. x).

Crossing the Streams. The contrast is clear between Hays's approach to inner-biblical interpretation and that of the more text-oriented critics nearer the Tel Aviv "school," which seeks to overcome such "pre-scientific" appeal to an informed intuition (Mintz 1984, p. 219). A willing ambiguity concerning the locus of an inner-biblical interpretation, and about key terms, might be argued to well suit a work in biblical studies that is at least as concerned with meanings generated by modern communities as with the meanings aimed at competent readers known to an alluding biblical author. At the same time, the more rigorously text-centered literary critic will judge that in any study of inner-biblical allusion where "so many terms are vague, so general and interchangeable," the reader might find "more and more brilliant meanings added to the heap," yet accomplish "no deepened understanding of the phenomenon of literature itself" (pp. 219–220).

These differences between the two trajectories, while vexing for the student of inner-biblical interpretation, need not mask their essential commensurability. Hays's "seven tests" for text-intended echo have been used selectively by later scholars to great effect (i.e., availability of evoked text to alluding author; volume; recurrence in alluding work; thematic coherence between texts; historical plausibility of intertextual meanings; history of interpretation; and satisfaction to today's reader). Hollander's "cave of resonant signification" (p. 65) corresponds well to the evoked text's larger literary context as understood in Ben-Porat's "fourth stage" of allusion (less clearly in Hays's use of the term, wherein it refers rather to the alluding author's unconscious memories and associations regarding the evoked text [Hays 1989, p. 43; so Willey, pp. 81–82]). Again, Hays's understanding of *metalepsis*, while clearly distinct from that of Hollander's, introduces the concept of Ben-Porat's "fourth stage" of allusion to readers not acquainted with Ben-Porat. Although Hays (along with most scholars on "the Old Testament in the New Testament") continues to use "allusion" in its nonfigurative sense of "indirect reference," he, nonetheless, distinguishes carefully where Paul's use of the Old Testament is figurative or "metaphorical," a "trope" (e.g., 1989, pp. 40, 44); in other words, where Ben-Porat and the literary critics indebted to her would recognize "allusion." Should the currently-distracting differences even in terminology alone be ameliorated, then "inner-biblical interpretation" might soon prove much less intractable to the newcomer interested in how biblical texts interpret or evoke, by design, older biblical texts, drawing on their authority, explaining their meaning, or appropriating them into figurative tropes.

Prospectus for the Future. The first task facing the study of inner-biblical interpretation is to follow a practice modeled in the late 1970s, eschewing the use of "allusion" in its mundane and inaccurate sense of "indirect (covert) reference," and using the term solely for proposed instances wherein the use of the older text by the newer constitutes a text-intended figurative trope akin to metaphor. Other landscapes of inquiry looking fruitful from such a vantage point include the union of historical and literary criticism in inner-biblical interpretation and attention to recent scholarship concerning scribal schools in ancient Israel.

The study of inner-biblical interpretation provides a strikingly generative ground on which some of the productive tensions common to academic biblical studies can be freshly explored. The felt need to choose between a historical approach and a literary critical one is acknowledged today as a false dichotomy and an artifact of literary criticism's "adolescence" in biblical studies. Inner-biblical interpretation, in its diachronic orientation and commitment to sensitive discernment of troping as a strategy intended by the text, reminds the scholar that study of literary poetics need not entail an abandoning of interest in the history reflected in the biblical text: "An appreciation of [an instance of inner-biblical interpretation]... contributes to the historian of Israelite religion as well as to the literary critic" (Sommer 1996, p. 483).

Finally, the study of inner-biblical interpretation in the Hebrew Bible has lagged behind New Testament (especially Pauline) scholarship regarding the role of scribal practice and memory in the crafting of inner-biblical interpretations. Interest in "scribal schools" in ancient Israel and the role of memory in scribal practice, has grown in recent scholarship (e.g., Van der Toorn 2007; Carr 2005 and 2011), and appears to be ripe for engagement by those interested in inner-biblical interpretation in the Hebrew Bible.

[*See also* Conservative Jewish Interpretation; Diachronic Interpretation; Intertextuality; Metaphor Theory and Biblical Texts; Midrash; Mimesis Criticism; Orthodox Jewish Interpretation; Rabbinic Exegesis; Reader-Response Criticism; Reform Jewish Interpretation; *and* Synchronic Interpretation.]

BIBLIOGRAPHY

Ben-Porat, Ziva. "The Poetics of Literary Allusion." *PTL: A Journal for Descriptive Poetics and Theory of Literature* 1 (1976): 105–128. This article distinguishes "allusion" as a metonymic figurative trope from "allusion" as mere tacit reference and proposes "four stages" in a reader's performance of interliterary allusion.

Bloom, Harold. *The Anxiety of Influence: A Theory of Poetry*. New York: Oxford University Press, 1973. Bloom's work establishes his theory of influence as the inspiring yet daunting effect that the artist suffers under the work of her predecessors.

Carr, David McLain. *The Formation of the Hebrew Bible: A New Reconstruction*. New York: Oxford University Press, 2011. The seminal work continues to give shape to reconstruction of Israelite scribal practice begun in *Writing on the Tablet of the Heart*.

Carr, David McLain. *Writing on the Tablet of the Heart: Origins of Scripture and Literature*. Oxford: Oxford University Press, 2005. Carr, examines practices of textuality and orality in Mesopotamian, Egyptian, and Hellenistic historical contexts, including a chapter on ancient Israel.

Collins, John Joseph. *Daniel: With an Introduction to Apocalyptic Literature*. Forms of the Old Testament Literature 20. Grand Rapids, Mich.: Eerdmans, 1984. The cited pages distinguish between inner-biblical "exegesis" and allusion.

Conte, Gian Biagio. *The Rhetoric of Imitation: Genre and Poetic Memory in Virgil and Other Latin Poets*. Translated by Charles Segal. Cornell Studies in Classical Philology. Vol. 44. Ithaca, N.Y.: Cornell University Press, 1986. Translation in part of *Memoria dei poeti e sistema letterario and 11 genere e i suoi confini*, first published in 1976. Chapters one and two explore the functions of interliterary allusion alongside those of metaphor, simile, and related devices. The work also attends to matters of "canon" in allusion.

Culler, Jonathan D. *The Pursuit of Signs: Semiotics, Literature, Deconstruction*. Ithaca, N.Y.: Cornell University

Press, 1981. This is an accessible work on the critical study of semiotics and signification, including intertextuality as derived from Kristeva's synchronic sense.

Elam, Helen Regueiro. "Influence." In *The New Princeton Handbook of Poetic Terms*, edited by T. V. F. Brogan, 131–135. Princeton, N.J.: Princeton University Press, 1994. This article is an excellent, reasonably recent survey of "influence" for the novice.

Elam, Helen Regueiro. "Intertextuality." *In The New Princeton Handbook of Poetic Terms*, edited by T. V. F. Brogan, 141–143. Princeton, N.J.: Princeton University Press, 1994. This work is an excellent survey of "intertextuality" for those not yet well acquainted with the concept.

Eslinger, Lyle. "Inner-Biblical Exegesis and Inner-Biblical Allusion: The Question of Category." *Vetus Testamentum* 42 (1992): 47–58. Eslinger distinguishes between inner-biblical "exegesis" and a program of synchronic intertextuality that the author—in a move rejected by later scholars and incongruent with some other literary criticism—calls "inner-biblical allusion."

Fewell, Danna Nolan. *Reading between Texts: Intertextuality and the Hebrew Bible.* Literary Currents in Biblical Interpretation. Louisville, Ky.: Westminster John Knox, 1992. The forward, glossary, and first section provide a representative look at inner-biblical interpretation as seeking to encompass theoretically the synchronic and diachronic alike.

Fishbane, Michael A. *Biblical Interpretation in Ancient Israel.* New York: Oxford University Press, 1985. Fishbane surveys examples of inner-biblical interpretation. Still relevant and instructive, this work, nonetheless, divides such texts into categories not since widely accepted: scribal, legal, aggadic, and mantological exegesis.

Garner, Richard. *From Homer to Tragedy: The Art of Allusion in Greek Poetry.* London: Routledge, 1990. Like Conte, Garner takes up relation of metaphor and simile to interliterary allusion and also explores the "gap" between texts and reader in which an allusive figure is generated.

Hatina, Thomas R. *In Search of a Context: The Function of Scripture in Mark's Narrative.* Vol. 232 of Journal for the Study of the New Testament Supplement Series. London: Sheffield Academic, 2002. This excellent work examines how the trope of literary allusion functions within a narrative, alongside that narrative's other rhetorical strategies, and briefly seeks to define "the intent of the text" in the hermeneutical landscape of the author, the reader, and their respective contexts.

Hays, Richard B. *The Conversion of the Imagination: Paul as Interpreter of Israel's Scripture.* Grand Rapids, Mich.: Eerdmans, 2005. This work is a set of essays comprising Hays's mature reflections on biblical allusion, both regarding its method and its value for confessional communities reading Paul. It is also valuable for the author's engagement with critics of his earlier works.

Hays, Richard B. *Echoes of Scripture in the Letters of Paul.* New Haven: Yale University Press, 1989. An enormously influential examination of Paul's use of the Hebrew Bible, this work is methodologically at once ambitiously detailed and terminologically free, as would be much of the work (especially in "the Old Testament in the New") that is inspired and influenced by it.

Hollander, John. *The Figure of Echo: A Mode of Allusion in Milton and After.* Berkeley: University of California, 1981. Hollander offers a series of essays exploring allusion through the lens of "echo" as a recurring figure in Milton.

Hutton, Jeremy. "Isaiah 51:9–11 and the Rhetorical Appropriation and Subversion of Hostile Theologies." *Journal of Biblical Literature* 126, no. 2 (2007): 271–303. This work concludes that, alluding to Canaanite hymn, Isaiah 51 "lampoons the Canaanite mythological *Chaoskampf.*" It adopts Ben-Porat's terminology as well as Hays's "seven tests."

Hylen, Susan. *Allusion and Meaning in John 6.* Beihefte zur Zeitschrift für die Neutestamentliche Wissenschaft und die Kunde der Älteren Kirche. Berlin: W. de Gruyter, 2005. This work is a valuable not only for its clarity of method but also as an example of a sustained study on allusion in a biblical text of manageable size.

Irwin, William. "What Is an Allusion?" *Journal of Aesthetics and Art Criticism* 59, no. 3 (2001): 287–297. Irwin gives the reader an up-to-date engagement with theory in allusive poetics, including roles of author, text, and reader.

Johnson, Anthony L. "Allusion in Poetry." *PTL: A Journal for Descriptive Poetics and Theory of Literature* 1 (1976): 579–587. Johnson's article is a sustained engagement with Conte's work (cited earlier), with independent proposals, in the form of a review.

Knowles, Michael P. "Scripture, History, Messiah: Scriptural Fulfillment and the Fullness of Time in Matthew's Gospel." In *Hearing the Old Testament in the New Testament*, edited by Stanley E. Porter, 59–82. Grand Rapids, Mich.: Eerdmans, 2006. Through examination of Matthew's use of scripture, Knowles arrives at Jesus as the eschatological "still point" around which Matthew's tumultuous, faction-ridden (narrative and historical) settings revolve.

Kristeva, Julia. "Word, Dialogue, and Novel." In *Desire in Language*, edited by Leon S. Roudiez, 64–91. New York: Columbia University Press, 1980. Original in *Σημειωτικη: Recherches Pour Une Sémanalyse*. Paris: Éditions du Seuil, 1969. In this article, Kristeva coins "intertextuality," understanding all language as (per Bakhtin) appropriated and dialogic.

Kronfeld, Chana. "Allusion: An Israeli Perspective." *Prooftexts* 5 (1985): 137–163. A continued engagement with Ben-Porat and Perri on allusion, this article is relevant to Hebrew Bible inner-biblical interpretation. Kronfeld forcefully argues a persuasive case that the study of allusion, properly a subfield of literary poetics, is wasted when used only for historical-critical ends.

Kugel, James L. "The Bible's Oldest Interpreters." *Prooftexts* 7 (1987): 269–305. Kugel reviews Fishbane (1985), with noteworthy independent reflections and proposals concerning inner-biblical interpretation.

Lennon, Paul. *Allusions in the Press: An Applied Linguistic Study*. Berlin: Mouton de Gruyter, 2004. This work examines the phenomenon of literary allusion in the non-"literary" British press. Specifically excludes mere indirect reference as a mode of allusion, and engages such multi-stage models of allusion as those of Ben-Porat and Perri.

Lyons, Michael A. *From Law to Prophecy: Ezekiel's Use of the Holiness Code*. Library of Hebrew Bible/Old Testament Studies. New York: T.&T. Clark, 2009. Valuable for exploring whether a biblical work alludes to earlier texts, this work also examines how such allusions function rhetorically in the alluding book.

Miller, Geoffrey David. "Intertextuality in Old Testament Research." *Currents in Biblical Research* 9, no. 3 (2011): 283–309. Miller reviews the academic history of the various uses and definitions of intertextuality in Hebrew Bible studies.

Miner, Earl. "Allusion." In *Princeton Encyclopedia of Poetry and Poetics*, edited by Alex Preminger, 18. Princeton, N.J.: Princeton University Press, 1965. An accessible and manageable starting place on "allusion" in literary criticism, this work engages such essays as those cited here from Ben-Porat, Perri, and Sommer.

Mintz, Alan. "On the Tel Aviv School of Poetics." *Prooftexts* 4, no. 3 (1984): 215–235. Mintz's article is a critical appraisal at the Tel Aviv "school," with its text-oriented approach to literature and its goal of a scientifically-grounded literary poetics.

Miscall, Peter D. "Isaiah: New Heavens, New Earth, New Book." In *Reading between Texts*, edited by Danna Nolan Fewell, 41–56. Louisville, Ky.: Westminster John Knox, 1992. Miscall uses "intertextuality" in a synchronic sense as an alternative to critique traditional critical claims of Israelite "borrowing" from Mesopotamian antecedents, illustrated by cross-reading of Isaiah and Genesis.

Moyise, Steve. *Evoking Scripture: Seeing the Old Testament in the New*. London: T.&T. Clark, 2008. The reader should find this work helpful in its engagement and critique of peers on intertextuality (broadly conceived). Every chapter explores how the understanding of intertextuality (or inner-biblical interpretation) illuminates a specific thesis question brought to a particular New Testament text.

Moyise, Steve. "Intertextuality and the Study of the Old Testament in the New Testament." In *Old Testament in the New Testament*, 14–41. Sheffield, UK: Sheffield Academic, 2000. In this work, Moyise preserves the term "intertextuality," acknowledging its problems and proposing subcategories of "intertextual echo," "dialogical intertextuality," and "postmodern intertextuality."

Perri, Carmela. "On Alluding." *Poetics* 7 (1978): 289–307. Perri takes up and develops Ben-Porat's rejection of the term "allusion" to signify any nonfigurative indirect reference. Demonstrates that the trope "allusion" may be crafted in the context of direct reference and even citation.

Porter, Stanley E. "The Use of the Old Testament in the New Testament: A Brief Comment on Method and Terminology." In *Early Christian Interpretation of the Scriptures of Israel*, Journal for the Study of the New Testament Supplementary Series 148, 79–96. Sheffield: Sheffield Academic, 1997.

Pucci, Joseph Michael. *The Full-Knowing Reader: Allusion and the Power of the Reader in the Western Literary Tradition*. New Haven, Conn.: Yale University, 1998. Pucci seeks to determine "the kind of reading occasioned by allusion" as a literary figure, and examines the competencies an allusion requires. Its trajectory is from the modern, to the medieval, to the classic.

Richards, I. A. *The Philosophy of Rhetoric*. New York: Oxford University, 1936. This seminal work is a series of essays often cited for its introduction of the often-adopted terms "vehicle" and "tenor" in metaphor. The essays demonstrate vitality, even omnipresence, of metaphor in language.

Sommer, Benjamin D. "Exegesis, Allusion and Intertextuality in the Hebrew Bible: A Response to Lyle Eslinger." *Vetus Testamentum* 46, no. 4 (1996): 479–489.

Sommer joins with Eslinger in an appraisal of Fishbane (1985), while demonstrating that Eslinger's "inner-biblical allusion" is a poor label for his proposal, in that what Eslinger calls for is more accurately described as a mode of synchronic, reader-oriented "intertextuality."

Sommer, Benjamin D. *A Prophet Reads Scripture: Allusion in Isaiah 40—66*. Stanford, Calif.: Stanford University Press, 1998. This is the first influential work in inner-biblical interpretation to appropriate Ben-Porat's understanding of allusion. It contributes a helpful and clear definition of "echo" that has been often, but not universally, accepted.

Toorn, K. van der. *Scribal Culture and the Making of the Hebrew Bible*. Cambridge, Mass.: Harvard University Press, 2007. Using biblical and comparative evidence, van der Toorn proposes a professional scribal class related to biblical Levites, and its role in the editing and creation of the texts of the Hebrew Bible.

Vassar, John S. *Recalling a Story Once Told: An Intertextual Reading of the Psalter and the Pentateuch*. Macon, Ga.: Mercer University, 2007. Synchronic in its method, but (as ably argued by Miller) this work is often diachronic in its presuppositions and conclusions.

Willey, Patricia Tull. *Remember the Former Things: The Recollection of Previous Texts in Second Isaiah*. Vol. 161. Society of Biblical Literature Dissertation Series. Edited by Michael V. Fox and Elizabeth Johnson. Atlanta: Scholars, 1997. Methodologically grounded in "intertextuality" and in Hays's "seven tests," this work is solidly diachronic in its orientation to Second Isaiah's creative appropriation of preexilic texts and traditions.

G. Brooke Lester

INTERTEXTUALITY

Intertextuality has been influential in the field of literary studies ever since Bulgarian philosopher Julia Kristeva coined the term in the late 1960s. It can be understood as the study of how a given text is connected with other texts outside itself and how those texts affect the interpretation of the given text. The outside texts are likewise connected with other texts that affect their respective interpretation. Texts are relational in nature and not isolated from other texts. The number of studies on the subject continues to escalate; among the reasons for this are its interdisciplinary emphasis and its postmodern character. In biblical studies intertextuality provides a creative way to understand thoughts, phrases, verses, or passages in relation to other texts. Biblical texts are read in light of other texts with the aim of adding new insight to their interpretation, and text relationships are not limited to canonical citations of earlier canonical references as is commonly done in studies entitled with variations of the phrase, "New Testament Quotations of the Old Testament."

Even so, intertextuality is theoretically complex, and a uniform definition for the term remains quite elusive. A number of its foremost theorists promote a diversity of meanings and methods (e.g., Plett 1991). This article considers intertextuality in relation to: (1) its origin; (2) metalepsis and echoes in biblical studies; (3) poststructural interpretation in biblical studies; (4) various intertextual approaches to biblical studies; and (5) prospects for further study.

Origin of Intertextuality. The original instances of the meaning and use of intertextuality begin with the *Tel Quel* ("as is") editorial group in Paris to which Julia Kristeva belonged. This group included thinkers such as Jacques Derrida, Philippe Sollers, and Roland Barthes (see e.g., Moi in Kristeva 1986, pp. 3–9). In this intellectual environment Kristeva introduced the Russian theorist Mikhail Bakhtin to a Western audience (see M. M. Bakhtin, *The Dialogic Imagination*; translated by C. Emerson and M. Holquist; Austin: University of Texas Press, 1981). Bakhtin had replaced the "static hewing" from texts with "a model where literary structure does not simply *exist* but is generated in relation to *another* structure. What allows a dynamic dimension to structuralism is his concept of the 'literary word' as an *intersection of textual surface* rather than a *point* (a fixed meaning), as a dialogue among several writings." These writings include those of the author, the author's addressee or character, and the cultural context, whether earlier or contemporary (Kristeva, pp. 35–36). Kristeva uses the term "intertextuality" when discussing that "any text is constructed as a mosaic of quotations;

any text is the absorption and transformation of another" (p. 37).

Kristeva developed intertextuality not only as a means of criticizing literary texts as independent units, but also as an attempt to overturn the political and ideological climate of her day, leading up to the student uprisings in France in 1968. Whereas traditional notions of structuralism affirmed scientific stability, objectivity, hierarchy, and "language used," Kristeva's poststructuralism challenged these ideas with uncertainty, subjectivity, relational networks, and "speaking beings." As an ideology, intertextuality was viewed as a deconstruction of texts and "semiotic lever to unhinge all bourgeois notions of an autonomous subject" (Manfred Pfister, "How Postmodern is Intertextuality?" In Plett, pp. 207–224 [212]). Kristeva wrote further that the term "denotes the transposition of one (or more) system(s) of signs into another," which is not to be confused with the "banal sense of 'study of sources'" (p. 111). The original conception of the term also encourages productivity, plural meanings, and a creative redistribution of language.

Barthes (1981, p. 39), Kristeva's mentor, likewise believed that intertextuality could not be mitigated to source or influence theory because its "anonymous formulae" are rarely ever located. The text assumes the presence of other texts and is a woven "tissue of past citations," a redistribution of language at various levels. The text is therefore not an independent unit of communication isolated from other texts; it is interconnected with others to the extent that it cannot be properly appreciated without recognition of other texts that are related to it.

Since the 1970s the trajectory of intertextuality has travelled both in the direction of poststructuralism/deconstruction, and, as it continues to be recontextualized, in the direction of more structural patterns of interpretation. Michael Riffaterre's *Semiotics of Poetry* (Bloomington: Indiana University Press, 1980) and Gérard Genette's *Palimpsests: Literature in the Second Degree* (Lincoln: University of Nebraska Press, 1997) provide alternative taxonomies of the latter pattern. Intertextuality, moreover, has extended beyond the boundaries of poetry and literary fiction into other disciplinary fields such as art, music, film, computer science, and religious studies. The last of these categories finds a large number of adherents in biblical studies.

Intertextual Metalepsis and Echoes in Biblical Studies. Although certain biblical interpreters merely adopt the term "intertextuality" to their historical-critical methods of inquiry, other interpreters explain their use of the term and support their task with a generally workable set of criteria. Similar to the literary field from which the term originated, intertextual biblical studies evince both structural and poststructural approaches. The former has been more influential than the latter.

The study of biblical sources prior to 1989 frequently focused on the pursuit of explicit citations and their location in earlier scripture in an attempt to distill a final, historical meaning to a given text. Since then a shift may be detected through the newer discipline of biblical intertextuality, which often pursues scripture's more subtle or latent references, whether communicated by the author consciously or unconsciously. The aim of such studies frequently centers on what the text might have evoked for the early readers and auditors. This shift contributes toward a trend advancing literary and relational models of reading scripture.

Richard Hays's *Echoes of Scripture in the Letters of Paul* (1989) is frequently addressed as perhaps the most influential study on the use of intertextuality and its criteria within the field of biblical studies. Hays sets out to pursue Paul's readings of Israel's scriptures, readings that are often puzzling to the contemporary person who studies Paul's letters. As an example, the Mosaic Law in Deuteronomy 30:11–14 is transformed by the apostle to mean the "word of faith" in Romans 10:5–10. Hays suggests that Paul, along with ancient rabbis, presupposed the validity of novel readings of the scriptures to unveil latent truths behind the texts they read.

Hays then proposes intertextuality as a productive way to encounter Paul's reading of earlier texts, and he defines the term as "the imbedding of fragments of an earlier text within a later one" (1989,

p. 14). Hays's method pays homage to John Hollander's *Figure of an Echo: A Mode of Allusion in Milton and After* (Berkeley: University of California Press, 1981), a work that advances continuity within poetic traditions by exhibiting the poet as "honoring the voices of the dead even while forming echoes that transform their words in new acoustical environments" (Hays 1989, p. 19). The first task of literary criticism in this regard draws attention to the echo so that others might hear it, and the second duty is to provide explanation of the new figures and distortions the echo might generate.

Along with Hollander, Hays understands as an important property of an echo the term *metalepsis*, a device that links texts together through an echo with the effect of recovering suppressed or unstated points that resonate between the texts: "Allusive echo functions to suggest to the reader that text B should be understood in light of a broad interplay with text A, encompassing aspects of A beyond those explicitly echoed" (p. 20). Hays provides an example through his interpretation of the phrase, "this will turn out for my deliverance" found in Philippians 1:19, which is said to echo Job 13:16 (Septuagint [LXX]). The neighboring verses in the context of the latter convey Job as a figurative prisoner suffering for the sake of righteousness. As such, Paul, who is imprisoned when he writes to the Philippians, takes on the subtle role of Job as a righteous sufferer. The echo from text B draws the reader into a delicate set of comparative ideas from text A that might enlighten the reader's perspectives of text B.

Scholars who interpret scripture along the lines of echoes and metalepsis consider the way this intertextual approach invites fresh and creative readings of the text. Another example from Paul's letters comes from Galatians 2:2. Scholars traditionally interpret the phrase, "run in vain" from this verse as agonistic discourse with an athletic footrace for its figurative background. A study of the phrase through its intertextual echoes, however, draws the reader to prophetic discourse from Israel's scriptures. The phrase "in vain" may be echoed from Habakkuk 2:2–4 (LXX) in which the herald or courier of the prophet's message runs from town to town and proclaims a vision that will come to pass and not be "in vain." The prophet's message includes a promise that "the righteous shall live by my faithfulness." That vision Paul reconfigures as the gospel fulfilled in his day and characterized by the righteous person living by faith(fulness), a message that the apostle as Christ's prophetic herald proclaims both to the Galatians and as a missionary who "runs" or travels from city to city (see B. J. Oropeza, "Running in Vain, but Not as an Athlete (Galatians 2:2): The Impact of Habakkuk 2:2–4 on Paul's Apostolic Commission"; in *Jesus and Paul: Global Perspectives in Honor of James D. G. Dunn*, edited by B. J. Oropeza, C. K. Robertson, and D. C. Mohrmann, pp. 139–150; London: T.&T. Clark, 2009). The echo of the words "run" and "in vain" from text B invites readers to ponder from text A the related notions of a prophet's courier and the message of faith and righteousness that is proclaimed in public gatherings. Paul ponders his own prophetic commission through the intertext, though perhaps only his opponents and the Galatian auditors possessing adequate knowledge from Israel's scriptures would be conscious of the latent ideas in the subtext.

Hays (1989, pp. 29–32) suggests seven tests for detecting intertextual echoes, which are not intended as ironclad rules but can be used as interpretative guidelines: (1) availability: was the source available to the author who allegedly echoes it and to the readers who read it? (2) volume: does the given text contain words and/or related syntax with the source text, how prominent is the source text, and is the given text rhetorically stressed by the author? (3) recurrence: does the author refer to the same source text elsewhere? (4) thematic coherence: does the reported echo fit with the author's use elsewhere, and does it illuminate the author's argument? (5) historical plausibility: could the author intend the meaning and the readers be assumed to know it? (6) history of interpretation: have other readers of later periods heard the same text behind the text? (7) satisfaction: does the echo make sense of the text and enlighten the contextual discourse? Of the seven points some propose that the first two are the only criteria essential for proper intertextual hermeneutics.

Hays's intertextual method finds both supporters (e.g., Wagner 2003; Watson, 2004) and critics (e.g., Evans and Sanders 1993). Responding to Hays's criteria, Stanley Porter (e.g., 1997, pp. 82–84, 92) argues that the notion of availability is too inadequate to explain whether an echo is present when the audience is not aware of it. Likewise, Hays's conceptualization of echoes is thought by Porter to be confusing because Hays does not make clear enough distinctions between echoes and allusions. Porter's criticisms raise awareness of the importance of properly defining one's terms. Both allusions and echoes remain distinct from the more explicit biblical references that quote earlier scriptures and use citation formulae such as "it is written" (Rom 3:10), "he says" (Heb. 1:6–8), and "to fulfill what was spoken" (Matt 1:22), but a consensus among biblical scholars regarding widely accepted meanings that clearly and consistently distinguish between allusions and echoes remains to be seen. Current discussions sometimes center on whether the terms are used consciously or unconsciously by the authors and the degree to which the authors' audiences would have been aware of them.

Hays, referencing Hollander, provides a generalized distinction between allusions and echoes: allusions depend on "authorial intention" and the assumption that the reader will recognize the allusion's source; an echo "finesses such questions" and is not dependent on the conscious intention of the author. But since one could only know the audience of scripture hypothetically, Hays wishes to be flexible with the terminology: "*allusion* is used of obvious intertextual references, *echo* of subtler ones" (Hays 1989, p. 29). Typically, for those who make minimal distinctions between the terms, the use of echo mainly identifies the activity of metalepsis, namely those reverberations from the larger context of the subtext referenced by the biblical author (Wagner, pp. 9–10; Fewell 1992, p. 21).

Christopher Stanley (2008, pp. 125–136) takes issue with Hays's intertextual approach for assuming that Paul's echoes of Israel's scriptures would be recognized by his predominantly Gentile audiences. Not only would they not be as familiar with Israel's scriptures as would Jewish audiences, but they lived in a world in which the literacy rate would be about 10 percent of the population, and mainly the wealthy and elitists would have access to the scriptures. For Stanley, in *Arguing with Scripture: The Rhetoric of Quotations in the Letters of Paul* (New York: T.&T. Clark, 2004), Paul uses quotations in his letters as rhetorical acts involving audience responses, and three levels of ancient hearers are determined: (1) the informed audience who was widely familiar with the Jewish scriptures; (2) the competent audience who possessed some basic knowledge of the scriptures, enough to grasp Paul's point through his citations; and (3) the minimal audience who had very little knowledge of scriptures. Among his conclusions Stanley suggests that Paul often directed his quotations to an implied audience that resembled the "competent audience." The actual audience, however, may have been more diverse than this, and Paul's rhetorical arguments from scripture may have been incomprehensible to the "minimal audience" hearing his letters, while his manner of manipulating texts to support his arguments might have been rejected or challenged by an "informed audience" (p. 178). Stanley's view adds complexity to the biblical audience and does not assume that this audience would have heard the same echoes we hear from the texts today.

Scholars such as J. Ross Wagner (2003, pp. 36–39) and Brian Abasciano ("Diamonds in the Rough: A Reply to Christopher Stanley Concerning the Reader Competency of Paul's Original Audiences," *Novum Testamentum* 49 [2007]: 153–183) respond that illiteracy should not be equated with the emergent Christian audience's ignorance of earlier scriptures. This is especially the case when congregations as corporate entities could possess scriptures and apostolic letters, hear repeated readings with regular discussions about those readings, and, as far as Pauline churches are concerned, possess a teaching office (1 Cor 12:28–29; cf. Eph 4:11).

Biblical Intertextuality and Poststructuralism. Thomas Hatina (1999) focuses on the poststructural framework from which intertextuality originated. He finds fault with the way biblical scholars adopt the term while at the same time neglecting its ideological matrix that arose in response to the type of historical-critical influence models these scholars attempt to maintain. His critique highlights the chasm between traditional influence criticisms and classic intertextuality. He challenges biblical scholars who wish to identify their study as intertextuality to be familiar with, and hopefully engaging in, this discussion.

Two scholars escaping his critique are George Aichele and Gary Phillips, who edit a volume from the academic journal *Semeia* 69/70 (1995) with the thematic title, *Intertextuality and the Bible.* They take seriously the poststructural framework that undergirds the original meaning of the term. The editors' leading article emphasizes Kristeva's approach and then suggests that, by such a measure, intertextuality ought to disturb the biblical reader whose task is to determine specific textual arrangements and study texts within the framework of history and societies ("Introduction: Exegesis, Eisegesis, Intergesis," pp. 6–18 [11]). "This means nothing less than a deconstructive search for the inherent conflicts, tensions, and aporias in the transposition of systems and subjectivities, in the violent juxtaposing, to borrow the Gospel of Matthew's words, what is new and what is old from the treasure room (Matt 13:52)." They continue that the approach scrutinizes the role readers play as "subjective agents" perpetrating such systems, and as such "intertextuality is not a matter of allusion or source tracking; it is a matter of transformation" (p. 11).

Timothy Beal (2000, p. 129) articulates shared sentiments for biblical studies after discussing Kristeva's method:

> The tracing out of intertextual relations is endless and, quite literally, pointless. Therefore, any interpretive conclusion is a matter of giving up, shutting down, or maybe petering out. The interpretant makes a decision, a cut, which cuts off other possible relations, positions roadblocks against other intersections. And where I make my cuts and set up my roadblocks is likely determined not only by accident and oversight but also by the hermeneutical and ideological norms—spoken and unspoken—established within my academic discipline and within my other networks of affiliation and accountability.

An important corollary for Beal is that intertextuality focuses on what is unstable and uncontainable in the biblical text as it exudes into the contemporary readers' clashing cultural and societal constructs, whether past, present, or future, and it "demands self-critical honesty, at least, about why and how we cut it off where and when we do" (p. 130). He suggests that the way for the reader to determine legitimate intertextual relationships is through the reader's own ideology.

In his essay entitled, "Ideology and Intertextuality: Surplus of Meaning and Controlling the Means of Production" (in Fewell, pp. 27–39 [36]) Beal lists three guideposts for methodological direction regarding intertextually-based studies: The first centers on how the interpreter imposes limitations on the countless number of intertextual possibilities for a biblical text. The second aims at the pursuance of which ideologies the production admits as containment strategies. Issues of canon, genre, form, and decisions about which voices are to be foregrounded and which ones marginalized come into play here. The third focuses on how the "established boundaries (or 'critical consensus') of intertextual relationship" might be "transgressed" for the purpose of uncovering new relationships and foregrounding other voices. An important goal of such an approach seeks to overturn "the established strategies of containment and loosen their control" over the "procession of production" (p. 36).

An example of poststructural intertextual exploration can be viewed in George Aichele's "Canon as Intertext: Restraint or Liberation?" (in Hays, Alkier, and Huizenga 2009, pp. 139–156). Aichele breaks the biblical texts free from the ideological control of canonical boundaries to engage with external texts as he produces an interface between scripture and scenes from the pulp fiction and popular film hero, Conan the Barbarian. Within such an environment, depictions of a hero who suffers by hanging on a tree takes on new cultural meaning and may speak back to the biblical texts about Jesus's crucifixion.

Such interpreters of biblical literature attempt to follow patterns akin with the *Tel Quel* originators of intertextuality, and their viewpoints implicitly and sometimes explicitly raise concerns against biblical interpreters who adopt the term "intertextuality" as a trendy banner under which to hang their old, historical-critical approaches to source materials.

Nevertheless, there are biblical scholars who maintain their interpretations as intertextual, and, although they recognize the importance of *Tel Quel*'s influence on the term, they prefer not to adopt poststructural ideologies. To support their view such scholars follow the lead of literary theorists who criticize the original approach. Jonathan Culler's *The Pursuit of Signs: Semiotics, Literature, Deconstruction* (Ithaca, N.Y.: Cornell University Press, 2001, p. 105), for example, suggests that when one assumes Kristeva's model, which claims that other discourses impose a "universe" on a given text, the study of intertextuality becomes impractical. The model is difficult to adopt on account of the immense and undefined space it appropriates, and "when one narrows it so as to make it more usable one either falls into source study of a traditional and positivistic kind (which is what the concept was designed to transcend) or else ends by naming particular texts as the pre-texts on grounds of interpretative convenience" (p. 109).

Others respond that a genetic fallacy is committed by those who insist that intertextuality must always be done within the confines of poststructuralism. Similarly, one's insistence on a stable and fixed meaning for the term based on its original use stands at odds with the unstable and decentralized nature of discourse supported by its originators. Susan Friedman (1991, p. 154) points out this problem when writing that "discourses of influence and intertextuality have not been and cannot be kept pure, untainted by each other." It might be expected that intertextuality can be reconfigured as it constantly travels to different locations within the vast constellation of text relationships, including biblical spaces. It can be suggested that Kristeva's idea of intertextuality is more descriptive than programmatic (Pfister, as cited earlier, in Plett, p. 210). The term is constantly being transformed, a development that seems compatible with the originator's thoughts on the instability of language. Steve Moyise (2002, p. 429) writes that the term "has taken on a life of its own, and now has to be interpreted (or abandoned) in light of current practice rather than the originating moment."

Biblical Intersections. Hays's influential work resulted in a surplus of Pauline intertextual studies. Other early biblical interpreters of intertextuality employ the term in relation to the Synoptic Gospels, Hebrews, and Revelation (Draisma 1989). Kenneth Litwak's *Echoes of Scripture in Luke-Acts: Telling the History of God's People Intertextually* (London: T.&T. Clark, 2005) works with criteria derived from Hays to examine passages from Luke-Acts, and Gary Manning's *Echoes of a Prophet: The Use of Ezekiel in the Gospel of John and in Literature of the Second Temple Period* (London: T.&T. Clark, 2004), studies at the intersection of Johannine tradition, Israel's scriptures, and Second Temple Literature. Jon Paulien's "Elusive Allusions in the Apocalypse: Two Decades of Research into John's Use of the Old Testament" (in Brodie, MacDonald, and Porter 2006, pp. 61–68) surveys the landscape of uses of scripture in Revelation. Quite often intertextual works establish their own criteria for determining intertexts. Dale Allison (2000, pp. 5–13), for example, distils scriptural allusions from Q, and to determine when allusions are "illusions," he establishes six criteria, the first of which considers the history of interpretation. An allusion can either intensify or diminish in presence based on whether it has been detected by some other readers throughout the centuries.

Although text relations in biblical studies frequently examine the New Testament's use of the Hebrew and Septuagint scriptures, intertextuality transcends the boundaries of traditional canonical readings to engage with intercanonical and noncanonical texts. Fewell compiles intertextual studies from scholars who start from the Hebrew scriptures and explore their relationship with other Hebrew scriptures including, among other comparisons, Isaiah's relation to Genesis, Judges 19 in relation to Genesis 19, and the golden calf of 1 Kings 12:28 in relation to Exodus 32:4. The antiquity of Genesis provides fertile subtexts for subsequent intertextual ventures, as does prophetic and wisdom literature when echoing earlier texts. Patricia Tull Willey's *Remember the Former Things: The Recollection of Previous Texts in Second Isaiah* (Atlanta: Scholars, 1997) provides one of many examples from the Hebrew prophets, and Jeremy Corley and Vincent Skemp's edited volume, *Intertextual Studies in Ben Sira and Tobit* (Washington D.C.: The Catholic Biblical Association of America, 2005) addresses studies in wisdom literature and the Apocrypha.

Regarding Hebrew poetry, John Vassar's study on the Psalms and Pentateuch (2007), for example, espouses a fourfold literary approach to allusions derived from Ziva Ben-Porat's "The Poetics of Literary Allusion" (*PTL: A Journal for Descriptive Poetics and Theory of Literature* 1 [1976]: 105–128). First, there is an activation of the alluding text (text that is read) and the evoked text (text alluded to by the alluding text). This takes place by means of a "marker" that signals or triggers the intertextual process. Second, there is recognition of the text that is being evoked, the "marked." Third, there is the recognition and modification of a pattern that results between the interaction of the texts. Fourth, there is a maximizing of patterns activated from the evoked text "as a whole," which formulates connections between texts apart from the marker and marked. The reading of the two texts together may generate novel interpretations in which not only the evoked text interprets the latter text, but the latter text can modify the interpretation of the evoked text. Vassar adopts this study to derive intertextual aspects between Psalms and the Pentateuch in which Psalms contains the "marker" of five books (Pss 1–41; 42–72; 73–89; 90–116; 107–150), which in turn triggers the thought of the five books of the Pentateuch.

Conversely, the Hebrew scriptures can become the intertext for later noncanonical texts. A growing number of studies of the Pseudepigrapha, Qumran literature, and other Second Temple sources suggest that these materials are illumined by their intertextual play with Israel's scriptures (e.g., Evans and Zacharias, 2009). Boyarin (1994) considers Kristeva's mosaic of texts being absorbed and transformed by other texts as a constructive hermeneutic for the use of Torah in Midrash. Lesleigh Cushing Stahlberg's *Sustaining Fictions: Intertextuality, Midrash, Translation, and the Literary Afterlife of the Bible* (New York: T.&T. Clark, 2008) works with ancient Jewish retellings of the scriptures under the aspects of approach (quantity of material retold), stance (attitude toward the retelling), and filter (interpretative lens for the retelling).

In his study of Pauline hermeneutics Francis Watson (pp. 2–6) opens up a three-way conversation between the New Testament author, the earlier texts referenced from Israel's scriptures, and Second Temple literature that appeals to the same subtexts. These writings along with Paul's letters are shaped by Israel's scriptures from which they derive theological interests that can be fruitfully compared. Paul's hermeneutic turns out to be intertextual, and he derives his Christological, ecclesiological, and soteriological foci through his reading of the scriptures. For Watson, Paul's seemingly contradictory way of speaking about Mosaic law in his letters is derived from his discovery of "the tension-laden dynamics of the scriptural narrative itself, in its diachronic unfolding—a discovery that serves to illuminate the logic of the gospel. Scriptural dissonance is both uncovered by the gospel and resolved by it, since its theological function is to testify to the gospel" (p. 24).

The socio-rhetorical method of Vernon Robbins (1996, pp. 40–70) positions intertextuality as the second of five major components of biblical interpretation (the other four are inner texture, social and cultural texture, ideological texture, and sacred texture). For Robbins (p. 40), intertexture involves the text's "representation of, reference to, and use of phenomena in the 'world' outside the text being interpreted." This takes place through oral-scribal, cultural, social, and historical intertextures. Oral-scribal intertexture includes the recitation, recontextualization, reconfiguration, amplification, or thematic elaborations of texts. Cultural intertexture centers on insider knowledge, which for Robbins includes allusions and the more subtle echoes. Social intertexture includes social roles, social institutions, social codes, and social relationships. Historical intertextures reference events at precise times and locations. From the socio-rhetorical perspective, intertexture reminds the reader that the text is not limited to canonical and noncanonical literature. Robbins's approach highlights the significance of looking at texts both inside and outside of the realm of literature. Ancient inscriptions and oral traditions are two such examples of noncanonical texts that are coded without the use of ink and pen, and yet they encourage audiences to ponder new spaces within a network of ideas.

Moyise presents five types of intertextuality: (1) the *intertextual echo* as characterized by Hays's use; (2) *narrative intertextuality*, which uses the framework of popular stories such as the Exodus; (3) *exegetical intertextuality*, which pursues the ancient author's exegesis of a scriptural passage; (4) *dialogical intertextuality*, which allows for the reshaping of the retold story; the influence of the text works both ways, with the old text affecting the new and new affecting the old; and (5) *postmodern intertextuality*, in which both the writer and reader, mindful of the text belonging to a web of texts, assign subjective meaning to the text. Moyise agrees most with the fourth type, which he addresses in more detail through his seminal work, *The Old Testament in the Book of Revelation* (Sheffield, UK: Sheffield Academic Press, 1995). Even so, he suggests that intertextuality should be used as an umbrella term for the complexity of interactions between texts. He hopes that his classification system will lead to further clarifications regarding the plurality of uses of the term intertextual.

The Future of Intertextuality. Prospective intertextual studies might include further resolutions about our discerning allusions and echoes, and either making plausible and consistent distinctions between the two, or finally establishing their interchangeable character. Although studies continue to increase on the canonical texts' echoes of earlier canonical texts, more studies on the biblical use of noncanonical materials might be in order. Such probing not only might include further ventures into ancient Near Eastern and Second Temple texts, but also Greco-Roman literature, progymnasmata, magical papyri, and so on. A method that justifies the interplay of social and culture dimensions of the text, such as Robbin's approach, would be complementary with this endeavor and allow for unwritten texts to enter the conversation. The blending of rhetorical and intertextual methods, especially as they engage with external textures, would also help increase the number of creative projects in the field. MacDonald (2001) focuses on intertextuality and *mimesis* (imitation of ancient writings taught to Greco-Roman students) and might provide one suitable starting point for studies comparing biblical and Greco-Roman literature.

More fusions of interpretative methods, new and old, also seem warranted for the intertextual horizon. Stefan Alkier's "New Testament Studies on the Basis of Categorical Semiotics" (in Hays, Alkier, and Huizenga 2009, pp. 223–248) presents a framework through semiotics that endeavors to bridge the gap between synchronic and diachronic readings of texts and allows for both historical-critical and post-structural approaches to have an intertextual voice.

Likewise, intertextuality as a method need not be irreconcilable with ancient Jewish hermeneutics. William Stegner's "Romans 9.6–29—A Midrash" (*Journal for the Study of the New Testament* 22 [1986]: 37–52) argues that midrashic texts often did not include the "catch words" (key words) in their citations of scripture; these key words would be found in the larger context of the source text, which the rabbis would know from memory. He suggests that Paul may be using such an approach when he cites Genesis 25:23 (Rom 9:12), where the key word "sonship" from Romans 9:6–7 does not appear in Genesis 25:23 but in 25:25, and when he cites Malachi 1:2–3 (Rom 9:13), where the key word "call" is found in Malachi 1:4. This technique may be similar to intertextual metalepsis and is grounded in a context and culture more compatible with the biblical authors than with postmodern literary theories. Hays's criticism of such methods (1989, p. 12; cf. 197) admits that even though they might produce some positive results, "the yield rarely seems to justify the investment of large sums of hope." Only further studies will determine the level of yield, however, and whether such a method, or others like it, could be thought of as an important precursor to metalepsis.

Biblical structural and poststructural methods of interpretation that venture into art, film, music, drama, and Internet hypertexts, to name several places, might find productive discussions that would generate cross disciplinary interest. Other interdisciplinary venues worthy of pursuit might center on how intertextual concepts interact with alternative patterns of biblical and literary references including allegory, typology, pastiche, parody, plagiarism, insider jargon, clichés, erratic references, form criticism, text variants, *Vorlage*, and oral performances. The future for intertextual studies seems promising as its interpretative methods continue to move throughout the vast space of textual connections and be transformed by them.

[*See also* Allegory and Allegorical Interpretation; Deconstruction; Inner-biblical Interpretation; Midrash; Mimesis Criticism; Poststructuralist Interpretation; Reception Criticism and Theory; Redaction Criticism, *subentry* Apocrypha and Deuterocanonical Books; Redaction Criticism, *subentry* Hebrew Bible; Redaction Criticism, *subentry* New Testament; Rhetorical Criticism; Socio-rhetorical Criticism; Structuralist Interpretation; *and* Synoptic Problem.]

BIBLIOGRAPHY

Aichele, George, and Gary A. Phillips, eds. *Intertextuality and the Bible. Semeia* 69/70 (1995). These volumes of the academic journal exemplify poststructural and postmodern approaches to the Bible focused on intertextuality. Various contributors work from the Hebrew scriptures, Christian scriptures, or texts beyond both scriptures.

Allen, Graham. *Intertextuality.* 2d ed. New Critical Idiom. London: New York: Routledge, 2011. This is one of the best introductions to literary intertextuality. The author covers Kristeva and her earlier influences, Barthes, Genette, Riffaterre, Harold Bloom, feminism, postcolonialism, and postmodernism.

Allison, Dale C. *The Intertextual Jesus: Scripture in Q.* Harrisburg, Pa.: Trinity Press International, 2000. This work provides an example on intertextual use derived from Matthew and Luke, and it establishes criteria for discerning allusions that are reminiscent of but distinct from Hays's criteria.

Barthes, Roland. "Theory of the Text." In *Untying the Text: A Post-Stucturalist Reader*, edited by Robert Young, 31–47. Boston, London, and Henley: Routledge & Kegan Paul, 1981. This article provides as good, succinct English introduction to Barthes's text theory. The more advanced reader may wish to consult his work entitled *S/Z* (Paris: Éditions du Seuil, 1970).

Beal, Timothy K. "Intertextuality." In *Handbook of Postmodern Biblical Interpretation*, edited by A. K. M. Adam, 128–130. St. Louis, Mo.: Chalice, 2000. This article addresses the use of intertextuality in scripture from a poststructural perspective.

Beale, G. K., and D. A. Carson, eds. *Commentary on the New Testament Use of the Old Testament.* Nottingham: Apollos/Grand Rapids, Mich.: Baker Academic, 2007. Although this work does not set out to advance the Intertextual method, it provides a compendium of New Testament scripture citations and allusions for further studies, and the various contributions in the work address the interpretation of Second Temple literature's references to the same sources referenced by the New Testament authors.

Boyarin, Daniel. *Intertextuality and the Reading of Midrash.* Bloomington: Indiana University Press, 1994. This is an influential work in the field that engages the Hebrew scriptures as the source text for intertextuality. Boyarin is conversant with Kristeva's theory.

Brodie, Thomas L., Dennis MacDonald, and Stanley E. Porter, eds. *The Intertextuality of the Epistles: Explorations of Theory and Practice.* Sheffield, UK: Sheffield Phoenix, 2006. This is a collection of intertextual articles that works with novel issues such as the New Testament readings of other New Testament texts, pseudepigraphy, the use of Greco-Roman sources, and the like.

Draisma, Sipke, ed. *Intertextuality in Biblical Writings: Essays in Honour of Bas van Iersel*, Kampen: Kok, 1989. This monograph exemplifies one of the earliest uses of intertextuality in the New Testament. Many of its contributors focus on texts from the Gospels.

Evans, Craig A., and James A. Sanders, eds. *Paul and the Scriptures of Israel. Journal for the Study of the New Testament: Supplement Series* 83. Studies in Scripture in Early Judaism and Christianity 1. Sheffield, UK: Sheffield Academic Press, 1993. This collection of essays from various scholars devotes a major section to Richard Hays's intertextual method, which is critiqued by Evans, Sanders, W. S. Green, and J. C. Beker, and includes Hays's response.

Evans, Craig A., and H. Daniel Zacharias. *Early Christian Literature and Intertextuality. Volume 1, Thematic Studies. Volume, 2, Exegetical Studies.* Library of New Testament Studies 391, 392. London; New York, N.Y.: T.&T. Clark, 2009. This two-volume collection of studies not only engages with biblical texts but also Second Temple literature such as Pseudepigrapha, Qumran, and Philo.

Fewell, Danna Nolan, ed. *Reading Between Texts: Intertextuality and the Hebrew Bible.* Literary Currents in Biblical Interpretation. Louisville, Ky.: Westminster/John Knox Press, 1992. This monograph collects a number of essays that discuss the theory of intertextuality for biblical interpretation in the Hebrew Scriptures.

Friedman, Susan Stanford. "Weavings: Intertextuality and the (Re)Birth of the Author." In *Influence and Intertextuality in Literary History,* edited by Jay Clayton and Eric Rothstein, 146–180. Madison: University of Wisconsin Press, 1991. This is an influential article in literary studies that provides a critique of early approaches to intertextuality.

Hatina, Thomas R. "Intertextuality and Historical Criticism in New Testament Studies," *Biblical Interpretation* 7 (1999): 28–43. This article explores the origin of intertextuality in light of the *Tel Quel* group, and it urges biblical scholars who use intertextual methodology to consider its poststructural ideology.

Hays, Christopher B. "Echoes of the Ancient Near East? Intertextuality and the Comparative Study of the Old Testament." In *The Word Leaps the Gap: Essays on Scripture and Theology in Honor of Richard B. Hays,* edited by J. Ross Wagner, C. Kavin Rowe, and A. Katherine Grieb, 20–43. Grand Rapids, Mich.: Eerdmans, 2008. The author examines intertextual theory, Richard Hays's criteria, and its reconfigured crossover into the Hebrew Scriptures and Ancient Near Eastern studies.

Hays, Richard B. *Echoes of Scripture in the Letters of Paul.* New Haven, Conn: Yale University Press, 1989. This monograph is essential for understanding the major intersection that has taken place between intertextual and biblical studies. Hays examines select passages from Paul's letters as they reference Israel's scriptures. He interprets the texts by using the concepts [of] echoes and metalepsis.

Hays, Richard B., Stefan Alkier, and Leroy A. Huizenga, eds. *Reading the Bible Intertextually.* Waco Tex.: Baylor University Press, 2009. This is an important collection of biblical intertextual perspectives whose contributors come from both ends of the intertextual divide. Some contributors work with synchronic models and cultural semiotics complimentary of poststructuralism, while others employ diachronic models and address traditional biblical criticisms.

Kristeva, Julia, with Toril Moi, eds. *The Kristeva Reader.* New York: Columbia University Press, 1986. This book is a good introduction to a variety of primary essays from Julia Kristeva that are translated into English. Crucial for intertextual theory are Kristeva's, "Word, Dialogue and Novel" and "Revolution in Poetic Language." The first article was translated from *Semeiotiké. Recherches pour une sémanalyse* (Collections Tel Quel. Paris: Le Seuil, 1969), portions of which were later translated in Kristeva's *Desire in Language: A Semiotic Approach to Literature and Art* (Introduction by Leon S. Roudiez; translated by Thomas Gora, Alice Jardine, and Leon S. Roudiez; New York: Columbia University Press, 1980). The second article compiles selections from Kristeva's *Revolution in Poetic Language* (Introduction by Leon S. Roudiez; translated by Margaret Waller; New York: Columbia University Press, 1984), which was derived from her work, *La Révolution du langage poétique* (Paris: Éditions du Seuil, 1974). In the Introduction, Toril Moi gives concise background information regarding Kristeva's years with the *Tel Quel* group.

MacDonald, Dennis R., ed. *Mimesis and Intertextuality in Antiquity and Christianity.* Harrisburg, Pa.: Trinity Press International, 2001. This collection of essays discusses Greco-Roman *mimesis* and intertextuality, including New Testament imitations of Homer's epics.

Moyise, Steve. "Intertextuality and Biblical Studies: A Review." *Verbum et Ecclesia* 23 (2002): 418–431. Written by one of the most prolific writers on biblical intertextuality, this article surveys intertextual approaches and identifies five different models for biblical interpretation.

Plett, Heinrich F., ed. *Intertextuality.* Research in Text Theory 15. Berlin: Walter de Gruyter, 1991. This work collects a number of important essays on the theory of intertextuality. The editor promotes a diversity of meanings and methods for literary intertextuality.

Porter, Stanley E. "The Use of the Old Testament in the New Testament: A Brief Comment on Method and Terminology." In *Early Christian Interpretation of Israel:*

Investigations and Proposals, edited by Craig Evans and James A. Sanders, 79–96. Journal for the Study of the Old Testament: Supplement Series 148. Studies in Scripture in Early Judaism and Christianity 5. Sheffield, UK: Sheffield Academic Press, 1997. The article raises criticisms and the problem of definition and categories related to the New Testament use of Israel's scriptures, including intertextual approaches.

Robbins, Vernon K. *Exploring the Texture of Texts: A Guide to Socio-Rhetorical Interpretation*. Harrisburg, Pa.: Trinity Press International, 1996. This study describes the socio-rhetorical method of intertextuality, which engages in oral-scribal, social, cultural, and historical intertextures.

Stanley, Christopher D. "Paul's 'Use' of Scripture: Why the Audience Matters." In *As it is Written: Studying Paul's Use of Scripture*, edited by Stanley E. Porter and Christopher D. Stanley, 125–155. Society of Biblical Literature Symposium Series 50. Atlanta/Leiden: Scholars Press/Brill, 2008. The article criticizes Hays's method and highlights the importance of our determining the audience in biblical writings.

Vassar, John S. *Recalling a Story Once Told: An Intertextual Reading of the Psalter and the Pentateuch*. Macon, Ga.: Mercer University Press, 2007. The method in this monograph is derived from a poetic-literary perspective of allusions. Intertextuality in this work centers on the Hebrew Scriptures.

Wagner, J. Ross. *Heralds of the Good News: Isaiah and Paul in Concert in the Letter to the Romans*. Leiden: Brill, 2003. This work provides an exemplary reading of Paul's letter to the Romans through the lens of intertextual echoes from Isaiah.

Watson, Duane F., ed. *The Intertexture of Apocalyptic Discourse in the New Testament*. Society of Biblical Literature Symposium Series 14. Atlanta: Society of Biblical Literature, 2002. This collection of New Testament articles exhibits the intertextual approach influenced by Vernon Robbins's socio-rhetorical method.

Watson, Francis. *Paul and the Hermeneutics of Faith*. London: T.&T. Clark, 2004. The work combines intertextuality with a three-way conversation between New Testament (Pauline letters), Second Temple sources, and Israel's scriptures (Torah).

B. J. Oropeza

J

JAPANESE INTERPRETATION

After the Meiji government of Japan repealed the ban on Christianity in 1873, Roman Catholic and Protestant missionaries began clerical training for Japanese citizens. From that time on, Japanese Christians have imported and closely followed Euro-American theology and biblical scholarship. It is natural in such scholarship, regardless of whether one is liberal or conservative (or even fundamentalist), to receive theological education in European or North American universities or seminaries before introducing their acquired methodologies to Japanese churches and academic spheres. Although it is said that Japanese Christians are "a Bible-reading people," few of them are actually interested in interpreting the Bible from their own context. There are, however, a few examples of readings from the Bible that are informed by the Japanese context. The features of Japanese biblical interpretation can be summed up in three overall trends: biblical scholarship outside the church (including historical criticism as a tool of critique and the interpretation of the Bible in dialogue with Buddhism); biblical scholarship inside of the church (i.e., canonical-theological hermeneutics); and new translations of the Bible from the margins.

Biblical Scholarship outside the Church. In Japan, historical criticism has been a tool to criticize the institutional church and its traditional dogma. Many of the so-called "academic biblical scholars" distance themselves from the church or stand "outside" the church. This is typical of national universities, specifically Tokyo University with its close ties with the *Mukyokai* (the nonchurch movement) tradition. Although such universities offer courses on the academic study of religions and philology, which include biblical studies, none of them provide clerical training. Many of these academic biblical scholars receive their training at these national universities and in German-speaking spheres that focus on philology.

The Mukyokai Tradition. Kanzo Uchimura founded the *Mukyokai* in 1900. Uchimura emphasized anti-institutionalism (antidenominationalism), antiritualism, and the pursuit of an indigenous expression of faith. Instead of forming another denominational church, Uchimura and his followers created independent Bible study groups. They claimed that any person who read the Bible had the privilege and responsibility to read and interpret the Bible free from any kind of authority, since the Bible was not merely the church's book but also a work of classic literature. They accepted historical criticism and philological studies of the scripture. As leaders of the *Mukyokai*, Toraji Tsukamoto (famous for his synopsis of the Synoptic Gospels) and Tateo Kanda (well known for his studies on Greek literature) left their mark on academic biblical scholarship in Japan. Subsequently, Masao Sekine (the Old Testament) and Goro Maeda (the New Testament), leaders of *Mukyokai* as well as professors at national universities, expanded academic studies of the scripture in postwar Japan and attracted many future students. Due to the efforts of these scholars, the Bible is now widely accepted by intellectuals not only as the canon for Christians but also as one of the Western classical texts, which has significance not only for Christians but for humanity in general.

The Criticism of Paul and "Paulinism." The criticism of Paul and "Paulinism" during the 1970s was an epoch-making controversy in the history of Japanese Christianity. The movement attracted many young pastors, laity, and NT scholars. In the context of the student movement that protested against the 1951 Japan-US Security Treaty, some young Christians opposed the sophisticated and authoritative nature of established Christianity in Japan. They claimed that the nature of the church derived from the thoughts of Paul. Some examples include his conformist attitude toward Rome (Rom 13), his compromising attitude toward slavery (e.g., 1 Cor 7:21), and his sexist remarks (e.g., 1 Cor 7:1–11). Above all, the "faith" that Paul advocates is non-practicing (cf. Rom 3:28). In other words, they argued that current Christians prayed about war and social injustice but did not practice the same ethic of love that Jesus taught his followers. They defined such practices as "Paulinism" and criticized Christians for making Christianity nothing more than an abstract idealistic religion.

Kenzo Tagawa, who was a fellow student of Goro Maeda at Tokyo University and gained his doctoral degree from Strasbourg University in France, was at the forefront of the criticism. According to Tagawa, early Christianity formed soon after Jesus's death when his followers deified Jesus and systematized a faith that centered on the mythological representation of Christ's (the Son of God) resurrection. Paul enforced such an abstract and idealistic dimension of Christianity. In addition, Tagawa argued that Paul reversed actual facts and transformed them into virtual conceptions (*Hihanteki Shutai no Keisei* 1980). Citing 1 Corinthians 7:29–31, Tagawa suggested that Paul did not actually deny "the world" based on facts but only pretended to deny it. For example, Paul did not ask that his readers give up their possessions but only pretend to give them up. Furthermore, citing 1 Corinthians 7:21–22, (freedom given by the Lord), Tagawa suggested that this freedom was acquired in a virtual sphere that willingly accepted slavery in "the world." This scope of Tagawa's criticism expanded from Paul to Christianity and finally to religion in general.

In 1980 Tagawa published *A Man Called Jesus*. According to Tagawa, Jesus was not a person of religion; he was a critic of religion. At that time Jesus stood on the side of the oppressed people and dared to offer a "paradoxical protest" to the Roman and Jewish rulers. When Jesus stated, "[t]he sabbath was made for humankind" (Mark 2:28), he admitted that, even though the sabbath law was originally founded to protect their labors, it ultimately dominated the Jewish people as a dogma. In this case, Jesus criticized the law because he believed that Judaism was an apparatus that only brought Jewish leaders into power. Furthermore, Jesus's statement of "[g]ive therefore the emperor the things that are the emperor's" (Matt 22:21) was an ironic criticism against both Jewish and Roman rulers. In this case, Jesus tried to liberate the poor who suffered from double taxation by both the Romans and the Temple in "the world." Tagawa suggests that Jesus, while facing the reality of the oppressed people, argued for liberation from this common "real world."

Biblical Interpretation as Interreligious Dialogue. Although a few scholars suggest parallelism between the theology of Jesus and Paul and Buddhist philosophers, specifically Shinran (1173–1263), any attempts to interpret the Christian scripture in a multifaith context are rare, particularly in regard to other Japanese religions (e.g., Shintoism). This is mostly because these religions do not have a systematic dogma or a process of systematizing their teachings.

Seeichi Yagi is the central figure of such interpretation. He completed his graduate work in the NT at Tokyo University under Goro Maeda before continuing his study at Göttingen University in

Germany. Since the publication of his initial principal work *The Formation of New Testament Thought* in 1963, he has attempted to synthesize NT thought and philosophy of religion in order to clarify a common ground between Buddhism and Christianity. This common connection between the two religions is known as *bashology* (topology), which is derived from the Japanese word *basho* (meaning "place"). This interpretation understands individuals as a set in the field of *Transzendenz* and expresses the activity thereof. For example, Yagi suggests that the NT had bashological thinking but it has forgotten it in the increasing personal view of God in Western Christianity.

Yagi claims that the Christ-kerygma of primitive Christianity, including that of Jesus's resurrection, should be understood as the interpretation of an "enlightenment" event peculiar to that time. In this enlightenment event, the absolutization of the ego is overcome, and the event itself is parallel to Zen Buddhism. In addition, Yagi grasps the NT as a whole with little regard to the differences of authors, time, and place; he identifies three theological types in it. "Type A" theology emphasizes that Jesus's death on the cross was for the redemption of our sins (e.g., Rom 3:24–25; 1 Cor 15:3; 1 John 4:10). In this case, the plural use of "sin(s)" represents the transgressions of the Law in the OT while "righteousness" represents the strict observance of the Law. Since it is impossible for all human beings to observe the Law perfectly on their own, redemption by Jesus's death on the cross is inevitable for everyone. Yagi assumes that this type of theology was formed in the primitive church in Jerusalem before Paul.

"Type B" theology emphasizes that Christ is the Son of God who arrives from heaven, becomes incarnate, lives a faithful and devoted life, dies on the cross, and is resurrected (Phil 2:6–11; 1 John 4:9, 14, 15). "Sin" (singular) in this case represents the power that dominates the present and future of all human beings (John 8:34; Rom 7:17), whereas "faith" is the most important aspect for believers. For those who have faith in Christ, they first share the power and work of Christ, and then belong to the so-called body of Christ. Yagi assumes that this type of theology was reformed by Hellenistic Christianity based on "Type A" theology. Examples of Type A theology are found in 1 Corinthians 15:3–4, Romans 3:24–25, and 1 Corinthians 11:23–25; whereas, Type B theology is shown in Philippians 2:6–11 and Romans 10:9.

Finally, "Type C" theology emphasizes love, particularly in regard to the personal relationships formed by human beings (1 John 4:7–16). In this case, Type C theology argues that the work of God is observed when humans love one another (John 1:13; 1 John 4:7). In other words, this type of theology is the manifestation of the existence of love. According to Yagi, 1 John belongs to "Type C" theology. In addition, the heart of historical Jesus's teaching is also Type C theology (Mark 2:27; 7:15; 10:17–22; 12:28–34; Luke 17:33).

In his book, Yagi compares Type B theology with the teachings of Shinran, the founder of Shin-Buddhism. According to Yagi, both Type B theology and Shinran's teaching attempt to solve an individual's existential matter (for instance; death and sinful life; cf. Gal 2:20b; Shinran, *Tannisho* 5), and teach that salvation of individuals is solely through entrusting the benevolence of Christ (Paul) or Amida Buddha (Shinran). Moreover, Yagi suggests a similarity between the relationship of the *law* (Type A) and *love* (Type C) in Christianity and that of *Funbetsu* (knowledge based on differentiation) and *Satori* (enlightenment) in Zen Buddhism.

In his book, *Paul/Shinran, Jesus/Zen* (1983), Yagi fully explores the parallelism between NT thought and Buddhist philosophy. He argues that Paul's teachings agree with Shinran and that Jesus's tradition reflects Zen. As stated in Galatians 2:19–20, the ego of Paul that seeks salvation of the "self" in observance of the Law has died. As a result, Paul is "crucified with Christ" and Christ lives in Paul. In other words, Christ had become Paul's ultimate subject. The "ego" of Paul, however, actually still exists and it proclaims that he believes in the Son of God who is the object of his faith. Such thoughts of Paul are similar to Shinran's teachings where a person can reach *Hosho Hosshin* (the highest aspect of reality) through *Shinjin* (entrusting to Amida

Buddha's Primal Vow). An individual can gain this level of *Shinjin* individually only by the *Ekou* (the loving power that can save all human beings) of Amida Buddha. According to Yagi, these comparisons lead both Christians and Buddhists to consider the question of whether Christ (or what Paul calls "Christ in Holy Spirit, Christ living in me") and Amida Buddha are two different "transcendent" existences or the same transcendent experience.

Biblical Scholarship Inside the Church. The members of the *Mukyokai* believed that they could still be Christians without the church by simply and faithfully studying the Bible. The critics of Paul or "Paulinism" as well as Bible interpreters who read the Christian scripture in the context of interreligious dialogue, tend to distance themselves from the church or stand "outside" the church. Contrary to that trend, Zenda Watanabe asserted that faithful study of the Bible did not exist outside the framework of the church, and he advocated canonical-theological hermeneutics in Christian scripture. Watanabe, a holiness pastor-turned-theologian, attempted to harmonize historical-critical methods and faithful readings of the Bible. He studied historical-critical methods in the United States and the phenomenological method (*zu der Sache selbst*) in Germany. The crux of his interpretation emphasizes how the entire Bible (Genesis to Revelation) is the canon of the church.

Watanabe published numerous works that further promoted his canonical-theological hermeneutics including three principal books on the doctrine of the Bible: *Canonicity of the Bible* (1949), *Interpretation of the Bible* (1954), and *Theology of the Bible* (1963). According to Watanabe, there are two dimensions of reading the Bible: (1) as classic literature from a diachronic and philological point of view, and (2) as canon of the church from a synchronic standpoint. Citing the philosopher Wilhelm Dilthey (1833–1911), Watanabe states that the goal of historical criticism is "to understand the author better than the author understood himself." On the other hand, citing Heidegger, he defines canonical-theological hermeneutics as "not a way of knowing those characteristics of entities which themselves are [*seinender Beschaffenheiten des Seienden*]; it is rather a determination of the structure of the Being which entities possess" (Heidegger, *Being and Time*).

Watanabe's hermeneutics include three overall perspectives. First, his definition of canonical-theological hermeneutics means reading the text from the perspective of today's church, with a sixty-six-book defined canon. Second, the entire Bible (Genesis to Revelation) should be interpreted as a witness to Christ. Third, the arrangement sequence of the Bible shows the salvation history of the chosen people ("the people of Israel" in the OT and the church in the NT). For example, Stephen's sermon in Acts 7 and the lives of eminent believers in Hebrews 11 reflect the fact that the early church determined the salvation history in the arrangement sequence of the OT where eschatology had cut across the vertical row of salvation history. The catastrophic end is designated as a sudden event to us by the primitive church (e.g., Matt 24:37).

An example of this canonical-theological hermeneutics can be seen in the book of Genesis. Genesis is divided into primeval history (Gen 1–11) and the narrative of Israel's ancestors (Gen 12–50). In the first section, the problem and tragedy of the "natural state" of human beings is shown through the myth in which they were initially based on the image of God (Gen 1). However, they ultimately lost relationship with God and the natural world (Gen 2–3). In the latter section, the solution for the problem of the "natural state" of human beings is shown in the case of individuals who simply believed in the grace of God.

Bible Translations from the Margins. A new trend of Japanese interpretation can be seen in the margins of Japanese society. Two translations of the NT are attempts to restore neglected viewpoints of the oppressed minorities and the exploited languages of the locals. People involved in translating projects of the existing translations of the Bible devote every effort to make their text understandable to everyone. Therefore, almost all existing Japanese translations of the Bible emphasize the viewpoint of the majority of the Japanese people who are comfortable using standard Japanese (*Hyojungo*) and neglect the viewpoint of people in rural areas who are uncomfortable with standard Japanese.

Tetsuro Honda. A Franciscan priest once at the top of his order in Japan, Tetsuro Honda now lives in Kamagasaki, Japan's largest concentration of day laborers. He published original translations of the four Gospels, the Acts of Apostles, and several Pauline letters from the standpoint of day laborers and homeless persons. He was trained at the Pontificio Istituto Biblico in Rome and participated in several Bible translation projects including the Franciscan version of the Bible (*Fransisukokai-yaku*) and the New Interconfessional Bible (*Shin-kyoudou-yaku*). However, he realized that these translations did not relate to day laborers or the homeless because the wording of these translations reflected a middle-class perspective. These translations viewed Jesus as a middle-class person who was concerned about the poor. If we reread the Bible from the viewpoint of the marginalized people, though, Jesus himself was actually one of the needy who stood in line at a soup kitchen.

In addition, we can understand Honda's Christology through his interpretation of the Christ hymn in Philippians 2:6–11, where Honda opposes the generally accepted view that the hymn represents Christ's humility. He points out the mistake of the New Interconfessional Bible (widely used in the churches of Japan), which translates the Greek word *morphē* into "status" in order to emphasize the condescension of Christ. It basically means "figure," "form," or "way of being." In this case, Paul does not mean that Jesus actually condescendingly traveled from heaven to the bottom of the world. Conversely, God is at the "bottom" and works there for the suffering people by God's nature (cf. Pss 113, 139). Jesus merely took human form and lived as a follower of God who dwells at the bottom of society's heap and worked for the people there. The ordinary interpretation of the Christ hymn as a glorification of Christ's humility reflects the mind-set of middle-class Christians, who assume that Jesus, too, was a middle-class person, and who extend a "helping hand" to day laborers and the homeless in order to imitate Christ's humility. On the other hand, they do not affirm day laborers and the homeless equally without religious conversion. Since God is on the side of the needy, middle-class Christians need conversion rather than the less fortunate (regardless of their faith).

Reviewing Honda's translation of Mark 1:15 may help us to further understand his thesis. The NRSV translates the phrase as follows: "The time is fulfilled, and the kingdom of God has come near, repent, and believe in the good news." Honda translates the same phrase as "The time is fulfilled, and the kingdom of God is very near, review from the underside, and begin walking while relying on the gospel." First of all, he translates *metanoeō* as "shift one's viewpoint from top-down to underside." The Greek prefix *meta* is the preposition implying "change" or "remove," and the Greek noun *nous* that simply means "mind" but more appropriately means "criteria, "track of thinking," and "making decisions;" hence, *metanoeō* signifies to "shift one's viewpoint." In addition, in the LXX, *metanoeō* is the translation for the Hebrew root *nḥm*, which means "to have compassion with." Therefore, *metanoeō* means "to shift one's viewpoint to the place where one can have compassion for pain, suffering, loneliness, and the anger of others." It is noteworthy that what Jesus and John the Baptist mean by *metanoeō* is not "religious conversion" but a review of a world that is compassionate toward individuals who suffer. Finally, Honda interprets the phrase *pisteuete en tō euaggeliō* based on his unique understanding of *metanoeō*. The Greek verb *pisteuō* means "believing with the heart," "confessing with the mouth," (cf. Rom 10:10) but also "doing the will of God" (cf. Matt 7:21). The word *euaggelion* here does not represent the propagation of Christianity, but rather what happened to the characters in the Gospels. These characters view the world from the standpoint of the least favored or the oppressed (*metanoeō*), which influences readers to side with the less fortunate. Thus, the justice of God who stands in the midst of the poor (cf. Ps 113) has come to liberate the oppressed to establish peace and a world where people truly share joy with one another. This ethereal world is what Honda calls the "kingdom of God."

Harutsugu Yamaura. From 2002 to 2004, Harutsugu Yamaura, a Roman Catholic layperson and a medical doctor, translated the four Gospels from original Greek texts (not via normative standard Japanese [*hyojungo*]) into *Kesen-go* (a language spoken in Japan's northeastern coastal region). When the Meiji imperial government attempted to unite Japan into a strong and unified nation, it formed the normative standard Japanese language based on the dialect spoken in the upper-class areas of Tokyo (*yamanote-kotoba*). This act forced locals to speak standard Japanese and attempted to eliminate additional dialects. For instance, schools taught this standard language and banned the use of dialects. In addition, the translation of the Bible unintentionally contributed toward this Japanese policy because almost all of the existing Bible translations were in standard Japanese.

Yamaura devoted more than 25 years restoring his native language of *Kesen-go* since he believed that it was an independent language on its own and not simply a dialect. He created orthography using two writing systems; the first based on the Latin script, and the second based on the Japanese writing system. He further supported the language by publishing a dictionary and introductory grammar textbooks.

During his process of translating the four Gospels into *Kesen-go*, he first attempted to do so from the normative standard Japanese. As he began, he realized that the familiar translations of the Bible were filled with unfamiliar theological jargon, which translators simply modernized in order to provide an appropriate translation. In one example, Greek terms such as *Agapē* ("love") or *agapaō* ("I love") are translated into *Ai* or *Aisuru* in standard Japanese. However, the Japanese people rarely say *Aisu* and instead say *Daijinisuru* ("cherish" or "be kind to"). In this case, the well-known statement of "love your enemy" should be translated (or interpreted) as "be kind to (even) your enemy" since it sounds more realistic. In another example, he translates the phrase from the Sermon on the Mount, "Blessed are the poor in spirit, for theirs is the kingdom of heaven" (Matt 5:3) into the following: "Those who are weak, hopeless, and lonely are happy for such people who are wrapped within God's arms." The Greek phrase *Oi ptochoi to pneumati* ("the poor in spirit") translated literally into Japanese is "those who breathe weakly," meaning those who feel hopeless and powerless due to the lack of money and status. In addition, "God's Reign" ("the kingdom of God" or "the kingdom of heaven") means the world under God's thumb. One in such a world feels safe just like a baby in a mother's arms. According to Yamaura, the people who suffer adversity know a true sense of deep grief and empathy. Jesus says here that mercy grown in such severe situations lead people in suffering to happiness. The image of God that Jesus proclaims is different from the God of Hosts in the OT but the source of mercy.

In 2011, several months after the March earthquake-tsunami disaster, Yamaura published the new translation of four Gospels in everyday language. In his translation, the words of characters in the Gospels are translated into various Japanese dialects, similar to everyday speech in Jesus's time when there were a variety of dialects and no normative language. In addition, his translation includes no unfamiliar theological jargons (e.g., *dikaiosunē* = being merciful and generous, and doing God's will; and *pistis* = relying on God's power). Thus, Yamaura's translation of the Bible in *Kesen-go* and everyday language is the disclosure about the significance of the Gospels, which is usually hidden by the jargon used in the traditional Bible.

Legacy. Reviewing the history of Japanese Interpretation, it is obvious that almost all Japanese biblical expositors study the Bible in their own context informed by the methodologies of Euro-American biblical scholarship. A unique feature of Japanese Interpretation is that the academic biblical studies play a role to criticize the status quo of institutional Christianity. Only more recently, interpretation has turned toward restoring the neglected perspectives of the minorities in Japan.

[*See also* Asian American Biblical Interpretation; Cross-Cultural Exegesis; Cultural Studies; Historical Criticism, *subentry* Hebrew Bible; Historical Criticism, *subentry* New Testament; Liberation Hermeneutics;

Postcolonial Biblical Interpretation; *and* Theological Interpretation.]

BIBLIOGRAPHY

Arai, Sasagu, ed. *Paulo o Doutoraeruka* [How Do We Think about Paul?]. Tokyo: Shinkyo Shuppansha, 1972.

Asano, Atsuhiro. "Uchimura and the Bible in Japan." In *The Oxford Handbook of the Reception History of the Bible*, edited by Michael Lieb, Emma Mason, and Jonathan Roberts, 323–339. Oxford: Oxford University Press, 2011.

Furuya, Yasuo, ed. *A History of Japanese Theology*. Grand Rapids, Mich.: Eerdmans, 1997.

Honda, Tetsuro. *Chiisakusaretahitobitonotameno Fukuin* [The Gospel for the least: the Four Gospels and the Acts of the Apostles]. Nagoya: Shinseisya, 2001.

Honda, Tetsuro. *Kamagasaki to Fukuin* [Kamagasaki and the Gospel]. Tokyo: Iwanami Shoten, 2006.

Honda, Tetsuro. *Seisyo o Hakkensuru* [Discovering the Bible]. Tokyo: Iwanami Shoten, 2010.

Maeda, Goro. *Maeda Goro Senshu* [The Selected Works of Goro Maeda]. 4 vols and Supplement. Tokyo: Kyobunkwan, 2007–2009.

Michalson, Carl. *Japanese Contributions to Christian Theology*. Philadelphia: Westminster, 1960.

Philips, James M. *From the Rising of the Sun: Christians and Society in Contemporary Japan*. Maryknoll, N.Y.: Orbis, 1981.

Sekine, Masao. *Sekine Masao Chosakushu* [The Complete Works of Masao Sekine]. 20 vols. and Supplement. Tokyo: Shinchi Syobou, 1979–2004.

Tagawa. Kenzo. *Hihanteki Shutai no Keisei* [The Formation of Critical-Subject]. Tokyo: Sanitsu Syobou, 1971.

Tagawa. Kenzo. *Iesu toiu Otoko* [A Man Called Jesus]. Tokyo: Sanitsu Syobou, 1980.

Uchimura, Kanzo. *Uchimura Kanzo Zenshu* [The Complete Works of Kanzo Uchimura]. 41 vols. Tokyo: Iwanami Shoten. 1980–2001.

Watanabe, Zenda. *Watanabe Zenda Zensyu* [The Complete Works of Zenda Watanabe]. 5 vols. and Supplement. Tokyo: Kirisutokyou Shinbun, 1965–1966.

Yagi, Seiichi. "Buddhist Philosophy and New Testament Theology." *Buddhist-Christian Studies* 19 (1999): 165–172.

Yagi, Seiichi. "'I'in the Words of Jesus." In *The Myth of Christian Uniqueness: Toward a Pluralistic Theology of Religions*, edited by John Hick and P. Knitter, 117–134. Maryknoll, N.Y.: Orbis, 1987.

Yagi, Seiichi. *Pauro/Shinran, Iesu/Zen* [Paul/Shinran, Jesus/Zen]. Kyoto: Houzoukan, 1983.

Yagi, Seiichi. *Sinyaku Sisou no Seiritsu* [The Formation of New Testament Thought]. Tokyo: Sinkyou Shuppansha, 1963.

Yamaura, Harutsugu. *Galilaya no Iesyu* [Jesus in Galilee: Japanese Translation of the Four Gospels]. Ofunato: Epix, 2011.

Yamaura, Harutsugu. *Kesen-go Yaku Shinyaku Seisyo* [the Kesen-go Translation of the New Testament], 4 vols. Ofunato: Epix, 2002–2004.

Tomohiro Omiya

K

KOREAN INTERPRETATION

The rapid growth and particular interpretation of Christianity among South Koreans is intimately tied to how the Bible was appropriated within in this religio-cultural and sociopolitical milieu from the eighteenth century onward. The spread of Christianity in Korea accelerated upon the arrival of the Jesuits in 1789 and Protestant missions in 1884. Today 30 percent of the nation's population adheres to Christianity. The Protestant share (19%) is the largest among Asian states, while the Catholic share (11%) is the third largest. Less noted and understood, though, is the tapestry of Korean biblical interpretation that emerged in the context of other religious traditions, war and post-war growth, and a Korean consciousness of struggle and suffering. These influences proffer a distinctive Koreanness of biblical interpretation that relates closely to God's liberating intervention for a people who perceive their need to move beyond oppression.

Foundational Attitude toward the Bible. Korean biblical interpretation follows a pervasive Asian religious ethos that focuses on "teachings" that influence the ways in which individuals, communities, and society function in relation to each other and the world beyond. Unlike Western categorization of religion as a particular aspect of life, these Asian teachings are more fluid and pervasive. They penetrate every part of life and are absorbed into other teachings. There are no social and religious boundaries unaffected.

Asian teachings are accepted as authoritative. They function canonically. Thus, no Shamanist, Buddhist, or Confucianist would question the credibility of his or her scriptures. The critical methods and hermeneutical approaches of Western academe are alien concepts to most adherents of these teachings. Instead, Koreans typically read their sacred texts repeatedly, memorize and recite them, and align their lives accordingly. The texts point to works of the spirits, the Truth, the Way, or the Principle of the universe. Studying a text is a stage of self-awakening or self-enlightenment. Textual meaning is revealed, not excavated. One meets reality beyond the text, not in critical analysis of it.

So as Jesuit and Protestant missionaries introduced the Bible into this socioreligious context, early Korean Christians approached the Bible as a religious text in the same manner as the other religious texts within Asian culture. Once they accepted it as sacred, the text was revered as the inspired Word of God, "the letter sent by God," and that from which they could hear God's voice, feel God's delights and sorrows, watch God's actions, and participate in God's life. This intimate embodiment of "teachings" wrought trust and obedience, not Western modes of critical study, historicism, or "scientific, detached and objective study" (Lee Moon-Jang, p. 281). Koreans immersed themselves in the Word of scripture until they could not distinguish themselves from the Word itself. Through reading, memorizing, reciting, and meditating on the Word, there was no dichotomy of text and reader. Koreans went beyond the linguistic, historical, and cultural conditions of the Bible and embodied its teachings for self-awakening. They ate and drank the Bible for nourishment to understand the relationships, history, and world that God created.

This intuitive reading of the Bible manifested itself in public collective interpretation and practices that continue today. Most well known is the one- to three-week-long *Sagyonghoe*, a collective intensive Bible study. Dating back to 1890 and institutionalized during the Great Revival of 1907, *Sagyonghoe* practice follows a standard pattern in which a lay leader or pastor interprets the texts only after individual and communal line-by-line readings, recitations, and acceptance of the text. The meeting includes the *Saebyok Kidohoe*, a daybreak prayer meeting of devotions, long prayers, and biblical exposition. These two rituals are integrated into the *Puhunghoe*, a revival meeting that played significantly into the phenomenal expansion of Christianity. Together these still shape normative Korean Christian worship services and daily life today.

Pre- and Early Translation of the Bible into the Korean Language (1780s–1911). The first full translation of the Bible into vernacular Korean (*Han Guel*) occurred in 1911 with revolutionary effect. Prior to this development, the Jesuit mission translated catechistic and devotional books into Korean. Simultaneously, Confucianists considered Christianity in light of their own sacred teachings and translated selected biblical passages into Chinese. The Jesuit instruction in Catholicism was labeled "western learning" and spread mainly among disaffected upper classes, who sought to reform the Confucian-based government with a new moral and spiritual belief system. Among the Confucianists, Yi Pyok was a leading figure of a pro-Christian Confucian group. His seminal work, "The Essence of Holy Teaching" (1779–86), drew on Old Testament texts in anticipation of a sage-king Jesus. And he rearranged New Testament selections to portray Jesus as an ideal person who fulfills human relationships completely and teaches the new way of "self-cultivation and governing of people"—typical Confucian scriptural themes. He recast the theocentric image of Jesus in the Bible as a Confucian anthropocentric image of master. In the same way, the Confucius's understanding of Taoist Truth or Ultimate Principle shifted from an investigation of things or accumulation of knowledge to an encounter with a person. Despite this fine example of Christian, Confucian, and Taoist cross-textual reading, this work had a limited effect on Catholics since he wrote in Chinese and did not engage the Bible entirely.

By contrast, Protestant missionaries began with the translation and distribution of the Bible in the Korean language. Prior to this, Confucian classics and Buddhist sacred texts were only available in Chinese for the benefit of the elite literati class (*Yang Ban*). These elites not only enjoyed the privileges of societal power but also disregarded Korean script altogether.

In such a divided society, the translation of the Bible into Korean was empowering for vast numbers of common people. Two brothers, Suh Sang-Yun and Suh Kyoung-Yun, converted in the course of their work with biblical translators J. Ross and J. Macintyre (1882–1887). This early work taught commoners Korean script via the Bible. Twin paths of empowerment followed. People gained literacy and embodied Christian teachings of justice and equality in their organization of local faith communities. This movement spread across Korea with the help of colporteurs and "the Bible women" who shared the gospel and participated in changing social structures (Park Jong-Chun, pp. 18–19). These early Korean Protestants were not satisfied with the teachings of self-enlightenment and moved from transformation of self to that of society. They appropriated the Bible in confronting the devastating politics of their time. Biblical translation helped revolutionize the function of Korean religious traditions.

From Biblical Translation to Interpretation amidst Turmoil (1912–1935). In the context of Japanese aggression and occupation, four prominent Korean biblical scholars presented textual interpretation methods that also empowered Koreans to challenge the Japanese colonizers. By the turn of the twentieth century, the long-standing Chosun dynasty, established in 1392, was crippled by its own internal discord. In the face of Japan's quest for economic-militaristic cultural hegemony, the Chosun forfeited Korean sovereignty to Japan from 1910 to 1945. During these 35 years, Japan seized more than 40 percent of Korean land, restricted the people's freedom of speech and publication, changed educational curricula, and eliminated the study of Korean language, culture, and history. In these oppressive times, Christian teachings with vernacular translations and literacy campaigns provided some interpretive, social, and political strength.

The first of four important theologians from this crucial period, Kil Sun-Joo (1869–1935), taught an interpretive method of biblical inerrancy as a means of spiritual renewal and pietism, as well as recovery of the Korean nation. Commonly considered the father of the Korean Church, Kil's cultivation of *Sagyonghoe*, *Saebyok Kidohoe*, and *Puhunghoe* embodied the principle of "let the Bible interpret itself." His teachings focused on the imminent second coming of Christ and normative behavior of repeated confessions, fervent prayer, and biblical literalism. Kil's teachings not only laid the foundation for Korean theological conservatism but also nurtured Korean identity vis-à-vis Japanese colonizers.

By contrast, the second leading theologian, Choi Byung-Hyun (1858–1927), wrestled with interreligious dialogue among ancient Korean religious traditions and the advent of Christianity. In his monumental work, "The Dialectic Relationship among Religious Traditions," published in Korea's first academic journal (*Shinhak Segye* [Theological World], 1916–1918), he argued for the supremacy of Christ rather than a new supreme religious tradition of Christianity. He posited that all religious traditions were cultural manifestations of divine activities in the created world. Christianity thus followed in a continuum of ancient religious phenomena. Still he set the distinguishing gospel truth of Christ as the criterion for determining the relative value of all religious traditions, including Christianity. For him, Christ was the fulfillment and completion of all truths. His focus was on the biblical testimony of Christ, not the defense of a new religion—Christianity—in opposition to other Asian teachings. Choi's teaching united rather than divided Koreans living under Japanese oppression.

The third of these theologians, Yang Joo-Sam (1879–?), was actually the first one trained as a biblical scholar. After studies at Vanderbilt and Yale, he became the first Korean editor of *Shinhak Segye*. In the seminal work, "The Comprehensive Summary of the Old and the New Testaments" (1916–1917), Yang rejected literal inspiration of the Bible, which was the standard belief of the time. Rather, he posited the absence of original biblical texts, the existence of numerous errors in manuscripts, and the complex history of composition and transmission of the text. Still he upheld the unique authority of the Christian Scripture on the basis of three unifying arguments for a nation under Japanese rule. First, the Bible presents a coherent theological theme of God's reconciliation with a broken world. Second, the Bible compels any reader to work for the well being of all humanity. And third, the Bible reveals a unique spiritual quality not found in other sacred texts. Yang argued that all available interpretive methods should help Koreans explicate the spiritual wisdom hidden in fallible human words. Consistent with Asian teachings, Yang posited that the Bible showed a path of obedient livelihood, not simply a religious book of study.

Finally, Namgung Hyuk (1882–?) taught the New Testament as the first Korean professor in Pyongyang Presbyterian Theological Seminary, established in 1901. His exegesis, published in another Korean academic journal, *Shinhak Jinam* (Direction of Theology, 1928–1938), concentrated on authorial intent through intratextual studies. His construct of Pauline theology was continuous with the teachings of

Jesus and the entire New Testament, presenting a coherent and unified theological message.

Regardless of these four theologian's interpretive principles—whether biblical inerrancy, inter-religious dialogue, or the authority and unity of the Bible—their greatest contribution to the emerging Korean Church was the provision of ways for Korean Christians to deal with Japanese occupation. These diverse methods of biblical interpretation empowered lay people to change their perceptions of their current political situation, and helped shape their dream of an independent nation once again. In particular, Kil Sun-Joo, despite being influenced by the nonpolitical engagement policy of Western missionaries, joined the independence movement and was one of the thirty-three signatories of the Declaration of Independence in 1919.

Decades of Controversy (1935–1950s). From 1930–1945, as Japan colonized Korea and then waged war on China, the United States, and other Allied forces, Korean Christians struggled with their own identity, leadership, and interpretation of the Bible. As part of its militarism, Japan forced Koreans to assume Japanese names, expunge Korean language in school, worship at Shinto shrines, and swear loyalty to Japan for all ages. Soon after Japan's unconditional surrender in 1945, Korea was divided according to the political maneuvering of three Cold War powers—the United States, the Soviet Union, and China. The north and south of Korea then endured a civil war from 1950–1953. At this time of particular peril and need, the Christian Church lost societal authority and leadership. It also split internally over biblical interpretive methods, gender, and denominationalism. Increasing numbers of well-trained Korean theologians authored biblical translations and commentaries but found they were at the vortex of a church divided over three lines of biblical interpretation: literalism and inerrancy, critical historical methods, and liberal existentialism.

Most prominent among these three lines of interpretation was a vigorous defense of biblical literalism. Denying the validity of higher criticism of the Bible, Byun Hong-Gyu (1899–1976) espoused the first and most popular of these lines of interpretation, the doctrine of plenary inspiration. By this understanding, God spoke directly to the human authors of the Bible and thus no errors existed in God's communication. Byun used the concept of holiness to understand the God of the Bible: ritual (Torah), ethical (Prophets), personal (Writings), and spiritual (New Testament). He argued for the unity of these four bodies of literature in the Old and New Testaments in terms of God's salvific act in Christ.

Park Hyeung-Ryong (1897–1979) went further to advocate the theological position of verbal plenary inspiration, which he derived from the Princeton Theological Seminary debate that had instigated antimodernist fundamentalism in the United States. Park defended the inspired nature of all of scripture, including statements of scientific, historical, or geographical fact. He insisted that "doing theology in the Korean Church meant not creating something new, but continuing to uphold the apostolic traditions [i.e., teachings of the early missionaries]" (Sebastian C. H. Kim 2008, p. 133). His methods are reflected in the work of Park Yun-Sun (1905–1989), who completed commentaries on all sixty-six books of the Bible. In these, he followed an interpretive principle that "the Bible ought to be interpreted by the Bible." No external scholarly disputes were pertinent to Park's commentaries. He also provided more than one thousand homilies addressing current issues before the Korean churches. Such a literalist approach to biblical interpretation remains in tune with the Korean ethos of religious teachings and a source of spiritual comfort for the majority of Korean Christians today.

The second line of biblical interpretation was the historical-critical method championed by Kim Chai-Choon (1901–1987), for whom biblical content determined its inspired status, not the other way around. Since there is a personal relationship between God and humanity, the Bible is best understood as the record of that dialogue between God and the world, as written by inspired humans. The eternal life-giving Word of God was, therefore, expressed in temporal, cultural, and historical terms by these biblical authors. Kim's ultimate task for biblical interpretation was to make God's Word alive to his contemporaries. For this, he concentrated on the Prophets, especially Amos, Isaiah, and Jeremiah, through whose writing Kim depicts the God at work in Israel's history as also at work in the unjust political and ideological turmoil of Kim's own time. Kim faced three challenges. First, there was militant opposition to his historical-critical methods within the Korean Church. Second, he struggled to awaken the historical conscience of Korean Christians whose fundamentalist theology was apolitical. And third, he wrote prophetically in an age of Cold War parameters of militarism and dictatorship.

A third line of biblical interpretation was the liberal-existentialism proposed by Jung Kyung-Ok (1903–1945). For Jung, the "liberal" label did not refer to a particular theological system but to a theological tendency encouraging continual reformulation of biblical truth within specific cultural and historical contexts. He understood the Bible as one of many ways in which God's saving act in Christ has been revealed. God is bigger than the God described in the Bible. This magnanimous God speaks not only through the Bible but also other cultures and history. He employed various critical methods for interpretation since the Bible is a collection of the testimonies of Israel and the early Church, which belong to the wider general stream of religious literature. Still he sought to discover the spiritual wisdom and vitality of each biblical author, not simply some cognitive knowledge. Without this existential dimension, reading the Bible would only be an intellectual exercise.

The internal church struggle among fundamentalists and historical-critical interpreters played out among Korean Presbyterians, resulting in separate conservative and progressive denominations by 1953. Meanwhile, the third approach, represented by Jung, laid a firm doctrinal basis for the Korean Methodist denomination. Jung's work, "The Principle of Christianity" (1935), influenced the efforts of Yang Joo-Sam (scholar of historical methods), Ryu Hyung-Ki (chief editor for the Korean translation of the Abingdon Bible Commentary), and Choi Byung-Hyun (advocate for inter-religious dialogue). Jung's acceptance of "general revelation" encouraged future Methodist theologians to engage passionately in the dialogue of Christians, Korean traditional religious traditions, and a variety of other religious experiences.

Decades of Contextualization (1960–1980). The devastating Korean War and its aftermath shaped new strains of biblical interpretation for a people whose country was torn asunder by harsh political and socioeconomic turmoil. No period in Korean history had ever experienced so much change so fast. Not surprisingly, this wrought profound shifts in Korean Christian hermeneutics. Quite surprisingly, the defining significance of this change is fully appreciated neither inside nor outside of Korea. First war, then postwar rebuilding, and now modern identification with struggle and suffering created a distinctive Korean-ness to biblical interpretation.

In the wake of civil and international war, there was no clear political or military resolution by 1953. More than five million people died and more than ten million families were separated. The nation's economy was ruined. No less a jolt of change was the ensuing South Korean postwar economic growth from 1960–1980. A series of four 5-year economic development plans and considerable US economic, military, and infrastructural "Cold War support" spurred South Korea's exponential growth. The national per capita income spiked from $75 to $1,000. But national averages concealed gaps between rich and poor. These two decades of postwar dynamism wrought wealth and birthed a new middle class, but so too they witnessed deplorable workers' conditions, pervasive political corruption, rapid urbanization, ruptured traditional family structure and core values, ever-present competition and anxiety, and recurrent student and citizen protests. In such contentious times, what religious traditions and means of textual interpretation prove useful, even salvific? While the majority of Korean Christians understandably upheld the Bible as normative and authoritative, a growing minority viewed the Bible as a reference point for further engagement with other religious traditions, an unearthed Korean spirituality, cruel socioeconomic conditions among laborers, and rampant political turmoil.

Chief among these struggles was the unbearable reality of poverty, which compelled distinctly different biblical interpretations of how marginalized people embedded in a context of oppression and suffering may relate to God. Interpretative solutions ranged from gospels of plentitude, to those of spirituality, and to diverse interpretations of *minjung*, which takes as its hermeneutical key the particular situation of oppression. One new strand began with the prosperity gospel of Cho Yong-Gi (b. 1936), who focused on biblical passages underscoring material blessing. As founder of the Full Gospel Church, the world's largest congregation with one million members as of 2007, Cho interpreted the Bible as a portrait of a God who grants spiritual salvation, bodily health, and material wealth for believers. This interpretation of tangible blessing spread widely across denominations. It provided a sense of comfort amidst harsh reality and prompted visions of a better life here and now. It drew on shamanistic beliefs that the spirits (especially those of dead ancestors) determine what happens in the present temporal world. This interpretation added to the already conservative reading of the Bible in the Korean Church, but with stronger antihistorical emphases than fundamentalism.

On the other hand, several theologians took spirituality as their hermeneutical key to contextualize "Korean" theologies. Ryu Dong-Sik (b. 1922) interpreted the New Testament, especially the Gospel of John, in light of his understanding of Korean spirit. This spirituality consists of three elements—*Han*, *Myeut*, *Sam*. Each persists in the lives of Korean people despite changes of religious traditions. For Ryu, *Han* refers to the essence of the universe. *Myeut* is the aesthetic excitement that arises from inner strength and quality. And *Sam* is culturally creative and productive living. Ryu posits that these three elements culminate in Christ. Jesus as Logos shares the essence of God (*Han*), is a full human being (*Myeut*), and unites divinity and humanity through his self-denial (*Sam*). In Christ's life, death, and resurrection, Koreans may fulfill their spirit. The gospel as proclaimed to Koreans is planted in the Korean soil of struggle, and now matures as an integral part of their identity.

Another contextualization comes from Yun Sung-Bum (1916–1980), who saw Korean Confucianism as the starting point of his theology. For him, the three concepts of Confucianism—*Hyou* (justification = righteousness), *In* (sanctification = love), and *Seong* (sincerity = Christian perfection)—are united as is the triune Christian God. This concept of a triune God reinforced the implied trinity of the ancient Korean national mythologies of the divine figures *Hwanin*, *Hwanung*, and *Dangun*. The three-in-one relationship is the authentic nature of humanity and is manifested in Christ. Jesus as Logos is the son of *Seong* or *Seong* itself. Similar to Ryu, the theology of Yun is based on the Gospel of John. Still Yun goes further to argue that the unchangeable gospel truth has always been embedded in Korean religious traditions, though it has only recently been unveiled.

Still other theologians have used the deplorable socioeconomic conditions of marginalized laborers as the starting point of biblical interpretations. For them, the Bible attends to the life stories, traditions, and histories of *minjung*, which are the common ordinary people who are socially isolated, economically exploited, politically oppressed, and culturally alienated in Korean history. Thus, Suh Nam-Dong (1918–1984) interpreted the entire testimony of the Bible in terms of the two historical events, the Exodus and the Crucifixion-Resurrection—each an account of God's intervention in the political and socioeconomic *minjung* history of humanity. These two liberating events progress from a one-off event of a particular people (the Israelites) to the model (Jesus event) that is perpetually emulated. Since Jesus identified himself with *minjung*, his death and resurrection are understood as the beginning of the death and resurrection of all *minjung* throughout history. Suh traces this eternal revolutionary event of God in Christ throughout Korean history of struggle and suffering such as the *Tonghak* movement of peasants rising up against landlords, government, and foreign powers (1894), the 1 March Independence movement against Japan (1919), and the 19 April Student Revolution that toppled the autocratic regime of Rhee Syng-Man (1960).

Several biblical scholars wrestled with *minjung* exegetically. Against the traditional historical-critical interpretation of the Gospel of Mark, Ahn Byung-Mu (1922–1996) underscored three significant points. First, the term *ochlos* denotes a marginalized social class of tax collectors, prostitutes, and the destitute. This *ochlos* is the central group of people surrounding the historical Jesus. Second, the *ochlos* group witnessed the Jesus event and expressed their own suffering and hope through his passion. Third, Jesus the Messiah shared the suffering of the *ochlos*, and they struggled together to usher in God's kingdom on earth. These led Ahn to conclude that the Gospel of Mark depicts a social biography of Jesus, not his personal life, death, and resurrection. The relationship between Jesus and the *ochlos* is analogous to the recurring presence of Christ among the Korean *minjung*. In their embodied interpretation of Jesus's passion, the *minjung* reclaim place, reconstruct identity, and become subjects of history.

Moon Hee-Suk (b. 1933) sees *minjung* subjectivity in his analysis of the exodus. The *habiru* (or Hebrews) were *minjung* of their time, confronting the oppression and injustices of the Egyptian Pharaohs. They were active participants in God's liberating acts and not just victims of oppression. Still Moon also identifies the unconscious passivity among *habiru minjung* when they balk in the costly course of liberation, pushing back against Moses's leadership and wavering in rising up to be subjects of their own destiny. Moon concludes that "human history should be of the *minjung*, by the *minjung*, and for the *minjung*, for they are the subjects of history" (Moon Hee-Suk 1985, p. 73).

Identifying an even broader *minjung* paradigm in the Bible, Kim Jeong-Joon (1914–1981) interprets the entire Old Testament from *minjung* perspective. He reads the Pentateuch as a summary of the confession of politically and economically oppressed wandering Israelites who seek God's protection and salvation. In the historical and prophetic books, he examines the social situation of the downtrodden. Even in the Wisdom literature, he attends to the life of *minjung*. So the Psalms of lamentation are the cries of *minjung* people with concrete struggles. Moreover, the book of Job exemplifies the suffering of the innocent, righteous, and powerless. And Proverbs provides antidotes for how *minjung* may live as subjects in their place in society.

In sum, *minjung* biblical interpretations take the socioeconomic and political realities of suffering in Korean society as the hermeneutical key, and regard the Bible as a reference of historical support for such interpretations. Methodologically they share common traits with liberation-focused interpretations in that they are inductive, descriptive, and biographical in narrating the stories of any *minjung*'s experiences of God. Yet their "Korean-ness" lies in the particularity of the content that they are not interpretations "of" Korea, but "for" Korean *minjung*. In other words, their "Korean-ness" does not depend on their hermeneutical originality so much as on their ability to address the localized, nationalistic *minjung* reality of Korea.

Reconfigurations of *minjung* Interpretations (1980–present). Over the last three decades, *minjung* interpretations have proliferated. While the wealthy elite and burgeoning middle class of South Korean society have enjoyed the "miracle on the Han River," signifying unprecedented postwar economic growth, all Koreans have had to endure harsh authoritarianism. Postwar governance denied democracy and appeased only a small constituency of the military elite. Wealth was not distributed fairly by *jaebuls*, the family-run industrial, monopolistic conglomerates backed by the central bank and government policies. The *jaebuls* and the military used the uncertain state of ceasefire with North Korea to quash dissent.

Material comfort in lieu of political freedom and spiritual well being continued until 1997. While the Asian financial crisis swept across many states, this economic meltdown sparked a South Korean pursuit of justice and reunification with the North. Even a few years earlier, the presidential change from former military generals to political activists in 1993 rekindled national policies seeking reunification.

Since the late 1990s, diverse *minjung* interpretations take as their starting point class-consciousness, gender, and reunification of North and South Korea. Theologians Park Sung-Joon and Kang Won-Don employed Marxist theory in identifying the working class as *minjung*. These theologians posit that the class of *minjung* must establish more just relations in material production. Such a Marxist-driven interpretation would revolutionize both society and the established church. Taking this argument a step further, theologian Kim Jin-Ho identifies *minjung* as all victims of globalization. The borderless flow of global capital creates severe imbalances in the distribution of goods, opportunities, and costs. Together, these interpretations are more theoretical than earlier *minjung* interpretations grounded in Korean history and the Bible narrative. Significant exegetical work from these theologians is yet to be seen.

Other scholars pay particular attention to the *minjung* of the *minjung*, the women of Korea. *Han* is a term that depicts the deep-seated anger and sadness that rises from prolonged oppression and exploitation. While *han* speaks to the general condition of *minjung*, it describes more acutely the layered oppression endured by Korean women in their struggle within the sexism of Confucianism and Asian society, let alone the limited roles they were allowed within the Korean Church. Feminist interpretations of *minjung* are explored through in the *Ewha*'s (the first university for women in Korea) *Journal of Feminist Theology*. It has devoted issues to *minjung* methodology and content, ranging from postcolonial perspectives to the "comfort women" sexual slavery of World War II. Importantly, Lee Kyung-Sook and Park Kyung-Mi note that these feminist interpretations find life-affirming, empowering *minjung* hermeneutics for all, and not just women.

Perhaps most striking (and potentially unifying) of all *minjung* interpretations is that which sees all of Korea—the people of the North and the South—as the oppressed, exploited, dominated, divided, and manipulated objects of external Cold War ideology. All Koreans suffered. More than 5 million casualties and 10 million separated families are just part of the pathos of a peripheral war zone of global forces and beliefs. Since 1953, the people of both Koreas have endured their respective government's indoctrination that each side of the Korean DMZ (Demilitarized Zone) faces its worst enemy, even though both peoples are of the same blood, culture, and history. Addressing the need for peaceful national reunification, Yim Tae-Soo (b. 1944) draws this lesson from the entire history of ancient Israel. For him, the Deuteronomistic accounting of the failure of Israel and Judah to reunify when they depended on the military might of foreign powers does not suit the Korean context. Rather, the model of Chronicles builds on notions of "all Israel," brotherly love," and one God for both Judah and Israel, even if they were divided. The Chronicles' postexilic construction of an ideal Israel is similar to the prophets' vision of a unified Israel (Isa 11:11–16; Hos 1:10–11; Jer 3:18; Ezek 37:15–28). This provides a positive trajectory for Korean reunification efforts.

Still other scholars, such as Min Young-Jin, Kang Sa-Moon, Ahn Byung-Mu, and Lee Kyung-Sook, turn to the concept of Jubilee in Leviticus 25 as a biblical foundation for peaceful reunification. Although they do not explain how all of Korean state-societal relations would adopt this conviction shared by just some of the 30 percent of Koreans who adhere to Christian beliefs, these theologians contend that a Korean Jubilee would acknowledge the following points and steps: God owns the land; reunification relies on the sovereignty of God; as a covenant people of God, Korean Christians must confess their hand in letting the nation be divided since 1953; as the slaves are liberated, Koreans must be liberated from the bondage of ideological, political, and military hostility toward each other; as debts are cancelled, the privileged must yield their vested interests for poorer neighbors; as the next kin plays a crucial role for family restoration, all people must participate actively in the decision-making process for the rebuilding the society; and as the unity of Israel society is restored, both Koreas must work together for reconciliation of the people and formation of one nation that shares a common identity and fate.

Clearly, the concept of *minjung* is multidimensional. As a new generation of *minjung* theologians expands the concept of *minjung* in this era of globalization, the Korean Church may address their society more holistically, including the plight of unemployed laborers, foreign migrant workers, those underserved by social welfare, and others facing ecological crises.

Korean Interpretation Still in the Making. Biblical interpretation in Korea remains traditionally *Wissenschaft* in its shape and scope because the majority of Korean biblical scholars studied in the West. They continue to introduce, refine, and engage in western academic enterprises. However, vestiges of particular "Korean-ness" arise in their collective work as they share a basic attitude toward the Bible. Ingrained in Korean norms of how to read the teachings of ancient religious traditions, these biblical scholars begin from the vantage point of the Bible's sacredness. They proceed with a combination of contemplative reflection and critical analysis. Their end product often nurtures believers as if they are the children of God on this life journey. So as diverse as the aforementioned trajectories of biblical exegesis are, they nonetheless create a tapestry of Korean interpretation.

For further study, one must investigate how these trajectories have related to one another over recent decades. As the back of a tapestry shows incongruous colors and strands of threads, the continuing discourse of these interpretive paths would helpfully consider the following. Was the dominant tendency of literal reading of the Bible influenced by Ryu Dong-Sik's and/or Ahn Byung-Mu's preference to take Korean spirit and economic condition as the starting points of interpretation? Why does Yi Pyok's cross-textual interpretation and reconceptualization of Confucian texts and the Bible not continue? Can *minjung* interpretations pay attention to the other *minjung* embedded in the story? So in the case of the exodus event, the true *minjung* were the people of the Canaanites, Hittites, the Amorites, the Perizzites, the Hivites, and the Jebusites, whose homes and lives the God of the Israelites destroyed? Such considerations may provide a clearer picture of Korean interpretation, just as the front side of this tapestry reveals creative art already in process.

[*See also* Asian American Biblical Interpretation; Chinese Interpretation; Cross-Cultural Exegesis; Cultural Studies; Liberation Hermeneutics; Postcolonial Biblical Interpretation; Race, Ethnicity, and Biblical Criticism; *and* Theological Interpretation.]

Bibliography

Ahn, Byung-Mu. "Jesus and the Minjung in the Gospel of Mark." In *Minjung Theology: People as the Subject of History*, edited by the Commission on Theological Concerns of the Christian Conference of Asia, 138–152. Toa Payoh, Singapore: Christian Conference of Asia, 1981.

Cheon, Samuel. "Biblical Interpretation in Korea: History and Issues." In *Ways of Being, Ways of Reading: Asian American Biblical Interpretation*, edited by Mary F. Foskett and Jeffrey Kah-Jin Kuan, 31–44. St. Louis, MO: Chalice, 2006.

Hwang, Jae-Buhm. "Rev. Kil Sŏn-ju's Theology Emphasizing Spiritual Endeavor, Revivalism and Biblical Inerrancy: Commemorating the Centenary of the Great Revival of 1907 in P'yŏngyang." *Acta Koreana* 10, no. 2 (2007): 101–119.

Kang, Sa-Moon. "*Kwangbok 50 Junyun (1995) ae daehan Heenyunbupjuk Jeokyong Moonjae* (A Study on how to apply the concept of biblical Jubilee to the fiftieth year of Korean liberation (1955) from Japanese colonization." *Jangshin Nondan* 11 (1995): 50–80.

Kim, Chai-Choon. "*Moonja Younggamsulgwa Sungsuh Muohsul* (Regarding verbal inspiration and biblical inerrancy)." *Shipjagoon* 3 (1950): 12–23.

Kim, In-Soo. "*Taksa Choi Byung-hyunui Kidockkyowa Jaere Jonggyuwaui Daewhae Dahan Yungu* (A Study on Religious Dialogue between Christianity and Traditional Religions according to Taksa Choi Byung-hyun)." *Jangshin Nondan* 25 (2006): 35–68.

Kim, Jeong-Joon. "*Minjung Shinhakui Gooyak Sungshujuk Geunguh* (References of Old Testament for Minjung Theology)." *Shinhak Sasang* 24 (1979): 5–32.

Kim, Sebastian C. H. "The Word and the Spirit: Over-Coming Poverty, Injustice and Division in Korea." In *Christian Theology in Asia*, edited by Sebastian C. H. Kim, 129–153. Cambridge, UK: Cambridge University Press, 2008.

Lee, Kyung-Sook, "The Biblical Hermeneutics of Liberation from the Perspective of Asian Christian Women: Recovering the Liberation-Tradition of early Christianity." In *Feminist Interpretation of the Bible and the Hermeneutics of Liberation*, edited by Silvia Schroer and Sophia Bietenhard, 164–170. London; New York: Sheffield Academic Press, 2003.

Lee, Mahn-Yol. "Korean Protestants and the Reunification Movement." In *Christianity in Korea*, edited by Robert E. Buswell Jr. and Timothy S. Lee, 238–257. Honolulu, HI: University of Hawai'i Press, 2006.

Lee, Moon-Jang. "A Post Critical Reading of the Bible as a Religious Text." *Asian Journal of Theology* 14, no. 2 (2000): 272–285.

Lee, Whan-Jin, "*Heachun Yun Sung-Byum kyusuui Hyowa Hebrew Sungsuhui Tochakwhah* (Relationship between Heachun Yun Sung-Byum's thought on Hyo and contextualization of the Hebrew Bible)." *Shinhakgwa Segye* 55 (2006): 5–36.

Lee, Yeong-Mee. "A Political Reception of the Bible: Korean Minjung Theological Interpretation of the Bible." October 2005. http://sbl-site.org//Article.aspx?ArticleID=457.

Moon, Cyris H. S. *A Korean Minjung Theology: An Old Testament Perspective*. Maryknoll, NY: Plough Publications, 1985.

Park, Jong-Chun. *Crawl with God, Dance in the Spirit! A Creative Formation of Korean Theology of the Spirit*. Nashville, TN: Abingdon Press, 1998.

Park, Yun-Sun. "*Sungkyungui kwonwii* (The authority of the Bible)." *Shinhak Jinam* 19 (1971): 6–19.

Ryu, Dong-Sik. *Hankook Shinhakui Gwangmaek* (The Treasure Veins of Korean Theology). Rev. ed. Seoul: Dasan Geulbang, 2000. The first edition was published in 1982.

Yang, Guen-Seok. "A Pre-critical Reading of the Bible in Korea: Its Hermeneutical and Methodological Implications." *CTC Bulletin* 16, no. 1 (1999): 12–29.

Yang, Joo-Sam. "*Gooshinyak Jeonsuh Chongron* (The Comprehensive Summary of the Old and New Testament)." *Shinhak Segye* (1916–1917): 69–88.

Yim, Tae-Soo. "*Sungkyungeul tonghae bon Tongilui Dangwiisung* (Biblical Justification for the Reunification)." *Mokhwaewah Shinhak* 43 (1993): 56–65.

Won W. Lee

L

Latina/o Interpretation

There is no single definition that can explain the totality of what Latina/o interpretation means. In the broadest sense, however, the term can refer to a variety of critical approaches undertaken by members of the Latina/o community who consciously utilize their *latinidad* as a hermeneutical lens to reread the Bible, usually with the intention of subverting totalitarian readings, advancing liberating and inclusive interpretations, and bringing about social and political transformation. As such, Latina/o interpretation is better characterized as a focus of analysis than as a particular methodology. The variety of approaches and reading strategies used and advanced by Latina/o interpreters mirrors the multiculturalism of the Latina/o community. Therefore, to fully appreciate the fluidity of methodologies, reading strategies, and hermeneutical perspectives used in Latina/o interpretation, one must understand the history of the Latina/o community and the origin of its name.

Name and History of the Community. "Latina/o" and "Hispanic" are the two main ethnonyms that have been in use since the 1980s to categorize the collective of inhabitants of the United States who can trace their historical and cultural roots to either Spain or the twenty Spanish-speaking countries from Latin America, including Puerto Rico. Although the two terms have been used interchangeably by the media, and there is extensive documentation arguing in favor of both, there is no consensus within the Hispanic/Latina/o population about which ethnonym better describes the community. The ongoing debate stresses the artificiality of both terms, their limitation to convey the complexity of the community and, to an extent, the sense that both are exonyms, externally imposed labels by the government or another segment of the population for the sake of politically identifying an amorphous ethnic group that seems to defy categorization. In fact, the first time the name Hispanic was officially used was during the 1980 census, when the US government established it to refer to people in the United States whose cultural or historical roots can be traced to Spain and the Spanish-speaking countries in Latin America. The new name was not well received by the liberal population. For many it was an offensive reminder of the colonial past of Latin America under the imperial power of Spain, originally named Hispania. Soon after it emerged, a new term began to circulate as an act of self-naming: Latino, a political alternative to the name Hispanic. By the 2000 census the name Latino was added to the ethnic category list: Spanish/Hispanic/Latino. Both terms, Hispanic and Latina/o, have continued to be scrutinized regarding their social, cultural, and political implications. Latino has transitioned into an intentionally gender-inclusive term adding the feminine ending "a" to Latina/o. Some differentiate the names by using Latina/o to refer to those born or raised and educated in the United States, as opposed to Hispanic to refer to those born or raised and educated in Latin America or Spain. Latinas/os, by and large, have experienced what it means to be a member of a socially and politically minoritized group, while Hispanics might have had a different experience of minoritization, growing up as part of the majority status in their countries of origin. Latina/o refers to those inhabitants in the United States who exclusively trace their cultural and historical roots to the Spanish-speaking countries of Latin America; it is a self-adopted name that intentionally cuts the colonial-imperial ties with Spain. Hispanic as a term continues to be used, and it is the choice of the conservative population on the East Coast. Of course, these categories are fluid and permeable, a fact that becomes evident when we review the life of real, flesh-and-blood Hispanics/Latinas/os. It is important to mention that most Latinas/os, when asked to self-identify themselves, usually tend to use their country of origin: Mexican American, Puerto Rican, Cuban American, Ecuadorian American, and so on.

History. Latina/o, as an all-encompassing ethnic label, includes people from a great variety of cultural backgrounds, nationalities, belief systems, religious practices, political affiliations, economic statuses, physical constitutions, complexions, educational systems, and other identity markers. There are no common visible identity markers that could help to differentiate or associate all Latinas/os as belonging to the community. Equally, the experiences of discrimination and marginalization often seen as a common ground within the Latina/o community are experiences that not all Latinas/os have lived. In fact, there are those who have never embraced their *latinidad* just to avoid rejection. Another important experience that makes it impossible to simplify the reality of the Latina/o community in the United States is the experience of immigration. There are many ways, documented and undocumented, to gain entry into the United States and many reasons for coming, and all of them have significant influence in the way Latinas/os relate to this country. Some have come to the country as political refugees, others for professional advancement, economic survival, to save their lives from persecution due to their religious beliefs or sexual preferences, to seek medical treatment, to reunite with family, or to seek an advanced education. Others never traveled: the border simply moved and they became part of the US population. There are countless other reasons and stories of immigration, many of them painful and violent, others joyful and full of hope. All of them have become crucial memories for the Latina/o community.

Another major force that has contributed in shaping the perceptions and representations of the Latina/o community is the political history between the United States and Latin America. A brief account of some of the main episodes of this political history can illuminate the emotional and ideological scars that have been imprinted in the cultural memory of the Latina/o community. The first critical event of the US-Latin American political history happened in 1848 when, guided by the ideology of a Manifest Destiny, the United States invaded Mexico and, through the Treaty of Guadalupe Hidalgo, annexed half of the Mexican territory and its inhabitants. This violent act has forever marked the identity of the Mexican Americans, Chicanos, and Latinas/os of Mexican descent. It has also affected US-Mexico political relations and their uncreative immigration policies that fail to acknowledge the deep interdependency of these two nations and how they need to work together for mutual economic and political survival. Too many lives have been lost at the borderlands; too much money has been wasted to guard and protect a border that should be a source of life, not death.

Fifty years later, in 1898, following the Spanish-US War and the Treaty of Paris, the United States gained temporary control of Cuba and annexed Puerto Rico, Guam, and the Philippines. Through this expansionist move, Puerto Ricans became US citizens in 1917, but they have been granted limited power as citizens since they cannot vote in presidential elections. This unique partial and ambiguous relationship that began with the annexation of the island has deeply marked the tentative and ever-changing relationships of the United States and Puerto Ricans. A few years later, in 1902, Cuba gained independence, but through the Platt Amendment signed in 1903, the United States acquired a perpetual lease of Guantánamo Bay to establish an American naval base. Years later, in 1961, the Bay of Pigs Invasion would also forever leave its mark in the Cuban-US affairs, fracturing the relations of the Latina/o Cuban community and their relatives who remained living in the island.

Between 1912 and 1973, four of the most brutal and oppressive tyrannies emerged after the US invasions to Dominican Republic, Nicaragua, Guatemala, and Chile. This brief chronological review of the political history of the United States and Latin America shows some of the historical scars and wounds that have marked their relationships and consequently have influenced the ways in which the Latina/o population is perceived and treated in the United States. Haunted by memories of political upheaval, invasions, dispossessions, exploitation, and oppression, minoritized Latina/o groups have struggled to make sense of their identity, their foreign context, and their hopes of a better world.

Models of Latina/o Interpretation. As a postmodern interpretive lens, Latina/o interpretation encompasses a variety of critical approaches undertaken by members of the Latina/o community. Latinas/os consciously engage in a continuous theorization of the self, critically defining their social and ideological location as members of the minoritized group in the United States who elect to use their self-defined *latinidad* as a hermeneutical lens to reread the Bible and reinvent society. With such politicized identity, forged in the heat of violent imperial wars, invasions, oppressive regimes, and exclusionary labels, it is no surprise that Latina/o interpretations of the Bible seek to confront totalitarian and imperializing readings, advance liberating and inclusive interpretations, and promote social and political transformation. The following hermeneutical models and reading strategies exemplify some of the diverse ways in which Latina/o scholars have been interpreting the Bible since the late 1970s.

A Hermeneutics of *Mestizaje*.

The Galilean Journey—*Virgilio Elizondo*. Bravely evoking the violent act of the Spanish-Indian *mestizaje* that gave birth to the *raza mestiza* of Latin America, Virgilio Elizondo chooses the concept of *mestizaje* (from *mestizo*, meaning mixed) as interpretive key to reread the Gospels and the mixed identity of the Mexican American community. Elizondo's theology of *mestizaje* comprises a pastoral theology grounded in the Mexican American experience of the borderlands between the United States and Mexico, a site of rupture and violence.

As a Latino theologian writing at the end of the 1970s, when the ethnic labels "Hispanic" and "Latina/o" had not yet joined the political conversations, Elizondo identifies himself as a Mexican American, born from Mexican parents in San Antonio, Texas. He acknowledges how his experience of mixture, being bilingual and bicultural in the context of the American Southwest, has historically and culturally conditioned the way he reads the Bible, particularly the Gospels. As a Roman Catholic priest, deeply committed to his Mexican American community, a community struggling for survival in the midst of discrimination from a society that perceives them as inferior because of their *mestizaje*, Elizondo wonders what to do about the future of his community. Then, propelled by the firm conviction that the identity and mission of the Mexican American people can be ennobled and strengthened through the identity and mission of Jesus of Nazareth, he develops his theology of *mestizaje:* an identity map and a call to action for his community to become agents of historical change by embracing Jesus's life as a model for social transformation.

Deliberately reading as a Mexican American, Elizondo re-theorizes the concept of *mestizaje*, a term usually associated with violence, suffering, and marginalization, into an empowering concept that speaks of new possibilities, prophetic power, new creation, and a source of unity. Working from a hermeneutics of *mestizaje*, Elizondo develops his reading strategy and theological model of *Galilean Journey* to not only reinterpret the Bible through the life of Jesus but also to reinterpret the life of the

Mexican American community in light of the identity and mission of Jesus, the Galilean *mestizo*. In this process, Elizondo calls for a serious cultural rereading of the Gospels from a historical perspective to discover how Jesus of Nazareth functioned in relation to his history and culture. Only by discovering how he functioned then, as a borderland reject in a *mestiza* Galilee, will we discover how he might function today, as a *mestizo* Mexican American living in the junction between Anglo-America and Latin America. By keeping in mind the present-day faith community during the reading process, the reader can find areas of convergence and divergence between the life of Jesus and the life of the local church, allowing Jesus to come alive in the faith community.

From his hermeneutics of *mestizaje*, Elizondo distinguishes three guiding principles in the life of Jesus that constitute the Galilean journey: (1) his Galilean identity, (2) the confrontation in Jerusalem as he goes there to die, and (3) the victory of the resurrection. From Jesus's Galilean identity, Elizondo derives the Galilee principle: "what human beings reject, God chooses as his very own" (1983, p. 91). Galilee, a region that experienced many invasions, was geographically located at a crossroads for international travel routes. The Galileans were continually exposed to diverse cultures and world trade; it was a cosmopolitan region. Because of its complex mixture and hybridity, Galilee became a symbol of rejection. When Mexican American Christians reread their identity in light of the cultural identity of Jesus the Galilean, the meaning of their cultural identity becomes clear. Their *mestizaje* becomes their Galilean identity and challenge. In Elizondo's second principle, "God chooses an oppressed people, not to bring them comfort in their oppression, but to enable them to confront, transcend, and transform whatever in the oppressor society diminishes and destroys the fundamental dignity of human nature" (p. 103). Jesus's liberating ministry did not stop in Galilee; he had to go to Jerusalem to culminate his mission. It is there that he faces and challenges the oppressive structures of his time. The call his Galileans followers received is the same call that his followers receive today to go with him and challenge the Jerusalems of today. In these days Mexican Americans are called by this principle to challenge oppressive systems and liberate those who are enslaved by oppressive structures, such as racism and liberal capitalism, to build a better society (p. 111). Elizondo's third principle, that of the resurrection, suggests that "only love can triumph over evil, and no human power can prevail against the power of unlimited love. Out of suffering and death, God will bring health and life" (p. 115). When Jesus concluded his ministry by confronting Jerusalem, he was willing to go all the way, even to the cross. If liberation is to become a reality, Mexican Americans have no other choice than to confront the Jerusalems of today. Elizondo affirms that by accepting and following Jesus, the *mestizo* Galilean, the Mexican American *mestizos* living in the borderland between Anglo-America and Latin America will be able to bring unity between the people of the Americas. Only by breaking away from negative stereotypes will they be able to unite and work for the common good. The principles of *Galilean Journey* offer to help in the transformation process of society by giving a new reading strategy of the Bible and a model to rejuvenate the reality of the Mexican American community.

Based on a hermeneutics of faith and liberation, Elizondo's theological and interpretive model is an invitation to the Mexican American community to use the life of Jesus as a powerful source for understanding their marginalized identity and claim it with pride. Their *mestizaje* is their Galilean identity. Ultimately, what Elizondo offers to his community through his hermeneutical model is a way of living, of fully embracing their identity as Mexican Americans, as contemporary marginalized Galileans who are called to embrace their mission of confronting the oppressive systems of society and bring about a better world.

Hermeneutics of *la lucha*.

Mujerista Biblical Interpretation—Ada María Isasi-Díaz. Grounded in a liberation hermeneutics of *la lucha* (struggle), *mujerista* biblical interpretation is the reading strategy of *mujerista* theology, a grassroots theology initially developed under the rubric "Hispanic women's liberation theology" in the mid 1980s by Ada María Isasi-Díaz, a pioneer of Hispanic/Latina/o theologies. Isasi-Díaz immigrated to the United States as a political refugee from Cuba in 1960 at the beginning of a decade that would have a profound effect in her theological work, particularly the last three years of which she spent working as a missionary among the poor and oppressed in Peru. From her missionary experience she learned to respect and admire the religious understandings and practices of the poor and oppressed whose lives were a constant struggle (*lucha*) to survive the everyday (*lo cotidiano*) hardships. These experiences, as well as her work with Gustavo Gutiérrez, founder of liberation theology, became the foundation of her *mujerista* theology.

As an activist theologian committed to the struggle for justice and peace, Isasi-Díaz elaborated her *mujerista* theology as a platform to give voice to Latina grassroots women and their everyday struggles for survival, to challenge oppressive religious teachings and practices, and to empower Latina women to become agents of radical change to transform society and eliminate oppression. Doing theology from her Catholic perspective and aware and respectful of the popular Christianity of her base community, Isasi-Díaz developed *mujerista* biblical interpretation as a reading strategy that embraces and responds to the reality of Latina grassroots women. As such, *mujerista* biblical interpretation operates, like *mujerista* theology, on the foundation of three central elements from the reality of Latina grassroots women. First, *mujerista* theology is based on Hispanic Christianity, a Christianity influenced and shaped by diverse religious understandings and practices. It is a *mestiza* and *mulata* Christianity that mixes religious practices and content from the Catholicism of the conquistadores, African and Amerindian religions, and Protestant and evangelical traditions. Because the role of the Bible is very different in each of these religious practices, for some of them inexistent and for others an authoritative text usually read from a patriarchal perspective, it is an urgent matter for *mujerista* theology to articulate a *mujerista* biblical interpretation to help Latina women to appropriate the Bible in a liberative way.

Second, the sources of *mujerista* theology are the experiences of Latina women and their struggle for survival, not the Bible. Equally, the starting point for interpreting the Bible from a *mujerista* perspective is the experience of Latina women. From her Catholic perspective and her experience, Isasi-Díaz explains how Latina women do not read the Bible in their daily life, and when they need help, they find it in praying to God and the saints, not in the Bible. And third, *mujerista* theology operates under the critical lens of liberation, a liberation that has to do with physical and cultural survival. Reading the Bible from this perspective means that the Bible can be accepted as divine revelation and as authoritative for life only as long as it contributes to the liberation of Latina women.

Out of the three foundational elements of *mujerista* theology, Isasi-Díaz defines three guiding elements in *mujerista* biblical interpretation: (1) the criterion for using the Bible is need. Latina grassroots women use the Bible when they need it, for what they need it, and in the manner in which they need it; (2) the central lens in *mujerista* biblical interpretation has to be the struggle for liberation, a hermeneutics of *la lucha*; and (3) Hispanic women's interpretation of the Bible is central for identifying and struggling for their *proyecto histórico*, their preferred future. The implementation of the *proyecto histórico* shapes *mujerista* biblical interpretation in four concrete ways. First of all, biblical exegesis is praxis. It is a communal task where all participants have a voice and is a way to claim their right to think. Second, Latina grassroots women live their faith within a functional religious pluralism, a "grassroots ecumenism," which Isasi-Díaz takes as an invitation to read the Bible beyond traditional doctrinal purity and in solidarity with Hispanic women, bringing to the text whatever tool is necessary from their diverse religious practices in order to understand the text in a liberative way. Third, the Bible should be read in ways that confront and defy elitism, demanding the elimination of its hierarchical understandings, structures, and ecclesiastical privileges. Fourth, *mujerista* biblical interpretation should reject the split between the personal and the political, respect the self-determination for the person, analyze and redefine power for a just society, respect the right of all groups to struggle and achieve liberation, and achieve the common good.

As a woman in the Catholic Church and a former Ursulina novice, Isasi-Díaz's main concern with the Bible is the exclusionary way in which it has been read and used to control women and prevent them from appropriating the text from their own views. Operating from a hermeneutics of suspicion, Isasi-Díaz seeks to subvert the patriarchal power of the Bible by questioning its authority and accepting it only as a liberating and authoritative text in as far as it enables and advances the liberation and survival of Latina women. By empowering Latina women to use their experience as the entry point into the Bible and by opening a forum where Latina women can read the Bible in any way they need in order to survive, Isasi-Díaz challenges the elitist views and hierarchical readings of those in power to authorize the correct interpretation of the Bible. By subverting all the authorized ways of reading the Bible, Isasi-Díaz de-patriarchalizes the biblical text and calls into question the solidarity of the church with the women who have to find their own liberative ways of reading the Bible in order to survive and struggle for a better world. *Mujerista* theology affirms that without liberation there cannot be justice and peace. Liberation is a communal endeavor, and no one can find liberation in isolation or at the expense of others. *Mujerista* biblical interpretation, therefore, is a communal endeavor that seeks the liberation of all.

Hermeneutics of Exile: Reading "in Spanish" and "Through Hispanic Eyes"—Justo L. González. Justo L. González, a Cuban American Methodist minister and historian who immigrated to the United States at the end of the 1950s, presents two reading strategies. The first model, reading "in Spanish," is the reading strategy of *mañana* theology, a Christian theology from a Hispanic perspective elaborated by González in the late 1980s. *Mañana* theology works from the perspective of a people "in exile," who, in their sufferings and struggles, hope for a better *mañana* in light of the reign of God. Using his experience of exile as a hermeneutical lens and a point of entry into the biblical text, González proposes reading the Bible "in Spanish" as a political reading. This means reading the Bible from the perspective of those who live in exile, the Hispanic people living as aliens in a strange land, marginalized and discriminated. For González, reading "in Spanish" means reading in the vernacular, the language of the exiles and not the language of those in power; thus the Bible becomes the book of the people, not the book of the powerful. To read the Bible from the reality of marginalization rather than from the perspective of the powerful turns the Bible into a political text. Reading in the vernacular requires some guidelines, which González calls a "grammar" for reading "in Spanish." First, one reading "in Spanish" must address issues of power and powerlessness when reading the Bible. The questions of who has the power and who does not and whose side God takes cannot be avoided. Second, given the fact that only a small portion of the Bible was written to be read in private, the Bible should be read remembering that God is addressing the whole community. Readers reading "in Spanish" must be careful not to privatize the faith. Third, reading "in Spanish" means to pay attention to what the children, the simple, and the poor have to say. The whole community is invited to interpret the Bible, and everyone's voice counts. Fourth, just as the community reads and interprets the Bible, the Bible reads and interprets the community and its situation. The community reads the Bible in order to understand itself better in light of the word of God.

In the mid-1990s, González developed a second reading model, "reading the Bible through Hispanic eyes." In this model, although the reading strategy is called "through Hispanic eyes," González uses interchangeably the terms "Hispanics" and "Latinos." In his first strategy, however, he uses the term "Hispanic" exclusively. This change in language speaks of the changes in the Latina/o community; with the diversification of the community new challenges emerge. While González uses his experience of exile as his hermeneutical lens in the first strategy, in the second he widens his hermeneutical lens by exploring five different entry points into the text to acknowledge the experiences of other Latina/o groups who enrich the complexity of the community. He addresses the Latina/o realities of marginality, poverty, *mestizaje y mulatez*, exiles and aliens, and solidarity. González affirms that regardless of their backgrounds, most Latinas/os identify their experience in society with the image of marginality. The vast majority of Latinas/os in the United States have experienced poverty. When it comes to the question of race/ethnicity, the experience of being mixed and hybrid, *mestizas/os* and *mulatas/os*, is a reality clearly written in the skin of most Latinas/os. For many Latinas/os the experience of finding themselves in a land not of their own, as aliens and exiles, is a reality of longing and separation. In the midst of all these realities of exclusion, oppression, discrimination, and alienation, there is, however, one reality that binds all together: the reality of solidarity, of standing together and being a family to all those excluded.

As a Latino scholar and Methodist minister González remains deeply committed to the theological education of the academic and Christian Latina/o communities. Thus, he finds himself living in a constant tension between a hermeneutics of faith and a hermeneutics of suspicion. On one hand, from the academic perspective of the Bible, González approaches the text from a postmodern perspective, acknowledging the historical and cultural gaps between him and the text, and the need to read the text well aware of its otherness. On the other hand, a hermeneutics of faith is well in place as he speaks of the proven authority of the Bible in the life of the church, an authority under which the community allows the Bible to interpret it in a new radical way.

Hermeneutics of the Diaspora: Intercultural criticism—*Fernando F. Segovia*. Reading from his experience of Diaspora, as one who was forced to leave his country for political reasons and permanently live in a foreign land, Fernando F. Segovia engages the biblical text from a hermeneutics of the Diaspora with its corresponding methodological approach of intercultural criticism. At the beginning of the 1960s, Segovia immigrated to the United States from Cuba, leaving behind all that was familiar to start life in a new reality, one he describes as the world of the colonizer. Coming from the world of the colonized into the world of the colonizer, he began to experience his new reality as a child of colonialism and neocolonialism, living within the traditional relationships marked by oppositional binaries such as center/margins, civilization/primitivism. This experience of being "thrown" (*arrojado*) into a new world, a different culture with a different language, created the inescapable reality of biculturalism. And it is from this reality of Diaspora—of being in two worlds yet not belonging to either one completely—that the experience of an alienating otherness emerges. However, this otherness, which can be at first expressed in terms of exclusion and discrimination when imposed by the colonizer, is an otherness that can be strategically used as a point of departure for a re-appropriation of the term, positively presented when used as a self-expression of self-determination. When Latinas/os claim their otherness and turn it into their own identity, the very source of their alienation becomes the source of a new identity, one creatively used for the purpose of liberation. From a position of not having a place to call home, having been "thrown" into a strange world and being displaced and disposed from the familiar, the experience of creatively claiming the self-expressed otherness gives Latinas/os an advantage of knowing two worlds and being able to move between them, by negotiating their identity accordingly. Well aware of the reality that both worlds are constructions, Latinas/os can learn what makes each world function and use it to their advantage to effectively navigate both worlds. This new way of constructing otherness should be used with caution. For this otherness to be used as a liberationist perspective, it should not become idealized or exclusionist. The process of constructing Latina/o otherness, therefore, should be one of self-appropriation, of self-definition and direction, with an active refusal to be bound by external definitions. This process of self-othering is also committed to the affirmation of the self-otherness of others and is engaged in respectful critical exchange with others and their self-affirmed otherness.

Two elements emerge as central from the experience of Diaspora: otherness, and engagement. A hermeneutics of the Diaspora is, at its core, one of otherness and engagement with a manifest destiny of liberation. Out of such hermeneutics of otherness and engagement emerges the reading strategy of intercultural criticism, the critical interaction between the various cultures at play in the process of reading texts, which calls for a full contextualization of the participating elements, texts, and readers. Speaking more specifically about the interplay of the participating elements in this reading strategy, Segovia identifies three basic dimensions at work. First, the biblical text, like any other culturally and historically conditioned social group, should be considered as "other." Guided by the hermeneutics of otherness and engagement, this means that the text should be treated with respect, like all "others" allowing distance between text and reader, acknowledging and valuing the contextuality and otherness of the text. The goal is to understand the text as a whole as a world of its own. Second, the reader should also be considered as a historically and culturally conditioned "other." There is no such thing as a universal or objective reader, but instead a self-conscious reader who should be acknowledged, valued, and analyzed according to one's context. Third, the interaction between text and reader should be considered not as a neutral encounter between two others but as an unavoidable filtering of the one world by and through the other, knowing that the remoteness of the text as other is ultimately a construction of the past from the present as presented by the reader. Segovia defines this interpretation of the Diaspora as one with a manifest destiny of liberation. It begins with contextualization and seeks to acknowledge, respect, and engage the other. Segovia offers this not as the Latina/o hermeneutic but as one more reading strategy with similar dreams of liberation for all.

As the primary voice of Latina/o biblical criticism in the academy, Segovia has been instrumental in the formation of *latinidad* within that community of biblical scholars and theologians. Deeply committed to the advancement of minoritized groups, Segovia has consistently engaged academic forums offering critical ways of the theorization of the Latina/o self, that is, *latinidad*. Segovia began to formulate his hermeneutics of the Diaspora with its corresponding reading strategy of intercultural criticism at the beginning of the 1990s. Informed by a hermeneutics of suspicion, this hermeneutics of Diaspora engages the biblical text as a historically and culturally conditioned "other," one that needs to be critically engaged to decode its message, a message which is never directly addressed to the reader and is always mediated by the present reconstructions of the past from the "otherness" of readers and critics.

The Legacy and Future of Latina/o Interpretation. Academically speaking, Latina/o interpretation could be considered a fairly new interpretive approach that formally emerged at the end of the 1960s and beginning of the 1970s, if only the written documentations of the approach were to be considered. If we think about the importance of community for Latina/o interpretation, though, the legacy of Latina/o interpretation has a longer story. This one began with the evangelization of the Americas by the *conquistadores* and the resistance of the indigenous people to give up their age-old beliefs and worldviews and which ultimately became an integral part of the Christianity of the Americas. The indigenous hermeneutics resisted the *conquistador* interpretations.

The number of Latinas/os in the academy engaged in theological and biblical criticism has noticeably increased since the beginning of the twenty-first century. New perspectives continue to emerge and have found a solid foundation in the pioneer models from the 1970s to 1990s. Some of the new readings incorporate postcolonial perspectives that engage the reality of colonization, like the reading from a Puerto Rican perspective of Philippians by Efraín Agosto. Others use the so-called border theory to speak from the reality of the borderlands between Mexico and the United States, like Leticia A. Guardiola-Sáenz who sees the representation of the Jesus in the Gospel of John as a "borderlander" who constantly crosses different borders, creating a new reality, a third space, like the reality of *la frontera*. Eventually, as more Latinas/os begin to theorize their *latinidad*, more reading models will be emerging in the coming years. What is admirable about the four models highlighted in this article is the distinct commitment on the part of the reader to address the Latina/o community with the similar task of advancing liberation, whether at the level of the faith community, the grassroots communities in general, or the academic community. The models engage the Bible in very different ways, some more compliant and others more resistant. In the end, when considered within the lens of cultural studies, all models are valid expressions of the ways in which Latinas/os engage their *latinidad* to critically read the Bible.

[*See also* Central and South American Interpretation; Class Criticism; Cross-Cultural Exegesis; Cuban Interpretation in the Cuban Diaspora; Cultural Studies; Diaspora Studies; Feminist Biblical Interpretation; Ideological Criticism; Race, Ethnicity, and Biblical Criticism; Theological Interpretation; *and* Womanist Interpretation.]

BIBLIOGRAPHY

Abalos, David T. *Latinos in the United States: The Sacred and the Political.* Notre Dame, Ind.: University of Notre Dame Press, 1986.

Aponte, Edwin David, and Miguel A. De La Torre, eds. *Handbook of Latina/o Theologies.* St. Louis: Chalice, 2006.

Aquino, María Pilar, Daisy L. Machado, and Jeanette Rodríguez, eds. *A Reader in Latina Feminist Theology: Religion and Justice.* Austin: University of Texas Press, 2002.

Bañuelas, Arturo J., ed. *Mestizo Christianity: Theology from Latino Perspective.* Maryknoll, N.Y.: Orbis, 1995.

Deck, Allan Figueroa, ed. *Frontiers of Hispanic Theology in the United States.* Maryknoll, N.Y.: Orbis, 1992.

Elizondo, Virgilio. *Galilean Journey: The Mexican-American Promise.* Maryknoll, N.Y.: Orbis, 1983.

González, Juan. *Harvest of Empire: A History of Latinos in America.* New York: Viking, 2000.

González, Justo L. *Mañana: Christian Theology from a Hispanic Perspective.* Nashville: Abingdon, 1990.

Gonzalez, Justo L. *Santa Biblia: The Bible Through Hispanic Eyes.* Nashville: Abingdon, 1996.

Isasi-Díaz, Ada María. *Mujerista Theology: A Theology for the Twenty-First Century.* Maryknoll, N.Y.: Orbis, 1996.

Isasi-Díaz, Ada María, and Fernando F. Segovia, eds. *Hispanic/Latino Theology: Challenge and Promise.* Minneapolis: Fortress, 1996.

Isasi-Díaz, Ada María, and Yolanda Tarango. *Hispanic Women: Prophetic Voice in the Church.* 1988. Reprint, Minneapolis: Fortress, 1992.

Rodríguez, José David, and Loida I. Martell-Otero, eds. *Teología en Conjunto: A Collaborative Hispanic Protestant Theology.* Louisville: Westminster/John Knox, 1997.

Segovia, Fernando F. *Decolonizing Biblical Studies: A View from the Margins.* Maryknoll, N.Y.: Orbis, 2000.

Leticia A. Guardiola-Sáenz

LATTER-DAY SAINTS (MORMON) INTERPRETATION

Mormons—the Latter-day Saints—are a Bible-believing people. They have foundational perspectives in common with the allegiance and usage that other believers bring to holy writ. The interpretive tradition through which the Saints engage the Bible, however, is uncommonly complex, even when they are not themselves aware of this complexity. This tradition harbors dimensions sufficiently distinct from those of more traditional Christians as to render the overall Mormon relation to the Bible unique. These dimensions must be taken into account before one can make sense of the Mormon interpretation of any given passage or of a general Mormon hermeneutic—explicit or implicit.

The Mormon Difference. One dimension contributing to this complex difference is the Mormon emphasis on the erratic history of textual transmission and translation: "We believe the Bible to be the word of God," says an LDS article of faith penned in the antebellum United States, "as far as it is translated correctly." The issues are taken for granted as resolved by some religious communities using a standard modern translation, or are addressed with keen focus by a class of biblical scholars. But in the realm of popular theology, which informs much of Mormon practice in a church without a professional clergy, this principle, by historical precedent from the 1820s and 1930s, is apt to engender skepticism of the integrity of the text whenever interpretive difficulties present themselves, even where practitioners are oblivious to the accomplishments of modern textual criticism.

Another difference between Mormons and others is the Mormon belief that new scripture has been added to the canon, most prominently in the form of the Book of Mormon but also in additional revelations received and taught by the founding prophet Joseph Smith. Indeed, the Mormon canon, which begins with the Bible, is not only expanded but open. "We believe all that God has revealed, all that He does now reveal, and we believe that He will yet reveal many great and important things pertaining to the kingdom of God," Smith wrote in an 1842 passage subsequently canonized itself. Mormon sensibility on this front—but not on this alone—shares something with Martin Buber's interpretation of Hasidic Judaism. Buber objected to those who construed the Torah as a closed world: "To you," he said, "God is One who created once and not again; but to us God is he who 'renews the work of creation every day.' To you God is One who revealed Himself once and no more; but to us He speaks out of the burning thorn bush of the present." Mormon faith in biblical scripture is foundational; without it the coherence of the Book of Mormon and Mormon history and theology more broadly would unravel and would not have come into existence in recognizable form. Subsequent claims of revelation are always called forth, directly or indirectly, in relation to the biblical text. The Bible is tethered to all that emerged in Mormonism. Yet it is a regard for the ongoing process of revelation itself, more than any single expression of it that especially evokes Mormon loyalty. *Sola scriptura* has no resonance in this tradition: a closed canon begets minds closed to God's ongoing call.

An open canon implies the presence of those who receive inspiration, revelation, and even new scripture (i.e., living prophets). In practice this belief in an open canon produces a complementary tension. But in Mormonism revelation received and issued from living prophets need not be canonized or even written to be genuine. Thus emerges an etymological oxymoron yielding religious potency—oral scripture. "Whatsoever [those who hold the priesthood] shall speak when moved upon by the Holy Ghost shall be scripture, shall be the will of the Lord, shall be the mind of the Lord, shall be the work of the Lord, shall be the voice of the Lord, and the power of God unto salvation" (Doctrine and Covenants [D&C] 68:4). Startling by the standards of contemporary Christian practice in technologically developed countries, the idea of oral scripture is common in other parts of the world, in other times, and in other religious traditions. Moreover, it is not only those held to be prophetic leaders (apostles) of the LDS church who are subject to revelation. All disciples are believed to have revelation available to them to address matters in their respective jurisdictions.

Whether oral or (with additional status) written, scripture was not, for Mormonism's founder, wholly static, final, or untouchable as the word of God. It was potentially provisional, given to humans "in their weakness, after the manner of their language," as one of Smith's revelations proclaimed (D&C 1:24). Revelation was subject to addition and refinement: "precept on precept; line upon line . . . ; here a little and there little," in the words of Isaiah (28:9–10; unless otherwise noted, all Bible references are to the King James Version, following Mormon custom). Whether biblical or extrabiblical, the record of God's encounter with humankind is sacred but not sacrosanct. The record of revelation is precious but not superior to direct experience with the divine—the life spring of such records. Revelation received by mortal minds, even canonized revelation, is subject to correction, clarification, and extension. Nor is every instance of holy writ of equal inspiration nor intended to apply beyond the temporal and local context in which it was given.

The Mormon use of the Bible is always conditioned by such perspectives. Interpretation of any given biblical passage is colored by the existence of the Book of Mormon and additional modern revelations, just as those revelations often hinge on the Bible, even when by contrast, for their meaning and elements of their form. Moreover, written scripture is ever received with a consciousness of the existence of inspired living interpreters—prophets and apostles.

Extensions of these distinctive dimensions in Mormon usage include other aspects. One instance is the production of private scripture (private blessings held to be inspired and pronounced orally [and later transcribed] upon individual Saints by designated church patriarchs, a practice patterned after the biblical blessings the patriarch Israel gave to each of his sons near the end of his life as recorded in Gen 49). Another example is temporary scripture. For example, a certain portion of the original Doctrine and Covenants (the "doctrine" section) was later de-canonized by church authorities, defined as theological speculation. Similarly, just as Martin Luther decommissioned the Epistle of James, among other biblical books (dismissing it as "an epistle of straw"), so Joseph Smith declared the Song of Solomon an "uninspired book."

Joseph Smith. Mormons are not made from cookie cutters and, thus, have developed over time a range of thinking about biblical interpretation. It was, nonetheless, the teaching and practice of Joseph Smith (1805–1844) that shaped the Mormon scriptural mind. It was he who laid the essential parameters within which the Mormon tradition developed and Mormon diversity in biblical thought expressed itself. It is he who most fundamentally requires attention if we are to come to terms with Mormon biblical perspectives.

By the standards of modern academic biblical scholarship, Smith's use of the biblical narrative is outrageous and crude. Yet if analysts are to account for the coherence and ongoing vibrancy of the religion he ushered into being, they can ill afford to miss a controlling character of his approach: while the Mormon prophet made up his own rules of biblical engagement, the crudity of his method and its result is akin to the crudity of a van Gogh painting. For millions, it works, and it changes one's point of view. To comprehend something of this, it is useful to examine some specifics of Smith's usage, including the sometimes awkward aspects, and then to stand back to gain perspective on the Mormon prophet's overall project, which was spectacular in scope. His use of the Bible, in turn, provides both a DNA strand of and a crucial influence upon his entire bewildering enterprise.

The movement's founder came of age in the Bible-soaked environs of antebellum New England and upstate New York. He thrived just as the authority of the Bible, that pillar of Western civilization, was undergoing a rift. On the one hand, its stature was challenged by Enlightenment thinkers and the nascent rise of the prestige of science. Thomas Paine, more colorful than most, decried the obscene stories, voluptuous debaucheries, the cruel revenge and executions "with which more than half of the Bible is filled." Thomas Jefferson famously excised from his own version of scripture the considerable portions he construed as morally unedifying or based on superstition. This erosion of biblical authority, only a hole in the dam at first, grew broad by the end of the nineteenth century, wider yet in the decades that followed. On the other hand, the more common current in Andrew Jackson's evangelical America was to elevate unmediated scripture—in theory unfiltered by clerical, creedal, or scholarly interpretation—to its historical summit. While clergy and creeds retained a measure of importance in some sectors, the ascendant watchword in much Christian discourse was "The Bible alone!" Democracy in the early republic was flowering; who needed a fancy preacher schooled at Yale or Andover Seminary to tell the people what the Bible said?

This shift in the tectonic plates of the Bible's prestige, along with the democratization of its interpretation that provoked a tumult of religious opinions and new sects, also created a vacuum of spiritual authority. The abrupt arrival of religious freedom in the new United States, including legal disestablishment at the federal level, helped spawn that vacuum. More locally, disestablishment in New York, where Joseph Smith grew up, preceded the federal statutes. In this atmosphere, Smith later reported, it was precisely the failure of the Bible to resolve the urgent disputes of the day that helped drive him to his knees in the woods in the spring of

1820. There his prayer over the state of his soul, in the context of religious cacophony, was answered by a theophany that presaged his call as a prophet. A decade later he had brought forth the Book of Mormon, with its biblical cast and links, and received "power from on high" to found a uniquely authorized church.

In certain respects, Smith's scriptural presumptions were common to his place and time. As with his peers, his religious notions and everyday speech were steeped in the language and images of the King James Bible. He seemed to share his culture's predominant assumptions about the historicity, literality, and inspired nature of the Bible. He took in its narratives by assuming the immutability of truth and the immediate relevance of its prophecies to him, his society, his nation, and his time. He was influenced by a surrounding Christian primitivism that sought to transcend historical corrosion by returning to the beliefs and ways of the first-century church. Along with many of his era, he anticipated the return of Christ in an imminent millennium, in a dispensationalist framework that laid bare God's coherent, even tidy, plan for human history.

The Book of Mormon. Smith also swam cross-current to his culture's biblical presuppositions. Most audaciously, he published a "second Bible." The Book of Mormon, Smith reported, was translated from ancient, long-buried gold plates given him by an angel. The language on the plates was a "reformed Egyptian," consisting of "the learning of the Jews and the [altered] language of the Egyptians" (1 Nephi 1:2). Its English form was expressed in "reformed Jacobean." That is, its prose was adapted to the early nineteenth rather than the early seventeenth century but was unmistakably patterned after the style of the King James Bible, the language Joseph Smith knew as sacred. Accomplished "in his weakness," as the Lord warned it would be, Smith's adaptation of Jacobean prose is imperfect, and his own vocabulary and grammar are also evident. The Mormon prophet did not pretend to translate the record as a trained scholar but by divine assistance through methods on which he never elaborated.

This new "gold Bible," as many began to call it, would have been incomprehensible without its readers presuming the existence of the Bible. Smith's record primarily conveyed the thousand-year history of a Jewish civilization of contending factions, whose originating family was first transplanted to the New World prior to the Babylonian conquest of Jerusalem and Judea. The long account is climaxed by a visit of the resurrected Christ to the peoples of the New World, and brought to a tragic half-end through a devastating civil war in the fifth century C.E. in which one of the factions, the Nephites, was destroyed. The record purported to prophesy about the Bible as a book (from a vantage of 600 B.C.E.) and yet, in the nineteenth century, to itself be a fulfillment of biblical prophecy, as per Isaiah:

> And thou shalt be brought down, and shalt speak out of the ground, and thy speech shall be low out of the dust, and thy voice shall be, as of one that hath a familiar spirit, out of the ground, and thy speech shall whisper out of the dust. (Isa 29:4)

The ultimate object of this record of "a remnant of the House of Israel" was "to the convincing of the Jew and Gentile that Jesus is the Christ."

The English rendition of the Book of Mormon was printed in biblical mode as a collection of books, divided into chapters and, later, verses. Without apparent embarrassment on the part of Joseph Smith, the book proffered two dozen chapters of material in common with the traditional Bible. The two books share more than fifty thousand phrases of three or more words, excluding definite and indefinite articles. Inhabitants of the narrative were descendants of biblical peoples, and the book's episodes often echoed biblical stories, including the archetypal Exodus (from opening chapters of the Book of Mormon and passim) and Paul's conversionary encounter with an angel of the road to Damascus (cf. Acts 9:1–9 to Alma the Younger's conversion in Mosiah 27:8–19).

Some of the volume's traits are impossible to miss. So transparent was the content of prophecy in the Book of Mormon rendition that the boundary between what amounts to its New and Old Testaments are eroded. Prophecies of Christ's coming are specific and detailed: centuries before his coming it is known that Christ will be born of a virgin from Nazareth at a specific time, centuries hence.

Other traits are equally anomalous but not cast as miracle and indeed are rarely noticed by scholars. Fifty years before theories of the multiple authorship and the ancient redaction of biblical books gained currency in the United States among any but a handful of specialists at Andover Seminary and at Harvard, the Book of Mormon presented an explicit and dramatic example of the documentary hypothesis in living action rather than by vestigial scholarly deduction. The Book of Mormon forthrightly portrayed the fourth-century prophet-historian Mormon freely appropriating, abridging, and editing the records of earlier writers in his account of the ancient Nephite peoples. Whereas the documentary hypothesis would contribute to a series of highly publicized heresy trials in many Christian denominations in the decades surrounding the turn of the twentieth century, Joseph Smith's book, recorded in the late 1820s and published in 1830, displays an ancient prophet-editor at work as a central premise of the Book of Mormon structure—central enough to account for the volume's name.

A core of believers—thirty thousand strong by the time of Smith's 1844 murder at the age of thirty-nine—gathered about the book and its young prophetic midwife. Thus arose in the antebellum United States a new religious movement, launched by a new scripture that was patterned after biblical language and themes—a book that challenged yet endorsed biblical authority, mirrored biblical style, interpreted biblical passages, shared its content, amended its errors, filled its lapses, and restored its mode—namely, the prophet voice.

The Bible Revised. Scarcely pausing after publishing the Book of Mormon, Smith took on an equally monumental task—a revision of the Bible itself. He never completed this task but worked heavily at it for several years and episodically thereafter under the ostensible notion that the ancient texts and meaning had often been marred by mistranslation and scribal omissions, additions, and errors. Thousands of verses were altered in small or significant ways. The original manuscript and the King James Bible on which Smith recorded his "translation" disclose that the work entailed prayerful experimentation. In some places, Smith makes a provisional change, and then crosses it out in favor of a second or third attempt. Sometimes he scraps the changes and resorts to the original. This process comports with an 1829 methodological revelation he received on behalf of his assistant, Oliver Cowdery, who had failed in his own attempt to translate: "Behold," the revelation has the Lord saying to Oliver:

> you have not understood; you have supposed that I would give it unto you, when you took no thought save it was to ask me. But, behold, I say unto you, that you must study it out in your mind; then you must ask me if it be right, and if it is right I will cause that your bosom shall burn within you; therefore, you shall feel that it is right. But if it be not right you shall have no such feelings, but you shall have a stupor of thought that shall cause you to forget the thing which is wrong.

In this "branch of my calling," Smith made six basic types of changes, and these types disclose "translation" here to have other than a traditional meaning. The prophet did not translate from Greek or Hebrew to English. He translated one world to another, time to eternity, as his vision allowed through both mundane and dramatic strokes.

By far the most common of his alterations are routine modernization of terms, grammatical improvements, and technical clarifications: not "such trust have we through Christ to God-ward" as per the KJV, but "such trust have we through Christ toward God" (2 Cor 3:4). John the Baptist's "meat" was not locusts and wild honey (Matt 3:4), but rather his "food."

A second type consists of changes informed by common sense and preexisting theological notions. For example, where God was portrayed in the KJV as "repenting" of the evil that he thought to do to some poor recalcitrant (Jer 18:8, variously in Exod and elsewhere), Smith reasoned that God, who is perfect, needs no repentance. Thus, God did not "repent," but "withheld" the evil (harm) he thought to perform toward the sinner. Similarly, Smith amended Jesus's prayer (Matt 6:13) from "And lead us not into temptation" (which the prophet knew God would never do) to "And suffer us not to be led into temptation." This is significant at a second level because the Book of Mormon parallel to this verse (where a resurrected Christ utters a similar prayer) is identical to the KJV rather than to Smith's revision. That Smith made later alterations shows how he experimented and sometimes refined a passage in progressive stages.

The third sort of change Smith enacted amounted to "interpretive additions," clarifying commentary, which he often signaled by the phrase "or in other words." To Jesus's instruction that disciples turn their other cheeks if struck (Luke 6:29), Smith appended "or, in other words, it is better to offer the other [cheek] than to revile again."

A fourth kind of change Smith produced entailed harmonization. Knowing that God's truth is not contradictory, the prophet reconciled passages that appeared to conflict with other passages or with his own experience and revelation. He squared and conflated the accounts of Judas Iscariot's death in Matthew 27:3–8 and the conflicting one in Acts 1:18–19. The KJV of John has Jesus say, "No man hath seen God at any time; the only begotten Son, which is in the bosom of the Father, he hath declared him" (John 1:18). This could not be allowed to stand, for it contradicted both Exodus 33:11, wherein Moses had seen God "face to face," and Smith's own visionary experience. Thus, John 1:18 became: "And no man hath seen God at any time, except he hath borne record of the Son; for except it is through him no man can be saved."

A fifth type of change is not easily classified. One simply observes that the meaning of some given text has been changed, seemingly idiosyncratically. Proverbs 18:22 morphs from "*whoso* findeth a wife findeth a good *thing*, and obtaineth favour of the Lord" to "whoso findeth a wife hath obtained favor of the Lord." Jesus no longer "marveled" at a centurion's faith in Matthew 8:10; the multitude, rather than Jesus, marveled, presumably because Smith gauged that the divine Savior, omniscient, could not be surprised.

The final and most consequential changes are comprised of long, revealed additions that have little or no biblical parallel. These include the dramatic passages of the Book of Abraham (especially chapter 3) that lay out Mormon cosmology and ontology. They include the visions of Moses that define God's purpose in creation: "to bring to pass the immortality and [the qualitative] eternal life of man"—that is, to invite and assist his human children to be "partakers of the divine nature" (2 Pet 1:4). They further include the startling visions of Enoch, who encountered a God capable of weeping at the travail of a sinful humanity—not a current notion in Smith's day—and who showed Enoch wherefore he wept:

> And it came to pass that the Lord spake unto Enoch, and told Enoch all the doings of the children of men; wherefore Enoch knew, and looked upon their wickedness, and their misery, and wept and stretched forth his arms, and his heart swelled wide as eternity; and his bowels yearned; and all eternity shook. (Moses 7:41)

In the process of this work of biblical "translation," Smith was pressed at many points into querying the Lord. Consequently he received revelations on diverse matters (including the practice of polygamy) that eventually were themselves canonized in the collection called the Doctrine and Covenants (D&C). These revelations are possessed of diverse biblical connections both in content and style. All are saturated with KJV words, phrases, and concepts. For every two verses of the revelations, approximately three phrases or clauses parallel some phrase or clause from the King James Bible.

Restoration. If we step back from the unconventional, even strange, particularities of the brush strokes on Joseph Smith's canvas, it is possible to discern that his use of the Bible, like the entirety of his new religion, was in service to something so large that it is not often grasped. It can be glimpsed by thinking about the Mormon term "restoration."

Scholars of Mormonism commonly think of Joseph Smith as one among many figures in antebellum

America who sought to "restore" primitive Christianity. Smith and Alexander Campbell became the best known of these, but there were many others, such as Barton W. Stone, among the Baptists and other groups. Smith is recognized as significant among these both for the marked, though controversial, success of his movement and because he coupled an aspiration to restore pristine Christianity with a labor to restore ancient Israel, thus creating a literal church-kingdom.

Yet the restoration that Smith brought encompassed more than the return of Christian-Hebrew principles, powers, doctrines, ordinances, and authority once allegedly lost through long-ago apostasies (as many Mormons think of it). With fabulous imagination inspired and directed by his claimed revelations, and in *Targum*-like mode, the Smithian restoration sought not merely the return of things as they *once were*, but *as they should have been*. His umbilical cord to the Bible remained in creative tension with his freedom from conventional usage of it. Smith's was the expression of a prophetic mythmaking capacity, the power not merely to describe reality but to shape it. Grasping this fact allows room for such extraordinary expansions of the Bible as embodied in the visions of Enoch in the book of Moses, noted earlier. The Mormon restoration went even further by including revealed meta-historical matters "kept hidden from before the foundation of the earth." These notions were radical and more multifaceted than those launched by Alexander Campbell or by any other restorationist in American history. These reformers, like Smith, sometimes borrowed the language of Acts 3:21 to speak of the "restitution of all things." Unlike them, however, Smith intended the phrase quite literally. He sought to bring back the lost, to complete the partial, and to repair the broken.

Joseph Smith's use of the Bible and his wider notion of revelation and "translation" served not so much to establish the correctness of any given text but as the building blocks for a more rare and seminal process—religion-making and the creation of *mythos*.

Assessment. Converts to early Mormonism inherited a deep and traditional biblicism in addition to the radical departures in biblical orientation in which their founding prophet led them, creating a certain tension in practice. Smith's successor, Brigham Young, assumed and remained loyal to the general biblical tradition but elevated the authority of living leaders and dismissed parts of the Bible as "baby stories." Apostle Orson Pratt, the leading intellectual among church leaders during Young's time, hued closer to a traditional biblicism and contested Young's theological migrations. While contemporary manuals of LDS Sunday schools and the church's religious education system seem innocent of a deliberate scriptural hermeneutic and oblivious to issues of historical-literary criticism, individual leaders and educators range widely in their awareness and stance. Even when America's culture wars swirled around Darwinism and biblical criticism in the early twentieth century, Mormonism's official response was a cautious "no comment." A minority of Saints today, including some who teach at Brigham Young University, make full, if discrete, use of current critical tools.

The status of the King James Bible evolved from being Mormonism's common translation, during its first century and a half, to its official version by the late twentieth century. This reactionary direction, against the tide of the rest of English-speaking Christianity excepting primarily fundamentalist Baptists and analogous groups, was fueled by a wide-ranging program of "correlation" in the Mormon church operative since the 1960s. The broader thrust of correlation was to bring under standardized central control the curriculum, finances, publications, and auxiliaries of the church in an era of vast international expansion. One manifestation of the church's effort was to integrate the four standard Mormon scriptures by way of publishing their own edition of the King James Bible (1979) and adding to it a vast annotation system entwined with the Book of Mormon, the Doctrine and Covenants, and the Pearl of Great Price. The rest of the Mormon canon, with similar cross-referencing, followed in 1981. The result militates against the sort of critical thought about the history and nature of the scriptural texts that informs mainstream Christian denominations such as Methodists and Presbyterians. It buffers the Saints from critical scriptural thinking and conveys an impression of complete theological harmony within the Bible, and between the Bible and other Mormon scriptures. It also buffers believers from the acids of modernity.

Exhibiting an internal diversity and a dose of inconsistency across time, Mormons have, relative to other Christians, tended at once to elevate and moderate the biblical revelation. On the one hand, Mormons' very real biblical devotion is tempered by their sense of its pockmarked textual history and the presence of additional scripture and living prophets. On the other hand, the Saints believe they have vividly recapitulated biblical experience and renewed the process of revelation in their own midst. Hence biblical authority and reality are plausible and alive for them despite the drift of a secularizing culture.

Since Joseph Smith's time, the Mormon use of scripture has combined a traditional faith in the Bible with more "conservative" tendencies (an extra dose of literalism), some liberal elements (such as Joseph Smith's insistence on the deep-seated limits of human language), and some radical ingredients (an open canon, an oral scripture, the relegating of biblical pronouncements to experiential truth or the pronouncements of living prophets). Taken as a whole, the package renders Mormons as Bible-believing Christians, but with a difference.

[*See also* Authority of the Bible; Canon of the Bible; Historical Criticism, *subentry* Hebrew Bible; Historical Criticism, *subentry* New Testament; *and* Literary Criticism, Literary Theory, and the Bible.]

BIBLIOGRAPHY

Barlow, Philip L. *Mormons and the Bible: The Place of the Latter-day Saints in American Religion.* 2d ed. New York: Oxford University Press, 2013. Traverses the entirety of Mormon history by treating key figures and by comparing other religious traditions. This edition reinterprets Joseph Smith and examines most recent decades.

The Book of Mormon, The Doctrine and Covenants of the Church of Jesus Christ of Latter-day Saints, and *The Pearl of Great Price* (published together in one binding). Salt Lake City: The Church of Jesus Christ of Latter-day Saints, 1989. The scriptures that Joseph Smith produced in their modern annotated form that correlates traditional Mormon understandings among the four Mormon works of scripture.

Brown, Jerry W. *The Rise of Biblical Criticism in America, 1800–1870.* Middletown, Conn.: Wesleyan University Press, 1969.

Brown, Samuel M. *In Heaven as It Is on Earth: Joseph Smith and the Early Mormon Conquest of Death.* New York: Oxford University Press, 2012. Illuminates the biblical usage of early Mormonism as a byproduct of interpreting the conquest of death as Mormonism's original thrust.

Bushman, Richard L. *Joseph Smith: Rough Stone Rolling.* New York: Alfred A. Knopf, 2005. The best biography for getting at the sources, including the Bible, of Joseph Smith's thought.

Clark, J. Reuben. *Why the King James Version?* Salt Lake City: Deseret Books, 1956. Both a primary and secondary source, in that it remains the most influential Mormon tome defending the KJV against more modern translations.

Denny, Frederick M., and Rodney L. Taylor, eds. *The Holy Book in Comparative Perspective.* Columbia: University of South Carolina Press, 1985. Aids the comparison of diverse religions' perspectives on their scriptures.

Faulring, Scott H., Kent P. Jackson, and Robert J. Matthews, eds. *Joseph Smith's New Translation of the Bible: Original Manuscripts.* Provo: Religious Studies Center, Brigham Young University Press, 2004.

Flake, Kathleen. "Translating Time: The Nature and Function of Joseph Smith's Narrative Canon." *Journal of Religion* 87 (October 2007): 497–527. Argues that Joseph Smith was not merely describing reality, but shaping it; translating not mere texts, but experience, history, and meta-history.

Fogarty, Gerald P. *American Catholic Biblical Scholarship: A History from the Early Republic to Vatican II.* San Francisco: Harper and Row, 1989.

Graham, William Albert. *Beyond the Written Word: Oral Aspects of Scripture in the History of Religion.* New York: Cambridge University Press, 1987. Dethrones the presumption that "scripture" is by definition a written religious text, noting that the majority of all people who have been religious could neither read nor write.

Givens, Terryl L. *By the Hand of Mormon: The American Scripture that Launched a New World Religion.* New York: Oxford University Press, 2002. Yields insight into Joseph Smith's use of the Bible by focusing on the Book of Mormon.

Hardy, Grant. "The King James Bible and the Future of Missionary Work." *Dialogue* 45 (Summer 2012): 1–44. A Mormon scholar argues that Mormonism's twenty-first-century insistence on the KJV as its official Bible inverts a mid-twentieth-century logic for the same practice, which will make dialogue with other faiths increasingly difficult.

Hatch, Nathan O., and Mark A. Noll, eds. *The Bible in America: Essays in Cultural History.* New York: Oxford University Press, 1982. Provides cultural and historical context against which to compare Mormon usage.

Hutchison, William R. *The Modernist Impulse in American Protestantism.* Cambridge, Mass.: Harvard University Press, 1976. The preeminent treatment of the Protestant grapple with faith and modernist thought, with implications for all other traditions.

The Joseph Smith Papers. Various editors. Salt Lake City: Church Historian's Press, 2009 and following. An ongoing project to publish and exhaustively annotate all extant Joseph Smith documents in a projected 20 volumes. Will include five series: Documents, Journals, Revelations and Translations, Histories, and Legal and Business Records. Six volumes + facsimile, from four of the series, published as of October 2012.

Matthews, Robert J. *A Plainer Translation of the Bible—A History and Commentary.* Provo: Brigham Young University Press. 1975. A faithful rather than critical analysis of Joseph Smith's revision of the Bible; it thus serves as both a primary and secondary source for studying how Smith's "new translation" functions in sectors of modern Mormonism.

Noll, Mark A. *Between Faith and Criticism: Evangelicals, Scholarship, and the Bible in America.* San Francisco: Harper and Row, 1986.

Snell, Heber C. *Ancient Israel: Its Story and Meaning.* Salt Lake City: Stevens and Wallis, 1948. The Chicago-trained Snell exemplifies early Mormon efforts to accommodate "higher criticism" of the Bible.

Stendahl, Krister. "The Sermon on the Mount and Third Nephi." In *Reflections on Mormonism: Judaeo-Christian Parallels,* edited by Truman G. Madsen. Provo: Religious Studies Center, Brigham Young University Press, 1978. A non-Mormon scholar finds the Christ portrayed in the Book of Mormon closer to the New Testament John than to the Synoptic Gospels.

Talmage, James E. *Jesus the Christ.* Salt Lake City: Bookcraft, 1972. Both a primary and a secondary source, Talmage's work, first published in 1915, has for generations shaped the image of Christ in the Mormon mind.

Philip L. Barlow

LESBIAN, GAY, BISEXUAL, AND TRANSGENDER INTERPRETATION

Beginning in the 1970s, self-acknowledged (i.e., "out") gays and lesbians began to offer vernacular and scholarly interpretations of biblical passages that many traditional interpreters used to condemn homosexual practices. The first concerns of gay and lesbian interpreters were self-defense, pastoral amelioration of self-condemnation, and identity formation. "Desperate for some consolation, I picked up my Bible," says Patricia Nell Warren's Harlan character in *Harlan's Race* (Beverly Hills: Wild Cat Press, 1994) after the death of his partner, Olympic runner Billy Sive. But as he continues to read, "that infamous passage in Leviticus 20:13 was staring up at me.... Almost breaking the pen, I made red marks through those lines." (pp. 16, 47)

Over a generation, gay and lesbian interpretation has advanced from its initial confrontation with the so-called "texts of terror" (Gen 19; Lev 18:22, 20:13; Rom 1:26–27; 1 Cor 6:9; and 1 Tim 1:10), first identified as key texts by Derrick Sherwin Bailey in 1955, to put on the full armor of biblical criticism including close reading of texts and contexts. Concern with context led in new directions: first, to a topical focus on sexuality, gender, the body, disease, and plague, issues at the core of lesbian and gay identity during the rise of the modern gay rights movement (1969–) and magnified by the initial public response to the HIV/AIDS crisis (1980s); and then to the use of these *topoi* as analytic lenses (through sexuality studies, gender studies, and body theology) to read the whole range of biblical and related literatures. This move, coupled with the rise of HIV/AIDS and transgender interpretations, paved the way to the ready adoption of queer theory as the dominant interpretive lens in the 2000s.

Terminology. Gay and lesbian interpretation, currently known as "lesbian, gay, bisexual, and transgender [LGBT] interpretation" fell under the rubric, "homosexuality and the Bible" in the 1970s (e.g., McNeill; Horner); or "lesbian and gay" (Alpert), "gay-affirmative" (Stone 1997), or "gay and lesbian interpretation" (Stone 1999) in the 1980s and 1990s.

It is often confused with (because it partially intersects) "queer interpretation," a set of hermeneutic approaches that gained steam in literary studies in the 1990s and entered biblical studies at the turn of the millennium (e.g., Stone 2001). "LGBT" conforms to a post-HIV/AIDS ordering of the communities of concern, although an earlier abbreviation, "GLBT," is still seen. Other communal designations include the neologism "translesbigay" and the alphabetically multiplicative "LGBTIQQAA" (adding intersexual, queer, questioning, asexual, and ally).

Principles of LGBT Interpretation. Beginning as apologetic defense, LGBT interpretation found its way to affirmation. Starting with texts that seemed to condemn homosexuality, LGBT interpreters ultimately placed the whole Bible under their purview. While demarcating personal identity, LGBT interpretation began to question the very boundaries of persona. Can one have more than one identity? Does identity have an essence? Such questions anticipated the rise of a new interpretive movement—queer biblical interpretation—that has partially displaced LGBT interpretation *per se.*

Gay and Lesbian Apologetics. Deirdre Good (1997) asserts, in her survey of apologetic approaches to the "texts of terror," that LGBT interpreters follow several reading strategies: one of "restoration," "omission," or "completion." By "restoration" she means that an interpreter argues that a particular text such as Romans chapter 1 as a whole does not address contemporary debates about homosexuality, but is really about something else (e.g., the consequences of idolatry, homosexual acts done by heterosexuals, purity regulations, pederasty, non-procreative sex, incest, and bestiality). This "displacement" restores the "proper way to view the biblical passage" and "exonerates" biblical authority, especially for the LGBT reader. The "strategy of omission" unfolds from this—it is an argument from silence (e.g., the Gospels say nothing about "homosexual" relations). To the degree that both strategies speak of "homo-" or "heterosexuals," they suffer from LGBT interpreters' anachronistic use of identity categories that first emerged in the late nineteenth century. While the Israelites, Greeks, Romans, and Jews were aware of the variety of sexual behaviors now subsumed under "homo-" or "heterosexual," they did not divide the landscape of "sexual identities" by them.

The "strategy of completion" takes a different tack: it admits that the texts of terror frankly condemn homosexuality. However, the larger textual context, for example, Paul's discussion in Romans of the "new creation," or the *de minimis* attention to homosexuality in the Bible as a whole, "completes" the biblical picture that cannot be seen when verses are decontextualized as prooftexts. This approach has the virtue of recognizing that biblical texts and ideas can stand in tension with each other as the result of drawing on multiple source documents and their historical development as a library. It also allows for inner-biblical exegesis and intertextuality—that is Bible interpreting or reusing the Bible.

Gay Affirmative Interpretation. When LGBT interpretation moves beyond apologetic responses to affirmation, it draws upon second-wave feminist (1960s–1980s) and "gay ideas" from its communities of interest and women's and gay liberation movements. For instance, LGBT people name themselves, by reclaiming pejoratives like *feygele,* "gay," "lesbian," and "queer," and by self-identifying or "coming out." Thus LGBT interpreters may well name their own interpretive practice and "out" themselves. LGBT interpretation "reclaims our history" by excavating biblical texts for LGBT characters and practices, "outing" them, or reading them into biblical gaps and erasures. It "honors our relationships" by observing same-sex, biblical relational models such as Ruth and Naomi or David and Jonathan. And LGBT interpretation attempts to build LGBT community by observing the biblical communities of eunuchs (as in Esther or Daniel), the same-gender pairings and communities of "single" Christians (Rom 16), or the welcome given to same-sex partners and eunuchs (Matt 8:13; Acts 8:25–39). From lesbian feminism and HIV/AIDS activism comes the notion that LGBT interpretation should have an activist component—indeed it should "act-up." Thus it resists "homophobic" interpretations and pushes back against bullying with texts. Finally, LGBT interpretation can assert, as a 1970 Gay Liberation Front protest sign emphatically did, "God is gay."

Gay and Lesbian Intersectionalities. Because LGBT interpretation focuses on identity issues—the formation, stabilization, and politics of individual and communal identity—it also intersects with other "nontraditional" hermeneutic approaches that have an identitarian component: for instance, African and African American, womanist, Latina/o, or postcolonial interpretation. This recognizes that most early interpreters were white North Americans, Australians, or northern Europeans from among the economic elites. Following the lead of "standpoint feminists," some LGBT interpreters refine their thinking to consider intersections with race, class, and empire.

LGBT versus Queer Hermeneutics. LGBT interpretation's most striking difference with Queer interpretation is precisely over identity—"queer," among other things, is about an unspecified "identity without an essence" that is a "zone of possibilities" (Jagose 1996, pp. 2, 90). Indeed, queer interpretation in practice attempts to leave a space for the other-not-thought-of and denaturalizes its focus on the sexuality, gender, and bio-sex of the body (e.g., asking the question, "Is gender innate, socially-constructed, or performative?"). Thus "queer" is "skeptical of the self-evident status of identity categories" (p. 101) dramatizing anomalies between bio-sex, gender, and sexuality and so, like disability studies, resists the notion of "normal."

Queer biblical interpretation also builds from the inner-LGBT critique of the limits of apologetics and identity politics in interpretation. Apologetics operates on the same playing field, and uses the same exegetical methods, as those who pursue antigay interpretations. This approach endlessly recapitulates the search for "correct meaning" while not following to conclusion the implications of examining "standpoint" and reader reception.

What are those implications? Identity cannot be reduced to two, or four, or nine statuses as well as the unmentioned status of "straight." The lengthening list of statuses in the string LGBTIQQAA illustrates the limits, and ultimate breakdown, of the dualities: heterosexual/homosexual, male/female, and abled/disabled. Even a continuum between two poles or a matrix is insufficient to show human diversity over the dimensions of sexuality, gender, and body. Ultimately, one must think in terms of a three-dimensional matrix to allow for human variability, with clusters of data points representing some of the more common occurrences. The gender/sexuality/body possibilities appear as rogue stars and galaxies in the larger universe. While LGBT interpretation decenters white-able-male, straight interpretation—what once was (and still is) the center and majority of all biblical interpretation—queer interpretation replaces the decentering move with a sense that there is no center to the universe. All standpoints are interpretive phenomena to be observed including the gaseous Magellanic clouds of patently false, racist, or homophobic interpretation. All intersectionalities are in play and contribute to the pleroma of what is contained in the text.

Memes from LGBT Interpretation. The meme is a semiotic concept, modeled after the biological gene, for a cultural unit that can carry cultural ideas or behaviors from one person to another. As the analogue of a gene, memes replicate, mutate, or otherwise vary in response to their environment. A number of LGBT interpretive ideas have taken on a life of their own between and outside of LGBT communities—and likewise LGBT communities have absorbed memes from without. Key interpretive memes are discussed below.

Lesbian Interpretation. Deryn Guest argues for a "lesbian-identified" hermeneutics that highlights the concerns particular to its community—a hermeneutics that should not be erased by the advance of queer studies. She prefers the rubric "lesbian-identified" as it partially sidesteps the question of earlier lesbian separatists as to who counts as a lesbian. Following Adrienne Rich's 1979 notion of a "lesbian continuum," a range of woman-identified experiences, not necessarily exclusively genital, women can find a place in a larger lesbian community crystallized around the ethnic minority model of group self-interest. Lesbian-identified hermeneutics builds on four principles: (1) "resistance" that transforms the feminist "hermeneutic of suspicion" into "hetero-suspicion." The hermeneut approaches the absence of female homoeroticism from male-centered and patriarchal texts suspecting "erasure," and so, problematizes it; (2) "rupture" of the gender and sexuality binaries (male/female; hetero-/homosexual) and their boundaries while also rejecting an "essence" for either. The Ruth-Naomi story, "a staple for lesbian-identified readings" (Guest 2005, p. 184), can retain its sexual ambiguities while bringing into play the notion of "lesbian continuum"; (3) "reclamation" "makes visible the absence of positive lesbian-identified representations" (p. 201) in the Bible and fills in the blank through "appropriation." For example, one might "cruise" existing characters, and, informed by the "reader's erotic knowledge," identify Lydia in Acts 16:14–16, a seller of purple who travels near the island of Lesbos, as a lesbian. Guest finds this reading an improbable stretch from the available details. As a classically trained biblical exegete, she prefers historical or midrashic reconstruction—one reads the embedded clues within a text (that point to another reality) to fill a story gap. For example, do the emotional sparks between Sarah and Hagar point to a richer woman-to-woman relationship? (4) Finally, "re-engagement" points to an activist component of lesbian-identified hermeneutics.

Bernadette Brooten reminds readers that Romans 1:26 is the only biblical verse that plausibly refers to female homoeroticism. Her 1996 book, *Love between Women: Early Responses to Female Homoeroticism*, has two foci. First, she documents at length women's history, subjectivity, and ancient understandings of women's eroticism in the context of early Christianity and its surrounding pagan world. She is careful here to avoid the use of "lesbian"—a term first used by a medieval scholiast—in favor of terms used by the texts themselves (e.g., *tribades*). She observes that nearly all writers of the time—even male elite authors who (by contemporary definition) are homosexual—condemn female same-sex behavior as "unnatural," yet tolerate it (p. 359). Second, she undertakes a careful study of Romans 1:18–32 to pursue Paul's notions about "unnatural intercourse." But unlike Boswell or McNeill who ameliorate Paul's teaching here, she plainly sees "Paul as condemning all forms of homoeroticism" (p. 244). Her critique of the Pauline text derives from her historical analysis: Paul adopted the concept of "natural intercourse" from his environment (p. 266). Therefore, it is culture-bound. The implication of Brooten's approach, that one should not deny any uncomfortable facts about the text supported by context, shifts apologetic discussion to the authority of the text and its cultural relevance (p. 302).

Just as Brooten's work pays attention to the recovery of erased "lesbian" history, another careful scholar, Mary Rose D'Angelo, draws attention to the New Testament partnerships of Tryphena and Tryphosa (Rom 16:12), Euodia and Syntyche (Phil 4:2), and Martha and Mary (Luke 10:38–42; John 11:1–12:8) as woman-loving-woman relationships. "Paired women" becomes something of a meme in lesbian interpretation, drawing not only on the obvious pairs such as Ruth and Naomi, but also exercising "critical imagination" to exorcise women characters from their "heteropatriarchal storyworld" (Guest, p. 154). The "bracketing" of that world allows Deborah, for instance, to meet Yael (Judg 4—5).

Gay Interpretation. Gay-identified interpretation has primarily taken an apologetic focus on the principal texts of terror. Gay interpreters have often embraced the best "scientific" results of the late twentieth century project of literary and historical criticisms. What do the inner-biblical exegetical texts say about Sodom? "Sodomy" has a history and how does the history-of-the-idea affect interpretation? Does the Sodom story evince a failure of hospitality, a prideful neglect of the poor (Ezek 16:49), or male-male lust? Is it a text about potential gang rape as its heterosexual mirror, the outrage at Gibeah (Judg 19), suggests? Or is the reader's horror really about sex with angels?

What do Leviticus 18:22 and 20:13 mean when they literally command that men should not lie with a male "the lyings of a woman?" One apologetic move argues that these texts are really about "idolatry" (when paired with Lev 18:20, *per* Countryman 1988); or about gay sex outside of a loving relationship. Olyan (1994) argues that Leviticus 18:22 condemns the insertive role in anal intercourse, a rule also found in Middle Assyrian Law A 20. Leviticus 20:13 extends the rule to both participants. Boyarin argues that these texts reject a specific sexual act—male anal intercourse—which functions like cross-dressing, a gender-deviance that "mixes kinds" (Lev 19:19). He points out, however, that the Babylonian Talmud permits heterosexual anal intercourse as the second of two possible "lyings with a woman" (cf. *b. Sanh* 54). Milgrom argues that the command applies only to Jews in the land of Israel (as suggested by the rhetorical frame (Lev 18:24–30). Stewart suggests that these texts only apply to male-male incest relations to the same degree of kinship for which male-female incest is forbidden. Nearly all commentators now note that lesbian sex is not mentioned: "You shall not lie with a male as with a woman; it is an abomination" (Lev 18:22). In contrast, some contemporary Bible translations are ready to draw conclusions beyond the Hebrew text: "Do not practice homosexuality" (New Living Translation); or "No man is to have sexual relations with another man; God hates that" (Good News Bible). Both translations enlarge the prohibition—but the latter personalizes and intensifies the meaning of the "diagnostic" term *tôʾēbâ*, "abhorrence," only here. It does not carry the sentiment forward to the peroration in Leviticus 18:26–30 where the term applies to all the prohibited behaviors of the chapter. If "God hates" the behavior in Leviticus 18:22, God must also hate sexual relations during menstruation by differently gendered married couples (v. 19).

With respect to Romans 1:26–27, some argue that Romans chapter one functions not only as intertextual interpretation of a chain of biblical texts (Gen 9; Lev 17–20), but also must be set in dialogue with the entire sexual system presented in the Torah—that is, in the relevant parts of the Purity Code (Lev 12–15) and Holiness Code (Lev 17–22) as well as elsewhere in biblical law, in the narratives of the Former Prophets from Joshua–2 Kings, in the prophetic texts concerning eunuchs and women from the Latter Prophets Isaiah and Jeremiah, and especially in the sex-positive book of the Song of Songs from the Writings. A fuller scholarly consideration of the ancient Israelite and Hebrew Bible contexts of Romans 1:18–32 is work that Brooten concedes needs to be done.

Excavative interpretation seeks to find textual evidence of gay, or at least, homophilic relationships in the Bible. David and Jonathan as the parade example turns on a passage from "The Song of the Bow" (2 Sam 1:26, New Jewish Publication Society): "I grieve for you,/ My brother Jonathan,/ You were most dear to me./ Your love was wonderful to me/ More than the love of women." Was this warrior-buddy love? The homosocial love of two very good friends? Or sexual love, too?

To this meme of "paired male-focused men" one could add the account of the "Centurion and his 'boy'" in Matthew 8:13. Some translate *pais* as "servant" (following the use of *doulos* for the same story at Luke 7:2) to capture the idea that the sick man is an adult and not a child. But this simultaneously disguises and acknowledges that *pais* can function as sexual slang for a submissive partner. The story is striking because Jesus responds without hesitation "I will come and cure him" (v. 7) and then marvels when the centurion asks him simply to give the command: "Truly I tell you, in no one in Israel have I found such faith" (v. 10). The double-outsider, gentile and homophile, stands for all on the outside including gays.

Likewise, even Jesus has his beloved disciple—sometimes thought to be John. Paul is part of an all-male community (Rom 16:21–23) and he travels with male companions, Timothy or Titus among them. These pairings and groups can be read as homophilic though always assumed celibate by non-LGBT readers. But celibacy, or asexuality, also represents a sexual minority position and the meme of "sexual difference."

This last suggests the most important meme for all LGBT interpretation—that of the Ethiopian eunuch (McNeill 1995, pp. 139–144; Wilson 1995, pp. 120–131). The eunuch, too, is a member of a sexual minority: alternately thrust from Israelite society (Deut 23:1 [Heb. v.2]), despised as unfruitful (Isa 56:3), yet promised a future (Isa 56:4–5), and shining like Shaashgaz, Hegai, and Hathach in Esther (2:14–15; 4:4–5). This eunuch is an African public official and also, as a eunuch, one who potentially could not be circumcised and thus perpetually cut off from the Israelite covenant. He asks the deacon-evangelist Philip about the meaning of Isaiah 53:7–8: "Like a sheep he was led to the slaughter, and like a lamb silent before its shearer so he does not open his mouth. In his humiliation justice was denied him. Who can describe his generation?" (Acts 8:33–34). Here the eunuch asks about someone who was "sheared," who had no offspring. So, while the African origins of the eunuch are noted in African American interpretation, and it is sometimes noted that he is the first gentile convert in Acts (before Cornelius)—two indicia of his outsider status—gay interpretation notices that he is part of a sexual minority drawn to the "Suffering Servant" by losses that resonate with his own. The Ethiopian-eunuch-as-sexual-minority stands in LGBT interpretation for all sexual minorities including gays.

Bisexual Interpretation. Bisexuality is one of three species in the twentieth century taxonomy of sexual orientation (homosexual—bisexual—heterosexual). After the rise of queer studies a more complex taxonomy or matrix of fluid sexual expressions has replaced this continuum. Bisexual biblical interpretation, as an identitarian phenomenon, barely exists, suffering from a lack of "bisexual-identified" interpreters. However, "defense against biphobia" has emerged as one interpretive meme. Michael Carden (2000) notes the rise of antibisexual interpretations of the outrage at Gibeah (Judg 19) among some Christian vernacular interpreters in the late 1990s—a text that had not entered the "homophobic imagination" since the failed attempt by Nicholas of Lyra (1265–1349) to associate the gang-rape of the Levite's concubine with the gang's initial threat of "sodomitic sex."

Gay interpretation that has biphobic uses is also possible. One interpretive strategy applied to Romans 1:26–27 displaces "blame" from male homosexuals to bisexuals: that is, properly heterosexual (gentile) men replace male-female sex with same-sex relations, "going beyond what was natural to them" (McNeill 1993, p. 56). As Brooten notes, the argument that Paul only rejects homosexual acts committed by heterosexuals cuts against both bisexuals and lesbians who feel they have chosen to love women (p. 244).

Transgender Interpretation. The term "transgender" can include persons who have "changed their gender but not their genitals," for instance, transsexuals, intersexuals, cross-dressers, drag kings and queens, androgynes. (Mollenkott 2001, p. 40). Or, as Kate Bornstein would argue, you are transgendered if "you're not perfectly gendered" according to normative models, or you are "transgressing gender" by studying it to gain a new perspective. For Bornstein, transgenderedness is a matter of degree (1988, p. 74).

Within this spectrum, as *per* Mollenkott, transsexuals are persons who hope for, plan, or have made changes to their genitals (as FTM [female-to-male] or MTF [male-to-female]) through voluntary gender-reassignment surgery. Intersexuals (formerly "hermaphrodites," about 1.7 percent of the general population) are persons who have genetic or hormonal conditions that disguise, change, or otherwise make ambiguous their bio-sex. For instance, the adrenal glands can produce a masculinizing hormone that affects an XX fetus (adrenal hyperplasia). Such are often subjected to involuntary gender-reassignment surgery. Cross-dressers (formerly known as "transvestites"), who are often heterosexually self-identified, dress in clothing from another gender for emotional or erotic purposes. Drag queens (usually gay) and drag kings (usually lesbian) will cross-dress for parody, entertainment, or personal satisfaction. Androgynes, formerly understood as persons who exhibited genitals or attributes of both bio-sexes (a variety of intersex), are now understood as people who simultaneously adopt the characteristics of both males and females, or wear gender-neutral clothing.

Transgender interpretation includes scholarly, pastoral, vernacular, and performance-artist practitioners such as Mollenkott, Tanis (who self-identifies as FTM), Kolakowski (as MTF), and Toscano. To the extent that it has identitarian foci, this interpretative approach is particularly concerned with the issues of all the various transgender subcategories. Its multiplication of gender categories (and movement between gender identifications) fits well with the three-dimensional matrix of gender/sexuality/bio-sex of the queer approaches mentioned above. Indeed, "trans"-positions illustrate the postulated indeterminancy that underlies queer interpretation.

The key biblical texts for trans-interpretation include the thirty-four-or-so passages in the Hebrew Bible and New Testament about eunuchs and castration (Lev 21:16–23, Deut 23:1 [Heb. v.2], multiple verses in Esth, Isa 56:3–5, Matt 19:10–12, Acts 8:25–39); and passages taking up the symbols or clothes of different genders (Deut 22:5), the creation of a new woman who "encompasses a man" (Jer 31:22), and the Pauline declaration of no male nor female in Christ (Gal 3:28). To these may be added all the gender anomalies and cross-positions such as the androgynous figure, *hā ʾādām*, "the Adam" (who mirrors the gender potentialities of the fetus; see 2:7–8, 18–24), circumcision as genital modification, Jesus as the fruit of virgin birth, Paul as mother (Gal 4:19), or men as part of the bride of Christ (Rev 19:7; 21:9). But as Toscano points out in the performance work "Transfigurations," transgender Bible stories appear throughout the Bible in its many accounts of gender subversion. For example, Joseph wears a *kĕtōnet passîm* (Gen 37:3), an "ornamented tunic" worn by virgin Israelite princesses (2 Sam 13:18). Trans-interpretation is not limited to explicit texts of hope or terror.

Interpretations of several biblical passages have risen to the level of active memes. In Isaiah 56:3–5 the covenant-faithful eunuch receives a "monument and a name" (*yad waššem*) better than sons and daughters—the famous phrase also names the Holocaust memorial in Israel, Yad Vashem. As Kolakowski notes, the promise of a name speaks to transsexuals looking for a new name to represent their whole self. It is also a promise that overcomes the law that excludes fully castrated eunuchs from the congregation; frames the heroic actions of eunuchs in Esther; makes it possible for Daniel to be "outed" (as Bar Kappara does in *b. Sanh.* 93b); and prepares New Testament readers for the first non-Jewish convert to the nascent Christian movement, the Ethiopian Eunuch (Acts 8:25–39).

It is the story of the Ethiopian eunuch who was readily baptized, coupled with Jesus's matter-of-fact "eunuch saying" concerning three types of eunuchs (Matt 19:10–12)—especially his noting ones who have made themselves eunuchs for the kingdom of heaven—that pushes some lesbian and gay interpreters to claim "eunuch" as a euphemism for "gay and lesbian" rather than simply analogizing them to transsexuals. As Kolakowski avers, the very power of the implicit argument of these passages—that eunuchs are not automatically condemned and excluded, but rather included in the faith community—leads to their appropriation by gay and lesbian interpreters.

Besides the memes of "monument and a name" and "communal inclusion of the eunuch," transgender interpretation naturally raises two more questions that also function as memes: "How many genders are there (biblically speaking)?" And, "What is God's gender?" Jaron Kanegson, following Rabbi David Seidenberg (2002, pp. 64–65), and Stewart (p. 93) take up the first question by a return to the categories elucidated in rabbinic literature: besides male and female, add (1) *andĕrôgînôs* ("androgyne" as both male and female; *m. Bik.* 1:5); *ṭûmṭûm* ("person of indeterminate gender; a person whose genitals are hidden or undeveloped" *m. ʿArak.* 1:1); (2) *sārîsʾādām* ("eunuch emasculated by men;" m. Yebam. 8:4); its opposite; (3) the *sārîs ḥammâ* ("eunuch from the time of seeing the sun, i.e., a natural eunuch born with a penis but without visible testicles or without other signs of sexual maturity by age 20"; *m. Yebam.* 8:4; *b. Yebam.* 80a); (4) a *sārîs mammāš* ("a real, tangible castrate" as Rav (175–247 C.E.) asserts of Daniel's companions, Hananiah, Mishael, and Azariah (*b. Sanh.* 93b; cf. Dan 1:1–7 with Isa 39:7); and finally; (5) the *ʾaylônît* ("metaphorically ram-like, barren, wombless woman incapable of conception"; *m. Yebam.* 8:5; *b. Ketub.* 11a). One can see that Jesus's three-kinds-of-eunuchs-saying (i.e., born so, made so by others, and made so by oneself for the kingdom of heaven) resonates with the multiplicity of the rabbinic categories above. This antique Jewish taxonomy also clarifies questions to ask about God's gender: Is it hidden? Or, does it reflect one or more of the gender categories Bible readers have found in the text?

Contribution. LGBT interpretation has focused its interpretive lenses on the sexual, gender, and body systems evident in the Bible. The "outsider" perspective of LGBT hermeneuts has aided the surfacing or rediscovery of overlooked textual elements. New questions asked of the biblical text draw out new coinage from its treasury. These findings represent more than just a contribution to the history of reader reception, or homiletical grist for the mill, but are a matter of urgency for LGBT readers. For the interpretive community-at-large, the challenge to readers' presuppositional categories may allow it to feast anew on the Bible's plenty.

[*See also* Feminist Biblical Interpretation; Masculinity Studies; *and* Queer Criticism and Queer Theory.]

BIBLIOGRAPHY

Alpert, Rebecca T. "In God's Image: Coming to Terms with Leviticus." In *Twice Blessed: On Being Lesbian, Gay, and Jewish*, edited by Christie Balka and Andy Ross, 61–70. Boston: Beacon, 1989.

Bailey, Derrick Sherwin. *Homosexuality and the Western Christian Tradition.* London: Longmans Green, 1955. Bailey's analysis, drawing on the early twentieth century sexologists, contrasts the invert (natural homosexual) with the pervert (heterosexual who does homosexual acts). His analysis of the six "texts of terror" may be thought of as "gay interpretation" *avant la lettre.*

Bornstein, Kate. *My Gender Workbook.* New York and London: Routledge, 1998. Approaches transgenderism through a series of exercises.

Boswell, John. *Christianity, Social Tolerance, and Homosexuality: Gay People in Western Europe from the Beginning of the Christian Era to the Fourteenth Century.* Chicago: University of Chicago Press, 1981.

Boyarin, Daniel. "Are There Any Jews in 'The History of Sexuality'?" *Journal of the History of Sexuality* 5, no. 3 (1995): 333–355. Focuses on Lev 18:22 as forbidding anal, but not oral, intercourse as supported by the Babylonian Talmud and other Late Antique Jewish literature.

Brooten, Bernadette J. *Love between Women: Early Christian Responses to Female Homoeroticism.* Chicago and London: University of Chicago Press, 1996.

Carden, Michael. "Bisexuality and Biblical Interpretation or How an Obscure Biblical Narrative Enters the Fundamentalist Imaginary as a Buttress of Biphobia." *Social Alternatives* [Brisbane] 19, no. 3 (2000): 31–35. One of the few interpreters who discusses bisexuality.

Countryman, L. William. *Dirt, Greed, and Sex: Sexual Ethics in the New Testament and Their Implications for Today.* Philadelphia: Fortress, 1988.

D'Angelo, Mary Rose. "Women Partners in the New Testament." *Journal of Feminist Studies in Religion* 6, no. 1 (1990): 65–86.

Good, Deirdre J. "Reading Strategies for Biblical Passages on Same-Sex Relations." *Theology and Sexuality* 7 (1997): 70–82. From an inner-LGBT position, analyzes and critiques lesbian and gay apologetics.

Goss, Robert. *Jesus Acted Up: A Gay and Lesbian Manifesto.* San Francisco: HarperSanFrancisco, 1994. Possibly the earliest work to speak of "queer biblical heremenutics" though here "queer" serves as a cover term for "gay and lesbian" as a coalition-building gesture for the HIV/AIDS crisis.

Guest, Deryn. *When Deborah Met Jael: Lesbian Biblical Hermeneutics.* London: SCM, 2005.

Horner, Thomas M. *Jonathan Loved David: Homosexuality in Biblical Times.* Philadelphia: Westminster Press, 1978.

Jagose, Annamarie. *Queer Theory: An Introduction.* New York: New York University Press, 1996.

Kanegson, Jaron. "A Young Man from Chelm: Or a Non-traditionally Gendered Hebrew School Teacher Tells All." In *Queer Jews*, edited by David Shneer and Caryn Aviv, 55–69. New York and London: Routledge, 2002.

Kolakowski, Victoria S. "Toward a Christian Ethical Response to Transsexual Persons." *Theology and Sexuality* 6 (1997): 10–31.

McNeill, John J. *The Church and the Homosexual.* 4th ed. Boston: Beacon, 1993. First published in 1976 by Pocket Books with the Roman Catholic Church's official *imprimi potest.*

McNeill, John J. *Freedom, Glorious Freedom: The Spiritual Journey to the Fullness of Life for Gays, Lesbians, and Everybody Else.* Boston: Beacon, 1995.

Milgrom, Jacob. *Leviticus 17–22.* Anchor Bible 3A; New York: Doubleday, 2000. The premier "straight" Leviticus commentator takes a generous stance on LGBT issues.

Mohr, Richard D. *Gay Ideas: Outing and Other Controversies.* Boston: Beacon, 1992.

Mollenkott, Virginia Ramey. *Omnigender: A Transreligious Approach.* Cleveland: Pilgrim Press, 2001.

Olyan, Saul M. "'And With a Male You Shall Not Lie the Lying Down of a Woman': On the Meaning and Significance of Leviticus 18:22 and 20:13." *Journal of the History of Sexuality* 5, no. 2 (1994): 179–206. Looks at the ancient Near Eastern context and applies an "active/passive" model of sexual behavior to explain key biblical texts.

Stewart, David Tabb. "Leviticus." In *The Queer Bible Commentary*, edited by Deryn Guest, Robert E. Goss, Mona West, and Thomas Bohache, 77–104. London: SCM, 2006.

Stone, Ken. "Gay/Lesbian Interpretation." In *Dictionary of Biblical Interpretation.* Vol. 1. Edited by John H. Hayes, 432–434. Nashville, Tenn.: Abingdon, 1999. Asserts that the next direction for "GLBT" interpretation is to advance beyond key texts to examine all biblical and related literature.

Stone, Ken. "The Hermeneutics of Abomination: On Gay Men, Canaanites, and Biblical Interpretation." *Biblical Theology Bulletin* 27, no. 2 (1997): 36–41. Argues for a "Gay-affirmative" hermeneutic.

Stone, Ken, ed. *Queer Commentary and the Hebrew Bible.* Journal for the Study of the Old Testament: Supplement Series. 334. Sheffield, UK: Sheffield Academic Press, 2001. Some contributors take "queer" as an umbrella term for "LGBT" as opposed to appropriating queer theory as a new lens.

Tanis, Justin. *Transgendered: Theology, Ministry, and Communities of Faith.* Cleveland: Pilgrim, 2003. A pioneer transsexual biblical interpreter.

Toscano, Peterson. "Transfigurations: Transgressing Gender in the Bible." *Transgender Bible Stories.* http://www.petersontoscano.com/transfigurations (accessed January 4, 2012).

Wilson, Nancy. *Our Tribe: Queer Folks, God, Jesus, and the Bible.* San Francisco: HarperSanFrancisco, 1995. Lesbian pastoral and vernacular interpretations.

David Tabb Stewart

Liberation Hermeneutics

In the latter part of the 1980s those working within the framework of liberation theologies began to explore other ways of talking about "liberation." While the term "liberation" was still of immense rhetorical importance, given its rich heritage (Bonino 1975), the terrain from within which the term had arisen was shifting. There was not the same hope that imagined socialist forms of political liberation would materialize. The collapse of the Soviet Union had much to do with this, as did the failure of socialist-inclined movements and parties to establish themselves politically and economically in nation states in Latin America, Africa, and Asia. So those working within this hermeneutic framework began to reimagine what "liberation" might look like, both in terms of what liberation was "from" and what liberation was "to." One way of talking about "liberation" which began to emerge during this time was to speak of "the God of life" and "idols of death" (Hinkelammert 1986). What liberation theology was about, it was argued, was taking sides with the God of life against the forces of death. The call and task of Christians was to "read the signs of the times," discerning where God was already at work bringing life in the midst of death, and then to become co-workers with God.

Liberation theology was to be done, within this revised terminology, in the context of the struggle for life in the midst of death. In the South African context, for example, the key concept became that of "struggle." The emphasis became less on the end product ("liberation") and more on the ongoing process of God's liberatory project. The advantage of this shift in emphasis and formulation has been that there is a place for liberation theologies after political liberation, as is the case in South Africa. As long as the God of life is engaged against the idols of death—whether these be the idols of neoliberal capitalism in the South African government's macroeconomic policy, or the idols of patriarchy within South African cultures and religions, or the idols of moral and medical discrimination in the context of South Africa's HIV and AIDS pandemic—there is a need for forms of liberation hermeneutics that work with and proclaim the God of life.

While liberation theologies continue to call for and hope for the fullness of liberation, what John calls "abundant life" (John 10:10), liberation theologians in South Africa and elsewhere recognized that for millions of people the reality is a daily struggle for survival, for basic life. "Struggle" is the reality of life for many, and a distinctive feature of "struggle" in South African and other liberation theologies is its systemic nature. "The struggle" is not primarily an internal struggle within individuals, though it does include this; the primary struggle within liberation theologies is, to rephrase Ephesians, against systems and structures that bring death (Eph 6:12). The struggle is fundamentally against structural sin. Given its systemic nature, the fundamental commitment of liberation theologies is the taking of sides. There is no neutral position in the contestation between the God of life and the idols of death. There may be more than one choice, as is argued in the landmark theological formulation of the *Kairos Document* (Kairos 1985), but there is always a choice and a stance to take. In what follows we will explore the cardinal choices that characterize liberation hermeneutics, focussing on the biblical dimensions of liberation theology, namely biblical liberation hermeneutics.

Biblical Liberation Hermeneutics. Biblical liberation hermeneutics has at its core five interrelated distinctive features, which can be found across a range of liberation theologies. The five distinctive features are, according to Per Frostin, "the choice of 'interlocutors', the perception of God, social analysis, the choice of theological tools, and the relationship between theory and practice" (Frostin 1988, p. 6). Frostin's analysis of liberation theologies is a useful starting point because it draws directly on a wide range of related liberation theologies in dialogue with each other. The data Frostin uses are drawn substantially from the self-constituted dialogue of Third World theologians working together in forums such as EATWOT, the Ecumenical Association of Third World Theologians.

Choice of Interlocutors. With respect to the first and fundamental feature, the choice of interlocutors, the emphasis in biblical liberation hermeneutics has been on social relations, not ideas or techniques, as has been the tendency in post-Enlightenment Western theology and biblical studies. This emphasis leads to the central question in biblical liberation hermeneutics, namely, "Who are the interlocutors of biblical interpretation?" Or, "Who are biblical scholars reading 'with,' when they read the Bible?" To these questions liberation hermeneutics gives a decisive answer: "a preferential option for the poor." Echoing the words of one of the founding liberation theologians, Gustavo Gutiérrez, we can say that while the primary interlocutor of Western biblical scholarship is the educated middle-class, the primary interlocutor of biblical liberation hermeneutics is "the poor, the exploited classes, the marginalized races, all the despised cultures" (Gutiérrez 1973, p. 241). This choice of interlocutors is more than an ethical commitment, it is also an epistemological commitment, requiring an interpretive starting point within the social experience and social analysis of the poor themselves. The other four emphases of liberation criticism each flow from this first, which is why biblical liberation hermeneutics must always be more than an interpretive technique. The actual presence and participation of the poor in any interpretive act is pivotal.

However, exactly how the poor are present in biblical interpretation is a matter of some debate in liberation hermeneutics. Clearly articulated by Juan Luis Segundo in the early 1980s (Segundo 1985), the debate has become even more polarized in recent years. Key to these disagreements and the debate is the role of the intellectual (in this case the socially engaged biblical scholar) and their assessment of the ideological (in classical Marxist terms) capacity of the poor and marginalized. Those who argue for the epistemological privilege of the poor and marginalized with respect to knowledge of their oppressive contexts work with thin conceptions of ideological hegemony. According to such thin notions, dominant ideologies never completely erase the knowledge they subjugate. Hegemony "is always threatened by the vitality that remains in the forms of life it thwarts." Hegemony "is always intrinsically unstable, always vulnerable" (Comaroff and Comaroff 1991, p. 27).

Furthermore, those who argue for the epistemological privilege of the poor and marginalized recognize that domination has a greater impact on the *sociopolitical opportunities* for resistance of the poor and marginalized than it does on the *religio-psychosocial capacity* of the poor and marginalized to resist domination. Subordinate classes, argues James Scott, are "*less* constrained at the level of thought and ideology, since they can in secluded settings speak with comparative safety, and *more* constrained at the level of political action and struggle, where the daily exercise of power sharply limits the options available to them" (Scott 1990, p. 91). Contending with traditional Marxist and early Latin American notions of hegemony, Scott argues that there are minimal constraints at the level of recognition, but more serious constraints at the level of action.

So the constraint on the poor and marginalized is not a recognition of their oppression nor a desire to resist but the social space in which to act. The poor already have a language, though the social space in which they can use their language is constrained by the structures of domination. But the *organized* poor, working class, and marginalized, Scott argues, do have their safe sequestered sites in which their dignity is given voice and where a thick and resilient "hidden transcript" is constructed. They have their heterotopias in which "all the other real sites that can be found within the culture, are simultaneously represented, contested, and inverted" (Foucault 1967, p. 3).

The role of the socially engaged biblical scholar in such *organized* contexts is that of the facilitator or animator, one who comes alongside those who are struggling to assert their dignity and its concomitant ideology/theology. Among *unorganized* individuals, the role of the intellectual may appear to be more interventionist, though it remains fundamentally faciliatory. Similarly, among those in poor and marginalized communities who have been atomized or kept under constant surveillance, it may appear that their human dignity has been so damaged that a "false-consciousness" has enveloped them. But this apparent silence is not the silence of consent to hegemony, but the silence of an embodied but yet-to-be-articulated ideology. Some socially engaged biblical scholars, working with a strong sense of the epistemological privilege of the poor and a weak sense of social hegemony, view their contribution as providing particular sets of critical analysis characteristic of biblical studies alongside the critical resources already being used by organized communities of the poor and marginalized. These additional critical resources, the tools of the biblical studies trade, are not primarily of use because they conscientize but because they offer other ways of forging lines of connection between the embodied struggle of the poor and the kindred struggles within and behind the biblical text.

However, there are also socially engaged biblical scholars and theologians, including Frostin and Segundo, who embrace strong notions of hegemony, arguing that the poor and marginalized have been "colonized" by the dominant ideology and are trapped in "a culture of silence" (Freire 1985, p. 72). Because it is the social sciences that provide the theologian who wants to carry out the de-ideologizing task with valuable cognitive tools, and because these are tools that are beyond the grasp of the majority of people, the role of the socially engaged theologian or biblical scholar must be seen as pivotal. In Frostin's terms, it is the socially engaged biblical scholar (whether an organic intellectual from among the poor or a socially engaged middle-class intellectual who works in solidarity with the poor) who enables the poor to break their "culture of silence" and go on to "create their own language" (Frostin, p. 10).

The Perception of God. Turning to the second distinctive feature of biblical liberation hermeneutics, the perception of God, Frostin notes that the first emphasis, the choice of interlocutors, has important consequences not only for the interpretation of social reality but also for the understanding of God. For while the interlocutors of many forms of progressive (including postcolonial) biblical hermeneutics question or bracket faith, the interlocutors of liberation hermeneutics "share" the same faith as their oppressors, but they do not share the same economic, social, or political life. The core "theological" question liberation hermeneutics asks is not whether God exists or not, but whose side God is on. As EATWOT so aptly expressed it, "The question about God in the world of the oppressed is not knowing whether God exists or not, but knowing on which side God is" (Frostin, p. 6). So the central problem in Third World countries is not atheism but an idolatrous submission to systems of oppression, and the central question posed to any faith tradition is whether and to what extent that tradition deifies the ideologies used to sacralize structures of oppression. So while oppressor and oppressed may be said to share the same faith, the faith tradition itself is a site of struggle, and is profoundly contested.

The South African *Kairos Document*, a prophetic theological response to the State of Emergency in 1985, is perhaps the clearest articulation of a faith tradition, in this case the church, as a site of struggle. However, while the document provides an incisive analysis of contestation within the Christian tradition in South Africa, there is no similar analysis of the Bible. The Bible is assumed to be on the side of the liberation struggle. The apartheid state, the *Kairos Document* argues, is "misusing theological concepts and biblical texts for its political purposes" (Kairos, §2). The "god" of the apartheid state is "the god of teargas, rubber bullets, sjamboks [whips], prison cells, and death sentences. Here is a god who exalts the proud and humbles the poor—the very opposite of the God of the Bible who 'scatters the proud of heart, pulls down the might from their thrones and exalts the humble'" (Luke 1:51–52) (Kairos, §2.4). This "hermeneutic of trust" with respect to the Bible is a feature of many forms of liberation hermeneutics, for liberation hermeneutics in its various forms has tended to work with the Bible as sacred scripture. While liberation practitioners may mean different things by the notion of "sacred scripture," there has been general agreement that the Bible is "substantive" rather than merely "instrumental" in its participation in the liberation project. Latin American forms of liberation hermeneutics have been clearest about the liberatory capacity of the Bible.

That the Bible has a substantive value is related to what Albert Nolan has called "the shape" of scripture (Nolan 1988). Liberation hermeneutics has tended to argue that the Bible has a liberatory "shape" or "semantic axis," to use the term used by J. Severino Croatto (Croatto 1987). Until recently, Latin American voices have been fairly insistent on a hermeneutics of trust, in which we can trust the basic liberatory trajectory of scripture. Any distortion of God's liberatory project was put down to the church's misuse of scripture, not to the inherent ideology of scripture itself.

But this consensus has been vigorously contested by black, feminist, and postcolonial biblical hermeneutics. From these perspectives, the Bible is itself a site of struggle, representing contending discourses, whether at the sociohistorical, or literary, or symbolic-metaphorical level. For some liberationists, albeit a minority, the voices of the marginalized within the text are so compromised by layers of dominating discourse that the Bible can only be an instrumentalist resource, not a substantive resource. Socially engaged biblical scholars who adopt an instrumentalist position only continue to use the Bible because the masses consider it a sacred and substantive resource, even though the biblical scholar or theologian does not (Mofokeng 1988).

The increasing attention given to the ideological agenda of biblical texts makes it difficult for biblical scholars to deny that the Bible has a multiplicity of often contending voices. It is also difficult to deny that the Bible is a sacred, significant, and substantive resource for the majority of those ordinary readers with whom socially engaged biblical scholars work. While ordinary readers do not usually have the particular critical capacities of the discipline, they have their own strategies for discerning liberatory strands among the more oppressive voices of scripture; they have forged their own ways of "conjuring" with scripture (Smith 1994). But while ordinary readers can and do either bracket or theologically reconstitute those details of scripture that do not fit within their ideo-theological orientations, scholarly readers are more constrained, being both accountable to the communities of struggle with whom they work and responsible to the ideological detail their discipline discerns in the Bible.

Social Analysis of Conflicts. The third distinctive feature, that of the necessity for social analysis, also derives from the first, for the option for the poor as the chief interlocutors of biblical liberation hermeneutics is based on a conflictual perception of social reality, affirming that there is a difference between the perspectives of the privileged "from above" and of the poor "from below." EATWOT reports characterize the world as "a divided world," where theology and biblical interpretation can only be done within the framework of an analysis of these conflicts.

As we have already stated, the root conflict for liberation hermeneutics is economic. The Dar es Salaam report of EATWOT (1976) was unequivocal, stating that "the division among rich and poor was perceived as the major phenomenon of contemporary history" (Frostin, p. 8). Central to the social analysis of liberation hermeneutics is the relationship between theology and economy. The struggle against Mammon is the core struggle for liberation hermeneutics. As Jesus put it, "You cannot serve God and Mammon" (Matt 6:23). The pursuit of economic profit, the kernel value of capitalism, it was argued, is incompatible with faith in God. The cult of Mammon distorts Christian faith, substituting faith in the true God with faith in the false gods of an idolatrous economic system. And it is the poor who have unsubstitutable insights into the difference between God and the idols, both in their own contexts and, as we will examine more fully below, in biblical contexts.

However, though subsequent EATWOT meetings confirmed the priority of the economic domain, other domains of struggle gradually forced their way onto the EATWOT agenda. By 1988 when Frostin published his analysis of liberation theology he discerned six "different levels of oppression": economic (rich-poor); classist (capitalists-proletariat; geographic (North-South); sexist (male-female), ethnic (e.g., white-black); and cultural (dominant-dominating cultures) (Frostin, p. 8). As is evident from these formulations, the social analysis of early forms of liberation hermeneutics tended to adopt a binary format.

While EATWOT consistently stressed the interrelatedness of these struggles, many of the debates within EATWOT centered on the priority given to and the relationships between different levels of oppression. Generally speaking, the discussion followed continental lines of divisions, where Latin Americans have emphasized the value of socioeconomic analysis while Africans and Asians have tended to stress religio-cultural analysis, and where women from each of these continents consistently emphasized the male-female contradiction (Oduyoye 1983). By the late 1970s the privileging of Marxist socio-economic analysis was being contested on a broad front, including the contributions of feminist biblical scholars, who argued that patriarchy was another foundational system of exploitation. Others soon joined women to contest the privileging of the economic, arguing for the inclusion of culture (both pre- and post- the emergence of "postcolonial" criticism), caste, nonwestern interreligious realities, disability, sexuality, and HIV and AIDS.

Land has been a key site of struggle in various forms of liberation hermeneutics, though it has usually been incorporated into other categories of social analysis. In Latin American liberation hermeneutics land issues have been represented as a component of economic struggles, and in South African liberation hermeneutics land issues have been represented as a component of racial struggles. Indeed, a familiar anecdote told throughout sub-Saharan Africa goes as follows: "When the white man came to our country he had the Bible and we (Blacks) had the land. The white man said to us "let us pray." After the prayer, the white man had the land and we had the Bible". But the issue of land has been given particular prominence in its own right by Palestinian liberation hermeneutics. In the recent *Kairos Palestine* document (2009), the last in a long line of "kairos" documents linked to the South African *Kairos Document*, the struggle for "the land" is central. The opening paragraph of this document sums up its message in these words:

> Our word is a cry of hope, with love, prayer and faith in God. We address it first of all to ourselves and then to all the churches and Christians in the world, asking them to stand against injustice and apartheid, urging them to work for a just peace in our region, calling on them to revisit theologies that justify crimes perpetrated against our people and the dispossession of the land. (*Kairos Palestine*, p. 3)

A few paragraphs later the document makes it clear that it rejects those forms of biblical and theological interpretation that legitimate the occupation of Palestinian land:

> In this historic document, we Palestinian Christians declare that the military occupation of our land is a sin against God and humanity, and that any theology that legitimizes the occupation is far from Christian teachings because true Christian theology is a theology of love and solidarity with the oppressed, a call to justice and equality among peoples. (*Kairos Palestine*, p. 3)

Given the importance of Marxist categories and concepts in the historical formation of liberation hermeneutics and the ongoing neocolonial economic profile of our globalized world, an economic orientation remains at the core of liberation hermeneutics, even though there is growing recognition of the many other forms of marginalization that intersect in various ways with class. Liberation hermeneutics has been impacted by postmodern, postcolonial, and queer modes of analysis that have deconstructed rigid binary forms of social analysis (Althaus-Reid 2000), but has been wary of any form of analysis that downplays the economic (Boer 2005).

Biblical Interpretive Tools. The fourth distinctive feature in Frostin's analysis of the methodology of biblical liberation hermeneutics has to do with the choice of interpretive tools with which to engage the theological tradition and the biblical text. With a different interlocutor and a different perception of God, liberation theologians need different tools for their theological reflection. There is a shift in liberation theologies from philosophy as the primary cognate discipline alongside theology to the social sciences. As we have seen above, among the first tasks of a theological deployment of the social sciences is economic analysis of contemporary contexts of struggle. A second, related task, for biblical liberation hermeneutics is the use of tools from the social sciences to analyze the biblical text.

A key relationship in liberation hermeneutics is that between the actual experience/knowledge of struggle of the poor and marginalized and the forms of social analysis provided by the social sciences. The starting point for biblical liberation hermeneutics, in the words of Itumeleng Mosala, are "eyes that are hermeneutically trained in the struggle for liberation today" as they probe "the kin struggles of the oppressed and exploited of the biblical communities" (Mosala 1986, p. 196). This primary experience is then resourced with sociohistorical tools (Gottwald 1979; Schüssler-Fiorenza 1983), which are used to interrogate past and present power structures. While sociohistorical modes of reading have been the preferred choice in liberation hermeneutics, literary and semiotic modes of reading have also found a place within biblical liberation hermeneutics (Trible 1984; Croatto).

The dominant modes of analysis in the discipline of biblical studies historically and institutionally have been historical and sociological, and so the formative years of liberation hermeneutics, whether in Brazil, South Africa, or the Philippines, were dominated by sociohistorical analysis of the Bible. The consequence of privileging sociohistorical analysis in liberation hermeneutics has been the foregrounding of the "scholarly" reader and the "marginalizing," to some extent, of the "ordinary" reader. However, partly in recognition of the nonegalitarian effects of sociohistorical modes of reading the Bible and partly because of poststructuralist critique, socially engaged biblical scholars have gradually embraced the full range of other modes of reading, including a diverse array of literary-semiotic and thematic-metaphoric modes. Such modes of reading resemble more closely "ordinary" modes of reading, and so provide important opportunities for interpretive collaboration between the socially engaged biblical scholar and the ordinary Bible readers. The text becomes a site of collaboration, with both bringing their respective resources to bear on the detail of the text as they read together.

Literary-semiotic-type and thematic-metaphoric-type scholarly modes of reading, while offering more egalitarian entry points for ordinary readers to participate on more equal terms with scholarly readers, also offer systematic and structured "critical" contributions to the reading process that are similar to sociohistorical modes of interpretation. For central to liberation hermeneutics is the sharing of structured and systematic—critical—modes of analyzing the Bible with ordinary readers. This is because biblical liberation hermeneutics is not only about an analogy of struggle (the biblical text in its context // we in our context) but also about an analogy of method (critical modes of interpreting text // critical modes of interpreting context). However, notwithstanding the importance of these scholarly critical resources, there seems to be a growing recognition in liberation hermeneutics not only of the agency of the poor and marginalized but also of the presence of critical forms of discourse among the poor and marginalized, so that socially engaged biblical scholars should understand their collaboration as offering their biblical critical reading resources alongside the local resources already present in communities of ordinary readers of the Bible (West 1995).

The Relationship between Theory and Practice. Frostin's fifth and final distinctive feature follows from this, focusing on the dialectics between praxis and biblical interpretation. In biblical liberation hermeneutics, biblical interpretation is "a second act." The first act is the praxis of action and reflection. The "action" envisaged here is actual action in a particular social struggle; integrally related to this action is reflection on the action; and integrally related to this action-induced reflection is further action, refined or reconstituted by the reflection on and reconsideration of theory (and so the cyclical process continues). Out of this first act of praxis, second order liberation biblical interpretation is constructed.

Liberation hermeneutics is fundamentally a process, and this process can be described as having three movements: See-Judge-Act. Shaped extensively by the "worker priest" movement championed by Fr. Joseph Cardijn in the 1930s in Belgium, and embodied in Latin America and South Africa by the Young Christian Workers movement, the threefold See-Judge-Act process provides a structure to liberation hermeneutics, reiterating and integrating each of the distinctive features discussed. The process of liberation hermeneutics begins with social analysis of a context of struggle (See), moves into a similar systemic analysis of the Bible, bringing text and context into dialogue (Judge), and then moves into community controlled action (Act). Community-based action provides a new site of contestation and struggle, such that further social analysis is required (See), and so the process continues.

This overall shape of liberation hermeneutics is relatively uncontested among practitioners, but, as we have indicated, there are differences in how each moment of the See-Judge-Act process is understood and practiced. Liberation hermeneutics begins with an analysis among the organized poor of the systems that oppress them, giving priority to the economic, but recognizing the multidimensional and interrelated character of structural domination. While local categories and concepts of social analysis are always the starting point for social analysis, the social sciences are brought alongside these local emic understandings by organic intellectuals and activist-intellectuals. Integral to the participatory process of liberation hermeneutics are forms of "liturgical" scaffolding (including prayer, singing, drama, music, and small group work) and collaborative community-based work (including the forms of social engagement that have led to this "new" moment of social analysis).

The reality "uncovered" by social analysis is then interrogated or "judged" by the shape of God's project of liberation that has been discerned within the biblical and theological tradition. Here too there is a place for both local and scholarly interpretive tools as the Bible is brought into dialogue with social reality. In this phase of the process the Bible is read more closely and carefully than is commonly done by people of faith (Riches et al. 2010, p. 41), which is part of the contribution of the sets of critical resources of biblical studies. More importantly, the resources of biblical scholarship provide additional access to the various ideological layers of and the structural systems in and behind the biblical text. The "Judge" moment in liberation hermeneutics enables a dialogue between a structural analysis of the context and a structural "reading" of the biblical text.

As Norman Gottwald has cautioned, there are limits to the analogies of struggle constructed by the "Judge" moment. "Given the reality that economic systems cannot be 'imported' from the Bible to meet our needs," he says, "the ethical force of the Bible on issues of economics will have to be perspectival and motivational rather than prescriptive and technical" (Gottwald 1993, p. 345). But as Gottwald goes on to argue, this kind of ethical force is considerable. Notwithstanding the very real differences and the distance between the economic systems of the ancient Near East/Greco-Roman world and our world, what connects the two "is a common thread of economic inequity and oppression and a common thread of struggle against needless economic suffering." Even if, as Mosala would argue, this trajectory is not as prominent as liberation theologians have imagined, recognizing and understanding the economic (and the other) systems that shape biblical texts assists communities of struggle from falling into what the *Kairos Document* refers to as "church theology," where an "unstructural understanding of the Bible" simply reinforces and confirms an "unstructural understanding of the present" (Mosala 1989, p. 32).

Having analyzed contextual realities, having judged these realities against the shape of God's redemptive project, liberation hermeneutics then moves to work toward the "kin-dom" of God (i.e., a less hierarchical "kingdom") "on earth, as it is in heaven" (Matt 6:10). Biblical liberation hermeneutics is not primarily about biblical interpretation, but about social transformation. Indeed, as the See-Judge-Act process demonstrates, biblical interpretation is merely one moment of a larger process, albeit a pivotal moment.

A Luta Continua ("The Struggle Continues"). Liberation hermeneutics "understands itself," Per Frostin reminds us, "as an unfinished process," and one that should be evaluated in relation to "the first act" of praxis (Frostin, p. 10). And while the debates of biblical scholars about liberation hermeneutics are potentially useful to the larger project (Sugirtharajah 2006, pp. 77–80), liberation hermeneutics should not, in the first instance, be evaluated by its biblical interpretation but by the effects of the praxis that biblical interpretation plays a part in producing.

[*See also* Central and South American Interpretation; Class Criticism; Economics and the Bible; Feminist Biblical Interpretation; Materialist Criticism; Postcolonial Biblical Interpretation; *and* Queer Criticism and Queer Theory.]

BIBLIOGRAPHY

Althaus-Reid, Marcella. *Indecent Theology: Theological Perversions in Sex, Gender and Politics.* London and New York: Routledge, 2000. An engagement with liberation theology from the perspective of queer theory.

Boer, Roland. "Marx, Postcolonialism, and the Bible." In *Postcolonial Biblical Criticism: Interdisciplinary Intersections*, edited by S. D. Moore and F. F. Segovia. London and New York: T.&T. Clark, 2005. An exploration of the economic hubris of postcolonial studies.

Bonino, Jose Miguez. *Doing Theology in a Revolutionary Situation.* Philadelphia: Fortress, 1975. The classic introduction to liberation theology.

Comaroff, Jean, and John L. Comaroff. *Of Revelation and Revolution: Christianity, Colonialism and Consciousness in South Africa.* Vol. 1. Chicago: University of Chicago Press, 1991. An in-depth historical-anthropological analysis of the early missionary-colonial project in southern Africa.

Croatto, J. Severino. *Biblical Hermeneutics: Toward a Theory of Reading as the Production of Meaning.* New York: Orbis, 1987. A literary-semiotic contribution to biblical liberation hermeneutics.

Foucault, Michel. *Of other spaces: heterotopias* 1967 cited 19/03/08 2008. Available from http://foucault.info/documents/heteroTopia/foucault.heteroTopia.en.html. A suggestive exploration of the role of alternative spaces in marginalized communities.

Freire, Paulo. *The Politics of Education: Culture, Power, and Liberation.* Westport, Conn.: Greenwood, 1985. The less well-known companion to *Pedagogy of the Oppressed.*

Frostin, Per. *Liberation Theology in Tanzania and South Africa: A First World Interpretation.* Lund, Sweden: Lund University Press, 1988. A remarkably incisive analysis of African forms of liberation hermeneutics.

Gottwald, Norman K. *How Does Social Scientific Criticism Shape Our Understanding of the Bible as a Resource for Economic Ethics?* Atlanta: Scholars Press, 1993. An incisive analysis of the relationship between biblical text and contemporary context.

Gottwald, Norman K. *The Tribes of Yahweh: A Sociology of the Religion of Liberated Israel, 1250–1050 B.C.*

Maryknoll, N.Y.: Orbis, 1979. The groundbreaking sociohistorical analysis of ancient Israel.

Gutiérrez, Gustavo. *A Theology of Liberation: History, Politics and Salvation.* Maryknoll, N.Y.: Orbis, 1973. The classic reference work on liberation theology.

Hinkelammert, Franz J. *The Ideological Weapons of Death: A Theological Critique of Capitalism.* Maryknoll, N.Y.: Orbis, 1986. An important reformulation of liberation hermeneutics in its second decade.

Kairos, the Theologians. *Challenge to the Church: The Kairos Document: A Theological Comment on the Political Crisis in South Africa.* Braamfontein, South Africa: The Kairos Theologians, 1985. One of the most significant theological reflections to come out of the South African struggle against apartheid.

Kairos Palestine. "A Moment of Truth: A Word of Faith, Hope and Love from the Heart of Palestinian Suffering: Kairos Palestine." www.kairospalestine.ps, 2009. This "kairos" document is the most recent in a long line of "kairos documents" inspired by the South African *Kairos Document.*

Mofokeng, T. "Black Christians, the Bible and Liberation." *Journal of Black Theology* 2 (1988): 34–42. One of the first voices from within black theology to argue that the Bible was itself a problem for liberation struggles.

Mosala, Itumeleng J. *Biblical Hermeneutics and Black Theology in South Africa.* Grand Rapids, Mich.: Eerdmans, 1989. The most incisive analysis of the limits of black theology's biblical hermeneutics.

Mosala, Itumeleng J. "The Use of the Bible in Black Theology." In *The Unquestionable Right to Be Free: Essays in Black Theology,* edited by I. J. Mosala and B. Tlhagale. Johannesburg: Skotaville, 1986. A searching critique of the biblical hermeneutical assumptions of black theology in South Africa and North America.

Nolan, Albert. *God in South Africa: The Challenge of the Gospel.* Cape Town: David Philip, 1988. An articulation of South African contextual/liberation theology.

Oduyoye, Mercy Amba. "Reflections from a Third World Woman's Perspective: Women's Experience and Liberation Theologies." In *Irruption of the Third World: Challenge to Theology,* edited by V. Fabella and S. Torres. Maryknoll, N.Y.: Orbis, 1983. One of the first published arguments for a feminist perspective within Third World theologies.

Riches, John, Helen Ball, Roy Henderson, Craig Lancaster, Leslie Milton, and Maureen Russell. *What is Contextual Bible Study? A Practical Guide with Group Studies for Advent and Lent.* London: SPCK, 2010. An analysis of how southern African forms of liberation hermeneutics have been appropriated in Scotland.

Schüssler-Fiorenza, Elizabeth. *In Memory of Her: A Feminist Theological Reconstruction of Christian Origins.* London: SCM, 1983. The pioneering sociohistorical perspective on feminist biblical hermeneutics.

Scott, James C. *Domination and the Arts of Resistance: Hidden Transcripts.* New Haven, Conn.: Yale University Press, 1990. A careful and insightful argument for the agency of the poor, and the limits of ideological hegemony.

Segundo, Juan Luis. "The Shift within Latin American Theology." *Journal of Theology for Southern Africa* 52 (1985): 17–29. An important analysis of the two contending viewpoints within liberation theology with respect to the role of the intellectual.

Smith, Theophus H. *Conjuring Culture: Biblical Formations of Black America.* Oxford and New York: Oxford University Press, 1994. An exploration of the biblical hermeneutics of ordinary African Americans, from slavery to the present.

Sugirtharajah, R.S. "Postcolonial Biblical Interpretation." In *Voices from the Margin: Interpreting the Bible in the Third World,* edited by R. S. Sugirtharajah. Maryknoll, N.Y.: Orbis, 2006. A detailed engagement between liberation and postcolonial hermeneutics.

Trible, Phyllis. *Texts of Terror: Literary-feminist Readings of Biblical Narratives.* Philadelphia: Fortress, 1984. The groundbreaking work on literary feminist biblical hermeneutics.

West, Gerald O. *Biblical Hermeneutics of Liberation: Modes of Reading the Bible in the South African Context.* 2d ed. Maryknoll, N.Y.: Orbis; Pietermaritzburg, South Africa: Cluster, 1995. An exploration of how the Bible is used in various liberation struggles, with a focus on the South African struggle.

Gerald West

LITERARY CRITICISM, LITERARY THEORY, AND THE BIBLE

The terms "literary criticism" and "literary theory" are used in biblical studies to indicate a range of literary and theoretical approaches to the Hebrew Bible and New Testament. Literary critical interpretations begin with the assumption that the Bible is literature and proceed using the tools, strategies, and methodologies of literary analysis. While literary criticism and literary theory come to biblical studies from other disciplines in the humanities (chiefly English and modern literatures), the relationship between fields is not often a close one, and the meanings associated with the terminology vary, sometimes greatly, between disciplines.

Literary criticism is often positioned against more traditional modes of biblical interpretation, in particular the historical-critical method. While literary criticism has occasionally been used to mean source criticism or form criticism, this usage is no longer generally accepted. Literary theory often signals a relationship to the forms of critique that occur in other disciplines, including English and modern literatures. At times, literary theory is used to mean "theory" as such, including poststructuralism, deconstruction, psychoanalysis, and other postmodern approaches (on this usage, see Terry Eagleton's introduction, *Literary Theory*, 2008). This usage occurs among both adherents and skeptics. Literary theoretical approaches employ the techniques of literary criticism, though often with a more pronounced poststructuralist or postmodern emphasis, and frequently take up questions that go beyond the interpretation of a specific unit of text.

A related term "Bible as literature," has largely fallen out of favor in biblical studies, mostly due to the ambiguity of the word "as," but persists primarily in English departments and popular accounts.

Early Literary Approaches. The literary approach to the Bible is at once a modern innovation, made possible by large-scale philosophical and critical transformations in the disciplines of history, literature, and biblical studies, and a recurring technique across the long history of biblical interpretation. In *The Idea of Biblical Poetry* (1981, 1998), James Kugel demonstrates that the Bible has been read as literature by a variety of interpreters since late antiquity; his particular focus is the Hebrew poetic texts. Kugel traces the influence of Greek conceptions of poetry on late antique and medieval biblical readers, arguing that an emphasis on Greek poetic features such as meter, rhyme, and a whole range of rhetorical devices leads to the creation of a category of "biblical poetry." For Kugel, this category, however common, is erroneous. This literary approach culminates in Robert Lowth's *Lectures on the Sacred Poetry of the Hebrews* (*De Sacra Poesi Hebraeorum Praelectiones*) in 1753 (London: Routledge/Thoemmes, 1995). After a spirited defense of poetry as a genre, Lowth turns to the biblical literature, arguing that "parallelismus membrorum," the parallel line, is the defining feature of biblical poetry. Lowth is widely recognized as the first to offer a so-called system of biblical poetry, but, as Kugel points out, his study encapsulates and reflects larger ongoing trends (*Idea of Biblical Poetry*, 1998, pp. 204–286). Nevertheless, Lowth remains a central figure in the history of biblical literary criticism.

In *The Enlightenment Bible* (2005), Jonathan Sheehan picks up the history of interpretation at the Enlightenment. Sheehan argues that modernity produces a "cultural Bible," which is distinct from the religious text that precedes it. For Sheehan, the cultural Bible of the Enlightenment includes an embrace of the literary Bible. This increased literary interest in the Bible, like the premodern interpretations that Kugel describes, is largely centered upon the question of poetry in the Hebrew Bible (HB). Sheehan demonstrates that the literary approach to the Bible offers a fruitful alternative to theological reading, even as it facilitates modes of reading that link the Hebrew nation to the modern project of nationalism in Germany, England, and elsewhere. This is especially clear in Johann Gottfried von Herder's *The Spirit of Hebrew Poetry* (1833; Aleph Press, 1971 [English]), a text that occupies roughly the same cultural space in German-language biblical studies as does Lowth's in English-language work.

Literary Criticism and the Bible as Literature. From the Enlightenment Bible on, the biblical text proved a compelling interpretive object for artists and critics alike. Among numerous others, Matthew Arnold, Samuel Coleridge, and T. S. Eliot all wrote about the Bible and its relationship to literature and culture. During the later twentieth century, influential literary critics such as Northrop Frye and Harold Bloom likewise took up the biblical text. In this turn to the Bible by literary scholars, the work of Frank Kermode deserves particular attention for bridging the disciplinary space between literary criticism and biblical studies. At the same time, the twentieth century saw courses on "The Bible as Literature" multiply across the academy, often taught out of English departments and by literature scholars.

The phrase "The Bible as literature" generally refers not to the practice of literary criticism in the discipline of biblical studies but rather to readings of the Bible in other literary and critical disciplines. These readings often privilege the content and form of the text over and against the questions of context, source, textuality, and redaction that are standard in biblical studies, even for literary-oriented biblical scholars. This approach frequently (if not exclusively) deals with the English translations of the Bible; the King James Version holds a special interest for scholars, especially but not exclusively in departments of English. Thus readings of the "Bible as literature" sometimes incorporate issues of translation and of literary resonances in the English-language literary tradition, even as traditional literary concerns such as sound play, rhythm, and rhyme are often neglected due to a lack of expertise in the original languages.

The most important literary reading of the Bible from the first half of the twentieth century comes from Erich Auerbach, author of *Mimesis* (1953, fiftieth anniversary ed., 2003). Though Auerbach discusses biblical narrative in detail in only a single chapter, "Odysseus' Scar," his analysis both illuminates a specific text (Gen 22) and demonstrates the potential of close readings as a literary and critical approach to the Bible. "Odysseus' Scar" opens with a close reading of Book 19 of the *Odyssey*, in which Odysseus, home at last, encounters an old woman who recognizes him by the scar on his thigh. Against this scene, Auerbach contrasts a biblical example, the binding of Isaac (Gen 22), directing attention to the terse narration and the paucity of detail. While Homer's text is elaborately descriptive, creating a "uniformly illuminated, uniformly objective present," the biblical text is "fraught with background"—spare, suggestive, and obscure (Auerbach, 7, 12). For Auerbach, these two texts represent two distinct modes of representing reality and, as such, represent rival literary forms throughout the Western literary tradition. Auerbach's reading influenced a large number of later readers, among them important biblical literary critics such as Alter and Kermode.

Literary Approaches Originating within Biblical Studies. The interest in bringing together the Bible with literary criticism did not flourish only in literature circles. Biblical scholars, too, were increasingly turning to forms of literary analysis. In the 1968 presidential address to the Society of Biblical Literature, James Muilenburg called on biblical studies to embrace new critical approaches. After praising the interpretive gains of form criticism, Muilenberg urged his colleagues to go "beyond" form criticism and to take up questions of aesthetics, style, and literary technique. Muilenberg's method, known as "rhetorical criticism," gained traction in the field and served as an important and perhaps necessary predecessor to literary criticism, as well as a significant interpretive method in its own right.

Taking up the imperative to move beyond form criticism, the journal *Semeia*, published by the Society of Biblical Literature from 1974 to 2002, served as an early forum for literary approaches to the Bible. For the following quarter-century, *Semeia* repeatedly engaged with topics in literary theory, among them narrative (*Semeia* 9, 15, 26, 46, and 63), Reader-Response Criticism (31, 48), textuality, (40, 50, 65), genre (43), intertextuality (69–70), semiotics (81), poststructuralism (50, 54), and the "ethics of reading" (77). *Semeia* also put out thematic issues addressing the work of literary theorists, including Paul Ricoeur (4, 19), Jacques Derrida (23, 54), René Girard (33), and Northrop Frye (89). Sometimes, the engagement with literary theory in *Semeia* preserved the relatively traditional biblical studies model of applying the theory to the text. At other points, however, *Semeia* produced innovative theoretical work that challenged both the reading of the biblical text and the field of knowledge in literary theory.

The Hebrew Bible and *The Art of Biblical Narrative*. In 1975 Robert Alter published an important article in *Commentary* titled "A Literary Approach to the Bible." In a revised form, the article appeared as the first chapter in *The Art of Biblical Narrative* (1981; 2d ed., 2011), Alter's guide to the literary reading of the HB. The book interweaves literary theory of the biblical text with a number of close readings that serve as applied examples. Alter emphasizes the "conscious artistry" of the biblical writer, arguing that even narratives constructed from inherited materials display "the kind of subtle cogency we associate with the conscious artistry of the narrative mode designated prose fiction" (Alter, p. 36). These parallels between biblical narrative and prose fiction appear repeatedly across Alter's work; he compares the biblical text to Fielding, Flaubert, and James, among others. His reading strategy treats the biblical text as closer to these modern works than to, for example, Ugaritic literature. Alter works to illuminate the meaningful literary choices that the biblical writer makes with the available material. Beyond turning the literary criticism of the novel onto the biblical text, he takes up as well a number of stylistic features specific to ancient Hebrew prose literature, including the type scene and the function of repeated *Leitwörter*, an idea developed earlier by Buber and Rosenzweig (Alter, pp. 92–93). And throughout the book, Alter stresses the "composite artistry" (Alter, 131ff.) of the final form of the text. Under Alter, the redactor, long familiar from source criticism, becomes an artist.

The Art of Biblical Narrative was an immediate—and lasting—success. Alter won the National Jewish Book Award and became an authoritative voice of the new literary criticism of the Bible. A proliferation of literary and narrative studies quickly appeared in biblical studies, many of them following Alter in adapting the practices of New Criticism and bracketing questions of history, authorship, and other traditional concerns of the historical-critical method in favor of close reading and immanent literary analysis of the biblical text. What accounted for this sudden success of the literary method? At the time of publication, biblical studies was increasingly drawn to literary studies; Steven Weitzman emphasizes the "timeliness" of Alter's approach in the 1970s and 1980s, noting that "it linked biblical study with literary theory at a time when the latter was a source of considerable cultural capital" ("Before and After *The Art of Biblical Narrative*," *Prooftexts* 27:2 [2007]: 193). That the specific literary approach Alter championed was in many ways at odds with the contemporaneous developments in literary theory—the 1970s and 1980s saw the ascendance of forms of theory very different from the New Critical practices that Alter advocates—did not really diminish the attraction of literary theory for biblical scholarship.

Other Literary Approaches to Hebrew Narrative. *The Art of Biblical Narrative* was not the only important work on biblical narrative of its time. Meir Sternberg's *The Poetics of Biblical Narrative* (1985) represents another significant literary approach to the HB. Sternberg's book expands upon earlier work done in collaboration with Menahem Perry, particularly the article "The King through Ironic Eyes: Biblical Narrative and the Literary Reading Process" (*Hasifrut* 1:2 [1968]: 263–292 [Hebrew]; *Poetics Today* 7:2 [1986]: 275–322 [English]). Sternberg describes biblical narrative as a "system of gaps" to be pieced together and filled in by the reader as the reading process unfolds. This does not, however, make meaning into an arbitrary and uncontrolled project of social construction; there are, he insists, both legitimate and illegitimate ways of filling gaps. The work of the reader is to determine the system of gaps specific to the narrative and then to fill them.

Sternberg also insists that the Bible is characterized by its "foolproof composition"—an idea that addresses, in part, the problem of "illegitimate" gap filling. According to Sternberg, the play between viewpoints and perspectives, temporal discontinuities, proleptic strategies of characterization, and repetition all contribute to a textual whole that is taken as foolproof. While Sternberg is astute at observing the workings of biblical ambiguity, his insistence on foolproof composition has met with significant resistance from critics, particularly insofar as it is at least implicitly theological. The distinction between "legitimate" and "illegitimate" gap filling, however, is problematic, even as he introduces a distinction between gaps, which the reader must fill, and "blanks," which can remain unfilled. The literary criticism of the Bible, however, largely followed Alter's approach more closely, even as the number of literary texts and readings proliferated.

Narrative and Parable: Literary Approaches to the New Testament. Literary methods appeared as well in New Testament (NT) Studies. While the literary approach to Hebrew narrative influenced this development, literary critics also drew on earlier NT scholarship—particularly on the Gospels—which appeared in the 1960s and 1970s. Much of this work began with questions of form, genre, and language and moved to embrace broader literary concerns. Amos Wilder's *The Language of the Gospel* (1964), for example, used language as an entry point into a literary treatment of the text. The parables were particularly important objects of study in this phase of literary inquiry. Frank Kermode, already the author of a study of apocalypticism and literature (*The Sense of an Ending*, Oxford, 1967), took up parables and narrative in *The Genesis of Secrecy* (1979), a study of the Gospel of Mark. Although Kermode was trained as a literary critic, his work increasingly addressed the Bible and influenced biblical scholars. Robert Funk's *Parables and Presence* (1982, containing a number of pieces published previously) represents another influential use of the parables to introduce literary questions into biblical studies. Funk also makes use of structuralism and poststructuralism, even referencing Lacan, and his work offers an early model for using literary theory to read the Bible. Both Wilder and Funk were also important figures in the journal *Semeia*. The first issue contains an introductory editorial by Wilder, while its topic is "A Structuralist Approach to the Parables," edited by Funk (*Semeia* 1:1, 1972). Kermode, meanwhile, went on to collaborate with Robert Alter as coeditors of the influential *The Literary Guide to the Bible* (1987).

An especially influential book on a NT narrative text is *Mark as Story*, jointly authored by the biblical scholar David Rhoads and the English professor Donald Michie; the biblical scholar Joanna Dewey also collaborates on the second and third editions. *Mark as Story* sets forth an accessible and convincing reading of that Gospel "as story," complete with narrator, setting, plot, characters, and readers. This accessible introduction to narrative criticism opened the gate to an outpouring of narrative critical studies of texts within the Gospels and in Acts, as well as the Gospels and Acts as wholes, with significant work taking place in the Society of Biblical Literature group on "The Literary Aspects of the Gospels and Acts," whose activity happened to be bounded by the first and second editions of *Mark as Story*. The literary approach to the Gospels spread to other biblical texts. More than ever before, the NT had become the object of literary critique, expressed not only in articles and monographs but also in entire commentaries and commentary series oriented to literary approaches to NT books. In addition, Rhoads, along with Dewey and others, has since helped pioneer the new—and related—approach of performance criticism, bringing to literary criticism concerns for media and audience (see Hearon and Ruge-Jones 2009).

Critical Assessments of the Literary Approach. An array of narrative and other literary studies quickly followed as literary approaches gained traction in biblical studies. Many of the first generation of biblical critics to engage seriously with literary criticism implicitly or explicitly emulated the approach of New Criticism, emphasizing formal analysis and literary tropes and devices over and against both historical approaches and the theoretical concerns of poststructuralism and deconstruction in ascendance in literary theory at large. This resistance to literary theory is often raised as an objection against the "literary approach to the Bible." Mieke Bal, for example, has criticized the refusal of the literary approach, in its early forms, to engage with questions such as ideology. Bal is especially critical of Sternberg's work; in an important review, published in *Diacritics*, she describes his approach as theology veiled as literary criticism ("The Bible as Literature: A Critical Escape," *Diacritics*, 16:4 [1986]). A related critique has also been levied against seemingly nonideological readings; critics argue that the literary approach goes too far in praising the merits of the text, allowing a basically theological attitude toward the text to endure under the cover of "literary" appreciation (Moore and Sherwood 2011, 92–94).

The literary approach has likewise been criticized for refusing to historicize the text or to acknowledge the significance of its cultural contexts, although more recent work does much to address these criticisms. Other critics object not simply to the form of literary analysis but to the starting premise that the literary provides a useful category through which to enter into the biblical text. Long before the literary approach gained traction, NT scholars debated the appropriateness of identifying the text as literature. In 1923, the form critic Karl-Ludwig Schmidt, for example, distinguished between the Gospels, which he named *Kleinliteratur,* and other, more consciously literary forms of *Hochliteratur* (*The Place of the Gospels in the General History of Literature,* Columbia, S.C.: University of South Carolina Press, 2002). James Kugel voiced this critique even more strongly with reference to the HB, though his argument can be applied to the NT as well. To take the Bible as literature, Kugel argued, was to commit a category mistake: the Bible is not "literature" at all. While Kugel grants that the Bible has been treated as a literary text since the Hellenistic period, he insists that postbiblical readers lack "literary competence" to understand and interpret the text properly. Without this competence, literary interpretation is at best anachronistic, and often disingenuous and distracting. Kugel's critique, however, found limited success, and the production of literary readings of the Bible only increased.

Kugel's general critique of anachronism in biblical literary criticism finds specific manifestation in his debate with Alter about biblical poetry. In *The Art of Biblical Poetry* (1985), Alter (1) affirms that biblical poetry is characterized by multiple, overlapping parallelisms; (2) traces the structures of intensification in the poetic line, theorizing the relationship between poetic repetition and history; and (3) concludes by arguing that understanding biblical poetry illuminates the Western poetic tradition. In *The Idea of Biblical Poetry* (1998), Kugel, in sharp resistance to Alter's work, argues that biblical poetry does not exist except as an unproductive and anachronistic distraction. Instead, poetry and prose exist on a continuum, varying chiefly in the degree of parallelism they exhibit. To speak of biblical poetry is to force nonnative categories, borrowed from classical Greek and Latin texts or from modern literature, onto the text. While many of the early studies of biblical poetry were, like Alter's work, implicitly New Critical in orientation, later work began to embrace poststructuralism, deconstruction, and other more contemporary literary theories.

From New Criticism to Literary Theory. Despite Kugel's critiques, the "literary approach to the Bible" quickly gained influence in the field of biblical studies. Though its first generation of practitioners did not always agree with each other's theoretical arguments or close readings, they shared a basic theoretical orientation. This "first generation" of literary critics of the Bible share an understanding of the "literary approach" as basically a formal one, an uncovering of literary structures and an explication of the workings of the text on a narrative, poetic, or structural level. From the perspective of literary theory, this approach has much in common with New Criticism, Russian formalism, and other formalist methods. This critical approach perhaps achieves its peak in the 1987 *The Literary Guide to the Bible,* edited by Alter together with Kermode and addressing both the HB and the NT.

The Literary Guide to the Bible is primarily a commentary, with essays on each of the books of the HB and the NT. The approaches taken by the essays vary, though they generally tend to emphasize form, structure, and other forms of immanent critique and close reading, instead of drawing on the social, material, and political concerns that had already begun to dominate the literary theory of the 1980s (see further Eagleton, *Literary Theory,* 2008). The commentaries are accompanied by several general essays, including Alter's description of "The Characteristics of Ancient Hebrew Poetry" and Kermode on the formation of the canon. Here, too, are several essays setting the biblical literature in its larger literary milieu—"The Hebrew Bible and Canaanite Literature" (Jonas C. Greenfield); "The New Testament and Greco-Roman Writing" (Helen Elsom); and "Midrash and Allegory" (Gerald L. Bruns). These essays, while only a portion of the volume, nevertheless signal an important shift toward bringing together close literary analysis with a thick awareness of the larger literary world in which this literature is conceived and executed.

A number of book-length studies and edited volumes began to appear, counterbalancing, like *Semeia*, literary criticism with literary theory. A good early example of this trend is *The Book and the Text: The Bible and Literary Theory* (1990), edited by Regina Schwartz. Published just three years after *The Literary Guide to the Bible*, it offers a collection of essays that bring together a range of literary readings of the HB and the NT. Alter and Sternberg are present, but they are joined by a number of critics whose work demonstrates an openness to literary theory in its "higher" and more abstracted forms. Schwartz's lucid introduction begins with Alter's 1975 essay but then deftly charts the movement beyond it. Schwartz acknowledges and sketches an introduction to the proliferation of new methods and approaches in the field of literary studies, even as she cautions that the task is not simply one of applying techniques to the text. The essays take up both the HB and the NT in a variety of ways, including feminist literary theory (Mieke Bal), psychoanalysis and the Hebrew prophets (Herbert Marks), and NT new historicism (Mary Ann Tolbert). The volume also includes, among others, contributions by the theorists Paul Ricoeur (on NT narrative) and Terry Eagleton (on speech act theory and Jonah); their inclusion signals a productive interdisciplinarity between biblical studies and other literary and theoretical disciplines.

Beyond the many specific insights into the texts, the real significance of Schwartz's *The Book and the Text* lies in its thoroughgoing engagement between the biblical text and literary theory. This is an engagement that continues, as well, in a pair of volumes published several years later, *The New Literary Criticism and the Hebrew Bible* (edited by Cheryl Exum and David Clines) and *The New Literary Criticism and the New Testament* (edited by Elizabeth Struthers Malbon and Edgar V. McKnight). Both volumes offer a number of examples of "the new literary criticism"—not New Criticism but post-structuralist, feminist, materialist, psychoanalytic, and reader-response approaches. Many of these approaches eventually develop into full-fledged methods of interpretation; it is worth noting that they originate in literary criticism and literary theory, as these volumes nicely demonstrate.

Alter and Kermode's New Critical literary approach, even as it claimed hegemony—or perhaps because of its hegemonic status—had been surpassed. The move beyond the "literary approach" to the realms of literary "theory" was sealed by the 1997 publication of *The Postmodern Bible*, at once a manifesto for new theoretical ways of reading the Bible and a primer on a variety of theoretical approaches. Authored by the Bible and Culture Collective, made up of a number of important biblical literary scholars and theorists, the text surveys a number of important theoretical methods, loosely paralleling the fields Eagleton discusses in *Literary Theory*. The volume makes a compelling argument for the use of theory in biblical scholarship.

Recent Developments: the Bible "After Theory". The possibilities for critical engagements between the Bible and theory (literary and otherwise) have been taken up by an increasing number of scholars in recent years, in forums including the "Reading, Theory, and the Bible" section of the Society of Biblical Literature and journals such as *Biblical Interpretation* and *The Bible and Critical Theory* (*Semeia* ceased publication in 2002). Among the most influential scholars in this evolving conversation are Stephen D. Moore and Yvonne Sherwood. Independently and together, Moore and Sherwood's works have long been central to the literary theory wing of biblical studies. Sherwood has explored deconstruction, feminist theory, and performance theory; Moore's work spans narrative theory, reader-response theory, autobiographical criticism, and masculinity studies, among others. Together, they authored the 2011 monograph *The Invention of the Biblical Scholar: A Critical Manifesto*, itself an outgrowth of an SBL session loosely focused on Terry Eagleton's *After Theory* (Moore and Sherwood, p. ix). Moore and Sherwood chart out—and critique—a detailed history of biblical studies' engagement with theory. The most interesting and provocative part of their work, however, is their future vision for the Bible and theory. Moore and Sherwood call on biblical scholars and theorists to move beyond the uneasy coexistence that has allowed theory to find a toehold in the biblical studies academy without, however, significantly influencing it in any way. Together with this embrace of theory, they call for a critical interrogation of the unquestioned hegemony of the historical critical method, and of "history" as privileged object of inquiry in biblical studies. They likewise call on biblical scholars, like literary scholars, to embrace a playfulness with language and to acknowledge scholarly writing, theoretical and otherwise, not as the transparent transmission of knowledge, but as an artful, constructed, and itself literary form.

The Invention of the Biblical Scholar ends by tracking the recent turn in literary theory toward "big, flabby, old-fashioned words" such as justice, truth, faith, and evil (Moore and Sherwood, p. 127). This turn is especially apparent in those forms of theory found within, or in conversation with, continental philosophy. The challenge for biblical studies is how to engage with this turn to religion on behalf of literary theory. As the authors note, such questions often feel "disturbingly intimate, proximate, or 'philosophical'" (Moore and Sherwood, 128); at the same time, they present a unique opportunity for biblical studies not simply to borrow from literary theory and then force it upon texts, cookie-cutter style, but rather to work on the front lines of production and critique. Bringing biblical studies and literary theory in closer conversation—if not always agreement—would open new possibilities in both fields.

Future Directions. The turn to Continental philosophy and to religious themes is not the only possible future direction for literary theory and criticism. The production of more traditional literary critical readings of the text, with an emphasis on such matters as form, rhythm, structure, genre, and narrative will no doubt continue to be an important part of biblical studies as a whole. These literary readings, however, are increasingly moving beyond straight New Critical analyses of the text to incorporate history, source criticism, performance criticism, and other textual approaches into a richly nuanced appreciation of the text. Thus biblical literary criticism seems primed to follow the movement in literary criticism more generally to incorporate and embrace an eclectic spectrum of hermeneutic methods.

The more theoretically oriented side of the literary approach also holds promise in biblical studies. The ideological criticism of texts often relies on literary methods at least in part; here feminist criticism in particular has shown great adeptness in adopting literary methods. Sherwood's *The Prostitute and the Prophet* (1996) remains a model of the engagement between literary criticism, feminist criticism, and theory; the two decades since its publication have seen a proliferation of similar and imitative approaches. Queer criticism of the Bible seems primed to follow; queer literary approaches have already appeared in a scattering of works, including work by Moore (most recently collected in *The Bible in Theory*, 2010). Marxist literary criticism, while an important force in literary theory as such, has made only limited inroads in biblical studies (*The Postmodern Bible* covers the topic briefly); Marxist historical criticism has also made occasional forays. The work of Roland Boer is perhaps the best example of Marxist theory of a literary bent in biblical studies. The journal *Bible and Critical Theory*, edited by Boer and Julie Kelso, consistently offers a range of innovative theoretical approaches (not at all limited to "Critical Theory" in the strict sense of the Frankfurt School). Psychoanalytic criticism, another important form of literary theory in nonbiblical fields, has likewise made only limited inroads into the biblical studies guild; the work of Ilona Rashkow offers a good starting place.

The future of each of these forms of literary theory remains open. It may be hoped, however, that new theoretical approaches to the biblical text informed by recent literary theory will increase, even as formal literary criticism remains a standard method of interpretation. In any number of forms, literary criticism and literary theory are important tools for biblical interpreters.

[*See also* Deconstruction; Feminist Biblical Interpretation; Formalist Interpretation; Ideological Criticism; Masculinity Studies; Materialist Criticism;

Narrative Criticism and Narrative Hermeneutics; Performance Criticism; Poststructuralist Interpretation; Postmodern Interpretation; Psychological Biblical Interpretation; Queer Criticism and Queer Theory; Reader-Response Criticism; Reception Criticism and Theory; Rhetorical Criticism; Structuralist Interpretation; *and* Synchronic Interpretation.]

BIBLIOGRAPHY

Alter, Robert. *The Art of Biblical Narrative.* 2d ed. New York: Basic Books, 2011. Originally published 1981. Still the classic introduction to the literary criticism of the HB, with an emphasis on the techniques of New Criticism. The 1975 *Commentary* article "A Literary Approach to the Bible" appears, in revised form, as the first chapter in the 1981 edition.

Alter, Robert. *The Art of Biblical Poetry.* New York: Basic Books, 1985. An influential and readable analysis of biblical poetry, combined with close readings of poetic texts from a number of books of the Hebrew Bible.

Alter, Robert, and Frank Kermode, eds. *The Literary Guide to the Bible.* Cambridge, Mass.: Belknap Press of Harvard University Press, 1987. An anthology of literary essays on the Bible, loosely reflecting the approaches of the editors. The volume includes essays on every book of the Hebrew Bible and the New Testament, as well as several thematic and theoretical contributions.

Auerbach, Erich. *Mimesis: The Representation of Reality in Western Literature.* 50th anniversary ed. Princeton: Princeton University Press, 2003. Originally published 1953. A classic study of the Western literary tradition; the first chapter, "Odysseus' Scar," sets forth a famous comparison of the *Iliad* and the sacrifice of Isaac to argue that Homer and the Bible represent two models for representing reality in literary texts.

Bible and Culture Collective. *The Postmodern Bible.* New Haven: Yale University Press, 1995. Introduces and assesses the value of a range of postmodern methods for biblical scholarship, including reader-response, structuralist, poststructuralist, rhetorical, psychoanalytic, feminist and womanist, and ideological criticism.

Eagleton, Terry. *Literary Theory: An Introduction.* 3d ed. University of Minnesota Press, 2008. An excellent introduction to literary theory by a preeminent practitioner. Surveys a number of important movements, including reception theory, structuralism and semiotics, poststructuralism, psychoanalysis, and political criticism.

Exum, J. Cheryl, and David J. A. Clines, eds. *The New Literary Criticism and the Hebrew Bible.* London: Continuum International Publishing Group, 1993. A collection of essays using "the new literary criticism," including poststructuralism, feminist critique, reader-response approaches, psychoanalysis, and deconstruction. The essays cover a range of texts in the Hebrew Bible, including both prose and poetry.

Funk, Robert Walter. *Parables and Presence: Forms of the New Testament Tradition.* Philadelphia: Fortress, 1982. A study of the New Testament, in particular the parables, that employs both literary criticism and interpretive methods such as structuralism.

Hearon, Holly, and Philip Ruge-Jones, eds. *The Bible in Ancient and Modern Media: Story and Performance.* Eugene, Ore.: Cascade Books, 2009. Offers an introduction to media studies and performance criticism as methods of literary interpretation. The emphasis is on NT material.

Kermode, Frank. *The Genesis of Secrecy: On the Interpretation of Narrative.* Cambridge, Mass.: Harvard University Press, 1979. An insightful study of biblical narrative by a nonbiblical literary critic. Kermode takes as a starting point the Gospel of Mark, particularly the parables.

Kugel, James. "On the Bible and Literary Criticism." *Prooftexts* 1, no. 3 (September 1, 1981): 217–236. Perhaps the most important critique of the use of literary methods to read the Bible. Kugel argues that the literary approach is anachronistic, unproductive, and misleading.

Kugel, James. *The Idea of Biblical Poetry: Parallelism and Its History.* Baltimore, Md.: The Johns Hopkins University Press, 1981, 1998. Kugel argues that "poetry" does not exist as a distinct genre in the Hebrew Bible, and that parallelism instead is the defining feature of texts commonly misunderstood as poetry. The second half of the book gives a history of poetry as an "idea" in late antique, medieval, and early modern interpretive traditions, ending with Robert Lowth.

Malbon, Elizabeth Struthers, and Edgar V. McKnight, eds. *The New Literary Criticism and the New Testament.* London: Sheffield Academic Press, 1994. Brings together essays on the New Testament that use the methods of "the new literary criticism" and offers literary and theoretical insight into a wide range of books and texts of the NT. This is the companion volume to Exum and Clines, *The New Literary Criticism and the Hebrew Bible.*

Moore, Stephen D. *The Bible in Theory: Critical and Postcritical Essays.* Atlanta, Ga.: Society of Biblical Literature, 2010. A collection of essays spanning much of Moore's scholarly career; a good introduction to both Moore's own important body of work and to the larger themes of postmodernity, textuality, autobiographical criticism, masculinity, sexuality, postcoloniality, and the end of theory in biblical studies.

Moore, Stephen D, and Yvonne Sherwood. *The Invention of the Biblical Scholar: A Critical Manifesto*. Minneapolis: Fortress, 2011. Combines a history of the discipline of biblical studies and its relationship to literary theory with a vigorous argument for innovative new critical and theoretical approaches, as well as a new relationship between biblical studies and theory.

Muilenburg, James. "Form Criticism and Beyond." *Journal of Biblical Literature* 88, no. 1 (March 1, 1969): 1–18. In the 1968 presidential address to the Society of Biblical Literature, published in the SBL, Muilenburg called for a movement "beyond" form criticism to what he termed "rhetorical criticism," an important step toward literary criticism.

Rhoads, David M., Joanna Dewey, and Donald Michie. *Mark as Story: An Introduction to the Narrative of a Gospel*. 2d ed. Minneapolis: Fortress, 1999. This jointly authored volume by a biblical scholar (Rhoads) and a literary scholar (Michie) reads Mark "as story." The second edition is significantly revised from the 1982 first edition and includes the collaboration of Dewey, another biblical scholar. Important for both literary criticism in general and New Testament narrative criticism in particular.

Schwartz, Regina, ed. *The Book and the Text: The Bible and Literary Theory*. Oxford: Blackwell, 1990. An edited volume that brings together literary readings from a variety of critical approaches, ranging from New Criticism and narratology to poststructuralist and postmodern approaches. The essays by Schwartz and Marks are especially recommended.

Sheehan, Jonathan. *The Enlightenment Bible: Translation, Scholarship, Culture*. Princeton: Princeton University Press, 2005. An account of the transformed understandings of the Bible in the Enlightenment, including a new recognition of the Bible as a literary text.

Sherwood, Yvonne. *The Prostitute and the Prophet: Hosea's Marriage in Literary-Theoretical Perspective*. Sheffield: Sheffield Academic Press, 1996. This study of Hosea 1—3 offers an excellent model for an approach to biblical text that combines a range of literary theoretical approaches, including semiotics, feminist criticism, and deconstruction.

Wilder, Amos N. *Early Christian Rhetoric: The Language of the Gospel*. Peabody, Mass.: Hendrickson, 1999. Originally published in 1964. A study of language in the Gospels that anticipates the use of literary criticism in modern New Testament studies.

Rhiannon Graybill

Lutheran Interpretation

What is identifiably Lutheran in the matter of biblical interpretation is quite specific: Luther, the Confessions, Lutheran scholasticism, and pietism. These shape the Lutheran tradition communally, and they are harkened back to repeatedly by Lutheran scholars. There are individual figures who loom large as interpreters of the Bible who happen to be Lutheran: Georg Wilhelm Friedrich Hegel (1770–1831, Søren Kierkegaard (1813–1855), Rudolf Bultmann (1884–1976), and Dietrich Bonhoeffer (1906–1945) to name just a few. But being Lutheran, while certainly part of their identity, is not essential to their contribution to biblical scholarship. So it is Luther, the Confessions, Lutheran scholasticism, and pietism that are the focus.

Martin Luther (1483–1546) and the Confessions. ***The Gospel as Oral Word.*** As an interpreter of the Bible, Martin Luther was above all dogmatic in his approach. The dynamic reality of his fundamental dogmatic principle of law and gospel holds greater authority in his theology than strict exposition of biblical passages. The law consists of the moral imperatives given by the righteous God to order society and especially to expose the sinner as a fallen creature. The gospel is the gracious love of God in Christ, which accepts the sinner even though fallen and unworthy. To read the Bible with the gospel as its heart is to "urge Christ" in each biblical text. "The Scriptures," asserts Luther in *Theses concerning Faith and Law* (1535), "must be understood in favor of Christ, not against him. For that reason they must either refer to him or must not be held to be true Scriptures." And again: "If one of them had to be parted with, Christ or the law, the law would have to be let go, not Christ" (*Luther's Works* [*LW*] 34.112).

Because of his fundamental dogmatic criterion of the gospel, Luther could be radically suspicious of certain elements within the Bible. The example of the letter of James is well known. Luther referred to it as a "strawy epistle" because of its dependence on works (*LW* 35.361–362). He believed that the Book of Hebrews errs on the matter of repentance:

> [Hebrews, James, Jude, and Revelation] have from ancient times had a different reputation [from John's and Paul's writings]. In the first place, the fact that Hebrews is not an epistle of St. Paul, or of any other apostle, is proved by what it says in chapter 2, that through those who had themselves heard it from the Lord this doctrine has come to us and remained among us.... Again, there is a hard knot in the fact that in chapters 6 and 10 it flatly denies and forbids to sinners any repentance after baptism.... This is contrary to all the gospels and to St. Paul's epistles.... We cannot put [Hebrews] on the same level with the apostolic epistles. (*LW* 35.394–395)

Even the Apostles themselves have no formal guarantied authority:

> All the genuine sacred books agree in this, that all of them preach and inculcate *[treiben]* Christ. And that is the true test by which to judge all books, when we see whether or not they inculcate Christ. For all the Scriptures show us Christ, Romans 3; and St. Paul will know nothing but Christ, I Corinthians 2. Whatever does not teach Christ is not yet apostolic, even though St. Peter or St. Paul does the teaching. Again, whatever preaches Christ would be apostolic even if Judas, Annas, Pilate, and Herod were doing it. (*LW* 35.395–396)

Luther could engage in biting sarcasm at scripture's expense. A famous example appears in his important late essay *On the Councils and the Church* (1539) when he discusses the very first council at Jerusalem described in the Book of Acts. In Acts 15:29 the Holy Spirit commands that Christians abstain "from blood and from what is strangled." In mock protest, Luther appeals to the German stomach: "We must teach and insist that henceforth no prince, lord, burgher, or peasant eat geese, doe, stag, or pork cooked in blood.... And burghers and peasants must abstain especially from red sausage and blood sausage" (*LW* 41.28). When the issue is sausage, the Holy Spirit must give way! Here Luther clearly anticipates the type of biting criticism that would later be commonly encountered in the Enlightenment.

Luther could take this apparently cavalier approach to the biblical text not only because of his dogmatic commitment to the gospel against the law, but also because he never equated the gospel with the written scriptures. On the contrary, he taught that the gospel is a "living voice" that reaches believers across time in the authentic form of oral propagation. The primary responsibility of the Christian community is the transmission of the living word of faith in the encounter of preaching and hearing. The gospel proclaims forgiveness and, together with the sacraments, brings divine grace to believers. It is the phrase *im Schwang* (in movement) as Luther puts it in the *Large Catechism* of 1529, an essential confessional document of the Lutheran confessional tradition (*Book of Concord* 189), making the church alive and providing its identity (*LW* 52.139). As Luther declares in a famous passage in the *Church Postil* (1522), this oral word holds a definite priority over written scripture. Jesus and the apostles were above all public proclaimers. Certainly they drew upon the scriptures—that is, the Old Testament—but they did so in living speech:

> In the New Testament, preaching must be done orally and publicly, with the living voice, to produce in speech and hearing what prior to this lay hidden in the letter and secret vision.... This is why Christ did not write his doctrine himself but transmitted it orally, and also commanded that it should be orally continued giving no command that it should be written. (*LW* 52.205)

Luther extracts the following lesson from this important fact:

> So it is not at all in keeping with the New Testament to write books on Christian doctrine. Rather in all places there should be fine, godly learned, spiritual, diligent preachers without books, who extract the living word from the old Scripture and unceasingly inculcate it into people, just as the apostles did. For before they wrote, they first of all preached to the people by word of mouth and converted them, and this was their real apostolic and New Testament work. (*LW* 52,205f.)

Because there "was a serious decline and a lack of the Spirit" in the church allowing "heretics" and "false teachers" to gain a foothold, God's word was necessarily set to writing (*LW* 52.206). The *gramma* of the New Testament, then, at least when considered in the specific terms of its origin (a crucial question for the mindset of tradition), is a tragic necessity of Christian experience that functions to stabilize the message of oral proclamation and to protect it precisely in its powerful spontaneity as human speech transparent to revelation. While *sola scriptura* is the watchword of the Reformation, and while no authority transcends the authority of scripture, nevertheless, it remains a fact that the *verbum Dei non scriptum* is prior, as even later Protestant scholasticism would acknowledge (see Fraenkel 1961, pp. 71–77). The gospel is essentially a proclaimed message, and upon it—rather than upon an inherited, formalized scriptural principle—does the authority and correct interpretation of the Bible depend.

Rejection of Catholic Authority. The essential oral nature of the gospel is also a critical principle with regard to Catholic tradition. Whatever antiquity the Catholic Church may claim in terms of creed ("one, holy, catholic, apostolic"—Nicene Creed) or apologetic ("everywhere, always and by all"—Vincent of Lerins [d. c. 445], *Commonitory* II/3), Luther refused to identify the church as instituted by Christ with the church of the papacy: "... the essence, life, and nature of Christendom is not a physical assembly, but an assembly of hearts in one faith.... This is what spiritual unity really means on the basis of which men are called a 'communion of saints'" (*LW* 39.65). This unity alone is sufficient to create Christendom, and without it, no unity—be it that of city, time, persons, work, or whatever else it may be—can create Christendom (*LW* 39.65). Thus: "There is not a single letter in Holy Scripture saying that such a church, where it is by itself, is instituted by God" (*LW* 39.70). In Luther's view, Catholicism collapses Christian tradition into the jurisdictional authority and pronouncements of the magisterium, justifying this move on the spurious notion that revelation is integrated sacramentally into the hierarchy of the priesthood and takes legal form. The resulting illusion—that somehow the priestly hierarchy, and especially the Papacy, guarantees revelation across time and represents Christ in a direct way—means in reality that the church has no independent critical measure by which to test the spirits and to judge its faithfulness. To accept this "tradition" is to accept the legal power of the priesthood, to allow the gospel to be overshadowed by ecclesiastical authority; in short, to make the community of faith hermeneutically impenetrable, hidden behind the gilded curtain of canon law. It is against this understanding of tradition that the full and positive power of *sola scriptura* asserts itself in Luther's theology. In order to free "true" tradition from the inflexible, juridical connection of canon law and place it under the sole authority of the gospel, scripture alone must show the way:

> The Romanists want to be the only masters of Holy Scripture, although they never learn a thing from the Bible all their life long.... Their claim that only the pope may interpret Scripture is an outrageous fancied fable. They cannot produce a single letter [of Scripture] to maintain that the interpretation of Scripture or the confirmation of its interpretation belongs to the pope alone. They themselves have usurped this power. And although they allege that this power was given to St. Peter when the keys were given him, it is clear enough that the keys were not given to Peter alone but to the whole community. (*Three Treatises* 12)

The "whole community" of the church is the priesthood of all believers, a teaching that Luther adhered to until at least 1525. There is no distinction between the laity and the clergy: "All Christians are truly of the spiritual estate, and there is no difference among them except that of office. Paul says in 1 Corinthians 12 [vv. 12–13] that we are all one body, yet every member has its own work by which it serves the others. This is because we all have one baptism, one gospel, one faith, and are all Christians alike; for baptism, gospel, and faith alone make us spiritual and a Christian people" (*Three Treatises* 12). The baptized Christian is called to *fides explicata* (explicit faith), which means the full knowledge of Christ, and not *fides implicate* (implicit faith), that is, the Catholic position of obedience to the church. This is why Luther translated the Bible into the vernacular and encouraged literacy for both men and women, boys and girls. This is the basis of lay authority:

> St. Paul gives every Christian the power to teach among Christians if there is a need, saying, "You can all prophesy one by one, so that all may learn and all be admonished" [1 Cor. 14:31]. Again, "You should earnestly desire to prophesy, and do not forbid speaking in tongues; but all things should be done decently and in order" [1 Cor. 14: 39–40].
>
> Let this passage be your sure foundation, because it gives such an overwhelming power to the Christian congregation to preach, to permit preaching, and to call. (*LW* 39.311)

In attacking the Roman Church in this way, Luther was far more radical than the late medieval criticism that preceded him. Luther was bold enough to assert that in the church itself Satan had begun to work, that error was being taught, and that the antichrist was allowed to reign. Against these demonic challenges, God's word alone is firm and unchanging. But God's word is mingled with and hidden under the forces of opposition that oppress the church at all times and places. That God's word is realized in the community of faith is only because the word itself forms a confessional response to divine grace from Adam to the present day. Knowledge of God's word is not a continuous, unbroken achievement of the church. That would make it the church's work. Rather, such knowledge is best understood as the spontaneous response of the Christian community to the gospel, a response created within the hearts of believers by the Holy Spirit. Certainly, insofar as the church adheres to its origin in Christ's sacrifice and to the articles of faith delivered in the scriptures, there may be seen a continuity in the witness of faith. But this is "the logic of the Holy Spirit, a logic which treats realities in their entirety rather than breaking them up" (*LW* 41.139). God is able to provide faithfulness in the church and not theological conclusions or the legal succession of bishops. Therefore, under the guidance of the Spirit, responsible faith requires critical discernment of the text of scripture as distinct from the tradition of the church.

Principles of Interpretation. This critical discernment demands a concentrated attention on the biblical text over against the "human traditions" of ecclesiastical interpretation. The artificial medieval system of allegorization, with its four senses of literal, allegorical, anagogical, and tropical interpretation, was largely, although not entirely, abandoned by Luther in favor of the right of the biblical text, literally interpreted, to speak for itself. Such a concentration on literal interpretation of the Bible not only provided what Hans Frei (1922–1988) calls "drastic relief" from exegetical custom (*The Eclipse of the Biblical Narrative*. New Haven, Conn., 1974, p. 19), but was vitally important in the reformer's struggle with church dogma and with the hierarchy. By means of literal exegesis, many ecclesiastical customs were exposed as being without biblical warrant.

Further, Luther sought to discern the meaning of biblical texts by paying close attention to the historical context of passages: "For before one learns the reason and the motive for what a man says, it is only letters, the shouts of choristers or the songs of nuns. . . . There are many passages in Holy Scripture that are contradictory according to the letters; but when that which motivates them is pointed out, everything is all right" (*LW* 41.53f). This sense of context even extends to individual authors of scripture and their differences. For example, commenting on Galatians 1:12 ("For I did not receive it from man, nor was I taught it, but it came through a revelation of Jesus Christ"), Luther declares:

> The histories in the Scriptures are often concise and confused so that they cannot be easily harmonized, as, for example, the denials of Peter and the history of Christ's Passion, etc. Thus Paul is not reciting the entire history here. Therefore I do not expend any labor or concern on harmonizing these things, but here pay attention to Paul's purpose and intention. (*LW* 26.62)

In these remarkable opinions, which go to the heart of the identity of the Reformation, the necessity of an historical criticism that candidly recognizes conflict among biblical texts—a necessity that we recognize as a hallmark of modern theology—is anticipated and affirmed. It is fair to say that the Reformation is an essential step in the formation of a theology that exercises its responsibility by employing historical criticism in its work.

Late nineteenth-century liberal Protestantism seized upon these insights of interpretation in Luther to argue that the true spirit of the Reformation was antithetical to all aspects of ecclesiastical tradition. "The rise of Protestantism," asserts Ferdinand Christian Baur (1792–1860), "can be thought of as an act of free self-determination that required the highest spiritual and moral energy" (Baur, *Lehrbuch der christlichen Dogmengeschichte.* Tübingen, 1867, p. 273). According to Adolf von Harnack (1851–1930), the Reformation did not simply reformulate the inherited "system of doctrine," but "uprooted the foundations of dogma" setting in motion an entirely new "principle" of Christian faith (Harnack, *History of Dogma.* 1907, 7:22). The basis of Luther's rebellion was the "gospel," which Harnack defines as both the dynamic experience of the forgiveness of sins and new life in the Kingdom of God. The gospel principle of the Reformation is a critical norm of faith that liberates Christians from all forms of external authority:

> The Reformation obtained a new point of departure for the framing of Christian faith in the Word of God, and it discarded all forms of infallibility which could offer an *external* security for faith, the infallible organization of the Church, the infallible doctrinal tradition of the Church, and the infallible Scriptural codex. (Harnack, 1907, 7:24)

Viewed historically, so this argument goes, it is precisely this criticism of external authority that engendered the modern temperament of Western culture.

There is no doubt that there are elements in Luther's hermeneutic that support this liberal Protestant position. It would be a serious mistake, however, to push the intriguing hermeneutical insights of the reformer too far. While Luther represents a signpost on the road to modernity, he is no modern biblical critic. By no means did Luther reject a precritical viewpoint toward the reading of the Bible. Indeed, in a certain sense, he even exaggerated it as he practiced what Wolfhart Pannenberg calls a "scripture-positivism" [*Schriftpositivismus*], inherited from late medieval nominalism. (Pannenberg, *Basic Questions in Theology.* 1970, 1:3). Since the biblical text was his primary weapon against the power of the church, Luther relied on what he perceived to be the ability of scripture to undergird his doctrinal formulations. His principles of exegesis and dogmatics were one. Standing against the might of the church and the weight of its hoary customs, Luther exalted the authority of scripture in no uncertain terms. He considered the Bible to be *fons et judex* of the church's life. He asserted that the Bible alone is to be trusted because it is the prime agent of the Holy Spirit. Leaders of the church, regardless of rank, must subordinate themselves to its witness: "The Pope, Luther, Augustine, Paul, an angel from heaven—these should not be masters, judges, or arbiters but only witnesses, disciples, and confessors of Scripture" (*LW* 26.56–57).

This is Luther's doctrine of the clarity of scripture. It has two important aspects. First, the literal sense of scripture is identical with its historical content. There is no going behind the text in order to discover a different event than the event reported. Indeed, the question does not even arise. This is why *sola scriptura* is the watchword of the Reformation and why Luther asserts that Scripture is "its own interpreter" (*sui ipsius interpres—Weimarer Ausgabe* (*WA*) 7:97.23). Second, the Bible has a universal and immediate sense, granted by the Holy Spirit and recognized by the eyes of faith, that transcends historical conditions and events. The meaning of the Bible is plain to the common reader:

> The Holy Spirit is the plainest writer and speaker in heaven and earth, and therefore his words cannot have more than one, and that the very simplest, sense, which we call the literal, ordinary, natural sense. That the things indicated by the simple sense of his simple words should signify something further and different, and therefore one thing should always signify another, is more than a question of words or of language. For the same is true of all other things

> outside of the Scriptures, since all of God's works and creatures are living signs and words of God, as St. Augustine and all the teachers declare. But we are not on that account to say that the Scriptures or the Word of God has more than one meaning. (Spaeth and Jacobs, 3.350)

On the basis of these assumptions, especially the second, Luther attacked the theology of his time and the church of the papacy. He did so with the confidence that his doctrine was identical with the doctrine of scripture, which is the doctrine of God. "*Doctrina est coelum, vita terra*": "Doctrine is heaven; life is earth" (*WA* 42.2, 51f; *LW* 27.41).

Thus, while the reformer's theological vision of the sharp distinction between law and gospel and his concentration on literal or historical exegesis led him to practice a nascent form of historical criticism, he did not surrender essential premodern assumptions about reality that had guided the church from ancient times. According to Luther's view of revelation, history—or at least "true" history, the history that brings knowledge of God—is sure and certain. This is the *historia sacra* of Bible and church that is eternal, unchanging, and ever-present. It is the word of God contained in the scriptures and the community of those who respond to this word. It may be hidden because of the ways of the world and the power of the church or the papacy, but it is there for the eyes of faith.

The Bible as Personal Encounter. Luther did not investigate the hermeneutical tension between what we would call modern and traditional elements in his understanding. The reformer was essentially an existential, imaginative, and spontaneous thinker not given to systematic exposition: "For Luther, theology as the object of intellectual inquiry and theology as the sphere of a personal encounter formed an individual unity" (Ebeling, 1970, pp. 95–96). Front and center for him was the question of personal salvation arising out of the anxiety of despair (*Anfechtung*). Humanity, Luther believed, is in total rebellion against God and is essentially evil. In his early *Scholastic Disputation* (1517), Luther goes so far as to border on Manichaeism. While he denies it, he seems to concede it, as is apparent in theses 7 through 10:

> 7.... without the grace of God the will produces of necessity an action which is wicked and wrong.
> 8. Nor does it therefore follow that the will is naturally evil, in other words that the will has the nature of being essentially evil as the Manichaeans maintain.
> 9. It is nevertheless innately and inevitably corrupt.
> 10. One must concede that the will is not free to strive toward whatever is declared good (*LW* 31.10).

In his *Lectures on Romans* (1515–1516), Luther introduced the idea that the human being is *simul iustus et peccator* (at the same time justified and sinner). We cannot earn the righteous of God or live up to its perfect standard. God grants us righteousness as a gift: "Give the king your justice, O God, and your righteousness to a king's son" (Ps 72:1). Thus we find ourselves in this situation *coram Deo* (before God):

> But it is by the mercy of God that this evil, though it remains, is not reckoned to those who fervently call upon him to set them free.... It is as with a sick man who believes his physician as he assures him that he will most certainly get well. In the meantime, he obeys his orders.... Can one say that this sick man is healthy? No; but he is at the same time both sick and healthy.
>
> Now can we say that he is perfectly righteous? No; but he is at the same time both a sinner and righteous, a sinner in fact but righteous by virtue of the reckoning and the certain promise of God that he will redeem him from sin in order, in the end, to make him perfectly sound and whole. (Luther: *Lectures on Romans*, tr. Pauck 1961, p. 127)

To be in this position is no excuse for complacency. While believers have faith in the promise of God, they must struggle against the temptations of the flesh and the devil. Struggle and discontent are signs that faith is genuine:

> The believers ... always have trials enough; they must wage war constantly. Those who are without faith and the Spirit do not feel this; or they fall behind, run away, and follow evil lust.... If you are a

> Christian, you must learn that you will undoubtedly feel all kinds of trials and evil inclinations in your flesh. For if faith is present, a hundred more evil thoughts and a hundred more new trials come than were there before. Only see to it that you are a man and do not let yourself be taken captive by them. Resist constantly and say: "I will not! I will not!" . . . [A] true Christian life is never at rest. (*LW* 30.70–71)

There is more medieval monk than modern person in this claim. Luther believed that the old Adam had all the power. He knew how far humanity had truly fallen. Jesus says, "If you want to be perfect, go, sell your possessions and give to the poor, and you will have treasure in heaven. Then come, follow me" (Mt 19:21). As a struggling Christian, Luther went deep into the self and confessed that he did not want to be perfect. "My will," Luther realized, "is the will to undo." In this terrible discovery, Luther goes even further into the dark night of the soul than St. Paul does in his honest agony about "not doing the good I want to do but doing what I hate to do" (Rom 7:19). He goes to that place in the sacred tradition of theology where St. Augustine went as a teenage boy, under the pear tree, to realize that he hates the good and loves to hate. Destroying the fruit of the tree along with his friends for no good reason, and then later reflecting on it, Augustine caught a glimpse of the human condition in its waste and void. He confesses to God: "It was filthy and I loved it. I loved my own destruction. I loved my own fault; not the object to which I directed my faulty action, but my fault itself, was what I loved, my vile soul leaping down from thy support into extinction" (*Confessions* II/4). This is the true self asserts Luther; this is what a person is at the base, a "furious and untamed beast" (*LW* 26.308), who "does not want God be God" because I want to be God alone (*LW* 31.10). It is this self that crucifies Christ because, as St. John tells us, we love the darkness and hate the light (John 3:19). In Luther's harsh view of the matter, people do not want to strive for perfection; instead, they want God out of the way. Luther discovered this in his own life. By his fame and notoriety, he brought it to the consciousness of the West in a new way. It is no accident that Shakespeare pays an offhand compliment to Luther in the creation of his greatest, most compelling abandoned, confused, lost character: Hamlet, we are told, is a student at Wittenberg.

Luther's insights regarding the hiddenness of Christian truth and the need for critical discernment of the scriptures stand side by side with assertions about the absoluteness of the word of God as a direct product of divine causality. The lack of thoroughgoing explication of his own position meant that Luther's most intriguing hermeneutical proposals, radical for their time, were unable to put into effect firm and immediate methodological consequences for the practice of theology as a whole.

Lutheran Scholasticism. The Reformation adopted its own form of scholasticism beginning in the following generation. The powerful urge to have Christian truth easily and publicly available returned as Protestant theologians, less confident than the original reformers in the independent power of the gospel, sought to link the presence of God to an enduring, visible structure that was both theological and metaphysical. Scholastic theology was taken over by the apologetic desire—ever present in the church—to secure the possession of philosophical truth for its cause. Those who came after Luther claimed that the absolute truth ascribed to the divine could also be found to reside in a specific human form: in this case, the text of the canonical scriptures. Protestant scholasticism refused to follow the reformers' often radical stance on the matter of biblical interpretation. Instead, it gravitated toward a doctrine that emphasized the majesty of the biblical text: "We believe what the Holy Scriptures declare, simply because *they* declare it, and it is they that beget faith in us, and they are the only source from which we derive our faith" (Schmid, 1899, p. 51). Luther's freewheeling approach to particular texts was interpreted to be peculiar to his volcanic personality. Rather than critical study of the content of the Bible, there was "*Theologica Biblica.*" According to this approach, scripture operated as an appendix to Protestant dogmatics, providing *dicta probantia,* that is, proof texts for individual *loci.* The method of using *dicta probantia* was complemented by the scholastic doctrine of the divine inspiration of scripture that concentrated on securing the Bible as a whole from attack so that it could function in its chief role of providing the underpinning of divine sanction for the dogmatic enterprise. If Roman Catholics claimed infallibility for the Pope, Protestant scholastics claimed infallibility for the Bible.

The age of scholasticism had a dual relationship to the reformers, both positive and negative. Positively, it was one with them in affirming the principle of *sola scriptura.* This it did powerfully in its doctrine of the perspicuity of scripture, which declared that the Bible is plain and clear in content. The Bible is open for all believers. It is not the property of an educated elite. The common person of common sense, under the guidance of the Holy Spirit, is able to discern scripture's truth. Scripture is a gift given to the whole church and empowers all of its members.

Negatively, Protestant scholasticism differed from the reformers in its unwillingness to acknowledge the complexity of the relation of the gospel to the biblical text. This difference was a major obstacle because it led Protestant scholasticism ultimately to be motivated by a spirit alien to the original impulse of the Reformation. While the reformers were confident and assertive, scholasticism was defensive and dogmatic. Whereas Luther had written daringly of Christ against the law, scholasticism made of the Bible an impregnable fortress defended by a theological theory in which every verse was the truth from God's own mouth whispered into the ear of his scribes. This is the doctrine of verbal inspiration. In short, the Bible was inerrant. It contained "no lie, no falsehood, not even the smallest error either in words or in matter, but everything, together and singly, that is handed on in them is most true, whether it be a matter of dogma or of morals or of history or of chronology or of topography or of nomenclature; no want of knowledge, no thoughtlessness or forgetfulness, no lapse of memory." (Johann Andreas Quenstedt (1617–1688), *Theologia didactico-polemica,* Wittenberg, 1685, I: 77; quoted and tr. in Arthur Carl Piepkorn, "What does "Inerrancy" Mean?" *Concordia Theological Monthly,* 26 [1965]: 578).

Pietism. It was Lutheran pietism that first recognized the theological insufficiency of Protestant scholasticism as well as the contrast between scholasticism and the reformers. Pietists such as Philip Jacob Spener (1635–1705) complained that, "the scholastic theology which Luther had thrown out the front door had been introduced by others through the back door" (Spener, 1964, p. 54). They lamented the dry rationalism of scholastic theology and its penchant for defensive debate. They sought to concentrate attention on the fundamentals of the Christian's spiritual condition before God: "Let us remember that in the last judgment we shall not be asked how learned we were and whether we displayed our learning before the world.... Instead, we shall be asked how faithfully and with how childlike a heart we sought to further the kingdom of God" (p. 36). Lutheran pietists appealed directly to the figure of Luther who had "restored the bright light of the gospel" (p. 36). by concentrating on the simple, clear word of God. What the church needed was not scholasticism, but "true biblical theology" (p. 55).

Pietism questioned the methodological presuppositions of scholastic theology. It was critical of scholasticism's defense of biblical inerrancy. Spener, for example, refused to proclaim the infallibility of scripture in matters of history, geography, and chronology. He spoke of the inspiration of biblical authors rather than biblical words. The authority of scripture flows from its center in Jesus Christ and the illumination of the Holy Spirit, not from strict allegiance to formal principle. Pietism helped to expose the Protestant scholastic movement as a self-conscious reactionary force and to turn the tide to new ways of thinking.

[*See also* Allegory and Allegorical Interpretation; Authority of the Bible; Catholic Biblical Interpretation; Evangelical Interpretation; Exegesis;

Historical Criticism, *subentry* Hebrew Bible; Historical Criticism, *subentry* New Testament; Homiletics; Reformed Christian Interpretation; *and* Theological Interpretation.]

BIBLIOGRAPHY

Bayer, Oswald. "Luther as an Interpreter of Holy Scripture," In *The Cambridge Companion to Martin Luther*, edited by Donald McKim, 73–85. New York: Cambridge University Press, 2003. The best encyclopedic treatment of the subject in English.

Bornkamm, Heinrich. *Das Wort Gottes bei Luther*. Munich: Kaiser, 1933.

Bornkamm, Heinrich. *Luther and the Old Testament*, translated by Eric Gritsch and Ruth Gritsch. Philadelphia: Fortress, 1969.

Ebeling, Gerhard. *Evangelische Evangelienauslegung*, 3d ed. Tübingen: ry, 1991. The classic work on Luther as biblical expositor.

Ebeling, Gerhard. *Luther: An Introduction to His Thought*, translated by R. A. Wilson. Philadelphia: Fortress, 1970.

Fraenkel, Peter. *Testimonium Patrum: The Function of the Patristic Argument in the Theology of Philip Melanchthon*. Geneva: E. Droz, 1961.

Gerrish, Brian. "The Word of God and the Words of Scripture: Luther and Calvin on Biblical Authority." In *The Old Protestantism and the New*, edited by Brian Gerrish, 51–68. Chicago: The University of Chicago Press, 1982.

Hagen, Kenneth. *Luther's Approach to Scripture as Seen in His 'Commentaries' on Galatians 1519–1538*. Tübingen: Mohr, 1993. Excellent close reading of the text.

Lohse, Bernhard. *Martin Luther's Theology: Its Historical and Systematic Development*, translated by Roy A. Harrisville, 187–195. Minneapolis: Fortress, 2000. Most recent comprehensive study of Luther's theology.

Luther, Martin. *Lectures on Romans*, translated and edited by Wilhelm Pauck. Philadelphia: Westminster, 1961.

Luther, Martin. *Luther's Works*. American ed., edited by Helmut T. Lehman et. al.; 55 vols. Philadelphia: Fortress, 1955–1986.

Luther, Martin. *Three Treatises*, translated by Charles M. Jacobs et. al. Philadelphia: Fortress, 1970.

Pelikan, Jaroslav. *Luther the Expositor*. St. Louis: Concordia, 1959. Standard work in English; highly dependent on Eberling.

Quanbeck, Warren. *The Hermeneutical Principles of Luther's Early Exegesis*. Dissertation: Princeton Theological Seminary, 1948. A pioneering account of the subject in English that never found its way to publication.

Schmid, Heinrich. *The Doctrinal Theology of the Evangelical Lutheran Church*. 3d ed., translated by Charles A. Hay and Henry E. Jacobs. Minneapolis: Augsburg, 1899.

Spaeth, Adolph and Henry Eyster Jacobs, eds. *Works of Martin Luther*, with an introduction and notes. 6 vols. Philadelphia: Muhlenberg, 1915–1943.

Spener, Philip Jacob. *Pia Desideria*. Translated by Theodore G. Tappert. Philadelphia: Fortress, 1964.

Tappert, Theodore. G., ed. and trans. *The Book of Concord*. Philadelphia: Fortress, 1959.

Weimarer Ausgabe. *Martin Luthers Kritische Gesammtausgabe*, edited by. J. C. F. Knaake et. al. Weimar: H. Böhlau. 1883–2009. The complete critical edition of Luther's works.

Walter Sunberg

M

Masculinity Studies

Masculinity studies is an emerging field in biblical studies that looks explicitly at how the male gender is portrayed in the text. Masculinity studies uses the tools for gender analysis that have been developed in feminist interpretation and by gender theorists, and shares many of the same goals of examining the role gender plays in the text. It explores the ways in which societies construct an understanding of what it is to be a man or masculine, focusing particularly on how gender and masculinity are embedded in power structures. Unlike feminist studies, masculinity studies does not need to search for male figures and voices in history and society, since the male and the masculine are the unmarked norm. The challenge instead has been to make those norms visible and to expose the multiple ways in which those norms permeate the ideas, structures, and assumptions of society. Feminist interpretation has made considerable progress in bringing light to those hidden assumptions, but has mostly focused on examining the construction of femininity and feminine gender roles within the texts. While feminist critics recognized that if femininity is a social construct, then masculinity must be as well, relatively little attention was given to the features of that construct. Masculinity studies arose to fill that gap. Like the feminist movement before it, masculinity studies uses a variety of types of analysis to understand how gender functions in a culture.

Terminology. One of the issues in describing masculinity studies is the lack of a useful and consistent vocabulary to discuss the issues. Masculinity studies, in the realm of gender studies, is usually contrasted with men's studies. The latter, including the mythopoetic men's groups, is more generally associated with popular culture and can often be seen as a backlash against feminism, promoting traditional gender roles and stereotypical masculine traits. These movements focus on helping men to understand their own identity and role in society, as well as taking an interest in men's rights, in cases such as child custody decisions. In contrast, academic masculinity studies as described here takes a more descriptive and analytic role, often seeking to deconstruct gender roles, or at least trying to articulate the many factors that have led to these particular social constructions.

Clarifying that masculinity studies is the examination of constructed gender and not a movement of men is helpful, but the problem of terminology remains. The lack of vocabulary that is parallel to *feminist* and *feminism* demonstrates the general unmarked nature of masculinity in cultural structures, including language. Femininity is contrasted not with the explicitly masculine, but with the norm, identifying masculinity as humanity. In an effort to make the discussion of masculinity syntactically less awkward and to make the vocabulary of masculinity more marked so that the embedded structural norms are further revealed, this article will use the terms *masculist* and *masculism* to refer to the interpretive strategy that studies masculinity as a constructed concept and recognizes multiple forms of valid masculinities (see Goldingay 1995, p. 161; Olson 2006, p. 77). Thus masculism as used here critiques the status quo dominated by hegemonic masculinity, rather than championing the promotion of men's interests over those of women.

History. Studies of masculinity started to emerge in the late 1970s and 1980s, sometimes as a response to the feminist movement. In this first wave of men's studies, the emphasis was on exploring the characteristics of men, especially in terms of reclaiming what was perceived as lost in the industrial age. The mythopoetic movement mentioned earlier, which flourished in the 1990s, is an example of this. This movement often decries the lack of ritual in industrial society to initiate males into full manhood. One prominent figure is the writer Robert Bly, whose most famous work in the area is *Iron John*. Bly and others draw on Jungian archetypes as manifested in myths like Grimms' fairy tales to restore a sense of traditional manhood. The Promise Keepers is another movement that tries to restore masculine identity in its members. This group functions more within Christianity rather than the broader spirituality of the mythopoetic movement. The Promise Keepers aims to instill the principles of responsibility, leadership, and faithfulness among its followers, but has been criticized for advocating strict gender roles with the man as the authority figure and head of the household. Some aspects of the movement, however, promote egalitarian values in the family, emphasizing the expressive component of masculinity and not just the instrumental.

In the academic world, men's studies programs began to develop alongside women's studies programs. Rather than focusing on reclaiming men's identities and traditional roles, men's studies programs looked at social constructions of masculinity. Robert W. Connell has been particularly influential in theorizing about masculinity on the basis of both anthropological and psychoanalytic perspectives.

Psychoanalytic Studies. Psychological approaches to masculinity first arose with Sigmund Freud and the development of psychoanalysis. Freud's work on the Oedipus complex initiated an exploration of the complexities of masculinity. In his studies of gender and homosexuality, Freud came to the conclusion that people contain both masculine and feminine elements, which are intertwined and expressed to different degrees, so that humans are inherently bisexual. Masculinity is a multilayered phenomenon that develops through the complex relationships of a man with his parents as objects of desire, his primordial masculinity and castration anxiety, and later social interactions, so that masculinity arises through constantly shifting emotional attachments. For Freud, there was no such thing as a pure, unfiltered masculinity. Later psychoanalysis, however, simplified the idea of masculinity, ignoring much of the complexity of development between masculine and feminine forces implicit in Freud's ideas. In this simplified approach, heterosexuality developed naturally and unproblematically while alternate expressions of gender were viewed as psychological disorders.

Carl Jung accepted the presence of masculine and feminine forces in all people, but related them in a different way than did Freud. He identified his ideas of the socially constructed persona with the masculine, and the repressed, subconscious anima with the feminine. The polarities between them were expressed by contrasting unconscious archetypes, which can be balanced, but never overcome. This idea of archetypes existing in the collective unconscious was expanded by later generations and forms the basis of many of the mythopoetic masculinity movements. Later theorists took these ideas a step further and formulated the concept of a core gender identity. Men either identified as masculine or feminine and the balance between masculine and feminine archetypes of Jung or the more complex relationships expressed by Freud were largely rejected.

Alfred Adler took gender ideas in a different direction than did his colleague Freud, focusing on the social implications. He understood the masculine and feminine elements existing in a person to be in tension, but also noted that the masculine was more highly valued in social institutions. Thus the feminine tended to be rejected through an excessive emphasis on the masculine. Adler saw this as harmful to society, since it was frequently associated with aggression, which was particularly problematic in the aftermath of World War I. In later developments, the Frankfort School applied similar theories of gender to the development of authoritarian or democratic personalities in society. Jacques Lacan envisioned masculinity as a concept fulfilling a particular social and symbolic space, in which the phallus plays a central dominant role, but is explicitly disassociated from the penis, an idea taken up by later theorists, such as Judith Halberstam, who explore the concept of female masculinities.

Anthropological Studies. The basis of the anthropological approach is ethnographic studies. Cross-cultural analysis has been particularly important in developing theories of masculinity. Several cultures have been objects of interest, but nonurban Mediterranean societies, especially in Spain and Greece, and Polynesian studies have figured prominently. Maurice Berger, Harry Brod, Andrea Cornwall, and Nancy Lindisfarne, among others, have contributed significant studies. While cross-cultural generalizations have their drawbacks, including glossing over features particular to a given culture and tending to focus on the "other," they are useful for drawing out certain elements of masculinity, some of which are discussed later.

Characteristics of Hegemonic Masculinity. The term hegemonic masculinity, coined by Tim Carrigan, is frequently employed in discussions of masculinity. It expresses the idea that masculinity is usually tightly entwined with power; thus studying masculinity is an important way to analyze the competing power structures in a given society. Hegemonic masculinity is that specific gender construction that is dominant in cultural and political power structures. It may not be fully embodied by any particular man, but the combination of traits is promoted because of its association with power. Thus a particular gender construction continues to be imitated and propagated by those who wish to rise in the hierarchy of status and power, whether this is conscious or not. Hegemonic masculinity is not a stable concept, however, but is shaped by the competing subversive masculinities and the political tensions these represent. Masculinity cannot be defined simply in a dichotomy with femininity, but rather is expressed along a continuum that must be continually contested with other men, according to the characteristics of the current hegemonic norms. Cross-cultural studies have demonstrated a number of typical components of hegemonic masculinity. While not being equally important or present in all patriarchal cultures, these features comprise a basic understanding of how masculinity is performed in many social contexts.

Military Might. Valor in warfare is an important display of masculinity in many cultures. Prowess on the field of battle often represents sexual prowess, as well. War has customarily been the domain of men, and the weapons of war are often associated with men's virility. In modern times guns are used either to refer to a man's strength (powerful biceps) or potency (as a phallic symbol). In ancient times and nonindustrial cultures, the equivalent characteristics were conveyed by bows and arrows or staffs and spears. For example, in the ancient Near East bows were a frequent metonym for warriors, and a warrior's fate could be ascertained by the fate of his bow. One such example occurs in the Assyrian friezes showing the king's defeat of a besieged city. The king is displayed with his bow taut and drawn, while the defeated soldiers are displayed as small figures, forced to cut their bows in half. Victory in battle thus increases masculinity, whereas loss is emasculating. A defeated man could maintain some degree of masculinity if he acted bravely in the face of severe opposition. Bravery was demonstrated by the position of scars in the Greco-Roman world. If a warrior had scars on his chest, it showed his willingness to face death in the face of close encounters with the enemy, rather than run away in fear. Scars on the back, however, bespoke cowardice and were thus an affront to masculinity.

Bodily Integrity. The inability to defend oneself from bodily penetration, from weapons, as in warfare, corporal punishment, as a slave, or sexual penetration severely compromised masculinity. Because the appearance of emasculation creates anxiety about a loss of power and prestige, males in power, or aspiring to power, strongly assert their dominance in defending their bodies from penetration or other abuse. While asserting one's role as the active partner in heterosexual intercourse was necessary, it was far more important in homosexual relations. The insertive partner can maintain or even increase his masculinity, because he is penetrating another man, but the masculinity of the passive partner is compromised. In the Greco-Roman context the typical status of the passive partner as a young man or slave underscores this point. The defense of bodily integrity extends to corporal punishment, which also penetrates the body. Being beaten or whipped was an affront to a man's masculinity in the Greco-Roman context, and it was unlawful to beat a Roman citizen, who as such, had a higher social status than the average person. Because slaves were both at the low end of the social hierarchy and were subject to being both beaten and used as sexual objects, the masculinity of male slaves was effectively effaced.

Honor. The honor and shame model, developed primarily from studies of Mediterranean cultures, has been a popular system to understand another aspect of masculinity, which is the ability of a man to show control of the sexuality of the women in his household. Although the model has been criticized as overly simplistic for linking honor and shame too closely to gender and for glossing over differences between the cultures, it has proved a useful way to look at certain features of social relations. In this model, women are expected to remain virgins before marriage and to be faithful after marriage. Men are expected to guard this sexual fealty. The honor of men is thus largely dependent on the shame, that is, the chastity, of the women in their household. Outside sexual activity is a threat to the honor of the males responsible for the women, because it constitutes a challenge to the masculinity of the father or husband by the male who is cavorting with the woman. Illicit sex, therefore, is largely viewed as a competition between males, with challenges requiring a strong response. That response is often directed at the woman, not only because she is easier to target, but also because she casts aspersion on the honor and masculinity of her guardian by going to another male without official consent. When a daughter has sex before betrothal, she dishonors her father. The worst dishonor a man can suffer, however, is if he is cuckolded by his wife. In part this is because when she turns to another man, she leaves her husband open to the implication that he was somehow deficient in his ability to provide for her, in material or sexual terms or both. The dishonor increases for the husband if he knows about the affair, but does nothing, which shows that he was not only unable to prevent the affair, but also to end it.

Virility. A visible sign of a man's masculinity is the ability to reproduce. The strong emphasis on female fidelity in marriage is often justified by a concern with paternity. In order for a man to know that his offspring are indeed his own, he must ensure that he is the only one having intercourse with his wife. The children themselves, especially sons, serve, among other things, as proof of their father's virility. Although the female who is childless is often castigated as barren, in many areas of the world the male is considered the real source of the child, while the mother serves as an incubator. The language of seed, sowing, insemination, and so forth is quite common cross-culturally. In this model the male provides the seed, while the female is the soil. Soil can be fertile or barren, but it ultimately plays a passive role. The active role of the male must be continually proven.

Provisioning. Another component of masculinity is a man's ability to provide for his household. Failure to do so can be grounds for divorce. Insufficient provisions could also provide a rationale for the women in his household to stray and increase a man's dishonor. Related to this, hospitality was an important component of honor. Hospitality not only shows a man's generosity, but also his ability to provide not only enough for his own family, but for visitors as well.

Spatiality. A man provides for his household and has authority over it, but the gendered nature of space in the household defines particular masculine and feminine roles. In most patriarchal societies, the interior space of the home, or the private realm, is where women have power, while the exterior or public space is the domain of men. Since politics, large scale economics, and communal religious rituals are usually performed in the public realm, men have the dominant visible power in a society. Thus men are expected to spend most of their time and energy in the public realm, and those who too often frequent the private realm are ridiculed as behaving like women.

Public Presentation. In the public realm a man is expected to demonstrate self-control. Displaying mastery of emotions and actions is a key feature of masculine status, especially in the Greco-Roman era. Senses and emotions were linked with women, while the exercise of self-control and rationality were associated with men. A second aspect of public presentation is the ability to engage successfully in debate, which comprises several factors. Debate involves the ability to defeat another man through *riposte*, thinking quickly and responding cleverly and eloquently to opposition. Skillful rhetoric, the way words are used and arguments deployed, is crucial, but delivery of the speeches is equally important. Good delivery requires an impressive bodily presence. A handsome, well-built body gives more weight to a man's words. A related characteristic is the tenor of the voice. Manly men have strong, low-pitched voices. Speeches delivered by those with high, squeaky voices are less effective, because their deliverers are less masculine. Thus physicality and intellect are intertwined in successful speech.

Masculinity Studies of the Bible. Masculist interpretation has been applied to biblical texts as a way to gain further insight into the motivations, relationships, and power structures embedded in the texts. The societies of ancient Israel and the Hellenistic world, like most societies, were patriarchal, and men dominated the public realm. The biblical texts were written, probably exclusively, by men and focused largely on male characters and concerns. Masculist biblical interpretation, like feminist interpretation, employs a broad range of approaches and methodologies, utilizing in particular psychological and anthropological perspectives.

Hebrew Bible. Many of the assumptions about masculinity in the Hebrew Bible, particularly hegemonic masculinity, are drawn from textual description and iconography throughout the ancient Near East, especially Assyria and Babylonia. Information specifically about Israelite masculinity has to be drawn from the biblical texts themselves through such approaches as psychoanalytical, literary, and cross-cultural studies.

Psychoanalytic Approaches. One of the earlier works in biblical studies that takes a psychoanalytic approach is Howard Eilberg-Schwartz's *God's Phallus and Other Problems for Men and Monotheism* (1994). The thesis of the book is that the maleness of God presents a problem to male worshippers, because males and females are naturally complementary. Logically then, women would be the natural worshippers of a male god. In order for men to take part in worship of a male deity, they must become feminized, an issue noted by a number of other scholars. One consequence of this feminization is that the patriarchs must subordinate their masculinity to God. Examples of this include the case of Moses's circumcision by Zipporah (Exod 4) and Jacob's "hip" wound in his wrestling with the angel (Gen 32), both of which represent a divine attack on the procreative organs of the men.

Literary Approaches. Other scholars examine normative masculinities primarily within the text. Dennis Olson examines how masculinity intersects with femininity in the Genesis creation narratives. In addition to analyzing how masculinity functions within the text, linking the story of Adam and Eve with that of Cain and Abel, he draws out implications for contemporary masculinity.

David Clines, an early contributor to masculist interpretation, has written several works exploring masculinity in particular biblical characters. His essay "David the Man" crystallizes several of these concepts and has been referenced by many later works. Taking David as an epitome of masculinity, he elucidates several characteristics of the ideal man.

Many of these correspond to the features of hegemonic masculinity listed earlier, including prowess on the battlefield, virility, persuasive speech, and spending time with men as opposed to women, while including less common features such as beauty and musicianship. Clines has also identified masculine traits that are also found in other biblical characters, including the prophets. One challenge for this method of analysis is that the prominent male figures in the text often do not represent the ideal of manhood in Israelite culture, but display subordinate masculinities, as they are men most willing to submit to God. The latter point illustrates the situational nature of masculinity. What is an appropriate expression of masculinity in one context may represent less power and prestige in another context.

Other scholars primarily following the literary approach focus more explicitly on how masculinity is entwined in the power structures of Israelite society. Ken Stone provides an example of this approach, exploring the connections between gender, sex, and power. As noted earlier, the display of virility has important connotations for leadership and ability to carry out the functions of state. Examples of this abound in the Deuteronomistic History in which men contest with each other for control of females, which symbolizes control of the kingdom. A lower status man (e.g., Absalom or Abner) challenges the masculinity and the power of his superior (David or Ishbosheth) by claiming women in his household. The response, or lack thereof, in these cases supports the fact that the superior is unable to hold onto temporal as well as sexual power.

Cross-cultural Approaches. Other scholars use cross-cultural studies to shed light on aspects of masculinity in the biblical texts. Susan Haddox has reconstructed a probable hegemonic masculinity functioning in Hosea using data from the biblical texts, Assyrian textual and iconographic sources, and contemporary anthropological studies. She investigates how Hosea uses a variety of metaphors, drawn from the cultural context, to critique the actions and attitudes of Israel's male elite by contrasting the standards of hegemonic masculinity to those required for a proper relationship with God.

A number of studies are emerging that utilize insights from both biblical and nonbiblical sources to analyze masculinity in the Hebrew Bible. Most of the work so far has been on specific texts, generating the data needed for more overarching analysis. Examples of these studies are included in *Men and Masculinity in the Hebrew Bible and Beyond* (2010), one of the first anthologies to focus on masculist interpretation of these texts. As the field progresses it will continue to develop methodologies and apply them to a variety of texts and genres.

New Testament. Masculinity in the New Testament is easier to classify than in the Hebrew Bible. There is a wealth of information from Hellenistic texts, which often explicitly deal with the characteristics and relationships within gender categories. A number of studies have applied these cultural characteristics to New Testament texts, particularly those pertaining to Jesus, and to a lesser extent, the disciples, and Paul.

The studies of the Gospels approach masculinity both from the perspective of psychoanalysis and by considering the context of Greco-Roman understandings of masculinity. Psychoanalytic studies have considered such things as the displacement of male anxieties about masculinity and the body. Jennifer Glancy's work on the beheading of John the Baptist discusses the projection of Herod's anxieties onto manipulative women. The problematic role of the body, in Jesus's incarnation, crucifixion, and resurrection is addressed by Graham Ward. Though Jesus is fully embodied in the flesh at the beginning of the Gospel narrative, the male body is gradually erased. The passion and crucifixion accelerate the effacement of both the body and Jesus's masculinity, until finally in the resurrected Christ, the body is almost entirely eliminated, taken up only in the communion bread and the church. Stephen Moore has considered the role of God's masculinity in and behind the text, as a motivator for understanding motivation and portrayal of the body, both divine and human.

Studies situating masculinity in the New Testament within the larger Greco-Roman context are more numerous and have shed considerable light on the complexities of the portrayal of Jesus and the other men in the texts. They draw on works by classicists as well as New Testament scholars to illuminate gender representations in the Bible. The anthology *New Testament Masculinities* (2003), edited by Stephen D. Moore and Janice Capel Anderson, is a significant contribution to the field. The essays therein cover the major parts of the canon. Most of the essays draw upon understandings of masculinity from the cultural and historical background. Colleen Conway's monograph *Behold the Man: Jesus and Greco-Roman Masculinity* (2008) undertakes a thorough examination of Jesus's masculinity from the writings of Paul through the Gospels and ending in Revelation. From these studies a variety of characteristics of New Testament masculinities can be ascertained.

Masculinity of Jesus. Jesus upholds the cultural constructions of masculinity in some ways and subverts them in others. Taken together, these studies construct a multifaceted portrait of Jesus's masculinity. One masculine characteristic that Jesus displays is his association with outdoor spaces, which are the realm of men, rather than indoor spaces, an idea explored by Jerome Neyrey. In Luke's description of his childhood, Jesus is born outside and speaks to the elders in the Temple, the domain of men. His interactions with his disciples and his teaching all take place in the out-of-doors with only occasional meals that take place indoors. Jesus is outdoors even more than would be typical for a Greco-Roman man, because he does not preside over a traditional household. While a man's masculinity comes into question if he spends too much time in the private space associated with women, a man is nevertheless expected to hold authority over his household to prove his masculinity. Jesus rejects this role in the traditional sense, by rejecting his biological family, but he does establish his own, redefined household, consisting of his followers.

A second masculine characteristic that Jesus displays is his skill in verbal debate through making and responding to challenges in the public arena. All of the Gospels show Jesus in conflict with the religious, and sometimes, civil authorities. They question his right to speak, pointing out, among other things, his inauspicious place of origin. The Gospels repeatedly assert, however, that Jesus teaches and speaks with authority, beyond that which is held by the scribes and Pharisees. The acknowledged leaders continually test Jesus on matters of religious and civil issues, and his answers leave them appeased (in a few cases), speechless, or resentful. None of them is able to best him in public argument, and the verbal challenges he makes to them go unanswered.

Jesus shows mastery over others throughout his ministry. This mastery is displayed on three levels: human, natural, and supernatural. At the human level his mastery comes out from the beginning. Even when he is baptized by John, most of the Gospels are very clear that John considers himself subservient to Jesus, not worthy even to untie his sandals. Jesus calls his disciples from their tasks, with almost no resistance, causing them to leave family and occupations with hardly a backward glance. When people do resist, the text indicates that they are not worthy of following Jesus, rather than that Jesus is powerlessness over them. In the Temple he overthrows the tables of the money changers and critiques the elders. At the natural level, he shows mastery over the chaotic sea, calming the storm and walking on water. He destroys a fig tree with just a word and can make fish assemble and jump into nets. His healing of physical wounds suggests his power over matter, as does his ability to multiply loaves and fish and to turn water into wine. In the realm of the supernatural, Jesus has authority over the demons, and is able to cast them out over their protests and resistance. They recognize him as Lord and Son of God even when no one else does. This success in casting out demons is not easily replicated by his disciples, which further underscores Jesus's special authority. His foreknowledge of his death and resurrection indicates that he has some mastery over his passion, especially in John, even though the events themselves subvert Jesus's masculinity.

Despite all of those masculine traits, Jesus subverts other aspects of Greco-Roman masculinity.

First, as mentioned earlier, he rejects the role of the traditional householder, and in his redefined family he does not set himself up as the father, but as the son and brother. He associates with people of a lower social status, and while he is the teacher, his words are persuasive only for those people. Those in authority cannot best him in an argument, but neither do they concede overall defeat, instead plotting to eliminate him. Most notably, in the passion, Jesus gives up nearly all claims to hegemonic masculinity. The scourging violates his bodily integrity, as does the crucifixion itself, which was not an honorable means of execution, further degrading Jesus's standing. The fact that his disciples abandon him at the end shows their disavowal of his leadership. Finally, Jesus submits himself fully to the will of God the father, refusing to claim mastery over himself. This final submission to God follows the pattern set up in the Hebrew Bible, in which the top masculine status is reserved for God. Through this submission, however, Jesus gains mastery over death and over humanity. The symbol of Jesus's power in Revelation is that of the slaughtered lamb, which represents the ultimate triumph of the subordinate masculinity favored by God. Jesus's power over the world is expressed through the Lamb's transformation into the warrior and the lion.

Masculinity of Paul. There have been a number of studies examining Paul's masculinity, many of which have shown that in contrast to the fairly masculine portrayal of Jesus in the Gospels, Paul tends to have a compromised masculinity both in his own self-portrayal and in the perception of others. Most unusually for a man in Hellenistic culture, he repeatedly states his willingness to suffer indignities in the service of Christ and the communities he founded. He does not hide his illness or his many scars from beatings with rods and whips. Jennifer Glancy thoroughly examined the verses in which Paul's boasts of these beatings. Unlike what modern interpreters may think, in the Greco-Roman context, the ability to withstand whippings could not be considered a sign of manly strength and valor, but were instead the marks of slaves, who by definition have severely compromised masculinity. The complexity of Paul's masculinity is further revealed because while he writes strong, authoritative letters, he seems to have a weak physical presence, and is willing to be all things to all people to lead them to Christ. Jennifer Larson observes that these are characteristics of the wimp and the flatterer, both of which are mocked by his opponents as unmanly. Yet Paul also asserts his authority over the communities he has founded, and strongly counters challenges put to him by his opponents, regarding his teaching of the gospel. Paul's masculinity is multifaceted, in that he asserts it when it will help his mission, but lets it be compromised when that demonstrates his faithfulness to Christ, whose example of suffering and self-sacrifice Paul emulates.

Masculinity in the Epistles. The epistles were important in shaping the early Christian community, and so what they say about the masculinity of the believers, as well as the masculinity of Paul, deserves attention. Brigitte Kahl studied the implications of the statement that in Christ there is no male and female (Gal 3:28) for the masculinity of followers of Christ. Galatians focuses extensively on the imagery of male genitalia, yet the bridge between the gospel of the foreskin and the gospel of the circumcised is couched in terms of maternal examples, which would seem to decenter traditional understandings of masculinity and lead to alternate understandings of gender in the Christian community. On the other hand, Conway counters that the loss of male and female in the context of Greco-Roman society results in an androgyny that is essentially male, so that masculinity retains its central place. She notes that in general Paul portrays Jesus as masculine, although he aligns that masculinity with the sometimes nonhegemonic ideals, such as endurance, lauded by the philosophers, in order to explain Jesus's unmanly death. In salvation Jesus grants his followers the masculine virtues of righteousness and self-control. The Pastoral Epistles continue the emphasis on righteousness and self-control, while reinscribing conventional gender roles and hierarchies in the early church.

Significance. Masculist interpretation is set to make a significant contribution to the study of biblical texts. It complements feminist criticism and queer theory in its concern with the constructed nature of gender. Because most of the texts are predominantly written by men, about men, and for men, there is an extensive field of potential analysis. Specific appeals to or critiques of the masculinity of the original audience and the impact of those appeals on later readers provide layers of meaning for a passage. Explicit attention to masculinity can reveal important elements of the rhetorical assumptions and aims of the texts that have generally been overlooked. The impact of the construction of masculinity for the men in the text, for those who have transmitted it, and for those who have and continue to interpret is beginning to be realized. Future studies of both individual texts and more overarching themes of masculinity and gender will open new avenues of understanding of masculine perspectives of the text that have previously been accepted as normative.

[*See also* Cultural Anthropology, *subentry* Hebrew Bible; Cultural Anthropology, *subentry* New Testament; Feminist Biblical Interpretation; Ideological Criticism; Lesbian, Gay, Bisexual and Transgender Interpretation; Psychological Biblical Interpretation; Queer Criticism and Queer Theory; Social Sciences, *subentry* Hebrew Bible; *and* Social Sciences, *subentry* New Testament.]

BIBLIOGRAPHY

Berger, Maurice, Brian Wallis, and Simon Watson, eds. *Constructing Masculinity.* New York: Routledge, 1995. An influential collection in shaping the contours of sociological approaches to masculinity studies.

Bly, Robert. *Iron John: A Book about Men.* Reading, Mass.: Addison-Wesley, 1990. A popular text from the mythopoetic men's movement, drawing on Jungian archetypes to help men reclaim a masculine identity.

Brod, Harry, ed. *The Making of Masculinities: The New Men's Studies.* Boston: Allen & Unwin, 1987. A collection of essays focusing on the sociological approach to masculinity studies, including Tim Carrigan's essay that defines hegemonic masculinity, a concept utilized extensively in later studies.

Chapman, Cynthia R. *The Gendered Language of Warfare in the Israelite-Assyrian Encounter.* Harvard Semitic Monographs 62. Winona Lake, Ind.: Eisenbrauns, 2004. An excellent analysis of masculinity in Assyrian royal annals and iconography as it applies to the gendered rhetoric of warfare in the biblical texts.

Clines, David J. *Interested Parties: The Ideology of Writers and Readers of the Hebrew Bible.* Journal for the Study of the Old Testament Supplement Series 205. Gender, Culture, Theory 1. Sheffield, UK: Sheffield Academic Press, 1995. Includes Clines's essay on "David the Man," which elucidates characteristics of masculinity in the Hebrew Bible and has been influential in many later studies.

Cornwall, Andrea and Nancy Lindisfarne, eds. *Dislocating Masculinity: Comparative Ethnographies.* Male Orders. New York: Routledge, 1994. An excellent collection of studies employing an anthropological approach to the study of masculinity.

Connell, R. W. *Masculinities.* 2d ed. Berkeley: University of California Press, 2005. A seminal work in masculinity studies, it lays out different approaches to the studies of masculinity, particularly in a sociological context.

Conway, Colleen M. *Behold the Man: Jesus and Greco-Roman Masculinity.* New York: Oxford University Press, 2008. A thorough study of Jesus's masculinity throughout the New Testament texts using a historical-cultural approach.

Creangă, Ovidiu. ed. *Men and Masculinity in the Hebrew Bible and Beyond.* The Bible in the Modern World 33. Sheffield, UK: Sheffield Phoenix, 2010. The first major anthology of masculinity studies of the Hebrew Bible. It includes an assessment of the field to date.

Eilberg-Schwarz, Howard. *God's Phallus: And Other Problems for Men and Monotheism.* Boston: Beacon, 1994. An early work on masculinity and biblical studies, employing a psychoanalytic approach.

Gilmore, David D. ed. *Honor and Shame and the Unity of the Mediterranean.* Special Publication of the American Anthropological Association 22. Washington, D.C.: American Anthropological Association, 1987. A collection of studies discussing how the honor and shame system functions in various cultures. Cross-cultural studies of honor have been very influential in analyzing biblical masculinity.

Glancy, Jennifer A. "Unveiling Masculinity: The Construction of Gender in Mark 6:17–29." *Biblical Interpretation* 11 (1994): 34–50. An early study of masculinity in the New Testament from a psychoanalytic perspective.

Glancy, Jennifer A. "Boasting of Beatings." *Journal of Biblical Literature* 123 (2004): 99–135. An examination of the effects of Paul's scarred body on his masculinity, placed in the context of Greco-Roman attitudes toward scars from battles and whippings.

Goldingay, John. "Hosea 1–3, Genesis 1–4 and Masculist Interpretation." In *A Feminist Companion to the Latter Prophets*, edited by Athalya Brenner, 161–168. Feminist Companion to the Bible 8. Sheffield, UK: Sheffield Academic, 1995. An early article applying a masculist interpretation to problematic texts for feminist interpretation.

Haddox, Susan E. *Metaphor and Masculinity in Hosea*. Studies in Biblical Literature 141. New York: Peter Lang, 2011. A monograph examining how the prophet draws his rhetorical images from the field of masculinity in the Ancient Near East, employing a historical and cross-cultural approach.

Hoffner, Harry A. Jr. "Symbols of Masculinity and Femininity: Their Use in Ancient Near Eastern Sympathetic Magic Rituals." *Journal of Biblical Literature* 85 (1966): 326–334. An example of using Assyrian literature and archaeology to provide insight on references to gender in the Hebrew Bible.

Kahl, Brigitte. "No Longer Male: Masculinity Struggles Behind Gal 3:28?" *Journal for the Study of the New Testament* 79 (2000): 47–69. A study of the implications of Paul's male and female imagery in Galatians for the masculinity of Gentile Christians.

Larson, Jennifer L. "Paul's Masculinity." *Journal of Biblical Literature* 123 (2004): 85–97. An analysis of how Paul's self-portrayal was situated in Greco-Roman constructions of masculinity.

Moore, Stephen D. *God's Beauty Parlor: And Other Queer Spaces around the Bible*. Contraversions. Stanford, Calif.: Stanford University Press, 2001. A collection of essays exploring issues of the divine body, sexuality, beauty, and violence.

Moore, Stephen D., and Janice Capel Anderson, eds. *New Testament Masculinities*. Semeia Studies 45. Atlanta: Society of Biblical Literature, 2003. The first major anthology of masculinity studies in the New Testament. It includes a helpful bibliography of general, classical, and biblical masculinity studies.

Neyrey, Jerome H. "Jesus, Gender, and the Gospel of Matthew." In *New Testament Masculinities*, edited by Stephen D. Moore and Janice Capel Anderson, 43–66. Semeia Studies 45. Atlanta: Society of Biblical Literature, 2003. A study of Jesus in the Gospel of Matthew in the light of Greco-Roman ideas of gendered spaces and components of public speech.

Olson, Dennis T. "Untying the Knot? Masculinity, Violence, and the Creation-Fall Story of Genesis 2–4." In *Engaging the Bible in a Gendered World*, edited by Linda Day and Carolyn Pressler, 73–86. Louisville, Ky.: Westminster John Knox, 2006. An interpretation of the J stories in Genesis, focusing on the masculine roles in the text and their implications for contemporary readers.

Stone, Ken. "Gender Criticism: The Un-Manning of Abimelech." In *Judges and Method: New Approaches in Biblical Studies*, edited by Gale A. Yee, 183–201. 2d ed. Minneapolis: Fortress, 2007. A good explanation of how to practice gender criticism, focusing on the masculinity of Abimelech in Judges.

Stone, Ken. *Sex, Honor, and Power in the Deuteronomistic History*. Journal for the Study of the Old Testament Supplement Series 234. Sheffield, UK: Sheffield Academic, 1996. An analysis of the interplay of gender and power in the texts, particularly how sex frequently symbolizes a power play among men.

Ward, Graham. "The Displaced Body of Jesus Christ. In *Radical Orthodoxy: A New Theology*, edited by John Milbank, Catherine Pickstock, and Graham Ward, 163–181. London: Routledge, 1999. An example of a study dealing with the problem of the divine male body.

Susan E. Haddox

MASORA AND MASORETIC INTERPRETATION

Masora, which in a broad sense is usually defined as "tradition, transmission," refers in a technical sense to the complete corpus of notes of a textual nature that were transmitted together with the biblical text or independently, with the aim of preserving its integrity.

The corpus of annotations which make up the Masora correspond to the three systems of Hebrew vocalization from which their names are derived: the Palestinian Masora, the Tiberian Masora, and the Babylonian Masora (Ofer 2001). The purpose of all three is the same, although they differ in their form and system of annotation. In all three systems the Masora was transmitted together with the biblical text and also in independent treatises. The difference between them lies mainly in the number of notes, which is far greater in the Tiberian Masora. There is also a fundamental difference between the Tiberian and Babylonian Masoras in their terminology, since the latter uses unique terms.

An additional Masora is attached to the text of Targum Onkelos (Klein 2000). The masoretic notes to this Targum are like the other three Masoras in form and layout, but quite different in their purpose, which is to try to establish precisely how to translate from the Hebrew original while preserving the translation choices made by the author. This fundamental difference determines the other differences of content and terminology.

The Tiberian system and its Masora eventually prevailed over the others, and it is therefore the best known and the one on which this article will concentrate.

Development. Little is still known about the emergence of the Masora, its development, and its creators. It is generally thought to have begun around the sixth to seventh century C.E., and the work of compiling the information contained in the Masoretic notes is normally attributed to the Masoretes, most of whom were anonymous men. From the information in the Masora itself, its history can be traced in outline and divided into two distinct periods, to which a third can be added to account for its transmission and those who worked on it.

Pre-Masoretic Period. References to names such as Dosa ben Eleazar, R. Yehuda ha-Babli, and Naqay, among others, are indications of the rabbinical world in the centuries preceding the emergence of the Masora, going back to the second century B.C.E. In this period some of the textual traditions that came to fruition in the Masora must have been formed, especially those relating to the consonantal text, though they could also have included certain traditions of reading. Rabbinical literature also echoes these traditions, referring to them, in many cases, in terminology similar to that of the Masora. Although one cannot speak in this period of a corpus of notes like that which forms the Masora nor of the existence of a group of people dedicated to this task, one can clearly detect a common impetus to maintain and preserve the biblical text unchanged.

Masoretic Period. The development of core Masoretic activity took place between the estimated date of emergence of the Masora and the mid-tenth century. The Masoretes compiled the textual information and wrote it down, either in the form of notes in the outer and inner margins (known as Masora Parva [MP]) and in the upper and lower margins of the biblical text (known as Masora Magna [MM]), or in the form of lists included mainly in separate treatises, which make up the Masora. The Masoretes were also responsible for adding vowels and cantillation marks to the biblical text.

The few names of Masoretes indicated in some notes are from the last generations. The "Teachers of Tiberias," the "Men of Tiberias," and "Phinehas, Head of the Academy," can be dated to around the first half of the ninth century. Reference is also made to members of the ben Asher family, regarded as the most prestigious Masoretes, whose activity spanned five generations, from the second half of the eighth century, with the work of Asher the Elder, down to Aaron ben Asher, the last of the dynasty, in the second half of the tenth century. Finally, there is mention of Moses ben David ben Naphtali, a contemporary of Moses ben Asher, who advocated a different system of vocalization and accentuation of the biblical text. With these two the Masoretic period is considered to have reached its conclusion.

The great Tiberian Masoretic codices known today come from this last period: the Cairo Codex of the Prophets (C), the Leningrad B19 manuscript (L), and the Aleppo Codex (A). Their Masoras and vocalization have been attributed to the ben Asher family, the first to Moses ben Asher and the other two to Aaron ben Asher.

Post-Masoretic Period. From the end of the Masoretic period right down to our own day there have always been those who have continued to work on the Masora, though not always on the same scale and with the same degree of interest. The type of work carried out in this period differs from that of the previous era in being concerned, first, with collecting, organizing, and systematizing existing Masoretic material, and in recent centuries, with editing and studying it.

The earliest exponents include Me'ir ben Todros ha-Levi Abulafia, author of *Masoret Seyag la-Torah*, a work in which the Masoretic information is arranged by roots; Menahem ben Shelomoh ha-Meiri, known for his work *Kiryat Sefer*, the second part of which contains a collection of Masoretic information; and finally Yequtiel ben Yehudah ha-Naqdan, author of *Ein ha-Qoré*, which formulates grammatical rules on the use of accents in the biblical texts and collects Masoretic notes on the Pentateuch, Lamentations, and Esther.

As early as the Renaissance period there are two key figures for the preservation and continuation of the Masora who must be mentioned: Jacob ben Hayyim ibn Adoniyah and Elias Levita. The former, who lived in the sixteenth and seventeenth centuries, has been credited with rescuing the Masora from extinction and restoring it to its original function of "the preservation of the textual tradition." He was the author of what is known as the Second Rabbinical Bible, published by Daniel Bomberg in Venice in 1524–1525, an eclectic edition of the Hebrew biblical text and its Masoras that became the *textus receptus* of Judaism until the edition of Leningrad MS B19 produced by Paul Kahle in 1937. Elias Levita also lived in the same period. This highly prolific author made numerous contributions to the study of the Masora, which led him to be regarded as the father of Masoretic studies. Two of his works in particular are worth mentioning here: the *Sefer Zik̲ronot*, where he sets out the laws and uses of the Masora and provides a list of Masoretic terms, and the *Massoreth ha-Massoreth*, his most important work, in which he presents the history of the Masora and his theory on its origin, denying the revealed nature of the vowels and crediting the Masoretes with inventing and writing them.

Apart from the work of Menahem de Lonzano and Jedidiah Solomon Rafael ben Abraham de Norzi in the second half of the sixteenth century and the early years of the seventeenth, work on the Masora declined notably until the nineteenth century, when a veritable revival took place. The first contributions in the field, begun in that century by Wolf Heidenheim, Joseph Derenbourg, Seligman Baer, William Wickes, and Solomon Frensdorff, were editions of the works of the first Masoretes. Although these works contain a large amount of information and reveal the rules their authors followed, they do not enable one to form a proper view of what Masoretic literature really is. It was Christian Ginsburg who initiated modern Masoretic studies at the end of the nineteenth century. The four volumes of his *The Massorah Compiled from Manuscripts* offer the largest collection of Masoretic lists and notes so far compiled and are regarded as an indispensable instrument for understanding, investigating, and using the Masora.

This upward trend continued in the twentieth century. In the first half, the outstanding figures are Henri Hyvernat, whose profound study of the language of the Masora is still the only existing work on the subject, and Paul Kahle. It was Kahle who, having recognized the value of the ben Asher tradition, decided to edit the biblical text on the basis of a single manuscript, Leningrad Codex B19, and therefore to publish only the Masora presented in this manuscript. This policy was followed in the third edition of Kittel's *Biblia Hebraica*. Kahle's friendship with Federico Pérez Castro led to the creation of the Madrid school (Fernández Tejero and Fernández Marcos 2008), with its ongoing and wide-ranging work in the field of the Masora.

Moving on to the second half of the century, Gerard Weil continued the work begun by Kahle and was responsible for editing the MP and MM for the *Biblia Hebraica Stuttgartensia*, although as a result of his editorial decisions what is presented is not really the Masora in the Leningrad manuscript but a version based on the set of indications of the MP in the manuscript. He was also the first to use computers to process the Hebrew biblical text and its Masoras.

The foundation of the International Organization for Masoretic Studies (IOMS) in 1972 by Harry M. Orlinsky gave a definitive boost to Masoretic studies worldwide. Since then, and continuing up to the present day, these studies have developed mainly in two geographical areas: Israel and Spain. In Israel, figures like Aron Dotan, Israel Yeivin, and Mordechai Breuer have contributed to illuminating the highly complex subject of Masoretic accents, which continues to be studied by new researchers such as Rachel Mashiah and Nurit Reich, among others. Of the numerous studies produced in that country, the most notable are those on the other Masoras (Babylonian and Palestinian), the presence and use of the Masora in medieval commentators, especially Rashi, and the editing work done on the Aleppo codex and its Masoras and on the Masoretic work of Norzi. These works have been carried out by Zvi Betzer, Lea Himmelfarb, David Lyons, Jordan S. Penkower, and Yosef Ofer, among others.

In Spain, the Masoretic activity undertaken by the Madrid school has been very wide-ranging and is characterized by methodological innovation in editing the Masoras that accompany the biblical text (Dotan 2010). In the edition of the Cairo codex, for example, the Masoras were edited exactly as they appear in the manuscript, with no attempt to systematize them, as Weil did in the edition of the MP in the Leningrad manuscript, and the *simanîm* ("catchwords") were identified. Work is currently underway on an edition of the Masoras in Madrid Complutense University manuscript M1 (M1), in which only the Masoras themselves are being edited, without the biblical text they accompany. Equally innovative are the comparative studies of the Masoras in the principal biblical codices. Among the members of the Madrid school, in addition to Pérez Castro, already referred to earlier, mention should be made of Emilia Fernández Tejero, María Josefa de Ázcarraga Servert, María Teresa Ortega Monasterio, Carmen Muñoz, Fernando Díaz Esteban, and more recently Elvira Martín-Contreras and Guadalupe Seijas de los Ríos-Zarzosa.

In addition, though on a smaller scale, there is an interest in Masoretic studies in America, which should be mentioned, with John Revell in Canada, David Marcus and Daniel S. Mynatt in the United States, and Edson de Faria Francisco in Brazil. There are also a great many researchers who have addressed the world of the Masora at some point and have contributed sporadically to advancing Masoretic studies.

Masoretic Interpretation. The first to draw attention to details of the textual tradition of the biblical text and use them in interpretation were the rabbis. Rabbinical literature frequently contains interpretations based on full or defective writing, the distinctive form and size of certain letters, the unusual spelling of a word, and so on. These interpretations are usually in two parts: a first part, indicating the textual information that is to be interpreted, normally in language similar to that of the Masora, and a second part, giving the exegetical explanation of the textual detail, derived using the traditional hermeneutical principles employed by rabbis, especially those of a textual nature (Martín-Contreras 2003). The explanations given for these details tend to be different in their aims from more common kinds of rabbinical interpretations, which seek to clarify, illuminate, or amplify the meaning of the text. In the former, the intention is rather to point out a textual feature or a numerical or other type of observation, and then to look for an explanation for that detail.

Other details of the textual tradition are also included in this literature, such as words that are read though not written in the biblical text, and conversely words that are written in the text but not read, as well as certain irregularities which affect the written form of the biblical text, such as the inverted *nun*, suspended letters, *puncta extraordinaria*, and so on. All these are included in the Masoretic sources. The exegesis that accompanies them in this literature is also incorporated into the Masora, albeit to a lesser extent, in notes which interpolate Midrashic explanations and which are usually known as Exegetical Masoras (Dotan 2010; Martín–Contreras 2006).

The Masora and the Interpretation of the Biblical Text. The Masora is an indispensable tool for correct interpretation of the biblical text. It constitutes a historical record that accompanies the actual text and is designed to preserve it and transmit it correctly. The addition of vowels and cantilation marks to the biblical text is in itself an exegesis of that text, since the former determine a particular reading among the various possible alternatives and the latter have syntactic value. However, the stereotypes surrounding the Masora and lack of knowledge of this source have resulted in its usefulness being ignored, and occasionally even denied.

Although the need to take account of the study of the function of accents in interpretation and exegesis of the biblical text has been recognized in recent years, as reflected in several works on the subject

(Revell 2000; Carasik 2001; Samuel 2005), its other "facets" for interpretation have yet to be explored.

One of the obstacles to using the Masora for interpretation is the Masora itself. Some of the features that have led it to be labelled as difficult and mysterious are the very ones that have hindered its widespread use as a source of interpretation. The way in which Masoretic notes are normally expressed makes it impossible, in most cases, to appreciate the content of the note and its possible relevance to interpretation on a first reading. It tends to be:

- concise: generally expressed using abbreviations. Many Masoretic notes consist only of a number and do not specify even the most basic information. And yet this does not necessarily mean that their object is to count words, letters, verses, etc. Some may contain information of a statistical nature, but most of them represent the briefest possible way of recording the information. They are similar to the notes that explicitly give more information. We can readily appreciate this in cases where the same information is given in different ways, formats, and forms, depending on the manuscript. For example, in Deuteronomy 15:9 the following information on the Word ורעה is found in the MP of the Leningrad and Aleppo manuscripts: "nine times." In the MM, the nine verses where that particular word appears are listed. At first sight, the note could be classified as numerical, stating the number of times the word appears in the Bible. However, the MP and MM in manuscript M1 seem to indicate something different. Together they give us more complete information and show that the intention of the note is not just to state how many times the word appears. The numerical information given this time is the same as in the other manuscripts: "nine times." However, the note continues: "seven of them are 'bad' and three 'good.'" This additional information provides the clue to understanding the true intention of the note. Having identified the *simanîm*, given in the MM, and having carefully examined the references, we can infer that: (1) The first six are from the root רעע "to be bad" (although the note says seven, only six *simanîm* are given); (2) The other three are from the root רעה "to shepherd." That is to say, the Word occurs nine times but from two different roots. This is the real meaning of the note; its purpose is not to give the number of times the Word appears in the Bible.
- elliptical: part of what is present in the notes is implicit, namely all the information that the Masoretes did not consider necessary to state explicitly because it was well known in their period. Lack of familiarity with this information and the time that has elapsed since the notes were written makes them difficult to understand. This, combined with a widespread lack of knowledge of the Masora among scholars devoted to the study of the biblical text, largely due to the need for additional specialized training, has contributed decisively to it being undervalued.

Methodology. All these difficulties can be solved by supplying the information that was left implicit and by formulating a clear methodology of how to analyze Masoretic notes, enabling us to identify and study them in order to apply them subsequently to the interpretation of the biblical text.

The following five steps should be followed when analyzing a Masoretic note (see Martín-Contreras, and Seijas de los Ríos 2010): (1) Find the words with a circellus and the MP note attached to that lemma; (2) Locate the MM; (3) Identify the *simanîm*; (4) Confirm the note; (5) Understand the note.

These five steps are proposed when working on the Masora from a manuscript. If an edition of a Masora is used, only steps four and five are necessary. The following two steps are also required to appreciate the value of Masoretic information for interpretation: (1) Understand the note, and (2) Translate the note.

As already mentioned, Masoretic notes are expressed in a very concise form, normally using abbreviations. We therefore need to understand what the Masorete is saying. The first task is to translate the note. In order to do so, until we know all the abbreviations and are familiar with them, we can use the lists of terms and corresponding abbreviations published in the most important editions and introductions. This will enable us to translate the note. But because Masoretic notes are so concise, translating them is not enough; we also need to understand them.

However, there are no steps or methodology that can be followed in order to try to understand what is not explicitly stated in the note. We have to "get into the mind of the Masorete": in other words, to develop a Masoretic mentality so as to be able to follow the implicit logical process behind the explicit notes. In order to acquire this mentality, the following may be helpful:

A. Some general theoretical notions of what a Masoretic note is, what it contains, and how it is formulated, before we embark on the analysis.

The most important aspect of Masoretic notes is the phenomena that they refer to. On the basis of years of analysis, we can say that the majority of Masoretic notes are concerned with spelling, vocalization, accentuation, meaning, grammatical rules, combinations of words, combinations of particles, and, less commonly, counting.

We can state explicitly the kind of information that can be found on each of these phenomena. For example, if we focus on the Masoretic notes related to spelling, we can list the following information: they may deal with (a) the *plene* or *defective* spelling of a word; or (b) orthographic peculiarities.

For each of these two groups, we can specify more detailed information. Plene or defective spelling may refer to: (a) *Matres lectionis*, with or without vowel letters *yod* and *waw*; (b) letters, with or without any other letter, usually those known as weak letters; (c) words, with or without one or more other words, usually in similar combinations of words.

Orthographic peculiarities may refer to: (a) exceptions to the usual form; (b) different spelling of a word; (c) substitution of letters, commonly *rêš* instead of *dalet* and *sin* instead of *samek*; (d) word division.

We can also state explicitly what terminology is used and how the information is presented in the notes. Continuing with the example of spelling, we can list it as follows:

- The most common technical terms are *ḥaser*, *male*ʾ, and *katab*.
- The information can be presented: (a) giving just the number of occurrences of the word; (b) giving a description of the spelling of the word; (c) giving the word together with other words that share the same phenomenon.

This prior classification of the phenomena and the notes can help us to decipher the information given in the notes, even when it is just a number. In this way, we develop a Masoretic way of thinking, which will assist our understanding.

B. An awareness of some of the characteristic features of the Masora: (a) MP notes highlight minority or less common forms; (b) there is no one single Masora; (c) the Masora is not numerical in nature. Even though the relationship between these features and the decoding of Masoretic notes has not always been sufficiently emphasized, they are crucial when approaching the Masora for the first time.

Once we have incorporated this perspective into our way of thinking, we can begin the task of solving the logical puzzle posed by the Masoretic note. We have the objective, which is all the information contained in the note, and also the clues: all the information we have collected in the process of analyzing the note (the MP, the MM, the identification of the *simanîm*, other evidence). They can help us to understand the overall meaning of the note, its purpose.

A good starting point is to formulate questions and hypotheses. The fact that we have to use working hypotheses to supply the implicit information might lead one to suppose that the interpretation of the notes is a subjective matter, at the whim of the researcher. However, the next step circumscribes the range of possible interpretations and enables us to confirm the true meaning of the note.

Confirming the Note. It is necessary to confirm that the information given in the notes is true: that the number of times it is stated matches the *simanîm* given, that the verses contain the phenomenon recorded, and so on.

In order to do so, it is important to consult the *masorot* of the principal Tiberian biblical manuscripts (C, A, and L) and the major Masoretic lists and treatises (Ginsburg 1975; Frensdorff 1864/1972; Díaz-Esteban 1975; Dotan 1967; Ognibeni 1995; Weil 1971) and to check whether they contain any information similar to the note. We have to be cautious before saying that a note is not correct. The Masora may be true even if it is not confirmed by other records.

The following example illustrates how the two steps are applied. The MP of manuscript M1 on the word וַיַּאַסְפוּ in 1 Samuel 5:11 says: "ten *paštîn*". The MM gives ten verses: Exodus 4:29; Numbers 11:32; 1 Samuel 5:8; 5:11; 17:1; 2 Samuel 21:13; 2 Kings 23:1; 2 Chronicles 24:11; 29:15; Jeremiah 40:12. So the first hypothesis is that the note relates to the *pašṭa*ʾ; in other words, to the ten times that the word appears with that accent. But if we check the word in each of the verses given in the MM, we can see that it does not have that accent in all of them.

It is therefore necessary to pursue other clues. The other sources contain only numerical information. The MP of A says "ten" and there is no MM. In list 1001 of Ginsburg's Masoretic compilation the lemma and the information match our note, "ten." Moreover, at the end of that list there is a reference to another list, number 1011, where the lemma is: "twelve times is written וַיֵּאָסְפוּ." This extra information could help us to understand the note. If we examine this last list in relation to our information and compare them, we can see that the two words share the same consonantal text but differ in their vocalization. The lemma has a *pataḥ* under the *yod* in list 1001 and a *ṣerê* under the *yod* in list 1011. The question arises: what does this mean? By investigating the differences between the words included in the two lists, it is possible to conclude that the words in list 1001 are third-person plural masculine imperfect *qal* and those in list 1011 are third-person plural masculine imperfect *nipal*. They are similar in all respects except conjugation. So the purpose of the note is to distinguish the *qal* from the *nipal* form.

Practical Uses. There are many possible ways in which the Masora may be used for interpretation of the biblical text. Among others, they include:

- Determining word roots. There are words that appear with different spellings in the text and even with one of the radical letters missing or altered, which makes it difficult to identify the root. Masoretic notes can help us to clarify what the root is. For example, in Jeremiah 19:11 we find the word להרפה; the MP to this passage in the Aleppo manuscript says: "unique written with *heh*," thereby indicating that this is the only time the *nipal* construct infinitive of the root רפא is written with *heh* instead of the ʾ*alep* of the root. Then there is the more complex case of the word הבי in Ruth 3:15. This is normally interpreted as a second-person feminine singular *qal* imperative of the root יהב "give." However, the information in the Aleppo, M1, and Rabbinical Bible Masoras indicates, among other things, that this word comes from the root בוא, that it is written defective of ʾ*alep* and that it is a feminine form but is written in the masculine form. This information obliges us to reconsider the usual interpretation of this word and to offer a new description, such as: second-person masculine singular *hipil* imperative of the root בוא used for the feminine (Martín-Contreras 2009).
- Distinguishing between homophonic forms. A case in point is לָחֶם in Judges 5:8, whose MP in C says: "unique." The note indicates that in this passage the word *laḥem* is from the root לחם "fight," and therefore means "war," not "bread" (*leḥem*), a word which in the pausal form is also vocalized as *laḥem*. These two homophonic roots would otherwise be easily confused.
- Differentiating meanings. For example, the MP to Numbers 33:27 in M1 says that *mittaḥat* is "unique as name of place." It thereby indicates that on this occasion it is not a preposition, as is the case the other forty-eight times *mittaḥat* appears in the Bible. Or Deuteronomy 19:11, where the MP in M1, commenting on the word *ha-*ʾ*el*, says: "eight times [in] profane

language in the Pentateuch and 1 [in] sacred language." It thus distinguishes the eight times *ha-ʾel* is a common noun from the only time it is the name of the divinity.

- Shedding light on problems of translation and interpretation. There are some problematic words in the biblical text, arising either from the corruption or the obscurity of the text, and these are sometimes explained using the researchers' own conjectures or on the basis of old versions and records. The Masora can also be used as one more piece of evidence with which to interpret the text and clarify these difficult cases. Some studies offer examples of how to incorporate the Masora into the investigation in these cases and the results achieved (Fernández Tejero 1984; Barthélemy 1992). An example is Psalm 22:17, where one of the problematic words, *kāʾărî,* is translated as "they pierce me," "they have run me through," "they kill me," in the light of old versions and records. However, according to the Masora there is another possibility. The word appears again in the Bible, in Isaiah 38:13, where the MP in C, A, and L indicate that it is the same word there and in Psalm 22:17. It could therefore be translated "like a lion" in Psalms, as it is in Isaiah 38:13, a lion which, moreover, had already appeared in verse 14 and reappears in verse 22.

Lines of Research: Suggestions for the Future. To take advantage of the benefits that the use of the Masora can bring to the interpretation and history of the biblical text, we need to encourage the pursuit of research in two fields: masoretic studies, on the one hand, and biblical studies and textual criticism on the other.

In the latter, the value of the Masora needs to be recognized as a prerequisite for developing a methodology to incorporate the Masora into that area of study.

In the field of masoretic studies, one of the principal objectives must be to continue making the Masora accessible, through manuals and also courses and complementary studies to facilitate the use of certain Masoretic works, as well as through the employment of new technologies to make them more widely available. It would be useful to develop a classification of known Masoretic information so as to provide a clear idea of the different subjects it addresses and thereby highlight its value for the study of grammar, the Hebrew language, and the interpretation of the biblical text.

Given that the great majority of Masoretic material remains unpublished, and our knowledge of its content and nature is therefore still incomplete, we need to continue editing this material, especially that which does not accompany the biblical text, and also the lists contained in various manuscripts and fragments of the Genizah, since this is where least work has been done.

Bearing in mind that there is no one single Masora and that information on a word can therefore appear in different forms, and also that not all the manuscripts present the same information, we need to carry out comparative studies of the Masoras in different manuscripts, as well as other studies on the various phenomena related to grammar, syntax, textual criticism, exegesis, and so on. Moreover, it would be a good idea to encourage interaction between the different fields by undertaking collaborative studies and exchanging ideas and methodologies.

[*See also* Midrash; *and* Rabbinic Exegesis.]

BIBLIOGRAPHY

Barthélemy, Dominique. *Ézéchiel, Daniel et les 12 Prophètes.* Vol. 3 of *Critique textuelle de l'Ancien Testament.* Orbis biblicus et orientalis 50:3. Fribourg/Göttingen: Éditions Universitaires/Vandenhoeck & Ruprecht, 1992.

Carasik, Michael. "Exegetical Implications of the Masoretic Cantillation Marks in Ecclesiastes." *Hebrew Studies* 42 (2001): 145–165. http://works.bepress.com/michael_carasik/15.

Díaz-Esteban, Fernando. *Sefer Oklah we Oklah: colección de listas de palabras destinadas a conservar la integridad del texto hebreo de la Biblia entre los judíos de la Edad Media.* Textos y Estudios "Cardenal Cisneros" 4. Madrid: CSIC, 1975.

Dotan, Aron. *The Diqduqé hatteʾamim of Aaron ben Moshe ben Asher, With a Critical Edition of the Original*

Text from New Manuscripts. Jerusalem: The Academy of the Hebrew Language, 1967.

Dotan, Aron. "The Contribution of the Modern Spanish School to Masoretic Studies." *Estudios Bíblicos* 68, no. 4 (2010): 411–418.

Dotan, Aron. "Masora's Contribution to Biblical Studies. Revival of an Ancient Tool." In *Congress Volume Ljubljana 2007*, edited by André Lemaire, 57–69. Leiden and Boston: Brill 2010.

Fernández Tejero, Emilia. "Masora y Exégesis." In *Simposio Bíblico Español (Salamanca, 1982)*, edited by Natalio Fernández Marcos, Julio Trebolle Barrera, and Javier Fernández Vallina, 183–191. Madrid: Universidad Complutense, 1984.

Fernández Tejero, Emilia, and Natalio Fernández Marcos. "Paul E. Kahle and Federico Pérez Castro: The Origins of the Madrid School of Biblical Text Criticism." *Sefarad* 68, no. 1 (2008): 5–14.

Frensdorff, Solomon. *Das Buch Ochlah W'ochlah*. Hannover: Hahn, 1864. Repr., New York: Ktav, 1972.

Ginsburg, Christian David. *The Massorah: Compiled from Manuscripts Alphabetically and Lexically Arranged*. New York: Ktav, 1975.

Klein, Michael L. *The Masorah to Targum Onqelos: As Preserved in Mss Vatican Ebreo 448, Rome Angelica Or. 7, Fragments on the Cairo Genizah in Earlier Editions by A. Berliner and S. Landauer/ Critical Edition with Comments and Introduction*. Binghamton, N.Y.: Targum Studies, 2000.

Martín-Contreras, Elvira. "Comments on Textual Details: Relationships between Masorah and Midrash." *Journal of Jewish Studies* 54 (2003): 62–70.

Martín-Contreras, Elvira. "Continuity of the Tradition: Masorah with Midrashic Explanations." *Journal of Semitic Studies* 50 (2005): 329–339.

Martín-Contreras, Elvira. "Masoretic and Rabbinic Lights on the word הבי, Ruth 3:15: יהב or בוא?." *Vetus Testamentum* 59 (2009): 257–265.

Martín-Contreras, Elvira and Guadalupe Seijas de los Ríos. *Masora. La transmisión de la tradición de la Biblia Hebrea*. Estella: Verbo Divino 2010.

Ofer, Yosef. *The Babylonian Masora of the Pentateuch its Principle and Methods*. Jerusalem: Hebrew University Magnes Press, 2001.

Ognibeni, Bruno. *La seconda parte del Sefer Oklah we Oklah: edizione del Ms. Halle, Universitätsbibliothek*. Textos y Estudios "Cardenal Cisneros" 57. Madrid/Fribourg: CSIC/Université De Fribourg, 1995.

Revell, John. "The Interpretative Value of the Massoretic Punctuation." In Part 2: The Middle Age. Vol. 1 of *Hebrew Bible / Old Testament. The History of Its Interpretation*, edited by Magne Saebo, 64–73. Göttingen: Vandenhoeck & Ruprecht, 2000.

Samuel, Leonora. "Accentuation: A Tool for Interpreting the Text of the Hebrew Bible." *Jewish Bible Quarterly* 33, no. 3 (2005): 174–183.

Weil, Gerard E. *Massorah Gedolah Iuxta codicem Leningradensem B19a.* Rome: Pontifical Biblical Institute, 1971.

Elvira Martín-Contreras

MATERIALIST CRITICISM

The basic sense of materialism as a philosophical position is that the only reality is matter and that all aspects of existence rely on material processes. Thus, observable, material processes determine what are usually regarded as immaterial, such as consciousness, beliefs, and ideas. Crucially, materialism denies the independent existence of these immaterial processes, and thus argues that there is no extra-material world of gods and spirits. However, precisely what constitutes "matter" is open to debate, especially if one places it within the context of the universe. Are gravity and antimatter also material or are they immaterial? Opposed to materialism are idealism (the position that ideas are real, historical causes) and dualism (allowing for material and immaterial realms). Most religions hold to versions of dualism or idealism, for the gods belong to the immaterial world.

In this light, materialist criticism of the Bible may be understood in two senses. First, the move to make biblical criticism a "scientific" discipline in late eighteenth and early nineteenth century Europe (especially Germany) entailed removing theological concerns. God was no longer an actor in history, and texts were analyzed in terms of material causes, whether in terms of politics, economics, or social dynamics. However, most biblical critics also held to some form of idealism, either as a personal religious belief that they quarantined from their academic criticism, or as an assumption that ideas also have a causative effect on history.

A more sophisticated materialism is found in Marxist materialism, although Marxism is often misunderstood as reducing idealist elements of the

Bible to material or economic causes. Marx is occasionally guilty of such a reduction, for example, the "religious world is but the reflex of the real world" (Marx 1867 [1976], p. 90). More often Marx develops a complex dialectical argument in which materialism and idealism interact with one another, so much so that a fully realized idealism ends in materialism. Thus, in relation to Hegel, the dialectic which is "standing on its head" must "be turned right side up again, if you would discover the rational kernel within the mystical shell" (Marx 1867 [1976], p. 22). This is known as dialectical materialism or historical materialism, for its approach is more inclusive than simplistic idealism or materialism.

For biblical critics the use of this more sophisticated approach means, on the one hand, an expansion of traditional concerns with the nature of the text, author's intention (which in its more recent form is described as "political ideology"), and religious matters, and, on the other hand, an effort to overcome disciplinary splintering into literary, historical, and theological concerns. Materialist interpretation therefore means expanding traditional concerns to include material infrastructure—economic production and social relations—as inescapably part of that total picture. The following survey deploys the Marxist distinction between superstructure and infrastructure or base, the former designating texts, culture, religion, and ideology, and the latter the means and relations of economic production. As dynamic concepts, they should be understood in terms of trains and railways, where infrastructure is the complex network of tracks, stations, and electronic monitoring, and superstructure is the rolling stock itself.

Superstructure: Literature and Culture. At this level, the impetus for materialist literary readings in biblical criticism has come from Terry Eagleton (1991, 1996, 2006 [1976]) and Fredric Jameson (1981, 1991). Despite differences, both argue that literature is semiautonomous, with distinct features, and yet integral to its socioeconomic context. Other Marxists have also contributed, such as Lefebvre on space (1991), Gramsci on power (1992, 1996, 2007), Bloch on the dialectic of revolution and reaction (1995, 2009), and Adorno and Horkheimer on myth and theological suspicion (2002).

Key biblical scholars who have deployed Eagleton include Gottwald's (1992a) reading of Deutero-Isaiah as propaganda to encourage a reluctant ruling elite back to Jerusalem from comfortable Babylonian exile, Mosala's (1989) interpretation of redactional layers of Micah and Luke in light of class and ideology, and Yee's (2003) study of ideological representations of woman as evil. Jameson's work, especially his three-level schema of immediate politics, class-conflict and ideology, and the historical clash of modes of production, has been more influential in biblical studies. It has inspired Penchansky's (1991) reading of Job, as well as Jobling's (1992, 1998) interpretations of the contradictions of royal ideology in Psalm 72 and of 1 Samuel in conjunction with feminism and deconstruction. Sneed (1998, 2004) has interpreted Qoheleth via Jameson's concern with ideological and class contradictions, and Burt (2009) deploys Jameson's insights into textual-cum-socioeconomic tensions to interpret the contradictory "Nehemiah Memoir." Boer uses that approach to interpret the Jeroboam narratives in Kings and Chronicles (1996), appropriations of the Bible in popular culture (1999), as well as contributions from Benjamin, Bloch, Gramsci, Althusser, Adorno and Lefebvre for biblical criticism (2003).

In New Testament work, Pippin (1992a, 1992b) deploys Eagleton and Jameson to reinterpret the Apocalypse in its ancient and postmodern conjunctions, Cadwallader (2007) brings together archaeology and materialist analysis of economic contradictions in his Gospel interpretations, and Bernier (2010) explores intersections between psychoanalysis (Julian Jaynes) and Jameson to read the cognitive forms of John's Gospel, as well as a materialist approach to the earliest Christologies (2012). All these works overlap with infrastructure, although they begin with detailed analysis of texts before considering questions of socioeconomics. The same approach is used in a recent collection of Marxist-feminist readings of the Bible, in which a range of materialist approaches, including those of Simone de Beauvoir, Rosemary Hennessy, Julie Kristeva, and Juliet Mitchell, are used to offer new readings of Proverbs, the Solomon narratives, Mark's Gospel, Paul, and the epistle of 1 Peter (Boer and Økland 2008).

Infrastructure: Economics and Society. Here we follow a pattern in which work done outside biblical criticism has influenced that discipline.

Hebrew Bible. Karl Kautsky (2007 [1908]) was the first to offer a sustained materialist, socioeconomic analysis of early Israel. He argues that the agricultural basis in Canaan set in train a process of differentiation, in which some—due to soil fertility, rainfall patterns, war, or happenstance—gained wealth at the expense of others. Such economic differentiation is the beginning of class, in which a certain group is disconnected from the production of food, clothing, and housing. Wealthy landowners appropriated land, which was rented out to landless but working peasants. When these peasants failed to meet exorbitant debt requirements, they became debt-slaves to the landowners. The inevitable result was in a slave-based mode of production.

In between Kautsky and serious materialist analysis of the Hebrew Bible is an important but largely ignored tradition of Soviet-era Russian scholarship. The little that is known has been mediated by Wittfogel's (1963) wayward argument that the key to the Ancient Near East's economies was in the oriental despot's control over irrigation (Krader 1975, pp. 290–291; Hindess and Hirst 1975, pp. 208–220; Butzer 1996). The key here is the Asiatic Mode of Production (AMP), a proposal drawn from Marx (Krader; Bailey and Llobera 1981; Lichtheim 1990; Marx 1964). In contrast to Wittfogel, its features were more extensive: common ownership of land, centralized control of public works by government, tensions between autonomous village-communes and cities, and religion as the central language for expressing political, philosophical, juridical, and political issues. Many of the debates taken up later in the West are already found in these Soviet-era discussions. One may delineate the following stages in Soviet research (Dunn 2011 [1982]; D'iakonoff 1969b; D'iakonoff and Kohl 1991). In that scholarship, the AMP gave way briefly to feudalism as the preferred mode of production, which then was overtaken in the 1930s by a slave-based mode of production under the influence of V. V. Struve (1969a, 1969b; Tyumenev 1969a, 1969b; Dandamaev 2009 [1974]), which then, in the face of increasing problems (D'iakonoff 1969a, 1974, 1991), fell beneath a revised and revitalized AMP in the 1970s. This happened precisely when it was attacked in the West, belatedly and without reference to Soviet research (Hindess and Hirst, pp. 178–220; Anderson 1974, pp. 462–549). The lessons from the Soviet debates have still to be learned, for they provide a remarkable example of the dialectical interaction between data and theory that is the core of historical materialist analysis. Specifically, the issues that remain include land ownership, different modes of extracting surplus, city-village tensions, indentured labor, class conflict, state formation, and socioeconomic transition.

Although both Kautsky's work and that of the Soviet-era are still ignored, they established mode of production as the key to materialist studies. In biblical criticism debates have turned on the nature of that mode of production, with Gottwald providing the benchmark (1999 [1979]). He argued that the context of ancient Palestine was a "tributary" mode of production, in which surplus was produced by extracting tribute, in produce and labor, from overtaxed peasants for a city-state ruling class (and then imperial center). These city-states were economically oppressive and socially hierarchical. Ancient Israel arose through a rebellion of disaffected peasants against the tributary mode in the thirteenth century B.C.E. and establishing a different, "communitarian" mode of production. It was cooperative, relatively egalitarian, and distributed surplus among the people. Gottwald traces this communitarian mode at various points in Israel's history, especially with the prophets, the Jesus movement, and reconstruction of Judaism by the Pharisees after the two revolts against Rome (67–74 C.E. and 132–135 C.E.) (Gottwald 1992b).

Until recently, Gottwald continued to set the agenda for materialist criticism, although not without modifications. Subsequent work has reshaped some of his categories. Carol Meyers and Gale Yee have argued that the communitarian mode of production should be reconsidered in light of Marshall Sahlins's familial or household mode of production (Sahlins 1968, 1972), a term that recognizes the role of women in the economy. In Meyers's appropriation, the household (*bet-av*) was the primary unit of economic and social production, and it includes many elements from Gottwald's communitarian mode: in the highlands an alternative society was formed, with allegiance given to Yahweh alone and no earthly master, and in which women played a much larger role. Although Meyers does not engage directly with Marxist studies, that task is undertaken by Yee. She agrees with Meyers concerning the nature of the domestic mode of production. Yee's concern is women, in which the domestic situation is one of the kin group loyalty controlled by a paterfamilias. By contrast, the later kings preferred a nuclear family that broke the control of the kin group and policed the sexual lives of women in a more restrictive manner. Jobling (1991, 1998) too works with the domestic mode of production, expanding it to include the primacy of the household, the architectural dominance of domestic buildings, and absence of fortifications, division of labor according to gender. Jobling offers a novel interpretation of familial structure, drawing on Bal's (1988) distinction between virilocal (the woman leaves her household to live in the man's) and patrilocal (the man leaves his household to live in the woman's father's). Thus, virilocal marriage characterizes the tributary mode of production in the era of kingship, while the domestic mode of production operates patrilocally. Simkins (1999a, 1999b, 2004) provides a unique variation on the familial tensions outlined by Yee and Jobling. He argues that these should be seen as clientalistic (nuclear family) and domestic (extended family) modes of production. The qualified egalitarianism of the domestic mode of production (as argued by those earlier) is actually a textual ideology that attempts to ameliorate economic and social inequality. In response to the domestic mode's inability to deal with inequality, the hierarchical and unequal patron-client mode (a reworking of Gottwald's tributary mode) replaces it under the Israelite kingship.

Relatively little work in historical materialist analysis of the infrastructure has taken place after these contributions, although Boer (2007b) attempts a preliminary sketch of what he calls the "sacred economy." It draws not only on the work outlined earlier, but also on neglected Russian Soviet-era scholarship, the Marxist-inspired Regulation School of economic theory, and Marxist approaches more generally. Assuming that all economic relations are socially determined and that crisis is the norm rather than equilibrium, Boer suggests that the primary economic source of tension was between allocative and extractive economic practices. While the former reallocated agricultural produce along kinship, patron-client, judicial, and military lines, the latter extracted its surplus through tribute and limited exchange. Each period of relative economic stability involved compromise between these tensions (a regime of allocation), the unravelling of which caused economic and political collapse. The role of religion, culture, and other institutions was to provide the necessary justifications (a mode of regulation) for each compromise. This sketch is the basis for a monograph to be published by Westminster John Knox. Recently, Nam (2012) has offered a critical re-engagement with Karl Polanyi (1971 [1968], 2001 [1944]; Polanyi, Arensberg, and Pearson 1957). Nam deploys Polanyi's distinctions between formal (identity between the ancient economic world and ours) and substantivist (difference) approaches, as well as the forms of exchange—reciprocal, redistributive, and market—to argue for a complex picture in Kings. Both Nam's and Boer's work takes place in the context of a revived interest in materialist questions in a new Society of Biblical Literature section, "Economics in the Biblical World" (from 2011), in which all of the key questions are being reassessed—economic theory, class, family, agriculture, tribute, and exchange.

New Testament. New Testament materialist analysis begins with Friedrich Engels (1894–1895 [1990], 1882 [1989], 1883 [1990]). Engels argued that "Christianity was originally a movement of oppressed people: it first appeared as the religion of slaves and freedmen, of poor people deprived of all rights, of peoples subjugated or dispersed by Rome" (1894–1895 [1990], p. 447). His proposal has influenced materialist analysis both within and without biblical criticism. Thus, both Luxemburg (1970 [1905]) and Kautsky (2007 [1908]) agree with Engels but go further, arguing that early Christianity was communist (following Acts 2:44–5 and 4:32–5). However, being urban, it was a communism of consumption and not production, thereby leaving the economic system intact. Modern communism therefore completes what was imperfectly begun in the early church. Despite the collapse of early Christian communism into a hierarchical organization comfortable with imperial power, Kautsky traces the communist impulse through monasticism and continual religiously-inspired revolutionary movements down to his own day (1947a [1895–1897], 1947b [1895–1897]; 1977 [1922]). While Luxemburg's text was neglected, Kautsky's position was simultaneously criticized and assumed by biblical scholars and sociologists (Deissman 1929; Troeltsch 1992 [1911]). By contrast, conservative or neoliberal scholars preferred to argue for a mixed social origin of Christianity, including upper and lower class members (Judge 2008 [1960]; Stark 1996; Meeks 2003).

Others sought to deepen the initial insights from Engels, Luxemburg, and Kautsky, often without explicit recognition. The breakthrough work by Belo (1975, 1981; Clévenot 1976, 1985) on the Gospel of Mark drew upon Marx, Roland Barthes, Jacques Lacan, Georges Bataille, and Louis Althusser to offer a complex literary reading with a specific materialist dimension. Following Dhoquois (1971), Belo argued that the context of early Christianity was a "subasiatic" mode of production, in which the local economy functions in its older fashion (AMP), but the state controls exchange in order to appropriate surplus value. The problem here is a multiplication of modes of production (a tendency also in Hebrew Bible scholarship), for Dhoquois also suggests Asiatic, subasiatic, para-asiatic, and Asiatic feudalist modes of production, along with slavery and European feudalism. Rather than such multiplication, it is more rigorous to deal with the complexity of transitions between modes of production (Foster-Carter 1978; Feiner 1986).

Another feature of Kautsky's study was the radically political nature of Jesus's teachings, especially in relation to property and wealth. Outside biblical criticism, the Marxist classicist Ste. Croix has emphasized this dimension (Ste. Croix 1981, pp. 427–438; 2006, pp. 355–368). This element connects with a long tradition in biblically-inspired revolutionary movements, for example, Thomas Müntzer and the Peasants Revolt in Germany, the Münster Revolution, and Gerrard Winstanley and the Diggers in England. But a specifically materialist approach is found not only in Belo, for whom Jesus's band become militants, the resurrection a revolutionary symbol, and the *ekklesia* a radical movement, but also in Myers (1989), Theissen (1978, 1987, 1999) and Horsley (Horsley and Hanson 1985; Horsley 1992, 1995, 1996, 2002, 2008).

While for Myers, Jesus is an exemplar of nonviolent revolutionary resistance in the context of the Jewish uprising of 66–70 C.E. and the sociopolitical matrix of the times, Theissen argues that the wandering charismatics of the Jesus movement were able to deal with a series of contradictions, such as the tensions between rich and poor, socioecological tensions between city and country, sociopolitical problems in the debate over love for one's enemy and theocracy, and sociocultural tensions between Hellenistic assimilation and Jewish identity. Horsley argues that the Jesus movement must be understood in the context of a Jewish peasantry militantly subversive before a brutal Roman Empire. The materialist context was a tension between a Roman-imposed slave-based mode of production in the cities and the Asiatic or tributary mode of production in the countryside, which exacted brutal tribute. The peasants resisted by means of slowdowns, sabotage, prophetic and messianic movements, scribal writings, counter-terrorism, and revolts.

A final feature of materialist New Testament readings once again gains its impetus from outside, now from Marxist philosophers who emphasize the radical nature of Paul. First was Alain Badiou (2003 [1997]), for whom Paul is the exemplar of the revolutionary event (Christ's resurrection), which he names and which inspires fidelity and hope in a militant band. Giorgio Agamben (2005 [2000]) replied with a different approach, arguing that Paul offers a radical approach to the "time that is left us," a seizing of a moment of kairos out of the stream of kronos and bringing it to fulfillment. There followed Slavoj Žižek (2000, 2001, 2003, 2008; Žižek and Milbank 2009), who is actually caught, seeking a genuine event that will change the coordinates of existence—whether a laicized grace or Christian love with a distinct psychoanalytic-cum-Leninist approach—but also toying with refusism (a refusal to engage at all) in order to block the tendency of revolutions to run into the mud. The debate that followed these interventions increases (Critchley 2000; Caputo and Alcoff 2009; Surin 2009; Blanton and De Vries Forthcoming; Boer 2007a, pp. 334–390; 2009, pp. 155–204), but Elliott (2008) offers the most significant contribution from biblical criticism. He develops a sophisticated Marxist approach to the issues of faith, mercy, piety, virtue, and hope within the context of Roman imperialism, power, and economics. Notably, Elliott finds Paul caught in contradictions as he tries to mediate an alternative position characterized as the "horizon of the possible."

To sum up, the attraction of Marxist-inspired materialist criticism is to enable one to connect fruitfully both superstructural and infrastructural dimensions, rather than separating culture, religion, ideology, politics, society, and economics into discrete fields. In the work of many of the scholars noted earlier, the social sciences, as well as history, archaeology, economics, and political science, are as crucial to analysis as literary and theoretical concerns.

[*See also* Class Criticism; Economics and the Bible; Social Sciences, *subentry* Hebrew Bible; *and* Social Sciences, *subentry* New Testament.]

BIBLIOGRAPHY

Agamben, Giorgio. *The Time That Remains: A Commentary on the Letter to the Romans.* Translated by P. Dailey. Stanford, Calif.: Stanford University Press, 2005 [2000]. An important Marxist-inspired engagement with Paul from a leading Italian philosopher.

Anderson, Perry. *Lineages of the Absolutist State.* London: New Left Books, 1974. An excellent work on the historical and economic shifts from ancient Greece and Rome to feudalism and the emergence of the absolute monarch.

Badiou, Alain. *Saint Paul: The Foundation of Universalism.* Translated by R. Brassier. Stanford, Calif.: Stanford University Press, 2003 [1997]. Another Marxist-inspired assessment of Paul, with a different position from Agamben.

Bailey, Anne M., and Josep R. Llobera, eds. *The Asiatic Mode of Production: Science and Politics.* London: Routledge and Kegan Paul, 1981. All of the crucial sources on the Asiatic mode of production are gathered here, along with a summary.

Bal, Mieke. *Death and Dissymetry: The Politics of Coherence in the Book of Judges.* Chicago: University of Chicago Press, 1988. A breakthrough work in Hebrew Bible criticism by the cultural critic, Mieke Bal.

Belo, Fernando. *Lecture matérialiste de l'évangile de Marx: Récit-Pratique-Idéologie.* Revised ed. Paris: Les Editions du Cerf, 1975.

Belo, Fernando. *A Materialist Reading of the Gospel of Mark.* Translated by M. J. O'Connell. Maryknoll: Orbis, 1981. One of the first consistently materialist (Marxist) readings of the Gospel of Mark.

Bernier, Jonathan. "The Consciousness of John's Gospel: A Prolegomenon to a Jaynesian-Jamesonian Approach." *Bible and Critical Theory* 6, no. 2 (2010): 1–11.

Bernier, Jonathan. "From Historical Criticism to Historical Materialism in the Study of Earliest Christology." *Bible and Critical Theory* 8, no. 3 (2012): 67–76. Two works in a project that seek to apply Marxist literary criticism to the New Testament.

Blanton, Ward, and Hent De Vries, eds. *Paul in Philosophy and Culture.* Chicago: University of Chicago Press, forthcoming. A major collection on the recent interpretations of by philosophers.

Bloch, Ernst. *Atheism in Christianity: The Religion of the Exodus and the Kingdom.* Translated by J. T. Swann. London: Verso, 2009. Bloch was one of the leading Marxists who found inspiration in the Bible and deeply influenced theology in the twentieth century.

Bloch, Ernst. *Principle of Hope.* Translated by N. Plaice, S. Plaice and P. Knight. Cambridge, Mass.: MIT Press, 1995.

Boer, Roland. *Criticism of Heaven: On Marxism and Theology.* Leiden: Brill, 2007a.

Boer, Roland. *Criticism of Religion: On Marxism and Theology II, Historical Materialism Book Series.* Leiden: Brill, 2009. Works that offer sustained engagements between Marxism, the Bible and theology.

Boer, Roland. *Jameson and Jeroboam.* Atlanta.: Scholars, 1996.

Boer, Roland. *Knockin' on Heaven's Door: The Bible and Popular Culture.* London: Routledge, 1999.

Boer, Roland. *Marxist Criticism of the Bible.* London: Continuum, 2003.

Boer, Roland. "The Sacred Economy of Ancient 'Israel'." *Scandinavian Journal of the Old Testament* 21, no. 1 (2007b): 29.

Boer, Roland, and Jorunn Økland, eds. *Marxist Feminist Criticism of the Bible.* Sheffield, UK: Sheffield Phoenix, 2008.

Burt, Sean. "The Contradictions of Genre in the Nehemiah-Memorial." Graduate Program in Religion, Duke University, Durham, N.C., 2009. A doctoral dissertation that applies the work of Fredric Jameson to the Hebrew Bible.

Butzer, Karl W. "Irrigation, Raised Fields and State Management." *Antiquity* 70, no. 267 (1996): 200–205. A critique of Wittfogel, with a focus on the Asiatic mode of production.

Cadwallader, Alan. "In Go(l)d we Trust: Literary and Economic Exchange in the Debate over Caesar's Coin (Mark 12:13–17)." *Biblical Interpretation* 14, no. 5 (2007): 486–507. A resolutely materialist reading focussing on economics.

Caputo, John D., and Linda M. Alcoff, eds. *St. Paul among the Philosophers.* Bloomington: Indiana University Press, 2009. A collection that deals with the philosophical engagements with Paul, drawing together philosophers and New Testament critics.

Clévenot, Michel. *Approches matérialistes de la Bible.* Paris: Les Editions du Cerf, 1976.

Clévenot, Michel. *Materialist Approaches to the Bible.* Translated by W. J. Nottingham. Maryknoll, N.Y.: Orbis, 1985. A popularizing work based on that of Belo.

Critchley, Simon. "Demanding Approval: On the Ethics of Alain Badiou." *Radical Philosophy* 100 (2009): 16–27. A philosophical critique of Alain Badiou's philosophy and engagement with Paul.

Dandamaev, Muhammad. *Slavery in Babylonia: From Nabopolassar to Alexander the Great (626–331 B.C.).* Translated by V. A. Powell. DeKalb: Northern Illinois University Press, 2009 [1974]. Another significant Soviet-era Russian scholar of the ancient Near East.

Deissmann, Adolf. *The New Testament in the Light of Modern Research.* Garden City, N.Y.: Doubleday, Doran, 1929. Early New Testament work that assumed Engels's and Kautsky's argument for the lower-class make-up of early Christianity, although at the same time criticizing the latter.

Dhoquois, Georges. *Pour l'histoire: Essai d'histoire matérialiste comparative.* Paris: Anthropos, 1971. A work dealing with the Asiatic mode of production and used by Belo.

D'iakonoff, Igor M, ed. *Ancient Mesopotamia: Socio-Economic History. A Collection of Studies by Soviet Scholars.* Moscow: "Nauka", 1969b.

D'iakonoff, Igor M. "The Commune in the Ancient East as Treated in the Works of Soviet Researchers." In *Introduction to Soviet Ethnography.* Vol. 2. edited by S. P. Dunn and E. Dunn, 519–48. Berkeley, Calif.: Highgate Road Social Science Research Station, 1974.

D'iakonoff, Igor M. "General Outline of the First Period of the History of the Ancient World and the Problem of the Ways of Development." In *Early Antiquity,* edited by I. M. Diakonoff and P. L. Kohl, 27–66. Chicago: University of Chicago Press, 1991.

D'iakonoff, Igor M. "The Rise of the Despotic State in Ancient Mesopotamia." In *Ancient Mesopotamia: Socio-Economic History. A Collection of Studies by Soviet Scholars,* edited by I. M. D'iakonoff, 173–203. Moscow: "Nauka", 1969a.

D'iakonoff, Igor M., and Philip L. Kohl, eds. *Early Antiquity.* Chicago: Chicago University Press, 1991. D'iakonoff was a leading Soviet-era Russian scholar of the ancient Near East and is well worth a read.

Dunn, Stephen P. *The Fall and Rise of the Asiatic Mode of Production.* London: Routledge, 2011 [1982].

Eagleton, Terry. *Criticism and Ideology: A Study in Marxist Literary Theory.* London: New Left Books, 2006 [1976]. Marxist cultural critical work that has influenced biblical criticism.

Eagleton, Terry. *Ideology: An Introduction.* London: Verso, 1991.

Eagleton, Terry. *Literary Theory: An Introduction.* Oxford: Blackwells, 1996.

Elliott, Neil. *The Arrogance of Nations: Reading Romans in the Shadow of Empire.* Minneapolis: Fortress, 2008. A leading work on the political readings of Paul by a biblical scholar.

Engels, Friedrich. "The Book of Revelation." In *Marx and Engels Collected Works.* Vol. 26. 112–117. Moscow: Progress Publishers, 1883 [1990].

Engels, Friedrich. "Bruno Bauer and Early Christianity." In *Marx and Engels Collected Works.* Vol. 24. 427–435. Moscow: Progress Publishers, 1882 [1989].

Engels, Friedrich. "On the History of Early Christianity." In *Marx and Engels Collected Works.* Vol. 27. 445–469. Moscow: Progress Publishers, 1894–1895 [1990]. Deeply influential works by Engels on early Christianity.

Feiner, Susan. "Property Relations and Class Relations in Genovese and the Modes of Production Controversy." *Cambridge Journal of Economics* 10, no. 1 (1986): 61–75.

An economist critiques the "mode of production controversy."

Foster-Carter, Aidan. "The Modes of Production Controversy." *New Left Review* 107 (1978): 47–77. Another critique of the "mode of production controversy."

Gottwald, Norman K. "Social Class and Ideology in Isaiah 40–55: An Eagletonian Reading." *Semeia* 59 (1992a): 43–57.

Gottwald, Norman K. "Sociology of Ancient Israel." In *Anchor Bible Dictionary*, Vol. 6. Edited by D. N. Freedman, 79–89. New York: Doubleday, 1992b.

Gottwald, Norman K. *The Tribes of Yahweh: A Sociology of Liberated Israel 1250–1050 B.C.E.* Sheffield, UK: Sheffield Academic, 1999 [1979]. Reprint with new Preface. Benchmark work on socioscientific and Marxist readings of the Hebrew Bible.

Gramsci, Antonio. *Prison Notebooks.* Translated by J. A. Buttigieg and A. Callari. Vol. 1. New York: Columbia University Press, 1992. Original edition, Quaderni del carcere, 1975.

Gramsci, Antonio. *Prison Notebooks.* Translated by J. A. Buttigieg. Vol. 2. New York: Columbia University Press, 1996. Original edition, Quaderni del carcere, 1975.

Gramsci, Antonio. *Prison Notebooks.* Translated by J. A. Buttigieg. Vol. 3. New York: Columbia University Press, 2007. Original edition, Quaderni del carcere, 1975. Italian Marxist philosopher whose importance for biblical criticism is yet to be realized.

Hindess, Barry, and Paul Q. Hirst. *Pre-capitalist Modes of Production.* London: Routledge and Kegan Paul, 1975. A staunch theoretical critique of the Asiatic mode of production and slave-based mode.

Horkheimer, Max, and Theodor W. Adorno. *Dialectic of Enlightenment: Philosophical Fragments.* Translated by E. Jephcott. Stanford, Calif.: Stanford University Press, 2002. Profound work that continues to influence philosophy and cultural theory and is beginning to leave its mark in biblical criticism.

Horsley, Richard. *Archaeology, History and Society in Galilee.* Philadelphia: Trinity Press International, 1996.

Horsley, Richard. *Galilee: History, Politics, People.* Philadelphia: Trinity Press International, 1995.

Horsley, Richard. "Jesus and Empire." In *In the Shadow of Empire: Reclaiming the Bible as a History of Faithful Resistance*, edited by R. Horsley, 75–96. Louisville, Ky.: Westminster John Knox, 2008.

Horsley, Richard. *Jesus and Empire: The Kingdom of God and the New World Order.* Minneapolis: Augsburg Fortress, 2002.

Horsley, Richard. *Jesus and the Spiral of Violence: Popular Jewish Resistance in Roman Palestine.* Philadelphia, Pennsylvania: Augsburg Fortress, 1992.

Horsley, Richard, and John S. Hanson. *Bandits, Prophets, and Messiahs: Popular Movements in the Time of Jesus.* Philadelphia: Trinity Press International, 1985. Horsley's works have led the way for historical materialist and political readings of the New Testament.

Jameson, Fredric. *The Political Unconscious: Narrative as a Socially Symbolic Act.* Ithaca, N.Y.: Cornell University Press, 1981.

Jameson, Fredric. *Postmodernism, or, the Cultural Logic of Late Capitalism.* Durham, N.C.: Duke University Press, 1991. Deeply influential and sophisticated Marxist literary criticism that has influenced biblical criticism.

Jobling, David. "Feminism and 'Mode of Production' in Ancient Israel: Search for a Method." In *The Bible and the Politics of Exegesis: Essays in Honor of Norman K. Gottwald on His Sixty-Fifth Birthday*, edited by D. Jobling, P. L. Day, and G. T. Sheppard, 239–251. Cleveland: Pilgrim, 1991.

Jobling, David. "'Forced Labor': Solomon's Golden Age and the Question of Representation." *Semeia* 54 (1992): 57–76.

Jobling, David. *1 Samuel.* Collegeville, Minn.: Liturgical, 1998. Insightful works that integrate Marxism, feminism, and poststructural criticism.

Judge, E.A. *Social Distinctives of the Christians in the First Century: Pivotal Essays.* Peabody, Mass.: Hendrickson, 2008 [1960]. A leading revisionist of the lower-class theory of Christian origins.

Kautsky, Karl. *Foundations of Christianity.* Translated by H. F. Mins. London: Socialist Resistance, 2007 [1908]. A leading Marxist theoretician after Marx and Engels, who made the first detailed historical materialist study of biblical societies.

Kautsky, Karl. *Vorläufer des neueren Sozialismus I: Kommunistische Bewegung im Mittelalter.* Berlin: Dietz, 1947a [1895–1897].

Kautsky, Karl. *Vorläufer des neueren Sozialismus II: Der Kommunismus in der Deutschen Reformation.* Berlin: Dietz, 1947b [1895–1897].

Kautsky, Karl, and Paul Lafargue. *Vorläufer des neueren Sozialismus.* Stuttgart: Dietz, 1977 [1922]. A work that traces the history of Christian revolutionaries.

Krader, Lawrence. *The Asiatic Mode of Production: Sources, Development and Critique in the Writings of Karl Marx.* Assen, the Netherlands: Van Gorcum, 1975. A thorough work on the Asiatic mode of production.

Lefebvre, Henri. *The Production of Space.* Translated by David Nicholson-Smith. Hoboken, N.J.: Wiley-Blackwell, 1992. A groundbreaking work from a leading French Marxist that has influenced many disciplines in the sciences and humanities.

Lichtheim, George. "Marx and the 'Asiatic Mode of Production'." In *Marxian Economics*. Vol. 2. Edited by J. E. King, 17–43. Aldershot, UK: Elgar, 1990. Part of the Marxist discussion of the Asiatic mode of production.

Luxemburg, Rosa. "Socialism and the Churches." In *Rosa Luxemburg Speaks*, edited by M.-A. Waters, 131–152. New York: Pathfinder, 1970 [1905]. Lesser known than Kautsky, but this work argues for an early Christian communism.

Marx, Karl. *Capital: A Critique of Political Economy*. Vol. 1. Translated by B. Fowkes. London: Penguin in association with New Left Books, 1867 [1976].

Marx, Karl. *Pre-Capitalist Economic Formations*. Translated by J. Cohen. New York: International Publishers, 1964. Two of Marx's key works with relevance for biblical societies.

Meeks, Wayne A. *The First Urban Christians: The Social World of the Apostle Paul*. New Haven, Conn.: Yale University Press, 2003. An example of socioscientific criticism that seeks to set itself apart from Kautsky.

Mosala, Itumeleng. *Biblical Hermeneutics and Black Theology in South Africa*. Grand Rapids, Mich.: Eerdmans, 1989. A Marxist-inspired study by a man who became a leading educational figure in postapartheid South Africa.

Myers, Ched. *Binding the Strong Man: A Political Reading of Mark's Story of Jesus*. Maryknoll, N.Y.: Orbis, 1989. An influential work in the churches on a radical reading of Mark.

Nam, Roger. *Portrayals of Economic Exchange in the Book of Kings*. Leiden: Brill, 2012. A thorough reengagement with Karl Polanyi's significance for biblical economics.

Penchansky, David. *The Betrayal of God: Ideological Conflict in Job*. Louisville, Ky.: Westminster John Knox, 1991. An earlier engagement with Fredric Jameson.

Pippin, Tina. *Death and Desire: The Rhetoric of Gender in the Apocalypse of John*. Louisville, Ky.: Westminster John Knox, 1992a.

Pippin, Tina. "Eros and the End: Reading for Gender in the Apocalypse of John." *Semiea* 59 (1992b.): 193–210. Readings of the Apocalypse by using intersections between Marxism, feminism, and poststructuralism.

Polanyi, Karl. *The Great Transformation: The Political and Economic Origins of Our Time*. Boston: Beacon, 2001 [1944]. Crucial work on ancient Near Eastern economies that still set the agenda today.

Polanyi, Karl. *Primitive, Archaic and Modern Economies*. Boston: Beacon, 1971 [1968].

Polanyi, Karl, Conrad M. Arensberg, and Harry W. Pearson, eds. *Trade and Market in the Early Empires: Economies in History and Theory*. New York: Free Press, 1957.

Sahlins, Marshall. *Stone Age Economics*. New York: de Gruyter, 1972. Works that have been deployed regarding the household or domestic mode of production in regard to ancient Israel.

Sahlins, Marshall. *Tribesmen*. Englewood Cliffs: Prentice-Hall, 1968.

Simkins, Ronald. "Class and Gender in Early Israel." In *Concepts of Class in Ancient Israel*, edited by M. Sneed, 71–86. Atlanta: Scholars, 1999a.

Simkins, Ronald. "Family in the Political Ecomony of Monarchic Israel." *Bible and Critical Theory* 1, no. 1 (2004): 36–42. Marxist readings, arguing for the importance of patron-client relations and the centrality of the family in ancient Israel.

Simkins, Ronald. "Patronage and the Political Economy of Ancient Israel." *Semeia* 87 (1999b.): 123–144.

Sneed, Mark. "Qohelet and his 'Vulgar' Critics: A Jamesonian Reading." *Bible and Critical Theory* 1, no. 1 (2004): 1–11. Marxist-inspired readings of the book of Qohelet.

Sneed, Mark. "The Social Location of the Book of Qoheleth." *Hebrew Studies* 39 (1998): 41–50.

Stark, Rodney. *The Rise of Christianity: A Socialist Reconsiders History*. Princeton, N.J.: Princeton University Press, 1996. A revisionist reading of early Christianity using "rational choice" theory.

Ste. Croix, G. E. M. de. *Christian Persecution, Martyrdom, and Orthodoxy*. Edited by M. Whitby and J. Streeter. Oxford: Oxford University Press, 2006. Important work on ancient Greece and early Christianity by a Marxist classicist, work that is only now being appreciated.

Ste. Croix, G. E. M. de. *The Class Struggle in the Ancient Greek World: From the Archaic Age to the Arab Conquest*. London: Duckworth, 1981.

Struve, V. V. "The Problem of the Genesis, Development and Disintegration of the Slave Societies in the Ancient Orient." In *Ancient Mesopotamia: Socio-Economic History. A Collection of Studies by Soviet Scholars*, edited by I. M. D'iakonoff, 17–69. Moscow: "Nauka", 1969a.

Struve, V. V. "Some New Data on the Organization of Labour and on Social Structure in Sumer During the Reign of the IIIrd Dynasty of Ur." In *Ancient Mesopotamia: Socio-Economic History. A Collection of Studies by Soviet Scholars*, edited by I. M. D'iakonoff, 127–172. Moscow: "Nauka", 1969b. Foundational work in Soviet-era Russian work on the ancient Near East, proposing a slave-based mode of production.

Surin, Kenneth. *Freedom Not Yet: Liberation and the Next World Order*. Durham, N.C.: Duke University Press, 2009. A recent Marxist engagement with economics and politics by a scholar trained as a theologian.

Theissen, Gerd. *The Religion of the Earliest Churches: Creating a Symbolic World*. Translated by J. Bowden. Philadelphia: Augsburg Fortress, 1999. Socio-psychological studies of the New Testament.

Theissen, Gerd. *The Shadow of the Galilean: The Quest of the Historical Jesus in Narrative Form*. Translated by J. Bowden. Philadelphia: Fortress, 1987.

Theissen, Gerd. *Sociology of Early Palestinian Christianity*. Translated by J. Bowden. Philadelphia: Fortress, 1978.

Troeltsch, Ernst. *The Social Teaching of the Christian Churches*. Translated by O. Wyon. 2 vols. Louisville, Ky.: Westminster John Knox, 1992 [1911]. A work that accepted the Engels-Kautsky theory of lower-class origins for early Christianity but also set itself apart by arguing for primarily religious causes.

Tyumenev, A. I. "The State Economy of Ancient Sumer." In *Ancient Mesopotamia: Socio-Economic History. A Collection of Studies by Soviet Scholars*, edited by I. M. D'iakonoff, 70–87. Moscow: "Nauka", 1969a.

Tyumenev, A. I. "The Working Personnel on the Estate of the Temple of dBa-Ú in Lagas During the Period of Lugalanda and Urukagina (25th–24th cent. B.C.)." In *Ancient Mesopotamia: Socio-Economic History. A Collection of Studies by Soviet Scholars*, edited by I. M. D'iakonoff, 88–126. Moscow: "Nauka," 1969b. A contributor to the Soviet-era Russian debate over ancient Near-Eastern economics.

Wittfogel, Karl. *Oriental Despotism*. New Haven, Conn.: Yale University Press, 1963. A misguided effort to argue that irrigation was the key to the Asiatic mode of production.

Yee, Gale A. *Poor Banished Children of Eve: Woman as Evil in the Hebrew Bible*. Minneapolis: Fortress, 2003. An important feminist-Marxist work on the Hebrew Bible.

Žižek, Slavoj. *On Belief*. London: Routledge, 2001.

Žižek, Slavoj. *In Defense of Lost Causes*. London: Verso, 2008.

Žižek, Slavoj. *The Fragile Absolute, or, Why is the Christian Legacy Worth Fighting For?* London: Verso, 2000.

Žižek, Slavoj. *The Puppet and the Dwarf: The Perverse Core of Christianity*. Cambridge, Mass.: MIT, 2003.

Žižek, Slavoj, and John Milbank. *The Monstrosity of Christ: Paradox or Dialectic?* Cambridge, Mas.: MIT, 2009. A leading contemporary philosopher who has sought to locate the revolutionary core of Christianity.

Roland Boer